The
GREEK TESTAMENT

Volume III
GALATIANS—PHILEMON

The GREEK TESTAMENT

WITH A CRITICALLY REVISED TEXT, A DIGEST OF
VARIOUS READINGS, MARGINAL REFERENCES TO VERBAL AND
IDIOMATIC USAGE, PROLEGOMENA,
AND A CRITICAL AND EXEGETICAL COMMENTARY

by

HENRY ALFORD, D.D.

with revision by

EVERETT F. HARRISON, Th.D., Ph.D.

Volume III
GALATIANS—PHILEMON

MOODY PRESS
CHICAGO

Printed in the United States of America

CONTENTS OF THE PROLEGOMENA.

CHAPTER I.

THE EPISTLE TO THE GALATIANS.

CHAPTER II.

THE EPISTLE TO THE EPHESIANS.

CHAPTER III.

THE EPISTLE TO THE PHILIPPIANS.

CHAPTER IV.

THE EPISTLE TO THE COLOSSIANS.

CONTENTS OF THE PROLEGOMENA

CHAPTER V.

THE FIRST EPISTLE TO THE THESSALONIANS.

CHAPTER VI.

THE SECOND EPISTLE TO THE THESSALONIANS.

CHAPTER VII.

ON THE PASTORAL EPISTLES.

CHAPTER VIII.

ON THE FIRST EPISTLE TO TIMOTHEUS.

CHAPTER IX.

THE SECOND EPISTLE TO TIMOTHEUS.

CHAPTER X.

THE EPISTLE TO TITUS.

CHAPTER XI.

THE EPISTLE TO PHILEMON.

CHAPTER XII.

APPARATUS CRITICUS.

PROLEGOMENA.

CHAPTER I.

THE EPISTLE TO THE GALATIANS.

SECTION I.

ITS AUTHORSHIP.

1. OF all the Epistles which bear the characteristic marks of St. Paul's style, this one stands the foremost. See below, on its style, § 4. So that, as Windischmann observes, whoever is prepared to deny the genuineness of this Epistle, would pronounce on himself the sentence of incapacity to distinguish true from false. Accordingly, its authorship has never been doubted.

2. But that authorship is also upheld by external testimony:

(a) Irenæus, adv. Hær. iii. 7. 2, p. 182, quotes the Epistle by name: " Sed in ea quæ est ad Galatas, sic ait : Quid ergo lex factorum ? posita est usque quo veniat semen, cui promissum est &c." (Gal. iii. 19.)

Many allusions to it are found.

(β) Polycarp, ad Phil. cap. iii. : p. 1008.

Παύλου . . . ὃς καὶ ἀπὼν ὑμῖν ἔγραψεν ἐπιστολάς, εἰς ἃς ἐὰν ἐγκύπτητε, δυνηθήσεσθε οἰκοδομεῖσθαι εἰς τὴν δοθεῖσαν ὑμῖν πίστιν, ἥτις ἐστὶ μήτηρ πάντων ἡμῶν (Gal. iv. 26). And again, cap. v., p. 1009: εἰδότες οὖν, ὅτι θεὸς οὐ μυκτηρίζεται . . . . (Gal. vi. 7).

(γ) Justin Martyr, or whoever was the author of the Oratio ad Græcos, printed among his works, seems to allude to Gal. iv. 12, in the words γίνεσθε ὡς ἐγώ, ὅτι κἀγὼ ἤμην ὡς ὑμεῖς : and to Gal. v. 20, in these, ἔχθραι, ἔρεις, ζῆλος, ἐριθεῖαι, θυμοί, κ. τὰ ὅμοια τούτοις, c. v., p. 5.

(δ) Besides these, there are many more distant allusions in the works of Ignatius, Polycarp, and Justin, which may be seen cited in Lardner and Windischmann, and Davidson, Introd. to N. T. vol. ii. pp. 318-19.

SECTION II.

FOR WHAT READERS IT WAS WRITTEN.

1. This Epistle was written ταῖς ἐκκλησίαις τῆς Γαλατίας (ch. i. 2).
GALATIA (Γαλλογραικία Strabo xii. 566, Gallogræcia Liv. xxxvii. 8,
xxxviii. 12) was a district of Asia Minor (once part of Phrygia, Strabo
xii. 571, ii. 130), bounded N. by Paphlagonia and Bithynia, E. by
Pontus and Cappadocia (divided from both by the Halys), S. by Cappadocia and Phrygia, W. by Phrygia and Bithynia. Notwithstanding its
mountainous character, it was fruitful, especially near the river Halys
(Strabo xii. 567). The principal cities were Ancyra, Pessinus, and
Tavium. Ancyra was declared the capital by Augustus. The inhabitants (Γαλάται, only a later form of Κέλται, Pausan. i. 3. 5,—also Gallo-
græci) were Gauls in origin. The Gallic tribes of the Trochmi and
Tolistoboii, with the German tribe of Tectosagi (or Toctosages), crossed
over from Thrace into Asia Minor, having formed part of the Gallic
expedition which pillaged Delphi, in the third century B.C. (cir. 280.)
In Asia they at first became mercenary troops under Nicomedes, king
of Bithynia, but soon overran nearly the whole of Asia Minor, till
Antiochus Soter and Eumenes drove them into its central portion,
afterwards called Galatia. There they were at first ruled by tetrarchs,
and afterwards (when their real independence had been taken from
them by the Consul Manlius Vulso, B.C. 189,—see Livy xxxviii. 16—
27) by kings ; of whom the two Deiotari, father and son, are known to
us, the former as having been defended by Cicero in a speech still extant,
the latter as also a friend of the great orator's (Epp. ad Attic. v. 17).
Amyntas, the successor of this latter, was their last king: at his death
(B.C. 26) Galatia was reduced to a Roman province. See for full accounts,
Strabo, book xiii. ch. 5 : Livy, as above : the Introductions to this Epistle
in Meyer, De Wette, and Windischmann : Winer's Realwörterbuch, art.
Galatia : Conybeare and Howson, vol. i. p. 284 ff., edn. 2 : and the learned
dissertation on the question whether the Galatians were Teutons or Celts,
appended to Prof. Lightfoot's edition of this Epistle.

2. The character of the people, as shewn in this Epistle, agrees
remarkably with that ascribed to the Gallic race by all writers[1]. They
received the Apostle at his first visit with extreme joy, and shewed him
every kindness : but were soon shaken in their fidelity to him and the
Gospel, and were transferring their allegiance to false teachers.

3. The Galatian churches were founded by St. Paul at his first visit,

---

[1] So Cæsar, B. G. iv. 5 : " infirmitatem Gallorum veritus, quod sunt in consiliis capi-
undis mobiles, et novis plerumque rebus student, nihil his committendum existimavit."
And Thierry, Hist. des Gaulois, Introd.: " un esprit franc, impétueux, ouvert à toutes
les impressions, éminemment intelligent : mais à côté de cela, une mobilité extrême,
point de constance, ... beaucoup d'ostentation, enfin une désunion perpétuelle, fruit
d'excessive vanité." C. & H. i. 285, note.

when he was detained among them by sickness (ch. iv. 13: see note and compare Acts xvi. 6), during his second missionary journey, about A.D. 51 (see chronol. table in Prolegg. to Acts, Vol. II.). Though doubtless he began his preaching as usual among the Jews (cf. Jos. Antt. xvi. 6. 2, for the fact of many Jews being resident in Ancyra), yet this Epistle testifies to the majority of his readers being Gentiles, not yet circumcised, though nearly persuaded to it by Judaizing teachers. At the same time we see by the frequent references to the O. T. and the adoption of the rabbinical method of interpretation by allegory (ch. iv. 21—31), that he had to do with churches which had been accustomed to Judaizing teaching, and familiarized with the O. T.   See Meyer, Einl. p. 3. In the manifold preparations for the Gospel which must have taken place wherever Jews were numerous, through the agency of those who had at Jerusalem heard and believed on Jesus, we need not wonder at any amount of judaistic influence apparent even in churches founded by St. Paul himself : nor need any hypotheses respecting his preaching be invented to account for such a phænomenon.

SECTION III.

WITH WHAT OBJECT IT WAS WRITTEN.

1. Judaizing teachers had followed, as well as preceded, the Apostle in Galatia, and had treated slightingly his apostolic office and authority (ch. i. 1, 11), giving out that circumcision was necessary (ch. v. 2 ; vi. 12). Their influence was increasing, and the churches were being drawn away by it (i. 6 ; iii. 1, 3 ; iv. 9—11 ; v. 7--12). Against these teachers he had already testified in person (i. 9 ; iv. 16, where see notes, and cf. Acts xviii. 23),—and now that the evil was so rapidly and seriously gaining ground, he writes this Epistle expressly to counteract it.

2. The object then of the Epistle was (1) to defend his own apostolic authority; and (2) to expose the judaistic error by which they were being deceived. Accordingly, it contains two parts, the apologetic (ch. i. ii.) and the polemic (ch. iii.—v. 12).   These are naturally followed by a hortatory conclusion (ch. v. 13—end). See these parts subdivided into their minor sections in the notes.

SECTION IV.

ITS MATTER, AND STYLE.

1. The matter of the Epistle has been partly spoken of in the last section. In the first, or apologetic portion, it contains a most valuable historical résumé of St. Paul's apostolic career, proving his independence of human authority, and confirming as well as illustrating the narrative in the Acts, by mentioning the principal occasions when he held intercourse with the other Apostles: relating also that remarkable interview

3]

with St. Peter, so important for its own sake, and giving rise to his own precious testimony to Christian truth in ch. ii. 14—21.

2. The polemical portion has much in common with the Epistle to the Romans. But this difference is observable; that whereas in that Epistle, the whole subject is treated, as belonging to the great argument there handled, logically, and without reference to any special circumstances,—*here* all is strictly controversial, with immediate reference to the judaizing teachers.

3. In style, this Epistle takes a place of its own among those of St. Paul. It unites the two extreme affections of his remarkable character: severity, and tenderness : both, the attributes of a man of strong and deep emotions. Nothing can be more solemnly severe than its opening, and ch. iii. 1—5; nothing more touchingly affectionate than some of its appeals, e. g. ch. iv. 18—20. It is therefore quite a mistake to characterize its tone as altogether overpowering and intimidating[2]. A half-barbarous people like the Galatians, known for their simplicity and impressibility, would be likely to listen to both of these methods of address : to be won by his fatherly pleading, as well as overawed by his apostolic rebukes and denunciations.

4. There are several points of similarity in this Epistle to the peculiar diction of the Pastoral Epistles. The student will find them pointed out in the reff., and for the most part remarked on in the notes. They seem to indicate, in accordance with our interpretation of ch. vi. 11, that he wrote this Epistle, as those, with his own hand, without the intervention of an amanuensis. This matter will be found more fully treated below, ch. vii. on the Pastoral Epistles, § i. 32.

SECTION V.

TIME AND PLACE OF WRITING.

1. We have no date in the Epistle itself, which may enable us to determine the time when it was written. This can only be gathered from indirect sources. And consequently, the most various dates have been assigned to it : some, as Marcion in old times, and Michaelis, al., in modern, placing it *first* among St. Paul's Epistles : and others, as Schrader and Köhler, *last*. The following considerations will narrow our field of uncertainty on the point :

2. If the reasoning in the note on the chronological table, Vol. II. Prolegg. pp. 26, 27, be correct,—the visit to Jerusalem mentioned Gal. ii. 1 ff. is identical with that in Acts xv. 1 ff. It will thence follow that the Epistle cannot have been written *before* that visit : i. e. (see Chron. Table as above) not before A.D. 50.

3. I have maintained, in the note on Gal. iv. 16, that the words

---

[2] See Jowett, Epistles to the Romans, Thessalonians, and Galatians, vol. i. p. 191.

there used most naturally refer to the Apostle's second visit to the churches of Galatia, when Acts xviii. 23, he went through τὴν Γαλατικὴν χώραν . . . . στηρίζων πάντας τοὺς μαθητάς.   If so, this Epistle cannot date *before that visit*: i. e. (Chron. Table as above) not before the autumn of the year 54.

4. The first period then which seems probable, is the Apostle's stay at Ephesus in Acts xix., from autumn 54, till Pentecost 57.   And this period is so considerable, that, having regard to the οὕτως ταχέως of ch. i. 6, it must be regarded as quite possible that our Epistle may have been written during it.   The above is the view of Hug, De Wette, Olsh., Usteri, Winer, Neander, Greswell, Anger, Meyer, Wieseler, and many others.

5. The next period during which it might have been written is, his stay at Corinth, Acts xx. 2, 3, where he spent the winter of the year 57-8, and whence he wrote the Epistle to the Romans.   This is the opinion of Conybeare and Howson (vol. ii. p. 162, edn. 2).   They support their view entirely by the similarity of this Epistle and that to the Romans.   "It is," they say (p. 165, note), "exactly that resemblance which would exist between two Epistles written nearly at the same time, while the same line of argument was occupying the writer's mind, and the same phrases and illustrations were on his tongue."   It has also been maintained with much skill and learning, since the first edition of this volume appeared, by Prof. Lightfoot, in an article in the Journal of Sacred and Classical Philology for Jan. 1857 : which article is reproduced in the Introduction to his edition of the Epistle, 1865. He traces the sequence of the lines of thought in the greater Epistles, and finds internal evidence enough to make him decide strongly that it is very improbable, that the two Epistles to the Corinthians intervened between those to the Galatians and Romans, or that to the Galatians between the second to the Thessalonians and the first to the Corinthians.

6. I own that these considerations seem to me weighty ones, and have caused me to modify the decided preference which I gave in my first edition to the earlier date.   Still, I do not feel Prof. Lightfoot's argument to have settled the question.   It might be that the elementary truths brought out amidst deep emotion, sketched, so to speak, in great rough lines in the fervent Epistle to the Galatians, dwelt long on St. Paul's mind (even though other subjects of interest regarding other churches intervened), and at length worked themselves out, under the teaching and leading of the Spirit, into that grand theological argument which he afterwards addressed, without any special moving occasion, but as his master exposition of Christian doctrine, to the church of the metropolis of the world.

7. I think then that it must always remain a question between these two periods.   In favour of the former of them it may be said that,

5]

considering the οὕτως ταχέως[3], we can hardly let so long a time elapse
as the second would pass over,—and that probability is in favour of
strong emotion having, in the prompting of God's Spirit, first brought
out that statement of Christian truth and freedom, which after-delibera-
tion expanded, and polished, and systematized, in the Epistle to the
Romans : and in favour of the latter may be alleged the interesting
considerations respecting the grouping of St. Paul's Epistles, and the
parallels between 2 Corinthians, Galatians, and Romans, which Prof.
Lightfoot has adduced.

8. Of course my objection to the date implied in the common subscription, ἐγράφη ἀπὸ Ῥώμης, adopted by Theodoret, Calov., Hammond,
al., is even stronger than that stated above. Those who wish to see the
matter discussed at more length, may refer to Davidson, Introd. ii.
p. 292 ff., and to Prof. Lightfoot's edition of the Epistle, pp. 35—55.

CHAPTER II.

THE EPISTLE TO THE EPHESIANS.

SECTION I.

ITS AUTHORSHIP.

1. THE ancient testimonies to the Apostle Paul having been the
author of this Epistle, are the following :

(α) Irenæus adv. Hær. v. 2. 36, p. 294 :

καθὼς ὁ μακάριος Παῦλός φησιν ἐν τῇ πρὸς Ἐφεσίους ἐπιστολῇ ὅτι
μέλη ἐσμὲν τοῦ σώματος, ἐκ τῆς σαρκὸς αὐτοῦ, καὶ ἐκ τῶν ὀστέων
αὐτοῦ (Eph. v. 30). Again i. 8. 5, p. 42, τοῦτο δὲ καὶ ὁ Παῦλος λέγει·
πᾶν γὰρ τὸ φανερούμενον, φῶς ἐστίν (Eph. v. 13).

(β) Clem. Alex. Strom. iv. § 65, p. 592 P. :

διὸ καὶ ἐν τῇ πρὸς Ἐφεσίους γράφει (cf. supra, § 61, φησὶν ὁ ἀπόστολος,
where 1 Cor. xi. 3, &c. is quoted, § 62, ἐπιφέρει γοῦν, citing Gal. v.
16 ff. : and infra, § 66, κἂν τῇ πρὸς Κολοσσαεῖς . . . . from which it
is evident that the subject of γράφει is 'St. Paul') ὑποτασσόμενοι
ἀλλήλοις ἐν φόβῳ θεοῦ κ.τ.λ. Eph. v. 21—25.

(γ) ib. Pæd. i. § 18, p. 108 P. :

ὁ ἀπόστολος ἐπιστέλλων πρὸς Κορινθίους φησίν, 2 Cor. xi. 2. . . .
σαφέστατα δὲ Ἐφεσίοις γράφων ἀπεκάλυψε τὸ ζητούμενον ὧδέ πως
λέγων· μέχρι καταντήσωμεν οἱ πάντες κ.τ.λ. Eph. iv. 13—15.

---

[3] For I cannot accept the suggestion of Prof. Lightfoot, which would make ταχέως
subjective to μετατίθεσθε, 'ye are so rapidly changing.' I have treated on this view
in my note on Rev. i. 1, where much depends on it.

2. Further we have testimonies to the Epistle being received as canonical Scripture, and therefore, by implication, of its being regarded as written by him whose name it bears : as e. g. :

(δ) Polycarp, ad Philippenses, c. xii., p. 1013 ff. :

"Ut his scripturis dictum est, 'Irascimini et nolite peccare,' et 'Sol non occidat super iracundiam vestram.'" Eph. iv. 26[4].

(ε) Tertullian adv. Marcion. v. 17, p. 512 (see below, § ii. 17 c).

(ζ) Irenæus several times mentions passages of this Epistle as perverted by the Valentinians : e. g. ch. i. 10 (Iren. i. 3. 4, p. 16): iii. 21 (Iren. i. 3. 1, p. 14) : v. 32 (Iren. i. 8. 4, p. 40) : and in many other places (see the Index in Stieren's edn.) cites the Epistle directly.

3. I have not hitherto adduced the testimony ordinarily cited from Ignatius, Eph. 12, p. 656, on account of the doubt which hangs over the interpretation of the words [5] :

πάροδός ἐστε τῶν εἰς θεὸν ἀναιρουμένων, Παύλου συμμύσται τοῦ ἡγιασμένου, τοῦ μεμαρτυρημένου, ἀξιομακαρίστου, οὗ γένοιτό μοι ὑπὸ τὰ ἴχνη εὑρεθῆναι ὅταν θεοῦ ἐπιτύχω, ὃς ἐν πάσῃ ἐπιστολῇ μνημονεύει ὑμῶν ἐν χριστῷ Ἰησοῦ.

I conceive however that there can be little doubt that these expressions are to be interpreted of the Epistle to the Ephesians. First, the expression συμμύσται seems to point to Eph. i. 9, as compared with the rest of the chapter,—to ch. iii. 3—6, 9. And it would be the very perversity of philological strictness, to maintain, in the face of later and more anarthrous Greek usage, that ἐν πάσῃ ἐπιστολῇ must mean, 'in every Epistle,' and not 'in all his Epistle.' Assuming this latter meaning (see note on Eph. ii. 21), the expression finds ample justification in the very express and affectionate dwelling on the Christian state and privileges of those to whom he is writing—making mention of them throughout all his Epistle[6].

---

[4] Meyer, Einl. p. 24, prefers to consider both these citations as made from the O. T. Ps. iv. 4, and Deut. xxiv, 15 (?), on the ground of the title 'Scripture' never occurring of the N. T. in the apostolic fathers.

[5] The chapter itself is wanting in the ancient Syriac version published by Mr. Cureton. But this will hardly be adduced as affecting its genuineness. Hefele's view, "pius ille monachus, qui versionem Syriacam elaboravit, omnia omisisse videtur quæ ipsi et usui suo ascetico minus congrua minusve necessaria putabat," seems to be the true one.

[6] Pearson's remarks on this point are worth transcribing : "Hæc a martyre non otiose aut frigide, sed vere, imo signanter et vigilanter dicta sunt. Tota enim Epistola ad Ephesios scripta, ipsos Ephesios, eorumque honorem et curam maxime spectat, et summe honorificam eorum memoriam ad posteros transmittit. In aliis epistolis apostolus eos ad quos scribit sæpe acriter objurgat aut parce laudat. Hic omnibus modis perpetuo se Ephesiis applicat, illosque tanquam egregios Christianos tractat, evangelio salutis firmiter credentes, et Spiritu promissionis obsignatos, concives sanctorum, et domesticos Dei. Pro iis sæpe ardenter orat, ipsos hortatur, obtestatur, laudat, utrumque sexum sedulo instruit, suum erga eos singularem affectum ubique prodit." Vindiciæ Ignatianæ, pt. ii. ch. 10, end.

4. In the *longer* recension of this Epistle of Ignatius, the testimony is more direct: in ch. vi., p. 737, we read,

ὡς Παῦλος ὑμῖν ἔγραφεν· ἓν σῶμα καὶ ἓν πνεῦμα κ.τ.λ. (Eph. iv. 4—6.)

And in ch. ix., p. 741,

δι᾽ οὓς ἀγαλλιώμενος ἠξιώθην δι᾽ ὧν γράφω προσομιλῆσαι τοῖς ἁγίοις τοῖς οὖσιν ἐν Ἐφέσῳ, τοῖς πιστοῖς ἐν χριστῷ Ἰησοῦ.

5. As we advance to the following centuries, the reception of the authorship of St. Paul is universal[7]. In fact, we may safely say that this authorship was never called in question till very recent times.

6. Among those critics who have repudiated our Epistle as not written by the Apostle, the principal have been De Wette and Baur. The ground on which they build their reasoning is, for the most part, the same. De Wette holds the Epistle to be a verbose expansion of that to the Colossians. He describes it as entirely dependent on that Epistle, and as such, unworthy of a writer who always wrote in freshness and fulness of spirit, as did St. Paul. He believes he finds in it every where expressions and doctrines foreign to his diction and teaching. This being so, he classes it with the Pastoral Epistles and the first Epistle of Peter, and ascribes it to some scholar of the Apostles, writing in their name. He is not prepared to go so far as Baur, who finds in it the ideas and diction of Gnostic and Montanistic times. On this latter notion, I will treat below: I now proceed to deal with De Wette's objections.

7. First of all, I would take a general view of their character, and say, that, on such a general view, they, as a whole, make *for*, rather than against, the genuineness of the Epistle. According to De Wette, a gifted scholar of the Apostles, in the apostolic age itself, writes an Epistle in imitation, and under the name, of St. Paul. Were the imitation close, and the imitator detected only by some minute features of inadvertent inconsistency, such a phænomenon might be understood, as that the Epistle found universal acceptance as the work of the Apostle: but according to our objector, the discrepancies are wide, the inconsistencies every where abundant. He is found, in his commentary, detecting and exposing them at every turn. Such reasoning may prove a passage objectively (as in the case of Mark xvi. 9—20, or John vii. 53—viii. 11) to be out of place among the writings of a particular author, all subjective considerations apart: but it is wholly inapplicable when used to account for the success of a forger among his contemporaries, and indeed acts the other way.

8. Let us view the matter in this light. Here is an Epistle *bearing the name* of St. Paul. Obviously then, it is no mere accidental inser-

[7] See Orig. contra Celsum, iii. 20, vol. i. p. 458; Tert. de Præscr. Hær. c. 36, vol. ii. p. 49; De Monog. c. 5, ib. p. 935; Cypr. Testim. iii. 7, p. 737; Ep. lxxv.

tion among his writings of an Epistle written by some other man, and
on purely objective grounds requiring us to ascribe it to that other
unknown author; but it is either a genuine production of the Apostle,
or a *forgery*.   Subjective grounds cannot be kept out of the question :
it is a successful forgery : one which imposed on the post-apostolic age,
and has continued to impose on the Church in every age.   We have
then a right *to expect in it the phænomena of successful forgery :* close
imitation, skilful avoidance of aught which might seem unlike him
whose name it bears ;—construction, if you will, out of acknowledged
pauline materials, but so as to shun every thing unpauline.

9. Now, as has been seen above, the whole of De Wette's reasoning
goes upon the exact opposite of all these phænomena.   The Epistle is
unpauline : strange and surprising in diction, and ideas.   Granting this,
it might be a cogent reason for believing an *anonymous* writing *not to be*
St. Paul's : but it is no reason why a forgery bearing his name should
have been successful,—on the contrary, is a very sufficient reason why it
should have been immediately detected, and universally unsuccessful.
Let every one of De Wette's positions be granted, and carried to its
utmost; and the more in number and the stronger they are, the more
reason there will be to infer, that the only account to be given of a
writing, so unlike St. Paul's, obtaining universal contemporary acceptance
as his, is, that it was his own genuine composition.   Then we should
have remaining the problem, to account for the Apostle having so far
departed from himself : a problem for the solution of which much acquaintance with himself and the circumstances under which he wrote
would be required,—and, let me add, a treatment very far deeper and
more thorough than De Wette has given to any part of this Epistle.

10. But I am by no means disposed to grant any of De Wette's
positions as they stand, nor to recognize the problem as I have put it
in the above hypothetical form.   The relation between our Epistle and
that to the Colossians, I have endeavoured to elucidate below (§ vi. and
Prolegg. to the Col., § iv.).   The reasonings and connexions which he
pronounces unworthy of the Apostle, I hold him, in almost every case, not
to have appreciated : and where he has appreciated them, to have hastily
condemned.   Here, as in the instance of 1 Tim., his unfortunate prejudgment of the spuriousness of the Epistle has tinged his view of every
portion of it: and his commentary, generally so thorough and able, so
fearless and fair, is worth hardly more than those of very inferior men,
not reaching below the surface, and unable to recognize the most obvious
tendencies and connexions.

11. The reader will find De Wette's arguments met in detail by
Rückert (Comm. p. 289 ff.), Hemsen (der Apostel Paulus, pp. 629—
38); and touched upon by Harless (Comm. Einleit. p. lxvi ff.), Neander (in a note to his Pfl. u. Leit. edn. 4, p. 521 ff.), and Meyer (Einl.
9]

p. 20 ff.). Davidson also treats of them in full (Introd. to N. T. vol. ii. pp. 352—60), and Eadie very slightly (Introd. p. xxx f.)[8].

12. Baur's argument will be found in his 'Paulus, der Apostel Jesu Christi, &c.' pp. 417—57. It consists, as far as it is peculiar to him, mainly in an attempt to trace in our Epistle, and that to the Colossians (for he holds both to be spurious), expressions and sentiments known to be those of Gnosticism and Montanism: and in some few instances to shew that it is not probable that these heresies took their terms from the Epistles, but rather the Epistles from them. This latter part, on which indeed the conclusiveness of the whole depends, is very slightly, and to me most inconclusively done. And nothing is said in Baur of the real account of the occurrence of such terms in the Epistle, and subsequently in the vocabulary of these heretics: viz. that the sacred writer laid hold of them and employed them, so to speak, high up the stream of their usage, before they became polluted by heretical additions and misconceptions,—the heretics, lower down the same stream, when now the waters were turbid and noxious: his use of them having tended to impress them on men's minds, so that they were ready for the purpose of the heretics when they wanted them. That those heretics used many other terms not known to these Epistles, is no proof that their account was the original one, and this of our Epistles borrowed from it, but simply proves nothing. Some of these terms were suited to the Apostle's purpose in teaching or warning: these he was led to adopt: others were not so suitable,—those he left alone. Or it may be that between his writing and their development, the vocabulary had received additions, which consequently were never brought under his notice. Eadie refers, for an answer to Baur, to Lechler, das apostolische u. nachapostolische Zeitalter, u. s. w. Haarlem, 1852, a work which I have not seen.

13. Taking then the failure of the above objections into account, and strengthening it by anticipation with other considerations which will come before the reader as we advance, we see no reason whatever against following the universal view of the Church, and pronouncing St. Paul to be, as he is stated to be (ch. i. 1), the author of our Epistle.

SECTION II.

FOR WHAT READERS IT WAS WRITTEN.

1. In treating of this part of our subject, that city and church seem first to deserve notice, to which the Epistle, according to our present text, is addressed. We will first assume, that it was an Epistle to the EPHESIANS.

[8] See also "Ad Ephesios revera dabatur Epistola illa canonica, Paulo non Pseudopaulo auctore:" a Prælectio which I read at Cambridge in 1849; the chronological view of which I have seen reason to modify, but not its argument respecting this Epistle.

2. EPHESUS, in Lydia, was situated in an alluvial plain (Herod. ii. 10) on the south side of and near the mouth of the Caÿstrus. "The city stood on the S. of a plain about five miles long from E. to W., and three miles broad, the N. boundary being Mount Gallesius, the E. Mount Pactyas, the S. Mount Coressus, and on the W. it was washed by the sea. The sides of the mountains were very precipitous, and shut up the plain like a stadium, or race-course." Lewin, i. p. 344. See his plan, p. 362 : and the view of the site of Ephesus in C. and H. vol. ii. p. 83, edn. 2. For its ancient history, see Lewin, and C. and H. ib., and the art. 'Ephesus,' in Smith's Dict. of Geography. It was a place of great commerce (Strabo xiv. 641), but was principally noted for its beautiful temple of Artemis (Herod. i. 26 ; ii. 148. Strabo. l. c. Plin. v. 37. Pausan. vii. 2. 4 ; iv. 31. 6, &c.), which was at the head of its harbour Panormus, and was from very ancient times the centre of the worship of that goddess. This temple was burnt down by Herostratus, in the night of the birth of Alexander the Great (B.C. 355 ; see Plut. Alex. c. 3 ; Cicero de Nat. Deor. ii. 27), but rebuilt at immense cost (Strabo, l. c.), and was one of the wonders of the ancient world. On the worship of Artemis there, &c., see Acts xix. 24 ff. and notes, and Winer Realw. 'Ephesus.' The present state of the site of the city, the stadium, theatre, supposed basement of the temple, &c., are described in Smith's Dict. of Geogr., his Bible Dict., and in C. and H., as above.

3. St. Paul's first visit to Ephesus is related Acts xviii. 19—21. It was very short, as he was hastening to reach Jerusalem by the next Pentecost. The work begun by him in disputations with the Jews, was carried on by Apollos (ib. 24—26), and by Aquila and Priscilla (ib. 26). After visiting Jerusalem, and making a journey in the Eastern parts of Asia Minor, he returned thither (ib. xix. 1) and remained there τριετίαν (ib. xix.; xx. 31): during which period the founding of the Ephesian church must be dated. From what is implied in Acts xix. and xx., that church was considerable in numbers : and it had enjoyed a more than usual portion of the Apostle's own personal nursing and teaching. It will be important to bear this in mind when we come to consider the question of this section.

4. On his last recorded journey to Jerusalem he sailed by Ephesus, and summoned the elders of the Ephesian church to meet him at Miletus, where he took what he believed to be his last farewell of them, in that most characteristic and wonderful speech, Acts xx. 18—35.

5. At some subsequent time (see Prolegg. to the Pastoral Epistles), he left Timotheus behind in Ephesus, at which place the first Epistle was addressed to him (1 Tim. i. 3), and perhaps (?) the second. The state of the Ephesian church at the time of these Epistles being written, will be found discussed in the Prolegomena to them.

6. Ecclesiastical tradition has connected the Apostle John with

Ephesus: see Vol. I. Prolegg. ch. v. § i. 9 ff.: and his long residence and death there may with safety be assumed.

7. To this church our Epistle is addressed, according to our present text. And there is nothing in its contents inconsistent with such an address. We find in it clear indications that its readers were mixed Jews and Gentiles[9],—that they were in an especial manner united to the Apostle in spiritual privilege and heavenly hope[10]:—that they resided in the midst of an unusually corrupt and profligate people[1].

8. Nor are minor indications wanting, which possess interest as connecting our Epistle with the narrative in the Acts. He had preached to them τὸ εὐαγγέλιον τῆς χάριτος τοῦ θεοῦ, Acts xx. 24 ; and he commits them τῷ λόγῳ τῆς χάριτος αὐτοῦ, ib. ver. 32. In this Epistle alone, not in the contemporary and in some respects similar one to the Colossians, do we find such expressions as δόξης τῆς χάριτος αὐτοῦ, ch. i. 6,—τὰ πλοῦτος τῆς χάριτος αὐτοῦ, ib. 7, and ii. 7,—and an unusual recurrence of χάρις in all its forms and energies. If he preached among them 'the good tidings of the grace of God,' this may well be called 'the Epistle of the grace of God.' In no other of his writings, not even in the Epistle to the Romans, is grace so magnified and glorified. Again in Acts xx. 22 f. we read δεδεμένος ἐγὼ τῷ πνεύματι πορεύομαι εἰς Ἰερουσαλήμ, τὰ ἐν αὐτῇ συναντήσοντά μοι μὴ εἰδώς, πλὴν ὅτι τὸ πνεῦμα τὸ ἅγιον κατὰ πόλιν διαμαρτύρεταί μοι λέγων ὅτι δεσμὰ καὶ θλίψεις με μένουσιν. And accordingly, here only in his Epistles addressed to churches[2], and not in that to the Colossians, do we find him calling himself ὁ δέσμιος (ch. iii. 1; iv. 1).

He had not shrunk from declaring to them πᾶσαν τὴν βουλὴν τοῦ θεοῦ (Acts xx. 27): and accordingly, in this Epistle alone is βουλή used by St. Paul of the divine purpose,—κατὰ τὴν βουλὴν τοῦ θελήματος αὐτοῦ, ch. i. 11.

In Acts xx. 28 it is said of God and the church, ἣν περιεποιήσατο διὰ τοῦ αἵματος τοῦ ἰδίου: and in Eph. i. 14, we have the singular expression εἰς ἀπολύτρωσιν τῆς περιποιήσεως, i. e. of that which He περιεποιήσατο (see note there).

In Acts xx. 32, he commits them to God and the word of His grace, τῷ δυναμένῳ οἰκοδομῆσαι καὶ δοῦναι τὴν κληρονομίαν ἐν τοῖς ἡγιασμένοις πᾶσιν. Not to lay any stress on the frequent recurrence of the image of οἰκοδομή, as being common in other Epistles,—the concluding words can hardly fail to recall Eph. i. 18, τίς ὁ πλοῦτος τῆς δόξης τῆς κληρονομίας αὐτοῦ ἐν τοῖς ἁγίοις,—Eph. i. 14, ὅ ἐστιν ἀρραβὼν τῆς κληρονομίας ἡμῶν,—and v. 5, οὐκ ἔχει κληρονομίαν ἐν τῇ βασιλείᾳ (see Acts xix. 8) τοῦ χριστοῦ καὶ θεοῦ.

9. I would not lay the stress which some have laid on the prevalence of the figure of 'the spiritual building' in this Epistle, as having any

[9] ch. ii. 14 ff. Compare Acts xix. 10.
[10] ch. i. 3 ff. and passim.　　　　[1] ch. iv. 17 ff.; v. 1–13.
[2] The other cases are in those addressed to individuals ; 2 Tim. i. 8. Philem. vv. 1, 9.

12]

connexion with the famous temple of Diana.   We should, I think, be suspicious of such supposed local and temporal references (see on 1 Cor. v. 7),
unless the context (as e. g. in 1 Cor. ix. 24, 25) plainly points them out.

10. But various objections have been brought against the view that
this Epistle was really addressed to the Ephesians.   I will take these
as recently summed up by Conybeare and Howson, Life and Epistles of
St. Paul, vol. ii. pp. 486 ff.

11. *"First, it would be inexplicable that St. Paul, when he wrote to
the Ephesians, amongst whom he had spent so long a time, and to whom he
was bound by ties of such close affection* (Acts xx. 17, &c.), *should not
have a single message of personal greeting to send.   Yet none such are
found in this Epistle."*   It may be well, in dealing with this, to examine
our Apostle's practice in sending these greetings.   They are found in
greatest abundance in the Epistle to the Romans, written to a church
which, as a church, he had never seen, but which, owing to its situation
in the great metropolis, contained many of his own friends and fellow-
labourers, and many friends also of those who were with him at Corinth.
In 1 Cor., written to a church which he had founded, and among whom
he had long resided (Acts xviii. 11), there is not one person saluted by
name[3];—and one salutation only sent, from Aquila and Priscilla.   In
2 Cor., not one personal salutation of either kind.   In Gal., not one: a
circumstance commonly accounted for by the subject and tone of the
Epistle: and if there, why not here also?   In Phil., not one: though
an approach may be said to be made to a personal greeting in μάλιστα
οἱ ἐκ τῆς Καίσαρος οἰκίας.   In Col., the Epistle sent at the same time as
this, and by the same messengers, several of both kinds.   In 1 Thess.
and 2 Thess., none of either kind.   In 1 Tim., *sent to Ephesus* (see
Prolegg. to Pastoral Epistles), none: in 2 Tim., several of both kinds:
in Philemon, salutations *from* brethren, but not *to* any.

The result at which we thus arrive, without establishing any fixed
law as to the Apostle's practice, shews us how little weight such an
objection as this can have.   The Philippians were his dearly beloved,
his joy and his crown: yet not one of them is saluted.   The Galatians
were his little children, of whom he was in labour till Christ should be
formed in them: yet not one is saluted.   The Thessalonians were imitators
of him and of the Lord, patterns to all that believed in Macedonia and
Achaia: yet not one of them is selected for salutation.   The general
salutations found in several of these cases, the total omission of all
salutation in others, seem to follow no rule but the fervour of his own
mind, and the free play of his feeling as he writes.   The more general

---

[3] It is plain that the salutations sent *from persons who were with the Apostle,*
would depend on his circumstances at the time, and on the connexion between those
with him and the church to which he was writing.   When he wrote from Corinth to
Rome they were abundant.

and solemn the subject, the less he seems to give of these individual notices : the better he knows those to whom he is writing, as a whole, the less he seems disposed to select particular persons for his affectionate remembrance. May we not then conceive it to be natural, that in writing to a church with which he had been so long and intimately acquainted, in writing too on so grand and solemn a subject as the constitution and prospects of Christ's universal church, he should pass over all personal notices, referring them as he does to Tychicus, the bearer of the Epistle? I own I am unable to see any thing improbable in this :—but it seems to me, as far as we can trace his practice, to be in accordance with it.

12. "*Secondly, he could not have described the Ephesians as a church whose conversion he knew only by report*" (ch. i. 15).

The answer to this is very simple. First, he nowhere says that he knew their *conversion* only by report, but what he does say is, ἀκούσας τὴν καθ᾽ ὑμᾶς πίστιν ἐν τῷ κυρίῳ Ἰησοῦ, καὶ τὴν [ἀγάπην τὴν] εἰς πάντας τοὺς ἁγίους : an expression having no reference whatever to their conversion, but pointing to the report which he had received of their abounding in Christian graces ;—and perfectly consistent with, nay, explained as it seems to me most simply on, the hypothesis of his having known their previous circumstances well. Any supposition of allusion to their conversion robs the καθ᾽ ὑμᾶς of its fine distributive force, and misses the point of the sentence. But, secondly, if there were any doubt on this point,—if any were disposed to charge us with thus understanding the words merely as a help out of the difficulty,—their meaning is decided for us by the Apostle himself. *Philemon* was his ἀγαπητός and συνεργός (Philem. 1). He was his son in the faith (ib. ver. 19). Yet he addresses him in almost the same words, and in the same connexion with εὐχαριστῶν κ.τ.λ. He says, ἀκούων σου τὴν ἀγάπην καὶ τὴν πίστιν ἣν ἔχεις εἰς τὸν κύριον Ἰησοῦν καὶ εἰς πάντας τοὺς ἁγίους. It is strange that after this had been pointed out, the objection should ever have been again raised.

13. "*Thirdly, he could not speak to them as only knowing himself (the founder of their church) to be an Apostle by hearsay (ch. iii. 2), so as to need credentials to accredit him with them*" (iii. 4).

This objection, as will be seen by the notes on iii. 2, is founded on inattention to the force of εἴ γε[4], and of the aorist ἠκούσατε. The meaning is not, as E. V., 'If ye have heard,' implying a doubt whether they ever had heard, but as given in my note in loc., 'If, that is, ye heard,'—i. e. 'assuming that, when I was with you, ye heard ;' and the words convey a reminiscence of that which they did hear. The *cre-*

---

[4] In Conybeare's version he gives the force of εἴ γε, but, as so often, renders the aorist by a perfect, ' for I suppose that you have heard.'

dential view of ver. 4 falls with this mistaken rendering of ver. 2: not to mention that it could not for a moment stand, even were that other possible, the reference being to what was before written in ch. i. [5]

14. *" Fourthly, he could not describe the Ephesians as so exclusively Gentiles* (ch. ii. 11 ; iv. 17), *and so recently converted"* (v. 8; i. 13 ; ii. 13).

To the former objection I reply, 1) that the Ephesian church, as other churches out of Judæa, would naturally be composed for the most part of Gentiles, and as such would be addressed in the main as Gentiles : so we have him writing to the Romans, xi. 13, ὑμῖν δὲ λέγω τοῖς ἔθνεσιν. And if exception be taken to this reference, and it be understood as rather marking off the Gentile portion of those to whom he was then writing, the same exception cannot be taken to 1 Cor. xii. 2, where, in writing to a mixed church (Acts xviii. 4, 8), he says, almost in the same words as in Eph. ii. 11, οἴδατε ὅτι ὅτε ἔθνη ἦτε, κ.τ.λ. : 2) that in this Epistle, of all others, we might expect to find the distinction between Jew and Gentile pass into the background, the subject being, the constitution and glories of the universal Church : 3) that, as before remarked (under 7), indications are not wanting of the mixed composition of the Ephesian Church. Surely the ἵνα τοὺς δύο κτίσῃ ἐν αὐτῷ εἰς ἕνα καινὸν ἄνθρωπον (ii. 15) would not have been written to a Church exclusively Gentile.

To the latter objection I answer, that in no one of the passages cited is there the slightest intimation of their having been recently converted; —but, if any temporal conclusion can be drawn from them, all three testify rather to a considerable period having elapsed since that event. In ch. v. 8 we have, ἦτε γὰρ ποτὲ σκότος, νῦν δὲ φῶς ἐν κυρίῳ : in i. 13, ἐν ᾧ καὶ πιστεύσαντες ἐσφραγίσθητε . . . : in ii. 13, ὑμεῖς οἱ ποτὲ ὄντες μακρὰν ἐγενήθητε ἐγγύς.

Of the first and third of these, we may observe that the same ποτέ designates *their* unconverted state, by which he designates *his own* in Gal. i. 13, 23 bis, Tit. iii. 3 : yet his conversion was by many years antecedent to that of the Ephesians. Of the second and third, that the aorists serve to remove both the things spoken out of the category of recent events. Had their conversion been recent, and its presence, as an act, still abiding, we should have read perfects here and not aorists [6].

15. Having endeavoured to give a reply to these internal objections to the *Ephesian* view of the Epistle, I go on to notice the *external* difficulties besetting the view which I have taken.

---

[5] This indeed is confessed in Conybeare's note, in loc. p. 497.

[6] The force of the former aorist is preserved in Conybeare's version, "you believed in him and received his seal:" but the latter is made into a perfect, "ye who were once far off have been brought near;" this not being one of those cases where νυνί makes such a rendering in English necessary. See note there.

15]

16. They may be summed up in a discussion of the various reading in ch. i. 1 (see var. readings), by which ἐν Ἐφέσῳ is omitted from the text. Basil the Great, contra Eunom. ii. 19, vol. i. p. 254 f., says : τοῖς Ἐφεσίοις ἐπιστέλλων ὡς γνησίως ἡνωμένοις τῷ ὄντι δι' ἐπιγνώσεως, ὄντας αὐτοὺς ἰδιαζόντως ὠνόμασεν εἰπών· τοῖς ἁγίοις τοῖς οὖσιν καὶ πιστοῖς ἐν χριστῷ Ἰησοῦ. οὕτω γὰρ οἱ πρὸ ἡμῶν παραδεδώκασι, καὶ ἡμεῖς ἐν τοῖς παλαιοῖς τῶν ἀντιγράφων εὑρήκαμεν. From this we infer, that Basil received our Epistle as really written to the Ephesians, but read ch. i. 1 without the words ἐν Ἐφέσῳ, both traditionally, and because he had seen it so read in ancient MSS. The testimony then *does not touch the recognition of the Epistle as written to the Ephesians*, but simply the insertion or omission of the words ἐν Ἐφέσῳ in the text : a matter with which we will deal below.

17. " *This assertion of Basil's is confirmed by Jerome, Epiphanius, and Tertullian.*" C. and H. vol. ii. p. 487.

(a) Jerome : "Quidam . . putant . . . eos qui Ephesi sunt sancti et fideles essentiæ vocabulo nuncupatos, ut . . . ab eo qui EST, hi qui SUNT appellentur. . . . . Alii vero simpliciter non ad eos qui sint (al. sunt), sed qui Ephesi sancti et fideles sint, scriptum arbitrantur." Ad Eph. i. 1, vol. vii. p. 545.

Doubtless this *may* point to the various reading, and I have allowed it in the Digest as a testimony that way · but it is by no means a decisive one. It may be fairly interpreted on the contrary hypothesis, as indeed Meyer takes it. " Eos qui Ephesi sunt sancti et fideles" represents τοῖς ἁγίοις τοῖς οὖσιν ἐν Ἐφέσῳ καὶ πιστοῖς. This he may be assumed to have read without dispute. Then he proceeds to say, that τοῖς οὖσιν was interpreted in two ways : either as an *essentiæ vocabulum*, or as belonging to ἐν Ἐφέσῳ. His whole sentence *need not point to any omission* of the words ἐν Ἐφέσῳ.

(b) " *Epiphanius quotes Eph. iv. 5, 6, from Marcion's* πρὸς Λαοδικέας.*" C. and H. ib., note.

But to this I must demur, for Epiphanius in reality does no such thing. Having cited the words, εἷς κύριος, μία πίστις κ.τ.λ., he proceeds, οὐ γὰρ ἔδοξε τῷ ἐλεεινοτάτῳ Μαρκίωνι ἀπὸ τῆς πρὸς Ἐφεσίους ταύτην τὴν μαρτυρίαν λέγειν, ἀλλ' ἀπὸ τῆς πρὸς Λαοδικέας (i. 3. 12, vol. i. p. 375). Therefore his testimony shews merely what he knew before, that Marcion, among his recognized Epistles of St. Paul, had καὶ πρὸς Λαοδικέας λεγομένης μέρη:—that this passage was one of such μέρη;—and that Epiphanius blames him for not quoting it from the Epistle to the Ephesians, where accordingly we infer that he himself read it.

(c) Tertullian. His testimony is the following, contra Marcion. v. 11, vol. ii. p. 500,—"Praetereo hic et de alia epistola quam nos ad Ephesios praescriptam habemus, haeretici vero ad Laodicenos :" and ib. c. 17, p. 512,—" Ecclesiæ quidem veritate epistolam istam ad Ephesios habemus emissam, non ad Laodicenos, sed Marcion ei titulum aliquando interpolare gestiit, quasi et in isto diligentissimus explorator : nihil autem de titulis interest, cum ad omnes apostolus scripserit, dum ad quosdam."

Hence it is commonly argued, and conceded even by Meyer (Einl. p. 4), that Tertullian did not read the words ἐν Ἐφέσῳ, or he would have charged Marcion with endeavouring to falsify the *text* as well as to supply a new title. Certainly, it might be so: but it might also be, that he used the word *titulum* in a wide sense, including the title and the corresponding portion of the text. It might be again, since, as Epiphanius tells us (see above), Marcion acknowledged only fragments of an Epistle to the Laodiceans, that the beginning of our Epistle was not among them.

18. If it be thought necessary to deal with the fact of the omission of ἐν Ἐφέσῳ in B and other ancient MSS., we may find at least an illustration of it in the words ἐν Ῥώμῃ (Rom. i. 7) being omitted in G al. It seems to have been done with reference to the catholic subject of the Epistle, very possibly by churches among whom it was read, and with a view to generalize the reference of its contents [7].

19. It is necessary now to deal with two hypotheses respecting the readers to whom our Epistle was addressed; both obviously falling to the ground with the genuineness of the words ἐν Ἐφέσῳ, but requiring also separate treatment. The first of these is, that it was to the *Laodiceans*. So (see above) Marcion: so Grot., Hammond, Mill, Pierce, Wetst., Paley, and many more. But this idea has not even tradition to stand on. All the consensus of the ancient Church is against it. It has nothing to rest on but conjecture, arising out of the mention of an Epistle ἐκ Λαοδικείας, in Col. iv. 16, which seems to have induced Marcion to alter the title. No single MS. fills in the gap produced by omitting ἐν Ἐφέσῳ with the words ἐν Λαοδικείᾳ. Again, if this had been really so, is it conceivable that the Laodicean church would without protest and without any remaining sign of their right to the Epistle, have allowed that right to be usurped by the Ephesians and universally acknowledged by the church as theirs? See other minor difficulties of the hypothesis alleged by Meyer, Einl. pp. 9, 10, 19, and Harless, Einl. p. xxxix. This failing, another way has been struck out, possessing much more plausibility, and gaining many more adherents [1]. It has been supposed that the Epistle was *encyclical*, addressed to more churches than Ephesus only. But I cannot help regarding this hypothesis as even less worthy

---

[7] See Meyer, Einl. p. 7.

[1] The hypothesis was started by Usher, in his Annals, on the year 64 ; and is upheld by Bengel, Benson, Michaelis, Schmidt, Eichhorn, Hug, Flatt, Hemsen, Schott, Feilmoser, Schrader, Guerike, Schneckenburger, Neander, Rückert, Credner, Matthies, Harless, Olshausen, Stier, Conybeare and Howson, and many more, with various subhypotheses as to the central church to which it was sent and the means by which it was to be circulated.]

of our acceptance than the other. It has against it, 1) and chiefly, its total discrepancy with the spirit of the Epistle, which, to whomsoever sent, is clearly addressed to one set of persons throughout, coexisting in one place, and as one body, and under the same circumstances: 2) the improbability that the Apostle,.who in two of his Epistles (2 Cor., Gal.) has so plainly specified their encyclical character, should have here omitted all such specification : 3) the even greater improbability that he should have, as on this hypothesis must be assumed, written a circular Epistle to a district of which Ephesus was the commercial capital[2], addressed to various churches within that district, yet from its very contents (as by the opponents' hypothesis) not admitting of application to the church of that metropolis, in which he had spent so long a time, and to which he was so affectionately bound : 4) the inconsistency of this hypothesis with the address of the Epistle, and the universal consensus of the ancient church, who, however they read that address, had no doubt of its being properly entitled. Nor is this objection removed by the form of the hypothesis suggested by C. and H., that copies were sent, differently superscribed, which superscriptions, perplexing the copyists, were left out, and then, as copies of the Epistle became spread over the world,—all imported from Ephesus, it was called 'the Epistle from Ephesus,' and so the name of Ephesus came into the text:—for this would, besides being very far-fetched and improbable, not account for the consensus throughout the church, in the Asiatic portion of which, at least, traces of the accurate addresses would be preserved. 5) Another objection, running counter to 1) but not therefore inconsistent with it, is that if it had been *encyclical*, some notice at least would have been found of special local (or rather *regional*) circumstances, as in those to the Corinthians and Galatians. The absence of such notice might easily be accounted for, if it were indeed written to the Ephesians alone : but not, if to various Asiatic churches, some of which were so far from having the Ephesians' intimacy with the Apostle, that they had never even seen him. There could be no reason for his addressing in common the churches of Laodicea, Hierapolis, Philadelphia, and others (I take the names from C. and H. ii. 489), except the existence of some common special dangers, and need of some common special exhortation, of neither of which do we find any hint. See various ramifications of this hypothesis dealt with and refuted in Meyer, Einl. pp. 11—13.

20. I infer then, in accordance with the prevalent belief of the Church in all ages, that this Epistle was VERITABLY ADDRESSED TO THE SAINTS IN EPHESUS, and TO NO OTHER CHURCH.

---

[2] See C. and H. ii. 489.

SECTION III.

ITS OCCASION, OBJECT, AND CONTENTS.

1. The contents of the Epistle afford no indication of its having sprung out of any *special circumstances* of the Ephesian church. Tychicus and Onesimus were being sent to Colossæ. The former was charged with a weighty Epistle to the church there, arising out of peculiar dangers which beset them; the latter, with a private apostolic letter of recommendation to his former master, also a resident at Colossæ. Under these circumstances, the yearning heart of St. Paul went forth to his Ephesians. He thought of them as a church in Christ of his own planting—as the mystic Body of Christ, growing onwards for an habitation of God through the Spirit. And, full of such thoughts, he wrote this Epistle to them at the same time with, or immediately subsequent to, his penning of that to the Colossians (on their relation, see below, § vi., and principally, Prolegg. to Col. § iv. 4 ff.).

2. This being so, the object of the Epistle is a general one—*to set forth the ground, the course, the aim and end, of the* CHURCH OF THE FAITHFUL IN CHRIST. He speaks to the Ephesians as a type or sample of the Church universal. He writes to them not as an ecclesiastical father, united with others, Timotheus or the like, directing and cautioning them,—but as their Apostle and prisoner in the Lord, bound for them, and set to reveal God's mysteries to them.

3. To this intent and this spirit the contents admirably correspond. Through the whole Epistle, without one exception, we read of ἡ ἐκκλησία in the singular, never of ἐκκλησίαι in the plural. Of this Church, through the whole, he describes the origin and foundation, the work and course, the scope and end. Every where, both in its larger and smaller portions, this threefold division is found. I have endeavoured, in the notes, to point it out, as far as my space would enable me : and those who wish to see it traced yet farther, will find this done even with more minuteness than I should be disposed in every particular to subscribe, in Stier's very elaborate and diffuse commentary. But in fact, the *trichotomy* respecting the Church rests upon another, and sublimer yet. Every where with him the origin and foundation of the Church is in the WILL OF THE FATHER, τοῦ τὰ πάντα ἐνεργοῦντος κατὰ τὴν βουλὴν τοῦ θελήματος αὐτοῦ,—the work and course of the Church is by the SATISFACTION OF THE SON, by our υἱοθεσίαν διὰ Ἰησοῦ χριστοῦ,—the scope and end of the Church is the LIFE IN THE HOLY SPIRIT,— δυνάμει κραταιωθῆναι διὰ τοῦ πνεύματος αὐτοῦ εἰς τὸν ἔσω ἄνθρωπον.

4. The various sections will be found indicated in the notes. I will here give only a general summary of the Epistle.—In ch. i., after the introduction of the subject by an ascription of praise to the Father,

19]

who chose us to be holy to Himself in Christ by the Spirit[3], he opens the counsel of the Father[4], whose will it was to sum up all things in Christ[5], and above all His Church[6], composed of Jews and Gentiles, believers in Christ, and sealed with His Spirit. Then with a sublime prayer, that the eyes of their hearts might be enlightened to see the magnitude of the matter[7], he brings in the PERSON OF CHRIST[8], exalted above all for His Church's sake, to which God hath given Him as Head over all things. Thence[9] he passes to the fact of their own vivification in and with Christ, and the fellowship of the mystery which he, the Apostle of the Gentiles, was set to proclaim to the world, viz. that spiritual life, by which, rooted and grounded in love, they might come to know the knowledge-passing love of Christ, that they might be filled up to all the fulness of God. Thus having laid forth the ground, course, and scope of the Church, he ends this first part of his Epistle with a sublime doxology[1].

The rest from ch. iv. 1, is principally hortatory : but here also we have the same tripartite division. For he begins by explaining[2] the constitution of the Church, in unity and charity and spiritual gifts, by Christ : then[3] he exhorts to all these graces which illustrate the Christian life,—laying the foundation of each in the counsel of God towards us,—and proposing to us their end, our salvation and God's glory. And this he carries[4] into the common duties of ordinary life—into wedlock, and filial and servile relations. After this, in a magnificent peroration[5], he exhorts to the putting on of the Christian armour, by which the great end of the militant Church may be attained, to withstand in the evil day, and having accomplished all things, to stand firm. And most aptly, when this is concluded, he sums up all with the Catholic benediction and prayer of ch. vi. 23, 24.

SECTION IV.

AT WHAT TIME AND PLACE IT WAS WRITTEN.

1. When St. Paul wrote our Epistle, he was a PRISONER ; ch. iii. 1; iv. 1; vi. 20. This narrows our choice of time to two occasions, supposing it to have been written before the period when the history in the Acts terminates :

A) his imprisonment at Jerusalem and Cæsarea (Acts xxi. 27—xxvi. 32), from Pentecost 58, to the autumn of 60 (see Chronological Table in Vol. II. Prolegg. pp. 23—25):

B) his imprisonment at Rome, commencing in February 61, and lasting to the end of the history in the Acts, and probably longer.

[3] ver. 3 ff.	[4] ver. 8 ff.	[5] ver. 10.	[6] ver. 11 ff.
[7] ver. 15 ff.	[8] ver. 20 ff.	[9] ch. ii. 1 ff.	[1] iii. 20 f.
[2] ch. iv. 1—16.	[3] iv. 17. v. 21.	[4] v. 22—vi. 9.	[5] vi. 10—20.

2. Further, the three Epistles, to the Colossians, Ephesians, and Philemon, it can hardly be questioned, were sent at one and the same time. The two former are connected as well by their great similarity of contents, as by the fact that Tychicus was the common bearer of both : the two latter, by the common mention of Onesimus as sent to Colossæ, and the common mention of Epaphras, Marcus, Aristarchus, Demas, Lucas, as sending salutations. In speaking therefore of the time and place of writing this Epistle, we are dealing with those others likewise.

3. The view (A) has been taken by some distinguished scholars of modern times in Germany ; Schulz (Stud. u. Krit. 1829, p. 612 f.), Schneckenburger (Beitr. p. 144 f.), Schott, Böttger, Wiggers (Stud. u. Krit. 1811, p. 436 ff.), Thiersch (die Kirche im apostol. Zeitalter, 1852, p. 176), and Meyer (Einl. p. 15 ff.).

4. The arguments by which it is supported are best and most compendiously stated by Meyer, and are as follows :—

a) Because it is more natural and probable that the slave Onesimus fled from Colossæ to Cæsarea, than that he undertook a long sea-voyage to Rome.

b) If our Epistle and that to the Colossians were sent from Rome, Tychicus and his fellow-traveller Onesimus would arrive first at Ephesus and then at Colossæ: in which case we might expect that St. Paul would, in his notice of Tychicus to the Ephesians (ch. vi. 21, 22), have named Onesimus also, as he has done in Col. iv. 8, 9, to gain for his beloved Onesimus a good reception in Ephesus also. Whereas, if Tychicus and Onesimus travelled from Cæsarea, they would come first, according to the purpose of Onesimus's journey, to Colossæ, where the slave would be left with his master,—and thence to Ephesus : in which case Onesimus would naturally be named in the Epistle to the Colossians, and not in that to the Ephesians.

c) In Eph. vi. 21, ἵνα δὲ εἰδῆτε καὶ ὑμεῖς—καί shews that, when Tychicus should arrive at Ephesus, he would already have reported the affairs of the Apostle to some others. These others are the Colossians, whom Paul knew that he would visit *first :* which again speaks for Cæsarea, and not for Rome, as the place of writing. Had it been the latter, the καί would have appeared in Col. iv. 8, not in Eph. vi. 21.

d) In Philem. 22, the Apostle begs Philemon to prepare him a lodging, and seems to anticipate occupying it soon ; which assumes a direct journey to Phrygia after his liberation, which he would reach almost contemporaneously with the arrival of Onesimus. Now it appears from Phil. ii. 24, that on his liberation from his *Roman* imprisonment, he intended to go to Macedonia, which is inconsistent with visiting Philemon.

5. The view (B) has been the general belief from ancient times

downwards. Its upholders urge that every circumstance of the Epistle fits it ; and reply to the considerations urged above,

a) That there is no weight in this : a fugitive slave would be in fact more likely than otherwise to get on board ship and take refuge in the great metropolis. And there, notwithstanding what Meyer says to the contrary, he would be more likely to escape the search of the 'fugitivarii,' whose knowledge and occupation, we may presume, were principally local, hardly in strict organization over the whole empire.

b) This evidently requires, to be good for any thing, the assumption, that it fell in with the Apostle's plan, to recommend Onesimus to the Ephesians. But in the absence of any allusion to personal matters in this Epistle,—in the reference of all such things to Tychicus,—accordant with the very *general* purpose and subject of the Epistle itself, this assumption cannot be received. Meyer argues that the *general* character of our Epistle cannot be pleaded with regard to the one passage in it which is individual and personal. But surely, it is perfectly legitimate to say, even with regard to such a passage, that the same plan, which induced the Apostle to insert only one such passage in the Epistle, would also induce him to insert one personal notice only in such passage. To found an argument on any such omission in our Epistle, would be unsafe.

c) This, it is maintained, falls entirely to the ground on the different rendering of καί, adopted in the following commentary (see note in loc.),— viz. referring it, not to another party who were to receive notices of the Apostle, besides those to whom he was writing, but to the reciprocal introduction of ὑμεῖς, 'you also concerning me, as I have been long treating concerning you.'

d) No argument can be raised on ground so entirely uncertain as this. It is very possible that altered circumstances may from time to time have changed the Apostle's plans ; and that, as we have some reason to believe his projected journey to Spain (Rom. xv. 22—24) to have been relinquished, or at all events postponed,—so also other projected journeys may have been, according as different churches seemed to require his presence, or new fields of missionary work to open before him. Besides which, it may be fairly said, that there is nothing inconsistent in the two expressions, of Phil. ii. 23 and Philem. 22, with the idea of the Apostle projecting a land journey through Greece to Asia Minor : or at all events a general visitation, by what route he may not as yet have determined, which should embrace both Philippi and Colossæ.

6. On the positive side of this view (B), it is alleged, that the circumstances of the Roman imprisonment suit those of these Epistles better than those of the Cæsarean. From Eph. vi. 19, 20, we gather that he had a certain amount of freedom in preaching the Gospel, which is

hardly consistent with what we read in Acts xxiv. 23 of his imprisonment at Cæsarea, where, from the necessity of the case, a stricter watch
was requisite (cf. Acts xxiii. 21), and none but those ascertained to be
his friends (οἱ ἴδιοι αὐτοῦ) were permitted to see him.　Among any such
multitude of Jews as came to his lodgings on the other occasion, Acts
xxviii. 23 ff., might easily be introduced some of the conspirators, against
whom he was being guarded.

　　Besides, we may draw some inference from his *companions*, as mentioned in these Epistles.　Tychicus, Onesimus, Aristarchus, Marcus,
Jesus Justus, Epaphras, Lucas, Demas, were all with him.　Of these
it is very possible that Lucas and Aristarchus may have been at
Cæsarea during his imprisonment, for we find them both accompanying
him to Rome, Acts xxvii. 1, 2.　But it certainly is not so probable that
all these were with him at one time in Cæsarea.　The two, Lucas and
Aristarchus, are confessedly common to both hypotheses.　Then we
may safely ask, In which of the two places is it more probable that six
other of his companions were found gathered round him ?　In the great
metropolis, where we already know, from Rom. xvi., that so many of
the brethren were sojourning,—or at Cæsarea, which, though the most
important place in Palestine, would have no attraction to gather so
many of his friends, except the prospect of sailing thence with him,
which we know none of them did ?

　　Perhaps this is a question which never can be definitely settled, so as
absolutely to preclude the Cæsarean hypothesis : but I own it appears
to me that the whole weight of probability is on the Roman side.
Those who firmly believe in the genuineness of this Epistle, will find
another reason why it should be placed at Rome, at an interval of from
three to five years after the Apostle's parting with the Ephesians in
Acts xx., rather than at Cæsarea, so close upon that event.　In this
latter case, the absence of all special notices would be far more surprising
than it is at present.

　　7. We may then, I believe, safely assume that our Epistle was
written FROM ROME,—and that probably during the period comprised
in Acts xxviii. 30, before St. Paul's imprisonment assumed that harsher
character which seems to come before us in the Epistle to the Philippians (see Prolegg. to that Epistle, § iii.).

　　8. This would bring the time of writing it within the limits A.D.
61—63 : and we should not perhaps be far wrong in dating it A.D. 62.

SECTION V.

ITS LANGUAGE AND STYLE.

　　1. As might be expected from the account given of the object of our

Epistle in § iii., the thoughts and language are elevated and sublime; and that to such a degree, that it takes, in this respect, a place of its own among the writings of St. Paul: ὑψηλῶν σφόδρα γέμει τῶν νοημάτων καὶ ὑπερόγκων· ἃ γὰρ μηδαμοῦ σχεδὸν ἐφθέγξατο, ταῦτα ἐνταῦθα δηλοῖ, Chrys., who subjoins examples of this from ch. iii. 10; ii. 6; iii. 5. Theophylact says, ἐπεὶ οὖν δεισιδαίμων τε ἦν οὕτως ἡ πόλις, καὶ οὕτω σοφοῖς ἐκόμα, πολλῇ σπουδῇ κέχρηται Παῦλος πρὸς τοὺς τοιούτους γράφων, καὶ τὰ βαθύτερα δὲ τῶν νοημάτων καὶ ὑψηλότερα αὐτοῖς ἐπίστευσεν, ἅτε κατηχημένοις ἤδη. So also Grotius, in his preface: "Paulus jam vetus in apostolico munere, et ob Evangelium Romæ vinctus, ostendit illis quanta sit vis Evangelii præ doctrinis omnibus: quomodo omnia Dei consilia ab omni ævo eo tetenderint, quam admiranda sit in eo Dei efficacia, rerum sublimitatem adæquans verbis sublimioribus quam ulla unquam habuit lingua humana." Witsius, in his Meletemata Leidensia (p. 192; cited by Dr. Eadie, Commentary on the Ephesians, Introd. p. xxxi) thus characterizes it: "Ita vero universam religionis Christianæ summam divina hac epistola exponit, ut exuberantem quandam non sermonis tantum evangelici παῤῥησίαν, sed et Spiritus Sancti vim et sensum, et charitatis Christianæ flammam quandam ex electo illo pectore emicantem, et lucis divinæ fulgorem quendam admirabilem inde elucentem, et fontem aquæ vivæ inde scaturientem, aut ebullientem potius, animadvertere liceat: idque tanta copia, ut superabundans illa cordis plenitudo, ipsa animi sensa intimosque conceptus, conceptus autem verba prolata, verba denique priora quæque subsequentia, premant, urgeant, obruant."

2. These characteristics contribute to make our Epistle *by far the most difficult of all the writings of St. Paul.* Elsewhere, as in the Epistles to the Romans, Galatians, and Colossians, the difficulties lie for the most part at or near the surface: a certain degree of study will master, not indeed the mysteries of redemption which are treated of, but the contextual coherence, and the course of the argument: or if not so, will at least serve to point out to every reader where the hard texts lie, and to bring out into relief each point with which he has to deal: whereas here the difficulties lie altogether beneath the surface; are not discernible by the cursory reader, who finds all very straightforward and simple. We may deduce an illustration from secular literature. Every moderately advanced schoolboy believes he can construe Sophocles; he does not see the difficulties which await him, when he becomes a mature scholar, in that style apparently so simple. So here also, but for a different reason. All on the surface is smooth, and flows on unquestioned by the untheological reader: but when we begin to enquire, why thought succeeds to thought, and one cumbrous parenthesis to another,— depths under depths disclose themselves, wonderful systems of parallel allusion, frequent and complicated underplots; every word, the more we search, approves itself as set in its exact logical place; we see every phrase contributing, by its

own similar organization and articulation, to the carrying out of the organic whole. But this result is not won without much labour of thought, —without repeated and minute laying together of portions and expressions,—without bestowing on single words and phrases, and their succession and arrangement, as much study as would suffice for whole sections of the more exoteric Epistles.

3. The student of the Epistle to the Ephesians must not expect to go over his ground rapidly ; must not be disappointed, if the week's end find him still on the same paragraph, or even on the same verse, weighing and judging,—penetrating gradually, by the power of the mind of the Spirit, through one outer surface after another,—gathering in his hand one and another ramifying thread, till at last he grasps the main cord whence they all diverged, and where they all unite,—and stands rejoicing in his prize, deeper rooted in the faith, and with a firmer hold on the truth as it is in Christ.

4. And as the wonderful effect of the Spirit of inspiration on the mind of man is nowhere in Scripture more evident than in this Epistle, so, to discern those things of the Spirit, is the spiritual mind here more than any where required. We may shew this by reference to De Wette, one of the ablest of Commentators. I have mentioned above, § i. 6, that he approaches this Epistle with an unfortunate and unworthy prejudgment of its spuriousness. He never thinks of applying to it that humble and laborious endeavour which rendered his commentary on the Romans among the most valuable in existence. It is not too much to say, that on this account he has missed almost every point in the Epistle : that his Handbuch, in this part of it, is hardly better than works of third-rate or fourth-rate men : and just for this reason—that he has never come to it with any view of learning from it, but with the averted eyes of a prejudiced man. Take, as a contrast, the two laborious volumes of Stier. Here, I would not deny, we have the opposite course carried into extreme : but with all Stier's faults of two minute classification,—of wearisome length in exegesis,—of unwillingness to lose, and attempts to combine, every divergent sense of the same passage,—we have the precious and most necessary endowment of spiritual discernment,—acquaintance with the analogy of the faith. And in consequence, the acquisition to the Church of Christ from his minute dissection of this Epistle has been most valuable ; and sets future students, with regard to it, on higher spiritual ground than they ever occupied before.

5. It is not to be wondered at, where the subject is *sui generis*, and treated of in a method and style unusually sublime, that the ἅπαξ λεγόμενα should be in this Epistle more in number than common, as well as the ideas and images peculiar to it. The student will find both these pointed out and treated of in the references and the notes. I would again impress on him, as against De Wette and others, that all such

phænomena, instead of telling against its genuineness, are in its favour, and that strongly. Any skilful forger would not perhaps make his work a mere cento from existing undoubted expressions of St. Paul, but at all events would write on new matter in the Apostle's well-known phraseology, avoiding all words and ideas which were in his writings entirely without example.

SECTION VI.

ITS RELATION TO THE EPISTLE TO THE COLOSSIANS.

1. I reserve the full discussion of this subject to the chapter on the Epistle to the Colossians. It would be premature, until the student is in full possession of the object and occasion of that Epistle, to institute our comparison between the two.

2. It may suffice at present to say what may be just enough, as regards the distinctive character of the Epistle to the Ephesians. And this may be done by remarking, that we have here, in the midst of words and images common to the two, an entire absence of all controversial allusion, and of all assertion as against maintainers of doctrinal error. The Christian state, and its realization in the Church, is the one subject, and is not disturbed by any looking to the deviations from that state on either hand, nor guarded, except from that fundamental and directly subversive error of impure and unholy practice.

CHAPTER III.

THE EPISTLE TO THE PHILIPPIANS.

SECTION I.

ITS AUTHORSHIP AND INTEGRITY.

1. IT has been all but universally believed that this Epistle was written by St. Paul. Indeed, considering its peculiarly Pauline psychological character, the total absence from it of all assignable motive for falsification, the spontaneity and fervour of its effusions of feeling, he must be a bold man who would call its authorship in question[1].

---

[1] Meyer quotes from Rilliet, Commentaire, Genève, 1841: "Si parmi les écrits de Paul il est vu, qui plus d'autres porte l'empreinte de la spontanéité, et repousse toute apparence de falsification motivée par l'intérêt d'une secte, c'est sans contredit l'épitre aux Philippiens."

2. Yet this has been done, partially by Schrader (der Apost. Paulus, vol. v.: see especially p. 233, line 14 from bottom, and following), who supposed ch. iii. 1—iv. 9 interpolated, as well as shorter passages elsewhere, conceding however the Pauline authorship in the main: and entirely by Baur (Paulus Ap. Jesu Christi u.s.w., pp. 458—475), on his usual ground of later Gnostic ideas being found in the Epistle. To those who would see an instance of the very insanity of hypercriticism, I recommend the study of these pages of Baur. They are almost as good by way of burlesque, as the "Historic Doubts respecting Napoleon Buonaparte" of Abp. Whately. According to him, all *usual* expressions prove its spuriousness, as being taken from other Epistles: all *unusual* expressions prove the same, as being from another than St. Paul. Poverty of thought, and want of point, are charged against it in one page: in another, excess of point, and undue vigour of expression. Certainly the genuineness of the Epistle will never suffer in the great common-sense verdict of mankind, from Baur's attack. There is hardly an argument used by him, that may not more naturally be reversed and turned against himself.

3. In external testimonies, our Epistle is rich.

(a) Polycarp, ad Philipp. iii. p. 1008, testifies to the fact of St. Paul having written to them,

. . . . Παύλου . . . . ὃς καὶ ἀπὼν ὑμῖν ἔγραψεν [2] ἐπιστολάς, εἰς ἃς ἐὰν ἐγκύπτητε, δυνηθήσεσθε οἰκοδομεῖσθαι εἰς τὴν δοθεῖσαν ὑμῖν πίστιν.

(β) And ib. xi., pp. 1013 f., he writes,

"Ego autem nihil tale sensi in vobis, vel audivi, in quibus laboravit beatus Paulus, qui estis (laudati) in principio epistolæ ejus. De vobis etenim gloriatur in omnibus ecclesiis quæ Deum solæ tunc cognoverant." Cf. Phil. i. 5 ff.

(γ) Irenæus, iv. 18. 4, p. 251:

"Quemadmodum et Paulus Philippensibus (iv. 18) ait: Repletus sum acceptis ab Epaphrodito, quæ a vobis missa sunt, odorem suavitatis, hostiam acceptabilem, placentem Deo."

(δ) Clement of Alexandria, Pædag. i. 6 (52), p. 129 P.:

αὐτοῦ ὁμολογοῦντος τοῦ Παύλου περὶ ἑαυτοῦ οὐχ ὅτι ἤδη ἔλαβον ἢ ἤδη τετελείωμαι κ.τ.λ. Phil. iii. 12—14.

In Strom. iv. 3 (12), p. 569 P., he quotes Phil. ii. 20: in id. 5 (19), p. 572, Phil. i. 13: in id. 13 (94), p. 604, Phil. i. 29, 30; ii. 1 ff., 17; i. 7; and ii. 20 ff., &c. &c.

(ε) In the Epistle of the Churches of Lyons and Vienne, in Euseb.

---

[2] Not necessarily to be understood of more than one Epistle. See Coteler and Hefele in loc.

H. E. v. 2, the words ὃς ἐν μορφῇ θεοῦ ὑπάρχων οὐχ ἁρπαγμὸν ἡγήσατο τὸ εἶναι ἴσα θεῷ are cited. Cf. Phil. ii. 6.

(ζ) Tertullian, de resurr. carnis, c. 23, vol. ii. p. 826:

"Ipse (Paulus, from the preceding sentence) cum Philippensibus scribit: siqua, inquit, concurram in resuscitationem quæ est a mortuis, non quia jam accepi aut consummatus sum," &c. &c. Phil. iii. 11 ff.

(η) The same author devotes the 20th chapter of his fifth book against Marcion (p. 522 f.) to testimonies from this Epistle, and shews that Marcion acknowledged it. And de præscr. c. 36, p. 49, among the places to which 'authenticæ literæ' of the Apostle's 'recitantur,' he says, 'habes Philippos.'

(θ) Cyprian, Testt. iii. 39, p. 756:

"Item Paulus ad Philippenses: Qui in figura Dei constitutus," &c. ch. ii. 6—11.

4. It has been hinted above, that Schrader doubted the *integrity* of our Epistle. This has also been done in another form by Heinrichs, who fancied it made up of two letters,—one to the Church, containing chaps. i. ii., to ἐν κυρίῳ iii. 1, and iv. 21—23: the other to private friends, beginning at τὰ αὐτὰ γράφειν, iii. 1, and containing the rest with the above exception. Paulus also adopted a modification of this view. But it is hardly necessary to say, that it is altogether without foundation. The remarks below (§ iv.) on its style will serve to account for any seeming want of exact juncture between one part and another.

SECTION II.

FOR WHAT READERS AND WITH WHAT OBJECT IT WAS WRITTEN.

1. The city of PHILIPPI has been described, and the πρώτη τῆς μερίδος τῆς Μακεδονίας πόλις, κολωνία discussed, in the notes on Acts xvi. 12 ff., to which the student is referred. I shall now notice only the foundation and condition of the Philippian Church.

2. The Gospel was first planted there by Paul, Silas, and Timotheus (Acts xvi. 12 ff.), in the second missionary journey of the Apostle, in A.D. 51. (See Chron. Table in Prolegg. to Acts.) There we read of only a few conversions, which however became a rich and prolific seed of future fruit. He must have visited it again on his journey from Ephesus into Macedonia, Acts xx. 1; and he is recorded to have done so (a third time), when, owing to a change of plan to avoid the machinations of his enemies, the Jews at Corinth, he returned to Asia through Macedonia; see Acts xx. 6. But we have no particulars of either of these visits.

3. The cruel treatment of the Apostle at Philippi (Acts xvi. l. c. 1 Thess. ii. 2) seems to have combined with the charm of his personal fervour of affection to knit up a bond of more than ordinary love between him and the Philippian Church. They alone, of all churches, sent subsidies to relieve his temporal necessities, on two several occasions, immediately after his departure from them (Phil. iv. 15, 16 ; 1 Thess. ii. 2) : and they revived the same good office to him shortly before the writing of this Epistle (Phil. iv. 10, 18 ; 2 Cor. xi. 9).

4. This affectionate disposition may perhaps be partly accounted for by the fact of *Jews* being so few at Philippi. There was no synagogue there, only a προσευχή by the river side : and the opposition to the Apostle arose not from Jews, but from the masters of the dispossessed maiden, whose hope of gain was gone. Thus the element which resisted St. Paul in every Church, was wanting, or nearly so, in the Philippian. His fervent affection met there, and almost there only, with a worthy and entire return. And all who know what the love of a warm-hearted people to a devoted minister is, may imagine what it would be between such a flock and such a shepherd. (See below, on the style of the Epistle.)

5. But while this can hardly be doubted, it is equally certain that the Church at Philippi was in danger from Jewish influence : not indeed among themselves [3], but operating on them from without (ch. iii. 2),— through that class of persons whom we already trace in the Epistle to the Galatians, and see ripened in the Pastoral Epistles, who insisted on the Mosaic law as matter of external observance, while in practice they gave themselves up to a life of lust and self-indulgence in depraved conscience.

6. The slight trace which is to be found in ch. iv. 2, 3, of the fact related Acts xvi. 13, that the Gospel at Philippi was first received by female converts, has been pointed out in the notes there.

7. The general state of the Church may be gathered from several hints in this Epistle and others. They were *poor*. In 2 Cor. viii. 1, 2, we read that ἡ κατὰ βάθους πτωχεία αὐτῶν ἐπερίσσευσεν εἰς τὸ πλοῦτος τῆς ἁπλότητος αὐτῶν. They were *in trouble*, and probably from persecution : compare 2 Cor. viii. 2 with Phil. i. 28—30. They were *in danger of*, if not already in, *quarrel and dissension* (cf. ch. ii. 1—4 ; and i. 27 ; ii. 12, 14 ; iv. 2) ; on what account, we cannot say ; it may be, as has been supposed by De W., that they were peculiarly given to spiritual pride and mutual religious rivalry and jealousy. This may have arisen out of their very progress and flourishing state as a Church engendering pride. Credner supposes (Davidson, p. 381), that it may have

---

[3] This has been supposed, by Eichhorn, Storr, Flatt, &c., but certainly without reason. De W. and Dr. Davidson refer (ii. 380) with praise to Schinz, Die christliche Gemeinde zu Philippi, ein exegetischer Versuch, 1833, which I have not seen.

been a spiritual form of the characteristic local infirmity, which led them to claim the title πρώτη πόλις for their city ; but this falls to the ground, if πρώτη be geographically explained : see note Acts xvi. 12.

8. The *object* of the Epistle seems to have been no marked and definite one, but rather the expression of the deepest Christian love, and the exhortation, generally, to a life in accordance with the Spirit of Christ. Epaphroditus had brought to the Apostle the contribution from his beloved Philippians ; and on occasion of his return, he takes the opportunity of pouring out his heart to them in the fulness of the Spirit, refreshing himself and them alike by his expressions of affection, and thus led on by the inspiring Spirit of God to set forth truths, and dilate upon motives, which are alike precious for all ages, and for every Church on earth.

SECTION III.

AT WHAT TIME AND PLACE IT WAS WRITTEN.

1. It has been believed, universally in ancient times (Chrys., Euthal., Athanas., Thdrt., &c.), and almost without exception (see below) in modern, that our Epistle was written *from Rome*, during the imprisonment whose beginning is related in Acts xxviii. 30, 31.

2. There have been some faint attempts to fix it at Corinth (Acts xviii. 11, so Oeder, in Meyer), or at Cæsarea (so Paulus and Böttger, and Rilliet hesitatingly ; see Meyer). Neither of these places will suit the indications furnished by the Epistle. The former view surely needs no refuting. And as regards the latter it may be remarked, that the strait between life and death, expressed in ch. i. 21—23, would not fit the Apostle's state in Cæsarea, where he had the appeal to Cæsar in his power, putting off at all events such a decision for some time. Besides which, the Καίσαρος οἰκία, spoken of ch. iv. 22, cannot well be the πραιτώριον τοῦ Ἡρώδου at Cæsarea of Acts xxiii. 35, and therefore it is by that clearer notice that the πραιτώριον of ch. i. 13 must be interpreted (see note there), not vice versâ. It was probably the barrack of the prætorian guards, attached to the palatium of Nero.

3. Assuming then that the Epistle was written from Rome, and during the imprisonment of Acts xxviii. ultt., it becomes an interesting question, to *which part of that imprisonment* it is to be assigned.

4. On comparing it with the three contemporaneous Epistles, to the Colossians, to the Ephesians, and to Philemon, we shall find a marked difference. In them we have (Eph. vi. 19, 20) freedom of preaching the Gospel implied : here (ch. i. 13—18) much more stress is laid upon his bondage, and it appears that others, not he himself, preached the Gospel, and made the fact of his imprisonment known. Again, from this same

passage it would seem that a considerable time had elapsed since his imprisonment: enough for "his bonds" to have had the general effects there mentioned. This may be inferred also from another fact: the Philippians had heard of his imprisonment,—had raised and sent their contribution to him by Epaphroditus,—had heard of Epaphroditus's sickness,—of the effect of which news on them he (Epaphroditus) had had time to hear, ch. ii. 26, and was now recovered, and on his way back to them. These occurrences would imply four casual journeys from Rome to Philippi. Again (ch. ii. 19, 23) he is expecting a speedy decision of his cause, which would hardly be while he was dwelling as in Acts xxviii. ultt.

5. And besides all this, there is a spirit of anxiety and sadness throughout this Epistle, which hardly agrees with the two years of the imprisonment in the Acts, nor with the character of those other Epistles. His sufferings are evidently not the chain and the soldier only. Epaphroditus's death would have brought on him λύπην ἐπὶ λύπην (ch. ii. 27): there was then a λύπη before. He is now in an ἀγών—in one not, as usual, between the flesh and the spirit, not concerning the long-looked for trial of his case, but one of which the Philippians had heard (ch. i. 29, 30), and in which they shared by being persecuted too: some change in his circumstances, some intensification of his imprisonment, which had taken place before this time.

6. And if we examine history, we can hardly fail to discover what this was, and whence arising. In February, 61, St. Paul arrived in Rome (see Chron. Table in Prolegg. to Acts, Vol. II.). In 62[4], Burrus, the prætorian præfect, died, and a very different spirit came over Nero's government: who in the same year divorced Octavia, married Poppæa[5], a Jewish proselyte[6], and exalted Tigellinus, the principal promoter of that marriage, to the joint prætorian præfecture. From that time, Nero began 'ad deteriores inclinare[7]:' Seneca lost his power: 'validior in dies Tigellinus[8]:' a state of things which would manifestly deteriorate the condition of the Apostle, and have the effect of hastening on his trial. It will not be unreasonable to suppose that, some little time after the death of Burrus (Feb., 63, would complete the διετία ὅλη of Acts xxviii. 30), he was removed from his own house into the πραιτώριον, or barrack of the prætorian guards attached to the palace, and put into stricter custody, with threatening of immediate peril of his life. Here it would be very natural that some of those among the prætorians who had had the custody of him before, should become agents in giving the publicity to "his bonds," which he mentions ch. i. 13. And

---

[4] Tacit. Annal. xiv. 51.   See Clinton's Fasti Romani, i. p. 44.
[5] Tacit. Annal. xiv. 60.   [6] Jos. Antt. xx. 8. 11.
[7] Tacit. Annal. xiv. 52.   [8] Tacit. Annal. xiv. 57.

such a hypothesis suits eminently well all the circumstances of our Epistle.

7. According to this, we must date it shortly after Feb., 63 : when now the change was fresh, and the danger imminent. Say for its date then, the summer of 63.

SECTION IV.

LANGUAGE AND STYLE.

1. The language of this Epistle is thoroughly Pauline. Baur has indeed selected some phrases which he conceives to savour of the vocabulary of the later Gnosticism, but entirely without ground. All those which he brings forward, οὐχ ἁρπαγμὸν ἡγήσατο,—ἑαυτὸν ἐκένωσεν,—μορφὴ θεοῦ,—σχῆμα,—καταχθόνιοι,—may easily be accounted for without any such hypothesis : and, as has been already observed in Prolegg. to Ephesians, peculiar expressions may just as well be held to have descended from our Epistles to the Gnostics, as vice versâ.

2. The mention of ἐπίσκοποι καὶ διάκονοι in ch. i. 1, has surprised some. I have explained in the note there, that it belongs probably to the late date of our Epistle. But it need surprise no one, however that may be: for the terms are found in an official sense, though not in formal conjunction, in speeches made, and Epistles written long before this : e. g. in Acts xx. 28 ; Rom. xvi. 1.

3. In style, this Epistle, like all those where St. Paul writes with fervour, is discontinuous and abrupt, passing rapidly from one theme to another [1] ; full of earnest exhortations [2], affectionate warnings [3], deep and wonderful settings-forth of his individual spiritual condition and feelings [4], of the state of Christians [5] and of the sinful world [6],—of the loving counsels of our Father respecting us [7], and the self-sacrifice and triumph of our Redeemer [8].

4. No Epistle is so warm in its expressions of affection [9]. Again and again we have ἀγαπητοί and ἀδελφοί recurring : and in one place, ch. iv. 1, he seems as if he hardly could find words to pour out the fulness of his love—ὥστε, ἀδελφοί μου ἀγαπητοὶ καὶ ἐπιπόθητοι, χαρὰ καὶ στέφανός

---

[1] e. g., ch. ii. 18, 19,—24, 25,—30, iii. 1,—2, 3, 4,—14, 15, &c.

[2] See ch. i. 27, iii. 16, iv. 1. ff., 4, 5, 8, 9.

[3] See ch. ii. 3, 4, 14 ff., iii. 2, 17—19.

[4] See ch. i. 21—26, ii. 17, iii. 4—14, iv. 12, 13.

[5] See ch. ii. 15, 16, iii. 3, 20, 21.

[6] See ch. iii. 18, 19.

[7] See ch. i. 6, ii. 13, iv. 7, 19.

[8] See ch. ii. 4—11.

[9] See ch. i. 7, 8, ii. 1, 2, iv. 1.

μου, οὕτως στήκετε ἐν κυρίῳ, ἀγαπητοί. We see how such a heart, penetrated to its depths by the Spirit of God, could love. We can see how that feeble frame, crushed to the very verge of death itself, shaken with fightings and fears, burning at every man's offence, and weak with every man's infirmity, had yet its sweet refreshments and calm resting-places of affection. We can form some estimate,—if the bliss of reposing on human spirits who loved him was so great,—how deep must have been his tranquillity, how ample and how clear his fresh springs of life and joy, in HIM, of whom he could write, ζῶ δὲ οὐκ ἔτι ἐγὼ, ζῇ δὲ ἐν ἐμοὶ χριστός (Gal. ii. 20) : and of whose abiding power within him he felt, as he tells his Philippians (ch. iv. 13), πάντα ἰσχύω ἐν τῷ ἐνδυναμοῦντί με.

CHAPTER IV.

THE EPISTLE TO THE COLOSSIANS.

SECTION I.

AUTHORSHIP.

1. THAT this Epistle is a genuine work of St. Paul, was never doubted in ancient times : nor did any modern critic question the fact, until Schrader[1], in his commentary, pronounced some passages suspicious, and led the way in which Baur[2] and Meyerhoff[3] followed. In his later work, Baur entirely rejects it[4]. The grounds on which these writers rest, are partly the same as those already met in the Prolegomena to the Ephesians. The Epistle is charged with containing phrases and ideas derived from the later heretical philosophers,—an assertion, the untenableness of which I have there shewn as regards that Epistle, and almost the same words would suffice for this. Even De Wette disclaims and refutes their views, maintaining its genuineness : though, as Dr. Davidson remarks, "it is strange that, in replying to them so well, he was not led to question his own rejection of the authenticity of the Ephesian Epistle."

2. The arguments drawn from considerations peculiar to this Epistle, its diction and style, will be found answered under § iv.

3. Among many external testimonies to its genuineness and authenticity are the following :

(a) Justin Martyr, contra Tryph. 85, p. 182, calls our Lord πρωτότοκος πάσης κτίσεως (Col. i. 15), and similarly § 84, p. 181 ; 100, p. 195.

---

[1] Der Apost. Paulus, v. 175 ff.
[2] Die sogenannt. Pastoralbr. p. 79 : Ursprung der Episcop. p. 35.
[3] Der Br. an die Col., &c. Berlin, 1838.
[4] Paulus, Apost. Jesu Christi, pp. 417-57.

(β) Theophilus of Antioch, ad Autolycum, ii. 22, p. 365, has : τοῦτον τὸν λόγον ἐγέννησε προφορικόν, πρωτότοκον πάσης κτίσεως.

These may perhaps hardly be conceded as direct quotations. But the following are beyond doubt :

(γ) Irenæus, iii. 14. 1, p. 201 :

"Iterum in ea epistola quæ est ad Colossenses, ait : 'Salutat vos Lucas medicus dilectus.'" (ch. iv. 14.)

(δ) Clement of Alexandria, Strom. i. 1 (15), p. 325 P. :

κἂν τῇ πρὸς Κολοσσαεῖς ἐπιστολῇ, "νουθετοῦντες," γράφει, "πάντα ἄνθρωπον καὶ διδάσκοντες κ.τ.λ." (ch. i. 28.)

In Strom. iv. 7 (56), p. 588, he cites ch. iii. 12 and 14 :—in Strom. v. 10 (61, ff.), p. 682 f.,—ch. i. 9—11, 28, ch. ii. 2 ff., ch. iv. 2, 3 ff. In id. vi. 8 (62), p. 771, he says that Παῦλος ἐν ταῖς ἐπιστολαῖς calls τὴν Ἑλληνικὴν φιλοσοφίαν ' στοιχεῖα τοῦ κόσμου ' (Col. ii. 8).

(ε) Tertullian, de præscr. hæret. c. 7, vol. ii. p. 20 :

"A quibus nos Apostolus refrænans nominatim philosophiam testatur caveri oportere, scribens ad Colossenses : videte, ne quis sit circumveniens vos &c." (ch. ii. 8.)

And de Resurr. carnis, c. 23, vol. ii. p. 825 f. :

"Docet quidem Apostolus Colossensibus scribens . . . ." and then he cites ch. ii. 12 ff., and 20,—iii. 1, and 3.

(ζ) Origen, contra Cels. v. 8, vol. i. p. 583 :

παρὰ δὲ τῷ Παύλῳ . . . . τοιαῦτ' ἐν τῇ πρὸς Κολασσαεῖς λέλεκται· μηδεὶς ὑμᾶς καταβραβευέτω θέλων κ.τ.λ. (ch. ii. 18, 19.)

4. I am not aware that the integrity of the Epistle has ever been called in question. Even those who are so fond of splitting and portioning out other Epistles, do not seem to have tried to subject this to that process.

SECTION II.

FOR WHAT READERS AND WITH WHAT OBJECT IT WAS WRITTEN.

1. COLOSSÆ, or (for of our two oldest MSS.,—א writes one (a) in the title and subscription, and the other (o) in ch. i. 2 ; and B has a with o written above by 1. m. in the title and subscription, and o in ch. i. 2) COLASSÆ, formerly a large city of Phrygia (ἀπίκετο (Xerxes) ἐς Κολοσσάς, πόλιν μεγάλην Φρυγίας, Herod. vii. 30 : ἐξελαύνει (Cyrus) διὰ Φρυγίας . . . . . εἰς Κολοσσάς, πόλιν οἰκουμένην, εὐδαίμονα καὶ μεγάλην, Xen. Anab. i. 2. 6) on the river Lycus, a branch of the Mæander (ἐν τῇ Λύκος ποταμὸς ἐς χάσμα γῆς ἐσβαλὼν ἀφανίζεται[5], ἔπειτα διὰ σταδίων ὡς μάλιστά κη

---

[5] See this chasm accounted for in later ages by a *Christian legend*, Conyb. and Hows., edn. 2, vol. ii. p. 480, note.

πέντε ἀναφαινόμενος, ἐκδιδοῖ καὶ οὗτος ἐς τὸν Μαίανδρον. Herod. ibid.).
In Strabo's time it had lost much of its importance, for he describes
Apamea and Laodicea as the principal cities in Phrygia, and then says,
περίκειται δὲ ταύταις καὶ πολίσματα, among which he numbers Colossæ.
For a minute and interesting description of the remains and neighbourhood, see Smith's Dict. of Ancient Geography, sub voce. From what is
there said it would appear, that Chonæ (*Khonos*), which has, since the
assertion of Nicetas, the Byzantine historian who was born there [6], been
taken for Colossæ, is in reality about three miles S. from the ruins of
the city.

2. The Church at Colossæ consisted principally of Gentiles, ch. ii. 13.
To whom it owed its origin, is uncertain. From our interpretation of
ch. ii. 1 (see note there), which we have held to be logically and contextually necessary, the Colossians are included among those who had
not seen St. Paul in the flesh. In ch. i. 7, 8, Epaphras is described as
πιστὸς ὑπὲρ ἡμῶν διάκονος τοῦ χριστοῦ, and as ὁ καὶ δηλώσας ἡμῖν τὴν
ὑμῶν ἀγάπην ἐν πνεύματι: and in speaking of their first hearing and
accurate knowledge of the grace of God in truth, the Apostle adds
καθὼς ἐμάθετε ἀπὸ Ἐπαφρᾶ τοῦ ἀγαπητοῦ συνδούλου ἡμῶν. As this is
not [7] καθὼς καὶ ἐμάθετε, we may safely conclude that the ἐμάθετε refers
to that first hearing, and by consequence that Epaphras was the founder
of the Colossian Church. The time of this founding must have been
subsequent to Acts xviii. 23, where St. Paul went καθεξῆς through
Galatia and Phrygia, στηρίζων πάντας τοὺς μαθητάς: in which journey
he could not have omitted the Colossians, had there been a Church
there.

3. In opposition to the above conclusion, there has been a strong
current of opinion that the Church at Colossæ *was founded by St. Paul.*
Theodoret seems to be the first who took this view (Introd. to his
Commentary). His argument is founded mainly on what I believe to
be a misapprehension of ch. ii. 1 [8], and also on a partial quotation of

---

[6] So also Theophylact on ch. i. 2, πόλις Φρυγίας αἱ Κολοσσαί, αἱ νῦν λεγόμεναι
Χῶναι.

[7] The rec. has the καί: see var. readd. Its insertion would certainly primâ facie
change the whole face of the passage as regards Epaphras, and make him into an accessory teacher, after the ᾗ ἡμέρᾳ ἠκούσατε. Still, such a conclusion would not be
necessary. It might merely carry on the former καθὼς καί, or it might introduce a
particular additional to ἐπέγνωτε, specifying the accordance of that knowledge with
Epaphras's teaching.

[8] His words are: ἔδει δὲ συνιδεῖν τῶν ῥητῶν τὴν διάνοιαν. βούλεται γὰρ εἰπεῖν, ὅτι
οὐ μόνον ὑμῶν ἀλλὰ καὶ τῶν μὴ τεθεαμένων με πολλὴν ἔχω φροντίδα. εἰ γὰρ τῶν μὴ
ἑωρακότων αὐτὸν μόνον τὴν μέριμναν περιέφερε, τῶν ἀπολαυσάντων αὐτοῦ τῆς θέας καὶ
τῆς διδασκαλίας οὐδεμίαν ἔχει φροντίδα. Leaving the latter argument to go for what
it is worth, it will be at once seen that the οὐ μόνον view falls into the logical difficulty
mentioned in the note in loc., and fails to account for the αὐτῶν.

Acts xviii. 23, from which he infers that the Apostle must have visited Colossæ in that journey, adducing the words διῆλθε τὴν Φρυγίαν καὶ τὴν Γαλατικὴν χώραν, but without the additional clause στηρίζων πάντας τοὺς μαθητάς.

4. The same position was taken up and very elaborately defended by Lardner, ch. xiv. vol. ii. p. 472. His arguments are chiefly these:

1) The improbability that the Apostle should have been twice in Phrygia and not have visited its principal cities.

2) The Apostle's assurance of the fruitful state of the Colossian Church, ch. i. 6, 23 ; ii. 6, 7.

3) The kind of mention which is made of Epaphras, shewing him not to have been their first instructor: laying stress on the καθὼς καί in ch. i. 7 (rec. reading, but see above, par. 2), and imagining that the recommendations of him at ch. i. 7, 8, iv. 12, 13, were sent to prevent his being in ill odour with them for having brought a report of their state to St. Paul,—and that they are inconsistent with the idea of his having founded their Church.

4) He contends that the Apostle does in effect say that he had himself dispensed the Gospel to them, ch. i. 21—25.

5) He dwells on the difference (as noted by Chrysostom in his Pref. to Romans, but not with this view) between St. Paul's way of addressing the Romans and Colossians on the same subject, Rom. xiv. 1, 2, Col. ii. 20—23 ; and infers that as the Romans were not his own converts, the Colossians must have been.

6) From ch. ii. 6, 7, and similar passages as presupposing his own foundership of their Church.

7) "If Epaphras was sent to Rome by the Colossians to enquire after Paul's welfare, as may be concluded from ch. iv. 7, 8, that token of respect for the Apostle is a good argument of personal acquaintance. And it is allowed, that he had brought St. Paul a particular account of the state of affairs in this Church. Which is another argument that they were his converts."

8) Ch. i. 8, "who declared unto us your love in the Spirit," is "another good proof of personal acquaintance."

9) Ch. iii. 16, as shewing that the Colossians were endowed with spiritual gifts, which they could have received only from an Apostle.

10) From ch. ii. 1, 2, interpreting it as Theodoret above.

11) From the ἄπειμι of ch. ii. 5, as implying previous presence.

12) From ch. iv. 7—9, as "full proof that Paul was acquainted with them, and they with him."

13) From the salutations in ch. iv. 10, 11, 14, and the appearance of Timotheus in the address of the Epistle, as implying that the Colossians were acquainted with St. Paul's fellow-labourers, and consequently with himself.

36]

14) From the counter salutations in ch. iv. 15.

15) From ch. iv. 3, 4, and 18, as "demands which may be made of strangers, but are most properly made of friends and acquaintance."

16) From the Apostle's intimacy with Philemon, an inhabitant of Colossæ, and his family; and the fact of his having converted him. "Again, ver. 22, St. Paul desires Philemon to prepare him a lodging. Whence I conclude that Paul had been at Colossæ before."

5. To all the above arguments it may at once be replied, that based as they are upon mere verisimilitude, they must give way before the fact of the Apostle never having once directly alluded to his being their father in the faith, as he does so pointedly in 1 Cor. iii. 6, 10 ; in Gal. i. 11 ; iv. 13 : Phil. ii. 16 ; iii. 17 ; iv. 9 : 1 Thess. i. 5 ; ii. 1, &c. Only in the Epistles to the Romans and Ephesians, besides here, do we find such notice wanting : in that to the Romans, from the fact being otherwise : in that to the Ephesians, it may be from the general nature of the Epistle, but it may also be because he was not entirely or exclu sively their founder : see Acts xviii. 19—28.

6. Nor would such arguments from verisimilitude stand against the logical requirements of ch. ii. 1. In fact, all the inferences on which they are founded will, as may be seen, full as well bear turning the other way, and ranging naturally and consistently enough under the other hypothesis. The student will find them all treated in detail in Dr. Davidson's Introduction, vol. ii. pp. 402—406.

7. It may be interesting to enquire, if the Church at Colossæ owed its origin not to St. Paul, but to Epaphras, why it was so, and at what period we may conceive it to have been founded. Both these questions, I conceive, will be answered by examining that which is related in Acts xix., of the Apostle's long sojourn at Ephesus. During that time, we are told, ver. 10,—τοῦτο δὲ ἐγένετο ἐπὶ ἔτη δύο, ὥστε πάντας τοὺς κατοικοῦντας τὴν Ἀσίαν ἀκοῦσαι τὸν λόγον τοῦ κυρίου, Ἰουδαίους τε καὶ Ἕλληνας : — and this is confirmed by Demetrius, in his complaint ver. 26,—θεωρεῖτε καὶ ἀκούετε ὅτι οὐ μόνον Ἐφέσου, ἀλλὰ σχεδὸν πάσης τῆς Ἀσιας ὁ Παῦλος οὗτος πείσας μετέστησεν ἱκανὸν ὄχλον. So that we may well conceive, that during this time Epaphras, a native of Colossæ, and Philemon and his family, also natives of Colossæ, and others, may have fallen in with the Apostle at Ephesus, and become the seeds of the Colossian Chu.ch. Thus they would be dependent on and attached to the Apostle, many of them personally acquainted with him and with his colleagues in the ministry. This may also have been the case with them at Laodicea and them at Hierapolis, and thus Pauline Churches sprung up here and there in Asia, while the Apostle confined himself to his central post at Ephesus, where, owing to the concourse to the temple, and the communication with Europe, he found so much and worthy occupation.

37]

8. I believe that this hypothesis will account for the otherwise strange phænomena of our Epistle, on which Lardner and others have laid stress, as implying that St. Paul had been among them : for their personal regard for him, and his expressions of love to them : for his using, respecting Epaphras, language hardly seeming to fit the proximate founder of their Church :—for the salutations and counter salutations.

9. The enquiry into the occasion and object of this Epistle will be very nearly connected with that respecting the state of the Colossian Church, as disclosed in it.

10. It will be evident to the most cursory reader that there had sprung up in that Church a system of erroneous teaching, whose tendency it was to disturb the spiritual freedom and peace of the Colossians by ascetic regulations : to divide their worship by inculcating reverence to angels, and thus to detract from the supreme honour of Christ.

11. We are not left to infer respecting the class of religionists to which these teachers belonged : for the mention of νουμηνία and σάββατα in ch. ii. 16, at once characterizes them as Judaizers, and leads us to the then prevalent forms of Jewish philosophy, to trace them. Not that these teachers were *merely Jews;* they were Christians : but their fault was, the attempt to mix with the free and spiritual Gospel of Christ the theosophy and angelology of the Jews of their time, in which they had probably been brought up. Of such theosophy and angelology we find ample traces in the writings of Philo, and in the notices of the Jewish sect of the Essenes given us by Josephus[9].

12. It does not seem necessary to mark out very strictly the position of these persons as included within the limits of this or that sect known among the Jews : they were infected with the ascetic and theosophic notions of the Jews of their day, who were abundant in Phrygia[1] : and they were attempting to mix up these notions with the external holding of Christianity.

13. There must have been also mingled in with this erroneous Judaistic teaching, a portion of the superstitious tendencies of the Phrygian character, and, as belonging to the Jewish philosophy, much of that incipient Gnosticism which afterwards ripened out into so many strange forms of heresy.

14. It may be noticed that the Apostle does not any where in this Epistle charge the false teachers with immorality of life, as he does the very similar ones in the Pastoral Epistles most frequently. The infer-

---

[9] Cf. B. J. ii. 8. 2—13, where, beginning τρία γὰρ παρὰ Ἰουδαίοις εἴδη φιλοσοφεῖται, he gives a full account of the Essenes. Among other things he relates that they took oaths συντηρήσειν τά τε τῆς αἱρέσεως αὐτῶν βιβλία, καὶ τὰ τῶν ἀγγέλων ὀνόματα.

[1] See Jos. Antt. xii. 3. 4, where Alexander the Great is related to have sent, in consequence of the disaffection of Lydia and Phrygia, two thousand Mesopotamian and Babylonian Jews to garrison the towns.

ence from this is plain. The false teaching was yet in its bud. Later down, the bitter fruit began to be borne; and the mischief required severer treatment. Here, the false teacher is εἰκῆ φυσιούμενος ὑπὸ τοῦ νοὸς τῆς σαρκὸς αὑτοῦ (ch. ii. 18) : in 1 Tim. iv. 2, he is κεκαυτηριασμένος τὴν ἰδίαν συνείδησιν : ib. vi. 5, διεφθαρμένος τὸν νοῦν, ἀπεστερημένος τῆς ἀληθείας, νομίζων πορισμὸν εἶναι τὴν εὐσέβειαν. Between these two phases of heresy, a considerable time must have elapsed, and a considerable development of practical tendencies must have taken place.

15. Those who would see this subject pursued further, may consult Meyer and De Wette's Einleitungen : Davidson's Introduction, vol. ii. pp. 407—424, where the various theories respecting the Colossian false teachers are mentioned and discussed : and Professor Eadie's Literature of the Epistle, in the Introduction to his Commentary.

16. The occasion then of our Epistle being the existence and influence of these false teachers in the Colossian Church, the object of the Apostle was, to set before them their real standing in Christ : the majesty of His Person, and the completeness of His Redemption : and to exhort them to conformity with their risen Lord : following this out into all the subordinate duties and occasions of common life.

SECTION III.

TIME AND PLACE OF WRITING.

1. I have already shewn in the Prolegg. to the Ephesians that that Epistle, together with this, and that to Philemon, were written and sent at the same time : and have endeavoured to establish, as against those who would date the three from the imprisonment at Cæsarea, that it is much more natural to follow the common view, and refer them to that imprisonment at Rome, which is related in Acts xxviii. ultt.

2. We found reason there to fix the date of the three Epistles in A.D. 61 or 62, during that freer portion of the imprisonment which preceded the death of Burrus : such freedom being implied in the notices found both in Eph. vi. 19, 20, and Col. iv. 3, 4, and in the whole tone and spirit of the three Epistles as distinguished from that to the Philippians.

SECTION IV.

LANGUAGE AND STYLE : CONNEXION WITH THE EPISTLE TO THE EPHESIANS.

1. In both language and style, the Epistle to the Colossians is peculiar. But the peculiarities are not greater than might well arise from the fact, that the subject on which the Apostle was mainly writing was

39]

one requiring new thoughts and words. Had not the Epistle to the Romans ever been written, that to the Galatians would have presented as peculiar words and phrases as this Epistle now does.

2. It may be well to subjoin a list of the ἅπαξ λεγόμενα in our Epistle:

ἀρέσκεια, ch. i. 10.	νουμηνία, ib. 16.
δυναμόω, ib. 11.	καταβραβεύω, ib. 18.
ὁρατός, ib. 16.	ἐμβατεύω, ib. 18.
πρωτεύω, ib. 18.	δογματίζω, ib. 20.
εἰρηνοποιέω, ib. 20.	ἀπόχρησις, ib. 22.
μετακινέω, ib. 23.	λόγον ἔχειν, ib. 23.
ἀνταναπληρόω, ib. 24.	ἐθελοθρήσκεια, ib. 23.
πιθανολογία, ch. ii. 4.	ἀφειδία, ib. 23.
στερέωμα, ib. 5.	πλησμονή, ib. 23.
συλαγωγέω, ib. 8.	αἰσχρολογία, ch. iii. 8.
φιλοσοφία, ib. 8.	μομφή, ib. 13.
θεότης, ib. 9.	βραβεύω, ib. 15.
σωματικῶς, ib. 9.	εὐχάριστος, ib. 15.
ἀπέκδυσις, ib. 11.	ἀθυμέω, ib. 21.
χειρόγραφον, ib. 14.	ἀνταπόδοσις, ib. 24.
προσηλόω, ib. 14.	ἀνεψιός, ch. iv. 10.
ἀπεκδύω, ch. ii. 15; ch. iii. 9.	παρηγορία, ib. 11.

δειγματίζω, ib 15 (?) (see Matt. i. 19).

3. A very slight analysis of the above will shew us to what they are chiefly owing. In ch. i. we have *seven*: in ch. ii., *nineteen* or *twenty*: in ch. iii., *seven*: in ch. iv., *two*. It is evident then that the nature of the subject in ch. ii. has introduced the greater number. At the same time it cannot be denied that St. Paul does here express some things differently from his usual practice: for instance, ἀρέσκεια, δυναμόω, πρωτεύω, εἰρηνο- ποιέω, μετακινέω, πιθανολογία, ἐμβατεύω, μομφή, βραβεύω, all are pecu- liarities, owing not to the necessities of the subject, but to *style*: to the peculiar frame and feeling with which the writer was expressing himself, which led to his using these unusual expressions rather than other and more customary ones. And we may fairly say, that there is visible throughout the controversial part of our Epistle, a loftiness and artificial elaboration of style, which would induce precisely the use of such expres- sions. It is not uncommon with St. Paul, when strongly moved or sharply designating opponents, or rising into majestic subjects and thoughts, to rise also into unusual, or long and compounded words: see for examples, Rom. i. 24—32; viii. 35—39; ix. 1—5; xi. 33—36; xvi. 25—27, &c., and many instances in the Pastoral Epistles. It is this σεμνότης of controversial tone, even more than the necessity of the subject handled, which causes our Epistle so much to abound with peculiar words and phrases.

4. And this will be seen even more strongly, when we turn to the Epistle to the Ephesians, sent at the same time with the present letter. In writing both, the Apostle's mind was in the same general frame— full of the glories of the Person of Christ, and the consequent glorious privileges of His Church, which is built on Him, and vitally knit to Him. This mighty subject, as he looked with indignation on the beggarly system of meats and drinks and hallowed days and angelic mediations to which his Colossians were being drawn down, rose before him in all its length and breadth and height ; but as writing to *them*, he was confined to one portion of it, and to setting forth that one portion pointedly and controversially. He could not, consistently with the effect which he would produce on them, dive into the depths of the divine counsels in Christ with regard to them. At every turn, we may well conceive, he would fain have gone out into those wonderful prayers and revelations which would have been so abundant if he had had free scope : but at every turn, οὐκ εἴασεν αὐτὸν τὸ πνεῦμα Ἰησοῦ : the Spirit bound him to a lower region, and would not let him lose sight of the βλέπετε μή τις, which forms the ground-tone of this Colossian Epistle. Only in the setting forth of the majesty of Christ's Person, so essential to his present aim, does he know no limits to the sublimity of his flight. When he approaches those who are Christ's, the urgency of their conservation, and the duty of marking the contrast to their deceivers, cramps and confines him for the time.

5. But the Spirit which thus bound him to his special work while writing to the Colossians, would not let His divine promptings be in vain. While he is labouring with the great subject, and unable to the Colossians to express all he would, his thoughts are turned to another Church, lying also in the line which Tychicus and Onesimus would take : a Church which he had himself built up stone by stone ; to which his affection went largely forth : where if the same baneful influences were making themselves felt, it was but slightly, or not so as to call for special and exclusive treatment. He might pour forth to his Ephesians all the fulness of the Spirit's revelations and promptings, on the great subject of the Spouse and Body of Christ. To them, without being bound to narrow his energies evermore into one line of controversial direction, he might lay forth, as he should be empowered, their foundation in the counsel of the Father, their course in the satisfaction of the Son, their perfection in the work of the Spirit.

6. And thus,—as a mere human writer, toiling earnestly and conscientiously towards his point, pares rigidly off the thoughts and words, however deep and beautiful, which spring out of and group around his subject, putting them by and storing them up for more leisure another day : and then on reviewing them, and again awakening the spirit which prompted them, playfully unfolds their germs, and amplifies their sug-

41]

gestions largely, till a work grows beneath his hands more stately and more beautiful than ever that other was, and carrying deeper conviction than it ever wrought :—so, in the higher realms of the fulness of Inspiration, may we conceive it to have been with our Apostle. His Epistle to the Colossians is his caution, his argument, his protest : is, so to speak, his working-day toil, his direct pastoral labour : and the other is the flower and bloom of his moments, during those same days, of devotion and rest, when *he* wrought not so much in the Spirit, as the Spirit wrought in *him*. So that while we have in the Colossians, system defined, language elaborated, antithesis, and logical power, on the surface—we have in the Ephesians the free outflowing of the earnest spirit, —to the mere surface-reader, without system, but to him that delves down into it, in system far deeper, and more recondite, and more exquisite : the greatest and most heavenly work of one, whose very imagination was peopled with the things in the heavens, and even his fancy rapt into the visions of God.

7. Thus both Epistles sprung out of one Inspiration, one frame of mind : that to the Colossians first, as the task to be done, the protest delivered, the caution given : that to the Ephesians, begotten by the other, but surpassing it : carried on perhaps in some parts simultaneously, or immediately consequent. So that we have in both, many of the same thoughts uttered in the same words [2] ; many terms and phrases peculiar to the two Epistles ; many instances of the same term or phrase, still sounding in the writer's ear, but used in the two in a different connexion. All these are taken by the impugners of the Ephesian Epistle as tokens of its spuriousness : I should rather regard them as psychological phænomena strictly and beautifully corresponding to the circumstances under which we have reason to believe the two Epistles to have been written : and as fresh elucidations of the mental and spiritual character of the great Apostle.

[2] See reff.: tables of these have been given by the Commentators. I will not repeat them here, simply because to complete such a comparison would require far more room and labour than I could give to it, and I should not wish to do it as imperfectly as those mere formal tables have done it. The student may refer to Davidson, vol. ii. p. 391.

CHAPTER V.

THE FIRST EPISTLE TO THE THESSALONIANS.

SECTION I.

ITS AUTHORSHIP.

1. This Epistle has been all but universally recognized as the undoubted work of St. Paul. It is true (see below) that no reliable citations from it appear in the Apostolic Fathers: but the external evidence from early times is still far too weighty to be set aside.

2. Its authorship has in modern times been called in question (1) by Schrader, and (2) by Baur, on internal grounds. Their objections, which are entirely of a subjective and most arbitrary kind, are reviewed and answered by De Wette, Meyer, and Dr. Davidson (Introd. to N. T. vol. ii. pp. 454 ff.)[1]: and have never found any acceptance, even in Germany.

3. The external testimonies of antiquity are the following:

Irenæus adv. Hær. v. 6. 1, p. 299 f.: "Et propter hoc apostolus seipsum exponens, explanavit perfectum et spiritualem salutis hominem, in prima epistola ad Thessalonicenses dicens sic: Deus autem pacis sanctificet vos perfectos," &c. (1 Thess. v. 23.)

---

[1] I must, in referring to Dr. Davidson, not be supposed to concur in his view of the Apostle's expectation in the words ἡμεῖς οἱ ζῶντες οἱ περιλειπόμενοι (1 Thess. iv. 15, 17). See my note there.

There is a very good statement of Baur's adverse arguments, and refutation of them, in Jowett's work on the Thessalonians, Galatians, and Romans, "Genuineness of the first Epistle," vol. i. 15—26. In referring to it, I must enter my protest against the views of Professor Jowett on points which lie at the very root of the Christian life: views as unwarranted by any data furnished in the Scriptures of which he treats, as his reckless and crude statement of them is pregnant with mischief to minds unaccustomed to biblical research. Among the various phænomena of our awakened state of apprehension of the characteristics and the difficulties of the New Testament, there is none more suggestive of saddened thought and dark foreboding, than the appearance of such a book as Professor Jowett's. Our most serious fears for the Christian future of England, point, it seems to me, just in this direction: to persons who allow fine æsthetical and psychological appreciation, and the results of minute examination of spiritual feeling and mental progress in the Epistles, to keep out of view that other line of testimony to the fixity and consistency of great doctrines, which is equally discoverable in them. I have endeavoured below, in speaking of the matter and style of our Epistle to meet some of Professor Jowett's assertions and inferences of this kind.

Clem. Alex. Pædag. i. 5 (19), p. 109 P. : τοῦτό τοι σαφέστατα ὁ μακάριος Παῦλος ὑπεσημήνατο, εἰπών· δυνάμενοι ἐν βάρει εἶναι κ.τ.λ. to ἑαυτῆς τέκνα (1 Thess. ii. 6).

Tertullian de resurr. carnis, § 24, vol. ii. p. 828 : "Et ideo majestas Spiritus sancti perspicax ejusmodi sensuum et in ipsa ad Thessalonicenses epistola suggerit : De temporibus autem . . . . . quasi fur nocte, ita adveniet." (1 Thess. v. 1 f.)

SECTION II.

FOR WHAT READERS AND WITH WHAT OBJECT IT WAS WRITTEN.

1. THESSALONICA was a city of Macedonia, and in Roman times, capital of the second district of the province of Macedonia (Liv. xlv. 29 f.), and the seat of a Roman prætor (Cic. Planc. 41). It lay on the Sinus Thermaicus, and is represented to have been built on the site of the ancient Therme (Θέρμη ἡ ἐν τῷ Θερμαίῳ κόλπῳ οἰκημένη, ἀπ' ἧς καὶ ὁ κόλπος οὗτος τὴν ἐπωνυμίην ἔχει, Herod. vii. 121), or peopled from this city (Pliny seems to distinguish the two : 'medioque flexu littoris Thessalonica, liberæ conditionis. Ad hanc, a Dyrrhachio cxv mil. pas., Therme.' iv. 10) by Cassander, son of Antipater, and named after his wife Thessalonice, sister of Alexander the Great (so called from a victory obtained by his father Philip on the day when he heard of her birth) [2]. Under the Romans it became rich and populous (ἡ νῦν μάλιστα τῶν ἄλλων εὐανδρεῖ, Strab. vii. 7: see also Lucian, Asin. c. 46, and Appian, Bell. Civ. iv. 118), was an 'urbs libera' (see Pliny, above), and in later writers bore the name of "metropolis." "Before the founding of Constantinople it was virtually the capital of Greece and Illyricum, as well as of Macedonia : and shared the trade of the Ægean with Ephesus and Corinth" (C. and H. edn. 2, vol. i. p. 380). Its importance continued through the middle ages, and it is now the second city in European Turkey, with 70,000 inhabitants, under the slightly corrupted name of Saloniki. For further notices of its history and condition at various times, see C. and H. i. pp. 378-83 : Winer, RWB. sub voce (from which mainly the above notice is taken) : Dr. Holland's Travels : Lewin, vol. i. p. 252.

2. The church at Thessalonica was founded by St. Paul, in company with Silas and Timotheus [3], as we learn in Acts xvii. 1—9. Very little

---

[2] So Strabo, vii. excerpt. 10 : μετὰ τὸν Ἄξιον ποταμόν, ἡ Θεσσαλονίκη ἐστὶν πόλις, ἡ πρότερον Θέρμη ἐκαλεῖτο· κτίσμα δ' ἐστὶν Κασσάνδρου· ὃς ἐπὶ τῷ ὀνόματι τῆς ἑαυτοῦ γυναικός, παιδὸς δὲ Φιλίππου τοῦ Ἀμύντου, ὠνόμασεν· μετῴκισεν δὲ τὰ πέριξ πολίχνια εἰς αὐτήν· οἷον Χαλάστραν, Αἰνείαν (see Dion. Hal., Antiq. i. 49), Κίσσον, καί τινα καὶ ἄλλα.

[3] That this latter was with Paul and Silas, though not expressly mentioned in the

is there said which can throw light on the origin or composition of the Thessalonian church. The main burden of that narrative is the rejection of the Gospel by the Jews there. It is however stated (ver. 4) that some of the Jews believed, and consorted with Paul and Silas ; and of the devout Greeks a great multitude, and of the chief women not a few.

3. But some account of the Apostle's employment and teaching at Thessalonica may be gathered from this narrative, connected with hints dropped in the two Epistles. He came to them, yet suffering from his persecution at Philippi (1 Thess. ii. 2). But they received the word joyfully, amidst trials and persecutions (ib. i. 6 ; ii. 13), and notwithstanding the enmity of their own countrymen and of the Jews (ii. 14 ff.). He maintained himself by his labour (ib. ii. 9), although his stay was so short [4], in the same spirit of independence which characterized all his apostolic course. He declared to them boldly and clearly the Gospel of God (ii. 2). The great burden of his message to them was the approaching coming and kingdom of the Lord Jesus (i. 10 ; ii. 12, 19 ; iii. 13 ; iv. 13—18 ; v. 1—11, 23, 24. Acts xvii. 7 : see also § iv. below), and his chief exhortation, that they would walk worthily of this their calling to that kingdom and glory (ii. 12 ; iv. 1 ; v. 23).

4. He left them, as we know from Acts xvii. 5—10, on account of a tumult raised by the unbelieving Jews ; and was sent away by night by the brethren to Berœa, together with Silas and Timotheus (Acts xvii. 10). From that place he wished to have revisited Thessalonica : but was prevented (1 Thess. ii. 18), by the arrival, with hostile purposes, of his enemies the Thessalonian Jews (Acts xvii. 13), in consequence of which the brethren sent him away by sea to Athens.

5. Their state after his departure is closely allied with the enquiry as to the object of the Epistle. The Apostle appears to have felt much anxiety about them : and in consequence of his being unable to visit them in person, seems to have determined, during the hasty consultation previous to his departure from Berœa, to be left at Athens, which was the destination fixed for him by the brethren, alone, and to send Timotheus back to Thessalonica to ascertain the state of their faith [5].

Acts, is inferred by comparing Acts xvi. 3, xvii. 14, with 1 Thess. i. 1 ; 2 Thess. i. 1 ; 1 Thess. iii. 1—6.

[4] We are hardly justified in assuming, with Jowett, that it was only three weeks. For " three Sabbaths," even if they mark the whole stay, may designate four weeks : and we are not compelled to infer that a Sabbath may not have passed at the beginning, or the end, or both, on which he did not preach in the synagogue. Indeed the latter hypothesis is very probable, if he was following the same course as afterwards at Corinth and Ephesus, and on the Jews proving rebellious and unbelieving, separated himself from them : at which, or something approaching to it, the προσεκληρώθησαν τῷ Παύλῳ κ. τῷ Σίλᾳ of Acts xvii. 4 may perhaps be taken as pointing.

[5] I cannot see how this interpretation of the difficulty as to the mission of Timotheus

6. The nature of the message brought to the Apostle at Corinth (Acts xviii. 5) by Timotheus on his arrival there with Silas, must be inferred from what we find in the Epistle itself. It was, in the main, favourable and consolatory (1 Thess. iii. 6—10). They were firm in faith and love, as indeed they were reputed to be by others who had brought to him news of them (i. 7—10), full of affectionate remembrance of the Apostle, and longing to see him (iii. 6). Still, however, he earnestly desired to come to them, not only from the yearnings of love, but because he wanted to fill up τὰ ὑστερήματα τῆς πίστεως αὐτῶν (iii. 10). Their attention had been so much drawn to one subject—his preaching had been so full of one great matter, and from the necessity of the case, so scanty on many others which he desired to lay forth to them, that he already feared lest their Christian faith should be a distorted and unhealthy faith. And in some measure, Timotheus had found it so. They were beginning to be restless in expectation of the day of the Lord (iv. 11 ff.),—neglectful of that pure, and sober, and temperate walk, which is alone the fit preparation for that day (iv. 3 ff. ; v. 1—9), —distressed about the state of the dead in Christ, who they supposed had lost the precious opportunity of standing before Him at His coming (iv. 13 ff.).

7. This being so, he writes to them to build up their faith and love, and to correct these defects and misapprehensions. I reserve further consideration of the contents of the Epistle for § iv., 'On its matter and style.'

SECTION III.

PLACE AND TIME OF WRITING.

1. From what has been said above respecting the state of the Thessalonian Church as the occasion for writing the Epistle, it may readily be inferred that no considerable time had elapsed since the intelligence of that state had reached the Apostle. Silas and Timotheus were with him (i. 1): the latter had been the bearer of the tidings from Thessalonica.

2. Now we know (Acts xviii. 5) that they rejoined him at Corinth, apparently not long after his arrival there. That rejoining then forms

---

lies open to the charge of "diving beneath the surface to pick up what is really on the surface," and thus of "introducing into Scripture a hypercritical and unreal method of interpretation, which may be any where made the instrument of perverting the meaning of the text." (Jowett, i. p. 120.) Supposing that at Berœa it was fixed that Timotheus should not accompany St. Paul to Athens, but go to Thessalonica, and that the Apostle should be deposited at Athens and left there alone, the brethren returning, what words could have more naturally expressed this than διὸ μηκέτι στέγοντες εὐδοκήσαμεν καταλειφθῆναι ἐν Ἀθήναις μόνοι?

our *terminus a quo*. And it would be in the highest degree unnatural
to suppose that the whole time of his stay at Corinth (a year and six
months, Acts xviii. 11) elapsed before he wrote the Epistle,—founded as
it is on the intelligence which he had heard, and written with a view to
meet present circumstances. CORINTH therefore may safely be assumed
as the place of writing.

3. His stay at Corinth ended with his setting sail for the Pentecost
at Jerusalem in the spring of 54 (see chron. table in Prolegg. to Acts,
Vol. II.). It would begin then with the autumn of 52. And in the
winter of that year, I should be disposed to place the writing of our
Epistle.

4. It will be hardly necessary to remind the student, that this date
places the Epistle *first*, in chronological order, *of all the writings of St.
Paul* that remain to us.

SECTION IV.

MATTER AND STYLE.

1. It will be interesting to observe, wherein the first-written Epistle
of St. Paul differs from his later writings. Some difference we should
certainly expect to find, considering that we have to deal with a temperament so fervid, a spirit so rapidly catching the impress of circumstances, so penetrated by and resigned up to the promptings of that
indwelling Spirit of God, who was ever more notably and thoroughly
fitting His instrument for the expansion and advance of His work of
leavening the world with the truth of Christ.

2. Nor will such observation and enquiry be spent in vain, especially
if we couple it with corresponding observation of the sayings of our
Lord, and the thoughts and words of his Apostles, on the various great
departments of Christian belief and hope.

3. The faith, in all its main features, was delivered once for all. The
facts of Redemption,—the Incarnation, and the Atonement, and the
glorification of Christ,—were patent and undeniable from the first. Our
Lord's own words had asserted them : the earliest discourses of the
Apostles after the day of Pentecost bore witness to them. It is true
that, in God's Providence, the whole glorious system of salvation by
grace was the gradual imparting of the Spirit to the Church : by occasion here and there, various points of it were insisted on and made
prominent. Even here, the freest and fullest statement did not come
first. "Repentance toward God, and faith toward our Lord Jesus Christ"
was ever the order which the apostolic proclamation took. The earliest
of the Epistles are ever moral and practical, the advanced ones more

doctrinal and spiritual. It was not till it appeared, in the unfolding of God's Providence, that the bulwark of salvation by grace must be strengthened, that the building on the one foundation must be raised thus impregnable to the righteousness of works and the law, that the Epistles to the Galatians and Romans were given through the great Apostle, reaching to the full breadth and height of the great argument. Then followed the Epistles of the imprisonment, building up higher and higher the edifice thus consolidated : and the Pastoral Epistles, suited to a more developed ecclesiastical condition, and aimed at the correction of abuses, which sprung up later, or were the ripened fruit of former doctrinal errors.

4. In all these however, we trace the same great elementary truths of the faith. Witness to them is never wanting : nor can it be said that any change of ground respecting them ever took place. The work of the Spirit as regarded them, was one of expanding and deepening, of freeing from narrow views, and setting in clearer and fuller light : of ranging and grouping collateral and local circumstances, so that the great doctrines of grace became ever more and more prominent and paramount.

5. But while this was so with these 'first principles,' the very view which we have taken will shew, that as regarded other things which lay at a greater distance from central truths, it was otherwise. In such matters, the Apostle was taught by experience ; Christ's work brought its lessons with it : and it would be not only unnatural, but would remove from his writings the living freshness of personal reality, if we found him the same in all points of this kind, at the beginning, and at the end of his epistolary labours : if there were no characteristic differences of mode of thought and expression in 1 Thessalonians and in 2 Timotheus : if advance of years had brought with it no corresponding advance of standing-point, change of circumstances no change of counsel, trial of God's ways no further insight into God's designs.

6. Nor are we left to conjecture as to those subjects on which especially such change, and ripening of view and conviction, might be expected to take place. There was one most important point on which our Lord Himself spoke with marked and solemn uncertainty. The TIME OF HIS OWN COMING was hidden from all created beings,—nay, in the mystery of his mediatorial office, from the Son Himself (Mark xiii. 32). Even after his Resurrection, when questioned by the Apostles as to the time of his restoring the Kingdom to Israel, his reply is still, that "it is not for them to know the times and the seasons, which the Father hath put in his own power" (Acts i. 7).

7. Here then is a plain indication, which has not, I think, been sufficiently made use of in judging of the Epistles. The Spirit was to *testify of Christ* : to take of the things of Christ, and shew them unto them. So that however much that Spirit, in His infinite wisdom, might be

pleased to impart to them of the details and accompanying circumstances of the Lord's appearing, we may be sure, that the truth spoken by our Lord, " Of that day and hour knoweth no man," would hold good with regard to them, and be traced in their writings. If they were true men, and their words and Epistles the genuine production of inspiration of them by that Spirit of Truth, we may expect to find in such speeches and writings tokens of this appointed uncertainty of the day and hour : expectations, true in expression and fully justified by appearances, yet corrected, as God's purposes were manifested, by advancing experience, and larger effusions of the Spirit of prophecy.

8. If then I find in the course of St. Paul's Epistles, that expressions which occur in the earlier ones, and seem to indicate expectation of His almost immediate coming, are gradually modified,—disappear altogether from the Epistles of the imprisonment,—and instead of them are found others speaking in a very different strain, of dissolving, and being with Christ, and passing through death and the resurrection, in the latest Epistles,—I regard it, not as a strange thing, not as a circumstance which I must explain away for fear of weakening the authority of his Epistles, but as exactly that which I should expect to find ; as the very strongest testimony that these Epistles were written by one who was left in this uncertainty,—not by one who wished to make it appear that Inspiration had rendered him omniscient.

9. And in this, the earliest of those Epistles, I do find exactly that which I might expect on this head. While every word and every detail respecting the Lord's coming is a perpetual inheritance for the Church, —while we continue to comfort one another with the glorious and heart-stirring sentences which he utters to us in the word of the Lord, —no candid eye can help seeing in the Epistle, how the uncertainty of " the day and hour " has tinged all these passages with a hue of near anticipation : how natural it was, that the Thessalonians receiving this Epistle, should have allowed that anticipation to be brought even yet closer, and have imagined the day to be actually already present.

10. It will be seen by the above remarks, how very far I am from conceding their point to those who hold that the belief, of which this Epistle is the strongest expression, was an idle fancy, or does not befit the present age as well as it did that one. It is God's purpose respecting us, that we should ever be left in this uncertainty, looking for and hasting unto the day of the Lord, which may be upon us at any time before we are aware of it. Every expression of the ages before us, betokening close anticipation, coupled with the fact that the day has not yet arrived, teaches us much, but unteaches us nothing: does not deprive that glorious hope of its applicability to our times, nor the

Christian of his power of living as in the light of his Lord's approach and the daily realization of the day of Christ[6].

11. In style, this Epistle is thoroughly Pauline,—abounding with phrases, and lines of thought, which may be paralleled with similar ones in his other Epistles[7]: not wanting also in insulated words and sentiments, such as we find in all the writings of one who was so fresh in thought and full in feeling ; such also as are in no way inconsistent with St. Paul's known character, but in every case finding analogical justification in Epistles of which no one has ever thought of disputing the genuineness.

12. As compared with other Epistles, this is written in a quiet and unimpassioned style, not being occasioned by any grievous errors of doctrine or defects in practice, but written to encourage and gently to admonish those who were, on the whole, proceeding favourably in the Christian life.   To this may be attributed also the fact, that it does not deal expressly with any of the great verities of the faith, rather taking them for granted, and building on them the fabric of a holy and pure life.   That this should have been done until they were disputed, was but natural : and in consequence not with these Epistles, but with that to the Galatians, among whom the whole Christian life was imperilled by Judaistic teaching, begins that great series of unfoldings of the mystery of salvation by grace, of which St. Paul was so eminently the minister.

[6] It is strange that such words as the following could be written by Mr. Jowett, without bringing, as he wrote them, the condemnation of his theory and its expression home to his mind : " *In the words which are attributed in the Epistle of St. Peter to the unbelievers of that day* (? surely it is to the unbelievers of *days to come*,—a fact which the writer, by altering the reference of the words, seems to be endeavouring to dissimulate), *we might truly say that, since the fathers fell asleep, all things remain the same from the beginning.   Not only do ' all things remain the same,' but the very belief itself (in the sense in which it was held by the first Christians) has been ready to vanish away.*" Vol. i. p. 97.

[7] Baur has most perversely adduced *both these* as evidences of spuriousness : among the former he cites ch. i. 5, as compared with 1 Cor. ii. 4 : i. 6, with 1 Cor. xi. 1 : i. 8, with Rom. i. 8 : ii. 4—10, with 1 Cor. ii. 4, iv. 3, 4, ix. 15, 2 Cor. ii. 17, v. 11, xi. 9 : for his discussion of the latter, see his " Paulus Apostel, u.s.w." pp. 489, 490.

CHAPTER VI.

THE SECOND EPISTLE TO THE THESSALONIANS.

SECTION I.

ITS AUTHORSHIP.

1. THE recognition of this Epistle has been as general,—and the exceptions to it for the most part the same,—as in the case of the last.

2. The principal testimonies of early Christian writers are the following :

(α) Irenæus, adv. Hær. iii. 7. 2, p. 182 :

"Quoniam autem hyperbatis frequenter utitur Apostolus (Paulus, from what precedes) propter velocitatem sermonum suorum, et propter impetum qui in ipso est Spiritus, ex multis quidem aliis est invenire. . . . . Et iterum in secunda ad Thessalonicenses de Antichristo dicens, ait : Et tunc revelabitur," &c. ch. ii. 8, 9.

(β) Clement of Alexandria, Strom. v. 3 (17), p. 655 P. :

οὐκ ἐν πᾶσι, φησὶν ὁ ἀπόστολος, ἡ γνῶσις, προσεύχεσθε δὲ ἵνα ῥυσθῶμεν ἀπὸ τῶν ἀτόπων καὶ πονηρῶν ἀνθρώπων· οὐ γὰρ πάντων ἡ πίστις (2 Thess. iii. 1, 2).

(γ) Tertullian, de resurr. carnis c. 24, vol. ii. p. 828 : following on the citation from the first Epistle given above, ch. v. § i. 3, ... "et in secunda, pleniore sollicitudine ad eosdem : obsecro autem vos, fratres, per adventum Domini nostri Jesu Christi," &c. (ch. ii. 1, 2.)

3. The objections brought by Schmidt (Einl. ii. p. 256 ff.), Kern (Tübing. Zeitschrift für 1839, 2 heft.), and Baur (Paulus, u.s.w. p. 488 ff.) against the genuineness of the Epistle, in as far as they rest on the old story of similarities and differences as compared with St. Paul's acknowledged Epistles, have been already more than once dealt with. I shall now only notice those which regard points peculiar to our Epistle itself.

4. It is said that this second Epistle is not consistent with the first : that directed their attention to the Lord's coming as almost immediate : *this* interposes delay,—the apostasy,—the man of sin, &c. It really seems as if no propriety nor exact fitting of circumstances would ever satisfy such critics. It might be imagined that this very discrepancy, even if allowed, would tell most strongly in favour of the genuineness.

5. It is alleged by Kern, that the whole prophetic passage, ch. ii. 1 ff.,

51]

does not correspond with the date claimed for the Epistle. It is assumed, that the man of sin is Nero, who was again to return, Rev. xvii. 10,— ὁ κατέχων, Vespasian,—the ἀποστασία, the falling away of Jews and Christians alike. This view, it is urged, fits a writer in A.D. 68—70, between Nero's death and the destruction of Jerusalem. But than this nothing can be more inconclusive. Why have we not as good a right to say, that *this interpretation* is wrong, because it *does not correspond to the received date* of the Epistle, as vice versâ ? To us (see below, § v.) the interpretation is full of absurdity, and therefore the argument carries no conviction.

6. It is maintained again, that ch. iii. 17 is strongly against the genuineness of our Epistle : for that there was no reason for guarding against forgeries ; and as for πάσῃ ἐπιστολῇ, the Apostle had written but one. For an answer to this, see note in loc., where both the reason for inserting this is adduced, and it is shewn, that almost all of his Epistles either are expressly, or may be understood as having been, thus authenticated.

7. See the objections of Schmidt, Schrader, Kern, and Baur, treated at length in Lünemann's Einleitung to his Commentary, pp. 161—167: and in Davidson, Introd. vol. ii. pp. 484, end.

SECTION II.

FOR WHAT READERS, AND WITH WHAT OBJECT IT WAS WRITTEN.

1. The former particular has been already sufficiently explained in the corresponding section of the Prolegomena to the first Epistle. But inasmuch as the condition of the Thessalonian Church in the mean time bears closely upon the object of the Epistle, I resume here the consideration of their circumstances and state of mind.

2. We have seen that there were those among them, who were too ready to take up and exaggerate the prevalence of the subject of Christ's coming among the topics of the Apostle's teaching. These persons, whether encouraged by the tone of the first Epistle or not, we cannot tell (for we cannot see any reference to the first Epistle in ch. ii. 2, see note there), were evidently teaching, as an expansion of St. Paul's doctrine, or as under his authority, or even as enjoined in a letter from him (ib. note), the actual presence of the day of the Lord. In consequence of this, their minds had become unsettled: they wanted directing into the love of God and the imitation of Christ's patience (ch. iii. 5). Some appear to have left off their daily employments, and to have been taking advantage of the supposed reign of Christ to be walking disorderly.

3. It was this state of things, which furnished the occasion for our Epistle being written. Its object is to make it clear to them that the day of Christ, though a legitimate matter of expectation for every Christian, and a constant stimulus for watchfulness, was not yet come : that a course and development of events must first happen, which he lays forth to them in the spirit of prophecy : shewing them that this development has already begun, and that not until it has ripened will the coming of the Lord take place.

4. This being the occasion of writing the Epistle, there are grouped round the central subject two other general topics of solace and confirmation : comfort under their present troubles (ch. i.) : exhortation to honesty and diligence. and avoidance of the idle and disorderly (ch. iii.).

SECTION III.

PLACE AND TIME OF WRITING.

1. In the address of the Epistle, we find the same three, Paul, Silvanus, and Timotheus, associated together, as in the first Epistle. This circumstance would at once direct us to Corinth, where Silas and Timotheus rejoined St. Paul (Acts xviii. 5), and whence we do not read that they accompanied him on his departure for Asia (ib. xviii. 18). And as we believe the first Epistle to have been written from that city, it will be most natural, considering the close sequence of this upon that first, to place the writing of it at Corinth, somewhat later in this same visit of a year and a half (Acts xviii. 11).

2. *How long* after the writing of the first Epistle in the winter of A.D. 52 (see above, ch. v. § iii. 3) we are to fix the date of our present one, must be settled merely by calculations of probability, and by the indications furnished in the Epistle itself.

3. The former of these do not afford us much help. For we can hardly assume with safety that the Apostle had received intelligence of the effects of his first Epistle, seeing that we have found cause to interpret ch. ii. 2 not of that Epistle, but of false ones, circulated under the Apostle's name. All that we can assume is, that more intelligence had arrived from Thessalonica : how soon after his writing to them, we cannot say. Their present state, as we have seen above, was but a carrying forward and exaggerating of that already begun when the former letter was sent : so that a very short time would suffice to have advanced them from the one grade of undue excitement to the other.

4. Nor do any hints furnished by our Epistle give us much more assistance. They are principally these. (a) In ch. i. 4, the Apostle speaks of his ἐγκαυχᾶσθαι ἐν ταῖς ἐκκλησίαις τοῦ θεοῦ concerning the en-

53]

durance and faith of the Thessalonians under persecutions. It would seem from this, that the Achæan Churches (see 1 Cor. i. 2; 2 Cor. i. 1; Rom. xvi. 1) had by this time acquired number and consistence. This however would furnish but a vague indication: it might point to any date after the first six months of his stay at Corinth.   (b) In ch. iii. 2, he desires their prayers ἵνα ῥυσθῶμεν ἀπὸ τῶν ἀτόπων καὶ πονηρῶν ἀνθρώπων. It has been inferred from this, that the tumult which occasioned his departure from Corinth was not far off: that the designs of the unbelieving Jews were drawing to a head: and that consequently our date must be fixed just before his departure. But this inference is not a safe one: for we find that his open breach with the Jews took place close upon the arrival of Silas and Timotheus (Acts xviii. 5—7), and that his situation immediately after this was one of peril: for in the vision which he had, the Lord said to him, οὐδεὶς ἐπιθήσεταί σοι τοῦ κακῶσαί σε.

5. So that we really have very little help in determining our date, from either of these sources. All we can say is, that it must be fixed, in all likelihood, between the winter of 52 and the spring of 54: and taking the medium, we may venture to place it somewhere about the middle of the year 53.

SECTION IV.

STYLE.

1. The style of our Epistle, like that of the first, is eminently Pauline. Certain dissimilarities have been pointed out by Baur, &c. (see above, § i. 3): but they are no more than might be found in any one undoubted writing of our Apostle. In a fresh and vigorous style, there will ever be, so to speak, librations over any rigid limits of habitude which can be assigned: and such are to be judged of, not by their mere occurrence and number, but by their subjective character being or not being in accordance with the writer's well-known characteristics. Professor Jowett has treated one by one the supposed inconsistencies with Pauline usage (vol. i. p. 139 f.), and shewn that there is no real difficulty in supposing any of the expressions to have been used by St. Paul. He has also collected a very much larger number of resemblances in manner and phraseology to the Apostle's other writings. The student who makes use of the references in this edition will be able to mark out these for himself, and to convince himself that the style of our Epistle is so closely related to that of the rest, as to shew that the same mind was employed in the choice of the words and the construction of the sentences.

2. One portion of this Epistle, viz. the prophetic section, ch. ii. 1—12,

54]

as it is distinguished from the rest in subject, so differs in style, being, as is usual with the more solemn and declaratory paragraphs of St. Paul, loftier in diction and more abrupt and elliptical in construction. The passage in question will be found on comparison to bear, in style and flow of sentences, a close resemblance to the denunciatory and prophetic portions of the other Epistles : compare for instance ver. 3 with Col. ii. 8, 16 ; vv. 8, 9 with 1 Cor. xv. 24—28 ; ver. 10 with Rom. i. 18, 1 Cor. i. 18, 2 Cor. ii. 15 ; ver. 11 with Rom. i. 24, 26 ; ver. 12 with Rom. ii. 5, 9, and Rom. i. 32.

SECTION V.

ON THE PROPHETIC IMPORT OF CH. II. 1—12.

1. It may be well, before entering on this, to give the passage, as it stands in our rendering in the notes [1].

"(1) But we entreat you, brethren, in regard of the coming of our Lord Jesus Christ, and our gathering together to Him,—(2) in order that ye should not be lightly shaken from your mind nor troubled, neither by spirit, nor by word, nor by epistle as from us, to the effect that the day of the Lord is present. (3) Let no man deceive you in any manner: for [that day shall not come] unless there have come the apostasy first, and there have been revealed the man of sin, the son of perdition, (4) he that withstands and exalts himself above every one that is called God or an object of adoration, so that he sits in the temple of God, shewing himself that he is God. (5) . . . . (6) And now ye know that which hinders, in order that he may be revealed in his own time. (7) For the MYSTERY ALREADY is working of lawlessness, only until he that now hinders be removed : (8) and then shall be REVEALED the LAWLESS ONE, whom the Lord Jesus will destroy by the breath of His mouth, and annihilate by the appearance of His coming : (9) whose coming is according to the working of Satan in all power and signs and wonders of falsehood, (10) and in all deceit of unrighteousness for those who are perishing, because they did not receive the love of the truth in order to their being saved. (11) And on this account God is sending to them the working of error, in order that they should believe the falsehood, (12) that all might be judged who did not believe the truth, but found pleasure in iniquity."

[1] I must caution the reader, that the rendering given in my notes is not in any case intended for a polished and elaborated version, nor is it my object to put the meaning into the best idiomatic English : but I wish to represent, as nearly as possible, the construction and intent of the original. The difference between a literal rendering, and a version for vernacular use, is very considerable, and has not been enough borne in mind in judging of our authorized English version.

2. It will be my object to give a brief résumé of the history of the interpretation of this passage, and afterwards to state what I conceive to have been its meaning as addressed to the Thessalonians, and what as belonging to subsequent ages of the Church of Christ. The history of its interpretation I have drawn from several sources : principally from Lünemann's Schlussbemerkungen to chap. ii. of his Commentary, pp. 204—217.

3. The first particulars in the history must be gleaned from the early Fathers. And their interpretation is for the most part well marked and consistent. They all regard it as a prophecy of the future, as yet unfulfilled when they wrote. They all regard the παρουσία as the personal return of our Lord to judgment and to bring in His Kingdom. They all regard the adversary here described as an individual person, the incarnation and concentration of sin[2].

[2] The following citations will bear out the assertion in the text:

IRENÆUS, adv. hær. v. 25. 1, p. 322: "Ille enim (Antichristus) omnem suscipiens diaboli virtutem, veniet non quasi rex justus nec quasi in subjectione Dei legitimus: sed impius et injustus et sine lege, quasi apostata, et iniquus et homicida, quasi latro, diabolicam apostasiam in se recapitulans: et idola quidem seponens, ad suadendum quod ipse sit Deus: se autem extollens unum idolum, habens in semetipso reliquorum idolorum varium errorem : ut hi qui per multas abominationes adorant diabolum, hi per hoc unum idolum serviant ipsi, de quo apostolus in Epistola quæ est ad Thessalonicenses secunda, sic ait " (vv. 3, 4).

Again, ib. 3, p. 323 : "'Usque ad tempus temporum et dimidium temporis' (Dan. vii. 25), hoc est, per triennium et sex menses, in quibus veniens regnabit super terram. De quo iterum et apostolus Paulus in secunda ad Thess., simul et causam adventus ejus annuntians, sic ait" (vv. 8 ff.).

Again, ib. 30. 4, p. 330: "Cum autem devastaverit Antichristus hic omnia in hoc mundo, regnabit annis tribus et mensibus sex, et sedebit in templo Hierosolymis: tum veniet Dominus de cœlis in nubibus, in gloria Patris, illum quidem et obedientes ei in stagnum ignis mittens: adducens autem justis regni tempora, hoc est requietionem, septimam diem sanctificatam ; et restituens Abrahæ promissionem hæreditatis : in quo regno ait Dominus, multos ab Oriente et Occidente venientes, recumbere cum Abraham, Isaac et Jacob."

TERTULLIAN, de Resurr. c. 24, vol. ii. p. 829, quoting the passage, inserts after ὁ κατέχων, " quis, nisi Romanus status? cujus abscessio in decem reges dispersa Antichristum superducet, et tum revelabitur iniquus." See also his Apol. c. 32, vol. i. p. 447.

JUSTIN MARTYR, dial. cum Tryph. c. 110, p. 203 : δύο παρουσίαι αὐτοῦ κατηγγελμέναι εἰσί, μία μὲν ἐν ᾗ παθητὸς καὶ ἄδοξος καὶ ἄτιμος καὶ σταυρούμενος κεκήρυκται, ἡ δὲ δευτέρα ἐν ᾗ μετὰ δόξης ἀπὸ τῶν οὐρανῶν πάρεσται, ὅταν καὶ ὁ τῆς ἀποστασίας ἄνθρωπος, ὁ καὶ εἰς τὸν ὕψιστον ἔξαλλα λαλῶν, ἐπὶ τῆς γῆς ἄνομα τολμήσῃ εἰς ἡμᾶς τοὺς Χριστιανούς.

ORIGEN, contra Cels. vi. 45 f. vol. i. p. 667 f.: ἐχρῆν δὲ τὸν μὲν ἕτερον τῶν ἄκρων, καὶ βέλτιστον, υἱὸν ἀναγορεύεσθαι τοῦ θεοῦ, διὰ τὴν ὑπεροχήν· τὸν δὲ τούτῳ κατὰ διάμετρον ἐναντίον, υἱὸν τοῦ πονηροῦ δαίμονος, καὶ Σατανᾶ, καὶ διαβόλου . . . λέγει δὲ ὁ Παῦλος, περὶ τούτου τοῦ καλουμένου ἀντιχρίστου διδάσκων, καὶ παριστὰς μετά τινος ἐπικρύψεως τίνα τρόπον ἐπιδημήσει, καὶ πότε τῷ γένει τῶν ἀνθρώπων, καὶ διὰ τί. He then quotes this whole passage.

4. Respecting, however, the minor particulars of the prophecy, they are not so entirely at agreement. Augustine says (de civ. Dei, xx. 19. 2, p. 685 : cf. also Jerome in the note),—' in *quo templo* Dei sit sessurus, incertum est : utrum in illa ruina templi quod a Salomone rege constructum est, an vero in Ecclesia. Non enim templum alicujus idoli aut dæmonis templum Dei Apostolus diceret [3].' And from this doubt about his ' session,' a doubt about his person also had begun to spring up ; for he continues, ' unde nonnulli non ipsum principem sed universum quodammodo corpus ejus, id est, ad eum pertinentem hominum multitudinem simul cum ipso suo principe hoc loco intelligi Antichristum volunt.'

5. The meaning of τὸ κατέχον, though, as will be seen from the note, generally agreed to be the Roman empire, was not by any means universally acquiesced in. Theodoret says, τινὲς τὸ κατέχον τὴν Ῥωμαϊκὴν ἐνόησαν βασιλείαν, τινὲς δὲ τὴν χάριν τοῦ πνεύματος. κατεχούσης γάρ, φησί, τῆς τοῦ πνεύματος χάριτος ἐκεῖνος οὐ παραγίνεται, ἀλλ' οὐχ οἷόν τε παύσασθαι παντελῶς τὴν χάριν τοῦ πνεύματος . . . . ἀλλ' οὐδὲ τὴν Ῥωμαϊκὴν βασιλείαν ἑτέρα διαδέξεται βασιλεία· διὰ γὰρ τοῦ τετάρτου θηρίου καὶ ὁ θειότατος Δανιὴλ

CHRYSOSTOM in loc. : τίς δὲ οὗτός ἐστιν ; ἆρα ὁ Σατανᾶς ; οὐδαμῶς· ἀλλ' ἄνθρωπός τις πᾶσαν αὐτοῦ δεχόμενος τὴν ἐνέργειαν. καὶ ἀποκαλυφθῇ ὁ ἄνθρωπός, φησιν, ὁ ὑπεραιρόμενος ἐπὶ πάντα λεγόμενον θεὸν ἢ σέβασμα. οὐ γὰρ εἰδωλολατρείαν ἄξει ἐκεῖνος, ἀλλ' ἀντίθεός τις ἔσται, καὶ πάντας καταλύσει τοὺς θεούς, καὶ κελεύσει προσκυνεῖν αὐτὸν ἀντὶ τοῦ θεοῦ, καὶ καθεσθήσεται εἰς τὸν ναὸν τοῦ θεοῦ, οὐ τὸν ἐν Ἱεροσολύμοις μόνον, ἀλλὰ καὶ εἰς τὰς πανταχοῦ ἐκκλησίας.

And below : καὶ τί μετὰ ταῦτα ; ἐγγὺς ἡ παραμυθία. ἐπάγει γάρ· ὃν ὁ κύριος Ἰησοῦς κ.τ.λ. καθάπερ γὰρ κ.τ.λ. See the rest cited in the note on ver. 8.

CYRIL OF JERUS., Catech. xv. 12, p. 229 : ἔρχεται δὲ ὁ προειρημένος ἀντίχριστος οὗτος, ὅταν πληρωθῶσιν οἱ καιροὶ τῆς Ῥωμαίων βασιλείας, καὶ πλησιάζει λοιπὸν τὰ τῆς τοῦ κόσμου συντελείας. δέκα μὲν ὁμοῦ Ῥωμαίων ἐγείρονται βασιλεῖς, ἐν διαφόροις μὲν ἴσως τόποις, κατὰ δὲ τὸν αὐτὸν βασιλεύοντες καιρόν. μετὰ δὲ τούτους ἑνδέκατος ὁ Ἀντίχριστος ἐκ τῆς μαγικῆς κακοτεχνίας τὴν Ῥωμαϊκὴν ἐξουσίαν ἁρπάσας.

Theodoret's interpretation agrees with the above as to the personality of Antichrist and as to our Lord's coming. I shall quote some portion of it below, on ὁ κατέχων, and τὸ μυστήριον.

AUGUSTINE, de civ. Dei, xx. 19. 4, vol. vii. p. 687 : "Non veniet ad vivos et mortuos judicandos Christus, nisi prius venerit ad seducendos in anima mortuos adversarius ejus Antichristus."

JEROME, Epist. cxxi., ad Algasiam, qu. 11, vol. i. p. 887 f. : "Nisi, inquit, venerit discessio primum . . . . ut omnes gentes quæ Romano imperio subjacent, recedant ab his, et revelatus fuerit, id est, ostensus, quem omnia prophetarum verba prænunciant, homo peccati, in quo fons omnium peccatorum est, et filius perditionis, id est diaboli : ipse est enim universorum perditio, qui adversatur Christo, et ideo vocatur Antichristus ; et extollitur supra omne quod dicitur Deus, ut cunctarum gentium deos, sive probatam omnem et veram religionem suo calcet pede : et in templo Dei, vel Hierosolymis (ut quidam putant), vel in ecclesia, ut verius arbitramur, sederit, ostendens se, tanquam ipse sit Christus et filius Dei : nisi, inquit, fuerit Romanum imperium ante desolatum, et Antichristus præcesserit, Christus non veniet : qui ideo ita venturus est, ut Antichristum destruat."

[3] Theodoret also : ναὸν δὲ θεοῦ τὰς ἐκκλησίας ἐκάλεσεν, ἐν αἷς ἁρπάσει τὴν προεδρείαν, θεὸν ἑαυτὸν ἀποδεικνύναι πειρώμενος.

τὴν Ῥωμαϊκὴν ἠνίξατο βασιλείαν. ἐν δὲ τούτῳ τὸ μικρὸν κέρας ἐβλάστησε τὸ
ποιοῦν πόλεμον μετὰ τῶν ἁγίων. αὐτὸς δὲ οὗτός ἐστι περὶ οὗ τὰ προρρηθέντα
εἶπεν ὁ θεῖος ἀπόστολος. οὐδέτερον τούτων οἶμαι φάναι τὸν θεῖον ἀπόστολον,
ἀλλὰ τὸ παρ᾽ ἑτέρων εἰρημένον εἶναι ἀληθὲς ὑπολαμβάνω. ἐδοκίμασε γὰρ ὁ
τῶν ὅλων θεὸς παρὰ τὸν τῆς συντελείας αὐτὸν ὀφθῆναι καιρόν. ὁ τοῦ θεοῦ
τοίνυν ὅρος νῦν ἐπέχει φανῆναι. And so also Theodor.-Mops.[4] Another
meaning yet is mentioned by Chrysostom, or rather another form of that
repudiated above by Theodoret, viz., that the continuance of ἡ τοῦ
πνεύματος χάρις, τουτέστι χαρίσματα, hindered his appearing. And
remarkably enough, he rejects this from a reason the very opposite of
that which weighed with Theodoret,—viz., from the fact that spiritual
gifts had ceased : ἄλλως δὲ ἔδει ἤδη παραγίνεσθαι, εἴ γε ἔμελλε τῶν χαρισμάτων ἐκλειπόντων παραγίνεσθαι· καὶ γὰρ πάλαι ἐκλέλοιπεν[5]. Augustine's
remarks (ubi supra) are curious : "Quod autem ait, et nunc quid deti-
neat scitis, ... quoniam scire illos dixit, aperte hoc dicere noluit. Et
ideo nos, qui nescimus quod illi sciebant, pervenire cum labore ad id
quod sensit Apostolus, cupimus, nec valemus : præsertim quia et illa
quæ addidit, hunc sensum faciunt obscuriorem. Nam quid est, ' Jam
enim,' &c. (ver. 7)? Ego prorsus quid dixerit, fateor me ignorare."
Then he mentions the various opinions on τὸ κατέχον, giving this as the
view of some, that it was said "de malis et fictis qui sunt in ecclesia,
donec perveniant ad tantum numerum qui Antichristo magnum populum faciat : et hoc esse mysterium iniquitatis quia videtur occultum . ."
then again quoting ver. 7, adds, "hoc est, donec exeat de medio ecclesiæ
mysterium iniquitatis, quod nunc occultum est."

6. This μυστήριον τῆς ἀνομίας was also variously understood. Chrysostom says, Νέρωνα ἐνταῦθά φησιν, ὡσανεὶ τύπον ὄντα τοῦ Ἀντιχρίστου· καὶ
γὰρ οὗτος ἐβούλετο νομίζεσθαι θεός. καὶ καλῶς εἶπε τὸ μυστήριον· οὐ γὰρ
φανερῶς ὡς ἐκεῖνος, οὐδ᾽ ἀπηρυθριασμένως. εἰ γὰρ πρὸ χρόνου ἐκείνου
ἀνευρεθῇ, φησίν, ὃς οὐ πολὺ τοῦ Ἀντιχρίστου ἐλείπετο κατὰ τὴν κακίαν, τί
θαυμαστὸν εἰ ἤδη ἔσται ; οὕτω δὴ συνεσκιασμένως εἶπε, καὶ φανερὸν αὐτὸν
οὐκ ἠθέλησε ποιῆσαι, οὐ διὰ δειλίαν, ἀλλὰ παιδεύων ἡμᾶς μὴ περιττὰς ἔχθρας
ἀναδέχεσθαι ὅταν μηδὲν ᾖ τὸ κατεπεῖγον· This opinion is also mentioned
by Augustine, al., but involves of course an anachronism. Theodoret,
also mentioning it, adds : ἐγὼ δὲ οἶμαι τὰς ἀναφυείσας αἱρέσεις δηλοῦν τὸν
ἀπόστολον· δι᾽ ἐκείνων γὰρ ὁ διάβολος πολλοὺς ἀποστήσας τῆς ἀληθείας,
προκατασκευάζει τῆς ἀπάτης τὸν ὄλεθρον. μυστήριον δὲ αὐτοὺς ἀνομίας
ἐκάλεσεν, ὡς κεκρυμμένην ἔχοντας τῆς ἀνομίας τὴν πάγην . . . . ὁ κρύβδην ἀεὶ
κατεσκεύαζε, τότε προφανῶς καὶ διαρρήδην κηρύξει.

[4] It is decisive against this latter view, as Lünemann has observed, that if τὸ κατέχον be God's decree, ὁ κατέχων must be *God Himself*, and then the ἕως ἐκ μέσου
γένηται could not be said.

[5] An ingenuous and instructive confession, at the end of the fourth century, from
one of the most illustrious of the fathers.

7.[6] The view of the fathers remained for ages the prevalent one in the Church. Modifications were introduced into it, as her relation to the state gradually altered; and the Church at last, instead of being exposed to further hostilities from the secular power, rose to the head of that power ; and, penetrating larger and larger portions of the world, became a representation of the kingdom of God on earth, with an imposing hierarchy at her head. Then followed, in the Church in general, and among the hierarchy in particular, a neglect of the subject of Christ's coming. But meanwhile, those who from time to time stood in opposition to the hierarchy, understood the Apostle's description here, as they did also the figures in the Apocalypse, of that hierarchy itself. And thus arose,—the παρουσία being regarded much as before, only as an event far off instead of near,—first in the eleventh century the idea, that the Antichrist foretold by St. Paul is the *establishment and growing power of the Popedom.*

8. This view first appears in the conflict between the Emperors and the Popes, as held by the partisans of the imperial power : but soon becomes that of all those who were opponents of the hierarchy, as wishing for a freer spirit in Christendom than the ecclesiastical power allowed. It was held by the Waldenses, the Albigenses, the followers of Wickliffe and Huss. The κατέχον, which retarded the destruction of the papacy, was held by them to be the *Imperial power*, which they regarded as simply a revival of the old Roman Empire.

9. Thus towards the time of the Reformation, this reference of Antichrist to the papal hierarchy became very prevalent : and after that event it assumed almost the position of a dogma in the Protestant Churches. It is found in Bugenhagen, Zwingle, Calvin, &c., Osiander, Baldwin, Aretius, Erasm.-Schmid, Beza, Calixtus, Calovius, Newton, Wolf, Joachim-Lange, Turretin, Benson, Bengel, Macknight, Zachariæ, Michaelis, &c. : in the symbolical books of the Lutheran Church, and in Luther's own writings : and runs through the works of our English Reformers[7].

10. The upholders of this view generally conceive that the Papacy will go on bringing out more and more its antichristian character, till at last the παρουσία will overtake and destroy it. The ἀποστασία is the *fall from pure evangelical doctrine* to the traditions of men. The singular, ὁ ἄνθρωπος τῆς ἁμαρτίας, is taken collectively, to signify a ' *series et successio hominum,*' inasmuch as it is a monarchical empire which is in question, which remains one and the same, though its individual

---

[6] What follows, as far as paragraph 24, is taken principally from Lünemann's Schlussbemerkungen, as above: with the exception of the citations made in full, and personal opinions expressed.

[7] See a very complete résumé of the passages on Antichrist in the Reformers, under the word, in the excellent Index to the publications of the Parker Society.

head may change. The godlessness of Antichrist, described in ver. 4, is justified historically by the Pope setting himself above all authority divine and human, the words πάντα λεγόμενον θεόν, &c. being, in accordance with Scriptural usage, taken to mean the princes and governments of the world, and an allusion being found in σέβασμα to σεβαστός, the title of the Roman Emperors. The ναὸς τοῦ θεοῦ is held to be the *Christian Church*, and the καθίσαι to point to the tyrannical power which the Pope usurps over it. By τὸ κατέχον is understood the *Roman Empire*, and by ὁ κατέχων the *Roman Emperor*,—and history is appealed to, to shew that out of the ruins of that empire the papacy has grown up. The declaration, τὸ μυστήριον ἤδη ἐνεργεῖται τῆς ἀνομίας, is justified by the fact, that the "semina erroris et ambitionis," which prepared the way for the papacy, were already present in the Apostle's time. For a catalogue of the τέρατα ψεύδους, ver. 9, rich material was found in relics, transubstantiation, purgatory, &c. The annihilation of Antichrist by the πνεῦμα τοῦ στόματος of the Lord, has been understood of the breaking down of his power in the spirits of men by the opening and dispersion of the word of God in its purity by means of the Reformation ; and the καταργήσει τῇ ἐπιφανείᾳ τῆς παρουσίας αὐτοῦ, of the final and material annihilation of Antichrist by the coming of the Lord Himself.

11. In the presence of such a polemical interpretation directed against them, it could hardly be expected that the Roman Catholics on their side would abstain from retaliation on their opponents. Accordingly we find that such writers as Estius, al., interpret the ἀποστασία of *the defection from the Romish Church and the Pope*, and understand by Antichrist the *heretics*, especially *Luther and the Protestant Church*.

12. Even before the reference to the papacy, the interpreters of the Greek Church took *Mohammed* to be the Antichrist intended by St. Paul, and the ἀποστασία to represent the *falling off* of many Oriental and Greek Churches *to Islamism*. And this view so far influenced the Protestant Church, that some of its writers have held a double Antichrist,—an Eastern one, viz. Mohammed and the Turkish power,—and a Western, viz. the Pope and his power. So Melancthon, Bucer, Bullinger, Piscator, &c.

13. Akin to this method of interpretation is that which in our own century has found the apostasy in the enormities of the French Revolution, Antichrist in *Napoleon*, and τὸ κατέχον in the *continuance of the German Empire:* an idea, remarks Lünemann, convicted of error by the termination of that empire in 1806.

14. One opinion of modern days has been, that it is objectionable to endeavour to assign closely a meaning to the single details of the imagery used by St. Paul. This has led to giving the whole description a general, ideal, or symbolic sense. So *Koppe*, who thinks that the Apostle

60

is only following the general import of the Jewish expectations, resting on the prophecy of Daniel, that there should be a season of godlessness before the time of the end, the full eruption of which he expects after his own death : he himself being ὁ κατέχων. Similarly *Storr*,—who sees in ἄνθρωπος τῆς ἁμαρτίας 'potestas aliqua, Deo omnique religioni adversaria, quæ penitus incognita et futuro demum tempore se proditura sit,' and in τὸ κατέχον, the 'copia hominum, verissimo amore inflammatorum in Christianam religionem.' *Nitzsch* again believes the 'man of sin to be the power of godlessness' come to have open authority, or the general contempt of all religion. *Pelt*, comm. in Thess. p. 204, sums up his view thus : " Mihi igitur cum Koppio adversarius ille *principium* esse videtur, sive vis spiritualis evangelio contraria, quæ huc usque tamen in Pontificiorum Romanorum operibus ac serie luculentissime sese prodiit, ita tamen, ut omnia etiam mala, quæ in ecclesiam compareant, ad eandem Antichristi ἐνέργειαν sint referenda. Ejus vero παρουσία, i. e. summum fastigium, quod Christi reditum, qui nihil aliud est nisi regni divini victoria[8], antecedet, futurum adhuc esse videtur, quum illud tempus procul etiam nunc abesse putemus, ubi omnes terræ incolæ in eo erunt ut ad Christi sacra transeant. κατέχον vero cum Theodoreto putarim esse Dei voluntatem illud Satanæ regnum cohibentem, ne erumpat, et si mediæ spectantur causæ, apostolorum tempore maxime imperii Romani vis, et quovis ævo illa resistentia, quam malis artibus, quæ religionem subvertere student, privati commodi et honoris augendorum cupiditas opponere solet." And Pelt thinks that the symptoms of the future corruption of the Christian Church were already discernible in the apostolic times, in the danger of falling back from Christian freedom into Jewish legality, in the mingling of heathenism with Christianity, in false γνῶσις and ἄσκησις, in angelolatry, in the "fastus a religione Christiana omnino alienus."

15. *Olshausen's* view is, that inasmuch as the personal coming of Christ is immediately to follow this revelation of Antichrist, such revelation cannot have yet taken place : and consequently, though we need not stigmatize any of the various interpretations as false, none of them has exhausted the import of the prophecy. The various untoward events and ungodly persons which have been mentioned, including the unbelief and godlessness of the present time, are all prefigurations of Antichrist, but contain only *some* of his characteristics, not *all:* it is the union of *all* in some one personal appearance, that shall make the full Antichrist, as the union in one Person, Jesus of Nazareth, of all the types and prophecies, constituted the full Christ. And the κατέχον is the *moral and conservative influence of political states,* restraining this great final outbreak. See more on this below.

[8] So again Pelt, p. 185 : "Tenentes, illum Christi adventum a Paulo *non visibilem* habitum."

16. On the other hand, some have regarded the prophecy as one already fulfilled. So Grotius, Wetstein, Le Clerc, Whitby, Schöttgen, Nösselt, Krause, and Harduin. All these concur in referring the παρουσία τοῦ κυρίου to the coming of Christ in the *destruction of Jerusalem.*

17. *Grotius* holds Antichrist to be the godless *Caligula*, who (Suet. Calig. 22, 33) ordered universal supplication to himself as the High God, and (Jos. Antt. xviii. 8. 2. Philo, Leg. ad Cai. § 81, vol. ii. p. 576) would have set up a colossal image of himself in the temple at Jerusalem: and in ὁ κατέχων he sees *L. Vitellius*, the proconsul of Syria and Judæa, whose term of office delayed the putting up of the statue,—and in ὁ ἄνομος, *Simon Magus.* This theory is liable to the two very serious objections, 1) that it makes ὁ ἄνθρ. τῆς ἁμαρτ. and ὁ ἄνομος into two separate persons : 2) that it involves an anachronism, our Epistle having been written after Caligula's time.

18. According to *Wetstein*, the ἄνθρ. τῆς ἁμαρτίας is *Titus*, whose army (Jos. B. J. vi. 6. 1), καιομένου αὐτοῦ τοῦ ναοῦ, καὶ τῶν πέριξ ἀπάντων, κομίσαντες τὰς σημαίας εἰς τὸ ἱερόν, καὶ θέμεναι τῆς ἀνατολικῆς πύλης ἄντικρυς, ἔθυσάν τε αὐταῖς αὐτόθι, καὶ τὸν Τίτον μετὰ μεγίστων εὐφημιῶν ἀπέφηναν αὐτοκράτορα. His κατέχων is *Nero*, whose death was necessary for the reign of Titus,—and his ἀποστασία, the *rebellion and slaughter of three princes,* Galba, Otho, and Vitellius, which brought in the Flavian family. But this is the very height of absurdity, and surely needs no serious refutation.

19. *Hammond* [9] makes the *man of sin* to be *Simon Magus*, and *the Gnostics*, whose head he was. The ἐπισυναγωγὴ ἐπ᾿ αὐτόν, ver. 1, he interprets as the "major libertas coëundi in ecclesiasticos coetus ad colendum Christum :" the ἀποστασία, the falling off of Christians *to Gnosticism* (1 Tim. iv. 1) : ἀποκαλυφθῆναι, the Gnostics "putting off their disguise, and revealing themselves in their colours, i. e. cruel, professed enemies to Christ and Christians :" ver. 4 refers to Simon "making himself the supreme Father of all, who had created the God of the Jews" (Iren. i. 24. 1, 2, p. 100 f.). By τὸ κατέχον, he understands the *union* yet subsisting more or less *between the Christians and the Jews* in the Apostle's estimation, which was removed when the Apostles entirely separated from the Jews : and ὁ κατέχων he maintains to be virtually the same with τὸ κατέχον, but if any masculine subject must be supplied, would make it ὁ νόμος. The μυστήριον τῆς ἀνομίας he refers to the *wicked lives* of these Gnostics, but mostly to their persecution of the Christians. Ver. 8 he explains of the *conflict at Rome* between Simon and the Apostles Peter and Paul, which ended in the death of the former. Lünemann adds, " The exegetical and historical monstrosity of this interpretation is at present universally acknowledged."

[9] On the New Test. in loc.

20. *Le Clerc* holds the ἀποστασία to be the *rebellion of the Jewish people* against the yoke of Rome: the man of sin, the *rebel Jews*, and especially their leader *Simon, son of Giora*, whose atrocities are related in Josephus :—πᾶς λεγόμ. θεὸς κ.τ.λ., denotes the *government:*—τὸ κατέχον is *whatever hindered the open breaking out of the rebellion*,— partly the influence of those Jews in office who dissuaded the war,— partly fear of the Roman armies: and ὁ κατέχων, on one side, the "*præses Romanus*,"—on the other, the "*gentis proceres, rex Agrippa et pontifices plurimi.*" The μυστήριον τῆς ἀνομίας is the *rebellious ambition*, which under the cloke of Jewish independence and zeal for the law of Moses, was even then at work, and at length broke openly forth.

21. *Whitby* takes the *Jewish people* for Antichrist, and finds in the apostasy the *falling away of the Jewish converts to their old Judaism*, alluded to in the Epistle to the Hebrews (iii. 12—14; iv. 11; vi. 4—6; x. 26, 27 al. fr.). His κατέχων is "the *Emperor Claudius*, who will let till he be taken away, i. e. he will hinder the Jews from breaking out into an open rebellion in his time, they being so signally and particularly obliged by him, that they cannot for shame think of revolting from his government."

22. *Schöttgen* (vol. i. p. 861 ff.) takes Antichrist to be the *Pharisees, Rabbis, and doctors of the law*, who set up themselves above God, and had impious stories tending to bring Him into contempt: the ἀποστασία, the *rebellion against Rome:* the κατέχον, "*Christiani*, qui precibus suis rem aliquando distulerunt, donec oraculo divino admoniti Hierosolymis abierunt, et Pellam secesserunt:" the μυστήριον τῆς ἀνομίας, "*ipsa doctrina perversa*," referring to 1 Tim. iii. 16.

23. *Nösselt* and *Krause* understand by Antichrist the *Jewish zealots*, and by the κατέχον, *Claudius*, as Whitby. Lastly, *Harduin* makes the ἀποστασία the *falling off of the Jews to paganism*,—the man of sin, the *High Priest Ananias* (Acts xxiii. 2),—the κατέχων, *his predecessor*, whose term of office must come to an end before he could be elected. From the beginning of his term, the ἄνθρωπος τῆς ἁμαρτίας was working as a prophet of lies, and was destroyed at the taking of Jerusalem by Titus.

24. All these *præterist* interpretations have against them one fatal objection:—that it is impossible to conceive of the destruction of Jerusalem as in any sense corresponding to the παρουσία in St. Paul's sense of the term: see especially, as bearing immediately on this passage, 1 Thess. ii. 19; iii. 13; iv. 15; v. 23.

25. A third class of interpretations is that adopted by many of the modern German expositors, and their followers in England. It is best described perhaps in the words of De Wette (Einl. Handb. ii. 132): "He goes altogether wrong, who finds here any more than the Apostle's

subjective anticipation from his own historical position, of the future of the Christian Church;" and expanded by Mr. Jowett (vol. ii. p. 178), " Such passages (Eph. vi. 12) are a much safer guide to the interpretation of the one we are considering, than the meaning of similar passages in the Old Testament. For they indicate to us the habitual thought of the Apostle's mind: 'a falling away first,' suggested probably by the wavering which he saw around him among his own converts, the grievous wolves that were entering into the Church of Ephesus (Acts xx. 29): the turning away of all them of Asia (2 Tim. i. 15). When we consider that his own converts, and his Jewish opponents, were all the world to him,—that through them, as it were in a glass, he appeared to himself to see the workings of human nature generally, we understand how this double image of good and evil should have presented itself to him, and the kind of necessity which he felt, that Christ and Antichrist should alternate with each other. It was not that he foresaw some great conflict, decisive of the destinies of mankind. What he anticipated far more nearly resembled the spiritual combat in the seventh chapter of the Romans. It was the same struggle, written in large letters, as Plato might have said, not on the tables of the heart, but on the scene around: the world turned inside out, as it might be described: evil as it is in the sight of God, and as it realizes itself to the conscience, putting on an external shape, transforming itself into a person."

26. This hypothesis is so entirely separate from all others, that there seems no reason why we should not deal with it at once and on its own ground, before proceeding farther. It will be manifest to any one who exercises a moment's thought, that the question moved by it simply resolves itself into this: *Was the Apostle, or was he not, writing in the power of a spirit higher than his own?* In other words, we are here at the very central question of *Inspiration or no Inspiration:* not disputing about any of its details, which have ever been matters of doubt among Christians: but just asking, for the Church and for the world, *Have we, in any sense, God speaking in the Bible, or have we not?* If we have,— then of all passages, it is in these which treat so confidently of futurity, that we must recognize His voice: if we have it not in these passages, then where are we to listen for it at all ? Does not this hypothesis, do not they who embrace it, at once reduce the Scriptures to books written by men,—their declarations to the assertions of dogmatizing teachers,— their warnings to the apprehensions of excited minds,—their promises to the visions of enthusiasts,—their prophecies, to anticipations which may be accounted for by the circumstances of the writers, but have in them no objective permanent truth whatever ?

27. On such terms, I fairly confess I am not prepared to deal with a question like that before us. I believe that our Lord uttered the words ascribed to Him by St. John (ch. xvi. 12, 13); I believe the

apostolic Epistles to be the written proof of the fulfilment of that promise, as the apostolic preaching and labours were the spoken and acted proof: and in writing such passages as this, and 1 Thess. iv. 13—17, and 1 Cor. xv., I believe St. Paul to have been giving utterance, not to his own subjective human opinions, but to truths which the Spirit of God had revealed to him: which he put forth indeed in writing and in speaking, as God had placed him, in a Church which does not know of the time of her Lord's coming,—as God had constituted his own mind, the vessel and organ of these truths, and gifted him with power of words,—but still, as being the truth for the Church to be guided by, not his own forebodings, for her to be misled by. What he may have meant by his expressions, is a question open to the widest and freest discussion: but that what he did mean, always under the above necessary conditions, is truth for us to receive, not opinion for us to canvass, is a position, the holding or rejecting of which might be very simply and strictly shewn to constitute the difference between one who receives, and one who repudiates, Christian revelation itself.

28. I now proceed to enquire, which, or whether any of all the above hypotheses, with the exception of the last, seems worthy of our acceptance. For the reason given above (24), I pass over those which regard the prophecy as fulfilled. The destruction of Jerusalem is inadequate as an interpretation of the coming of the Lord here: He has not yet come in any sense adequate to such interpretation: therefore the prophecy has yet to be fulfilled.

29. The interpretations of the ancient Fathers deserve all respect, short of absolute adoption *because they were* their interpretations. We must always in such cases strike a balance. In living near to the time when the speaking voice yet lingered in the Church, they had an advantage over us: in living far down in the unfolding of God's purposes, we have an advantage over them. They may possibly have heard things which we have never heard: we certainly have seen things which they never saw. In each case, we are bound to enquire, which of these two is likely to preponderate?

30. Their consensus in expecting a *personal* Antichrist, is, I own, a weighty point. There was nothing in their peculiar circumstances or temperament, which prevented them from interpreting all that is here said as a personification, or from allegorizing it, as others have done since. This fact gives that interpretation a *historical* weight, the inference from which it is difficult to escape. The subject of the coming of Antichrist must have been no uncommon one in preaching and in converse, during the latter part of the first, and the second century. That no echoes of the apostolic sayings on the matter should have reached thus far, no savour of the first outpouring of interpretation by

the Spirit penetrated through the next generation, can hardly be conceived. So far, I feel, the patristic view carries with it some claim to our acceptance.

31. The next important point, the interpretation of τὸ κατέχον and ὁ κατέχων, rests, I would submit, on different grounds. Let us for a moment grant, that by the former of these words was imported the *temporal political power*, and by the latter, *he who wielded it*. Such being the case, the concrete interpretation most likely to be adopted by the Fathers would be, the *Roman Empire*, which existed before their eyes as that political power. But *we* have seen that particular power pass away, and be broken up : and that very passing away has furnished us with a key to the prophecy, which they did not possess.

32. On the μυστήριον τῆς ἀνομίας, as has been seen, they are divided : but even were it otherwise, their concrete interpretations are just those things in which we are not inferior to them, but rather superior. The prophecy has since their time expanded its action over a wide and continually increasing historic field : it is for us to observe what they could not, and to say what it is which could be thus described,—then at work, ever since at work, and now at work ; and likely to issue in that concentration and revelation of evil which shall finally take place.

33. On looking onward to the next great class of interpretations, that which makes the man of sin to be the *Papal power*, it cannot be doubted, that there are many and striking points of correspondence with the language of the prophecy in the acts and professions of those who have successively held that power. But on the other hand it cannot be disguised that, in several important particulars, the prophetic requirements are very far from being fulfilled. I will only mention two, one subjective, the other objective. In the characteristic of ver. 4, the Pope does not and never did fulfil the prophecy. Allowing all the striking coincidences with the latter part of the verse which have been so abundantly adduced, it never can be shewn that he fulfils the former part, nay so far is he from it, that the abject adoration of and submission to λεγόμενοι θεοί and σεβάσματα has ever been one of his most notable peculiarities[1]. The second objection, of an external and historical character, is even more decisive. If the Papacy be Antichrist, then has the manifestation been made, and endured now for nearly 1500 years,

---

[1] It must be plain to every unbiassed mind, that the mere logical inference, that the Pope sets himself up above all objects of worship, because he *creates* objects of worship, and *the maker must be greater than the thing made*, is quite beside the purpose. It entirely fails in shewing *hostility to, and lifting himself above, every one that is called God or an object of worship*. The Pope is the *devoted servant* of the false gods whom he creates, not their antagonist and treader-down. I should not have noticed so irrelevant an argument, had it not been made much of as against my view.

and yet that day of the Lord is not come, which by the terms of our prophecy such manifestation is immediately to precede [2].

34. The same remarks will apply even more forcibly to all those minor interpretations which I have enumerated above. None of them exhausts the sense of the prophecy: and the taking any one of them to be that which is here designated, would shew the failure of the prophecy, not its fulfilment: for they have been and have passed away, and the Lord is not yet come.

35. We are thus directed to a point of view with regard to the prophecy, of the following kind. The ἄνομος, in the full prophetic sense, is not yet come. Though 1800 years later, we stand, with regard to him, where the Apostle stood : the day of the Lord not present, and not to arrive until this man of sin be manifested : the μυστήριον τῆς ἀνομίας still working, and much advanced in its working : the κατέχον still hindering. And let us ask ourselves, what does this represent to us ? Is it not indicative of a state in which the ἀνομία is working on, so to speak, underground, under the surface of things,—gaining, throughout these many ages, more expansive force, more accumulated power, but still hidden and unconcentrated ? And might we not look, in the progress of such a state of things, for repeated minor embodiments of this ἀνομία,—ἄνομοι, and ἀντίχριστοι πολλοί (1 John ii. 18) springing up here and there in different ages and countries,—the ἀποστασία going onward and growing,—just as there were of Christ Himself frequent types and minor embodiments before He came in the flesh ? Thus in the Papacy, where so many of the prophetic features are combined, we see as it were a standing embodiment and type of the final Antichrist—in the remarkable words of Gregory the Great, the 'præcursor Antichristi:' and in Nero, and every persecutor as he arose, and Mohammed, and Napoleon, and many other forms and agencies of evil, other more transient types and examples of him. We may, following out the parallelism, contrast the Papacy, as a type of Antichrist, having its false priesthood, its pretended sacrifices, its 'Lord God' the Pope, with that standing Jewish hierarchy of God's own appointing, and its High Priesthood by which our Lord was prefigured : and the other and personal types, with those typical persons, who appeared under the old covenant, and set forth so plainly the character and sufferings and triumphs of the Christ of God.

36. According then to this view, we still look for the man of sin, in the fulness of the prophetic sense, to appear, and that immediately before the coming of the Lord. We look for him as the final and central embodiment of that ἀνομία, that resistance to God and God's law, which has been for these many centuries fermenting under the crust of human society, and of which we have already witnessed so many

---

[2] For surely this is the only possible understanding of our ver. 8 on the ordinary acceptance of words.

partial and tentative eruptions. Whether he is to be expected personally, as one individual embodiment of evil, we would not dogmatically pronounce: still we would not forget, that both ancient interpretation, and the world's history, point this way. Almost all great movements for good or for ill have been gathered to a head by one central personal agency. Nor is there any reason to suppose that this will be otherwise in the coming ages. In proportion as the general standard of mental cultivation is raised, and man made equal with man, the ordinary power of genius is diminished, but its extraordinary power is increased ; its reach deepened, its hold rendered more firm. As men become familiar with the achievements and the exercise of talent, they learn to despise and disregard its daily examples, and to be more independent of mere men of ability; but they only become more completely in the power of gigantic intellect, and the slaves of pre-eminent and unapproachable talent. So that there seems nothing improbable, judging from these considerations, and from the analogy of the partial manifestations which we have already seen, that the centralization of the antichristian power, in the sense of this prophecy, may ultimately take place in the person of some one of the sons of men.

37. The great ἀποστασία again will receive a similar interpretation. Many signal apostasies the world and the Church have seen. Continually, those are going out from us, who were not of us. Unquestionably the greatest of these has been the Papacy, that counterfeit of Christianity, with its whole system of falsehood and idolatry. But both it, and Mohammedanism, and Mormonism, and the rest, are but tentamina and foreshadowings of that great final apostasy (ἡ ἀποστασία), which shall deceive, if it were possible, even the very elect.

38. The particulars of ver. 4 we regard variously, according as the ἄνομος is a person or a set of persons, with however every inclination to take them literally of a person, giving out these things respecting himself, and sitting as described in the temple of God, whether that temple is to be taken in the strictly literal signification of the Jerusalem-temple (to which we do not incline), or as signifying a Christian place of assembly, the gathering-point of those who have sought the fulfilment of the divine promise of God's presence,—and so called the temple of God.

39. The κατέχον and κατέχων, the one the *general hindrance*, the other the *person in whom that hindrance is summed up*, are, in this view, very plain. As the Fathers took them of the Roman Empire and Emperor, standing and ruling in their time, repressing the outbreak of sin and enormity,—so have we been taught by history to widen this view, and understand them of the *fabric of human polity*, and *those who rule that polity*, by which the great up-bursting of godlessness is kept down and hindered. I say, we have been taught this by history : seeing that as often as these outbursts have taken place, their course and devastations

have been checked by the knitting up again of this fabric of temporal power : seeing that this power, wherever the seeds of evil are most plentiful, is strictly a *coercive* power, and that there only is its restraining hand able to be relaxed, where the light and liberty of the Gospel are shed abroad : seeing that especially has this temporal power ever been in conflict with the Papacy, restraining its pretensions, modifying its course of action, witnessing more or less against its tyranny and its lies.

40. The explanation of the μυστήριον τῆς ἀνομίας has been already anticipated. It, the ἀνομία, in the hearts and lives, in the speeches and writings of men, is and ever has been working in hidden places, and only awaits the removal of the hindering power to issue in that concentrated manifestation of ὁ ἄνομος, which shall usher in the times of the end.

41. *When* this shall be, is as much hidden from us, as it was from the Apostles themselves. This may be set, on the one hand, as a motive to caution and sobriety ; while on the other let us not forget, that every century, every year, brings us nearer to the fulfilment,—and let this serve to keep us awake and watchful, as servants that wait for the coming of their Lord. We are not to tremble at every alarm ; to imagine that every embodiment of sin is the final one, or every falling away the great apostasy : but to weigh, and to discern, in the power of Him, by whom the prince of this world is judged : that whenever the Lord comes He may find us ready,—ready to stand on His side against any, even the final concentration of His adversaries ; ready, in daily intercourse with and obedience to Him, to hail His appearance with joy.

42. If it be said, that this is somewhat a dark view to take of the prospects of mankind, we may answer, first, that we are not speculating on the phænomena of the world, but we are interpreting God's word : secondly, that we believe in One in whose hands all evil is working for good,—with whom there are no accidents nor failures,—who is bringing out of all this struggle, which shall mould and measure the history of the world, the ultimate good of man and the glorification of His boundless love in Christ : and thirdly, that no prospect is dark for those who believe in Him. For them all things are working together for good ; and in the midst of the struggle itself, they know that every event is their gain ; every apparent defeat, real success ; and even the last dread conflict, the herald of that victory, in which all who have striven on God's part shall have a glorious and everlasting share.

CHAPTER VII.

ON THE PASTORAL EPISTLES.

SECTION I.

THEIR AUTHORSHIP.

1. THERE never was the slightest doubt in the ancient Church, that the Epistles to Timothy and Titus were canonical, and written by St. Paul.

(α) They are contained in the Peschito Syriac version, which was made in the second century.

(β) In the fragment on the Canon of Scripture first edited by Muratori and thence known by his name, generally ascribed to the end of the second century or the beginning of the third (see Routh, Reliq. Sacr. i. pp. 397 ff.), we read, among the Epistles of St. Paul " verum ad Philemonem una, et ad Timotheum duas (duæ ?) pro affectu et dilectione, in honore tamen Ecclesiæ catholicæ, in ordinatione ecclesiasticæ disciplinæ, sanctificatæ sunt."

(γ) Irenæus begins his preface, p. 1, with a citation of 1 Tim. i. 4, adding καθὼς ὁ ἀπόστολός φησιν : in iv. 16. 3, p. 246, cites 1 Tim. i. 9 : in ii. 14. 7, p. 135, 1 Tim. vi. 20 : in iii. 14. 1, p. 201, quotes 2 Tim. iv. 9—11:

"Lucas . . . . quoniam non solum prosecutor, sed et co-operarius fuerit apostolorum, maxime autem Pauli, et ipse autem Paulus manifestavit in epistolis, dicens : Demas me dereliquit et abiit Thessalonicam, Crescens in Galatiam, Titus in Dalmatiam : Lucas est mecum solus :"

In i. 16. 3, p. 83, quotes Titus iii. 10 :

οὓς ὁ Παῦλος ἐγκελεύεται ἡμῖν μετὰ μίαν καὶ δευτέραν νουθεσίαν παραιτεῖσθαι.

And again, with ὡς καὶ Παῦλος ἔφησεν, iii. 3. 4, p. 177. In iii. 2. 3, p. 176, he says, τούτου τοῦ Λίνου Παῦλος ἐν ταῖς πρὸς Τιμόθεον ἐπιστολαῖς μέμνηται.

(δ) Clement of Alexandria, Strom. ii. 11 (52), p. 457 P. :

περὶ ἧς ὁ ἀπόστολος γράφων, ὦ Τιμόθεέ, φησιν, τὴν παρακαταθήκην φύλαξον ἐκτρεπόμενος τὰς βεβήλους κενοφωνίας κ.τ.λ. 1 Tim. vi. 20.

Strom. iii. 6 (51), p. 534 P. :

αὐτίκα περὶ τῶν 'βδελυσσομένων τὸν γάμον Παῦλος ὁ μακάριος λέγει . . .
1 Tim. iv. 1.

Ib. (53), p. 536 P. :

ἴσμεν γὰρ καὶ ὅσα περὶ διακόνων γυναικῶν ἐν τῇ ἑτέρᾳ πρὸς Τιμόθεον ἐπιστολῇ ὁ γενναῖος διατάσσεται Παῦλος.

Strom. i. 14 (59), p. 350 P. :

τὸν δὲ ἕβδομον οἱ μὲν . . . οἱ δὲ Ἐπιμενίδην τὸν Κρῆτα . . . οὗ μέμνηται ὁ ἀπόστολος Παῦλος ἐν τῇ πρὸς Τίτον ἐπιστολῇ λέγων οὕτως· Κρῆτες ἀεὶ κ.τ.λ. (Tit. i. 12).

These are only a few of the direct quotations in Clement.

(ε) TERTULLIAN :

De præscript. hæret. c. 25, vol. ii. p. 37 : " Et hoc verbo usus est Paulus ad Timotheum : O Timothee, depositum custodi (1 Tim. vi. 20). Et rursum : Bonum depositum serva " (2 Tim. i. 14). And he further proceeds to quote 1 Tim. i. 18, vi. 13 ff. ; 2 Tim. ii. 2 (twice).

Ib. c. 6, p. 18: "Nec diutius de isto, si idem est Paulus, qui et alibi hæreses inter carnalia crimina enumerat scribens ad Galatas, et qui Tito[3] suggerit, hominem hæreticum post primam correptionem recusandum, quod perversus sit ejusmodi et delinquat, ut a semetipso damnatus." (Tit. iii. 10, 11.)

Adv. Marcion. v. 21, p. 524, speaking of the Epistle to Philemon : " Soli huic epistolæ brevitas sua profuit, ut falsarias manus Marcionis evaderet. Miror tamen, cum ad unum hominem literas factas receperit, quod ad Timotheum duas et unam ad Titum de ecclesiastico statu compositas recusaverit."

(ζ) Eusebius includes all three Epistles among the universally confessed canonical writings (ὁμολογούμενα), H. E. iii. 25.

It is useless to cite further testimonies, for they are found every where, and in abundance.

2. But we must notice various allusions, more or less clear, to these Epistles, which occur in the *earlier* Fathers.

(η) CLEMENT OF ROME (end of Cent. I.): Ep. 1 ad Cor. ch. 29, p. 269 : προσέλθωμεν οὖν αὐτῷ ἐν ὁσιότητι ψυχῆς, ἁγνὰς καὶ ἀμιάντους χεῖρας αἴροντες πρὸς αὐτόν. See 1 Tim. ii. 8[4].

(θ) IGNATIUS (beginning of Cent. II.): Ep. to Polycarp, § 6, p. 724 : ἀρέσκετε ᾧ στρατεύεσθε. See 2 Tim. ii. 4.

(ι) POLYCARP (beginning of Cent. II.): Ep. ad Philipp. ch. 4, p. 1008 : ἀρχὴ δὲ πάντων χαλεπῶν φιλαργυρία· εἰδότες οὖν ὅτι οὐδὲν εἰσηνέγκαμεν εἰς τὸν κόσμον, ἀλλ' οὐδὲ ἐξενεγκεῖν τι ἔχομεν, ὁπλισώμεθα τοῖς ὅπλοις τῆς δικαιοσύνης : 1 Tim. vi. 7, 10.

---

[3] Dr. Davidson, Introd. iii. 109, omits the word 'Tito,' as it would appear, from inadvertency.

[4] Two other supposed references may be seen in Lardner, ii. p. 39, and Davidson, iii. p. 101; but they are too slight to authorize their introduction here.

Ib. ch. 9, p. 1013: οὐ γὰρ τὸν νῦν ἠγάπησαν αἰῶνα. See 2 Tim. iv. 10[5].

(κ) HEGESIPPUS (end of Cent. II.), as cited by Eusebius (H. E. iii. 32), says that, while the ἱερὸς τῶν ἀποστόλων χορός remained, the Church παρθένος καθαρὰ καὶ ἀδιάφθορος ἔμεινεν : but that, after their withdrawal, and that of those who had been ear-witnesses of inspired wisdom, ἡ σύστασις τῆς ἀθέου πλάνης began, διὰ τῆς τῶν ἑτεροδιδασκάλων ἀπάτης: who, as no apostle was left, γυμνῇ λοιπὸν ἤδη τῇ κεφαλῇ τῷ τῆς ἀληθείας κηρύγματι τὴν ψευδώνυμον γνῶσιν ἀντικηρύττειν ἐπεχείρουν. See 1 Tim. vi. 3, 20[6].

(λ) ATHENAGORAS (end of Cent. II.): Legat. pro Christianis 16, p. 291 : πάντα γὰρ ὁ θεός ἐστιν αὐτὸς αὑτῷ, φῶς ἀπρόσιτον : 1 Tim. vi. 16.

(μ) THEOPHILUS OF ANTIOCH (end of Cent. II.): ad Autolyc. iii. 14, p. 389 : ἔτι μὴν καὶ περὶ τοῦ ὑποτάσσεσθαι ἀρχαῖς καὶ ἐξουσίαις, καὶ εὔχεσθαι περὶ αὐτῶν, κελεύει ἡμᾶς θεῖος λόγος ὅπως ἤρεμον καὶ ἡσύχιον βίον διάγωμεν. 1 Tim. ii. 1, 2. Tit. iii. 1[7].

ii. p. 95 (Lardner) : διὰ ὕδατος καὶ λουτροῦ παλιγγενεσίας πάντας τοὺς προσιόντας τῇ ἀληθείᾳ.

(ν) To these may be added Justin Martyr (middle of Cent. II.), Dial. c. Tryph. c. 47, p. 143 : ἡ χρηστότης καὶ ἡ φιλανθρωπία τοῦ θεοῦ. Tit. iii. 4.

3. Thus the Pastoral Epistles seem to have been from the earliest times known, and continuously quoted, in the Church. It is hardly possible to suppose that the above coincidences are all fortuitous. The only other hypothesis on which they can be accounted for, will be treated farther on.

4. Among the Gnostic heretics, however, they did not meet with such universal acceptance. Clement of Alexandria, Strom. ii. 11 (p. 457 P.), after having quoted 1 Tim. vi. 20 ff., adds : ὑπὸ ταύτης ἐλεγχόμενοι τῆς φωνῆς, οἱ ἀπὸ τῶν αἱρέσεων τὰς πρὸς Τιμόθεον ἀθετοῦσιν ἐπιστολάς. Tertullian (see above, under ϵ) states that Marcion rejected from his canon (recusaverit) the Epistles to Timothy and Titus. And Jerome, Prol. ad Titum, vol. vii. p. 685, says : "Licet non sint digni fide qui fidem primam irritam fecerunt, Marcionem loquor et Basilidem et omnes hæreticos qui vetus laniant testamentum: tamen eos aliqua ex parte ferremus, si saltem in novo continerent manus suas, et non auderent Christi (ut ipsi jactitant) boni Dei Filii, vel Evangelistas violare, vel Apostolos ..... ut enim de cæteris Epistolis taceam, de quibus quicquid contrarium suo dogmati viderant, eraserunt, nonnullas integras repudiandas

---

[5] See other slighter parallels in Lardner and Davidson, ubi supra. The μέγα τῆς θεοσεβείας μυστήριον, commonly adduced from Justin (in Eus. H. E. iii. 27), is not his, but forms part of the text of Eusebius. See Huther, Einl. p. 35.

[6] See on Baur's attempt to meet this, below, par. 14 note.

[7] Lardner gives ὃς διδάσκει ἡμᾶς δικαιοπραγεῖν, καὶ εὐσεβεῖν καὶ καλοποιεῖν, as an allusion to Tit. ii. 11, 12: but it is far too slight.

crediderunt, ad Timotheum videlicet utramque, ad Hebræos, et ad Titum, quam nunc conamur exponere. . . . . Sed Tatianus, Encratitarum patriarches, qui et ipse nonnullas Pauli Epistolas repudiavit, hanc vel maxime, id est, ad Titum, Apostoli pronunciandam credidit, parvipendens Marcionis et aliorum, qui cum eo in hac parte consentiunt, assertionem." This last fact, Tatian's acceptance of the Epistle to Titus, Huther thinks may be accounted for by the false teachers in that Epistle being more expressly designated as *Jews*, ch. i. 10, 14; iii. 9.

5. From their time to the beginning of the present century, the authenticity of the Pastoral Epistles remained unquestioned. At that time, Schmidt (J. E. C.) first, and afterwards Schleiermacher (in his Letters to Gass, 1807) attacked the genuineness of the first Epistle to Timothy: which on the other hand, was defended by *Planck, Wegscheider,* and *Beckhaus.* It soon began however to be seen, that from the close relation of the three Epistles, the arguments which Schleiermacher had used against one, would apply to all: and accordingly first *Eichhorn,* and then not so decidedly *De Wette,* denied the genuineness of all three.

6. The latter Commentator, in his Introduction (1826), combined the view of Schleiermacher, that 1 Tim. was a compilation from the other two, with that of Eichhorn, that all three were not the genuine productions of St. Paul: but at the same time allowed to the consent of the Church in all ages so much weight, that his view influenced only the historical origin of the Epistles, not their credit and authority.

7. This mere negative ground was felt to be unsatisfactory: and Eichhorn soon put forth a positive hypothesis, that the Epistles were written by some disciple of St. Paul, with a view of collecting together his oral injunctions respecting the constitution of the Church. This was adopted by Schott, with the further conjecture that St. Luke was the author.

8. The defenders of the Epistles [8] found it not difficult to attack such a position as this, which was raised on mere conjecture after all: and Baur, on the other hand, remarked [9], "We have no sufficient resting-place for our critical judgment, as long as we only lay down that the Epistles are not Pauline: we must have established some positive data which transfer them from the Apostle's time into another age." Accordingly, he himself has laboured to prove them to have been written in the time of the Marcionite heresy; and their author to have been one who, not having the ability himself to attack the Gnostic positions, thought to uphold the Pauline party by putting his denunciations of it into the mouth of the Apostle.

[8] Hug, Bertholdt, Feilmoser, Guerike, Böhl, Curtius, Klug, Heydenreich, Mack. See Huther, Einleitung, p. 38, from which many of the particulars in the text are taken.

[9] Die sogenn. Pastoralbriefe des Apostel Paulus aufs neue kritisch untersucht, 1835.

9. This view of Baur's has been, however, very far from meeting with general adoption, even among the impugners of the genuineness of our Epistles. The new school of Tübingen have alone accepted it with favour. De Wette himself, in the later editions of his Handbuch (I quote from that of 1847), though he is stronger than ever against the three Epistles, does not feel satisfied with the supposed settling of the question by Baur. He remarks, "According to Baur, the Epistles were written after the middle of the second century, subsequently to the appearance of Marcion and other Gnostics. But, inasmuch as the allusions to Marcion, on which he builds this hypothesis, are by no means certain, and the testimonies of the existence of the Pastoral Epistles stand in the way (for it is hardly probable that the passage in Polycarp, c. 4 (see above, par. 2), can have been the original of 1 Tim. vi. 7, 10): it seems that we must assume an earlier date for the Epistles,—somewhere about the end of the first century[1]."

10. With this last dictum of De Wette's, adverse criticism has resumed its former uncertain footing, and is reduced to the mere negative complexion which distinguished it before the appearance of Baur's first work. We have then merely to consider it as a negation of the Pauline origin of the Epistles, and to examine the grounds on which that negation rests. These may be generally stated under the three following heads:

I. The historical difficulty of finding a place for the writing of the three Epistles during the lifetime of St. Paul:

II. The apparent contact with various matters and persons who belong to a later age than that of the Apostles: and

III. The peculiarity of expressions and modes of thought, both of which diverge from those in St. Paul's recognized Epistles.

11. Of the first of these I shall treat below, in the section "On the times and places of writing." It may suffice here to anticipate merely the general conclusion to which I have there come, viz. that they belong to the latest period of our Apostle's life, after his liberation from the imprisonment of Acts xxviii. Thus much was necessary in order to our discussion of the two remaining grounds of objection.

12. As regards objection II., three subordinate points require notice:

(a) *The heretics, whose views and conduct are opposed in all three Epistles.*

It is urged that these belonged to later times, and their tenets to systems undeveloped in the apostolic age. In treating of the various places where they are mentioned, I have endeavoured to shew that the tenets and practices predicated of them will best find their explanation by regarding them as the marks of a state of transition between Judaism,

---

[1] Handbuch: Allgemeine Bemerkungen über die Pastoralbriefe, p. 121.

through its ascetic form, and Gnosticism proper, as we afterwards find it developed[2].

13. The traces of Judaism in the heretics of the Pastoral Epistles are numerous and unmistakable. They professed to be νομοδιδάσκαλοι (1 Tim. i. 7) : commanded ἀπέχεσθαι βρωμάτων (ib. iv. 3) : are expressly stated to consist of μάλιστα οἱ ἐκ περιτομῆς (Tit. i. 10) : caused men προσέχειν Ἰουδαϊκοῖς μύθοις (ib. 14): brought in μάχας νομικάς (ib. iii. 9).

14. At the same time, the traces of incipient Gnosticism are equally apparent. It has been thought best, in the notes on 1 Tim. i. 4, to take that acceptation of γενεαλογίαι, which makes it point to those lists of Gnostic emanations, so familiar to us in their riper forms in after history : in ch. iv. 3 ff., we find the seeds of Gnostic dualism ; and though that passage is prophetic, we may fairly conceive that it points to the future development of symptoms already present. In ib. vi. 20, we read of ψευδώνυμος γνῶσις, an expression which has furnished Baur with one of his strongest objections, as betraying a post-apostolic origin[3]. But, granted the reference to *gnosis*, Gnostically so called, neither Baur nor any one else has presumed to say, when the term began to be so used. For our present purpose, the reference is clear. Again in 2 Tim. ii. 17, 18, we read of some of them explaining away the resurrection of the body, saying that it has passed already,—a well-known error of the Gnostics (see note in loc.).

15. It remains that we should shew two important facts, which may influence the reader's mind concerning both the nature of these heretics, and date of our Epistles. First, they are not the Judaizers of the Apostle's earlier Epistles. These his former opponents were strong upholders of the law and its requirements : identify themselves plainly with the 'certain men from Judæa' of Acts xv. 1, in spirit and tenets : uphold circumcision, and would join it with the faith in Christ. Then as we proceed, we find them retaining indeed some of their former features, but having passed into a new phase, in the Epistle to the Colossians. There, they have added to their Judaizing tenets, various excrescences of will-worship and superstition : are described no longer as persons who would be under the law and Christ together, but as vain,

[2] See 1 Tim. i. 3, 4, 6, 7, 19; iv. 1—7; vi. 3 ff.; 2 Tim. ii. 16—23; iii. 6—9, 13; iv. 4; Titus i. 10, 11, 14, 16; iii. 9, 10,—and notes.
[3] Baur makes much of the passage of Hegesippus quoted above, par. 2, κ, in which he says that this ψευδών. γνῶσις first became prevalent after the Apostles were removed from the Church. On this he founds an argument that our Epistle could not have appeared till that time. But the passage as compared with the Epistle proves the very reverse. The ψευδών. γν. was secretly working in the Apostles' time, and for that reason this caution was given: but after their time it began to be openly professed, and came forth, as Hegesippus says, with uncovered head.

puffed up in their carnal mind, not holding the Head (see Prolegg. to Col., § ii. 10 ff.).

16. The same character, or even a further step in their course, seems pointed out in the Epistle to the Philippians. There, they are not only Judaizers, not only that which we have already seen them, but κύνες, κακοὶ ἐργάται, ἡ κατατομή : and those who serve God in the power of His Spirit are contrasted with them. And here (Phil. iii. 13), we seem to find the first traces becoming perceptible of the heresy respecting the resurrection in 2 Tim. ii. 18, just as the preliminary symptoms of unsoundness on this vital point were evident in 1 Cor. xv.

17. If now we pass on to our Epistles, we shall find the same progress from legality to superstition, from superstition to godlessness, in a further and riper stage. Here we have more decided prominence given to the abandonment of the foundations of life and manners displayed by these false teachers. They had lost all true understanding of the law itself (1 Tim. i. 7): had repudiated a good conscience (ib. 19): are hypocrites and liars (ib. iv. 2), branded with the foul marks of moral crime (ib.) : are of corrupt minds, using religion as a means of bettering themselves in this world (ib. vi. 5 ; Tit. i. 11) : insidious and deadly in their advances, and overturning the faith (2 Tim. ii. 17) : proselytizing and victimizing foolish persons to their ruin (ib. iii. 6 ff.) : polluted and unbelieving, with their very mind and conscience defiled (Tit. i. 15) : confessing God with their mouths, but denying Him in their works, abominable and disobedient, and for every good work worthless (ib. i. 16).

18. I may point out to the reader, how well such advanced description of these persons suits the character which we find drawn of those who are so held up to abhorrence in the later of the Catholic Epistles, and in the Epistle to the Hebrews : how we become convinced, as we pass down the apostolic age, that all its heresies and false teachings must be thought of as gradually converging to one point,—and that point, godlessness of life and morals. Into this, Judaism, once so rigid, legality, once so apparently conscientious, broke and crumbled down. I may state my own conviction, from this phænomenon in our Pastoral Epistles, corroborated indeed by all their other phænomena, that we are, in reading them, necessarily placed at a point of later and further development than in reading any other of the works of St. Paul.

19. The *second* important point as regards these heretics is this : as they are not the Judaizers of former days, so *neither are they the Gnostics of later days.* Many minor points of difference might be insisted on, which will be easily traced out by any student of church history : I will only lay stress on one, which is in my mind fundamental and decisive.

20. The Gnosticism of later days was eminently *anti-judaistic.* The Jewish Creator, the Jewish law and system, were studiously held in con-

tempt and abhorrence. The whole system had migrated, so to speak, from its Jewish standing-point, and stood now entirely over against it. And there can be little doubt, whatever other causes may have co-operated to bring about this change, that the great cause of it was the break-up of the Jewish hierarchy and national system with the destruction of Jerusalem and the temple. The heretical speculations had, so to speak, no longer any mooring-place in the permanence of the old law, and thus, rapidly drifting away from it, soon lost sight of it altogether, and learned to despise it as a thing gone by. Then the oriental and Grecian elements, which had before been in a state of forced and unnatural fusion with Judaism, cast it out altogether, retaining only those traces of it which involved no recognition of its peculiar tenets.

21. The false teachers then of our Epistles seem to hold a position intermediate to the Apostle's former Judaizing adversaries and the subsequent Gnostic heretics, distinct from both, and just at that point in the progress from the one form of error to the other, which would suit the period subsequent to the Epistle to the Philippians, and prior to the destruction of Jerusalem. There is therefore nothing in them and their characteristics, which can cast a doubt upon the genuineness of the Epistles.

22. (b) (See above, par. 12), *the ecclesiastical order subsisting when they were written.* Baur and De Wette charge the author of these Epistles with hierarchical tendencies. They hold that the strengthening and developing of the hierarchy, as we find it aimed at in the directions here given, could not have been an object with St. Paul. De Wette confines himself to this general remark: Baur goes farther into detail. In his earlier work, on the Pastoral Epistles, he asserts, that in the genuine Pauline Epistles there is found no trace of any official leaders of the Churches (it must be remembered that with Baur, the genuine Epistles are only those to the Galatians, Corinthians, and Romans): whereas here those Churches are found in such a state of organization, that ἐπίσκοποι, πρεσβύτεροι, and διάκονοι are significantly put forward: πρεσβύτεροι according to him being the name for the collective body of church-rulers, and ἐπίσκοπος for that one of them who was singly entrusted with the government. In his later work ('Paulus' u.s.w.), he maintains that the Gnostics, as the first heretics proper, gave the first occasion for the foundation of the episcopal government of the Churches. But even granting this, the very assumption would prove the earlier origin of our Epistles: for in them there is not the slightest trace of episcopal government, in the later sense. Baur's own explanation of ἐπίσκοπος differs entirely from that later sense.

23. The fact is, that the form of Church government disclosed in our Epistles is of the simplest kind possible. The diaconate was certainly, in some shape or other, coæval with the very infancy of the Church:

and the presbyterate was almost a necessity for every congregation. No Church could subsist without a government of some kind : and it would be natural that such an one as that implied in the presbyterate should arise out of the circumstances in every case.

24. The directions also which are here given, are altogether of an ethical, not of an hierarchical kind. They refer to the selection of men, whose previous lives and relations in society afford good promise that they will discharge faithfully the trust committed to them, and work faithfully and successfully in their office. The fact that no such directions are found in the other Epistles, is easily accounted for : partly from the nature of the case, seeing that he is here addressing persons who were entrusted with this selection, whereas in those others no such matter is in question : partly also from the late date of these letters, the Apostle being now at the end of his own course,—seeing dangerous heresies growing up around the Church, and therefore anxious to give those who were to succeed him in its management, direction how to consolidate and secure it.

25. Besides which, it is a pure assumption that St. Paul could not, from his known character, have been anxious in this matter. In the Acts, we find him ever most careful respecting the consolidation and security of the churches which he had founded : witness his journeys to inspect and confirm his converts (Acts xv. 36; xviii. 23), and that speech uttered from the very depth of his personal feeling and desire, to the presbytery of the Ephesian Church (ib. xx. 18—38).

26. We must infer then, that there is nothing in the hints respecting Church-government which these Epistles contain, to make it improbable that they were written by St. Paul towards the close of his life.

27 (c) (See above, par. 12.) *The institution of widows*, referred to 1 Tim. v. 9 ff., is supposed to be an indication of a later date. I have discussed, in the note there, the description and standing of these widows : holding them to be not, as Schleiermacher and Baur, deaconesses, among whom in later times were virgins also, known by the name of χῆραι (τὰς παρθένους τὰς λεγομένας χήρας, Ign. ad Smyrn. c. 13, p. 717), but as De W., al., an especial band of real widows, set apart, but not yet formally and finally, for the service of God and the Church. In conceiving such a class to have existed thus early, there is no difficulty : indeed nothing could be more natural : we already find traces of such a class in Acts ix. 41; and it would grow up and require regulating in every portion of the Church. On the ἑνὸς ἀνδρὸς γυνή, which is supposed to make another difficulty, see note, 1 Tim. iii. 2.

28. Other details belonging to this objection II. are noticed and replied to in treating of the passages to which they refer. They are founded for the most part in unwarranted assumptions regarding the apostolic age and that which followed it : in forgetting that there

must have been a blending of the one age into the other during that later section of the former and earlier section of the latter, of both of which we know so little from primitive history : that the forms of error which we find prevalent in the second century, must have had their origin and their infancy in an age previous : and that here as elsewhere, 'the child is father of the man :' the same characteristics, which we meet full-grown both in the heretics and in the Church of the second century, must be expected to occur in their initiative and less consolidated form in the latter days of the Apostles and their Church [4].

29. We come now to treat of objection III.,—*the peculiarity of expressions and modes of thought, both of which diverge from those in St. Paul's recognized Epistles.* There is no denying that the Pastoral Epistles do contain very many peculiar words and phrases, and that the process of thought is not that which the earlier Epistles present. Still, our experience of men in general, and of St. Paul himself, should make us cautious how we pronounce hastily on a phænomenon of this kind. Men's method of expression changes with the circumstances among which they are writing, and the persons whom they are addressing. Assuming the late date for our Epistles which we have already mentioned, the circumstances both of believers and false teachers had materially changed since most of those other Epistles were written. And if it be said that on any hypothesis it cannot have been many years since the Epistles of the imprisonment, we may allege on the other hand the very great difference in subject, the fact that these three are addressed to his companions in the ministry, and contain directions for Church management, whereas none of the others contain any passages so addressed or of such character.

30. Another circumstance here comes to our notice, which may have modified the diction and style at least of these Epistles. Most of those others were written by the hand of an amanuensis; and not only so, but probably with the co-operation, as to form of expression and putting out of the material, of either that amanuensis or some other of his fellow-helpers. The peculiar character of these Pastoral Epistles forbids us from imagining that they were so written. Addressed to dear friends and valued colleagues in the ministry, it was not probable that he should have written them by the agency of others. Have we then, assuming that he wrote them with his own hand, any points of comparison in the other Epistles? Can we trace any resemblance to their peculiar diction in portions of those other Epistles which were undoubtedly or probably also autographic?

---

[4] See the objection regarding the *youth of Timotheus* assumed in these Epistles, treated below in § ii., 'On the places and times of writing.'

31. The first unquestionably autographic Epistle which occurs to us is that to Philemon : which has also this advantage for comparison, that it is written to an individual, and in the later portion of St. Paul's life. And it must be confessed, that we do not find here the resemblance of which we are in search. The single word εὔχρηστος is the only point of contact between the unusual expressions of the two. It is true that the occasion and subject of the Epistle to Philemon were totally distinct from those of any of the Pastoral Epistles : almost all their ἅπαξ λεγόμενα are from the very nature of things excluded from it. Still I must admit that the dissimilarity is striking and not easily accounted for. I would not disguise the difficulty which besets this portion of our subject : I would only endeavour to point out in what direction it ought to guide our inference from the phænomena.

32. We have found reason to believe (see note on Gal. vi. 11) that the Epistle to the Galatians was of this same autographic character. Allowing for the difference of date and circumstances, we may expect to find here some points of peculiarity in common. In both, false teachers are impugned : in both, the Apostle is eager and fervent, abrupt in expression, and giving vent to his own individual feelings. And here we do not seek in vain[5]. We find several unusual words and phrases common only to the two or principally occurring in them. Here again, however, the total difference of subject throughout a great portion of the Epistle to the Galatians prevents any very great community of expression.

33. We have a very remarkable addition to the Epistle to the Romans in the doxology, ch. xvi. 25, 26 ; appended to it, as we have there in-

---

[5] I set down a list of the principal similarities which I have observed between the diction of the Gal. and the Pastoral Epp. :

1. τοῦ δόντος ἑαυτὸν περὶ κ.τ.λ., Gal. i. 4 : compare ὁ δοὺς ἑαυτὸν ἀντίλυτρον ὑπὲρ κ.τ.λ., 1 Tim. ii. 6 ; ὃς ἔδωκεν ἑαυτὸν ὑπὲρ ἡμῶν, Tit. ii. 14. These are the only places where this expression is used of our Lord.

2. εἰς τοὺς αἰῶνας τῶν αἰώνων, Gal. i. 5 : compare the same expression in 1 Tim. i. 17, 2 Tim. iv. 18. The only other place where it occurs is in the last Epistle of the imprisonment, Phil. iv. 20.

3. προέκοπτον, Gal. i. 14, found in 2 Tim. ii. 16, iii. 9, 13, and Rom. xiii. 12 only in St. Paul.

4. ἰδοὺ ἐνώπιον τοῦ θεοῦ, Gal. i. 20 : the expression ἐν. τ. θ. occurs elsewhere frequently in St. Paul, but in this asseverative sense is found only in the Past. Epp. : 1 Tim. v. 21, vi. 13, 2 Tim. ii. 14 (κυρίου), iv. 1.

5. στύλος, Gal. ii. 9 : in St. Paul, 1 Tim. iii. 15 only.

6. ἀνόητοι, Gal. iii. 1 : in St. Paul (Rom. i. 14), 1 Tim. vi. 9, Tit. iii. 3 only.

7. μεσίτης, Gal. iii. 20 : in St. Paul (three times in Hebrews), 1 Tim. ii. 5 only.

8. ἐλπίς, objective, Gal. v. 5 : compare Tit. ii. 13.

9. πνεύματι ἄγεσθε, Gal. v. 18 : construction, with ἄγομαι (Rom. viii. 14), 2 Tim. iii. 6 only.

10. καιρῷ ἰδίῳ, Gal. vi. 9 : found 1 Tim. ii. 6, vi. 15, Tit. i. 3 only.

ferred, in later times by the Apostle himself, as a thankful effusion of his fervent mind. That addition is in singular accordance with the general style of these Epistles. We may almost conceive him to have taken his pen off from writing one of them, and to have written it under the same impulse[6].

34. There remain, however, many expressions and ideas not elsewhere found. Such are πιστὸς ὁ λόγος, 1 Tim. i. 15; iii. 1; iv. 9: 2 Tim. ii. 11: Tit. iii. 8,—a phrase dwelling much at this time on the mind of the writer, but finding its parallel at other times in his favourite πιστὸς ὁ θεός, and the like: cf. 1 Cor. i. 9; x. 13: 2 Cor. i. 18: 1 Thess. v. 24: 2 Thess. iii. 3 :—εὐσέβεια, εὐσεβῶς, 1 Tim. ii. 2; iii. 16; iv. 7; vi. 11: 2 Tim. iii. 5, 12: Tit. i. 1; ii. 12,—of which we can only say that occurring as it does in this peculiar sense only here and in 2 Peter, we should be disposed to ascribe its use to the fact of the word having at the time become prevalent in the Church as a compendious term for the religion of Christians :—σώφρων and its derivatives, 1 Tim. ii. 9, 15; iii. 2: 2 Tim. i. 7: Tit. i. 8; ii. 2, 4 ff., 12,—a term by no means strange to the Apostle's other writings, cf. Rom. xii. 3: 2 Cor. v. 13, but probably coming into more frequent use as the necessity for the quality itself became more and more apparent in the settlement of the Church (cf. also 1 Pet. iv. 7):—ὑγιής, ὑγιαίνειν, of right doctrine, 1 Tim. i. 10; vi. 3: 2 Tim. i. 13; iv. 3: Tit. i. 9, 13; ii. 1 f., 8,—one of the most curious peculiarities of our Epistles, and only to be ascribed to the prevalence of the image in the writer's mind at the time, arising probably from the now apparent tendency of the growing heresies to corrupt the springs of moral action:—μῦθοι, 1 Tim. i. 4; iv. 7: 2 Tim. iv. 4: Tit. i. 14,—to be accounted for by the fact of the heretical legends having now assumed such definite shape as to deserve this name, cf. also 2 Pet. i.

---

[6] The actual verbal accordances are frequent, but even less striking than the general similarity :

ver. 25. εὐαγγέλιόν μου: (Rom. ii. 16) 2 Tim. ii. 8 only.

κήρυγμα (1 Cor. i. 21, ii. 4, xv. 14): 2 Tim. iv. 17, Tit. i. 3 only.

χρόνοις αἰωνίοις: 2 Tim. i. 9, Tit. i. 2 only.

ver. 26. φανερωθέντος in this sense, St. Paul elsewhere, but also 1 Tim. iii. 16, 2 Tim. i. 10, Tit. i. 3.

κατ᾽ ἐπιταγὴν . . . θεοῦ, (1 Cor. vii. 6, 2 Cor. viii. 8,) 1 Tim. i. 1, Tit. i. 3 only.

μόνῳ σοφῷ θεῷ: 1 Tim. i. 17, var. readd.

I may add to these instances, those of accordance between the Pastoral Epistles and the speech of St. Paul in Acts xx. : viz.

δρόμος, found only Acts xiii. 25, xx. 24, 2 Tim. iv. 7.

περιποιεῖσθαι, Paul, only Acts xx. 28, 1 Tim. iii. 13.

ἱματισμός, Paul, only Acts xx. 33, 1 Tim. ii. 9.

ἐπιθυμέω, with a gen., only Acts xx. 33, 1 Tim. iii. 1.

λόγοι τοῦ κυρίου, Acts xx. 35, 1 Tim. vi. 3.

ἀντιλαμβάνεσθαι, Paul, only Acts xx. 35, 1 Tim. vi. 2.

for προσέχειν, with a dative, see next paragraph.

16:—ζητήσεις, 1 Tim. i. 4; vi. 4: 2 Tim. ii. 23: Tit. iii. 9,—which expression, if not exactly applied to erroneous speculations, is yet used elsewhere of disputes about theological questions; cf. Acts xv. 2; xxv. 20 (John iii. 25); the difference of usage is easily accounted for by the circumstances :—ἐπιφάνεια, instead of παρουσία, 1 Tim. vi. 14: 2 Tim. iv. 1, 8: Tit. ii. 13,—which has a link uniting it to 2 Thess. ii. 8, and may have been, as indeed many others in this list, a word in familiar use among the Apostle and his companions, and so used in writing to them : —δεσπότης, for κύριος, in the secular sense of *master*, 1 Tim. vi. 1, 2: 2 Tim. ii. 21: Tit. ii. 9,—which is certainly remarkable, St. Paul's word being κύριος, Eph. vi. 5, 9: Col. iii. 22; iv. 1,—and of which I know no explanation but this possible one, that the Eph. and Col. being written simultaneously, and these three also near together, there would be no reason why he might not use one expression at one time and the other at another, seeing that the idea never occurs again in his writings :—ἀρνεῖσθαι, 1 Tim. v. 8: 2 Tim. ii. 12 f.; iii. 5: Tit. i. 16; ii. 12,—common to our Epistles with 2 Pet., 1 John, and Jude, but never found in the other Pauline writings ; and of which the only account that can be given is, that it must have been a word which came into use late as expressing apostasy, when the fact itself became usual, being taken from our Lord's own declarations, Matt. x. 33, &c. :— παραιτεῖσθαι, 1 Tim. iv. 7; v. 11: 2 Tim. ii. 23: Tit. iii. 10,—a word the links of whose usage are curious. It is confined to St. Luke and St. Paul and the Epistle to the Hebrews. We have it thrice in the parable of the great supper, Luke xiv. 18, 19: then in the answer of Paul to Festus, in all probability made by himself in Greek, Acts xxv. 11: and Heb. xii. 19, 25 bis. We may well say of it, that the *thing* introduced the word: had the Apostle had occasion for it in other Epistles, he would have used it: but he has not (the same may be said of γενεαλογίαι, 1 Tim. i. 4: Tit. iii. 9 ;—ματαιόλογος, -γία, 1 Tim. i. 6: Tit. i. 10;—κενοφωνίαι, 1 Tim. vi. 20: 2 Tim. ii. 16;—λογομαχίαι, -εῖν, 1 Tim. vi. 4: 2 Tim. ii. 14;—παραθήκη, 1 Tim. vi. 20: 2 Tim. i. 12, 14):—σώτηρ, spoken of God,—1 Tim. i. 1; ii. 3; iv. 10: Tit. i. 3; ii. 10; iii. 4, common also to Luke (i. 47) and Jude (25): the account of which seems to be, that it was a purely Jewish devotional expression, as we have it in the Magnificat,—and not thus absolutely used by the Apostles, in their special proclamation of the Son of God in this character ;—we may observe that St. Jude introduces it with the limitation διὰ Ἰησοῦ χρ. τοῦ κυρίου ἡμῶν;—but in familiar writing one to another, when there was no danger of the mediatorship of Jesus being forgotten, this true and noble expression seems still to have been usual :—βέβηλος, 1 Tim. i. 9; iv. 7; vi. 20: 2 Tim. ii. 16,—common only to Heb. (xii. 16),—an epithet interesting, as bringing with it the fact of the progress of heresy from doctrine to practice, as also does ἀνόσιος, 1 Tim. i. 9;

2 Tim. iii. 2 :—διαβεβαιοῦσθαι, 1 Tim. i. 7 : Tit. iii. 8, a word but slightly differing in meaning, and in its composition with διά (a natural addition in later times), from βεβαιοῦν, which is a common expression with our Apostle, Rom. xv. 8 : 1 Cor. i. 6, 8 : 2 Cor. i. 21 : Col. ii. 7 (Heb. ii. 3 ; xiii. 9) :—προςέχειν, with a dat., 1 Tim. i. 4 ; iii. 8 ; iv. 1, 13 : Tit. i. 14,—found also frequently in St. Luke, Luke xii. 1 ; xvii. 3 ; xxi. 34 : Acts v. 35 ; viii. 6, 10, 11 ; xvi. 14 : xx. 28 (Paul), and Heb. ii. 1 ; vii. 13 : 2 Pet. i. 19 : a word testifying perhaps to the influence on the Apostle's style of the expressions of one who was so constantly and faithfully his companion :—ὑπομιμνήσκειν, 2 Tim. ii. 14 : Tit. iii. 1 (2 Pet. i. 12 : 3 John 10 : Jude 5) :—a word naturally coming into use rather as time drew on, than " in the beginning of the Gospel :" —ἀποτρέπεσθαι, ἐκτρ., 2 Tim. iii. 5 : 1 Tim. i. 6 ; v. 15 ; vi. 20 : 2 Tim. iv. 4 (Heb. xii. 13),—words owing their use to the progress of heresy ; which may be said also of ἀστοχεῖν, 1 Tim. i. 6 ; vi. 21: 2 Tim. ii. 18,— and of τυφοῦσθαι, 1 Tim. iii. 6 ; vi. 4 : 2 Tim. iii. 4 :—&c. &c.

35. There seems no reason why any of the above peculiarities of diction should be considered as imperilling the authenticity of our Epistles. The preceding paragraph will have shewn, that of many of them, some account at least may be given : and when we reflect how very little we know of the circumstances under which they were used, it appears far more the part of sound criticism to let such difficulties stand unsolved, under a sense that we have not the clue to them, than at once and rashly to pronounce on them, as indicative of a spurious origin.

36. Another objection brought by De Wette against our Epistles seems to me to make so strikingly and decisively *for* them, that I cannot forbear giving it in his own words before commenting upon it : " In the composition of all three Epistles we have this common peculiarity,— that from that which belongs to the object of the Epistle, and is besides for the most part of general import, the writer is ever given to digress to general truths, or so-called common-places (1 Tim. i. 15 ; ii. 4—6 ; iii. 16 ; iv. 8—10 : 2 Tim. i. 9 f.; ii. 11—13, 19—21; iii. 12—16 : Tit. ii. 11—14; iii. 3—7), and that even that which is said by way of contradiction or enforcing attention, appears in this form (1 Tim. i. 8—10 ; iv. 4 f. ; vi. 6—10 : 2 Tim. ii. 4—6: Tit. i. 15). With this is combined another peculiarity common to them, that after such digressions or general instructions, the writer's practice is to recur, or finally to appeal to and fall back on previous exhortations or instructions given to his correspondent (1 Tim. iii. 14 f. ; iv. 6, 11 ; vi. 2, 5 (rec.) : 2 Tim. ii. 7, 14 ; iii. 5 : Tit. ii. 15 ; iii. 8)." In commenting on this, I would ask, what could be more natural than both these phænomena, under the circumstances, supposing St. Paul their author ? Is it not the tendency of an instructor writing to his pupil to make these compendious references to truths well known and established between them ? Would not

83]

this especially be the case, as age drew on, and affectionate remembrance took the place of present and watchful instruction ? We have hardly a stronger evidence for the authenticity of our Epistles, than our finding them so exactly corresponding with what we might expect from Paul the aged towards his own sons in the faith. His restless energies are still at work : we see that the ἐνδυνάμωσις will keep him toiling to the end in his οἰκονομία : but those energies have changed their complexion : they have passed from the dialectic character of his former Epistles, from the wonderful capacity of intricate combined ratiocination of his subsequent Epistles, to the urging, and repeating, and dilating upon truths which have been the food of his life : there is a resting on former conclusions, a stating of great truths in concentrated and almost rhythmical antithesis, a constant citation of the '*temporis acti*,' which lets us into a most interesting phase of the character of the great Apostle. We see here rather the succession of brilliant sparks, than the steady flame : burning words indeed and deep pathos, but not the flower of his firmness, as in his discipline of the Galatians, not the noon of his bright warm eloquence, as in the inimitable Psalm of Love (1 Cor. xiii.).

37. We may also notice, as I have pointed out in the notes on 1 Tim. i. 11 ff., a habit of going off, not only at a word, or into some collateral subject, as we find him doing in all his writings, but on the mention of any thing which reminds him of God's mercies to himself, or of his own sufferings on behalf of the Gospel, into a digression on his own history, or feelings, or hopes. See 1 Tim. i. 11 ff.; ii. 7: 2 Tim. i. 11 ff., 15 ff. ; ii. 9, 10; iii. 10 f.; iv. 6 ff. These digressions do not occur in the Epistle to Titus, perhaps on account of the less intimate relation which subsisted between him and the Apostle. I cannot help considering them also as deeply interesting, betokening, as I have there expressed it in the note, advancing age, and that faster hold of individual habits of thought, and mannerisms, which characterizes the decline of life.

38. De Wette brings another objection against our Epistles, which seems to me just as easily to bear urging on the other side as the last. It is, the constant *moral* reference of all that is here said respecting the faith : the idea that error is ever combined with evil conscience, the true faith with good conscience. From what has been already said, it will be seen how naturally such a treatment of the subject sprung out of the progress of heresy into ethical corruption which we have traced through the later part of the apostolic age : how true all this was, and how necessary it was thus to mark broadly the line between that faith, which was the only guarantee for purity of life, and those perversions of it, which led downwards to destruction of the moral sense and of practical virtue.

39. When however in his same paragraph (Allgem. Bemerkungen üb. die Pastoralbriefe, p. 117 c) he assumes that the writer gives a validity to *moral desert*, which stands almost in contradiction to the Pauline doctrines of grace, and cites 1 Tim. ii. 15; iii. 13; iv. 8; vi. 18 ff.: 2 Tim. iv. 8, to confirm this,—I own I am quite unable to see any inconsistency in these passages with the doctrine of grace as laid down, or assumed, in the other Epistles. See Rom. ii. 6—10: 1 Cor. iii. 14; ix. 17, 25; xv. 58: Phil. i. 19, and many other places, in which the foundation being already laid of union with Christ by faith, and salvation by His grace, the carrying on and building up of the man of God in good works, and reward according to the measure of the fruits of the Spirit, are quite as plainly insisted on as any where in these Epistles.

40. De Wette also finds what he calls, 'an *apology for the law*, and an admission of its possessing an ethical use,' in 1 Tim. i. 8. In my notes on that passage, I have seen reason to give it altogether a different bearing: but even admitting the fact, I do not see how it should be any more inconsistent with St. Paul's measure of the law, than that which he says of it in Rom. vii. And when he objects that the *universalism* of these Epistles (1 Tim. ii. 4; iv. 10; Tit. ii. 11), although in itself Pauline, does not appear in the same polemical contrast, as e. g. in Rom. iii. 29,—this seems very trifling in fault-finding: nothing on the contrary can be more finely and delicately in accordance with his former maintenance against all impugners of God's universal purpose of salvation to all mankind, than that he should, even while writing to one who did not doubt of that great truth, be constant to his own habit of asserting it.

41. There are many considerations pressed by the opponents of the Pauline authorship, which we can only mention and pass by. Some of them will be found incidentally dealt with in the notes: with others the student who has hitherto followed the course of these remarks will know how himself to deal. As usual, the similarities to, as well as discrepancies from, the other Epistles, are adduced as signs of spuriousness[7]. The three Epistles, and especially the first to Timothy, are charged with poverty of sentiment, with want of connexion, with unworthiness of the Apostle as author. On this point no champion of the Epistles could so effectually defeat the opponents, as they have defeated themselves. Schleiermacher, holding 1 Tim. to be compiled out of the other two, finds it in all these respects objectionable and below the mark: Baur will not concede this latter estimate, and De Wette charges Schleier-

[7] Huther gives a list of parallels against which this objection has been brought, and I transcribe it, that the reader may judge and refute for himself: 1 Tim. i. 12—14, as compared with 1 Cor. xv. 9, 10: 1 Tim. ii. 11, 12, with 1 Cor. xiv. 34, 35: 2 Tim. i. 3—5, with Rom. i. 8 ff.: ii. 5, with 1 Cor. ix. 24: ii. 6, with 1 Cor. ix. 7 ff.: ii. 8, with Rom. i. 3: ii. 11, with Rom. vi. 8: ii. 20, with Rom. ix. 21: iii. 2 ff., with Rom. i. 29 ff.: iv. 6, with Phil. ii. 17: Tit. i. 1—4, with Rom. i. 1 ff.

macher with having failed to penetrate the sense of the writer, and found faults, where a more thorough exposition must pronounce a more favourable judgment. These differences may well serve to strike out the argument, and indeed all such purely subjective estimates, from the realms of biblical criticism.

42. A word should be said on the smaller, but not less striking indications of genuineness, which we here find. Such small, and even trifling individual notices, as we here meet with, can hardly have proceeded from a forger. Of course a careful *falsarius* may have taken care to insert such, as would fall in with the known or supposed state of the Apostle himself and his companions at the time: a shrewd and skilful one would invent such as might further any views of his own, or of the Churches with which he was connected: but I must say I do not covet the judgment of that critic, who can ascribe such a notice as that of 2 Tim. iv. 13, τὸν φελόνην ὃν ἀπέλιπον ἐν Τρωάδι παρὰ Κάρπῳ ἐρχόμενος φέρε, καὶ τὰ βιβλία, μάλιστα τὰς μεμβράνας, to either the caution or the skill of a forger. What possible motive there could be for inserting such minute particulars, unexampled in the Apostle's other letters, founded on no incident in history, tending to no result,—might well baffle the acutest observer of the phænomena of falsification to declare.

43. A concession by Baur himself should not be altogether passed over. St. Paul in his farewell discourse, Acts xx. 29, 30, speaks thus: ἐγὼ οἶδα ὅτι εἰσελεύσονται μετὰ τὴν ἄφιξίν μου λύκοι βαρεῖς εἰς ὑμᾶς μὴ φειδόμενοι τοῦ ποιμνίου, καὶ ἐξ ὑμῶν αὐτῶν ἀναστήσονται ἄνδρες λαλοῦντες διεστραμμένα τοῦ ἀποσπᾶν τοὺς μαθητὰς ὀπίσω ἑαυτῶν. Baur confesses that here the defenders of the Epistles have firm ground to stand on. "Here we see," he continues, "the Apostle anticipating just what we find more in detail in the Pastoral Epistles." But then he proceeds to set aside the validity of the inference, by quietly disposing of the farewell discourse, as written "post eventum." For those who look on that discourse very differently, his concession has considerable value.

44. I would state then the general result to which I have come from all these considerations:

1. External testimony in favour of the genuineness of our Epistles is so satisfactory, as to suggest no doubt on the point of their universal reception in the earliest times.

2. The objections brought against the genuineness by its opponents, on internal grounds, are not adequate to set it aside, or even to raise a doubt on the subject in a fair-judging mind.

45. I therefore rest in the profession of the Epistles themselves, and the universal belief of Christians, that they were VERITABLY WRITTEN BY ST. PAUL[8].

---

[8] I have preferred in this section giving those considerations which influence most

SECTION II.

TIME AND PLACE OF WRITING.

1. A difficult problem yet remains: to assign, during the life of the Apostle, a time for the writing, which will suit the phænomena of these Epistles.

2. It will have been abundantly seen by what has preceded, that I cannot consent to place them in any portion of St. Paul's apostolic labours recorded in the Acts. All the data with which they themselves furnish us, are against such a supposition. And most of all is the state of heresy and false teaching, as indicated by their common evidence. No amount of ingenuity will suffice to persuade us, that there could have been during the long sojourn of the Apostle at Ephesus in Acts xix., such false teachers as those whose characters have been examined in the last section. No amount of ingenuity again will enable us to conceive a state of the Church like that which these Epistles disclose to us, at any time of that period, extending from the year 54 to 63, during which the other Epistles were written. Those who have attempted to place the Pastoral Epistles, or any of them, in that period, have been obliged to overlook all internal evidence, and satisfy themselves with fulfilling the requirements of external circumstances.

3. It will also be seen, that I cannot consent to separate these Epistles widely from one another, so as to set one in the earlier, and the others in the later years of the Apostle's ministry. On every account, they must stand together. Their style and diction, the motives which they furnish, the state of the Church and of heresy which they describe, are the same in all three: and to one and the same period must we assign them.

4. This being so, they necessarily belong to the latest period of the Apostle's life. The concluding notices of the Second Epistle to Timotheus forbid us from giving an earlier date to that, and consequently to the rest. And no writer, as far as I know, has attempted to place that Epistle, supposing it St. Paul's, at any date except the end of his life[9].

my own mind, to entering at full length on all the bearings of the subject. The reader will find a very good and terse compendium of the objections and their answers in Conybeare and Howson, vol. ii. pp. 657—660, edn. 2 : and a full and elaborate discussion of both in Dr. Davidson's Introduction to the N. T. vol. iii. pp. 100—153. That portion of Dr. Davidson's work is very well and thoroughly done, in which he shews the insuperable difficulties which beset the hypothesis of a scholar of St. Paul having forged the Epistles at the end of the first century, as De Wette supposes. Huther's and Wiesinger's Einleitungen also contain full and able discussions of the whole question; especially the latter.

[9] De Wette has fallen into a curious blunder in carrying out his own hypothesis. He argues that 1 Tim. must have been written after 2 Tim., because we find Hyme-

5. The question then for us is, What was that latest period of his life? Is it to be placed at the end of the first Roman imprisonment, or are we to conceive of him as liberated from that, and resuming his apostolic labours?

6. Let us first try the former of these hypotheses. It has been adopted by chronologers of considerable note: lately, by Wieseler and Dr. Davidson. We approach it, laden as it is with the weight of (to us) the insuperable objection on internal grounds, stated above. We feel that no amount of chronological suitableness will induce us complacently to put these Epistles in the same age of the Church with those to the Ephesians, Colossians, and Philippians. But we would judge the hypothesis here on its own merely external grounds.

7. In order for it to stand, we must find some occasion, *previous to the imprisonment*, when St. Paul may have left Timotheus at Ephesus, himself proceeding to Macedonia. And this time must of course be subsequent to St. Paul's first visit to Ephesus, Acts xviii. 20, 21, when the Church there was founded, if indeed it can be said to have been then founded. On his departure then, he did not go into Macedonia, but to Jerusalem; which alone, independently of all other considerations, excludes that occasion[1].

8. His second visit to Ephesus was that long one related in Acts xix., the τριετία of Acts xx. 31, the ἔτη δύο of xix. 10, which latter, however, need not include the whole time. When he left Ephesus at the end of this time, after the tumult, ἐξῆλθε πορευθῆναι εἰς τὴν Μακεδονίαν, which seems at first sight to have a certain relation to πορευόμενος εἰς Μακεδονίαν of 1 Tim. i. 3. But on examination, this relation vanishes: for in Acts xix. 22, we read that, intending to go to Jerusalem by way of Macedonia and Achaia, he sent off from Ephesus, before his own departure, Timotheus and Erastus: so that he could not have left Timotheus behind in Ephesus. Again, in 1 Tim. iii. 14, he hopes to return to Ephesus shortly. But we find no trace of such an intention, and no attempt to put it in force, in the history. And besides, even if Timotheus, as has sometimes been thought from 1 Cor. xvi. 11, did return to Ephesus before the Apostle left it, and in this sense might have been left there on his departure, we must then suppose him to have almost immediately deserted the charge entrusted to him; for he is again, in the autumn of

næus, who is mentioned with reprobation, apparently for the first time, in 2 Tim. ii. 17 f.,—in a further stage of reprobation, judged and condemned, in 1 Tim. i. 20. He forgets that, the two Epistles being according to him forgeries, with no real circumstances whatever as their basis, such reasoning is good for nothing. He is in fact arguing from their genuineness to their spuriousness.

[1] This was however supposed by Calvin to have been the time of writing 1 Tim.: on ch. iii. 14,—"omnino enim sperabat se venturum: ut venisse probabile est, si hanc epistolam scripsit quo tempore Phrygiam peragrabat: sicuti refert Lucas Act. xviii. 23."

57, with St. Paul in Macedonia in 2 Cor. i. 1, and in Corinth in the winter (Rom. xvi. 21), and returned to Asia thence with him, Acts xx. 4: and thus, as Wieseler remarks, the whole scope of our Epistle, the ruling and ordering of the Ephesian Church during the Apostle's absence, would be defeated. Grotius suggested, and Bertholdt adopted, a theory that the Epistle might have been sent on St. Paul's return from Achaia to Asia, Acts xx. 4, and that Timotheus may, instead of remaining in Troas on that occasion, as related Acts xx. 5, have gone direct to Ephesus, and there received the Epistle. But, apart from all other difficulties [2], how exceedingly improbable, that such an Epistle should have preceded only by a few weeks the farewell discourse of Acts xx. 18—35, and that he should have sent for the elders to Miletus, though he himself had expressed, and continually alluded to in the Epistle, an intention of visiting Ephesus shortly!

9. These difficulties have led to a hypothesis that the journey from Ephesus is one unrecorded in the Acts, occurring during the long visit of Acts xix. That during that time a journey to Corinth did take place, we have inferred from the data furnished in the Epistles to the Corinthians: see Prolegg. to Vol. II. ch. iii. § v. During that journey, Timotheus may have been left there. This conjecture is at least worthy of full discussion: for it seems to fulfil most of the external requirements of the first Epistle.

10. Mosheim, who was its originator, held the journey to Greece to have taken place very early in the three years' visit to Ephesus, and to have lasted nine months,—thus accounting for the difference between the *two years and three months* of Acts xix. 8, 10, and the *three years* of Acts xx. 31. Wieseler [3], however, has so far regarded the phænomena of the Epistle itself, as to shew that it would be very unlikely that the false teachers had early in that visit assumed such consistency and acquired such influence: and besides, we must assume, from the intimation in 1 Tim. i. 3 ff., that the false teachers had already gained some notoriety, and were busy in mischief, *before* the Apostle's departure.

11. Schrader [4], the next upholder of the hypothesis, makes the Apostle remain in Ephesus up to Acts xix. 21, and then undertake the journey there hinted at, through Macedonia to Corinth, thence to Crete (where he founded the Cretan Churches and left Titus), to Nicopolis in Cilicia (see below, in the Prolegg. to Titus: sending from thence the first Epistle to Timotheus and that to Titus), Antioch, and so through Galatia back to Ephesus. The great and fatal objection to this hypothesis is, the insertion in Acts xix. 21—23 of so long a journey, lasting, according to

---

[2] See Wieseler, Chronologie, vol. ii. p. 291 ff.

[3] Ib. p. 296 f.

[4] Der Apostel Paulus, vol. i. pp. 100 ff.

Schrader himself[5], two years (from Easter 54 to Easter 56), not only without any intimation from St. Luke, but certainly against any reasonable view of his text, in which it is implied, that the intention of ver. 21 was not then carried out, but afterwards, as related in ch. xx. 1 ff.

12. Wieseler himself has adopted, and supported with considerable ingenuity, a modified form of Schrader's hypothesis. After two years' teaching at Ephesus, the Apostle, he thinks, went, leaving Timotheus there, on a visitation tour to Macedonia, thence to Corinth, returning by Crete, where he left Titus, to Ephesus. During this journey, either in Macedonia or Achaia, he wrote 1 Tim.,—and after his return to Ephesus, the Epistle to Titus: 2 Tim. falling towards the end of his Roman imprisonment, with which, according to Wieseler, his life terminated. This same hypothesis Dr. Davidson adopts, rejecting however the unrecorded visit to Corinth, which Wieseler inweaves into it: and placing the voyage to Crete during the same Ephesian visit, but separate from this to Macedonia.

13. It may perhaps be thought that some form of this hypothesis would be unobjectionable, if we had *only the first Epistle to Timotheus* to deal with. But even thus, it will not bear the test of thorough examination. In the first place, as held by Davidson, in its simplest form, it inserts into the Apostle's visit to Ephesus, a journey to Macedonia and back entirely for the sake of this Epistle[6]. Wieseler's form of the hypothesis avoids, it is true, this gratuitous supposition, by connecting the journey with the unrecorded visit to Corinth: but is itself liable to these serious objections (mentioned by Huther, p. 17), that 1) it makes St. Paul write the first Epistle to the Corinthians a very short time after the unrecorded visit to Corinth, which is on all accounts improbable. And this is necessary to his plan, in order to give time for the false teachers to have grown up at Ephesus:—2) that we find the Apostle, in his farewell discourse, prophetically anticipating the arising of evil men and seducers among the Ephesians: whereas by any placing of this Epistle during the three years' visit, such must have already arisen, and drawn away many[7]. 3) The whole character of the first Epistle shews that it belongs, not to a very brief and casual absence of this kind, but to one originally intended to last some time, and not unlikely to be prolonged beyond expectation. The hope of returning very soon (iii. 14)

---

[5] See his Chronological Table at the end of his Apostel Paulus, vol. i.

[6] "Why the Apostle went into Macedonia from Ephesus, cannot be discovered." Davidson, vol. iii. p. 13.

[7] Dr. Davidson (iii. p. 14) refers for a refutation of this objection, to his subsequent remarks (pp. 32 f.) on the state of the Ephesian Church. But no sufficient refutation is there found. Granting the whole account of the Ephesian Church there given, it would be quite impossible to conceive that subsequently the Apostle should have spoken of the λύκοι βαρεῖς as altogether future.

is faint : the provision made, is for a longer absence. Had the Apostle intended to return in a few weeks to Ephesus and resume the government of the Church there, we may safely say that the Epistle would have presented very different features. The hope expressed in ch. iii. 14, quite parenthetically, must not be set against the whole character of the Epistle[8], which any unbiassed reader will see provides for a lengthened superintendence on the part of Timothy as the more probable contingency.

14. Thus we see that, independently of graver objections, independently also of the connexion of the three Epistles, the hypothesis of Wieseler and Davidson does not suit the requirements of this first Epistle to Timotheus. When those other considerations come to be brought again into view,—the necessarily later age of all three Epistles, from the heresies of which they treat, from the Church development implied by them, from the very diction and form of thought apparent in them,—the impossibility, on any probable psychological view of St. Paul's character, of placing writings, so altogether diverse from the Epistles to the Corinthians, in the same period of his life with them,—I am persuaded that very few students of Scripture will be found, whose mature view will approve any form of the above hypothesis.

15. It will not be necessary to enter on the various other sub-hypotheses which have been made, such as that of Paulus, that the first Epistle was written from Cæsarea ; &c. &c. They will be found dealt with in Wieseler and Davidson, and in other introductions.

16. Further details must be sought in the following Prolegomena to each individual Epistle. I will mention however two decisive notices in 2 Tim., which no advocate of the above theory, or of any of its modifications, has been able to reconcile with his view. According to that view, the Epistle was written at the end of the first (and only) Roman imprisonment. In ch. iv. 13, we have directions to Timotheus to bring a cloak and books which the Apostle left at Troas. In ib. ver. 20 we read " *Erastus remained in Corinth, but Trophimus left I in Miletus sick.*" To what these notices point, I shall consider farther on : I would now only call the reader's attention to the following facts. Assuming as above, and allowing only the two years for the Roman imprisonment, —the last time he was at Troas and Miletus was *six years before* (Acts xx. 6, 17) ; on that occasion *Timotheus was with him :* and he had repeatedly seen Timotheus since : and, what is insuperable, even supposing these difficulties overcome, *Trophimus did not remain there,* for he was at Jerusalem with St. Paul at the time of his apprehension, Acts xxi. 29. It will be easily seen by reference to any of the supporters of the one imprisonment, how this point presses them. Dr. Davidson tries to account for it by supposing Trophimus to have sailed with St. Paul from Cæsarea in Acts xxvii., and to have been left at Myra, with the

[8] See Davidson, ib. vol. iii. p. 14.

understanding that he should go forward to Miletus, and that under this impression, the Apostle could say Trophimus I left at Miletus (ἀπέλιπον ἐν Μιλήτῳ) sick. Any thing lamer, or more self-refuting, can hardly be conceived: not to mention, that thus also some years had since elapsed, and that the above insuperable objection, that Timotheus had been with him since, and that Trophimus *the Ephesian* must have been talked of by them, remains in full force.

17. The whole force then of the above considerations, as well of the internal character of the Epistles, as of their external notices and requirements, compels us to look, for the time of their writing, to a period subsequent to the conclusion of the history in the Acts, and consequently, since we find in them the Apostle at liberty, *subsequent to his liberation from the imprisonment with which that history concludes.* If there were no other reason for believing that he was thus liberated, and undertook further apostolic journeyings, the existence and phænomena of these Epistles would enforce such a conclusion upon us. I had myself, some years since, on a superficial view of the Pauline chronology, adopted and vindicated the one-imprisonment theory[9] : but the further study of these Epistles has altogether broken down my former fabric. We have in them, as I feel satisfied any student who undertakes the comparison will not fail to discover, a link uniting St. Paul's writings with the Second Epistle of Peter and with that of Jude, and the Epistles of St. John : in other words, with the later apostolic age. There are *two ways only* of solving the problem which they present: one of these is, by believing them to be spurious ; the other, by ascribing them to a period of St. Paul's apostolic agency subsequent to his liberation from the Roman imprisonment of Acts xxviii. ultt.

18. The whole discussion and literature of this view, of a liberation and second imprisonment of our Apostle, would exceed both the scope and the limits of these Prolegomena. It may suffice to remind the reader, that it is supported by an ancient tradition by no means to be lightly set aside : and to put before him the principal passages of early ecclesiastical writers in which that tradition is mentioned.

19. Eusebius, H. E. ii. 22, relates thus :

καὶ Λουκᾶς δὲ ὁ τὰς πράξεις τῶν ἀποστόλων γραφῇ παραδούς, ἐν τούτοις κατέλυσε τὴν ἱστορίαν, διετίαν ὅλην ἐπὶ τῆς Ῥώμης τὸν Παῦλον ἄνετον διατρίψαι, καὶ τὸν τοῦ θεοῦ λόγον ἀκωλύτως κηρύξαι ἐπισημηνάμενος. τότε μὲν οὖν ἀπολογησάμενον, αὖθις ἐπὶ τὴν τοῦ κηρύγματος διακονίαν λόγος ἔχει στείλασθαι τὸν ἀπόστολον, δεύτερον δ᾽ ἐπιβάντα τῇ αὐτῇ πόλει, τῷ κατ᾽ αὐτὸν τελειωθῆναι μαρτυρίῳ. ἐν ᾧ δεσμοῖς ἐχόμενος τὴν πρὸς Τιμόθεον δευτέραν ἐπιστολὴν συντάττει κ.τ.λ.

20. Clement of Rome, Ep. i. ad Corinth. c. 5, p. 17 ff. (the lacunæ in the text are conjecturally filled in as in Hefele's edition) :

[9] In pp. 5—7 of the Prælectio referred to above, ch. ii. § i. 11 note.

διὰ ζῆλον (καὶ ὁ) Παῦλος ὑπομονῆς βραβεῖον ὑ(πέσχ)εν, ἑπτάκις δεσμὰ φορέσας, φ(υγα)δ ευθείς, λιθασθείς. κῆρυξ γ(ενό) μενος ἔν τε τῇ ἀνατολῇ καὶ ἐν (τῇ) δύσει, τὸ γενναῖον τῆς πίστεως αὐτοῦ κλέος ἔλαβεν, δικαιο- σύνην διδάξας ὅλῳ τῷ κόσμῳ, κα(ὶ ἐπὶ) τὸ τέρμα τῆς δύσεως ἐλθών, καὶ μαρτυρήσας ἐπὶ τῶν ἡγουμένων. οὕτως ἀπηλλάγη τοῦ κόσμου, καὶ εἰς τὸν ἅγιον τόπον ἐπορεύθη, ὑπομονῆς γενόμενος μέγιστος ὑπογραμμός[1].

21. The fragment of Muratori on the canon contains the following passage[2]:

"Lucas optime Theophile comprehendit quia sub præsentia ejus singula gerebantur, sicuti et semote passionem Petri evidenter decla- rat, sed profectionem Pauli ab urbe ad Spaniam proficiscentis . ."

This passage is enigmatical, and far from easy to interpret. But all that we need dwell on is, that *the journey of St. Paul into Spain is taken as a fact;* and in all probability, the word 'omittit' being sup- plied, the writer means to say, that St. Luke in the Acts does not relate that journey.

22. This liberation and second imprisonment being assumed, it will naturally follow that the First Epistle to Timotheus and that to Titus were written during the interval between the two imprisonments ;—the second to Timotheus during the second imprisonment. We shall now proceed to enquire into the probable assignment and date of each of the three Epistles.

23. The last notice which we possess of the first Roman imprison- ment, is the Epistle to the Philippians. There (i. 26) the Apostle evidently intends to come and see them, and (ii. 24) is confident that it will be before long. The same anticipation occurred before in his Epistle to Philemon (ver. 22). We may safely then ascribe to him the inten- tion, in case he should be liberated, of visiting the Asiatic and the Macedonian Churches.

24. We suppose him then, on his hearing and liberation, which cannot have taken place before the spring of A.D. 63 (see chronological table in Prolegg. to Acts), to have journeyed Eastward: visiting perhaps Philippi, which lay on the great Egnatian road to the East, and passing into Asia. There, in accordance with his former desires and intentions, he would give Colossæ, and Laodicea, and Hierapolis, the benefit of his apostolic counsel, and confirm the brethren in the faith. And there perhaps, as before, he would fix his head-quarters at Ephesus. I would not however lay much stress on this, considering that there might well

[1] By some of those who deny a second imprisonment, τὸ τέρμα τῆς δύσεως is inter- preted as if the gen. were one of apposition, 'his τέρμα, *which was* ἡ δύσις;' by others it is rendered the *goal* or *centre* of the West: by others, the *Eastern* boundary of the West: and by all it is taken to mean *Rome.* By those who hold a second imprisonment, it is taken to mean *Spain* or even *Britain.*

[2] See Routh, Reliq. Sacr. iv. p. 4.

have been a reason for his not spending much time there, considering the cause which had driven him thence before (Acts xix.). But that he did *visit* Ephesus, must on our present hypothesis be assumed as a certain fact, notwithstanding his confident anticipation expressed in Acts xx. 25 that he should never see it again. It was not the first time that such anticipations had been modified by the event[3].

25. It would be unprofitable further to assign, except by the most distant indications, his course during this journey, or his employment between this time and that of the writing of our present Epistles. One important consideration, coming in aid of ancient testimony, may serve as our guide in the uncertainty. The contents of our Epistles absolutely require as late a date as possible to be assigned them. The same internal evidence forbids us from separating them by any considerable interval, either from one another, or from the event which furnished their occasion.

26. Now we have traditional evidence well worthy of note, that our Apostle suffered martyrdom in the last year, or the last but one, of Nero. Euseb., Chron. anno 2083 (commencing October A.D. 67) says, "Neronis 13°. Nero ad cætera scelera persecutionem Christianorum primus adjunxit: sub quo Petrus et Paulus apostoli martyrium Romæ consummaverunt."

And Jerome, Catalog. Scriptorum Ecclesiasticorum (c. 5, vol. ii. p. 838), under Paulus, "Hic ergo, *decimo quarto* Neronis anno, eodem die quo Petrus, Romæ pro Christo capite truncatus, sepultusque est in via Ostiensi, anno post passionem Domini tricesimo septimo."

27. I should be disposed then to agree with Conybeare and Howson in postponing both the occasions and the writing of the Pastoral Epistles to very near this date. The interval may possibly have been filled up, agreeably to the promise of Rom. xv. 24, 28, and the tradition of Clement of Rome (quoted above, par. 20), by a journey to Spain, the τέρμα τῆς δύσεως: or it may have been spent in Greece and Asia and the interjacent islands.

As we approach the confines of the known ground again furnished by our Epistles, we find our Apostle again at Ephesus. However the

---

[3] Compare 2 Cor. v. 4, 5, with Phil. i. 23. Dr. Davidson (iii. pp. 16 ff.) lays great stress on the οἶδα of Acts xx. 25, as implying certain apostolic foresight in the power of the Spirit, and argues thence that a subsequent visit to Ephesus cannot have taken place. For argument's sake, let it be so, and let us turn to Phil. i. 25, written, according to Dr. Davidson, at the close of the Roman imprisonment, from which he was not liberated but by death. There we read, οἶδα ὅτι μενῶ καὶ παραμενῶ πᾶσιν ὑμῖν εἰς τὴν ὑμῶν προκοπὴν καὶ χαρὰν τῆς πίστεως, ἵνα τὸ καύχημα ὑμῶν περισσεύῃ ἐν χριστῷ Ἰησοῦ ἐν ἐμοὶ διὰ τῆς ἐμῆς παρουσίας πάλιν πρὸς ὑμᾶς. Surely what is good on one side is good on the other: and I do not see how Dr. Davidson can escape the force of his own argument. He must take his choice, and give up one οἶδα or the other. He has surrendered the latter: why may not we the former?

intervening years had been spent, much had happened which had wrought changes on the Church, and on himself, since his last visit. Those heresies which were then in the bud, had borne bitter fruit. He had, in his own weak and shattered frame, borne about, for four or five more years of declining age, the dying of the Lord Jesus. Alienation from himself had been spreading wider among the Churches, and was embittering his life. Supposing this to have been in A.D. 66 or 67, and the 'young man Saul' to have been 34 or 35 at his conversion, he would not now be more than 64 or 65: but a premature old age would be every way consistent with what we know of his physical and mental constitution. Four years before this he had affectionately pleaded his advancing years in urging a request on his friend Philemon (Philem. 9).

28. From Ephesus, leaving Timotheus there, he went into Macedonia (1 Tim. i. 3). It has been generally assumed, that the first Epistle was written from that country. It may have been so; but the words παρεκάλεσά σε προσμεῖναι ἐν Ἐφέσῳ πορευόμενος εἰς Μακεδονίαν, rather convey to my mind the impression that he was *not in Macedonia* as he was writing. He seems to speak of the whole occurrence as one past by, and succeeded by other circumstances. If this impression be correct, it is quite impossible to assign with any certainty the place of its being written. Wherever it was, he seems to have been in some field of labour where he was likely to be detained beyond his expectations (1 Tim. iii. 14, 15): and this circumstance united with others to induce him to write a letter full of warning and exhortation and direction to his son in the faith, whom he had left to care for the Ephesian Church.

29. Agreeably with the necessity of bringing the three Epistles as near as may be together, we must here place a visit to Crete in company with Titus, whom he left there to complete the organization of the Cretan Churches. From the indications furnished by that Epistle, it is hardly probable that those Churches were now founded for the first time. We find in them the same development of heresy as at Ephesus, though not the same ecclesiastical organization (cf. Tit. i. 10, 11; 15, 16; iii. 9, 11, with i. 5). Nor is the former circumstance at all unaccountable, even as combined with the latter. The heresy, being a noxious excrescence on Judaism, was flourishing independently of Christianity,—or at least required not a Christian Church for its place of sustenance. When such Church began, it was at once infected by the error. So that the Cretan Churches need not have been long in existence. From Tit. i. 5, they seem to have sprung up σποράδην, and to have been on this occasion included by the Apostle in his tour of visitation: who seeing how much needed supplying and arranging, left Titus there for that purpose (see further in Prolegg. to Titus, § ii.).

30. The Epistle to Titus, evidently written very soon after St. Paul left Crete, will most naturally be dated from Asia Minor. Its own

95]

notices agree with this, for we find that he was on his way to winter at Nicopolis (ch. iii. 12), by which it is most natural to understand the well-known city of that name in Epirus[4]. And the notices of 2 Tim. equally well agree with such an hypothesis: for there we find that the Apostle had, since he last communicated with Timotheus, been at Miletus and at Troas, probably also at Corinth (2 Tim. iv. 13, 20). That he again visited Ephesus, is on every account likely: indeed, the natural inference from 2 Tim. i. 18 is, that he had spent some time (possibly of weakness or sickness—from the expression ὅσα διηκόνησεν: but this inference is not necessary, see note there) at that city in the companion-ship of Timotheus, to whom he appeals to confirm what he there says of Onesiphorus.

31. We may venture then to trace out this his last journey as having been from Crete by Miletus, Ephesus, Troas, to Corinth (?): and thence (or perhaps direct by Philippi without passing up through Greece: or he may have gone to Corinth from Crete, and thence to Asia) to Nico-polis, where he had determined to winter (Tit. iii. 12). Nicopolis was a Roman colony (Plin. iv. 1 or 2: Tacit. Ann. v. 10), where he would be more sure against tumultuary violence, but at the same time more open to direct hostile action from parties plotting against him in the metro-polis. The supposition of Mr. Conybeare (C. and H. ii. 573, edn. 2), that being known in Rome as the leader of the Christians, he would be likely, at any time after the fire in 64, to be arrested as implicated in causing it, is not at all improbable. In this case, as the crime was alleged to have been committed at Rome, he would be sent thither for trial (C. and H. ib. note) by the duumviri of Nicopolis.

32. Arrived at the metropolis, he is thrown into prison, and treated no longer as a person charged with matters of the Jewish law, but as a common criminal: κακοπαθῶ μέχρι δεσμῶν ὡς κακοῦργος, 2 Tim. ii. 9. All his Asiatic friends avoided him, except Onesiphorus, who sought him out, and was not ashamed of his chain (2 Tim. i. 16). Demas,

---

[4] See a complete account of Nicopolis in Wordsworth's Pictorial Greece, pp. 310—312; Conybeare and Howson, vol. ii. p. 572, edn. 2; Smith's Dict. of Geography, sub voce.

It is very improbable that any of the comparatively insignificant places elsewhere called by this name is here intended. An enumeration of them will be found in Smith's Dict. of Geogr. as above. The only two which require mention are, 1) Nicopolis in *Thrace*, on the Nessus (Νικόπολις ἡ περὶ Νέσσον, Ptol. iii. 11, 13), supposed by Chry-sostom and Theodoret (ἡ δὲ Ν. τῆς Θράκης ἐστί, Chrys.: τῆς Θράκης ἐστὶν ἡ Ν., τῇ δὲ Μακεδονίᾳ πελάζει, Thdrt.) to be here intended. This certainly *may* have been, for this Nicopolis is not, as some have objected, the one founded by Trajan, see Schrader, vol. i. p. 117: but it is hardly likely to have been indicated by the word thus absolutely put: 2) Nicopolis in *Cilicia*, which Schrader holds to be the place, to suit his theory of the Apostle having been (at a totally different time, see above, par. 11) on his way to Jerusalem.

I may mention that both Winer (RWB.) and Dr. Smith (Dict. of Geogr. as above: not in Bibl. Dict.) fall into the mistake of saying that *St. Paul dates the Epistle from Nicopolis.* No such inference can fairly be drawn from ch. iii. 12.

Crescens, and Titus had, for various reasons, left him. Tychicus he had sent to Ephesus. Of his usual companions, only the faithful Luke remained with him. Under these circumstances he writes to Timotheus a second Epistle, most likely to Ephesus (ii. 17; iv. 13), and perhaps by Tychicus, earnestly begging him to come to him before winter (iv. 21). If this be the winter of the same year as that current in Tit. iii. 12, he must have been arrested immediately on, or perhaps even before, his arrival at Nicopolis. And he writes from this his prison, expecting his execution (ἐγὼ γὰρ ἤδη σπένδομαι, καὶ ὁ καιρὸς τῆς ἐμῆς ἀναλύσεως ἐφέστηκεν, 2 Tim. iv. 6).

33. We hear, 2 Tim. iv. 16, 17, of his being brought up before the authorities, and making his defence. If in the last year of Nero, the Emperor was absent in Greece, and did not try him in person. To this may perhaps point the μαρτυρήσας ἐπὶ τῶν ἡγουμένων of Clement of Rome (see above, par. 20): but it would be manifestly unwise to press an expression in so rhetorical a passage. At this his hearing, none of his friends was bold enough to appear with or for him: but his Christian boldness was sustained by Him in whom he trusted.

34. The second Epistle to Timotheus dates after this his first apology. How long after, we cannot say: probably some little time, for the expression does not seem to allude to a *very recent* occurrence.

35. After this, all is obscurity. That he underwent execution by the sword, is the constant tradition of antiquity, and would agree with the fact of his Roman citizenship, which would exempt him from death by torture. We have seen reason (above, par. 26) to place his death in the last year of Nero, i. e. late in A.D. 67, or A.D. 68. And we may well place the Second Epistle to Timotheus a few months at most before his death [5].

---

[5] One objection which is brought against the view taken above of the date of the Pastoral Epistles, is drawn from 1 Tim. iv. 12, μηδείς σου τῆς νεότητος καταφρονείτω. It is argued (recently by Dr. Davidson, vol. iii. p. 30 f.) that supposing Timotheus to have been twenty when the Apostle first took him for his companion,—at the date which we have assigned to the first Epistle, he would not be less than thirty-four or thirty-five when the Epistle was written; "an age," adds Dr. Davidson, "at which it was not likely he should be despised for his youth." But surely such an age would be a very early one at which to be set over such a Church as that of Ephesus: and at such an age, an ecclesiastical officer whose duty was to rebuke elders, unless he comported himself with irreproachable modesty and gravity, would be exceedingly liable to be slighted and set aside for his youth. The caution seems to me quite to stand in its place, and to furnish no valid objection whatever to our view.

CHAPTER VIII.

ON THE FIRST EPISTLE TO TIMOTHEUS.

THE AUTHORSHIP, and TIME AND PLACE OF WRITING, have been already discussed : and much has been said on the style and diction of this in common with the other Pastoral Epistles. It only remains to consider, 1. The person to whom the Epistle was written : 2. Its especial occasion and object.

SECTION I.

TO WHOM WRITTEN.

1. TIMOTHEUS is first mentioned Acts xvi. 1 ff. as dwelling either in Derbe or Lystra (ἐκεῖ, after both places have been mentioned), but probably in the latter (see on Acts xx. 4, where Δερβαῖος cannot be applied to Timotheus): at St. Paul's second visit to those parts (Acts ib. cf. xiv. 6 ff.). He was of a Jewish mother (Euniké, 2 Tim. i. 5) and a Gentile father (Acts xvi. 1, 3): and had probably been converted by the Apostle on his former visit, for he calls him his γνησίον τέκνον ἐν πίστει (1 Tim. i. 2). His mother, and his grandmother (Lois, 2 Tim. i. 5), were both Christians,—probably also converts, from having been pious Jewesses (2 Tim. iii. 14, 15), during that former visit.

2. Though as yet young, Timotheus was well reported of by the brethren in Lystra and Iconium (Acts xvi. 2), and hence, forming as he did by his birth a link between Jews and Greeks, and thus especially fitted for the exigencies of the time (Acts ib. ver. 4), St. Paul took him with him as a helper in the missionary work. He first circumcised him (ib. 3), to remove the obstacle to his access to the Jews.

3. The next time we hear of him is in Acts xvii. 14 ff., where he with Silas remained behind in Berœa on occasion of the Apostle being sent away to Athens by sea. From this we infer that he had accompanied him in the progress through Macedonia. His youth would furnish quite a sufficient reason why he should not be mentioned throughout the occurrences at Philippi and Thessalonica. That he had been at this latter place, is almost certain : for he was sent back by St. Paul (from Berœa, see Prolegg. to 1 Thess. § ii. 5 f.) to ascertain the state of the Thessalonian Church (1 Thess. iii. 2), and we find him rejoining the Apostle, with Silas, at Corinth, having brought intelligence from Thessalonica (1 Thess. iii. 6).

4. He remained with the Apostle at Corinth, and his name, together with that of Silas (Silvanus), appears in the addresses of both the Epistles

to the Thessalonians, written (see Prolegg. to 1 Thess. § iii.) at Corinth. We have no express mention of him from this time till we find him "ministering" to St. Paul during the long stay at Ephesus (Acts xix. 22): but we may fairly presume that he travelled with him from Corinth to Ephesus (Acts xviii. 18, 19), either remaining there with Priscilla and Aquila, or (which is hardly so probable) going with the Apostle to Jerusalem, and by Antioch through Galatia and Phrygia. From Ephesus (Acts xix. 22) we find him sent forward with Erastus to Macedonia and Corinth (1 Cor. iv. 17 ; xvi. 10: see on this whole visit, Vol. II. Prolegg. to 2 Cor. § ii. 4). He was again with St. Paul in Macedonia when he wrote the Second Epistle to the Corinthians (2 Cor. i. 1 : Vol. II. Prolegg. ibid.). Again, in the winter following we find him in his company in Corinth, where he wrote the Epistle to the Romans (Rom. xvi. 21) : and among the number of those who, on his return to Asia through Macedonia (Acts xx. 3, 4), went forward and waited for the Apostle and St. Luke at Troas.

5. The next notice of him occurs in three of the Epistles of the first Roman imprisonment. He was with St. Paul when he wrote to the Colossians (Col. i. 1), to Philemon (Philem. 1), and to the Philippians (Phil. i. 1). How he came to Rome, whether with the Apostle or after him, we cannot say. If the former, we can only account for no mention of him being made in the narrative of the voyage (Acts xxvii., xxviii.) by remembering similar omissions elsewhere when we know him to have been in company, and supposing that his companionship was almost a matter of course.

6. From this time we know no more, till we come to the Pastoral Epistles[1]. There we find him left by the Apostle at Ephesus to take care of the Church during his absence : and the last notice which we have in 2 Tim. makes it probable that he would set out (in the autumn of A.D. 67 ?), shortly after receiving the Epistle, to visit St. Paul at Rome.

7. Henceforward, we are dependent on tradition for further notices. In Eus. H. E. iii. 42, we read Τιμόθεός γε μὴν τῆς ἐν Ἐφέσῳ παροικίας ἱστορεῖται πρῶτος τὴν ἐπισκοπὴν εἰληχέναι : an idea which may well have originated with the Pastoral Epistles, and seems inconsistent with the very general tradition, hardly to be set aside (see Prolegg. Vol. I. ch. v. § i. 9 ff.), of the residence and death of St. John in that city. Nicephorus (H. E. iii. 11) and the ancient martyrologies make him die by martyrdom under Domitian. See Winer, sub voce : Butler's Lives of the Saints, Jan. 24.

8. We learn that he was set apart for the ministry in a solemn manner by St. Paul, with laying on of his own hands and those of the presbytery (1 Tim. iv. 14 ; 2 Tim. i. 6), in accordance with prophetic utterances of the Spirit (1 Tim. ib. and i. 18): but at what time this

---

[1] On the notice of him in Heb. xiii. 23, see Proleg. to Vol. IV. ch. i. § i. 160; ii. 34.

took place, we are not informed: whether early in his course, or in Ephesus itself, as a consecration for his particular office there. This latter seems to me far the more probable view.

9. The character of Timotheus appears to have been earnest and self-denying. We may infer this from his leaving his home to accompany the Apostle, and submitting to the rite of circumcision at his hands (Acts xvi. 1 ff.),—and from the notice in 1 Tim. v. 23, that he usually drank only water. At the same time it is impossible not to perceive in the notices of him, signs of backwardness and timidity in dealing with the difficulties of his ministerial work. In 1 Cor. xvi. 10 f., the Corinthians are charged, ἐὰν δὲ ἔλθῃ Τιμόθεος, βλέπετε ἵνα ἀφόβως γένηται πρὸς ὑμᾶς· τὸ γὰρ ἔργον κυρίου ἐργάζεται ὡς κἀγώ· μήτις οὖν αὐτὸν ἐξουθενήσῃ, προπέμψατε δὲ αὐτὸν ἐν εἰρήνῃ. And in the notes to the two Epistles the student will find several cases, in which the same traits seem to be referred to[2]. They appear to have increased, in the second Epistle[3], where the Apostle speaks earnestly, and even severely, on the necessity of Christian boldness in dealing with the difficulties and the errors of the day.

10. I subjoin a chronological table of the above notices in the course of Timotheus, arranging them according to that already given in the Prolegg. to Acts, and to the positions taken in the preceding chapter :

A.D.	
45.	Converted by St. Paul, during the first missionary journey, at Lystra.
51. Autumn.	Taken to be St. Paul's companion and circumcised (Acts xvi. 1 ff.).
	Sent from Berœa to Thessalonica (Acts xvii. 14; 1 Thess. iii. 2).
52.	With Silas, joins St. Paul at Corinth (Acts xviii. 5; 1 Thess. iii. 6).
Winter, see above, ch. v. § iii.	With St. Paul (1 Thess. i. 1; 2 Thess. i. 1).
57. Spring.	With St. Paul at Ephesus (Acts xix. 22): sent thence into Macedonia and to Corinth (Acts ib.; 1 Cor. iv. 17, xvi. 10).
Winter.	With St. Paul (2 Cor. i. 1).
58, beginning.	With St. Paul (Rom. xvi. 21).
Spring.	Journeying with St. Paul from Corinth to Asia (Acts xx. 4).
62 or 63.	With St. Paul in Rome (Col. i. 1; Philem. 1; Phil. i. 1).
63—66.	Uncertain.
66 or 67.	Left by St. Paul in charge of the Church at Ephesus. (First Epistle.)
67 or 68.	(Second Epistle.) Sets out to join St. Paul at Rome.
Afterwards.	Uncertain.

[2] See notes on 1 Tim. v. 23; 2 Tim. i. 5, 7; iii. 10; and cf. besides 1 Tim. iv. 12.

[3] It is possible that there may have been a connexion between these indications and the tone of the message in Rev. ii. 1—6: see note there.

SECTION II.

OCCASION AND OBJECT.

1. The Epistle declares its own occasion. The Apostle had left the Ephesian Church in charge to Timotheus: and though he hoped soon to return, was apprehensive that he might be detained longer than he expected (1 Tim. iii. 14, 15). He therefore despatched to him these written instructions.

2. The main object must be described as personal: to encourage and inform Timotheus in his superintendence at Ephesus. But this information and precept regarded two very different branches of his ecclesiastical duty.

3. The first was, the making head against and keeping down the growing heresies of the day. These are continually referred to: again and again the Apostle recurs to their mention: they evidently dwelt much on his mind, and caused him, in reference to Timotheus, the most lively anxiety. On their nature and characteristics I have treated in the preceding chapter.

4. The other object was, the giving directions respecting the government of the Church itself: as regarded the appointing to sacred offices, the selection of widows to receive the charity of the Church, and do service for it,—and the punishment of offenders.

5. For a compendium of the Epistle, and other details connected with it, see Davidson, vol. iii.

CHAPTER IX.

THE SECOND EPISTLE TO TIMOTHEUS.

SECTION I.

TO WHAT PLACE WRITTEN.

1. It has been very generally supposed, that this Epistle was written to Timotheus while the latter was still at Ephesus.

2. The notices contained in it seem partially to uphold the idea. In ch. i. 16—18, Onesiphorus is mentioned as having sought out the Apostle

at Rome, and also having ministered to him at Ephesus : and in ch. iv. 19, the household of Onesiphorus is saluted. Such a notice, it is true, *decides* nothing : but comes in aid of the supposition that St. Paul was writing to Ephesus. Our impression certainly is, from ch. i. 18, that Onesiphorus resided, when living, at Ephesus.

3. Again, in ch. ii. 17, we find Hymenæus stigmatized as a teacher of error, who can hardly be other than the Hymenæus of 1 Tim. i. 20 (see notes there). Joined with this latter in 1 Tim. appears an Alexander : and we again have an Alexander ὁ χαλκεύς mentioned as having done the Apostle much mischief in our ch. iv. 14 : and there *may be* a further coincidence in the fact that an Alexander is mentioned as being put forward by the Jews during the tumult at Ephesus, Acts xix. 33 [1].

4. Besides, the whole circumstances, and especially the character of the false teachers, exactly agree. It would be very difficult to point out any features of difference, such as change of place would be almost sure to bring out, between the heretical persons spoken of here, and those in the first Epistle.

5. The *local* notices come in aid, but not with much force. Timotheus is instructed to bring with him matters which the Apostle had left at *Troas* (ch. iv. 13), which he would pass in his journey from Ephesus to Rome. Two other passages (ch. iv. 12, 20) present a difficulty : and Michaelis, who opposes this view, urges them strongly. St. Paul writes, Τυχικὸν δὲ ἀπέστειλα εἰς Ἔφεσον. This could hardly have been so written, as a simple announcement of a fact, if the person to whom he was writing was himself in that city. This was also felt by Theodoret,— δῆλον ἐντεῦθεν ὡς οὐκ ἐν Ἐφέσῳ διῆγεν ἀλλ’ ἑτέρωθί που κατὰ τουτονὶ τὸν καιρὸν ὁ μακάριος Τιμόθεος. The only answer that I can give, may be derived from the form and arrangement of the sentence. Several had been mentioned, who had left him of their own accord : then, with δέ, introducing a contrast, he states that *he had sent* Tychicus to Ephesus. If any stress is meant to be laid on this circumstance, the notice might still consist with Timotheus himself being there : " but do not wonder at Tychicus being at Ephesus, for I sent him thither." This however is not satisfactory : nor again is it, to suppose with Dr. Davidson (iii. 63) that for some reason Tychicus would not arrive in Ephesus so soon as the Epistle. He also writes, Τρόφιμον δὲ ἀπέλιπον ἐν Μιλήτῳ ἀσθε-νοῦντα. This would be a strange thing to write from Rome to Timotheus in Ephesus, within a few miles of Miletus itself, and respecting Tro-phimus, who was an Ephesian (Acts xxi. 29). It certainly may be said that there might be reasons why the notice should be sent. It might

---

[1] See note there. The latter hypothesis mentioned in it, that he was put forward to clear the Jews, is at least possible : and then he might well have been an enemy of the Apostle.

be intended to clear Trophimus from the charge which appears to be laid against Erastus, that he had remained behind of his own accord in his native land. With the Apostle's delicate feeling for all who were connected with him, he might well state this (again with a δέ) respecting Trophimus, though the fact of his remaining at Miletus might be well known to Timotheus, and his own profession of sickness as the reason.

6. There is a very slight hint indeed given in ch. iv. 11, which may point the same way. Timotheus was to take up Mark and bring him to Rome. The last notice we have had of Mark, was a recommendation of him to the Colossian Church (Col. iv. 10), and that in a strain, which *may* import that he was to be a resident labourer in the Gospel among them. If Mark was at Colossæ, he might be easily sent for from Ephesus to accompany Timotheus.

SECTION II.

OCCASION AND OBJECT.

1. It only remains to enquire respecting this Epistle, what special circumstances occasioned it, and what objects are discernible in it.

2. The immediately moving occasion seems to have been one personal to the Apostle himself. He was anxious that Timotheus should come to him at Rome, bringing with him Mark, as soon as possible (ch. i. 4 ; iv. 9, 11, 21).

3. But he was uncertain how it might be with himself: whether he should live to see his son in the faith, or be 'offered up' before his arrival. He sends to him therefore, not merely a message to come, but a letter full of fatherly exhortations and instructions, applicable to his present circumstances. And these seem not to have been unneeded. Many of his former friends had forsaken him (ch. i. 15 ; iv. 10), and the courage and perseverance of Timotheus himself appeared to be giving way (see above, Prolegg. to 1 Tim. § i. 9). The letter therefore is calculated in some measure to supply what his own mouth would, if he were permitted to speak to him face to face, still more fervently urge on him. And thus we possess an Epistle calculated for all ages of the Church : in which while the maxims cited and encouragements given apply to all Christians, and especially ministers of Christ, in their duties and difficulties,—the affecting circumstances, in which the writer himself is placed, carry home to every heart his earnest and impassioned eloquence.

4. For further notices, I again refer to Dr. Davidson, vol. iii. pp. 48 —75.

EXCURSUS ON PUDENS AND CLAUDIA [2].

1. In 2 Tim. iv. 21, we read as follows:

ἀσπάζεταί σε Εὔβουλος καὶ Πούδης καὶ Λῖνος καὶ Κλαυδία καὶ οἱ ἀδελφοὶ πάντες.

2. Martial, lib. iv. Epigr. 13, is inscribed 'ad Rufum, de nuptiis Pudentis et Claud peregrinæ:' and the first lines run thus:

> "Claudia, Rufe, meo nubit peregrina Pudenti:
> Macte esto tædis, o Hymenææ, tuis."

3. An inscription was found at Chichester in the early part of the last century, and is now in a summer-house in the gardens at Goodwood, running thus, the lacunæ being conjecturally filled in:—

> (N)eptuni et Minervæ templum
> (pr)o salute d(omu)s divinæ
> (ex) auctoritat(e Tib.) Claud.
> (Co)gidubni r. leg. aug. in Brit.
> (colle)gium fabror. et qui in eo
> (a sacris) sunt d. s. d. donante aream
> (Pud)ente Pudentini fil.

4. Now in Tacitus, Agricol. 14, we read, " quædam civitates (in Britain) Cogidubno regi donatæ (is ad nostram usque memoriam fidissimus mansit) vetere ac jampridem recepta populi R. consuetudine, ut haberet instrumenta servitutis et reges." From this inscription these 'civitates' appear to have constituted the kingdom of Sussex. We also gather from the inscription that Cogidubnus had taken the name of his imperial patron, (Tiberius) Claudius: and we find him in close connexion with a Pudens.

5. It was quite natural that this discovery should open afresh a point which the conjectures of British antiquarians appeared before to have provisionally closed. It had been imagined that Claudia, who was identified with the Claudia Rufina of Martial, xi. 53 ('Claudia cæruleis quum sit Rufina Britannis Edita, quam Latiæ pectora plebis habet!'), was a native of *Colchester*, and a daughter of Caractacus, whom they supposed to have been admitted into the Claudian gens.

6. A new fabric of conjecture has been now raised, more ingenious and more probable [3]. The Pudens of Martial is (i. 32) a centurion, aspiring to the "meriti præmia pili," i. e. to be made a primipilus: which ambition we find accomplished in lib. v. 48: and his return to Rome from the North to receive the honour of equestrian rank is anticipated in lib. vi. 58. He may at some time have been stationed in Britain—possibly attached in capacity of adjutant to King Cogidubnus. His presentation of an area for a temple to Neptune and Minerva may have been occasioned by escape from shipwreck, the college of carpenters (shipbuilders) being commissioned to build it to their patrons, Neptune and Minerva; or, as Archdn. Williams (p. 24) seems to think, by a desire to introduce Roman arts among the subjects of the client king. If the British maiden

---

[2] See further on this subject a paper by J. H. Parker, Esq., F.S.A., on "the House of Pudens at Rome" in the Archæological Journal, Vol. xxviii. (No. 109), pp. 41 ff., in which he confirms by architectural evidence the tradition that the church of Sta. Pudentiana occupies a portion of the site of the house of this Pudens.]

[3] In Archdeacon Williams's pamphlet on Pudens and Claudia. I have also consulted an article in the Quarterly Review for July, 1855, entitled "the Romans at Colchester," in which Archdeacon Williams's view is noticed.

Claudia was a daughter of King Tiberius Claudius Cogidubnus, there would be no great wonder in her thus being found mentioned with Pudens.

7. But conjecture is led on a step further by the other notices referred to above Claudia is called *Rufina*. Now Pomponia, the wife of the late commander in Britain Aulus Plautius, belonged to a house of which the Rufi were one of the chief branches. If she were a Rufa, and Claudia were her protégée at Rome (as would be very natural, seeing that her father was received into alliance under Aulus Plautius), the latter would naturally add to her very undistinguishing appellation of Claudia the cognomen of Rufina. Nor is the hypothesis of such a connexion purely arbitrary. A very powerful link appears to unite the two ladies—viz. that of Christianity. Pomponia, we learn from Tacitus (Ann. xii. 32), was (in the year 57) ' superstitionis externæ rea,' and being ' mariti judicio permissa,' was by him tried, ' prisco instituto, propinquis coram,' and pronounced innocent. Tacitus adds, that after many family sorrows, ' per XL annos non cultu nisi lugubri, non animo nisi mæsto, egit. Idque illi imperitante Claudio, impune, mox ad gloriam vertit.' Now it is not at all an improbable explanation of this, that Pomponia may have been a Christian : and the remarkable notice with which our citation from Tacitus concludes may point to the retirement of a Christian life, for which the garb of sorrow would furnish an excuse and protection [4].

8. If then such a connexion as this subsisted, it would account for the conversion of the British maiden to Christianity: and the coincidences are too striking to allow us to pass over the junction of Pudens with her in this salutation. They apparently were not married at this time, or the Apostle would hardly have inserted a third name, that of Linus, between theirs. And this is what we might expect : for the last year of Nero, which is the date we have assigned to the Epistle, is the earliest that can be assigned to any of Martial's pieces, being the year in which he came to Rome.

9. Two of the Epigrams of Martial, i. 32 and v. 48, mention facts which involve Pudens in the revolting moral licence of his day. But there is no reason for supposing them to refer to dates subsequent to his conversion and marriage. Martial's Epigrams are by no means in chronological order, and we cannot gather any indications of this fact with certainty from them.

10. Again, a difficulty has been found in the heathen invocation in the marriage epigram. But, as remarked in the article referred to in the note, we have no allusion to Christian marriage rites during the first three or four centuries, and it is not at all improbable that the heathen rites of the *confarreatio* may, at this early period at least, have been sought by Christians to legalize their unions. When we do find a Christian ceremonial, it is full of the symbolism of the confarreatio. And it seems to be shewn that this was so in the case before us, by the epithet of *sancto*, (in the line ' Di bene, quod sancto peperit fecunda marito,' Mart. xi. 53,) implying that all rites had been duly observed [5].

11. If the above conjectural but not purely arbitrary fabric of hypothesis is allowed to stand, we have the satisfaction of knowing that Claudia was a woman not only of high character, but of mental acquirement (' Romanam credere matres Italides possint, Atthides esse suam,' Mart. ib.), and the mother of a family of three sons, and possibly daughters as well (Mart. ib.).

---

[4] Archdeacon Williams (p. 38) fancies he sees in this *cultus lugubris* and *animus mæstus* signs that she gave way in the trial, and thus saved herself, and that the same circumstance may account for so noble a lady not being mentioned by St. Paul.

[5] This ' *sancto* ' Archdeacon Williams thinks represents ἁγίῳ, and implies the Christianity of Pudens. Surely this is very improbable.

CHAPTER X.

THE EPISTLE TO TITUS.

SECTION I.

TO WHOM WRITTEN.

1. The time and place of writing this Epistle have been before discussed (see above, ch. vii. § ii. 29 f.). It appears to have been sent from Ephesus, or perhaps from Macedonia, during the last year of the Apostle's life (A.D. 67), to Titus, who was left in charge with the Churches in the island of Crete. We shall now gather up the notices which remain to us respecting Titus himself.

2. It is by no means easy to construct an account of Titus. At first sight, a strange phænomenon presents itself. The narrative in the Acts never once mentions him. And this is the more remarkable, because of all the companions of St. Paul he seems to have been the most valued and trusted. No adequate reason has ever been given for this omission. There must be some, it is thought, which we cannot penetrate. Was he identical with some one or other of St. Paul's companions, known to us in the Acts under another name? None seems to satisfy the conditions. Or are we to regard the notice in 2 Tim. iv. 10 as indicative of his ultimate desertion of the Apostle, and thus to seek for a solution of the problem? But even with such a supposition, we shall not touch the narrative of the Acts, which we believe to have been published some years previous to the writing of that Epistle. So that we must be content to leave the problem unsolved, and to put together the few notices which we possess, as given of a person distinct from any mentioned in the Acts.

3. The first notice of Titus, in respect of time, occurs in Gal. ii. 1, 3. We there learn that he was of Gentile origin; and that he was taken by Paul and Barnabas to the council of the Apostles and elders which was convened at Jerusalem to consider of the question of the obligation of the Mosaic law. The narrative in the Acts speaks merely of τινὲς ἄλλοι being sent with the two Apostles. But we see clearly the reason why Titus should be marked out in Gal. ii. for separate mention. He was an uncircumcised Gentile, and the independence of action of St. Paul is shewn by his refusing to listen for a moment to the proposal, which appears to have been urged, for his circumcision. In the Acts, no such reason for special mention of him existed. And this considera-

tion will shew, that we are perhaps not justified in assuming from this incident that Titus held any position of high confidence or trust *at this time.* We find him in close companionship with the Apostles, but that is all we can say. He was certainly converted by means of St. Paul himself, from the γνησίῳ τέκνῳ of Tit. i. 4.

4. Our next notice of him is found in 2 Cor., where it appears (ch. xii. 18) that he, with two other brethren, whose names are not mentioned, was sent forward by St. Paul from Ephesus, during his long visit there, to Corinth, to set on foot a collection (ch. viii. 6) for the poor saints at Jerusalem, and also to ascertain the effect of the first Epistle on the Corinthians. St. Paul, on his departure from Ephesus, waited at Troas, where great opportunities of usefulness were opening before him (ch. ii. 12) : but so anxious was he for the return of Titus (Τίτον τὸν ἀδελφόν μου), that he "left them and passed into Macedonia" (ib. 13). There he met with Titus, who brought him a satisfactory account of the effect of the first Epistle (ch. vii. 6—15) : and from that which St. Paul there says of him, his effective zeal and earnestness in the work of the Gospel is sufficiently shewn. Further proof of these is given in his undertaking of his own accord the delicate task of completing the collection (ch. viii. 6, 16, 17 ff.) : and proof also of the Apostle's confidence in him, in the terms in which he commends him to the Corinthians. He calls him his own κοινωνός (ch. viii. 23) : appeals to his integrity, and entire unity of action with himself (ch. xii. 18).

5. From this time (A.D. 57 : see Vol. II. Prolegg. to 2 Cor. § ii. 3), to the notices furnished by our Epistle (A.D. 67), we know nothing of Titus. At this latter date we find him left in Crete by St. Paul, obviously for a temporary purpose : viz. to "carry forward the correction of those things which are defective" (ch. i. 5), and among these principally, to establish presbyteries for the government of the various Churches, consisting of ἐπίσκοποι (ib. ver. 7). His stay there was to be very short (ch. iii. 12), and he was, on the arrival of Tychicus or Artemas, to join the Apostle at Nicopolis. Not the slightest trace is found in the Epistle, of any intention on the part of St. Paul to place Titus permanently over the Cretan Churches : indeed, such a view is inconsistent with the date furnished us in it.

6. Titus appears to have accordingly rejoined the Apostle, and afterwards to have left him for Dalmatia (2 Tim. iv. 10). Whether from this notice we are to infer that he had been with him in Rome, is quite uncertain. It would seem more probable that he had gone from Nicopolis, or at all events from some point on the journey. We can hardly, on mature consideration of the expressions in 2 Tim. iv. 10, entirely get rid of the impression, that Titus had left the Apostle of his own accord. There is, as has been above observed, an apparent contrast intended between those who are classed with Demas,—they being even included

under his ἐπορεύθη, without another verb expressed—and Tychicus, who had been sent on a mission by the Apostle. Still, it would be unfair to lay any stress on this, in a matter so well admitting of charitable doubt: and we may be well permitted, with Mr. Conybeare, to "hope that his journey to the neighbouring Dalmatia was undertaken by desire of St. Paul."

7. The traditionary notices of the after life of Titus are too evidently grounded on a misunderstanding of our Epistle, to be worth much. Eus. H. E. iii. 4, says, Τιμόθεός γε μὴν τῆς ἐν Ἐφέσῳ παροικίας ἱστορεῖται πρῶτος τὴν ἐπισκοπὴν εἰληχέναι (see on this above, Prolegg. to 1 Tim. § i. 7), ὡς καὶ Τίτος τῶν ἐπὶ Κρήτης ἐκκλησιῶν. And so Theodoret assumes, on 1 Tim. iii. 1.

8. Butler informs us (Lives of the Saints, Jan. 4) that Titus is honoured in Dalmatia as its principal Apostle: that he again returned from Dalmatia to Crete, and finished a laborious and holy life by a happy death in Crete, in a very advanced old age, some say in his 94th year: that he is looked on in Crete as the first archbishop of Gortyna, which metropolitical see is now fixed at Candia, the new capital, built by the Saracens after the destruction of Gortyna. But all this fabric too manifestly bears the appearance of having been raised on the above misapprehension, to possess any traditional worth.

SECTION II.

THE CHURCHES OF CRETE.

1. When, and by whom, these Churches were founded, is quite uncertain. Crete abounded with Jews of wealth and influence. We find proof of this in Jos. Antt. xvii. 12. 1, Κρήτῃ προσενεχθεὶς (the Pseudo-Alexander) Ἰουδαίων ὁπόσοις εἰς ὁμιλίαν ἀφίκετο, ἐπήγαγεν εἰς πίστιν, καὶ χρημάτων εὐπορηθεὶς δόσει τῇ ἐκείνων ἐπὶ Μήλου διῆρεν: and again B. J. ii. 7. 1, τοὺς ἐν Κρήτῃ Ἰουδαίους ἐξαπατήσας καὶ λαμπρῶς ἐφοδισθείς, διέπλευσεν εἰς Μῆλον: Philo, leg. ad Caium, § 36, vol. ii. p. 587,—οὐ μόνον αἱ ἤπειροι μεσταὶ τῶν Ἰουδαϊκῶν ἀποικιῶν εἰσιν, ἀλλὰ καὶ νήσων αἱ δοκιμώταται Εὔβοια, Κύπρος, Κρήτη. In Acts ii. 11 Cretans are named among those who heard the utterance of the Spirit on the day of Pentecost. It is probable therefore, that these Churches owed their origin to the return of individuals from contact with the preaching of the Gospel, and had therefore as yet been unvisited by an Apostle, when they first come before us towards the end of St. Paul's ministry.

2. It is plain that no certain evidence can be deduced, as to the existence of these Churches, from no mention being made of them when St. Paul passed by Crete on his voyage to Malta in Acts xxvii. We have no reason to suppose that he was at liberty to go where he pleased

while remaining in port, nor can we reason, from the analogy of Julius's permission at Sidon, that similar leave would be given him where perhaps no personal relation subsisted between him and the inhabitants. Besides which, the ship was detained by a contrary wind, and probably expecting, during a good part of the time, to sail every day.

3. The next point requiring our attention is, the state of those Churches at the date of our Epistle. If it appear, on comparison, that the false teachers in them were more exclusively Jewish than those at Ephesus, it must be remembered, that this would be a natural consequence, the origin of the Churches being that which we have supposed. And in that case the Apostle's visit, acting as a critical test, would separate out and bring into hostility this Judaistic element, and thus lead to the state of things which we find in this Epistle.

4. Various objections are brought by De Wette against the Epistle, as not corresponding with the facts, in its assumptions and expressions. The first of them, that " it professes to have been written shortly after the founding of the Churches, but sets forth a ripeness and abundance of heretical teaching quite inconsistent with such recent foundation," falls to the ground on our hypothesis of their origin. They were old in actual date of existence, but quite in their infancy of arrangement and formal constitution.

5. With our hypothesis also falls his second objection : viz. that " the great recent success of the Apostle there makes the severity of his characterization of the inhabitants, and that upon another's testimony (ch. i. 12), quite inexplicable. We should rather have looked for thankful recognition, as in other Epistles." But, supposing Christianity to have grown up there in combination with the national vices, and a thorough work of purification to be wanted, then we need not be surprised at the Apostle reminding Titus of the character of those with whom he had to deal, appealing to the testimony of their own writers to confirm the fact.

6. His *third* objection, that " the heretical teachers must have grown up under the eyes of Titus since the Apostle's absence, and thus must have been better known to him than to St. Paul, whereas here we have St. Paul informing him about them,"—is grounded on pure assumption, arising from mistake. The false teachers had been there throughout, and, as we have said, had been awaked into activity by the Apostle's presence and teaching. He knew, from long and bitter experience, far more of them than Titus could do : and his notices and warnings are founded on this longer experience and more thorough apostolic insight.

7. His *fourth*, that " in relation to the moral and ecclesiastical state of the Cretan Christians, as disclosed in the Epistle, a duration of the Gospel among them of some length must be assumed,—from the stress laid on previous purity of character in those to be chosen to church-

offices,"—also falls to the ground on our hypothesis of the origin and previous duration of the Churches.

8. The *fifth* is,—that "it is most unnatural and startling to find not one reference to what the Apostle had taught and preached in Crete, when in 1 Thess., an Epistle written under similar circumstances, we find so many." But we entirely deny the parallelism. The Thessalonian Church had been founded by himself; he was torn away from it in the midst of his teaching: every reason existed for constantly recalling what he had said to them, either to enforce it, or to guard it from misunderstanding. Such was not the case here. He was writing of a Church which he had not himself founded: whose whole situation was different: and writing not to the Church itself, but to one whom he had commissioned to set it in order, and who knew, and needed not reminding of, what he had preached there.

9. It only remains under this head, that we should say something of the character of the Cretans which St. Paul has quoted from Epimenides, ch. i. 12,— Κρῆτες ἀεὶ ψεῦσται, κακὰ θηρία, γαστέρες ἀργαί.

10. Meursius, in his very complete and elaborate treatise on Crete, has accumulated nearly all the testimonies of the ancients respecting them. From his pages I take a few, that the student may be able to illustrate the character by them.

11. On their *avarice*, we have the testimony of Livy, xliv. 45, "Cretenses spem pecuniæ secuti: et quoniam in dividendo plus offensionum quam gratiæ erat, quinquaginta talenta iis posita sunt in ripa diripienda :"—of Plutarch, Paul. Æmil. c. 23, τῶν δὲ στρατιωτῶν, ἐπηκολούθησαν οἱ Κρῆτες, οὐ δι' εὔνοιαν, ἀλλὰ τοῖς χρήμασιν, ὥσπερ κηρίοις μέλιτται, προσλιπαροῦντες :—of Polybius, vi. 46. 3, ὁ περὶ τὴν αἰσχροκέρδειαν καὶ πλεονεξίαν τρόπος οὕτως ἐπιχωριάζει παρ' αὐτοῖς, ὥστε παρὰ μόνοις Κρηταιεῦσι τῶν ἁπάντων ἀνθρώπων μηδὲν αἰσχρὸν νομίζεσθαι κέρδος.

12. On their *ferocity and fraud*, Polybius vi. 46. 9, Κρηταιεῖς ἐν πλείσταις ἰδίᾳ τε καὶ κατὰ κοινὸν στάσεσι καὶ φόνοις καὶ πολέμοις ἐμφυλίοις ἀναστρεφομένους : and iv. 8. 11, Κρῆτες δὲ καὶ κατὰ γῆν καὶ κατὰ θάλατταν πρὸς μὲν ἐνέδρας καὶ λῃστείας καὶ κλοπὰς πολεμίων, καὶ νυκτερινὰς ἐπιθέσεις καὶ πάσας τὰς μετὰ δόλου καὶ κατὰ μέρος χρείας ἀνυπόστατοι, πρὸς δὲ τὴν ἐξ ὁμολόγου καὶ κατὰ πρόσωπον φαλαγγηδὸν ἔφοδον, ἀγεννεῖς καὶ πλάγιοι ταῖς ψυχαῖς :—Strabo, x. c. 4, περὶ δὲ τῆς Κρήτης ὁμολογεῖται διότι . . . ὕστερον πρὸς τὸ χεῖρον μετέβαλεν ἐπὶ πλεῖστον. μετὰ γὰρ τοὺς Τυῤῥηνούς, οἳ μάλιστα ἐδῄωσαν τὴν καθ' ἡμᾶς θάλατταν, οὗτοι εἰσὶν οἱ διαδεξάμενοι τὰ λῃστήρια :—an Epigram of Leonides, Anthol. iii. 22,—αἰεὶ λῃσταὶ καὶ ἁλιφθόροι οὔτε δίκαιοι Κρῆτες· τίς Κρητῶν οἶδε δικαιοσύνην ;

13. On their *mendacity*, Polybius vi. 47. 5, καὶ μὴν οὔτε κατ' ἰδίαν ἤθη δολιώτερα Κρηταιέων εὕροι τις ἄν, πλὴν τελείως ὀλίγων, οὔτε καθόλου ἐπιβουλὰς ἀδικωτέρας :—again, the proverb, Κρὴς πρὸς Αἰγινήτην, is thus

110]

explained by Diogenianus, Cent. v. prov. 92,—ἐπὶ τῶν πανούργοις χρω-
μένων πρὸς ἀλλήλους λέγεται:—Psellus, de operat. Dæm., πλὴν ἴσθι μηδ᾽
αὐτὸν ἐρραψῳδηκέναι με ταῦτα τερατευόμενον, κατὰ τοὺς Κρῆτας καὶ Φοίνι-
κας. And the word κρητίζειν was an expression for 'to lie.' Suidas
has κρητίζειν πρὸς Κρῆτας, ἐπειδὴ ψεῦσται καὶ ἀπατεῶνές εἰσι: see also
Polyb. viii. 21. 5. And their *general depravity* was summed up in the
proverb, quoted by Constant. Porphyrogen. de them. lib. i., τρία κάππα
κάκιστα· Καππαδοκία, Κρήτη, Κιλικία.

CHAPTER XI.

THE EPISTLE TO PHILEMON.

SECTION I.

ITS AUTHORSHIP.

1. THE testimonies to the Pauline authorship of this Epistle are
abundant.

(α) Tertullian, in enumerating the Epistles of St. Paul with which
Marcion had tampered, concludes his list thus (adv. Marc. v. 21, vol. ii.
p. 524):

"Soli huic epistolæ brevitas sua profuit ut falsarias manus Marcionis evaderet. Miror tamen, cum ad unum hominem litteras
factas receperit, quod &c." (see the whole passage cited above, ch.
vii. § i. 1. ε.)

(β) Origen, Hom. xix. in Jer. 2: vol. iii. p. 263:

ὅπερ καὶ ὁ Παῦλος ἐπιστάμενος ἔλεγεν ἐν τῇ πρὸς Φιλήμονα ἐπιστολῇ
τῷ Φιλήμονι περὶ 'Ονησίμου· ἵνα μὴ κατ᾽ ἀνάγκην τὸ ἀγαθὸν ᾖ, ἀλλὰ
καθ᾽ ἑκούσιον (Philem. ver. 14).

And again in Matth. Comm. series, § 72, p. 889:

"Sicut Paulus ad Philemonem dicit: Gaudium enim magnum
habuimus et consolationem in caritate tua, quia viscera sanctorum
requieverunt per te, frater." (Philem. ver. 7.)

And again in id. § 66, p. 884:

"A Paulo autem dictum est ad Philemonem: hunc autem ut Paulus
senex, &c." (ver. 9.)

(γ) Eusebius, H. E. iii. 25, reckons this Epistle among the ὁμολογούμενα.

(δ) Jerome, prooem. in Philem. vol. vii. pp. 743, 4, argues at some

111]

length against those who refuse to acknowledge this Epistle for St. Paul's because it was simply on personal matters and contained nothing for edification.

2. That neither Irenæus nor Clement of Alexandria cites our Epistle, is easily accounted for, both by its shortness, and by the fact of its containing nothing which could illustrate or affirm doctrinal positions. Ignatius seems several times to allude to it:

Eph. c. ii., p. 645; ὀναίμην ὑμῶν διὰ παντός, ἐάνπερ ἄξιος ὦ (Philem. ver. 20).

Magnes. c. xii., p. 672; the same expression; which also occurs in the Ep. to Polycarp, c. i., p. 720, and c. vi., p. 725.

3. The internal evidence of the Epistle itself is so decisive for its Pauline origin,—the occasion and object of it (see below, § ii.) so simple, and unassignable to any fraudulent intent, that one would imagine the impugner of so many of the Epistles would at least have spared this one, and that in modern times, as in ancient, according to Tertullian and Jerome, "sua illam brevitas defendisset." But Baur has rejected it, or, which with him is the same thing practically, has placed it in his second class, of *antilegomena*, in common with the other Epistles of the imprisonment.

4. In doing so, he confesses ("Paulus, u.s.w." pp. 475 ff.) to a feeling of subjecting himself to the imputation of hypercritical scepticism as to authenticity: but maintains that the Epistle must stand or fall with those others: and that its very insignificance, which is pleaded in its defence, all the more involves it in their fate. Still, he professes to argue the question on the ground of the Epistle itself.

5. He finds in its diction several things which strike him as unpauline[1]: several which establish a link between it and those other Epistles. The latter position we should willingly grant him, and use against him. But the former is here, as so often, taken up by him in the merest disregard to common sense and probability. Such expressions, occurring in a familiar letter, such as we do not elsewhere possess, are no more than are perfectly natural, and only serve to enlarge for us the Apostle's vocabulary, instead of inducing doubt, where all else is so thoroughly characteristic of him.

6. The contents also of the Epistle seem to him objectionable. The incident on which it is founded, he says, of itself raises suspicion. He then takes to pieces the whole history of Onesimus's flight and conversion, and the feeling shewn to him by the Apostle, in a way which, as I observed before (ch. iii. § i. 2) respecting his argument against

---

[1] I subjoin Baur's list: συνστρατιώτης, ver. 2: ἀνῆκον, ἐπιτάσσειν, ver. 8: πρεσβύτης, ver. 9: ἄχρηστος and εὔχρηστος, ver. 11: ἀπέχω in the sense of '*receive back*' (but see note there), ver. 15: ἀποτίω, προσοφείλω, ver. 19: ὀνίνασθαι, ver. 20: ξενία, ver. 22: the *frequent recurrence* (vv. 7, 12, 20) of the expression σπλάγχνα, not otherwise unpauline.

the Epistle to the Philippians, only finds a parallel in the pages of burlesque: so that, I am persuaded, if the section on the Epistle to Philemon had been first published separately and without the author's name, the world might well have supposed it written by some defender of the authenticity of the Epistle, as a caricature on Baur's general line of argument.

7. On both his grounds of objection—the close connexion of this with the other Epistles of the imprisonment, and its own internal evidence,—fortified as these are by the consensus of the ancient Church, we may venture to assume it as certain that this Epistle was written by St. Paul.

SECTION II.

THE PLACE, TIME, OCCASION, AND OBJECT OF WRITING.

1. The Epistle is connected by the closest links with that to the Colossians. It is borne by Onesimus, one of the persons mentioned as sent with that Epistle (Col. iv. 9). The persons sending salutation are the same, with the one exception of Jesus Justus. In Col. iv. 17, a message is sent to Archippus, who is one of those addressed in this Epistle. Both Epistles are sent from Paul and Timotheus; and in both the Apostle is a prisoner (Col. iv. 18; Philem. vv. 1, 9).

2. This being so, we are justified in assuming that it was written at the same place and time as the Epistles to the Colossians and Ephesians, viz. at Rome, and in the year 61 or 62.

3. Its occasion and object are plainly indicated in the Epistle itself. Onesimus, a native of Colossæ [2], the slave of Philemon, had absconded, after having, as it appears, defrauded his master (ver. 18). He fled to Rome, and there was converted to Christianity by St. Paul. Being persuaded by him to return to his master, he was furnished with this letter to recommend him, now no longer merely a servant, but a brother also, to favourable reception by Philemon. This alone, and no didactic or general object, is discernible in the Epistle.

SECTION III.

TO WHAT PLACE ADDRESSED, &c.

1. From comparing Col. iv. 9, with ib. 17 and Philem. 2, we infer that Philemon was a resident at Colossæ. The impression on the

---

[2] ἐξ ὑμῶν can hardly in Col. iv. 9 bear any other meaning: he could surely not be described, under the circumstances, as "belonging to the Colossian Church," as supposed by Dr. Davidson, Introd. ii. p. 138. The case of Epaphras in Col. iv. 12 is not strictly parallel; but even there, there is no reason why the words should not bear their proper sense.

reader from Philem. 1, 2, is that Apphia was his wife, and Archippus (a minister of the church there, Col. iv. 17), their son, or some near relative dwelling with them under the same roof. A letter on a matter so strictly domestic would hardly include strangers to the family in its address.

2. An hypothesis has been advanced, recently by Wieseler, that our present Epistle is alluded to in Col. iv. 16, as ἡ ἐκ Λαοδικείας, and that the message to Archippus in the next verse favours the view that he, and consequently Philemon, dwelt at Laodicea. And this is corroborated, by Archippus being called bishop of Laodicea in the Apostolic Constitutions (vii. 46, p. 1056, Migne).

3. The objection to this hypothesis is not so much from any evidently false assumption or inference in the chain of facts, all of which may have been as represented, but from the improbability, to my view, that by the latter limb of the parallelism—"*this Epistle*," "*that from Laodicea*,"—can be meant a private letter, even though it may have regarded a member of the Colossian church. We seem to want some Epistle corresponding in weight with that to the Colossians, for such an order, in such a form, to receive its natural interpretation[3].

4. Of Onesimus we know nothing for certain, except from the notices here and in Col. iv. 9. Tradition reports variously respecting him. In the Apostolical Canons (73) he is said to have been emancipated by his master, and in the Apostolical Constitutions (vii. 46, p. 1056) to have been ordained by St. Paul himself bishop of Berœa in Macedonia, and to have suffered martyrdom in Rome, Niceph. H. E. iii. 11. In the Epistle of Ignatius to the Ephesians, we read, cap. i. p. 645, ἐπεὶ οὖν τὴν πολυπληθίαν ὑμῶν ἐν ὀνόματι θεοῦ ἀπείληφα ἐν Ὀνησίμῳ, τῷ ἐν ἀγάπῃ ἀδιηγήτῳ, ὑμῶν δὲ ἐν σαρκὶ ἐπισκόπῳ· ὃν εὔχομαι κατὰ Ἰησοῦν χριστὸν ὑμᾶς ἀγαπᾶν, καὶ πάντας ὑμᾶς ἐν ὁμοιότητι εἶναι. εὐλογητὸς γὰρ ὁ χαρισάμενος ὑμῖν ἀξίοις οὖσι τοιοῦτον ἐπίσκοπον κεκτῆσθαι[4]. It is just possible that this may be our Onesimus. The earliest date which can be assigned to the martyrdom of Ignatius is A.D. 107, i. e. thirty-five years after the date of this Epistle. Supposing Onesimus to have been thirty at this time, he would then have been only sixty-five. And even setting Ignatius's death at the latest date, A.D. 116, we should still be far within the limits of possibility. It is at least singular that in ch. ii. p. 645, immediately after naming Onesimus, Ignatius proceeds ὀναίμην ὑμῶν διὰ παντός (cf. Philem. ver. 20; and above, § i. 2).

---

[3] In the Prælectio above referred to, Prolegg. to Eph., § i. 11, note, I had adopted Wieseler's hypothesis. Maturer consideration led me to abandon it, solely on the ground of the improbability stated in the text. We must regard the Epistle to the Laodiceans as one now lost to us (see Prolegg. to Vol. II. ch. iii. § iv. 3).

[4] See also id. chapters ii., vi., pp. 645, 649.

SECTION IV.

CHARACTER AND STYLE.

1. This Epistle is a remarkable illustration of St. Paul's tenderness and delicacy of character. Dr. Davidson well remarks, "Dignity, generosity, prudence, friendship, affection, politeness, skilful address, purity, are apparent. Hence it has been termed with great propriety, *the polite Epistle.* The delicacy, fine address, consummate courtesy, nice strokes of rhetoric, render the letter an unique specimen of the epistolary style." Introd. vol. iii. p. 160.

2. Doddridge (Expositor, introd. to Philem.) compares it to an Epistle of Pliny to Sabinianus, ix. 21, written as an acknowledgment on a similar occasion of the reception of a libertus by his master [5]: and justly gives the preference in delicacy and power to our Epistle. The comparison is an interesting one, for Pliny's letter is eminently beautiful, and in terseness, and completeness, not easy to surpass.

3. Luther's description of the Epistle is striking, and may well serve to close our notice of it, and this portion of our prolegomena to the Epistles.

" This Epistle sheweth a right noble lovely example of Christian love. Here we see how St. Paul layeth himself out for the poor Onesimus, and with all his means pleadeth his cause with his master; and so setteth himself, as if he were Onesimus, and had himself done wrong to Philemon. Yet all this doeth he not with power or force, as if he had right thereto; but he strippeth himself of his right, and thus enforceth Philemon to forego his right also. Even as Christ did for us with God the Father, thus also doth St. Paul for Onesimus with Philemon: for Christ also stripped Himself of His right, and by love and humility enforced the Father to lay aside His wrath and power, and to take us to His grace for the sake of Christ, who lovingly pleadeth our cause, and with all His heart layeth Himself out for us. For we are all His Onesimi, to my thinking."

---

[5] The Epistle runs thus :

"C. Plinius Sabiniano suo S.

" Bene fecisti quod libertum aliquando tibi charum, reducentibus epistolis meis, in domum, in animum recepisti. Juvabit hoc te : me certe juvat : primum quod te talem video, ut in ira regi possis : deinde, quod tantum mihi tribuis, ut vel autoritati meæ pareas, vel precibus indulgeas. Igitur et laudo et gratias ago : simul in posterum moneo, ut te erroribus tuorum, etsi non fuerit qui deprecetur, placabilem præstes. Vale."

CHAPTER XII.

APPARATUS CRITICUS.

SECTION I.

LIST OF MSS. CONTAINING THE EPISTLES OF ST. PAUL.

NOTE.—It is intended to include in this Table the mention of those MSS. only which contain, and of those particulars which concern, the portion of the N. T. comprehended in this Volume.

	Designation.	Date.	Name of Collator and other information.	Gosp.	Cath.	Apoc.
A	Alexandrinus.	V.	*See Vol. I.*	A	A	A
B	Vatican 1209.	IV.	*See Vol. I.*	B	B	—
C	Ephræmi.	V.	*See Vol. I.*	C	C	C
D	Claromontanus.	VI.	*See Vol. II.*	—	—	—
E	Sangermanensis.	IX.	A faulty transcript of D.	—	—	—
F	Augiensis.	IX.	*See Vol. II.*	—	—	—
G	Boernerianus.	IX.	Cited only when it differs from F.	Δ	—	—
H	Paris, Coisl. 202, A.	VI.	Only fragments. *See Vol. II.*	—	—	—
I$_b$	Frag. Tischendorf.	V.	*See Vol. I.*	—	I$_b$	—
K	Moscow Synod, 98.	IX.	*See Vol. II.*	—	K	—
L	Passionei.	IX.	*See Vol. II.*	—	L	—
[P]	[Porphyrii.]	[VIII]	[*See Vol. II.* (Def. Col. iii. 16—iv. 8. 1 Thess. iii. 5—iv. 17.)]	—	[P]	[P]
ℵ	Sinaiticus.	IV.	*See Vol. I.*	ℵ	ℵ	ℵ
a	Lambeth 1182.	XII.	Scrivener.	—	a	—
b	Lambeth 1183.	1358	Scrivener.	—	b	—
c	Formerly Lambeth 1184.	XV.	Sanderson in Scrivener.	—	c	—
d	Lambeth 1185.	XV.	Scrivener.	—	d	—
e	Lambeth 1186.	XI.	Scrivener.	—	—	a
f	Theodori.	1295	Scrivener.	q	f	—
g	Wordsworth.	XIII.	Scrivener.	l	g	—
(h)	*See 104 below.*	1357	*Cited as* h *in this edition.*	m	h	b
k	Trin. Coll. Camb., B. x. 16.	1316	Scrivener.	w	k	—
(l)	*See 29 below.*	—	*Cited as* l.	—	—	—
(m)	*See 37 below.*	—	*Cited as* m *Acts Epp.,* 69 *in the Gospels.*	—		
(n)	*See 30 below.*	—	*Cited as* n *in this edition.*	—	—	—
(o)	*See 61 below.*	—	*Cited as* o *in this edition.*	—	—	—
1	Basle, K. iii. 3. (late B. vi. 27.)	X.	Tregelles and Roth in Gosp.	1	1	—
2	Basle (late B. ix. ult.).	XV.	Mill (*B.* 2). Belonged to Amerbach. Mutilated.	—	2	—
3	Vienna, Theol. 5 (Kol.)	XII.	Alter. Known as Corsendoncensis.	3	3	—
4	Basle (late B. x. 20).	XV.	Mill's *B.* 3. Wetstein, throughout Epp.	—	4	—
5	Paris 106.	XII.	Stephens' δ′. Scholz.	5	5	—
6	Paris 112.	XIII.	Stephens' ε′. (Def. Tit. ii. 1—Philem. 12.)	6	6	—
7	Basle (late B. vi. 17).	X. ?	Readings given in Wetstein. Text surrounded by various scholia from Thdrt., Gennad., Œc., Sevrn., &c. On parchment.	--	—	—

	Designation.	Date.	Name of Collator and other information.	Gosp.	Cath.	Apoc.
(8)	. . . .	—	Stephens' ζ'. *Identified by some with* 132 *below.*	—	50	—
9	Paris 102.	X.	Stephens' ι'. No lacunæ.	—	7	—
10)	*Not identified.*	—	Stephens' ια'.	—	8	—
11	Univ. Lib. Camb., MS. Kk. 6. 4.	XI.	Stephens' ιγ'. (Def. 1 Tim. iv. 12 —2 Tim. iv. 3.)	—	9	—
12	Paris 237.	X.	Stephens (ιε'). Wetstein, "de integro." Scholia.	—	10	2
(13)	. . . .	—	*See note* a.			
(14)	Jacobi Fabri Daventriensis.	XVI.	*See note* b.	90	47	—
(15)	Amandi.	—	*See note* c.	—	—	—
16	Paris 219.	XI.	Wetstein. Variorum scholia. Inspected by Reiche. Belonged to J. Lascaris.	—	12	4
17	Paris 14. (Colb. 2844.)	XI.	Tregelles. *See* 33, *Vol. I.*	33	13	—
18	Paris, Coisl. 199.	XI.	Wetstein.	35	14	17
19	Paris, Coisl. 26.	XI.	Wetstein. Variorum comm.	—	16	—
20	Paris, Coisl. 27.	X.	Wetstein. Variorum comm. Mutilated.	—	—	—
21	Paris, Coisl. 205.	XI.	Wetstein.	—	17	19
22	Paris, Coisl. 202, A.	XIII.	Wetstein. Variorum comm.	—	18	18
23	Paris, Coisl. 200.	XIII.	Wetstein. Stephens' θ. "Continet totum N. T. præter Apoc. (nam in Catalogo hujus Bibliothecæ Apoc. per errorem pro Ep. Paul. ponitur.)" Wetstein.	38	19	—
24	Bodleian, Misc. 136.	XII.	Cited by Wetstein on Joh. vii. Ebnerianus.	105	48	—
25	Brit. Mus., King's Lib. 1. B. 1.	XIV.	Wetstein (Westmonasteriensis 935). Mutilated.	—	20	—
26	Camb.Univ. Lib., MS. Dd. 11. 90.	XIII.	(Def. 2 Tim. i. 1—ii. 4; Tit. i. 9—ii. 15. Ends Philem. ver. 2.)	—	21	—
27	Camb.Univ. Lib., MS. Ff. 1. 30.	XI.	The following portions were supplied in XIIth century. Gal. i. 1—8; Eph. i. 1—13; Col. i. 1, 2; 2 Thess. iii. 16—end; 1 Tim. i. 1—4; Philem. 24, 25. Of these Gal. (or Eph.?) i. 1—4; Col.			

a Jacobus Faber Stapulensis, i. e. Jacques le Fevre d'Estaples, a native of Etaples in Picardy, collated five Greek MSS. of St. Paul's Epistles which he sometimes appeals to in his Commentary (Paris, 1512). These citations, whenever it is necessary to refer to them, should not be quoted as if they came from some one MS. distinct from the others in the list, but as " var. read. in comm. Fab. Stap." or the like.

b A ms. which once belonged to J. C. Wolf of Hamburg. It was procured by Wetstein from Wolf's library, and collated by him. It consists of two square paper volumes, containing the whole N. T. exc. Apoc., copied by Jas. Faber, of Daventer (a brother scholar of Erasmus), from a ms. written A.D. 1293 on Mt. Athos, by the scribe Theodore, who wrote also Gosp. 74, and Scrivener's Gosp. q Epp. f. The Epistle of St. Jude occurs twice, the 2nd copy is entered as Cath. 55.

c " We know nothing more of it than that Amandus, who lived at Louvain, had it in his possession, that Zeger appealed to it," on Rom. i. 32 (as reading ου συνηκαν), "and that Erasmus supposed it to be a latinizing manuscript. How many books of the N.T. it contains, where it is at present preserved, whether it has been used in modern times under another name, are questions which I am unable to answer." (Michaelis.)

	Designation.	Date.	Name of Collator and other information.	Gosp.	Cath.	Apoc.
			i. 1, 2, are also found in the older portion. Catena chiefly from Photius.	—		
28	Bodleian, Baroc. 3.	XI.	Mill (*Baroc.*). Scholia.	—	23	6
29	Chr. Coll. Camb. F. i. 13.	XII.	Mill (*Cant.* 2). Scrivener (l, *so cited in this ed.*).	—	24	
30	Em. Coll. Camb. i. 4. 35.	XII.	Mill (*Cant.* 3). Scrivener (n, *so cited in this ed.*).	—	53	—
31	Brit. Mus., Harl. 5537.	1087	Mill (*Cov.* 2).	—	25	7
32	Brit. Mus., Harl. 5557.	XII.	Mill (*Cov.* 3).	—	26	—
33	Brit. Mus., Harl. 5620.	XV.	Mill (*Cov.* 4). No lacuna (Griesb. Symb. Crit.).	—	27	—
34	Brit. Mus., Harl. 5778.	XIII.	Mill (*Sin.*). Very much mutilated.	—	28	8
35	Geneva 20.	XII.	Mill (*Genev.*).	—	29	—
36	Bodleian, Misc. 74.	XIII.	Mill (*Hunt.* 1). Formerly known as Huntingdon 131. " Perlegi . . . Gal. i., ii." (Griesbach.)	—	30	9
37	The Leicester MS.	XIV.	Scrivener. *Cited as* " m " *in this vol.,* " f " *in Apoc.,* 69 *in the Gospels. See* 69, *Vol. I.*	69	31	14
38	Bodleian, Laud. 31.	XIII.	Mill (*Laud.* 2).	51	32	—
39	Linc. Coll. Oxf. 82.	XI.	Mill (*Lin.* 2).	—	33	—
40	Dublin, Montfort MS.	XVI.	Barrett and Dobbin.	61	34	92
41	Magd. Coll. Oxf. 9.	XI.	Mill (*Magd.* 1).	57	35	—
43	New Coll. Oxf. 59.	XIII.	Mill (*N.* 2).	—	37	—
44	Leyden, Voss. 77.	XIII.	Sarrau. Mill's *Pet.* 1. Wetstein, Dermout.	—	38	—
d(45)	*Situation unknown.*	—	Sarrau. Mill's *Pet.* 2. Belonged (with *Pet.* 1 and 3) to Paul Petavius.	—	39	11
46	Vatican, Alex. 179.	XI.	Zacagni. Mill's *Pet.* 3. Birch. (Def. Tit. iii. 3 to end of Philem.)	—	40	12
47	Bodleian, Roe 16.	XII.	Mill (*Roe* 2). Marginal scholia.	—	—	—
48	Frankfort on Oder, Seidel MS.	XI.	Middeldorpf.	—	42	13
49	Vienna, Theol. 300 (Nessel).	XII.	Alter. Mill's *Vien.*	76	43	—
d(50)	*Situation unknown.*	—	A MS. brought from Rhodes, occasionally referred to by Stunica, one of the Complutensian editors.	—	52	—
(51)	. . . .	—	*See note* e.	—	—	—
d(52)	Hamburg.	XV.	Bengel's Uffenbachianus.	—	45	16
(53)	*See M in Vol. II.*					
55	Munich 375.	XI.	Bengel (*Augsburg,* 6). Œc.-comm.	—	46	—
f(56)						

d These numbers are bracketed because it is perfectly possible that the MSS. denoted by them may be entered in the list under other numbers.

e Under this number Wetstein and succeeding editors have entered " *Codices Laur. Vallæ.*" " Laurentius Valla, a learned Roman, who was born in 1417, and died in 1467, published in 1440, *Annotationes in N. T.*, in which he collected the readings of three Greek and three Latin MSS., and took particular pains to amend the Latin version. The book was published at Paris in 1505, and gave occasion to the Complutensian Polyglott." (Michaelis' Introductory Lectures, 4to, London, 1761, p. 66.)

f Under this number Wetstein and succeeding editors have entered a Zürich MS.,

	Designation.	Date.	Name of Collator and other information.	Gosp.	Cath.	Apoc.
57	Vienna, Theol. 23 (Nessel).	XIII.	Edited by Alter.	218	65	33
58	Vatican 165.	XII.	Edited by Zacagni. Called Crypto-ferratensis.	—	—	—
59	Paris, Coisl. 204.	XI.	Inspected. Catena.	—	—	—
g(60)						
61	Camb.Univ. Lib., MS. Mm. 6. 9.	XII.	Mill's *Hal.*, identified by Scrivener with 221 below. *Cited as* "o" from Scrivener's Collation.	440	61	—
62	Brit. Mus.,Harl.5588.	XIII.	Eph. collated by Griesbach.	—	59	—
63	Brit. Mus.,Harl.5613.	1407	Eph. collated by Griesbach.	—	60	29
(64)	*See M in Vol. II.*					
65	Paris 60.	XIV.	Inspected by Griesbach.	—	62	
h(66)						
67	Vienna, Theol. 302 (Nessel).	XII.	Alter and Birch. The readings inserted by a corrector (67^2) are very valuable.	—	66	34
68	Vienna, Theol. 313 (Nessel).	XIII.	Alter and Birch.	—	63	—
69	Vienna, Theol. 303 (Nessel).	XIII.	Alter and Birch.	—	64	—
70	Vienna, Theol. 221 (Nessel).	1331	Alter and Birch.	—	67	—
71	Vienna, Theol. 10 (Kollar).	XII.	Alter and Birch.	—	—	—
72	Copenhagen 1.	1278	Hensler. Cited by Bengel and Birch.	234	57	—
73	Upsala, Sparwenfeld, 42.	XI.	Aurivilius. Catena. (Part of this MS. is XIIth cent.)	—	68	—
74	Wolfenbüttel xvi. 7.	XIII.	Knittel (collation given in Matthæi).	—	69	30
75	Brit. Mus., Addl. MS. 5115-7.	1326?	(Epp. Cent. xii. Scrivener.) "Lectt. ex 1 Tim. mecum communicavit Rev. Paulus." (Griesbach.)	109	22	—
76	Bibl. Paul. Leipsic.	XIII.	Readings of Gal. Eph. given by Matthæi, p. 203.	—	—	—
77	Vatican 360.	XI.	Birch (cursorily inspected).	131	70	66
78	Vatican 363.	XI.	Inspected by Birch and Scholz.	133	71	—
79	Vatican 366.	XIII.	Birch (cursorily).	—	72	37
80	Vatican 367.	XI.	Birch " per omnia contuli."	—	73	—
81	Vatican 761.	XII.	Inspected by Birch. Œc.-comm.	—	—	—
83	Vatican 765.	XI.	Inspected by Birch. Comm. on marg.	—	—	—
84	Vatican 766.	XII.	Ditto ditto.	—	—	—
85	Vatican 1136.	XIII.	Epp. inspected by Birch. (Def. from 1 Tim. vi. 5.) Apoc. bef. Epp.	—	—	39
86	Vatican 1160.	XIII.	Inspected by Birch and Scholz.	141	75	40
87	Vatican 1210.	XI.	1, 2 Thess.; 1, 2 Tim. Tit. Philem. " exacte contuli " Birch.	142	76	—
88	Vatican, Palat. 171.	XIV.	Zacagni.	149	77	25

which consists merely of the Epistles of St. Paul, transcribed for his own benefit by the reformer Zwingle from Erasmus' 1st edition.

g Under this number Wetstein cites " Codices Græci, quorum fit mentio in *Correctorio Bibliorum Latinorum seculo xiii.* scripto."

h Another transcript of Erasmus' 1st edition, Harl. 5552 in the British Museum. Griesbach copied certain various readings found on the margin.

	Designation.	Date.	Name of Collator and other information.	Gosp.	Cath.	Apoc.
89	Vatican, Alex. 29.	XII.	Birch "accurate exam." Contains Gal., Eph. i. 1—9 only of this vol.	—	78	—
90	Vatican, Urb. 3.	XI.	Inspected by Birch.	—	79	—
91	Vatican, Pio 50.	XII.	Birch "per omn. diligenter bis coll."	—	80	42
92	Propaganda Lib. Rome 250.	1274	Engelbreth in Birch (once *Borg.* 4).	180	82	44
93	Naples i. B. 1'.	XI.	1 Tim. collated by Birch.	—	83	—?
94	Laur. Lib. Florence iv. 1.	X.	Inspected by Birch. Mutilated at end. Marginal commentary.	—	84	—
95	Laur. Lib. Florence iv. 5.	XIII.	Inspected by Birch. Thl.'s comm.	—	85	—
96	Laur. Lib. Florence iv. 20.	XI.	Inspected by Birch. Marg. comm.	—	86	75
97	Laur. Lib. Florence iv. 29.	X.	Inspected by Birch.	—	87	—
98	Laur. Lib. Florence iv. 31.	XI.	Inspected by Birch.	—	88	—
99	Laur. Lib. Florence iv. 32.	XI.	Inspected by Birch.	—	89	45
100	Laur. Lib. Florence x. 4.	XII.	Inspected by Birch. Comm.	—	—	—
101	Laur. Lib. Florence x. 6.	XI.	Inspected by Birch. Comm.	—	—	—
102	Laur. Lib. Florence x. 7.	XI.	Inspected by Birch. Var. comm.	—	—	—
103	Laur. Lib. Florence x. 19.	XII.	Inspected by Birch. Catena.	—	—	—
104	Brit. Mus. Addl. 11837.	1357	Scrivener. *Cited as* "h."	201	91	—
105	Bologna Can. Reg., 640.	XI.	Inspected by Scholz.	204	92	—
106	St. Mark's Venice, 5.	XV.	Rinck.	205	93	88
107	St. Mark's Venice, 6.	XV.	Rinck.	206	94	—
108	St. Mark's Venice, 10.	XV.	Rinck.	209	95	46
109	St. Mark's Venice, 11.	XI.	Rinck. (Philem. wanting.)	—	96	—
110	St. Mark's Venice, 33.	XI.	Rinck. Comm.	—	—	—
111	St. Mark's Venice, 34.	XI.	Rinck. Comm.	—	—	—
112	St. Mark's Venice, 35.	XI.	Rinck. Comm. (Def. 1 Thess. iv. 13—2 Thess. ii. 14.)	—	—	—
[i]113	(Moscow ?)	XI.	Matthæi (a). Belonged to Matthæi himself.	—	98	—
114	Moscow Synod, 5.	1445	Matthæi (c).	—	99	—
115	Moscow Synod, 334.	XI.	Matthæi (d). Thl.'s comm.	—	100	—
116	Moscow Synod, 333.	XIII.	Matthæi (f). Scholia.	—	101	—
(117)	*The MS. called* "K" *above.*					
118	Moscow Synod, 193.	XII.	Matthæi (h).	—	103	—
120	Dresden, Cod. Matth.	XI.	Matthæi (k).	241	104	47
121	Moscow Synod, 380.	XII.	Matthæi (l).	242	105	48
122	Moscow Synod, 328.	XI.	Matthæi (m).	—	106	—
123	Moscow Synod, 99.	XI.	Matthæi (n). Scholia.	—	—	—
125	Munich 504.	1387	Inspected by Scholz. Philem. wanting.	—	—	—
126	Munich 455.	XIV.	Inspected by Scholz. Philem. wanting. Prob. copied from same MS. as preceding.	—	—	—
128	Munich 211.	XI.	Inspected by Scholz.	—	179	82

[i] Rinck uses this number for St. Mark's Venice 36.

	Designation.	Date.	Name of Collator and other information.	Gosp.	Cath.	Apoc.
129	Munich 35.	XVI.	Inspected by Scholz. Thl.'s comm. (So Hardt.)	—	—	—
130	Paris, Bibl. de l'Arsenal 4.	XI.	Inspected by Scholz.	43	54	—
131	Paris, Coisl. 196.	XI.	Inspected by Scholz.	330	132	—
132	Paris 47.	1364	Reiche.	18	113	51
133	Paris 56.	XII.	Inspected by Scholz.	—	51	52
134	Paris 57.	XIII.	Reiche.	—	114	—
135	Paris 58.	XIII.	Inspected by Scholz. (Def. 2 Tim. ii. to end, Tit.)	—	115	—
136	Paris 59.	XVI.	Inspected by Scholz.	—	116	53
137	Paris 61.	XIII.	Reiche. (Def. Philem. 21—25.)	263	117	—
138	Paris 101.	XIII.	Coll. 1 Tim.; 1 and 2 Thess. by Scholz.	—	118	55
139	Paris 102 A.	X.	Reiche.	—	119	56
140	Paris 103.	X.	Reiche. (in Epp. Paul). Marginal Schol.		11	—
141	Paris 103 A.	XI.	Inspected by Scholz. (Def. Phil. i. 5—end; Col.; 1 Thess. i. 1—iv. 1, v. 26—end; 2 Thess. i. 1—11.)	—	120	—
142	Paris 104.	XIII.	Inspected by Scholz.	—	121	—
143	Paris 105.	XI.	Inspected by Scholz. Contains Gal. i. 1—10, ii. 4—end; Eph. i. 1—18; 1 Tim. i. 14—v. 5.	—	122	—
144	Paris 106 A.	XIV.	Inspected by Scholz.	—	123	—
145	Paris 108.	XVI.	Inspected by Scholz. Contains Phil., Col., Thess., Tim.	—	—	—
148	Paris 111.	XVI.	Inspected by Scholz. Contains Tit., Philem.	—	—	—
149	Paris 124.	XVI.	Inspected by Scholz.	—	124	57
150	Paris 125.	XIV.	Inspected by Scholz.	—	125	—
151	Paris 126.	XVI.	Inspected by Scholz.	—	—	—
153	Paris 216.	X.	Reiche. Scholia.	—	126	—
154	Paris 217.	XI.	Inspected by Scholz and Reiche. Thdrt.'s Comm. on Epp. Paul.	—	127	—
155	Paris 218.	XI.	Inspected by Scholz. Catena.	—	128	—
156	Paris 220.	XIII.	Inspected by Scholz. Comm., txt often omitted.	—	129	—
157	Paris 222.	XI.	" Coll. magna codicis pars." Scholz. (Def. Col. i. 1—6.)	—	—	—
158	Paris 223.	1045	Inspected by Scholz and Reiche. Catena.	—	131	—
159	Paris 224.	XI.	Inspected by Scholz. Catena.	—	—	64
160	Paris 225.	XVI.	Inspected by Scholz. Fragments w. Thl.'s comm.	—	—	—
164	Paris 849.	XVI.	Inspected by Scholz. Thdrt.'s comm. w. txt on marg.	—	—	—
165	Turin, C. I. 39.	XVI.	Inspected by Scholz. Contains 1 and 2 Thess., Tim., Tit., Philem.	—	—	—
166	Turin, C. I. 40.	XIII.	Scholz " accurate coll."	—	133	—
167	Turin, C. II. 17 (19).	XI.	Inspected by Scholz.	—	134	—
168	Turin, C. II. 38 (325).	XII.	Inspected by Scholz. Comm.	—	—	—
169	Turin, C. II. 31 (1).	XII.	Inspected by Scholz.	—	136	—
170	Turin, C. II. 5 (302).	XIII.	Inspected by Scholz.	339	135	83
171	Ambros. Lib. Milan 6.	XIII.	Inspected by Scholz.	—	—	—
172	Ambros. Lib. Milan 15.	XII.	Inspected by Scholz. Comm. after Chr.	—	—	—
173	Ambros. Lib. Milan 102.	XIV.	Inspected by Scholz.	—	138	—

	Designation.	Date.	Name of Collator and other information.	Gosp.	Cath.	Apoc.
174	Ambros. Lib. Milan 104.	1434	Inspected by Scholz.	—	139	—
175	Ambros. Lib. Milan 125.	XV.	Inspected by Scholz. Continuous comm.	—	—	—
176	Ambros. Lib. Milan 97.	XI.	"Coll. loca Ep. Paul. plurima." Scholz.	—	137	—
177	Modena 14 (MS. II. A. 14).	XV.	"Coll. cod. integer." Scholz.	—	—	—
178	Modena 243 (MS. III. B. 17).	XII.	"Coll. cod. integer." Scholz under Paul.	—	142	—
(179)	Cursive portion of H of the Acts.	XII.	Scholz. *Cited as* H[r].	—	H	—
180	Laur. Lib. Florence vi. 13.	XIII.	Inspected by Scholz.	363	144	—
181	Laur. Lib. Florence vi. 36.	XIII.	Inspected by Scholz.	365	145	—
182	Laur. Lib. Florence 2708 (?).	1332	Inspected by Scholz.	367	146	—
183	Laur. Lib. Florence iv. 30.	XII.	Inspected by Scholz.	—	147	76
184	Laur. Lib. Florence 2574 (?).	984	Inspected by Scholz.	—	148	—
185	Vallicella Lib. Rome, E. 22.	XVI.	Inspected by Scholz.	393	167	—
186	Vallicella Lib. Rome, F. 17.	1330	Inspected by Scholz.	394	170	—
188	Vatican 1430.	XII.	Inspected by Scholz.	—	155	—
189	Vatican 1649.	XIII.	Inspected by Scholz. Thdrt.'s comm.	—	—	—
190	Vatican 1650.	1073	Inspected by Scholz. Comm. on Epp. Paul.	—	156	—
192	Vatican 1761.	XI.	Inspected by Scholz. Past. Epp. edited by Mai, as supplementary to B.	—	158	—
193	Vatican 2062.	XI.	Inspected by Scholz. Scholia.	—	160	24
194	Vatican 2080.	XII.	Inspected by Scholz.	175	41	20
195	Vatican, Ottob. 31.	X.	Inspected by Scholz.	—	—	—
196	Vatican, Ottob. 61.	XV.	Inspected by Scholz.	—	—	—
197	Vatican, Ottob. 176.	XV.	Inspected by Scholz.	—	—	78
198	Vatican, Ottob. 258.	XIII.	Inspected by Scholz. Latin version.	—	161	69
199	Vatican, Ottob. 66.	XV.	Inspected by Scholz.	386	151	70
200	Vatican, Ottob. 298.	XV.	Inspected by Scholz. Latin version.	—	162	—
201	Vatican, Ottob. 325.	XIV.	Inspected by Scholz.	—	163	—
203	Vatican, Ottob. 381.	1252	Inspected by Scholz.	390	164	71
204	Vallicella Lib. Rome, B. 86.	XIII.	Inspected by Scholz.	—	166	22
205	Vallicella Lib. Rome, F. 13.	XIV.	Inspected by Scholz.	—	168	—
206	Ghigi Lib. Rome, R. v. 29.	1394	Inspected by Scholz.	—	169	—
207	Ghigi Lib. Rome, R. v. 32.	XV.	Inspected by Scholz. Comm.	—	—	—
208	Ghigi Lib. Rome, R. viii. 55.	XI.	Inspected by Scholz. Thdrt.'s comm.	—	—	—
209	Two MSS. in the Library of the Collegio Romano.	XVI.	Inspected by Scholz.	—	171	—
210		XVI.	Inspected by Scholz.	—	172	—

	Designation.	Date.	Name of Collator and other information	Gosp.	Cath.	Apoc.
(211)	Naples (no number).	XI.	Inspected by Scholz. *Apparently the same as 93 above.*	—	(173)	—
212	Naples 1 C. 26.	XV.	Inspected by Scholz.	—	174	—
213	Barberini Lib. Rome 29.	1338	Inspected by Scholz. Scholia.	—	—	—
215	Venice 546.	XI.	(Part Cent. XIII.) Inspected by Scholz. Comm.	—	140	74
216	Mon. of S. Bas. Messana 2.	XII.	Inspected by Münter.	—	175	—
217	Palermo.	XII.	Inspected by Scholz. (Def. 2 Tim. i. 8—ii. 14.)	—	—	—
218	Syracuse.	XII.	Inspected by Münter.	421	176	—
219	Leyden, Meerm. 116	XII.	Dermout.	122	177	—
220	Berlin, Diez. 10.	XV.	(Def. 1 Tim. iv. 1—end.)	400	181	—
k(221)	*The same MS. as 61 above.*					
k(222)	Camb. Univ. Lib., MS. Nn. 5. 27.	—	A folio copy of the Greek Bible, printed " Basileæ per. Joan. Hervagium 1545." A few notes are written on the margin.	441	110	—
k(223)	Camb. Univ. Lib., MS Nn. 3. 20, 21.	—	A copy of the Greek Test., 8vo., London, 1728, interleaved and bound up in two volumes. Contains MS. notes by John Taylor.	442	152	—
224	Bodleian, Clarke 9.	XIII.	On parchment. Inspected by Scholz.	—	58	—
k(225)	*The same MS. as 11 above.*					
k(226)	*The same MS. as 27 above.*					

k Scholz has run into great confusion with the manuscripts in the Cambridge University Library from not understanding the signs in his memoranda respecting them. The following explanation may be sufficient to clear up the matter. All the MSS. in the Library have since 1753 been denoted by a double-letter class mark, a number for the shelf, and a number for the volume. Nasmith, in writing out a list of the MSS. as thus arranged, added numbers on the margin to indicate merely the position which each MS. held in his catalogue. Nasmith's classified index contains references to this catalogue by these marginal numbers, ψ being prefixed if the reference is to a printed book with MS. notes, an asterisk if to a Greek MS. Similar marginal numbers have been inserted in the printed catalogue now in course of publication; they are not the same as Nasmith's, and it is as misleading to refer to MSS. by these numbers without stating what catalogue is meant, as to the pages of a book more than once edited, without stating the edition used. This may be seen in the following examples:—

MS. Ff. 1. 30, is 1152 on Nasmith's margin, and 1163 on that of the new Printed Catalogue.

MS. Kk. 6. 4, is 2068 on Nasmith's margin, and 2084 on that of the new Printed Catalogue.

MS. Mm. 6. 9, is 2423 on Nasmith's margin, and 2468 on that of the new Printed Catalogue.

MS. Nn. 3. 20, is ψ 2537 in Nasmith's index.

MS. Nn. 5. 27, is ψ 2622 in Nasmith's index.

It is right to prefix MS. to the double letter to indicate that the volumes meant belong to the Cases so marked in the Library, and to prevent any confusion with the classes of Printed Books alone known by the same letters.

	Designation.	Date.	Name of Collator and other information.	Gosp.	Cath.	Apoc.
227	Bodleian, Clarke 4.	XII.	On parchment. Inspected by Scholz.	—	56	—
228	Escurial χ. iv. 17.	XI.	Moldenhauer. (See Birch, Gospels.)	226	108	—
229	Escurial χ. iv. 12.	XIV.	Moldenhauer. (See Birch, Gospels.)	228	109	—
230	Riccardi Lib. Florence 84.	XV.	Inspected by Scholz. (= lect.-37.)	368	150	84
231	Gr. Mon. Jerusalem 8.	XIV.	Inspected by Scholz.	—	183	—
232	Gr. Mon. Jerusalem 9.	XIII.	Inspected by Scholz.	—	184	85
233	Mon. S. Saba, nr. Jerus. 1.	XI.	Inspected by Scholz.	—	185	—
234	Mon. S. Saba, nr. Jerus. 2.	XIII.	Inspected by Scholz.	457	186	—
235	Mon. S. Saba, nr. Jerus. 10.	XIII.	Inspected by Scholz.	462	187	86
236	Mon. S. Saba, nr. Jerus. 15.	XII.	Inspected by Scholz.	—	188	—
237	Mon. S. Saba, nr. Jerus. 20.	XIII.	Inspected by Scholz.	466	189	89
238	Strasburg, Molsheimensis.	XII.	Various readings of Gospels given by Arendt in the German Theol. quarterly for 1833. Those of Acts and Epp. communicated to Scholz.	431	180	—
239	Laur. Lib. Florence vi. 27.	XII.	Inspected by Scholz.	189	141	—
240	Brit. Mus., Harl. 5796.	XV.	Inspected by Scholz.	444	153	—
241	Wolfenbüttel, Gud. 104.	XII.	(Inspected by Scholz?) Scholia.	—	97	—
242	Middlehill Worcestersh. 1461.	XI.	(Inspected by Scholz?) Once Meermann 118.	—	178	87
243 243ᵃ	Two MSS. in a monastery in the Island of Patmos.	XII. XIII.	Inspected by Scholz.	—	182	—
244	Ch. Ch. Oxf., Wake 34 [2 (Scholz)].	XI.	Inspected by Scholz.	—	190	27
245	Ch. Ch. Oxf., Wake 38 [3 (Scholz)].	XI.	(Inspected by Scholz?) Catena.	—	191	—
246	Ch. Ch. Oxf., Wake 37 [4 (Scholz)].	XI.	(Inspected by Scholz?)	—	192	—
8-pe	St. Petersburgh xi. 1. 2. 230.	XII.	Muralto.	8-pe	8-pe	—

The following is a List of Lectionaries.

	Designation.	Date.	Name of Collator and other information.
lect-1	Leyden 243. Scaligeri.	XI.	Wetstein and Dermout. Contains Col. i. 12—23; 1 Thess. iv. 13—v. 10; 1 Tim. iv. 9—v. 10. (= ev-6)
lect-2	Brit. Mus., Cotton. Vesp. B. 18.	XI.	" Contains the portions of Acts and Epp. appointed to be read throughout the whole year. Casley collated it in 1735, and Wetstein inserted his extracts." (Michaelis.) Mutilated at beg. and end.
lect-3	Bodleian, Baroc. 202?	995	(Quoted by Mill. Heb. x. 22, 23 qu.?)
lect-4	Brit. Mus., Harl. 5731.	XIV.	Griesbach. Contains the following fragments:—Gal. iii. 23—29; iv. 4—7;

	Designation.	Date.	Name of Collator and other information.
lect-5	Bodleian, Cromwell 11. (Olim 296.) A liturgy book, containing 5thly (pp. 149—290), εὐαγγελοαποστόλων τῶν μεγάλων ἑορτῶν.	1225	id. 22—27; v. 22—vi. 2; Phil. ii. 5—11; Col. ii. 8—12; iii. 4—11; id. 12 —16; 2 Tim. ii. 1—10. (= Gosp. 117) Griesbach, who says "Variantes lectiones collegi e . . . Gal. iv. 4—7; Phil. iv. 4—9; Col. ii. 8, 9 . . ."
lect-6	Göttingen (C. de Missy).	XV.	Matthæi (v). See his appendix to Thess. Contains a large number of the usual lections.
lect-7	Copenhagen 3.	XV.	Hensler in Birch. (= ev-44)
lect-8	Propaganda Lib. Rome 287.	XI.	Birch. (= ev-37)
lect-9	Paris 32.	XII.	Inspected by Scholz. (= ev-84)
lect-10	Paris 33.	XII.	Inspected by Scholz. (= ev-85)
lect-11	Paris 34.	XII.	Inspected by Scholz.
lect-12	Paris 375.	1022	Scholz. An important MS. (= ev-60)
lect-13	Moscow Synod, 4.	X.	Matthæi (b).
lect-14	Moscow Synod, 291.	XII.	Matthæi (e).
lect-16	Moscow Synod, 266.	XV.	Matthæi (ξ). (= ev-52)
lect-17	Moscow Synod 267.	XV.	Matthæi (χ). (= ev-53)
lect-18	Moscow Synod, 268.	1470	Matthæi (ψ). (= ev-54)
lect-19	Moscow Typogr., 47.	XVII.	Matthæi (ω). (= ev-55)
lect-20	Moscow Typogr., 9.	XVI.	Matthæi (16). Contains 2 Tim. ii. 1—10. (= ev-56)
lect-21	Paris 294.	XI.	Inspected by Scholz. (= ev-83)
lect-22	Paris 304.	XIII.	Inspected by Scholz.
lect-23	Paris 306.	XII.	Inspected by Scholz.
lect-24	Paris 308.	XIII.	Mostly O. T. lections; only a few from N. T.
lect-25	Paris 319.	XI.	Inspected by Scholz.
lect-26	Paris 320.	XII.	Inspected by Scholz. Mutilated.
lect-27	Paris 321	XIII.	Inspected by Scholz. Defective.
lect-28	Bodleian, Selden 2.	XV.	Griesbach. (= ev-26)
lect-29	Paris 370.	XII.	Some lections from Gospp. and Epp. (= ev-94)
lect-30	Paris 373.	XIII.	
lect-31	Paris 276.	XV.	Inspected by Scholz. (= ev-82)
lect-32	Paris 376.	XIII.	Entered in list of MSS. of Gospels as 324. (Lections in) 1 and 2 Tim. collated by Matthæi.
lect-33	Paris 382.	XIII.	"Cursim coll. magna codicis pars." Scholz.
lect-34	Paris 383.	XV.	Inspected by Scholz.
lect-35	Paris 324.	XIII.	Inspected by Scholz. (ev-92)
lect-36	Paris 326.	XIV.	Inspected by Scholz. (ev-93)
lect-37	Riccardi Lib. Florence 84.	XV.	See ms 230 above.
lect-38	Vatican 1528.	XV.	
lect-39	Vatican, Ottob. 416.	XIV.	(ev-133)
lect-40	Barberini Lib. Rome 18.	XIV.	Some parts of Cent. X.
lect-41	Barberini Lib. Rome (no number).	XI.	The first 114 leaves are lost.
lect-42	Vallicella Lib. Rome, C. 46.	XVI.	
lect-43	Riccardi Lib. Florence 2742	?	(Inspected by Scholz ?)
lect-44	Glasgow (MissyBB).	?	Manuscript collations by Missy were once in Michaelis' possession.
lect-45	Glasgow (MissyCC).	1199	
lect-46	Ambros. Lib. Milan 63.	XIV.	Inspected by Scholz.
lect-47	Ambros. Lib. Milan 72.	XII.	Inspected by Scholz. (ev-104)
lect-48	Laur. Lib. Florence 2742.	XIII.	Inspected by Scholz. (ev-112)

	Designation.	Date.	Name of Collator and other information.
lect-49	Mon. St. Saba, nr. Jerus. 16.	XIV.	(Inspected by Scholz?)
lect-50	St. Saba 18.	XV.	Inspected by Scholz.
lect-51	St. Saba 26.	XIV.	Inspected by Scholz.
lect-52	St. Saba (no number).	1059	Inspected by Scholz.
lect-53	St. Saba (no number).	XIV.	Inspected by Scholz. (ev-160)
lect-54	St. Saba (no number).	XIII.	
lect-57	Ch. Ch. Oxf., Wake 12 (1, Scholz).	XI.	(26 Apoc.)
lect-58	Ch. Ch. Oxf., Wake 33 (5, Scholz).	1172	

For VERSIONS *and* FATHERS, *see Vol. II.*

SECTION II.

LIST, AND SPECIFICATION OF EDITIONS, OF BOOKS QUOTED, REFERRED
TO, OR MADE USE OF IN THIS VOLUME.

(Works mentioned in the lists given in the Prolegg. to Vols. I. and II.
are not here again noticed.)

BAUR, Paulus, der Apostel Jesu Christi, u.s.w., Stuttgart, 1845.

Ditto, Die sogenannte Pastoral-briefe u.s.w. (this latter work is
quoted second hand.)

BISPING, Erklärung der Briefe an die Ephesier, Philipper, Colosser, u. des
ersten Briefes an d. Thessalonicher, Münster 1855. (Rom. Catholic.)

DAVIDSON, DR. S., Introduction to the New Testament, vol. iii.:
1 Timothy—Revelation, Lond. 1851.

DE WETTE, Exegetisches Handbuch, u.s.w.: Gal. and Thess., 2nd ed.,
Leipzig 1845 : Eph., Phil., Col., Philem., 2nd ed., Leipzig 1847 :
1 Tim., 2 Tim., and Titus, 2nd ed., Leipzig 1847.

EADIE, PROF., Commentary on the Epistle to the Ephesians, Lond. and
Glasgow 1854.

Ditto, Commentary on the Epistle to the Colossians, Lond. and
Glasgow 1856.

ELLICOTT, C. J. (now Bishop of Gloucester and Bristol), a Critical and
Grammatical Commentary on St. Paul's Epistle to the Galatians,
&c., London 1854. 2nd edition, 1859.

Ditto, on the Epistle to the Ephesians, London 1855. 2nd edition,
1859.

Ditto, on the Pastoral Epistles, London 1856. 2nd edition, 1861.

Ditto, on the Epistles to the Philippians, Colossians, and Philemon,
London 1857.

Ditto, on the Epistles to the Thessalonians, London 1858 [1].

---

[1] I cannot forbear recording my very deep sense of the service rendered by Bishop
Ellicott to students of the Greek Testament by these laborious, conscientious, and

126]

FRITZSCHE, Pauli ad Romanos Epistola, 3 voll., Hal. Sax. 1836.

FRITZSCHIORUM Opuscula Academica, Lipsiæ 1838.

HARLESS, Commentar über den Brief Pauli an die Ephesier, Erlangen 1834.

HEFELE, Patrum Apostolicorum Opera, ed. 3, Tübingen 1847.

HOFMANN, Der Schriftbeweis, 2 voll., Nördlingen 1855.

JOWETT, PROF., the Epistles of St. Paul to the Thessalonians, Galatians, Romans : with critical Notes and Illustrations, Lond. 1856.

KRÜGER, Griechische Sprachlehre für Schulen, Berlin 1852.

MACK, Commentar über die Pastoralbriefe des Apostels Paulus, Tübingen 1836. (Rom. Catholic.)

MEYER, H. A. W., Kritisch-exegetischer Commentar über das neue Testament :—Gal., 2nd ed., Göttingen 1851 : Eph., Göttingen 1853 : Col., and Philem., Göttingen 1848 : Thess., continuation by Lünemann, Göttingen 1850 : 1 Tim., 2 Tim., and Titus, continuation by Huther, Göttingen 1850.

PASSOW, Handwörterbuch der Griechischen Sprache : neu bearbeitet und zeitgemäss umgestaltet von Dr. Rost u. Dr. Palm, Leipzig 1841—1857 [2].

PELT, Epist. Pauli Ap. ad Thessalonicenses &c., Griefswald 1830.

STIER, DR. RUDOLF, Die Gemeinde in Christo Jesu: Auslegung des Briefes an die Epheser, 2 voll., Berlin 1848.

USTERI, der Paulinische Lehrbegriff, Zurich 1851.

WINDISCHMANN, Erklärung des Briefes an die Galater, Mainz 1843. (Rom. Catholic.)

WINER, Pauli ad Galatas Epistolam latine vertit et perpetua annotatione illustravit Dr. G. B. Winer, ed. tertia, Lips. 1829.

scholarlike volumes. They have set the first example in this country of a thorough and fearless examination of the grammatical and philological requirements of every word in the sacred text. I do not know any thing superior to them, in their own particular line, in Germany : and they add what, alas, is so seldom found in that country, profound reverence for the matter and subjects on which the author is labouring Nor is their value lessened by Bishop Ellicott having confined himself for the most part to one department of a Commentator's work—the grammatical and philological. No student ought to be without these books, nor ought he to spare himself in making them his own by continual study.

[2] This Lexicon (which has now all appeared) is as superior to all other editions of Passow, German and English, as Passow was to all that went before. A comparison of any important words will shew the difference at once. The immense labour requisite will, it is to be feared, deter our lexicographers from giving the English public a translation : but it would be a great boon to the scholarship of our country. [It is understood that a new edition of Liddell and Scott's Lexicon, now long promised, will contain all the valuable improvements and additions from Rost and Palm. A translation was in progress, but was broken off by the lamented death of Dr. Donaldson in the spring of 1861.]

ERRATA.

Page 88, reference o, *for* Rom. viii. 1, 4 *read* Rom. viii. 4
— 111, reference o, *for* Rom. xi. 30 *read* Rom. xi. 33.
— 117, reference z, *for* † *read* ‡, and in the bracket following *insert* Esth. vi. 3 A.
— 192, reference u, *for* iii. 14 *read* iii. 16.
— 215, reference r, *dele* (bis).
— 289, reference h, *after* 2 Cor. xii. 7 *insert* [bis].
— 292, reference v, *for* Rom. ii. 18 *read* Rom. i. 18.
— 295, reference k, *for* Matt. xvii. 43 *read* Matt. xxvii. 43.

Readings of the Codex Vaticanus (B) in the text of this volume, which have been ascertained by the Editor's personal inspection of the MS. at Rome, February, 1861.

Gal. i. 4. του ενεστωτος, not ενεστωτος as Bentley.

5. των αιωνων as in Mai ed. 1, not τω αι. as in ed. 2.

15. αφωρισας is in codex.

ii. 4. καταδουλουσουσιν is 1. m.

14. Κηφα is in codex.

iii. 16. ερρεθησαν is 1. m.

21. οντως εν νομω, not εν ν. οντως as Bentley.

iv. 4. ο θεος is in codex, not omitted as in Bentley.

17. υμας θελουσιν is in codex without correction, not ημας.

25. το δε αγαρ, not το αγαρ as Bentley.

vi. 11. ηλικοις is in codex, all from 1. m. [Tischdf. ascribes π to his B³.]

Eph. i. 1. ουσιν is at the end of a line, and εν εφεσω in margin, but it is very doubtful whether it is 2. m., and not rather 1. m., as some of its letters seem to have the double ink of 1. and 2. m.

23. του τα παντα, not του παντα as Mai.

iv. 2. εν αγαπη, not αγαπη as Bentley.

20. εμαθετε as Mai ed. 1, not εμαθητε as ed. 2.

23. δε is not omitted as in Bentley.

32. ημιν is not "added by another hand" as Bentley asserts, but in the codex, 1. m.

Phil. i. 22. αιρησωμαι as Bentley, not -σομαι as Mai.

Phil. ii. 9. αυτω το ονομα is in codex.

30. παρακολευσαμενος, not -βολ-. [e contra Tischdf.]

Col. Title. κολασσαεις, both letters being 1. m. [Tischdf. assigns ο to his B³.]

i. 2. κολοσσ- is 1. m.

4. εις παντας, not τη εις as Muralto.

16. εν τοις, not τα εν τοις as Muralto.

18. η αρχη, not αρχη as Muralto.

20. επι γης, not επι της γης as Muralto.

27. ο εστιν, not ος εστιν as Muralto.

ii. 1 and 2. Vercellone's marginal notes are right: cod. has εωρ-, and του θεου χριστου. εορ- is 1 m. in ver. 18.

iii. 8. νυνει 1. m.

end. κολασσ. is here plainly 1. m.

1 Thess. i. 2. 1st υμων is not omitted as in Bentley.

iii. 8. στηκετε as in Mai ed. 2, not -ητε as in ed. 1.

iv. 1. λοιπον αδελφοι is 1. m.: το λ. ουν αδ. 2. m.

[4. "ειδεναι ends a line, and is followed by ενα written by the 2da manus." — Mr. Cure, April, 1862.]

v. 13. ηγεισθε is in codex.

2 Thess. ii. 3. η αποστασ. is in codex.

iii. 14. συναναμιγνυσθαι as Bentley, not -σθε as Mai.

ΠΡΟΣ ΓΑΛΑΤΑΣ.

ABDFK
LPℵ a b
c d e f g
h k l m n
o 17. 47 I. ¹ Παῦλος ἀπόστολος οὐκ ᵃἀπ᾽ ἀνθρώπων οὐδὲ ᵇδι᾽ ἀνθρώπου, ἀλλὰ διὰ Ἰησοῦ χριστοῦ καὶ ᶜθεοῦ ᶜπατρὸς

ᵃ = Rom. xiii.
1. so ἐκ,
Matt. xxi. 25.
ᵇ = 1 Cor. i. 9.
2 Cor. i. 11.

ᶜ Eph. vi. 23.   1 Thess. i. 1.   2 Thess. i. 1, 2.   1 Pet. i. 2.   2 John 3.   Jude 1.   see 1 Cor. viii. 6.

TITLE. rec η προς γαλατας επιστολη παυλου: elz παυλου του αποστολου η προς γαλατας επιστολη : του αγιου και πανευφημου αποστολου παυλου επ. πρ. γαλ. L: πρ. γαλ. επ. τ. αγ. απ. παυλ. h : [παυλου επ. πρ. γαλ. P k:] επ. πρ. γαλ. l: txt ABKℵ m n o 17 [47], and (prefixing αρχεται) DF.

CHAP. I. 1—5.] ADDRESS AND GREET-ING. πολλοῦ τὸ προοίμιον γέμει θυμοῦ κ. μεγάλου φρονήματος· οὐ τὸ προοίμιον δὲ μόνον, ἀλλὰ καὶ πᾶσα, ὡς εἰπεῖν, ἡ ἐπιστολή. Chrys. In the very opening sentence of the Epistle, we see the fervour of the Apostle's mind and the weightiness of his subject betraying themselves. The vindication of his own apostolic calling,— and the description of the work and pur-pose of Christ towards us, shew him to be writing to those who had disparaged that apostleship, and were falling from their Saviour. 1.] It is better not to join ἀπόστολος (here of course used in its strict and highest sense: see Ellicott, and an interesting note in Jowett) with ἀπ᾽, but to let it stand by itself, and take the two prepositions as indicating, ἀπό the remote originating cause, διά the nearer instru-mental one. In St. Paul's case, neither of these was merely human; the Lord Jesus was both the original Sender, and Himself the Announcer of the mission. Perhaps however the prepositions must not be so strictly pressed,—see ref. 1 Cor.,—and observe that the following διά belongs to θεοῦ πατρός as well as to Ἰησοῦ χριστοῦ.— ἀνθρώπου is perhaps (as Mey., De W., Ellic., al.) singular, for the sake of contrast to Ἰησ. χρ. following; but more probably for solemnity's sake, the singular making even

a more marked exclusion of human agency than the plural. Luther's view of the sen-tence is: "The Judaizing teachers could shew their credentials as disciples of Apos-tles or messengers of churches, and de-spised Paul as having none such. To this he answers that he had not indeed any commission from men, but derived his authority from a higher source." But (1) this was not the fact, for he had a regular mission from the church at An-tioch: (2) the words do not express it. κ. θεοῦ πατρός] If by Jesus Christ. then also by God the Father, in and by whose appointment all the me-diatorial acts of Christ in the Headship of His Church are done. The inferences of Chrys. al. as to the equality of the Father and the Son from this juxtaposition, ap-pear far-fetched, and according to "the mind, not of the apostolic, but of the Ni-cene age," as Jowett: but we may say at least this, that the strongest possible con-trast is here drawn between man, in the ordinary sense, on the one side, and Jesus Christ, and God the Father, on the other. Had not the Apostle regarded Jesus Christ as one with the Father in the Godhead, he never could have written thus. On the use of διά here where ἀπό might be expected, see Ellicott's note. He refers it to the brevity with which St. Paul ex-

d Matt. xvii. 9.
Luke ix. 7.
John ii. 22.
xii. 1, 9, 17.
xxi. 14. Acts
iii. 15 al2.
Paul, Rom.
iv. 24 and
passim. Heb.
xi. 19. 1 Pet.
i. 21.
g = Rom. viii. 3. τοῦ ^d ἐγείραντος αὐτὸν ^d ἐκ ^d νεκρῶν, **2** καὶ οἱ σὺν ἐμοὶ ABDFK
LPℵ a b
c d e f g
h k l m n
o 17. 47
πάντες ἀδελφοί, ταῖς ἐκκλησίαις τῆς Γαλατίας. ^{3 e} χάρις
ὑμῖν καὶ ^e εἰρήνη ἀπὸ ^c θεοῦ ^c πατρὸς καὶ κυρίου ἡμῶν
Ἰησοῦ χριστοῦ, ⁴ τοῦ ^f δόντος ἑαυτὸν ^g περὶ τῶν ἁμαρτιῶν

e Rom. i. 7 al.   f = 1 Tim. ii. 6.   Tit. ii. 14.   1 Macc. vi. 44. (= παραδ., ch. ii. 20 reff.)
Heb. x. 6, from Ps. xxxix. 6.

3. ημων bef και κυριου (as in Rom i. 7, 1 Cor i. 3, 2 Cor i. 2, &c) A[P]ℵ d 17 fuld (with demid hal) [copt(sic, Treg)] Chr-txt lat-ff : om ημων a l (not 67) : ins in both places æth.

4. rec (for περι) υπερ, with Bℵ³ rel Chr Thdrt Damasc Œc-comm : txt ADFKL[P]ℵ¹

presses himself : I should rather say that he states our Lord Jesus and God the Father to have been the *causa medians*, in bringing down divine agency even to the actual *fact* of his mission—and leaving it therefore to be inferred à fortiori that the *causa principalis* was the will of God.

It is important to remember that the mission of Paul to the actual work of the ministry was by the command of the *Holy Spirit*, Acts xiii. 2,—proceeding from, and expressing the will of, the Father and the Son. πατρός is better taken generally, as in reff., **the Father**, than supplied with ἡμῶν (as De W. al.) or αὐτοῦ (as Meyer al.). τοῦ ἐγ. αὐτ.] Why specified here? Not, I think, because (Meyer) Paul was called to be an Apostle *by the risen Saviour*,—nor merely (De W.) to identify the Father as the Originator of the Son's work of Redemption (which is so in Rom. iv. 24,—but here would not immediately concern Paul's calling to be an Apostle),—nor (Calvin, al.) to meet the objection that he had never seen Christ, and turn it into an advantage, in that (Aug. (but cf. his Retractations), Erasm., Beza, al.) he alone was commissioned by the already risen and ascended Jesus,—for in this case we should not find τοῦ ἐγείραντος κ.τ.λ. stated as a predicate of the Father, but τοῦ ἐγερθέντος κ.τ.λ. as one of the Son, —nor as asserting the Resurrection against the Jews and Judaizing Galatians (Chrys., Luther), which is far-fetched, —nor again (Jowett) as expressing an attribute of the Father, without which He can hardly be thought of by the believer, —for this is too loose a relevancy for a sentence so pointed as the present : but because the Resurrection, including and implying the Ascension, was the Father's bestowal on Christ of gifts for men, by virtue of which (ἔδωκεν τοὺς μὲν ἀποστόλους, κ.τ.λ. Eph. iv. 11) Paul's *Apostleship had been received*. Cf. a similar sentiment in Rom. i. 4, 5. ἐκ νεκρῶν = ἐκ τῶν ν.,—see note on Rom. iv. 24. In Matt. xiv. 2 ; xxvii. 64 ; xxviii. 7 ; Eph. v. 14 ; Col. i. 18 (ii. 12 ?) ; 1 Thess. i. 10,

the article is expressed : otherwise it is always omitted. **2.** ἀδελφοί] Who ✻ these were, may best be inferred by the Apostle's usage in the addresses of other Epistles, where we have Σωσθένης ὁ ἀδελφός (1 Cor. i. 1), Τιμόθεος ὁ ἀδ. (2 Cor. i. 1. Col. i. 1. Philem. 1). They were his colleagues in the work of the Gospel, his companions in travel, and the like (not all the members of the church where he was, as Erasm., Grot., Jowett, al., who would hardly be specified as being σὺν αὐτῷ,— besides that such an address would be unprecedented) : and their unanimity (πάντες) is here stated, as Chrys., Luther, al., to shew that he was not alone in his doctrine, but joined by all the brethren who were present. At the same time πάντες would seem to imply that just now he had many of these ἀδελφοί with him. But we cannot draw any inference from this as to the date of our Epistle : for we do not know who were his companions on many occasions. At Ephesus, where probably it was written, we hear only of Gaius and Aristarchus (Acts xix. 29), but we cannot say that there were not others : in all likelihood, several more of those mentioned Acts xx. 4, were with him.

ταῖς ἐκκλ.] πανταχοῦ γὰρ εἴρψεν ἡ νόσος. Thdrt. The principal cities of Galatia were Pessinus and Ancyra : but this plural seems to imply more than two such churches. See 1 Cor. xvi. 1, and Acts xvi. 6 ; xviii. 23. That we have here barely ταῖς ἐκκλ., without any honourable adjunct (as in 1 Cor., 2 Cor., 1 Thess., 2 Thess., &c.), must be explained as Chrys. al.: θέα δέ μοι καὶ ἐνταῦθα τ. πολλὴν ἀγανάκτησιν. οὐ γὰρ εἶπε Τοῖς ἀγαπητοῖς, οὐδὲ Τοῖς ἡγιασμένοις, ἀλλὰ Τ. ἐκκλ. τ. Γαλ. Meyer denies this, alleging (carelessly, which is not usual with him) 1 Thess. and 2 Thess. as addressed barely τῇ ἐκκλησίᾳ, whereas in both we have added ἐν θεῷ πατρὶ κ. κυρίῳ Ἰησ. χρ.

3.] See introductory note on Rom. i. 1—7. **4.**] He thus *obiter* reminds the Galatians, who wished to return to the bondage of the law, of the

Η ημων ἡμῶν, ὅπως g ἐξέληται ἡμᾶς ἐκ τοῦ h αἰῶνος τοῦ i ἐνεστῶτος
ABDFH πονηροῦ κατὰ τὸ θέλημα τοῦ j θεοῦ καὶ j πατρὸς ἡμῶν,
KLP℠ a
b c d e f 5 ᾧ ἡ k δόξα εἰς τοὺς l αἰῶνας τῶν αἰώνων. ἀμήν.
g h k l m
n o 17.47 6 m Θαυμάζω ὅτι οὕτως ταχέως n μετατίθεσθε ἀπὸ τοῦ

g = Acts vii.
10. xii. 11.
xxiii. 27
xxvi. 17 only.
Exod. iii. 8.
Polyb. xv.
22. 4,
ἐξελούμενοι
τοὺς Κια-

νοὺς ἐκ τῶν περιεστώτων κακῶν.
i ⇒ Rom. viii. 38. 1 Cor. vii. 26 al. 1 Macc. xii. 44.
Isa. lxiii. 16. k ellips., Rom. xi. 36. Eph. iii. 21.
17. 2 Tim. iv. 18. Dan. vii. 18. see Ps. cx. 10.
13. Eccl. v. 7. Demosth. 349. 3. w. ὅτι, Luke xi. 38. John iii. 7. iv. 27.
16. (Heb. vii. 12. xi. 5 pass.) Jude 4 only. Deut. xxvii. 17 (= 2 Macc. vii. 24. Polyb. xvii. 13. 5,
μετατιθέναι τὰς ἐκείνων πατρίδας ἀπὸ τινων ὑποκειμένων εἰς ἑτέρας συμμαχίας).

h ⇐ Matt. xii. 32. xiii. 40. Rom. xii. 2. 1 Cor. i. 20 al.
j Phil. iv. 20. 1 Thess. i. 3. iii. 11, 13. see
1 Phil. iv. 20. 1 Tim. i.
m = Mark vi. 6. John vii. 21. 1 John iii
n Acts vii

a c e f m n [47] Orig Thl. (67² is given on difft sides by Bch and Alter.) rec ενεστωτος
hef αιωνος(omg 3rd του), with DFHKL[P]℠³ rel latt goth Orig₁ Chr Thdrt Œc-comm
Victorin: om αιωνος e¹: txt AB℠¹ 17 [47] æth Orig₃ Did. om το ℵ¹.
6. om ουτως F [115].

great object of the Atonement, which they
had forgotten. Ch. iii. 13 is but a re-
statement, in more precise terms, of this.

δόντος ἑαυ.] viz. as an offering, unto
death : an expression only found (in N. T.)
here and in the Pastoral Epistles. Several
such will occur; see the inference, in
Prolegomena to Past. Epistles, § i. 32, note.

περί, in this connexion, has much
the same sense as ὑπέρ: see reff., and
note on Eph. vi. 19; also Ellic.'s note
here. ὅπ. ἐξέληται] ἐξαιρεῖσθαι is
the very word used by the Lord of St.
Paul's own great deliverance, see reff.

τ. αἰῶνος τ. ἐνεστ. πονηροῦ] the present
(not, as Mey., 'coming.' The word will
not bear this meaning in 1 Cor. vii. 26,
nor apparently (see note) in 2 Thess. ii. 2,
much less in Rom. viii. 38) evil age (state
of things; i. e. the course of this present
evil world ;—and, as understood, make us
citizens and inheritors of a better αἰῶνος,
τοῦ μέλλοντος. So Luther : "vocat hunc
totum mundum, qui fuit, est et erit, præsens seculum, ad differentiam futuri et
æterni sæculi." The allusion (Jowett) to
the Jewish expressions, "the present age,"
"the age to come," as applying to the
periods before and after the Messiah's
coming, is very faint,—indeed hardly
traceable, in the change which the terms
had undergone as used in a spiritual sense
by Christians.' See however the rest of
his note, which is full of interest).

κατὰ τὸ θέλημα . . ,] And this, (1) not
according to our own plan, in proportion
to our legal obedience or any quality in
us, but according to the Father's sovereign will, the prime standard of all the
process of redemption: and (2) not so that
we may trifle with such rescuing purpose
of Christ by mixing it with other schemes
and fancies, seeing that it is according to
a procedure prescribed by Him, who doeth
all things after the counsel of His own
will. And this, not as the lord merely
of His works, but as πατρὸς ἡμῶν, bound

to us in the ties of closest love—for our
good, as well as to fulfil His own eternal
purpose. On the question, whether the
genitive ἡμῶν depends on both, or only on
the latter of the two nouns θεοῦ κ. πατρός,
I agree in Ellicott's conclusion, that as
πατρός is regularly anarthrous, and thus
purely grammatical considerations are confounded,—as θεός conveys one absolute
idea, while πατήρ might convey many relative ones, it is natural to believe that
the Apostle may have added a defining
genitive to πατήρ, which he did not intend
to be referred to θεός. Render therefore, God and our Father, not 'our God
and Father.' 5. ᾧ ἡ δόξα] So (reff.)
on other occasions, when speaking of the
wonderful things of God, St. Paul adds a
doxology. "In politeia, quando regum aut
principum nomina appellamus, id honesto
quodam gestu, reverentia, et genuflexione
facere solemus. Multo magis cum de Deo
loquimur, genu cordis flectere debemus."
Luther. In ἡ δόξα,—the glory κατ' ἐξοχήν, or 'the glory which is His,'—the
article is probably inserted for solemnity.
"In this and similar forms of doxology,—
excepting the angelic doxology, Luke ii.
14, and that of the multitude, Luke xix.
38,—δόξα regularly takes the article when
used alone: see Rom. xi. 36; xvi. 27;
Eph. iii. 21; Phil. iv. 20; 2 Tim. iv. 18;
Heb. xiii. 21; 2 Pet. iii. 18. When joined
with one or more substantives, it appears
sometimes with the article (1 Pet. iv. 11;
Rev. i. 6; vii. 12) : sometimes without it
(Rom. ii. 10; 1 Tim. i. 17; Jude 25)."
Ellicott. τοὺς αἰῶν. τ. αἰών.] See
note on Eph. iii. 21. 6—10.] Announcement of the occasion of the
Epistle, in his amazement at their
speedy falling away from the Gospel. Assertion of that Gospel's exclusive claim to their adhesion, as
preached by him, who served God in
Christ, and not popularity among
men. We have none of the usual expres-

o = ver. 15.
Rom. viii. 30.
ix. 24 al. fr.
p 1 Cor. vii. 15.
Eph. iv. 4.
1 Thess. iv. 7.
t = Acts xv. 24. constr. w. art., Luke xviii. 9. Col. ii. 8. Ps. xxi. 11. Xen. Anab. vi. 5. 9.

ᵒκαλέσαντος ὑμᾶς ᵖἐν ᑫχάριτι ᑫχριστοῦ εἰς ἕτερον εὐαγ-
γέλιον· 7 ὃ οὐκ ἔστιν ἄλλο, ˢεἰ μή τινές εἰσιν οἱ ⁺τα-

q Rom. v. 15. Acts xv. 11.   r = 2 Cor. xi. 4 al.   s see note.

ABDFH
KLPℵ a
b c d e f
g h k l m
n o 17. 47

ins ιυ̅ bef χυ̅ D [39] vss.   om χριστου F¹[and G] Tert₂ Cypr₂ Lucif.

sions of thankfulness for their faith, &c. ; but he hurries vehemently into his subject, and, as Chrys. says, σφοδρότερον τῷ μετὰ ταῦτα κέχρηται λόγῳ, καθάπερ πυρωθεὶς σφοδρῶς ὑπὸ τῆς ἐννοίας τῶν εὐεργεσιῶν τοῦ θεοῦ. 6.] θαυμάζω in this sense (see reff.) is a word of mildness, inasmuch as it imports that better things were expected of them,—and of condescension, as letting down the writer to the level of his readers and even challenging explanation from them. Still, like many other such mild words, it carries to the guilty conscience even sharper rebuke than a harsher one would. οὕτως ταχέως] either (1) 'so soon after your conversion' (Calv., Olsh., Meyer, &c.), or (2) 'so quickly,'—'after so little persuasion,' when the false teachers once came among you (Chr., De W., &c.), or (3) 'so soon after my recent visit among you' (Bengel, &c.). Of these I prefer (1), as more suiting the dignity of the passage, and as the more general and comprehensive reason. But it does not exclude (2) and (3) : 'so soon,' might be, and might be intended to be, variously supplied. See Prolegomena, on the time and place of writing this Epistle. μετατίθ.] are passing over, pres. : not as E. V. 'are removed,' which is doubly wrong, for μετ. is not passive but middle, in the common usage of the word, according to which the Galatians would understand it. So Plato, Theog. 122 c, σμικρὸν γάρ τι μετατίθεμαι, 'I am beginning somewhat to change my opinion:' see also Gorg. 493 c : Demosth. 379. 10: Ἴβηρες, ὅσοι ... ἐς Ῥωμαίους μετέθεντο, Appian, Hisp.c.17; &c. See also examples in Wetst. Chrys. says well, οὐκ εἶπε Μετέθεσθε, ἀλλὰ Μετατίθεσθε· τουτέστιν, οὐδέπω πιστεύω, οὐδὲ ἡγοῦμαι ἀπηρτισμένην εἶναι τὴν ἀπάτην· ὃ καὶ αὐτὸ πάλιν ἐστὶν ἀνακτωμένου. It is interesting to notice, in connexion with οὕτως ταχέως μετατίθεσθε, the character given by Cæsar of the Gauls: "ut ad bella suscipienda Gallorum alacer ac promtus est animus : sic mollis ac minime resistens ad calamitates mens ipsorum est." B. G. iii. 19 :—" Cæsar ... infirmitatem Gallorum veritus, quod sint in consiliis capiendis mobiles, et novis plerumque rebus student :" ib. iv. 5 : see also ib. ii. 8 ; iii. 10. τοῦ καλέσ. ὑμ.] not to be taken with χριστοῦ, as Syr., Jer., Luth.

(gives both constructions, but prefers this), Calv., Grot., Bengel, &c., nor understood of Paul, as al. and recently by Bagge,—but, as almost always with the Apostle (see note on Rom. i. 6), of GOD the Father (see ver. 15 ; and cf. Rom. viii. 30 ; ix. 24, 25 : 1 Cor. i. 9 ; vii. 15, 17 : 1 Thess. ii. 12 : 2 Thess. ii. 14 : 2 Tim. i. 9. Also 1 Pet. v. 10). ἐν χάρ. χρ.] in (as the element, and hence the medium ; not into, as E. V.; see for construction 1 Cor. vii. 15. In the secondary transferred sense of local prepositions, so often found in later Greek, it is extremely difficult to assign the precise shade of meaning: see Jowett's and Ellic.'s notes here. But we may safely lay down two strongly marked regions of prepositional force, which must never be confounded, that of motion, and that of rest. ἐν, for example, can never be strictly rendered ' into,' nor εἰς, ' in.' Where such appears to be the case, some logical consideration has been overlooked, which if introduced would right the meaning) the grace of Christ. Christ's grace is the elementary medium of our ' calling of God,' as is set forth in full, Rom. v. 15, ἡ δωρεὰ (τοῦ θεοῦ) ἐν χάριτι τῇ τοῦ ἑνὸς ἀνθρ. Ἰησ. χρ.:—see also Acts xv. 11. And ' Christ's grace' is the sum of all that He has suffered and done for us to bring us to God;—whereby we come to the Father,—in which, as its element, the Father's calling of us has place. εἰς ἕτερ. εὐαγγ.] to a different (in kind : not ἄλλο, another of the same kind, which title he denies it, see below) gospel (so called by its preachers ; or said by way of at once instituting a comparison unfavourable to the new teachers, by the very etymology of εὐαγγέλιον). 7.] Meyer's note appears to me well to express the sense: " the preceding εἰς ἕτερον εὐαγγέλιον was a paradoxical expression, there being in reality but one Gospel. Paul appeared by it to admit the existence of many Gospels, and he therefore now explains himself more accurately, how he wishes to be understood—ὃ οὐκ ἔστιν ἄλλο, εἰ μὴ &c.," i. e. which " different Gospel," whereto you are falling away, is not another, not a second, besides the one Gospel (ἄλλο, not ἕτερον again ; see above), except that there are some who trouble you &c. That is : 'This ἕτερον εὐαγγ. is only in so far another, that there are certain, who &c.'

ράσσοντες ὑμᾶς καὶ θέλοντες ᵘμεταστρέψαι τὸ εὐαγγέλιον
τοῦ χριστοῦ. ⁸ ἀλλὰ καὶ ἐὰν ἡμεῖς ἢ ˙ἄγγελος ἐξ
οὐρανοῦ ᵛεὐαγγελίζηται ὑμῖν ᵂπαρ᾽ ὃ ᵛεὐηγγελισάμεθα

u Acts ii. 20
(from Joel
ii. 31). James
iv. 9 only.
Deut. xxiii.
5. 1 Kings
x. 9. Sir. xi.
31.

v absol. w. dat., ch. iv. 13. Luke iv. 18, from Isa. lxi. 1. Rom. i. 15. (1 Cor. xv. 1.) pass., 1 Pet. iv. 6.
w = Acts xviii. 13. Rom. i. 26. iv. 18. xvi. 17 al.

7. om και θελοντες א¹(ins א-corr¹ obl).
8. καν B Dial Chr Thl. ευαγγελιζεται K[P] c d k n [47] Thdrt-ms Œc : ευαγγε-
λισηται AN æth Eus Ath Cyr-jer Cyr Thdrt₁ Procl, *evangelizaverit* latt Tert₂ Cypr.
υμιν bef ευαγγ. BH Chr Archel Victorin Aug : om υμιν Fא¹ Dial Eus Damasc
Tert₂(elsw₁ om 2nd υμ.) Cypr Lucif. for 1st υμιν, υμας D¹ f l Cyr-jer Chron.
ευαγγελισαμεθα D(ed Tischdf) FH.

Notice that the stress is on οὐκ; so that
Paul, though he had before said εἰς ἔτερον
εὐαγγ., yet *guards the unity* of the Gospel,
and explains what he meant by ἔτερον
εὐαγγέλιον to be *nothing but a corruption
and perversion of the one Gospel of
Christ.* Others, as Chrys., Œc., Thdrt.,
Luther, De Wette, &c., take ὃ οὐκ ἔστιν
ἄλλο as all referring to εὐαγγέλιον, "*which
is* (admits of being) *no other*" (= μὴ
ὄντος ἄλλου): and then εἰ μή is merely
adversative, '*but*,' or '*only*,' a meaning
which it will hardly bear, but which, as
De W. remarks, is not necessarily involved in his interpretation: 'except that'
answering for it quite as well. The objection to his view is (1) that the meaning assigned to ὃ οὐκ ἔστιν ἄλλο is very
harsh, taking the relative from its application to the concrete (ἔτερον εὐαγγ.),
and enlarging it to the abstract (τὸ εὐαγγ.
in general) (2) that the juxtaposition of
ἔτερον and ἄλλο in one sentence seems to
require, as in 1 Cor. xv. 40, 41, that the
strict meaning of each should be observed.
Others again (Winer, Olsh., &c.) refer the
ὃ to the whole sentence from ὅτι &c. to
εὐαγγέλιον—'*which* (viz. your falling
away) *is nothing else but* (has no other
cause, but that) *&c.*' To this the objection (2) above applies, and it is besides
very unlikely that St. Paul would thus
have shifted all blame from the Galatians
to their false teachers ('hanc culpam non
tam vobis imputo quam perturbatoribus
illis,' &c. Luther), and, as it were, wiped
out the effect of his rebuke just after uttering it. Lastly, Schött., and Cornel.-a-
Lapide, take ὃ οὐκ ἄλλο as a parenthesis, and refer εἰ μή to θαυμάζω,
which should thus have been ἐθαύμαζον
(ἄν). This would besides make the sentence a very harsh and unnatural one.
The nature of this 'different Gospel,' as
gathered from the data in our Epistle,
was (1), though recognizing Jesus as the
Christ, it insisted on circumcision and the
observance of the Mosaic ordinances as to
times, &c.: (2) it professed to rest on the

authority of some of the other Apostles
see Chrys. quoted below. οἱ ταρ.]
The article points out in a more marked
manner the (notorious) occupation of these
men, q. d. '*certain your disturbers, &c.*'
Add to reff., Herodot. ix. 70, τὴν σκηνὴν
τ. Μαρδονίου οὗτοι ἔσαν οἱ διαρπάσαντες.
Xen. An. ii. 4. 5, ὁ ἡγησόμενος οὐδεὶς
ἔσται : and compare the common expression εἰσὶν οἱ λέγοντες. τὸ εὐαγγ. τ.
χρ.] perhaps here not '*Christ's Gospel*,'
but the Gospel of (i. e. relating to, preaching) Christ. The context only can determine in such expressions whether the
genitive is subjective or objective.

8.] **But** (no matter who they are οἱ ταρ.
&c.) **even though** (in καὶ εἰ, καὶ ἐάν, &c.,
the force of the καί is distributed over the
whole supposition following, see Hartung,
Partikell. i. 139; and ἐάν is distinguished
from εἰ, in supposing a case which has
never occurred, see 1 Cor. xiii. 1, and a
full explanation in Herm. on Viger, p. 832)
we (i. e. usually, '*I, Paul*:' but perhaps
used here on account of οἱ σὺν ἐμοὶ πάντες
ἀδελφοί, ver. 2) **or an angel from heaven**
(ἄγγ. ἐξ οὐρ. to be taken together, not
ἐξ οὐρ. εὐαγγ.: introduced here as the
highest possible authority, next to a divine Person : even were this possible, were
the highest rank of created beings to furnish the preacher, &c. See 1 Cor. xiii. 1.
Perhaps also, as Chrys., there is a reference to the new teachers having sheltered
themselves under the names of the great
Apostles : μὴ γάρ μοι Ἰάκωβον εἴπης, φησί,
καὶ Ἰωάννην· κἂν γὰρ τῶν πρώτων ἀγγέλων ᾖ τις τῶν ἐξ οὐρανοῦ διαφθειρόντων
τὸ κήρυγμα κ.τ.λ. Then he adds : ταῦτα
δὲ οὐχ ὡς καταγινώσκων τ. ἀποστόλων
φησίν, οὐδὲ ὡς παραβαινόντων τὸ κήρυγμα, ἄπαγε· εἴτε γὰρ ἡμεῖς, εἴτε ἐκεῖνοι, φησίν, οὕτω κηρύσσομεν· ἀλλὰ δεῖξα.
βουλόμενος ὅτι ἀξίωμα προσώπων οὐ προς-
ίεται, ὅταν περὶ ἀληθείας ὁ λόγος ᾖ).
preach (evangelize : it is impossible to
preserve in English the εὐαγγέλιον, and
in it the reference back to vv. 6, 7) **to
you other than what** (παρά (reff.) as in

ὑμῖν, ˣ ἀνάθεμα ἔστω. º ὡς ʸ προειρήκαμεν, καὶ ἄρτι πάλιν λέγω, εἴ τις ὑμᾶς ᶻ εὐαγγελίζεται ʷ παρ᾽ ὃ ᵃ παρελάβετε, ˣ ἀνάθεμα ἔστω. 10 ἄρτι γὰρ ἀνθρώπους ᵇ πείθω ἢ τὸν θεόν ; ἢ ζητῶ ἀνθρώποις ᶜ ἀρέσκειν ; εἰ ἔτι ἀνθρώποις ᶜ ἤρεσκον, ᵈ χριστοῦ ᵈ δοῦλος οὐκ ἂν ᵉ ἤμην. 11 ᶠ Γνωρίζω γὰρ ὑμῖν, ἀδελφοί, τὸ εὐαγγέλιον τὸ εὐ-

9. προειρηκα אˡ k.
10. [for ἤ, ει P.]   rec aft ει ins γαρ (for connexion), with D².³KL[P] rel syrr Chr Thdrt Thl Œc: om ABD¹Fא 17. 67² latt copt arm Cyr₃ Damasc [Orig-int₃] lat-ff.
11. rec (for γαρ) δε, with AD².³KL[P]א¹·³ d(in red) rel syrr copt Chr Cyr₂ Thdrt [Orig-int₁] Ambrst: om æth : txt BD¹F א-corr¹ 17 latt Damasc Jer [Victorin] Aug. [om αδελφοι P (a) 67².   το ευαγγελιον is written 3ce by B¹.]

παρὰ δόξαν, παρὰ τοὺς ὅρκους, παραβαίνειν, &c. not merely 'against,' nor merely 'besides,' but indicating 'beyond,' in the sense of overstepping the limit into a new region, i. e. it points out specific difference. The preposition is important here, as it has been pressed by Protestants in the sense of 'besides,' against Roman Catholic tradition, and in consequence maintained by the latter in the sense of 'against.' It in fact includes both) we preached (evangelized) to you, let him be accursed (of God : no reference to ecclesiastical excommunication : for an angel is here included. See note, Rom. ix. 3, and compare ch. v. 10 : also Ellic.'s and Bagge's notes here). 9.] As we said before (referring, not to ver. 8 as most Commentators ; for the word more naturally, as in 2 Cor. xiii. 2 (so προείπαμεν, 1 Thess. iv. 6), relates to something said on a former occasion,—and the plural seems here to bind it to εὐηγγελισάμεθα, —but to what he had said during his presence with them : see a similar reference, ch. v. 3, 21), I also now say again, —If any one is (no longer now a supposition, but an assumption of the fact : see Hermann, ut supra ; and Ellic.'s note) evangelizing you (reff.) other (with another gospel) than that which ye received (from us), let him be accursed (see above). 10.] For (accounting for, and by so doing, softening, the seeming harshness of the last saying, by the fact which follows) am I NOW (ἄρτι takes up the ἄρτι of the last verse, having here the principal emphasis on it,—q. d. 'in saying this,'—'in what I have just said ;' 'is this like an example of men-pleasing ?') persuading (seeking to win over to me, ζητῶν ἀρέσκειν nearly ; see reff.) MEN (see 1 Cor. iv. 3 ; 2 Cor. v. 11 :

not, as Erasm. (al. not Luther), 'num res humanas suadeo, an divinas ?'—nor as Calvin, 'suadeone secundum homines an secundum Deum ?') or (am I conciliating) (πείθω losing its more proper meaning, as of course, when thus applied) God ? or am I seeking to please MEN (a somewhat wider expression than the other, embracing his whole course of procedure) ? (Nay) if I any longer (implying that such is the course of the world before conversion to Christ ; not necessarily referring back to the time before his own conversion, any more than that is contained by implication in the words, but rather perhaps to the accumulated enormity of his being, after all he had gone through, a man-pleaser) were pleasing men (either (1) imperf., = 'seeking to please :' so that the fact, of being well-pleasing to men, does not come into question ; or (2) as Mey., 'the fact of pleasing, result of seeking to please :' 'if I were popular with men :' the construction will bear both), I were not (ἤμην is a late form, found however in Xen. Cyr. vi. 1. 9 : see Ellic. here) the (or a, but better 'the') servant of Christ. Some interpret χρ. δου. οὐκ ἂν ἤμην as Chr., ἔτι μετὰ Ἰουδαίων ἤμην, ἔτι τὴν ἐκκλησίαν ἐδίωκον. But this would more naturally be expressed by οὐκ ἂν ἐγενόμην, and, as Mey. remarks, would give a very flat and poor sense : it is better therefore to take δοῦλος in its ethical, not its historical meaning.

11—CHAP. II. 21.] FIRST, or APOLOGETIC PART OF THE EPISTLE ; consisting in an historical defence of his own teaching, as not being from men, but revealed to him by the Lord,—nor influenced even by the chief Apostles, but of independent authority. 11, 12.] Enunciation of this subject. γν. γάρ] The γάρ

αγγελισθὲν ὑπ' ἐμοῦ, ᵍὅτι οὐκ ἔστιν ʰ κατὰ ʰ ἄνθρωπον·
12 ⁱ οὐδὲ ⁱ γὰρ ἐγὼ παρὰ ἀνθρώπου ᵃ παρέλαβον αὐτό,
οὔτε ἐδιδάχθην, ἀλλὰ δι' ʲ ἀποκαλύψεως Ἰησοῦ χριστοῦ.
13 ᵏ ἠκούσατε γὰρ τὴν ἐμὴν ˡ ἀναστροφήν ᵐ ποτε ἐν τῷ
ⁿ Ἰουδαϊσμῷ, ὅτι ᵒ καθ' ᵒᵖ ὑπερβολὴν ᑫ ἐδίωκον τὴν ʳ ἐκκλησίαν τοῦ ʳ θεοῦ καὶ ˢ ἐπόρθουν αὐτήν, 14 καὶ ᵗ προέκοπτον

g constr., 1 Cor. xvi. 15 al. see Winer, edn. 6, § 66. 5. a.
h Rom. iii. 5. 1 Cor. iii. 3. ix. 8. xv. 32. ch. iii. 15. 1 Pet. iv. 6.
i John v. 22. vii. 5. viii. 42. Rom. viii. 7.

j ch. ii. 2. 1 Cor. xiv. 6, 26. 2 Cor. xii. 1, 7. Rev. i. 1. 32. 3 Kings x. 1. l = Eph. iv. 22 reff.
n here only †. 2 Macc. viii. 1 al. (-ίζειν, -ικῶς, ch. ii. 14.) 2 Cor. i. 8. iv. 17 only. v. 10, 11, &c. Ps. vii. 1. 2 Macc. v. 8. 21. ver. 23 only †. 17. Jos. Vita § 2, εἰς μεγάλην παιδείας προύκοπτον ἐπίδοσιν.
k = Matt. xi. 2. Luke xxiii. 6. Acts xvii. m = John ix. 13. Rom. vii. 9. xi. 30 al. o Rom. vii. 13. 1 Cor. xii. 31. p as above (o). 2 Cor. iv. 7. xii. 7 only†. r 1 Cor. i. 2 al. (xv. 9 esp.) t Luke ii. 52. Rom. xiii. 12. 2 Tim. ii. 16. iii. 9, 13 only. q = Matt. s Acts ix. see Sir. li.

12. for ουτε, ουδε (mechanical repetition) AD¹F[P]ℵ m Eus Chr Cyr₁ : txt BD³KL rel Œc. for δι', δια A a².
13. for επορθ., επολεμ. F, expugnabam latt lat-ff(exc Aug). (here and in ver 23.)

seems to have been corrected to δέ, as not applying immediately to the foregoing,— or perhaps in reminiscence of 1 Cor. xv. 1; 2 Cor. viii. 1. It refers back to vv. 8, 9. On γνωρ., see note, 1 Cor. xv. 1. κατὰ ἄνθρωπον] according to man, as E. V. (see reff.): i. e. measured by merely human rules and considerations, as it would be were it of human origin: so βελτίονος ἢ κατ' ἄνθρωπον νομοθέτου, Xen. Mem. iv. 4. 24, κατά cannot itself express the origin (as Aug., a-Lapide, Est., al.), though it is included by implication: see note ver. 4, on κατὰ τὸ θέλημα. 12.] proof of this. For neither (οὐδὲ γάρ in negative sentences, answers to καὶ γάρ in positive; e.g. in Herod. i. 3, ἐπιστάμενον πάντως ὅτι οὐ δώσει δίκας· οὐδὲ γὰρ ἐκείνους διδόναι:— omit the οὐ, and substitute καί for οὐδέ, and the sentence becomes affirmative. So that οὐδέ has nothing to do, except in ruling the negative form of the clause, with οὔτε following, but belongs to this clause only. See on the whole, Ellic.'s note) did I (ἐγώ strongly emphatic, —see example from Herodot. above: 'neither did I, any more than the other Apostles.' Thus this clause stands alone; the 'neither' is exhausted and does not extend to the next clause) receive it (historically) from man (i. e. 'any man;' not 'a man,' but generic, the article being omitted after the preposition as in ver. 1), nor was taught it (dogmatically); but through revelation of (i. e. from, genitive subjective: see reff. Thdrt. (but not altogether: for he subjoins, αὐτὸς αὐτὸν ἔσχε διδάσκαλον) al. take the genitive as objective, 'revelation of,' i. e. revealing) Jesus Christ. WHEN did this revelation take place?—clearly, soon after his conversion, imparting to him as it did the knowledge of the Gospel which he afterwards preached; and therefore in all pro-

bability it is to be placed during that sojourn in Arabia referred to in ver. 17. It cannot be identical with the visions spoken of 2 Cor. xii. 1 ff.,—for 2 Cor. was written in A.D. 57, and fourteen years before that would bring us to A.D. 43, whereas his conversion was in 37 (see Chron. Table in Prolegomena, Vol. II.), and his subsequent silence, during which we may conceive him to have been under preparation by this apocalyptic imparting of the Gospel, lasted but three years, ver. 18. Nor can it be the same as that appearance of the Lord to him related Acts xxii. 18,—for that was not the occasion of any revelation, but simply of warning and command. He appears to refer to this special revelation in 1 Cor. xi. 23 (where see on the supposed distinction between ἀπό and παρά); xv. 3. 1 Thess. iv. 15; see notes in those places. 13—II. 21.] Historical working out of this proof: and first (vv. 13, 14) by reminding them of his former life in Judaism, during which he certainly received no instruction in the Gospel from men. 13. ἠκούσ.] ye heard, viz. when I was among you: from myself: not as E. V., 'ye have heard.' γάρ binds the narrative to the former verses, as in the opening of a mathematical proof. ἀναστρ.] Wetst. cites Polyb. iv. 82. 1, κατά τε τὴν λοιπὴν ἀναστροφὴν καὶ τὰς πράξεις τεθαυμασμένος ὑπὲρ τὴν ἡλικίαν. This meaning of the word seems (Mey.) to belong to post-classical Greek. There is no article before nor after ποτε, perhaps because the whole, ἀναστ.-ποτε-ἐν-τῷ-Ἰουδ., is taken as one, q. d. τὸν ἐμόν ποτε Ἰουδαϊσμόν: or better, as Donaldson in Ellicott, "the position of ποτε is due to the verb included in ἀναστροφήν. As St. Paul would have said ἀνεστρεφόμην ποτε, he allows himself to write τὴν ἐμ. ἀναστροφήν ποτε."

u here only †. Dion. Hal.
Antt. x. 49.
(-Δικος,
Dan. i. 10
Theod.)
v = Acts xviii.
2. 2 Cor. xi.
26 al. Esth.
ii. 10.
w 2 Cor. i. 12
al⁶. Phil. i.
14. 1 Thess.
ii. 17. Heb.
ii. 1. xiii. 19
(Mark xv. 14
v. r.) only †.
x = Tit. ii. 14 (reff.).
8. Levit. xxii. 13 al.
4. xli. (xxxiv.) 2 only.
c Acts xiii. 2. Rom. i. 1. Levit. xx. 26.
e ver. 6.
iii. 21.

ABDFK
LPℵ a b
c d e f g
h k l m n
o 17. 47

ἐν τῷ ᵒἸουδαϊσμῷ ὑπὲρ πολλοὺς ᵘσυνηλικιώτας ἐν τῷ
ᵛγένει μου, ʷπερισσοτέρως ˣζηλωτὴς ʸὑπάρχων τῶν
ᶻπατρικῶν μου ᵃπαραδόσεων. ¹⁵ ὅτε δὲ ᵇεὐδόκησεν ὁ
ᶜἀφορίσας με ᵈἐκ κοιλίας μητρός μου καὶ ᵉκαλέσας
ᶠδιὰ τῆς χάριτος αὐτοῦ ¹⁶ ᵍἀποκαλύψαι τὸν υἱὸν αὐτοῦ
ἐν ἐμοί, ἵνα εὐαγγελίζωμαι αὐτὸν ἐν τοῖς ἔθνεσιν, εὐθέως
οὐ ʰπροσανεθέμην ⁱσαρκὶ καὶ ⁱαἵματι, ¹⁷ οὐδὲ ἀπῆλθον

y = Acts viii. 16. xvi. 3, 20, 37. Rom. iv. 19 al.
a =ₘMatt. xv. 2 ¦ Mk. 1 Cor. xi. 2. 2 Thess. ii. 15. iii. 6‡.
b constr., Luke xii. 32. Rom. xv. 26. 1 Cor. i. 21. 1 Macc. xiv. 46.
f = Rom. xii, 3.
h ch. ii. 6 only †. Diod. Sic. xvii. 116, τοῖς μάντεσι προσανατιθέμενος περὶ τοῦ σημείου.
Lucian. Jup. Trag. ∤ 1, ἐμοὶ προσανάθου, λάβε με σύμβουλον πόνων.
50. Eph. vi. 12. Heb. ii. 14 only. Sir. xiv. 18.

z here only. Gen. l.
Jer. xxxix. (xxxii.)
d Matt. xix. 12. Luke i. 15. Isa. xlix. 1. see Jer. i. 5.
g Matt. xi. 25. 1 Cor. ii. 10. Phil. iii. 15. 1 Pet. i. 12. 1 Kings
i Matt. xvi. 17. 1 Cor. xv

15. rec aft ευδοκησεν ins ο θεος, with ADKL[P]ℵ rel syr-w-ast copt [æth arm] Orig₁ (and int₁) Chr₁ Thdrt₃ Iren-int₁ Aug: om BF vulg Syr Chr₁ Thdrt₂ Iren-int₁ Orig-int [Victorin] Faust(in Aug) Ambrst Jer. αφωρισας B(ita cod. see table at end of prolegg. to this vol) D³ m n 47¹.

[16. ευαγγελισωμαι D¹ : -λιζομαι LP c f k.]

17. rec (for 1st απηλθον) ανηλθον, with AKL[P]ℵ rel latt syr[-txt] copt Chr Thdrt

Mey. cites as a parallel construction, ἡ τῆς Τροίας ἅλωσις τὸ δεύτερον, Plato, Legg. iii. 685 D. τ. ἐκκλ. τ. θεοῦ] for solemnity, to set himself in contrast to the Gospel, and shew how alien he then was from it (1 Cor. xv. 9). ἐπόρθ.] τουτέστι, σβέσαι ἐπεχείρει τ. ἐκκλησίαν, καταστρέψαι κ. καθελεῖν, ἀφανίσαι· τοῦτο γὰρ πορθοῦντος ἔργον. Chrys. But more than the mere attempt is to be understood: he was verily destroying the Church of God, as far as in him lay. Nor must we think of merely laying waste; the verb applies to men, not only to cities and lands, cf. Acts ix. 21,—κεῖνος γὰρ ἔπερσεν ἀνθρώπους, Soph. Aj. 1177, and σὲ παρακαλῶ, μὴ ἡμῖν ὁ Πρωταγόρας τὸν Σιμωνίδην ἐκπέρσῃ, Plato, Protag., p. 340.

14. συνηλικιώτας] "The compound form (compare συμμέτοχος, Eph. iii. 6; v. 7 : συγκοινωνός, 1 Cor. ix. 23 al.) is condemned by the Atticists : Attic writers using only the simple form." Ellicott. ἐν τῷ γένει μ.., in my nation, see reff. περισσ.] viz. than they. ζηλ. τ. πῷ μ. παρ.] a zealous assertor (or defender) of my ancestral traditions (i. e. those handed down in the sect of the Pharisees, Paul being Φαρισαῖος, υἱὸς Φαρισαίων, Acts xxiii. 6,—not, the law of Moses. This meaning is given by the μου: without it the παραδόσεις of the whole Jewish nation handed down from οἱ πατέρες, might be meant : cf. Acts xxvi. 5). 15—17.] After his conversion also, he did not take counsel with MEN. 15.] It was God's act, determined at his very birth (cf. especially Acts xiii. 2), and effected by a special calling : viz., that on the road to Damascus, carried out by the instrumentality of

Ananias. To understand κολέσας of an act in the divine Mind, as Rückert, is contrary to our Apostle's usage of the word, cf. ver. 6 ; Rom. viii. 30 al. This calling first took place, then the revelation, as here. 16.] ἀποκαλ. belongs to εὐδόκησεν, not to καλ. (Erasm.), nor to ἀφορ. and καλ. (Est., al.),—to reveal his Son (viz. by that subsequent revelation, of which before, ver. 12 : not by his conversion, which, as above, answers to καλέσας) in me (strictly : 'within me,' τῆς ἀποκαλύψεως καταλαμπούσης αὐτοῦ τὴν ψυχήν, Chrys. : not 'through me' (Jer., Erasm., Grot., &c.), which follows in ἵνα εὐαγγ. κ.τ.λ., nor in my case (Rückert, al.), as manifested by me as an example to myself or to others, as in 1 John iv. 9 : the context here requires that his own personal illumination should be the point brought out ;—nor 'to me' (Calv., al.), which though nearly equivalent to ' in me,' weakens the sense), &c. Notice the present εὐαγγελίζωμαι, the ministry being not a single act, but a lasting occupation. ἐν τ. ἔθν.] the main object of his Apostleship : see ch. ii 7, 9. ' εὐθέως is really connected with ἀπῆλθον : but the Apostle, whose thoughts outrun his words, has interposed the negative clause, to anticipate his purpose in going away.' Jowett. προσανεθ.] See reff. The classical sense is, ' to lay on an additional burden:' and in middle voice, 'on oneself:' cf. Xen. Mem. ii. 1. 8. The later sense, 'to impart to,' τινί τι, either, as here, with the view of getting, or as in ch. ii. 6, with that of conferring. The πρός in composition does not signify addition, but direction : see Acts xxvii. 7, note. σαρκὶ κ. αἵμ.] i. e. with man-

εἰς Ἱεροσόλυμα πρὸς τοὺς πρὸ ἐμοῦ ἀποστόλους, ἀλλὰ ^j Luke chiefly, i. 56. Acts viii. 25 al. fr. elsw. Heb. vii. 1. 2 Pet. ii. 21. (Matt. viii. 13. Mark xiv. 40 v. r.) Gen. xliii. 10. k John vi. 3 only. Judg. xxi. 8 Ald. 3 Kings xiii. m Acts n = Matt. ἀπῆλθον εἰς Ἀραβίαν καὶ πάλιν ^j ὑπέστρεψα εἰς Δαμασκόν. ¹⁸ ἔπειτα μετὰ ἔτη τρία ^k ἀνῆλθον εἰς Ἱεροσόλυμα ^l ἱστορῆσαι Κηφᾶν, καὶ ^m ἐπέμεινα ⁿ πρὸς αὐτὸν ἡμέρας δεκαπέντε· ¹⁹ ἔτερον δὲ τῶν ἀποστόλων οὐκ

12 only (?).   1 here only †.   Esdr. i. 33 (31) bis. 42 (40) only.   ἀνὴρ ὃν ἐγὼ...ἱστόρησα,
Jos. B. J. vi. 1. 8.   ἱστόρησα γάρ τινα Ἐλεάζαρον, Antt. viii. 2. 5 (see Ellicott's note).
x. 48. xii. 16 al. L.P. [John viii. 7.]   Exod. xii. 39 B.   w. πρός, 1 Cor. xvi. 7.
xiii. 56.   John i. 1, 2.   1 Cor. xvi. 6, 7 al.

txt BDF a Syr syr-mg Bas Thl-mg.   (αλλα, so ABDFL[P]א.)
18. τρια bef ετη A[P]א a b o 17 Syr copt Chr Damasc.   rec (for κηφαν) πετρον, with DFKL[P]א³ rel latt syr-txt [arm Victorin]: txt ABא¹ 17. 67² Syr syr-mg copt æth. (Cf ch ii. 11, 14.)   [υπεμεινα P.]
19. for ουκ ειδον, ειδον ουδενα D¹F latt lat-ff(exc Aug Sedul).

kind, "generally with the idea of weakness and frailty," Ellic. whose note see, and also reff.   **17.**] ἀπῆλθον both times refers to his departure from Damascus: q. d. 'when I left Damascus, I did not go . . . . . but when I left Damascus, I went.' The repetition of ἀπῆλθον is quite in the Apostle's manner; Meyer adduces as examples Rom. viii. 15 (Heb. xii. 13, 22. We may add Heb. ii. 16).   εἰς Ἀραβ.] On the place which this journey holds in the narrative of Acts ix., see notes on vv. 19, 22 there. Its object does not seem to have been (as Chrys., al., Meyer, al.) the preaching of the gospel, —nor are the words ἵνα εὐαγγελ. κ.τ.λ. necessarily to be connected with it,—but preparation for the apostolic work; though of course we cannot say, that he did not preach during the time, as before and after it (Acts ix. 20, 22) in the synagogues at Damascus. Into *what part* of Arabia he went, we have no means of determining. The name was a very vague one, sometimes including Damascus ('Damascus Arabiæ retro deputabatur, antequam transcripta erat in Syrophœnicem ex distinctione Syriarum.' Tert. adv. Marcion., iii. 13, vol. ii. p. 339: so also (verbatim) adv. Judæos 9, p. 619. ὅτι δὲ Δάμασκος τῆς Ἀραβικῆς γῆς ἦν κ. ἔστιν, εἰ καὶ νῦν προσνενέμηται τῇ Συροφοινίκῃ λεγομένῃ, οὐδ' ὑμῶν τινες ἀρνήσασθαι δύνανται, Justin Mart. c. Trypho, 78, p. 176),—sometimes extending even to Lebanon and the borders of Cilicia (Pliny, Hist. Nat. vi. 32). It was however more usually restricted to that peninsula now thus called, between the Red Sea and the Persian Gulf. Here we must apparently take it in the wider sense, and understand that part of the Arabian desert which nearly bordered on Damascus. (From C. and H. edn. 2, i. p. 117, f.) *How long* he remained there we are equally at a loss to say. Hardly for any considerable portion of the three

years: Acts ix. 23 will scarcely admit of this: for those ἡμέραι ἱκαναί were manifestly passed at Damascus. The journey is mentioned here, to account for the time, and to shew that he did not spend it in conferring with *men*, or with the other Apostles.   καὶ πάλ. ὑπέστρ.] cf. Acts ix. 22, 25.   **18—24.**] *But after a very short visit to Peter at Jerusalem, he retired to Syria and Cilicia.* **18.**] At first sight, it would appear as if the three years were to be reckoned from his *return to Damascus:* but on closer examination we see that μετὰ ἔτη τρ. stands in opposition to εὐθέως above, and the ἀνῆλθον κ.τ.λ. here answers to ἀπῆλθον κ.τ.λ. there. So that we must reckon them from his *conversion:* ὅτε δὲ εὐδόκησεν κ.τ.λ. ruling the whole narrative. See also on ch. ii. 1. This is the journey of Acts ix. 26,—where see note. There is no real discrepancy between that account and this. The incident which led to his leaving Damascus (Acts ix. 25. 2 Cor. xi. 32, 33) has not necessarily any connexion with his purpose in *going to Jerusalem:* a purpose which may have been entertained before, or determined on after, that incident. To this visit must be referred the vision of Acts xxii. 17, 18.   ἱστορ. Κηφ.] to make the acquaintance of Cephas—not to get information or instruction from him: see reff., and Ellic. here. Peter was at this early period the prominent person among the Apostles; see note on Matt. xvi. 18.   ἐπέμ. πρός] originally a pregnant construction, but from usage become idiomatic. See reff.   ἡμέρ. δεκαπ.] mentioned to shew how little of his institution as an Apostle he could have owed to Peter. *Why no longer,* see in Acts ix. 29; xxii. 17—21. [On the form δεκαπέντε see Moulton's Winer, p. 313, note 5.]   **19.**] This verse admits of two interpretations, between which other con-

o Matt. xii. 4.
1 Cor. viii. 4. εἶδον, °εἰ μὴ Ἰάκωβον τὸν ἀδελφὸν τοῦ κυρίου. 20 ᵖ ἃ

see ver. 7.
p constr., Luke δὲ γράφω ὑμῖν, ἰδοὺ �q ἐνώπιον τοῦ θεοῦ ὅτι οὐ ʳ ψεύδομαι.
xxi. 6. 2 Cor.
xii. 17. 21 ἔπειτα ἦλθον εἰς τὰ ˢ κλίματα τῆς Συρίας καὶ τῆς Κιλι- c ἔπειτα
q = 1 Tim. v. ...
21. vi. 13.
2 Tim. ii. 14. κίας. 22 ᵗᵘ ἤμην δὲ ᵘᵛ ἀγνοούμενος τῷ ʷ προσώπῳ ταῖς ABCDF
iv. 1. KLPℵ a
r Rom. ix. 1. ἐκκλησίαις τῆς Ἰουδαίας ταῖς ˣ ἐν χριστῷ, 23 μόνον δὲ b c d e f
2 Cor. xi. 31. g h k l m
1 Tim. ii. 7. ᵘ ἀκούοντες ᵘ ἦσαν ὅτι ὁ ʸ διώκων ἡμᾶς ᶻ ποτὲ νῦν ᵃᵇ εὐαγ- n o 17.47
Prov. xiv. 5.
s Rom. xv. 23.

2 Cor. xi. 10 only. (Judg. xx. 2 A.?) t ver. 10. u constr., Luke i. 10, 20 al. fr. Prov. vi. 3. v Paul,
Acts xiii. 27. xvii. 23. Rom. i. 13 al13. Mark ix. 32 ‖ L. Heb. v. 2. 2 Pet. ii. 12. Lev. iv. 13. w dat., see
1 Thess. ii. 17. x Rom. xvi. 7. Eph. i. 13 al. y = ver. 13 reff. partic., Eph. iv. 28 al. fr.
ı ver. 13. a here only. b pres., Matt. ii. 22. John i. 40. ii. 9. iv. 1. Acts iv. 13. viii. 18 al. fr. Winer, § 40. 2. c.

[20. for του θεου, κυριου P 17 syr-txt.]
21. om 2nd της ℵ¹(ins ℵ-corr¹ ᵒᵇˡ) [17. 47].
22. om τω F [108¹(Sz.)] [εκκλησιας B¹(Tischdf).] for 2nd ταις, της D¹
(not lat), της εκ . . . της εν χῶ d.

siderations must decide. (1) That James, the Lord's brother, was one of the Twelve, and the only one besides Peter whom Paul saw at this visit: (2) that he was one τῶν ἀποστόλων, but not necessarily of the Twelve. Of these, (1) apparently cannot be: for after the choosing of the Twelve (John vi. 70), the ἀδελφοί of our Lord did not believe on Him (John vii. 5): an expression (see note there) which will not admit of *any* of His brethren having then been His disciples. We must then adopt (2): which is besides in consonance with other notices respecting the term ἀπόστολος, and the person here mentioned. I reserve the subject for full discussion in the prolegomena to the Ep. of James. See also notes, Matt. x. 3; xiii. 55; John vii. 5. 20.] This asseveration (cf. 2 Cor. xi. 31) applies most naturally to the important fact just asserted—his short visit to Jerusalem, and his having seen only Peter and James, rather than to the whole subject of the chapter. If a report had been spread in Galatia that after his conversion he spent years at Jerusalem and received regular institution in Christianity at the hands of the Apostles, this last fact would naturally cause amazement, and need a strong confirmatory asseveration. As regards the construction, ἃ . . . . . ὑμῖν stands alone, (with regard to) the things which I am writing to you,—and the word necessary to be supplied to carry on the sense from ἰδοὺ ἐνώπ. τ. θεοῦ to ὅτι, lies under the ἰδού, which here answers to such words as διαμαρτύρομαι, 1 Tim. v. 21; 2 Tim. ii. 14; iv. 1,—παραγγέλλω, 1 Tim. vi. 13. Meyer would supply γράφω, which seems harsh: others take ὅτι as '*for*,' which is worse still (cf. 2 Cor. xi. 21, ὁ θεὸς οἶδεν . . . . ὅτι οὐ ψεύδομαι),—and this too, understanding ἐστίν after θεοῦ (Bengel). 21.] The beginning only of this journey is related in

Acts ix. 30, where see note. Dean Howson suggests (edn. 2, i. p. 129, f.) that he may have gone at once from Cæsarea to Tarsus by sea, and Syria and Cilicia may afterwards have been the field of his activity, —these provinces being very generally mentioned together, from their geographical affinity, Cilicia being separated from Asia Minor by Mount Taurus. (See also note on Luke ii. 1, 2.) Winer, al. have understood by Syria here, Phœnicia: but as Meyer has shewn, inconsistently with usage. In Acts xv. 23, 41, we find churches in Syria and Cilicia, which may have been founded by Paul on this journey. The supposition is confirmed by our ver. 23: see below. 22, 23.] 'So far was I from being a disciple of the Apostles, or tarrying in their company, that the churches of Judæa, where they principally laboured, did not even know me by sight.' τῷ προσώπῳ, the referential, or adverbial dative: Donalds., Gramm. § 457. τῆς Ἰουδαίας excludes Jerusalem, where he *was known*. Jowett doubts this: but it seems to be required by Acts ix. 26—29. Chrys. seems to mistake the Apostle's purpose, when he says, ἵνα μὴ θῇς, ὅτι τοσοῦτον ἀπεῖχε τοῦ κηρύξαι αὐτοῖς περιτομήν, ὅτι οὐδὲ ἀπὸ ὄψεως γνώριμος ἦν αὐτοῖς: and Olshausen, in supposing him to be refuting the idea that he had learned the Gospel from other Christians in Palestine. 23. ἀκ. ἦσαν] They (the members of the churches: cf. Eurip. Hec. 39, πᾶν στράτευμ' Ἑλληνικὸν, πρὸς οἶκον εὐθύνοντας ἐναλίαν πλάτην) heard reports (not '*had heard*,' as Luth.: the resolved imperfect gives the sense of *duration*: see reff. and passim) that (not the recitative ὅτι, but the explicative, following ἀκ. ἦσαν. Mey. remarks that no example is found of the former use of ὅτι by St. Paul, except in O. T. citations, as ch. iii. 8) our (better taken as a change of person into the *oratio directa*, than with

γελίζεται τὴν ^{ac} πίστιν ἣν ποτὲ ^d ἐπόρθει. ²⁴ καὶ ^{ef} ἐδόξαζον c = Rom. i. 5.
ch. iii. 23, 25.

^{fg} ἐν ἐμοὶ τὸν θεόν.   II. ¹ ἔπειτα ^h διὰ δεκατεσσάρων ἐτῶν d ver. 13. Acts
ix. 21 only †.

πάλιν ⁱ ἀνέβην εἰς Ἱεροσόλυμα μετὰ Βαρνάβα, ^k συνπαρα- e = Matt. v. 16.
f John xiii.31,32.
xiv.13.xvii.10.

g = 1 Cor. iv. 2, 6.   h = Matt. xxvi. 61 ‖ Mk. Acts xxiv. 17 al. Deut. ix. 11. xv. 1.

i Matt. xx. 18. Acts xv. 2 al. Ezra vii. 6, 7.   k Acts xii. 25. xv. 37, 38 only. Gen. xix. 17. Jot i. 4 only.

24. εν εμοι bef εδοξαζον DF latt goth [arm] Victorin Ambrst.

CHAP. II. 1. ανεβην bef παλιν DF goth [æth] : om παλιν copt Chr Iren-int [Tert]. ανηλθον (*from ch* i. 18) C Chron.

Mey. to understand ἡμᾶς as '*us Christians*,' the Apostle including himself as he writes) **former persecutor** (not, as Grot., for διώξας, but as ὁ πειράζων, taken as a substantive : see reff.) **is preaching the faith** (objective, as in reff., and 1 Tim. i. 19 b; iii. 9; iv. 1, &c.; but not = the doctrine of the Gospel) **which he once was destroying** (see on ver. 13). **And they glorified God in me** ('in my case :' i. e. my example was the cause of their glorifying God :—not, '*on account of me*,' see reff., and cf. ἐν ἀρεταῖς γέγαθε, Pind. Nem. iii. 56,—ἐν σοὶ πᾶσ' ἔγωγε σώζομαι, Soph. Aj. 519. Bernhardy, Syntax, p. 210). By thus shewing the spirit with which the churches of Judæa were actuated towards him, he marks more strongly the contrast between them and the Galatian Judaizers. Thdrt. says strikingly : μανθάνοντες γὰρ τὴν ἀθρόαν μεταβολήν, κ. ὅτι ὁ λύκος τὰ ποιμένων ἐργάζεται, τῆς εἰς τὸν θεὸν ὑμνῳδίας τὰ κατ' ἐμὲ πρόφασιν ἐλάμβανον.   **II. 1—10.]** *On his subsequent visit to Jerusalem, he maintained equal independence, was received by the Apostles as of co-ordinate authority with themselves, and was recognized as the Apostle of the uncircumcision.*   **1. διὰ δεκατ. ἐτῶν]** First, *what does this διά imply?* According to well-known usage, διά with a genitive of time or space signifies 'through and beyond :' thus, ὁ μὲν χρόνος δὴ διὰ χρόνου προὔβαινέ μοι, Soph. Philoct. 285, —διὰ δέκα ἐπάλξεων πύργοι ἦσαν μεγάλοι, Thuc. iii. 21, and then τῶν πύργων ὄντων δι' ὀλίγου : see reff., and Bernhardy, Syntax, p. 235. Winer, Gramm. edn. 6, § 51. (The *instrumental* usage, διὰ δακρύων, διὰ νυκτός, &c. is derived from this, the instrument being regarded as the means, passed through before the end is attained : but obviously has no place here, where a *definite* time is mentioned.)   See more in Ellic. **διὰ δεκ. ἐτ.** then is **after fourteen ★ years,** δεκατεσσάρων παρελθόντων ἐτῶν, Chrys.   Next, *from what time* are we to reckon?   Certainly at first sight it would appear,—*from the journey last mentioned.*   And Meyer maintains that we are bound to accept this first impression without enquiring any further.   But why?   Is the *prima facie* view of a construction always right?   Did we, or did he, judge thus in ch. i. 18 ?   Are we not bound, in all such cases, should any reason *ab extra* exist for doing so, to re-examine the passage, and ascertain whether our *prima facie* impression may not have arisen from neglecting some indication furnished by the context?   That this is the case here, I am persuaded.   The ways of speaking, in ch. i. 18, and here, are very similar.   The ἔπειτα in both cases may be well taken as referring back to the same *terminus a quo*, διά being used in this verse as applying to the *larger* interval, or even perhaps to prevent the fourteen years being counted from the event last mentioned, as they would more naturally be, had a second μετά been used. What would there be forced or unnatural in a statement of the following kind? "After my conversion (ὅτε δέ, &c. ch. i. 15) my occasions of communicating with the other Apostles were these : (1) after three years I went up, &c.   (2) after fourteen years had elapsed, I again went up, &c. ?" This view is much favoured, if not rendered decisive, by the change in position of ἐτῶν and the numeral, in this second instance.   In ch. i. 18, it is μετὰ ἔτη τρία : ἔτη, in the first mention of the interval, having the emphatic place.   But now, it is not δι' ἐτῶν δεκατεσσάρων, but διὰ δεκατεσσάρων ἐτῶν—ἐτῶν now passing into the shade, and the numeral having the emphasis—a clear indication to me that the ἔτη have the same reference as before, viz. to the *time of his conversion.*   A list, and ample discussion, of the opinions on both sides, will be found in Anger, de ratione temporum, ch. iv.   · This (cf. Chronol. Table in Prolegg. Vol. II.) would bring the visit here related to the year 50 : see below.   **πάλιν ἀνέβην]** I again **went up :** but nothing is said, and there was no need to say any thing, of another visit during the interval.   It was the object of the Apostle to specify, *not all his visits to Jerusalem*, but *all his occasions of intercourse with the other Apostles* : and it is mere trifling, when Meyer, in his love of creating discrepancies, maintains that in such a narration as this, St. Paul

l = Phil. iv. 11.
m = (Rom. xvi. 25.) Eph. iii. 3 only.
n = 1 Cor. xiv. 6, 26 al. ‡ (1 Kings xx. 29 al.) 23. 2 Cor. ii. 13. v. 19 al.

λαβὼν.καὶ Τίτον· 2 ¹ ἀνέβην δὲ ˡᵐ κατὰ ᵐⁿ ἀποκάλυψιν, καὶ ᵒ ἀνεθέμην ᵖ αὐτοῖς τὸ εὐαγγέλιον ὃ ᑫ κηρύσσω ἐν τοῖς ἔθνεσιν,

o Acts xxv. 14 only. 2 Macc. iii. 9. 2 Macc. iii. 9.
q = Matt. iv. 23. ix. 35 al. Acts viii. 5. xx. 25.
p so Matt. iv.

ABCDF KLPℵ a bcdef ghklm no 17.47

2. for ανεθεμην (contuli D-lat vulg[and lat col of F]), αναβαλομην exposui F.

would be putting a weapon into the hands of his opponents by omitting his second journey. That journey was undertaken (Acts xi. 30) in pursuance of a mission from the church at Antioch, to convey alms to the elders of the suffering church at Jerusalem. It was at a period of persecution, when James the son of Zebedee and Peter were under the power of Herod, —and in all probability the other Apostles were scattered. Probably Barnabas and Saul did not see any of them. They merely (Acts xii. 25) fulfilled their errand, and brought back John Mark. If in that visit he had no intercourse with the Apostles, as his business was not with them, the mention of it here would be irrelevant: and to attempt, as Mey., to prove the Acts inaccurate, because that journey is not mentioned here, is simply absurd. That the visit here described is in all probability the THIRD related in the Acts (A.D. 50) on occasion of the council of Apostles and elders (Acts xv.), I have shewn in a note to the chronological table, Prolegomena to Acts, Vol. II. The various separate circumstances of the visit will be noticed as we proceed. συνπ. καὶ Τίτον] In Acts xv. 2, ἔταξαν ἀναβαίνειν Π. κ. Βαρν. καί τινας ἄλλους ἐξ αὐτῶν. Titus is here particularized by name, on account of the notice which follows, ver. 3: and the καί serves to take him out from among the others. On Titus, see Prolegg. to Ep. to Titus. 2.] δέ not only carries on the narrative, emphatically repeating the verb (Mey.), but carries on the refutation also—but I went up (not for any purpose of learning from or consulting others, but) &c.:—So Il. ω. 484, ὡς Ἀχιλεὺς θάμβησεν ἰδὼν Πρίαμον θεοειδέα· θάμβησαν δὲ καὶ ἄλλοι,—and other examples in Hartung, i. p. 168. Of his undertaking the journey κατ' ἀποκάλυψιν, nothing is said in the Acts, all that is related there being, the appointment by the church of Paul and Barnabas and others to go. What divine intimation Paul may have received, inducing him to offer himself for the deputation, we cannot say: that some such occurred, he here assures us, and it was important for him to assert it, as shewing his dependence only on divine leading, and independence of any behests from the Jerusalem church. Meyer well remarks that the history itself of the Acts furnishes an instance of such a double prompting: Peter was induced by a vision, and at the same time by the messengers of Cornelius, to go to Cæsarea. Schrader would give a singular meaning to κατ' ἀποκάλυψιν; that his visit was for the purpose of making known the Gospel which he preached, &c. Hermann (de ep. ad Gal. trib. prim. capp., cited by Meyer) agrees: "explicationis causa, i.e. ut patefieret inter ipsos quæ vera esset Jesu doctrina." But it is against this sense, that (1) the N. T. usage of ἀποκάλυψις always has respect to revelation from above, and (2) this very phrase, κατ' ἀποκάλυψιν, is found in ref. Eph. used absolutely as here, undoubtedly there signifying by revelation. Hermann's objection that for this meaning, κατά τινα ἀποκ. would be required, is nugatory: not the particular revelation (concrete) which occasioned the journey, but merely the fact that it was by (abstract) revelation, is specified. ἀνεθέμην] (reff.): so Aristoph. Nub. 1436, ὑμῖν ἀναθεὶς ἅπαντα τἀμὰ πράγματα. See more examples in Wetst. αὐτοῖς] to the Christians at Jerusalem, implied in Ἱεροσόλ. above: see reff. This wide assertion is limited by the next clause, κατ' ἰδ. &c. Œc., Calv., Olsh., al. take αὐτοῖς to mean the Apostles: in which case, the stress by and by must be on κατ' ἰδίαν,—I communicated it (indeed,—μέν would more naturally stand here on this interpretation) to them, but privately (i.e. more confidentially,—but how improbable, that St. Paul should have thus given an exoteric and esoteric exposition of his teaching) τοῖς δοκοῦσιν. Chrys. is quoted for this view by Mey., but not quite correctly; ἐπειδὴ γὰρ ἐν τοῖς Ἱεροσολύμοις πάντες ἐσκανδαλίζοντο, εἴ τις παραβαίη τὸν νόμον, εἴ τις κωλύσειε χρήσασθαι τῇ περιτομῇ .... παῤῥησίᾳ μὲν παρελθεῖν κ. τὸ κήρυγμα ἀποκαλύψαι τὸ ἑαυτοῦ οὐκ ἠνείχετο, κατ' ἰδίαν δὲ τοῖς δοκοῦσιν ἀνέθετο ἐπὶ Βαρνάβα κ. Τίτου, ἵνα οὗτοι μάρτυρες ἀξιόπιστοι γένωνται πρὸς τοὺς ἐγκαλοῦντας, ὅτι οὐδὲ τοῖς ἀποστόλοις ἔδοξεν ἐναντίον εἶναι, ἀλλὰ βεβαιοῦσι τὸ κήρυγμα τὸ τοιοῦτον. Estius, characteristically enough, as a Romanist; 'publice ita contulit, ut ostenderet gentes non debere circumcidi et servare legem Mosis,—privato autem et secreto colloquio cum apostolis habito placuit ipsos quoque Ju-

^r κατ᾽ ἰδίαν δὲ τοῖς ^s δοκοῦσιν, ^t μή ^t πως ^u εἰς ^{uv} κενὸν ^w τρέχω r Matt. xiv. 13, 23. xvii. 1
ἢ ^w ἔδραμον. 3 ^x ᾽Αλλ᾽ ^x οὐδὲ Τίτος ὁ σὺν ἐμοὶ ῞Ελλην al.† 2 Macc. iv. 5.
ὢν ^y ἠναγκάσθη ^z περιτμηθῆναι· 4 διὰ ^a δὲ τοὺς ^b παρεις- s = ver. 6 b only‡. Eur. Hec. 292. see

vv. 6 a, 9. Mark x. 42.　　t Rom. xi. 21 al9.　Paul (Acts xxvii. 29 rec.) only.　　u 2 Cor.
vi. 1.　Phil. ii. 16 bis.　1 Thess. iii. 5.　Isa. lxv. 23.　　v 1 Thess. ii. 1 reff.　　w = ch. v. 7.
Phil. ii. 16.　see 1 Cor. ix. 24—26.　Ps. cxviii. 32.　　x Luke xxiii. 15.　Acts xix 2.　　y = Acts
xxvi. 11. xxviii. 19. ver. 14. ch. vi. 12‡.　(Prov. vi. 4.)　1 Macc. ii. 25 al.　　z Luke i. 59 al. fr.
L.P., exc. John vii. 22.　Gen. xvii. 10.　　a so ver. 2.　Rom. iii. 22.　Phil. ii. 8.　　b here
only †.　Strabo 17, p. 794.　Moulton's Winer, p. 296, note i (-άγειν, 2 Pet. ii. 1. see also Jude 4.)

3. [ουτε F.]　　om ὁ B.

dæos ab observantia Mosaicæ legis . . . .
esse liberandos.'　　κατ. ἰδ. δέ] but
(limits the foregoing αὐτοῖς; q. d., "when
I say 'to them,' I mean." Ellic. ed. 2,
questions this, and understands δέ to introduce *another* conference, more private
than that just mentioned) **in private** (in
a private conference : not to be conceived
as separate from, but as specifying, the
former ἀνεθέμην) **to those that were eminent** (more at length ver. 6, οἱ δοκοῦντες εἶναί τι. These were James, Cephas,
and John, ver. 9,—who appear to have
been the only Apostles then at Jerusalem. Olsh. supposes the words to imply
blame, not in the mind of the Apostle
himself, but as reflecting on the unworthy
exaltation of these Apostles by the Judaizing teachers. He illustrates this by
οἱ ὑπερλίαν ἀπόστολοι, 2 Cor. xi. 5 ; but
an expression of such feeling here seems
out of place, and it is better to understand
οἱ δοκοῦντες as describing mere matter of
fact ; see examples in Kypke and Elsner),
lest by any means I should (seem to)
be running, or (to) **have run, in vain.**
οὐ περὶ ἑαυτοῦ τέθεικεν, ἀλλὰ περὶ τῶν
ἄλλων· τουτέστιν, ἵνα μάθωσιν ἅπαντες
τὴν τοῦ κηρύγματος συμφωνίαν, κ. ὅτι
κ. τοῖς ἄλλοις ἀρέσκει τὰ ὑπ᾽ ἐμοῦ κηρυτ-
τόμενα, Thdrt.: so also Chrys., Thl., Calv.,
al. The construction of two moods after
the same conjunction is found elsewhere
in Paul : cf. 1 Thess. iii. 5. The present subjunctive τρέχω implies continuance in the course ; the 2 aorist indicative ἔδραμον, the course already run. It
is quite out of the question, that this last
clause should express a bonâ fide fear, lest
his ministry should really be, or have
been, in vain, without the recognition of
the church at Jerusalem (De W., al.) :
such a sentiment would be unworthy of
him, and, besides, at variance with the
whole course of his argument here. The
reference must be (as Thdrt. above) to
the *estimation* in which his preaching
would be held by those to whom he imparted it. When we consider the very
strong prejudices of the Jerusalem church,
this feeling of anxiety, leading him to
take measures to prevent his work from

being tumultuously disowned by them, is
surely but natural. On εἰς κενόν and
τρέχω, see reff. (The grammatical difficulty is well discussed in Ellicott's note.)
　　3.] **But** (so far were they from
regarding my course to have been in
vain, that) **neither** (ἀλλ᾽ οὐδέ introduces a climax, see reff.) **was Titus,
who was with me, being a Greek** (i. e.
though he was a Gentile, and therefore
liable to the demand that he should
be circumcised), **compelled to be circumcised** (i. e. we did not allow him to be
thus compelled : the facts being, as here
implied, that the church at Jerusalem
(and the Apostles? apparently not, from
Acts xv. 5) demanded his circumcision,
but on account of the reason following,
the demand was not complied with, but
resisted by Paul and Barnabas. So Meyer,
with Piscator and Bengel, and I am persuaded, rightly, from what follows. But
usually it is understood, that the circumcision of Titus was *not even demanded*,
and that Paul alleged this as shewing his
agreement with the other Apostles. So
Chrys.: ἀκρόβυστον ὄντα οὐκ ἠνάγκασαν
περιτμηθῆναι οἱ ἀπόστολοι, ὅπερ ἀπό-
δειξις ἦν μεγίστη τοῦ μὴ καταγινώσκειν
τῶν ὑπὸ τοῦ Παύλου λεγομένων ἢ πρατ-
τομένων : so also Thdrt., Thl., Œc., &c.,
and Winer and De W. Had this been so,
besides that the following could not have
stood as it does, not the strong word
ἠναγκάσθη, but the weakest possible word
would have been used—'*the circumcision of Titus was not even mentioned*') :
　　4.] **but** (i. e. '*and this?*'—the
construction of the sentence is (against
Ellic.) precisely as ver. 2 : this δέ restricts and qualifies the broader assertion
which went before. '*Titus was not compelled . . . . : and that*,' &c. To connect
this with ver. 2, supposing ver. 3 to be
parenthetical, as Mr. Bagge, seems harsh,
and unnecessary. A second δέ would
hardly be found in the same sentence in
this restrictive sense) **on account of the
false brethren who had been foisted in
among us** (the Judaizers in the church
at Jerusalem, see Acts xv. 1. The word
παρείσακτος is not found elsewhere. It

c 2 Cor. xi. 26 only†.
d = Acts x. 41, 47. xiii. 31, 43. Rom. i. 25 al.
e Rom. v. 20 only†.
f here only.
2 Kings x. 3. 1 Chron. xix. 3. Ezek. xxi. 21 Ed.-vat. [ἡπατοσκοπ. AB &c.]

ἄκτους ᶜ ψευδαδέλφους, ᵈ οἵτινες ᵉ παρεισῆλθον ᶠ κατασκο-
πῆσαι τὴν ᵍ ἐλευθερίαν ἡμῶν ἣν ἔχομεν ἐν χριστῷ Ἰησοῦ,
ἵνα ἡμᾶς ʰ καταδουλώσουσιν, 5 οἷς ⁱ οὐδὲ ᵏ πρὸς ὥραν
ˡ εἴξαμεν τῇ ᵐ ὑποταγῇ, ἵνα ἡ ⁿ ἀλήθεια τοῦ ⁿ εὐαγγελίου
ᵒ διαμείνῃ ᵖ πρὸς ὑμᾶς. 6 ἀπὸ δὲ τῶν ᑫ δοκούντων εἶναί

ABCDF
KLPℵ a
b c d e f
g h k l m
n o 17. 47

(-πεύειν, Josh. ii. 2, 3. -πος, Heb. xi. 31.)
h 2 Cor. xi. 20 only. Gen. xlvii. 21. constr., see note.
35. 2 Cor. vii. 8. Philem. 15 only. (1 Thess. ii. 17.)
m 2 Cor. ix. 13. 1 Tim. ii. 11. iii. 4 only†. (-τάσσειν, Eph. v. 21, 22.)
o Luke i. 22. xxii. 28. Heb. i. 11 (from Ps. ci. 26). 2 Pet. iii. 4 only. Jer. xxxix. (xxxii.) 14.
i. 18 reff. q = ver. 9. Mark x. 42. Susan. 5. see ver. 2.

g = 1 Cor. x. 29. ch. v. 1, 13.
i = 1 Cor. v. 1. xiv. 21 al.
l here only†. Wisd. xviii. 25 only.
n ver. 14. Col. i. 5.
k John v.
p = ch.

4. aft ινα ins μη F(not F-lat). rec καταδουλωσωνται, with K [47, appy] rel Chr(δουλωσωντ.) Thdrt, -σονται L [116-22]: txt AB¹CDℵ; -σωσιν B²F 17 Damasc. [P def.]

5. om οις ουδε D¹ Iren-int Tert(who attributes "nec" to Marcion) Ambrst (Græci e contra: "nec...") Victorin Primas: om ουδε hal, lat-mss-mentioned-by-Jer-and-Sedul: ins ABCDᶠFKL[P]ℵ rel vulg syrr copt goth gr-mss-in-Jer-Ambrst Orig Epiph Chr Thdrt Mcion-t Ambr Aug₂. for διαμεινη, διαμενη [A]F [47]. (C defective.)

occurs in the title of the "prologus incerti auctoris" to Sirach: πρόλογος παρείσακτος ἀδήλου. It is found however in the lexicons of Hesych., Photius, and Suidas, and interpreted ἀλλότριος. The verb παρεισάγειν is common in Polybius, without any idea of surreptitious introduction: see Schweigh.'s Index: but such an idea certainly seems here to be attached to it, by the repetition of παρεις-, in παρεισῆλθον immediately after), men who (οἵτινες classifies) crept in to spy (in a hostile sense: so Chrys., ὁρᾷς πῶς καὶ τῇ τῶν κατασκόπων προσηγορίᾳ ἐδήλωσε τὸν πόλεμον ἐκείνων,—reff., and Eur. Helen. 1607, ὅποι νοσοῖεν ξυμμάχων κατασκοπῶν) our freedom (from the ceremonial law: to see whether, or how far, we kept it) which we have in Christ Jesus, with intent to enslave us utterly (the future after ἵνα is found John xvii. 2; Rev. iii. 9; viii. 3; xxii. 14. Hermann, on Œd. Col. 156, says— "futuro non jungitur ἵνα, ut." The construction of the future with ὅπως and ὅπως μή is common enough in the classics. Winer remarks, Gr. edn. 6, § 41. b. 1. b, that it denotes continuance, whereas the aorist subjunctive is used of something transitory: but qu.? I should rather say that it signifies the certain sequence, in the view of the agent, of that which follows, not merely that it is his intent,—and that it arises from the mingling of two constructions, beginning as if ἵνα with the subjunctive were about to be used, and then passing off to the direct indicative); to whom not even for one hour (reff.) did we (Barnabas, Titus, and myself) yield with the subjection required of us (dative of the manner: the article giving the sense,

'with the subjection claimed.' Fritzsche takes it, 'yield by complying with the wish of the Apostles:' but this is manifestly against the context: Hermann, and similarly Bretschneider, 'quibus ne horæ quidem spatium Jesu obsequio segnior fui,'—absurdly enough, against the whole drift of the passage, and the Apostle's usage of ὑποταγη abstractedly), that the truth of the Gospel (as contrasted with the perverted view which they would have introduced: but not to be confounded with τὸ ἀληθὲς εὐαγγέλιον. Had they been overborne in this point, the verity of the Gospel would have been endangered among them,—i. e. that doctrine of justification, on which the Gospel turns as the truth of God) might abide (reff.: and note on ch. i. 18) with you ('you Galatians:' not, 'you Gentiles in general:' the fact was so,—the Galatians, specially, not being in his mind at the time: it is only one of those cases where, especially if a rhetorical purpose is to be served, we apply home to the particular what, as matter of fact, it only shares as included in the general).

The omission of οἷς οὐδέ in this sentence (see var. readd.) has been an attempt to simplify the construction, and at the same time to reconcile Paul's conduct with that in Acts xvi. 3, where he circumcised Timothy on account of the Jews. But the circumstances were then widely different: and the whole narrative in Acts xv. makes it extremely improbable that the Apostle should have pursued such a course on this occasion. 6.] He returns to his sojourn in Jerusalem, and his intercourse with the δοκοῦντες. The construction is difficult, and has been very variously given. It seems best (and so most Commentators) to regard it as an anacolu-

[r]τι, [s]ὁποῖοί ποτε ἦσαν [t]οὐδέν μοι [tu]διαφέρει· [v]πρόςωπον
θεὸς ἀνθρώπου οὐ [v]λαμβάνει· ἐμοὶ γὰρ οἱ [w]δοκοῦντες
οὐδὲν [x]προσανέθεντο, [7] ἀλλὰ [y]τοὐναντίον ἰδόντες ὅτι
[z]πεπίστευμαι τὸ εὐαγγέλιον τῆς [a]ἀκροβυστίας καθὼς

r = Acts 7. 36.
1 Cor. iii 7.
x. 19. ch. vi.
3, 15.
Demosth.
s Acts xxvi. 29.
582. 27.
1 Cor. iii. 13.
1 Thess. i. 9.
James i. 24

only †.　　t = here (ch. iv. 1) only.　　u see 1 Cor. xv. 41.　　v Luke xx. 21. Ps. lxxxi.
2. (see Acts x. 34. Eph. vi. 9.)　　w = ver. 2 only ‡. Eur. Hec. 292.　　x ch. i. 16 only †.
y 2 Cor. ii. 7. 1 Pet. iii. 9 only †. 3 Macc. iii. 22.　　　　z = Rom. iii. 2. 1 Cor. ix. 17. constr.,
Acts xxi. 3.　　a Rom. iii. 30 al17. Paul only, exc. Acts xi. 3. Gen. xvii. 11.

6. ποτ ℵ[1]. ins ο bef θεος A[P]ℵ 17. θεος ανθρωπου bef προσωπον D[1.3]F
Victorin Aug. aft δοκουντες ins τι ειναι (repetition of foregoing) F vulg(ed, agst
am Jer) Ambrst Pel.

7. for ιδοντες, ειδοτες C[P] f 17 Œc-txt, ιδοτες m n.

thon. The Apostle begins with ἀπὸ δὲ τῶν δοκούντων εἶναί τι, having it in his mind to add οὐδὲν προσελαβόμην or the like: but then, going off into the parenthesis ὁποῖοί ποτε ἦσαν &c., he entirely loses sight of the original construction, and proceeds with ἐμοὶ γάρ &c., which follows on the parenthesis, the γάρ rendering a reason (this is still my view, against Ellic. whose note see) for the οὐδέν μοι διαφέρει &c. De Wette and others think that the parenthesis ends at λαμβάνει, and the construction is resumed from ἀπὸ δέ &c. in an active instead of in a passive form: but it seems better, with Meyer, to regard the parenthesis as never formally closed, and the original construction not resumed. Other ways are ; (1) most of the Greek Fathers (Chrys. hardly says enough for this to be inferred as his opinion), and others (e. g. Olsh., Rückert) take ἀπό as belonging to διαφέρει, as if it were περί: so Thl., οὐδεμία μοι φροντὶς περὶ τῶν δοκούντων, &c. The preposition seems capable, if not exactly of this interpretation, of one very nearly akin to it, as in βλέπετε ἀπό and the like expressions: but the objection is, that it is unnatural to join διαφέρει with ἀπό which lies so far from it, when ὁποῖοί ποτε ἦσ. so completely fills up the construction. (2) Homberg (Parerg. p. 275: Meyer) renders,—'ab illis vero, qui videntur esse aliquid, non differo.' But as Meyer remarks, though διαφέρω ἀπό τινος may bear this meaning, certainly διαφέρει μοι ἀπό τινος cannot. (3) Hermann assumes an aposiopesis, and understands 'what should I fear ?' but an aposiopesis seems out of place in a passage which does not rise above the fervour of narrative. See other interpretations in Meyer and De Wette. οἱ δοκοῦντ. εἶναί τι may be either subjective ('those who believe themselves to be something'), or objective ('those who have the estimation of being something'). The latter is obviously the meaning here. ποτε is understood by some to mean 'once,' 'olim:' 'whatever

they once were, when Christ was on earth:' so vulg. ('quales aliquando fuerint'), Pelag., Luth., Beza, al. But this is going out of the context, and unnecessary. The emphasis is on μοι, and is again taken up by the ἐμοὶ γάρ below. Phrynichus (p. 384) condemns τίνι διαφέρει as not used by the best writers, but Lobeck (note, ibid.) has produced examples of it, as well as of the more approved construction τί διαφέρει, from Xenophon, Plato, and Aristotle. πρόςωπ. . . . λαμβ.] q. d. 'I wish to form all my judgments according to God's rule—which is that of strict unbiassed justice.' See Eph. vi. 9. προσανέθεντο] as in ch. i. 16, —imparted. As I, at my first conversion, did not impart it to flesh and blood, so they now imparted nothing to me: we were independent the one of the other. The meaning 'added' (οὐκ ἐδίδαξαν, οὐ διώρθωσαν, οὐδὲν προσέθηκαν ὧν ᾔδειν, Chrys.; so Thdrt., and most Commentators, and E. V. 'in conference added') is not justified by the usage of the word: see note, as above. Rückert, Bretschneider, Olsh., al. explain it: 'laid on no additional burden.' But this is the active, not the middle, signification of the verb: see Xen. Mem. ii. 1. 8, where προσαναθέσθαι is not 'to impose on another additional duties,' but 'to take them on a man's self.' 7.] Not only did they impart nothing to me, but, on the contrary, they gave in their adhesion to the course which I and Barnabas had been (independently) pursuing. "In what does this opposition (ἀλλὰ τοὐναντίον) consist ? Apparently in this, that instead of strengthening the hands of Paul, they left him to fight his own battle (practically: but they added the weight of their approval: see Ellic.). They said, 'Take your own course : preach the Gospel of the uncircumcision to Gentiles, and we will preach the Gospel of the circumcision to Jews.'" Jowett. ἰδόντες, viz. by the communication mentioned ver. 2, coupled with the now manifest results of

Πέτρος τῆς ^b περιτομῆς (⁸ ὁ γὰρ ^c ἐνεργήσας Πέτρῳ ^d εἰς ^e ἀποστολὴν τῆς ^b περιτομῆς, ^c ἐνήργησεν καὶ ἐμοὶ εἰς τὰ ἔθνη) ⁹ καὶ γνόντες τὴν ^f χάριν τὴν ^f δοθεῖσάν μοι 'Ιάκωβος καὶ Κηφᾶς καὶ 'Ιωάννης, οἱ ^g δοκοῦντες ^h στύλοι εἶναι, ⁱ δεξιὰς ¹ ἔδωκαν ἐμοὶ καὶ Βαρνάβᾳ ^k κοινωνίας, ἵνα ἡμεῖς εἰς τὰ ἔθνη, αὐτοὶ δὲ εἰς τὴν ^l περιτομήν, 10 ^m μόνον τῶν πτωχῶν ⁿ ἵνα ^o μνημονεύωμεν, ὃ καὶ ^p ἐσπούδασα ^q αὐτὸ

Margin left:
b = Rom. iii. 30. see Phil. iii. 3.
c w. dat., here bis only. Prov. xxxi. 12.
w. ἐν, Rom. vii. 5. 1 Cor. xii. 6. Phil. ii. 13 al. (Isa. xli. 4.) (-γῆς w. εἰς, of the object, Philem. 6.)
d = 2 Cor. ii. 12. Col. i. 29.
e Acts i. 25. Rom. i. 5. 1 Cor. ix. 2 only. Deut. xxii. 7.
4. iii. 10. 2 Cor. viii. 1. Eph. iii. 2, 8. iv. 7 (29). 2 Tim. i. 9. (James iv. 6. 1 Pet. v. 5.)
h = here only. 1 Tim. iii. 15. Rev. iii. 12. x. 1 only. 3 Kings vii. 41.
45, 50 only. Jos. Antt. xviii. 9. 3.
l = ver. 7. ellips., ch. v. 13. Rom. iv. 16.
words, John xiii. 29. Acts xix. 4. Rom. xi. 31. 1 Cor. ix. 15. xiv. 9. 2 Cor. ii. 4.
1 Macc. xii. 11.
p Eph. iv. 3 reff.

Margin right:
H καὶ βαρναβα
ABCDF HKLPN abcde fghkl mno 17. 47

f = (Paul) Rom. xii. 3, 6. xv. 15. 1 Cor. i. g ver. 6 reff.
i here only. 1 Macc. xi. 62. xiii.
k = Acts ii. 42. Levit. vi. 2. arrangt. of words, 1 Thess. ii. 13.
m 1 Cor. vii. 39. ch. i. 23. v. 13 al. n inversion of
o = Col. iv. 18.
q Acts xxiv. 15, 20. 2 Cor. ii. 3. vii. 11 al.

8. om ο γαρ το περιτομης (homœot) N¹(ins N-corr^{1a}). καμοι ACD¹F[P] a f k m 17 [47] Chr₂ Damasc : txt BD³KLN rel Chr Thl Œc.
9. for ιακωβ. κ. κηφας, πετρος κ. ιακωβ. DF fuld goth Thdrt₄ Nys Iren-int Tert : ιακωβος (omg και κηφ.) A Epiph : txt BCKL[P]N rel vulg syrr copt Ath Chr Thdrt₂ Damasc Aug Pel Bede. aft ημεις ins μεν (to correspond to δε follg) ACD N-corr¹ obl a b d² f h o [47] 67² syr copt Naz Bas Chr₂ Thdrt₂ Damasc : om BFHKL [P]N¹ rel latt goth Orig₂ Chr Thl Œc lat-ff.
10. ινα bef των πτωχων DF vss lat-ff.
[μνημονευομεν DP d¹.]

his preaching among the Gentiles. Compare Acts xv. 12. πεπίστ. (for construction see reff. Acts and 1 Cor. and other examples in Winer, Gram., § 39. 1. a) has the emphasis : **they saw that I was** (lit. am : the state being one still abiding) ENTRUSTED **with the Gospel of the uncircumcision, as Peter with that of the circumcision**; therefore they had only to accede to the appointment of God. τῆς ἀκροβ.] i. e. belonging to, addressed to, the uncircumcised (οὐ τὰ πράγματα λέγων αὐτά, ἀλλὰ τὰ ἀπὸ τούτων γνωριζόμενα ἔθνη, Chrys.). Peter was not the Apostle of the circumcision *only*, for he had opened the door to the Gentiles (Acts x., to which he refers, ib. xv. 7), but in the ultimate assignment of the apostolic work, he wrought less among the Gentiles and more among the Jews than Paul : see 1 Pet. i. 1, and note. But his own Epistles are sufficient testimonies that, in his hands at least, the Gospel of the circumcision did not differ in any essential point from that of the uncircumcision. Cf., as an interesting trait on the other side, Col. iv. 11. **8.**] Parenthetic explanation of πεπίστευμαι κ.τ.λ. Πέτρῳ and ἐμοί are datives commodi, not governed by the ἐν in ἐνεργ., the meaning of this preposition being already expressed in the word ἐνεργεῖν, and having therefore no force to pass on : cf. ref. Prov. ἐνήργ. applies to the ἀπακολουθοῦντα σημεῖα with which the Lord accompanied His word spoken by them, and to the power with which they spoke that word. The agent in ἐνεργ. is GOD,—the Father : see 1 Cor. xii. 6; Phil. ii. 13;

Rom. xv. 15, 16. εἰς ἀποστ.] towards, with a view to, the Apostleship,—reff. εἰς τὰ ἔθνη] The fuller construction would be, εἰς ἀποστολὴν τ. ἐθνῶν : so τάων οὔτις ὁμοία νοήματα Πηνελοπείῃ | ἤδη, Od. β. 120 : and frequently. **9.**] resumes the narrative after the parenthesis. Ἰάκωβος] placed first, as being at the head of the church at Jerusalem, and presiding (apparently) at the conference in Acts xv. δοκοῦντες alludes to vv. 2 and 6; see there. στύλοι] pillars, i. e. principal supporters of the church, men of distinction and weight; see reff., and examples in Wetst. : and Suicer, sub voce. Clem.rom. ad Cor. i. 5, p. 217, uses the word directly, without metaphor : οἱ δικαιότατοι στύλοι ἐδιώχθησαν. δεξ. ἔδωκ. κοιν.] On the separation of the genitive from its governing noun, see Winer, § 30. 3, remark 2. It is made here, because what follows respects rather κοινωνίας than ἔδωκαν. ἵνα κ.τ.λ.] There is an ellipsis of some verb; πορευθῶμεν and -θῶσιν, or perhaps εὐαγγελιζώμεθα, -ζωνται, which might connect with εἰς (see 1 Thess. ii. 9; 1 Pet. i. 25. But Meyer objects that it is not found with εἰς in St. Paul) : or as Beza, ἀπόστολοι γενώμεθα. Similar ellipses occur Rom. iv. 16; ch. v. 13. This division of labour was not, and could not be, strictly observed. Every where in the Acts we find St. Paul preaching 'to the Jews first,' and every where the Judaizers followed on his track; see Jowett's note.
10. μόν. τ. πτ. ἵνα μν.] The genitive is put before the conjunction for emphasis : see reff., and 2 Thess. ii. 7, and

τοῦτο ποιῆσαι. [11] ὅτε δὲ ἦλθεν Κηφᾶς εἰς Ἀντιόχειαν, [rs] κατὰ πρόσωπον αὐτῷ [st] ἀντέστην, ὅτι [u] κατεγνωσμένος ἦν.

r Luke ii. 31.
Acts iii. 13.
xxv. 16.
2 Cor. x. 1.
2 Chron. xiii.
u 1 John iii.

8.   s Deut. vii. 24.   t Acts vi. 10. xiii. 8.   Job xli. 2 al.
20, 21 only.   Deut. xxv. 1.

11. rec (for κηφας) πετρος, with DFKL rel demid goth Chr Thl Œc [Victorin] Tert: petrus cephas fuld : txt ABCH[P]‍א 17. 67² vulg Syr syr-mg copt [æth arm] Clem(in Eus) Chron Damasc Pel Ambrst.

John xiii. 29, where remarkably enough it is the same word which precedes ἵνα, ... τοῖς πτωχοῖς ἵνα τὶ δῷ. The construction is complete without supplying any participle (αἰτοῦντcς or παρακαλοῦντες), depending upon ἔδωκαν.   ὃ καὶ ἐσπ. αὐτὸ τ. ποι.] which was the very thing that I also was anxious to do,—viz., then and always: it was my habit. So that ἐσπούδασα has not a pluperfect sense. He uses the singular, because the plural could not correctly be predicated of the whole time to which the verb refers: for he parted from Barnabas shortly after the council in Acts xv. Meyer understands ἐσπούδ. of the time subsequent to the council only: but this does not seem necessary. The proofs of this σπουδή on his part may be found, Rom. xv. 25—27; 1 Cor. xvi. 1—4; 2 Cor. viii. ix.; Acts xxiv. 17: which, though they probably happened after the date of our Epistle, yet shewèd the bent of his habitual wishes on this point.   αὐτὸ τοῦτο is not merely redundant, as in ἧς εἶχεν τὸ θυγάτριον αὐτῆς πνεῦμα ἀκάθαρτον, Mark vii. 25,—but is an emphatic repetition of that to which ὅ refers, as in the version above. So that ὃ ἐσπ. αὐτὸ τοῦτο ποι. = καὶ ἐσπ. τὸ αὐτὸ τοῦτο ποι. Cf. Thuc. i. 10,—'Ἀθηναίων δὲ τὸ αὐτὸ τοῦτο παθόντων. Cf. Ellicott's note.   11—17.] He further proves his independence, by relating how he rebuked Peter for temporizing at Antioch. This proof goes further than any before: not only was he not taught originally by the Apostles,—not only did they impart nothing to him, rather tolerating his view and recognizing his mission,—but he on one occasion stood aloof from and reprimanded the chief of them for conduct unworthy the Gospel : thus setting his own Apostleship in opposition to Peter, for the time.   11. ὅτε δὲ ἦλθ.] This visit of Peter to Antioch, not related in the Acts, will fall most naturally (for our narrative follows the order of time) in the period described, Acts xv. 35, seeing that (ver. 13) Barnabas also was there. See below.   Κηφᾶς] ἡ ἱστορία παρὰ Κλήμεντι κατὰ τὴν πέμπτην τῶν ὑποτυπώσεων, ἐν ᾗ καὶ Κηφᾶν, περὶ οὗ φησὶν ὁ Παῦλος "Ὅτε δὲ ἦλθ. Κ. εἰς Ἀντ. κατ. πρ. αὐτ. ἀντέστην, ἕνα φησὶ γεγονέναι τῶν ἑβδομήκοντα μαθητῶν, ὁμώνυμον Πέτρῳ τυγχάνοντα τῷ

ἀποστόλῳ. Eus. H. E. i. 12. This story was manifestly invented to save the credit of St. Peter. See below.   κατὰ πρόσωπον] to the face,—see reff. : not 'before all,' which is asserted by and by, ver. 14. One of the most curious instances of ecclesiastical ingenuity on record has been afforded in the interpretation of this passage by the fathers. They try to make it appear that the reproof was only an apparent one—that ὁ θεῖος Πέτρος was entirely in the right, and Paul withstood him, κατὰ πρόσωπον, 'in appearance merely,' because he had been blamed by others. So Chrys.: so Thdrt. also: and Jerome,— "Paulus ... nova usus est arte pugnandi, ut dispensationem Petri, qua Judæos salvari cupiebat, nova ipse contradictionis dispensatione corrigeret, et resisteret ei in facie, non arguens propositum, sed quasi in publico contradicens, ut ex eo quod Paulus eum arguens resistebat, hi qui crediderant e gentibus servarentur." In Ep. ad Gal. ad loc. This view of his met with strong opposition from Augustine, who writes to him, nobly and worthily, Ep. 40. 3, vol. ii. p. 155, ed. Migne : "In expositione quoque Ep. Pauli ad Gal., invenimus aliquid, quod nos multum moveat. Si enim ad Scripturas sanctas admissa fuerint velut officiosa mendacia, quid in eis remanebit auctoritatis ? Quæ tandem de Scripturis illis sententia proferetur, cujus pondere contentiosæ falsitatis obteratur improbitas ? Statim enim ut protuleris : si aliter sapit qui contra nititur, dicet illud quod prolatum erit honesto aliquo officio scriptorum fuisse mentitum. Ubi enim hoc non poterit, si potuit in ea narratione, quam exorsus Apostolus ait, Quæ autem scribo vobis, ecce coram Deo quia non mentior, credi affirmarique mentitus, eo loco ubi dixit de Petro et Barnaba, cum viderem, quia non recte ingrediuntur ad veritatem Evangelii? Si enim recte illi ingrediebantur, iste mentitus est : si autem ibi mentitus est, ubi verum dixit ? Cur ibi verum dixisse videbitur, ubi hoc dixerit quod lector sapit ; cum vero contra sensum lectoris aliquid occurrerit, officioso mendacio deputabitur ? . . . . Quare arripe, obsecro te, ingenuam et vere Christianam cum caritate severitatem, ad illud opus corrigendum et emendandum, et παλινῳδίαν, ut

v Luke xv. 2.
Acts x. 41.
xi. 3. 1 Cor.
v. 11 only.
Gen. xliii. 32.
w = but mid.,
Heb. x. 38,
from Hab. ii.
4. (Acts xx.
20, 27 only.
Deut. i. 17.)
y Acts x. 45. xi. 2.

12 πρὸ τοῦ γὰρ ἐλθεῖν τινας ἀπὸ Ἰακώβου μετὰ τῶν
ἐθνῶν ᵛ συνήσθιεν· ὅτε δὲ ἦλθον, ʷ ὑπέστελλεν καὶ ˣ ἀφώριζεν ἑαυτόν, φοβούμενος τοὺς ʸ ἐκ ʸ περιτομῆς, 13 καὶ
ᶻ συνυπεκρίθησαν αὐτῷ καὶ οἱ λοιποὶ Ἰουδαῖοι, ὥστε καὶ

ABCDF
HKLPℵ
a b c d e
f g h k l
m n o 17.
47

Deut. i. 17.) see 2 Thess. iii. 6. Demosth. 54 ult.   x = Acts xix. 9. 2 Cor. vi. 17, from Isa. lii. 11 (ch. i. 15) al.
y Acts x. 45. xi. 2. Rom. iv. 12. Col. iv. 11. Tit. i. 10 only.   z here only †. Polyb. iii. 92. 5, Φάβιος...
συνυπεκρίνετο τοῖς...φιλοκινδύνως διακειμένοις : & al.

12. ηλθεν BD¹Fℵ e k Orig(ελθοντος ιακωβου), venisset D-lat G-lat some-mss-of-vulg : txt ACD²·³HKL[P] rel vss gr-lat-ff, venissent am(with fuld F-lat), venirent vulg-ed (and demid).

13. om 2nd και B 67² vulg(and F-lat) copt goth [Orig₁].   aft ιουδαιοι ins παντες

dicitur, cane. Incomparabiliter enim pulchrior est veritas Christianorum, quam Helena Græcorum ....'" (Similarly in several other Epistles in vol. ii. ed. Migne, where also Jerome's replies may be seen.) Afterwards, Jerome abandoned his view for the right one : 'Nonne idem Paulus in faciem Cephæ restitit, quod non recto pede incederet in Evangelio?' Apol. adv. Ruf. iii. 2, vol. ii. p. 532: see also cont. Pelag. i. 22, p. 718. Aug. Ep. 180. 5, vol. ii. p. 779. ὅτι κατεγνωσμένος ἦν] (not, as vulgate, quia reprehensibilis erat ('because he was to be blamed,' E. V.: similarly Calv., Beza, al.): no such meaning can be extracted from the perfect participle passive; nor can Hebrew usage be alleged for such a meaning in Greek. The instance commonly cited from Lucian de saltat., p. 952, ἀληθῶς, ἐπὶ μανίᾳ κατεγνωσμένος, is none whatever; nor is Iliad, α. 388, ὃ δὴ τετελεσμένος ἐστί : the perfect participle having in both its proper sense. Nor again is ψηλαφωμένῳ (ὄρει), Heb. xii. 18, at all to the purpose : see note there) because he was condemned ('a condemned man,' as we say : by whom, does not appear: possibly, by his own act : or, by the Christians in Antioch : but St. Paul would hardly have waited for the prompting of others to pronounce his condemnation of him. I therefore prefer the former : he was (self) convicted : convicted of inconsistency by his conduct). 12.] These τινες ἀπὸ Ἰακώβου have been softened by some Commentators into persons who merely gave themselves out as from James (Winer, &c. and even Ellicott, edn. 2), or who merely came from Jerusalem where James presided (Beza, Grot., Olsh., &c.). But the candid reader will I think at once recognize in the words a mission from James (so Thl., De W., Estius (doubtfully), Rückert, Meyer, De W.): and will find no difficulty in believing that that Apostle, even after the decision of the council regarding the Gentile converts, may have retained (characteristically, see his recommendation to St. Paul, in Acts xxi. 18 ff.) his strict view of the duties of Jewish converts,—for that is perhaps all that the present passage requires. And this mission may have been for the very purpose of admonishing the Jewish converts of their obligations, from which the Gentiles were free. Thus we have no occasion to assume (with De W.) that James had in the council been over-persuaded by the earnestness and eloquence of Paul, and had afterwards undergone a reaction : for his course will be consistent throughout. And my view seems to me to be confirmed by his own words, Acts xv. 19, where the emphatic τοῖς ἀπὸ τῶν ἐθνῶν ἐπιστρέφουσιν tacitly implies, that the Jews would be bound as before. συνήσθιεν] As he had done, Acts x., on the prompting of a heavenly vision; and himself defended it, Acts xi. See below. ὑπέστελλεν] as well as ἀφώριζεν, governs ἑαυτόν: withdrew himself. So Polyb. i. 16. 10, ὁ δὲ βασιλεὺς Ἱέρων, ὑποστείλας ἑαυτὸν ὑπὸ τὴν Ῥωμαίων σκέπην, and al. freq. The imperfects express that there were more cases than one where he did this—it was the course he took. φοβούμενος] being afraid of. Chrys., to bear out his interpretation of the whole incident, says, οὐ τοῦτο φοβούμενος, μὴ κινδυνεύσῃ· ὁ γὰρ ἐν ἀρχῇ μὴ φοβηθείς (witness his denial of his Lord), πολλῷ μᾶλλον τότε· ἀλλ' ἵνα μὴ ἀποστῶσιν. ἐπεὶ καὶ αὐτὸς λέγει Γαλάταις, φοβοῦμαι ὑμᾶς μή πως εἰκῆ κεκοπίακα κ.τ.λ. And so Piscator, Grot., Estius, al. The whole incident is remarkably characteristic of Peter—ever the first to recognize, and the first to draw back from, great principles and truths : see this very ably enlarged on in Jowett's note on ver. 11. 13. συνυπεκρ.] were guilty of like hypocrisy. The word is not (as De W.) too strong a one to describe their conduct. They were aware of the liberty in Christ which allowed them to eat with Gentiles, and had practised it : and now, being still aware of it, and not convinced to the contrary, from mere fear of man they adopted a contrary course. The case bore

Βαρνάβας ^aσυναπήχθη αὐτῶν τῇ ^bὑποκρίσει. 14 ἀλλ'
ὅτε εἶδον ὅτι οὐκ ^cὀρθοποδοῦσιν ^dπρὸς τὴν ^eἀλήθειαν
τοῦ ^eεὐαγγελίου, εἶπον τῷ Κηφᾷ ^fἔμπροσθεν πάντων Εἰ

...αλη-
θειαν H.
ABCDF
KLPℵ a
b c d e f
g h k l m
n o 17. 47

a Rom. xii. 16.
2 Pet. iii. 17
only. Exod.
xiv. 6 only.
constr., John
iii. 16 only.
see Winer,

§ 41. 5, remark 1.   b Matt. xxiii. 28.   Mark xii. 15.   Luke xii. 1.   1 Tim. iv. 2.   (James
v. 12 v. r.)   1 Pet. ii. 1 only †.   2 Macc. vi. 25 only.   c here only †. pres., ch. i. 23 reff.
d = Luke xii. 47.   2 Cor. v. 10.   e ver. 5.   f = Matt. v. 16 al.   2 Kings iii.
31 A. see 1 Tim. v. 20.

ℵ¹(ℵ³ disapproving).   συνυπηχθη partly written by ℵ³ : συνυπαχθηναι a[: βαρναβα
συναπαχθηναι P (67²)].   τη υποκρ. bef αυτων DFH[P] b m o 17 latt [Victorin]:
txt ABCKL[ℵ] rel Chr Damasc.
14. for ειδ., ιδον AD²FL m.   rec (for κηφα) πετρω, with DFKL[P] rel fuld-
vict syr goth Chr Victorin: txt ABCℵ 17. 67²(Bch) vulg Syr copt æth arm Clem(in

but very little likeness to that discussed
in 1 Cor. viii.—x.; Rom. xiv. There, it
was a mere matter of *licence* which was in
question : here, the very foundation itself.
It was not now a question of using a
liberty, but of asserting a truth, that of
justification by the faith of Christ, and
not by the works of the law.   ὥστε
. . . . συναπήχθη] The indicative usually
follows ὥστε, when the result is matter
of fact : the infinitive usually, when it is
matter of course as well. So Herod. vi.
83,—'Αργος δὲ ἀνδρῶν ἐχηρώθη οὕτω,
ὥστε οἱ δοῦλοι αὐτέων ἔσχον πάντα τὰ
πρήγματα, where it was not a necessary
consequence of the depopulation, but a
result which followed as matter of fact
(so also John iii. 16, where the sending
the Son to be the Saviour of the world
was not a necessary consequence of the
Father's love, but followed it as its result
in fact : so that it is (against Ellic. edn. 1)
an instance in point): Plato, Apol. 37 c,—
οὕτως ἀλόγιστός εἰμι, ὥστε μὴ δύνασθαι
λογίζεσθαι, where the degree of ἀλογία
supposed involves the result of not being
able to reason at all. See Krüger, Gram.
§ 65, 3. 1; Kühner, ii. p. 563. But the
distinction does not seem always to be accurately observed.   On συναπ., see ref.
Rom., and note. Understand αὐτοῖς after
συναπ., and take τῇ ὑπ. as ·the instrumental dative : '*was carried away (with
them) by their hypocrisy :*' or possibly
the dative of the state *into* which &c. : see
2 Pet. iii. 17 : but this construction seems
questionable : see Ellic. edn. 2. Fritz.
cites Zosimus, Hist. v. 6, καὶ αὐτὴ δὲ
ἡ Σπάρτη συναπήγετο τῇ κοινῇ τῆς
'Ελλάδος ἁλώσει: add Clem. Alex. Strom.
i. 17, p. 368 P., τῇ ἡδονῇ συναπαγόμενος
(Ellicott). " Besides the antagonism in
which this passage represents the two great
Apostles, it throws an important light
on the history of the apostolic church
in the following respects :—1] As exhi-
biting Peter's relation to James, and his
fear of those who were of the circumcision, whose leader we should have naturally supposed him to have been. 2]

Also, as pourtraying the state of inde-
cision in which all, except St. Paul, even
including Barnabas, were in reference to
the observance of the Jewish law." Jowett.
14.] ὀρθοποδεῖν apparently not occurring elsewhere, its meaning must be got
from cognate words. We have ἀτραπὸν
ὀρθοβατεῖν, Anthol. ix. 11, ὀρθοπραγεῖν,
Arist. Eth. Eud. iii. 2, and ὀρθοτομέω,
ὀρθοδρομέω, &c.: **to walk straight** is
therefore undoubtedly its import, and
metaphorically (cf. περιπατεῖν, στοιχεῖν
frequently in Paul), **to behave uprightly.**
πρός] It is best, with Meyer, to
take ἀλήθεια as in ver. 5, and render
connecting πρός with ὀρθοποδοῦσιν, **towards (with a view to) maintaining
and propagating the truth** (objectively,
the unadulterated character) **of the Gospel.** Others (De W., al.) render πρός
'*with reference to,*' ('*according to,*' E.V.,)
and take τ. ἀλήθ. τ. εὐ. to mean '*the truth
(fulness of character) required by the
Gospel.*' Mey. remarks, that St. Paul does
not express *nouns* after verbs of motion by
πρός, but by κατά, cf. Rom. viii. 4 ; xiv.
15; 1 Cor. iii. 3. Ellic. however answers,
that in all these instances, περιπατέω, St.
Paul's favourite verb of moral motion, is
used, and that ὀρθοποδέω does not so
plainly express motion as περιπατέω.
Still, I prefer the former meaning, as
better suiting the expression ἡ ἀλήθεια
τ. εὐαγγ.: cf. ver. 5.   ἔμπρ. πάντ.]
'before the church assembled.' The words
require this, and the reproof would otherwise have fallen short of its desired effect
on the Jewish converts.   The speech
which follows, and which I believe to extend
to the end of the chapter, must be regarded
as a compendium of what was said, and a
free report of it, as we find in the narra-
tives by St. Paul himself of his conversion. See below. **If thou, being (by
birth, originally, cf. Acts xvi. 20 and note)
a Jew, livest** (as thy usual habit. **As**
Neander (Pfl. u. Leit., p. 114) remarks,
these words shew that Peter had long
been himself convinced of the truth on
this matter, and lived according to it:

σὺ Ἰουδαῖος g ὑπάρχων h ἐθνικῶς καὶ οὐκ i Ἰουδαϊκῶς ζῇς,
k πῶς τὰ ἔθνη l ἀναγκάζεις m Ἰουδαΐζειν; 15 ἡμεῖς n φύσει
Ἰουδαῖοι καὶ οὐκ o ἐξ o ἐθνῶν p ἁμαρτωλοί, 16 εἰδότες δὲ
ὅτι οὐ q δικαιοῦται ἄνθρωπος q ἐξ ἔργων νόμου, r ἐὰν
r μὴ διὰ s πίστεως s Ἰησοῦ χριστοῦ, καὶ ἡμεῖς t εἰς χριστὸν

ABCDF
KLPℵ a
b c d e f
g h k l m
n o 17.47

g = ch. i. 14 reff.
h here only †. (-κός, Matt. v. 47.)
i here only †. (-κός, Tit. i. 14.)
k = Rom. vi. 2. 1 Cor. xv. 12. ch. iv. 9.
l = ver. 3 reff.
m here only. Esth. viii. 17 (ix. 4) only. (-ισμός, ch. i. 13, 14.) Rom. i. 26 al.† Wisd. vii. 20 only.) Rom. ii. 12. 1 Cor. vi. 1. ix. 21. Eph. ii. 12.
n Rom. ii. 14. ch. iv. 8. Eph. ii. 3 only. (-σις, o Acts xv. 14, 23. Rom. ix. 24. 1 Kings xv. 18.
p = Tobit xiii. 6. see q Rom. iii. 20. iv. 2. James ii. 21, 24, 25.
r = here only. see note. = εἰ μή, Matt. xii. 4. Rev. ix. 4. 12 and passim. Acts x. 43. xix. 4. Rom. x. 14 al.
s obj. gen., Rom. iii. 22, 26 al. t John i.

Eus) Ps-Ath Did₂ Thdrt Dial-trin Philo-carp Pel. for υπαρχ., ων Dʹ. rec
ζης bef και ουκ ιουδαικως, with DKL rel syrr goth Chr Thdrt Damasc Thl Œc : txt
ABCF[P]ℵ m 17 am(with demid fuld F-lat) arm Orig Philo-carp lat-ff(but D-lat
Ambrst Sedul Agap om και ουκ ιουδ.).—ουχ ACℵ¹ m 17 Chr₁ : ουχι [B]D¹ℵ³ d² l
Damasc : om ουκ c d¹.—om και α. rec (for πως) τι, with KL rel syr Chr Thdrt
Thl Œc : txt ABCDF[P]ℵ m 17 latt Syr copt [goth] æth [arm] Orig Damasc lat-ff.
16. rec om δε, with AD³K[P] rel vss gr-ff [Victorin]: ins BCD¹FLℵ [47] latt goth
Cyr Thdrt₁ lat-ff, ουν f. χριστου bef ιησ. AB 17 Victorin Aug_{h.l.} : txt CDFKL[P]ℵ

see further on ver. 18) **as a Gentile** (*how*,
is shewn by μετὰ τῶν ἐθνῶν συνήσθιεν
above) **and not as a Jew, how (is it that
(reff.)) thou art compelling the Gentiles**
(i. e. virtually and ultimately; for the
high authority of Peter and Barnabas
would make the Gentile converts view
their course as necessary to all Christians.
There is no need, with De W. and Wieseler, to suppose that the τινες ἀπὸ Ἰακ.
actually compelled the Gentile converts
to Judaize, as necessary to salvation, and
Peter upheld them : nor is there any
difficulty in the expression: the present
may mean, as it often does, ' *art compelling to the best of thy power*,' ' *doing
thy part to compel*,'—for such certainly
would be the *ultimate result*, if Jews and
Gentiles might not company together in
social life—"his principle logically involved this, or his influence and example
would be likely to effect it." Jowett) **to
Judaize** (observe the ceremonial law)?
15.] Some (Calv., Beza, Grot., Hermann, al.) think that the speech ends
with ver. 14 : Calov., al., with ver. 15 :
Luther, al., with ver. 16 : Flatt, Neander,
al., with ver. 18 : Jowett, that the conversation gradually passes off into the
general subject of the Epistle. "Ver.
14," he says, "is the answer of St. Paul
to St. Peter : what follows, is more like
the Apostle musing or arguing with himself, with an indirect reference to the
Galatians." But it seems very unnatural
to place any break before the end of the
chapter. The Apostle recurs to the Galatians again with ὦ ἀνόητοι Γαλάται, ch.
iii. 1 : and it is harsh in the extreme to
suppose him to pass from his speech to
Peter into an address to them with so
little indication of the transition. I therefore regard the speech (which doubtless is

freely reported, and gives rather the bearing of what was said, than the words
themselves, as in Acts xxii. and xxvi.) as
continuing to the end of the chapter, as do
Chr., Thdrt., Jer., Est., Beng., Rosenm.,
Winer, Rückert, Usteri, Olsh., B.-Crus.,
Meyer, De W. **We** (thou and I) **by
nature** (birth) **Jews and not sinners from
among the Gentiles** (he is speaking to
Peter from the common ground of their
Judaism, and using (ironically ?) Judaistic
language, in which the Gentiles were
ἔθεοι, ἄνομοι, ἄδικοι, ἁμαρτωλοί (reff.).
The putting a comma after ἐθνῶν, and
taking ἁμαρτωλοί with ἡμ. φύσ. Ἰουδ.
(Prim. in Est., Elsner, Er.-Schmid, al.),
' *We, by birth Jews, and, though not
from the Gentiles, yet sinners*,' is absurd), **knowing nevertheless** (this seems,
against Ellic. ed. 2, the proper force of δέ
here, and is the same in sense as his
" *but as we know*," but clearer) **that a
man is not justified by** (as the ground
of justification : see Ellic.'s note on the
sense of ἐκ) **the works of the law** (not
' *by works of law*,' or ' *on the score of
duty done*' (Peile) : this, though following as an inference, and a generalization
of the axiom, was not in question here.
' *The works of the law*,' just as 'the faith
of Jesus Christ ;' the genitives in both
cases being objective—the works which
have the law (ceremonial and moral) for
their object,—which are wrought to fulfil
the law : Meyer compares ἁμαρτήματα
νόμου, Wisd. ii. 12,—faith which has
Jesus Christ for its object,—which is reposed in or on Him. On δικαιόω, see
note, Rom. i. 17),—(supply, nor is any
man justified, and see reff.) **except by**
(as the medium of justification. Ellic. observes that two constructions seem to be
mixed—οὐ δικ. ἄνθ. ἐξ ἔργ. ν., and οὐ

Ἰησοῦν [tu] ἐπιστεύσαμεν, ἵνα [qv] δικαιωθῶμεν [q] ἐκ [s] πίστεως
[s] χριστοῦ καὶ ουκ [q] ἐξ ἔργων νόμου, ὅτι [q] ἐξ ἔργων
νόμου οὐ [q] δικαιωθήσεται [w] πᾶσα σάρξ.   17 εἰ δὲ ζητοῦντες
δικαιωθῆναι [x] ἐν χριστῷ [y] εὑρέθημεν καὶ αὐτοὶ ἁμαρτωλοί,
[z] ἆρα χριστὸς ἁμαρτίας [a] διάκονος; [b] μὴ γένοιτο. 18 εἰ

u aor., = Acts
xix. 2. Rom.
xiii. 11. 1 Cor.
iii. 5.
v Rom. iii. 30.
v. 1. ch. iii.
8, 24.
w constr.,Rom.
iii. 20. Matt.
xxiv.22. Acts
x. 14. Exod.
xv. 26.

x = Col. i. 16 reff.   y = Matt. i. 18. Rom. vii. 10. Neh. ix. 8.   z Luke xviii. 8. Acts
  viii. 30 only. Gen. xxvi. 9 Ed-vat. (ἆρα F.)   a see Rom. xv. 8. 2 Cor. xi. 15.   b Gospp.
  Luke xx. 16 only. Rom. iii. 4, 6, 31 al6. 1 Cor. vi. 15 only. L.P. Josh. xxii. 29.

rel vss Chr Cyr Thdrt Ambr Jer Aug₂.   ιησουν bef χριστον B a¹ 17 syrr copt æth
Thdrt₁ Aug₂ : om ιησ. d¹ l.   om 2nd χριστου F Thdrt₁ Tert [Victorin] Tich (see
Rom iii. 28 al) : ιησ. χ. K syr-w-ast [æth].   rec διοτι, with CD³KL[P] rel : txt
ABD¹FℵＮ 17. 67² Damasc.   rec ου δικαιωθησεται bef εξ εργ. νομ., with KL rel goth
Thdrt₁ Thl Œc : ουκ εξ εργ. ν. δικ. a : txt ABCDF[P]ℵ m 17 latt syrr copt [æth] arm
Thdrt₁ Damasc₂ lat-ff.

δικ. ἄνθ. ἐὰν μὴ διὰ π. Ἰ. χ. ἐὰν μή in
this elliptical construction is not elsewhere found : but εἰ μή repeatedly (reff.).
The ἐάν seems to remove further off the
hypothesis, which arises in the mind, of
the two being united) the faith of (see
above) Jesus Christ,—we also (as well as
the Gentile sinners, q. d., casting aside
our legal trust) believed (reff.) on Christ
Jesus (notice Ἰησ. χρ. above, χρ. Ἰησ.
here. This is not arbitrary. In the
general proposition above, Ἰησ. χρ., as
the name of Him on whom faith is to be
exercised : here, when Jews receive Him
as their Messiah, χρ. Ἰησ., as bringing
that Messiahship into prominence. Perhaps, however, such considerations are but
precarious. For example, in this case,
the readings are in some confusion. It
may be remarked, that the Codex Sinai-
ticus agrees throughout with our text)
that we might be justified by (this time,
faith is the ground) the faith of Christ,
and not by the works of the law : because
(it is an axiom in our theology that) by
the works of the law shall all flesh find
no justification (Angl. : 'shall no flesh be
justified :' our language not admitting of
the logical form of the Greek : but by this
transposition of the negative, the sense
is not accurately rendered).   There is
a difference between Commentators in the
arrangement of the foregoing sentence.
Meyer follows Lachmann in placing a
period after χριστοῦ, and understanding
ἐσμέν at Ἰουδ. or ἁμαρτωλοί. Beza,
Hermann, Rückert, Usteri, Ellicott, al.,
begin a new sentence at εἰδότες δέ, also
understanding ἐσμέν. But it seems much
better, as above (with De W., al.), to
carry on the sentence throughout. Meyer's
objection, that thus it would not represent the matter of fact, for Peter and
Paul were not converted as εἰδότες κ.τ.λ.,
would apply equally to his own arrangement, for they were not converted ἵνα
δικαιωθῶσιν κ.τ.λ.   17.] Continues

the argument. But if, seeking (put first
for emphasis—in the course of our earnest
endeavour) to be justified in Christ (as
the element—the Body, comprehending
us the members. This is lost sight of by
rendering 'through Christ'), we ourselves
also (you and I, addressed to Peter) were
found to be sinners (as we should be,
if we regarded the keeping of the law as
necessary ; for we should be just in the
situation of those Gentiles who in the
Judaistic view are ἁμαρτωλοί, faith having
failed in obtaining righteousness for us,
and we having cast aside the law which
we were bound to keep) is therefore
Christ the minister of sin (i. e. are we
to admit the consequence which would in
that case be inevitable, that Christ, having
failed to obtain for his own the righteousness which is by faith, has left them sinners, and so has done all His work only to
minister to a state of sin)?   Whether we read ἄρα or ἆρα matters little ;
either will express the meaning, but the
latter more pungently than the former.
The clause must be interrogative, as μὴ
γένοιτο always follows a question in St.
Paul ; see reff. Those who would take
ἆρα for ἆρ' οὐ (qu. can it ever be so taken,
in spite of Matthiæ (Gr. Gr. § 641), Winer
(comm. h. l., but not in Gr. ed. 6, § 57.
2, where he allows the translation given
above), Monk (on Eur. Alcest. 353), and
Porson (pref. to Hec. p. x)?) seem to
me to miss altogether the fine irony of the
question, which, as it stands, presupposes
the ἆρ' οὐ question already asked, the inevitable answer given, and now puts the
result, 'Can we believe, are we to hold
henceforth, such a consequence?' The
same might be said of all the passages alleged by the above scholars in support of
their view. Theodoret expresses well the
argument : εἰ δὲ ὅτι τὸν νόμον κατα-
λιπόντες τῷ χριστῷ προσεληλύθαμεν, διὰ
τῆς ἐπ' αὐτῷ πίστεως τῆς δικαιοσύνης
ἀπολαύσασθαι προσδοκήσαντες, παράβασις

c = Matt. xxvi.
61. Acts vi.
14. 2 Cor. v.
1. Ezra v. 12.
d = Rom. xv.
20.
e Rom. ii. 25,
27. James
ii. 9, 11
only †. Ps.
xvi. 4 Symm.
f = Paul only,
Rom. iii. 5.
v. 8. 2 Cor.
vi. 4. Susan.

γὰρ ἃ ᶜ κατέλυσα, ταῦτα πάλιν ᵈ οἰκοδομῶ, ᵉ παραβάτην
ἐμαυτὸν ᶠ συνιστάνω. ¹⁹ ἐγὼ γὰρ διὰ νόμου ᵍ νόμῳ ʰ ἀπέθανον, ἵνα ᵍ θεῷ ζήσω. ²⁰ χριστῷ ⁱ συνεσταύρωμαι· ζῶ
δὲ οὐκ ἔτι ἐγώ, ζῇ δὲ ἐν ἐμοὶ χριστός· ᵏ ὃ δὲ νῦν ζῶ ˡ ἐν
σαρκί, ἐν πίστει ζῶ τῇ τοῦ ᵐ υἱοῦ τοῦ θεοῦ τοῦ ἀγαπή-
σαντός με καὶ ⁿᵒ παραδόντος ⁿ ἑαυτὸν ὑπὲρ ἐμοῦ. ²¹ οὐκ

ABCDF
KLPℵ a
b c d e f
g h k l m
n o 17.47

61 Theod. -άνειν, 2 Cor. iii. 1. v. 12. x. 12, 18 only.   g dat. = Rom. vi. 2, 11.   h = Col. ii. 20.
i Matt. xxvii. 44 ┤ Mk. J.   Rom. vi. 6 only †.   k accus. of object, Rom. vi. 10.   l = 1 Tim. iii. 16 reff.
m gen., ver. 16.   n Eph. v. 25 only.   o = Rom. iv. 25.   Isa. liii. 12.

18. rec συνιστημι, with D³KL rel : txt ABCD¹F[P]ℵ 17. 67² Cyr.
20. ins ο bef χριστος F Ign.   om 3rd ζω A.   for του υι. τ. θ., του θεου
κ. χριστου BD¹F : txt ACD²·³KL[P]ℵ rel vulg(and F-lat) syrr copt goth [æth arm]
Clem Dial Chr Cyr₄ Thdrt Damasc Ambrst.

τοῦτο νενόμισται, εἰς αὐτὸν ἡ αἰτία χωρήσει τὸν δεσπότην χριστόν· αὐτὸς γὰρ ἡμῖν τὴν καινὴν ὑπέδειξε διαθήκην· ἀλλὰ μὴ γένοιτο ταύτην ἡμᾶς τολμῆσαι τὴν βλασφημίαν.

18.] **For** (substantiates the μὴ γένοιτο, and otherwise deduces the ὑρέθημεν ἁμαρτωλοί) **if the things which I pulled down, those very things** (and no others) **I again build up** (which thou art doing, who in Cæsarea didst so plainly announce freedom from the law, and again here in Antioch didst practise it thyself. The *first person* is chosen *clementiæ causa*; the *second* would have placed Peter, where the first means that he should place *himself*), **I am proving** (reff.) **myself a transgressor** (παραβάτης is the species, bringing me under the genus ἁμαρτωλός. So that παραβ. ἐμ. συνιστ. is the explanation of ἁμαρτωλοὶ εὑρέθημεν). The *force* of the verse is,—'You, by now reasserting the obligation of the law, are proving (*quoad te*) that your former step of setting aside the law was in fact a *transgression* of it:' viz. in that you neglected and set it aside,—not, as Chrys., Thl., and Meyer (from ver. 19), because the law itself was leading you on to faith in Christ : for (1) that point is not yet raised, not belonging to this portion of the argument, and (2) by the hypothesis of this verse the ἐγώ has *given up* the faith in Christ, and so cannot be regarded as acknowledging it as the end of the law. See against this view, but to me not convincingly, Ellicott, ed. 2.

19.] For (the γὰρ (agst Ellic.) retains, on our view of παραβάτης, its full exemplifying force) **I** (ἐγώ, for the first time expressed, is marked and emphatic. The first person of the *last* verse, serves as the transition point to treating, as he now does, of HIS OWN state and course. And this ἐγώ, as that in Rom. vii., is purely and bona fide 'I Paul;' not 'I and all believers') **by means of the law died to the law** (Christ was the end of

the law for righteousness : the law itself, properly apprehended by me, was my παιδαγωγός to Christ : and in Christ, who fulfilled the law, I died to the law : i. e. satisfied the law's requirements, and passed out of its pale : the dative, as Ellic. remarks, is a sort of dativus commodi, as also in ⟨ἦν θεῷ⟩ that I should live to God (the end of Christ's work, LIFE unto God. ζήσω is 1 aor. subj. in subordination to the aor. preceding : not fut., as stated in former edd. [before 1865]. See Ellic.). Many of the Fathers (some as an *alternative*), Luther, Bengel, al., take the first νόμος here to mean the Gospel (the νόμος τοῦ πνεύματος τῆς ζωῆς of Rom. viii. 2); but it will be manifest to any who follow the argument, that this cannot be so. This διὰ νόμου νόμῳ ἀπέθανον is in fact a compendium of his expanded experience in Rom. vii.: and also of his argument in ch. iii. iv. below.

I am ('*and have been*,' perf.) **crucified with Christ** (specification of the foregoing ἀπέθανον : the way in which I died to the law, was by being united to, and involved in the death of, that Body of Christ which was crucified): **but it is no longer I that live, but** (it is) **Christ that liveth in me** (the punctuation—χρ. συνεσταύρωμαι, ζῶ δέ· οὐκέτι ἐγώ, ζῇ δὲ ἐν ἐμ. χρ.,—as in E. V., &c.—is altogether wrong, and would require ἀλλά before οὐκέτι. The construction is one not without example, where the emphatic word is repeated in two parallel clauses, each time with δέ. Thus Eur. Iph. Taur. 1367, φιλεῖς δὲ καὶ σὺ τὸν κασίγνητον, θεᾶ· φιλεῖν δὲ κἀμὲ τοὺς ὁμαίμονας δόκει: Xen. Cyr. vi. 2. 22, ἔνθα πολὺς μὲν οἶνος, πολλὰ δὲ σῦκα, πολὺ δὲ ἔλαιον, θάλαττα δὲ προσκλύζει. So that our second δέ is not ﬁonﬃern,—'*not I, but*,'—but a﬇er, as the first—q. d. 'but the life is not mine,—but the life is Christ's within me.' Notice, not ὁ ἐν ἐμοὶ χρ.: Christ is the vine, we the branches: He lives, He, the same Christ, through and in every one of His believing

^p ἀθετῶ τὴν χάριν τοῦ θεοῦ· εἰ γὰρ διὰ νόμου ^q δικαιοσύνη, p 1 Cor. i. 19.
ch. iii. 15.
ἄρα χριστὸς ^r δωρεὰν ἀπέθανεν. Isa. xxxi. 2.
see 1 Thess.
iv. 8.

III. ¹ Ὦ ^s ἀνόητοι Γαλάται, τίς ὑμᾶς ^t ἐβάσκανεν, q ellips., ch. iii.
21.
οἷς ^{uv} κατ᾽ ^v ὀφθαλμοὺς Ἰησοῦς χριστὸς ^w προεγράφη r = John xv.
25, from
Ps. xxxiv.

19. (Matt. x. 8. Rom. iii. 24 al.)   s ver. 3. Luke xxiv. 25. Rom. i. 14. 1 Tim. vi. 9. Tit. iii.
3 only. L.P. Prov. xvii. 28.   t here only. Deut. xxviii. 54, 56. Sir. xiv. 6, 8 only.   u = ch. ii.
11 reff.   v here only. see note.   w Rom. xv. 4. Eph. iii. 3. Jude 4 only†.   Esdr. vi.
31 F (προσγρ. A) only. 1 Macc. x. 36.

CHAP. III. 1. rec aft εβασκανεν add τη αληθεια μη πειθεσθαι (*from ch* v. 7), with
CD³KL[P] rel vulg syr goth æth arm[-usc] Ath Cyr₁ Thdrt₂ Damasc : om ABD¹FℵK
17¹. 67² fuld Syr coptt Orig(in Jer) Chr₂ Cyr₁[?] Thdrt₁ lat-ff.   rec aft προε-
γραφη ins εν υμιν, with DFKL rel vulg syr goth Ath Chr Thdrt₂ Damasc lat-ff : om
ABC[P]ℵ 17¹ am(with tol F-lat) Syr coptt æth arm Cyr₂ Thdrt₁ Eus-int Archel Aug.

people)—but (taken up again, parallel with
ζῶ δὲ . . . . (ῇ δέ) that which (i. e. 'the
life which,' as E. V.) I now (since my conversion, as contrasted with the time before :
not, as Rück., al., the *present* life contrasted with the *future*) live in the flesh
(in the fleshly body ;—which, though it
appear to be a mere animal life, is not. So
Luth. : "in carne quidem vivo, sed ego
hanc vitam quantulacunque est, quæ in me
agitur, non habeo pro vita. Non enim est
vere vita, sed tantum larva vitæ, sub qua
vivit alius, nempe Christus, qui est vere
vita mea") I live in (not '*by*,' as E. V.,
Chr. (διὰ τὴν πίστιν), Œc., Thl., Thdrt.
(διὰ τῆς πίστεως) : ἐν π. corresponds to
ἐν σαρκί : *faith*, and *not the flesh*, is the
real element in which I live) faith, viz.
that (the article particularizes, what sort
of faith) of (having for its object, see on
ver. 16) the Son of God (so named for
solemnity, and because His eternal Sonship is the source of His life-giving power,
cf. John v. 25, 26) who loved me (the
link, which binds the eternal Son of God
to me) and (proved that love, in that He)
gave Himself up (to death) for me (on
my behalf. 21.] I do not (as thou
(Peter) art doing, and the Judaizers)
frustrate (reff. : not merely '*despise*,' as
Erasm., al.) the grace of God : for (justification of the strong expression ἀθετῶ)
if by the law (comes) righteousness (not
justification—but *the result of justification*), then Christ died without cause (not
'*in vain*,' with reference to the *result* of
His death (for which meaning Lidd. and
Scott's Lex. refers to LXX : but it does
not appear to occur in that sense), but
gratuitously, causelessly (reff.) ;—' *Christ
need not have died.*' εἰ γὰρ ἀπέθανεν ὁ
χριστός, εὔδηλον ὅτι διὰ τὸ μὴ ἰσχύειν τὸν
νόμον ἡμᾶς δικαιοῦν· εἰ δὲ ὁ νόμος δικαιοῖ,
περιττὸς ὁ τοῦ χριστοῦ θάνατος. Chr.).
οὕτω ταῦτα διεξελθὼν ἐκ τῆς πρὸς τὸν
τρισμακάριον (truly so in this case, in
having found such a faithful reprover)
Πέτρον διαλέξεως, πρὸς αὐτοὺς λοιπὸν

ἀποτείνεται, κ. βαρυθυμῶν ἀποφθέγγεται.
Thdrt.

CH. III. 1—V. 12.] SECOND, or PO-
LEMICAL PART OF THE EPISTLE.   1.]
The Apostle exclaims indignantly, moved
by the fervour and truth of his rebuke of
Peter, against the folly of the Galatians,
for suffering themselves to be bewitched
out of their former vivid apprehension of
Christ's work and Person.   ἀνόητοι
must not, with Jer., be taken as an allusion to any supposed national stupidity of
the Galatians (Wetst. on ch. i. 6, cites from
Themistius a very different description :
οἱ ἄνδρες . . . ὀξεῖς κ. ἀγχίνοι κ. εὐμα-
θέστεροι τῶν ἄγαν Ἑλλήνων) : it merely
springs out of the occasion : see ref. Luke.

ὑμᾶς has the emphasis—'YOU, to
whom,' &c.   ἐβάσκανεν] Not with
Chr. al., '*envied*,' in which sense the verb
usually takes a dative : so Thom. Mag.,
βασκαίνω, οὐ μόνον ἀντὶ τοῦ φθονῶ, ὅπερ
πρὸς δοτικὴν συντάσσεται, ἀλλὰ καὶ ἀντὶ
τοῦ μέμφομαι κ. διαβάλλω παρὰ τοῖς παλαιοῖς εὕρηται, κ. συντάσσεται μετὰ αἰτια-
τικήν (not always, cf. Sir. xiv. 6) ; but, as
E. V. bewitched,—fascinated : so Aristot.
Probl. xx. 34, διὰ τί τὸ πήγανον βασκα-
νίας φασὶ φάρμακον εἶναι ; ἢ διότι βασ-
καίνεσθαι δοκοῦσι λάβρως ἐσθίοντες ; . . .
ἐπιλέγουσι γοῦν, ὅταν τῆς αὐτῆς τραπέ-
ζης ἰδίᾳ τι προσφέρωνται, μεταδιδόντες,
"ἵνα μὴ βασκάνῃς με."   κατ᾽ ὀφθ.]
openly,—before your eyes : so ἵνα σοι
κατ᾽ ὀφθαλμοὺς λέγῃ, Aristoph. Ran. 625 ;
cf. κατ᾽ ὄμμα, Eur. Androm. 1040, κρυπτὸς καταστάς, ἢ κατ᾽ ὄμμ᾽ ἐλθὼν μάχῃ ;
προεγράφη] was described before,
as in reff. It has been variously explained,
(1) '*depicted before you.*' So Œc., Thl.
(Chrys. ?), Erasm., Luth., Calv., Winer,
Rückert, Jowett, &c. But προγράφειν
cannot be shewn to have any such meaning ; nor (see below) is it required (as
Jow.) by the context. (2) '*palam scriptus
est :*' so Estius, Elsner, Bengel, al. But
this, although an allowable meaning (τῆς
δίκης προγεγραμμένης αὐτῷ, διὰ πένθος

x = Acts xxiii.
27. Esth.iv.
5. 2 Macc.
vii. 2.
y = ch. ii. 16
reff.
z Acts viii. 15,
17, 19. xix. 2
al.
a = Rom. x.

ἐσταυρωμένος; ² τοῦτο μόνον θέλω ˣ μαθεῖν ἀφ᾽ ὑμῶν, ᵞ ἐξ ἔργων νόμου τὸ ᶻ πνεῦμα ᶻ ἐλάβετε ἢ ἐξ ᵃ ἀκοῆς πίστεως; ³ ᵇ οὕτως ᶜ ἀνόητοί ἐστε; ᵈ ἐναρξάμενοι ᵉ πνεύματι νῦν ᵉ σαρκὶ ᶠ ἐπιτελεῖσθε; ⁴ τοσαῦτα ᵍ ἐπάθετε ʰ εἰκῆ;

ABCDF
KLPℵ a
b c d e f
g h k l m
n o 17. 47

16 (from Isa. liii. 1), 17.   1 Thess. ii. 13 al].   b = Heb. xii. 21.   c ver. 1 reff.   d Phil. i. 6
only.   Deut. ii. 24, 25, 31,   e dat. of manner, 1 Cor. ix. 7. x1. 5 al.   Winer, § 31. 7.   f Rom. xv.
28.   2 Cor. vii. 1.   Phil. i. 6 al.   1 Kings iii. 12.   g Paul, 1 Cor. xii. 26.   2 Cor. i. 6.   Phil. i.
29.   1 Thess. ii. 14.   2 Thess. i. 5.   2 Tim. i. 12 only. see note.   h here bis.   ch. iv. 11.   Matt. v.
22.   Rom. xiii. 4.   1 Cor. xv. 2.   Col. ii. 18 only.   Prov. xxviii. 25 only.

2. μαθειν bef θελω D¹·³F.

οἰκούρει, Plut. Camill. 11), would not suit ἐν ὑμῖν (see below). (3) '*prosoriptus est.*' So Vulg., Ambr., Aug., Lyra. (προΰγραφεν αὐτοὺς φυγάδας, Polyb. xxxii. 21. 12; οἱ προγεγραμμένοι, ib. 22. 1.) But this is quite irrelevant to the context. It is best therefore to keep to St. Paul's own meaning of προγράφειν, and understand it to refer to the time when he preached Christ among them, which he represents as a previous description in writing of Christ, in their hearts and before their eyes. Jerome, Hermann, al., understand it as above, '*olim scriptus est*,' interpreting it, however, of the prophecies of the O. T. But not to mention that no prophecy sets Him forth as ἐσταυρωμένος, the whole passage (cf. vv. 2—5) evidently refers to the time when the Apostle preached among them. (See more in De W. and Meyer, from whom the above is mainly taken.) (The ἐν ὑμῖν of the rec. could hardly belong to ἐσταυρωμένος; for if so, it would more naturally be ἐσταυρ. ἐν ὑμῖν, the emphasis, as it now stands, being on ἐν ὑμῖν: but it must belong to προεγράφη, as above, and as in 2 Cor. iii. 2,— 'in animis vestris.' So Mey. Among the various meanings proposed,—'among you' (E. V., &c., De W., Rück.), 'on account of you' (Koppe, but wrongly, see ch. i. 24, note),—Luther's is the most remarkable : "jam non solum abjecistis gratiam Dei, non solum Christus frustra vobis mortuus est, sed turpissime in vobis crucifixus est. Ad eum modum loquitur et Epistola ad Ebr. vi. 6: denuo crucifigentes sibimetipsis filium Dei, &c." This again is condemned by the context, and indeed by the aor. προεγράφη.) ἐσταυρωμένος, as expressing the whole mystery of redemption by grace, and of freedom from legal obligation. ' It has an echo of συνεσταύρωμαι in ch. ii. 20.' Jowett. 2.] τ. μόνον,—not to mention all the *other* grounds on which I might rest my argument, '*this only*,' &c. διὰ συντόμου λόγου κ. ταχίστης ἀποδείξεως ὑμᾶς πεῖσαι βούλομαι. Chr. μαθεῖν, be informed: not to be pressed, as Luther, al. (" Agite nunc, respondete mihi discipulo vestro, tam subito enim facti estis docti, ut mei

jam sitis praeceptores et doctores"), but taken in its ordinary sense, see reff. **Did ye from** (as its ground, see ch. ii. 16) the **works of the Law** (not a Law) **receive the Spirit** (evidently here to be taken as including *all His gifts*, spiritual and external : not as Chr., Thl., Jer., χαρίσματα only : for the two are distinguished in ver. 5), **or from the hearing of faith** (meaning either, '*that preaching which proclaimed faith*,' or '*that hearing, which received (the) faith*.' The first is preferable, because (1) where their first receiving the Gospel is in question, the *preaching* of it would probably be hinted at, as it is indeed taken up by the οὖν below, ver. 5 : (2) where the question is concerning the power of faith as contrasted with the works of the law, faith would most likely be *subjective*. But certainly we must not understand it '*obedience* (ὑπακ. Rom. i. 5; xvi. 26. See 1 Kings xv. 22) *to the faith*,' as Wahl, al., which would spoil the contrast here)? 3.] **Are ye so** (to such an extent, emph.) **foolish** (as viz. the following fact would prove)? **Having begun** (see Phil. i. 6, where the same two verbs occur together, and 2 Cor. viii. 6, where προενήρξατο is followed by ἐπιτελέσῃ. Understand, ' the Christian life') **in the Spirit** (dative of the manner in which, reff. The Spirit, i. e. the Holy Spirit, guiding and ruling the spiritual life, as the 'essence and active principle' (Ellic.) of Christianity,—contrasted with the flesh,—the element in which the law worked), **are ye now being completed** (passive here, not mid., cf. Phil. i. 6, where the active is used: and for the passive, Luke xiii. 32. The middle does not appear to occur in the N. T., though it does in classical Greek, e.g. Polyb. ii. 58. 10, μηθὲν ἀσεβὲς ἐπιτελεσαμένοις. Diod. Sic. xii. 54, μεγάλας πράξεις ἐπιτελεσάμενοι) in (dative, as above) **the flesh**? 4.] **Did ye suffer** (not, '*have ye suffered*,' as almost all Commentators, E. V., &c.,— i. e. πεπόνθατε, Heb. ii. 18; Luke xiii. 2) **so many things in vain**? There is much controversy about the meaning. (1) Chrys., Aug., and the ancients, Grot., Wolf, Rück., Olsh., &c., understand it of the sufferings

[i] εἴ γε καὶ [h] εἰκῆ. 5 ὁ οὖν [k] ἐπιχορηγῶν ὑμῖν τὸ πνεῦμα
καὶ [l] ἐνεργῶν [m] δυνάμεις ἐν ὑμῖν [y] ἐξ ἔργων νόμου ἢ ἐξ
[a] ἀκοῆς πίστεως ; 6 καθὼς Ἀβραὰμ [n] ἐπίστευσεν τῷ θεῷ,

i = 2 Cor. v. 3. Col. i. 23.
k 2 Cor. ix. 10. Col. ii. 19.
2 Pet. i. 5, 11 only †.
Sir. xxv. 22

only. (-γία, Eph. iv. 16. Phil. i. 19.)
22. xix. 11. 1 Cor. xii. 10, 28 ‡.

l ch. ii. 8 reff.
n w. dat., GEN. xv. 6. John v. 24.

m = Matt. vii. 22. Acts ii.
Acts xvi. 34.

5. aft νομου ins (see ver 2) το πνευμα ελαβετε A.
6. καθως γεγραπται Επιστευσεν αβρ. F.

which the Galatians underwent at the time of their reception of the Gospel. And, I believe, rightly. For (a) πάσχω occurs (see reff.) seven times in St. Paul, and always in the strict sense of 'suffering,' by persecution, or hardship (similarly in Heb., 1 Pet., &c.): (b) the historic aorist here marks the reference to be to some definite time. Now the time referred to by the context is that of their conversion to the Gospel, cf. τὸ πν. ἐλάβετε,—ἐναρξάμενοι πνεύματι above. Therefore the meaning is, **Did ye undergo all those sufferings** (not specially mentioned in this Epistle, but which every convert to Christ must have undergone as a matter of course) **in vain** (Schomer first, and after him many, and Winer, B.-Crus., De Wette, understand παθεῖν here in a good sense, in reference to divine grace bestowed on them. But πάσχω seems never to be thus used in Greek without an indication in the context of such a meaning, e. g. εὖ πάσχειν, or as in Jos. Antt. iii. 15. 1, ὅσα παθόντες ἐξ αὐτοῦ κ. πηλικῶν εὐεργεσιῶν μεταλαβόντες, where the added clause defines the παθόντες; and never in N. T., LXX nor Apocrypha at all. (3) Bengel refers it to their patience with Paul (patientissime sustinuistis pertulistisque me); but this, as Meyer remarks, would be expressed by ἀνέχειν, hardly by πάσχειν. (4) Meyer, to the troubles of their bondage introduced by the false and judaizing teachers. But not to dwell on other objections, it is decisive against this, (a) that it would thus be present, πάσχετε (see ch. iv. 10), not past at all, and (b) that even if it might be past, it must be the perfect and not the aorist. I therefore hold to (1); οὐ γὰρ ὑπὲρ τοῦ νόμου ἀλλ' ὑπὲρ τοῦ χριστοῦ τὰ παθήματα, Thdrt.: πάντα γὰρ ἐκεῖνα, φησίν, ἅπερ ὑπεμείνατε, ζημιῶσαι ὑμᾶς οὗτοι βούλονται, κ. τὸν στέφανον ὑμῶν ἁρπάσαι. Chrys. (So Ellic. ed. 2.) When Meyer says that this meaning is ganz isolirt vom Context, he is surely speaking at random: see above. (Ellic. ed. 1 took ἐπάθετε in a neutral sense, as applying to both persecutions and blessings, and nearly so Jowett: 'Had ye all these experiences in vain ?' objecting to (1) that it is unlike the whole spirit of the Apostle. But we find surely a trace of the same spirit in

Phil. 29, i. 30; as there suffering is represented as a special grace from Christ, so here it might well be said, 'let not such grace have been received in vain')) ? **if it be really in vain** (on εἴ γε καί, see note on 2 Cor. v. 3 : the construction is, 'if, as it must be, what I have said, εἰκῆ, is really the fact.' The Commentators all take it as a supposition,—some, as Chr., &c., E.V., 'if it be yet in vain,' as a softening of εἰκῆ, others, as Meyer, De W., al., as an intensification of it, 'if it be only in vain (and not something worse)'). 5.] οὖν takes up again the question of ver. 2, and asks it in another form. There is a question whether the participles ἐπιχορηγῶν and ἐνεργῶν are present, referring to things done among them while the Apostle was writing, or imperfect, still spoken of the time when he was with them ? Chrys., Thdrt., &c., and Bengel, al., maintain the latter : Luth., Calv., Rück., Meyer, De W., &c., the former. It seems to me, that this question must be settled by first determining who is the agent here spoken of. Is it the Apostle ? or is it not rather GOD, and is not this indicated by the reference to Abraham's faith in the next verse, and the taking up the passive ἐλογίσθη by δικαιοῖ ὁ θεός in ver. 8 ? If it be so, then the participles here must be taken as present, but indefinite, in a substantive sense (Winer), as ὁ διώκων ἡμᾶς ποτέ, ch. i. 23. And certainly God alone can be said (and so in ref. 2 Cor.) ἐπιχορηγεῖν τὸ πνεῦμα, and ἐνεργεῖν (ch. ii. 8) δυνάμεις ἐν ὑμῖν (see below). ἐπιχορ.] The ἐπί does not imply addition, but as so often with prepositions of motion in composition, the direction of the supply : see notes on Acts xxvii. 7; Rom. viii. 16.

δυνάμεις] here, not merely miracles or χαρίσματα, though those are included : nor is ἐν ὑμῖν, 'among you;' but δυν. are the wonders wrought by divine Power **in you** (cf. θεὸς ὁ ἐνεργῶν τὰ πάντα ἐν πᾶσιν, 1 Cor. xii. 6. θεὸς γάρ ἐστιν ὁ ἐνεργῶν ἐν ὑμῖν τὸ θέλειν κ.τ.λ. Phil. ii. 13. Eph. ii. 2; also Matt. xiv. 2), viz. at your conversion and since. ἐξ ἔργ.] (supply **does He it**) **in consequence of** ("as the originating or moving cause," Ellic.) **the works of the law, or in consequence of the hearing** (see above,

o = Rom. ii. 26
al. Prov.
xvii. 28.
p = Acts x. 4.
xix. 27.
Rom. ix. 8
& passim.
Wisd. ix. 6.
q Rom. ii. 8.
iii. 26. iv. 12,
14 al.
r Acts ii. 31

καὶ ᵒ ἐλογίσθη αὐτῷ ᴾ εἰς δικαιοσύνην. ⁷ γινώσκετε ἄρα
ὅτι οἱ ᑫ ἐκ πίστεως, οὗτοί εἰσιν υἱοὶ 'Αβραάμ. ⁸ ʳ προ-
ιδοῦσα δὲ ἡ ˢ γραφὴ ὅτι ᑫ ἐκ πίστεως ᵗ δικαιοῖ τὰ ἔθνη ὁ
θεός, ᵘ προευηγγελίσατο τῷ 'Αβραὰμ ὅτι ᵛ ἐνευλογηθήσονται ἐν σοὶ πάντα τὰ ἔθνη. ⁹ ὥστε οἱ ᑫ ἐκ πίστεως ʷ εὐλο-

ABCDF
KLPℵ a
b c d e f
g h k l m
n o 17. 47

only. = Ps. cxxxviii. 3. Wisd. xix. 1. see Gen. xxxvii. 18.
17. John vii. 38 al. t ch. ii. 16 reff.
only. GEN. xii. 3 Ed-vat. xxii. 18. xxvi. 4.

s γρ., personified, Rom. iv. 3. ix.
u here only †. see note. v Acts iii. 25
w = Acts iii. 26. Eph. i. 3. Heb. vi. 14 al. Gen. xii. 3.

7. [for αρα, γαρ P.]   om οἱ C¹(appy).   υιοι bef εισιν Bℵ¹ Chr Thdrt Iren-int₁
[Victorin] Ambr.

8. [for δε, γαρ P.]   τα εθνη bef δικαιοι ℵ m.   προευηγγελισται D¹ 67².
elz (for ενευλ.) ευλογηθ., with F h n : txt ABCDKL[P]ℵ rel Cyr Thdrt Damasc Œc

ver. 2) of faith ?   6—9.] *Abraham's
faith was his entrance into righteousness before God : and Scripture, in recording this, records also God's promise to him, by virtue of which all the
faithful inherit his blessing.*   6.] The
reply to the foregoing question is understood : it is ἐξ ἀκοῆς πίστεως. And then
enters the thought of God's ἐνεργεῖν as
following upon Abraham's faith. The
fact of justification being now introduced,
whereas before the ἐπιχορηγεῖν τὸ πνεῦμα
was the matter enquired of, is no real
departure from the subject, for both these
belong to the ἐνάρξασθαι of ver. 3,—are
concomitant, and inseparable. On the
verse, see note, Rom. iv. 3.   7.]
γινώσκ. is better taken indicatively, with
Jer., Ambr., Beza, Rück., al., than imperatively, with most Commentators (and
Mey., De W., Olsh., Ellic.). It is no objection to the indicative that such knowledge could not well be predicated of the
Galatians : it is not so predicated, but is
here set before them as a thing which
they ought to be acquainted with—**from
this then you know** (q. d. 'omnibus
patet.' The imperative seems to me to
lose the fine edge of the Apostle's argumentative irony : besides that the usage
of that mood with ἄρα is not frequent :
indeed apparently only to be found in
Homer ; cf. Il. κ. 249 ; ω. 522. See on
the other side, Ellicott's note here).
οἱ ἐκ πίστεως] see Rom. ii. 8 ; iii. 26,
and notes, **those who are of faith**, as
the origin and the ἀφορμή of their spiritual life.   οὗτοι] emphatic ; **these**,
and these only (see Rom. viii. 14), not
οἱ ἐξ ἔργων. Chrys. says οὐχ οἱ τὴν
φυσικὴν ἔχοντες πρὸς αὐτὸν συγγένειαν :
but this point is not here raised : besides, they might be, as well as others,
if they were ἐκ πίστεως, see Rom. iv. 16.
υἱοὶ 'Αβρ.] see Rom. iv. 11—17,
and notes.   8.] **But** (transitional
(see Ellicott's note)) **the Scripture** (as
we say, Nature : meaning, the Author

of the Scripture ; see reff.) foreseeing
(Schöttgen, Hor. Hebr. i. 732, gives examples of 'quid vidit Scriptura ?' and the
like, as common sayings among the Jews)
that of faith (emphatic,—'*and not of
works*') **God justifieth** (present, not merely
as Mey., De W., al., because the time
foreseen was regarded as present, nor
'respectu Pauli scribentis,' as Bengel,—
but because it was God's *one* way of
justification—He never justified in any
other way—so that it is the normal present, q. d. 'is a God that justifieth') **the
Gentiles** (observe, there is no *stress* here
on τὰ ἔθνη,—it is not ἐκ πίστεως καὶ τὰ
ἔθνη δικαιοῖ ὁ θ. : so that, as is remarked
above, no question is raised between the
carnal and spiritual seed of Abraham,—
nor, as Bengel, 'δέ vim argumenti ex-
tendit etiam ad *gentes :*' the question is
between those who were ἐκ πίστεως, and
those who wanted to return to the ἔργα
νόμου, whether Jews or Gentiles. So
that in fact τὰ ἔθνη must be here taken
in its widest sense, as in the Abrahamic
promise soon to be quoted) **announced
the good news beforehand** (the word is
found only in Philo, and in this sense :—
ἑσπέρα τε καὶ πρωΐα, ὧν ἡ μὲν προευαγ-
γελίζεται μέλλοντα ἥλιον ἀνίσχειν, de
Mundi Opif. § 9, vol. i. p. 7, and de mut.
nom. § 29, p. 602, ὃς (viz. ὁ νεοττὸς)
. . . . . τοὺς ταρσοὺς διασείειν φιλεῖ, τὴν
ἐλπίδα τοῦ πέτεσθαι δυνήσεσθαι προευαγ-
γελιζόμενος) **to Abraham :** (ὅτι recitative) **In thee** (not, '*in thy seed*,' which
is a point not here raised ; but strictly
in thee, as followers of thy faith, it
having first shewn the way to justification before God. That the words
will bear that other reference, does not
shew that it must be introduced here)
shall all the Gentiles (see above : not
to be restricted with Meyer, al., to
its narrower sense, but expressing, from
Gen. xviii. 18 ; xxii. 18, in a form suiting
better the Apostle's present argument,
the πᾶσαι αἱ φυλαὶ τῆς γῆς of Gen.

γοῦνται σὺν τῷ ˣ πιστῷ 'Αβραάμ. 10 ὅσοι γὰρ ᑫ ἐξ ἔργων
νόμου εἰσίν, ʸ ὑπὸ ᶻ κατάραν ʸ εἰσίν· γέγραπται γὰρ ὅτι
ᵃ ἐπικατάρατος πᾶς ὃς οὐκ ᵇ ἐμμένει ἐν πᾶσιν τοῖς γεγραμμένοις ἐν τῷ βιβλίῳ τοῦ νόμου, ᶜ τοῦ ποιῆσαι αὐτά.
11 ᵈ ὅτι δὲ ᵉ ἐν νόμῳ οὐδεὶς ᵉ δικαιοῦται ᶠ παρὰ τῷ θεῷ
ᵈᵍ δῆλον, ὅτι ʰ ὁ δίκαιος ἐκ πίστεως ζήσεται· 12 ὁ δὲ νόμος
οὐκ ἔστιν ἐκ πίστεως, ἀλλ' ⁱ ὁ ποιήσας αὐτὰ ζήσεται ἐν
αὐτοῖς. 13 χριστὸς ἡμᾶς ʲ ἐξηγόρασεν ἐκ τῆς ᵏ κατάρας

x = John xx. 27. so δίκαιον Λώτ, 2 Pet. ii. 7.
y Rom. iii. 9. 1 Cor. ix. 20.
z ver. 13 bis. Heb. vi. 8. James iii. 10. 2 Pet. ii. 14 only. Gen. xxvii. 12, 13.
a DEUT. xxvii. 26. (John vii. 49 v. 7.) 13 only.
b constr., Heb. viii. 9, from Jer. xxxviii. (xxxi.) 32

only. w. dat., Acts xiv. 22. absol., Acts xxviii. 30 only.
12. vii. 19 al. 3 Kings xvi. 19. Winer, § 44. 4.
39. Rom. v. 9. 1 Cor. vi. 11.
only. Num. xxvii. 21. h HAB. ii. 4.
v. 16. Col. iv. 5 only. Dan. ii. 8 only.)
k ver. 10.
c constr., Matt. xxi. 32. Acts iii.
d 1 Cor. xv. 27 only.
f = Rom. ii. 13. 1 Cor. iii. 19 al.
i LEVIT. xviii. 5.
e = Acts xiii.
g Matt. xxvi. 73
j = ch. iv. 5 only. (Eph.

10. rec om οτι, with KL rel vulg syrr [Orig₁] Chr Thdrt: ins ABCDF[P]א 17 arm Cyr₁
Damasc. om 1st εν Bא¹ m 17. 67² [Cyr₄-p] Damasc. εγγεγραμμενοις B[: om 47].
11. [P def.] om τω [bef θεω] D¹F. om δηλον F. ins γεγραπται γαρ bef
2nd οτι D¹F.
12. αλλα D¹א. rec aft αυτα ins ανθρωπος, with D³KL rel [syr-mg]: om A(appy)
BCD¹F[P]א 17. 67² latt syrr copt æth arm Mcion-e Chr Cyr Damasc Ambrst Aug
Jer. εν αυτω F. (not F-lat.)

xii. 3) be blessed. 9.] Consequence
of ἐνευλογηθήσονται above, substantiated
by ver. 10 below. A share in Abraham's
blessing must be the accompaniment of
faith, not of works of the law
πίστεως has the emphasis. σύν, to
shew their community with him in the
blessing: τῷ πιστῷ, to shew wherein the
community consists, viz. FAITH.
10.] substantiation of ver. 9: they ἐξ
ἔργων νόμου cannot be sharers in the
blessing, for they are accursed; it being
understood that they do not and cannot
ἐμμένειν ἐν πᾶσιν &c.: see this expanded
in Rom. iii. 9—20. The citation is freely
from the LXX. On τοῦ ποιῆσαι, not a
Hebraism, but a construction common
in later Greek, see Ellic.'s note.
11, 12.] 'contain a perfect syllogism, so
that ὁ δίκ. ἐκ πίστ. ζήσεται is the major
proposition, ver. 12 the minor, and ἐν
νόμῳ οὐδ. δικ. παρὰ τ. θεῷ the consequence.' Meyer. It is inserted to
strengthen the inference of the former
verse, by shewing that not even could a
man keep the law, would he be justified—
the *condition* of justification, as revealed
in Scripture, being that it is *by faith.*
But (= moreover) that in (not merely
the *elemental* in, but the *conditional* as
well: 'in and by:' not 'through') the
law no man is justified (the *normal*
present: is, in God's order of things)
with God (not emphatic as Bengel, 'quicquid sit apud homines:' this would require οὐδεὶς παρὰ τῷ θεῷ δικαιοῦται:
but δικαιοῦται-παρὰ-τῷ-θεῷ is simply
predicated of οὐδείς) is evident, for (it is
written, that) the just by faith shall live

(not '*the just shall live by his faith*,' as
Winer, De W., al. The order of the words
would indeed suggest this rendering, seeing that ὁ ἐκ π. δ. ζ. would properly represent the other: but we must regard
St. Paul's logical use of the citation: and
I think, with Meyer, that he has abstained from altering the order of the
words as being well known. He is not
seeking to shew *by what* the righteous
shall live, but the *ground itself* of *that
righteousness* which shall *issue in life;*
and the contrast is between ὁ δίκαιος ἐκ
πίστεως and ὁ ποιήσας αὐτά. It is right
to say that Ellic. (both edd.) prefers the
other rendering, and supports it by the
fact that the original Hebrew will not bear
this one, and that St. Paul adopts the
words of the LXX as they stand; and by
the contrast between ζήσεται ἐκ πίστεως,
and ζήσεται ἐν αὐτοῖς. Jowett doubts
whether ζήσεται could be used absolutely:
but see Heb. xii. 9. I still however prefer
rendering as above. The construction
desiderated by Bp. Middleton to suit our
rendering,—ὁ δίκαιος ὁ ἐκ π.,—would stultify the sentence, by bringing into view
other δίκαιοι, who were not ἐκ πίστεως):
but (logical, introducing the minor of
the syllogism: see above) the law (not
'law, as such,' Peile: no such consideration appears here, nor any where, except
in so far as the law of Moses is treated
of as possessing the qualities of law
in general) is not of (does not spring
from nor belong to: 'non agit fidei
partes,' Beng.) faith: but (ſondern) (its
nature is such that) he who has done them
(viz. πάντα τὰ προστάγματά μου κ. π.

l = John vi.
51. xvii. 19.
Rom. v. 6.
m (Deut. xxi.
23, κεκατη-
ραμένος
ὑπὸ θεου.)
ver. 10, from
Deut. xxvii.
26.
n Acts v. 30.
x. 39 only.
Gen. xl. 19.

τοῦ νόμου, γενόμενος ¹ὑπὲρ ἡμῶν ᵏκατάρα, ὅτι γέγραπται ᵐἘπικατάρατος πᾶς ὁ ⁿᵒκρεμάμενος ἐπὶ ⁿ ξύλου, ¹⁴ ἵνα
ᵖ εἰς τὰ ἔθνη ἡ qʳ εὐλογία τοῦ ʳˢἈβραὰμ ᵗγένηται ἐν
χριστῷ Ἰησοῦ, ἵνα τὴν ᵘἐπαγγελίαν τοῦ πνεύματος λά-
βωμεν διὰ τῆς πίστεως.

ABCDF
KLPℵ a
b c d e f
g h k l m
n o 17. 47

o = as above (n). Luke xxiii. 39. (Matt. xviii. 6. xxii. 40. Acts xxviii. 4 only.)   p = Rom.
iii. 22. 2 Cor. viii. 14 (see Acts xxi. 17. xxv. 15).   q 1 Cor. x. 16. Heb. vi. 7 al.   r Gen. xxviii. 4.
s gen. obj., Rom. xv. 8.   t = 2 Cor. viii. 14. Matt. xviii. 19.   u Luke xxiv. 49. Acts i. 4.
ii. 33, 39 al. fr. Amos ix. 6.

13. rec (for οτι γεγρ.) γεγρ. γαρ, with D³KL[P]ℵ rel syrr copt Iren-gr Did Chr Cyr
Thdrt: txt ABCD¹F 17 latt, Eus Damasc Iren-int Jer Ambrst Hil Aug.
14. ιησ. bef χρ. Bℵ Syr [æth].   for επαγγ., ευλογιαν D¹F k Tert Ambrst Vig.
(not F.-lat.)

τὰ κρίματά μου of Levit. xviii. 5) **shall
live in** (conditional element) **them** (see
Rom. x. 5).   **13.**] But this curse has
been removed by the redemption of Christ.
The joyful contrast is introduced abruptly,
without any connecting particle : see an
asyndeton in a similar case in Col. iii. 4.
The ἡμᾶς is emphatic, and applies solely
to the JEWS. *They only* were under the
curse of ver. 10,—and they being by Christ
redeemed from that curse, the blessing of
Abraham (justification by faith), which was
always destined by God to flow through
the Jews to the Gentiles, was set at liberty
thus to flow out to the Gentiles. This,
which is Meyer's view, is certainly the
only one which suits the context. To
make ἡμᾶς refer to Jews and Gentiles, and
refer ἡ κατ. τοῦ νόμ. to the law of conscience, is to break up the context altogether.   ἐξηγόρ.] See, besides reff.,
1 Cor. vi. 20; vii. 23; 2 Pet. ii. 1; Rev.
v. 9. Ellicott remarks, 'the ἐξ- need not
be very strongly pressed, see Polyb. iii. 42
2, ἐξηγόρασε παρ᾽ αὐτῶν τά τε μονόξυλα
πλοῖα κ.τ.λ. . . . . The tendency,' he continues, 'to use verbs compounded with
prepositions without any obvious increase
of meaning, is one of the characteristics of
later Greek: so Thiersch, de Pentat. vers.
alex. ii. 1, p. 83.'   The form of the idea
is,—the Law (personified) held us (Jews)
under its curse; (**out of this**) **Christ
bought us,** BECOMING (emphatic, standing
first) **a curse** (not ἐπικατάρατος, concrete,
but κατάρα, abstract, to express that he
became not only accursed, but the curse,
coextensive with the disability which
affected us) **for us** (the JEWS again. Not,
as many older Commentators, and Rück..
Olsh., Peile, &c., '*instead of us,*' but '*on
our behalf.*' It *was* in our stead; but
that circumstance is not expressed by
ὑπέρ used of Christ's death for us—see
reff. and Ellic.'s note; and Usteri, Paulin.
Lehrbegriff, p. 115 ff.).   **ὅτι γέγρ.**
κ.τ.λ. is a parenthesis, justifying the formal

expression γενόμ. ὑπ. ἡμ. κατάρα. The
citation omits the words ὑπὸ θεοῦ of the
LXX. They were not to the point here,
being understood as matter of course, the
law being *God's* law. The article ὁ is
not in the LXX. The words are spoken
of hanging *after death by stoning;* and
are given in l. c. as a reason why the body
should not remain on the tree all night,
because one hanging on a tree is accursed
of God. Such formal curse then extended
to Christ, who *died* by hanging on a tree.
     14.] **in order that** (the intent of
γενόμ. ὑπ. ἡμ. κατάρα) **the blessing of
Abraham** (promised to Abraham : i. e.
justification by faith ; ver. 9) **might be**
(come) **upon the Gentiles** (not, all nations,
but strictly the Gentiles: see above on
ver. 13) **in** (in and by, *conditional element*) **Jesus the Christ, that** (ἵνα, parallel
with, not dependent on and included in,
the former ἵνα : for this clause has no
longer to do with τὰ ἔθνη, see below. We
have a second ἵνα co-ordinate with a first
in Rom. vii. 13 ; 2 Cor. ix. 3 ; Eph. vi.
19, 20) **we** (not emphatic, nor is ἡμεῖς expressed: no longer the Jews, as Beza and
Bengel, but all Christians: see Jowett's
note, which perhaps is too finely drawn)
might receive (in full, as fulfilled, aor.)
through the (or, but not so usually, *our*)
faith (as the subjective medium : but rendered objective by the article, as so often
by St. Paul : no *stress* on διὰ τ. π.) **the
promise of the Spirit** (viz. that made
Joel ii. 28. See Acts ii. 17, 33; Luke
xxiv. 49,—THE PROMISE of the new covenant). The genitive τοῦ πν. is objective,
—the Spirit being the thing promised.
But let me guard tiros against the old
absurdity, " ἐπαγγελία τοῦ πνεύματος pro
τὸ πνεῦμα τὸ ἐπηγγελμένον," which would
destroy, here and every where else, the
logical form of the sentence. This ' receiving the promise of the Spirit' distinctly refers back to ver. 2, where he
asked them whether they received the

¹⁵ Ἀδελφοί, ᵛʷκατὰ ᵛʷἄνθρωπον ʷ λέγω· ˣὅμως ἀνθρώπου ᵞ κεκυρωμένην ᶻ διαθήκην οὐδεὶς ᵃἀθετεῖ ἢ ᵇἐπιδιατάσσεται. ¹⁶ τῷ δὲ Ἀβραὰμ ᶜἐρρέθησαν αἱ ᵈἐπαγγελίαι καὶ τῷ ᵉσπέρματι αὐτοῦ. οὐ ᶠλέγει Καὶ τοῖς σπέρμασιν, ὡς ᵍἐπὶ πολλῶν, ἀλλ' ὡς ᵍἐφ' ἑνὸς Καὶ τῷ σπέρματί σου,

v ch. i. 11.
w Rom. iii. 5.
(1 Cor. ix. 8.)
x (=) John xii. 42. 1 Cor. xiv. 7 only.
2 Macc. xv.5.
y 2 Cor. ii. 8 only. Gen. xxiii. 20. Levit. xxv. 30 only.
c Matt. v.
e Acts iii.
g = Heb. vii.

z 1 Cor. xi. 25 al. fr. Deut. ix. 5 al. 21, &c. 25. Gen. xiii. 15. xvii. 8. 11 (?) only (see 2 Cor. vii. 14).
a ch. ii. 20 reff. d plur., = Rom. ix. 4. xv. 8. 2 Cor. i. 20. vii. 1. Heb. vi. 13 al⁵. f = Rom. xv. 10 [11]. see 1 Cor. vi. 16. = w. acc., Mark ix. 12.
b here only †.

15. κατα ανθρωπον λεγω bef αδελφοι A arm Damasc. προκεκυρωμενην (see ver 17) C 17 Chr·ms. επιτασσεται D¹.

16. om δε D¹F latt [Iren] Chr lat-ff. (ερρεθησαν, so AB¹(ita cod) CD¹F[P]‭א‬ c (d) e f h 17 Cyr₂ Thdrt₃ Damasc.) aft σπερμασιν ins σου D¹ [copt æth]. αλλα B.

Spirit by the works of the law, or by the hearing of faith? "Here is a pause, at which the indignant feeling of the Apostle softens, and he begins the new train of thought which follows with words of milder character, and proceeds more quietly with his argument." Windischmann.

15—18.] But what if the law, coming after the Abrahamic promise, *abrogated* that promise? These verses contain the refutation of such an objection: *the promise was not abrogated by the law.*

15.] τί ἐστι κατ' ἄνθρ. λέγω; ἐξ ἀνθρωπίνων παραδειγμάτων. Chr. But (see 1 Cor. xv. 32) the expression refers not only to the character of the example chosen, but to the temporary standing-point of him who speaks: I put myself for the time on a level with ordinary men in the world. ὅμως is out of its logical place, which would be after οὐδεὶς; see on ref. 1 Cor. To make it '*even*' and take it with ἀνθρώπου, is contrary to its usage. A (mere) **man's covenant** (not 'testament,' as Olsh., after Aug., al.; for there is here no introduction of that idea: the promise spoken to Abraham was strictly a *covenant*, and designated διαθήκη in the passages which were now in the Apostle's mind, see Gen. xv. 18; xvii. 7. On the general meaning, see Mr. Bagge's note) **when ratified** (reff.), **no one notwithstanding** (that it is merely a human covenant) **sets aside or supplements** (with new conditions, Jos. Antt. xvii. 9. 4 describes Archelaus as ὁ ἐν ταῖς **ἐπιδιαθήκαις** ὑπὸ τοῦ πατρὸς ἐγγεγραμμένος βασιλεύς,—'in his father's subsequent testament:' and again says of Antipas, B. J. ii. 2. 3, ἀξιῶν τῆς **ἐπιδιαθήκης** τὴν διαθήκην εἶναι κυριωτέραν, ἐν ᾗ βασιλεὺς αὐτὸς ἐγέγραπτο. Nothing is implied as to the nature of the additions, whether consistent or inconsistent with the original covenant: the simple fact that *no additions are made*, is enounced). **16.**] This verse is not, as commonly supposed, the minor proposition

of the syllogism, applying to Abraham's case the general truth enounced in ver. 15: for had it been so, (1) we should certainly find ὑπὸ θεοῦ contrasted with the ἀνθρώπου before, and (2) the parenthesis οὐ λέγει . . . . χριστός would be a mere irrelevant digression. This minor proposition does not follow till ver. 17. What is *now* said, in a parenthetical and subsidiary manner, is this: The covenant was not merely nor principally made with Abraham, but with Abraham *and* HIS SEED, and that seed referred, not to the Jewish people, but to CHRIST. The covenant then was not fulfilled, but awaiting its fulfilment, and He to whom it was made was yet to appear, when the law was given. αἱ ἐπ.] because the promise was many times repeated: e. g. Gen. xii. 7; xv. 5, 18; xvii. 7, 8; xxii. 18. κ. τῷ σπ. αὐ.] These words, on which, from what follows, the stress of the whole argument rests, are probably meant to be a formal quotation. If so, the promises quoted must be Gen. xiii. 15; xvii. 8 (Jowett supposes xxi. 12, but qu.?), where the words occur as here. οὐ λέγει] viz. He who gave the promises —God. ἐπὶ πολ., ἐφ' ἑνός] of many, of one, as E. V. Plato has very nearly this usage, βούλομαι δέ μοι μὴ ἐπὶ θεῶν (de diis) λέγεσθαι τὸ τοιοῦτον, Legg. p. 662 d. See also Rep. 524 e. Cf. Ellic.'s note. τοῖς σπέρμασιν . . . τῷ σπέρματι] The central point of the Apostle's argument is this: The seed to whom the promises were made, was Christ. To confirm this position,—see Gen. xxii. 17, 18, where the collective σπέρμα of ver. 17 is summed up in the individual σπέρμα of ver. 18, he alleges a philological distinction, recognized by the Rabbinical schools (see Wetst. and Schöttgen ad loc.). This has created considerable difficulty: and all sorts of attempts have been made to evade the argument, or to escape standing committed to the dis-

h attr., Mark xv. 16. Eph. i. 14. 1 Tim. iii. 15 al. Winer, § 24. 3. i 1 Cor. i. 12. x. 29. see 1 Cor. vii. 29. xv. 50.

h ὅς ἐστιν χριστός. 17 ᵢ τοῦτο δὲ λέγω, διαθήκην k προ- κεκυρωμένην ὑπὸ τοῦ θεοῦ ὁ μετὰ τετρακόσια καὶ τριά-

k here only †.

ABCDF KLPℵ a b c d e f g h k l m n o 17. 47

for ὅς, ο D¹F², quod Iren-int Tert: ου F¹G, quo G-lat. (qui D-lat F-lat.)

17. rec aft θεου ins εις χριστον, with DFKL rel syrr arm(ed ven) Chr Thdrt Chron Ambrst: om ABC[P]ℵ 17. 67² vulg copt æth [Cyr₃-p] Damasc Jer Aug꜀ₐₑₚₑ Pel Bede. rec ετη bef τετρ. κ. τρ., with KL rel Thdrt Chron: txt ABCDF[P]ℵ a m 17

tinction. Jerome (ad loc.), curiously and characteristically, applies the κατὰ ἄνθρω- πον λέγω to this distinction especially, and thinks that the Apostle used it as adapted to the calibre of those to whom he was writing: "Galatis, quos paulo ante stultos dixerat, factus est stultus." The Roman-Catholic Windischmann, one of the ablest and most sensible of modern expositors, says, "Our recent masters of theology have taken up the objection, which is as old as Jerome, and forgetting that Paul knew Hebrew better than themselves, have severely blamed him for urging the singular σπέρματι here, and thus justify-ing the application to Christ, seeing that the word זָרַע, which occurs here in the Hebrew text, has no plural (Wind. is not accurate here: the plur. זְרָעִים is found 1 Sam. viii. 15, in the sense of 'grains of wheat'), and so could not be used. Yet they are good enough to assume, that Paul had no fraudulent intent, and only followed the arbitrary exegesis of the Jews of his time (Rückert). The argu-ment of the Apostle does not depend on the grammatical form, by which Paul here only puts forth his meaning in Greek,—but on this, that the Spirit of God in the promise to Abraham and the passage of Scripture relating that pro-mise, has chosen a word which implies a collective unity, and that the promise was not given to Abraham *and his children*. Against the prejudice of the carnal Jews, who held that the promise applied to the plurality of them, the individual descend-ants of the Patriarch, as such,—the Apostle maintains the truth, that only the Unity, Christ, with those who are in-corporated in Him, has part in the in-heritance." On these remarks I would observe, (1) that the Apostle's argument is independent of his philology: (2) that his philological distinction must not be pressed to mean more than he himself intended by it: (3) that the *collective and indi-vidual* meanings of σπέρμα are both un-doubted, and must have been evident to the Apostle himself, from what follows, ver. 29. We are now in a position to inter-pret the words ὅς ἐστιν χριστός. Meyer says 'χριστός is the personal Christ Jesus, not, as has been held (after Aug.), Christ

and His Church.' This remark is true, and untrue. χρ. certainly does not mean 'Christ *and* His Church:' but if it im-ports only the personal Christ Jesus, why is it not so expressed, χριστὸς Ἰησοῦς? For the word does not here occur in pass-ing, but is the predicate of a very definite and important proposition. The fact is, that we must place ourselves in St. Paul's position with regard to the idea of Christ, before we can appreciate all he meant by this word here. Christians are, not by a figure, but really, the BODY OF CHRIST: Christ contains His people, and the men-tion even of the personal Christ would bring with it, in the Apostle's mind, the in-clusion of His believing people. This seed is, CHRIST: not merely in the narrower sense, the man Christ Jesus, but Christ the Seed, Christ the Second Adam, Christ the Head of the Body. And that this is so, is plain from vv. 28, 29, which are the key to ὅς ἐστιν χριστός: where he says, πάντες γὰρ ὑμεῖς ΕΙΣ ἐστε ἐν χριστῷ Ἰησοῦ (notice Ἰησοῦ here carefully in-serted, where the Person is indicated). εἰ δὲ ὑμεῖς χριστοῦ, ἄρα τοῦ Ἀβραὰμ ΣΠΕΡΜΑ ΕΣΤΕ, κατ' ἐπαγγελίαν κλη-ρονόμοι. So that while it is necessary for the form of the argument here, to express Him to whom the promises were made, and not the aggregate of his people, after-wards to be identified with Him (but not here in view), yet the Apostle has intro-duced His name in a form not circum-scribing His Personality, but leaving room for the inclusion of His mystical Body.

17.] Enthymematical inference from vv. 15, 16, put in the form of a restate-ment of the argument, as applying to the matters in hand. **This however I say** (this is my meaning, the drift of my previous statement): **the covenant** (better than *a* covenant, as most Commentators; even Meyer and De W.: the emphatic substantive is often anarthrous: cf. the different arrangement in ver. 15) **which was previously ratified by God** (εἰς χρ. being inserted by some to complete the correspondence with ver. 16: the *fact was so*, it was '*to Christ*,' as its second party, that the covenant was ratified by God), **the Law, which took place** (was constituted) **four hundred and thirty**

κοντα ἔτη γεγονὼς νόμος οὐκ [l]ἀκυροῖ [m]εἰς τὸ [n]καταρ-   l Matt. xv. 6 |
γῆσαι τὴν [o]ἐπαγγελίαν. [18] εἰ γὰρ [p]ἐκ νόμου ἡ [q]κληρο-   Mk. only †.
νομία, [r]οὐκ ἔτι [p]ἐξ ἐπαγγελίας· τῷ δὲ ᾿Αβραὰμ [s]δι᾿   Esdr. vi. 32
ἐπαγγελίας [t]κεχάρισται ὁ θεός. [19] [u]τί οὖν ὁ νόμος;   only. (ἄκυ-
                                                     ρον ποιεῖν,
                                                     Prov. i. 25.
                                                     v. 7.)
                                               m Acts iii. 19.
                                               vii. 19 al.
                                               n Rom. iii. 3. iv.

14. 1 Cor. xiii. S. P. only, exc. Luke xiii. 7.   Heb. ii. 14.   Ezra iv. 21, 23. v. 5. vi. 8 only.   o ver. 14.
p ver. 2.   q Acts vii. 5. xx. 32 al.   Isa. liv. 17.   r = Rom. vii. 17, 20. xi. 6.   s = Rom. xii. 3.
t act. signif. & = Acts xxvii. 24. (2 Cor. ii. 10.)   2 Macc. iii. 33.   u so ταῦτα τί ἐστιν, Æschin.
Ctes. p. 77.

latt syrr copt Chr Cyr Damasc Ambrst Jer.

years after, does not abrogate, so as to do away the promise. As regards the interval of 430 years, we may remark, that in Exod. xii. 40, it is stated, "The sojourning of the children of Israel who dwelt in Egypt, was four hundred and thirty years." (In Gen. xv. 13, Acts vii. 6, the period of the oppression of Israel in Egypt is roundly stated at 400 years.) But to this, in order to obtain the entire interval between the covenant with Abraham and the law, must be added the sojourning of the patriarchs in Canaan,—i. e. to the birth of Isaac, 25 years (Gen. xii. 4; xxi. 5),—to that of Jacob, 60 more (Gen. xxv. 26),—to his going down into Egypt, 130 more (Gen. xlvii. 9); in all = 215 years. So that the time really was 645 years, not 430. But in the LXX (and Samaritan Pentateuch) we read, Exod. xii. 40, ἡ δὲ κατοίκησις (παροίκ., A.) τῶν υἱῶν ᾿Ισραὴλ, ἣν κατῴκησαν (παρῴκ., A.) ἐν γῇ Αἰγύπτῳ καὶ ἐν γῇ Χαναάν (A. adding αὐτοὶ καὶ οἱ πατέρες αὐτῶν) ἔτη τετρακόσια τριάκοντα : — and this reckoning St. Paul has followed. We have instances of a similar adoption of the LXX text, in the apology of Stephen: see Acts vii. 14, and note. After all, however, *the difficulty* lies in the 400 years of Gen. xv. 13 and Acts vii. 6. For we may ascertain thus the period of the sojourn of Israel in Egypt: Joseph was 39 years old when Jacob came into Egypt (Gen. xli. 46, 47; xlv. 6): therefore he was born when Jacob was 91 (91 + 39 = 130 : see Gen. xlvii. 9). But he was born 6 years before Jacob left Laban (compare ib. xxx. 25 with xxxi. 41), having been with him 20 years (ib. xxxi. 38, 41), and served him 14 of them for his two daughters (xxx. 41). Hence, seeing that his marriage with Rachel took place when he was 78 (91—20—7; the marriages with Leah and Rachel being contemporaneous, and the second seven years of service occurring *after*, not, as I assumed in the first edition, before, the marriage with Rachel); Levi, the *third* son of Leah, whose *first* son was born after Rachel's marriage (xxix. 30—32), must have been born not

earlier than Jacob's 81st year,—and consequently was about 49 (130—81) when he went down into Egypt. Now (Exod. vi. 16) Levi *lived in all* 137 years : i. e., about 88 (137—49) years in Egypt. But (Exod. vi. 16, 18, 20) Amram, father of Moses and Aaron, married his father Kohath's sister, Jochebed, who was therefore, as expressly stated Num. xxvi. 59, 'the daughter of Levi, whom *her mother* bare to Levi in Egypt.' Therefore Jochebed must have been born within 88 years after the going down into Egypt. And seeing that Moses was 80 years old at the Exodus (Exod. vii. 7),—if we call x his mother's age when he was born, we have $88 + 80 + x$ as a maximum for the sojourn in Egypt, which clearly therefore cannot be 430 years, or even 400 ; as in the former case x would = 262,—in the latter 232. If we take x = cir. 47 (to which might be added in the hypothesis any time which 88 and x might have had in common) we shall have the sojourn in Egypt = 215 years, which added to the previous 215, will make the required 430. Thus it will appear that the LXX, Samaritan Pent., and St. Paul, have the right chronology,—and as stated above, the difficulty lies in Gen. xv. 13 and Acts vii. 6,—and in the Hebrew text of Exod. xii. 40.   18.] See Rom. iv. 14. For if the inheritance (the general term for all the blessings promised to Abraham, as summed up in his Seed who was to inherit the land,—in other words, for the Kingdom of Christ: see 1 Cor. vi. 9, 10) is of the law (i. e. by virtue of the law, having as its ground the covenant of the law) it is no more (οὐκ ἔτι, as νῦν in argumentative passages, not of time, but logical—the οὐκ *follows* on the hypothesis) of (by virtue of) promise: but (the 'but' of a demonstration, appealing to a well-known fact) to Abraham by promise hath God granted (it) (and therefore it is not of the Law).   19—24.] *The use and nature of the Law.* What (ref.) then (is) the Law ('ubi audimus Legem nihil valere ad conferendam justitiam, statim obrepunt variæ cogitationes : aut igitur esse inutilem, aut contrariam fœderi Dei,

iv. 15. v. 14.
1 Tim. ii. 14.
Heb. ii. 2.
ix. 15. Ps.
c. 3. Wisd. xiv. 31 only. w. gen., Rom. ii. 23. 2 Macc. xv. 10 only.
ii. 41 al. fr. Paul, here only. Heb. xii. 19. Deut. iv. 2.
z pass. sign., here only. 2 Macc. iv. 27. act., Rom. iv. 21. Heb. xii. 26.
b LEVIT. xxvi. 46.

τῶν ᵛπαραβάσεων ʷχάριν ˣπροσετέθη, ʸἄχρις οὗ ἔλθῃ ABCDF
τὸ σπέρμα ᾧ ᶻἐπήγγελται, ªδιαταγεὶς δι᾽ ἀγγέλων ᵇἐν

w Eph. iii. 1 reff.   x Acts
y constr., Rom. xi. 25. 1 Cor. xi. 26.
a = Acts vii. 44 (-γή, Acts vii. 53).

ABCDF
KLPℵ a
b c d e f
g h k l m
n o 17. 47

19. for παραβασ., παραδοσεων D¹: πραξεων F, *factorum* D-lat Iren-int₂ Ambrst, *prævaricationum aut factorum* G-lat. (*propter transgressionem* F-lat.) om χαριν F [Clem] Iren-int₂ Ambrst.   for προσετ., ετεθη D¹F (*posita est* latt) Clem Orig Eus [Iren-int].   for οὗ, αν B 17 Clem [Eus].   αγγελου C¹(appy) d Thdrt₁-ms

aut tale quippiam.' Calv.)? **For the sake of the transgressions [of it]** (the words τῶν παραβάσεων χάριν have been variously understood. (1) Aug., Calv., Beza, Luth., al., explain it of the *detection* of transgressions, as in Rom. vii. (2) Chrys., Œc., Thl., Jer., Erasm., Grot., Rück., Olsh., B.-Crus., De Wette, al., of their *repression*: μὴ ἐξῇ Ἰουδαίοις ἀδεῶς ζῆν . . . ἀλλ᾽ ἀντὶ χαλινοῦ ὁ νόμος αὐτοῖς ἐπικείμενος ᾖ, παιδεύων, ῥυθμίζων, κωλύων παραβαίνειν. Chrys. (3) Luth., Est., Bengel, al., combine (1) and (2). But it is hardly possible that either of these should be the true explanation. For the Apostle is not now treating of the detection of sin, or of the repression of sin (which latter was besides *not the office* of the Law, see Rom. v. 20), but of the Law as a preparation for Christ, vv. 23, 24: and therefore it must be regarded in its propædeutic office, not in its detective or (?) repressive. Now this propædeutic office was, to *make sin into* TRANSGRESSION,— so that what was before not a transgression might now become one. The law then was added (to the promise, which had no such power), for the sake of (in order to bring about *as transgressions*) the transgressions (of it) which should be, and thus (ver. 23) to shut us up under sin, viz. the transgression of the law. This is nearly Meyer's view, except that he makes this the exclusive meaning of χάριν, which usage will not sustain, cf. 1 John iii. 12. Ellic.'s view is very close to mine, which he has mistaken) **it was superadded** ("προσετέθη does not contradict the assertion of ver. 15, οὐδεὶς . . . . ἐπιδιατάσσεται. For the Law was not given as an ἐπιδιαθήκη, but came in as another institution, additional to that already existing." Meyer) **until the seed shall have come** (he places himself at the giving of the law and looks on into the future: hence the subjunctive, not the optative: and without ἄν, because the time is a certain and definite one), **to whom** (ver. 16) **the promise has been** (see above) **made** (the vulgate renders ἐπήγγελται *promiserat*, sc. Deus: and so Bengel prefers, from reff. active. But the

passive suits ver. 16 (ἐῤῥέθησαν) better, and is justified by reff. Macc. Bretschneider understands it *cui demandatum est*, viz. *to put an end to the law*: but this is against N. T. usage of ἐπαγγέλλω, and absurd, where ἐπαγγελίαι is so often used in the context. This Seed is of course Christ), **being enjoined** (the aorist participle does not here denote previous occurrence, but is merely part of an aorist sentence: so Herod. i. 14, Γύγης δὲ τυραννεύσας ἀνέπεμψεν ἀναθήματα . . . : Diod. Sic. xi. 31, γενναίως ἀγωνισάμενος πολλοὺς ἀνεῖλε τῶν Ἑλλήνων. See Hermann on Viger, pp. 772-3. For διατάσσω, cf. note on Acts vii. 53, and Hesiod, Op. 274, τόνδε γὰρ ἀνθρώποισι νόμον διέταξε Κρονίων: it is not *promulgate*, as Winer) **by means of** (not, *under the attestation of*, as Peile, nor *in the presence of*, as Calov., al.) **angels** (angels were, according to the Rabbinical view, the enactors and enjoiners of the Law: so Jos. Antt. xv. 5. 3, ἡμῶν τὰ κάλλιστα τῶν δογμάτων κ. τὰ ὁσιώτατα τῶν ἐν τοῖς νόμοις δι᾽ ἀγγέλων παρὰ τοῦ θεοῦ μαθόντων: see also the citations in Wetst.: Heb. ii. 2; and note on Col. ii. 15. Of course no explaining away of ἄγγελοι into men (Moses, Aaron, &c.) as Chrys. (altern.: ἢ τοὺς ἱερέας ἀγγέλους λέγει, ἢ καὶ αὐτοὺς τοὺς ἀγγέλους ὑπηρετήσασθαί φησι τῇ νομοθεσίᾳ), al., can be allowed. Observe, the angels are not the *givers* of the Law, but its *ministers*, and *instrumental enactors*: the Law, with St. Paul, is always *God's* Law; see especially Rom. vii. 22) **in the hand of a mediator** (viz. MOSES, who came from God to the people with the tables of the law in his hands. Cf. his own words, Deut. v. 5, κἀγὼ εἱστήκειν ἀναμέσον κυρίου κ. ὑμῶν ἐν τῷ καιρῷ ἐκείνῳ ἀναγγεῖλαι ὑμῖν τὰ ῥήματα κυρίου, ὅτι ἐφοβήθητε ἀπὸ προσώπου τοῦ πυρὸς κ. οὐκ ἀνέβητε εἰς τὸ ὄρος, λέγων . . . : Philo, *vita Mos.* iii. 19, vol. ii. p. 160, οἷα **μεσίτης** κ. διαλλακτὴς οὐκ εὐθὺς ἀνεπήδησεν, ἀλλὰ πρότερον τὰς ὑπὲρ τοῦ ἔθνους ἱκεσίας κ. λιτὰς ἐποιεῖτο. Schöttgen gives numerous examples from the Rabbinical books, in which the name *Mediator* is given to Moses.— But most of the Fathers (not Thdrt.),

χειρὶ ^cμεσίτου· ²⁰ ὁ δὲ ^cμεσίτης ^dἑνὸς οὐκ ἔστιν, ὁ δὲ ^c here bis.
1 Tim. ii. 5.
Heb. viii.

6. ix. 15. xii. 24 only.   Job ix. 33 (only ?).   d gen., = Rom. iii. 29.

Bede, Lyra, Calvin, Calov., al., understand *Christ* to be meant : Schmieder and Schneckenburger, *the Angel of the Covenant,*—the Metatron. Neither of these interpretations however will hold against the above evidence).   *Why* does the Apostle add this last clause ? I am inclined to think with Meyer that it is,—not to disparage the law in comparison with the Gospel (as Luth., Elsn., Flatt, Rück., Jowett, &c. &c.) or with the promise (Estius, Schneckenb., De Wette), but to enhance the solemnity of the giving of the law as a preparation for Christ, in answer to the somewhat disparaging question τί οὖν ὁ νόμος; If the δι᾽ ἀγγέλων had been here disparaging, as in Heb. ii. 2, διὰ τοῦ κυρίου or the like must have been expressed, as there, on the other side. And ἐν χειρὶ μεσίτου is certainly no disparagement of the old covenant in comparison with the new, for this it has in common with the other. The fact is (see below on ver. 20), that no such comparison is in question here.   **20.**] "The explanations of this verse, so obscure from its brevity, are so numerous (Winer counted 250 : Jowett mentions 430) that they require a bibliography of their own." De Wette. I believe we shall best disentangle the sense as follows. (1) Clearly, ὁ μεσίτης and ὁ θεός are opposed. (2) As clearly, ἑνὸς οὐκ ἔστιν and εἷς ἐστιν are opposed. (3) From this contrast arises an apparent opposition between the law and the promises of God, which (not alone, but as the conclusion of the whole τί οὖν to εἷς ἐστιν) gives occasion to the question of ver. 21. Taking up therefore again (1),— ὁ μεσίτης, by whose hand the law was enacted, stands opposed to ὁ θεός, the giver of the promises. And that, in this respect (2) ;—(a) ὁ μεσίτης is not ἑνός, but (b) ὁ θεός is εἷς. And herein lies the knot of the verse ; that is, in (b),—for the meaning of (a) is pretty clear on all hands ; viz. that ὁ μεσίτης (generic, so ref. Job ; 'quæ multa sunt cunctis in unum colligendis,' Hermann ad Iph. in Aul. p. 15, præf. cited by Meyer) does not belong to *one party* (masculine) (but to *two,* as going between one party and another). Then to guide us to the meaning of (b), we must remember, that the numerical contrast is the primary idea : ὁ μεσίτης belongs not to *one,* but ὁ θεός *is one.* Shall we then say, that all reference of εἷς (as applied to ὁ θεός) beyond this numerical one is to be repudiated ? I cannot think

so. The proposition ὁ θεὸς εἷς ἐστιν would carry to the mind of every reader much more than the mere *numerical* unity of God—viz. His Unity as an *essential attribute,* extending through the whole divine Character. And thus, though the proposition ὁ μεσίτης ἑνὸς οὐκ ἔστιν would not, by itself, convey any meaning but that a mediator belongs to more than one, it would, when combined with ὁ θεὸς εἷς ἐστιν, receive a shade of meaning which it did not bear before,—of a state of things involved in the fact of a μεσίτης being employed, which was not according to the ἑνότης of God, or, so to speak, in the main track of His unchanging purpose. And thus (3), the law, administered by the μεσίτης, belonging to a state of οὐχ εἷς, two at variance, is apparently opposed to the ἐπαγγελίαι, belonging entirely to ὁ εἷς, the one (faithful) God. And observe, that the above explanation is deduced entirely from the *form of the sentence itself,* and from the idea which the expression ὁ θεὸς εἷς ἐστιν must necessarily raise in the mind of its reader, accustomed to the proposition as the foundation of the faith ;—not from any preconceived view, to suit which the words, or emphatic arrangement, must be forced. Notice by the way, that the objection, that the Gospel too is ἐν χειρὶ μεσίτου, does not apply here : for (α) there is no question here of the *Gospel,* but only of the *promises,* as direct from God : (β) the μεσίτης of the Gospel is altogether different, and His work different : He has absolutely reconciled the parties at variance, and MADE THEM ONE in Himself. Remember St. Paul's habit of *insulating* the matter in hand, and dealing with it irrespective of all such possible objections. To give even an analysis of the various opinions on this verse would far exceed the limits of this commentary : I will only take advantage of Meyer's long note, and of other sources, to indicate the main branches of the exegesis. (I) The Fathers, for the most part, pass lightly over it, as easy in itself,—and do not notice its pragmatic difficulty. Most of them understand by the μεσίτης, Christ, the mediator between God and man. In interpreting ἑνὸς οὐκ ἔστιν and εἷς ἐστιν, they go in omnia alia. It may suffice to quote one or two samples. Chrys. says, τί ἂν ἐνταῦθα εἴποιεν αἱρετικοί ; εἰ γὰρ τὸ "μόνος ἀληθινός," οὐκ ἀφίησι τὸν υἱὸν εἶναι θεὸν ἀληθινόν, οὐκ ἄρα οὐδὲ θεόν, διὰ τὸ

θεὸς εἷς ἐστιν.　²¹ ὁ οὖν νόμος ᵉ κατὰ τῶν ᶠ ἐπαγγελιῶν ABCDF
KLPℵ a
b c d e f
g h k l m
n o 17.47

λέγεσθαι "ὁ δὲ θεὸς εἷς ἐστιν.".....
ὁ δὲ μεσίτης, φησί, δύο τινῶν γίνεται
μεσίτης. τίνος οὖν μεσίτης ἦν ὁ χριστός; ἢ δῆλον ὅτι θεοῦ κ. ἀνθρώπων;
ὁρᾷς πῶς δείκνυσιν ὅτι καὶ τὸν νόμον
αὐτὸς ἔδωκεν; εἰ τοίνυν αὐτὸς ἔδωκε,
κύριος ἂν εἴη καὶ λῦσαι πάλιν. And
Jerome, 'manu mediatoris potentiam
et virtutem ejus debemus accipere, qui
cum secundum Deum unum sit ipse cum
patre, secundum mediatoris officium alius
ab eo intelligitur.' Theodoret, having explained the μεσίτης of Moses, proceeds,
on ὁ δὲ θεὸς εἷς ἐστιν,—ὁ καὶ τὴν ἐπαγγελίαν τῷ Ἀβραὰμ δεδωκώς, καὶ τὸν
νόμον τεθεικώς, καὶ οὖν τῆς ἐπαγγελίας
ἡμῖν ἐπιδείξας τὸ πέρας. οὐ γὰρ ἄλλος
μὲν ἐκεῖνα θεὸς ᾠκονόμησεν, ἄλλος δὲ
ταῦτα. (II) The older of the modern
Commentators are generally quite at fault :
I give a few of them : Grotius says, 'Etsi
Christus mediator Legem Judæis tulerit,
ut ad agnitionem transgressionum addu-
ceret, eoque ad fœdus gratiæ præpararet,
non tamen unius est gentis Judaicæ mediator, sed omnium hominum : quemadmodum Deus unus est omnium.' Luther
(1519), ' Ex nomine mediatoris concludit,
nos adeo esse peccatores, ut legis opera
satis esse nequeant. Si, inquit, lege justi
estis, jam mediatore non egetis, sed neque
Deus, cum sit ipse unus, secum optime
conveniens. Inter duos ergo quæritur
mediator, inter Deum et hominem ; ac si
dicat, impiissima est ingratitudo, si mediatorem rejicitis, et Deo, qui unus est,
remittitis, &c.' Erasmus, in his paraphrase : ' Atqui conciliator, qui intercedit,
inter plures intercedat oportet, nemo enim
secum ipse dissidet. Deus autem unus
est, quocum dissidium erat humano ge-
neri. Proinde tertio quopiam erat opus,
qui naturæ utriusque particeps utramque
inter sese reconciliaret, &c.' Calvin, as
the preferable view, ' diversitatem hic
notari arbitror inter Judæos et Gentiles.
Non unius ergo mediator est Christus,
quia diversa est conditio eorum quibuscum
Deus, ipsius auspiciis, paciscitur, quod ad
externam personam. Verum Paulus inde
æstimandum Dei fœdus negat, quasi secum pugnet, aut varium sit pro hominum
diversitate.' (III) The later moderns
begin to approach nearer to the philological and contextual requirements of the
passage, but still with considerable errors
and divergences. Bengel, on the first
clause, ' Medius terminus est in syllogismo,
cujus major propositio et minor expri-

mitur, conclusio subauditur. *Unus non
utitur mediatore illo* : atqui *Deus est
unus.* Ergo Deus non prius sine mediatore, deinde per mediatorem egit. Ergo
is cujus erat mediator non est unus idem-
que cum Deo sed diversus a Deo, nempe
ὁ νόμος, Lex. .... ergo mediator Sinai-
ticus non est Dei sed legis : Dei autem,
promissio.' Locke (so also Michaelis):
" God is but one of the parties concerned
in the promise : the Gentiles and Israelites together made up the other, ver. 14.
But Moses, at the giving of the law, was
a mediator only between the Israelites
and God : and therefore could not transact
any thing to the disannulling the promise, which was between God and the
Israelites and Gentiles together, because
God was but one of the parties to that
covenant : the other, which was the Gentiles as well as Israelites, Moses appeared
or transacted not for." (IV) Of the
recent Commentators, Keil (Opusc. 1809—
12) says : 'Mediatorem quidem non unius
sed duarum certe partium esse, Deum
autem qui Abrahamo beneficii aliquid pro-
miserit, unum modo fuisse : hincque apostolum id a lectoribus suis colligi voluisse,
in lege ista Mosaica pactum mutuum
Deum inter atque populum Israeliti-
cum mediatoris opera intercedente initum
fuisse, contra vero in promissione rem ab
unius tantum (Dei sc. qui solus eam dederit) voluntate pendentem transactam,—
hincque legi isti nihil plane cum hac rei
fuisse, adeoque nec potuisse ea novam
illius promissionis implendæ conditionem
constitui, eoque ipso promissionem omnino
tolli.' And similarly Schleiermacher (in
Usteri's Lehrbegriff, p. 186 ff.), but giving
to εἷς the sense of freedom and independence ;—and Meyer, only repudiating the
second part of Keil's explanation from
' hincque,' as not belonging to an abstract
sentence like this, but being historical, as
if it had been ἦν, and besides contrary to
the Apostle's meaning, who deduces from
our verse a consequence the contrary to
this (' hincque ..... fuisse'), and obviates
it by the question in ver. 21. For the
numerous other recent interpretations and
their refutations I must refer the reader
to Meyer's note (as also to Ellicott's (in his
ed. 1 : see his present view in his ed. 2), who
preferred Windischmann's interpretation of
εἷς, ' One, because He was both giver and
receiver united : giver, as the Father ;
receiver, as the Son, the σπέρμα ᾧ ἐπήγγελται.' But this seems going too deep—

τοῦ ^gθεοῦ; ^hμὴ γένοιτο. εἰ γὰρ ⁱἐδόθη νόμος ^kὁ δυνά- ^{g ellips., ch. ii. 21.}
μενος ^lζωοποιῆσαι, ^mὄντως ἐκ νόμου ἂν ἦν ἡ δικαιοσύνη· ^{h ch. ii. 17 reff. i = John i. 17.}
²² ἀλλὰ ⁿσυνέκλεισεν ἡ γραφὴ ^oτὰ πάντα ὑπὸ ἁμαρτίαν, ^{vii. 19, 22. Acts vii. 8. Ezek. xx. 11 al.}

k so Acts iv. 12. x. 41 (μάρτ. τοῖς προκεχ.). Winer, § 20. 4. l John v. 21. Rom. iv. 17. 1 Pet.
iii. 18 al. Eccl. vii. 13. m Mark xi. 32. Luke xxiii. 47. 1 Cor. xiv. 25 al. Num. xxii. 37
only. n Luke v. 6. Rom. xi. 32 only. Josh. vi. 1 al. o (= τοὺς πάντας, Rom. xi.
32.) so neut., 1 Cor. i. 27, 28. Heb. vii. 7 al. Winer, § 27. 5.

21. om του θεου B D-lat [Victorin] Ambrst-ed[: om του F]. for οντως, αληθεια
F. rec αν bef εκ νομου, with D²·³KL[P] rel Chr Thdrt : om αν D¹ Damasc : om
ην a : om αν ην F : txt A B[but εν νομω] Cℵ 17 (but ην bef αν ℵ 17) Cyr₂.
22. om τα FK Damasc. υφ AD¹F m Damasc.

almost, we may say, arriving at the conclusion by a *coup de main*, which would not have borne any meaning to the readers) : see also Jowett's note, which seems to me further to complicate the matter by introducing into it God's unity of dealing with man, and man's unity with God in Christ. (V) We may profitably lay down one or two canons of interpretation of the verse. (a) Every interpretation is wrong, which understands *Christ* by ὁ μεσίτης. The context determines it to be abstract, and its reference to be to Moses, the mediator of the Law. (β) Every interpretation is wrong, which makes εἷς mean ' one party ' in the covenant. ὁ θεὸς εἷς ἐστιν itself confutes any such view, being a well-known general proposition, not admitting of a concrete interpretation. (γ) Every interpretation is wrong, which confines εἷς (as Meyer) to its mere numerical meaning, and does not take into account the ideas which the general proposition would raise. (δ) Every interpretation is wrong, which deduces from the verse the *agreement* of the law with the promises : because the Apostle himself, in the next verse, draws the very opposite inference from it, and refutes it on other grounds. (ε) Every attempt to set aside the verse as a gloss is utterly futile. 21.] The Law being thus set over against the promises,—being given through a mediator between two,—the promises by the one God,—it might seem as if there were an inconsistency between them. The nature of the contrariety must not (as De W.) be deduced from the following disproof of it : this disproof proceeds on τῶν παραβάσεων χάριν προσετέθη, which is *not* the ground of the apparent contrariety, but its explanation. The appearance of inconsistency lay in the whole paragraph preceding—the οὐκ ἀκυροῖ of ver. 17, the εἰ ἐκ νόμου, οὐκέτι ἐξ ἐπαγγελίας of ver. 18,—and the contrast between the giving of the two in ver. 20. " τοῦ θεοῦ is not without emphasis: the promises which rest immediately on God, and were attested (? sic still in ed. 2) by no me-

diator." Ellic. εἰ γάρ] Notwithstanding all the above features of contrast between the Law and the promises, it is not against them, for it does not pretend to perform the same office ; *if it did*, then there would be this rivalry, which now does not exist. νόμος ὁ δυν. is best expressed in English, as in E. V., a law which could . . . . . for the article circumscribes the νόμος to some particular quality indicated in the defining participle which follows : see reff. Peile's rendering, " if that which (ὁ δυνάμενος !) should have power to give life had been given in the form of law," is in the highest degree ungrammatical. ζωοποιῆσαι takes for granted that we by nature are *dead* in trespasses and sins. ὄντως has the emphasis : in very truth, and not only in the fancy of some, by the law (as its ground) would have been righteousness (which is the condition of life eternal,— ὁ δίκαιος . . . . ζήσεται. If life, the result, had been given by the law, then righteousness, the *condition* of life, must have been by it also : reasoning from the whole to its part). 22.] But on the contrary (ἀλλά, not δέ: comp. Ellic. This not being the case,—no law being given out of which could come righteousness) the Scripture (not the Law, as Chrys. and most of the Fathers, also Calv., Beza, al. ; but as in ver. 8, the Author of Scripture, speaking by that His witness) shut up (not subjective, as Chrys., ἤλεγξεν . . . . κ. ἐλέγξας κατεῖχεν ἐν φόβῳ,—for it is their objective state of incapacity to attain righteousness which is here brought out : —nor ' conclusit omnes simul,' as Bengel, al. : the preposition enhances the force of κλείειν, as in ' contraho,' συμπνίγειν, &c.: see note Rom. xi. 32, where the same expression occurs. " The word συγκλείειν is beautifully chosen, to set off more clearly the idea of Christian freedom by and by." Windischmann : cf. ch. v. 1. Nor has συγκλ. merely a declaratory sense, as Bull, Examen Censuræ xix. 6, ' conclusos involutos declaravit,' al.) all (neuter, as indicating the entirety of mankind and man's

p ver. 14 reff.
q gen., = ch.
ii. 16. Rom.
iii. 22, 26.
r = Rom. vii.
9.
s = ch. i. 23.
Rom. i. 5.
Jude 3.
t 2 Cor. xi. 32.
Phil. iv. 7.   1 Pet. i. 5 only †.   Judith iii. 6.   u see Wisd. xvii. 16.   v transp. of words, Rom
viii. 18.   1 Cor. xii. 22.   w = Matt. xi. 25.   Rom. i. 17.   Cor. ii. 10.   Isa. lvi. 1.   x he
bis.   1 Cor. iv. 15 only †.

ἵνα ἡ ᵖ ἐπαγγελία ἐκ � πίστεως �ۤ Ἰησοῦ χριστοῦ δοθῇ τοῖς
πιστεύουσιν. ²³ πρὸ τοῦ δὲ ʳ ἐλθεῖν τὴν ˢ πίστιν, ὑπὸ
νόμον ᵗ ἐφρουρούμεθα ᵘ συγκλειόμενοι ᵘ εἰς τὴν ᵛ μέλλουσαν ˢ πίστιν ʷ ἀποκαλυφθῆναι. ²⁴ ὥστε ὁ νόμος ˣ παιδ-

ABCDF
KLPℵ a
b c d e f
g h k l m
n o 17. 47

23. rec συγκεκλεισμενοι, with CD³KL rel Clem₁ Cyr₂[?] Thdrt Thl Œc: txt
ABD¹F[P]ℵ 17 [47] Clem₁ Chr₂ Cyr₃.

world: 'humana omnia,' as Jowett: cf. reff. I think (against Ellic. ed. 2) that we must hold fast this) under sin, in order that (the *intention* of God, as in Rom. xi. 32: *not the mere result*, here or any where else. Beware of such an assertion as Burton's, quoted also by Peile;—"ἵνα here implies, not the cause, but the consequence, as in many places." ἵνα never implies any thing of the sort; nor does any one of the examples he gives bear him out) the promise (i. e. the things promised—the κληρονομία, cf. vv. 16, 18) (which is) by (depends upon, is conditioned by) faith of (which has for its object and its Giver—is a matter altogether belonging to) Jesus Christ (q. d. ἡ ἐπαγγ. ἡ ἐκ π.: but the article in such sentences is frequently omitted, especially where no distinction is intended between the subject and another of the same kind: cf. τῆς πίστεως ἐν χρ. Ἰησ. below, ver. 26,—τοῖς κυρίοις κατὰ σάρκα, Eph. vi. 5, &c.   The words ἐκ πίστ. cannot well be taken with δοθῇ without harshness, especially as Ἰησοῦ χριστοῦ intervenes, and τοῖς πιστεύουσιν is already expressed. Besides, in this case they would most naturally come first,—ἵνα ἐκ πίστεως Ἰ. χρ. ἡ ἐπαγγ. δοθῇ τ. π.) might be given (be a *free gift*—δοθῇ has the emphasis) to them that believe (δοθῇ having the emphasis, τοῖς πιστ. does no more than take up ἐκ πίστ. above; q. d. 'to those who fulfil that condition').
23.] But (δέ carries us on to a further account of the rationale and office of the law. "When the noun, to which the particle is attached, is preceded by a preposition, and perhaps the article as well, δέ may stand the third or fourth word in the sentence. So ἐν τοῖς πρῶτοι δὲ Ἀθηναῖοι, Thuc. i. 6: οὐχ ὑπὸ ἐραστοῦ δέ, Plato, Phædr. 227 d, &c." Hartung, Partikell. i. 190) before (this) faith (not, *the faith*, in the sense of *the objects of faith*, but the faith just mentioned, viz. πίστις Ἰησοῦ χρ., which did not exist until Christ) came (was found, or was possible, in men: cf. ref., where however it is more entirely subjective), we (properly, we Jewish believers —but not here to be pressed, because he is speaking of the divine dealings with men

generally—the Law was for τὰ πάντα, the only revelation) were kept in ward (not simply '*kept*' as E. V., but as Chrys., ὥσπερ ἐν τειχίῳ τινί,—though not as he proceeds, τῷ φόβῳ κατεχόμενοι—for, as above, our objective state is here treated of: see Rom. vii. 6. But we must not yet, with Chrys., al., introduce the παιδαγωγός, or understand ἐφρουρ. as conveying the idea of '*safely kept*' (οὐδὲν ἕτερον δηλοῦντός ἐστιν, ἢ τὴν ἐκ τῶν ἐντολῶν τοῦ νόμου γενομένην ἀσφάλειαν): συγκλειόμενοι is quite against this, and the pædagogic figure does not enter till the next verse, springing out of the preparation implied in εἰς, joined to the fact of our sonship, see below. Our present verse answers to ch. iv. 2, where we find ἐπίτροποι and οἰκονόμοι, not the παιδαγωγός. See Jowett's beautiful illustration), shut up under the law, in order to (εἰς of the preparatory *design*, not merely of the *result*, or the arrival of the time: and it may belong either to συγκλειόμ. (not to συγκεκλεισμένοι, if that be read, as that would betoken the act completed when the Law was given), or to the imperfect ἐφρουρούμεθα) the faith (as in ver. 22) about to be revealed (on the order of the words see on ref. Rom. "As long as there was no such thing as faith in Christ, this faith was *not yet revealed*, was as yet an element of life hidden in the counsel of God." Meyer).   24.] So that (taking up the condition in which the last verse left us, and *adding to it the fact* that we are the SONS of God, cf. γάρ, ver. 26) the Law has become (has turned out to be) our tutor (pedagogue, see below) unto (ethically; for) Christ (the παιδαγωγός was a faithful slave, entrusted with the care of the boy from his tender years till puberty, to keep him from evil physical and moral, and accompany him to his amusements and studies. See Dict. of Gr. and Rom. Antt. sub voce. The E. V. '*schoolmaster*' does not express the meaning fully: but it disturbs the sense less than those have done, who have selected one portion only of the pedagogue's duty, and understood by it, '*the slave who

αγωγὸς ἡμῶν γέγονεν εἰς χριστόν, ἵνα ᵞ ἐκ πίστεως ᵞ δι-
καιωθῶμεν· ²⁵ ʳ ἐλθούσης δὲ τῆς ˢ πίστεως οὐκ ἔτι ὑπὸ
ˣ παιδαγωγὸν ἐσμέν. ²⁶ πάντες γὰρ ᶻ υἱοὶ θεοῦ ἐστε διὰ
τῆς ᵃ πίστεως ᵃ ἐν χριστῷ Ἰησοῦ· ²⁷ ὅσοι γὰρ ᵇ εἰς
χριστὸν ᵇ ἐβαπτίσθητε, χριστὸν ᶜ ἐνεδύσασθε. ²⁸ οὐκ
ᵈ ἔνι ᵉ Ἰουδαῖος οὐδὲ ᵉ Ἕλλην, οὐκ ᵈ ἔνι ᶠ δοῦλος οὐδὲ

y ch. ii. 16 reff.
z Matt. v. 9.
Luke (vi. 35)
xx. 36. Rom.
viii. 14, 19.
a Eph. i. 15.
Col. i. 4.
1 Tim. iii. 13.
2 Tim. iii. 15.
εἰς, Acts xx.
21. ἐπί, Heb.
vi. 1. πρός,
b Matt. xxviii.
19. Acts xix.

5. Rom. vi. 3. 1 Cor. x. 2. xii. 13.   c = Rom. xiii. 14.   Eph. iv. 24.   Col. iii. 10.   Ps. cxxxi. 9.
d here 3ce. 1 Cor. vi. 5.   Col. iii. 11.   James i. 17 only. see Luke xi. 41.   e see Rom. i. 16.   f Eph. vi. 8 al.

24. for γεγονεν, εγενετο B Clem₁.   aft χρ. ins ιησουν D¹(and lat) F fuld(and
F-lat) [copt arm] Ambrst.
26. aft υιοι ins οι א¹(marked for erasure by א¹ or א-corr).   [om της and εν
χριστω P.]
28. for 2nd ουδε, η D¹-gr: και lect-17.

leads a child to the house of the schoolmaster' (οἷόν τινι σοφῷ διδασκάλῳ προσφέρει τῷ δεσπότῃ χριστῷ, Thdrt.: so also
Thl.: see Suicer, νόμος, b), thus making
Christ the schoolmaster, which is inconsistent with the imagery. On the contrary,
the whole schoolmaster's work is included
in the παιδαγωγός, and Christ represents
the ἐλευθερία of the grown-up son, in
which he is no longer guarded or shut up,
but justified by faith, the act of a free
man ; and to Christ *as a Teacher* there is
here no allusion), **in order that by faith
we might be justified** (which could only
be done when Christ had come): **but** (adversative) **now that the faith** (see above)
**has come, we are no longer under a
tutor** (pedagogue). **26.**] *Reason of
the negation in last verse.* **For ye all**
(Jews and Gentiles alike) **are** SONS (no
longer παῖδες, requiring a παιδαγωγός) **of
God by means of the** (or, but not so well,
your) **faith in Christ Jesus** (some (Usteri,
Windisch., al.) would join ἐν χρ. Ἰησ. with
υἱοὶ θεοῦ ἐστε, but most unnaturally,—and
unmeaningly, for the idea of ἐν χρ. Ἰησ.
in that case has been already given by διὰ
τῆς πίστεως. The omission of τῆς before
ἐν will stagger no one : see Col. i. 4, where
the same expression occurs). **27.**] **For**
(substantiates and explains the assertion
of ver. 26 : see below) **as many of you as
were baptized into** (see Rom. vi. 3 and
notes) **Christ, put on Christ** (at that time,
compare the aorists in Acts xix. 2 : not
"*have been baptized,*" and "*have put
on,*" as E. V., which leaves the two actions
only concomitant : the aorists make them
identical : as many as were baptized into
Christ, did, in that very act, put on, clothe
yourselves with, Christ : see Ellicott's
note). The force of the argument is well
given by Chrys.: τίνος ἕνεκεν οὐκ εἶπεν,
ὅσοι γὰρ εἰς χριστὸν ἐβαπτίσθητε, ἐκ τοῦ
θεοῦ ἐγεννήθητε; τὸ γὰρ ἀκόλουθον τοῦ
δεῖξαι υἱοὺς τοῦτο ἦν. ὅτι πολὺ φρικω-

δέστερον αὐτὸ τίθησιν. εἰ γὰρ ὁ χριστὸς
υἱὸς τοῦ θεοῦ, σὺ δὲ αὐτὸν ἐνδέδυσαι, τὸν
υἱὸν ἔχων ἐν ἑαυτῷ κ. πρὸς αὐτὸν ἀφο-
μοιωθείς, εἰς μίαν συγγένειαν κ. μίαν ἰδέαν
ἤχθης. Observe here how boldly and
broadly St. Paul asserts the effect of
Baptism on all (πάντες γὰρ . . . and
ὅσοι ἐβαπτ.) the baptized. Luther remarks: "Hic locus diligenter observandus
est contra fanaticos spiritus, qui majesta-
tem baptismi extenuant, et sceleste et im-
pie de eo loquuntur. Paulus contra mag-
nificis titulis baptismum ornat, appellans
lavacrum regenerationis ac renovationis
Sp. sancti (Tit. iii. 5), et hic dicit omnes
baptisatos Christum induisse, quasi dicat :
non accepistis per baptismum tesseram,
per quam adscripti estis in numerum christianorum, ut nostro tempore multi fana-
tici homines senserunt, qui ex baptismo
tantum tesseram fecerunt, hoc est, breve
et inane quoddam signum, sed 'quotquot'
inquit etc.: id est, estis extra legem rapti
in novam nativitatem, quæ facta est in
baptismo." But we may notice too, as
Meyer remarks, that the very putting on
of Christ, which as matter of standing and
profession is done in baptism, forms a subject of exhortation to those already baptized, in its ethical sense, Rom. xiii. 14.

28.] The absolute equality of all
in this sonship, to the obliteration of all
differences of earthly extraction or position. See Col. iii. 11 ; Rom. x. 12 ; 1 Cor.
xii. 13. οὐκ ἔνι = οὐκ ἔνεστιν—'il n'y
a pas:' De Wette quotes Plato, Gorg. 507,
ὅτῳ δὲ μὴ ἔνι κοινωνία, φιλία οὐκ ἂν εἴη.
Buttmann (ii. 299), Kühner (i. 671),
Winer (§ 14. 2, remark), maintain ἔνι to
be a form of the preposition ἐν, and the
same of ἔπι, πάρα, &c. But Meyer replies, that all those passages are against
this view, where ἔνι and ἐν occur together, as 1 Cor. vi. 5 ; Xen. Anab. v. 3.
11. Observe, Ἰουδ. **οὐδὲ** Ἕλλ., δοῦλος **οὐδὲ**
ἐλεύθ.,—but ἄρσεν **καὶ** θῆλυ: the two

g Matt. xix.
4 ‖ Mk. (from
Gen. i. 27).
Rom. i. 27
only.
h as above (g).
Luke ii. 23.
Rev. xii. 5
only.
i as above (g).
Rom. i. 26
only.
k gen., Rom.
xiv. 8.
1 Cor. i. 12.
iii. 22, 23 al.
7. Isa. xli. 8.
i. 2 al. Micah i. 15.
i. 13. Deut. xii. 19.
only ‡. Dan. vii. 3 (Theod.).

ᶠ ἐλεύθερος, οὐκ ᵈ ἔνι ᵍʰ ἄρσεν καὶ ᵍⁱ θῆλυ· ἅπαντες γὰρ
ὑμεῖς εἷς ἐστε ἐν χριστῷ Ἰησοῦ.   ²⁹ εἰ δὲ ὑμεῖς ᵏ χριστοῦ,
ˡ ἄρα τοῦ ᵐ Ἀβραὰμ ᵐ σπέρμα ἐστέ, ⁿ κατ᾽ ⁿ ἐπαγγελίαν
ᵒ κληρονόμοι.

IV. ¹ ᵖ Λέγω δέ, ᑫ ἐφ᾽ ὅσον ᑫ χρόνον ὁ ᵒ κληρονόμος
ʳ νήπιός ἐστιν, οὐδὲν ˢ διαφέρει δούλου κύριος πάντων ὤν,

ABCDF
KLPℵ a
b c d e f
g h k l m
n o 17. 47

1 1 Cor. xv. 14.   2 Cor. v. 15. see Rom. vii. 3, 25.   m John viii. 33.   Rom. ix.
n Acts xiii. 23 (Paul).   2 Tim. i. 1 only.   o Rom. iv. 13, 14. viii. 17.   Heb.
p Rom. xv. 8. ch. v. 16.   q Rom. vii. 1.   1 Cor. vii. 39. see 2 Pet.
r = 1 Cor. xiii. 11 (5 times).   Ps. viii. 2.   s = and constr., 1 Cor. xv. 41

αρρεν ℵ [Clem].   rec παντες (from ver 26, where there is no variation: Ellic
wrong), with B¹CDFKL[P] rel Clem₂ Orig Chr Thdrt Damasc : txt AB²ℵ.   om
εἰς Aℵ¹ [fuld¹]: for εἰς, ἐν F 17 latt copt goth Orig Ath₁ Ps-Ath Dial-trin Thdrt₁
Philo-carp lat-ff.   for εν χρ. ιησ., χριστου ιησου A; so ℵ¹, εν having been written
before χῡ, and marked for erasure : the marks have been removed by ℵ³ which reads
as text : om ιησ. c.

  29. for χριστου, εις εστε ἐν χῶ ῑῡ D¹F(with [besides F-lat] harl) Ambrst.   aft
αρα ins ουν D¹F.   σπερματος B copt.   rec ins και bef κατ᾽, with FKL[P] rel
syrr goth Chr Thdrt : om ABCDℵ 17 vulg copt [æth] arm Thdor-mops Damasc Ambrst
Victorin Aug.   κατα ℵ.

CHAP. IV. [1. aft δε ins αδελφοι F.   om ων C¹(appy).]

former being accidental distinctions which
may be entirely put off in falling back on
our humanity,—but the latter a necessary
distinction, absorbed however in the higher
category : q. d. "there is no distinction
into male and female." ἄρσεν κ. θῆλυ,
generalized by the neuter, as being the
only gender which will express both.
γάρ, reason why there is neither, &c.—viz.
our unity in Christ. On the unavoidable
inference from an assertion like this, that
Christianity did alter the condition of
women and slaves, see Jowett's note.
εἷς, more forcible and more strict
than ἔνι: for we are one, in Him, εἷς
καινὸς ἄνθρωπος, as he says in Eph. ii. 15,
speaking on this very subject.   29.]
Christ is 'Abraham's seed' (ver. 16) : ye
are one in and with Christ, have put on
Christ; therefore ye are Abraham's seed;
consequently heirs by promise; for to
Abraham and his seed were the promises
made.   The stress is on ὑμεῖς, τοῦ Ἀβραάμ,
and κατ᾽ ἐπαγγελίαν, especially on the
latter,—carrying the conclusion of the
argument, as against inheritance by the
law. See on this verse, the note on ver.
16 above.   "The declaration of ver. 7
is now substantiated by 22 verses of the
deepest, the most varied, and most comprehensive reasoning that exists in the
whole compass of the great Apostle's
writings." Ellicott.
IV. 1—7.] The Apostle shews the correspondence between our treatment under
the law and that of heirs in general : and
thus, by God's dealing with us, in sending
forth His Son, whose Spirit of Sonship we

have received, confirms (ver. 7) the conclusion that WE ARE HEIRS.   1.] λέγω
δέ refers to what follows (reff.), and does
not imply, 'What I mean, is.'
ὁ κληρ., generic, as ὁ μεσίτης, ch. iii. 20.
The question, whether the father of the
κληρονόμος here is to be thought of as
dead, or absent, or living and present, is
in fact one of no importance : nor does it
belong properly to the consideration of
the passage.   The fact is, the antitype
breaks through the type, and disturbs it :
as is the case, wherever the idea of inheritance is spiritualized.   The supposition in our text is, that a father (from
what reason or under what circumstances
matters not.   Mr. Bagge quotes from Ul-
pian, speaking of the right of a testator
appointing guardians, "Tutorem autem
et a certo tempore dare et usque ad cer-
tum tempus licet." Digest. xxvi. 2. 8)
has preordained a time for his son and
heir to come of age, and till that time, has
subjected him to guardians and stewards.
In the type, the reason might be absence,
or decease, or even high office or intense
occupation, of the father : in the antitype, it is the Father's sovereign will :
but the circumstances equally exist.
οὐδὲν διαφ. δούλου] διὰ τοῦτο γὰρ κ.
παίειν κ. ἄγχειν κ. στρεβλοῦν, κ. ἃ τῶν
δεσποτῶν πρὸς τοὺς οἰκέτας, ταῦτα τῶν
νιέων τοῖς ἐφεστῶσιν ἀξιοῦσιν ὑπάρχειν.
Libanius (Wetst.).   See below on ver. 3 :
and Plato, Lysis, pp. 207. 8, cited at
length in Bagge.   κύριος πάντων ὤν
must be understood essentially, rather
than prospectively.   It is said of him in

² ἀλλὰ ὑπὸ ᵗἐπιτρόπους ἐστὶν καὶ ᵘ οἰκονόμους ᵛ ἄχρι τῆς
ᵂ προθεσμίας τοῦ πατρός. ³ οὕτως καὶ ἡμεῖς ὅτε ἦμεν
ʳ νήπιοι, ὑπὸ τὰ ˣ στοιχεῖα τοῦ κόσμου ἦμεν ʸ δεδουλω-
μένοι· ⁴ ὅτε δὲ ἦλθεν τὸ ᶻ πλήρωμα τοῦ χρόνου, ᵃ ἐξαπέστειλεν ὁ θεὸς τὸν υἱὸν αὐτοῦ, ᵇ γενόμενον ἐκ γυναικός,

t Matt. xx. 8.
Luke viii. 3
only †.
2 Macc. xi. 1.
xiii. 2. xiv.
2.
u Luke xii. 42.
xvi. 1, 3, 8.
1 Cor. iv. 1,
2 al. 3 Kings
iv. 6.
v Rom. viii.

22.　1 Cor. iv. 11.　2 Cor. iii. 14 al.
τῆς προθ. ἐνισταμένης, καθ' ἣν ἔδει . . .
10, 12 only †.　Wisd. vii. 17. xix. 18 only.
19.　Tit. ii. 3.　2 Pet. ii. 19 only.　Gen. xv. 13.
51.　Acts ii. 1.　Ezek. v. 2.)
al6. L.P.　Mal. iii. 1.

w here only †.　Job xxxviii. 3 Symm.　Jos. Antt. xii. 4. 7,
x ver. 9.　Col. ii. 8, 20.　Heb. v. 12.　2 Pet. iii.
y Acts vii. 6.　Rom. vi. 18, 22.　1 Cor. vii. 15. ix.
z = Eph. i. 10 only. (comp. Luke i. 57. ix.
a Paul, here (bis) only.　Luke i. 53. xx. 10, 11.　Acts vii. 12
b see Matt. xi. 11.　Job xiv. 1.　ἐξ ἧς σὺ ἐγένου, Xen. Cyr. viii. 5. 19.

2. ins τῆς bef του πατρος B.　　**3.** [υμεις P.]　　for ημεν, ημεθα D¹Fℵ 17.
4. for 1st γενομ., γενωμενον k¹ : γεννομενον K [71. 109-15] : γεννωμενον a d e f g (26
others and correctors of 4 more in Reiche) æth Clem-ms Eus Ath₁ Thdrt₅ Damasc
Phot, natum fuld(with demid tol harl²) Iren-int₁ Cypr : txt ABCDFLℵ rel syrr copt
goth Clem Orig Eus Ath₁ Ps-Ath Meth Cyr-jer Chr Cyr₂ Thdrt, factum latt Iren-int₃
Tert Victorin Hil.

virtue of his rank, rather than of his
actual estate: *in posse*, rather than *in
esse*.　　**2.**] ἐπιτρόπους, overseers of
the person ; **guardians: οἰκονόμους,** overseers of the property, **stewards.** See Ellicott's and Bagge's notes.　　**προθεσμία,**
the time (previously) **appointed.** The
word (an adjective used substantively :
scil. ἡμέρα or ὥρα. See for the classical
meaning, 'the time allowed to elapse before bringing an action,' Smith's Dict. of
Antt. sub voce) is a common one : Wetst.
gives many examples. The following clearly
explain it : ὁρίσαι προθεσμίαν, ἐν ᾗ ᾗ τὸ
ἱερὸν συντελεσθήσεται, Polyæn. p. 597 :—
εἰ δὲ ὁ τῆς ζωῆς τῶν ἀνθρώπων χρόνος
εἰκοσαετὴς ἦν . . . . τὴν δὲ τῶν κ. ἐτῶν
προθεσμίαν ἐκπληρώσαντα, Plut. ad Apol-
lon. p. 113 e. It is no objection to the
view that the father is dead, that the
time was *fixed by law* (Hebrew as well as
Greek and Roman) : nor on the other
hand any proof of it, that **προθεσμία** will
hardly apply to a living man's arrangement : see on the whole, above.
3.] ἡμεῖς—are Jews only here included,
or Jews and Gentiles ?　Clearly, *both :*
for ἵνα τ. υἱοθεσ. ἀπολάβωμεν is spoken
of all believers in Christ.　He regards the
Jews as, for this purpose, including all
mankind (see note on ch. iii. 23), God's
only positive dealings by revelation being
with them—and the Gentiles as partakers
both in their infant-discipline, and in
their emancipation in Christ.　　**ὅτε**
ἦμεν νήπιοι refers, not to any immaturity
of capacity in *us*, but to the lifetime of
the church, as regarded in the προθεσμία
τοῦ πατρός : see below on ver. 4.
τὰ στοιχεῖα τοῦ κόσμου] Aug. interprets
this physically, of the worship of the elements of nature by the Gentiles : Chrys.,
Thdrt., al., of the Jewish new moons and
sabbaths : Neander (Pfl. u. Leit. p. 370),
of a religion of sense as opposed to that of

the spirit.　But it is more natural to take
στοιχεῖα in its simpler meaning, that of
letters or symbols of the alphabet, and
τοῦ κόσμου not in its worst sense, but as
in Heb. ix. 1, ἅγιον κοσμικόν,—' belonging
to the unspiritual outer world.'　Thus (as
in reff. Col.) the words will mean, the
elementary lessons of outward things
(as Conybeare has rendered it in his note :
' outward ordinances,' in his text, is not
so good).　Of this kind were all the enactments peculiar to the Law; some of which
are expressly named, ver. 10.　See στοιχεῖα well discussed in Ellicott's note ;
and some useful remarks in Jowett, in loc.
　　Meyer prefers taking ἦμεν and δε-
δουλωμένοι separate : ' we were under the
elements of the world, enslaved :' as answering better to ὑπὸ ἐπιτρόπους ἐστίν
above.　**4.**] **τὸ πλήρωμα τ. χρόνου**
('that whereby the time was filled up :'
see note on Eph. i. 23,—Fritzsche's note
on Rom. xi. 12, and Stier's, Eph. i.
p. 199 ff. for a discussion of the meanings
of πλήρωμα) answers to the προθεσμία τ.
πατρός, ver. 2 : see reff.　The Apostle
uses this term with regard not only to
the absolute will of God, but to the preparations which were made for the Redeemer on this earth : partly as Thl., ὅτε
πᾶν εἶδος κακίας διεξελθοῦσα ἡ φύσις ἡ
ἀνθρωπίνη ἐδεῖτο θεραπείας, partly as
Bengel, ' suas etiam ecclesia ætates habet.'
The manifestation of man's guilt was complete :—and the way of the Lord was prepared, by various courses of action which
He had brought about by men as his instruments.　**ἐξαπέστ.** cannot,—however little, for the purposes of the present
argument, the divine side of our Lord's
mission is to be pressed,—mean any thing
less than **sent forth** from Himself (reff.).
　　γενόμ. ἐκ γυν. will not bear being
pressed, as Calv., Grot., Estius, al., have
done ("discernere Christum a reliquis vo-

c ver. 21. Rom. γενόμενον ^c ὑπὸ ^c νόμον, 5 ἵνα τοὺς ^c ὑπὸ ^c νόμον ^d ἐξ- ABCDF
vi. 14, 15.
1 Cor. ix. 20. αγοράσῃ, ἵνα τὴν ^e υἱοθεσίαν ^f ἀπολάβωμεν. 6 ^g ὅτι δέ KLPℵ a
d = ch. iii. 13 b c d e f
only. (Eph.
v. 16. Col. ἐστε υἱοί, ^a ἐξαπέστειλεν ὁ θεὸς τὸ πνεῦμα τοῦ υἱοῦ αὐτοῦ g h k l m
iv. 5 only. n o 17. 47
Dan. ii. 8 only.) e Rom. viii. 15, 23. ix. 4. Eph. i. 5 only †. (not found elsw.) f = Luke (vi. 34)
xvi. 25. Num. xxxiv. 14. g so 1 Cor. xii. 15.

6. aft υἱοι add του θεου DF fuld(with [besides F-lat] demid hal tol) goth lat-ff(not
Aug₁). om ο θεος B.

luit hominibus: quia ex semine matris
creatus sit, non viri et mulieris coitu,"
Calv.): it is Christ's HUMANITY which is
the point insisted on, not His being born of
a virgin. On the other hand, the words
cannot for an instant be adduced as *inconsistent* with such birth: they state gene-
rically, what all Christians are able, from
the Gospel record, to fill up specifically.
γενόμ. ὑπὸ νόμον] '*born of a woman,*'
identified Him with all mankind: **born
under** (the idea of motion conveyed by the
accusative after ὑπό is accounted for by the
transition implied in γενόμενος) **the law,**
introduces another condition, in virtue of
which He became the Redeemer of those
who were under a special revelation and
covenant. A Gentile could not (humanly
speaking, as far as God has conditioned
His own proceedings) have saved the
world: for the Jews were the representative nation, to which the representative man must belong. γενόμ. is both
times emphatic, and therefore not to be
here rendered 'legi subjectum,' as Luther,
'unter das Gesetz gethan.' **5.**] See
above. Christ, being born under the law,
a Jewish child, subject to its ordinances,
by His perfect fulfilment of it, and by
enduring, as the Head and in the root of
our nature, its curse on the tree, bought
off (from its curse and power, but see on
ch. iii. 13) those who were under the law:
and if them, then the rest of mankind,
whose nature He had upon Him. Thus
in buying off τοὺς ὑπὸ νόμον, He effected
that ἡμεῖς, all men, τὴν υἱοθεσίαν ἀπολάβωμεν—**should receive** (not '*recover,*' as
Aug., al., and Jowett ('receive back'):
there is no allusion to the innocence which
we lost in Adam, nor was redemption by
Christ in any sense a *recovery* of the state
before the fall, but a far more glorious
thing, the bestowal of an adoption which
Adam never had. Nor is it, as Chrys.,
καλῶς εἶπεν, ἀπολάβωμεν, δεικνὺς ὀφει-
λομένην: it is true, it *was* the subject of
promise, but it is the mere act of *reception,* not how or why it was received,
which is here put forward. Nor again,
with Rückert and Schött., must we render
ἀπο-'*therefrom,*' as a fruit of the redemption. This again it *is,* but it is not
expressed in the word) **the adoption** (the

place, and privileges) **of sons.** The word
υἱοθεσία occurs only in the N. T. In
Herod. vi. 57 we have θετὸν παῖδα ποιέ-
εσθαι, and the same expression in Diod.
Sic. iv. 39. **6.**] Meyer interprets this
verse with Chrys.: καὶ πόθεν δῆλον ὅτι
γεγόναμεν υἱοί, φησίν; εἶπε τρόπον ἕνα,
ὅτι τὸν χριστὸν ἐνεδυσάμεθα τὸν ὄντα
υἱόν· λέγει κ. δεύτερον, ὅτι τὸ πνεῦμα
τῆς υἱοθεσίας ἐλάβομεν· οὐ γὰρ ἂν ἐδυ-
νήθημεν καλέσαι πατέρα, εἰ μὴ πρότερον
υἱοὶ κατέστημεν. And so Thdrt., Thl.,
Ambr., Pel., al., Koppe, Flatt, Rückert,
Schött., and Ellicott. [Jowett combines
both interpretations: but this can hardly
be.] If so, we must assume a very unusual
ellipsis after ὅτι δέ ἐστε υἱοί,—one hardly
justified by such precedents as Rom. xi.
18,—εἰ δὲ κατακαυχᾶσαι, οὐ σὺ τ. ῥίζαν
βαστάζεις, κ.τ.λ., Rom. xi. 15, and supply,
'God hath given you this proof, that....'
Meyer urges in defence of his view the
emphatic position of ἐστε, on which see
below. I prefer the ordinary rendering
because it suits best (1) the simplicity of
construction,—the causal ὅτι thus beginning a sentence followed by an apodosis,
as in ref.,—whereas we have no example
of the demonstrative ὅτι followed by the
ellipsis here supposed: cf. ch. iii. 11, where
δῆλον follows:—(2) the context;—it is
not in *corroboration* of the fact that we
are sons, but as a *consequence* of that fact,
that the Apostle states what follows: to
shew the completeness of the state of sonship. In Rom. viii. 16, the order of these
is inverted, and the witness of the Spirit
proves our sonship: but that does not
affect the present passage, which must
stand on its own ground. (3) The aorist
ἐξαπέστειλεν is against Meyer's view—it
would be in that case ἐξαπέσταλκεν. Ἱ
is now used of the time of the gift of the
Spirit. Render then: **Because moreover
ye are sons** (the stress on ἐστε is hardly to
be urged: υἱοί ἐστε would certainly give
a very strong emphasis on the *noun*: all
we can say of ἐστε υἱοί, where so insignificant a word as a verb substantive is concerned, is that there is now no such strong
stress on υἱοί, but that the *whole fact,* of
the state of sonship having been brought
in, and actually existing, is alleged) **God
sent forth** (not, '*hath sent forth*'—see

εἰς τὰς καρδίας ἡμῶν, [hi] κράζον [ij] Ἀββᾶ ὁ [ij] πατήρ.
7 ὥςτε οὐκ ἔτι εἶ δοῦλος, ἀλλὰ υἱός· εἰ δὲ υἱός, καὶ [k] κληρονόμος διὰ θεοῦ. 8 ἀλλὰ τότε μὲν οὐκ [l] εἰδότες θεὸν
[m] ἐδουλεύσατε τοῖς [n] φύσει μὴ οὖσιν θεοῖς· 9 νῦν δὲ [o] γνόντες [o] θεόν, [p] μᾶλλον δὲ [q] γνωσθέντες ὑπὸ θεοῦ, [r] πῶς [s] ἐπι-

h Mark x. 48 ‖ L. Ps. cvi. 6.
i Rom. viii. 15.
j as above (i). Mark xiv. 36 only.
k ver. 1.
l 1 Thess. iv. 5. 2 Thess. i. 8. (Exod. v. 2.)
m Matt. vi. 24. Acts xx. 19 al. Ps. ii. 11.
n here bis. Rom. ii. 14. ch. ii. 15 (reff.). Eph. ii. 3 only.
o Rom. i. 21. 1 Cor. i. 21. 1 John iv. 6, 7. (Jer. xxxviii. [xxxi.] 34.)
p = Rom. viii. 34. Eph. iv. 28. v. 11.
q 1 Cor. viii. 3. 2 Tim. ii. 19, from Num. xvi. 5. see Matt. vii. 23.
r = Rom. vi. 2. 1 Cor. xv. 12. ch. ii. 14.
s = 2 Pet. ii. 22. Jer. xi. 10.

rec υμων, with D³KL rel vulg syrr copt [æth] Chr Cyr Thdrt [Victorin] Aug: txt ABCD¹F[P]א c l n am(with [besides F-lat] flor hal) [arm] Ps-Justin Ath_2(and elsw-mss_2) Bas Did Ps-Ath [Cyr_1-ms Orig-int_1] Tert Hil Ambrst Jer. [for κραζον, εν ω κραζομεν F arm-mss Victorin.]

7. om εἶ F copt. (αλλα, so ABCD¹FL[P]א b g n o 17.) rec (for δια θεου) θεου δια χριστου (*see note*), with C³DKL[P]א³ rel goth Chr $Thdrt_4$ Œc Damasc: txt ABC¹א¹ 17 vulg copt Clem Ath Bas_{expr} Cyr_2 Did Ambrst Ambr [Victorin] Aug Pel Bede, δια θεον F.

8. rec μη bef φυσει, with D²FL rel syr Chr Cyr_1 Dial-trin Thdrt Ps-Ath [Tert]: om φυσει K D-lat lat-mss-in-Ambr [æth] Iren-int Ambrst [Victorin]: om μη o: txt ABCD¹·³ [P]א k 17 [47] vulg Syr copt goth Ath_4 Bas_2 Nys_4 $Cyr_{sæpe}$ Damasc Jer. εδουλευσατε at end of ver D¹F latt goth [Iren-int Victorin]: txt ABCD²·³KL[P]א rel Ambr Jer.

9. νυνει D¹F[: νυνι Cyr_2-p]. ins τον bef θεον F. aft υπο ins του K Orig

above) **the Spirit of His Son** (you being now fellows with that Son in the communion of the Spirit, won for you as a consequence of His atonement: called, Rom. viii. 15, πνεῦμα υἱοθεσίας, and ib. 9, πνεῦμα χριστοῦ, where participation in Him is said to be the necessary condition of belonging to Christ at all) **into our hearts** (as he changed from the third person to the first in the foregoing verse, so now from the second: both times from the fervour of his heart, wavering between logical accuracy and generous largeness of sympathy), **crying** (in Rom. viii. 15, it is ἐν ᾧ κράζομεν. Here the Spirit being the main subject, is regarded as the agent, and the believer merely as His organ) **Abba Father.** ὁ πατήρ is not a mere Greek explanation of Ἀββᾶ, but an address by His name of relation, of Him to whom the term Ἀββᾶ was used more as a token of affection than as conveying its real meaning of 'my father:' see notes on Mark xiv. 36, Rom. viii. 15. Aug. gives a fanciful reason for the repetition: "Eleganter autem intelligitur non frustra duarum linguarum verba posuisse idem significantia propter universum populum, qui de Judæis et de Gentilibus in unitatem fidei vocatus est: ut Hebræum verbum ad Judæos, Græcum ad gentes, utriusque tamen verbi eadem significatio ad ejusdem fidei spiritusque unitatem pertineat." And so Luther, Calvin, and Bengel. **7.**] Statement of the conclusion from the foregoing, and corroboration, from it, of ch. iii. 29. The second person singular individualizes and points home the inference. Meyer remarks that this individualization has been gradually proceeding from ver. 5—ἀπολάβωμεν,—ἔστε,—εἶ.

διὰ θεοῦ] The rec. θεοῦ διὰ χριστοῦ seems to have been an adaptation to the similar passage, Rom. viii. 17. On the text, Windischmann remarks, "διὰ θεοῦ combines, on behalf of our race, the whole before-mentioned agency of the Blessed Trinity: the Father has sent the Son and the Spirit, the Son has freed us from the law, the Spirit has completed our sonship; and thus the redeemed are heirs through the tri-une God Himself, not through the law, nor through fleshly descent."

8—11.] *Appeal to them*, as the result of the conclusion just arrived at, *why, having passed out of slavery into freedom, they were now going back again.* **8.**] **τότε** refers back for its time, not to ver. 3, as Windischmann, but to οὐκέτι εἶ δοῦλος, ver. 7. In οὐκ εἰδότ. θ., there is no inconsistency with Rom. i. 21: there it is the knowledge which the Gentile world might have had: here, the matter of fact is alleged, that they *had it not.* **τοῖς φύσει μὴ οὖσιν θ.**] **to gods, which by nature exist not**: see 1 Cor. viii. 4; x. 19, 20 and note. The rec. would be, "*to those which are not by nature gods,*" i. e. only made into gods by human fancy: but this is not the Apostle's way of conceiving of the heathen deities. Meyer compares 2 Chron. xiii. 9, ἐγένετο εἰς ἱερέα τῷ μὴ ὄντι θεῷ. Notice μή—giving the Apostle's judgment of their non-existence —and see 2 Cor. v. 21 note, where however I cannot hold with Ellic., that μὴ γνόντα expresses '*God's judgment*' (?).

9.] "The distinction which Olsh. attempts to set up between εἰδότες as the mere outward, and γνόντες as the inner

t – Heb. vii.
18. (so · εἰν,
Rom. viii. 3.)
u = here only.
v ver. 3.
w Wisd. xix. 6.
x = here only.
(Luke vi. 7 ‖
Mk. xiv. 1.
xx. 20. Acts

στρέφετε πάλιν ἐπὶ τὰ ^tἀσθενῆ καὶ ^uπτωχὰ ^vστοιχεῖα, ABCDF KLPℵ a
οἷς ^wπάλιν ^wἄνωθεν ^mδουλεύειν θέλετε ; ¹⁰ ἡμέρας ^xπαρα- b c d e f g h k l m
τηρεῖσθε καὶ ^yμῆνας καὶ ^zκαιροὺς καὶ ἐνιαυτούς. ¹¹ ᵃᵇ φο- n o 17. 47
βοῦμαι ᵃ ὑμᾶς, ᵃᵇ μή ᵃᵇ πως ᶜ εἰκῇ ᵈ κεκοπίακα ᵈ εἰς ὑμᾶς.

ix. 24 only.) ὁ δὲ τέταρτος, παρατηρεῖν τὰς ἑβδομάδας, Jos. Antt. iii. 5. 5.   y Levit. xxiii. 24.
z absol., Acts xvii. 26. Gen. i. 14.   a constr., see Col. iv. 17.   b 2 Cor. xi. 3. xii. 20.   c ch. iit.
4 reff.   d Rom. xvi. 6. indic., see Col. ii. 8. 1 Thess. iii. 5. Winer, ὃ 56. 2. b. α.

Dial-trin Ps-Ath.   ἐπιστρεφεσθαι D¹: ἐπιστρεφεται F.   δουλευσαι Bℵ.
10. transp καιρους and ενιαυτους DF Aug[: om και καιρους P].

knowledge, is mere arbitrary fiction: see John vii. 26, 27; viii. 55; 2 Cor. v. 16." Meyer.   μᾶλλον δὲ γν. ὑπ. θ.] See note on 1 Cor. viii. 3. Here the propriety of the expression is even more strikingly manifest than there: the Galatians did not so much acquire the knowledge of God, as they were taken into knowledge, recognized, by Him,—προσληφθέντες ὑπὸ θεοῦ, Thl.: οὐδὲ γὰρ ὑμεῖς καμόντες εὕρετε τὸν θεόν, . . . αὐτὸς δὲ ὑμᾶς ἐπεσπάσατο, Chrys. And this made their fall from Him the more matter of indignant appeal, as being a resistance of His will respecting them.   No change of the meaning of γνωσθ. must be resorted to, as 'approved,' 'loved' (Grot., al.: see others in De W. and Mey.): cf. Matt. xxv. 12; 2 Tim. ii. 19. Cf. also Phil. iii. 12.   πῶς] how is it that . . . ? see reff.   ἀσθ.] so the προάγουσα ἐντολή is called in Heb. vii. 18, ἀσθενὲς κ. ἀνωφελές. Want of power to justify is that to which the word points here.   πτωχ.] in contrast with the riches which are in Christ. Or both words may perhaps refer back to the state of childhood hinted at in ver. 6, during which the heir is ἀσθενής, as immature, and πτωχός, as not yet in possession. But this would not strictly apply to the elements as the Gentiles were concerned with them: see below.   On στοιχεῖα, see note, ver. 3.   πάλιν] These Galatians had never been Jews before : but they had been before under the στοιχεῖα τοῦ κόσμου, under which generic term both Jewish and Gentile cultus was comprised: so that they were turning back again to these elements.   ἄνωθεν] from the beginning,—afresh ; not a repetition of πάλιν: Mey. quotes πάλιν ἐξ ἀρχῆς, Barnab. Ep. 16, p. 773 Migne: and Wetstein gives, from Plautus, Cas. Prol. 33, 'rursum denuo.'   θέλετε, as in E. V., ye desire : but if thus expressed here by our translators, why not also in John v. 40, where it is still more emphatic ?
10.] The affirmative form seems best, as (see Ellic.) supplying a verification of the charge just brought against them interrogatively: explaining τίς τῆς δουλείας τρόπος, Thdrt. Wishing to shew to them in its most contemptible light

the unworthiness of their decadence, he puts the *observation of days* in the forefront of his appeal, as one of those things which they already practised. Circumcision he does not mention, because they were not yet drawn into it, but only in danger of being so (ch. v. 2, al.):—nor abstinence from meats, to which we do not hear that they were even tempted.   ἡμέρας, emphatic, as the first mentioned, and also as a more general predication of the habit, under which the rest fall. The days would be sabbaths, new moons, and feast days: see Col. ii. 16, where these are specified.   παρατηρ.] There does not seem to be any meaning of superstitious or inordinate observance (as Olsh., Winer, &c.), but merely a statement of the fact: see ref. Joseph., where, remarkable enough, the word is applied to the very commandment (the fourth) here in question. "When παρά is ethical, i. e. when the verb is used in a bad sense, e. g. ἐνεδρεύειν κ. παρατηρεῖν, Polyb. xvii. 3. 2, the idea conveyed is that of *hostile observation.*" Ellicott.   μῆνας] hardly new moons, which were *days :* but perhaps the seventh month, or any others which were distinguished by great feasts.   καιρούς] any festal seasons: so Levit. xxiii. 4, αὗται αἱ ἑορταὶ τῷ κυρίῳ κληταὶ ἅγιαι, ἃς καλέσετε αὐτὰς ἐν τοῖς καιροῖς αὐτῶν.   ἐνιαυτούς] can hardly apply to the sabbatical or jubilee years, on account of their rare occurrence, unless indeed with Wieseler, Chron. der Apost. Zeitalt. p. 286 note, we are to suppose that they were then celebrating one : perhaps those observations may be intended which especially regarded the *year,* as the *new* year. But this is not likely (see above on μῆνας): and I should much rather suppose, that each of these words is not minutely to be pressed, but all taken together as a rhetorical description of those who observed times and seasons. Notice how utterly such a verse is at variance with any and every theory of a *Christian sabbath,* cutting at the root, as it does, of ALL obligatory *observance of times as such :* see notes on Rom. xiv. 5, 6; Col. ii. 16. "These periodical solemnities of the

¹² Γίνεσθε ὡς ἐγώ, ὅτι κἀγὼ ὡς ὑμεῖς, ἀδελφοί, δέομαι ὑμῶν. οὐδέν με ἠδικήσατε· ¹³ οἴδατε δὲ ὅτι δι᾽ ἀσθένειαν

law shewed, by the fact of their periodical repetition, the imperfection of the dispensation to which they belonged : typifying each feature of Christ's work, which, as one great and perfect whole, has been performed once for all and for ever,—and were material representations of those spiritual truths which the spiritual Israel learn in union with Christ as a risen Lord. To observe periods then, now in the fulness of time, is to deny the perfection of the Christian dispensation, the complete and finished nature of Christ's work : to forsake Him as the great spiritual teacher of His brethren, and to return to carnal pædagogues : to throw aside sonship in all its fulness, and the spirit of adoption : and to return to childhood and the rule of tutors and governors." Bagge : who however elsewhere maintains the perpetual obligation of the Sabbath. **11.**] There is no attraction in the construction (φοβ. ὑμᾶς, μή πως ....), as Winer (comm. in loc.) holds: in that case ὑμεῖς must be the subject of the next clause (so in Diod. Sic. iv. 40 (Meyer), τὸν ἀδελφὸν εὐλαβεῖσθαι, μή ποτε .... ἐπίθηται τῇ βασιλείᾳ): but φοβ. ὑμᾶς stands alone, and the following clause explains it. So Soph. Œd. Tyr. 760, δέδοικ᾽ ἐμαυτὸν ... μὴ πόλλ᾽ ἄγαν εἰρημέν᾽ ᾖ μοι. The indicative assumes the fact which μή πως deprecates :—see reff. **12—16.**] *Appeal to them to imitate him, on the ground of their former love and veneration for him.* **12.**] This has been variously understood. But the only rendering which seems to answer the requirements of the construction and the context, is that which understands εἰμι or γέγονα after ἐγώ, and refers it to the Apostle having in his own practice cast off Jewish habits and become as the Galatians : i. e. a Gentile : see 1 Cor. ix. 20, 21. And so Winer, Neander, Fritz., De W., Meyer, Jowett (alt.), &c. (2) Chrys., Thdrt., Thl., Erasm.-par., al., regard it as said to Jewish believers, and explain,— τοῦτον εἶχον πάλαι τὸν ζῆλον· σφόδρα τὸν νόμον ἐπόθουν· ἀλλ᾽ ὁρᾶτε πῶς μεταβέβλημαι. ταύτην τοίνυν καὶ ὑμεῖς ζηλώσατε τὴν μεταβολήν (Thdrt.). But to this Meyer rightly objects, that ἤμην, which would in this case have to be supplied, must have been *expressed*, as being emphatic, and cites from Justin ad Græcos, c. 2, where however I cannot find it, γίνεσθε ὡς ἐγώ, ὅτι κἀγὼ ἤμην ὡς ὑμεῖς. (3) Jerome, Erasm.-not., Corn.-a-lap., Estius, Michaelis, Rückert, Olsh., ᾽.... as also I have accom-

modated myself to you.' But thus the second member of the sentence will not answer to the first. (4) Luther, Beza, Calvin, Grot., Bengel, Morus, Peile, al., would understand it, 'love me, as I love you' ("accipite hanc meam objurgationem eo animo quo vos objurgavi: ... sit in vobis is affectus erga me, qui est in me erga vos," Luth.). But nothing has been said of a want of *love :* and certainly had this been meant, it would have been more plainly expressed. The words ἀδελφοί, δέομαι ὑμῶν are by Chrys., Thdrt., al., Luther, Koppe, al., joined to the following: but wrongly, for there is no δέησις in what follows. οὐδέν με ἠδικήσατε] The key to rightly understanding these words is, their apposition with ἐξουθενήσατε, ... ἐξεπτύσατε ... ἐδέξασθε below. To that period they refer : viz. to the time when he first preached the Gospel among them, and the first introduction of this period seems to be in the words, ὅτι κἀγὼ ὡς ὑμεῖς. Then I became as you : and at that time you did me no wrong, but on the contrary shewed me all sympathy and reverence. Then comes in the inference, put in the form of a question, at ver. 16,—I must then have *since* become your enemy by telling you the truth. The other explanations seem all more or less beside the purpose : δηλῶν ὅτι οὐ μίσους, οὐδὲ ἔχθρας ἦν τὰ εἰρημένα .. Chrys., and similarly Thl., Aug., Pel., Luth., Calv. ('non excandesco mea causa, nec quod vobis sim infensus'), Estius, Winer, al., which would be irrelevant, and indeed preposterous without some introduction after the affection of the foregoing words : ᾽ *ye have done me no wrong,*' i. e. ᾽ ex animo omnia condonabat si resipiscerentur,' Beza : so Bengel, Rückert, al.,—which is refuted by the aorist ἠδικήσατε, of some definite *time.* The same is true of ᾽ ye have wronged not me but yourselves ' (Ambr., Corn.-a-lap., Schött.), —᾽ ... not me, but God, or Christ ' (Grot. al.). **13.**] δι᾽ ἀσθένειαν τῆς σαρκός can surely bear but one rendering,—on **account of bodily weakness** : all others (e. g. '*in weakness,*' as E. V., μετὰ ἀσθενείας, as Œc., Thl., ᾽ *per infirmitatem,*' as vulg., Luth., Beza, Grot., Estius, Jowett (comparing Phil. i. 15, where see note), '*during a period of sickness,*' as Mr. Bagge) are ungrammatical, or irrelevant, as ᾽ *on account of the infirmity of* (your) *flesh* ' (Jer., Estius, Hig., Rettig), which would require some qualifying adverb such as οὕτως with εὐηγγελισάμην, and would be-

e constr., ch. i. 8. Rom. i.
15. pass.,
1 Pet. iv. 6.
f John vi. 62.
ix. 8. 1 Tim. i. 13 only.
Gen. xiii. 3.
g Luke xxii.
28. Acts xx.
19. 1 Cor. x.
13 al. Deut.
iv. 34.

τῆς σαρκὸς ᵉ εὐηγγελισάμην ὑμῖν ᶠτὸ ᶠπρότερον, ¹⁴ καὶ
τὸν ᵍ πειρασμὸν ὑμῶν ʰ ἐν τῇ σαρκί μου οὐκ ⁱ ἐξουθενήσατε οὐδὲ ᵏ ἐξεπτύσατε, ἀλλὰ ὡς ἄγγελον θεοῦ
ˡ ἐδέξασθέ με, ὡς χριστὸν Ἰησοῦν. ¹⁵ ποῦ οὖν ὁ ᵐ μακα-
ρισμὸς ὑμῶν; ⁿ μαρτυρῶ γὰρ ὑμῖν ὅτι εἰ δυνατὸν τοὺς

ABCDF
KLPℵ a
b c d e f
g h k l m
n o 17. 47

h see 2 Cor. xii. 7.   i Rom. xiv. 3.   1 Cor. i. 28. vi. 4 al.   Prov. i. 7.   k here only †.
l = Matt. x. 14, 40.   Luke ix. 53.   2 Cor. vii. 15.   Wisd. xix. 14.   m Rom. iv. 6, 9 only †.
n constr., Acts xxii. 5.   Rom. x. 2.   Col. iv. 13.

13. om δε D¹F goth Damasc [Victorin] Aug.   om της F a.

14. rec (for υμων) μου τον, with D³KL[P] rel syr Chr Thdrt Damasc Œc : τον ℵ³ m
Syr goth arm Bas Thl : txt ABD¹Fℵ¹ 17. 67²(Bch) latt copt Cyr lat-ff, υμων τον C²
[Orig]. (C¹ illegible.)   om ουκ ℵ¹(ins ℵ-corr¹ ᵒᵇ¹).   (αλλα, so BF.)   [εξεδεξ. C.]

15. rec (for που) τις, with DKL rel syr goth æth-rom Thdor-mops Thl Œc [Victorin]
Aug₂ Ambrst : txt ABCF[P]ℵ 17 [47] 67² vulg Syr syr-mg copt arm Damasc Jer Pel
Bede. ("τὸ τίς ἀντὶ τοῦ ποῦ τέθεικεν" Chr Thdrt.)   rec aft ουν ins ην, with DK vss
Chr [Victorin]; η F : fuit aut est G-lat; εστιν 115 vulg Jer Sedul; νυν 122: om

sides be wholly out of place in an Epistle in
which he is recalling them to the substance
of his first preaching.   The meaning then
will be, that it was *on account of an illness*
that he first preached in Galatia : i. e. that
he was for that reason detained there, and
preached, which otherwise he would not
have done. On this, see Prolegomena, § ii.
3 : the fact itself, I cannot help thinking,
is plainly asserted here. Beware of conjectural emendation, such as δι' ἀσθενείας
of Peile, for which there is neither warrant nor need. τὸ πρότερον may
mean 'formerly,' but is more probably
'the first time,' with reference to that
second visit hinted at below, ver. 16, and
ch. v. 21. See Prolegomena, § v. 3.   **14.**]
I had in some former editions retained the
rec., feeling persuaded that out of it the
other readings have arisen. The whole
tenor of the passage seeming to shew that
the Apostle's weakness was spoken of as a
trial to the Galatians, μου appeared to
have been altered to ὑμῶν,—or to have
been omitted by some who could not see
its relevance, or its needfulness. But
the principles of sounder criticism have
taught me how unsafe is such ground
of arguing, and have compelled me to
adopt the text of the most ancient
mss. The **temptation** seems to have
been the 'thorn in the flesh' of 2 Cor.
xii. 1 ff., whatever that was: perhaps
something connected with his sight, or
some nervous infirmity: see below, and
notes on Acts xiii. 9 ; xxiii. 1.   ἐξ-
επτύσατε] "expresses figuratively and in
a climax the sense of ἐξουθ. Cf. the Latin
despuere, respuere. In other Greek writers
we have only καταπτύειν τινός, ἀποπτύ-
ειν τινά (Eur. Troad. 668; Hec. 1265.
Hes. ἔργ. 724), and διαπτύειν τινά in this
metaphorical sense,—but ἐκπτύειν always
in its literal sense (Hom. Od. ε. 322), as

also ἐμπτύειν τινί. Even in the passage
cited by Kypke from Plut., Alex. i. p.
328, it is in its literal sense, as ὥσπερ
χαλινόν follows. We must treat this
then as a departure from Greek usage,
and regard it as occasioned by ἐξουθ., as
Paul loves to repeat the same prepositions
in composition (Rom. ii. 17 ; xi. 7 al.),
not without emphasis." Meyer.
ὡς ἄγγελ. θ., ὡς χρ. Ἰησ.] a climax:—
besides the freedom of angels from fleshly
weakness, there is doubtless an allusion to
their office as messengers—and to His
saying, who is above the angels, Luke x.
16. No inference can be drawn from
these expressions being used of *the Galatians' reception* of him, that they were
already Christians when he first visited
them : the words are evidently not to be
pressed as accurate in point of chronology,
but involve an ὕστερον πρότερον : not,
'as you *would have* received,' &c., but 'as
you would (now) receive.'   **15.**] **Where
then** (i. e. where in estimation, holding
what place) (**was**) **your congratulation**
(of yourselves)? i. e. considering your
fickle behaviour since. 'Quæ causa fuit
gratulationis, si vos nunc pœnitet mei ?'
Bengel. Various explanations have been
given: ' quæ (reading τίς) *erat beatitudo
vestra*,' neglecting the οὖν, and making
μακαρισμός into *beatitudo*, which it will
not bear: so Œc., Luth., Beza, &c. All
making the words into an *exclamation*
(even if τίς be read) is inconsistent with
the context, and with the logical precision
of οὖν, and ὥστε below. ' *Where is then
the blessedness ye spake of ?*' (E. V.) is
perhaps as good a rendering as the words
will bear. μαρτυρῶ γὰρ . . .] a proof
to what lengths this μακαρισμός, and consequently their high value for St. Paul
ran, at his first visit. In seeking for a
reference for this expression, τ. ὀφθ. ὑμῶν

ὀφθαλμοὺς ὑμῶν ° ἐξορύξαντες ᵖ ἐδώκατέ μοι. 16 ὥστε °= here (Mark
ii. 4) only.
ᑫ ἐχθρὸς ὑμῶν γέγονα ʳ ἀληθεύων ὑμῖν; 17 ˢ ζηλοῦσιν Judg. xvi. 21
A. 1 Kings
ὑμᾶς οὐ ᵗ καλῶς, ἀλλὰ ᵘ ἐκκλεῖσαι ὑμᾶς θέλουσιν, ἵνα xi. 2. (Prov.
xix. 22 only.)
see note.

John ix. 33. xv. 22. xix. 11. Rom. vii. 7. Winer, § 42. 2.　　ᵖ ἄν omitted
iv. 15 only. Gen. xlii. 16.　　　　　　　　　　q = Rom. xi. 28.　　ʳ Eph.
ἐπαινούμενος κ. ζηλούμενος ὑπὸ τ. ἄλλων.　　s = 2 Cor. xi. 2. Zech. i. 14. pass., see Xen. Mem. ii. 1. 19,
al. 2 Macc. xv. 38.　　u Rom. iii. 27 only. Exod. xxiii. 2 B.　t John xviii. 23. 1 Cor. vii. 37. ch. v. 7
　　　　　　　　　　　　　　　　　　　　　　　2 Macc. xiii. 21 Ald. only.

ABCL[P]א m o 17 [47] 67² æth Thdrt-ms Damasc Thl.　　rec ins αν bef εδωκατε,
with D³KL[P]א³ rel: και, F; add et latt: om ABCD¹א¹ 17 [47] Damasc.
　　16. aft ωστε add εγω D¹(and lat) F Cypr.
　　17. elz (for 2nd υμας) ημας (apparently, from a conjecture of Beza's): txt A B(sic,
see table) CDFKL[P]א rel vss Eus Chr Thdrt Damasc lat-ff.　　[θελοντες P.]

ἐξορ. ἐδώκ. μοι, the right course will be,
not at once to adopt the conclusion, that
they point to ocular weakness on the part
of the Apostle, nor because they form a
trite proverb in many languages, therefore to set down (as Meyer, De W., Windischmann, al., have done) at once that
no such allusion can have been intended,
but to judge from the words themselves
and our information from other sources
whether such an allusion is likely. And
in doing so, I may observe that a proverbial expression so harsh in its nature, and
so little prepared by the context, would
perhaps hardly have been introduced without some particle of climax. Would not
the Apostle have more naturally written,
ὅτι εἰ δυνατόν, καὶ τοὺς ὀφθ. ὑμ. . . . . ?
Had the καί been inserted, it would have
deprived the words of all reference to a
matter of fact, and made them purely
proverbial. At the same time it is fair to
say that the order τοὺς ὀφθ. ὑμῶν rather
favours the purely proverbial reference.
Had the Apostle's eyes been affected, and
had he wished to express " You would, if
possible, have pulled out your own eyes,
and have given them to me," he would
certainly have written ὑμῶν τοὺς ὀφθ., not
τοὺς ὀφθ. ὑμῶν. In other words, the
more emphatic τοὺς ὀφθαλμούς is, the
more likely is the expression to be proverbial merely : the less emphatic τ. ὀφθ.
is, the more likely to refer to some fact,
in which the eyes were as matter of
notoriety concerned. The inference then
of any ocular disease from these words
themselves seems to me precarious. Certainly Acts xxiii. 1 ff. receives light from
such a supposition; but with our very
small knowledge on the subject, many conjectures may be hazarded with some shew
of support from Scripture, while none of
them has enough foundation to make it
probable on the whole. The proverb is
abundantly illustrated by Wetst. ἐξορύσ-
σω is the regular classic word : cf. Herod.
viii. 116: this however is doubted by
Ellic. See on the whole passage, Jow-

ett's most interesting "fragment on the
character of St. Paul," Epp. &c. vol. i.
pp. 290—303. 16.] So that (as
things now stand; an inference derived
from the contrast between their former
love and their present dislike of him. See
Klotz, Devar. ii. 776) have I become your
enemy (' hated by you;'—ἐχθρ. in passive
sense : or perhaps it may be active, as
Ellic.) by speaking the truth (see Eph.
iv. 15 note) to you? When did he thus
incur their enmity by speaking the truth ?
Not at his first visit, from the whole tenor
of this passage : nor in this letter, as some
think (Jer., Luther, al.), which they had
not yet read ; but at his second visit, see
Acts xviii. 23, when he probably found the
mischief beginning, and spoke plainly
against it. Cf. similar expressions in
Wetst. : especially ' obsequium amicos,
veritas odium parit,' Ter. Andr. i. 1. 40:
ὀργίζονται ἅπαντες τοῖς μετὰ παρρησίας
τ' ἀληθῆ λέγουσι, Lucian, Abdic. 7.
17.] 'My telling you the truth may have
made me seem your enemy : but I warn
you that these men who court you so
zealously (see ref. 2 Cor., and cf. Plut. vii.
762, cited by Fritz. ὑπὸ χρείας τὸ πρῶτον
ἕπονται κ. ζηλοῦσιν, ὕστερον δὲ καὶ φιλοῦ-
σιν) have no honourable purpose in so
doing : it is only in order to get you away
from the community as a separate clique,
that you may court them.' Thus the verse
seems to fit best into the context. As regards particular words, ἐκκλείω must bear
the meaning of exclusion from a larger and
attraction to a smaller, viz. their own,
party. (Our very word ' exclusive ' conveys the same idea.) I have therefore not
adopted Mey.'s rendering, ' from all other
teachers,'—nor that of Luther (1538),
Calv., Grot., Beng., Rück., Olsh., Winer,
al., ' from me and my communion,'—nor
that of Chrys., Œc., Thl., τῆς τελείας
γνώσεως ἐκβαλεῖν,—nor that of Erasm.,
Corn.-a-lap., ' from Christian freedom.'
The mood of ζηλοῦτε has been disputed : and it must remain uncertain here,
as in 1 Cor. iv. 6, where see note. Here as

v indic. (?) αὐτοὺς ^{sv} ζηλοῦτε. ¹⁸ καλὸν δὲ ^s ζηλοῦσθαι ἐν καλῷ ABCDF
pres., 1 Cor.
iv. 6. Tit. ii. πάντοτε, καὶ μὴ μόνον ^w ἐν τῷ ^x παρεῖναί με ^x πρὸς ὑμᾶς.
4. 1 John v.
20. (see Rev. ¹⁹ ^y τεκνία μου, ^z οὓς πάλιν ^{za} ὠδίνω, ^b ἄχρις οὗ ^c μορφωθῇ
iii. 9 al.)
w Matt. xiii. 4

KLℵ a
b c d e f
g h k l m
n o 17.47

al. Ezek. ix.
8.   x here bis. Acts xii. 20. 2 Cor. xi. 8.   y Paul, here only. John xiii. 33 al6. only†.   z constr.,
here only. ἡ πρὶν ὠδίνουσ' ἐμέ, Iph. Aul. 1234. ὠδίνουσα καλὰς πράξεις, Philo, Deus immut. 29, vol. i. p.
293.   a ver. 27. Rev. xii. 2 only. Isa. xxiii. 4 al.   b constr., Rom. xi. 25. 1 Cor. xi. 26.
c here only. Isa. xliv. 13 F (not ABℵ) only.

at end ins ζηλουτε δε τα κρειττω χαρισματα (see 1 Cor xii. 31) D¹F Victorin Ambrst Sedul.
18. for δε, γαρ 17 : quoque F-lat: om D¹F h Victorin Ambr₂.   rec ins το bef ζη-
λουσθαι, with DFKL[P] rel Chr Thdrt Thl Œc : om ABCℵ 17 Damasc.—ζηλουσθε
(itacism) Bℵ 17 vulg(and F-lat) Damasc Jer Ambrst : txt ACDFKL[P] rel [syr copt
goth æth arm] Chr Thdrt Thl Œc Aug Ambr.   for εν καλ. παν., παν. εν τω αγαθω
F(not F-lat).   for μη, ον DF.
19. for τεκνια, τεκνα B D¹(sic) Fℵ¹ Eus₂ Marcell [Orig-int₃ Hil₁ Victorin]: txt ACD²·³
KL[P]ℵ³ rel Clem Meth [Eus] Bas₂ Chr Cyr Thdrt₄ Damasc Phot [Orig-int₃ Hil₁].
for αχρ., μεχρις Bℵ¹ m.

there Meyer would give ἵνα the meaning
of ' in which case :' but it is surely far better where the sentence so plainly requires
ἵνα of the purpose, to suppose some peculiar
usage or solœcism in formation of the subjunctive on the part of the Apostle.
18.] Two meanings are open to us : (1) as
E. V. (apparently : but perhaps ' zealously
affected' may be meant for the passive—for
' earnestly courted ') and many Commentators taking ζηλοῦσθαι as middle—or passive with a signification nearly the same,
' it is good to be zealously affected in a
good cause, and not only during my presence with you :' in which case the sense
must be referred back to vv. 13—15, and the
allusion must be to their zeal while he was
with them. But, considering that this context is broken at ver. 17,—that the words
ζηλοῦσθαι ἐν καλῷ are an evident reference
to ζηλοῦσιν ὑμ. οὐ καλῶς, and that the
wider context of the whole passage adduces
a contrast between their conduct when he
was with them and now, I think it much
better (2) to explain thus : ' I do not
mean to blame them in the abstract for τὸ
ζηλοῦν ὑμᾶς : any teacher who did this
καλῶς, preaching Christ, would be a cause
of joy to me (Phil. i. 15—18) : and it is
an honourable thing (for you) to be the
objects of this zeal ('ambiri') ἐν καλῷ, in a
good cause (I still cannot see how this rendering of ἐν καλῷ ' alters the meaning of
the verb ' (Ellic.) : it rather seems to me
that the non-use of καλῶς, while the paronomasia is retained, leads to this meaning), at all times and by every body, not
only when I am (or was) present with
you :' q. d. ' I have no wish, in thus
writing, to set up an exclusive claim to
ζηλοῦν ὑμᾶς—whoever will really teach
you good, at any time, let him do it and
welcome.' Then the next verse follows
naturally also, in which he narrows from
relation between himself and them, from

the wide one of a mere ζηλωτής, to the
closer one of their parent in Christ, much
as in 1 Cor. iv. 14 f.,—ὡς τέκνα μου
ἀγαπητὰ νουθετῶ· ἐὰν γὰρ μυρίους παιδ-
αγωγοὺς ἔχητε ἐν χριστῷ, ἀλλ' οὐ πολλοὺς
πατέρας· ἐν γὰρ χρ. Ἰησοῦ διὰ τ. εὐαγγελίου ἐγὼ ὑμᾶς ἐγέννησα.   On other
interpretations, I may remark, (α) that
after ζηλοῦσιν, the strict passive meaning
is the only suitable one for ζηλοῦσθαι, as
it is indeed the only one justified by
usage : (β) that ζηλόω must keep its
meaning throughout, which will exclude
all such renderings as ' invidiose tractari '
here (Koppe) : (γ) that all applications of
the sentence to the Apostle himself as its
object (ἐν καλῷ, in the matter of a good
teacher, as Estius, Corn.-a-lap., al.) are
beside the purpose.   **19.**] belongs to
what follows, not to the preceding. Lachmann, (I suppose on account of the δέ
following, but see below,) with that want
of feeling for the characteristic style of
St. Paul which he so constantly shews in
punctuating, has attached this as a flat
and irrelevant appendage to the last verse
(so also Bengel, Knapp, Rückert, al.) :
and has besides tamed down τεκνία into
τέκνα, thus falling into the trap laid by
some worthless corrector. **My little chil-**
dren (the diminutive occurs only here in
St. Paul, but is manifestly purposely, and
most suitably chosen for the propriety of
the metaphor. It is found (see reff.)
often in St. John, while our Apostle has
τέκνον, 1 Tim. i. 18 ; 2 Tim. ii. 1), **whom**
(the change of gender is common enough.
Meyer quotes an apposite example from
Eur. Suppl. 12, θανόντων ἑπτὰ γενναίων
τέκνων . . . . οὓς ποτ' . . . . ἤγαγε) **I again**
(a second time ; the former was ἐν τῷ
παρεῖναί με, ver. 18) **travail with** (bear,
as a mother, with pain and anxiety, till
the time of birth) **until Christ shall have**
been fully formed within you (for Christ

χριστὸς ἐν ὑμῖν, 20 ᵈ ἤθελον δὲ ˣ παρεῖναι ˣ πρὸς ὑμᾶς ἄρτι καὶ ᵉ ἀλλάξαι τὴν φωνήν μου, ὅτι ᶠ ἀπορούμαι ἐν ὑμῖν. 21 Λέγετέ μοι οἱ ᵍ ὑπὸ ᵍ νόμον θέλοντες εἶναι, τὸν νόμον οὐκ ʰ ἀκούετε; 22 ⁱ γέγραπται γὰρ ὅτι Ἀβραὰμ δύο υἱοὺς ἔσχεν, ἕνα ἐκ τῆς ᵏ παιδίσκης καὶ ἕνα ἐκ τῆς ˡ ἐλευθέρας. 23 ἀλλ᾽ ὁ μὲν ἐκ τῆς ᵏ παιδίσκης ᵐ κατὰ ᵐⁿ σάρκα γεγέννηται, ὁ δὲ ἐκ τῆς ˡ ἐλευθέρας ᵒ διὰ τῆς ἐπαγγελίας. 24 ᴾ ἅτινά ἐστιν ᑫ ἀλληγορούμενα· αὗται γάρ ʳ εἰσιν δύο

d imperf., = Acts xxv. 22.
Rom. ix. 3.
Winer, § 41.
a. 2.
e Acts vi. 14.
Rom. i. 23.
1 Cor. xv. 51, 52. Heb. i.
12, from Ps. ci. 26 only.
Levit. xxvii. 33.
f Luke xxiv. 4.
John xiii. 22.
Acts xxv. 20.
2 Cor. iv. 8.
g Gen. xxxii. 7.
g vv. 4, 5.

h = Matt. x. 14. Luke xvi. 29. Isa. xlviii. 18. i Gen. xvi. 15. xxi. 1, 2. k = Matt.
xxvi. 69. Acts xii. 13 al. Gen. xvi. 1. xx. 17. l = 1 Cor. vii. 21. Neh. xiii. 17.
m Rom. i. 3. iv. 1. ix. 35. 1 Cor. x. 18 al. P. see John viii. 15. n = Rom. ix. 8. o = Rom. xii. 3.
p = Col. ii. 23. q here only †. (see note.) r = Matt. xxvi. 26. xiii. 38. John xv.
1. 1 Cor. x. 4. Gen. xli. 26, 27.

21. for ακουετε, αναγινωσκετε DF latt coptt arm Orig₁ Cyr₁[txt₂-p] Jer₁ Ambr₁ Ambrst [Victorin] Bede.
23. om μεν B vulg Tert Hil. γεγενηται D¹ m¹ 17 [syr-mg-gr] Orig₂. ελευθεριας(sic) ℵ. δι᾽ επαγγ., omg της, ACℵ b¹ o 17 Cyr₂ Damasc Thdrt₁.
24. for αυται, αντα F. rec ins αι bef δυο, with ℵ¹ 67 [Orig₂]: om ABCDFKL [P]ℵ³ rel [Orig₁].

dwelling in a man is the secret and principle of his new life, see ch. ii. 20),
20.] yea, I could wish (see note on Rom. ix. 3. There is a contrast in the δέ between his present anxiety in absence from them and his former παρεῖναι ver. 18: similar constructions with δέ are frequent, especially after vocatives, when some particular is adduced more or less inconsistent with the *address* which has preceded: thus Hom. Il. o. 244, Ἕκτορ, υἱὲ Πριάμοιο, τίη δὲ σὺ νόσφιν ἀπ᾽ ἄλλων | ἧσ᾽ ὀλιγηπελέων; Eur. Hec. 372, μῆτερ, σὺ δ᾽ ἡμῖν μηδὲν ἐμποδὼν γένῃ . . . al. freq.) **to be present with you now, and to change my voice** (from what, to what? Some say, from mildness to severity. But surely such a change would be altogether beside the tone of this deeply affectionate address. I should rather hold, with Meyer, —from my former severity, when I became your enemy by ἀληθεύων ὑμῖν, to the softness and mildness of a mother, still ἀληθεύων, but in another tone. The great majority of Commentators understand ἀλλάξαι as Corn.-a-lap. (Mey.): 'ut scilicet quasi mater nunc blandirer, nunc gemerem, nunc obsecrarem, nunc objurgarem vos.' But so much can hardly be contained in the mere word ἀλλάξαι without some addition, such as πρὸς τὸν καιρόν, πρὸς τὸ συμφέρον (1 Cor. xii. 7), or the like): **for I am perplexed about you** (not '*I am suspected among you*,' but ἐν ὑμῖν as in 2 Cor. vii. 16, θαρρῶ ἐν ὑμῖν,— the element in which: the other is irrelevant, and inconsistent with the N. T. usage of ἀπορούμαι: see reff. The verb is passive: Meyer quotes Demosth. p. 830. 2, πολλὰ τοίνυν ἀπορηθεὶς περὶ τούτων

κ. καθ᾽ ἕκαστον ἐξελεγχόμενος, and Sir. xviii. 7, ὅταν παύσηται, τότε ἀπορηθήσεται). **21—30.**] *Illustration of the relative positions of the law and the promise, by an allegorical interpretation of the history of the two sons of Abraham*: "intended to destroy the influence of the false Apostles with their own weapons, and to root it up out of its own proper soil" (Meyer). **21.** θέλοντες] καλῶς εἶπεν οἱ θέλοντες, οὐ γὰρ τῆς τῶν πραγμάτων ἀκολουθίας, ἀλλὰ τῆς ἐκείνων ἀκαίρου φιλονεικίας τὸ πρᾶγμα ἦν. Chrys. **τ. νόμον οὐκ ἀκούετε**] do ye not **hear** (heed) the **law**, listen to that which the law imparts and impresses on its hearers? Meyer would understand, 'do ye not hear the law read?' viz. in the synagogues, &c. But the other seems to me more natural. **22.**] γάρ answers to a tacit assumption of a negative answer to the foregoing question—'nay, ye do not: *for*,' &c. Phrynichus says on **παιδίσκη**, τοῦτο ἐπὶ τῆς θεραπαίνης οἱ νῦν τιθέασιν, οἱ δ᾽ ἀρχαῖοι ἐπὶ τῆς νεανίδος, οἷς ἀκολουθητέον. **23.**] κατὰ **σάρκα**, according to nature, in her usual course: δι᾽ ἐπαγγελίας, by virtue of (the) **promise**, as the efficient cause of Sara's becoming pregnant contrary to nature: see Rom. iv. 19. **24.**] which things (on ὅς and ὅστις see Ellic.'s note: here ἅτινα seems to enlarge the allegory beyond the mere births of the two sons to all the circumstances attending them) **are allegorical**: i. e. to be understood otherwise than according to their literal sense. So Suidas: ἀληγορία, ἡ μεταφορά, ἄλλο λέγον τὸ γράμμα, κ. ἄλλο τὸ νόημα: Hesych., ἀλληγορία, ἄλλο τι παρὰ τὸ

s ch. iii. 15, 17 reff.   s διαθῆκαι· μία   t μὲν ἀπὸ ὄρους Σινᾶ, εἰς   u δουλείαν   ABCDF
KLPℵ a
t μέν solita-
rium, Col. ii. 23 reff.   u ch. v. 1 reff.   b c d e f
g h k l m
n o 17.47

ἀκουόμενον ὑποδεικνύουσα : and gloss. N. Τ., ἀλληγορούμενα, ἑτέρως κατὰ μετάφρασιν νοούμενα, καὶ οὐ κατὰ τὴν ἀνάγνωσιν. The word is often used, as the thing signified by it is exemplified, by Philo. It was the practice of the Rabbinical Jews to allegorize the O. T. history. "Singula fere gesta quæ narrantur, allegorice quoque et mystice interpretantur. Neque hac in parte labores ipsorum plane possumus contemnere. Nam eadem Paulus habet, qualia sunt de Adamo primo et secundo, de cibo et potu spirituali, de Hagare, etc. Sic Joannes memorat Sodomum et Ægyptum mysticam, plagas item Ægyptias per revelationem hostibus Ecclesiæ immittendas prædicit," Schöttgen. How various persons take this allegorical comment of the Apostle, depends very much on their views of his authority as a Scripture interpreter. To those who receive the law as a great system of prophetic figures, there can be no difficulty in believing the events by which the giving of the law was prepared to have been prophetic figures also : not losing thereby any of their historic reality, but bearing to those who were able to see it aright, this deeper meaning. And to such persons, the fact of St. Paul and other sacred writers adducing such allegorical interpretations brings no surprise and no difficulty, but only strong confirmation of their belief that there are such deeper meanings lying hid under the O. T. history. That the Rabbis and the Fathers, holding such deeper senses, should have often missed them, and allegorized fancifully and absurdly, is nothing to the purpose : it is surely most illogical to argue that because they were wrong, St. Paul cannot be right. The only thing which really does create any difficulty in my mind, is, that Commentators with spiritual discernment, and appreciation of such a man as our Apostle, should content themselves with quietly casting aside his Scripture interpretation wherever, as here, it passes their comprehension. On their own view of him, it would be at least worth while to consider whether his knowledge of his own Scriptures may not have surpassed ours. But to those who believe that he had the Spirit of God, this passage speaks very solemnly ; and I quite agree with Mr. Conybeare in his note, edn. 2, vol. ii. p. 178, "The lesson to be drawn from this whole passage, as regards the Christian use of the O. T., is of an

importance which can scarcely be overrated." Of course no one, who reads, marks, learns, and inwardly digests the Scriptures, can subscribe to the shallow and indolent dictum of Macknight, 'This is to be laid down as a fixed rule, that *no ancient history is to be considered as allegorical, but that which inspired persons have interpreted allegorically :* but at the same time, in allegorizing Scripture, he will take care to follow the analogy of the faith, and proceed soberly, and in dependence on that Holy Spirit, who alone can put us in possession of His own mind in His word.' Calvin's remarks here are good : "Quemadmodum Abrahæ domus tunc fuit vera Ecclesia : ita minime dubium est quin præcipui et præ aliis memorabiles eventus qui in ea contigerunt, nobis totidem sint typi. Sicut ergo in circumcisione, in sacrificiis, in toto sacerdotio levitico allegoria fuit : sicuti hodie est in nostris sacramentis, ita etiam in domo Abrahæ fuisse dico. Sed id non facit ut a literali sensu recedatur. Summa perinde est ac si diceret Paulus, figuram duorum testamentorum in duabus Abrahæ uxoribus, et duplicis populi in duobus filiis, veluti in tabula, nobis depictam." As to the objection of Luther, repeated by De Wette, that this allegory shews misapprehension of the history (die Allegorie von Sara und Hagar, welche .... zum Stich zu schwach ist, denn sie weichet ab vom historischen Verstand. Luth., cited by De W.), because Ishmael had nothing to do with the law of Moses, the misapprehension is entirely on the side of the objectors. Not the bare literal historical fact is in question here, but the inner character of God's dealings with men, of which type, and prophecy, and the historical fact itself, are only so many exemplifications. The difference between the children of the bond and the free, of the law and the promise, has been shewn out to the world before, by, and since the covenant of the law. See an excellent note of Windischmann's ad loc., exposing the shallow modern critical school. See also Jowett's note, on the other side : and while reading it, and tracing the consequences which will follow from adopting his view, bear in mind that the question between him and us is not affected by any thing there said on the similarity between St. Paul and the Alexandrians as interpreters of Scripture,— but remains as it was before,—was the O. T. dispensation a system of typical

ᵛγεννῶσα, ᵖἥτις ἐστὶν Ἄγαρ· ²⁵ τὸ * γὰρ Ἄγαρ Σινᾶ
ὄρος ἐστὶν ἐν τῇ Ἀραβίᾳ· ᵂσυστοιχεῖ δὲ τῇ νῦν Ἱερου-
σαλήμ, ˣδουλεύει γὰρ μετὰ τῶν τέκνων αὐτῆς. ²⁶ ἡ δὲ

ᵛ Luke i. 13 al.
fr. Prov.
xvii. 17.
ᵂ here only †.
Polyb. x. 21.
ˣ absol., 1 Tim.
vi. 2.

25. *δὲ A B[sic, see table] D m [17¹(appy) harl(with demid)] copt Cyr₁: γαρ CFKL
[P]א [rel] vulg syrr æth arm Epiph Chr Cyr₂ Thdrt Damasc Orig-int [Victorin] Jer.—
om αγαρ CFא [17¹(Treg)] vulg [sah goth] æth arm Epiph Cyr_alic Damasc Orig-int
[Victorin] Jer. (*The variation appears to have sprung from the juxtaposition of*
γαρ αγαρ: *hence one or other was omd, and* δε *insd for connexion.*) aft εστιν ins
ον א. for συστοιχ. δε, (ἡ) συνστοιχουσα D¹F latt goth. (om ἡ D¹.) rec (for
2nd γαρ) δε, with D³KL rel syr-mg goth: *et servit* vulg(and F-lat) Syr [æth Orig-int
Hil] Jer Aug₃: txt ABCD¹F[P]א 17 [47] coptt [arm] Cyr Orig-int Aug₄.

events and ordinances, or is all such typical
reference fanciful and delusive? For these
(women (αὗται), not as Jowett, Ishmael
and Isaac, which would confuse the whole:
the mothers are the covenants;—the sons,
the children of the covenants) are (import
in the allegory, see reff.) two covenants
(not '*revelations*,' but literally covenants
between God and men): one (covenant)
indeed from Mount Sina (taking its origin
from,—or having Mount Sina as its centre,
as ὁ ἐκ Πελοποννήσου πόλεμος) gendering
(bringing forth children: De W. compares
υἱοί .... τῆς διαθήκης, Acts iii. 25) unto
(with a view to) bondage, which one is
(identical in the allegory with) Agar.
25.] (No parenthesis: συστοιχεῖ δέ begins
a new clause.) For the word Agar (when
the neuter article precedes a noun of another gender, not the *import* of that noun,
but the *noun itself*, is designated,—so
Demosth. p. 255. 4, τὸ δ' ὑμεῖς ὅταν εἴπω,
τὴν πόλιν λέγω. Kühner ii. 137) is (imports) Mount Sina, in Arabia (i. e. among
the Arabians. This rendering, which is
Chrysostom's,—τὸ δὲ Σινᾶ ὄρος οὕτω μεθ-
ερμηνεύεται τῇ ἐπιχωρίῳ αὐτῶν γλώττη
(so also Thl., Luther), is I conceive necessitated by the arrangement of the sentence, as well as by τὸ Ἄγαρ. Had the
Apostle intended merely to localize Σινᾶ
ὄρος by the words ἐν τῇ Ἀρ., he could
hardly but have written τὸ ἐν τῇ Ἀρ., or
have placed ἐν τ. Ἀρ. before ἐστιν. Had
he again, adopting the reading τὸ γὰρ
Σινᾶ ὄρος ἐστὶν ἐν τῇ Ἀραβίᾳ, intended
to say (as Windischmann), '*for Mount
Sina is in Arabia, where Hagar's de-
scendants likewise are,*' the sentence would
more naturally have stood τὸ γὰρ Σινᾶ ὄρ.
ἐν τῇ Ἀρ. ἐστίν, or καὶ γὰρ Σινᾶ ὄρ. ἐν τ.
Ἀρ. ἐστίν. As it is, the law of emphasis
would require it to be rendered, '*For Sina
is a mountain in Arabia*,' information
which the judaizing Galatians would hardly
require.   As to the fact itself, Meyer
states, "جَر in Arabic, is a stone: and

though we have no further testimony
that Mount Sina was thus named κατ'
ἐξοχήν by the Arabians, we have that of
Chrysostom; and Büsching, Erdbeschrei-
bung, v. p. 535, adduces that of the
traveller Haraut, that they to this day
call Sinai, *Hadschar*. Certainly we have
Hagar as a geographical proper name
in Arabia Petræa: the Chaldee paraphrast
always calls the wilderness of Shur, חגר."
So that Jowett certainly speaks too
strongly when he says, "the old explanations, that Hagar is the Arabic word for a
rock or the Arabic noun for Mount Sinai,
are destitute of foundation." As to the
improbability at which he hints, of St.
Paul quoting Arabic words in writing to
the Galatians, I cannot see how it is
greater than that of his making the covert
allusion contained in his own interpretation. We may well suppose St. Paul to
have become familiarized, during his
sojourn there, with this name for the
granite peaks of Sinai), but (δέ marks the
latent contrast that the addition of a new
fact brings with it: so Ellic.) corresponds
(viz. Agar, which is the subject, not Mount
Sina, see below. "συστοιχεῖν is '*to stand
in the same rank*:' hence '*to belong to the
same category,*' '*to be homogeneous with*:'
see Polyb. xiii. 8. 1, ὅμοια κ. σύστοιχα."
Mey., Chrys., all., and the Vulg. (*con-
junctus est*), take it literally, and understand it, γειτνιάζει, ἅπτεται, ' is joined, by
a continuous range of mountain-tops,' understanding *Sina* as the subject) with the
present Jerusalem (i. e. Jerusalem under
the law, the Jerusalem of the Jews, as
contrasted with the Jerusalem of the Messiah's Kingdom), for she (ἡ νῦν Ἱερουσ.,
not Ἄγαρ) is in slavery with her children.   26.] But (opposes to the last
sentence, not to μία μέν, ver. 24, which, as
Meyer observes, is left without an apodosis,
the reader supplying that the other covenant is Sara, &c.) the Jerusalem above (i. e.
the heavenly Jerusalem = Ἱερ. ἐπουράνιος
Heb. xii. 22, ἡ καινὴ Ἱερ. Rev. iii. 12;

y Phil. iii. 14.
Col. iii. 1.
z Isa. liv. 1.
Luke xv. 23.
Acts ii. 26.
Rom. xv. 10 al.
a Luke i. 7.
xxiii. 29 only.
Gen. xi. 30.
b = here only.
(Matt. vii. 6.
ix. 17 ‖.
Mark ix. 18 ‖ L. only.) see Isa. xlix. 13. lii. 9.
c ver. 19.
d = here only.
e w. posit., Mark ix. 42. Acts xx. 35. 1 Cor. ix. 15 (xii. 22) only. 1. c. only.
f = John iv. 17, 18.
g = Eph. iv. 24. Col. iii. 10. 1 Pet. i. 15. Lam. i. 12.
h Rom. ix. 8.

y ἄνω Ἰερουσαλὴμ ἐλευθέρα ἐστίν, p ἥτις ἐστὶν μήτηρ ABCDF
ἡμῶν· 27 γέγραπται γὰρ z Εὐφράνθητι a στεῖρα ἡ οὐ
τίκτουσα, b ῥῆξον καὶ βόησον ἡ οὐκ c ὠδίνουσα, ὅτι πολλὰ
τὰ τέκνα τῆς d ἐρήμου e μᾶλλον ἢ τῆς f ἐχούσης τὸν f ἄνδρα.
28 ὑμεῖς δέ, ἀδελφοί, g κατὰ Ἰσαὰκ h ἐπαγγελίας h τέκνα

KLPℵ a
b c d e f
g h k l m
n o 17. 47

26. om ητις εστιν (homœot) ℵ1(ins ℵ-corr1) [Victorin]. rec ins παντων bef ημων, with AC3KL[P]ℵ3 rel [arm Eus2] Mac Cyr-jer Thdrtpersæpe Damasc Iren-int [Orig-int2 Victorin] Jer Aug2: om BC1DFℵ1 17. 672 latt syrr coptt goth æth-mss Origsæpe Eus3 Chr Cyr5 Thdrt1(mss vary) Isid Tert Hil Ambrst Augsæpe.

27. for ου, μη DF.

28. rec ημεις and εσμεν (from ver 26), with ACD3KL[P]ℵ rel vulg(and F-lat) syrr copt goth æth-pl [arm] Chr Cyr Thdrt Aug : txt BD1F 17. 672 sah æth Orig(in Jer) Iren-int Victorin Ambrst Tich Ambr. (Υμεις [Υ in red] k o.)

xxi. 2, and see reff. on ἄνω. Michaelis, al., suppose *ancient Jerusalem* (Melchisedek's) to be meant. Vitringa, al., *Mount Zion*, as ἡ ἄνω πόλις means the Acropolis. But Rabbinical usage, as Schöttgen has abundantly proved in his Dissertation de Hierosolyma cœlesti (Hor. Heb. vol. i. Diss. v.), was familiar with the idea of a Jerusalem in heaven. See also citations in Wetst. This latter quotes a very remarkable parallel from Plato, Rep. ix. end, —ἐν ᾗ νῦν δὴ διήλθομεν οἰκίζοντες πόλει λέγεις, τῇ ἐν λόγοις κειμένῃ, ἐπεὶ γῆς γε οὐδαμοῦ οἶμαι αὐτὴν εἶναι. Ἀλλ᾽ ἦν δ᾽ ἐγὼ ἐν οὐρανῷ ἴσως παράδειγμα ἀνάκειται τῷ βουλομένῳ ὁρᾶν καὶ ὁρῶντι ἑαυτὸν κατοικίζειν. διαφέρει δὲ οὐδὲν εἴτε που ἐστὶν εἴτε ἔσται· τὰ γὰρ ταύτης μόνης ἂν πράξειεν, ἄλλης δὲ οὐδεμιᾶς. Εἰκός γ᾽, ἔφη. The expression here will mean, "the *Messianic Theocracy*, which before the παρουσία is the *Church*, and after it Christ's Kingdom of glory." Mey.) **is free, which** (which said city, which heavenly Jerusalem) **is our mother** (the emphasis is not on ἡμῶν as Winer: nay rather it stands in the least emphatic place, as indicating a relation taken for granted by Christians. See Phil. iii. 20. The rendering adopted by Mr. Bagge, "*which* (Jerusalem the free) *is* (answers to, as ἥτις ἐστὶν Ἄγαρ above) *our mother* (viz. Sarah)," is untenable from the absence of the article before μήτηρ, besides that it would introduce confusion, and a *double* allegory). **27.]** *Proof of this relation from Prophecy.* The portion of Isaiah from which this is taken, is directly Messianic : indicating in its foreground the reviviscence of Israel after calamity, but in language far surpassing that event. See Stier, Jesaias nicht pseudo-Jesaias, vol. ii. p. 512. The citation is from the LXX, verbatim. **ῥῆξον**] sc. φωνήν :

cf. many examples in Wetst. Probably the rule of supplying ellipses from the context (following which Kypke and Schött. here supply εὐφ. οσύνην, from εὐφράνθητι, and Isa. xlix. 13 ; lii. 9 ; cf. also 'erumpere gaudium, Ter. Eun. iii. 5. 2 (Ellie.)) need hardly be applied here ; the phrase with φωνήν was so common, as to lead at last to the omission of the substantive. The Hebrew רִנָּה, 'into joyful shouting,' seems not to have been read by the LXX. St. Paul here interprets the barren of Sara, who bore not according to the flesh (= the promise), and the fruitful of Agar (= the law). Clem. Rom., Ep. ii. ad Cor. 2, p. 333, takes the στεῖρα of the Gentile Church, ἐπεὶ ἔρημος ἐδόκει εἶναι ἀπὸ τοῦ θεοῦ, ὁ λαὸς ἡμῶν, νυνὶ δὲ πιστεύσαντες πλείονες ἐγενόμεθα τῶν δοκούντων ἔχειν θεόν (the Jewish Church), and similarly Origen (in Rom., lib. vi. 7, vol. iv. p. 578), . . . 'quod multo plures ex gentibus quam ex circumcisione crediderint.' And this has been the usual interpretation. It only shews how manifold is the 'perspective of prophecy :' this sense neither is incompatible with St. Paul's, nor surely would it have been denied by him. (So Chrys., al., in *this* passage, which is clearly wrong : for ἡμῶν, even without πάντων, must apply to *all* Christians for the argument to hold.) **ὅτι πολ**] not, as E. V., "*many more* &c.," which is inaccurate : but, **many are the children of the desolate, more than** (rather than ; both being numerous, hers are the *more* numerous) **of her,** &c. **τὸν ἄνδρα**] The E. V. has perhaps done best by rendering '*an husband*,' though thus the force of the Greek is not given. 'The husband' would mislead, by pointing at the one husband (Abraham) who was common to Sara and Agar, which might

ἐστέ. ²⁹ ἀλλ' ὥσπερ τότε ὁ ¹ κατὰ ¹ σάρκα γεννηθεὶς
ᵏ ἐδίωκεν τὸν ¹ κατὰ ¹ πνεῦμα, οὕτως καὶ νῦν. ³⁰ ἀλλὰ ᵐ τί
λέγει ἡ γραφή; ⁿ"Ἔκβαλε τὴν ᵒπαιδίσκην καὶ τὸν υἱὸν
αὐτῆς. οὐ γὰρ μὴ ᵖ κληρονομήσῃ ὁ υἱὸς τῆς ᵒπαιδίσκης
μετὰ τοῦ υἱοῦ τῆς ᵒ ἐλευθέρας. ³¹ �q διό, ἀδελφοί, οὐκ

i ver. 23.
k = Matt. v.
10, 11, 12.
Ps. vii. 1.
l Rom. i. 4.
m so Rom. iv. 3.
x. 8. xi. 2, 4.
n Acts xvi. 37.
Gen. xxi. 10.
o ver. 22.
p absol., here
only. (Matt.
v. 5 al.) Numb. xviii. 24.
q see Rom. ii. 1. Eph. ii. 11 al.

30. aft παιδισκην ins ταυτην (so LXX[not A]) A [copt]. om μη F m [Clem].
κληρονομησει (so LXX) BD[P]א k¹ m n 17 [47]. om του υιου א¹ : ins
א-corr¹ : ins υιον א³. for της ελευθ., μου ισαακ (from LXX) D¹F demid [Victorin]
Ambrst Jer Aug_aliq.

31. rec (for διο) αρα, with KL rel syr Chr Thl Œc : αρα ουν F Thdrt : ημεις δε
(see ver 28 var read) AC[P] copt Cyr₁ Damasc Jer₁ Aug₃ : txt BD¹א 17. 67² (sah
goth) Cyr₁[?], itaque latt Ambrst Jer₁.

do in this passage, but would not in Isaiah : whereas ἐχ. τὸν ἄνδρα means, 'her (of the two) who has (the) husband,' the other having none : a fineness of meaning which we cannot give in English.

28.] But (transitional : or rather perhaps adversative to the children of her who had an husband, which were last mentioned. With ἡμεῖς, it would be resumptive of ver. 26) ye (see var. readd.), **brethren,** like (the expression in full, κατὰ τ. ὁμοιότητα Μελχισεδέκ, occurs Heb. vii. 15. Wetst. quotes from Galen, ὁ ἄνθρωπος οὐ κατὰ λέοντά ἐστι τὴν ῥώμην, and from Arrian, Hist. Gr. ii., τιμώμενος ὑπὸ τοῦ δήμου κατὰ τὸν πατέρα Ἄγνωνα : see also reff.) **Isaac, are children of** pro- **MISE** (ἐπαγγ. emphatic :— are children, not κατὰ σάρκα, but διὰ τῆς ἐπαγγελίας, see ver. 23, and below, ver. 29).

29.] ὁ κατ. σάρ. γεν., see ver. 23. It has been thought that there is nothing in the Hebrew text to justify so strong a word as ἐδίωκεν. It runs, 'and Sarah saw the son of Hagar . . . . מְצַחֵק' (παίζοντα μετὰ Ἰσαὰκ τοῦ υἱοῦ αὐτῆς, LXX); and some deny that צחק ever means 'he mocked.' But certainly it does : see Gen. xix. 14. And this would be quite ground enough for the ἐδίωκεν, for the spirit of persecution was begun. So that we need not refer to tradition, as many have done (even Ellic., whom see; Jowett, as unfortunately usual with him when impugning the accuracy of St. Paul, asserts rashly and confidently, that the sense in which the Apostle takes the Hebrew is inadmissible), to account for St. Paul's expression. **τὸν κατὰ πνεῦμα,** sc. γεννηθέντα, **him that was born after the Spirit,** i.e. in virtue of the promise, which was given by the Spirit. Or, '*by virtue of the Spirit's agency:*' but the other is better.

οὕτως καὶ νῦν] "nec quicquam est quod tam graviter animos nostros vulnerare debeat, quam Dei contemptus, et adversus ejus gratiam ludibria : nec ullum magis exitiale est persequutionis genus, quam quum impeditur animæ salus." Calv.

30.] ἀλλά, as in E. V., '*nevertheless:*' notwithstanding the fact of the persecution, just mentioned. The quotation is adapted from the LXX, where μου Ἰσαάκ stands for τῆς ἐλευθέρας. We need hardly have recourse (with Ellic.) to the fact that God confirmed Sarah's words, in order to prove this to be *Scripture:* the Apostle is allegorizing the whole history, and thus every part of it assumes a significance in the allegory. **κληρονομήσῃ**] See Judg. xi. 2 (LXX), κ. ἐξέβαλον τὸν Ἰεφθάε, κ. εἶπον αὐτῷ, οὐ κληρονομήσεις ἐν τῷ οἴκῳ τοῦ πατρὸς ἡμῶν, ὅτι υἱὸς γυναικὸς ἑταίρας σύ. "The distinction drawn by Hermann on Œd. Col. 853, between οὐ μή with future indicative (duration or futurity) and with aorist subjunctive (speedy occurrence), is not applicable to the N. T. on account of (1) various readings (as here): (2) the decided violations of the rule where the MSS. are unanimous, as 1 Thess. iv. 15 : and (3) the obvious prevalence of the use of the subjunctive over the future, both in the N. T. and 'fatiscens Græcitas:' see Lobeck, Phryn. p. 722." Ellicott.

31.] I am inclined to think, against Meyer, De W., Ellic., &c., that this verse is, as commonly taken, the conclusion from what has gone before : and that the διό is bound on to the κληρονομήσῃ preceding. For that we are κληρονόμοι, is an acknowledged fact, established before, ch. iii. 29; ver. 7. And if we are, we are not the children of the handmaid, of whom it was said οὐ μὴ κληρονομ., but of the freewoman, of whose son the same words asserted that he should inherit. Observe in the first clause παιδίσκης is anarthrous : most likely because emphatically prefixed to its governing noun (cf. ἐθνῶν ἀπόστολος, Rom. xi. 13): but possibly, as

r =1 Cor. x. 29.
ch. ii. 4 al.
s John viii. 32, 36. Rom. vi. 18, 22. viii.
2, 21 only †.
(Sir. l. 21 Tromm. [but qu.? δευτε- ροῦν ABℵ &c.]) 2 Macc. i. 27. ii. 22 only.

ABCDF KLPℵ a b c d e f g h k l m n o 17. 47

ἐσμὲν °παιδίσκης τέκνα, ἀλλὰ τῆς °ἐλευθέρας· [V.] ¹ τῇ
ʳἐλευθερίᾳ ἡμᾶς χριστὸς ˢἠλευθέρωσεν. ᵗστήκετε οὖν,
καὶ μὴ πάλιν ᵘζυγῷ ᵛδουλείας ʷἐνέχεσθε. ² ἴδε ˣἐγὼ
ˣΠαῦλος λέγω ὑμῖν ὅτι ἐὰν ʸπεριτέμνησθε χριστὸς ὑμᾶς
οὐδὲν ᶻὠφελήσει· ³ ᵃμαρτύρομαι δὲ πάλιν παντὶ ἀνθρώπῳ

t Mark iii. 31. xi. 25. Rom. xiv. 4. 1 Cor. xvi. 13. Phil. i. 27. iv. 1. 1 Thess. iii. 8. 2 Thess.
ii. 15 only. Exod. xiv. 13 A. constr., 2 Cor. i. 24. u = Matt. xi. 29, 30. Acts xv. 10. 1 Tim. vi. 1 (Rev.
vi. 5) only. Jer. xxxv. (xxviii.) 14. v Rom. viii. 15, 21. ch. iv. 24. Heb. ii. 15 only. Exod. xx. 2 al.
w = here (Mark vi. 19. Luke xi. 53) only. (Gen.xlix. 23. Ezek.xiv.4 only.) Herod. ii. 121, τῇ παγῇ ἐνέχεσθαι. Plut.
Symp. ii. 3, ἐνέχεσθαι δόγμασιν Πυθαγορικοῖς. x 2 Cor. x. 1. Eph. iii. 1. Col. i. 23. 1 Thess.
ii. 18. Philem. 19. y Luke i. 59. ch. ii. 3 al. fr. Gen. xvii. 10. z = 1 Cor. xiv. 6. Heb. iv.
2. Prov. x. 2. a constr., Acts xx. 26. -ρομαι, Acts xxvi. 22. Eph. iv. 17. 1 Thess. ii. 12 only †.

CHAP. V. 1. rec aft ελευθερια ins ουν, omg it aft στηκετε, with C³KL rel Damasc
Thl Œc : om D m [47] latt syr Thdrt₂ Jer Ambrst : txt ABC¹F[P]ℵ 17. 67² (Syr) copt
goth Cyr₁ Aug. (An eccles. lect. ended with ηλευθερωσεν, C³ marks this by insg τελος.)
rec ins ᾗ bef ημας, with D²·³(F)KL rel Marc Chr Thdrt₂ Thl Œc (ᾗ ελευθερίᾳ
ἡμ. F latt Syr lat-ff) : om ABCD¹[P]ℵ m 17 copt [Cyr₁-p]. rec χριστος bef ημας,
with CKLℵ³ rel vss (Chr) Thdrt Damasc₁ Mcion-t [Tert] Victorin : txt ABDF[P]ℵ 17
am goth Cyr₁ Damasc₁ (Orig-int). δουλειας bef ζυγω DF goth Aug.
ανεχεσθε D¹·³ (1 ?) m Thdrt-ms Œc.
2. om παυλος ℵ¹(ins ℵ-corr¹ obl). περιτεμνησθε B n¹.
3. om παλιν D¹F a goth [arm] Chr Thl [Victorin] Jer Ambrst Aug. om οτι ℵ¹
(ins ℵ³).

indefinite, q. d. we are the children of no bondwoman, but of the freewoman. I prefer the former reason, as most consonant to N. T. diction. **V. 1—12.**] De W. calls this the *peroration* of the whole second part of the Epistle. It consists of *earnest exhortation to them, grounded on the conclusion of the foregoing argument, to abide in their evangelical liberty, and warning against being led away by the false teachers.*

1.] It is almost impossible to determine satisfactorily the reading (see var. readd.). In the fourth Edition I adopted that in the text, as being best attested by the most ancient authorities. **With liberty did Christ make you free** (i.e. ἐλεύθεροι is your rightful name and ought to be your estimation of yourselves, seeing that ἐλευθερία is your inheritance by virtue of Christ's redemption of you). **Stand fast, therefore** (reff. στήκω is unknown in classical Greek), **and be not again** (see note on ch. iv. 9: in fact, the whole world was under the law in the sense of its being God's only revelation to them) **involved** (reff.) **in the yoke of bondage** (better than 'a yoke;' an anarthrous noun or personal pronoun following another noun in the genitive often deprives that other noun of its article: e.g., τίς ἔγνω νοῦν κυρίου; 1 Cor. ii. 16: see numerous instances in Cant. v. 1. Cf. Winer, § 19. 2, most of whose examples however are after prepositions. [See also Moulton, p. 155, note 6.] Wetst. quotes from Soph. Aj. 944, πρὸς οἷα δουλείας ζυγὰ χωροῦμεν). **2.**] ἴδε, not ἰδέ, in later

Greek: see Winer, § 6. 1. a:—it draws attention to what follows, as a strong statement. ἐγὼ Παῦλος ἄντικρυς ὑμῖν λέγω κ. διαρρήδην, κ. τὸ ἐμαυτοῦ προστίθημι ὄνομα, Thdrt. τὴν τοῦ οἰκείου προσώπου ἀξιοπιστίαν ἀντὶ πάσης ἀποδείξεως τίθησι, Theophyl., and so Chrys. There hardly seems to be a reference (as Wetst. "ego quem dicunt circumcisionem prædicare") to his having circumcised Timothy. Calvin says well : "Ista locutio non parvam emphasin habet ; coram enim se opponit, et nomen dat, ne videatur causam dubiam habere. Et quanquam vilescere apud Galatas cœperat ejus auctoritas, tamen ad refellendos omnes adversarios sufficere asserit."
The *present*, ἐὰν περιτέμνησθε, implies the continuance of a habit, q. d. **if you will go on being circumcised.** He does not say, '*if you shall have been circumcised :*' so that Calv.'s question, 'quid hoc vult? Christum non profuturum omnibus circumcisis?' does not come in. On χρ. ὑμ. οὐδ. ὠφελήσει, Chrys. remarks: ὁ περιτεμνόμενος ὡς νόμον δεδοικὼς περιτέμνεται, ὁ δὲ δεδοικὼς ἀπιστεῖ τῇ δυνάμει τῆς χάριτος, ὁ δὲ ἀπιστῶν οὐδὲν κερδαίνει παρὰ τῆς ἀπιστουμένης. Nothing can be more directly opposed than this verse to the saying of the Judaizers, Acts xv. 1. The exception to the rule in Paul's own conduct, Acts xvi. 3, is sufficiently provided for by the *present tense* here : see above. **3.**] δέ, moreover, introduces an addition, and a slight contrast—'not only will Christ not profit . . . . . . but . . . . . .' On μαρτύρομαι (usually, in

ʸ περιτεμνομένῳ ὅτι ᵇ ὀφειλέτης ἐστὶν ὅλον τὸν νόμον
ποιῆσαι. ⁴ ᶜᵈ κατηργήθητε ᵈ ἀπὸ [τοῦ] χριστοῦ ᵉ οἵτινες
ᶠ ἐν νόμῳ ᶠ δικαιοῦσθε, ᵍ τῆς χάριτος ʰ ἐξεπέσατε. ⁵ ἡμεῖς
γὰρ ⁱ πνεύματι ᵏ ἐκ πίστεως ˡ ἐλπίδα δικαιοσύνης ᵐ ἀπεκδεχόμεθα. ⁶ ἐν γὰρ χριστῷ Ἰησοῦ οὔτε ⁿ περιτομή
τι ᵒ ἰσχύει οὔτε ᵖ ἀκροβυστία, ἀλλὰ πίστις δι' ἀγάπης
�q ἐνεργουμένη. ⁷ ʳ ἐτρέχετε ˢ καλῶς· τίς ὑμᾶς ᵗ ἐνέκοψεν

ᵇ Matt. vi. 12. xviii. 24.
Luke xiii. 4. Rom. i. 14. viii. 12. xv. 27 only †.
Soph. Aj. 590.
ᶜ ch. iii. 17 reff.
ᵈ Rom. vii. 2, 6. see 2 Cor. xi. 3.
ᵉ = Acts x. 41, 47 al.
ᶠ ch. iii. 11 reff.
ᵍ = Rom. v. 2. Jude 4.
ⁱ = ch. iii. 3. ver. 16. 1 Cor. ii. 4.
ᵐ Rom. viii. 19, 23, 25. 1 Cor.
ⁿ John vii. 22, 23. Rom. ii. 25 al.

h = 2 Pet. iii. 17. (Acts xii. 7. 1 Pet. i. 24. from Isa. xl. 8 al.)
k ch. ii. 16. iii. 8, 22. l = Col. i. 5. Tit. ii. 13. Heb. vi. 18.
i. 7. Phil. iii. 20. Heb. ix. 28. 1 Pet. iii. 20 only †.
fr. Exod. iv. 26. o = Heb. ix. 17. James v. 16. = ἐστιν, 1 Cor. vii. 19. ch. vi. 15.
p Rom. iv. 9, &c. 1 Cor. vii. 19. Col. iii. 11. P. only, exc. Acts xi. 3. Gen. xvii. 11. q mid., Rom.
vii. 5. 2 Cor. i. 6. iv. 12. Eph. iii. 20. (ch. ii. 8 reff.) r ch. ii. 2 reff. Rom. xi. 16.
s = 1 Cor. vii. 37. John xviii. 23 al. Prov. xxiii. 24. t Acts xxiv. 4. Rom. xv. 22. 1 Thess.
ii. 18. 1 Pet. iii. 7. Dan. ix. 26 Theod.-Ald. only. (ἐκκόπτ. AB.)

4. om του BCD¹F[P]א [Cyr₃-p] Thl: ins AD³KL rel Chr Thdrt Damasc. εξε-
πεσετε D³ a b² c d e f g h k m.
5. εκδεχ. א¹(txt א³). 6. om ιησου B copt.
7. rec ανεκοψε: [εβασκανεν 47:] txt ABCDFKL[P]א rel.

this sense, -ροῦμαι;— -ρομαι having an
accusative, whence Bretschn., al., supply
τὸν θεόν here, but wrongly), see reff. πάλιν,
once more: applies to the verb, not to
the μαρτυρία which follows, for that is
not a repetition. Thus it will refer to
παντὶ ἀνθρ. as 'a more extended application of ὑμῖν' (Ellic.), not, as Meyer, to a
former inculcation of this by word of
mouth at his second visit. περιτεμνομένῳ,
not -τμηθέντι, see above—to every man
who receives circumcision,—'submits to
be circumcised,' as Ellic. The emphasis
is on παντί, substantiating, and carrying
further, the last verse. ὅλον has the
stress. The circumcised man became a
'proselyte of righteousness,' and bound
to keep the whole law. "This true and
serious consequence of circumcision the
false Apostles had probably at least dis-
sembled." Mey. 4.] Explains and
establishes still further the assertion of ver.
2. Ye were annihilated from Christ
(literally: the construction is a pregnant
one, 'ye were cut off from Christ, and
thus made void:' see ref. 2 Cor. 'were,'
viz. at the time when you began your
course of ἐν νόμῳ δικ.), ye who are being
justified ('endeavouring to be justified,'
'seeking justification:' such is the force
of the subjective present. So Thl. ὡς
ὑπολαμβάνετε) in (not 'by:' it is the
element in which, as in the expression
ἐν κυρίῳ) the law,—ye fell from (reff.:
see 1 Cor. xiii. 8, note. Wetst. quotes
from Plut., Agis and Cleom. p. 796, τῶν
πλείστων ἐξέπεσεν ἡ Σπάρτη καλῶν:
Gracch. p. 834, ἐκπεσεῖν κ. στέρεσθαι τῆς
πρὸς τὸν δῆμον εὐνοίας: 'So Plato, Rep.
vi. 496, ἐκπεσεῖν φιλοσοφίας: Polyb. xii.
14. 7, ἐκπίπτειν τοῦ καθήκοντος,' Ellic.)
grace. 5.] Proof (hence γάρ) of

ἐξεπ. τ. χάρ., by statement e contrario
of the condition and hope of Christians.
Emphasis (1) on ἡμεῖς, as opposed to
οἵτινες ἐν νόμῳ δικαιοῦσθε,—(2) on πνεύματι (not 'mente' (Fritz.), nor 'spiritually,' Middleton, al., but by the (Holy)
Spirit, reff.), as opposed to σαρκί, the
fleshly state of those under the law, see
ch. iv. 29,—(3) on ἐκ πίστεως, as opposed
to ἐν νόμῳ, which involves ἐξ ἔργων.
ἐλπίδα δικαιοσύνης] Is this genitive objective, the hope of righteousness, i. e. the
hope whose object is perfect righteousness,
—or subjective, the hope of righteousness, i. e. the hope which the righteous
entertain—viz. that of eternal life? Certainly I think the former: for this reason,
that ἐλπίδα has the emphasis, and ἐλπίδα
δικ. ἀπεκδεχ. answers to δικαιοῦσθε above
—'Ye think ye have your righteousness
in the law: we, on the contrary, anxiously
wait for the hope of righteousness (full
and perfect).' The phrase ἀπεκδέχεσθαι
ἐλπίδα may be paralleled, Acts xxiv. 15;
Tit. ii. 13; Eur. Alcest. 130, τίν' ἔτι βίον
ἐλπίδα προσδέχωμαι: Polyb. viii. 21. 7,
προσδοκωμέναις ἐλπίσιν. 6.] Confirmation of the words ἐκ πίστεως, ver. 5.
ἐν χριστῷ, in Christ, as an element, in union with Christ,—in the
state of a Christian: notice χρ. Ἰησ., not
Ἰησ. χρ.:—in Christ, and that Christ,
Jesus of Nazareth. ἐνεργουμένη, not
passive, but middle, as always in N. T.
See reff. and notes on those places: also
Fritzsche's note on Rom. vii. 5. " ἐνεργεῖν, vim exercere de personis, ἐνεργεῖσθαι,
ex se (aut suam) vim exercere de rebus
collocavit, Gal. v. 6; Col. i. 29; 1 Thess.
ii. 13 al., ut h. l. Passivo (cf. ἐνεργεῖται
πόλεμος, Polyb. i. 13. 5; Jos. Antt. xv.
5. 3) nunquam Paulus usus est." The

u = Rom. ii. 8. 1 Pet. i. 22. [τῇ] u ἀληθείᾳ μὴ v πείθεσθαι ; 8 ἡ w πεισμονὴ οὐκ ἐκ τοῦ ABCDF KLPℵ a

v Acts xxviii. 24. Rom. ii. 8. x καλοῦντος ὑμᾶς. 9 μικρὰ yza ζύμη ὅλον τὸ yb φύραμα b c d e f g h k l m

w here only †. only used by Chrys. on yzc ζυμοῖ. 10 ἐγὼ πέποιθα d εἰς ὑμᾶς ἐν κυρίῳ ὅτι οὐδὲν n o 17. 47

1 Thess. i. 3 (De W.), and Eustath. (see Wetst.)
y 1 Cor. v. 6. z 1 Cor. as above. Matt. xiii. 33 ‖.
xii. 1. 1 Cor. v. 7, 8 only. Exod. xii. 15.
c as above (z) only—always w. ὅλον. Exod. xii. 39.
3. 2 Thess. iii. 4.)

x ch. i. 6 reff. particip., as 1 Thess. v. 24.
a as above (y z). Matt. xvi. 6 ‖, 11, 12. Luke
b Rom. ix. 21. xi. 16. 1 Cor. v. 6, 7 only. Exod xii. 34.
d 2 Cor. ii. 9, 12. viii. 23. ix. 8. (ἐπί, 2 Cor. ii.

om τη ABℵ¹ : ins CDFKL[P]ℵ³ rel [Jer, expr]. at end add μηδενι πειθεσθαι F lat-mss-in-Jer vulg-sixt(with demid hal) Victorin Lucif Ambrst-comm Pel Bede. (Gloss to account for η πεισμονη follg.)

8. om ουκ D¹ [32] lat-mss-in-Jer(who says " abstulerunt non ")-in-Sedul(who says male) Orig₁ Lucif [Victorin]. καλουντας(sic) ℵ.

9. for ζυμοι, δολοι D¹ vulg(and F-lat) lat-mss('male')-in-Jer-and-Sedul Mcion-e Constt Bas-mss Lucif [Victorin] Ambrst Pel : corrumpit fermentat G-lat.

10. aft εγω ins δε C¹F[P] demid syr arm Damasc Œc-comm. om εν κυριω B

older Romanist Commentators (Bellarm., Est.) insisted on the passive sense as favouring the dogma of fides formata, for which it is cited by the Council of Trent, sess. vi. cap. 7, de justific. And the modern Romanist Commentators, though abandoning the passive sense, still claim the passage on their side (e. g. Windischmann); but without reason ; love is the modus operandi of faith, that which justifies, however, is not love, but faith ; nor can a passage be produced, where St. Paul says we are justified by 'faith working by love,' but it is ever by faith only. One is astonished at the boldness of such a generally calm and fair writer as Windischmann, in claiming the passage for the Tridentine doctrine, even when the passive interpretation, which was all it had to lay hold on, is given up. As parallels to our passage, see Rom. xiv. 17 ; 1 Cor. vii. 19.

7—12.] He laments their deflexion from their once promising course, and denounces severely their perverters. Ye were running well ('hoc est, omnia apud vos erant in felici statu et successu, vivebatis optime, contendebatis recta ad vitam æternam quam vobis pollicebatur verbum,' &c. Luther): who (see ch. iii. 1, the question expresses astonishment) hindered you (Polyb. xxiv. 1. 12, uses ἐγκόπτειν with a dative, διὰ τὸ τὸν Φίλιππον ἐγκόπτειν τῇ δικαιοδοσίᾳ: Ellic. quotes, in connexion with the view of the primary notion being that of hindering by breaking up a road,—Greg. Naz. Or. xvi. p. 260, ἡ κακίας ἐγκοπτομένης δυσπάθεια τῶν πονηρῶν, ἡ ἀρετῆς ὁδοποιουμένης εὐπάθεια τῶν βελτιόνων) that ye should not (μὴ before πείθεσθαι is not pleonastic, but the construction, so often occurring, of a negative after verbs of hindering, is in fact a pregnant one, μὴ πείθεσθαι being the result of the hindrance: q. d. ὥστε μὴ π. or καὶ ἐποίησε μὴ π. See Bern-

hardy, Syntax, ix. 6 b, who quotes one example very apposite to this,—ἐμποδὼν ἡμῖν γένηται τὴν θεὸν μὴ 'ξελκύσαι, Aristoph. Pac. 315) obey the truth (i. e. submit yourselves to the true Gospel of Christ. These words, which Chrys. omits here, have been transferred hence to ch. iii. 1. See var. readd. there. On that account they are certainly genuine here) ?

8.] The persuasion (to which you are yielding—active ; not your persuasion, passive. πεισμονή may mean either. Ellic. says : " As the similar form πλησμονή means both satietas (the state) and also expletio (the act), Col. ii. 23 ; Plato, Sympos. 186 c. πλ. καὶ κένωσις,—so πεισμονή may mean the state of being persuaded, i. e. conviction, or the act of persuading, 'persuadendi sollertia' (Schött.) : cf. Chrys. on 1 Thess. i. 3, οὐ πεισμονὴ ἀνθρωπίνη . . . ἦν ἡ πείθουσα." But here, ἡ πεισμ. being connected with ὁ καλῶν ὑμᾶς, and answering to the act of ἐγκόπτειν in the last verse, is better taken actively) is not from (does not come from, is not originated by) Him who calleth you (i. e. God : see ch. i. 6 and note).

9.] ζύμη may allude either to men (Jer., Aug., Grot., Est., Beng., De W., al.), or to doctrine. In the parallel place in 1 Cor. v. 6, it is moral influence; so also where our Lord uses the same figure, Matt. xvi. 12, where ζύμη = διδαχή. Nor can there be any objection to taking it as abstract, and φύραμα concrete :—a little false doctrine corrupts the whole mass (of Christians). So Chrys. (οὕτω καὶ ὑμᾶς ἰσχύει τὸ μικρὸν τοῦτο κακόν, μὴ διορθωθέν, καὶ εἰς τέλειον ιουδαϊσμὸν ἀγαγεῖν), Thl., Luth., Calv., all. 10.] "After the warning of vv. 8, 9, Paul assures his readers that he has confidence in them, but that their perverters shall not escape punishment. Divide et impera !" Meyer.

ἐγώ, emphatic, I, for my part ; 'quod me attinet, ...' εἰς, with

ἄλλο ᵉφρονήσετε· ὁ δὲ ᶠταράσσων ὑμᾶς ᵍβαστάσει τὸ
ʰκρῖμα, ὅστις ἐὰν ᾖ. ¹¹ἐγὼ δέ, ἀδελφοί, εἰ ⁱπεριτομὴν
ἔτι ᵏκηρύσσω, ˡτί ἔτι ᵐδιώκομαι ; ἄρα ⁿκατήργηται τὸ
ᵒσκάνδαλον τοῦ ᵖσταυροῦ. ¹²qὄφελον καὶ ʳἀποκόψον-
ται οἱ ˢἀναστατοῦντες ὑμᾶς.

e = Acts
xxviii. 22.
Rom. xii. 3
al. 2 Macc.
xiv. 26.
f = Acts xv.
24. ch. i. 7.
1 Chron. ii. 7
Ald. parti-
cip., 2 Cor.
xi. 4. ver. 8
al.

g = Luke xiv. 27. John xix. 17. Acts xv. 10. ch. vi. 2, 5 al. 4 Kings xviii. 14. h = 1 Cor. xi.
29. 1 Tim. v. 12. James iii. 1. 2 Pet. ii. 3. i ver. 6 reff. k constr., Mark i. 4. Luke
iv. 49 (from Isa. lxi. 1) al. 1 Rom. iii. 7. ix. 19. m = ch. iv. 29 reff. n ch. iii. 17 reff.
o Rom. xiv. 13. 1 Cor. i. 23. Rev. ii. 14 al. 1 Kings xxv. 31. p = 1 Cor. i. 17. ch. vi. 12, 14. Phil.
iii. 18. q 1 Cor. iv. 8. 2 Cor. xi. 1. Rev. iii. 15 only. 4 Kings v. 3. Job xiv. 13. Ps. cxviii.
5 only. r Mark ix. 43, 45. John xviii. 10, 26. Acts xxvii. 32 only. = (see note) Deut. xxiii. 1.
s Acts xvii. 6. xxi. 38 only. L.P. Dan. vii. 23 LXX only. Ps. x. 1 Aq.

Chr(in Niceph ; elsw has it : εν χριστω Chr-txt). rec (for εαν) αν, with CDFKL
rel Dial : txt AB[P]‌ℵ b o 17. 67² Damasc.

11. om 1st ετι D¹F f 67² demid goth arm [Victorin] Jer Ambrst. (ἄρα D³.)
aft σταυρου ins του χριστου AC copt æth.

12. ωφελον D³KL l n. αποκοψωνται DF Œc.

regard to, see reff., and Bernhardy, p. 220.
On ἐν κυρίῳ, see 2 Thess. iii. 4 :—it is the
element or sphere in which his confidence is
conditioned. οὐδὲν ἄλλο φρον.] See
ἑτέρως, Phil. iii. 15 : of which this ἄλλο is
a kind of softening. We take the meaning
here to be, ye will be of no other mind
than this, viz. which I enjoin on you,—not
in vv. 8, 9 only, but in this Epistle, and in
his preaching generally. ὁ δὲ ταράσ-
σων need not be interpreted as referring
necessarily to any one ἐπίσημος among the
Judaizers (as Olsh., al.), but simply as individualizing the warning, and carrying
home the denunciation to each one's heart
among the perverters. Cf. οἱ ἀναστατοῦντες below, and ch. i. 7 ; iv. 17.
τὸ κρῖμα, the sentence, understood to be
unfavourable, is a burden laid on the judged
person, which he βαστάζει, bears. The
ὅστις ἐὰν ᾖ generalizes the declaration to
the fullest extent : see ch. i. 8, 9.
11.] The connexion appears to be this :
the Apostle had apparently been charged
with being a favourer of circumcision in
other churches ; as shewn e. g. by his
having circumcised Timothy. After the
preceding sharp denunciation of ὁ ταράσ-
σων ὑμᾶς, and ὅστις ἐὰν ᾖ, it is open to
the adversaries to say, that Paul himself
was one of their ταράσσοντες, by his inconsistency. In the abruptness then of
his fervid thoughts he breaks out in this
self-defence. ἐγώ, emphatic as before.
περιτομὴν has the chief emphasis,
as the new element in the sentence, and
not κηρύσσω, as Chrys. (οὐ γὰρ εἶπεν ὅτι
περιτομὴν οὐκ ἐργάζομαι, ἀλλά, οὐ κηρύσσω, τουτέστιν, οὐχ οὕτω κελεύω πιστεύειν),
al.,—its position not allowing this. The
first ἔτι is best understood, as referring,
not to any change in his preaching as an
Apostle (for he appears always to have been
of the same mind, and certainly was from

the first persecuted by the Jews), but to
the change since his conversion, before
which he was a strenuous fautor of Judaism.
Olsh. objects to this, that κηρύσσω could
not be used of that period. But this (even
if it be necessary to press κηρύσ. so far
into matter of fact) cannot be said with
any certainty :—the course of Saul as a
zealot may have often led him even to
preach, if not circumcision in its present
debated position, yet that strict Judaism
of which it formed a part. τί ἔτι
διώκ.] ἔτι is logical, as in reff. (De W.) :
i. e., what further excuse is there for my
being (as I am) persecuted (by the Jews)?
For, if this is so, if I still preach
circumcision, ἄρα, then is brought to
nought, is done away, the OFFENCE (reff.
stumbling-block, σκάνδ. has the emphasis)
of the cross—because, if circumcision, and
not faith in Christ crucified, is the condition of salvation, then the Cross has lost
its offensive character to the Jew : οὐδὲ
γὰρ οὕτως ὁ σταυρὸς ἦν ὁ σκανδαλίζων
τοὺς Ἰουδαίους, ὡς τὸ μὴ δεῖν πείθεσθαι
τοῖς πατρῴοις νόμοις. καὶ γὰρ τὸν Στέφανον προσενέγκοντες, οὐκ εἶπον ὅτι οὗτος
τὸν ἐσταυρωμένον προσκυνεῖ, ἀλλ᾽ ὅτι
κατὰ τοῦ νόμου κ. τοῦ τόπου λέγει τοῦ
ἁγίου. Chrys. 12.] The καί introduces a climax—I would (reff.) that
they who are unsettling you would even
. . . As to ἀποκόψονται, (1) it cannot be passive, as E. V., 'were even cut
off.' (2) It can hardly mean 'would cut
themselves off from your communion,' as
the καί is against so mild a wish, besides
that this sense of the word is unexampled.
(3) There is certainly an allusion to ἐνέκοψεν in ver. 7, so that in reading aloud
the Greek, the stress would be, ὄφελ. κ.
ἀποκόψονται οἱ ἀν. ὑμ. But (4) this allusion is one only of sound, and on account
of the καί, all the more likely to be to

t = Eph. ii. 10. 13 Ὑμεῖς γὰρ ^t ἐπ' ^u ἐλευθερίᾳ ἐκλήθητε, ἀδελφοί· ^v μό- ABCDF
1 Thess. iv. 7.
u = ver. 1 reff. νον μὴ ^w τὴν ^u ἐλευθερίαν εἰς ^x ἀφορμὴν τῇ σαρκί, ἀλλὰ KLP א a
v ch. ii. 10. b c d e f
Phil. i. 27.
w ellips., ch. ii. y διὰ τῆς ἀγάπης ^z δουλεύετε ἀλλήλοις. 14 a ὁ γὰρ ^a πᾶς g h k l m
9. Matt. no 17. 47
xxvi. 5 al.
x Rom. vii. νόμος ἐν ἑνὶ ^b λόγῳ ^c πεπλήρωται, ἐν ^d τῷ ^e Ἀγαπήσεις
8, 11. 2 Cor.
v. 12. xi. 12 bis. 1 Tim. v. 14 only. P. Ezek. v. 7 only. y so ver. 6. z see Rom. vi. 18,
22. 1 Cor. ix. 19. a order, Acts xix. 7. xxvii. 37. b Rom. xiii. 9. c = Matt. iii.
15. Acts xii. 25. xiv. 26 al. Ps. xix. 4. d Matt. xix. 18. Rom. xiii. 9 bis. e LEVIT. xix. 18.

13. for γαρ, δε F [syrr] Chr Aug₁ Pac. της σαρκος D¹ 17 vulg copt goth [Victorin] Ambr Ambrst Aug Pel. for δια τ. αγαπ., τη αγαπη του πνευματος DF vulg-ed copt goth Bas [Victorin] Ambrst.

14. for νομος, λογος KL. ins εν υμιν bef εν ενι λογω (*to refer the sentence to the Galatians*) D¹F [goth Tert Victorin] Ambrst: υμιν Mcion-e: *in paucis* syr(but txt in marg). rec πληρουται (*corrn, in ignorance of true sense of perfect*), with DFKL[P] rel [vulg] Chr Thdrt Damasc.h.l. [Victorin] Jer: txt ABCא m 17 Mcion-e Damasc₂ Aug. om εν τω D¹F latt arm Mcion-e [Tert Victorin] Ambrst Jer Pel

some well-known and harsh meaning of the word, *even as far as to which* the Apostle's wish extends. And (5) such a meaning of the word is that in which (agreeably to its primitive classical sense, of hewing off limbs, see Lidd. and Scott) it is used by the LXX, ref. Deut., by Arrian, Epict. ii. 20, by Hesych., ὁ ἀπόκοπος, ἤτοι ὁ εὐνοῦχος—by Philo, de legg. special. ad vi. vii. dec. cap. § 7, vol. ii. p. 306, τὰ γεννητικὰ προσαπέκοψαν,—de vict. offerent. § 13, p. 261, θλαδίας κ. ἀποκεκομμένος τὰ γεννητικά (Wetst.). It seems to me that this sense *must be adopted*, in spite of the protests raised against it; e. g. that of Mr. Bagge recently, who thinks it "involves a positive insult to St. Paul" (?). And so Chrys., and the great consensus of ancient and modern Commentators: and, as Jowett very properly observes, "the common interpretation of the Fathers, confirmed by the use of language in the LXX, is not to be rejected only because it is displeasing to the delicacy of modern times."
ὄφελον is used in the N. T. as a mere particle: see reff.: also Hermann on Viger, p. 756-7, who says: "omnino observandum est, ὄφελον nonnisi tunc adhiberi, quum quis optat ut fuerit aliquid, vel sit, vel futurum sit, quod non fuit aut est aut futurum est." The construction with a future is very unusual; in Lucian, Soloec. 1, ὄφελον καὶ νῦν ἀκολουθῆσαι δυνήσῃ is given as an example of a soloecism. I need hardly enter a caution against the punctuation of a few mss. and editions, by which ὄφελον is taken alone, and the following future supposed to be assertive, as βαστάσει above, ver. 10. The reff. will shew, how alien such an usage is from the usage of the N. T. ἀναστατοῦντες, ἀνατρέποντες, Hesych. It belongs to later Greek: the classical expression is ἀνάστατον ποιεῖν, Polyb. iii. 81. 6

al.: or τιθέναι, Soph. Antig. 670: and it is said to belong to the Macedonian dialect. Ellic., referring to Tittmann, p. 266: where however I can find no such assertion.

13—CH. VI. 5.] THE THIRD or HORTATORY PORTION OF THE EPISTLE, not however separated from the former, but united to it by the current of thought :— and, 13—15.] *Though free, be one another's servants in love.* γάρ gives the reason why the Apostle was so fervent in his denunciation of these disturbers; because they were striking at the very root of their Christian calling, which was for (on condition of ; hardly, for the purpose of ; see reff.) freedom. Only (make not) (so μή with the verb omitted and an accusative in μή 'μοιγε μύθους, Aristoph. Vesp. 1179; μὴ τριβὰς ἔτι, Soph. Antig. 577 ; μή μοι μυρίους μηδὲ δισμυρίους ξένους, Demosth. Phil. i. § 19. See more examples in Hartung, ii. 153) your liberty into (or, use it not for) an occasion (opportunity) for the flesh (for giving way to carnal passions), but by means of (your) love, be in bondage (opposition to ἐλευθερίᾳ) to one another. Chrys. remarks, πάλιν ἐνταῦθα αἰνίττεται, ὅτι φιλονεικία κ. στάσις κ. φιλαρχία κ. ἀπόνοια ταύτης αἰτία τῆς πλάνης αὐτοῖς ἐγένετο· ἡ γὰρ τῶν αἱρέσεων μήτηρ ἡ τῆς φιλαρχίας ἐστὶν ἐπιθυμία. 14.] See Rom. xiii. 8, 9. The rec. reading πληροῦται would mean merely '*is in course of being fulfilled,*' whereas now it is, 'is fulfilled:' not '*comprehended*' (Luth., Calv., Olsh., Winer, al.). "The question, how the Apostle can rightly say of the *whole* law, that it is fulfilled by loving one's neighbour, must not be answered by understanding νόμος of the *Christian* law (Koppe), or of the *moral* law only (Estius, al.), or of the *second* table of the decalogue (Beza, al.), or of every divinely revealed law in general (Schött.);—for ὁ πᾶς νόμος cannot

τὸν πλησίον σου ὡς σεαυτόν. ¹⁵ εἰ δὲ ἀλλήλους ᶠδά-
κνετε καὶ ᵍκατεσθίετε, ʰβλέπετε μὴ ὑπὸ ἀλλήλων ⁱἀνα-
λωθῆτε.

¹⁶ ᵏΛέγω δέ, πνεύματι ˡπεριπατεῖτε, καὶ ᵐἐπιθυμίαν
ᵐσαρκὸς οὐ μὴ ⁿτελέσητε. ¹⁷ ἡ γὰρ σὰρξ ᵒἐπιθυμεῖ ᵖκατὰ
τοῦ πνεύματος, τὸ δὲ πνεῦμα ᵖκατὰ τῆς σαρκός· ταῦτα

ᶠ here only. = Hab. ii. 7.
ᵍ Mark xii. 40 ‖ L. 2 Cor. xi. 20. Rev. xi. 5 only. Isa. ix. 12.
ʰ = Matt. xxiv. 4 ‖. 1 Cor. viii. 9. x. 12 al.
ⁱ Luke ix. 54 (2 Thess. ii. 8 v. r.) only. Joel ii. 3.
ᵐ (Rom. xiii.
ⁿ = Rom. ii. 27. James ii. 8.

k ch. iv. 1. Rom. xv. 8.   l constr., Acts (ix. 31) xxi. 21.   2 Cor. xii. 18.   14.) Eph. ii. 3.   2 Pet. ii. 18.   1 John ii. 16.   see 1 Pet. ii. 11.   o absol., James iv. 2.   2 Kings xxiii. 15.   p = ch. iii. 21 reff.

(not Aug₃).   rec (for σεαυτον) εαυτον, with FL[P] rel Chr Thl Œc : txt ABCDKℵ b c g h n o 17 Mcion-e Thdrt Damasc. (*Simly Rom* xiii. 9.)
   15. δακ. κ. κατεσθ. bef αλληλους, and αναλωθ. bef υπ. αλληλ. D¹·³F Cypr₂ Victorin. υπ' (for υπο) BDFℵ¹ a g m [47] Bas Chr Thl : txt ACD²·³L[P]ℵ³ rel [Orig₂] Thdrt Damasc Œc.

from the circumstances of the whole Epistle, mean any thing but '*the whole law of Moses:*'—but by placing ourselves on the lofty spiritual level from which St. Paul looked down, and saw all other commands of the law so far subordinated to the law of love, that whoever had fulfilled *this* command, must be treated as having fulfilled the whole." Meyer: who also remarks that τὸν πλησίον σου applies to fellow-Christians; cf. ἀλλήλους below.

15.] ἀλλήλους has both times the emphasis. The form of the sentence is very like Matt. xxvi. 52,—πάντες οἱ λαβόντες μάχαιραν, ἐν μαχαίρᾳ ἀπολοῦνται, except that there λαβόντες, as having the stress, precedes. Chrys. says, ταῖς λέξεσιν ἐμφαντικῶς ἐχρήσατο. οὐ γὰρ εἶπε **δάκνετε** μόνον, ὅπερ ἐστὶ θυμουμένου, ἀλλὰ καὶ **κατεσθίετε**, ὅπερ ἐστὶν ἐμμένοντος τῇ πονηρίᾳ. ὁ μὲν γὰρ δάκνων, ὀργῆς ἐπλήρωσε πάθος· ὁ δὲ κατεσθίων, θηριωδίας ἐσχάτης παρέσχεν ἀπόδειξιν, δήγματα δὲ κ. βρώσεις οὐ τὰς σωματικάς φησιν, ἀλλὰ τὰς πολὺ χαλεπωτέρας. οὐ γὰρ οὕτως ὁ ἀνθρωπίνης ἀπογευσάμενος σαρκὸς ἔβλαψεν, ὡς ὁ δήγματα εἰς τὴν ψυχὴν πηγνύς· ὅσον γὰρ ψυχὴ τιμιωτέρα σώματος, τοσούτῳ χαλεπωτέρα ἡ ταύτης βλάβη.
ἀναλωθ.] The literal sense must be kept, —consumed (by one another),—your spiritual life altogether annihilated: ἡ γὰρ διάστασις κ. ἡ μάχη φθοροποιὸν κ. ἀναλωτικὸν καὶ τῶν δεχομένων αὐτὴν κ. τῶν εἰσαγόντων, καὶ σητὸς μᾶλλον ἅπαντα ἀνατρώγει. Chrys.   **16—26.]** *Exhortation to a spiritual life, and warning against the works of the flesh.* **16.]**
λέγω δέ refers to ver. 13—repeating, and explaining it—q. d., 'What I mean, is this.' **πνεύματι**, the *normal* dative, of the rule, or manner, after or in which: Meyer quotes Hom. Il. o. 194, οὔτι Διὸς βέομαι φρεσίν:—**by the Spirit**. But **πν.** is not man's '*spiritual part*,' as Beza,

Rück., De W., al.; nor is **πνεύματι** '*after a spiritual manner,*' Peile,—nor will ἡ ἐνοικοῦσα χάρις give the force of πνεῦμα (Thdrt.): it is (as in ver. 5) **the Holy Spirit of God**: this will be clear on comparing with our vv. 16—18, the more expanded parallel passage, Rom. vii. 22—viii. 11. The history of the verbal usage is, that πνεῦμα, as χριστός and θεός, came to be used as a proper name: so that the supposed distinction between τὸ πν. as the objective (the Holy Ghost), and πν. as the subjective (man's spirit), does not hold.
   σαρκός] the natural man:—that whole state of being in the flesh, out of which spring the practices and thoughts of ver. 19.   **οὐ μὴ τελέσητε]** Is this (1) merely *future* in meaning, and a sequence on πνεύματι περιπ., 'and ye shall not fulfil,'—or is it (2) *imperative*, 'and fulfil not?' Ellic. in his note has shewn that this latter meaning is allowable, it being doubtful even in classical Greek whether there are not some instances of οὐ μή with the second person subjunctive imperatively used, and the tendency of later Greek being rather to use the subjunctive aorist for the future. And Meyer defends it on exegetical grounds. But surely (1) is much to be preferred on these same grounds. For the next and following verses go to shew just what this verse will then assert, viz. that the Spirit and the flesh *exclude one another.*   **17.]** *Substantiation of the preceding,—that if ye walk by the Spirit, ye shall not fulfil the lusts of the flesh.* The second **γάρ** (see var. readd.) gives a reason for the continual ἐπιθυμεῖν of these two against one another: viz., that they are opposites.
   ἵνα] not '*so that:*'—this *is* the *result:* but more is expressed by ἵνα. Winer gives the meaning well: "Atque hujus luctæ hoc est consilium, *ut* &c. Scil. τὸ πν. impedit vos, quo minus perficiatis

γὰρ ἀλλήλοις [q] ἀντίκειται, [r] ἵνα μὴ [s] ἃ ἐὰν θέλητε [s] ταῦτα
ποιῆτε. 18 εἰ δὲ [t] πνεύματι [t] ἄγεσθε, οὐκ ἐστὲ [u] ὑπὸ νόμον.
19 [v] φανερὰ δέ ἐστιν τὰ [w] ἔργα τῆς σαρκός, [x] ἅτινά ἐστιν
[y] πορνεία, [z] ἀκαθαρσία, [ab] ἀσέλγεια, 20 [c] εἰδωλολατρεία,
[d] φαρμακεία, [e] ἔχθραι, [bf] ἔρις, [bg] ζῆλος, [bh] θυμοί, [bi] ἐριθεῖαι,

ABCDF KLPℵ a b c d e f g h k l m n o 17. 47

q Luke xiii. 17. xxi. 15. 1 Cor. xvi. 9. Phil. i. 28. 2 Thess. ii. 4. 1 Tim. i. 10. v. 14 only. L.P. Zech. iii. 1.
r = 1 Thess. v. 4. (see note.)
s constr., Rom. vii. 15.
t Rom. viii. 14. constr., 2 Tim. iii. 6.
u ch. iv. 4, 5 reff.
v Rom. i. 19 al.
w see Rom. xiii. 12.
x = ch. iv. 24. Col. ii. 23.
y Matt. v. 32 al. fr. Gen. xxxviii. 24.
z Rom. i. 24. vi. 19 al. P., exc. Matt. xxiii. 27. Prov. vi. 16.
y z a 2 Cor. xii. 21.
y a m Mark vii. 21, 22.
z a Eph. iv. 19.
a 2 Pet. ii. 2. Jude 4 al.+ Wisd. xiv. 26 only.
b Rom. xiii. 13.
a c o 1 Pet. iv. 3.
c 1 Cor. x 14. Col. iii. 5. 1 Pet. iv. 3 only +.
d here (-ία, Rev. xviii. 23) only. Exod. vii. 11, 22. Isa. xlvii 9, 12.
e Eph. ii. 15 reff.
f 1 Cor. i. 11. Tit. iii. 9+. Sir. xxviii. 11 al.
f g 1 Cor. iii. 3.
f g h i 2 Cor. xii. 20. (Sir. xl. 5.)
f l m Rom. i. 29.
h plur., 2 Cor. xii. 20. (Wisd. vii. 20.)
i Rom. ii. 8. 2 Cor. xii. 20. Phil. i. 17. ii. 3. James iii. 14, 16 only +.

17. rec for (2nd) γαρ, δε (*prob to avoid recurrence of* γαρ *which introduced the former clause: the recurrence of* δε *would not be simly felt*), with ACD^{3}KL[P]ℵ^3 rel Chr Thdrt Damasc: txt BD^{1}Fℵ^1 17 latt copt [Cyr$_3$-p] lat-ff. rec αντικειται bef αλληλοις, with KL[P]ℵ rel syrr copt: txt ABCDF m 17 [47] latt goth [Cyr$_1$-p] Damasc$_1$ [Orig-int$_3$] lat-ff. for ἅ, ὃ D^{1}F goth: οσα 31. rec (for εαν) αν, with C^{2}DF K(e sil) L[P] rel Clem Chr Thdrt Damasc$_2$: om C^1: txt A B[μη αν was at first written, but εα added above] ℵ a.

18. aft ουκ ins ετι Cℵ^3 [47] syr Aug$_1$.

19. rec ins μοιχεια bef πορνεια (*from places such as Mt* xv. 19, *Mk* vii. 21, *cf Hos* ii. 2), with D F[-ειαι] KLℵ^3 rel syr [goth arm] gr-lat-ff: om ABC[P]ℵ^1 17 [47] vulg Syr copt æth Clem Mcion-e Cyr Eph Damasc$_1$ Tert Jer$_{expr}$ [Orig-int$_2$] Aug Fulg Pel.

20. rec ερεις (*the mss vary much between the sing and plur forms*), with CD$^{2.3}$ FKL[P] rel latt [Clem] Justin [Iren Orig-int$_2$ Cypr Lucif]: txt ABD^{1}ℵ b f g h k o. rec ζηλοι, with CD$^{2.3}$KLℵ rel vss gr-lat-ff: txt BD^1[P] 17 [Syr] goth Justin Damasc Concil-Carthag-in-Cypr, ζηλους F. (A defective.)

τὰ τῆς σαρκός (ea, quæ ἡ σάρξ perficere cupit), contra ἡ σάρξ adversatur vobis ubi τὰ τοῦ πνεύματος peragere studetis;" and Bengel: "Spiritus obnititur carni et actioni malæ: caro, Spiritui et actioni bonæ, *ut* (ἵνα) neque illa neque hæc peragatur." The necessity of supposing an ecbatic meaning for ἵνα in theology is obviated by remembering, that with God, results are all purposed. See this verse expanded in Rom. vii. viii. as above: in vii. 20 we have nearly the same words, and the same construction. It is true that θέλειν there applies only to one side, the better will, striving after good: whereas here it must be taken 'sensu communi,' for 'will' in general, to whichever way inclined. So that our verse requires expansion, both in the direction of Rom. vii. 15—20,—and in the other direction, οὐ γὰρ ὃ θέλω (after the natural man) ποιῶ κακόν· ἀλλ' ὃ οὐ θέλω ἀγαθόν, τοῦτο ποιῶ,—to make it logically complete. **18.**] By this verse, the locus respecting the flesh and the Spirit is interwoven into the general argument, thus (cf. ver. 23): the law is made for the flesh, and the works of the flesh: the Spirit and flesh ἀντίκεινται: **if** (δέ bringing out the contrast between the treatment of *both* in ver. 17, and the selection of *one side* in this verse) **then ye are led by** (see Rom. ref., ὅσοι . . . . πνεύματι θεοῦ ἄγονται, οὗτοι υἱοί εἰσιν θεοῦ) **the Spirit, ye are not under the law.** This he proceeds to substantiate, by specifying the works of the flesh and of the Spirit. This interpretation is better than the merely practical one of Chrys., al., ὁ γὰρ πνεῦμα ἔχων ὡς χρή, σβέννυσι διὰ τούτου πονηρὰν ἐπιθυμίαν ἅπασαν· ὁ δὲ τούτων ἀπαλλαγεὶς οὐ δεῖται τῆς ἀπὸ τοῦ νόμου βοηθείας, ὑψηλότερος πολλῷ τῆς ἐκείνου παραγγελίας γενόμενος,—for it is a very different thing οὐ δεῖσθαι νόμου, from οὐκ εἶναι ὑπὸ νόμον. **19—23.**] *substantiates* (see above) *ver.* 18. **19.**] **φανερά** (emphatic), **plain to all,** not needing, like the more hidden fruits of the *Spirit*, to be educed and specified: and therefore more clearly amenable to law, which takes cognizance of τὰ φανερά. **ἅτινά ἐστιν**] almost = 'for example:' 'qualia sunt:' see on ch. iv. 24. **ἀκαθ., impurity** in general. **ἀσέλγ.,** ἑτοιμότης πρὸς πᾶσαν ἡδονήν, Etym. Mag. It does not seem to include necessarily the idea of lasciviousness: "Demosthenes, making mention of the blow which Meidias had given him, characterizes it as in keeping with the well-known ἀσέλγεια of the man (Meid. 514). Elsewhere he joins δεσποτικῶς and ἀσελγῶς and προπετῶς." Trench, New Test. Synonyms, p. 64. The best word for it seems to be **wantonness,** '*protervitas.*' **20.**] **εἰδωλ.,** in its

ʲ διχοστασίαι, ᵏ αἱρέσεις, ²¹ ˡ φθόνοι, [ᵐ φόνοι,] ⁿ μέθαι, ᵇᵒ κῶ-
μοι, καὶ τὰ ὅμοια τούτοις, ἃ ᵖ προλέγω ὑμῖν καθὼς καὶ
�qπροεῖπον, ʳ ὅτι οἱ τὰ ˢ τοιαῦτα ˢ πράσσοντες ᵗ βασιλείαν
θεοῦ οὐ ᵗ κληρονομήσουσιν. ²² ὁ δὲ ᵘ καρπὸς τοῦ πνεύματός ἐστιν ἀγάπη, χαρά, εἰρήνη, ᵛʷˣ μακροθυμία, ᵛʷʸ χρηστότης, ᶻ ἀγαθωσύνη, πίστις, ²³ ᵛᵃ πραΰτης, ᵇ ἐγκράτεια·

j Rom. xvi. 17 (1 Cor. iii. 3 v. r.) only †.
l 1 Macc. iii. 29.
k 1 Cor. xi. 19. Acts v. 17 al5.
2 Pet. ii. 1 only.
1 Macc. vii.
30.
l m see above, with y a and f.
n Luke xxi. 34. Rom. xiii. 13

only. L.P. Hag. i. 6. Judith xiii. 15.   o Rom. xiii. 13. 1 Pet. iv. 3 only †. Wisd. xiv. 23. 2 Macc.
vi. 4 only.   p 2 Cor. xiii. 2. 1 Thess. iii. 4 only. Isa. xli. 26 only.   q Acts i. 16. 1 Thess. iv.
6 only †.   r constr., John xiii. 54. ix. 19. x. 36.   s Rom. i. 32. ii. 2, 3.   t 1 Cor. vi. 9, 10.
xv. 50. (see Eph. v. 5. James ii. 5.)   u = Rom. xv. 28. Eph. v. 9. Heb. xii. 11. James iii.
18. Prov. xi. 30.   v Col. iii. 12.   w as above (v). Rom. ii. 4. 2 Cor. vi. 6.
x as above (v w). Rom. ix. 22. 1 Tim. i. 16. Heb. vi. 12. James v. 10 al. Prov. xxv. 15.   y as above
(v w). Rom. iii. 12. xi. 22(3ce). Eph. ii. ι. Tit. iii. 4 only. Ps. xiii. 1, 3.   z Rom. xv. 14. Eph.
v. 9. 2 Thess. i. 11 only. Neh. ix. 35.   a Paul, 1 Cor. iv. 21 al7. James i. 21. iii. 13. 1 Pet.
iii. 15 only. Ps. xliv. 4.   b Acts xxiv. 25. 2 Pet. i. 6(bis) only †. Sir. xviii. 30(title) only

21. om φονοι (*prob from homœotel, but see Rom* i. 29) Bℵ 17 demid F-lat¹ Clem
Mcion-e Iren-int Cypr Jer₂(and elsw expressly) Ambrst Aug: ins ACDFKL[P] rel
lat-mss-in-Jer Chr Thdrt₂ Damasc Lucif. [κωμαι ℵ m¹.] om 2nd και BFℵ¹
67² vulg æth Chr₁ Tert [Cypr] Lucif: ins ACDKL[P]ℵ³ rel vss Clem Chr_{h.l.} Thdrt
Damasc Iren-int Jer. for προειπ., ειπον ℵ¹: προειρηκα D¹F.

23. rec πραοτης, with DFKL[P] rel: txt ABCℵ 17 [47] Cyr-jer. aft εγκρατ.
ins αγνεια D¹F latt(not am harl) [goth] Bas Pallad Iren-int [Orig-int₁] Cypr Ambrst
Pel Sedul (not Jer Aug).

proper meaning of **idolatry**: not, as Olsh.,
'*sins of lust,*' because of the unclean
orgies of idolatry. **φαρμ.,** either
'*poisonings,*' or '*sorceries.*' The latter is
preferable, as more frequently its sense in
the LXX and N. T. (reff.), and because
(Mey.) Asia was particularly addicted to
sorceries (Acts xix. 19). **θυμοί**] pas-
sionate outbreaks. θυμὸς μέν ἐστι πρόσκαιρος, ὀργὴ δὲ πολυχρόνιος μνησικακία,
Ammonius. διαφέρει δὲ θυμὸς ὀργῆς, τῷ
θυμὸν μὲν εἶναι ὀργὴν ἀναθυμιωμένην κ. ἔτι
ἐκκαιομένην, ὀργὴν δὲ ὄρεξιν ἀντιτιμωρήσεως.
Orig. sel. in Ps. ii., vol. ii. 541: both cited
by Trench, Syn. p. 146. **ζῆλος,**
jealousy (in bad sense)—reff. **ἐριθεῖαι**] not '*strife,*' as E. V. and commonly,
in error: see note on Rom. ii. 8,—but
cabals, unworthy compassings of selfish
ends. Wetst. N. T. ii. p. 147, traces in a
note the later meanings of **αἵρεσις.** Here
διχοστ., **divisions,** seems to lead to αἱρέσ.,
parties, composed of those who have *chosen*
their self-willed line and adhere to it.
Trench quotes Aug. (cont. Crescon. Don.
ii. 7 (9), vol. ix. p. 471): "*Schisma* est
recens congregationis ex aliquâ senten-
tiarum diversitate dissensio: *hæresis* autem
schisma inveteratum." But we must not
think of an ecclesiastical meaning only,
or chiefly here. **21.** φθόν., (φόν.)]
see Rom. i. 29, where we have the same
alliteration. **ἃ προλ.**] The construction of **ἃ** is exactly as John viii. 54, ὃν
ὑμεῖς λέγετε ὅτι θεὸς ὑμῶν ἐστιν:—it is
governed, but only as matter of reference,
by προλέγω,—not to be joined by attrac-

tion with πράσσοντες, as Olsh., al.
προλ. κ. προεῖπον] I forewarn you (now),
and did forewarn you (when I was with
you): the προ- in both cases pointing on
to the great day of retribution. **τὰ
τοιαῦτα**] The article generalizes τοιαῦτα,
the things of this kind, i. e. all such
things. See Ellic.'s note. **βασ. θ.
οὐ κλ.**] See reff. **22.**] **καρπός,** not
ἔργα, **τοῦ πνεύματος.** The works of the
flesh are no καρπός, see Rom. vi. 21.
These are the only real *fruit* of men: see
John xv. 1—8: compare also John iii. 20,
note. They *are,* or are manifested in,
ἔργα: but they are much more: whereas
those others are nothing more, as to any
abiding result for good. **ἀγάπη**—at
the head, as chief—1 Cor. xiii. See Rom.
xii. 9. **χαρά,** better merely **joy,** than
as Winer, al., '*voluptas ex aliorum com-
modis percepta,*' as opposed to φθόνος.
We must not seek for a detailed logical
opposition in the two lists, which would
be quite alien from the fervid style of
St. Paul. **χρηστότης, ἀγαθωσ.**]
Jerome, comm. in loc., says, "Benignitas
sive suavitas, quia apud Græcos χρηστότης utrumque sonat, virtus est lenis,
blanda, tranquilla, et omnium bonorum
apta consortio: invitans ad familiaritatem
sui, dulcis alloquio, moribus temperata.
Non multum bonitas (ἀγαθωσύνη) a be-
nignitate diversa est, quia et ipsa ad bene-
faciendum videtur exposita. Sed in eo
differt; quia potest bonitas esse tristior, et
fronte severis moribus irrugata bene quidem facere et præstare quod poscitur: non

c ch. iii. 21.
 ver. 17.
d gen., 1 Cor.
 iii. 22, 23 al.
e = ch. vi. 14.
 see Rom. vi.
 6.
f = Rom. vii. 5
 (viii. 18 al7.,
 Paul. Heb. ii.
 9, 10. x. 32.
 1 Pet. i. 11
 al3.) only †.

 ^c κατὰ τῶν τοιούτων οὐκ ἔστιν νόμος. ²⁴ οἱ δὲ τοῦ ^d χριστοῦ Ἰησοῦ τὴν σάρκα ^e ἐσταύρωσαν σὺν τοῖς ^f παθή- μασιν καὶ ταῖς ^g ἐπιθυμίαις. ²⁵ εἰ ζῶμεν ^h πνεύματι, πνεύ- ματι καὶ ⁱ στοιχῶμεν. ²⁶ μὴ ^j γινώμεθα ^k κενόδοξοι, ἀλλή- λους ^l προκαλούμενοι, ἀλλήλοις ^m φθονοῦντες. VI. ¹ ἀδελ-

ABCDF
KLPℵ a
b c d e f
g h k l m
n o 17. 47

g = ver. 16 reff. Rom. i. 24 al. Sus. 11, &c.   h dat., Rom. xii. 12 al. Winer, § 31. 6, 7. i (=) Acts xxi.
 24. Rom. iv. 12. ch. vi. 16. Phil. iii. 16 only. (Eccles. xi. 6 only.) j = ch. iv. 12. Eph. v. 17 al.
k here only †. (-ξία, Phil. ii. 3.) l here only †.   m here only †. Tobit iv. 16 only.

24. ins κυριου bef χριστου ℵ¹(but erased).   rec om ιησου, with DFKL rel latt syrr [goth arm Mcion-e] Chr Thdrt Ps-Ath [Orig-int₁] Cypr Jer : ins ABC[P]ℵ 17 [47¹] coptt æth Cyr_persæpe Bas Procop Damasc Aug. aft σαρκα ins αυτων F vulg Cypr.
25. πνευματι bef ζωμ. DF latt(not am demid al) [Orig₁] Aug : ζ. ουν εν πν. κ. πν. στοιχ. syrr Chr.   om και F Ambrst-ed.   στοιχουμεν D³KL e 67².
26. αλληλους (for -λοις) BG¹[P] c d k l [Clem₁] Chr Thdrt₁-ms₁ Œc : αλληλοιυς(sic) a : txt ACDFKLℵ rel Clem₂ Thdrt₂ Damasc.

tamen suavis esse consortio, et sua cunctos invitare dulcedine." Plato, deff. 412 e, defines χρηστότης, ἤθους ἀπλαστία μετ' εὐλογιστίας. ἀγαθωσ. is a Hellenistic word, see reff. Perhaps kindness and goodness would best represent the two words. πίστις, in the widest sense: ∗ faith, towards God and man : of love it is said, 1 Cor. xiii. 7, πάντα πιστεύει.
23.] πραΰτης seems to be well re- presented by meekness,—again, towards God and man : and ἐγκρ. by temperance, —the holding in of the lusts and desires. τῶν τοιούτ. answers to τὰ τοιαῦτα above, and should therefore be taken as neuter, not masculine, as Chrys., al. This verse (see above on ver. 18) substantiates οὐκ ἐστὲ ὑπὸ νόμον—for if you are led by the Spirit, these are its fruits in you, and against these the law has nothing to say : see 1 Tim. i. 9, 10. 24.] Fur- ther confirmation of this last result, and transition to the exhortations of vv. 25, 26. But (contrast, the one universal choice of Christians, in distinction from the two catalogues) they who are Christ's cruci- fied (when they became Christ's,—at their baptism, see Rom. vi. 2: not so well, 'have crucified,' as E. V.) the flesh, with its passions and its desires,—and there- fore are entirely severed from and dead to the law, which is for the fleshly, and those passions and desires—on which last he founds,— 25.] If (no connecting particle—giving more vividness to the in- ference) we LIVE (emphatic—if, as we saw, having slain the flesh, our life depends on the Spirit) in (said to be a species of in- strumental dative; but such usage is of very rare occurrence, and hardly ever undoubted. Here the dative is probably employed more as corresponding to the dative in the other member, than with

strict accuracy. But it may be justified thus: our inner life, which is hid with Christ in God, Col. iii. 3, is lived πνεύματι (normal dative), the Spirit being its gene- rator and upholder) the Spirit,—in the Spirit (emphatic) let us also walk (in our conduct in life : let our practical walk, which is led κατὰ προαιρεσιν of our own, be in harmony with that higher life in which we live before God by faith, and in the Spirit). 26.] connected with στοιχῶμεν above, by the first person,— and with ch. vi. 1, by the sense; and so forming a transition to the admonitions which follow. μὴ γινώμ., let us not become—efficiamur, vulg., Erasm.,— a mild, and at the same time a solemn method of warning. For while it seems to concede that they were not this as yet, it assumes that the process was going on which would speedily make them so. 'Let us not be,' of the E. V., misses this. κενόδοξοι would include, as De W. ob- serves, all worldly honour, as not an object for the Christian to seek, 1 Cor. i. 31 ; 2 Cor. x. 17. ἀλλήλ. προ- καλ.] εἰς φιλονεικίας κ. ἔρεις, Chrys. So ἐς δίκας προκαλουμένων τῶν Ἀθηναίων, Thuc. vii. 18: εἰς μάχην προὐκαλεῖτο, Xen. (Wetst.) "φθονεῖν is the correla- tive act on the part of the weak, to the προκαλεῖσθαι on the part of the strong. The strong vauntingly challenged their weaker brethren : they could only reply with envy." Ellicott. These words are addressed to all the Galatians:—the danger was common to both parties, the obedient and disobedient, the orthodox and the Judaizers.
VI. 1—5.] Exhortation to forbearance and humility. Brethren (bespeaks their attention by a friendly address; marking also the opening of a new subject, con-

φοί, ἐὰν καὶ [n]προλημφθῇ [o]ἄνθρωπος ἔν τινὶ [p]παραπτώματι, ὑμεῖς οἱ [q]πνευματικοὶ [r]καταρτίζετε [s]τὸν [s]τοιοῦτον ἐν [tu]πνεύματι [uv]πραΰτητος, [w]σκοπῶν σεαυτόν, μὴ καὶ σὺ [x]πειρασθῇς. 2 ἀλλήλων τὰ [y]βάρη [z]βαστάζετε, καὶ [a]οὕτως [b]ἀναπληρώσατε τὸν [c]νόμον τοῦ χριστοῦ. 3 εἰ

[n] = here only. (Mark xiv. 8.
[o] = 1 Cor. xi. 21 only †.)
Wisd. xvii.
17 only.
o = 1 Cor. iv. 1. xi. 28.
p Matt. vi. 14.
Rom. iv. 25
al. Ps. xviii.
12. Ezek.
xviii. 26.

q = 1 Cor. iii. 1. xiv. 37 al. † r 1 Cor. i. 10. Matt. iv. 21 al. Ezra iv. 13. s Acts xxii.
22. 1 Cor. v, 5, 11. 2 Cor. ii. 6, 7. x. 11. Tit. iii. 11. t Rom. viii. 15 bis. xi. 8 (from Isa.
xxix. 10). 2 Cor. iv. 13. Eph. i. 17 al. u 1 Cor. iv. 21. v ch. v. 23 reff.
w = & constr., Luke xi. 35. (Rom. xvi. 17. 2 Cor. iv. 18. Phil. ii. 4. iii. 17 only †. 2 Macc. iv. 5 only.)
x = 1 Cor. vii. 5. 1 Thess. iii. 5. James i. 13 al. y Matt. xx. 12. Acts xv. 28. 2 Cor. iv.
17. 1 Thess. ii. 6. Rev. ii. 24 only. Sir. xiii. 2. z = Rom. xv. 1. (ch. v. 10 reff.) a = Acts
xvii 33. 1 Cor. xi. 28. xiv. 25 al. b Matt. xiii. 14. 1 Cor. xiv. 16. xvi. 17. Phil. ii. 30. 1 Thess.
ii. 16 only. Gen. xxix. 28. imper. aor., John xiv. 15. 1 Cor. vi. 20. c see Rom. viii.
2. 1 Cor. ix. 21.

CHAP. VI. 1. om 1st καὶ K o [Syr goth]: forsan arm.   προκαταληφθη K.   rec
πραοτ., with ACDFKL rel : txt B[P]א 17. (See ch v. 23.)   for συ, αυτος D¹—σκ.
εκαστος σεαυτ. μη κ. αυτος πειρασθη F [Victorin].
    2. βαστασετε א¹(txt א³) : [-σατε P].   αναπληρωσετε (prob corrn, the imper aor
being unusual: see reff) BF latt Syr sah æth Thdrt-ms Procl lat-ff : txt ACDKL[P]א
rel syr [arm] Clem Ath Chr Thdrt Damasc, impletis goth.

nected however with the foregoing: see above), **if a man be even surprised** (προλημφθῇ has the emphasis, on account of the καί. This makes it necessary to assign a meaning to it which shall justify its emphatic position. And such meaning is clearly not found in the ordinary renderings. E. g. Chrysostom,—ἐὰν συναρπαγῇ,—so E. V. ' overtaken,' and De Wette, al., which could not be emphatic, but would be palliative: Grotius,—' si quis antea (h. e. antequam hæc ep. ad vos veniat) deprehensus fuerit:' Winer,—' etiam si (si vel) quis antea deprehensus fuerit in peccato, eum tamen (iterum peccantem) corrigite:' Olsh., who regards the προ- almost as expletive, betokening merely that the λαμβάνεσθαι comes in time before the καταρτίζειν. The only meaning which satisfies the emphasis is that of being caught in the fact, 'flagrante delicto,' before he can escape: which, though unusual, seems justified by ref. Wisd.: and so Meyer, Ellic., al.) **in any transgression** (with the meaning 'overtaken' for προλημφθῇ, falls also that of 'inadvertence' for παράπτωμα. The stronger meaning of 'sin,' is far commoner in St. Paul: see ref. Rom. and ib. v. 15, 16, 20; 2 Cor. v. 19; Eph. i. 7, ii. 1, 5; Col. ii. 13 bis), **do ye, the spiritual ones** (said not in irony, but bonâ fide: referring not to the clergy only, but to every believer), **restore** (Beza, Hammond, Bengel, al., have imagined an allusion to a dislocated limb being reduced into place: but the simple ethical sense is abundantly justified by examples: see Herodot., cited on 1 Cor. i. 10; Stob. i. 85, καταρτίζειν φίλους

διαφερομένους (Ellic.)) **such a person** (see especially 1 Cor. v. 5, 11) **in the spirit of meekness** (beware of the silly hendiadys: Chrys. gives the right allusion, —οὐκ εἶπεν " ἐν πραότητι," ἀλλ' " ἐν πνεύματι πραότητος·" δηλῶν ὅτι καὶ τῷ πνεύματι ταῦτα δοκεῖ, καὶ τὸ δύνασθαι μετ' ἐπιεικείας διορθοῦν τοὺς ἁμαρτάνοντας, χαρίσματός ἐστι πνευματικοῦ: and Ellic., "πν. here seems immediately to refer to the state of the inward Spirit as wrought upon by the Holy Spirit, and ultimately to the Holy Spirit, as the inworking power. Cf. Rom. i. 4, viii. 15; 2 Cor. iv. 13; Eph. i. 17: in all of which cases πι. seems to indicate the Holy Spirit, and the abstract genitive the specific χάρισμα"),—**looking to thyself** (we have the same singling out of individuals from a multitude previously addressed in Thucyd. i. 42, ὧν ἐνθυμηθέντες, καὶ νεώτερός τις παρὰ πρεσβυτέρου μαθών, ἀξιούτω .... ἡμᾶς ἀμύνεσθαι. See more examples in Bernhardy, p. 421), **lest thou also be tempted** (on a similar occasion: notice the aorist). **2.]** ἀλλήλων, prefixed and emphatic, has not been enough attended to. You want to become disciples of that Law which imposes heavy burdens on men: if you will bear burdens, **bear** ONE ANOTHER'S **burdens, and thus fulfil** (see var. readd.: notice aorist: by this act fulfil) **the law of Christ,**—a far higher and better law, whose only burden is love. The position of ἀλλήλων I conceive fixes this meaning, by throwing τὰ βάρη into the shade, as a term common to the two laws. As to the βάρη, the more general the meaning we give to it, the better it will accord with the sense of the command. The matter men-

γὰρ ᵈ δοκεῖ τις ᵉ εἶναι τὶ μηδὲν ὤν, ᶠ φρεναπατᾷ ἑαυτόν. 4 τὸ δὲ ᵍ ἔργον ἑαυτοῦ ʰ δοκιμαζέτω ἕκαστος, καὶ τότε ⁱ εἰς ἑαυτὸν μόνον τὸ ʲᵏ καύχημα ᵏ ἕξει, καὶ οὐκ ⁱ εἰς ˡ τὸν ἕτερον· 5 ἕκαστος γὰρ τὸ ἴδιον ᵐ φορτίον ᶻ βαστάσει. 6 ⁿ κοινωνείτω δὲ ὁ ᵒ κατηχούμενος τὸν λόγον τῷ ᵒ κατηχοῦντι ἐν

3. [om τι B¹ 32-8.]   rec εαυτον bef φρεναπατα, with DFKL[P] rel latt gr-lat-ff: txt ABCℵ m 17 coptt Chr.

4. om εκαστος B sah.

tioned in the last verse led on to this: but this grasps far wider, extending to *all* the burdens which we can, by help and sympathy, bear for one another. There are some which we *cannot :* see below. ἀναπληρ., **thoroughly fulfil** : Ellic. quotes Plut. Poplicol. ii., ἀνεπλήρωσε τὴν βουλὴν ὀλιγανδροῦσαν, 'filled up the Senate.' 3.] The chief hindrance to sympathy with the burdens of others, is self-conceit: that must be got rid of.   **εἶναι τί**, see reff. **μηδὲν ὤν**] there is (perhaps : but this must not be over-pressed, see Ellic.) a fine irony in the subjective μηδέν— 'being, if he would come to himself, and look on the real fact, nothing :' —whereas οὐδὲν ὤν expresses more the objective fact,—his real absolute worthlessness. See examples of both expressions in Wetst. h. l.   **φρεναπατᾷ**] not found elsewhere : see ref. and James i. 26. The word seems to mean just as ἀπατῶν καρδίαν αὑτοῦ there : I should hardly hold Ellic.'s distinction : both are subjective deceits, and only to be got rid of by testing them with plain matter of fact.   **4.**] *The test applied :* emphasis on τὸ ἔργον, which (as Mey.) is the complex, the whole practical result of his life, see reff. **δοκ.**] put to the trial (reff.) : not '*render* δόκιμον,' which the word will not bear.   **κ. τότε**] And then (after he has done this) **he will have his matter of boasting** (the article makes it subjective : the καύχημα, that whereof to boast, not without a slight irony,—whatever matter of boasting he finds, after such a testing, will be) **in reference to himself alone** (εἰς ἑαυ. μόν. emphatic—corresponds to εἰς τὸν ἕτ. below), **and not** (as matter of *fact :* not μή) **in reference to the other,** (or, **his neighbour**—the man with whom he was comparing himself : general in its meaning, but particular in each case of comparison).   **5.**] And this is the more advisable, because in the nature of

things, **each man's own load** (of infirmities and imperfections and sins: not of '*responsibility*,' which is alien from the context) **will** (*in ordinary life :* not '*at the last day*,' which is here irrelevant, and would surely have been otherwise expressed : the **βαστάσει** must correspond ＊ with the βαστάζετε above, and be a taking up and carrying, not an ultimate bearing the consequences of) **come upon himself to bear.**   **φορτίον** here, hardly with any allusion to Æsop's well-known fable (C. and H. ii. 182, edn. 2),—but,—as distinguished from βάρος, in which there is an idea of grievance conveyed,—the load imposed on each by his own fault. The future, in this sense of that which must be in the nature of things, is discussed by Bernhardy, pp. 377-8.   **6—10.**] *Exhortation* (in pursuance of the command in ver. 2, see below), *to liberality towards their teachers, and to beneficence in general.* **6.**] **κοινωνείτω** most likely intransitive, as there does not appear to be an instance of its transitive use in the N. T. (certainly not Rom. xii. 13). But the two senses come nearly to the same : he who shares in the necessities of the saints, can only do so by making that necessity partly his own, i. e., by depriving himself to that extent, and communicating to them. On κατηχούμ. and κατηχῶν, see Suicer, Thes. sub voce. This meaning, of '*giving oral instruction*,' is confined to later Greek : see Lidd. and Scott.   **δέ**, as bringing out a contrast to the individuality of the last verse. **τὸν λόγον**, in its very usual sense of **the Gospel,—the word of life.** It is the accusative of reference or of second government, after κατηχούμενος, as in Acts xviii. 25.   **ἐν πᾶσ. ἀγ.**] **in all good things:** *the things of this life* mainly, as the context shews. Nor does this meaning produce an abrupt break between vv. 5 and 6, and 6 and 7, as Meyer (who understands ἀγαθά of moral

πᾶσιν ἀγαθοῖς. 7 ᵖ μὴ ᵖ𐞥 πλανᾶσθε, θεὸς οὐ ʳ μυκτηρίζεται.
ὃ γὰρ ἐὰν ˢ σπείρῃ ἄνθρωπος, τοῦτο καὶ ˢ θερίσει· 8 ὅτι ὁ
ˢ σπείρων εἰς τὴν σάρκα ἑαυτοῦ ἐκ τῆς σαρκὸς ˢ θερίσει
ᵗ φθοράν· ὁ δὲ ˢ σπείρων εἰς τὸ πνεῦμα ἐκ τοῦ πνεύματος
ˢ θερίσει ζωὴν αἰώνιον. 9 ᵘ τὸ δὲ ᵘ καλὸν ποιοῦντες μὴ
ᵛ ἐγκακῶμεν· ʷ καιρῷ γὰρ ʷ ἰδίῳ θερίσομεν μὴ ˣ ἐκλυ-

p 1 Cor. vi. 9.
xv. 33.
James i. 16.
Isa. xliv. 8.
q Matt. xxii.
29 al.
r here only. =
Prov. i. 30.
xv. 20 al.
s Matt. vi. 26 ‖.
xxv. 24 ‖.
John iv. 36,
37 al. Job
iv. 8.
t Rom. viii.
u Rom. vii. 18,
Tit. i. 3 only.

21. 1 Cor. xv. 42, 50.   Col. ii. 22.   2 Pet. i. 4. ii. 12 (bis), 19 only.   Micah ii. 10.
21.   2 Cor. xiii. 7..   v Eph. iii. 13 reff.   w 1 Tim. ii. 6. vi. 15.   Tit. i. 3 only.
x Matt. xv. 32 ‖ Mk.   Heb. xii, 3, 5 (from Prov. iii. 31) only. = Deut. xx. 3.   2 Kings iv. 1.

7. for εαν, αν BD¹F m Dial Thl : txt ACD³KL[P]א rel [Orig₂(om₁)] Clem Chr Thdrt Damasc.   for τουτο, ταυτα D¹F (latt [Victorin]).

8. τη σαρκι F : in carne latt.   for εαυτου, αυτου D¹F a¹ Thdrt Thl : txt ABCD³KL[P]א rel [Clem].   aft σαρκος ins αυτου DF copt æth Chr Thdrt Zeno. θερισισει(sic) א¹(corrd by א-corr¹).   for εις τ. πν. (in spiritu latt [Victorin]), εκ του πν. D¹ sah [εις το πνευματι F].

9. rec εκκακ., with CD³KL[P] rel Clem Chr Thdrt, εκκακησωμεν F : txt ABD¹א m 17 Chr-wlf.   θερισωμεν CFL[P]א d h¹ k m 17 [47].

good ; 'share with your teachers in all virtues:' i. e. 'imitate their virtues') maintains. From the mention of bearing one another's burdens, he naturally passes to one way, and one case, in which those burdens may be borne—viz. by relieving the necessities of their ministers (thus almost all Commentators) and then, 7.] regarding our good deeds done for Christ as a seed sown for eternity, he warns them not to be deceived: in this, as in other seed-times, God's order of things cannot be set at nought: whatever we sow, that same shall we reap.   οὐ μυκτηρ.] is not mocked:—though men subjectively mock God, this mocking has no objective existence : there is no such thing as mocking of God in reality. μυκτηρίζειν λέγομεν τοὺς ἐν τῷ διαπαίζειν τινὰς τοῦτό πως τὸ μέρος (μυκτῆρα) ἐπισπῶντας, Etym. Mag. (cited by Ellic.) Pollux quotes the word from Lysias : in medicine it is used for bleeding at the nose (Hippocrat. p. 1240 D).   γάρ, 'and in this it will be shewn.'   σπείρῃ, present subjunctive (cf. σπείρων below).   τοῦτ. κ. θ.] this (emphatic, this and nothing else) shall he also (by the same rule) reap, viz. eventually, at the great harvest. The final judgment is necessarily now introduced by the similitude (ὁ θερισμὸς—συντέλεια αἰῶνός ἐστιν, Matt. xiii. 39), but does not any the more belong to the context in ver. 5.   8.] ὅτι, for —i. e. and this will be an example of the universal rule.   ὁ σπείρων, he that (now) soweth,—is now sowing. εἰς, unto,—with a view to—not local, 'drops his seed into,' 'tanquam in agrum,' Bengel: this in the N. T. is given by ἐν (Matt. xiii. 24, 27. Mark iv. 15), or ἐπί (Matt. xiii. 20, 23. Mark iv. 16, 20, 31):

εἰς τὰς ἀκάνθας (Matt. xiii. 22. Mark iv. 18) rather being 'among the thorns' (see Ellic.).   ἑαυτοῦ, not apparently with any especial emphasis—to his own flesh. φθοράν] (not ἀπώλειαν—as Phil. iii. 19) corruption—because the flesh is a prey to corruption, and with it all fleshly desires and practices come to nothing (De W.) : see 1 Cor. vi. 13 ; xv. 50 :—or perhaps in the stronger sense of φθορά (see 1 Cor. iii. 17 ; 2 Pet. ii. 12), destruction (Meyer).   ἐκ τ. πν.] See Rom. viii. 11, 15—17.   9.] But (in our case, let there be no chance of the alternative : see Hartung, Partikell. i. 166) in well-doing (stress on καλόν) let us not be faint-hearted (on ἐγκ. and ἐκκ., see note, 2 Cor. iv. 1. It seems doubtful, whether such a word as ἐκκακέω exists at all in Greek, and whether its use by later writers and place in lexicons is not entirely due to these doubtful readings. See Ellic.'s note) : for in due time (an expression of the pastoral Epistles, see reff.,—and Prolegomena to those Epistles, § i. 32, and note) we shall reap, if we do not faint (so reff., and Isocr., p. 322 a, ἵν' οὖν μὴ παντάπασιν ἐκλυθῶ, πολλῶν ἔτι μοι λεκτέων ὄντων). Thdrt., al., join μὴ ἐκλ. with θερίσομεν,—πόνου δίχα θερίσομεν τὰ σπειρόμενα· . . . ἐπὶ μὲν γὰρ τῶν αἰσθητῶν σπερμάτων καὶ ὁ σπόρος ἔχει πόνον, κ. ὁ ἀμητὸς ὡσαύτως· διαλύει γὰρ πολλάκις τοὺς ἀμῶντας κ. τὸ τῆς ὥρας θερμόν· ἀλλ' ἐκεῖνος οἱ τοιοῦτος ὁ ἀμητὸς πόνου γάρ ἐστι κ. ἱδρῶτος ἐλεύθερος. But though such a rendering would be unobjectionable (not requiring οὐ for μή, as Rück., al., for as Mey. rightly, the particle being subjective, μή would be in place), it would give a very vapid sense : whereas the other eminently suits the exhortation

x Rom. v. 18
all0. P.
y = Luke xii.
58. John xii.
35. Rev.
xxii. 12.
z = Acts xxiv.
25. 1 Cor.
vii. 29. Eccl.
iii. 1, &c.
a Rom. ii. 10.
Eph. iv. 28.
b Rom. ii. 10.
vii. 13. xiii.
3,4. 1 Thess.
v. 15.
c Eph. ii. 19.
1 Tim. v. 8

όμενοι. 10 ˣ ἄρα ˣ οὖν ʸ ὡς ᶻ καιρὸν ἔχομεν, ᵃ ἐργαζώμεθα ᵇ τὸ ἀγαθὸν πρὸς πάντας, μάλιστα δὲ πρὸς τοὺς ᶜ οἰκείους τῆς πίστεως. 11 ᴺἼδετε ᵈ πηλίκοις ὑμῖν ᵉ γράμμασιν ᶠ ἔγραψα ᶠᵍ τῇ ἐμῇ ᵍ χειρί. 12 ὅσοι θέλουσιν ʰ εὐπροσωπῆσαι ἐν ⁱ σαρκί, οὗτοι ʲ ἀναγκάζουσιν ὑμᾶς ᵏ περιτέμνεσθαι, μόνον ἵνα τῷ ˡ σταυρῷ τοῦ χριστοῦ μὴ ᵐ διώκωνται. 13 οὐδὲ γὰρ οἱ

ABCDF
KLPℵ a
b c d e f
g h k l m
n o 17. 47

only. Isa. lii. 6. 2 Macc. xv. 12 B. οἰκεῖοι φιλοσοφίας, Strabo i. p. 13. οἰκεῖος γεωγραφίας, ib. p. 25. (Wetst.)
d Heb. vii. 4 only. Zech. ii. 2. e see note and Acts xxviii. 21. 1 Macc. v. 10. dat., Matt. viii. 8.
f Philem. 19. g 1 Cor. xvi. 21. Col. iv. 18. 2 Thess. iii 17. h here only †. (-πος, Gen. xii.
11. Xen. Mem. i. 3. 10. -πίζειν, Ps. cxl. 6 Symm.) i Rom. ii. 28. 1 Tim. iii 16 reff. j = ch.
ii. 3 reff. k Luke i. 59 al. m ch. xvii. 10. l = ch. v. 11 reff. dat., Rom. xi 20. 2 Cor.
ii. 13. Bernhardy, p. 370. m ch. iv. 29 reff.

10. εχωμεν Bᴵℵ [m 17]. εργαζομεθα AB²L[P] c d m n [47] goth Œc: txt B¹CDFℵ rel vss Clem, -σωμεθα K 49.

11. γραμμασιν bef υμιν DF Aug.

12. rec μη bef τω στ. τ. χρ., with FKL rel Chr Thdrt Ambrst: txt ABCD[P]ℵ 17 vulg Syr goth Victorin Aug Jer Pel. διωκονται ACFKL[P] a d f k m [47]: txt BDℵ rel.

μὴ ἐγκ. 10.] ἄρα οὖν, so then: "the proper meaning of ἄρα, 'rebus ita comparatis,' is here distinctly apparent: its weaker ratiocinative force being supported by the collective power of οὖν." Ellic.

ὡς] not 'while' (Olsh., al.), nor, 'according as,' i. e. 'quotiescunque,' nor, 'since,' causal (De W., Winer, al.),—but as, i. e. in proportion as: let our beneficence be in proportion to our καιρός—let the seed-time have its καιρὸς ἴδιος, as well as the harvest, ver. 9. Thus καιρός is a common term between the two verses. τὸ ἀγ.] the good thing: as we say, 'he did the right thing:' that which is (in each case) good. τ. οἰκείους τ. πίστ.] those who belong to the faith: there does not seem to be any allusion to a household, as in E. V. In Isa. lviii. 7 'thy fellow-men' are called οἱ οἰκεῖοι τοῦ σπέρματός σου: so also in the examples from the later classics in Wetst., οἰκεῖοι φιλοσοφίας, — γεωγραφίας, — ὀλιγαρχίας, τυραννίδος,—τρυφῆς.

11—end.] POSTSCRIPT AND BENEDICTION. 11.] See in how large letters (in what great and apparently unsightly characters: see note on next verse. πηλίκοις will not bear the rendering (1) 'how many,' πόσοις,—or (2) 'what sort,' ποίοις:—but only (3) how great (reff.). Nor can (3) be made to mean (1) by taking γράμματα for 'Epistle,' a sense unknown to St. Paul) I wrote (not strictly the epistolary scribebam, nor referring to the following verses only: but the aorist spoken as at the time when they would receive the Epistle, and referring I believe to the whole of it, see also below) with my own hand. I do not see how it is possible to avoid the inference that

these words apply to the whole Epistle. If they had reference only to the passage in which they occur, would not γράφω have been used, as in 2 Thess. iii. 17? Again, there is no break in style here, indicating the end of the dictated portion, and the beginning of the written, as in Rom. xvi. 25; 2 Thess. iii. 17 al. I should rather believe, that on account of the peculiar character of this Epistle, St. Paul wrote it all with his own hand, —as he did the pastoral Epistles: and I find confirmation of this, in the partial resemblance of its style to those Epistles. (See Prolegomena, as above on ver. 9.) And he wrote it, whether from weakness of his eyes, or from choice, in large characters. 12.] As my Epistle, so my practice: I have no desire to make a fair show outwardly: my γράμματα are not εὐπρόσωπα (is there a further allusion to the same point in ὅσοι τῷ κανόνι τούτῳ στοιχήσουσιν, and even in στίγματα, below?) and I have no sympathy with these θέλοντες εὐπροσωπῆσαι ἐν σαρκί. The word εὐπροσωπεῖν occurs only here: but we have φαινοπροσωπεῖν, Cic. Att. vii. 21; xiv. 21: σεμνοπροσωπεῖν, Aristoph. Nub. 363. ἐν σαρκί, not merely 'in the flesh,' but in outward things, which belong to man's natural state: see ch. v. 19. οὗτοι, it is these who: see ver. 7. ἀναγκάζουσιν] are compelling:—go about to compel. τῷ σταυρῷ] dative of the cause, see reff. Winer would understand 'should be persecuted with the Cross (i. e. with sufferings like the Cross) of Christ.' But apart from other objections (which I do not feel, however, so strongly as Ellic.), surely this would have been otherwise expressed—by

^k περιτεμνόμενοι αὐτοὶ ⁿνόμον ⁿφυλάσσουσιν, ἀλλὰ θέ- n Acts vii. 53.
xxi. 24.
Rom. ii. 26.
λουσιν ὑμᾶς περιτέμνεσθαι, ἵνα ^oἐν τῇ ὑμετέρα σαρκὶ o Rom. ii. 17.
v. 3. 2 Cor.
^oκαυχήσωνται. ¹⁴ ^pἐμοὶ δὲ μὴ ^pγένοιτο ^oκαυχᾶσθαι, εἰ x. 15 al.
Jer. ix. 23,
24.
μὴ ^oἐν τῷ σταυρῷ τοῦ κυρίου ἡμῶν Ἰησοῦ χριστοῦ, δι' p Mark v. 16.
Acts xx. 16.
οὗ ^qἐμοὶ κόσμος ^rἐσταύρωται κἀγὼ κόσμῳ. ¹⁵ οὔτε γὰρ Gen. xliv. 7,
17.
stπεριτομή ^uτι ^tἔστιν οὔτε stἀκροβυστία, ἀλλὰ ^vκαινὴ q dat., Heb. vi.
6.
^vκτίσις. ¹⁶ καὶ ὅσοι τῷ ^wκανόνι τούτῳ ^xστοιχήσουσιν, r = ch. v. 24.
see Rom. vi.
6.

s ch. v. 6 reff.   t 1 Cor. vii. 19.   u ch. ii. 6 reff.   v 2 Cor. v. 17.   w 2 Cor.
x. 13, 15, 16 (Phil. iii. 16 v. r.) only. Micah iv. 4. Judith xiii. 6 only. = Job xxxviii. 5 Aq. (σπάρτιον
LXX.) dat., ch. v. 16. Phil. iii. 16.   x & constr., ch. v. 25 (reff.).

13. περιτετμημενοι BL rel 67² copt goth [æth] lat-ff : txt ACDK[P]ℵ d h l 17 syrr [sah arm] Mcion-e Chr Thdrt Damasc Bede.   for θελουσιν, βουλονται AC.
περιτεμεσθαι B.   καυχησονται DG¹[P 47] c d.

14. καυχησασθαι AD¹[K 47¹].   ins o bef κοσμος F (Clem Bas₄) Thl.   rec ins τω bef κοσμω, with C³D³KL rel Clem Orig₈ Ath₁ Mac Bas₅ Epiph Chr Cyr Thdrt Damasc : om ABC¹D¹F[P]ℵ 17 Orig₅ Ath₁.

15. rec (for ουτε γαρ) εν γαρ χ. ιησ. ουτε (from ch v. 6), with ACDFKL[P]ℵ rel latt syr-w-ast(εν to ιησ.) copt æth-pl Thdrt Damasc Victorin Ambrst : txt B 17 [47] Syr syr(altern) sah goth æth arm(ed 1805) Chr Sync Jer Aug.   rec (for εστιν) ισχνει (from ch v. 6), with D³KL[P]ℵ³ rel vulg Chr Thdrt : txt ABCD¹Fℵ¹ 17 [47] 67² Syr syr-mg coptt æth Orig Thl_alic Sync Jer Aug Ambrst.

16. στοιχουσιν (corrn to pres, as more usual and simpler. No reason can be given why the fut should have been substituted, and it belongs to the nervous style of this conclusion) AC¹DF syrr copt(appy) goth [æth] arm Chr Cyr Victorin Jer Aug₂ Ambrst Ruf : txt BC²KL[P]ℵ rel vulg(and F-lat) Chr Thdrt Hil Bede.

τοῖς παθήμασιν or the like.   **13.**]
For (proof that they wish only to escape
persecution) **not even they who are being
circumcised** (who are the adopters and in-
stigators of circumcision, cf. ἀναγκάζουσιν
above) **themselves keep the law** (νόμον emphatic : the words contain a matter of
fact, not known to us otherwise,—that
these preachers of legal conformity extended it not to the whole law, but
selected from it at their own caprice),
but wish you (emphatic) **to be circumcised, that in your** (emphatic) **flesh they
may make their boast** (ἵνα ἐν τῷ κατα-
κόπτειν τὴν ὑμετέραν σάρκα καυχήσων-
ται ὡς διδάσκαλοι ὑμῶν, i. e., μαθητὰς
ὑμᾶς ἔχοντες, Thl. In this way they escaped the scandal of the Cross at the
hands of the Jews, by making in fact
their Christian converts into Jewish proselytes).   **14.**] **But to me let it not
happen to boast** (on the construction, see
reff. Meyer quotes Xen. Cyr. vi. 3. 11,—
ὦ Ζεῦ μέγιστε, λαβεῖν μοι γένοιτο αὐτόν),
except in the Cross (the atoning death,
as my means of reconcilement with God)
of our Lord Jesus Christ (the full name
for solemnity, and ἡμῶν to involve his
readers in the duty of the same abjura-
tion), **by means of whom** (not so well,
'of which' (τοῦ σταυροῦ) as many Commentators ; the greater antecedent, **τοῦ**

κυρ. ἡμ. 'Ι. χ., coming after the σταυρῷ,
has thrown it into the shade. Besides, it
could hardly be said of the Cross, δι' οὗ)
the world (the whole system of unspiritual
and unchristian men and things. Notice
the absorption of the article in a word
which had become almost a proper name :
so with ἥλιος, γῆ, πόλις, &c.) **has been
(and is) crucified** (not merely 'dead :' he
chooses, in relation to σταυρός above, this
stronger word, which at once brings in his
union with the death of Christ, besides his
relation to the world) **to me** (ἐμοί, dative
of ethical relation : so μόνῳ Μαικήνᾳ καθ-
εύδω, Plut. Erot. p. 760 A : see other examples in Bernhardy, p. 85), **and I to the
world.** Ellic. quotes from Schött., 'alter
pro mortuo habet alterum.'   **15.**] See
ch. v. 6. *Confirmation of last verse :* so
far are such things from me as a ground
of boasting, that they are *nothing :* the
new birth by the Spirit is all in all.
κτίσις (see note on 2 Cor. v. 17), **creation :**
and therefore the result, as regards an
individual, is, that he is a **new creature :**
so that the word comes to be used in both
significations.   **16.**] **And as many**
(reference to the ὅσοι of ver. 12 ; and in
κανόνι to the εὐπροσωπ. and πηλίκοις
γράμμ.? see above) **as shall walk by this
rule** (of ver. 15. κανών is a 'straight
rule,' to detect crookedness : hence a *nor-*

y = Rom. ii. 2, 9.
z = 1 Cor. iii. 5. viii. 12.
xv. 38.
a = Rom. ix. 6.
b gen. of time, John iii. 2.
χειμῶνος, Thuc. iii. 104, & passim.
e Matt. xxvi. 10 ‖ Mk. Luke xviii. 5. Sir. xxix. 4.
d here only. Cant. i. 11 only.
e = (1) ver. 2. Rom. xi. 18.

εἰρήνη ᵞἐπ᾽ αὐτοὺς καὶ ἔλεος, ᶻκαὶ ᵞἐπὶ τὸν ᵃἸσραὴλ
τοῦ θεοῦ. ¹⁷ᵇτοῦ λοιποῦ ᶜκόπους μοι μηδεὶς ᶜπαρεχέτω·
ἐγὼ γὰρ τὰ ᵈστίγματα τοῦ Ἰησοῦ ἐν τῷ σώματί μου
ᵉβαστάζω.
¹⁸ Ἡ χάρις τοῦ κυρίου ἡμῶν Ἰησοῦ χριστοῦ μετὰ τοῦ
ᶠπνεύματος ὑμῶν, ἀδελφοί. ἀμήν.

ABCDF KLPℵ a
bcdef
ghklm
no17.47

ΠΡΟΣ ΓΑΛΑΤΑΣ.   ...C.

xv. 1. or (2) Acts ix. 15. εἰκόνα θεοῦ βαστάζειν, Clem. Rom. (Coteler. i. 692—Ellic.)   f Phil. iv.
23. 2 Tim. iv. 22. Philem. 25.

om 3rd καὶ D³[æth].   for θεου, κυριου D¹F (G-lat has both).
17. το λοιπον D¹.   μηδεις μοι κοπους D.   rec ins κυριου bef ιησου, with C³D³KL rel vulg D-lat syrr goth æth-pl : του χρ. Euthal-ms al : τ. κυ ιυ χυ ℵ [Victorin] : του κυρ. ημων ιησ. χρ. D¹F : [χριστου(only) P 47 copt-wilk æth arm Clem₁ Tert₁ :] alii aliter : txt ABC¹ 17 am(with demid F-lat) Petr Dial Euthal Epiph.
18. om ημων [P]ℵ m.   [om χριστου P e.]   om αμην G Victorin Ambrst.

SUBSCRIPTION. rec adds εγραφη απο ρωμης, with B²K(L)[P] rel syrr copt Thdrt Euthal Jer, απο εφεσου Thl₁ Œc : some add δια τιτου, or δια τιτ. κ. λουκα, or δια τυχικου : δια χειρος παυλου al₁ : 1 has no subscr· τελος της επ. πρ. γαλ. L (d) : txt AB¹C¹ℵ(adding στιχ τιβ´) 17, and D(addg επληρωθη) F(prefixing ετελεσθη επιστολη).

---

ma vivendi. The dative is *normal*), **peace be** (not ' *is* :' it is the apostolic blessing, so common in the *beginnings* of his Epistles : see also Eph. vi. 23) **upon them** (come on them from God ; reff., and Luke ii. 25, 40 al. freq.) **and** (and indeed, ' und zwar :' the καί explicative, as it is called : see reff.) **upon the Israel of God** (the subject of the whole Epistle seems to have given rise to this expression. Not the Israel after the flesh, among whom these teachers wish to enrol you, are blessed : but the ISRAEL OF GOD, described ch. iii. ult., εἰ δὲ ὑμεῖς χριστοῦ, ἄρα τοῦ Ἀβραὰμ σπέρμα ἐστέ. Jowett compares, though not exactly parallel, yet for a similar apparent though not actual distinction, 1 Cor. x. 32). **17.**] τοῦ λοιποῦ, as E. V., **henceforth**: scil., χρόνου. So Herod. iii. 15, ἔνθα τοῦ λοιποῦ διαιτᾶτο :—see numerous other examples in Wetstein. "τὸ λοιπόν continuum et perpetuum tempus significat,—ut apud Xen. Cyr. viii. 5. 24 ; τοῦ λοιποῦ autem repetitionem ejusdem facti reliquo tempore indicat, ut apud Aristoph. in Pace, v. 1684 (1050 Bekk.)." Hermann ad Viger., p. 706. But the above example from Herod. hardly seems to bear this out. Rather is a thing happening in time regarded as *belonging* to the period including it, and the genitive is one of possession. Against this Ellic., viewing the gen. as simply partitive, refers to Donalds. Gram. § 451 : who however defines his meaning by saying "partitive, or, what is the same thing,

possessive." This indeed must be the clear and only account of a partitive genitive. **κόπ. παρεχ.**] How ? Thdrt. (hardly Chrys.), al., understand it of the trouble of writing more epistles —οὐκέτι, φησί, γράψαι τὶ πάλιν ἀνέξομαι· ἀντὶ δὲ γραμμάτων τοὺς μώλωπας δείκνυμι, κ. τῶν αἰκισμῶν τὰ σημεῖα. But it seems much more natural to take it of giving him trouble by rebellious conduct and denying his apostolic authority, seeing that it was stamped with so powerful a seal as he proceeds to state. **ἐγὼ γάρ**] **for it is I** (not the Judaizing teachers) **who carry** (perhaps as in ver. 5, and ch. v. 10,—bear, as a burden : but Chrys.'s idea seems more adapted to the 'feierlich' character of the sentence: οὐκ εἶπεν, ἔχω, ἀλλά, βαστάζω, ὥσπερ τις ἐπὶ τροπαίοις μέγα φρονῶν ἢ σημείοις βασιλικοῖς : see reff. (2)) **in** (on) **my body the marks of Jesus. τὰ στίγματα** —the marks branded on slaves to indicate their owners. So Herod. vii. 233, τοὺς πλεῦνας αὐτέων, κελεύσαντος Ξέρξεω, ἔστιζον στίγματα βασιλήϊα : and in another place (ii. 113) is a passage singularly in point : ὅτεῳ ἀνθρώπων ἐπιβάληται στίγματα ἱρά, ἑωυτὸν διδοὺς τῷ θεῷ, οὐκ ἔξεστι τούτου ἄψασθαι. See many more examples in Wetst. These marks, in St. Paul's case, were of course the *scars of his wounds received in the service of his Master*—cf. 2 Cor. xi. 23 ff. **Ἰησοῦ** is the genitive of possession,—answering to the possessive βασιλήϊα in the extract above. There is no allusion whatever to any similarity between himself and our Lord, 'the marks which Jesus bore;' such an allusion would be quite irrelevant: and with its irrelevancy falls a whole fabric of Romanist superstition which has been raised on this verse, and which the fair and learned Windischmann, giving as he does the honest interpretation here, yet attempts to defend in a supplemental note. Neither can we naturally suppose any comparison intended between these his στίγματα as Christ's servant, and *circumcision :* for he is not now on that subject, but on his *authority as sealed by Christ :* and such a comparison is alien from the majesty of the sentence. **18.**] THE APOSTOLIC BLESS-ING. No special intention need be suspected in πνεύματος (ἀπάγων αὐτοὺς τῶν σαρκικῶν, Chrys.), as the same expression occurs at the end of other Epistles (reff.). I should rather regard it as a deep expression of his Christian love, which is further carried on by ἀδελφοί, the last word,—parting from them, after an Epistle of such rebuke and warning, in the fulness of brotherhood in Christ.

ΠΡΟΣ ΕΦΕΣΙΟΥΣ.

a Rom. xv. 32.
1 Cor. i. 1.
2 Cor. i. 1.
viii. 5. Col.
i. 1. 2 Tim.
i. 1 only.
v. 16. Rev. xvii. 14.

I. ¹ Παῦλος ἀπόστολος χριστοῦ Ἰησοῦ ᵃ διὰ θελήματος θεοῦ, τοῖς ᵇ ἁγίοις τοῖς οὖσιν [ἐν Ἐφέσῳ] καὶ ᶜ πιστοῖς ἐν

ABDFK
LPℵ a b
c d e f g
h k l m n
o 17. 47

b = Acts ix. 13, 32, 41. Rom. i. 7 al. fr. Dan. vii. 18. Wisd. iii. 9.   c = Acts x. 45. 1 Tim.

TITLE. elz παυλου του αποστολου η προς εφεσιους επιστολη : Steph προς εφεσιους επιστολη παυλου, with al : προς εφ. επ. του αγιου αποστολου παυλου h : του αγ. απ. π. επιστ. πρ. εφ. L : τοις εφεσιοις μυσταις ταυτα διδασκαλος εσθλος f : αρχεται προς εφεσιους DF : incipit epistula ad ephesios am : [π. επ. πρ. εφ. P :] πρ. εφ. επ. k : επ. πρ. εφ. l : txt ABKℵ m n o 17 [47].

CHAP. I. 1. rec ιησ. bef χρ., with AFKLℵ rel vulg-ed(with fuld F-lat) Syr [æth arm] gr-lat-ff : txt BD[P] 17 am syr copt goth Orig-cat Damasc Ambrst.   aft αγιοις ins πασιν Aℵ³ vulg copt Cyr Jer-txt.   om 2nd τοις D.   om εν εφεσω B¹ℵ¹ 67². (supplied in margin B¹[? see table]², so also ℵ³.)   Basil says, οὕτω γὰρ καὶ οἱ πρὸ ἡμῶν παραδεδώκασι καὶ ἡμεῖς ἐν τοῖς παλαιοῖς τῶν ἀντιγράφων εὑρήκαμεν : Marcion is accused by Tert of inserting ad Laodicenos, and so does not seem to have read εν εφ. here.   Also Tert and Jerome seem to have found it omd in other MSS. "quidam . . . putant . . . eos qui Ephesi sunt sancti et fideles essentiæ vocabulo nuncupatos ut . . . ab Eo qui EST, hi qui SUNT appellentur . . . Alii vero simpliciter non ad eos qui sint(al sunt), sed qui Ephesi sancti et fideles sint, scriptum arbitrantur." Jerome ad Eph. i. 1, vol. vii. p. 545. (See prolegomena, § ii. 17 a.)

CHAP. I. 1, 2.] ADDRESS AND GREETING. 1.] χρ. Ἰησ., as in the case of δοῦλος Ἰησ. χρ., seems rather to denote possession, than to belong to ἀπόστολος and designate the person from whom sent. διὰ θελ. θεοῦ] See on 1 Cor. i. 1. As these words there have a special reference, and the corresponding ones in Gal. i. 1 also, so it is natural to suppose that here he has in his mind, hardly perhaps the especial subject of vv. 3—11, the will of the Father as the ground of the election of the church, but, which is more likely in a general introduction to the whole Epistle, the great subject of which he is about to treat, and himself as the authorized expositor of it.   τ. οὖσιν ἐν Ἐφ.] On this, and on Ephesus, see Prolegomena. On ἁγίοις, see Ellicott's note. It is used

here in its widest sense, as designating the members of Christ's visible Church, presumed to fulfil the conditions of that membership : cf. especially ch. v. 3. καὶ πιστοῖς ἐν χ. Ἰ.] These words follow rather unusually, separated from τ. ἁγ. by the designation of abode : a circumstance which might seem to strengthen the suspicion against ἐν Ἐφέσῳ, were not such transpositions by no means unexampled in St. Paul. See the regular order in Col. i. 2. The omission of the article before πιστ. shews that the same persons are designated by both adjectives. Its insertion would not, however, prove the contrary.
ἐν χρ. Ἰησ. belongs only to πιστοῖς : see Col. i. 2 : faithful, i. e. believers, in (but ἐν does not belong to πιστός, as it often does to πιστεύω : see also Col. i. 4)

χριστῷ Ἰησοῦ. ² ᵈ χάρις ὑμῖν καὶ εἰρήνη ἀπὸ θεοῦ
πατρὸς ἡμῶν καὶ κυρίου Ἰησοῦ χριστοῦ.

³ ᵉ Εὐλογητὸς ὁ θεὸς καὶ πατὴρ τοῦ κυρίου ἡμῶν
Ἰησοῦ χριστοῦ, ὁ ᶠ εὐλογήσας ἡμᾶς ᵍ ἐν πάσῃ ʰ εὐλογίᾳ

d Gal. i. 3 al.
e Mark xiv. 61.
  Luke i. 68.
  Rom. i. 25.
  ix. 5. 2 Cor.
  i. 3. xi. 31.
  1 Pet. i. 3
  only. Gen.
  ix. 26.
f = Acts iii.
g constr., here only. see James iii. 9.

26. Gal. iii. 9. Heb. vi. 14 al. Gen. xxii. 17.
h = Rom. xv. 29. Heb. vi. 7. Ps. xxiii. 5.

2. [for ημ., υμων P.]   χρ. bef ιησ. B.
3. om και πατηρ B.   aft κυριου ins και σωτηρος (completing the familiar phrase:
see 2 Pet i. 11; ii. 20; iii. 2) א¹(א³ disapproving).   om ημας א¹(ins א-corr¹):

Christ Jesus. This, in its highest sense, 'qui fidem præstant,' not mere truth, or faithfulness, is imported: see reff. The ἁγίοις and πιστοῖς denote their spiritual life from its two sides—that of God who calls and sanctifies,—that of themselves who believe. So Bengel, 'Dei est, sanctificare nos et sibi asserere; nostrum, ex Dei munere, credere.' Stier remarks that by πιστ. ἐν χ. Ἰ.,—ἁγίοις gets its only full and N. T. meaning. He also notices in these expressions already a trace of the two great divisions of the Epistle—God's grace towards us, and our faith towards Him.   2.] After χάρις ὑμ. κ. εἰρ. supply rather εἴη than ἔστω; see 1 Pet. i. 2; 2 Pet. i. 2; Jude 2. On the form of greeting, cf. Rom. i. 7; 1 Cor. i. 3; 2 Cor. i. 2; Gal. i. 3, &c.   The Socinian perversion of the words, 'from God, who is the Father of us and of our Lord Jesus Christ,' is decisively refuted by Tit. i. 4, not to mention that nothing but the grossest ignorance of St. Paul's spirit could ever allow such a meaning to be thought of.   We must not fall into the error of refining too much, as Stier, on χάρις and εἰρήνη, as referring respectively to ἁγίοις and πιστοῖς: see ‖ above, where these last epithets do not occur.

3—III. 21.] FIRST PORTION OF THE EPISTLE: THE DOCTRINE OF THE CHURCH OF CHRIST. And herein, I. 3—23.] GROUND AND ORIGIN OF THE CHURCH, IN THE FATHER'S COUNSEL, AND HIS ACT IN CHRIST, BY THE SPIRIT. And herein again, (A) the preliminary IDEA OF THE CHURCH, set forth in the form of an ascription of praise vv 3—14:—thus arranged:—vv. 3—6] The FATHER, in his eternal Love, has chosen us to holiness (ver. 4),—ordained us to sonship (ver. 5),—bestowed grace on us in the Beloved (ver. 6):—vv. 7—12] In the SON, we have,—redemption according to the riches of His grace (ver. 7), knowledge of the mystery of His will (vv. 8, 9),—inheritance under Him the one Head (vv. 10—12):—vv. 13, 14] through the SPIRIT we are sealed,—by hearing the word of salvation (ver. 13),—by receiving

the earnest of our inheritance (ver. 14),—to the redemption of the purchased possession (ib.).   3.] Blessed (see note on Rom. ix. 5. Understand εἴη (Job i. 21; Ps. cxii. 2; or ἔστω, 2 Chron. ix. 8. Ellicott)—'Be He praised.' See a similar doxology, 2 Cor. i. 3. Almost all St. Paul's Epistles begin with some ascription of praise. That to Titus is the only exception (not Gal.: cf. Gal. i. 5). See also 1 Pet. i. 3) be the God and Father of our Lord Jesus Christ (cf. Rom. xv. 6; 2 Cor. i. 3; xi. 31; Col. i. 3—also 1 Cor. xv. 24. Such is the simplest and most forcible sense of the words—as Thl., ἰδοὺ κ. θεὸς κ. πατὴρ τοῦ αὐτοῦ κ. ἑνὸς χριστοῦ· θεὸς μέν, ὡς σαρκωθέντος· πατὴρ δέ, ὡς θεοῦ λόγου. See John xx. 17, from which saying of our Lord it is not improbable that the expression took its rise. Meyer maintains, 'God who is also the Father of . . . .:' on the ground that only πατήρ, not θεός, requires a genitive supplied. But we may fairly reply that, if we come to strictness of construction, his meaning would require ὁ θεός, ὁ καὶ πατήρ. Harless's objection, that on our rendering it must be ὁ θεός τε καὶ π., is well answered by Meyer from 1 Pet. ii. 25, τὸν ποιμένα κ. ἐπίσκοπον τῶν ψυχῶν ἡμῶν. Ellicott prefers Meyer's view, but pronounces the other both grammatically and doctrinally tenable), who blessed (aor.: not 'hath blessed:' the historical fact in the counsels of the Father being thought of throughout the sentence. εὐλογητός—εὐλογήσας——εὐλογία—such was the ground-tone of the new covenant. As in creation God blessed them, saying, 'Be fruitful and multiply,'—so in redemption,—at the introduction of the covenant, "all families of the earth shall be BLESSED,"—at its completion,—" Come ye BLESSED of my Father."   But God's blessing is in facts—ours in words only) us (whom? not the Apostle only: nor Paul and his fellow-Apostles—but, ALL CHRISTIANS—all the members of Christ. The καὶ ὑμεῖς of ver. 13 perfectly agrees with this: see there: but the κἀγώ of ver. 15 does not agree with the other views) in (instrumental or medial: the element in

i = Rom. i. 11.
1 Cor. ix. 11.
Col. i. 9.
1 Pet. ii. 5 †.
k = ver. 20. ch.
ii. 6. iii. 10. vi. 12 only. 2 Macc. iii. 39. (Matt. xviii. 35 al. fr. Ps. lxvii. 14 only. Dan. iv. 23 Theod.·A. Compl.
Ald. [οὐράν., BF.])
18 al. (1 Cor. i. 27 bis, 28. James ii. 5 only in epp.) Deut. vii. 7.
Matt. xiii. 35 al.   o as above (n) †. 2 Macc. ii. 29 only.
1 = Col. i. 16 reff. see Acts xv. 7.
m Mark xiii. 20. John vi. 70. xiii.
n John xvii. 24. 1 Pet. i. 20 only. ἀπό,
ABDFK
LPℵ ab
c d e f g
h k l m n
o 17.47

^{i} πνευματικῇ ἐν τοῖς ^{k} ἐπουρανίοις ^{l} ἐν χριστῷ, ^{4} καθὼς ^{m} ἐξελέξατο ἡμᾶς ^{l} ἐν αὐτῷ ^{n} πρὸ ^{no} καταβολῆς κόσμου,

υμας c d.   aft χριστω ins ιησου D$^{2.3}$[K 47] syr æth Thl [Victorin].
4. for εν αυτω, εαυτω F Did.

which, and means by which, the blessing is imparted) all (i. e. all possible—all, exhaustive, in all richness and fulness of blessing: cf. ver. 23 note) **blessing of the Spirit** (not merely, '*spiritual* (inward) *blessing:*' πνευματικός in the N. T. always implies the working of the Holy Spirit, never bearing merely our modern inaccurate sense of spiritual as opposed to bodily. See 1 Cor. ix. 11, which has been thus misunderstood) **in the heavenly places** (so the expression, which occurs five times in this Epistle (see reff.), and no where else, can only mean: cf. ver. 20. It is not probable that St. Paul should have chosen an unusual expression for the purposes of this Epistle, and then used it in several different senses. Besides, as Harless remarks, the preposition ἐπί in composition with adjectives gives usually a local sense: e. g. in ἐπίγειος, ἐπιχθόνιος, ἐπουράνιος, as compared with γήϊνος, χθόνιος, οὐράνιος. Chrys., al., would understand it '*heavenly blessings,*' in which case the Apostle would hardly have failed to add χαρίσμασιν, or ἀγαθοῖς, or the like. But, with the above rendering, *what is the sense?* Our country, πολίτευμα, is *in heaven*, Phil. iii. 20: there our High Priest stands, blessing us. There are our treasures, Matt. vi. 20, 21, and our affections to be, Col. iii. 1 ff. : there our hope is laid up, Col. i. 5: our inheritance is reserved for us, 1 Pet. i. 4. And there, in that place, and belonging to that state, is the εὐλογία, the gift of the Spirit, Heb. vi. 4, poured out on those who τὰ ἄνω φρονοῦσιν. Materially, we are yet in the body: but in the Spirit, we are in heaven —only waiting for the redemption of the body to be entirely and literally there. I may once for all premise, that it will be impossible, in the limits of these notes, to give even a synopsis of the various opinions on the rich fulness of doctrinal expressions in this Epistle. I must state in each case that which appears to me best to suit the context, and those variations which must *necessarily* be mentioned, referring to such copious commentaries as Harless or Stier for further statement) **in Christ** ("the threefold ἐν after εὐλογήσας, has a meaning ever deeper and more precise: and

should therefore be kept in translating. The blessing with which God has blessed us, consists and expands itself in all *blessing of the Spirit*—then brings in *Heaven*, the heavenly state in us, and us in it— then finally, CHRIST, *personally*, He Himself, who is set and exalted into Heaven, comes by the Spirit down into us, so that He is in us and we in Him of a truth, and thereby, and in so far, we are with Him in heaven." Stier).   **4.] According as** (καθώς explains and expands the fore-going—shewing wherein the εὐλογία consists as regards us, and God's working towards us. Notice, that whereas ver. 3 has summarily included in the work of blessing the Three Persons, the FATHER bestowing the SPIRIT in CHRIST,—now the threefold cord, so to speak, is unwrapped, and the part of each divine Person separately described: cf. argument above) **He selected us** (reff. I render *selected*, in preference to *elected*, as better giving the middle sense,—'chose for himself,'—and the ἐξ, that it is a choosing *out of* the world. The word (ref. Deut.) is an O. T. word, and refers to the spiritual Israel, as it did to God's elect Israel of old. But there is no *contrast* between their election and ours: it has been but one election throughout—an election in Christ, and to holiness on God's side—and involving accession to God's people (cf. πιστεύσαντες, ver. 13, and εἴγε ἐπιμένετε τῇ πίστει, Col. i. 23) on ours. See Ellicott's note on the word, and some excellent remarks in Stier, p. 62, on the divine and human sides of the doctrine of election as put forward in this Epistle) **in Him** (i. e. in Christ, as the second Adam (1 Cor. xv. 22), the righteous Head of our race. In Him, in one wide sense, were all mankind elected, inasmuch as He took their flesh and blood, and redeemed them, and represents them before the Father: but in the proper and final sense, this can be said only of His faithful ones, His Church, who are incorporated in Him by the Spirit. But in any sense, all God's election is *in* HIM only) **before the foundation of the world** (πρὸ κατ. κ. only here in St. Paul: we have ἀπὸ κατ. κ. in Heb. iv. 3; his expressions elsewhere are πρὸ

p εἶναι ἡμᾶς ἁγίους καὶ qr ἀμώμους qs κατενώπιον αὐτοῦ ἐν p constr., Col.
i. 10, 22.
q Col. i.

22. Jude 24 only.   r as above (q).   ch. v. 27.   Phil. ii. 15.   Heb. ix. 24.   1 Pet. i. 19.   Rev. xiv.
5 only.   2 Kings xxii. 24.   s as above (q).   Josh. xxi. 42 (44).   Levit. iv. 17 B.

τῶν αἰώνων, 1 Cor. ii. 7,—ἀπὸ τ. αἰ., Eph. iii. 9. Col. i. 26,—πρὸ χρόνων αἰωνίων, 2 Tim. i. 9,—χρόνοις αἰωνίοις, Rom. xvi. 25,—ἀπ᾽ ἀρχῆς, 2 Thess. ii. 13. Stier remarks on the necessary connexion of the true doctrines of creation and redemption : how utterly irreconcilable pantheism is with this, God's election before laying the foundation of the world, of His people in His Son), **that we should be** (infinitive of the purpose, see Winer, edn. 3, p. 267, § 45. 3. (In edn. 6, the treatment of the inf. of the purpose without the art. τοῦ, seems to have been inadvertently omitted.) The Apostle seems to have Deut. vii. 6; xiv. 2, before his mind; in both which places the same construction occurs) **holy and blameless** (the positive and negative sides of the Christian *character*—ἅγιοι, of the general positive category,—ἄμωμοι, of the non-existence of any exception to it. So Plut. Pericl., p. 173 (Mey.), βίος καθαρὸς κ. ἀμίαντος. This holiness and unblamableness must not be understood of that justification by faith by which the sinner stands accepted before God : it is distinctly put forth here (see also ch. v. 27) as an ultimate *result* as regards us, and refers to that sanctification which follows on justification by faith, and which is the will of God respecting us, 1 Thess. iv. 7. See Stier's remarks against Harless, p. 71) **before Him** (i. e. in the deepest verity of our being—throughly penetrated by the Spirit of holiness, bearing His searching eye, ch. v. 27 : but at the same time implying an especial nearness to His presence and dearness to Him—and bearing a foretaste of the time when the elect shall be ἐνώπιον τοῦ θρόνου τοῦ θεοῦ, Rev. vii. 15. Cf. Col. i. 22, note) **in love.** There is considerable dispute as to the position and reference of these words. Three different ways are taken. (1) Œcum., &c., join them with ἐξελέξατο. I do not see, with most Commentators, the extreme improbability of the qualifying clause following the verb after so long an interval, when we take into account the studied solemnity of the passage, and remember that ἐν χριστῷ in the last verse was separated nearly as far from its verb εὐλογήσας. My objection to this view is of a deeper kind : see below. (2) The Syr., Chrys., Thdrt., Thl., Bengel, Lachm., Harless, Olsh., Mey., De W., Stier, Ellic., all., join them with προορίσας in the following verse. To this,

in spite of all that has been so well said in its behalf, there is an objection which seems to me insuperable. It is, that in the whole construction of this long sentence, the verbs and participles, as natural in a solemn emphatic enumeration of God's *dealings* with His people, *precede* their qualifying clauses : e. g. εὐλογήσας ver. 3, ἐξελέξατο ver. 4, ἐχαρίτωσεν ver. 6, ἐπερίσσευσεν ver. 8, γνωρίσας ver. 9, προέθετο ib., ἀνακεφαλαιώσασθαι ver. 10. In no one case, except the necessary one of a *relative* qualification (ἧς ver. 6, and again ver. 8), does the verb *follow* its qualifying clause : and for this reason, that the verbs themselves are emphatic, and not the conditions under which they subsist. "Blessed be God who DID all this, &c." He may have fore-ordained, and did fore-ordain, *in love :* and this is implied in what follows, from κατὰ τ. εὐδ. to ἠγαπημένῳ : but the point *brought out,* as that for which we are to bless Him, is not that *in love* He fore-ordained us, but the *fact* of *that fore-ordination itself :* not His attribute, but His act. It is evidently no answer to this, to bring forward sentences elsewhere in which ἐν ἀγάπῃ stands first, such as ch. iii. 18, where the spirit of the passage is different. (3) The vulg., Ambrst., Erasm., Luth., Castal., Beza, Calvin, Grot., all., join them, as in the text, with εἶναι . . . . ἀμώμους κατ. αὐτοῦ. This has been strongly impugned by the last-mentioned set of Commentators : mainly on the ground that the addition of ἐν ἀγάπη to ἁγ. κ. ἀμώμ. κατ. αὐτοῦ, is ungrammatical,—is flat and superfluous,—and that in neither ch. v. 27, nor Col. i. 22, have these adjectives any such qualification. But in answer, I would submit, that in the first place, as against the *construction* of ἐν ἀγ. with ἀμώμ., the objection is quite futile, for our arrangement does not thus construct it, but adds it as a qualifying clause to the whole εἶναι . . . . αὐτοῦ. Next, I hold the qualification to be in the highest degree solemn and appropriate. ἀγάπη, that which man lost at the Fall, but which God is, and to which God restores man by redemption, is the great element in which, as in their abode and breathing-place, all Christian graces subsist, and in which, emphatically, all perfection before God must be found. And so, when the Apostle, ch. iv. 16, is describing the glorious building up of the body, the Church,

t ver. 11 reff.
u Rom. viii. 15,
23. ix. 4.
Gal. iv. 5
only †.
v = Col. i. 20.

ἀγάπῃ, ⁵ ^t προορίσας ἡμᾶς εἰς ^u υἱοθεσίαν διὰ Ἰησοῦ ABDFK
χριστοῦ ^v εἰς αὐτόν, κατὰ τὴν ^w εὐδοκίαν τοῦ θελήματος LPℵ a b
c d e f g
h k l m n

w Matt. xi. 26.   Luke ii. 14. x. 21.   Phil. i. 15. ii. 13.   2 Thess. i. 11.   Ps. v. 12.   o 17. 47

5. προωρίσας D¹[P], προωρησας d. (simly D¹ d m in ver 11.)   χριστου bef ιησου
B : om χρ. c.

he speaks of its increasing εἰς οἰκοδομὴν ἑαυτοῦ ἐν ἀγάπῃ. And it is his practice, in this and the parallel Epistle, to add ἐν ἀγάπῃ as the completion of the idea of Christian holiness—cf. ch. iii. 18 ; Col. ii. 2, also ch. iv. 2 ; v. 2. With regard to the last objection,—in both the places cited, the adjectives are connected with the verb παραστῆσαι, expressed therefore in the abstract as the ultimate result of sanctification in the sight of the Father, not, as here, referring to the *state* of sanctification, as consisting and subsisting in love.   **5.] Having predestined us** (subordinate to the ἐξελέξατο: see Rom. viii. 29, 30, where the steps are thus laid down in succession;—οὓς προέγνω, καὶ προώρισεν—οὓς προώρισεν, τούτους καὶ ἐκάλεσεν. Now the ἐκλογή must answer in this rank to the προέγνω, and precede the προώρισεν. Stier remarks well, " In God, indeed, all is one; but for our anthropomorphic way of speaking and treating, which is necessary to us, there follows on His first decree to adopt and to sanctify, the nearer decision, how and by what this shall be brought about, because it *could* only be thus brought about." προ,—as Pelagius (in Harless),—" ad eos refertur qui antea non fuerunt, et priusquam fierent, de his cogitatum est et postea substiterunt ") **unto adoption** (so that we should become His sons, in the blessed sense of being reconciled to Him and having a place in His spiritual family,—should have the remission of our sins, the pledge of the Spirit, the assurance of the inheritance) **through Jesus Christ** (THE SON of God, in and by whom, elementally and instrumentally, our adoption consists, cf. Rom. viii. 29, προώρισεν συμμόρφους τῆς εἰκόνος τ. υἱοῦ αὐτοῦ, εἰς τὸ εἶναι αὐτὸν πρωτότοκον ἐν πολλοῖς ἀδελφοῖς) **to Him** (the Father : see Col. i. 20, δι᾽ αὐτοῦ (Christ) ἀποκαταλλάξαι τὰ πάντα εἰς αὐτόν (the Father). So Thdrt., all., Harl., Olsh., Meyer, Stier : and rightly, for the Son could not be in this sentence the *terminus ultimus* (the whole reference being to the work and purpose of the Father) ; and had this been intended, as Harl. remarks, we must have had καὶ εἰς αὐτόν. De W., who, after Anselm, Tho.-Aq., Castal., all., refers it to the Son, fails to answer this objection of Harl.'s. But now arise two questions: (1) the meaning.

Does it merely represent ἑαυτῷ, a dativus commodi ? So Grot., al., but it cannot be, after the insertion of the *special* διὰ Ἰ. χ., that the sentence should again return to the general purpose. It seems much better, to join it with διὰ Ἰ. χ. as in Col. i. 20, above : and so Harl., but too indefinitely, taking it only as a phrase common with the Apostle and not giving its full import. As in Col. i. 20, the εἰς αὐτόν, though thus intimately connected with δι᾽ αὐτοῦ, depends on ἀποκαταλλάξαι, so here it must depend on υἱοθεσίαν, and its import must be 'to (*into*) Himself,'—i. e. so that we should be partakers of the divine nature : cf. 2 Pet. i. 4. (2) Should we read αὐτόν or αὑτόν ? It will depend on whether we refer this clause, from διὰ to κατά, to the Father as its subject, or consider it as a continuation of the Apostle's thanksgiving. And the latter is much the most likely; for had the former been the case, we should probably have had, instead of διὰ Ἰησ. χριστοῦ, διὰ τοῦ υἱοῦ αὐτοῦ Ἰ. χρ., so that reference to the Father might still be kept up. I decide therefore for αὑτόν, as Thdrt. certainly read, or his remark, τὸ δὲ εἰς αὑτόν, τὸν πατέρα λέγει, would have been needless. And so Erasm., Wetst., Lachm., Harl., Olsh., Meyer. Then αὐτοῦ in ver. 6 naturally takes it up again) **according to** (in pursuance of) **the good pleasure** (it is disputed whether εὐδοκία has here merely this general meaning of *beneplacitum*, or that of *benevolentia*. Harl. (see also Ellicott) examines thoroughly the use of the word by the LXX, and decides in favour of the *latter*, alleging especially, that a mere assertion of doctrine would be out of place in an ascription of thanksgiving. But surely this is a most unfortunate position. The facts on which doctrines rest are here the very subjects of the Apostle's thanksgiving : and the strict parallels of Matt. xi. 26, Luke x. 21, should have kept him from adducing it. Granting, as we must, *both senses* to εὐδοκεῖν and εὐδοκία, the context must in each case determine which is meant. And its testimony here is clear. It is, as De W. remarks, not in προωρισμένοι, but in προορίσας, that the object, to which εὐδοκία refers, is to be sought : and the subsequent recurrences to the same idea in ver. 9 and ver. 11 point out that it is not the Father's

αὐτοῦ, ⁶ εἰς ^x ἔπαινον ^y δόξης τῆς χάριτος αὐτοῦ, ^z ἧς   x Phil. i. 11. 1 Pet. i. 7.
^a ἐχαρίτωσεν ἡμᾶς ^b ἐν τῷ ἠγαπημένῳ, 7 ^c ἐν ᾧ ἔχομεν   Sir. xxxix. 10.

y = ver. 18. Col.

i. 27. see Ps. cxliv. 12.   z constr., 2 Cor. i. 4. ch. iv. 1. Winer, § 24. 1.   a Luke
i. 28 only †. Sir. xviii. 17 only. Ps. xvii. 25 Symm.   b vv. 3, 4 reff.   c Col. i. 14. 1 Cor.
i. 30.

6. ins της bef δοξης D.   rec (for ἧς) εν η, with DFKLℵ³ rel latt syr goth arm
Bas Chr_{h.l.} Thdrt Damasc [Victorin] Jer Aug : txt AB[P]ℵ¹ 17 [47] 67² Syr æth Orig-
cat Chr₁ : η Thl Ambrst.   aft ηγαπημενω ins υιω αυτου (explanatory addition) D¹F
vulg(but not am¹ al) lat-mss-in-Jer syr-w-ast goth æth Dial [Victorin] Aug Oros
Ambrst Pel.

7. εσχομεν D¹(not D-lat) ℵ¹ copt(accepimus) Iren-int.

benevolentia, but His beneplacitum, which
is in the Apostle's mind. And so Meyer,
De W., Stier, and Ellic. This beneplacitum WAS benevolentia, ver. 6; but that
does not affect the question. See, besides
Harl., a long note in Fritz. on Romans ii.
p. 369) **of His will,**   6.] to (with a
view to, as the purpose of the predestination) **the praise** (by men and angels—all
that can praise) **of the glory of His grace**
(beware of the miserable hendiadys, 'His
glorious grace,' by which all the richness
and depth of meaning are lost. The end,
God's end, in our predestination to adoption, is, that the glory,—glorious nature,
brightness and majesty, and kindliness and
beauty,—of His grace might be an object
of men and angels' praise : both as it is
in HIM, ineffable and infinite,—and exemplified in us, its objects ; see below, ver.
12. "Owing to the defining genitive, the
article (before δόξης) is not indispensable :
see Winer, edn. 6, § 19. 2, b : compare
Madvig, Synt. § 10. 2." Ellic.) **which**
(there is some difficulty in deciding
between the readings, ἐν ᾗ, and ἧς. The
former would be the most naturally substituted for an attraction found difficult : and the existence of ᾗ, as a reading,
seems to point this way. The latter, on
the other hand, might perhaps be written
by a transcriber carelessly, χάριτος having
just preceded. But I own this does not
seem to me very probable. A relative following a substantive, is as often in a different case, as in the same : and there could
be no temptation to a transcriber to write
ἧς here, which could hardly occur at all
unless by attraction, a construction to
which transcribers certainly were not
prone. I therefore, with Lachm., Mey.,
Rück., al., adopt ἧς. Considerations of
the exigencies of the sense, alleged by
Harl., al., do not come into play unless
where external authorities are balanced
(which is the case here), and probabilities
of alteration also (which is not)) **He bestowed upon us** (the meaning of χαριτόω
is disputed. The double meaning of χάρις,
—favour, grace bestowed, and that which

ensures favour, viz. grace inherent, beauty,
—has been supposed to give a double meaning to the verb also,—to confer grace, and
to render gracious, or beautiful, or acceptable. And this latter sense is adopted,
here and in Luke i. 28 (where see note),
by many,—e. g. by Chrys., τουτέστιν, οὐ
μόνον ἁμαρτημάτων ἀπήλλαξεν, ἀλλὰ καὶ
ἐπεράστους ἐποίησε,—Erasm., Luth., all.
But the meaning of χάρις, on which this
is founded, does not seem to occur in
the N. T., certainly not in St. Paul. And
χαριτόω, both here and in l. c., according
to the analogy of such verbs, will be 'to
bestow grace.' Another reason for this
sense is the indefinite aorist, referring to
an act of God once past in Christ, not to
an abiding state which He has brought
about in us. This, as usual, has been
almost universally overlooked, and the
perfect sense given. Another still is, the
requirement of the context. Harl. well
remarks, that, according to the sense
'bestowed grace,' ver. 7 is the natural
answer to the question, 'How hath He
bestowed grace?' whereas, on the other
rendering, it has only a mediate connexion
with this verse. Stier would unite both
meanings ; but surely this is impossible.
The becoming χαρίεντες may be a consequence of being κεχαριτωμένοι, but must
be quite independent of its verbal meaning. Conyb. remarks that it may be literally rendered 'His favour, wherewith He
favoured us :' but 'favour' would not
reach deep enough for the sense) **in** (see
above on ἐν χριστῷ, ver. 3. Christ is our
Head and including Representative) **the
Beloved** (i. e. Christ : = υἱὸς τῆς ἀγάπης
αὐτοῦ, Col. i. 13. He is God's ἠγαπημέ-
νος κατ' ἐξοχήν,—cf. Matt. iii. 17 ; John
iii. 16 ; 1 John iv. 9—11).   7.] Now
the Apostle passes, with ἐν ᾧ, to the
consideration of the ground of the church
in the SON (7—12): see the synopsis
above. But the Father still continues the
great subject of the whole ;—only the reference is now to the Son. **In whom**
(see on ἐν χρ. ver. 3—cf. Rom. iii. 24) **we
have** (objective—'there is for us.' But

d Luke xxi. 28.
Rom. iii. 24.
1 Cor. i. 30.
Col. i. 14.
Heb. ix. 15.
xi. 35. Dan.
iv. 32 (LXX).
only. (-τρουν, Exod. xxi. 8.
f Gal. vi. 1 reff.
i trans., 2 Cor. iv. 15. ix. 8 (a).

τὴν ᵈἀπολύτρωσιν διὰ τοῦ αἵματος αὐτοῦ, τὴν ᵉἄφεσιν
τῶν ᵉᶠπαραπτωμάτων, κατὰ τὸ ᵍπλοῦτος τῆς χάριτος
αὐτοῦ, 8 ʰἧς ⁱἐπερίσσευσεν εἰς ἡμᾶς ᵏἐν πάσῃ σοφίᾳ καὶ

ABDFK
LPℵ a b
c d e f g
h k l m n
o 17. 47

Zeph. iii. 1. see also Ps. lxviii. 18. Isa. lxiii. 4.)   e here only. see Gol. i. 14.
g neut., ch. ii. 7. iii. 8, 16. Phil. iv. 19. Col. i. 27. ii. 2.   h attr., ver. 6 reff.
l Thess. iii. 12 only ‡.   k = ver. 17. Col. i. 9, 28.

rec τον πλουτον, with D³KLℵ³ rel Orig-cat Cyr-jer: txt ABD¹(F)[P]ℵ¹ [47] 67²
[Cyr-mss₁-p].—το πληθος 17.   for χαριτος, χρηστοτητος A copt.

not without a subjective implied import, as spoken of those who truly *have* it—have laid hold of it : "are ever needing and ever having it," Eadie) the Redemption (from God's wrath—or rather from that which brought us under God's wrath, the guilt and power of sin, Matt. i. 21. The article expresses notoriety—'of which we all know,'—'of which the law testified, and the prophets spoke') through (as the instrument :—a further fixing of the *ἐν ᾧ*) His blood (which was the price paid for that redemption, Acts xx. 28 ; 1 Cor. vi. 20; both the ultimate climax of His obedience for us, Phil. ii. 8, and, which is most in view here,—the *propitiation,* in our nature, for the sin of the world, Rom. iii. 25 ; Col. i. 20. It is a noteworthy observation of Harless here, that the choice of the word, the BLOOD of Christ, is of itself a testimony to the idea of *expiation* having been in the writer's mind. Not the *death* of the victim, but its BLOOD, was the typical instrument of expiation. And I may notice that in Phil. ii. 8, where Christ's *obedience,* not His atonement, is spoken of, there is no mention of His shedding His Blood, only of the act of His Death), the remission (not "*overlooking*" (*πάρεσιν*) ; see note on Rom. iii. 25) of (our) transgressions (explanation of τ. ἀπολύτρωσιν: not to be limited, but extending to all riddance from the practice and consequences of our transgressions : at least equipollent with ἀπολύτρωσις :—so Thdrt., δι' ἐκείνου γὰρ τὰς τῶν ἁμαρτημάτων ἀποθέμενοι κηλῖδας, κ. τῆς τοῦ τυράννου δουλείας ἀπαλλαγέντες, τοὺς τῆς εἰκόνος τῆς θείας ἀπελάβομεν χαρακτῆρας. This against Harless), according to the riches (Ellic. compares Plato, Euthyphr. 12 A, τρυφᾷς ὑπὸ πλούτου τῆς σοφίας) of His grace (this alone would prevent ἄφεσις applying to merely the *forgiveness* of sins. As Passavant (in Stier), "We have in this grace not only redemption from misery and wrath, not only forgiveness,—but we find in it the liberty, the glory, the inheritance of the children of God,—the crown of eternal life : cf. 2 Cor. viii. 9 "), 8.] which he shed abundantly ('caused to abound :'

ἀφθόνως ἐξέχεε, Thl. : Thdrt. has the same idea, ἀναβλύζει γὰρ τὰς τοῦ ἐλέους πηγάς, κ. τούτοις ἡμᾶς περικλύζει τοῖς ῥεύμασιν. The E. V. is wrong, '*wherein He hath abounded :*' no such construction of attraction of a dative being found in the N. T. Calvin and Beza would take ἧς not as an attraction, but as the genitive after ἐπερίσ. as in Luke xv. 17, 'of which He was full, &c.' But this does not agree well with the γνωρίσας, &c. below. As little can the '*quæ superabundavit*' of the Vulg. (and Syr.) stand : the attraction of the nominative being scarcely possible, and this being still more inconsistent with γνωρίσας forth to us in all (possible) wisdom and prudence (with E. V., De Wette, &c., I would refer these words to God. On the other hand, Harless (with whom are Olsh., Stier, Ellic., al.) maintains, that neither πάσῃ nor φρονήσει will allow this. "πᾶς," he says, "never = *summus,*—never betokens the *intension,* but only the *extension,* never the power, but the frequency,—and answers to our 'every,' i. e. all possible ;—so that, when joined to abstracts, it presents them to us as concrete : πᾶσα δύναμις, 'every power that we know of,' 'that exists ;'—πᾶσα ὑπομονή, every kind of endurance that we know of;—πᾶσα εὐσέβεια, &c. Now it is allowable enough, to put together all excellences of one species, and allege them as the motive of a human act, because we can conceive of *men* as wanting in any or all of them : but not so with God, of whom the Apostle, and all of us, conceive as the Essence of all perfection. We may say of God, '*in Him is all wisdom,*' but not, '*He did this or that in all wisdom.*'" "Again," he continues, "*φρόνησις* cannot be ascribed to God." And this he maintains,—not by adopting the view of Wolf, al., that it is *practical knowledge,* which suits neither the context nor usage,—nor that of Anselm, Bengel, al., that σοφ. is '*de præsentibus,*' φρον. '*de futuris,*'—but by understanding σοφία of the normal collective state of the spirit, with reference especially to the *intelligence,* which last is expressed accord-

[l] φρονήσει
9 [mn] γνωρίσας ἡμῖν τὸ [mo] μυστήριον τοῦ θελήματος αὐτοῦ, κατὰ τὴν [p] εὐδοκίαν αὐτοῦ, ἣν [q] προέθετο [r] ἐν αὐτῷ
10 [s] εἰς [t] οἰκονομίαν τοῦ [u] πληρώματος τῶν [v] και-

l Luke i. 17 only. 3 Kings iii. 28. m ch. iii. 3. vi. 19. Col. i. 27 al. n as above (m). John xvii. 26. ch. iii. 5. vi. 21. Col. iv. 7, 9. Ezek. xliv. 23. o as above (m). Mark iv. 11. Rom. xi. 25. xvi. 25. 1 Cor. ii. 7. Dan. ii. 39 al. p ver. 5 reff. q Rom. i. 13. iii. 25 only ‡. Exod. xl. 4. r vv. 3, 4 reff. s = Matt. x. 18. t ch. iii. 2, 9. Luke xvi. 2, 3, 4. 1 Cor. ix. 17. Col. i. 25. 1 Tim. i. 4 only. Isa. xxii. 19, 21 only. u = Gal. iv. 4 only. v see note, and Mark i. 15. 1 Thess. v. 1.

9. γνωρισαι F latt goth Hil lat-ff (not Jer). om 2nd αυτου DF goth copt Tert Hil Victorin.

ing to its various sides, by the words so often found conjoined with σοφία,—σύνεσις, φρόνησις, γνῶσις. So that φρόνησις, as a one-sided result of σοφία, cannot be predicated of God, but only of men. According to this then, ἐν πάσ. σ. κ. φρ. must refer to that *in the bestowal of which on us* He hath made His grace to abound, so that *we should thereby become* σοφοὶ κ. φρόνιμοι:—as Olsh., ἵνα ἐν πάσῃ σοφίᾳ κ. φρονήσει περιπατῶμεν. Chrys. joins the words with γνωρίσας, understanding them, however, of *us*, not of God: ἐν π. σοφ. κ. φρ., φησί, γνωρίσας ἡμ. τὸ μ. τ. θ. αὐτ.· τουτέστι, σοφοὺς κ. φρονίμους ποιήσας τὴν ὄντως σοφίαν, τὴν ὄντως φρόνησιν. But see, on such arrangement, the note on ἐν ἀγάπῃ ver. 4.

Stier quotes from Passavant: "In the living knowledge of the thoughts and ways of God we first get a sure and clear light upon ourselves and our ways, a light cast from above upon the import and aim of this our earthly life in the sight of God and His eternity. Here is the true wisdom of the heart, the true prudence of life." But against this view, De W. alleges, (1) that φρόνησις can be as well predicated of God as γνῶσις, Rom. xi. 33, and is actually thus predicated, Prov. iii. 19; Jer. x. 12 LXX, of His *creative* wisdom, which is analogous to His *redemptive* wisdom. (2) that God's *absolute* wisdom is not here treated of, but His relative wisdom, as apparent in the use of means subservient to its end: so that ἐν πάσῃ would mean 'in all wisdom thereto belonging,' as Jer.: 'Deus in omni sapientia sua atque prudentia, juxta quod consequi poterant, mysterium revelavit.' And he compares ἡ πολυποίκιλος σοφία τ. θ. ch. iii. 10. These last arguments are weighty, as shewing the *legitimacy* of the application to God: but even beyond them is that which construction and usage furnish. It would be hardly possible, did no other consideration intervene, to refer this ἐν π. σ. κ. φρ. to other than the subject of the sentence,—cf. ἧς ἐχαρ. ἡμᾶς ἐν τῷ ἠγαπ. above. I therefore decide (still; after reconsideration of Ellicott's note) for the application to God, not to us. It was in His manifold wisdom and prudence, manifested in all ways possible for us, that He poured out His grace upon us: and this wisdom and prudence was especially exemplified in that which follows, the notification to us of His hidden will, &c. In Col. i. 9, the reference is clearly different: see note there), **having made known** (γνωρίσας is explicative of ἐπερίσσευσεν, just as προορίσας is of ἐξελέξατο above:—'in that He made known.' This 'making known,' is not merely the information of the understanding, but the revelation, in its fulness, to the heart) **to us** (not, the Apostles, but Christians in general, as throughout the passage) **the mystery** (reff. and Rom. xvi. 25. St. Paul ever represents the redemptive counsel of God as a mystery, i. e. *a design hidden in His counsels*, until revealed to mankind in and by Christ. So that his use of μυστήρ. has nothing in common, except the facts of concealment and revelation, with the mysteries of the heathen world, nor with any secret tradition over and above the gospel as revealed in the Scriptures. All who vitally know that, i. e. all the Christian church are the initiated: and all who have the word, read or preached, *may vitally* know it. Only the *world* without, the unbelieving, are the uninitiated) **of** (objective genitive, 'the material of which mystery was, &c.') **His will** (that which He purposed), **according to His good pleasure** (belongs to γνωρίσας, and specifies it: not to θελήμ. (τοῦ κατὰ τ. ε. αὐ.): i. e. so that the revelation took place in a time and manner consonant to God's eternal pleasure—viz. εἰς οἰκον., &c. On εὐδοκ., see above ver. 5) **which He purposed** (reff.) **in Himself** (ἐν αὐτῷ is read, and referred (1) to *Christ*, by Chrys. and the ff., Anselm, Bengel, Luther, all. But this is impossible, because ἐν τῷ χριστῷ is introduced with the proper name below, which certainly would not occur on the *second* mention after ἐν αὐτῷ, in the same reference: (2) to *the Father*, by Harless. But this is equally impossible. For αὐτῷ to refer to the subject of the sentence, we must have the mind of the reader removed one step from that subject by an

w Rom. xiii. 9
only †. Ps.
lxxi. 20
Theod.

ρῶν, w ἀνακεφαλαιώσασθαι τὰ πάντα ἐν τῷ χριστῷ, τὰ ABDFK
LPℵab
cdefg
hklmn
o 17. 47

10. for εις, κατα την A: εις is written twice, but the first marked for erasure, by ℵ[1].
rec aft 2nd τα ins τε, with ℵ[3] m [arm] Epiph [Cyr₂-p Victorin]: om ABDFKL
[P]ℵ[1] rel vss [Iren] Eus Cyr₁ [Tert].

intermediate idea supervening, as in κατὰ
τὴν εὐδοκίαν αὐτοῦ. Had this been κατὰ
τ. πρόθεσιν αὐτοῦ, the reference would
have been legitimate. But when, as here,
no such idea intervenes,—ἣν προέθετο
ἐν αὐτῷ—the subject is directly before
the mind, and αὐτός, not being reflective
but demonstrative, must point to some
other person: who in this case can only be
Christ. Our only resource then is to read
αὐτῷ) in order to (belongs to προέθετο,
not to γνωρίσας. Very many ancient
Commentators and the Vulg. and E. V.,
take εις wrongly as = ἐν, by which the
whole sense is confused. Hardly less confusing is the rendering of Erasm., Calv.,
Est., al., usque ad tempus dispensationis,
thereby introducing into προέθετο the
complex idea of decreed and laid up, instead of the simple one which the context requires) the œconomy of the fulfilment of the seasons (after long and careful search, I am unable to find a word
which will express the full meaning of
οικονομια. The difficulty of doing so will
be better seen below, after τὸ πλήρ. τῶν
καιρ. has been dealt with. This expression is by ro means = τὸ πλ. τοῦ χρόνου
in Gal. iv. 4, nor to be equalized with it,
as Harl. attempts to do, by saying that
many καιροί make up a χρόνος. The mistake which has misled almost all the Commentators here, and which as far as I know
Stier has been the only one to expose, has
been that of taking τὸ πλ. τῶν καιρῶν as a
fixed terminus a quo, = the coming of
Christ, as Gal. iv. 4,—whereas usage, and
the sense, determine it to mean, the whole
duration of the Gospel times; cf. especially
ch. ii. 7, ἐν τοῖς αἰῶσιν τοῖς ἐπερχομένοις:
1 Cor. x. 11, τὰ τέλη τῶν αἰώνων, and
Luke xxi. 24, καιροὶ ἐθνῶν, Acts i. 7; iii.
19, 21; 1 Tim. ii. 6. Thus τὸ πλ. τ. καιρῶν
will mean, the filling up, completing,
fulfilment, of the appointed seasons, carrying on during the Gospel dispensation.
Now, belonging to, carried on during, this
fulfilling of the periods or seasons, is the
οἰκονομία here spoken of. And, having
regard to the derivation and usage of the
word, it will mean, the giving forth of the
Gospel under God's providential arrangements. First and greatest of all, HE is
the οἰκονόμος: then, above all others, His
divine Son: and as proceeding from the
Father and the Son, the Holy Spirit—and

then in subordinate degrees, every one who
οἰκονομίαν πεπίστευται, i. e. all Christians,
even to the lowest, as οἰκονόμοι ποικίλης
χάριτος θεοῦ, 1 Pet. iv. 10. So that our
best rendering will be, œconomy, leaving
the word to be explained in teaching. The
genitive καιρῶν is one of belonging or ap-
purtenance as in κρίσις μεγάλης ἡμέρας,
Jude 6), to sum up (the infinitive belongs
to and specifies εὐδοκίαν;—ἣν . . . . καιρῶν having been logically parenthetical,—
and explains what that εὐδοκία was. The
verb, here as in the only other place in
the N. T. where it occurs (ref.), signifies
to comprehend, gather together, sum up.
As there the whole law is comprehended
in one saying, so here all creation is comprehended, summed up, in Christ. But
it can hardly be supposed that the ἀνακεφαλαιώσασθαι has express reference here
to Him as the κεφαλή: for 1) this is not
predicated of Him till below, ver. 22;—
2) the verb is from κεφάλαιον, not from
κεφαλή; so that such reference would be
only a play on the word:—3) the compound verb, as here, is used in Rom. l. c.
in the simple ordinary sense. The ἀνα-
applies to the gathering of all individuals,
not to any restoration (Syr., vulg., Olsh.
(Ellic. in part), al.), in which τὰ ἐπὶ τοῖς
οὐρανοῖς would have no share. See more
below: and cf. the ||, Col. i. 19, 20, and
note there) all things (neuter, and to be
literally so taken: not as a masculine,
which, when a neuter is so understood,
must be implied in the context, as in Gal.
iii. 22 :—the whole creation, see Col. i. 20)
in the Christ (q. d., His Christ. The
article is not expressed with χριστός after
a preposition, unless with some such special
meaning: see below ver. 12), the things
in (lit. on; see below) the heavens (universal—not to be limited to the angels
(Chrys., &c.), nor spirits of the just
(Beza, al.), still less to be understood of
the Jews, τὰ ἐπὶ τ. γῆς being the Gentiles (Locke, &c.). Chrys.'s words are so
far true, μίαν κεφαλὴν ἅπασιν ἐπέθηκε
τὸ κατὰ σάρκα χριστόν, κ. ἀγγέλοις κ.
ἀνθρώποις . . . τοῖς μὲν τὸ κατὰ σάρκα,
τοῖς δὲ τὸν θεὸν λόγον—but the Apostle's
meaning extends much further. The rec.
ἐν τ. οὐρ. seems to have been adopted
from Col. i. 20. There also ἐπί is read,
but by L and a few mss. only, and evidently from our passage. The construc-

ἐπὶ τοῖς οὐρανοῖς καὶ τὰ ἐπὶ τῆς γῆς· [11] ἐν αὐτῷ, ἐν ᾧ
καὶ [x] ἐκληρώθημεν [y] προορισθέντες [za] κατὰ [a] πρόθεσιν τοῦ
τὰ πάντα [b] ἐνεργοῦντος κατὰ τὴν [c] βουλὴν τοῦ θελήμα-

x here only.
1 Kings xiv.
41 (only ?).
y Acts iv. 28.
Rom. viii. 29,
30. 1 Cor. ii.
7. ver. 5

a = Phil. ii. 3 reff.
17. Ps. xxxii. 11.
only †.
z = Rom. viii. 28. ix. 11. ch. iii. 11.   2 Tim. i. 9.   Acts xxvii. 13 ‡.
b Gal. ii. 8 reff.
2 Macc. iii. 8.
c = Acts ii. 23. iv. 28. xiii. 36. Heb. vi.

rec for 1st ἐπι) εν, with AFK[P]א³ rel copt Orig-cat Epiph₂ Chr Cyr Thdrt Thl Iren-
int Victorin : txt BDLא¹ a c d e h l n goth [Eus] Thdrt Œc Tert.

11. for εκληρωθημεν, εκληθημεν (gloss) ADF syr : txt BKL[P]א rel vulg(and F-lat)
syr-w-ob goth [Eus] Chr Thdrt Damasc [Orig-int₁ Victorin] Ambrst Jer.   ins την
bef προθεσιν D¹F l.   aft προθεσιν ins του θεου DF [47] copt goth æth Ambrst.
om τα D¹F : for τα παντα, παντας d.

tion is a common one : cf. ἐπὶ χθονί Il. γ.
195, ἐπὶ πύλησι, ib. 149.   It is strange
to find in Ellicott a defence of the rec. ἐν,
grounded on the fact that " ἐπὶ is never
joined in the N. T. with οὐρανός or οὐρανοί, and that ἐν οὐρανῷ and ἐπὶ γῆς
are invariably found in antithesis."   Such
an argument would sweep away all the ἅπαξ
λεγόμενα of construction, and break down
the significance of all exceptional usage)
and the things on the earth (general, as
before τὰ πάντα.   All creation is summed
up in Christ : it was all the result of the
Love of the Father for the Son (see my
Doctrine of Divine Love, Serm. i.), and in
the Son it is all regarded by the Father.
The vastly different relation to Christ of
the different parts of creation, is no objection to this union in Him : it affects, as
Beng. on Rom. viii. 19, " pro suo quodque
genus captu."   The Church, of which the
Apostle here mainly treats, is subordinated
to Him in the highest degree of conscious
and joyful union : those who are not His
spiritually, in mere subjugation, yet con-
sciously ; the inferior tribes of creation,
unconsciously : but objectively, all are
summed up in Him) ;   **11.**] **in Him**
(emphatic repetition, to connect more
closely with Him the following relative
clause), **in whom we** (Christians, all, both
Jews and Gentiles ; who are resolved below
into ἡμεῖς and ὑμεῖς : see on ver. 12)
were also (besides having, by His purpose, the revelation of His will, ver. 9.
Not ' we also,' καὶ ἡμεῖς, as vulg. "in
quo etiam nos . . . ," nor as E. V. 'in
whom also') **taken for His inheritance**
(κληρόω, in its ordinary meaning, ' to appoint by lot,'—then ' to appoint' generally :
κληροῦμαι, mid. ' to get, or possess any
thing by such appointment.'   The aorist
passive, if ever taken in a middle sense,
cannot be thus understood here, on account of εἰς τὸ εἶναι following.   Confining
ourselves therefore to the strict passive
sense, we have three meanings apparently
open to us : (1) ' we were appointed by
lot.'   So Chrys., Thl., vulg. (sorte vocati
sumus), Erasm. (sorte electi sumus).

Chrys. supposes this apparently fortuitous
choice to be corrected by προορ. κ.τ.λ.
following : ' we were allotted, yet not by
chance :' others justify it, as Estius, 'quia
in ipsis electis nulla est causa cur eli-
gantur præ aliis.'   But to this Meyer
properly opposes the fact, that we are
never by St. Paul said to be chosen by
any such θεία τύχη, but only by the
gracious purpose of God : cf. Plato, Legg.
vi. p. 759 c: κληροῦν οὕτω τῇ θείᾳ τύχῃ
ἀποδιδόντα.   (2) ' we were made partakers of the inheritance,' i. e. of the
Kingdom of God, as Israel of Canaan,—
Acts xxvi. 18 : Col. i. 12.   This is adopted
by Harl., and Mey., and many others.
But it seems without authority from
usage : the instance which Mey. quotes
from Pind., Ol. viii. 19, κληροῦν τινι, not
bearing this rendering.   And besides, the
context is against it : ἐκληρώθημεν being
followed, as Stier observes, not by εἰς τὸ
ἔχειν ἡμ., but by εἰς τὸ εἶναι ἡμ., and
thus pointing at something which ' we'
are to become, not to possess.   Another
reason, see below.   (3) ' we were made an
(God's) inheritance.'   This (Grot., Beng.,
Olsh., De W., Stier, Ellic., al.) seems to
me the only rendering by which philology
and the context are alike satisfied.   We
thus take the ordinary meaning of κληρόω,
to assign as a κλῆρος : and the prevalent
idea of Israel in the O. T. is as a people
whom the Lord chose for His inheritance ;
cf. Deut. iv. 20, ὑμᾶς ἔλαβεν ὁ θεὸς . . . .
εἶναι αὐτῷ λαὸν ἔγκληρον : ib. ix. 29 ;
xxxii. 9 ; 3 Kings viii. 51, al.   Flatt cites
from Philo (qu. ref. ?), ᾧ προσκεκλήρωνται,
διότι τοῦ σύμπαντος ἀνθρώπων γένους
ἀπενεμήθη οἷα τις ἀπαρχὴ τῷ ποιητῇ κ.
πατρί.   Olsh. calls this ' the realization in
time of the ἐκλογὴ ἐν χριστῷ spoken of
before,' viz. by God taking to Himself a
people out of all nations for an inheritance
—first in type and germ in the O. T., then
fully and spiritually in the N. T.   This
interpretation will be further substantiated
by the note on ver. 12 below), having been
predestined (why mention this again ?
Harl. maintains that it here applies to the

78   ΠΡΟΣ ΕΦΕΣΙΟΥΣ.   I.

d Acts iii. 19.   *τος αὐτοῦ,* [12] *d εἰς τὸ εἶναι ἡμᾶς εἰς e ἔπαινον δόξης αὐτοῦ*   ABDFK
vii. 19. Rom.   LPℵ a b
i. 11, 20 al.   *τοὺς f προηλπικότας g ἐν τῷ χριστῷ.*   [13] *ἐν ᾧ καὶ ὑμεῖς,*   c d e f g
e ver. 6 reff.   h k l m n
f here only †.   o 17. 47
g 1 Cor. xv. 19. Ps. xxxii. 21.

12. rec ins *της* bef *δοξης*, with A h Chr Thdrt Œc: om BDFKL[P]ℵ rel Eus Cyr Damasc Thl.   om *αυτου* D¹F (not F-lat) flor Tert.

Jews only, and refers to their selection (according to him to *possess* the inheritance) by God: but this cannot be, because as remarked above, *ἡμᾶς,* which first brings up the difference, does not occur yet. The true answer to the question lies in this,—that here first the Apostle comes to the idea of the universal Church, the whole Israel of God, and therefore here brings forward again that fore-ordination which he had indeed hinted at generally in ver. 5, but which properly belonged to Israel, and is accordingly predicated of the Israel of the Church) **according to** (in pursuance of) **the purpose** (repeated again (see above) from ver. 9: cf. also ch. iii. 11) **of Him who works** (energizes; but especially in and among material previously given, as here, in His material creation, and in the spirits of all flesh, also His creation) **all things** (not to be restricted, as Grot., to the matter here in hand, but universally predicated) **according to the counsel of His will** (the *βουλή* here answers to the *εὐδοκία* ver. 5, —the definite shape which the will assumes when decided to action—implying in this case the union of sovereign will with infinite wisdom),   **12.**] **in order that we** (here first expressed, as distinguished from *ὑμεῖς,* ver. 13: see below) **should be to the praise of His glory** (see on ver. 6 and ver. 14 below), **namely, we who have before hoped in the Christ** (we Jewish-Christians who, before the Christ came, looked forward to His coming, waiting for the consolation of Israel: cf. especially Acts xxviii. 20, *ἕνεκεν γὰρ τῆς ἐλπίδος τοῦ Ἰσραὴλ τὴν ἅλυσιν ταύτην περίκειμαι*—and xxvi. 6, 7. The objection, that *so few* thus looked, is fully met by the largeness of St. Paul's own expression in this last passage. But this whole interpretation requires defending against opponents. First, the verse is variously punctuated. Harl., and Olsh. even more decidedly, read it *εἰς τὸ εἶναι ἡμᾶς, εἰς ἔπαινον δόξ. αὐ., τοὺς προηλπ. ἐν τῷ χρ.* But to this it may be objected, (1) that *εἰς ἔπ. δόξης αὐ.,* occurring as it does again at the end of the whole passage as the final aim of all, cannot with any probability be here merely parenthetical: (2) that above, ver. 6, and

below, ver. 14, it, as well as the predestination, has reference to the fulness of the Gospel, not to incomplete prefatory hope in Christ (this would be no objection to De W.'s view : see below) : (3) that thus we should require some demonstrative expression preceding, to mark out these *ἡμᾶς,* such as *ἐν ᾧ καὶ ἐκληρώθημεν ἡμεῖς οἱ προορισθέντες.* The objections which Harl. brings against the ordinary construction are implicitly answered in this exposition. They rest mainly on the mistake of referring *ἐκληρώθ. προορισθέντες* to the Jewish Christians : see above. De W. denies all reference to Jews and Gentiles,—(1) from the analogy of words compounded with *προ-* (*προ-ακούειν* Col. i. 5, *προλέγειν* Gal. v. 21; 1 Thess. iii. 4, *προγράφειν* Rom. xv. 4, *προεπαγγέλλεσθαι* Rom. i. 2), which he says indicate always priority as to the thing spoken of (in his idea here merely, 'hope previous to the fulfilment of that hope,' i. e. *προ-* has no meaning, for all hope must be this), not in comparison with other persons : but (a) this is not true—cf. *προελθόντες* Acts xx. 13, *προέχεσθαι, προηγεῖσθαι, προτιθέναι, προάγειν, προπορεύεσθαι,*—and (b) if it were, it does not touch our interpretation—hoped before (Christ's coming) :—(2) from ver. 13 saying nothing peculiar to Gentile Christians (but see there) : (3) from *καὶ ὑμᾶς,* in ch. ii. 1, and Col. i. 21, not meaning Gentile Christians, but being merely addressed to the readers generally. But in both these places it is so, merely because other things or persons have just been treated of : whereas here he would understand this *ἡμᾶς* as including the *ὑμεῖς,* thus depriving it of the force which it has there).

13.] What is the construction? Have we but one sentence, *ἐν ᾧ . . . . ἐσφραγίσθητε,* the two participial clauses being parallel, and both belonging to the verb ? so the ff., Beng., De W., Ellic., (by whom the view is well defended and explained,) &c. But this seems to me impossible, from the arrangement. It would require the omission of the second *ἐν ᾧ,* or the placing of the *καὶ ὑμεῖς* after *ἀκούσαντες.* As the sentence now stands, the second *ἐν ᾧ καὶ* must begin a new sentence, and surely cannot be the mere rhetorical repetition of the first. This being so, we must un-

ἀκούσαντες τὸν ʰ λόγον τῆς ʰ ἀληθείας, τὸ εὐαγγέλιον
τῆς σωτηρίας ὑμῶν, ἐν ᾧ καὶ πιστεύσαντες ¹ ἐσφραγίσθητε
τῷ ᵏ πνεύματι τῆς ᵏ ἐπαγγελίας τῷ ἁγίῳ, ¹⁴ ὅ ἐστιν

h 2 Cor. vi. 7.
2 Tim. ii. 15.
James i. 18.
i = 2 Cor. i.
22. ch iv. 30.
see Rev. vii.
3 al.

k here only. see Rom. i. 4. viii. 15. xi. 8.   2 Cor. iv. 13.   2 Tim. i. 7.   Heb. x. 29.

13. ημεις AKLℵ³(but ν restored) e f g¹ h k   n o Thl-ms [Victorin₁(txt₁)].   om
2nd και DF copt [goth arm] Did₂ Iren-int Tert [Victorin] Pel Aug.   εσφραγισθη
(for -θητε) B.

14. rec (for ὃ) ος, with DKℵ rel Chr-comm Thdrt Damasc Thl Œc : οστις, omg εστιν,

derstand some verb to complete ἐν ᾧ καὶ ὑμεῖς. Nothing can be more usual or more simple than to supply ἐστέ: nothing commoner than ἐν χριστῷ εἶναι: nothing better suited to the context than, after putting forward the Jewish believers, to turn to the Gentiles, 'Ye also have your part in Christ—our prominence does not exclude you.' Some supply ἠλπίκατε (Erasm.-ver., Calv., Est., al.), some ἐκληρώθητε (Erasm.-par., Harl., Olsh., al.); but the other is far simpler; and I cannot see how it deserves the charge which Ellicott brings against it, of being "a statement singularly frigid and out of harmony with the linked and ever-rising character of the context." It is quite accounted for as above, as forming a link in the context, whose character is well thus described. **In whom are ye also** (ye Gentile believers) **since ye heard** (from the time when . . . . . Their *hearing* was the *terminus a quo*) **the word of the truth** (the word whose character and contents are the truth of God: "quasi extra ipsum nulla esset proprie veritas," Calv.: see reff. This word is the instrument of the new birth, James i. 18. See Col. i. 5, and, above all, John xvii. 17), (viz.) **the Gospel of your salvation** (the Gospel whose contents, whose good tidings are your salvation : not a genitive of apposition, as Harl.,—cf. the expressions εὐαγγ. τῆς χάριτος τ. θεοῦ, Acts xx. 24,—τῆς εἰρήνης, ch. vi. 15,—τ. βασιλείας, Matt. ix. 35,—᾽Ιησοῦ χριστοῦ, Mark i. 1); **in whom** (belongs to *Christ*, as the former ἐν ᾧ—not to λόγον nor to εὐαγγέλιον,—nor is ἐν ᾧ to be taken with πιστεύσαντες, see below: but with ἐσφραγίσθητε—in whom ye not only are, but were sealed. The ἐν ᾧ καὶ . . . . . ἐσφραγίσθητε answers exactly to ἐν ᾧ καὶ ἐκληρώθημεν above; πιστεύσαντες not being by this construction rendered superfluous (Mey.) ; see below) **also** (belongs to πιστεύσαντες ἐσφραγίσθητε, not to either word alone) **on your believing** (*terminus a quo*, as ἀκούσαντες above. Not to be taken with ἐν ᾧ (as = εἰς ὅν, an usage unknown to St. Paul), for see Acts xix. 2, εἰ πνεῦμα ἅγ. ἐλάβετε **πιστεύσαντες** ;—'did ye receive

the Holy Ghost when ye believed ?'—and Rom. xiii. 11, νῦν . . . ἐγγύτερον ἡμῶν ἡ σωτηρία ἢ ὅτε **ἐπιστεύσαμεν**: see also 1 Cor. iii. 5; xv. 2,11; Heb. iv. 3. This use of the aorist marks the time when the act of belief first took place—and it must naturally therefore stand absolutely) **ye were sealed** (the fact followed on baptism, which was administered on belief in Christ. See the key-passage, Acts xix. 1—6.   **πιστεύσαντες** is, and is not, contemporaneous with **ἐσφραγίσθητε**: it is not, inasmuch as in strict accuracy, faith preceded baptism, and baptism preceded the gift of the Spirit : but it is, inasmuch as on looking back over a man's course, the period of the commencement of his faith includes all its accidents and accompaniments. See Ellic.'s note. The figure of *sealing* is so simple and obvious, that it is perhaps mere antiquarian pedantry, with Schöttgen, Grot., and Wetst., to seek for an explanation of it in Gentile practices of branding with the names of their deities, or even in circumcision itself.   The sealing was objective, making manifest to others (ὥστε εἶναι δῆλον, ὅτι θεοῦ ἐστε λάχος κ. κλῆρος, Thl.; so Chr., al.) : see John iii. 33 ; Rev. vii. 3,—but also subjective, an approval and substantiation of their faith (τὴν βεβαίωσιν ἐδέξασθε, Theod. Mops.), see Rom. viii. 16; 2 Cor. i. 22; 1 John iii. 24 b) **by the spirit of the promise** (i. e. who was ἡ ἐπαγγελία τοῦ πατρός, Luke xxiv. 49; Acts i. 4; Gal. iii. 14, 22 ; and I therefore insert the article. This, and not the other alternative, that the Spirit confirms God's promises to us, is the true rendering : He was the promise of the O. T. as well as of the N. T.: as Chr.: δύο εἰσὶν ἐπαγγελίαι, μία μὲν διὰ τῶν προφητῶν, ἑτέρα δὲ ἀπὸ τοῦ υἱοῦ. To unite together both alternatives as Stier does, weakens the force of the reference of ἐπαγγελίας back to God, so necessary to the context. The fact, that the Spirit is *to us* the Spirit of promise, is abundantly expressed in the following clause, **the Holy One** (I have preferred giving the ἁγίῳ separately, feeling with Meyer that there is an emphatic pathos in it which

2 Cor. i. 22.
v. 5 only.
Gen. xxxviii.
17, 18, 20
only.
m = Acts xx. 32.　Col. iii. 24.　1 Pet. i. 4.
14.　Heb. x. 39.　1 Pet. ii. 9 only.　2 Chron. xiv. 13.　Mal. iii. 17 only.

¹ ἀρραβὼν τῆς ᵐκληρονομίας ἡμῶν εἰς ⁿἀπολύτρωσιν τῆς
ᵒ περιποιήσεως, εἰς ᵖ ἔπαινον τῆς δόξης αὐτοῦ.

ABDFK
LPℵ a b
c d e f g
h k l m n
o 17. 47

n ver. 7 reff.　　　　o 1 Thess. v. 9.　2 Thess. ii.
p ver. 6 reff.

d : txt ABFL 67² Ath Euthal Chr-txt[, ω P].　　　[υμων P 17.]　　　om last της ℵ.

should not be lost in the usual prefix,
'the Holy Spirit.' The Spirit with whom
He sealed you is even *His own* Holy
Spirit—what grace, and mercy, and love,
is here!) **which** (if the ὅς of the rec. be
retained, it is not for a moment to be
referred to Christ,—nor to be insisted on
as agreeing with the understood gender
of the personal πνεῦμα,—but as so very
often, a relative agreeing in gender with
the subject (ἀρραβών) of the relative
clause : see ch. iii. 18 reff. and many more
examples in Brüder) **is the** (not ' an ')
earnest (" the word signifies the first in-
stalment paid as a pledge that the rest will
follow. It is used by the Greek orators,
and by the earlier Latin writers, especially Plautus and Terence. A. Gellius
[xvii. 2] speaks of it as a word considered
in his time [A.D. 120—50] to be vulgar,
and superseded by ' arra,' which is the
substitute for it in later Latinity. It is remarkable that the same word עֵרָבוֹן is used
in the same sense in Hebrew, Gen. xxxviii.
17, 18, from עָרַב, to *mix* or *exchange*, and
thence to *pledge*, as Jer. xxx. 21 ; Neh. v.
3. It was therefore probably derived by
the Greeks from the language of Phenician
traders, as *tariff, cargo,* are derived, in
the English and other modern languages,
from Spanish traders." Stanley, on 2 Cor.
i. 22. And so here—the Spirit is the
ἀπαρχή, Rom. viii. 23,—the μέρος τοῦ
παντός, as Chrys., or πρόδομα, as Hesych. :
the pledge and assurer to us of τὰ ὑπὸ
τοῦ θεοῦ. χαρισθέντα ἡμῖν, 1 Cor. ii. 12,
which eye hath not seen, &c.) **of our inheritance** (here the first person comes in
again, and not without reason. The inheritance (see above on ἐκληρώθημεν,
which involved the converse idea) belongs
to both Jew and Gentile—to all who are
the children of Abraham by faith, Gal. iii.
28, 29), **for** (' in order to,'—not ' *until*,' as
E. V. ; nor in ch. iv. 30 : nor does εἰς
belong to ὅ ἐστιν . . ., but to ἐσφραγίσθητε. These two final clauses express
the great purpose of all—not any mere
intermediate matter—nor can the Holy
Spirit be said to be any such intermediate
gift) **the full redemption** (ἀπολ. is often
used by the Apostle in this sense, e. g.
ch. iv. 30 ; Rom. viii. 23, of the full and
exhaustive accomplishment of that which
the word imports) **of His purchased possession** (the sense of περιποίησις has been

much disputed, and many ungrammatical
and illogical renderings of the words given.
A full discussion may be seen in Harless's note. The senses to be avoided
are (1) the nonsensical *antiptosis,* that
ἀπολ. τ. περιπ. = περιποίησιν τῆς ἀπο-
λυτρώσεως : (2) the equally absurd hendiadys, taking τ. περιποιήσεως for τὴν
περιποιηθεῖσαν, which fits neither the true
sense of εἰς, nor the context : (3) the
taking περιποιήσεως as *active* in meaning
—'redemptio qua contingat certa vitæ possessio.' Bucer. But this it could not convey to the Apostle's readers, unless constructed with some substantive to indicate
such a meaning, as in 1 Thess. v. 9, where
see note. A variety of this is proposed by
Grot.—'rescuing,' i. e. salvation—and defended by Heb. x. 39, where περιποίησις
ψυχῆς is opposed to ἀπώλεια. But besides that there the genitive ψυχῆς fixes
the meaning,—the article τῆς here, in my
view, is an insuperable objection. (4) the
taking περιπ. in a *passive* sense, as *res
acquisita*—making it therefore = κληρονομία, and giving to ἀπολύτρωσιν the
sense of *entire bestowal,* which it cannot
have. It remains then, that we seek some
technical meaning of περιποίησις, since
the obvious etymological ones fail. And
such a meaning is found by considering its
uses in the O. T. It, and its cognate word
περίειμι, are found applied to the people
of God, in the sense of a people whom He
preserves for Himself as His possession.
So Exod. xix. 5, ἔσεσθέ μοι λαὸς περιού-
σιος ἀπὸ πάντων τῶν ἐθνῶν, Deut. vii. 6 ;
xiv. 2 ; xxvi. 18 ;—Ps. cxxxiv. 4, τὸν
Ἰακὼβ ἐξελέξατο ἑαυτῷ ὁ κύριος, Ἰσραὴλ εἰς
περιουσιασμὸν ἑαυτῷ,—Isa. xliii. 21, λαόν
μου ὃν περιεποιησάμην τὰς ἀρετάς μου
διηγεῖσθαι,—Mal. iii. 17, ἔσονταί μοι, λέγει
κύριος παντοκρ., εἰς ἡμέραν, ἣν ἐγὼ ποιῶ,
εἰς περιποίησιν, κ. αἱρετιῶ αὐτοὺς . . . .
κ.τ.λ. In ref. 2 Chron. we have the
wider meaning of a *remnant* generally.
The above sense as applied to the people
of the Lord, was adopted by the N. T.
writers : e. g. St. Paul, Acts xx. 28, τὴν
ἐκκλησίαν τ. θεοῦ, ἣν περιεποιήσατο διὰ
τ. αἵματος τ. ἰδίου,—St. Peter, 1 Pet. ii.
9, ὑμεῖς . . . . λαὸς εἰς περιποίησιν. And
such seems to be the meaning here : though
no other case can be alleged in which the
word stands so absolutely. We must suppose, that it would explain itself to the

¹⁵ Διὰ τοῦτο κἀγώ, ^q ἀκούσας τὴν ^r καθ᾽ ὑμᾶς ^s πίστιν q constr., Matt. xi. 2. Acts
^s ἐν τῷ κυρίῳ Ἰησοῦ καὶ τὴν [^t ἀγάπην τὴν] ^t εἰς πάντας
τοὺς ^u ἁγίους, ¹⁶ οὐ ^v παύομαι ^w εὐχαριστῶν ὑπὲρ ὑμῶν,
^{xy} μνείαν ^x ποιούμενος ^z ἐπὶ τῶν ^z προσευχῶν μου, ¹⁷ ἵνα

q constr., Matt. xi. 2. Acts xxiii. 16. Gal. i. 13. Col. i. 4. Philem. 5. r constr., Acts xvii. 28. xviii. 15. xxvi. 3. u = ver. w = John xi. x Rom. i. 1 Thess. iii. 1 Thess. i. 2. Philem. 4 only.

s Gal. iii. 26. Col. i. 4. 1 Tim. iii. 13. 2 Tim. iii. 15. P.   t Col. i. 4 reff.
1 reff.   v = Acts vi. 13. xiii. 10. xx. 31. Col. i. 9 al.   Isa. xxxviii. 20.
41. Rom. i. 8.   1 Cor. i. 4 al. fr.^t   Judith viii. 25.   Wisd. xviii. 2.   2 Macc. i. 11 only.
9. 1 Thess. i. 2.   Philem. 4 only.   Job xiv. 13.   y as above (x).   Phil. i. 3.   1 Thess. iii.
6. 2 Tim. i. 3 (Rom. xii. 13 v. r.) only. P.   z Rom. i. 9.   1 Thess. i. 2.   Philem. 4 only.

15. aft ιησ. ins χριστω D¹(χυ) F vss.   om αγαπην την (*possibly from homœotel ?*)
AB[P]א¹ 17 [Orig-cat] Cyr[?] Jer Aug_{alic} : om την D¹F : ins KLא³ rel latt syrr copt
goth Chr Cyr₁ Thdrt Damasc Ambrst Aug₁.—κ. τ. ε. π. αγαπην τ. αγιους n¹ : κ. τ. ε. π.
τ. αγ. αγαπ. m 80 [Cyr₁-p].
16. παυσομαι D Victorin.   rec (aft μνειαν) ins υμων, with D³KL[P] rel vulg
syrr copt [arm Orig-cat] Chr Thdrt Damasc [Victorin] Jer Ambrst : aft ποιουμ. F : om
ABDא¹ m 17 goth Hil.

readers, from their familiarity with O. T. expressions, or with the Apostle's own use of it. This view is taken by the Syr., Œc., Erasm., Calv., Grot., and most Commentators, also by De Wette, Harless, Olsh., Meyer, Stier, Ellic. Stier endeavours, as so often, to unite the meanings regarding God, and ourselves,—for that we in being God's possession, reserved for survivorship to others, do, in the root of the word, thus survive, are thus saved: and undoubtedly this is so, but is not the leading idea) for the praise of His glory (as before, ver. 6 : but as Stier well remarks, χάριτος does not appear here, grace having *done its work*. αὐτοῦ is the Father: cf. ver. 17, ὁ πατὴρ τῆς δόξης. This, the thorough and final redemption of the Church which He hath acquired to Himself, is the greatest triumph of His glory: as Grot. well says, 'Plus aliquanto est in voce περιποιήσεως quam in voce κλήρου quam antea habuimus. κλῆρος, sors, jus proprium perpetuumque significat: περιποίησις, acquisitio, et hoc, et modum acquirendi gravem et laboriosum. Solemus autem plurimi ea facere quæ magno nobis constant'). See the typico-historical connexion of this wonderful passage with the patriarchal, legal, and prophetic periods, unfolded in Stier, i. pp. 129—136. I would not be understood to subscribe to all there advanced : but though his parallelism sometimes borders on the fanciful, the connexion is too striking to be altogether set aside by the real student of Scripture.

(B) vv. 15—23.] *The* IDEA OF THE CHURCH *carried forward, in the form of a prayer for the Ephesians, in which the fulfilment of the Father's counsel through the Son and by the Spirit, in His people, is set forth, as consisting in the* KNOW-

LEDGE *of the hope of His calling, of the riches of His promise, and the power which He exercises on His saints as first wrought by Him in Christ, whom He has made Head over all to the Church.*

15, 16.] INTRODUCTION TO THE PRAYER. **Wherefore** (i. e., on account of what has gone before since ver. 3 : but especially of what has been said since ver. 13, where καὶ ὑμεῖς first came in :—because ye are in Christ, and in Him were sealed, &c.) **I also** (κἀγώ, either as resuming the first person after the second, going back to the ἐκληρώθημεν ver. 11,—or as corresponding to καὶ ὑμεῖς above :—not, as Mey., al., because he is sensible that in thus praying for them he is helping *their* prayers for themselves) **having heard of** (on the indication supposed to be furnished by this respecting the readers, see Prolegg. § ii. 12) **the faith among you in the Lord Jesus** (καθ᾽ ὑμᾶς is not = ὑμετέραν, as ordinarily rendered (even by Meyer), either here or any where else : cf. the example which Mey. quotes from Thuc. vi. 16, τῷ κατ᾽ αὐτοὺς βίῳ, 'the life which prevails among them :' Ellic. compares, for the distinction, τῷ νόμῳ τῷ ὑμετέρῳ, addressed to Pharisees, John viii. 17, with νόμου τοῦ καθ᾽ ὑμᾶς, said with reference to Jews in Achaia, Acts xviii. 15 : nor is 'among you' merely local (*chez vous*), but is *partitive*, implying the possibility of some not having this faith, and thus intensifying the prayer which follows) **and [your love which is]** towards all the saints (on the reading, see digest. Taking the bracketed words as genuine, τὴν specifies τὴν ἀγ. which might be general : τ. καθ᾽ ὑμ. πίστιν wants no such specification, *all our faith* being ἐν τ. κυρ. Ἰησ., grounded in Him. Chrys. remarks : πανταχοῦ συνάπτει κ. συγκολλᾷ τ. πίστιν κ. τ. ἀγάπην

a here only.   ὁ ᵃθεὸς ᵃτοῦ κυρίου ἡμῶν Ἰησοῦ χριστοῦ, ὁ ᵇπατὴρ   ABDFK
w. πατήρ,
ver. 3. Rom.   τῆς ᶜδόξης, ᵈδῴη ὑμῖν ᵉᶠπνεῦμα ᶠσοφίας καὶ ᵍἀποκα-   LP℘ a b
xv. 6.   2 Cor.   c d e f g
i. 3. xi. 31.   h k l m n
Col. i. 3.   λύψεως ʰἐν ⁱἐπιγνώσει ᵏαὐτοῦ, 18 ˡπεφωτισμένους τοὺς   o 17.47
1 Pet. i. 3
only.   b =. 2 Cor. i. 3.   James i. 17.   c Acts vii. 2.   Ps. xxiii. 9, 10.   d (form) Rom. xv.
5.   2 Tim. i. 16, 18 al.   Gen. xxvii. 28. see Winer, edn. 6, § 14. l. g.   e Gal. vi. 1 reff.   f Exod.
xxviii. 3 Ed.-vat. (not AB.)   Isa. xi. 2.   g = ch. iii. 3.   h = ver. 8 reff.   i = ch. iv.
13. Col. i. 9, 10.   ii. 2.   1 Tim. in. 4 al.   2 Pet. i. 2, 3, 8. ii. 20.   Paul & 2 Pet. only, exc. Heb. x. 26.   Prov. ii. 5.
k obj. gen. aft. ἐπ. always.   l = ch. iii. 9   Heb. vi. 4. x. 32.   Ps. xviii. 8.

---

17. δω (for δωη) B.

θαυμαστήν τινα ξυνωρίδα) **cease not giving thanks for you, making mention (of them,**—viz. your faith and love) **in** (see reff. 'In ἐπί with a genitive, the apparent *temporal* reference partakes somewhat of the *local* reference of juxtaposition.' Bernhardy, p. 216) **my** (ordinary, see Rom. i. 9 note) **prayers.**   **17.**]
purpose (including also the *purport*, see note on 1 Cor. xiv. 13, and Ellicott's note here) *of the prayer :*—**that** (depends on the sense of μνείαν ποι. ἐπὶ τ. προσευχῶν, implying that a *prayer for them* took place) **the God of our Lord Jesus Christ** (see on ver. 3. The appellation is here solemnly and most appropriately given, as leading on to what is about to be said in vv. 20 ff. of God's *exaltation of Christ* to be Head over all things to His Church. To His God, Christ also in the days of His Flesh prayed, πάτερ, δόξασόν σου τὸν υἱόν : and even more markedly in that last cry, θεέ μου, θεέ μου), **the Father of glory** (not merely the *auctor, fons,* of glory, Grot., Olsh. : still less = πατὴρ ἔνδοξος : nor with Chrys. to be explained ὁ μεγάλα ἡμῖν δεδωκὼς ἀγαθά· ἀπὸ γὰρ τῶν ὑποκειμένων ἀεὶ αὐτὸν καλεῖ, ὡς, ὅταν λέγῃ ὁ πατὴρ τῶν οἰκτιρμῶν : nor is δόξης to be understood of the divine nature of Christ, as Thdrt. : θεὸν μὲν ὡς ἀνθρώπου, πατέρα δὲ ὡς θεοῦ, δόξαν γὰρ τὴν θείαν φύσιν ὠνόμασεν : for this would require τ. δόξης αὐτοῦ : but God is the Father,—by being the God and Father of our Lord Jesus Christ,—of that glory, the true and all-including glory, and *only glory,* of the Godhead, which shone forth in the manhood of the only-begotten Son (John i. 14),—the true Shechinah, which His saints beheld in the face of Christ, 2 Cor. iv. 4, 6, and into which they are changed by the Lord the Spirit, ib. iii. 18. In fact, 2 Cor. iii. 7—iv. 6, is the key to this sublime expression), **would give** (the account of the optative after ἵνα, when a present (παύομαι) has preceded, is very simple. It is used when the purpose is not that of the writer *as he is writing,* but is described as that of himself or some one else *at another time.* Thus Herod. ii. 93, καταπλώουσι ἐς θάλασσαν, κ. ἀναπλώ-

οντες ὀπίσω τῆς αὐτῆς ἀντέχονται, ... ἵνα δὴ μὴ **ἁμάρτοιεν** τῆς ὁδοῦ διὰ τὸν ῥόον. See Klotz, Devar. p. 622) **to you the Spirit** (certainly it would not be right to take πνεῦμα here as solely the Holy Spirit, nor as solely the spirit of man : rather is it the complex idea, of the spirit of man indwelt by the Spirit of God, so that as such, it is His special gift, see below) **of wisdom** (not, which *gives* wisdom, but which possesses it as its character—q. d. to which appertains wisdom) **and of revelation** (i. e. that revelation which belongs to all *Christians :* see 1 Cor. ii. 10 ff. : not the χαρίσματα of the early Church, as Olsh.,—nor could the Apostle be alluding to any thing so trivial and fleeting, see 1 Cor. xiii. xiv. To those who are taught of God's Spirit, ever more and more of His glories in Christ are revealed, see John xvi. 14, 15) **in** (belongs to δῴη : as the element and sphere of the working of this gift of the Spirit) **the full knowledge** (for the distinction between γνῶσις and ἐπίγνωσις, see 1 Cor. xiii. 12) **of Him** (Chr., Thl., Olsh., al., strangely connect ἐν ἐπιγνώσει αὐτοῦ with the following sentence, πεφωτισμ. κ.τ.λ. The whole parallelism is against this, in which πνεῦμα σοφ. κ. ἀποκ. is ‖ πεφωτ. τ. ὀφθ. τ. κ. ὑμ. and ἐν ἐπιγνώσ. αὐτοῦ is ‖ εἰς τὸ εἰδέναι κ.τ.λ. ;—and the object being to exalt the gifts of the Spirit, ἐν ἐπ. αὐτ. would hardly come first in the sentence, and thus monopolize the emphasis. See also on a similar proposal, ver. 4, end. **αὐτοῦ** (not αὐτοῦ) refers to the Father, — not to Christ, as Beza, Calv , al. ; cf. αὐτοῦ four times in vv. 18, 19 : Christ first becomes thus designated in ver. 20), **having the eyes of your heart enlightened** (the construction is as in Soph. Electr. 479, ὕπεστί μοι θράσος ἀδυπνόων κλύουσαν ἀρτίως ὀνειράτων,—Æsch. Choëph. 396, πέπαλται δ' αὖτέ μοι φίλον κέαρ τόνδε κλύουσαν οἶκτον : see also Acts xxvi. 3,—Kühner ii. p. 381 : so that πεφωτισμένους belongs to ὑμῖν, and τοὺς ὀφθαλμούς is the accusative of reference. So Beza, Beng., Koppe, Meyer, Ellic. : and such is the simpler and more forcible construction. But Grot., Rück., Harl., Olsh., De W.,

m ὀφθαλμοὺς τῆς m καρδίας ὑμῶν, n εἰς τὸ εἰδέναι ὑμᾶς τίς
ἐστιν ἡ o ἐλπὶς τῆς op κλήσεως p αὐτοῦ, τίς ὁ qr πλοῦτος
τῆς rs δόξης τῆς tu κληρονομίας u αὐτοῦ ἐν τοῖς v ἁγίοις,

m here only. see Matt. xiii. 15. n ver. 12 reff. o ch. iv. 4 only. constr., see Col. i. 23. p Rom. xi. 29. Phil. iii. 14. q Rom. ii. 4. ch. iii. 8 al. r Rom. ix. 23. ch. iii. 16. Col. i. 27. see Phil. iv. 19. s ver. 6. t ver. 14 reff. u constr., here only. v ver. 1 reff.

18. rec (for *καρδιας*) *διανοιας*, with d Cyr-jer Thdrt Œc: txt A ?]א rel. om *υμων* B 17 [Cyr_1-p]. for *εις το υμας*, *ινα οιδατε* F. for 1st *τις*, *τι* F [Orig-cat] Ephr. rec (aft *αυτου*) ins *και*, with D[3]KL[P]א[3] rel vulg(not am fuld tol) syrr copt [æth arm] $Orig\text{-}cat_2$ Chr Thdrt Damasc Ambrst-ms Jer: om ABD[1]Fא[1] 17 goth Ambrst-ed Victorin. *κληρον. της δοξης* א.

Stier, all., take *πεφ. τ. ὀφθ.* together, and govern it by *δῴη*, to which the article before *ὀφθ.* is no objection (as Beng.), but the logic of the passage *is*. The *enlightening as regards* (or *of*) *the eyes of the heart*, is a *condition, subordinate* to the *πνεῦμα σοφ. κ. ἀποκ.*, not another gift, correlative with it. Besides which, the sentence, even after all the grammatical vindications of Harl., al.,—*δῴη ὑμῖν . . . . πεφωτισμένους τοὺς ὀφθ. τῆς καρδίας ὑμῶν*, is clumsy and unpauline in the last degree. On *πεφωτισμ.*, cf. Matt. iv. 16: ch. iii. 9 (v. 14): Harl. gives an elaborate analysis, as usual, of the meaning, and remarks well that *φωτίζω* has the double meaning of 'belehren und beleben'—'*enlightening and enlivening.*' He cites from Greg. Naz.: *φῶς ὡς λαμπρότης ψυχῶν κ. λόγῳ κ. βίῳ καθαιρομένων. εἰ γὰρ σκότος ἡ ἄγνοια κ. ἡ ἁμαρτία, φῶς ἂν εἴη ἡ γνῶσις κ. ὁ βίος ὁ ἔνθεος.* The expression **τ. ὀφ. τῆς καρδίας** is somewhat unusual. The *καρδία* of Scripture is, as Harl., the Mittelpunkt des Lebens, the very core and centre of life, where the intelligence has its post of observation, where the stores of experience are laid up, and the thoughts have their fountain. Similarly the Homeric *κραδίη*, see Damm. Lex.: the Latin '*cor*'—cf. Cic. Tusc. i. 9,—'aliis cor ipsum animus videtur, ex quo excordes, vecordes, concordesque dicuntur.' Thus the *ὀφθ. τῆς καρδίας* would be those pointed at in Matt. vi. 22, 23,—that inner eye of the heart, through which light is poured in on its own purposes and motives, and it looks out on, and perceives, and judges things spiritual: the eye, as in nature, being both receptive and contemplative of the light), **that you may know** (purpose of the *πεφωτισμ.*, not of the *πνεῦμ. σοφ. κ. ἀποκ.* This which is now to be described, to the end of the chapter, is *involved in* the *πν. σοφ. κ. ἀποκ.*, not its *object*: but it *is* the object of the *enlightening*, which will endue us with the knowledge) **what** (the dispute among the Commentators, whether *τίς* implies *quality* or *quantity*, seems hardly worth entering into. The fulness of the simple meaning, '*what*,' embraces all categories under which the things mentioned can be contemplated. In the passage to which both sides appeal, ch. iii. 18, *τί τὸ πλάτος κ.τ.λ.* of course implies, '*how great is the breadth*, &c.:' but it implies this by the simple meaning '*what* is the breadth, &c.,' not by making *τί* = quantum, quantity being already involved in the substantives) **is the hope** (again, it is mere trifling to enquire whether *ἐλπίς* is the hope (subjective) or the thing hoped for (objective), in this case. For the *τίς* involves in itself both these. If I know WHAT the hope is, I know both its essence and its accidents. Undoubtedly such an objective sense of *ἐλπίς* does occur,—see on Col. i. 5; but certainly the meaning here is far wider than in that passage. As well might the subjective sense of Col. i. 23, be alleged on that side) **of** (belonging to, see on ch. iv. 4) **His calling** (i. e. the calling wherewith He called us. All the matters mentioned, *κλῆσις, κληρονομία, δύναμις*, are *αὐτοῦ, His*,—but not all in the same sense: see below. On *κλῆσις*, see notes, Rom. viii. 28—30), **what the riches of the glory of His inheritance** ("what a rich, sublime cumulation, setting forth in like terms the weightiness of the matters described;—and not to be weakened (verwässert) by any resolution of the genitives into adjectives." Mey. See Col. i. 27) **in** (in the case of, as exemplified in; not so weak as '*among*,'—nor merely '*in*,' so as to refer to its subjective realization in them) **the saints** (much dispute has arisen on the construction of **ἐν τ. ἁγ.** Koppe and Winer (Gram. § 19. 2. b, edn. 3: not appy in edn. 6), with whom Meyer and De Wette agree, connect it with *ἐστίν* understood, so as to mean 'what the richness of, &c. is among the saints.' To mention no other objection to this awkward construction, the context and sense are decisive against it. As Stier well says, 'Paul does not pray for their eyes to be enlightened, to see what great and rich things are already among Christians.' No: nor is it easy to conceive how any

w 2 Cor. iii. 10. 19 καὶ τί τὸ ᵂ ὑπερβάλλον ˣ μέγεθος τῆς δυνάμεως αὐτοῦ ABDFK
ix. 14. ch. ii.   LPℵ a b
7. iii. 19   ʸ εἰς ἡμᾶς τοὺς πιστεύοντας ᶻ κατὰ τὴν ᵃ ἐνέργειαν τοῦ c d e f g
only †. P.
2 Macc. iv.   h k l m n
13 al. (-λόν-   ᵇ κράτους τῆς ᵇ ἰσχύος αὐτοῦ, ²⁰ ἣν ᶜ ἐνήργηκεν ἐν τῷ o 17. 47
τως, 2 Cor.
xi. 23.)   x here only.   Exod. xv. 16.   y = 2 Cor. ix. 13. ch. iii. 2. see ἐφ'. ch. ii. 7.
z = ver. 5.   Col. i. 11.   a ch. iii. 7. iv. 16. Phil. iii. 21.   Col. i. 29. ii. 12.   2 Thess. ii. 9, 11. P. †   Wisd. vii.
18, 26 al.   b ch. vi. 10 only.   Isa. xl. 26.   Dan. iv. 27(30 Theod. F). see Col. i. 11.   2 Thess. i. 9.
c ver. 11 reff.

19. om υπερβαλλον F.   εις υμας D¹F[P] d m 17 [Victorin] Ambrst.

20. rec ενηργησεν, with DFKL[P]ℵ rel (vss and lat-ff ambiguous) [Orig·cat₁] Eus

intelligent reader of the Epistle could ever maintain such a rendering. The other construction is, to take ἐν τ. ἁγ. as belonging either to πλοῦτος, or to δόξης, or to κληρονομίας, as if it had been ὁ (or τῆς) ἐν τοῖς ἁγ. And this is the only one allowed by the context: cf. vv. 19, 20, where εἰς ἡμᾶς, ἐν χριστῷ, form objects of reference precisely similar. Again there is manifestly a distinction between οἱ ἅγιοι here, and ἡμεῖς οἱ πιστεύοντες in the next verse: the former being the *perfected*, the latter the *militant* saints. And this decides for the joining ἐν τ. ἁγ. to κληρονομίας αὐτοῦ,—'*His inheritance in*, whose example and fulness, and embodying is in *the saints.*' The objection to this is supposed to be the want of the article before ἐν, which is urged by Meyer (see also Ellicott's note here), because αὐτοῦ has intervened, thereby preventing κληρ. ἐν τ. ἁγ. being considered as one idea. But surely this is not so. If, *before* αὐτοῦ *was inserted*, ἡ κληρ. ἐν τ. ἁγίοις was sufficiently *one* to prevent the necessity of a *specification* of the genus κληρονομία that it was *the* κληρ. which was ἐν τ. ἁγ. (for such is the force of the inserted article), how can this logical fact be altered by the insertion of Him, *whose* κληρ. it is,—who originated and bestowed it,—and who is therefore necessarily *prior* to the κληρονομία, not intervening between it and its example? I therefore join it to κληρ., and so Rück., Harless, Olsh., Stier, al. This latter, as usual, combines the senses of κληρ. αὐτοῦ, including the inheritance which *God* has in *His people*, and that which they have in Him. His whole note is well worth attention), 19.] and **what the surpassing** (a word only pauline in N. T., see reff.) **greatness of His power to usward who believe** (construction as before, ver. 18, τῆς δυνάμ. αὐτ. εἰς ἡμ., not τί τὸ ὑπ. . . . . (ἐστὶν) εἰς ἡμ. Not His future power in the actual resurrection only is spoken of, but THE WHOLE of His energizing to usward from first to last, principally however His *present* spiritual work, cf. πιστεύοντας, not, as in 2 Thess. i. 10, πιστεύσασιν: see also Col. ii. 12,

und 1 Pet. i. 3—5. This power is exerted to *usward*, which expression of the E. V. I retain as giving better the prominence to *us* in the fact of its *direction*, than the more usual but tamer '*toward us.*' But it is not, as Matth., Flatt, the power which works faith in us, except in so far indeed as faith is a portion of its whole work: here, the πιστεύοντες are the material on which the power works), **according to** (in proportion to,—as might be expected from: but more than this—His power to usward is a part of, a continuation of, or rather included as a consequence in, the other. All the shallower interpretations must be avoided here:—Grot., 'rei similitudinem significat:' Van Ess., gleich der Werkung: nor must we join, as Erasm. al., κατὰ τ. ἐν. with πιστεύοντας, which is beside the Apostle's purpose: nor, with Mey., understand it as a qualification of εἰς τὸ εἰδέναι (Erkenntnißgrund des vorherigen Momentes): nor, with Harless, refer it to all three, ἐλπίς, πλοῦτος, μέγεθος: but with Chrys., Calv., Est., Grot., De W., Ellic., take it as an amplification, or explanation, or grounding, of—τὸ ὑπερβ. . . . to πιστεύοντας) **the working** (putting forth in action, in an object) **of the strength of His might** (κράτος the actual measure of ἰσχύς, His might. The latter is the attribute, subjectively considered: the former the weight of that attribute, objectively esteemed: the ἐνέργεια, the operation, in matter of fact, of the strength of that might. Calvin's distinction, though not quite accurate, is worth noting: "Inter tria nomina quæ hic posuit, hoc interest: quod *robur* est quasi radix, *potentia*, autem, arbor (qu. *vice versâ?*): *efficacia*, fructus, est enim extensio divini brachii, quæ in actum emergit"), **which** (viz. ἐνέργειαν: cf. ver. 6, note) **He hath wrought in Christ** (our ἀπαρχή, as Œc.: nor only this, but our Head, in virtue of God's ἐνέργεια in whom, His power to usward is made possible and actual. No shallower view, such as that of Grot. that 'Deus oculis humanis quantum posset, in Christo, capite et duce nostro, *ostendit*,' must be for a moment admitted) **in that He raised**

χριστῷ, [d] ἐγείρας αὐτὸν [d] ἐκ νεκρῶν, καὶ [e] καθίσας [f] ἐν [f] δεξιᾷ
αὐτοῦ ἐν τοῖς [g] ἐπουρανίοις 21 [h] ὑπεράνω πάσης [ikl] ἀρχῆς
καὶ [ilm] ἐξουσίας καὶ [kln] δυνάμεως καὶ [n] κυριότητος καὶ παντὸς
[o] ὀνόματος [p] ὀνομαζομένου οὐ μόνον ἐν τῷ [qrs] αἰῶνι [qr] τούτῳ

d Paul, 1 Cor.
xv. 12, 20
al. fr. Matt.
xvii. 9.
Luke ix. 7.
John ii. 22 al.
e trans., Acts
ii. 30. 1 Cor.
vi. 4 only.
1 Kings xxx.
f = Rom. viii. 34. Col. iii. 1. Heb. i. 3. viii.
g ver. 3 reff.
i = Luke xii. 11. ch. vi. 12. 1 Cor xv.
k Rom. viii. 38. l Rom. xiii. 1. m 1 Pet. ii 22.
o = Acts iv. 12. Phil. ii. 9. Heb. i. 4. Rev. iii. 5.
r Mt. L. (Mark iv. 19 v. r.) not John. Rom. xii. 2 al. fr.

21. intrans., 2 Thess. ii. 4 reff.
1. x. 12. xii. 2. 1 Pet. iii. 22 only. Ps. xv. 11. see Mark xvi. 5.
h ch. iv. 10. Heb. ix. 5 only. Deut. xxvi. 19.
24. Col. i. 16. ii. 15. Tit. iii. 1. k Rom. viii. 38.
n Col. i. 16. 2 Pet. ii. 10. Jude 8 only†.
p Luke vi. 13, 14. Acts xix. 13. Rom. xv. 20. 1 Cor. v. 11. ch. iii. 15. v. 3. 2 Tim. ii. 19 only. Josh. xxiii.
7 al. q Matt. xii. 32.
s Heb. vi. 5 only. Isa. ix. 6 AΝ³⁴.

Chr Thdrt Damasc: txt AB [Cyr₁-p] Procop.　　rec (for καθισας) εκαθισεν, with
DFKL[P] rel copt goth [Orig-cat] Chr Thdrt Damasc Thl Œc [Hil]: txt ABΝ 17 [47]
Eus Cyr Procop Tert [Victorin] Jer Ambr Pel.　　ins αυτον bef εν δεξια AΝ d 17. 67²
copt [Orig-cat] Eus Procop lat-ff.—(for εκ δεξιας, εν(sic, altered to εκ quite recently)
δεξιων A.)　　for επουρ., ουρανοις B Hil [Victorin].
21. εξουσιας και αρχης B.

(as γνωρίσας above, ver. 9) **Him from the dead** (the resurrection of Christ was not a mere bodily act, an earnest of our bodily resurrection, but was a spiritual act, the raising of His humanity (which is ours), consisting of body and soul, from infirmity to glory, from the curse to the final triumph. In that He died, HE DIED UNTO SIN once; but in that He liveth, HE LIVETH UNTO GOD. And so ἡμεῖς οἱ πιστεύοντες, knit to Him, have died unto sin and live unto God. It is necessary to the understanding of the following, thoroughly to appreciate this—or we shall be in danger of regarding, with the shallower expositors, Christ's resurrection as merely a *pledge* of our *bodily* resurrection, or as a mere *figure representing* our *spiritual* resurrection,—not as *involving* the resurrection of the Church in both senses); **and setting Him at His right hand** (see especially Mark xvi. 19) **in the heavenly places** (see on ver. 3: and Matt. vi. 9, note. But the fact of the universal idea, of God's dwelling being in heaven, being only a symbolism common to all men, must not for a moment induce us to let go the verity of Christ's bodily existence, or to explain away the glories of His resurrection into mere spiritualities. As Stephen saw Him, so He veritably is: in human form, locally existent) **over above** (not, as in my former editions [before 1865], '*far above*.' Ellicott says, "The intensive force which Chrys. and Thl. find in this word, ἵνα τὸ ἀκρότατον ὕψος δηλώσῃ, and which has recently been adopted by Stier and Eadie, is very doubtful: as is also the assertion (Eadie) that this prevails in the majority of passages in the LXX: cf. Ezek. i. 26; viii. 2; x. 19; xi. 22; xliii. 15; and even Deut. xxvi. 19; xxviii. 1. Such distinct instances as Ezek. xliii. 15, and in the N. T., Heb. ix. 5, the simi-

larly unemphatic use of the antitheton ὑποκάτω, John i. 51, Luke viii. 16, and the tendencies of Alexandrian and later Greek to form duplicated compounds, make it highly probable that ὑπεράνω, both here and ch. iv. 10, implies little more than simple local elevation. So too Syr. and apparently all the ancient versions") **all government** (cf. Matt. xxviii. 18) **and power and might and lordship** (see similar combinations in reff. The most reasonable account of the four words seems to be this: ὑπ. πάσ. ἀρχῆς gives the highest and fullest expression of exaltation: κ. ἐξουσίας is added as filling out ἀρχῆς in detail: ἐξουσία being not only government, but every kind of official power, primary and delegated: cf. Matt. viii. 9; x. 1; xxi. 23 ff.; Luke xx. 20; xxiii. 7. Then in the second pair, δύναμις is mere *might*, the raw material, so to speak, of power: κυριότης is that pre-eminence or lordship, which δύναμις establishes for itself. So that in the first pair we descend from the higher and concentrated to the lower and diffused: in the second we ascend from the lower and diffused to the higher and concentrated. The following shews that in this enumeration not only earthly, nor only heavenly authorities are meant to be included, but both together,—so as to make it perfectly general. That the *evil spirits* are included, is therefore manifest: see also ch. vi. 12; 1 Cor. xv. 24—26) **and every name that is named** (further generalization: indicating not merely titles of honour (cf. ὀνομάζομ.), nor persons but, as Stier, a transition from the ἀρχαί, &c. to πάντα below: answering to οὔτε τις κτίσις ἑτέρα, cf. Rom. viii. 39. And this transition passes into still wider meaning in the following words) **not only in this present state, but also in that which is to come** (= ἐνεστῶτα and

t Luke ii. 51.
1 Cor. xv. 27,
28. Heb. ii.
5, 8 al. fr.
Psa. viii. 6.
u John iii. 16,
35. ch. iv. 11.
Heb. viii. 10.
x. 16. Rev.
passim.

ἀλλὰ καὶ ἐν τῷ qs μέλλοντι· 22 καὶ πάντα t ὑπέταξεν ὑπὸ ABDFK LPℵ a b
τοὺς πόδας αὐτοῦ, καὶ αὐτὸν u ἔδωκεν v κεφαλὴν ὑπὲρ πάντα c d e f g h k l m n
τῇ w ἐκκλησίᾳ, 23 ἥτις ἐστὶν τὸ x σῶμα αὐτοῦ, τὸ y πλήρωμα o 17. 47
τοῦ τὰ πάντα z ἐν πᾶσιν y πληρουμένου.

v = 1 Cor. xi. 3. ch. iv. 15. v. 23. Col. i. 18. ii. 10, 19 only.   w absol., Acts viii. 3. see Matt. xvi.
18. epp. passim.   x = Rom. xii. 5. 1 Cor. xii. 27 ch. iv. 4, &c.   Col. i. 18 al.   y see notes.
z = ch. v. 18.   Col. i. 9 (note).   Gal. v. 14.

23. rec om τα, with e: ins AB[sic, see table]DFKL[P]ℵ rel [Orig-cat].

μέλλοντα of Rom. viii. 38—not only *time* present and to come, but the present (earthly) condition of things, and the future (heavenly) one. And forasmuch as that heavenly state which is for us *future*, is now, to those in it, present, *it* is by the easiest transition denoted by the μέλλων αἰών: cf. Luke xx. 35, and especially Heb. ii. 5, τὴν οἰκουμένην τ. μέλλουσαν. So that the meanings seem combined,—' every name now named in earth and heaven:' and, 'every name which we name,—not only now, but hereafter.' And in this last view Thdrt.: προστέθεικεν, ὅτι καὶ εἴ τινας τούτων ἀγνοοῦμεν, μετὰ δὲ ταῦτα γνωσόμεθα ἐν τῷ μέλλοντι βίῳ. Chrys.: ἆρα ἐστὶ δυνάμεών τινων ὀνόματα ἡμῖν ἄσημα κ. οὐ γνωριζόμενα. Grot., 'quæ noscemus in altero sæculo:' Beng., 'quamvis non omnes nominare possumus.' Wesley, beautifully expanding Bengel (Stier, p. 183): ' We know that the king is above all, though we cannot name all the officers of his court. So we know that Christ is above all, though we are not able to name all His subjects'), **22.**] **and subjected all things under His feet** (from the Messianic Ps. viii.; not without an allusion also in καθίσας, &c. above to Ps. cx. 1: not merely cited, as Thdrt., καὶ τ. προφητικὴν ἐπήγαγε μαρτυρίαν, but interwoven into the context, πάντα being a summing up of all mentioned before), **and gave** ('*presented;*' keep the literal sense: not '*appointed;*' see below) **HIM** (emphatic, from its position: HIM, thus exalted, thus glorified, the Father not only raised to this supereminence, but gave Him to His redeemed as their Head, &c.) **as Head over all things to the Church** (not as Chrys.,—in either of his alternatives: ἢ τὸν ὄντα ὑπὲρ πάντα τὰ ὁρώμενα κ. τὰ νοούμενα χριστόν (which would be τὴν κεφ., or τὸν ὑπὲρ πάντα), ἢ ὑπὲρ πάντα τὰ ἀγαθὰ τοῦτο πεποίηκε, τὸ τὸν υἱὸν δοῦναι κεφαλήν,—which is beside the context, in which no comparison is made between the gift of Christ and other blessings: nor as Beng., ' Ecclesia, super omnia, super imperia, &c., quorum caput (?) 'Christus est,

potest dicere, Christus est caput meum: ego sum corpus ejus,'—for this sense cannot possibly be extracted out of the words themselves ὑπὲρ πάντα: nor as Baumgarten, ὑπὲρ πάντα = μάλιστα πάντων, *præcipue, potius quam cæteris,*—for, not to mention other objections, πάντα must surely be the same in meaning as πάντα before: nor can πάντα be masculine, as Jer., Anselm, al., and Wahl: nor, as Calv., 'quia *simul* plena rerum omnium potestas et administratio illi sit commissa:' nor, with Harl., does πάντα find its limitation within the Church, so as not to apply to other things without it: nor is ὑπὲρ πάντα to be taken with κεφ., *summum caput,* as Olsh., all. : nor as Meyer, Stier, and Ellicott (edn. 1: in edn. 2, he interprets nearly as below), is another κεφαλήν to be supplied before τῇ ἐκκλ., 'gave Him, as Head over all things, as Head to the Church:' nor is the dative a dat. commodi, as De W.: but the meaning is thus to be gained, from what follows: CHRIST is Head over all things: the Church is the BODY of Christ, and as such is the fulness of Him who fills all with all: the Head of such a Body, is Head over all things; therefore when God gives Christ as *Head* to the church, He gives Him as *Head over all things* to the church, from the necessity of the case. Thus what follows is epexegetical of this), **which same** (Church, '*quæ quidem;*' hardly '*ut quæ,*' "in virtue of her being," as Meyer) **is His BODY** (not in a figure merely: it is veritably His Body: not that which in our glorified humanity He personally bears, but that in which He, as the Christ of God, is manifested and glorified by spiritual organization. He is its Head; from Him comes its life; in Him, in it, He is exalted: in it, He is lived forth and witnessed to; He possesses nothing for Himself,—neither His communion with the Father, nor His fulness of the Spirit, nor His glorified humanity,—but all for His Church, which is in the innermost reality, HIMSELF; His flesh and His bones—and therefore) **the fulness** (πλήρ. is in apposition with τὸ σῶμα αὐτ.,

II. [1] Καὶ ὑμᾶς ὄντας [a] νεκροὺς τοῖς [bc] παραπτώμασιν

a = John v. 25.
Rom. xi. 15.
Col.ii.13.Rev.
iii. 1.   b Gal. vi. 1 reff.   c here only.

and is a fresh description of ἡ ἐκκλησία. It would pass my limits, even to notice summarily what has been written on πλήρωμα. I will endeavour to give an account of the word itself. Like other derivatives in -μα from the perfect passive, it would appear primarily to designate either (1) concrete, that thing on which the action denoted by the verb has passed : e. g. ποίημα, the thing made, πρᾶγμα, the thing done, σπέρμα, the thing sown, πλή- ρωμα, the thing filled : or (2) abstract, that occurrence whereby the action de- noted has been exemplified : e. g. τρῶμα, the effect of τιτρώσκειν, not the thing wounded, but the wound inflicted : so κλάσμα, ἀρίθμημα, and the like; πλήρωμα, the fulness. From this latter, the transi- tion is very easy to the meaning the thing whereby the effect is produced, as where πλήρωμα is used for the crew of a ship (see also Matt. ix. 16 ‖ ; Mark vi. 43; 1 Cor. x. 26 ; Gal. iv. 4 ; ver. 10), ζεῦγμα for a bridge or yoke, &c. Hence arises the so-called active sense of such nouns, which is not in fact an active sense at all, but a logical transference from the effect to that which exemplifies the effect. Here, the simple and primary meaning is by far the best,—' the thing filled,'—" the filled up receptacle" (cf. κατοικητήριον, ch. ii. 22), as Eadie expresses it (see also Ellicott), the meaning being, that the church, being the Body of Christ, is dwelt in and filled by God : it is His πλήρωμα in an especial manner—His fulness abides in it, and is exemplified by it. The nearest approach to any one word in English which may express it, is made by fulness, though it, as well as πλ., requires explaining, as im- porting not the inherent plenitude of God Himself, but that communicated pleni- tude of gifts and graces wherein He infuses Himself into His Church. I would refer those who wish to enter more fully into this matter, to the long and laboured notes of Harless, and Stier : and to Fritzsche on Rom. vol. ii. pp. 469 ff.) of Him who filleth (it is doubted whether πληρου- μένου is passive, or middle in an active sense. Those who take πλήρωμα above, actively, " the filling up," generally (Har- less is an exception) defend the passive sense here, " of Him who is (being) filled, &c." So Chrys : πλήρωμα, φησίν· οἷον κεφαλὴ πληροῦται παρὰ τοῦ σώματος . . . . διὰ πάντων οὖν πληροῦται τὸ σῶμα αὐτοῦ. τότε πληροῦται ἡ κεφαλή, τότε τέλειον σῶμα γίνεται, ὅταν ὁμοῦ πάντες

ὦμεν συνημμένοι κ. συγκεκολλημένοι. Jer. : "Sicut adimpletur imperator, si quotidie ejus augeatur exercitus, et fiant novæ provinciæ, et populorum multitudo suc- crescat, ita et Christus, in eo, quod sibi credunt omnia, ipse adimpletur in omni- bus;" and Estius : "Qui secundum omnia, sive quoad omnia in omnibus sui corporis membris adimpletur. Nisi enim essent hic quidem pes ejus, ille vero manus, alius autem aliud membrum . . . . . non perficeretur Christus secundum rationem capitis." But to this it is difficult to assign any satisfactory sense, especially on account of τὰ πάντα ἐν πᾶσιν. It cer- tainly cannot be said that Christ awaits His completion, in any such meaning as this, by the completion of his Church. And it is not probable that if such had been the meaning, τὰ πάντα ἐν πᾶσιν would have thus barely and emphatically preceded the participle which itself con- veyed so new and startling an idea. We should have had some such arrangement as this—τὸ πλήρωμα τοῦ καὶ αὐτοῦ τὰ πάντα (κ.) ἐν πᾶσιν πληρουμένου. If now we take πληρουμένου in an active reflective sense, both meaning and ar- rangement will be satisfactory—' the ful- ness (receptacle, filled and possessed) of Him who filleth' τὰ πάντα ἐν πᾶσιν. But are we justified in thus taking it? It seems so, from Xen. Hell. vi. 2. 14, ὁ στρατηγὸς μάλα ὀξέως τὰς ναῦς ἐπλη- ροῦτο κ. τοὺς τριηράρχους ἠνάγκαζε. See likewise Plato, Gorg. § 106 ; Xen. Hell. v. 4. 56 ; vi. 2. 35 : Demosth. p. 1208. 14 : Plut. Alcib. 35 : Pollux i. 99 : in all of which the 1 aor. middle is thus used. Having then this authority as far as gram- matical usage is concerned, we are further inclined to this rendering by ch. iv. 10, where it is said of Christ, ὁ ἀναβὰς ὑπερ- άνω πάντων τῶν οὐρανῶν, ἵνα πληρώσῃ τὰ πάντα, and the Apostle proceeds to enumerate the various gifts bestowed by Him on His Church. See further in note there) all things (the whole universe: not to be restricted in meaning. The Church is the special receptacle and abiding-place—the πλήρωμα κατ' ἐξοχήν, of Him who fills all things) with all things (i. e. who is the bestower of all, wherever found. ἐν πᾶσιν has been rendered ' every where' (B.-Crus.): 'in every way' (De W.): 'in every case' (Harl.) and al.: but the Apostle's own usage is our best guide,—πληροῦσθε ἐν πνεύματι, ch. v. 18, and other reff., and directs us to the in-

d ver. 10 reff.
e = Gal. i. 13
reff.
f Rom. viii. 1, 4. xiv. 15.   1 Cor. iii. 3.   2 John 6 al.

καὶ ταῖς ᶜ ἁμαρτίαις [ὑμῶν], ² ᵈ ἐν αἷς ᵉ ποτὲ ᵈᶠ περιεπατή- ABDFK

LPℵ a b
c d e f g
h k l m n
o 17. 47

CHAP. II. 1. for αμαρτιαις, επιθυμιαις B.   rec om υμων, with KL rel Chr-comm
Damasc Thl Œc : ins BDF[P]ℵ m 17 [47] 67² vss Thdrt Lucif Victorin, εαυτων A.

strumental or elemental meaning—the thing with, or by, or in which as an element, the filling takes place. So that the expression will mean, *with all*, not only gifts, not only blessings, but *things* : who fills all creation with whatever it possesses—who is the Author and Giver of all things. The reference is, I think, to the Father, not to Christ. The latter has been imagined (see especially Ellicott), principally from strictly parallelizing the two clauses,—τὸ σῶμα | αὐτοῦ ‖, τὸ πλή-ρωμα | τοῦ τ. π. ἐν π. πληρουμένου ‖. But this is by no means conclusive : the second definitive clause may assert more than the first;—may be, not subordinate to the first, but inclusive of it. In ch. iv. 10, where Christ's filling all things is spoken of, we have the active voice, denoting the bare objective fact : whereas here the reciprocal middle implies a filling for Himself, which can hardly be predicated of any but the Father, for whom are all things, even the Son himself).

II. 1—22.] (See on ch. i. 3.) COURSE AND PROGRESS OF THE CHURCH THROUGH THE SON ; consisting mainly in the receiving of believers in the new man Christ Jesus—setting forth on one side the death and ruin in which they were;—on the other, the way to life opened to them by the finished work of Christ. This throughout the chapter, which is composed (as ch. i.) of two parts—the first, more doctrinal and assertive (vv. 1—10), the second more hortative and reminiscent (vv. 11—22). In both, the separate cases of Gentiles and Jews, and the present union in Christ, are treated of. And herein

A. 1—10.] THE POWER OF THE FATHER IN QUICKENING US, BOTH GENTILES AND JEWS, IN AND WITH CHRIST (1—6) ; —HIS PURPOSE IN MANIFESTING THIS POWER (7) ; — INFERENCE RESPECTING THE METHOD OF OUR SALVATION (8—10).

1, 2.] *Actual state of the Gentiles —dead in trespasses and sins, living under the power of the devil.* 1.] You also (καί is much more than merely copulative. It selects and puts into prominence ὑμᾶς, from among the recipients of God's grace implied in vv. 19—23 of the former chapter. See below), who were ("ὄντας clearly marks the state in which they were at the time when God quickened them : this in

ver. 5 is brought prominently forward by the καί : here however καί is joined with and gives prominence to ὑμᾶς. A simple indication, then, of their state, without any temporal or causal adjunct, 'when,' 'whereas,' &c., seems in the present case most satisfactory, as less calling away the attention from the more emphatic ὑμᾶς." Ellicott, edn. 1) dead (certainly not, as Meyer, '*subject to* (physical) *death :*' the whole of the subsequent mercy of God in His quickening them is *spiritual*, and therefore of necessity the death also. That it *involves* physical death, is most true ; but as I have often had occasion to remark (see e. g. on John xi. 25, 26), this latter is so subordinate to spiritual death, as often hardly to come into account in Scripture) in (not exactly as in Col. ii. 13, νεκροὺς ὄντας ἐν τοῖς παραπτώμασιν, where the *element* is more in view, whereas here it is the causal dative—we might render, were the expression good in serious writing, 'dead *of* your trespasses,' as we say ' he lies dead of cholera.' I use 'in' as giving nearly the same causal sense : we say, indiscriminately, 'sick *of* a fever,' and 'sick *in* a fever') [your] trespasses and sins (it seems difficult to establish universally any distinction such as has been attempted, e. g. by Tittm. Synon. p. 47,—" licet non satis vera Hieronymi distinctio videatur, qui παράπτωμα primum ad peccatum lapsum esse dicit, ἁμαρ-τίαν, quum ad ipsum facinus perventum est ; tamen in v. παράπτωμα proprie inest notio peccati quod temere commissum est, i. e. a nolente facere injuriam ; sed in ἁμαρ-τία et ἁμάρτημα cogitatur facinus quod, qui fecit, facere voluit, sive imprudens erraverit, recte se facere existimans, sive impetu animi et libidine obreptus fecerit. . . . Levius est παράπτωμα quam ἁμαρ-τία, si ἁμαρτία de singulo peccato dicitur." Where however, as here, the two occur together, it may be accepted as correct. If we take merely that of Ellicott, al., that " παραπτώματα are the particular, special acts of sin,—ἁμαρτίαι the more general and abstract, viz. all forms, phases, and movements of sin, whether entertained in thought or consummated in act," we shall not provide for the whole case : for ἁμαρτίαι are unquestionably used for special acts (= ἁμαρτήματα): and we want a distinction which shall embrace

σατε ᶠκατὰ τὸν ᵍαἰῶνα τοῦ ᵍκόσμου τούτου, ᶠκατὰ τὸν ᵍ here only.
ʰἄρχοντα τῆς ⁱἐξουσίας τοῦ ʲἀέρος, τοῦ ᵏπνεύματος τοῦ

g here only.
  see Gal. i. 4.
h = John xii.
  31. xiv. 30.
  xvi. 11.
i ch. i. 21 reff.   j Acts xxii. 23. 1 Cor. ix. 26. xiv. 9. 1 Thess. iv. 17. Rev. ix. 2. xvi. 17
  only. Ps. xvii. 11.   k = Luke ix. 55. Rom. viii. 15. 1 Cor. iv. 21. 2 Tim. i. 7. 1 John iv. 1 ff.

this case.   Another question concerns the construction of this accusative clause. Some (Beng., Lachm., Harl.) consider it as a continuation of ch. i. 23, and place a comma only at πληρουμένου. But (see our division of the sense) the sentence evidently finishes with πληρουμένου, and a new subject is here taken up. The simplest view seems to be the usual one, that the Apostle began with the accusative, intending to govern it by συνεζωοποίησεν τῷ χριστῷ, but was led away by the relative clauses, ἐν αἷς ποτὲ . . . . , ἐν οἷς καὶ ἡμεῖς . . . . , and himself takes up the dropped thread of the construction by ὁ δὲ θεὸς . . . . , ver. 4. So Erasm.: "hyperbati longioris ambitum ipse correxit Apostolus dicens ' Deus autem qui dives est' . . ." At all events, the clause should be left, in translation, pendent, as it stands, and not filled in conjecturally),

2.] **in which** (ἁμαρτίαις, the last substantive, but applying in fact to both) **ye once walked** (we hardly need, as Eadie, al., go back every time to the figure in περιπατεῖν—the word has become with the Apostle so common in its figurative sense. See Fritzsche's note, Rom. vol. iii. p. 140) **according to** (after the leading of, conformably to) **the course** (so E. V.: the very best word, as so often. The meaning of **αἰών** here is compounded of its temporal and its ethical sense: it is not exactly ' lifetime,' ' duration,' nor again ' fashion,' ' spirit,' but some common term which will admit of being both temporally and ethically characterized,—' career ' or ' course.' Beware 1) of taking **αἰῶνα** and **κόσμου** as synonymous, and the expression as a pleonasm ("utrumque nominat, seculum et mundum, cum sufficeret alterum dixisse," Estius), 2) of imagining, as Michaelis and Baur, that the expression is a gnostic one, the æon being the devil: for, as Meyer remarks, the ordinary sense of αἰών gives a good meaning, and one characteristic of St. Paul. See Gal. i. 4, for a use of αἰών—somewhat similar, but more confined to the temporal meaning) **of this world** (St. Paul generally uses ὁ κόσμος, but has ὁ κ. οὗτος in 1 Cor. iii. 19; v. 10; vii. 31. It designates the present system of things, as alien from God, and lying in the evil one), **according to the ruler of the power of the air** (the devil – the θεὸς τοῦ αἰῶνος τούτου, 2 Cor. iv. 4, is clearly meant: but it is difficult

exactly to dissect the phrase, and give each word its proper meaning. **ἐξουσία** appears to be used here as ὁμηλικίη in Homer, ἡλικία, ἑταιρία, δουλεία, ὑπηρεσία, συμμαχία, and the like, to represent the aggregate of those in power: as we say, ' the government.' So that all such renderings as ' princeps potentissimus ' are to be at once dismissed. So also is every explanation which would ascribe to the Apostle a polemical, or distantly allusive tendency, in an expression which he manifestly uses as one of passage merely, and carrying its own familiar sense to his readers. This against Michaelis, and all who have imagined an allusion to the gnostic ideas — and Wetst., who says, "Paulus ita loquitur ex principiis philosophiæ Pythagoreæ, quibus illi ad quos scribit imbuti erant." Not much better are those who refer the expression to Rabbinical ideas for its source. The different opinions and authorities (which would far exceed the limits of a general commentary) may be seen cited and treated in Harless, Stier, and Eadie. I am disposed to seek my interpretation from a much more obvious source: viz. the persuasion and common parlance of mankind, founded on analogy with well-known facts. (Ellic., edn. 2, disapproves this, but without sufficiently attending to my explanation which follows, which, as in so many cases where he imagines a difference between our interpretations, is practically the same as his own.) We are tempted by evil spirits, who have access to us, and suggest thoughts and desires to our minds. We are surrounded by the air, which is the vehicle of speech and of all suggestions to our senses. Tried continually as we are by these temptations, what so natural, as to assign to their ministers a dwelling in, and power over that element which is the vehicle of them to us ? And thus our Lord, in the parable of the sower, when He would represent the devil coming and taking away the seed out of the heart, figures him by τὰ πετεινὰ τοῦ οὐρανοῦ. The Apostle then, in using this expression, would be appealing to the common feeling of his readers, not to any recondite or questionable system of dæmonology. That traces are found in such systems, of a belief agreeing with this, is merely a proof that they have embodied the same general feeling, and may be used

νῦν [l] ἐνεργοῦντος ἐν τοῖς [mn] υἱοῖς τῆς [no] ἀπειθειας, 3 ἐν οἷς
καὶ ἡμεῖς πάντες [p] ἀνεστράφημεν ποτὲ ἐν ταῖς [q] ἐπιθυμίαις
τῆς [r] σαρκὸς ἡμῶν, ποιοῦντες τὰ [rs] θελήματα τῆς [s] σαρκὸς

ABDFK LPℵ a b c d e f g h k l m n o 17. 47

l ch. i. 11 reff. m = John xvii. 12. 2 Thess. ii. 3. see Isa. lvii. 4. n ch. v. 6 (Col. iii. 6 v. r.) only. o Rom. xi. 30, 32. Heb. iv. 6, 11 +. p = Matt. xvii. 22. 2 Cor. i. 12 (& constr.). 1 Tim. iii. 15. 1 Pet. i. 17. 2 Pet. ii. 18. Ezek. xix. 6. see Heb. x. 33. q (Rom. xiii. 14.) Gal. v. 16. 2 Pet. ii. 18. 1 John ii. 16. see 1 Pet. ii. 11. r plur., Acts xiii. 22 (from Isa. xliv. 28?) only. Jer. xxiii. 26 al. s John i. 13 only.

3. om *και ημεις* FL : for *ημ.*, *υμ.* A(but nearly erased) D[1].

in illustration, not as the ground, of the Apostle's saying. All attempts to represent **ἀήρ** as meaning '*darkness*,' or '*spirit*,' are futile, and beside the purpose. The word occurs (see reff.) six more times in the N. T. and no where in any but its ordinary meaning), **of the spirit** (*τῆς ἐξουσίας* being used as designating (see above) the personal aggregate of those evil ones who have this power, **τοῦ πνεύματος**, in apposition with it, represents their aggregate character, as an influence on the human mind, a spirit of ungodliness and disobedience,—the *πνεῦμα τοῦ κόσμου* of 1 Cor. ii. 12,—the aggregate of the *πνεύματα πλάνα* of 1 Tim. iv. 1. So that (against Harless) the meaning of *πνεύματος*, though properly and strictly objective, almost passes into the subjective, when it is spoken of as *ἐνεργοῦντος ἐν κ.τ.λ.* And this will account for the otherwise harsh conjunction of *ἄρχοντα τοῦ πνεύματος.* As he (the devil) is the ruler of *τὰ πνεύματα*, whose aggregate *τὸ πνεῦμα* is,—so he is the *ἄρχων* of the thoughts and ways of the ungodly,—of that *πνεῦμα* which works in them. The genitive, *πνεύματος*, must not be taken, as by many Commentators and by Rückert, as in apposition with *ἄρχοντα*, by the Apostle's negligence of construction. No such assumption should ever be made without necessity; and there is surely none here) **which is now** (i. e '*still*:' contrast to *ποτέ*,—to *you*, who have escaped from his government: no allusion need be thought of to the interval before the *παρουσία* being that of the hottest conflict between the principles (2 Thess. ii. 7. Rev. xii. 12), as De W.) **working in the sons of** (the expression is a Hebraism, but is strictly reproduced in the fact: that of which they are sons, is the source and spring of their lives, not merely an accidental quality belonging to them) **disobedience** (the vulg. renders it *diffidentia*, but unfortunately, as also Luther Unglaube; for both here and in ch. v. 6, it is practical conduct which is spoken of. Doubtless unbelief is the root of disobedience: but it is not here expressed, only implied. In Deut. ix. 23, **ἠπειθήσατε τῷ** *ῥήματι κυρίου τ. θεοῦ ὑμῶν*, and the allusion to it in Heb. iv. 6, *οἱ πρότερον εὐαγγελισθέντες οὐκ εἰσῆλθον δι'* **ἀπείθειαν,** we have the disobedience in its root—here, in its fruits—cf. ver. 3, *ποιοῦντες τὰ θελήματα κ.τ.λ.*): **3.] among whom** (the *υἱοὶ τ. ἀπειθείας*: not merely local, but 'numbered among whom,'—*ὧν καὶ αὐτοὶ ὄντες*, as Rückert: not '*in which*,' viz. *παραπτώμασιν*, as Syr., Jer., Grot., Bengel, al., and Stier, who would divide off *ἁμαρτίαι*, allotting them to the Gentiles, and to ver. 2,—and *παραπτώματα*, assigning them to the Jews, and to ver. 3. See further on this below: but meantime, besides its very clumsy treatment of the *ἁμαρτ.* and *παραπτ.* which both belong to *ὑμεῖς* in ver. 1, it ascribes to the Apostle an unusual and unnatural precision in distinguishing the two words which he had used without any such note of distinction, such as *τε—καί*) **we also all** (WHO? The usage of **ἡμεῖς πάντες** by St. Paul must decide. It occurs Rom. iv. 16, *ὅς ἐστιν πατὴρ πάντων ἡμῶν*, undeniably for Jews and Gentiles included (for the slight difference arising from *πάντων* being first, and therefore emphatic, need not be insisted on): viii. 32, *ὑπὲρ ἡμῶν πάντων παρέδωκεν αὐτόν*, where the universal reference is as undeniable: 1 Cor. xii. 13, where it is still more marked: *ἡμεῖς πάντες· . . . . εἴτε Ἰουδαῖοι εἴτε Ἕλληνες, εἴτε δοῦλοι εἴτε ἐλεύθεροι*: 2 Cor. iii. 18, equally undoubted. It can hardly then be that here he should have departed from his universal usage, and placed an unmeaning *πάντες* after *ἡμεῖς* merely to signify, 'we Jews, every one of us.' I therefore infer that by **ἡμεῖς πάντες**, he means, we all, Jews and Gentiles alike; all, who are now Christians) **lived our life** (reff. especially 2 Cor.) **once, in** (as in ref. 1 Pet., of the element, in which: in 2 Cor. i. 12, the same double use of *ἐν*, of the place, and the element, is found) **the desires of our flesh** (of our unrenewed selves, under the dominion of the body and the carnal soul. See a contrast, Gal. v. 16), **doing the wishes** (the instances in which *τὸ θέλημα* manifested itself: see reff.) **of our flesh and of our thoughts** (the plural use is remarkable. There appears to be a refer-

καὶ τῶν ᵗ διανοιῶν, καὶ ἤμεθα ᵘ τέκνα ᵛ φύσει ὀργῆς ὡς ᵗ₋ ch. iv.
18. Col. i.
21. plur., here (Heb. x. 16 v. r.) only. see note.
8. 1 Pet. i. 14. 2 Pet. ii. 14. Isa. lvii. 4.
26 al.)
u = Matt. xi. 19. Rom. ix 8. ch. v.
v Rom. ii. 14. Gal. ii. 15. iv. 8 only. (·σις, Rom. i.

rec (for ημεθα) ημεν, with ADFKL[P] rel Clem Did [Cyr-p] Chr Thdrt Damasc:
txt B❡ 17 Orig₄[and cat₁].   φυσει bef τεκνα ADFL[P] m latt arm Orig₁ Did Thdrt
lat-ff: om φυσει 109 æth Clem: txt BK❡ rel Orig₃[and int₁] [Cyr₂-p] Chr Thl Œc [Tert].

ence to Num. xv. 39, οὐ διαστραφήσεσθε ὀπίσω τῶν διανοιῶν ὑμῶν. In Isa. lv. 9, a distinction is made, ἀπέχει ... τὰ διανοήματα ὑμῶν ἀπὸ τῆς διανοίας μου, which is useful here, as pointing to διάνοιαι as an improper use for διανοήματα, —the instrument for its results. Thus 'thoughts' will be our nearest word— those phases of mind which may or may not affect the will, but which then in our natural state we allowed to lead us by the desires they excited), and were (the change of construction has been remarked by the best Commentators as intentional, not of negligence,—" to give emphasis to the weighty clause that follows, and to disconnect it from any possible relation to present time, ' we *were* children of wrath by nature,—it was once our state and condition, it is now so no longer.' " Ellicott. And Eadie remarks : " Had he written καὶ ὄντες, as following out the idea of ποιοῦντες, there might have been a plea against the view of innate depravity (see below)—'fulfilling the desires of the flesh and of the mind, and being,' or 'so being, children of wrath.' But the Apostle says καὶ ἤμεθα—'and we were,' at a point of time prior to that indicated in ποιοῦντες") children (not = υἱοί, but implying closer relation. The effect of the expression is to set those of whom it is predicated, beneath, in subjection to, as it were, the products of, ὀργή. So in the passages adduced by Harl.;—Deut. xxv. 2, בִּן נֵכָה הַכּוֹת, 'if he be the son of stripes,' i. e. not as LXX and E. V. ἄξιος πληγῶν, but actually beaten:—1 Sam. xx. 31, בֶּן־מָוֶת הוּא, 'he is the son of death,'—i. e. as we express it, ' he is a dead man,' anticipating the effect of that which seems to be certain) by nature (the meaning of φύσει is disputed. Some of the ancients (Cyr., Œc., Thl.), and Grot. took it as = ὄντως, ἀληθῶς, which meaning it never bears; see on Gal. iv. 8. Others (Holzhausen, Hoffm.) would join it with ὀργῆς, —'anger, which arises from the ungodly natural life:' but as Mey. remarks, even granting this use of φύσις, this would require τῆς τῇ φύσει ὀργῆς or τῆς ἐκ τῆς φύσ. ὀργῆς. It can then only mean, 'by nature.' And what does this imply? Harl., in loc., seems to have given the distinctive

sense well : " φύσις, in its fundamental idea, is that which has *grown* as distinguished from that which has been *effected* (das Gewordene in Gegensatz zum Gemachten), i. e. it is that which according to our judgment has the ground of its existence in individual development, not in accessory influence of another. Accordingly, φύσις, in its concrete idea, as the sum total of all growth, is ' rerum natura:' and in its abstract philosophical idea, φύσις is the contrast to θέσις. The φύσις of an individual thing denotes the peculiarity of its being, which is the result of its being, as opposed to every accessory quality: hence φύσει εἶναι or ποιεῖν τι means, 'sua sponte facere, esse aliquid' and 'natura esse aliquid:' to be and do any thing by virtue of a state (εἶναι) or an inclination (ποιεῖν), not acquired, but inherent : ἔξοιδα καὶ φύσει σε μὴ πεφυκότα | τοιαῦτα φωνεῖν, μηδὲ τεχνᾶσθαι κακά, Soph. Philoct. 80." If this be correct, the expression will amount to an assertion on the part of the Apostle of the doctrine of original sin. There is from its secondary position (cf. Plutarch de frat. am. p. 37, in Harl., ὀργάνων φύσει τοιούτων ἔτυχεν) no emphasis on φύσει: but its doctrinal force as referring to a fundamental truth otherwise known, is not thereby lessened. And it is not for Meyer to argue against this by assuming original sin not to be a pauline doctrine. If the Apostle asserts it here, this place must stand on its own merits, not be wrested to suit an apparent preconceived meaning of other passages. But the truth is, he cites those other passages in a sense quite alien from their real one. It would be easy to shew that every one of them (Rom. i. 18; ii. 8, 9; v. 12; vii. 9; xi. 21. Gal. ii. 15) is consistent with the doctrine here implied. The student will do well to read the long notes in Harl., De W., Stier, and Eadie) of wrath (WHOSE wrath, is evident : the meaning being, we were all concluded under and born in sin, and so actual objects of that wrath of God which is His mind against sin. ὀργή must not be taken as = τιμωρία, κόλασις, as Chrys., Thdrt., Basil, Thl., al. : this would in fact make the expression mean, *actually punished :* see above on τέκνα;—just as it now means, the

καὶ ᵂ οἱ ᵂ λοιποί· ⁴ ὁ δὲ θεός, ˣ πλούσιος ὢν ʸ ἐν ᶻ ἐλέει, διὰ τὴν πολλὴν ᵃ ἀγάπην αὑτοῦ ᵃἣν ᵃἠγάπησεν ἡμᾶς, ⁵ καὶ ὄντας ἡμᾶς ᵇ νεκροὺς τοῖς ᵇ παραπτώμασιν ᶜ συνεζωοποί- ησεν τῷ χριστῷ (ᵈ χάριτί ἐστε σεσωσμένοι) ⁶ καὶ ᵉ συν-

4. *o* is written twice in ℵ, but the first partly rubbed out.   om εν ℵ¹(ins ℵ³).
om αυτου D¹F [goth].

5. ins εν bef τοις παραπτωμασιν B syrr copt: om ℵ &c.   for τοις παραπτ., ταις αμαρτιαις D¹: τη αμαρτια F.   aft παραπτωμασιν ins και επιθυμιαις (*see ver* 1, *var read*) B.   aft συνεζ. ins εν (*see note*) B 17. 118 vulg(not am demid al) G-lat(altern) copt Chr Damasc lat-ff.   ins ου τη bef χαριτι D¹; ου F latt(not am) [Victorin] Aug.

actual objects of God's wrath against sin), **as also are** (not, were) **the rest** (of mankind : not Gentiles, as those hold who take the ἡμεῖς πάντες of Jews,— see above : nor, as Stier, the rest of the Jews who disbelieved : but, *all others, not like us, Christians*).   **4.**] The construction is resumed, having been interrupted (see above on ver. 1) by the two relative sentences, ἐν αἷς . . . ἐν οἷς. But (contrast to the preceding verse,—the ἔλεος and ἀγάπη, to the ὀργή just mentioned. **δέ** is, however, often used after a parenthesis, where no such logical contrast is intended, the very resumption of the general subject being a contrast to its interruption by the particular clauses : see examples in Klotz, Devarius, II. 376, 7) **God, being rich** (the participial clause states the general ground, and the following διὰ τ. πολλ. ἀγ., the special or peculiar motive, of συνεζωοπ., De W.) **in compassion** (for ἐν, see reff. οὐχ ἁπλῶς ἐλεήμων, ἀλλὰ πλούσιος· καθάπερ καὶ ἐν ἑτέρῳ (Ps. v. 7 ; lxviii. 13) φησὶν Ἐν τῷ πλήθει τοῦ ἐλέους σου· κ. πάλιν (Ps. l. 1) Ἐλέησόν με κατὰ τὸ μέγα ἔλεός σου, Chrys. **ἔλεος**, properly, as applying to our wretchedness before : cf. Ezek. xvi. 6),—**on account of His great love wherewith** (the construction may be attractive : but it would appear from ref. 2 Kings, to be rather a Hellenistic idiom) **He loved us** (the clause belongs, not to πλού. ὢν ἐν ἐλ., as Calv., al., and E. V. necessarily, by '*hath quickened*' following ; but to the verb below. ἡμᾶς are *all Christians ;* = ἡμεῖς πάντες in the last verse) **even when we were dead** (the καὶ belongs to, and intensifies, the *state predicated by* ὄντας νεκρούς ; and is therefore placed before the participle. It is not to be taken as a mere resumption of ver. 1 (Rück., al.), nor as the copula only (Meyer). His objection to the above rendering, that a quickening to life can happen only in and from a state of death, and therefore no emphasis on such a state

is required, is entirely removed by noticing that the emphasis is not on the mere fact ἐζωοποίησεν,—but on συνεζ. τῷ χριστῷ, with all its glorious consequences) **in our** (τοῖς, the π. which we committed) **trespasses** (see on ver. 1), **vivified** (not '*hath* vivified'—a definite act in time, not an abiding consequence is spoken of) **us together with Christ** (the reading ἐν τ. χρ. (see var. readd.) seems to have arisen either from repetition of the -εν in συνεζωοποίησεν, or from conformation to ver. 6.   It is clearly not allowable to render χριστῷ, *in Christ*, as Beza,—without the preposition. It is governed by the συν-, and implies not exactly as Chrys., ἐζωοποίησε κἀκεῖνον καὶ ἡμᾶς,—but that Christ was THE RESURRECTION and the Life, and we follow in and because of Him. The disputes about the meaning of ἐζωοποίησεν have arisen from not bearing in mind the relation in N. T. language between natural and spiritual death. We have often had occasion to observe that spiritual death in the N. T. includes in it and bears with it natural death as a consequence, to such an extent that this latter is often not thought of as worth mentioning : see especially John xi. 25, 26, which is the key-text for all passages regarding life in Christ. So here—God vivified us together with Christ : in the one act and fact of His resurrection He raised all His people—to spiritual life, and in that to victory over death, both spiritual, and therefore necessarily physical also. To dispute therefore whether such an expression as this is past (spiritual), or future (physical), is to forget that the whole includes its parts. Our *spiritual life* is the primary subject of the Apostle's thought : but this includes in itself our share in the resurrection and exaltation (ver. 6) of Christ.   The three aorists, συνεζωοποίησεν, συνήγειρεν, συνεκάθισεν, are all proleptical as regards the actuation in each man, but equally describe a past

ἤγειρεν καὶ [f] συνεκάθισεν ἐν τοῖς [g] ἐπουρανίοις ἐν χριστῷ
Ἰησοῦ, 7 ἵνα [h] ἐνδείξηται ἐν τοῖς [i] αἰῶσιν τοῖς [ik] ἐπερχομένοις τὸ [l] ὑπερβάλλον [m] πλοῦτος τῆς χάριτος αὐτοῦ ἐν
[n] χρηστότητι [o] ἐφ᾽ [o] ἡμᾶς ἐν χριστῷ Ἰησοῦ. 8 τῇ γὰρ

[f] trans., here
only ‡. intr.,
Luke xxii. 55
only. Exod.
xviii. 13.
[g] ch. i. 3 reff.
[h] Paul (Rom.
ix. 17, from
Exod. ix. 16.
1 Tim. i. 16.
[k] = Luke xxi.
v. 22 reff. P. Ps.
[n] Gal.

al.) only, exc. Heb. vi. 10, 11.　　　[i] here only. (see Mark x. 30 ‖ L.)
26. James v. 1.　　　1 ch. i. 19 reff.　　　[m] ch. i. 7 reff.
xxx. 19.　　　[o] Rom. xi. 22. see εἰς ἡμ., ch. i. 19.

6. om εν χ. ι. F [Orig₃(and int₄)] Hil Victorin Aug₂(ins₁).
7. om ver (homœotel) א¹(ins א-corr¹).　　　rec τον υπερβαλλοντα πλουτον, with
D³KL[P] rel : txt ABD¹Fא-corr¹ 17. 67² Orig₁ Eus.　　　ins τη bef χρηστοτητι D.
om ιησου D¹F æth-rom. (not F-lat.)

and accomplished act on God's part when He raised up Christ)—**by grace ye are saved** (this insertion in the midst of the mention of such great unmerited mercies to us sinners, is meant emphatically to call the reader's attention to so cogent a proof of that which the Apostle ever preached as the great foundation truth of the Gospel. Notice the perf. 'are saved,' not σώζεσθε, 'are *being* saved,' because we have passed from death unto life: salvation is to the Christian not a future but a past thing, realized in the present by faith)—**and raised us together with Him** (the Resurrection of Christ being the next event consequent on His vivification in the tomb) **and seated us together with Him** (the Ascension being the completion of the Resurrection. So that all three verbs refer strictly to the same work wrought on Christ, and in Christ on all His mystical Body, the Church) **in the heavenly places** (see on ch. i. 3, 20. "Obiter observa, non dixisse Apostolum : ' *et consedere fecit ad dexteram suam,*' sicut superiori capite de Christo dixerat : sedere enim ad dexteram Patris Christo proprium est ; nec cuiquam alteri communicatur : tametsi in throno Christi dicantur sessuri qui vicerint, Apoc. iii. in fine." Estius : and so Bengel) **in Christ Jesus** (as again specifying the element in which, as united and included in which, we have these blessings which have been enumerated—ἐν χρ. as in ch. i. 3, does not (Eadie) belong to τ. ἐπουρ. but to the verb, as an additional qualification, and recalling to the fact of our union in Him as the medium of our resurrection and glorification. The disputes as to whether these are to be taken as present or future, actual or potential, literal or spiritual, will easily be disposed of by those who have apprehended the truth of the believer's union in and with Christ. All these we have, in fact and reality (see Phil. iii. 20), in their highest, and therefore in all lower senses, in Him : they were ours, when they were His : but for their fulness in possession we are waiting till He come, when we shall be like and with Him),

7.] that **He might shew forth** (see Rom. ix. 23 : and for ἐνδείξηται, reff. The middle voice gives the reference which the English sentence itself implies, that the exhibition is for His own purpose, for His own glory (see ch. i. 6, 12, 14) —see note on Col. ii. 15. This meaning of *præ se ferre* is illustrated by Liddell and Scott sub voce : or far better by Palm and Rost, Lex. Beware of the rendering 'might give a specimen of' (Rückert, Eadie), which the word will not bear either here or in reff.) **in the ages which are hereafter to come** (what are they ? the future periods of the Church's earthly career,—or the ages of the glorified Church hereafter ? The answer must be given by comparing this with the very similar expression in Col. i. 26, 27, ... τὸ μυστήριον τὸ ἀποκεκρυμμένον ἀπὸ τῶν αἰώνων κ. ἀπὸ τῶν γενεῶν, νυνὶ δὲ ἐφανερώθη τοῖς ἁγίοις αὐτοῦ, οἷς ἠθέλησεν ὁ θεὸς γνωρίσαι τίς ὁ πλοῦτος τῆς δόξης αὐτοῦ κ.τ.λ. Here it is manifest (1) that the αἰῶνες from which the mystery was hidden are the past ages of this world ; (2) that those to whom, as here, God will make known the riches of His glory, are His saints, i. e. His church on earth. Therefore I conceive we are compelled to interpret analogously : viz. to understand the αἰῶνες ἐπερχόμενοι of the coming ages of the church, and the persons involved in them to be the future members of the church. Thus the meaning will be nearly as in ch. i. 12. The supposed reference to the future state of glory seems not to agree with αἰῶνες, nor with ἐπερχόμενοι :—nor with the fact that the second coming and future kingdom of Christ are hardly ever alluded to in this Epistle) **the exceeding riches of His grace in** (of the material of which this display of His grace will consist, the department in which it will find its exercise) **goodness** (see especially Rom. ii. 4) **towards us in** (not ' *through,*' as E. V.)

p ver. 5 reff.
q Rom. iii. 22,
30. 2 Cor. v.
7. Gal. ii. 16
iii. 26. Phil.
iii. 9. Col. ii
12 al., Paul.
1 Pet. i. 5.
r = Acts xv.
9.
s Rom. xiii. 11.
1 Cor. vi. 6,
8. Phil. i. 28.

ᵖ χάριτί ἐστε σεσωσμένοι ᑫ διὰ [τῆς] ᑫʳ πίστεως, ˢ καὶ
ᵗοῦτο οὐκ ᵗ ἐξ ὑμῶν, θεοῦ τὸ ᵘ δῶρον· ⁹ οὐκ ᵗ ἐξ ἔργων,
ἵνα μή τις ᵛ καυχήσηται. ¹⁰ αὐτοῦ γάρ ἐσμεν ʷ ποίημα,
ˣ κτισθέντες ἐν χριστῷ Ἰησοῦ ʸ ἐπὶ ᶻ ἔργοις ᶻ ἀγαθοῖς, ᵃ οἷς
ᵇ προητοίμασεν ὁ θεὸς ἵνα ᶜ ἐν αὐτοῖς ᶜ περιπατήσωμεν.

ABDFK
LPℵ a b
c d e f g
h k l m n
o 17.47

3 John 5.   t 1 Cor. i. 30.   2 Cor. iii. 5.   u = (& Paul) here
only. (Matt. ii. 11 al. Rev. xi. 10.) δωρεά, John iv. 10. 2 Cor. ix. 15 al.   v Paul (Rom. ii. 17
al³³., not Col.) only, exc. James i. 9. iv. 16. (so also καύχημα & καύχησις, exc. Heb. iii. 6.   James iv. 16.) Jer.
ix. 23, 24.   w Rom. i. 20 only.   Eccl. viii. 17.   x = ch. iii. 9. iv. 24.   Col. i. 16. iii. 10 al.
y = Gal. v. 13.   1 Thess. iv. 7.   z Paul (Rom. ii. 7. xiii. 3 al¹⁰.) only, exc. Acts ix. 36.   Heb. xiii. 21.
a attr., ch. i. 6 reff.   b Rom. ix. 23 only.   Isa. xxviii. 24.   Wisd. ix. 8 only.   c Rom. vi. 4.   2 Cor.
iv. 2. x. 3.   ch. v. 2   Col. ii. 6. iv. 5.   1 John i. 6, 7 al.   Prov. viii. 20.

8. αυτου χαριτι σεσ. εσμεν D¹ Syr copt æth.   om της (bef πιστεως) BD¹F[P]ℵ
17. 67² Chr: ins AD³KL rel Thdrt₂ Damasc Thl-comm Œc.   ημων DF d [Orig-cat
Petr] (Chrys Thl Œc in comm) Damasc.
9. καυχησεται B(Mai[not Tischdf Cod-Vat]) F.
10. for αυτου, θεου ℵ¹(txt ℵ-corr¹).   for χ. ιη., κυριω F.   for επι, επ F a c
g k m Chr₁ Thdrt Damasc : εν 73-4. 109 latt Aug lat-ff.

Christ Jesus (again and again he repeats
this "in Christ Jesus:" HE is the great
centre of the Epistle, towards whom all the
rays of thought converge, and from whom
all blessings flow; and this the Apostle
will have his readers never forget).

8.] For by grace (the article shews us the
import of the sentence—to take up and
expand the parenthetic clause χάριτί ἐστε
σεσωσμένοι above : but not barely so: that
clause itself was inserted on account of the
matter in hand being a notable example of
the fact, and this γάρ takes up also that
matter in hand—the ὑπερβάλλον πλοῦτος
κ.τ.λ.) ye are (perf.) saved, through [your]
(or [the], but the possessive article is preferable, see below: 'the' would make both
objective. The abstract, 'through faith,'
must be the rendering if the article be
omitted) faith (the dative above expressed
the objective instrumental condition of
your salvation,—this διά the subjective
medial condition: it has been effected by
grace and apprehended by faith): and this
(not your faith, as Chrys. οὐδὲ ἡ πίστις,
φησίν, ἐξ ὑμῶν : so Thdrt., al., Corn.-a-
lap., Beza, Est., Grot., Beng., all.;—this
is precluded (not by the gender of τοῦτο,
but) by the manifestly parallel clauses
οὐκ ἐξ ὑμῶν and οὐκ ἐξ ἔργων, of which
the latter would be irrelevant as asserted
of πίστις, and the reference of ver. 9 must
therefore be changed :—but, as Calv.,
Calov., Rück., Harl., Olsh., Mey., De W.,
Stier, al., 'your salvation ;' τὸ σεσωσμένοι
εἶναι, as Ellic.) not of yourselves, GOD'S
(emphatic) is the gift (not, as E. V. 'it
is the gift of God' (θεοῦ δῶρον),—τὸ δῶρον, viz. of your salvation : so that the
expression is pregnant—q. d., 'but it is a
gift, and that gift is God's.' There is
no occasion, as Lachm., Harl., and De W.,

to parenthesize these words : they form a
contrast to οὐκ ἐξ ὑμ., and a quasi-parallel
clause to ἵνα μή τις καυχήσ. below): not
of works (for ἐξ ἔργων, see on Rom. iii.
iv., and Gal. ii. 16), that no man should
boast (on the proposition implied, see on
Rom. iv. 2. ἵνα has in matter of fact its
strictest telic sense. With God, results
are all purposed ; it need not be understood, when we predicate of Him a purpose
in this manner, that it was His main or
leading aim ;—but it was one of those
things included in His scheme, which
ranked among His purposes).   10.]
For (substantiates vv. 8, 9. The English
reader is likely to imagine a contrast between 'not of works' and 'for we are His
workmanship,' which can hardly have been
in the mind of the Apostle) his handywork
are we (ποίημα, not, as Tert. and al., of
our original creation: "quod vivimus,
quod spiramus, quod intelligimus, quod
credere possumus, ipsius est, quia ipse con-
ditor noster est," Pelagius, in Harl.: this
is clearly refuted by the defining clause
below, κτισθ. κ.τ.λ., and the ποίημα shewn
to be the spiritual creation treated of in
vv. 8, 9), created in Christ Jesus (see ver.
15, ἵνα τοὺς δύο κτίσῃ ἐν αὐτῷ εἰς ἕνα
καινὸν ἄνθρωπον, and cf. Tit. iii. 5, where
the beginning of the new life is called
παλιγγενεσία. See also 2 Cor. v. 17 ;
Gal. vi. 15) for (see reff.: so Xen. Anab.
vii. 6. 3, καλεῖ αὐτοὺς ἐπὶ ξενίᾳ. See
Winer, edn. 6, § 48, c. e; Phrynichus, ed.
Lobeck, p. 475) good works (just as a tree
may be said to be created for its fruit:
see below), which (attraction for ἅ: not
'for which,' which would require ἡμᾶς
after the verb) God before prepared
(' ante paravit, quam conderet.' Fritz. in
Ellic. So Philo, de Opif. 25, vol. i. p. 18,

¹¹ Διὸ ^d μνημονεύετε ^d ὅτι ^e ποτὲ ὑμεῖς τὰ ἔθνη ^f ἐν ^f σαρκί, d Paul only.
Acts xx. 31.

οἱ ^g λεγόμενοι ^h ἀκροβυστία ὑπὸ τῆς ^g λεγομένης ⁱ περιτο- 2 Thess. ii. 5.
e = John ix.
13. Rom. vii.

μῆς ^f ἐν ^f σαρκὶ ^k χειροποιήτου, ¹² ὅτι ἦτε τῷ καιρῷ ἐκείνῳ 9. xi. 30 al.
f 1 Tim. iii. 16
reff.

^l χωρὶς χριστοῦ ^m ἀπηλλοτριωμένοι τῆς ⁿ πολιτείας τοῦ g Matt. x.

2. Acts iii. 2.   1 Cor. viii. 5.   2 Thess. ii. 4 al.   h Paul (Rom. ii. 25, &c.   1 Cor. vii. 17 al.) only,
   exc. Acts xi. 3.   Gen. xvii. 11, &c.   i Paul (Rom. as above [h].   1 Cor. vii. 19 al.) only, exc. John
vii. 22, 23.   Acts vii. 8. x. 45. xi. 2.   Exod. iv. 26.   k Mark xiv. 58.   Acts vii. 48. xvii. 24.   Heb.
ix. 11, 24 only.   Isa. ii. 18, of idols.   l John x. 5.   Rom. iii. 21 al.   m ch. iv. 18.   Col.
i. 21 only.   Ps. lxviii. 8.   n = here (Acts xxii. 28) only †.   2 Macc. iv. 11.

11. δια τουτο μνημονευοντες υμ. οι ποτε κ.τ.λ. F Dial₁.   rec υμεις bef ποτε (for euphony), with D³ [F, see above] KL[P]ℵ³ rel vss ff : txt ABD¹ℵ¹ m 17 vulg Dial₁ Cyr Did Ambr Jer.

12. rec ins εν bef τω καιρω (explanatory), with D³KL[P] rel vulg copt goth Orig-cat Dial Tert : om ABD¹Fℵ 17 tol(and F-lat) [Mcion₂] Chr-comm Epiph Cyr [Orig-

ὁ θεὸς τὰ ἐν κόσμῳ πάντα προητοίμασεν : Wisd. ix. 8, μίμημα σκηνῆς ἁγίας ἣν προητοίμασας ἀπ᾽ ἀρχῆς. The sentiment is the same as that in John v. 36, τὰ ἔργα ἃ ἔδωκέν μοι ὁ πατὴρ ἵνα τελειώσω αὐτά. To recur to the similitude used above, we might say of the trees,—they were created for fruits which God before prepared that they should bear them : i.e. defined and assigned to each tree its own, in form, and flavour, and time of bearing. So in the course of God's providence, our good works are marked out for and assigned to each one of us. See the doctrine of præ-existence in God explained in Delitzsch's biblische Psychologie, p. 23 ff. Stier's view, after Bengel, is that the verb προητ. is *neuter*, having no accusative after it,—'*for which God made preparation*, &c. :' but this usage of the compound verb wants example) **that we should walk in them.** Thus the truth of the maxim "bona opera non præcedunt justificandum, sed sequuntur justificatum" (see Harl.) is shewn. The sentiment is strictly pauline (against De W. and Baur), —in the spirit of Rom. xii., Gal. v. 22, 25, &c.

B. 11—22.] HORTATORY EXPANSION OF THE FOREGOING INTO DETAIL : REMIND-ING THEM, WHAT THEY ONCE WERE (vv. 11, 12); WHAT THEY WERE NOW IN CHRIST (vv. 13 - 22).   **11.] Where-fore** (since so many and great blessings are given by God to His people, among whom ye are) **remember, that once ye, the** (i. e. who belonged to the category of the) **Gentiles in the flesh** (i. e. in their corporeal condition of uncircumcision : 'præputium profani hominis indicium est,' Calv.—construction see below), **who are called (the) uncircumcision by that which is called (the) circumcision in the flesh wrought by hands** (this last addition ἐν σαρκὶ χειρ. seems made by the Apostle, not to throw discredit on circumcision, but as a reserve, περιτομή having a higher

and spiritual application : q.d.—'but they have it only in the flesh, and not in the heart.' As Ellic. well states the case— "The Gentiles were called, and *were* the ἀκροβυστία : the Jews were called, but were not truly the περιτομή." See Col. ii. 11),   **12.]** that ye were (the ὅτι takes up again the ὅτι in ver. 11, after the relative clause,—and the τῷ κ. ἐκείνῳ takes up the ποτέ there. It is not a broken construction, but only a repeti-tion; 'that, I say . . . .') **at that time** (when ye were,—not τὰ ἔθνη ἐν σαρκί, which ye are now, and which is carefully divided from ποτέ above by ὑμεῖς,—but that which is implied in ποτέ,—heathens, before your conversion to Christ. On the dative of time without the preposition ἐν, see Kühner, vol. ii. § 569, and remarks on its difference from the genitive and accusative) **without Christ** (separate from, having no part in, the promised Messiah. That this is the sense, is evident from ver. 13 : see below. The words χωρ. χρ. are not a defining clause to ἦτε ἀπηλ-λοτρ., as Lachmann points them, and De W. and Eadie render : 'that ye were, being without Christ, &c.' The arrange-ment would thus be harsh and clumsy beyond all precedent) **alienated from** (οὐκ εἶπε, κεχωρισμένοι . . . . . πολλὴ τῶν ῥημάτων ἡ ἔμφασις, πολὺν δεικνύσα τὸν χωρισμόν. ἐπεὶ καὶ Ἰσραηλῖται τῆς πολιτείας ἦσαν ἐκτός, ἀλλ᾽ οὐχ ὡς ἀλλότριοι ἀλλ᾽ ὡς ῥάθυμοι, κ. τῶν δια-θηκῶν ἐξέπεσον, ἀλλ᾽ οὐχ ὡς ξένοι, ἀλλ᾽ ὡς ἀνάξιοι, Chr. Gentiles and Jews were once united in the hope of re-demption—this was constituted, on the apostasy of the nations, into a definite πολιτεία for the Jews, from which and its blessings the Gentiles were alienated) **the commonwealth** (πολιτεία is both *polity*, *state* (objective),—τῶν τὴν πόλιν οἰκούν-των τάξις τις, Aristot. Polit. iii. 1,—and *right of citizenship*, ref. Acts. The former appears best here, on account of

o – & constr., here only.
Soph. Œd. Tyr. 219, 220.
p Acts iii. 25.
Heb. vii. 22 al. fr. Ezek. xxxiv. 25. plur., Rom. ix. 4. Gal. iv. 24 only.

Ἰσραὴλ καὶ º ξένοι τῶν ᵖ διαθηκῶν τῆς ᑫ ἐπαγγελίας, ᵃᴮᴰᶠᴷ
ἐλπίδα μὴ ἔχοντες καὶ ʳ ἄθεοι ἐν τῷ κόσμῳ· 13 ˢ νυνὶ δὲ
ᵗ ἐν χριστῷ Ἰησοῦ ὑμεῖς οἱ ᵘ ποτὲ ὄντες ᵛ μακρὰν ἐγενήθητε ʷ ἐγγὺς ˣ ἐν τῷ αἵματι τοῦ χριστοῦ. 14 αὐτὸς γάρ

ᴸᴾℵ a b
c d e f g
h k l m n
o 17. 47

q Gal. iv. 23. Heb. iv. 1 al. Amos ix. 6.   r here only †.   s Paul (Acts xxii.
1. xxiv. 13. Rom. vi. 22 al.) only, exc. Heb. viii. 6. Deut. x. 22.   t Rom. xvi. 7. Gal. i. 22.
u ver. 11 reff.   v ver. 17. Matt. viii. 30. Luke xv. 20. Acts ii. 39. xvii. 27. xxii. 21 (Paul). Isa. lvii.
19. Dan. ix. 7 Theod.   w abs., John xix. 42. Phil. iv. 5. Jer. xxxii. (xxv.) 26.   x Luke
xxii. 20. Rom. iii. 25. v. 9. Heb. x. 19. Rev. i. 5. v. 9.

intᵗ] Victorin Jer Aug.   [at end add τουτω F vulg Orig₃(and int₁).]

13. [om ιησ. L Iren Orig-int₁ Tert₁ Victorin.]   rec εγγυς bef εγενηθητε, with
DFKL[P] rel Chr Thdrt Damasc : txt ABℵ m 17 [47] vulg(and F-lat) goth Dial
Epiph [Cyr-p] Iren-int [Orig-int] Tert [Victorin].

ἀπηλλοτρ., which seems to require as its reference an objective external reality) of Israel (either as synonymous genitive, 'that commonwealth which is designated by the term Israel,' or possessive (as Ellic.) 'that commonwealth which Israel possessed.' I prefer the former, as more simple) and strangers from (so Soph. Œd. Tyr. 219, ἄʼγὼ ξένος μὲν τοῦ λόγου τοῦδʼ ἐξερῶ, ξένος δὲ τοῦ πραχθέντος. The genitive may be explained either 1) as one of the quality, as in μέλεος ἥβης, εὐδαίμων μοίρας,—or as 2) one of privation = negative of possession, ξένος being resolved into οὐ μέτοχος. This latter is perhaps the best. See Bernhardy, p. 171 ff.; Kühner, ii. 163) the covenants of the promise (τίνες ἦσαν αἱ δ. τ. ἐπ.; "Σοὶ κ. τῷ σπέρματί σου δώσω τ. γῆν ταύτην," κ. ὅσα ἕτερα ἐπηγγείλατο, Chrys. See note on Rom. ix. 4. The meaning here, as there, has been mistaken (Calv. al.) to be 'the two tables of the law.' Cf. Wisd. xviii. 22; Sir. xliv. 11), not having (μή on account of the subjective colouring given to the whole sentence by μνημονεύετε. So in ἀπιστοῦντες αὐτὸν μὴ ἥξειν, Thuc. ii. 101 : ὃ ἂν γνῶσι δυνάμενον μὲν χάριν ἀποδιδόναι, μὴ ἀποδιδόντα δέ, Xen. Cyr. i. 2. 7 : ψυχὴν σκοπῶν φιλόσοφόν τε καὶ μή, Plato, Rep. p. 486 B. See Winer, § 55. 5; Kühner, ii. § 715. 3) hope (not 'covenanted hope' (τὴν ἐλπ.),—but 'hope' at all. The emphatic position of ἐλπίδα makes this the more necessary) and without God (this is the best rendering, as it leaves ἄθεος in its latitude of meaning. It may be taken either 1) actively, 'denying God,' 'atheist,' 2) in a neuter sense (see Ellic.)—'ignorant of God' (ἔρημοι θεογνωσίας, Thdrt.: see Gal. iv. 8; 1 Thess. iv. 5, where the Gentiles are described as οὐκ εἰδότες τ. θεόν), or 3) passively, 'forsaken of God' (so Soph. Œd. Tyr. 661, ἐπεὶ ἄθεος ἄφιλος ὅ τι πύματον ὀλοίμαν : ib. 254, τῇσδέ τε γῆς, ὧδʼ ἀκάρπως καθέως ἐφθαρμένης). This latter meaning is best

here, on account of the passive character of the other descriptive clauses) in the world (contrast to the πολιτεία τοῦ Ἰσρ. "He subjoins to the godless 'How,' the godless 'Where,'" Mey. Olsh. understands, 'in this wicked world, in which we have so much need of divine guidance,' which is hardly in the simple words: Rück., 'in God's world,' contrast to ἄθεοι. These words must not be separated, as some, from ἄθεοι). 13.] But now (contrast to ἐν τῷ καιρῷ ἐκείνῳ) in Christ (not merely ἐν χριστῷ as you were χωρὶς χριστοῦ, but more—in a personal Messiah, whom you know as) Jesus (there is hardly a reference to the meaning of Jesus —much rather to its personal import— q. d. 'Now in Jesus the Christ') ye who once were far off were brought (keep the historic tense : it is the effect of a definite event of which he is speaking. The passive sense of the passive form ἐγενήθητε is well kept where the context justifies it, but must not always be pressed : see Ellic.'s note on ch. iii. 7) near (it was a common Jewish way of speaking, to designate the Gentiles as 'far off.' So Bereshith rabba, in Schöttg., Hor. Heb. in locum, 'Quicunque gentilem appropinquare facit, eumque ad religionem Judaicam perducit, idem est ac si creasset ipsum.' See also reff. Isa. and Dan.) in (or the instrument by which, but more—the symbol of a fact in which —the seal of a covenant in which,—your nearness to God consists. I prefer 'in' to 'by,' as wider, and better representing the Apostle's idea. The difference between ἐν here and διά in ch. i. 7 is, that there the blood of Christ is spoken of specifically, as the medium of our ἀπολύτρωσις—here inclusively, as representing the ἀπολύτρωσις. ἐν would have served there, and διά here, but the logical exactness of both would have been weakened by the change) the blood of Christ (see remarks on ch. i. 7). 14.] For He (there certainly is an emphasis on αὐτός, as Rück., Harl., Mey., Ellic., Eadie, 'He and none

ἔστιν ἡ ^y εἰρήνη ἡμῶν, ὁ ποιήσας τὰ ἀμφότερα ἓν καὶ τὸ ^z μεσότοιχον τοῦ ^a φραγμοῦ ^b λύσας, 15 _rἣν ^c ἔχθραν, ἐν τῇ σαρκὶ αὐτοῦ, τὸν ^d νόμον τῶν ^d ἐντολῶν ἐν ^e δόγμασιν ^f καταργήσας, ἵνα τοὺς δύο ^g κτίσῃ ^h ἐν ^h αὐτῷ ⁱ εἰς

y = here only. see Rom. v. 1.
z here only †.
a Matt. xxi. 33
‖ Mk. Luke xiv. 23 only.
Num. xxii. 24.
b = John ii. 19.
2 Pet. iii. 10,

11, 12. Esdr. i. 55 (52). c ver. 16. Luke xxiii. 12. Rom. viii. 7. Gal. v.20. James iv. 4
only. Gen. iii. 15. d here only. see Rom. iii. 27. vii. 2. viii. 2. Sir. xxxix. 8. e Luke
ii. 1. Acts xvi. 4. xvii. 7. Col. ii. 14 only. Ezek. xx. 26 B(but appy error) only. Dan. vi. 9 al. Theod.
f Luke xiii. 7. but = Paul (Rom. iii. 3 al. fr.) only, exc. Heb. ii. 14. Ezra iv. 21, 23. v. 5. vi. 8 only.
g ver. 10 reff. h = ch. i. 11 al. fr. i = Matt. xxvii. 51 ‖ Mk. Rev. xvi. 19. Judg. ix. 43.

15. rec εαυτω [see note], with DKLℵ³ rel Eus Epiph Ath₂ Chr Cyr₃ Thdrt Damasc Thl Œc: txt ABF[P]ℵ¹ m 17 Procop.

other.' This can hardly be denied by any one who will read through the whole from ver. 11, and mark the repetitions, χριστοῦ —χριστῷ Ἰησοῦ—τοῦ χριστοῦ, which this αὐτός takes up) is our peace (not by metonymy for εἰρηνοποιός, but in the widest and most literal sense, our peace. He did not make our peace and then retire, leaving us to enjoy that peace,—but is Himself its medium and its substance; His making both one was no external reconciliation, but the taking both, their common nature, on and into Himself,—see ver. 15. Bear in mind the multitude of prophetic passages which connect peace with Him, Isa. ix. 5, 6; lii. 7; liii. 5; lvii. 19; Micah v. 5; Hag. ii. 9; Zech. ix. 10: also Luke ii. 14; John xiv. 27; xx. 19, 21, 26. And notice that already the complex idea of the whole verse, that of uniting both Jews and Gentiles in one reconciliation to God, begins to appear: for He is our Peace, not only as reconciling Jew to Gentile, not as bringing the far-off Gentile near to the Jew, but as reconciling both, united, to God; as bringing the far-off Gentile, and the near Jew, both into peace with God. For want of observing this the sense has been much obscured: see below) who made (specification, how He is our peace. Better 'made,' than 'hath made:' the latter is true, but it is the historic fact which is here brought out) both (Jews and Gentiles; not 'man and God,' as Stier: cf. vv. 15, 16. Neuter, as abstract,—both things, both elements) one, and (epexegetic—'namely, * in that he') threw down the middle wall of the fence (i. e. the middle wall which belonged to—was a necessary part of the carrying out of—the φραγμός. The primary allusion seems to be to the rending of the veil at the crucifixion: not that that veil separated Jew and Gentile, but that it, the chief symbol of separation from God, included in its removal the admission to Him of that one body into which Christ made Jew and Gentile. This complex idea is before the Apostle throughout the sentence: and necessarily; for the reconcilia-

tion which Christ effected between Jew and Gentile was in fact only a subordinate step of the great reconciliation of both to God, which He effected by His sacrifice in the flesh,—and in speaking of one he speaks of the other also. The φραγμός, from what has been said above, is more general in sense than the μεσότοιχον; is in fact the whole arrangement, of which that was but an instrument—the separation itself, consequent on a system of separation: it = therefore the whole legal system, ceremonial and moral, which made the whole separation,—of Jew from Gentile,—and in the background, of both from God), the enmity (not, of Jew and Gentile: so strong a term is not justified as applying to their separation, nor does such a reference satisfy ver. 16,—see there;— but, the enmity in which both were involved against God, see Rom. viii. 7. τὴν ἔχθ. is in apposition with τὸ μεσότ. This enmity was the real cause of separation from God, and in being so, was the inclusive, mediate cause of the separation between Jew and Gentile. Christ, by abolishing the first, abolished the other also: see below) in His flesh (to be joined not with καταργήσας, as most Commentators, which is very harsh, breaking the parallelism, and making the instrumental predication precede the verb, which is not the character of this passage;—but with λύσας. Christ destroyed the μεσ., i. e. the ἔχθρα, in, or by, His flesh; see on ver. 16, where the same idea is nearly repeated. It was in His crucified flesh, which was ἐν ὁμοιώματι σαρκὸς ἁμαρτίας, that He slew this enmity. The rendering, 'the enmity which was in His flesh,' would certainly in this case require the specifying article τήν, besides being very questionable in sense), — having done away the law of decretory commandments (this law was the φραγμός,—the great exponent of the ἔχθρα. Its specific nature was that it consisted in commandments, decretorily or dogmatically expressed; — in ἐντολαὶ-ἐν-δόγμασιν. So

only. see
2 Cor. v. 17.
Gal. vi. 15.
1 James iii. 18
only. Isa.
xlv. 7. see
Matt. v. 9.
m Col. i. 20, 21
only †.
n Rom. xii. 4,
5. 1 Cor. x.
17 al.
23. iv. 13 al.   o Col. i. 20.
u here only. Esth. i. 14.

ἕνα ᵏ καινὸν ᵏ ἄνθρωπον, ¹ ποιῶν ¹ εἰρήνην, ¹⁶ καὶ ᵐ ἀπο-
καταλλάξῃ τοὺς ἀμφοτέρους ἐν ⁿ ἑνὶ ⁿ σώματι τῷ θεῷ ᵒ διὰ
τοῦ σταυροῦ, ᵖ ἀποκτείνας τὴν ᑫ ἔχθραν ἐν αὐτῷ. ¹⁷ καὶ
ʳ ἐλθὼν ˢ εὐηγγελίσατο ˢ εἰρήνην ὑμῖν τοῖς ᵗ μακρὰν καὶ
ˢ εἰρήνην ᵘ τοῖς ᵗᵘ ἐγγύς, ¹⁸ ὅτι δι' αὐτοῦ ἔχομεν τὴν ᵛ προς-

ABDF
KLPℵ a
b c d e f
g h k l m
n o 17. 47

p = here only.   q ver. 15 reff.   r = Matt. ii. 8. 9,
s Acts x. 36 [Rom. x. 15 (from Isa. lii. 7)] only.   t ver. 13 reff.
v Rom. v. 2. ch. iii. 12 only †.

16. εν εαυτω F 115 lat-mss-in-Jer latt syr (Syr om) lat-ff(not Tert Jer al).
17. rec om 2nd ειρηνην (as superfluous), with KL rel syrr Dial₂ Constt Eus Chr
Thdrt Tert : ins ABDF[P]ℵ 17 latt copt æth arm Eus Procop Cypr Hil.

that we do not require τὸν ἐν δόγ. or τῶν ἐν δόγ. This law, moral and ceremonial, its decalogue, its ordinances, its rites, was entirely done away in and by the death of Christ. See Col. ii. 13—15, notes. And the end of that κατάργησις was) **that He might create the two** (Jew and Gentile) **in Him** (it is somewhat difficult to decide between ἑαυτῷ and αὐτῷ. On the one hand, αὐτῷ is the *harder* reading : on the other, we have the constant confusion of αὐτ., αὑτ., and ἑαυτ., complicating the question. Whichever be read, the reference clearly must be to Christ, which, with αὐτῷ, is, to say the least, a harsh recurrence to the αὐτός of ver. 14) **into one new man** (observe, not that He might reconcile the two *to each other* only, nor is the Apostle speaking merely of any such reconciliation : but that He might incorporate the two, reconciled in Him to God, into one *new* man,—the old man to which both belonged, the enemy of God, having been slain in His flesh on the Cross. Observe, too, ONE new man : we are all in God's sight but one in Christ, as we are but one in Adam), **making peace** (not, between Jew and Gentile : He is ἡ εἰρήνη ἡμῶν, of us all : see below on ver. 17), **and** (parallel with the former purpose : not *'second* purpose' (Ellic., De W.), which yet must thus be the *first*. The καί is in fact just as in ver. 14) **might reconcile again** (most likely this is implied in the ἀπο. We have it only in Col. i. 20, 21, where the same sense, of *reinstating* in the divine favour, seems to be intended) **both of us in one body** (not His own human body, as Chrys. (who however seems to waver,—cf. ἕως ἂν μένωμεν ἐν τῷ σώματι τοῦ χριστοῦ,—between this and His mystical body), al.—but the Church, cf. the same expression Col. iii. 15) **to God** (if this had not been here expressed, the *whole* reference of the sentence would have been thought to be to the uniting Jews and Gentiles. That it is expressed, now shews that throughout, that union has been thought of only as a

subordinate step in a greater reconciliation) **by means of the cross** (the cross regarded as the symbol of that which was done on and by it), **having slain the enmity** (ἔχθρα has been taken here to mean the enmity between Jew and Gentile. But see on ver. 15 : and let us ask here, was this the enmity which Christ slew at His death ? Was this the ἔχθρα, the slaying of which brought in the ἀποκατάλλαξις, as this verse implies ? Does such a meaning of ἔχθρα at all satisfy the solemnity of the sentence, or of the next two verses ? I cannot think so : and must maintain ἔχθρα here (and if here, then in ver. 15 also) to be that between man and God, which Christ did slay on the cross, and which being brought to an end, the separation between Jew and Gentile, which was a result of it, was done away. Ellicott, who maintained the above opinion in his 1st edn., now agrees with that here insisted on) **on it** (on the cross : compare Col. ii. 15, notes : not in His body : see above) : **and having come, He preached** (how ? when ? Obviously after his death, because by that death the peace was wrought. We seek in vain for any such announcement made by Him in person after his resurrection. But we find a key to the expression in John xiv. 18, οὐκ ἀφήσω ὑμᾶς ὀρφανούς· ἔρχομαι πρὸς ὑμᾶς : see also ver. 28. And this coming was, by his Spirit poured out on the Church. There is an expression of St. Paul's, singularly parallel with this, and of itself strongly corroborative of the genuineness of our Epistle, in Acts xxvi. 23, εἰ παθητὸς ὁ χριστός, εἰ πρῶτος ἐξ ἀναστάσεως νεκρῶν φῶς μέλλει καταγγέλλειν τῷ τε λαῷ κ. τοῖς ἔθνεσιν. This coming therefore is by His Spirit (see on ver. 18), and ministers, and ordinances in the Church) **peace to you who were far off, and peace to those** (not "*to us*," for fear of still upholding the distinction where he wishes to merge it altogether) **that were nigh** (this εἰρήνη is plainly then not mere mutual reconciliation, but that

ἀγωγὴν οἱ ἀμφότεροι ἐν [w] ἑνὶ [w] πνεύματι πρὸς τὸν [x] πατέρα. [w ch. iv. (3) 4. Phil. i. 27.]

19 [y] ἄρα [y] οὖν οὐκέτι ἐστὲ [z] ξένοι καὶ [a] πάροικοι, ἀλλὰ ἐστὲ [x = Rom. vi. 4. 1 Cor. viii. 6. John, passim.]

[b] συνπολῖται τῶν [c] ἁγίων καὶ [d] οἰκεῖοι τοῦ θεοῦ, 20 [e] ἐποικο- [y Rom. v. 18. vii. 3. viii. 12. ix. 16, 18. Gal. vi. 10 al.]

δομηθέντες ἐπὶ τῷ [f] θεμελίῳ τῶν [g] ἀποστόλων καὶ [gh] προ- [P.]

Coι αμ-φοτεροι
...
ABCDF
KLPN a
b c d e f
g h k l m
n o 17. 47

z = Matt. xxv. 35, &c. xxvii. 7. Acts xvii. 21. Heb. xi. 13. 3 John 5 only. Ruth ii. 10.   a Acts vii.
6, 29. 1 Pet. ii. 11 only. Gen. xxiii. 4.   b here only †. Jos. Antt. xix. 2. 2.   c ch. i.
1 reff.   d (=) Gal. vi. 10. 1 Tim. v. 8 only. Isa. iii. 6.   e 1 Cor. iii. 10, &c. Col. ii.
7. Jude 20 only. Num. xxxii. 38 Ald. (οἰκ., AB) only.   f = Rom. xv. 20. 1 Cor. iii. 10, 11. 2 Tim.
ii. 19. Heb. vi. 1.   g Luke xi. 49. 1 Cor. xii. 28, 29. ch. iii. 5. iv. 11. Rev. xviii. 20.
h = as above (g). Acts xi. 27. xiii. 1. xv. 32. xxi. 10. 1 Cor. xiv. 29, &c. only.

19. aft αυτου ins οι αμφοτεροι εν ενι ℵ[1] (marked for erasure by ℵ-corr[1]). ℵ-corr[1]. εσχομεν rec om 2nd εστε (as superfluous), with D[3]KL[P] rel syrr copt gr-ff Tert Jer Ambr₁ : ins ABCD[1]Fℵ 17 latt goth Bas Victorin.

far greater peace which was effected by Christ's death, peace with God, which necessitated the union of the far off and the near in one body in Him. This is shewn especially by the repetition of εἰρήνην. See Isa. lvii. 19. Then follows the empowering reason, why He should preach *peace* to us both: and it is this ver. 18 especially which I maintain cannot be satisfied on the ordinary hypothesis of mere reconciliation between Jew and Gentile being the subject in the former verses. Here clearly the union (not reconciliation, nor is enmity predicated of them) of Jew and Gentile is subordinated to the blessed fact of an access TO GOD having been provided for both through Christ by the Spirit); **for** (not epexegetic of εἰρήνην, 'viz. that . . . .,' as Baumg.-Crus.) through Him we have our access (I prefer this intransitive meaning to that maintained by Ellic., al., '*introduction*,'—some (Mey.) say, by Christ (1 Pet. iii. 18) as our προσαγωγεύς (*admissionalis*, a word of Oriental courts), —not as differing much from it in meaning, but as better representing, both here and in Rom. v. 2, and ch. iii. 12, the *repetition*, the *present* liberty of approach, which ἔχομεν implies, but which '*introduction*' does not give), **both of us, in** (united in, 1 Cor. xii. 13) one Spirit (not '*one frame of mind*' (Anselm, Koppe, al.): the whole structure of the sentence, as compared with any similar one, such as 2 Cor. xiii. 13, will shew what spirit is meant, viz. the Holy Spirit of God, already alluded to in ver. 17; see above. As a parallel, cf. 1 Cor. xii. 13) **to the Father.** 19.] So then (ἄρα οὖν is said by Hermann (Viger, art. 292) not to be classical Greek. It is frequent in St. Paul, but confined to him: see reff. Cf. on Gal. vi. 10) **ye no longer are strangers and sojourners** (see ref. Acts, where certainly this is the sense. "πάροικος is here simply the same as the

classic μέτοικος (a form which does not occur in the N. T., and only once, Jer. xx. 3, in the LXX), and was probably its Alexandrian equivalent. It is used frequently in the LXX,—in eleven passages as a translation of גֵּר, and in nine of הֹשָׁב." Ellicott. 'Sojourners,' as dwelling among the Jews, but not numbered with them. Bengel opposes ξένοι to 'cives' and πάροικοι to 'domestici,'—and so Harless: but this seems too artificial), **but are fellowcitizens with the saints** (συμπολίτης is blamed by Phrynichus (ed. Lob. p. 172: see Lobeck's note) and the Atticists as a later word. But it occurs in Eur. Heraclid. 821, and the compound verb συμπολιτεύω is found in pure Attic writers: see Palm and Rost's Lex. πολῖται would not here express the meaning of *comrades, co-citizens*, of the saints. οἱ ἅγιοι are not *angels*, nor *Jews*, nor *Christians then alive* merely, but the saints of God in the widest sense,—all members of the mystical body of Christ,—the commonwealth of the spiritual Israel) **and of the household** (οἰκεῖοι, not as Harl., 'stones of which the house is built,' which is an unnatural anticipation here, where all is a political figure, of the material figure in the next verse: but 'members of God's family,' in the usual sense of the word) **of God,—having been built** (we cannot express the ἐπ-: the '*superædificati*' of the Vulg. gives it: we have the substantive 'superstructure,' but no verb corresponding. There is, though Harl. (see above) denies it, a transition from one image, a political and social, to another, a material) **upon the foundation** (dative as *resting upon* : * in 1 Cor. iii. 12, where we have εἴ τις ἐποικοδομεῖ ἐπὶ τὸν θεμέλιον . . . . ., the idea of *bringing and laying upon* is prominent, and therefore the case of motion is used. Between the genitive and dative of rest with ἐπί there is the distinction, that the genitive implies more **partial**

ABCDF
KLPℵ a
b c d e f
g h k l m
n o 17.47

φητῶν, ὄντος ⁱ ἀκρογωνιαίου αὐτοῦ χριστοῦ Ἰησοῦ, ²¹ ἐν

20. aft ακρογωνιαιου ins λιθου DF Orig₁ Eus Chr-txt.   for αυτου, του ℵ¹(txt ℵ-
corr¹): om Syr [copt] Orig_alie Chr-comm [Victorin].   rec ιησ. bef χρ., with
CDFKL[P] rel syrr [arm] Ps-Just Orig₁ Eus Victorin Jer₂: om ιησου (ℵ¹) m [æth]
Chr-txt [Tert]: txt ABℵ-corr 17 [47] vulg(and F-lat) copt goth Orig₄[and int₂] Thl
Ambrst Jer₂ Aug_sæpe.

overhanging, looser connexion,—the dative, a connexion of close fitting attachment. So in Xen. we have, ἐπὶ τῆς κε-
φαλῆς τὰ ὅπλα ἔφερον, partial, 'over,'—
οἱ Θρᾷκες ἀλωπεκίδας ἐπὶ ταῖς κεφαλαῖς
φοροῦσι, close, 'on:' see Donaldson's
Greek Gr. § 483) of the Apostles and
Prophets (how is this genitive to be understood? Is it a genitive of apposition,
so that the Apostles and Prophets themselves are the foundation? This has been
supposed by numerous Commentators, from
Chrys. to De Wette. But, not to mention the very many other objections which
have been well and often urged against
this view, this one is to my mind decisive,
—that it entirely destroys the imagery
of the passage. The temple, into which
these Gentiles were built, is the mystical
body of the Son, in which the Father
dwells by the Spirit, ver. 22. The Apostles
and Prophets (see below), yea, Jesus
Christ Himself, as the great inclusive
Head Corner Stone (see again below), are
also built into this temple. (That He
includes likewise the foundation, and is
the foundation, is true, and must be
remembered, but is not prominent here.)
Clearly then the Apostles and Prophets
cannot be the foundation, being here
spoken of as parts of the building, together with these Gentiles, and with
Jesus Christ Himself. But again, does
the genitive mean, the foundation which
the Apostles and Prophets have laid?
So also very many, from Ambrst., to
Rück., Harl., Mey., Stier, Ellic., both
edd. As clearly,—not thus. To introduce there here as agents, is as inconsistent as the other. No agents are here
spoken of, but merely the fact of the
great building in its several parts being
built up together. The only remaining
interpretation then is, to regard the genitive as simply possessive: 'the foundation
of the Apostles and Prophets,' = 'the
Apostles' and Prophets' foundation'—
that upon which they as well as yourselves are built. This exegesis, which I
find ascribed to Bucer only (in De W.),
seems to me beyond question the right
one. See more below.   But (2) who
are προφῆται? They have commonly

been taken, without enquiry, as the O. T.
Prophets. And certainly, the sense, with
some little straining, would admit of this
view. They may be said to be built upon
Christ, as belonging to that widest acceptation of His mystical body, in which
it includes all the saints, O. T. as well as
N. T. But there are several objections:
first, formal: the order of the words has
been urged against this view, in that
προφ. should have come first. I should
not be inclined to lay much weight on
this; the Apostles might naturally be
spoken of first, as nearest, and the
Prophets second—'the Apostles, yea and
of the Prophets also.' A more serious
formal objection is, the omission of the
article before προφ., thereby casting τῶν
ἀποστόλων κ. προφητῶν together as belonging to the same class. But weightier
objections are behind. In ch. iii. 5, we
have ὃ ἑτέραις γενεαῖς οὐκ ἐγνωρίσθη
τοῖς υἱοῖς τῶν ἀνθρώπων, ὡς νῦν ἀπεκα-
λύφθη τοῖς ἁγίοις ἀποστόλοις αὐτοῦ κ.
προφήταις ἐν πνεύματι, where unquestionably the προφῆται are N. T. Prophets; and again ch. iv. 11, καὶ αὐτὸς
ἔδωκεν τοὺς μὲν ἀποστόλους, τοὺς δὲ
προφήτας. And it is difficult to conceive
that the Apostle should have used the two
words conjoined here, in a different sense.
Even stronger is the consideration arising
from the whole sense of the passage. All
here is strictly Christian,—post-Judaic,
consequent on Christ's death, and triumph,
and His coming preaching peace by the
Spirit to the united family of man. So
that we must decide for προφ. being N. T.
Prophets: those who ranked next to the
Apostles in the government of the church:
see Acts xi. 27, note. They were not in
every case distinct from the Apostles:
the apostleship probably always including
the gift of prophecy: so that all the
Apostles themselves might likewise have
been προφῆται), Christ Jesus Himself
(the αὐτοῦ exalts the dignity of the
temple, in that not only it has among its
stones Apostles and prophets, but the
Lord Himself is built into it. The attempt of Bengel, al., to render αὐτοῦ,
'its,' and refer it to θεμελίῳ, will be seen,
by what has been said, to be foreign to

ᾧ πᾶσα ^k οἰκοδομὴ ^l συναρμολογουμένη ^{mn} αὔξει ⁿ εἰς ναὸν ἅγιον ^o ἐν κυρίῳ, ²² ἐν ᾧ καὶ ὑμεῖς ^p συνοικοδομεῖσθε ^q εἰς ^r κατοικητήριον τοῦ θεοῦ ^s ἐν πνεύματι.

k — Matt. xxiv. 1 ‖ Mk.
1 Cor. iii. 9.
2 Cor. v. 1.
(ch. iv. 29
al.) Ezek.
xvii. 17.

1 ch. iv. 16 only †.
o Rom. xvi. 11, 12 al. fr. P.
1 Cor. viii. 10.
18. vi. 18.   Col. i. 8.

m (-ξειν.) Col. ii. 19 only.   Isa. lxi. 11.
p here only †.   Esdr. v. 68 (65).
r Rev. xviii. 2 only.   Ps. lxxv. 2.
1 Pet. i. 12.   Jude 20.

n ch. iv. 15.   Gen. xxx. 30.
q = Matt. x. 18 al. fr. see
s Rom. ix. 1. ch. iii. 5. v.

21. rec aft πασα ins η (see note), with AC[P]ℵ-corr [arm Orig-cat₁] Thl : om BDFKLℵ¹ rel Ps-Just Clem [Orig-cat₁].
22. for θεου, χριστου B.

the purpose. Besides, it would more naturally be ὄντος αὐτοῦ ἀκρογ. . . . . . Bengel's idea, that on our rendering, it must be αὐτοῦ τοῦ, is refuted by such passages as καὶ αὐτὸς Δαυείδ, Luke xx. 42) **being the Head corner stone** (see, besides reff., Ps. cxvii. 22 ; Jer. xxviii. (li.) 26 ; Matt. xxi. 42; Acts iv. 11. The reference here is clearly to that Headstone of the Corner, which is not only the most conspicuous but the most important in the building : "qui, in extremo angulo (fundamenti, but qu. ?) positus, duos parietes ex diverso venientes conjungit et continet," Est. Builders set up such a stone, or build such a pillar of brick, before getting up their walls, to rule and square them by. I must again repeat, that the fact of Jesus Christ being Himself the *foundation*, however it underlies the whole, is not to be brought in as interfering with this portion of the figure),
21.] in whom (ὁ τὸ πᾶν συνέχων ἐστὶν ὁ χριστός, Chr. : not only so, but He is in reality the inclusive Head of the building : it all ἐν αὐτῷ συνέστηκεν, is squared and ruled by its unity to and in Him)· **all the building** (more properly πᾶσα ἡ οἰκοδ. : and to a *classical Greek ear*, any other rendering of πᾶσα οἰκ. than '*every building*,' seems preposterous enough. But 'every building' here is quite out of place, inasmuch as the Apostle is clearly speaking of but one vast building, the mystical Body of Christ : and πᾶσα οἰκ. cannot have Meyer's sense 'every congregation thus built in :' nor would it be much better to take refuge in the proper sense of οἰκοδομή, and render 'all building,' i. e. 'every process of building,' for then we should be at a loss when we come to αὔξει below. Are we then to render ungrammatically, and force words to that which they cannot mean ? Certainly not : but we seem to have some light cast here by such an expression as πρωτότοκος πάσης κτίσεως, Col. i. 15, which though it may be evaded by rendering 'of every creature,' yet is not denied by most Commentators to be intended to

bear this sense 'of all creation :' cf. also ib. ver. 23, ἐν πάσῃ κτίσει τῇ ὑπ' οὐρανόν. The account to be given of such later usages is, that gradually other words besides proper names became regarded as able to dispense with the article after πᾶς, so that as they said first πᾶσα Ἱεροσόλυμα (Matt. ii. 3), and then πᾶς οἶκος Ἰσραήλ (Acts ii. 36), so they came at length to say πᾶσα κτίσις (as we ourselves 'all creation,' for 'all *the* creation') and πᾶσα οἰκοδομή, when speaking of one universal and notorious building. Ellic. adds to the examples, πᾶσα γῆ, Thucyd. ii. 43, πᾶσα ἐπιστολή, Ignat. Eph. § 12, p. 656.
οἰκοδομή itself is a late form, censured by Phryn. (Lob. p. 421) and the Atticists) **being framed exactly together** (the verb (= συναρμόζω) sufficiently explains itself, being only found in these two places (ref.). Wetst. quotes ἡρμολόγησε τάφον from Anthol. iii. 32. 4, and Palm and Rost refer for ἁρμολογέω to Philip of Thessalonica, Ep. 78) **is growing** (there seems no reason why the proper sense of the present should not be retained. Both participle and verb imply that the fitting together and the growing are still going on : and the only way which we in English have to mark this so as to avoid the chance of mistake, is by the auxiliary verb substantive, and the participle. The bare present, 'groweth,' is in danger of being mistaken for the abstract quality, and the temporal development is thus lost sight of : whereas the other, in giving prominence to that temporal development, also necessarily implies the 'normal, perpetual, unconditioned nature of the organic increase' (Ellic.)) **to** (so 'crescere in cumulum,' Claudian in Piscator) **an holy temple in the Lord** (i. e. according to apostolic usage, and the sense of the whole passage, '*in Christ.*' The **ἐν ᾧ — ἐν κυρίῳ.** — ἐν ᾧ,—like the frequent repetitions of the name χριστός in vv. 12, 13, are used by the Apostle to lay all stress on the fact that Christ is the inclusive Head of all the building, the element in which it has its being and its growth. I would join

t Luke vii. 47.
Gal. iii. 19.
ver. 14. Tit.
i. 5, 11. 1 John iii. 12. Jude 16 only. Prov. xvii. 17.
i. 8. Philem. 1, 9. Heb. xiii. 3. Zech. ix. 12.

u Gal. v. 2 reff.

v Acts xxiii. 18. 2 Tim.

III. [1] Τούτου [t] χάριν [u] ἐγὼ [u] Παῦλος ὁ [v] δέσμιος τοῦ

ἐν κυρίῳ with ναὸν ἅγιον, as more accordant with the Apostle's style than if it were joined with αὔξει (αὔξει ἐν κυρ. εἰς ναὸν ἅγ.), or with ἅγιον (εἰς ναὸν ἐν κυρίῳ ἅγ.). The increase spoken of will issue in its being a holy temple in Christ), **22.] in whom** (not '*in which*,' viz. the temple—it is characteristic (see above) of this part of the epistle to string together these relative expressions, all referring to the same) **ye also** (not, as Eadie, '*even you:*' there is no depreciation here, but an exaltation, of the Gentiles, as living stones of the great building) **are being built in together** (with one another, or with those before mentioned. An imperative sense (' Ephesios hortatur ut crescant in fide Christi magis et magis postquam in ea semel fuerunt fundati,' Calv.) is not for a moment to be thought of: the whole passage is descriptive, not hortatory) **for** (Griesb. parenthesizes with two commas, ἐν ᾧ . . . . συνοικοδομεῖσθε, and takes this εἰς as parallel with the former **εἰς**. But this unnecessarily involves the sentence, which is simple enough as it stands) **an habitation of God** (the only true temple of God, in which He dwells, being the Body of Christ, in all the glorious acceptation of that term) **in the Spirit** (it is even now, in the state of imperfection, by the Spirit, dwelling in the hearts of believers, that God has His habitation in the Church : and then, when the growth and increase of that Church shall be completed, it will be still in and by the Holy Spirit fully penetrating and possessing the whole glorified Church, that the Father will dwell in it for ever. Thus we have the true temple of the Father, built in the Son, inhabited in the Spirit : the offices of the Three blessed Persons being distinctly pointed out: God, THE FATHER, in all His fulness, dwells in, fills the Church : that Church is constituted an holy Temple to Him in THE SON,—is inhabited by Him in the ever-present indwelling of the HOLY SPIRIT. The attempt to soften away ἐν πνεύματι into πνευματικῶς (ναὸς πνευματικός, Chrys., and so Thl., Œc., al., and even Olsh.) is against the whole sense of the passage, in which not the present spiritual state of believers, but their ultimate glorious completion (**εἰς**) is spoken of. See reff.).

III. 1—21.] AIM AND END OF THE CHURCH IN THE SPIRIT. And herein, *the revelation to it of the mystery*

of Christ, through those ministers who wrought in the Spirit : primarily, as regarded the Ephesians, through himself. *Thus first, of* HIS OFFICE AS APOSTLE OF THE GENTILES (1—13): *secondly,* under the form of a prayer for them, THE AIM AND END OF THAT OFFICE AS RESPECTED THE CHURCH : *its becoming strong in the power of the Spirit* (14—19). Then (20, 21) *doxology*, concluding this first division of the Epistle. 1—13.] (See above.) **On this account** (in order to explain this, something must be said on the construction. (a) Chrys. says :—εἶπε τοῦ χριστοῦ τὴν κηδεμονίαν τὴν πολλὴν ἐκβαίνει λοιπὸν κ. ἐπὶ τὴν ἑαυτοῦ, μικρὰν μὲν οὖσαν κ. σφόδρα οὐδὲν πρὸς ἐκείνην, ἱκανὴν δὲ καὶ ταύτην ἐπισπάσασθαι. διὰ τοῦτο καὶ ἐγὼ δέδεμαι, φησίν. This supplying of εἰμί after ὁ δέσμιος, and making the latter the predicate, is the rendering of Syr., and adopted by very many. It has against it, 1) that thus τούτου χάριν and ὑπὲρ ὑμῶν become tautological : 2) that thus ver. 2 and the following are unconnected with the preceding, serving for no explanation of it ('legationis, non vinculorum rationem explicat,' Castalio in Harl.) : 3) that the article ὁ with the predicate δέσμιος gives it undue prominence, and exalts the Apostle in a way which would be very unnatural to him,—'sum captivus *ille* Christi,' as Glass.,—and inconsistent with εἴ γε ἠκούσατε, &c. following. (ὐ) Erasm.-Schmidt, Hammond, Michael., Winer (and so E. V.) regard the sentence, broken at ἐθνῶν, as resumed at ch. iv. 1. Against this is the decisive consideration, that ch. iii. is no parenthesis, but an integral and complete portion of the Epistle, finished moreover with the doxology vv. 20, 21, and altogether distinct in subject and character from ch. iv. (c) Œc. says (and so Estius and Grot.) : ἀνταπόδοσίς ἐστι τούτου χάριν, οἷον· τούτου χ. ἐμοὶ τῷ ἐλ. π. ἁγ. ἐδόθ. κ.τ.λ. (ver. 8) σκόπει δὲ ὅτι ἀρξάμενος τῆς περιόδου κατὰ τὸ ὀρθὸν σχῆμα ἐν τῇ ἀποδόσει ἐπλαγίωσε, σχηματίσας τ. ἀνταπόδοσιν πρὸς τὸν περιβολῶν τύπον. But as Harl. remarks, this deprives τούτου χάριν of meaning : for it was not *because they were built in*, &c., that this grace was given to him : and, besides, thus the leading thought of the antapodosis in ver. 8 is clumsily forestalled in vv. 6, 7. (d) The idea that ver. 13 resumes the sentence (Camerar., Cramer, al.) is refuted by the

χριστοῦ [Ἰησοῦ] ὑπὲρ ὑμῶν τῶν ἐθνῶν, ² ^wεἴ ^wγε ^xἠκού-
...της d. σατε τὴν ^yοἰκονομίαν τῆς ^zχάριτος τοῦ θεοῦ τῆς ^zδοθείσης
ABCDF
KLPℵ a μοι ^aεἰς ὑμᾶς, ³ ὅτι ^bκατὰ ^bἀποκάλυψιν ^cἐγνωρίσθη μοι
bcefg
hklmn τὸ ^cμυστήριον, καθὼς ^dπροέγραψα ^eἐν ^eὀλίγῳ, ⁴ ^fπρὸς
o17.47

w Col. i. 23.
ch. iv. 21.
2 Cor. v. 3.
Gal. iii. 4
only. P.
x ch. i. 15 reff.
y = 1 Cor. ix.
17. (ch. i. 10
reff.)
z Gal. ii. 9 reff.
d = here

a = ch. i. 19 reff.   b = Gal. ii. 2 only.   (Rom. xvi. 25.)   c ch. i. 9 reff.
only. Rom. xv. 4.   Gal. iii. 1. Jude 4 only†.   Esdr. vi. 31 F (προσγρ. A). 1 Macc. x. 36 only.
e = here only. (Acts xxvi. 28, 29.) see 1 Pet. v. 12.   f = Luke xii. 47. 2 Cor. v. 10. Gal. ii. 14.

CHAP. III. 1. for χριστ., κυριου C.   om ιησου D¹Fℵ¹ o D-lat G-lat æth [Victorin₄]: ins ABCD²·³KL[P] ℵ-corr rel vulg [Orig-cat₁ Hil] : ιησ. bef χρ. Syr.   aft εθνων add πρεσβευω D 10 Ambrst-comm, *postulo* D-lat : something erased in 67.

2. for τ. θεου, αυτου A: [τ. χριστου P:] του θεου bef της χαριτος D¹·²F: om τ. θ. 115 Thl Ambrst-txt.

3. om οτι B D-lat [Victorin] Ambrst : κατ. απ. γαρ F goth.   rec εγνωρισε (*connecting with* τ. θεου *above*), with D³KL rel æth Damasc-txt Thl Œc: txt ABCD¹F[P]ℵ 17 [47] 67² latt syrr copt goth [arm] Clem [Hipp₁ Orig-cat₁] Chr Cyr Damasc-comm Jer Ambrst Pel.

insufficiency of such a secondary sentiment as that in ver. 13 to justify the long parenthesis full of such solemn matter, as that vv. 2—12; and by the improbability that the Apostle would resume τούτου χάριν by διό, with τούτου χάριν occurring again in the next verse, and not rather have expressed this latter in that case by καί. (e) It remains that with Thdrt. (on ver. 1, βούλεται μὲν εἰπεῖν ὅτι ταύτην ὑμῶν τὴν κλῆσιν εἰδὼς κ.τ.λ. δέομαι κ. ἱκετεύω τὸν τῶν ὅλων θεόν, βεβαιῶσαι ὑμᾶς τῇ πίστει κ.τ.λ., then on ver. 14, ταῦτα πάντα ἐν μέσῳ τεθεικὼς ἀναλαμβάνει τὸν περὶ προσευχῆς λόγον), Luth., Pisc., Corn.-a-lap., Schöttg., Beng., Rück., Harl., De W., Stier, Ellic., al., we consider ver. 14 as taking up the sense, with its repetition of τούτου χάριν, and the weighty prayer which it introduces, and which forms a worthy justification for so long and solemn a parenthesis. τούτου χάριν will then mean, 'seeing ye are so built in,' —stand in such a relation to God's purposes in the church) I Paul (he mentions himself here, as introducing to them the agent in the Spirit's work who was nearest to themselves, and setting forth that work as the carrying on of his enlightenment on their behalf, and the subject of his earnest prayer for them : see argument to this chapter above), the prisoner (but now without any prominence, or the very slightest: cf. Τιμόθεος ὁ ἀδελφός : it is rather generic, or demonstrative, than emphatic) of Christ [Jesus] (see ref. ; χρ. first, because it is not so much personal possession, as the fact of the Messiahship of Jesus having been the cause and origin of his imprisonment, which is expressed by the genitive) on behalf of you Gentiles (see ver. 13, where this ὑπὲρ ὑμῶν is repeated. The matter of fact was so :— his preaching to Gentiles aroused the

jealousy of the Jews, and led to his imprisonment. But he rather thinks of it as a result of his great office and himself as a sacrifice for those whom it was his intent to benefit),—if, that is (εἴ γε, 'assuming that:' see note on 2 Cor. v. 3. The Ephesians *had heard* all this, and St. Paul was now delicately reminding them of it. So that to derive from εἴ γε ἠκούσατε an argument against the genuineness of the Epistle, as De Wette does, is mere inattention to philology), ye heard of (when I was among you: his whole course there, his converse (Acts xx. 18—21) and his preaching, were just the imparting to them his knowledge) the œconomy (see note on ch. i. 10. It is not the apostolic office,—but the dispensation—*munus dispensandi*, in which he was an οἰκονόμος, of that which follows) of the grace of God which was given me (the χάρις δοθεῖσα (beware of joining δοθείσης with οἰκονομίαν by any of the so-called figures) was the material with respect to which the dispensation was to be exercised : so that the genitive is objective as in ch. i. 10) towards you (to be dispensed in the direction of, to, you)   3.] that (epexegesis of the fact implied in ἠκούσατε τὴν οἰκ. 'viz. of the fact that:' as we say, 'how that') by revelation (see reff.; the stress is on these words, from their position) was made known to me the mystery (viz. of the *admission of the Gentiles* (ver. 6) to be fellow-heirs, &c. See ch. i. 9, directly referred to below) even as I before wrote (not, 'have before written,' though this perhaps better marks the reference. 'Before wrote,' viz. in ch. i. 9 ff.) briefly (διὰ βραχέων, Chrys.: " Habet locutionem hanc Aristoteles rhet. iii. 2, p. 716, ubi de acuminibus orationis, quæ ex unius aut plurium vocum similium oppositione oriuntur, dicit, ea tanto ele-

g Matt. xii. 3.
2 Cor. i. 13 al.
fr. Isa.
xxxvii. 14.
h Matt. xxiv.
15. Rom. i.
20. 1 Tim.
i. 7. 2 Tim.
ii. 7. Prov.
i. 2.
i = Luke ii.
47. 1 Cor. i.
19 (from Isa.
xxix. 14).
Col. i. 9. ii.
2. 2 Tim. ii. 7 (Mark xii. 33) only.

ὃ δύνασθε g ἀναγινώσκοντες h νοῆσαι τὴν i σύνεσίν μου
k ἐν τῷ c μυστηρίῳ τοῦ χριστοῦ, 5 ὃ ἑτέραις l γενεαῖς
οὐκ c ἐγνωρίσθη τοῖς m υἱοῖς τῶν m ἀνθρώπων, ὡς νῦν n ἀπ-
εκαλύφθη τοῖς o ἁγίοις op ἀποστόλοις αὐτοῦ καὶ p προφήταις q ἐν q πνεύματι, 6 εἶναι τὰ ἔθνη r συγκληρονόμα καὶ
s σύνσωμα καὶ t συμμέτοχα τῆς u ἐπαγγελίας ἐν χριστῷ

ABCDF KLPℵ a b c e f g h k l m n o 17. 47

k constr., 2 Chron. xxxiv. 12. Neh. xiii. 7. Esdr. i. 33 (31).
l Acts xiv. 16. xv. 21. ver. 21. Col. i. 26. Isa. xli. 4.　　m here only. Ps. xxxv. 7 al.　　n & constr.,
Matt. xi. 25. 1 Cor. ii. 10. Phil. iii. 15. 1 Pet. i. 12. 1 Kings iii. 7.　　o Rev. xviii. 21 v. r. only.
p 1 Cor. xii. 28. Rev. xviii. 20, ch. ii. 20. iv. 11.　　q ch. ii. 22 reff.　　r Rom. viii. 17. Heb. xi. 9. 1 Pet.
iii. 7 only †.　　(-μεῖν, Sir. xxii. 26.)　　s here only †.　　t ch. v. 7 only †.　　u Gal. iii. 14 reff.

5. rec ins εν bef ετεραις (*on account of the double dative*), with syrr copt: om ABCD FKL[P]ℵ rel latt goth arm Clem₂ Orig Cyr-jer Chr Cyr₂ [Hil Victorin] Jer.　　αυτου bef αποστολοις DF copt Thl Hil [om αποστ. B].　　ins τω bef πνευματι F Chr. aft πν. ins αγιω D a b c o æth Vig: pref g.

6. [συνσωμα, so AB¹DFℵ 17. 47.]　　rec aft επαγγελιας ins αυτου, with D²·³FKL rel syr [goth] Thdrt Damasc Hil [Victorin]: om ABCD¹[P]ℵ 17 [47] demid(with tol) D-lat Syr copt [æth] arm Orig₃ Chr Cyr Jer Pel Sedul.　　rec [for χρ. ιησ.] τω χριστω, with DFKL rel [Hil Victorin]: txt ABC[P]ℵ 17 [47] vulg syr-w-ast copt goth [æth arm] Ambrst Pel.

gantiora esse, ὅσῳ ἂν ἐλάττονι, quanto brevius proferantur, et id ideo dicit sic se habere, ὅτι ἡ μάθησις, διὰ μὲν τὸ ἀντικεῖσθαι μᾶλλον, διὰ δὲ τὸ ἐν ὀλίγῳ θᾶττον γίνεται, quoniam ea ob oppositionem eo magis, ob brevitatem vero eo celerius percipiantur." Kypke, obss. sacræ, ii. p. 293),

4.] **by** (or, '*in accordance with ;*' perhaps '*at*' is our word nearest corresponding. The use of πρός is as in πρὸς τὸ ἀδόκητον τεταραγμένους) **which** (viz., *that which I wrote :* not the fact of my having written briefly, as Kypke) **ye can, while reading** (ἀναγ. absolute), **perceive** (aorist, because the act is regarded as one of a series, each of which, when it occurs, is sudden and transitory) **my understanding in** (construction see reff., and compare σύνεσιν ἐν πάσῃ σοφίᾳ, Dan. i. 17, also Dan. x. 1, LXX and Theod.) **the mystery of Christ** (by comparing Col. i. 27, it will clearly appear that this genitive is one of apposition :—the mystery IS Christ in all His fulness ; not of the object, '*relating to Christ*'), 5.] **which in other generations** (dative of time : so Luke xii. 20, ταύτῃ τῇ νυκτὶ τὴν ψυχήν σου ἀπαιτοῦσιν ἀπὸ σοῦ,—Matt. xvi. 21 al. : for the temporal meaning of γενεά, see reff.) **was not made known to the sons of men** ('latissima appellatio, causam exprimens ignorantiæ, ortum naturalem, cui opponitur Spiritus,' Beng. ; and to which, remarks Stier, ἁγίοις and αὐτοῦ are further contrasted) **as** (ἐγνωρίσθη μὲν τοῖς πάλαι προφήταις, ἀλλ' οὐχ ὡς νῦν· οὐ γὰρ τὰ πράγματα εἶδον, ἀλλὰ τοὺς περὶ τῶν πραγμάτων προέγραψαν λόγους, Thdrt.) **it has been now revealed** (we are com-

pelled in the presence of νῦν, to desert the aorist rendering 'was revealed,' which in our language cannot be used in reference to present time. The Greek admits of combining the two. We might do it by a paraphrastic extension of νῦν,—'as in this present age it was revealed') **to His holy** (see Stier's remark above. Olshausen says, "It is certainly peculiar, that Paul here calls the Apostles, and consequently himself among them, 'holy Apostles.' It is going too far when De W. finds in this a sign of an unapostolic origin of the Epistle : but still the expression remains an unusual one. I account for it to myself thus,—that Paul here conceives of the Apostles and Prophets, as a corporation (cf. ch. iv. 11), and as such, in their official character, he gives them the predicate ἅγιος, as he names believers, conceived as a whole, ἅγιοι or ἡγιασμένοι, but never an individual") **Apostles and Prophets** (as in ch. ii. 20, the N. T. Prophets—see note there) **in** (as the conditional element ; in and by) **the Spirit** (Chrys. remarks, ἐνόησαν γάρ· ὁ Πέτρος, εἰ μὴ παρὰ τοῦ πνεύματος ἤκουσεν, οὐκ ἂν ἐπορεύθη εἰς τὰ ἔθνη. ἐν πν. must not be joined with προφ. as Koppe, al. (not Chrys., as the above citation shews) ; for, as De W. remarks, the words would thus either be superfluous, or make an unnatural distinction between the Apostles and Prophets) —**that** ('namely, that'—giving the purport of the mystery) **the Gentiles are** (not, '*should be :*' a mystery is not a secret design, but a secret fact) **fellow-heirs** (with the Jews) **and fellow-members**

Ἰησοῦ διὰ τοῦ εὐαγγελίου, 7 οὗ ἐγενήθην ᵛδιάκονος · κατὰ
τὴν ʷˣδωρεὰν τῆς ˣʸχάριτος τοῦ θεοῦ τῆς ʸδοθείσης μοι
κατὰ τὴν ᶻᵃἐνέργειαν τῆς ᵃδυνάμεως αὐτοῦ. 8 ἐμοὶ τῷ
ᵇἐλαχιστοτέρῳ πάντων ᶜἁγίων ʸἐδόθη ἡ ʸχάρις αὕτη, τοῖς
ἔθνεσιν ᵈεὐαγγελίσασθαι τὸ ᵉἀνεξιχνίαστον ᶠπλοῦτος
τοῦ χριστοῦ, 9 καὶ ᵍφωτίσαι πάντας τίς ἡ ʰοἰκονομία

v = 1 Cor. iii.
5. 2 Cor. iii.
6. Col. i. 7, 23, 25 al.
w John iv. 10. Acts viii. 20. Wisd. xvi. 25.
x Rom. v. 15.
y Gal. ii. 9 reff.
z ch. i. 19 reff.
a here only.
b here only †. μειζό-
τερος, 3 John 4. only. Job v. 9. ix. 10. xxxiv. 24 only. i. 18 reff.
c ch. i. 1 reff.
h ch. i. 10 reff.
d ch. ii. 17 reff.
f neut., ch. i. 7 reff.
e Rom. xi. 33
g John i. 9. ch.

7. rec εγενομην (*more usual form*), with CD³KL rel : txt ABD¹F[P]א 17.   rec
την δοθεισαν, with D³KL rel syrr[?] goth Chr Thdrt Damasc Thl Œc: txt ABCD¹
F[P]א 17 [47] latt copt lat-ff.
8. rec aft παντων ins των, with [P] goth Cyr₁ Thdrt Thl: om ABCDFKLא rel
Orig [Cyr₁-p].   aft αυτη ins του θεου F.   rec ins εν bef τοις εθνεσι (*from* ||,
Gal i. 16, *where none omit it*), with DFKL rel latt syrr goth Dial Chr Cyr₁ Did Thdrt
Damasc lat-ff : om ABC[P]א o copt [Cyr₁-p].   rec τον α. πλουτον, with
D³KL[P]א³ rel Dial Cyr : txt ABCD¹Fא¹ 17. 67².
9. om παντας Aא¹ 67² Hil Jer Aug (not Tert all).   rec (for οικονομια) κοινωνια
(*explanatory gloss*), with e : txt ABCDFKL[P]א rel vss gr-lat-ff.

(of the same body) **and fellow-partakers
of the promise** (in the widest sense; the
promise of salvation :—the complex, including all other promises, even that chief
promise of the Father, the promise of the
Spirit itself) **in** (not to be referred to
τῆς ἐπαγγ., which would be more naturally, though not necessarily, τῆς ἐν,—
but to the three foregoing adjectives,—
in Christ Jesus, as the conditional element in which their participation consisted) **Christ Jesus** (see above on ch. ii. 13)
through the Gospel (He Himself was the
objective ground of their incorporation;
the εὐαγγέλιον, the joyful tidings of Him,
the *subjective medium* by which they apprehended it): **of which** (Gospel) **I became** (a reference to the event by which.
"The passive form, however, implies no corresponding difference of meaning (Rück.,
Eadie): γίγνομαι in the Doric dialect was
a deponent passive: ἐγενήθην was thus
used for ἐγενόμην, and from thence occasionally crept into the language of later
writers. See Buttm., Irregular Verbs, s. v.
ΓΕΝ—, Lobeck, Phryn. pp. 108-9." Ellic.)
a minister (see the parallel, Col. i. 23 :
and the remarks in Mey., and Ellic. on
διάκονος and ὑπηρέτης) **according to** (in
consequence of and in analogy with) **the
gift of the grace** (genitive of apposition,
as clearly appears from the definition of
the grace given in the next verse: the
grace *was* the gift) **of God which was
given to me** (δοθ., not tautological, or
merely pleonastic after δωρεάν, but to be
joined with what follows) **according to
the working in me of his power** (be-

cause, and in so far as, His Almighty
power wrought in me, was this gift of the
χάρις, the ἀποστολή, the office of preaching among the Gentiles, &c., bestowed
upon me).   **8.**] Instead of going
straight onward with ἐν τοῖς ἔθνεσιν κ.τ.λ.,
he calls to mind his own (not past, but
present and inherent, see 1 Tim. i. 15)
unworthiness of the high office, and resumes the context with an emphatic
declaration of it. **To me, who am less
than the least** (thus admirably rendered
by E. V. Winer, edn. 6, § 11. 2. b,
adduces ἐλαχιστότατος from Sext. Empir.
ix. 406, and μειότερος from Apoll. Rhod.
ii. 368—and Wetst. χερειότερος from Il.
β. 248, and other examples (Ellic. remarks
that Thuc. iv. 118 must be removed from
Wetst.'s examples, as the true reading
is κάλλιον)) **of all saints** (οὐκ εἶπε, τῶν
ἀποστόλων, Chrys. : and herein this has
been regarded as an expression of far
greater depth of humility than that in
1 Cor. xv. 8: but each belongs to the
subject in hand — each places him far
below all others with whom he compared
himself), **was given this grace** (viz.) **to
preach to the Gentiles** (τ. ἔθν. is emphatic, and points out *his* distinguishing
office.   There is no parenthesis of ἐμοί to
αὕτη as Harl. has unnecessarily imagined)
the unsearchable (reff.; " in its nature,
extent, and application." Ellic.) **riches of
Christ** (i.e. the fulness of wisdom, righteousness, sanctification, and redemption—
all centred and summed up in Him)
9.] **and to enlighten** (reff. ; not merely
externally to teach, referred to *his work*,—

i ch. i. 9 reff.
k (Matt. xi. 25.
xxv. 18 v. r.)
Luke x. 21.
1 Cor. ii. 7.
Col. i. 26
only. 4 Kings
iv. 27.
2. xi. 3 al. fr.
i. 21 reff.

τοῦ ᶦ μυστηρίου τοῦ ᵏ ἀποκεκρυμμένου ἀπὸ τῶν ˡ αἰώνων
ᵐ ἐν τῷ θεῷ τῷ τὰ πάντα ⁿ κτίσαντι, 10 ἵνα ᵒ γνωρισθῇ νῦν
ταῖς ᵖ ἀρχαῖς καὶ ταῖς ᵖ ἐξουσίαις ἐν τοῖς ᑫ ἐπουρανίοις διὰ

ABCDF
KLPℵ a
bcefg
hklmn
o 17.47

1 Col. i. 26. plur., Rom. i. 25. ix. 5. 1 Cor. ii. 7. x. 11. ch. ii. 7. 1 Tim. i. 17. Heb. i.
Ps. cxliv. 13. m Col. iii. 3. n ch. ii. 10 reff. o ch. i. 9 reff. p ch.
q ch. i. 3 reff.

aft των αιωνων ins και απο των γενεων F syr. om εν ℵ1. om τα D1F
Chr-ms. rec aft κτισαντι ins δια ιησου χριστου, with D3KL rel syr-w-ast Chr
Thdrt Thl Œc [Victorinappy]: om ABCD1F[P]ℵ 17 [47] latt Syr copt [goth] æth
arm Dial Bas Cyr Tert Jer Ambr Aug Ambrst Vig Pel.
10. om νυν F vulg D-lat Syr Orig Mcion-t Victorin.

but internally to enlighten the hearers, referred to *their apprehension :* as when the Apostles gave witness *with great power* of the resurrection of the Lord Jesus, Acts iv. 33. On St. Paul's mission to enlighten, see especially Acts xxvi. 18) all (no emphasis on πάντας, as Harl.—"not the Gentiles only, but all men,"—or as Mey. observes it would be πάντας (or τοὺς π. ?) φωτίσαι) **what** (the ellipse is supplied by εἰς τὸ εἰδέναι in ch. i. 18) **is the œconomy** (see on ch. i. 10) **of the mystery** ("the dispensation (arrangement, regulation) of the mystery (the union of Jews and Gentiles in Christ, ver. 6) was now to be humbly traced and acknowledged in the fact of its having secretly existed in the primal counsels of God, and now having been revealed to the heavenly powers by means of the Church." Ellicott) **which has been hidden from** (the beginning of) **the ages** (ἀπὸ τ. αἰώνων gives the temporal limit from which the concealment dated : so χρόνοις αἰωνίοις σεσιγημένου, Rom. xvi. 25. The decree itself originated πρὸ καταβολῆς κόσμου, ch. i. 4, πρὸ τῶν αἰώνων 1 Cor. ii. 7 : the αἰῶνες being the spaces or reaches of *time* necessary for the successive acts of created beings, either physical or spiritual) (in join with ἀποκεκρ.—hidden within,—humanly speaking, 'in the bosom or the mind of') **God who created all things** ("rerum omnium creatio fundamentum est omnis reliquæ œconomiæ, pro potestate Dei universali liberrime dispensatæ." Beng. The stress is on τὰ πάντα—this concealment was nothing to be wondered at—for God of His own will and power created ALL THINGS, a fact which involves His perfect right to adjust all things as He will. τὰ π., in the widest sense, embracing physical and spiritual alike), **10.**] **that** (general purpose of the whole : more properly to be referred perhaps to ἐδόθη than to any other one word in the last two verses. For this sublime cause the humble Paul was raised up,—to bring about,—he, the least worthy of the saints,—that to the

heavenly powers themselves should be made known, by means of those whom he was empowered to enlighten, &c. Cf. Chrys.: καὶ τοῦτο δὲ χάριτος ἦν, τὸ τὸν μικρὸν τὰ μείζονα ἐγχειρισθῆναι, τὸ γενέσθαι τούτων εὐαγγελιστήν) **there might be made known** (emphatic, as opposed to ἀποκεκρ. above—'no longer hidden, but ....') **now** (has the secondary emphasis : opposed to ἀπὸ τῶν αἰώνων) **to the governments and to the** (Stier notices the repetition of the article. It perhaps here does not so much separate the two ἀρχαί and ἐξ. as different classes, but serve to elevate the fact for solemnity's sake) **powers** (see ch. i. 21 and note) **in the heavenly places** (see ch. i. 3 note. The ἀρχ. and ἐξ. are those of the holy angels in heaven ; not, as has been vainly imagined, *Jewish rulers* (Locke, Schöttg.): *Christian rulers* (Pel.) : *good and bad angels* (Beng., Olsh.). These are excluded, not by ἐν τοῖς ἐπουρανίοις, see ch. vi. 12, but by the general tenor of the passage, as Ellic., who adds well : "evil angels more naturally recognize the *power*, good angels the *wisdom* of God") **by means of the Church** (ὅτε ἡμεῖς ἐμάθομεν, τότε κἀκεῖνοι δι' ἡμῶν, Chrys. See also Luke xv. 10 ; 1 Pet. i. 12 : and cf. Calvin's note here. "That the holy angels are capable of a specific increase of knowledge, and of a deepening insight into God's wisdom, seems from this passage clear and incontrovertible." Ellic. "Vide, quantus honos hominum, quod hæc arcana consilia per ipsos, maxime per apostolos, Deus innotescere angelis voluit. Ideo angeli post hoc tempus nolunt ab apostolis coli tanquam in ministerio majore collocatis, Apoc. xix. 10, et merito." Grot. But as Stier well notices, it is not by the Apostles directly, nor by human preaching, that the Angels are instructed in God's wisdom, but by the Church ;—by the fact of the great spiritual body, constituted in Christ, which they contemplate, and which is to them the θέατρον τῆς δόξης τοῦ θεοῦ) **the manifold** (πολυποίκιλος, so far from

τῆς [r] ἐκκλησίας ἡ [s] πολυποίκιλος [t] σοφία τοῦ θεοῦ, 11 κατὰ
[u] πρόθεσιν τῶν [v] αἰώνων ἣν ἐποίησεν [wx] ἐν τῷ [x] χριστῷ Ἰησοῦ
τῷ κυρίῳ ἡμῶν, 12 ἐν ᾧ [y] ἔχομεν τὴν [yz] παῤῥησίαν καὶ

r ch. i. 22 reff.
s here only †.
t = Rom. xi.
33. 1 Cor. i.
21, 24.
Rev. v. 12 al.
Dan. v. 11
w = Col. i. 16
1 John ii. 28. iii.
1. ch. vi. 19. Phil.
adverbially only

Theod.-compl.
reff.
21. iv. 17. v. 14.
i. 20. Col. ii. 15.
in Gospels.

u ch. i. 11 reff.
x 2 Cor. ii. 14. ch. i. 12, 20.
Prov. xiii. 5.
1 Tim. iii. 13. Philem. 8.

v gen. = here only. see note.
y Paul, here only. Heb. x. 19.
z Acts ii. 29 al4. 2 Cor. iii. 12. vii. 4.
Heb. iii. 6 al3. 1 John ii. 28 al. as above.

11. rec om 1st τω, with C³DKL[P]ℵ¹·³ rel Ath Chr Thdrt Damasc: ins ABC¹ℵ-
corr¹ m 17.—om τω χριστω ιησου F.

being a word found only here (Harl.,
Stier), occurs in Eur., Iph. Taur. 1149,
πολυποίκιλα φάρεα: in a fragment of
Eubulus, Ath. xv. 7, p. 679, στέφανον
πολυποίκιλον ἀνθέων, and twice in the
Orphic hymns, in this figurative sense:
πολυποίκιλος τελετή, v. 11; π. λόγος,
lx. 4) **wisdom of God** (*how* is the wisdom
of God πολυποίκιλος? It is all *one* in
sublime unity of truth and purpose: but
cannot be apprehended by finite minds in
this its unity, and therefore is by Him
variously portioned out to each finite race
and finite capacity of individuals—so that
the Church is a mirror of God's wisdom,
—chromatic, so to speak, with the rain-
bow colours of that light which in itself is
one and undivided. Perhaps there was in
the Apostle's mind, when he chose this
word, an allusion to the πτέρυγες περι-
στερᾶς περιηργυρωμέναι καὶ τὰ μετάφρενα
αὐτῆς ἐν χλωρότητι χρυσίου, the adornment of the ransomed church, in Ps. lxvii.
13. See Heb. i. 1; 1 Pet. iv. 10),
11.] **according to** (depends on γνωρισθῇ—
this imparting of the knowledge of God's
manifold wisdom was in accordance with,
&c.) **the** (not, '*a:*' after a preposition,
especially when a limiting genitive, as
here, follows, the omission of the article
can hardly be regarded as affecting the
sense) **purpose of (the) ages** (the genitive
is apparently one of time, as when we
say, 'it has been an opinion of years:'
the duration all that time giving the
αἰῶνες a kind of possession. If so, the
sense is best given in English by '*eternal*'
as in E. V.), **which** (πρόθεσιν) **He made**
(constituted, ordained. So Calv., Beza,
Harl., Rück. On the other hand, Thdrt.,
Grot., Koppe, Olsh., Mey., De W., Stier,
Ellic., would apply it to the *carrying out,
executing, in its historical realization.*
I can hardly think that so indefinite a
word as ποιέω would have been used to
express so very definite an idea, now introduced for the first time, but believe the
Apostle would have used some word like
ἐπετέλεσεν. Further, we should thus
rather expect the perfect; whereas the
aorist seems to refer back the act spoken

of to the origination of the design. Both
senses of ποιέω are abundantly justified:
see, for our sense, Mark xv. 1; Isa. xxix.
15: for the other, ch. ii. 3; Matt. xxi.
31; John vi. 38; 1 Thess. v. 24 al.) **in
Jesus our Lord the Christ** (or, '*in the
Christ,*' (namely) *Jesus our Lord.*' The
former is official, the latter personal. It
was in his Christ that He made the purpose: and that Christ is Jesus our Lord.
The words do not necessarily refer ἐποίησεν to the *carrying out* of the design.
They bind together God's eternal purpose
and our present state of access to Him by
redemption in Christ, and so close the
train of thought of the last eleven verses,
by bringing us again home to the sense of
our own blessedness in Christ. That he
says, ἐν τ. χριστῷ Ἰησ., does not, as Olsh.
and Stier, imply that the act spoken of
must necessarily be subsequent to the Incarnation: see ch. i. 3, 4: it is the complex
personal appellation of the Son of God,
taken from, and familiar to us by His incarnation, but applied to Him in His præ-
existence also), **12.]** **in whom** (for the
connexion, see note on last verse: in whom,
as their element and condition) **we have
our boldness** (not '*freedom of speech*'
merely, nor boldness *in prayer:* παῤῥησία
is used in a far wider sense than these, as
will appear by the reff.: viz., that of the
state of mind which gives liberty of speech,
cheerful boldness, 'fꞃeimuthigꜩeit,' Palm
and Rost's Lex.) **and (our) access** (see note
on ch. ii. 18: here the intransitive sense
is even more necessary, from the union
with παῤῥησίαν. We may confidently
say, that so important an objective truth
as our *introduction to God by Christ*
would never have been thus coupled to a
mere subjective quality in ourselves. Both
must be subjective if one is: the second
less purely so than the first—but both referring to our own feelings and privileges)
in confidence (τουτέστι, μετὰ τοῦ θαῤῥεῖν,
Chrys. Meyer remarks what a noble example St. Paul himself has given of this
πεποίθησις in Rom. viii. 38 f. πεποίθησις
is a word of late Greek; see Lobeck's
Phrynichus, p. 294) **through the faith**

a ch. ii. 18 reff.
b 2 Cor. i. 15.
iii. 4. viii. 22.
x. 2. Phil.
iii. 4 only. P.
4 Kings xviii.
19 only.
c ch. ii. 8 reff.
d obj. gen.
Acts iii. 16.
Gal. ii. 16 al.
fr.

[τὴν] ᵃπροσαγωγὴν ἐν ᵇπεποιθήσει ᶜδιὰ τῆς πίστεως ᵈαὐτοῦ. 13 διὸ ᵉαἰτοῦμαι μὴ ᶠἐγκακεῖν ᵍἐν ταῖς ʰθλίψεσίν μου ὑπὲρ ὑμῶν, ⁱἥτις ἐστὶν ᵏδόξα ὑμῶν. 14 τούτου ˡχάριν ᵐκάμπτω τὰ ⁿγόνατά μου ᵒπρὸς τὸν πατέρα, 15 ᵖἐξ οὗ πᾶσα q πατριὰ ἐν οὐρανοῖς καὶ ἐπὶ γῆς ʳὀνομάζεται, 16 ἵνα

ABCDF
KLPℵ a
bcefg
hklmn
o17. 47

e ver. 20. Col. i. 9. 1 John v. 14, &c. Ps. xxvi. 4.   f Luke xviii. 1. 2 Cor. iv. 1, 16. Gal. vi. 9. 2 Thess. iii. 13
only. L.P.† Prov. iii. 11 Theod.   g = John v. 35. Rom. ii. 23. 1 Thess. iii. 3 al.   h = Rom. v.
3. 2 Cor. vi. 4. Phil. iv. 14. Ps. xix. 1.   i attr., Mark xv. 16. Gal. iii. 16. ch. vi. 17. Phil. i. 20 al. fr.
k = 1 Cor. ii. 7. xi. 15. Phil. iii. 19. 1 Thess. ii. 20. Prov. xx. 29.   l ver. 1 reff.   m (in N.T.
always w. γόνυ.) Rom. xi. 4. xiv. 11. Phil. ii. 10 only. Isa. xlv. 24.   n see above (m). Mark iv.
19. Heb. xii. 12 al.   o = Luke xii. 3. 1 Cor. xiii. 12.   p = here only. Xen. Mem. iv. 6 12.
q Luke ii. 4. Acts iii. 25 only. Num. i. 18.   r ch. i. 21 reff.

12. [transp παρρησ. and προσαγ. D¹(F).] om 2nd την ABℵ¹ 17 : ins CDFKL [P]ℵ³ rel Ath Chr Thdrt Damasc.   for εν πεποιθησει, εν τω ελευθερωθηναι D¹.
13. rec εκκακειν, with CD³FKL[P] rel : txt ABD¹ℵ m 17 [47]. (See note on Gal vi. 9.)   for last υμων, ημων C c 17. 71-2. 80 copt arm.   [om last clause (hom.) 47.]
14. rec aft πατερα ins του κυριου ημων ιησ. χριστου (from ch i. 3, and simr passages; cf θεον και above. It wd hardly have been erased, as De W., as coming between πατ. and πατρια), with DFKLℵ³ rel latt syrr goth [arm Valent] Ps-Just [Hipp Orig₁(and int₄)] Chr Thdrt Damasc ₕ ₗ. Phot Tert Victorin Lucif: om ABC[P]ℵ¹ 17. 67² demid copt æth Thdot [Clem] Orig Did Meth Synod-ancyr-in-Epiph Cyr-jer₂ Cyr₃ Damasc Elias-cret Thl-comm_appy Jer_expr("non, ut in latinis codd. additum est, 'ad Patrem Dom. nostri J. C.,'—sed simpliciter 'ad Patrem' legendum") Aug₁ Cassiod-comm Vig.
[15. ουρανω P 47 Syr syr-mg goth Meth Orig-int₃.]

("ἐν χρ. points to the objective ground of the possession, διὰ τῆς πίστ., the subjective medium by which, and ἐν πεποιθ. the subjective state in which, it is apprehended." Ellic.) of (objective : = 'in:' of which He is the object: see reff.) Him.

13.] Wherefore ('quæ cum ita sint,' viz. the glorious things spoken of vv. 1—12: and especially his own personal part in them, ἐγὼ π., ἐμοὶ ἐδόθη, ἐγενήθην διάκονος:—since I am the appointed minister of so great a matter) I beseech you (not, beseech God,—which would awkwardly necessitate a new subject before ἐγκακεῖν: see below) not to be dispirited (not, 'that I may not be dispirited,' as Syr., Thdrt., Beng., Rück., Harl., Olsh. Such a reference is quite refuted by the reason rendered below, ἥτις ἐσ. δόξα ὑμῶν, and by the insertion of μου after θλ., which in this case would be wholly superfluous: not to mention its inconsistency with all we know of the Apostle himself) in (of the element or sphere, in which the faint-heartedness would be shewn : 'in the midst of') my tribulations for you (the grammatical Commentators justify the absence of the article before ὑπέρ by the construction θλίβομαι ὑπέρ τινος. This surely is not necessary, in the presence of such expressions as τοῖς κυρίοις κατὰ σάρκα, ch. vi. 5. The strange view of Harl., that ὑπὲρ ὑμῶν is to be joined with αἰτοῦμαι, needs no refutation), seeing that they are (not 'which is;' ἥτις is not = ἥ, but = 'quippe qui,' 'utpote qui :' see examples in Palm and Rost's Lex. ὅς, p. 547) your

glory (πῶς ἐστι δόξα αὐτῶν; ὅτι οὕτως αὐτοὺς ἠγάπησεν ὁ θεός, ὥστε καὶ τ. υἱὸν ὑπὲρ αὐτῶν δοῦναι, κ. τοὺς δούλους κακοῦν. ἵνα γὰρ αὐτοὶ τύχωσι τοσούτων ἀγαθῶν, Παῦλος ἐδεσμεῖτο, Chrys. Bengel compares ὑμεῖς ἔνδοξοι, ἡμεῖς δὲ ἄτιμοι, 1 Cor. iv. 10 : and this certainly seems against Stier's notion that δόξα ὑμῶν means 'your glorification,' 'the glory of God in you'). 14—19.] His prayer for them, setting forth the aim and end of the ministerial office as respected the Church, viz. its becoming strong in the power of the Spirit.

14.] On this account (resumes the τούτου χάριν of ver. 1 (see note there) :—viz. 'because ye are so built in, have such a standing in God's Church') I bend my knees (scil. in prayer: see reff.; and cf. 3 Kings xix. 18) towards (directing my prayer to Him : see Winer, § 49, h) the Father (on the words here interpolated, see var. readd.), from whom (as the source of the name: so Hom. Il. κ. 68, πατρόθεν ἐκ γενεῆς ὀνομάζων ἄνδρα ἕκαστον :—Soph., Œd. Tyr. 1036, ὥστ' ὠνομάσθης ἐκ τύχης ταύτης, ὃς εἶ :— Xen. Mem. iv. 5. 8, ἔφη δὲ καὶ τὸ διαλέγεσθαι ὀνομασθῆναι ἐκ τοῦ συνιόντας κοινῇ βουλεύεσθαι διαλέγοντας :—Cic. de Amicitia, 8, 'amor, ex quo amicitia nominata') every family (not 'the whole family' (πᾶσα ἡ πα. ἥ, or, less strictly, πᾶσα πατρ. ἥ), as E. V. The sense, see below) in the heavens and on earth is named (it is difficult to convey in another language any trace of the deep

ˢ δῷ ὑμῖν κατὰ τὸ ᵗᵘ πλοῦτος τῆς ᵘ δόξης αὐτοῦ ᵛ δυνάμει   s = Matt. xiii. 11.
ᵂ κραταιωθῆναι ˣ διὰ τοῦ πνεύματος αὐτοῦ ʸ εἰς τὸν ᶻ ἔσω   Acts ii. 4 al.
   t neut., ch. i. 7 reff.
   u ch. i. 18 reff.

v = Col. i. 11.   w Luke i. 80. ii. 40.   1 Cor. xvi. 13 only.   Neh. ii. 18.   x Acts xxi. 4.   Rom.
v. 5.   1 Cor. ii. 10 al.   y = ch. ii. 21 al.   z Rom. vii. 22. see 2 Cor. iv. 16.

16. rec (for δω) δωη, with DKL[P] rel Valent Ps-Just [Hipp] Orig-cat₁ Ath Mac Chr Cyr₂ Thdrt Damasc Thl Œc : txt ABCFℵ m 17 Orig-cat₂ Meth Bas Cyr₁.   rec τον πλουτον, with D³KL rel Ps-Just [Meth] Cyr₂: txt ABCD¹F[P]ℵ 67² [Orig-cat₂] Ath-ms Ephr, το πληθος 17.   ins εν bef δυναμει F copt.

connexion of πατήρ and πατριά here expressed. Had the sentence been 'the *Creator*, after whom every *creature* in heaven and earth is named,' all would be plain to the English reader. But we must not thus render ; for it is not in virtue of God's creative power that the Apostle here prays to Him, but in virtue of His adoptive love in Christ. It is best therefore to keep the simple sense of the words, and leave it to exegesis to convey the idea. πατριά is the *family*, or in a wider sense the *gens*, named so from its all having one πατήρ. Some (Est., Grot., Wetst., al.) have supposed St. Paul to allude to the rabbinical expression, 'the family of earth and the family of heaven :' but as Harl. observes, in this case he would have said π. ἡ πατρ., ἡ ἐν οὐρ. κ. ἡ ἐπὶ γ. Others (Vulg., Jer., Thdrt.,—ὃς ἀληθῶς ὑπάρχει πατήρ, ὃς οὐ παρ' ἄλλου τοῦτο λαβὼν ἔχει, ἀλλ' αὐτὸς τοῖς ἄλλοις μεταδέδωκε τοῦτο, — Corn.-a-lap.) have attempted to give πατριά the sense of *paternitas*, which it can certainly never have. But it is not so easy to say, to what the reference is, or why the idea is here introduced. The former of these will be found very fully discussed in Stier, pp. 487—99 : and the latter more shortly treated. The Apostle seems, regarding God as the Father of us His adopted children in Christ, to go forth into the fact, that He, in this His relation to us, is in reality the great original and prototype of the paternal relation, wherever found. And this he does, by observing that every πατριά, compaternity, body of persons, having a common father, is thus named (in Greek), *from that father*, —and so every earthly (and heavenly) family reflects in its name (and constitution) the being and sourceship of the great Father Himself. But then, what are πατριαί *in heaven?* Some have treated the idea of paternity *there* as absurd : but is it not necessarily involved in *any* explanation of this passage ? He Himself is the Father of spirits, Heb. xii. 9, the Father of lights, James i. 17 :— may there not be fathers in the heavenly Israel, as in the earthly ? May not the

holy Angels be bound up in spiritual πατριαί, though they marry not nor are given in marriage ? Observe, we must not miss the sense of ὀνομάζεται, nor render, nor understand it, as meaning '*is constituted*.' This is the fact, but not brought out here),   16.] that (see on ἵνα after words of beseeching, &c., note, 1 Cor. xiv. 13. The purpose and purport of the prayer are blended in it) He may give you, according to the riches of His glory (specifies δῷ, not what follows : give you, in full proportion to the abundance of His own glory—His own infinite perfections), to be strengthened with might (the dative has been taken in several ways : 1) adverbially, '*mightily*,' as βίᾳ εἰς οἰκίαν παριέναι, Xen. Cyr. i. 2. 2,— to which Meyer objects, that thus δύναμις would be strength on the side of the bestower rather than of the receiver, whereas the contrast with ἐγκακεῖν (?) requires the converse. This hardly seems sufficient to disprove the sense : 2) dative of the *form* or *shape* in which the κρατ. was to take place (Harl., al.), as in χρήμασι δυνατοὶ εἶναι, Xen. Mem. ii. 7. 7,—to which Meyer replies that thus the κραταιωθῆναι would only apply to one department of the spiritual life, instead of to all. But this again seems to me not valid : for '*might*,' '*power*,' is not one faculty, but a qualification of all faculties. Rather I should say that such a meaning would involve a tautology—'strengthened in strength.' 3) the instrumental dative is maintained by Mey., De W., al., and this view seems the best : '*with* (His) *might*,' imparted to you) by His Spirit (as the instiller and imparter of that might) into (not merely '*in*,' but '*to and into*,' as Ellic. : importing "the direction and destination of the prayed for gift of infused strength." κραταιοῖ, κατοικίζων εἰς τὸν χωρίζοντα ἔσω ἄνθρωπον τὸν χριστόν, Schol. in Cramer's Catena. Similarly Orig., ὥστε εἰς τ. ἔσ. ἄνθ. κατοικῆσαι τ. χριστὸν διὰ τῆς πίστεως, ib. Both rightly, as far as the idea of infusing into is concerned : but clearly wrong, as are the Gr.-ff. in general, in taking εἰς τ. ἔσ. ἄνθ. with what follows,

a Col. i. 19. ii. 9.
b ch. iv. 2. Col. ii. 2.
c Col. ii. 7 only. Isa. xl. 24.
d Matt. vii. 25. (Luke vii. 48 v. r.) Col. i. 23.

z ἄνθρωπον, 17 ᵃ κατοικῆσαι τὸν χριστὸν διὰ τῆς πίστεως
ἐν ταῖς καρδίαις ὑμῶν, 18 ᵇ ἐν ᵇ ἀγάπῃ ᶜ ἐρρἰζωμένοι καὶ
ᵈ τεθεμελιωμένοι, ἵνα ᵉ ἐξισχύσητε ᶠ καταλαβέσθαι ᵍ σὺν
πᾶσιν τοῖς ʰ ἁγίοις τί τὸ ⁱᵏ πλάτος καὶ ⁱˡ μῆκος καὶ ⁱᵐⁿ ὕψος

ABCDF KLPℵ a
b c e f g h k l m n o 17. 47

Heb. i. 10, from Ps. ci. 25.   1 Pet. v. 10 only.   e here only †.   Sir. vii. 6 B (ἰσχ., ACℵ) only.   f Acts
iv. 13. x. 34. xxv. 25.   Phil. iii. 12, 13.   Obad. 6.   g = Acts x. 2. xiv. 13 al. fr.   h = ch. i. 1 reff.
i Rev. xxi. 16.   Gen. vi. 15.   k Rev. xx. 9. xxi. 16 bis only.   l Rev. xxi. 16 bis only.
m Luke i. 78.   xxiv. 49. ch. iv. 8 (from Ps. lxvii. 19).   James i. 9.   Rev. xxi. 16 only.   n see Rom. viii. 39.

18. [for εξισχ., ισχυσητε D¹P.]   rec βαθος και υψος, with AKLℵ rel syr
Orig[-cat₂(and int₁) Eus] Mac Chr Thdrt Jer : txt BCDF[P] m 17 latt Syr copt [goth]
æth arm [Orig-cat₁(and int₁)] Ath Cyr [Victorin] Lucif Ambrst Pel Jer. (Tischdf
[Ed. 7] states the readings vice versa, appy by mistake.)

thus making ἐν ταῖς καρδ. ὑμ. tautological, or giving to διὰ τῆς πίστεως ἐν
ταῖς καρδίαις ὑμῶν the meaning, 'through
the faith which is in your hearts,' which
it cannot bear) the inner man (the spiritual man—the noblest portion of our
being, kept, in the natural man, under
subjection to the flesh (reff.), but in the
spiritual, renewed by the Spirit of God)—
that (continuation, not of the prayer
merely,—not from δῷ,—as the strong
word κατοικῆσαι, emphatically placed,
sufficiently shews,—but from κραταιωθῆναι,—and that as its result (see Orig.
above : not its purpose,—τοῦ κατ.). See
a similar construction Col. i. 10) Christ
may dwell (emphatic ; abide, take up His
lasting abode : ' summa sit, non procul
intuendum esse Christum fide, sed reci-
piendum esse animæ nostræ complexu, ut
in nobis habitet,' Calv.) by your faith
(apprehending Him, and opening the door
to Him,—see John xiv. 23 ; Rev. iii. 20—
and keeping Him there) in your hearts
(" partem etiam designat ubi legitima est
Christi sedes ; nempe cor : ut sciamus,
non satis esse, si in lingua versetur, aut
in cerebro volitet." Calv.),—ye having
been (Beza, Grot., al., and Meyer (and
so E. V.), join the participles with the
following ἵνα, justifying the trajection by
Gal. ii. 10 ; 2 Thess. ii. 7 ; Acts xix. 4 al.
But those cases are not parallel, as in
every one of them the prefixed words carry
especial emphasis, which here they cannot do. We must therefore regard the
clause as an instance of the irregular nominative (see ch. iv. 2 ; Col. ii. 2, and
reff. there) adopted to form an easy
transition to that which follows. Meyer
strongly objects to this, that the participles
are perfect, not present, which would be
thus logically required. But surely this
last is a mistake. It is upon the completion, not upon the progress, of their
rooting and grounding in love, that the
next clause depends. So Orig., Chrys.,
all., and Harl., De W., and Ellic.) rooted
and grounded (both images, that of a

tree, and that of a building, are supposed
to have been before the Apostle's mind.
But ῥιζόω was so constantly used in a
figurative sense (see examples in Palm
and Rost sub voce) as hardly perhaps of
necessity to suggest its primary image.
Lucian uses both words together, de
Saltat. 34 (Wetst.),—ὥσπερ τινὲς ῥίζαι
κ. θεμέλιοι τῆς ὀρχήσεως ἦσαν) in love
(love, generally—not merely αὐτοῦ, as
Chrys., nor ' qua diligimur a Deo,' Beza ;
nor need we supply ' in Christ ' after
the participles, thus disconnecting them
from ἐν ἀγ., as Harl. : but as Ellic.
well says, " This (love) was to be their
basis and foundation, in (on ?) which
alone they were to be fully enabled to
realize all the majestic proportions of
Christ's surpassing love to man "),—that
ye may be fully able (ref. : ἡ ἐπιμέλεια πολλάκις καὶ τῆς φύσεως ἐξίσχυσεν
ἐπιλειπούσης, Strabo, xvii. p. 788 (417
Tauchn.)) to comprehend (reff. " many
middle forms are distinguished from their
actives only by giving more the idea of
earnestness or spiritual energy : ἠριθμοῦντο
πολλοὶ ἅμα τὰς ἐπιβολάς, Thucyd. iii. 20 :
οὕτω δεῖ περὶ παντὸς σκοπεῖν· ὅταν γάρ
τι ταύτῃ σκοπούμενος ἔλῃς, οὕτως ἔμφρων
περὶ τοῦτο γέγονας. Plato." Krüger.
griech. Sprachlehre, § 52. 4) with all the
saints (all the people of God, in whom is
fulfilled that which is here prayed for)
what is the breadth and length and
height and depth (all kinds of fanciful
explanations have been given of these
words. One specimen may be enough :
ἐσχημάτισεν ὥσπερ τυπικώτερον εἰς σταυροῦ τύπον. βάθος γὰρ καὶ ὕψος καὶ
μῆκος καὶ πλάτος, τί ἕτερον ἂν εἴη, ἢ
τοῦ σταυροῦ φύσις ; διπλοῦν δέ που ἔοικε
τὸν σταυρὸν λέγειν, οὐχ ἁπλῶς· ἀλλ'
ἐπειδὴ ἡ μὲν τοῦ κυρίου οἰκονομία θεότης
ἐστὶν ἄνωθεν, καὶ ἀνθρωπότης κάτωθεν,
τὸ δὲ κήρυγμα ἀποστολικὸν διέτεινεν ἀπὸ
ἄρκτου εἰς μεσημβρίαν καὶ ἀπὸ ἀνατολῆς
εἰς δύσιν, συναγαγὼν καὶ κυρίου τὴν
οἰκονομίαν καὶ τῶν ἀποστόλων ὑπηρεσίαν·
τὸ διπλοῦν τῆς οἰκονομίας, ὡς ἐν διπλῷ

καὶ ᵖᵒ βάθος, ¹⁹ γνῶναί τε τὴν ᵖ ὑπερβάλλουσαν τῆς ᑫ γνώσεως ʳ ἀγάπην τοῦ ʳ χριστοῦ, ἵνα ˢ πληρωθῆτε ᵗ εἰς πᾶν τὸ
ᵘ πλήρωμα τοῦ θεοῦ. ²⁰ τῷ δὲ δυναμένῳ ᵛ ὑπὲρ πάντα
ποιῆσαι ʷ ὑπερεκπερισσοῦ ὧν ˣ αἰτούμεθα ἢ ʸ νοοῦμεν κατὰ
τὴν δύναμιν τὴν ᶻ ἐνεργουμένην ἐν ἡμῖν, ²¹ ᵃ αὐτῷ ἡ ᵃ δόξα

o = Rom. xi. 30.
p ch. i. 19 reff.
q = 1 Cor. viii.
1. xiii. 2, 8.
Hos. iv. 6.
(see 1 Tim. vi. 20.)
r = Rom. viii.
35. 2 Cor. v. 14.
s = Rom. i.

29. xv. 13. 2 Cor. vii. 4 al.   t = ch. ii. 21 al.   u = Rom. xv. 29. Col. i. 19. ii. 9.
v = Philem. 21.   w 1 Thess. iii. 10 only†.   Dan. iii. 22 Theod.-Ald.-compl. (-σσῶς, 1 Thess. v. 13.
x ver. 13 reff.   y ver. 4 reff.   z = Matt. xiv. 2 ‖. Rom. vii. 5. 1 Cor. xii. 6. 2 Cor. i.
6. iv. 12.   Gal. ii. 8. iii. 5 al., Paul chiefly.   a Rom. xi. 36. 2 Pet. iii. 18. Rev. i. 6.

19. om τε D¹F copt [æth].   αγαπην bef της γνωσεως A a 115 syr Jer(*scientiam
caritatis* Aug)₁.   πληρωθη, omg εις, B 17. 73. 116.
20. om υπερ DF latt lat-ff(exc Jer).

τῷ σταυρῷ ἐπιδεικνύμενος, οὕτως εἶπεν.
Severianus, in Cramer's Catena. Similarly
Origen, ib., Jer., Aug., Anselm, Aquin.,
Est. ('longitudo temporum est, latitudo
locorum, altitudo gloriæ, profunditas dis-
cretionis'). Numerous other explanations,
geometrical, architectural, and spiritual,
may be seen in Corn.-a-lap., Pole's Synops.,
and Eadie. The latter, as also Bengel and
Stier, see an allusion to the Church as the
temple of God—Chandler and Macknight
to the temple of Diana at Ephesus. Both
are in the highest degree improbable. Nor
can we quite say that the object of the
sentence is *the love of Christ* (Calv., Mey.,
Ellicott, al.) : for that is introduced in a
subordinate clause by and by (see on τε
below) : rather, with De W., that the genitive after these nouns is left indefinite—
that you may be fully able to comprehend
every dimension—scil., of all that God has
revealed or done in and for us (= τὸ μυστήριον τ. θεοῦ, Col. ii. 2)—though this is
not a genitive *to be supplied*, but lying in
the background entirely) and (τε introduces not a parallel, but a subordinate
clause. Of this Hartung, i. p. 105, gives
many examples. Eur. Hec. 1186,—ὅτ'
εὐτύχει | Τροία, πέριξ δὲ πύργος εἶχ' ἔτι
πτόλιν, | ἔζη τε Πρίαμος, Ἕκτορός τ'
ἤνθει δόρυ : Med. 642, ὦ πατρίς, δῶμά τ'
ἐμόν. So that the knowledge here spoken
of is not identical with the καταλαβέσθαι
above, but forms one portion of it, and by
its surpassing excellence serves to exalt
stiӀI more that great whole to which it belongs) **to know the knowledge-passing**
(τῆς γνώσεως, genitive of comparison after
ὑπερβ., as in διπλήσιος ἑωυτοῦ, Herod.
viii. 137,—οὐδενὸς ὕστερος, Plato, Tim.
p. 20 ᴀ. See Kühner, ii. § 540. γνῶναι
. . . γνώσεως are chosen as a paradox,
γνώσεως being taken in the sense of '*mere*,'
'*bare*' *knowledge* (ref.), and γνῶναι in the
pregnant sense of that knowledge which
is rooted and grounded in love, Phil. i. 9)
Love of Christ (subjective genitive; *Christ's
Love to us*—see Rom. v. 5 note, and viii.

35—39—not '*our love to Christ*.' Nor
must we interpret with Harl. (and Olsh.),
"*to know the Love of Christ more and
more as an unsearchable love.*" It is not
this *attribute* of Christ's Love, but the
Love itself, which he prays that they may
know), **that ye may be filled even to all
the fulness of God** (πᾶν τὸ πλήρωμα τῆς
θεότητος abides in Christ, Col. ii. 9.
Christ then abiding in your hearts, ye,
being raised up to the comprehension of
the vastness of God's mercy in Him and of
His Love, will be filled, even as God is full
—each in your degree, but all to your
utmost capacity, with divine wisdom and
might and love. Such seems much the
best rendering : and so Chrys. (altern.),
ὥστε πληροῦσθαι πάσης ἀρετῆς ἧς πλήρης
ἐστὶν ὁ θεός. τοῦ θ. then is the possessive
genitive. The other interpretation taking
θεοῦ as a genitive of origin, and **πλήρωμα**
for πλῆθος, 'ut omnibus Dei donis abun-
detis,' Est., is not consistent with **εἰς** (see
above), nor with the force of the passage,
which having risen in sublimity with every
clause, would hardly end so tamely).

20, 21.] DOXOLOGY, ARISING FROM THE
CONTEMPLATION OF THE FAITHFULNESS
AND POWER OF GOD WITH REGARD TO
HIS CHURCH. **20.]** **But to Him**
(δέ brings out a slight contrast to what
has just preceded—viz. *ourselves*, and our
need of strength and our growth in knowledge, and fulness) **who is able to do beyond all things** (ὑπέρ is not adverbial, as
Bengel, which would be tautological), **far
beyond** (reff. : ὧν is not governed by
πάντα : but this second clause repeats the
first in a more detailed and specified form.
" It is noticeable that ὑπέρ occurs nearly
thrice as many times in St. Paul's Epistles and the Epistle to the Hebrews as in
the rest of the N. T., and that, with a few
exceptions (Mark vii. 37. Luke vi. 38,
&c.), the compounds of ὑπέρ are all found
in St. Paul's Epistles." Ellic.) **the things
which** (genitive as γνώσεως above, ver.
19) **we ask or think** ('*cogitatio* latius

b 1 Cor. xiv. 19,
28.
c Luke i. 48.
(ver. 5 reff.)
d here only.
Dan. vii. 18.
e = Matt. viii.
5. Rom. xii.
1 al. fr.
Prov. viii. 4.
f ch. iii. 1 reff.
g & constr.,
Rom. xvi. 2. Phil. i. 27. Col. i. 10. 1 Thess. ii. 12. Paul only, exc. 3 John 6 †. Wisd. vii. 15 (xvi. 1. Sir. xiv.
11) only. h = Acts xxi. 21 al. fr. princ. Paul(31) & John(19). i Rom. xi. 29. 1 Cor. i. 26. ch.
i. 18 al(6). Paul only, exc. Heb. iii. 1. 2 Pet. i. 10. k 1 Cor. vii. 20. l attr., ch. i. 7 reff.
m = Matt. xxviii. 8. 1 Chron. xxix. 22 al. fr. n Acts xx. 19 (Paul). Phil. ii. 3. Col. ii. 18, 23. iii.
12. Paul only, exc. 1 Pet. v. 5 † (-φρων, 1 Pet. iii. 8. -φρονεῖν, Ps. cxxx. 2.) o Gal. v.
23. vi. 1 reff.

b ἐν τῇ ἐκκλησίᾳ [καὶ] ἐν χριστῷ Ἰησοῦ εἰς c πάσας τὰς
c γενεὰς τοῦ d αἰῶνος τῶν d αἰώνων, ἀμήν.

IV. 1 e Παρακαλῶ οὖν ὑμᾶς ἐγὼ ὁ f δέσμιος ἐν κυρίῳ,
g ἀξίως h περιπατῆσαι τῆς ik κλήσεως l ἧς k ἐκλήθητε,
2 m μετὰ πάσης n ταπεινοφροσύνης καὶ o πραΰτητος, μετὰ

ABCDF
KLPℵa
bcefg
hklmn
o 17.47

21. om καὶ D²KL[P] rel syrr goth [æth] Chr Thdrt Thl Œc Vig: ins ABC(D¹F)ℵ
17 vulg copt arm[?] Damasc-comm lat-ff.—εν χ. ι. και τη εκκλ. D¹F Victorin Ambrst.
om του αιωνος F tol.

CHAP. IV. 1. for κυριω, χριστω ℵ [æth. P uncertain].
2. rec πραοτητος, with ADFL rel : υπακοης K : txt BCℵ 17. [P def.]

patet quam preces: gradatio.' Beng.)
according to the power which is working
(not passive : see on Gal. v. 6 : the power
is the might of the indwelling Spirit ;
see Rom. viii. 26) **in us,** 21.] to
Him (solemn and emphatic repetition of
the personal pronoun) **be the glory** (the
whole glory accruing from all His dealings which have been spoken of : His own
resulting glory) **in the Church** (as its
theatre before men, in which that glory
must be recognized and rendered) [**and**]
in Christ Jesus (as its inner verity, and
essential element in which it abides. If
the καί be omitted, beware of rendering
' *in the Church which is in Christ Jesus,*'
which would not only require the article
(cf. Gal. i. 22, ταῖς ἐκκλ. τῆς Ἰουδαίας
ταῖς ἐν χριστῷ), but would make **ἐν**
χριστῷ Ἰησοῦ superfluous. As the text
stands, we need not say that ἐν χρ. Ἰησ.
is a second independent clause : it belongs
to **ἐν τῇ ἐκκ.** as inclusive of it, though not
as descriptive of ἐκκλ.: ' in the Church
and (thus) in Christ Jesus ') **to all the**
generations of the age of the ages (probably as Grot., ' augendi causa duas locu-
tiones Hebraicas miscuit Apostolus, quarum prior est ἀπὸ γενεᾶς εἰς γενεάν,
לְדֹר וָדֹר, Ps. x. 6, altera ἕως τοῦ αἰῶνος
עוֹלָמֵי עַד, Isa. xlv. 17.' Probably the account of the meaning is, that the *age of*
ages (eternity) is conceived as containing
ages, just as our ' age ' contains years :
and then those ages are thought of as
made up, like ours, of generations. Like
the similar expression, αἰῶνες τῶν αἰώνων,
it is used, by a transfer of what we know
in time, to express, imperfectly, and indeed improperly, the idea of Eternity).
IV. 1—VI. 20.] SECOND (hortatory)
PORTION OF THE EPISTLE : and herein
[A] (IV. 1—16) *ground of the Christian's*
duties as a member of the Church, viz. the

unity of the mystical Body of Christ (vv.
1—6) *in the manifoldness of grace given*
to each (7—13), *that we may come to per-*
fection in Him (14—16). 1.] **I ex-**
hort (see reff. παρακαλῶ, τὸ προτρέπω,
ὡς ἐπὶ τὸ πολύ. Thom.-Mag. in Ellic.)
you therefore (seeing that this is your
calling : an inference from all the former
part of the Epistle, as in Rom. xii. 1 ; but
here perhaps also a resumption of τούτου
χάριν of ch. iii. 1, 14, and thus carried
back to the contents of ch. i. ii.),—**the**
prisoner in the Lord (who am, as regards,
and for the sake of the cause, of the Lord,
a prisoner ; so that my captivity is *in the*
Lord, as its element and sphere, and therefore to be regarded as an additional in-
ducement to comply with my exhortation.
" Num quicquid est Christi, etiamsi coram
mundo sit ignominiosum, summo cum honore suscipiendum a vobis est." Calv. τοῖς
διὰ τὸν χριστὸν δεσμοῖς ἐναβρύνεται μᾶλλον ἢ βασιλεὺς διαδήματι. Thdrt. Beware
of joining **ἐν κυρ.** with **παρακαλῶ,** as in
2 Thess. iii. 12 (see ver. 17), which the
arrangement of the words here will not
permit), **to walk worthily of the calling**
(see ch. i. 18, and note Rom. viii. 28, 30)
wherewith (see ch. i. 6. The attracted
genitive may stand either for the dative
ᾗ or the accusative ἥν. Both constructions are legitimate attractions : cf. for
the dative, Xen. Cyr. v. 4. 39, ἤγετο δὲ
καὶ τῶν ἑαυτοῦ τῶν τε πιστῶν, οἷς ἥδετο,
κ. ὧν ἠπίστει πολλούς.—ὧν, for ἐκείνων,
οἷς ; and for the accusative, ch. i. 6, and
Hom. Il. χ. 649,—τιμῆς ἧστέ μ' ἔοικε
τετιμῆσθαι. De W. denies the legitimacy
of **κλῆσιν καλεῖν** ; but Raphel produces
from Arrian, Epict. p. 122, καταισχύνειν
τὴν κλῆσιν ἣν κέκληκεν) **ye were called,**
with (not ' *in,*' as Conyb., which, besides
not expressing **μετά,** the association of
certain dispositions to an act,—confuses

ᵖ μακροθυμίας, ᑫ ἀνεχόμενοι ἀλλήλων ἐν ἀγάπῃ, ³ ʳ σπουδάζοντες ˢ τηρεῖν τὴν ᵗ ἑνότητα τοῦ πνεύματος ἐν τῷ
ᵘ συνδέσμῳ τῆς εἰρήνης.   ⁴ ᵛ ἐν ᵛ σῶμα καὶ ʷ ἐν ʷ πνεῦμα,

p Rom. ii. 4 *
(al8. Paul).
Heb. vi. 12.
James v. 10.
1 Pet. iii. 20.
2 Pet. iii. 15.
Prov. xxv.
15.

n o p Col. iii. 12.   o p Gal. v. 22, 23.   q & constr., Matt. xvii. 17 ‖.   Acts xviii. 14.   1 Cor.
  iv. 12.   2 Cor. xi. 1, &c.   Col. iii. 13 (al7. Paul).   Isa. lxiii. 15.   r Gal ii. 10.   1 Thess. ii.
  17 (al4. Paul).   Heb. iv. 11.   2 Pet. i. 10, 15. iii. 14.   Isa. xxi. 3.   s = (Paul) 2 Tim. iv. 7 only.
t ver. 13 only †.   u Acts viii. 23.   Col. ii. 19. iii. 14 only.   Isa. lviii. 6.   v ch. ii. 16 reff.
w ch. ii. 18 reff.

3. for ειρηνης, αγαπης K 1 : αγαπης ειρηνης a¹.

the ἐν which follows) all (see on ch. i. 8)
lowliness (read by all means Trench's
essay on ταπεινοφροσύνη and πραότης,
in his N. T. Synonymes (xlii.).   I can
only extract one sentence here, to put the
reader on his guard : "Chrys. is in fact
bringing in pride again under the disguise
of humility, when he characterizes it
as a making of ourselves small *when we
are great* (ταπεινοφροσύνη τοῦτό ἐστιν,
ὅταν τις μέγας ὤν, ἑαυτὸν ταπεινοῖ : and
he repeats this often : see Suicer, Thes.
s. v.) : it is rather the esteeming ourselves
small, *inasmuch as we are so* : the thinking truly, and because truly, lowlily of
ourselves ") and meekness (before God,
accepting His dealings in humility, and
before men, as God's instruments, 2 Sam.
xvi. 11 : resting therefore on ταπεινοφρ.
as its foundation.   See Trench, as above),
with long-suffering (μακροθυμία consists
in not taking swift vengeance, but leaving
to an offender a place for repentance.
From this, its proper meaning, it is easily
further generalized to forbearance under
all circumstances of provocation.   Some,
as Est., Harl., Olsh., al., join these words
with ἀνεχόμενοι.   But thus (1) we should
have an emphatic tautology—for how
could the ἀνέχεσθαι be otherwise than
μετὰ μακροθυμίας ? and (2) the parallelism, μετὰ πάσης ταπ. κ. πραΰτ., μετ.
μακρ.,—would be destroyed.   Still less
should we, with Thdrt., Œc., and Bengel,
make all one sentence from μετὰ πάσ. to
ἀγάπ. : for thus (Mey.) we should lose
the gradual transition from the general
ἀξίως περιπ. τ. κλ. to the special ἀνεχ.
ἀλλ.),—forbearing (see reff. and Rom.
ii. 4; on the nom. part., see ch. iii. 18)
one another in love (it is very unnatural,
as Lachm. and Olsh. have done, to join
ἐν ἀγ. with σπουδάζοντες, making thereby
an exceedingly clumsy clause of the following), earnestly striving (reff.) to maintain the unity of the Spirit (that unity,
in which God's Holy Spirit in the Church
τοὺς γένει κ. τρόποις διαφόροις διεστηκότας
ἑνοῖ, as Chr.: not *animorum inter vos con-
junctionem*, as Est.,—and so Ambr., Anselm, Erasm., Calv., al.   The genitive is

in fact a possessive—*the Spirit's unity*,
that unity which the Spirit brings about,
ἣν τὸ πν. ἔδωκεν ἡμῖν, Thl.) in (united
together by : *within*) the bond of peace
(again Lachm. joins the qualifying clause
to the following sentence : here again most
unnaturally, both as regards what has
preceded, and the general truths which are
afterwards enounced : see below.   The
σύνδ. *is* εἰρήνη, not *that which brings
about* εἰρήνη, 'vinculum quo pax reti-
netur, id est, *amor*.' Beng.   So Thl., Rück.,
Harl., Stier.   Col. iii. 14, which is quoted
to support this meaning, is not applicable,
because love there is *expressly named*,
whereas here it certainly would not occur
to any reader, especially after ἐν ἀγάπῃ
has just occurred.   The genitive of apposition is the simplest—peace binds together the Church as a condition and
symbol of that inner unity which is only
wrought by the indwelling Spirit of
God).   4.] Lachm., joining ἐν σῶμα
κ.τ.λ. as far as ἐν πᾶσιν, with what has
gone before, makes these words hortatory : 'as one Body and one Spirit, even
as, &c.'   Certainly the reference to ἡ
κλῆσις ὑμῶν seems to tell for this.   But,
on the other hand, it is very unlikely
that the Apostle should thus use ἐν
σῶμα and ἐν πνεῦμα, and then go on
in the same strain, but with a different reference.   I therefore prefer the
common punctuation and rendering.
(There is) (better than '*ye are*,' which
will not apply to the following parallel
clauses.   The assertion of the unity of
the Church, and of our Lord in all His
operations and ordinances, springs immediately out of the last exhortation, as
following it up to its great primal ground
in the verities of God.   To suppose it connected by a γάρ understood (Eadie) is to
destroy the force and vividness with which
the great central truth is at once introduced without preface) one Body (reff. :
viz. Christ's mystical Body.   τί δ' ἐστιν,
ἐν σῶμα; οἱ πανταχοῦ τῆς οἰκουμένης
πιστοί, καὶ ὄντες κ. γενόμενοι κ. ἐσόμενοι.
πάλιν καὶ οἱ πρὸ τῆς τοῦ χριστοῦ παρουσίας εὐηρεστηκότες, ἐν σῶμά εἰσι.   Chrys.

x 1 Cor. vii. 15.
Gal. i. 6.
1 Thess. iv. 7.
y ch. i. 18.
z 1 Cor. viii. 6.
(1 Tim. ii. 5.)
a Rom. ix. 5 al.
b = Acts ix. 32.
2 Cor. viii. 8.
c ver. 16 reff.
d Gal. ii. 9 reff.

καθὼς καὶ ἐκλήθητε ˣ ἐν μιᾷ ʸ ἐλπίδι τῆς ⁱʸ κλήσεως ὑμῶν· 5 ᶻ εἷς ᶻ κύριος, μία πίστις, ἐν βάπτισμα, 6 ᶻ εἷς ᶻ θεὸς καὶ ᶻ πατὴρ πάντων, ὁ ᵃ ἐπὶ πάντων καὶ ᵇ διὰ πάντων καὶ ἐν πᾶσιν. 7 ᶜ ἑνὶ δὲ ᶜ ἑκάστῳ ἡμῶν ᵈ ἐδόθη [ἡ] ᵈ χάρις κατὰ

ABCDF
KLPℵ a
b c e f g
h k l m t
o 17. 47

4. om 2nd και B k 114 vulg(not fuld tol) syr goth [æth] Chr₁ [Victorin] Ambrst.
6. om 3rd και B 114 [Victorin]. rec aft πασιν ins υμιν (*the pronouns appear to be mere glosses to confine the assertion to Christians*), with k Chr-comm Thdrt : ημιν DFKL rel latt syrr goth [arm] Did Damasc Iren-int [Firmilian-in-Cypr Hil] : om ABC[P]ℵ 17. 67² copt æth Ign [Orig-cat₁] Eus Ath Naz Epiph Cyr Victorin Ambr Jer Aug Sedul.
7. υμων B k 120 Thdrt. om ἡ BD¹FL[P¹] k Damasc : ins ACD³K[P²]ℵ rel [Orig-cat₁] Chr Thdrt.—aft η χαρις ins αυτη C² 31 Cyr₁. (*The art was prob absorbed by the precedg* η, *or omitted as superfluous.*)

But these last hardly *sensu proprio* here) **and one Spirit** (viz. the Holy Spirit, who dwells in, and vivifies, and rules that one body : see ch. ii. 18, 22; 1 Cor. xii. 13 al.: not as Chrys., ἐν πν. καλῶς εἶπε, δεικνὺς ὅτι ἀπὸ τοῦ ἑνὸς σώματος ἐν πνεῦμα ἔσται, ἢ ὅτι ἐστὶ μὲν σῶμα εἶναι ἕν, οὐχ ἓν δὲ πνεῦμα· ὡς ἂν εἴ τις καὶ αἱρετικῶν φίλος εἴη· ἢ ὅτι ἀπ᾽ ἐκείνου δυσωπεῖ, τουτέστιν, οἱ ἐν πνεῦμα λαβόντες, καὶ ἐκ μιᾶς ποτισθέντες πηγῆς οὐκ ὀφείλετε διχονοεῖν· ἢ πν. ἐνταῦθα τὴν προθυμίαν φησίν), as also (τὸ καθὰ οἱ Ἀττικοὶ χρῶνται, τὸ δὲ καθὼς οὐδέποτε, ἀλλ᾽ ἢ τῶν Ἀλεξανδρέων διάλεκτος, καθ᾽ ἣν ἡ θεία γραφὴ γέγραπται. Emm. Moschop. a Byzantine grammarian, cited by Fabricius, vi. 191. See also Phryn. p. 426, and Lobeck's note : and Ellic. on Gal. iii. 6) **ye were called in** (elemental—the condition and sphere in which they were called to live and move, see reff. Mey. referring to Gal. i. 6, takes the instrumental sense: see there) **one hope of** (belonging to: you were called *in it* as the element, see above : it is then an accident of the κλῆσις. Or perhaps it may be the genitive of the *causa efficiens,* 'which the calling works,' as Ellic. Cf. 1 Thess. i. 6, μετὰ χαρᾶς πνεύματος ἁγίου) **your calling :** 5.] **one Lord** (as the Head of the Church : in this verse he grounds the co-existence of the ἐν σῶμα κ. ἐν πνεῦμα in the three great facts on which it rests—the first objective,— εἷς κύριος—the second subjective,—μία πίστις —the third compounded of the two,— ἐν βάπτισμα), **one faith** (in that one Lord : the subjective medium by which that one Lord is apprehended and appropriated : not 'fides *quæ* creditur,' but 'fides *quâ* creditur :' but it is necessarily understood, that this subjective faith has for its object the One Lord just mentioned) **one baptism** (the objective seal of the subjective faith, by which, as a badge, the members

of Christ are outwardly and visibly stamped with His name. The other sacrament, being a matured act of subsequent participation, a function of the incorporate, not a seal of incorporation (a symbol of *union,* not of *unity :* so Ellicott), is not here adduced. In 1 Cor. x. 17, where an act was in question which was a clear breach of union, it forms the rallying-point),
6.] **one God** (the unity is here consummated in its central Object: 'hoc est præcipuum, quia inde manant reliqua omnia,' Calv. But we must not miss the distinct witness to the doctrine of the Holy Trinity in these verses :—going upwards, we have 1st, the One Spirit dwelling in the one body :—2nd, the One Lord appropriated by faith and professed in baptism :—3rd, One God and Father supreme, in whom all find their end and object) **and Father of all** (masculine : 'of all within the Church,' for so is clearly the *primary* meaning, where he is speaking distinctly of the Church :—of all (Mey.) who have the υἱοθεσία. But it can hardly be doubted, that there is a further reference—to the universal Fathership of all men—which indeed the Church only inherits in its fulness, others having fallen out of it by sin,—but which nevertheless is just as absolutely true), **who is over all** (men, primarily ; and from the following,—men only, in this place. He is over all, in his *sovereignty as the* FATHER), **and through all** (men : in the co-extensiveness of Redemption by the Son with the whole nature of man : see on ver. 10 below, and ch. ii. 20, 21) **and in all** (men : by the indwelling of the Spirit, see ch. ii. 22. So that I cannot but recognize, in these three carefully chosen expressions, a distinct allusion again to the Three Persons of the blessed Trinity. All these are the work of the Father :—it is He who in direct sovereignty is over all

τὸ ᵉ μέτρον τῆς ᶠ δωρεᾶς τοῦ χριστοῦ. ⁸ διὸ ᵍ λέγει
ʰ’Αναβὰς εἰς ⁱὕψος ᵏἠχμαλώτευσεν ˡαἰχμαλωσίαν καὶ

e Rom. xii. 3.
2 Cor. x. 13.
vv. 13, 16. =
Paul only.
f ch. iii. 7 reff.

g Gal. iii. 16. James iv. 6. Heb. x. 5. see 1 Cor. vi. 16.　　h John iii. 13. Psa. lxvii. 18.
i = Luke i. 78. xxiv. 49. (ch. iii. 18 reff.)　　k here only. Amos i. 6. (-τίζειν, 2 Tim. iii. 6.)
l = Rev. xiii. 10 bis only. Num. xxi. 1. Judg. v. 12. 2 Chron. xxviii. 17. Diod. Sic. xvii. 70, τ. αἰχμαλωσίαν δουλαγωγοῦντες.

8. ηχμαλωτευσας [as LXX] AL a¹ c k [47] 114 æth.　om και (see LXX) AC²D¹FℵҀ¹
17 latt copt [arm Eus Orig-int₁] Iren-int Tert Hil Jer Ambrst [Lucif] : ins BC¹˒³D³KL
[P]ℵ³ rel syrr goth [æth] Orig Chr Thdrt Cyr Victorin.

—He who is glorified in the filling of all things by the Son :—He who is revealed by the witness of the indwelling Spirit. Many Commentators deny such a reference. Almost all agree in ἐν πᾶσιν representing the indwelling of the Spirit : the διὰ πάντων has been the principal stumbling-block : and is variously interpreted :—by some, of God's Providence,—τουτέστιν, ὁ προνοῶν καὶ διοικῶν, Chrys., al. : by others, of His pervading presence by the Spirit,—'Spiritu sanctificationis diffusus est per omnia ecclesiæ membra,' Calv.: by others, to the creation by the Son, 'per quem omnia facta sunt' (Aquin. in Ellic.): but this seems to be a conversion of διὰ πάντων into δι' οὗ πάντες, as indeed Olsh. expressly does, 'als Werkzeug, durch das sie sind.' Irenæus, v. 18. 2, p. 315, gives the meaning thus, adopting the Trinitarian reference, but taking the πάντων both times as *neuter*, and reading ἐν πᾶσιν ἡμῖν : 'super omnia quidem Pater, et ipse est caput Christi : per omnia autem verbum, et ipse est caput ecclesiæ : in omnibus autem nobis Spiritus, et ipse est aqua viva,' &c.). **7.] But** (the contrast is between ἐν πᾶσιν and ἑνὶ ἑκάστῳ—the general, and the particular. And the connexion is—as a motive to keep the unity of the Spirit—'none is overlooked :—each has his part in the distribution of the gifts of the One Spirit, which part he is bound to use for the well-being of the whole') **to each one of us was given** (by Christ, at the time of His exaltation—when He bestowed gifts on men) **[the] grace** (which was then bestowed : *the* unspeakable gift, — or, if the art. be omitted, grace, absolutely, — was distributed to each κατά &c.) **according to the measure of** (subjective genitive : the amount of : cf. Rom. xii. 3, ἑκάστῳ ὡς ὁ Θεὸς ἐμέρισεν μέτρον πίστεως) **the gift of Christ** ('*Christ's gift ;*'—the gift bestowed by Christ, 2 Cor. ix. 15: not, 'the gift which Christ received,'— for He is the subject and centre here—so Calv.,—'porro Christum facit auctorem, quia sicut a Patre fecit initium, ita in ipsum vult nos et nostra omnia colligere.' Still less must we with Stier, suppose both senses of

the genitive included). **8.] Wherefore** ('quæ cum ita sint :' viz.—the gift bestowed by Christ on different men according to measure) **He** (viz. God, whose word the Scriptures are. See reff. and notes : not merely 'it,' es ḫeiṗt, as De W. al. : nor, ἡ γραφή : had it been the subject, it must have been expressed, as in Rom. iv. 3 ; ix. 17 al.) **says** (viz. in Ps. lxviii. 18, see below : not, in some Christian hymn, as Flatt and Storr,—which would not agree with λέγει, nor with the treatment of the citation, which is plainly regarded as carrying the weight of Scripture. With the question as to the occasion and intent of that Psalm, we are not here concerned. It is a song of triumph, as ver. 1 (cf. Num. x. 35) shews, at some bringing up of the ark to the hill of Zion. It is *therefore* a Messianic Psalm. Every part of that ark, every stone of that hill, was full of spiritual meaning. Every note struck on the lyres of the sweet singers of Israel, is but part of a chord, deep and world-wide, sounding from the golden harps of redemption. The partial triumphs of David and Solomon only prefigured as in a prophetic mirror the universal and eternal triumph of the Incarnate Son of God. Those who do not understand this, have yet their first lesson in the O. T. to learn. With this caution let us approach the difficulties of the citation in detail) **He ascended up on high** (viz. Christ, at His Ascension : not '*having* ascended :' the aorist participle denotes an action not preceding, but parallel to, that expressed in the finite verb which it accompanies : see Bernhardy, Synt. p. 383. The ascending in the Psalm is that of God, whose presence was symbolized by the ark, to Zion. The Apostle changes the words from the 2nd person to the 3rd ; the *address* asserting a *fact*, which fact he cites), **he led captive a captivity** (i. e. 'those who *suffer* captivity :' a troop of captives : such is the constant usage of the abstract αἰχμαλωσία for the concrete in LXX: cf. reff. : and it is never put for *captivatores*, 'those who *cause* captivity,' as some would interpret it. In the Psalm, these would be, the captives from the then war, what-

116 ΠΡΟΣ ΕΦΕΣΙΟΥΣ. IV.

Luke xi. 13.
Phil. iv. 17
only. Gen.
xxv. 6.
n = Rom. x. 7.   Ps. cxxxviii. 8.

ἔδωκεν ᵐ δόματα τοῖς ἀνθρώποις. ⁹ τὸ δὲ ἀνέβη, τί ἐστιν
εἰ μὴ ὅτι καὶ ⁿ κατέβη εἰς τὰ ᵒ κατώτερα μέρη τῆς γῆς;

o here only.   Ps. lxii. 9 (but superl.).

ABCDF
KLPℵ a
b c e f g
h k l m n
o 17. 47

9. rec aft κατεβη ins πρωτον, with BC³KL [P(appy, from the space)] ℵ³ rel vulg(and
F-lat) syrr goth [arm] Eus₁ Thdrt Damasc Ambrst-ms Œc-comm : om AC¹DFℵ¹ 17.
67² am¹ coptt æth [Thdot₁ Orig₃(and int₁) Eus₁] Chr-comm Cyr Iren-int [Tert]
Lucif Hil [Victorin] Jer Aug.   om μερη D¹F Syr [goth æth] Thdot Orig₂ Eus₁
Iren-int₂ Tert Lucif Hil Ambrst Jer Avit : ins ABCD³KL[P]ℵ rel vulg(and F-lat)
[syr-mg-gr copt arm] Orig₁ Eus₁ Cyr Aug₂.

ever it was: in the interpretation, they
were God's enemies, Satan and his hosts,
as Chr., ποίαν αἰχμαλωσίαν φησί; τὴν
τοῦ διαβόλου. αἰχμάλωτον τὸν τύραννον
ἔλαβε, τὸν διάβολον καὶ τὸν θάνατον καὶ
τὴν ἀρὰν καὶ τὴν ἁμαρτίαν), he gave gifts
to mankind (Heb.: לְקַחְתָּ מַתָּנוֹת בָּאָדָם—
LXX, ἔλαβες δόματα ἐν ἀνθρώπῳ (-ποις [ℵ]
F [A def.]). The original meaning is obscure. There seems to be no necessity to
argue for a sense of ἔλαβες—'thou receivedst in order to give;' as the qualifying ἐν ἀνθρώποις will shew for what purpose, in what capacity, the receipt took
place. But certainly such a sense of לָקַח
seems to be substantiated : see Eadie's
note here, and his examples, viz. Gen. xv.
9; xviii. 5 (where the sense is very marked,
E. V. 'I will fetch'),—xxvii. 13 (ib.
'fetch me them'), xlii. 16,—Exod. xxvii.
20 ('that they bring thee'),—1 Kings
xvii. 10 ('fetch me,' λαβὲ δή μοι), al.
Then, what is בָּאָדָם? First, אָדָם is clearly
used in a collective sense: we have Jer.
xxxii. 20, יִשְׂרָאֵל וְאָדָם, 'Israel and the rest
of mankind,' see also Isa. xliii. 4 al. In
Prov. xxiii. 28, we have בָּאָדָם used for
'inter homines,' which is evidently its simplest meaning. If then we render here,
'hast taken gifts among men,' hast, as a
victor, surrounded by thy victorious hosts,
brought gifts home, spoils of the enemy,—
the result of such reception of gifts would
be naturally stated as the distribution of
them among such hosts, and the people,—
as indeed ver. 12 of the Psalm has already
stated. And so the Chaldee paraphrast
(and Syr. and Arabic vss.: but their testimony, as Christian, is little worth) understood the words, interpreting the passage
of Moses (which does not invalidate his
testimony : against Harl.) : 'thou hast
given gifts to the sons of men.' The literature of the passage may be seen in De
W. and Meyer: and more at length in
Stier, Eadie, and Harless. To give even a
synopsis of it here would far exceed our
limits).   9.] Further explanation of
this text. But that He ascended (τὸ ἀν.
does not here mean, 'the word' ἀνέβη,

which does not occur in the text cited),
what is it (does it imply) except that he
also (as well) descended to the lower
parts of the earth (the argument seems
to be this : the Ascension here spoken of
was not a first exaltation, but a return to
heaven of one who dwelt in heaven—οὐδεὶς
ἀναβέβηκεν εἰς τὸν οὐρανόν, εἰ μὴ ὁ ἐκ
τοῦ οὐρανοῦ καταβάς, ὁ υἱὸς τ. ἀνθρώπου
ὁ ὢν ἐν τῷ οὐρανῷ, John iii. 13, which is
in fact the key to these verses. The ascent
implied a previous descent. This is the
leading thought. But it is doubted how
far the words κατώτερα μέρη τῆς γῆς
carry that descent, whether to earth
merely, so that τῆς γῆς is the genitive of
apposition,—or to Hades, so that it is
genitive of possession. Usage will not
determine—for 1) it is uncertain whether
the Apostle meant any allusion to the corresponding Hebrew expression : 2) that
expression is used both for Hades, Ps. lxiii.
9, and for earth (θεμέλια, LXX), Isa. xliv.
23 (and for the womb, Ps. cxxxix. 15).
Nor can it be said (as Harl., Mey.) that
the descent into hell would be irrelevant
here—or that our Lord ascended not from
Hades but from the earth : for, the fact of
descent being the primary thought, we
have only to ask as above, how far that
descent is carried in the Apostle's mind.
The greater the descent, the greater the
ascent : and if the αἰχμαλωσία consisted
of Satan and his powers, the warfare in
which they were taken captive would
most naturally be contemplated in all
its extent, as reaching to their habitation itself :—'this ascent, what does
it imply but a descent, and that even
to the lower parts of the earth from which
the spoils of victory were fetched?' And
this meaning seems to be upheld by the ἵνα
πληρώσῃ τὰ πάντα which follows, as well
as by the contrast furnished by ὑπεράνω
πάντων τῶν οὐρανῶν.   This interpretation is upheld by most of the ancients,
Iren., Tert., Jer., Pelag., Ambrst.; also by
Erasm., Est., Calov., Bengel, Rück., Olsh.,
Stier, Baur (uses it as a proof of the gnostic
origin of the Epistle), Ellicott, al.: that of
the Incarnation merely, descent on earth,

10 ὁ καταβὰς αὐτός ἐστιν καὶ ὁ ἀναβὰς [p] ὑπεράνω πάντων
τῶν οὐρανῶν, ἵνα [q] πληρώσῃ τὰ πάντα. 11 καὶ αὐτὸς
[r] ἔδωκεν τοὺς μὲν [st] ἀποστόλους, τοὺς δὲ [st] προφήτας, τοὺς
δὲ [u] εὐαγγελιστάς, τοὺς δὲ [v] ποιμένας καὶ [tw] διδασκάλους,
12 πρὸς τὸν [x] καταρτισμὸν τῶν ἁγίων, εἰς [y] ἔργον [yz] διακονίας, εἰς [a] οἰκοδομὴν τοῦ [b] σώματος τοῦ [b] χριστοῦ,

p ch. i. 21 reff. q = ch. iii. 19 reff. (Acts ii. 2. v. 28.) r ch. i. 22 reff. s ch. iii. 5 reff. t 1 Cor. xii. 28. u Acts xxi. 8. 2 Tim. iv. 5 only †. v John x. 2 &c. but = here only. see Jer. iii. 15. Ezek. xxxiv. passim. w Acts xiii. 1. 1 Cor. xii. 28, 29. 2 Tim. iv. 3. Heb. v. 12. James iii. 1. x here only †. (-τισις, -τίζειν, 2 Cor. xiii. 9, 13.) y here only. z = Acts i. 17, 25. Rom. xi. 13 al. fr. † (1 Macc. xi. 58 only.) a = (Paul only) Rom. xiv. 19. xv. 2 al[9]. (ch. ii. 12 al.) b = 1 Cor. xii. 27. Col. ii. 17.

[**10.** om παντων P a[1] Thdot[1] Eus[1]. **12.** ins της bef διακονιας D[1]F.]

by Beza, Calv., Grot., Schöttg., Mich., Storr, Winer, Harl., B.-Crus., Meyer, De W., al.: that of Christ's *death* (and burial), by Chr., Thdrt., Œc., al.: that corresponding to Ps. cxxxix. 15, by Beza (alt.), Witsius, al.)? **10.**] **He that descended, He** (and no other: οὐ γὰρ ἄλλος κατελήλυθεν κ. ἄλλος ἀνελήλυθεν, Thdrt. αὐτός is the subject, and not the predicate (ὁ αὐτός)) **is also he that ascended** (see again John iii. 13) **up above** (reff.) **all the heavens** (cf. Heb. vii. 26, ὑψηλότερος τῶν οὐρανῶν γενόμενος: and ib. iv. 14, διεληλυθότα τοὺς οὐρανούς. It is natural that one who, like St. Paul, had been brought up in the Jewish habits of thought, should still use their methods of speaking, according to which the heaven is expressed in the plural, '*the heavens*.' And from such an usage, πάντες οἱ οὐρανοί would naturally flow. See, on the idea of a threefold, or sevenfold division of the heavens, the note on 2 Cor. xii. 2. Ellicott quotes from Bishop Pearson,—'whatsoever heaven is higher than all the rest which are called heavens, into that place did he ascend.' Notice the subjunctive after the aorist participle, giving the present and enduring sense to the verb: used, when "res ita comparata est, ut actione præterita tamen eventus nondum expletus sit, sed etiam nunc duret: . . . . Eur. Med. 215, Κορίνθιαι γυναῖκες, ἐξῆλθον δόμων, μή μοί τι μέμφησθ'." Klotz, Devar. ii. 618), **that He may fill** (not as Anselm, al., '*fulfil*') **all things** (the whole universe: see ch. i. 23, note: with His presence, His sovereignty, His working by the Spirit: not, with His glorified Body, as some have thought. "Christ is perfect God, and perfect and glorified man: as the former He is present every where, as the latter He can be present any where." Ellicott).

11.] Resumption of the subject—the diversity of gifts, all bestowed by Him, as a motive to unity. **And HE** (emphatic; 'it is He, that') **gave** (not for ἔθετο, any more than in ch. i. 22:—*the gifts which He gave* to His Church are now enumerated. "The idea is, that the men who filled the office, no less than the office itself, were a divine gift." Eadie) **some as Apostles** (see 1 Cor. xii. 28, and note; and a good enumeration of the essentials of an Apostle, in Eadie's note here), **some as prophets** (see on 1 Cor. xii. 10: and cf. ch. ii. 20; iii. 5, notes), **some as evangelists** (not in the narrower sense of the word, writers of gospels, but in the wider sense, of itinerant preachers, usually sent on a special mission: οἱ μὴ περιϊόντες πανταχοῦ, ἀλλ' εὐαγγελιζόμενοι μόνον, ὡς Πρίσκιλλα κ. Ἀκύλας. Chr. See note on Acts xxi. 8), **some as pastors and teachers** (from these latter not being distinguished from the pastors by the τοὺς δέ, it would seem that the two offices were held by the same persons. The figure in **ποιμένες**, if to be pressed, would imply that they were entrusted with some special flock, which they tended, καθήμενοι καὶ περὶ ἕνα τόπον ἠσχολημένοι, as Chr.; and then the διδασκαλία would necessarily form a chief part of their work. If this view be correct, this last class includes all the stationary officers of particular Churches), **in order to** (ultimate aim of these offices, see below) **the perfecting of the saints,—for** (immediate object, see below) **(the) work of (the) ministry** (of διάκονοι in God's Church. The articles give completeness in English, but do not affect the sense),—**for building up of the body of Christ** (the relation of these three clauses has been disputed. Chr., al., regard them as parallel: ἕκαστος οἰκοδομεῖ, ἕκαστος καταρτίζει, ἕκαστος διακονεῖ: but this is to confound the distinct prepositions, **πρός** and **εἰς**, after the unsupported notion that St. Paul uses prepositions almost indifferently. Others, as De W., regard **εἰς . . . εἰς** as dependent on **πρός**, and thus are obliged to give to **διακονία** a wider sense (*genus omnium functionum in ecclesia*) than it will bear. The best way certainly seems to be, with Mey. and Ellic., to regard **πρός** as the ultimate end, **εἰς** as the immediate use, as in Rom. xv. 2, *

118   ΠΡΟΣ ΕΦΕΣΙΟΥΣ.   IV.

Mark xiii. 30.
d Acts xvi. 1
a16. 1 Cor.
xiv. 36. Phil.
iii. 11 only.
L.P. (2 Kings
iii. 29.) 2 Macc. iv. 21.
f ver. 3 only †.
i ver. 7 reff.
l ch. i. 23 note.

13 ᶜ μέχρι ᵈ καταντήσωμεν ᵉ οἱ ᵉ πάντες ᵈ εἰς τὴν ᶠ ἑνότητα
τῆς πίστεως καὶ τῆς ᵍ ἐπιγνώσεως τοῦ υἱοῦ τοῦ θεοῦ, εἰς
ʰ ἄνδρα ʰ τέλειον, εἰς ⁱ μέτρον ᵏ ἡλικίας τοῦ ˡ πληρώματος

ABCDF
KLPℵ a
b c e f g
h k l m n
o 17. 47

e 1 Cor. x. 17.   2 Cor. v. 10.   Phil. ii. 21.   ὁ πᾶς, Gal. v. 14.   τὰ πάντα passim.
g ch. i. 17 reff.   h James iii. 2.   2 Kings xxii. 26.   see Col. i. 28. iv. 12.
k = Luke ii. 52. xix. 3 only.   Ezek. xiii. 18.   (see Matt. vi. 27 note.   John ix. 21.   Heb. xi. 11.)

13. om οι D¹F Clem₁ Orig₁.   om τ. υιου F Clem₁ Lucif.

ἕκαστος ἡμῶν τῷ πλησίον ἀρεσκέτω εἰς τὸ ἀγαθὸν πρὸς οἰκοδομήν), until (marks the duration of the offices of the ministry) we (being thus κατηρτισμένοι by virtue of the ἔργον διακονίας and the οἰκοδομή) arrive (see reff.: no sense of 'meeting,' but simply of 'attaining.' Ellicott well remarks, that we must be careful of applying to later Greek the canons of the grammarians respecting the omission of ἄν, as giving an air of less uncertainty to subjunctives in such constructions as this; and he adds, "the use of the subjunctive (the mood of conditioned but objective possibility), not future (as Chrys.), shews that the καταντᾶν is represented, not only as the eventual, but as the expected and contemplated result of the ἔδωκεν"), all of us (Christians, Jews as well as Gentiles: first person, because he himself was among the number. The article brings out the πάντες, as belonging to one class), at the unity of the faith ("How so? have not all Christians the same faith? . . . . No doubt they have, as regards its substance, but not as regards clearness and purity; because the object of faith may be diversely known, and knowledge has ever such a powerful influence on faith. Therefore he adds to this unity of faith καὶ τῆς ἐπιγνώσεως κ.τ.λ.: true and full unity of faith is then found, when all thoroughly know Christ, the object of faith, alike, and that in His highest dignity as the Son of God." De Wette) and of the knowledge (further result of the faith, ch. iii. 17, 19; 2 Pet. i. 5) of the Son of God (this objective genitive belongs to both τῆς πίστεως and τῆς ἐπιγνώσεως), at a perfect man (an awkwardness is given by the coupling of an abstract (εἰς ἑνότητα) to a concrete (εἰς ἄνδρα τέλειον). The singular not only denotes unity (Beza), but refers to the summation of us all in the one perfect Man Christ Jesus. The maturity of the ἀνὴρ τέλειος is contrasted with the νηπιότης which follows. Among curiosities of exegesis may be adduced that which Aug. mentions, de Civ. Dei xxii. 17, vol. vii. p. 778: "Nonnulli, propter hoc quod dictum est, Eph. iv. 13, nec in sexu foemineo resurrecturas foeminas credunt, sed in virili omnes aiunt") to the measure of the sta-

ture (or, 'age?' this is doubtful. The similitude in ἄνδρα τέλειον seems to be derived from age: that in ver. 16, from stature. The fact seems to be, that ἡλικία is a comprehensive word, including both ideas—answering to the German 'Erwachsenheit,' but having no corresponding word in our language. We have μέτρον ἥβης in Hom. Il. λ. 225. Od. λ. 317, σ. 217. The expression itself occurs in Lucian, Imag. 7 (Wetst.), τῆς ἡλικίας δὲ τὸ μέτρον, ἡλίκον ἂν γένοιτο· κατὰ τὴν ἐν Κνίδῳ ἐκείνην μάλιστα . . . μεμετρήσθω,—and Philostratus, vit. Sophist. p. 543, τὸ δὲ μέτρον τῆς ἡλικίας ταῖς μὲν ἄλλαις ἐπιστήμαις γήρως ἀρχή. Clearly, none of these passages settles the question. In Homer, the meaning is 'the measure of youth,'—the size and ripeness of youth: in Lucian, as decidedly 'the measure of the stature,' as in Philostr., 'the ripeness of manly age.' The balance must here be inclined by the prevalence of the image of growth and extension, which can hardly be denied as pervading the passage) of the fulness of Christ (see note on ch. i. 23; iii. 19. χρ. is a genitive subjective:—the fulness which Christ has: 'Christ's fulness.' Cf. Gal. iv. 19),—that (apparently another, and subordinate, aim of the bestowal of gifts on the church is here adduced. For we cannot go forward from the finished growth of ver. 13, and say that its object is ἵνα μηκ. ὦμεν νήπιοι, but must go back again to the growth itself and its purpose; that purpose being mainly the terminal one of ver. 13, and subordinately the intermediate one of our ver. 14. See Meyer's note) we be no more (having been so once: τὸ μηκέτι δείκνυσι πάλαι τοῦτο παθόντας. Chr.) children, tossed (like waves: see James i. 6: Jos. Antt. ix. 11. 3, ἔσται Νινευὴ κολυμβήθρα ὕδατος κινουμένη, οὕτως κ. ὁ δῆμος ἅπας ταρασσόμενος κ. κλυδωνιζόμενος οἰχήσεται φεύγων) and borne about by every wind of teaching (τῇ τροπῇ ἐμμένων καὶ ἀνέμους ἐκάλεσε τὰς διαφόρους διδασκαλίας. Thl. Wetst. quotes from Plut. de Audiend. Poetis, p. 28 D, μὴ παντὶ λόγῳ πλάγιον, ὥσπερ πνεύματι, παραδιδοὺς ἑαυτόν. The article before διδασκαλίας gives a greater definiteness to the abstract word, but cannot be ex-

τοῦ χριστοῦ, ¹⁴ ἵνα μηκέτι ὦμεν ᵐ νήπιοι, ⁿ κλυδωνιζόμενοι
καὶ ᵒ περιφερόμενοι παντὶ ᵖ ἀνέμῳ τῆς ᑫ διδασκαλίας ἐν τῇ
ʳ κυβείᾳ τῶν ἀνθρώπων, ἐν ˢ πανουργίᾳ πρὸς τὴν ᵗ μεθο-
δείαν τῆς ᵘ πλάνης, ¹⁵ ᵛ ἀληθεύοντες δὲ ἐν ἀγάπῃ ʷ αὐξήσωμεν ʷ εἰς αὐτὸν τὰ πάντα, ὅς ἐστιν ἡ ˣ κεφαλή,

m Matt. xi. 25.
xxi. 16, from
Ps. viii. 2.
1 Cor. iii. 1.
xiii. 11 (5
times) al3.,
Paul.(1Thess.
ii. 7 v. r.)
Ps. xviii. 7.
n here only.
Isa. lvii. 20
only. Jos.

Antt. ix. 11. 3.
iv. 10 only.)
9 ‖ Mk. Prov. ii. 17.
2. xi. 3 only. Josh. ix. 4.
27. Polycarp. ad Phil. § 7, p. 1012.)
v Gal. iv. 16 only. Gen. xlii. 16.

o = here only. [Heb. xiii. 9 v. r.   Jude 12 v. r.] Eccl. vii. 8. (Mark vi. 43. 2 Cor.
p Matt. xi. 7 ‖. Jude 12.   q 1 Tim. i. 10 reff. Paul on!y, exc. Matt. xv.
r here only †.   s (=) Luke xx. 23. 1 Cor. iii. 19. 2 Cor. iv.
t ch. vi. 11 only †.   (-δος, 2 Macc. xiii. 18. -δεύειν, 2 Kings xix.
u Matt. xxvii. 64. Rom. i. 27 al7. Prov. xiv. 8.
w ch. ii. 21.   x ch. i. 22 reff.

14. for νηπ., ηπιοι A.   την μεθοδιαν [B¹]D¹FKL[P]א e m n [47 Orig₁] : την
μεθοδον 17 : τας μεθοδιας A [copt] : remedium old-lat [Orig-int₁] Lucif [Victorin]
Ambrst Pel-comm.   aft πλανης ins του διαβολου A.
15. for αληθευοντες δε, αληθειαν δε ποιουντες F.   om η D¹F Clem.

pressed in English. So ἅπαξ προσουρή-
σαντα τῇ τραγῳδίᾳ, Aristoph. Ran. 95)
in (elemental : "the evil atmosphere, as
it were, in which the varying currents
of doctrine exist and exert their force."
Ellic. This is better than *instrumental*,
which, as we have just had παντὶ ἀνέμῳ,
would be a repetition) **the sleight** ('*dice-
playing*,' from κύβος. The word, as well
as κυβεύω, was naturally and constantly
used to signify 'entrapping by deceit :'
κυβείαν τὴν πανουργίαν καλεῖ πεποί-
ηται δὲ ἀπὸ κύβων τὸ ὄνομα· ἴδιον δὲ
τῶν κυβευόντων, τὸ τῇδε κἀκεῖσε μετα-
φέρειν τὰς ψήφους, καὶ πανούργως τοῦτο
ποιεῖν. Thdrt. See examples in Wetst.
The word was borrowed by the Rabbinical writers, and used in this sense : see
Schöttg. h. l.) **of men** (as contrasted with
τοῦ χριστοῦ, ver. 13), **in craftiness** (reff.)
furthering (tending or working towards :
or perhaps, but not so well,—*after*, *according to*, gemäß) **the system** (see reff.
and especially ch. vi. 11, note, and Chr.'s
explanation) **of error** (not, *deceit*, though
in fact the sense is so : πλάνη, even in
the passages generally alleged for this
active meaning, is best taken as 'error.'
The genitive πλάνης is subjective—the
plans are those which error adopts. τῆς
πλ., as τῆς διδασκαλίας : see above),
15.] **but** (opposition to the *whole* last
verse; introducing as it does, not only
ἀληθεύοντες ἐν ἀγάπῃ, but the αὐξήσωμεν below) **being followers of truth** (ἀληθεύειν cannot here mean merely to *speak
the truth*, as the whole matter dealt with
is more general; the particular follows,
ver. 25. The verb has the widest meaning of *being ἀληθής*—and (as Stier remarks) not without a certain sense of
effort, '*sectari veritatem*.' The Vulg.
gives it well, but perhaps with too exclusively practical a bearing, '*veritatem
facientes* :' Bengel, '*verantes* :' the old
English versions, '*folowe the truth*,' which

gives too much the objective sense to
truth. It is almost impossible to express
it satisfactorily in English. I have somewhat modified this last rendering, restoring the general sense of 'truth.' The
objection to 'followers of truth' is that
it may be mistaken for 'searchers after
truth'—but I can find no expression
which does not lie open to equal objection) **in love** (must be joined with
ἀληθεύοντες, not with αὐξήσωμεν. For
1) the mere participle with δέ would stand
most feebly and awkwardly at the beginning of the sentence : and 2) we have
already observed the habit of the Apostle
to be, to subjoin, not to prefix, his qualifying clauses. ἐν ἀγάπῃ is added, as the
element in which the Christian ἀληθεύειν
must take place : it is not and cannot be
an ἀληθεύειν at all hazards—a 'fiat justitia, ruat cœlum' truthfulness : but must
be conditioned by love : a true-seeking
and true-being with loving caution and
kind allowance — not breaking up, but
cementing, brotherly love by walking in
truth) **may grow up into** (increase towards the measure of the stature of ;—to
the perfect man in Him. Again an allusion to the incorporation of all the Church
in Christ : see below) **Him in all things**
(accusative of reference ; the article implying, in every department of our growth,
'in all things wherein we grow,' as Meyer)
who is the Head (see ch. i. 22), **namely,
Christ** (the nominative **is** best regarded
as an attraction to the *foregoing* relative,
just as in 'urbem quam statuo vestra est'
the substantive is attracted to the *following* relative. So we have, Eur. Hecub.
754, πρὸς ἄνδρ', ὃς ἄρχει τῆσδε Πολυ-
μήστωρ χθονός : and Plato, Apol. p. 41 A,
εὑρήσει τοὺς ὡς ἀληθῶς δικαστάς, οἵπερ
κ. λέγονται ἐκεῖ δικάζειν, Μίνως τε καὶ
Ῥαδάμανθυς κ. Αἴακος. In the face of
these examples, there is no occasion, with
De W. and Ellic., to suppose that the

χριστός, ¹⁶ ἐξ οὗ πᾶν τὸ ^y σῶμα ^z συναρμολογούμενον καὶ ^a συμβιβαζόμενον διὰ πάσης ^b ἁφῆς τῆς ^c ἐπιχορηγίας ^d κατ᾽ ^d ἐνέργειαν ἐν ^e μέτρῳ ^f ἑνὸς ^f ἑκάστου ^g μέρους τὴν ^h αὔξησιν τοῦ σώματος ⁱ ποιεῖται εἰς ^j οἰκοδομὴν ἑαυτοῦ ἐν ἀγάπῃ.

¹⁷ Τοῦτο οὖν λέγω καὶ ^k μαρτύρομαι ^l ἐν κυρίῳ, μηκέτι

y ch. i. 23 reff.
z ch. ii. 21 only †.
a Acts ix. 22. xvi. 10. (xix. 33 v. r.) 1 Cor. ii. 16, from Isa. xl. 14. Col. ii. 2, 19 only.
b Col. ii. 19 only ‡. (Lev. xiii. 2 al. fr. = יַד, plague.)
c Phil. i. 19 only †. (-γεῖν, Gal. iii. 5.)
29. 2 Thess. ii. 9 only.   e ver. 7 reff.
ii. 11 al. 1 Kings xiii. 20 Ald.
κάλλους τῶν τοῦ σώματος αὐτοῦ μελῶν κ. μερῶν.
i constr., Luke v. 33. Phil. i. 4. 1 Tim. ii. 1 al.
12. Acts xx. 26. xxvi. 22 (Paul only) †.
d ch. i. 19 (reff.). iii. 7. Phil. iii. 21. Col. i.
f Luke iv. 40. Acts ii. 3, 6. xx. 31. ver. 7. Col. iv. 6. 1 Thess.
g Luke xi. 36. Plato, Legg. vii. p. 795 e, ἐλαφρότητός τε ἕνεκα κ.
h Col. ii. 19 only †. 2 Macc. v. 16 only.
j ver. 12 reff.   k = Gal. v. 3. 1 Thess. ii.
1 1 Thess. iv. 1 al. fr. P.

...αγαπη C.
ABDFK LPℵ a b c e f g h k l m n o 17. 47

rec ins ο ͻef χριστος, with DFKL[P]ℵ³ rel : om ABCℵ¹ 17. 67² Bas Cyr Did Damasc.   **16.** om κατ᾽ ενεργειαν F D-lat arm(not ed-1805) Iren-int Lucif [Victorin].   for μερους, μελους (corrn to suit τ. σωματος) AC vulg Syr copt arm[?] Chr Cyr Jer Pel : txt BDFKL[P]ℵ rel syr[and -mg-gr] goth [æth] Bas-mss Thdrt Iren-int Lucif Victorin.   for εαυ., αυτου D¹Fℵ a m.

Apostle places χρ. at the end to give force to ἐξ οὗ which follows. Beware of Eadie's rendering, 'who is the Head, the (ὁ χρ.) Christ,' as alien from any design apparent in the argument, or indeed in the Epistle),

16.] **from whom** (see Col. ii. 19, an almost exact parallel, from which it is clear that ἐξ οὗ belongs to τὴν αὔξησιν ποιεῖται — He being the source of all growth) **all the body** (see on Col.), **(which is) being closely framed together** (note the present participle—the framing is not complete but still proceeding. For the word, see on ch. ii. 21) **and compounded** ('notat simul firmitudinem et consolidationem,' Bengel),—**by means of every joint** (to be joined, not with the participles preceding, but (see below) with τ. αὔξ. ποι., as Chr., Thdrt., Beng., Mey., except that they understand ἁφή to mean αἴσθησις—the perception of the vital energy imparted from the head (τὸ πνεῦμα τὸ ἀπὸ τ. ἐγκεφάλου καταβαῖνον, τὸ διὰ τῶν νεύρων), which is the cause of all growth to the body. But it seems hardly controvertible that ἁφή does signify 'joint' (συναφή) in the parallel Col. ii. 19; it is there (see note) joined with συνδεσμῶν so closely, as necessarily to fall into the same class of anatomical arrangements, and cannot mean αἴσθησις. Also in Damoxenus in Athenæus, iii. 102 E, we have it in this sense—καὶ συμπλεκομένης οὐχὶ συμφώνους ἁφάς. Indeed the meaning Berührung, 'point d'appui,' would naturally lead to that of joint) **of the** (article just as παντὶ ἀνέμῳ τῆς διδασκ. above: see note there) **supply** (the joints are the points of union where the supply passes to the different members, and by means of which the body derives the supply by which it grows. The genitive, as σῶμα

τῆς ἁμαρτίας, σκεύη τῆς λειτουργίας : "a kind of genitive *definitivus*, by which the predominant use, purpose, or destination of the ἁφή is specified and characterized." Ellic.),—**according to vital working in the measure of each individual part,**—**carries on** (remark the intensive middle ποιεῖται, denoting that the αὔξησις is not carried on ab extra, but by functional energy within the body itself) **the growth of the body** (I thus render, preferring to join as well διὰ π. ἁφ. τ. ἐπιχ. as κατ᾽ ἐν. κ.τ.λ. with τ. αὔξ. ποιεῖται rather than with the preceding participles, 1) to avoid the very long awkward clause encumbered with qualifications, πᾶν τὸ σῶμα σ. κ. σ. διὰ πᾶσ. ἁφ. τῆς ἐπιχ. κατ᾽ ἐνέργ. ἐν μέτρ. ἑν. ἑκ. μέρους : 2) because the repetition of τοῦ σώματος is much more natural in a cumbrous apodosis, than in a simple apodosis after a cumbrous protasis : 3) for perspicuity : the whole instrumentality and modality here described belonging to the growth (ἐπιχορ., ἐνέργ., ἐν μέτρῳ), and not merely to the compaction of the body. τοῦ σώματος is repeated, rather than ἑαυτοῦ used, perhaps for solemnity, perhaps (which is more likely) to call back the attention to the subject σῶμα after so long a description of its means and measure of growth) **for the building up of itself in love** (Meyer would join ἐν ἀγ. with τ. αὔξ. τ. σώμ. ποι. as suiting better ver. 15. This is hardly necessary, and encumbers still further the already sufficiently qualified αὔξ. ποιεῖται. Love is just as much the element in which the edification, as that in which the growth, takes place).

[B] (See on ver. 1.) **IV. 17—VI. 9.]** *Exhortations to a course of walking and conversation, derived from the ground just*

ὑμᾶς ᵐπεριπατεῖν καθὼς καὶ τὰ ἔθνη ᵐπεριπατεῖ ἐν ⁿμα-
ταιότητι τοῦ νοὸς αὐτῶν, 18 ᵒἐσκοτωμένοι τῇ ᵖδιανοίᾳ
ὄντες, ᑫἀπηλλοτριωμένοι τῆς ʳζωῆς τοῦ ʳθεοῦ, διὰ τὴν
ˢἄγνοιαν τὴν οὖσαν ἐν αὐτοῖς διὰ τὴν ᵗᵘπώρωσιν τῆς

m ver. 1 reff.
n Rom. viii. 20.
2 Pet. ii. 18
only. Ps.
xxx. 6.
o Rev. ix. 2.
xvi. 10 only.
Jer. xiv. 2.
(-τίζειν,

Matt. xxiv. 29 ‖ Mk. Luke xxiii. 45. Rom. i. 21. xi. 10, from Ps. lxviii. 23. Rev. viii. 12 only.)
p ch. ii. 3 reff. q ch. ii. 12 reff. r here only. s Acts iii. 17. xvii. 30. 1 Pet.
i. 14. Lev. xxii. 14. t Mark iii. 5 only. u as above (t). Rom. xi. 25 only †.

17. rec ins λοιπα bef εθνη (see note), with D³KL[P]ℵ³ rel syrr goth [arm] Chr
Damasc Thdrt Thl Œc : om ABD¹Fℵ¹ 17 [47] 67² latt coptt æth Clem Cyr lat-ff.
18. rec εσκοτισμενοι, with DFKL[P] rel Clem [Orig-cat₂] Chr Thdrt : txt ABℵ 17
Ath. om οντες F Thl. [αγνωσιαν F.]

---

laid down, and herein (iv. 17—v. 21) *general duties of Christians as united to Christ their Head*. **17.**] **This** (which follows) **then** (resumptive of ver. 1; as Thdrt., πάλιν ἀνέλαβε τῆς παραινέσεως τὸ προοίμιον. This is shewn by the fact that the μηκέτι περιπατ. here is only the negative side of, and therefore subordinate to, the ἀξίως περιπ. of ver. 1. Vv. 4—16 form a digression arising out of τ. ἑνότητα τ. πν. in ver. 3. Still this must not be too strictly pressed : the digression is all in the course of the argument, and μηκέτι here is not without reference to μηκέτι in ver. 14. The fervid style of St. Paul will never divide sharply into separate logical portions—each runs into and overlaps the other) **I say** (see Rom. xii. 3. There is no need to understand δεῖν before the infinitive which follows. The μηκ. ὑμ. περιπατεῖν is the object of λέγω expressed in the infinitive, just as regularly as in βούλομαί σε λέγειν. That an imperative sense is involved, lies in the context) **and testify** (see reff. : cf. Plato, Phileb. p. 47 D, ταῦτα δὲ τότε μὲν οὐκ ἐμαρτυράμεθα, νῦν δὲ λέγομεν : Thuc. vi. 80 ; viii. 53, Duk.) **in the Lord** (element ; not 'formula jurandi,' see 1 Thess. iv. 1, note), **that ye no longer** ('*as once :*' implied also by καί below) **walk as also** (besides yourselves : though the Ephesians did not walk so now, their returning to such a course is made the logical hypothesis) **the Gentiles** (ye being now distinguished from them by being members of God's church, though once Gentiles according to the flesh. Perhaps from this not being seen, λοιπά was inserted) **walk in** (element) **vanity** (see Rom. i. 21 : they ἐματαιώθησαν in their downward course from God. But we must not restrict the word to idolatry : it betokens the *waste* of the whole rational powers on worthless objects. See also on Rom. viii. 20) **of their mind** (their rational part), **being** (beware of referring ὄντες to ἀπηλλ. with Eadie. Besides its breaking the force of the sentence, I doubt

if such an arrangement is ever found) **darkened** (see again Rom. i. 21, and the contrast brought out 1 Thess. v. 4, 5, and ch. v. 8) **in** (the dative gives the sphere or element in which. The difference between it and the accusative of reference (τὴν διάνοιαν ἐσκοτισμένους, Jos. Antt. ix. 4. 3) is perhaps this, that the dative is more subjective—The man is dark :—wherein ? in his διάνοια : the accusative more objective—Darkness is on the man : —in him, whereon ? on his διάνοια) **their understanding** (perceptive faculty : intellectual discernment : see note, ch. ii. 3), **alienated** (reff. : objective result of the subjective 'being darkened') **from the life of God** (not 'modus vivendi quem Deus instituit,' as the ancients (Thdrt., Thl., and Grot., al.), for ζωή in N. T. never has this meaning (see the two clearly distinguished in Gal. v. 25), but always *life*, as opposed to death. Thus '*the life of God*' will mean, as Beza beautifully says, 'vita illa qua Deus vivit in suis :' for, as Beng., 'vita spiritalis accenditur in credentibus ex ipsa Dei vita.' Stier makes an important remark : " The Apostle is here treating, not so much of the life of God in Christ which is regenerated in believers, as of the original state of man, when God was his Life and Light, before the irruption of darkness into human nature ") **on account of the ignorance** (of God : see ref. 1 Pet.) **which is in them** (not, by nature : cf. Rom. i. 21—28 : they did not *choose to retain* God in their knowledge, and this loss of the knowledge of Him alienated them from the divine Life), **on account of** (second clause, subordinate to ἀπηλλ. : not subordinate to and rendering a reason for τὴν ἄγν. τ. οὖσαν, as Meyer, which would be awkward, and less like St. Paul) **the hardening** ('πώρωσις est obduratio, callus. Rem quæ hac voce significatur, eleganter describit Plutarchus, *de auditione* p. 46, ubi nullo monitorum ad vitam emendandam sensu duci, negotium esse dicit ἀνελευθέρου τινὸς δεινῶς κ.

v = Rom. i. 25.
vi. 2. 2 Cor.
viii. 10 al. fr.
w here only †.
x = Rom. i. 24,
&c. 1 Cor. v.
5. 1 Tim. i.
20. 2 Pet. ii.
4.

ᵗκαρδίας αὐτῶν, ¹⁹ ᵛοἵτινες ᵂἀπηλγηκότες ἑαυτοὺς ˣπαρ-
ἔδωκαν τῇ ʸᶻἀσελγείᾳ εἰς ᵃἐργασίαν ᶻᵇἀκαθαρσίας πάσης
ἐν ᶜπλεονεξίᾳ. ²⁰ ὑμεῖς δὲ οὐχ οὕτως ᵈἐμάθετε τὸν

ABDFK
LPℵ a b
c e f g h
k l m n o
17. 47

y Mark vii. 22. Rom. xiii. 13 al.† Wisd. xiv. 26 only.　　　z 2 Cor. xii. 21. Gal. v. 19.
a = here only. (Luke xii. 58. Acts xvi. 16, 19. xix. 24, 25 only. Jonah i. 8.)　b Rom. i. 24 al(7). Paul
only, exc. Matt. xxiii. 27. Prov. vi. 16.　c Col. iii. 5 reff.　d constr., Matt. xxiv. 32 ∥ Mk. Rom.
xvi. 17. 1 Cor. xiv. 35. Phil. iv. 9. Rev. xiv. 3. Isa. xxvi. 9, 10

19. for απηλγ., απηλπικοτες D : αφηλπ. F : *desperantes* latt Syr arm Iren-in-Epiph
Iren-int Jer(notices the variation) Ambrst Gild Pel.　ε(ις ακα)θαρσιαν A.
[πασης bef ακαθ. DF m.]　　　for εν πλ., και πλεονεξιας DF [æth] Clem [Victorin]
Ambrst Aug Gild Sedul Pel-comm.

ἀπαθοὺς πρὸς τὸ αἰδεῖσθαι νέου διὰ συνήθειαν ἁμαρτημάτων κ. συνέχειαν, ὥσπερ
ἐν σκληρᾷ σαρκὶ κ. τυλώδει τῇ ψυχῇ,
μώλωπα μὴ λαμβάνοντος.' Kypke. The
sense '*blindness*' is said by Fritzsche, on
Rom. xi. 7, to be invented by the grammarians. Thdrt. says πώρωσιν τὴν ἐσχάτην ἀναλγησίαν λέγει· καὶ γὰρ αἱ τῷ
σώματι ἐγγινόμεναι πωρώσεις οὐδεμίαν αἴσθησιν ἔχουσι διὰ τὸ παντελῶς νενεκρῶ-
σθαι) of their heart,　19.] who
as (οἵτινες, see ch. i. 23 note) being
past feeling (ὥσπερ τῶν ἀπὸ πάθους τινὸς μέρη πολλάκις τοῦ σώματος νενε-
κρωμένων οἷς οὐ μόνον ἄλγος οὐδὲν ἐκεῖθεν ἐγγίνεται, ἀλλ' οὐδὲ ἡ τοῦ μέρους
ἀφαίρεσις αἴσθησιν ἐμποιεῖ. Theod. Mops.
in Stier. From the '*desperatio*' of the
Vulg. Syr., seems to have come the reading ἀπηλπικότες, see var. readd. The ob-
duration described may spring in ordinary
life from despair :—so Cicero, Ep. fam. ii.
16, in Bengel, 'diuturna desperatione rerum obduruisse animum ad dolorem novum,'—and Polyb. ix. 40. 9, ἀπαλγοῦντες
ταῖς ἐλπίσι (where see Ernesti's note), but
may also result from other reasons. Certainly despair has nothing to do with the
matter here, but rather the carrying on
of the πώρωσις to positive ἀπάλγησις by the
increasing habit of sin) gave up themselves (" ἑαυτ., with terrific emphasis. It
accorded here with the hortatory object of
the Apostle to bring into prominence that
which happened on the side of their own
free will. It is otherwise in Rom. i. 24,
παρέδωκεν αὐτοὺς ὁ θεός : and the two
treatments of the fact are not inconsistent,
but parallel, each having its vindication
and its full truth in the pragmatism of the
context." Meyer) to wantonness (see Gal.
v. 19 note) in order to (conscious aim, not
merely incidental result of the παραδοῦναι
—see below) the working (yes and more—
the being ἐργάται—the working as at a
trade or business—but we have no one
word for it : cf. Chrys., ὁρᾷς πῶς αὐτοὺς
ἀποστερεῖ συγγνώμης ἐργασίαν ἀκαθαρσίας εἰπών ; οὐ παραπεσόντες, φησίν, ἥμαρ-

τον, ἀλλ' εἰργάζοντο αὐτὰ τὰ δεινά, κ.
μελέτῃ τῷ πράγματι ἐκέχρηντο) of impurity of every kind (see Rom. i. 24—27.
Ellic. remarks, "As St. Paul nearly invariably places πᾶς before, and not as here
after the abstract (anarthrous) substantive, it seems proper to specify it (that
circumstance) in translation ") in greediness (such is the meaning, and not '*with
greediness*,' i. e. greedily, as E. V., Chr.
(appy), Thdrt., Œc., Erasm., Calv., Est.,
al., nor '*certatim*, quasi agatur de lucro,
ita ut alius alium superare contendat,' as
Beza, nor as Harl. '*in gluttony*' (which
meaning his citation from Chrys. does not
bear out). πλεονεξία, the desire of
having more, is obviously a wider vice than
mere covetousness, though this latter is
generally its prominent form. It is self-
seeking, or *greed :* in whatever direction
this central evil tendency finds its employment. So that it may include in itself as
an element, as here, lustful sins, though it
can never actually mean '*lasciviousness*.'
In 1 Cor. v. 10 it (πλεονέκταις) is disjoined from πόρνοις by ἤ, and joined by
καί to ἅρπαξιν—clearly therefore meaning covetous persons. See also ch. v. 3, and
Col. iii. 5 : and compare Ellicott's note
here).　20.] But YOU (emphatic) did
not thus (οὐκ ἐπὶ τούτοις, Chr.—not on
these conditions, nor with such prospects.
Beza suggests that a stop might be put at
οὕτως—'ye are not thus : ye learned,'
&c. : but the sense is altogether marred by
it) learn Christ (Christ personal—not to
be explained away into ὀρθῶς βιοῦν, as
Chr., or any thing else : cf. 1 Cor. i. 23,
ἡμεῖς κηρύσσομεν χριστόν : Phil. i. 15—
18 ; Col. ii. 6. CHRIST Himself is the
subject of all Christian preaching and all
Christian learning — τὸ γνῶναι αὐτόν
(Phil. iii. 10) is the great lesson of the
Christian life, which these Ephesians began
to learn at their conversion : see next
verse), if, that is (see ch. iii. 2 note, and
2 Cor. v. 3. He does not *absolutely* assume the fact, but implies that he then
believed and still trusts it was so), it was

^d χριστόν, ²¹ ^e εἴ γε αὐτὸν ^f ἠκούσατε καὶ ^g ἐν αὐτῷ
ἐδιδάχθητε καθώς ἐστιν ^h ἀλήθεια ⁱ ἐν τῷ ⁱ Ἰησοῦ, ²² ^j ἀποθέσθαι ὑμᾶς ^k κατὰ τὴν προτέραν ^l ἀναστροφὴν τὸν
^m παλαιὸν ^m ἄνθρωπον τὸν ⁿ φθειρόμενον κατὰ τὰς ^o ἐπι-

e ch. iii. 2 reff.
f ch. i. 15 reff.
g = ch. i. 15.
h = John viii.
44. Rom. ix.
1.
i see 1 Thess.
iv. 14. 2 Cor.
iv. 11.
j ver. 25. Acts

vii. 58. Rom. xiii. 12. Col. iii. 8. Heb. xii. 1. James i. 21. 1 Pet. ii. 1 only. 2 Chron. xviii. 26.
k = Rom. ix. 3, 5. 1 Gal. i. 13. 1 Tim. iv. 12. Heb. xiii. 7. James iii. 13. 1 Pet. i. 15
al(7)†. Tobit iv. 14. 2 Macc. v. 8 Ed-vat. (καταστρ. AB) only. m Rom. vi. 6. Col. iii. 9.
n = 1 Cor. xv. 33. 2 Cor. xi. 3. Jude 10. Gen. vi. 11. o Mark iv. 19 al. fr.

Him that ye heard (if ye really heard at your conversion the voice of the Shepherd Himself calling you as his sheep —τὰ πρόβατα τὰ ἐμὰ τῆς φωνῆς μου ἀκούει, John x. 27, see also John v. 25) and in Him that ye were taught (if it was in vital union with Him, as members of Him, that ye after your conversion received my teaching. Both these clauses are contained in ἐμάθετε τὸν χρ.,—the first hearing of the voice of the Son of God, and growing in the knowledge of Him when awakened from spiritual death), as is truth in Jesus (the rendering and connexion of this clause have been much disputed. I will remark, 1) that it seems by its form to be subordinate to ἐν αὐτῷ ἐδιδάχθητε, and the καθώς to express the quality of the διδαχή: 2) that in this case we have ἐστιν ἀλήθεια ἐν τῷ Ἰησ. answering to ἐν αὐτῷ ἐδιδάχθητε. 3) to take the easier members first, ἐν τῷ Ἰησοῦ is a closer personal specification of ἐν αὐτῷ—in Jesus—that one name recalling their union in both in His Person, and, which is important here, in His example also: 4) καθώς ἐστιν ἀλήθεια expands ἐδιδάχθητε — if the nature of the teaching which you received was according to that which is truth (in Him). So that the meaning will amount to this— if ye were taught in Him according to that which is truth in Jesus:—if you received into yourselves, when you listened to the teaching of the Gospel, that which is true (respecting you—and Him) in your union with and life in Jesus, the Son of God manifest in the flesh. See Ellicott's note), 22.] namely (the infinitive depends on ἐδιδάχθητε (not on λέγω, ver. 17, as Bengel and Stier), and carries therefore (not in itself, but as thus dependent) an imperative force—see on ver. 17) that ye put off (cf. ἐνδύσασθαι ver. 24: aorist, because the act of putting off is one and decisive, so also of ἐνδύσασθαι below: but ἀνανεοῦσθαι, because the renewal is a gradual process. Beware of rendering, with Eadie and Peile, 'that ye have put off,' which is inconsistent with the context (cf. ver. 25), and not justified by ὑμᾶς being expressed. This latter is done merely to resume the subject after

the parenthetical ver. 21), as regards your former conversation (explains the reference of ἀποθέσθαι: q. d. (for you were clothed with it in your former conversation): and must not, as by Œc., Jer., Grot., Est., al., be joined with τὸν παλ. ἄνθρ.: on ἀναστρ., see note, Gal. i. 13), the old man (your former unconverted selves, see note on Rom. vi. 6) which is ("almost, 'as it is, &c.,' the participle having a slight causal force, and serving to superadd a further motive." Ellic.) being corrupted (inasmuch as the whole clause is subjectively spoken of the παλ. ἄνθρ., it is better to take φθ. (as usually) of inward 'waxing corrupt,' as in reff. (especially Jude), than of destination to perdition, as Mey., which would be introducing an outward objective element) according to (in conformity with ; as might be expected under the guidance of) the lusts of deceit (ἡ ἀπάτη is personified —the lusts which are the servants, the instruments of deceit: cf. ἐκ χειλέων ἀπάτης μου, Judith ix. 10. Beware of the unsatisfactory hendiadys, 'deceitful lusts,' E. V., which destroys the whole force and beauty of the contrast below to ὁσιότητι τῆς ἀληθείας), 23.] and undergo renewal (both should be marked,—the gradual process implied in the present, and the passive character of the verb. Of this latter there can be no doubt: the middle ἀνανεοῦσθαι having always an active force: so we have ἀνανεοῦσθαι τ. συμμαχίαν, Polyb. xxiii. 1. 5 : see many more examples in the Lex. Polybianum, and in Harl.'s note here: and we have even, in Antonin. iv. 3 (Harl.), ἀνανέου σεαυτόν. Stier's arguments in favour of the middle sense seem to me to be misplaced. ἐνδύσασθαι is middle, but that refers to a direct definite reflexive act; whereas the process here insisted on is one carried on by the Spirit of God, not by themselves. And it is not to the purpose to ask, as Stier does, 'How can the Apostle say and testify by way of exhortation, that they should be renewed as they ought to walk?' for we have perpetually this seeming paradox, of God's work encouraged or checked by man's co-operation or counteraction. The distinction between ἀνακαίνωσις and ἀνανέωσις

θυμίας τῆς ᵖ ἀπάτης, ²³ �q ἀνανεοῦσθαι δὲ τῷ ʳ πνεύματι ABDFK
τοῦ ʳˢ νοὸς ὑμῶν ²⁴ καὶ ᵗ ἐνδύσασθαι τὸν ᵘ καινὸν ᵘ ἄνθρω- cefgh
πον τὸν ᵛ κατὰ ᵛ θεὸν ᵂ κτισθέντα ἐν δικαιοσύνῃ καὶ ˣ ὁσιό- klmno
τητι τῆς ἀληθείας.

p Matt. xiii.
22 ‖ Mk. Col.
ii. 8. 2 Thess.
ii. 10. Heb.
iii. 13. 2 Pet.
ii. 13. (Jude
12 v.r.) only†.
Judith
ix. 10, 13.
xvi. 8 only.

LPℵ a b
17. 47

constr., 2 Pet. ii. 10.   q here only.   Job xxxiii. 24.   r here only.   s = Rom. i. 28. vii.
23. xii. 2 al.   t = Rom. xiii. 12, 14.   1 Cor. xv. 53, 54.   Col. iii. 10.   Ps. cxxxi. 9.   u ch. ii. 15
reff.   v Rom. viii. 27.   2 Cor. vii. 9, 10, 11.   1 Pet. iv. 6 only. see note.   w ch. ii. 10 reff.
x Luke i. 75 only.   Deut. ix. 5 al.

23. [ανανεουσθε D² m 17. 47 vulg syrr coptt Clem₂ lat-ff.]   om δε F [æth].
add εν B.

24. ενδυσασθε [B¹D²]K[P]ℵ k m [47 vulg syrr copt Clem₂ Eus₁ lat-ff].   οσιοτ.
και δικαιοσ. ℵ¹.   for της αλ., και αληθεια D¹F Cypr Hil Lucif (not Tert).

is not (as Olsh.) beside the purpose here,
but important. The reference in **καινός**
(*novus*) to the objective is prominent, in
νέος (*recens*) to the subjective. The
καινός is used as opposed to the former
self; the **νέος**, as regards the new nature
and growth in it: cf. Col. iii. 10, τὸν νέον,
τὸν ἀνακαινούμενον. Thus in Rom. xii. 2
it would not be said μεταμορφ. τῇ ἀνα-
νεώσει τ. νοός, because it is not by nor in
the ἀνανέωσις, but by or in the ἀνακαίνωσις, that the μεταμορφ. takes place.
Whereas here, where a process of growing up in the state of ἀνακαίνωσις is in
question, ἀνανεοῦσθαι is properly used.
ἀνακαινοῦσθαι is more 'renewal from the
age of the old man;' ἀνανεοῦσθαι, 'renewal in the youth of the new man.' See
Tittmann, Syn. p. 60 ff.) **by** (though (see
more below) the expression **τῷ πν. τοῦ
νοὸς ὑμ.** stands contrasted with **ἐν μα-
ταιότητι τοῦ νοὸς αὐτῶν**, ver. 17, yet the
omission of ἐν here serves to mark that
not merely the sphere in which, but the
agency by which, is now adduced) **the
Spirit of** *your* (emphatic) **mind** (the expression is unusual, and can only be understood by reference to the N. T. meaning
of **πνεῦμα**, as applied to men. First,
it is clearly here not exclusively nor properly 'the Holy Spirit of God,' because it
is called τὸ πν. τοῦ νοὸς ὑμῶν. It is a
πνεῦμα, in some sense belonging to, not
merely indwelling in, **ὑμεῖς**. The fact is,
that in the N. T. the πνεῦμα of man is
only then used 'sensu proprio,' as worthy
of its place and governing functions, when
it is one Spirit with the Lord. We read
of no πνεῦμα παλαιόν: the πνευματικός
is necessarily a man dwelt in by the Spirit
of God: the ψυχικός is the 'animal' man
led by the ψυχή, and πνεῦμα μὴ ἔχων,
Jude 19. Thus then the disciples of Christ
are ἀνανεούμενοι, undergoing a process of
renewal in the life of God, by the agency
of the **πνεῦμα** of their minds, the restored
and divinely-informed leading principle of
their **νοῦς**, just as the children of the

world are walking in the ματαιότης of *their*
minds. νοῦς, see above, ver. 17), **24.**]
and put on (see on ἀποθέσθαι above) **the
new man** (as opposed to παλαιόν; not
meaning *Christ*, any further than as He
is its great Head and prototype, see on
κτισθ.), **which was created** (mark the
aorist, as historical fact, once for all, in
Christ. In each individual case, it is not
created again, but put on: cf. Rom. xiii.
14) **after God** (= κατ' εἰκόνα τοῦ κτίσαντος αὐτόν, Col. iii. 10: also κατ' εἰκόνα
θεοῦ ἐποίησεν αὐτόν, Gen. i. 27: so 1 Pet.
i. 15, κατὰ τὸν καλέσαντα ὑμᾶς ἅγιον καὶ
αὐτοὶ ἅγιοι κ.τ.λ. The doctrine of the
restoration to us of the divine image in
Christ, as here implied, is not to be overlooked. Müller, 'Lehre von der Sünde,'
ii. p. 485 ff., denies any allusion to it here,
but on insufficient grounds, as indeed he
himself virtually allows. Not the bare
fact of Gen. i. 27, but the great truth
which that fact represents, is alluded to.
The image of God in Christ is a far more
glorious thing than Adam ever had, or
could have had: but still the κατ' εἰκόνα
θεοῦ, = κατὰ θεόν, is true of both: and,
as Müller himself says, 'jenes ist erst die
wahrhafte Erfüllung von diesem') **in** (element, or sphere, of the character of the
new man) **righteousness and holiness of
truth** (again, beware of '*true holiness*,'
E. V.—as destroying the whole antithesis
and force of the words. The genitive,
too, belongs to both substantives.
ἡ **ἀλήθεια**, God's essence, John iii. 33;
Rom. i. 25; iii. 7; xv. 8, opposed to ἡ
ἀπάτη above. "δικαιοσύνη and ὁσιότης
occur together, but in contrary order, in
ref. Luke, and Wisd. ix. 3. The adjectives and adverbs are connected, 1 Thess.
ii. 10: Tit. i. 8. δικαιοσύνη betokens a
just relation among the powers of the soul
within, and towards men and duties without. But ὁσιότης, as the Heb. חֶסֶד (Prov.
ii. 21. Amos v. 10), betokens the integrity
of the spiritual life, and the piety towards
God of which that is the condition. Hence

²⁵ Διὸ ^y ἀποθέμενοι τὸ ^z ψεῦδος ^a λαλεῖτε ^a ἀλήθειαν ^b ἕκα-
στος μετὰ τοῦ ^b πλησίον αὐτοῦ, ὅτι ἐσμεν ἀλλήλων ^c μέλη.
^{26 d} ὀργίζεσθε καὶ μὴ ἁμαρτάνετε. ὁ ἥλιος μὴ ^e ἐπιδυέτω
ἐπὶ [τῷ] ^f παροργισμῷ ὑμῶν, ²⁷ μηδὲ ^g δίδοτε ^{gh} τόπον τῷ

y ver. 22 reff.
z John viii. 44.
Rom. i. 25 al.
Ps. v. 6.
a John viii. 40
only. (elsw.
λέγειν, John
viii. 45, 46;
ἐρεῖν, 2 Cor.

xii. 6 only.) ZECH. viii. 16.
xii. 5.   1 Cor. xii. 27.
only. PSA. iv. 4.
f here only.   3 Kings xv. 30.
5. xxxviii. 12.

b Rom. xv. 2. Heb. viii. 11. Micah vii. 2.
d Matt. v. 22. xviii. 34. xxii. 7. Luke xiv. 21. xv. 28. Rev. xi. 18
e here only. DEUT. xxiv. 15. Josh. viii. 29. Jer. xv. 9 only, always w. ἥλιος.
4 Kings xix. 3 al. see note.
h = Heb. xii. 17.

c = Rom.
xii. 5.
g Luke xiv. 9. Rom. xii. 19. Sir. iv.

25. εκαστος bef αληθειαν א¹ [Clem₁].   for μετα του, προς τον (LXX) א¹(txt
א-corr¹·³).

26. aft οργ. ins δε F [goth Tert₁].   for επι, εν D¹.   om τω ABא¹: ins
DFKL[P]א³ rel Clem Ath Ps-Ath Chr Thdrt₂ Damasc.

27. rec μητε, with rel Chr₁ Thdrt: txt ABDFKL[P]א c f g h k l m n o 17 Clem₁.

both expressions together complete the
idea of moral perfection (Matt. v. 48). As
here the *ethical side* of the divine image
is brought out, Col. iii. 10 brings out the
intellectual. The new birth alone leads
to ἐπίγνωσις: all knowledge which proceeds not from renewal of heart, is but
outward appearance: and of this kind
was that among the false Colossian teachers. On the other hand, in Wisd. ii. 23
(ὁ θεὸς ἔκτισεν τὸν ἄνθρωπον ἐπ' ἀφθαρσίᾳ,
καὶ εἰκόνα τῆς ἰδίας ἰδιότητος (ἀϊδιότ.
F. (not A.)) ἐποίησεν αὐτόν) the physical
side of the divine image is brought out."
Olsh. Stier suggests that there is perhaps
a slight contrast in δικαιοσύνη to πλεονεξία ver. 19, and in ὁσιότης (τὸ καθαρόν,
Chr.) to ἀκαθαρσία).   25.] Wherefore (because of the general character of
the καινὸς ἄνθρωπος as contrasted with
the παλαιός, which has been given: εἰπὼν
τὸν παλαιὸν ἄνθρωπον καθολικῶς, λοιπὸν
αὐτὸν κ. ὑπογράφει κατὰ μέρος, Chr.)
having put off (the aorist should be noticed here: it was open to the Apostle to
write ἀποτιθέμενοι, but he prefers the
past—because the man must have once
for all put off falsehood as a characteristic
before he enters the habit of speaking
truth) **falsehood** (abstract, see reff.), **speak
truth each one with his neighbour** ('sciamus de Zacharia propheta sumptum,' Jer.:
see ref. 'We allow ourselves the remark,
hoping it may not be over-refining, that
the Apostle instead of πρὸς τὸν πλησίον
with the LXX, prefers following the Hebrew text and writing μετά, to express by
anticipation our inner connexion with one
another as ἀλλήλων μέλη.' Stier): **for
we are members of one another** (Rom.
xii. 5. The ἀλλήλων brings out the relation between man and man more strongly
than if he had said, *of one body*: at the
same time it serves to remind them that all
mutual duties of Christians are grounded
on their union to and in Christ, and not on
mere ethical considerations).   **26.**]

Be ye angry and sin not (citation: see
ref. Psa.: and that from the LXX, not
from the Hebrew, which (see Hupfeld on
the Psalms in loc.) means '*tremble* ('stand
in awe,' E. V.) and sin not.' The first
imperative, although jussive, is so in a
weaker degree than the other: it is rather
assumptive, than permissive. 'Be angry
(if it must be so):' as if he had said, 1 Cor.
vii. 31, χρᾶσθε τῷ κόσμῳ τούτῳ (for that
must be), καὶ μὴ καταχρᾶσθε. As Chr.,
εἴ τις ἐμπέσοι ποτὲ εἰς τὸ πάθος, ἀλλὰ μὴ
εἰς τοσοῦτον. Thus Tholuck's question,
Bergpred., p. 186, is answered:—" If Paul
speaks of culpable anger, how can he distinguish sinning from being angry? If
of allowable anger, how can he expect not
to retain it over the night?"—the answer
being, that he speaks of anger which *is* an
infirmity, but by being cherished, may
become a sin): **let the sun not set upon
(so Thuc. has, νὺξ ἐπεγένετο τῷ ἔργῳ)
your irritation** (i. e. set to your wrath
with a brother (in every case: the omission of the art. gives the sense '*upon any
παροργισμός*') a speedy limit, and indeed
that one which nature prescribes—the
solemn season when you part from that
brother to meet again perhaps in eternity.
The Commentators quote from Plut. de
am. frat., p. 488 B, a custom of the Pytha-
goreans, εἴποτε προσαχθεῖεν εἰς λοιδορίας
ὑπ' ὀργῆς, πρὶν ἢ τὸν ἥλιον δῦναι, τὰς
δεξιὰς ἐμβάλλοντες ἀλλήλοις κ. ἀσπασά-
μενοι διελύοντο.   **παροργισμός** is a
late word, apparently not found beyond
the N. T. and LXX: the verb -ίζω occurs
ch. vi. 4, where see note. The **παρ-** implies, irritation *on occasion given*, as in
παρορμάω, παροξύνω),   **27.**] **nor
again** (there is a slight climax: see below.
The rec. μήτε would require that μή before should be capable of being taken as
μήτε, which it clearly cannot, on account
of its position after ὁ ἥλιος) **give scope**
(opportunity of action, which you would
do by continuing in a state of παρορ-

i διαβόλῳ. 28 ὁ jk κλέπτων μηκέτι k κλεπτέτω, l μᾶλλον
δὲ m κοπιάτω no ἐργαζόμενος ταῖς χερσὶν τὸ o ἀγαθόν, ἵνα
ἔχῃ p μεταδιδόναι τῷ q χρείαν ἔχοντι. 29 πᾶς λόγος
r σαπρὸς ἐκ τοῦ s στόματος ὑμῶν μὴ s ἐκπορευέσθω, ἀλλ'
t εἴ t τις ἀγαθὸς πρὸς u οἰκοδομὴν τῆς v χρείας, ἵνα w δῷ
χάριν τοῖς ἀκούουσιν. 30 καὶ μὴ x λυπεῖτε τὸ y πνεῦμα τὸ
y ἅγιον τοῦ y θεοῦ, ἐν ᾧ z ἐσφραγίσθητε a εἰς b ἡμέραν bc ἀπο-

ABDFK LPℵ a b c e f g h k l m n o 17. 47

i = Matt. iv. 1, &c. ‖ L. al. fr. Job i. 6, &c. (adj., 1 Tim. iii. 11. 2 Tim. ii. 3. Tit. ii. 3 only.)
j particip., Gal. i. 23. Rev. xv. 2 al. fr.
k Matt. vi. 19. Rom. ii. 21 al. Obad. 5.
l Gal. iv. 9 reff.
m Paul, Rom. xvi. 6 al12. Matt. vi. 28 al. Jer. xvii. 16.
n Matt. vii. 23. xxvi. 10. Acts x. 35. Ps. xiv. 2.
o Rom. ii. 10. Gal. vi. 10.
p Luke iii. 11. Rom. i. 11. xii. 8. 1 Thess. ii. 8 only. Job xxxi. 17.
q Matt. iii. 14. Gospels passim. 1 Cor. xii. 21 bis, 24. 1 Thess. i. 8 (al3. Paul). Heb. v. 12 bis. x. 36. 1 John ii. 27. iii. 17. Rev. iii. 17 al. Prov. xviii. 2.
r Matt. vii. 17, 18. xii. 33 bis. xiii. 48. Luke vi. 43 bis only †.
s Matt. iv. 4 (from Deut. viii. 3). xv. 11, &c. Luke iv. 22. Rev. passim. Paul, here only. Num. xxxii. 24.
t = Phil. iv. 8 bis.
u = ver. 12 reff.
v abs., Acts xxviii. 10. Sir. xxxix. 33. see Phil. ii. 25. iv. 16.
w = James iv. 6. 1 Pet. v. 5. see Exod. iii. 21. (Ps. lxxxiv. 12.)
x = Rom. xiv. 15 al. act., 2 Cor. ii. 2, 5 bis, vii. 8 bis only. Job xxxi. 39.
y here only.
z ch. i. 13 reff.
a = Phil. ii. 16 b. 2 Tim. i. 12.
b here only.
c ch. i. 7 reff.

28. rec *το αγαθον* bef *ταις χερσιν*, with L rel Chr Damasc Thl Œc: om *ταις χερσιν* [P] 17. 67² Clem₂: *το αγ. τ. ιδ. χ.* K a f 71-2. 80 syr Thdrt: *ταις ιδιαις χ. το αγαθ.* (*see* 1 *Cor.* iv. 12) ADFℵ¹ m [47, omg *χερσιν*] latt coptt goth æth arm Bas Naz Epiph Damasc Jer Aug Pel: txt Bℵ³ am Ambrst. *εχηται* ℵ¹: *εχει* L[P 17]. *μεταδουναι* D¹F [Clem₁(txt₁)].
29. [*αλλα* BD¹.] for *χρειας*, *πιστεως* D¹F latt lat-mss-in-Jer [goth] Bas$_{sæpe}$ Naz Anton-and-Max Tert Cypr Hil Aug Ambrst Pel. for *δω*, *δοι* D¹F: *μεταδιδω* K.
30. *το αγ. πν.* D¹·³F goth.

γισμός) **to the devil** (not, *to the slanderer*, as Erasm., al.: **διάβολος** as a substantive *always* has this personal meaning in the N. T.; see reff.). **28.**] **Let him that stealeth** (not '*that stole*,' as E. V.; '*qui furabatur*,' Vulg.: cf. reff., and Winer, § 45. 7. Stier remarks well, that the word lies between *κλέψας* and *κλέπτης*: the former would be too mild, the latter too strong) **steal no longer, but rather** (*οὐ γὰρ ἀρκεῖ παύσασθαι τῆς ἁμαρτίας, ἀλλὰ καὶ τὴν ἐναντίαν αὐτῆς ὁδὸν μετελθεῖν*, Thl.: similarly Chr.) **let him labour, working** (cf. besides reff., John vi. 27 and note) **with his hands** (contrast to his former idleness for good, and bad use of those hands) **that which is good** (*τὸ ἀγ.* 'antitheton ad furtum prius manu piceata commissum.' Beng.), **in order that** (as a purpose to be set before every Christian in his honest labour) **he may have to impart to him that has need.** **29.**] **Let every worthless** (*ὃ μὴ τὴν ἰδίαν χρείαν πληροῖ*, Chr. (in Mey.: not in Hom. h. l.): not so much '*filthy*,'—see ch. v. 4) **saying not come forth from your mouth,—but whatever** (saying) **is good for edification of the** (present) **need** (the **χρεία** is *the deficiency:* the part which needs *οἰκοδομεῖσθαι*, = the defect to be supplied by edification; and so is the regular objective genitive after **οἰκοδομήν**, which has no article, because it has a more general reference than merely to *τῆς χρείας*, which afterwards limits it. The renderings '*quâ sit opus*' (Erasm., Peile, al.), '*use of edifying*' (Syr., Beza, E. V.), are manifestly wrong), **that it may give grace** (minister spiritual benefit: be a means of conveying through you the grace of God. Such, from the context (cf. **οἰκοδ. τῆς χρ.**), must be the meaning, and not '*may give pleasure*,' as Thdrt., Kypke, al.) **to them that hear:** **30.**] **and** (Thl. finely gives the connexion: *ἐὰν εἴπῃς ῥῆμα σαπρὸν κ. ἀνάξιον τοῦ χριστιανοῦ στόματος, οὐκ ἄνθρωπον ἐλύπησας, ἀλλὰ τὸ πν. τ. θεοῦ*) **grieve not** (the expression is anthropopathic,—but as Meyer remarks, truly and touchingly sets forth the *love* of God, which (Rom. v. 5) is shed abroad in our hearts by His Spirit) **the Holy Spirit of God** (the repetition of the articles gives solemnity and emphasis), **in whom** (as the element, condition, of the sealing: not *by* whom; the sealing, both of the Lord and of us His members, is the act of the Father, John vi. 27: the Spirit *being the seal*, ch. i. 13) **ye were sealed unto** (in reservation for) **the day of redemption** (the day when redemption shall be complete in glory—see again ch. i. 13. On the genitive, see Winer, § 30. 2,—so *ἡμέρα ὀργῆς*, Rom. ii. 5, &c. So far from the doctrine of final perseverance, for which Eadie more sharply than reasonably contends, being involved here, there could hardly be a plainer denial of it by implication. For in what would issue the *grieving* of the Holy Spirit, if not in quenching His testimony and causing Him to depart * from them? The caution of Thl., *μὴ λύσῃς τὴν σφραγῖδα*, is a direct inference

λυτρώσεως. ³¹ πᾶσα ^d πικρια καὶ ^e θυμὸς καὶ ^e ὀργὴ καὶ ^f κραυγὴ καὶ ^{eg} βλασφημία ^h ἀρθήτω ἀφ᾽ ὑμῶν σὺν πάσῃ ^{ei} κακίᾳ, ³² γίνεσθε δὲ εἰς ἀλλήλους ^j χρηστοί, ^k εὔσπλαγχνοι, ^{lm} χαριζόμενοι ⁿⁿ ἑαυτοῖς καθὼς καὶ ὁ θεὸς ἐν χριστῷ ^l ἐχαρίσατο * ὑμῖν.

d Acts viii. 23. Rom. iii. 14, from Ps. ix. 7 (28). Heb. xii. 15 only. e Col. iii. 8. f = Acts xxiii. 9 (Matt. xxv. 6. Heb. v. 7. Rev. xiv. 18. xxi. 4) only. Isa.

v. 7. (-γάζειν, Matt. xii. 19.)   g = Col. iii. 8. 1 Tim. vi. 4.   h = (in epp.) 1 Cor. vi. 15. Col. ii. 14 only. Matt. xiii. 12 & Gospp. passim. Acts xxii. 22. Isa. v. 23.   i. Rom. i. 29. Tit. iii. 3. 1 Pet. ii. 1 al. Gen. xxxi. 52.   j of men, here only. (Matt. xi. 30. Luke v. 39. vi. 35. Rom. ii. 4. 1 Cor. xv. 33. 1 Pet. ii. 3 [from Ps. xxxiii. 8] only.) Ps. cxi. 5. (-ότης, ch. ii. 7 reff.) k 1 Pet. iii. 8 only †. see note.   l = Luke vii. 42, 43. 2 Cor. ii. 7, 10. xii. 13. Col. ii. 13. L.P.† (Sir. xii. 3 al.)   m Col. iii. 13.   n = 1 Cor. vi. 7. see note, Col. iii. 13.

31. οργη και θυμος DF [m] latt copt Clem₁ Ps-Ath Cypr₂.

32. om δε B k [47] 177 Clem₁ [Orig-cat₁] Damasc₂ Œc : for δε, ουν D¹F 114 : txt AD³KL[P]א rel vulg(and F-lat) syr coptt Chr Thdrt Damasc Thl Tert [Victorin] Jer.

* ημιν B(sic 1. m., see table) DKL rel am syrr [arm] Orig-cat Chr-comm Thdrt Thl : υμιν AF[P]א d h m latt coptt goth [æth] Clem Cyr Thl-marg Œc [Orig-int₁] Tert [Victorin] Ambrst.

from the passage). **31.**] **Let all bitterness** (οἱ δὲ πικροὶ δυσδιάλυτοι, κ. πολὺν χρόνον ὀργίζονται, κατέχουσι γὰρ τὸν θυμόν, Aristot. Eth. Nic. iv. 11. ὁ τοιοῦτος κ. βαρύθυμός ἐστι κ. οὐδέποτε ἀνίησι τὴν ψυχήν, ἀεὶ σύννους ὢν κ. σκυθρωπός, Chrys. So that it is not only of speech, but of disposition) **and wrath and anger** (θυμὸς μέν ἐστι πρόσκαιρος, ὀργὴ δὲ πολυχρόνιος μνησικακία, Ammon. Both are effects of πικρία, considered as a rooted disposition. See Trench, Synon., § 37) **and clamour** ('in quem erumpunt homines irati,' Est. Chrys. quaintly says, ἵππος γάρ ἐστιν ἀναβάτην φέρων ἡ κραυγὴ τὴν ὀργήν· συμπόδισον τὸν ἵππον, κ. κατέστρεψας τὸν ἀναβάτην. His reproofs to the ladies of Constantinople on this head give a curious insight into the domestic manners of the time) **and evil speaking** (the more chronic form of κραυγή—the reviling another not by an outbreak of abuse, but by the insidious undermining of evil surmise and slander. Chrys. traces a progress in the vices mentioned : ὅρα πῶς πρόεισι τὸ κακόν. ἡ πικρία τὸν θυμὸν ἔτεκεν, ὁ θ. τὴν ὀργήν, ἡ ὀρ. τὴν κραυγήν, ἡ κρ. τὴν βλασφημίαν, τουτέστι τὰς λοιδορίας) **be put away from you, with all malice** (the inner root, out of which all these spring. ἡ οὐκ οἶδας, ὅτι αἱ πυρκαϊαὶ μάλιστά εἰσι χαλεπώταται, αἵπερ ἂν ἔνδον τρεφόμεναι μὴ φαίνωνται τοῖς περιεστηκόσιν ἐκτός ; Chrys.): **32.**] **but be ye** (it is very difficult to mark the distinction between γίνεσθε and ἐστέ in a translation. *Become ye* (Ellic.) is certainly too far off the time present ; *be ye*, too immediately belonging to it. The difficulty is best seen in such a command as that in John xx. 27, μὴ γίνου ἄπιστος ἀλλὰ πιστός) **towards one another kind** (see note, Gal. v. 22), **tender-hearted**

("εὔσπλ. profanis animosum, fortem, cordatum notat (see Eurip. Rhes. 192). At res ipsa docet h. l. esse, misericordem, benignum (ref.). In testament. xii. patriarch. p. 644, de Deo dicitur : ἐλεήμων ἐστὶ καὶ εὔσπλαγχνος, ibid. paulo post ; piis ἴασις κ. εὐσπλαγχνία, 'salus et misericordia futura' dicitur, ibid. p. 641, ἔχετε εὐσπλαγχνίαν κατὰ παντὸς ἀνθρώπου." Kypke. So also in the prayer of Manasseh, ὁ, εὔσπλαγχνος, μακρόθυμος κ. πολυέλεος ; see also the parallel, Col. iii. 12), **forgiving** (see Luke vii. 42. Bengel notices that the three, **χρηστοί, εὔσπλαγχνοι, χαριζόμενοι ἑαυτοῖς,** are opposed respectively to **πικρία, θυμός,** and **ὀργή**) each other (this idiom is found in classical Greek—καθ᾽ αὑτοῖν δικρατεῖς λόγχας στήσαντ᾽ ἔχετον κοινοῦ θανάτου μέρος ἄμφω, Soph. Antig. 145. See Matthiæ, Gr. § 489. See remarks on its especial propriety as distinguished from ἀλλήλοις, on ref. Col.), **even as** (argument from His example whom we ought to resemble—also from the mingled motives of justice and gratitude, as Matt. xviii. 33, οὐκ ἔδει καὶ σε ἐλεῆσαι τὸν σύνδουλόν σου, ὡς κἀγώ σε ἠλέησα ;) **God in Christ** (not *'for Christ's sake,'* as E. V., see 2 Cor. v. 19, 20. God IN Christ, manifested in Him, in all He has done, and suffered : Christ is the sphere, the conditional element in which this act took place. Chrys. appears to take ἐν as *'at the cost of,'* as (?) Josh. vi. 26 ; Matt. xvii. 21 : for he says, ἵνα σοι συγγνῷ, τὸν υἱὸν ἔθυσε) **forgave you** (not *'has forgiven'* (κεχάρισται), as E. V. It is the historical fact of Christ once for all putting away sin by the sacrifice of Himself, which is alluded to. So that we are not 1) to attempt to change the meaning into a future ("even as thou, Lord, for

o 1 Cor. iv. 16.
xi. 1. 1 Thess.
i. 6. ii. 14.
Heb. vi. 12
only †.
p 1 Cor. iv. 14,
17.   2 Tim. i.
2. see Phil.
ii. 15.
q ch. ii. 10 reff.
r Gal. ii. 20.
ver. 25 only.
s (=) Acts xxi.
26. xxiv. 17.   Rom. xv. 16.   Heb. x. 5, &c. only.   t Heb. x. 5, from Ps. xxxix. 6.   u Matt. ix. 13
al. fr. esp. Heb.   v ch. ii. 22 reff.   w Phil. iv. 18 only.   Gen. viii. 21.   Levit. i. 9.   x John xii.
3. 2 Cor. ii. 14, 16 bis.   Phil. as above (w) only.   Exod. v. 21.   y 2 Cor. ii. 15.   Phil. as above (w)
only.   Ezra vi. 10.   z Col. iii. 5 (reff.).   Gal. v. 19.   2 Cor. xii. 21.   a see 1 Cor. v. 10. ver. 5.

V. ¹ Γίνεσθε οὖν ° μιμηταὶ τοῦ θεοῦ ὡς ᵖ τέκνα ᵖ ἀγα-
πητά, ² καὶ �q περιπατεῖτε q ἐν ἀγάπῃ, καθὼς καὶ ὁ χριστὸς ἠγάπησεν ὑμᾶς καὶ ʳ παρέδωκεν ʳ ἑαυτὸν ὑπὲρ ὑμῶν
ˢᵗ προσφορὰν καὶ ᵗᵘ θυσίαν τῷ θεῷ ᵛ εἰς ʷˣ ὀσμὴν ʷʸ εὐωδίας.
³ ᶻ πορνεία δὲ καὶ ᶻ ἀκαθαρσία πᾶσα ᵃ ἢ ᶻᵃ πλεονεξία μηδὲ

ABDFK
LPℵ a b
c e f g h
k l m n o
17. 47

CHAP. V. 2. rec ημας, with DFKLℵ³ rel vss Chr Thdrt lat-ff: txt AB[P]ℵ¹ m sah
æth Clem₂ Thl Victorin Ambr-ms.   rec ημων, with ADFKL[P]ℵ rel Clem (Orig):
txt B m 116 spec sah æth Victorin Ambr-ms.—προσφοραν bef υπ. ημ. D: om υπ. υμ.
115 Chr-comm₁ Thl Leo₁.   θυσιαν και προσφοραν ℵ.

3. rec πασα bef ακαθαρσια (see ch iv. 31), with DFKL rel latt Clem₁ Chr Thdrt
[Victorin] Jer: om πασα m Thdrt₂ Thl-ms: txt AB[P]ℵ 17 copt Clem₁ Ephr Tert.

Christ's sake, hast promised to forgive
us." Family Prayers by Bishop Blomfield,
p. 43): nor 2) to render χαριζόμενοι and
ἐχαρίσατο, with Erasmus, 'largientes'
and 'largitus est,' a meaning clearly at
variance with the context).   V. 1, 2.]
These verses are best taken as transitional,
—the inference from the exhortation which
has immediately preceded, and introduction to the dehortatory passage which
follows.   Certainly Stier seems right in
viewing the περιπατεῖτε as resuming περιπατῆσαι ch. iv. 1, and indicating a beginning, rather than a close, of a paragraph.
Be ye (γίνεσθε, see on last verse) therefore (seeing that God forgave you in Christ,
see next verse) imitators of God (viz. in
walking in love, see below), as children
beloved (see next verse: and 1 John iv. 19,
ἡμεῖς ἀγαπῶμεν, ὅτι αὐτὸς πρῶτος ἠγάπησεν ἡμᾶς) and (shew it by this, that
ye) walk in love, as Christ also (this
comes even nearer: from the love of the
Father who gave His Son, to that of the
Son, the Personal manifestation of that
love in our humanity) loved (not, 'hath
loved' as E. V.) you (the ὑμᾶς . . . ὑμῶν
is more a personal appeal: the ἡμᾶς . . .
ἡμῶν of the rec. is a general one, deduced
from the universal relation of us all to
Christ), and gave up Himself (absol.: not
to be joined with τῷ θεῷ) for you (see
note on Gal. iii. 13:—'on your behalf:'
in fact, but not necessarily here implied,
'in your stead') an offering and a sacrifice (beware of προσφ. κ. θυσ. =
θυσίαν προσφερομένην (Conyb.): it is our
duty, in rendering, to preserve the terms
coupled, even though we may not be able
precisely to say wherein they differ.   The
ordinary distinction, that προσφορά is an
unbloody offering, θυσία a slain victim,
cannot be maintained, see Heb. x. 5, 18;
xi. 4.   I believe the nearest approach to
the truth will be made by regarding προσφ.

as the more general word, including all
kinds of offering,—θυσία as the more special one, usually involving the death of a
victim.   The great prominent idea here is
the one sacrifice, which the Son of God
made of Himself in his redeeming Love,
in our nature—bringing it, in Himself,
near to God—offering Himself as our representative Head: whether in perfect righteousness of life, or in sacrifice, (properly so
called, at his Death) to God (to be joined,
as a dat. commodi, with πρ. κ. θυσ.: not
with παρέδωκεν (as De W. and Mey.),
from which it is too far removed: still less
(as Stier, who would apply the clause τῷ
θ. . . . . εὐωδίας, to us) with what follows)
for an odour of sweet smell (the question
so much discussed, whether these words
can apply to a sin-offering strictly so called,
is an irrelevant one here.   It is not [see
above] the death of Christ which is treated
of, but the whole process of His redeeming
Love.   His death lies in the background
as one, and the chief, of the acknowledged
facts of that process: but it does not give
the character to what is here predicated of
Him.   The allusion primarily is to ref.
Gen., where after Noah had brought to
God a sacrifice of every clean beast and
bird, ὠσφράνθη κύριος ὁ θεὸς ὀσμὴν
εὐωδίας,—and the promise followed, that
He would no more destroy the earth for
man's sake).   3—21.] Dehortation
(for the most part) from works unbecoming
the holiness of the life of children and
imitators of God.   3.] But (not transitional merely: there is a contrast brought
out by the very mention of πορνεία after
what has just been said) fornication and
all impurity or (see ch. iv. 19 note) covetousness (ib.), let it not be even named
('ne nomen quidem audiatur.' Calv.   So
Dio Chrys. p. 360 B (Mey.), στάσιν δὲ
οὐδὲ ὀνομάζειν ἄξιον παρ' ὑμῖν: Herod. i.
138, ἅσσα δέ σφι ποιέειν οὐκ ἔξεστι, ταῦτα

^b ὀνομαζέσθω ἐν ὑμῖν, καθὼς ^c πρέπει ^d ἁγίοις, ⁴ καὶ ^e αἰσ- χρότης καὶ ^f μωρολογία, ἢ ^g εὐτραπελία ἃ οὐκ ^h ἀν- ῆκεν, ἀλλὰ μᾶλλον ⁱ εὐχαριστία. ⁵ τοῦτο γὰρ ^j ἴστε

b ch. i. 21 reff.
c constr.,
1 Tim. ii. 10.
Tit. ii. 1.
Heb. ii. 10.
Ps. xxxii.
vii. 26 only.

1. Sir. xxx. (xxxiii.) 28. d ch. i. 1 reff. e here only †. see ver. 12. Col. iii. 8.
f here only †. see Isa.' xxxii. 6. g here only †. see note. h Col. iii. 18. Philem.
8 only †. 1 Macc. xi. 35 (3ee) al. but not =. i = Acts xxiv. 3. Phil. iv. 6. Col. ii. 7 al. Luke & Paul
only, exc. Rev. iv. 9. vii. 12 †. Wisd. xvi. 28. Sir. xxxviii. 11. 2 Macc. ii. 28 only. j Acts
xxvi. 4. Heb. xii. 17. James i. 19 only.

4. for 1st and 2nd και, η (to suit η before) AD¹F latt sah Bas Ephr Antch Iren-int Orig-int [Victorin : 2nd only Pא¹] : transp 2nd και and η c: txt BD³KLא-corr¹ rel copt Clem Chr Thdrt Damasc Jer.   rec (for ἃ ουκ ανηκεν) τα ουκ ανηκοντα, with DFKL rel (Clem₁) Chr Thdrt Damasc : txt AB[P]א 17(omg ἅ) [47] 67² Clem₁ Ephr Antch Cyr.

5. rec (for ιστε) εστε, with D³KL rel syr Thdrt Damasc Thl : txt ABD¹F[P]א h 17

οὐδὲ λέγειν ἔξεστι. Cf. Ps. xv. 4) among you, as becometh saints (meaning, that if it were talked of, such conversation would be unbecoming the holy ones of God): and obscenity (not in word only (αἰσχρολογία, ref. Col.) : cf. Plato, Gorg. p. 525 Α, ὑπὸ ἐξουσίας κ. τρυφῆς κ. ὕβρεως κ. ἀκρατίας τῶν πράξεων ἀσυμμετρίας τε καὶ αἰσχρό- τητος γέμουσαν τὴν ψυχὴν εἶδεν) and foolish talking ('stultiloquium,' Vulg. Wetst. quotes from Antigonus de Mirabi- libus, 126, τὰ μεγάλα κ. ἐπανεστηκότα μωρολογίας κ. ἀδολεσχίας. Trench well maintains, Syn. § 34, that in Christian ethics, it is more than mere 'random talk :' it is that talk of fools, which is folly and sin together : including not merely the πᾶν ῥῆμα ἀργόν of our Lord (Matt. xii. 36), but in good part also the πᾶς λόγος σαπρός of his Apostle (Eph. iv. 29)) or (disjunc- tive, marking off εὐτραπελία as πλεονεξία before) jesting (much interest attaches to this word, which will be found well dis- cussed in Trench, as above. It had at first a good signification : Aristot. Eth. Nic. iv. 8, deals with the εὐτράπελος—οἱ ἐμμελῶς παίζοντες εὐτράπελοι προσαγο- ρεύονται,—and describes him as the mean between the βωμολόχος and ἄγροικος. So too Plato, Rep. viii. p. 563 Α,—οἱ δὲ γέροντες ξυγκαθιέντες τοῖς νέοις εὐτραπε- λίας τε κ. χαριεντισμοῦ ἐμπίπλανται, . . . ἵνα δὴ μὴ δοκῶσιν ἀηδεῖς εἶναι μηδὲ δεσποτικοί. But Trench remarks that there were indications of a bad sense of the word : e. g. Pind. Pyth. i. 178,—μὴ δο- λωθῇς, ὦ φίλε, κέρδεσιν εὐτραπέλοις, where he quotes from Dissen—' primum est de facilitate in motu, tum ad mores transfertur, et indicat hominem temporibus inservientem, diciturque tum de sermone urbano, lepido, faceto, imprimis cum levi- tatis et assentationis, simulationis notione.' I may add, as even more apposite here, Pyth. iv. 185, οὔτε ἔργον οὔτ' ἔπος εὐ- τράπελον κείνοισιν εἰπών. Aristotle him- self, Rhet. ii. 12 end, defines it as πεπαι- δευμένη ὕβρις. "The profligate old man

in the 'miles gloriosus' of Plautus, iii. 1. 42—52, who at the same time prides himself, and with reason, on his wit, his elegance, and his refinement (cavil- latus, lepidus, facetus), is exactly the εὐτράπελος : and remarkably enough, when we remember that εὐτραπελία being only expressly forbidden once in Scripture, is forbidden to Ephesians, we find him bringing out, that all this was to be expected from him, seeing that he was an Ephesian : 'Post Ephesi sum natus : non enim in Apulis, non Animulæ.'" Trench : whose further remarks should by all means be read), which are not be- coming (the reading τὰ οὐκ ἀνήκοντα has perhaps come into the text from the τὰ μὴ καθήκοντα of Rom. i. 28, the οὐκ of the text being preserved through inadvertence. If, however, the participial clause be re- tained in the text, it may be grammati- cally justified by remembering that, where the various objects are specified which as matter of fact are οὐκ ἀνήκοντα, the ob- jective negative particle οὐκ may be used: whereas in Rom. i. 28, where no such objects are specified, we have ποιεῖν τὰ μὴ καθήκοντα, 'si quæ essent indecora,' as Winer, § 55. 5 : see Hartung, vol. ii. p. 131): but rather thanksgiving (not, as Jer., Calv., al., 'sermo qui gratiam apud audientes habet,' which the word cannot mean. It is a question, what verb is to be supplied : Beng. supposes ἀνήκει, which is perhaps most likely, as suiting the simplicity of the construction of these hortatory verses better than going back to ὀνομαζέσθω (De W., Mey., al.),—and as finding a parallel in ch. iv. 29, where the ellipsis is to be supplied from the sentence itself. There is a play perhaps on the similar sound of εὐτρα- πελία and εὐχαριστία, which may ac- count for the latter not finding so com- plete a justification in the sense as we might expect : the connexion being ap- parently, 'your true cheerfulness and play of fancy will be found, not in buffoonery,

k constr., here only. see
Luke iv. 44 & pass. in Gospp.
Gen. i. 6.
11 Cor. v. 9, 10, 11. vi. 10.
1 Tim. i. 10.
Heb. xii. 16.
xiii. 4. Rev. xxi. 8. xxii.

k γινώσκοντες, ὅτι πᾶς ¹πόρνος ἢ ᵐἀκάθαρτος ἢ ⁿπλεον-
έκτης, °ὅ ἐστιν ᴾεἰδωλολάτρης, οὐχ ἔχει ᑫκληρονομίαν ἐν
τῇ βασιλείᾳ τοῦ ʳχριστοῦ καὶ ʳθεοῦ. ⁶ μηδεὶς ὑμᾶς
ˢἀπατάτω ᵗκενοῖς λόγοις· διὰ ταῦτα γὰρ ἔρχεται ἡ
ὀργὴ τοῦ θεοῦ ἐπὶ τοὺς ᵘυἱοὺς τῆς ᵘἀπειθείας. ⁷ μὴ

ABDFK
LℵN a b
c e f g h
k l m n o
17. 47

15†. Sir. xxiii. 16, 17 only.　　　　m = Rev. xvii. 4 only. in Gospp., only with πνεῦμα.　so also Acts v.
16. viii. 7.　Rev. xvi. 13. xviii. 2 a.　legal, Acts x. 14, 28. xi. 8.　1 Cor. vii. 14.　2 Cor. vi. 17.　Rev. xviii. 2 b.
n 1 Cor. v. 10, 11. vi. 10 only †.　Sir. xiv. 9 only.　　　　o constr. (see note), Mark xii. 42. xv. 42.　John i. 42,
43. Acts iv. 36.　　　　p 1 Cor. v. 10, 11. vi. 9. x. 7.　Rev. xxi. 8. xxii. 15 only †.　　　　q ch. i. 14 reff.
r Rev. xx. 6. see 1 Tim. v. 21.　Rev. xi. 15.　　　　s 1 Tim. i. 14.　James i. 26 only.　Isa. xxxvi. 14.
t 1 Cor. xv. 10, 14, 58.　Col. ii. 8.　James ii. 20.　Exod. v. 9.　Job vi. 6.　　　　u ch. ii. 2 reff.

latt coptt goth arm Clem Chr Cyr Œc Suid Cypr Jer Vig Pel.　rec (for ὅ) ὅς (*cf
constr in the* ‖ *Col* iii. 5, *where* ητις *follows the gender of* πλεονεξιαν : *the readg of* F
&c is another form of the same corrn, retaining the origl ὅ), with ADKL[P] rel syr
copt Clem Chr Thdrt₂ : txt Bℵ 17. 67² Cyr Jer₂, also with ιδωλολατρια F latt Cypr
Victorin Jer Ambrst.

　6. καινοις (*itacism*) ℵ.　　om γαρ ℵ¹(ins ℵ-corr¹) [Tert].

but in the joy of a heart overflowing
with a sense of God's mercies').

5.] *Appeal to their own knowledge that
such practices exclude from the kingdom
of God:* see below. **For this ye know**
(indicative, not imperative : this to my
mind is decided 1) by the context, in
which an appeal to their own consciousness of the fact is far more natural than a
communication of the fact to them : 2)
by the position of the words, which in the
case of an imperative would more naturally
be ἴστε γὰρ τοῦτο γινώσκοντες : 3) by the
use of the construction ἴστε γινώσκοντες,
which almost necessitates a matter of
fact underlying γινώσκοντες.—ἴστε γιν.
is not an example of the γινώσκων γνώσῃ
(Gen. xv. 13 al.) of Hebrew usage, the two
verbs being different) **being aware that
every fornicator or** (ἢ now, not καί, for
individualization of each) **unclean man,
or covetous man, which is** (i. e. 'that
is to say,'—'quod;' meaning, *the word*
πλεονέκτης. This reading necessarily confines the reference to *that one word*) **an
idolater** (cf. Col. iii. 5, which shews that
even ὅς ἐστιν would apply to the πλεονέκτης only, not, as Stier, al., to the *three :*
see Job xxxi. 24 ; Ps. lii. 7 ; Matt. vi. 24.
Mey. remarks well, that it was very natural for St. Paul, whose forsaking of all
things (2 Cor. vi. 10 ; xi. 27) so strongly
contrasted with selfish greediness, to mark
with the deepest reprobation the sin of
πλεονεξία), **hath not inheritance** (the *present* implying more the fixedness of the
exclusion, grounded on the eternal verities
of that Kingdom,—than mere future certainty : see 1 Cor. xv. 25) **in the Kingdom of Christ and God** (not '*and of God*'
(κ. τοῦ θ.) as E. V. No *distinction* is to
be made, χριστοῦ καὶ θεοῦ being in the
closest union. Nor is any specification
needed that the Kingdom of Christ is

also the Kingdom of God, as would be
made with the second article. This follows as matter of course : and thus the
words bear no legitimate rendering, except on the substratum of our Lord's Divinity. But on the other hand, we cannot safely say here, that the same Person
is intended by χριστοῦ κ. θεοῦ, merely on
account of the omission of the article.
For 1) any introduction of such a predication regarding Christ would here be
manifestly out of place, not belonging to
the context : 2) θεός is so frequently and
unaccountably anarthrous, that it is not
safe to ground any such inference from
its use here). 　　6.] **Let no one deceive
you with vain** (empty—not containing
the kernel of truth, of which words are
but the shell—words with no underlying
facts. Æschines, de Corona, p. 288, says
that Demosthenes had drawn up a decree,
κενώτερον τῶν λόγων οὓς εἴωθε λέγειν, κ.
τοῦ βίου ὃν βεβίωκε. See other examples in Kypke h. l.) **sayings** (the persons
pointed at are heathen, or pretended
Christian, palliators of the fore-mentioned
vices. The caution was especially needed,
at a time when moral purity was so generally regarded as a thing indifferent.
Harl. quotes from Bullinger, — " Erant
apud Ephesios homines corrupti, ut hodie
apud nos plurimi sunt, qui hæc salutaria
Dei præcepta cachinno excipientes obstre-
punt : humanum esse quod faciant ama-
tores, utile quod fœneratores, facetum
quod joculatores, et idcirco Deum non
usque adeo graviter animadvertere in
istiusmodi lapsus"); **for** (let them say what
they will, it is a fact, that) **on account of
these things** (the above-mentioned crimes,
see Col. iii. 6, δι' ὃ ἔρχεται ἡ ὀργ. κ.τ.λ. :
not the ἀπάτη just spoken of, to which
the objection is not so much the plural
ταῦτα, as the τοὺς υἱοὺς τ. ἀπειθείας

οὖν γίνεσθε ᵛ συμμέτοχοι αὐτῶν. ⁸ ʷ ἦτε γάρ ποτε ˣ σκότος, νῦν δὲ ˣ φῶς ἐν κυρίῳ· ὡς ʸ τέκνα φωτὸς ᶻ περιπατεῖτε ⁹ (ὁ γὰρ ᵃ καρπὸς τοῦ φωτὸς ἐν πάσῃ ᵇ ἀγαθωσύνῃ
καὶ δικαιοσύνῃ καὶ ἀληθείᾳ), ¹⁰ ᶜ δοκιμάζοντες τί ἐστιν
ᵈ εὐάρεστον τῷ κυρίῳ· ¹¹ καὶ μὴ ᵉ συγκοινωνεῖτε τοῖς

v ch. iii. 6 only †.
w Rom. vi. 17.
x Acts xxvi. 18. Rom. ii. 19. xiii. 12. 2 Cor. iv. 6
al. Isa. ix. 2.
y ch. ii. 3 reff.
z ch. iv. 1 reff.
a Gal. v. 22 reff.

b Rom. xv. 14. Gal. v. 22. 2 Thess. i. 11 only. Neh. ix. 35. c 1 Thess. ii. 4 reff. constr., Rom.
xii. 2. d Rom. xii. 1, 2. Phil. iv. 18. Col. iii. 20 al3. only. P.H.† Wisd. iv· 10. ix. 10 only. (-τως,
Heb. xii. 28. -τεῖν, Heb. xi. 5.) e Phil. iv. 14. Rev. xviii. 4 only †. (-ος, Phil. i. 7.)

9. rec (for φωτος) πνευματος (*from Gal* v. 25), with D³KL rel syr Chr Thdrt Damasc : txt ABD¹F[P]א 17 [47] 67² latt Syr coptt æth arm Mcion lat-ff.

10. for κυριω, θεω D¹F latt lat-ff(exc Aug).

which follows, shewing that the carrying out of their ἀπείθεια are the things spoken of; and the μὴ οὖν γίν. κ.τ.λ. of ver. 7) **cometh** (present, as ἔχει, ver. 5) **the wrath of God** (not merely, or chiefly, His ordinary judgments, 'quorum exempla sunt ante oculos,' as Calv. : nor the 'antitheton reconciliationis,' as Beng., for that is on all who are not in Christ (John iii. 36) : but His *special* wrath, His vengeance *for these sins*, over and above their state of ἀπείθεια) **on the sons of** (see on ch. ii. 2) **disobedience** (the active and practical side of the state of the ἀπειθῶν (John iii. 36) is here brought out. The word is a valuable middle term between unbelief and disobedience, implying their identity in a manner full of the highest instruction).

7.] **Be not** (the distinction ' *Become not*' ('nolite effici,' Vulg.: so Stier, Ellic., al.) is unnecessary and indeed unsuitable : it is not a gradual 'becoming,' but 'being,' like them, which he here dehorts from. See on γίνεσθε not bearing the meaning "become," note, ch. iv. ult.) **therefore** (since this is so—that God's wrath comes on them) **partakers** (see ch. iii. 6) **with them** (the υἱοὶ τ. ἀπ., not the *sins* :—sharers in that which they have in common, viz. these practices : their *present* habitude, not, *their punishment*, which is future: nor can the two senses be combined, as Stier characteristically tries to do). **8.]** **For** (your state (present, see above) is a totally different one from theirs—*excluding* any such participation) **ye** WERE (emphatic, see ref.) **once** (no μέν. "The rule is simple : if the first clause is intended to stand in connexion with and prepare the reader for the opposition to the second, μέν is inserted : if not, not : see the excellent remarks of Klotz, Devar. ii. p. 356 sq. : Fritz., Rom. x. 19, vol. ii. p. 423." Ellic.) **darkness** (stronger than ἐν σκότει, Rom. ii. 19 ; 1 Thess. v. 4 : they were *darkness itself*—see on φῶς below), **but now** (the ἐστέ is not expressed—perhaps, as Stier

suggests, not only for emphasis, but to carry a slight tinge of the coming exhortation, by shewing them what they *ought* to be, as well as were by profession) **light** (not πεφωτισμένοι—light has an active, illuminating power, which is brought out in ver. 13) **in** ('*in union with*'—conditioning element—not '*by*'—διὰ τῆς θεοῦ χάριτος, Chr.) **the Lord** (Jesus) : **walk** (the omission of οὖν makes the inference rhetorically more forcible) **as children of light** (not τοῦ φωτός, as in Luke xvi. 8, where τὸ φῶς is contrasted with ὁ αἰὼν οὗτος, and in next verse, where τοῦ φωτός is the figurative φῶς—q. d. 'the light of which I speak :' here it is light, *as light*, which is spoken of. The omission of the article *may* be merely from the rules of correlation, as Ellic. : but I much prefer here to treat it as significant) ; **for** (gives the reason of the introduction of the comparison in the context, connecting this with the moral details which have preceded) **the fruit of the light** (τοῦ, see above) **is in** (is borne within the sphere of, as its condition and element) **all goodness and righteousness and truth** (in all that is good (Gal. v. 22), right, and true. As Harl. observes, the opposites are κακία, ἀδικία, ψεῦδος) : **proving** (to be joined with περιπατεῖτε as its modal predicate, ver. 9 having been parenthetical. The Christian's whole course is a continual proving, testing, of the will of God in practice : investigating not what pleases himself, but what pleases Him) **what is well-pleasing to the Lord ;** **11.]** **and have no fellowship with** (better than '*be not partakers in*,' as De W., which would require a genitive, see Demosth. p. 1299. 20, συγκεκοινωνήκαμεν τῆς δόξης ταύτης οἱ κατεστασιασμένοι : whereas the person *with whom*, is regularly put in the dative, e. g. Dio Cass. xxxvii. 41, συγκοινωνήσαντός σφισι τῆς συνωμοσίας,—ib. lxxvii. 16, συνεκοινώνησαν αὐτῇ κ. ἕτεραι τρεῖς τῆς καταδίκης. And Phil. iv. 14 furnishes no objection to this rendering) **the unfruit-**

f Rom. xiii. 12
only. see
1 Cor. v. 5.
Isa. xxix. 15.
g Matt. xii. 22
‖ Mk. 1 Cor.
xiv. 14. Tit.
iii. 14. 2 Pet.
i. 8. Jude
12 only. Jer.
ii. 6. Wisd.
xv. 4 only.
h Gal. iv. 9 reff.

f ἔργοις τοῖς g ἀκάρποις τοῦ f σκότους, h μᾶλλον δὲ καὶ ἐλέγχετε. 12 τὰ γὰρ j κρυφῇ γινόμενα ὑπ᾿ αὐτῶν k αἰσχρόν ἐστιν καὶ λέγειν· 13 τὰ δὲ πάντα h ἐλεγχόμενα ὑπὸ τοῦ φωτὸς l φανεροῦται· πᾶν γὰρ τὸ l φανερούμενον φῶς ἐστιν. 14 διὸ m λέγει no Ἔγειρε ὁ op καθεύδων καὶ q ἀνάστα

ABDFK
LP‎‎‎‎‎‎‎‎ a b
cefgh
klmno
17. 47

i = John iii. 20.
only. 1 Kings xix. 2.
l Mark iv. 22. John iii. 21. Paul, Rom. i. 19 al. fr.
n Isa. lx. 1 Heb. Rom xiii. 11. Isa. xxvi. 19.
q Mark vi. 14. ix. 9, 10. xii. 25. Luke xvi. 31. John xx. 9. Acts x. 41. xvii. 3.

1 Cor. xiv. 24.　2 Tim. iv. 2.　Tit. i. 9, 13. ii. 15.　Ps. xlix. 21.　Xen. Symp. viii. 43.
k 1 Cor. xi. 6. xiv. 35.　Tit. i. 11 only. P.　Gen. xli. 3, &c. only.
Jer. xl. (xxxiii.) 6 only.　　　　　　m ch. iv. 8 reff.
o Dan. xii. 2 Theod.　　　　　　　　p 1 Thess. v. 6 reff.
j here

13. φανερουνται ΑΚ²L c m.
14. rec εγειραι, with rel [Hipp₂ Orig-cat₁] : txt ABDFKL[P]‎‎‎‎‎‎‎ e n [47 Mcion-e₂

ful works of darkness (see Gal. v. 19, 22 ; on which Jer., vol. vii. p. 505, says 'vitia in semetipsa finiuntur et pereunt, virtutes frugibus pullulant et redundant.' See also the distinction in John iii. 20, 21; v. 29, between τὰ φαῦλα πράσσειν and τὰ ἀγαθὰ or τὴν ἀλήθειαν ποιεῖν), but rather even reprove them (see reff.,—in words : not only abstain from fellowship with them, but attack them and put them to shame). 12.] For (the connexion seems to be, 'reprove them—this they want, and this is more befitting you—for to have the least part in them, even in speaking of them, is shameful') the things done in secret by them, it is shameful even to speak of (so καί in Plato, Rep. v. p. 465 B, τά γε μὴν σμικρότατα τῶν κακῶν δι᾿ ἀπρέπειαν ὀκνῶ καὶ λέγειν, see Hartung ii. p. 136. Klotz, Devar. ii. p. 633 f. : the connexion being—'I mention not, and you need not speak of, these deeds of darkness, much less have any fellowship with them—your connexion with them must be only that which the act of ἔλεγξις necessitates') :　13.] but (opposition to τὰ κρυφῇ γιν.) all things (not only, all the κρυφῇ γινόμενα, as Ellic. after Jer. al. : the Apostle is treating of the general detecting power of light, as is evident by the resumption of the πᾶν in the next clause) being reproved, are made manifest by the light : for every thing which is made manifest is light (the meaning being, 'the light of your Christian life, which will be by your reproof shed upon these deeds of darkness, will bring them out of the category of darkness into light' (ἐπειδὰν φανερωθῇ, γίνεται φῶς, Chr.). They themselves were thus 'once darkness,' but having been 're-proved' by God's Spirit, had become 'light in the Lord.' There is in reality no difficulty, nor any occasion for a long note here. The only matters to be insisted on are, 1) ὑπὸ τοῦ φωτός belongs to φανεροῦται, not to ἐλεγχόμενα : for it is not the fact of φανεροῦται that he is insisting

on, but the fact that if they reproved the works of darkness, these would become no longer works of darkness, but would be ὑπὸ τοῦ φωτὸς φανερούμενα. And 2) φανερούμενον is passive, not middle, in which sense it is never used in N. T. ; 'every thing which is made manifest, is no longer darkness, but light : and thus you will be, not compromised to these works of darkness, but making an inroad upon the territory of darkness with the ὅπλα τοῦ φωτός.' And thus the context leads on easily and naturally to the next verse. The objection to this (Eadie) that 'light does not always exercise this transforming influence, for the devil and all the wicked are themselves condemned by the light, without becoming themselves light,' is null, being founded on misapprehension of the φῶς ἐστιν. Objectively taken, it is universally true : every thing shone upon IS LIGHT. Whether this tend to condemnation or otherwise, depends just on whether the transforming influence takes place. The key-text to this is John iii. 20, πᾶς γὰρ ὁ φαῦλα πράσσων μισεῖ τὸ φῶς, κ. οὐκ ἔρχεται πρὸς τὸ φῶς, ἵνα μὴ ἐλεγχθῇ τὰ ἔργα αὐτοῦ,—His works being thus brought into the light,—made light, and he being thus put to shame. Notice also φανερωθῇ in the next verse, which is the desire of him who ποιεῖ τὴν ἀλήθειαν. The E. V. is doubly wrong— 1) in 'all things that are reproved' (π. τὰ ἐλεγχόμενα) : 2) in 'whatsoever doth make manifest is light' (πᾶν τὸ φανεροῦν) : besides that such a proposition has absolutely no meaning in the context. The meaning is discussed at length in Harl., Eadie, who however fall into the error of rendering φανερούμενον active (not middle),—Stier, Ellicott,—and best of all, Meyer) :　14.] wherefore (this being so—seeing that every thing that is made manifest becomes light,—is shone upon by the detecting light of Christ,—objectively,—it only remains that the man should be shone upon inwardly by the

ἐκ τῶν q νεκρῶν, r καὶ s ἐπιφαύσει σοι ὁ χριστός.　15 t βλέπετε οὖν u πῶς v ἀκριβῶς περιπατεῖτε, μὴ ὡς w ἄσοφοι,
ἀλλ᾽ ὡς σοφοί, 16 xy ἐξαγοραζόμενοι τὸν y καιρόν, ὅτι αἱ
za ἡμέραι ab πονηραί εἰσιν. 17 διὰ τοῦτο μὴ γίνεσθε c ἄφρονες,

r = John ii. 19.
James iv. 7, 8.
Rev. ii. 10.
s here only.
(-σκειν, Job
xxv. 5. xxxi.
26. xli. 9 BCℵ
[-φωσκ. A]
only.)
u = (see
note)
v = here (1 Thess. v. 2 reff.) only.　(-ής, Acts xxvi. 5.)
y Col. Dan. as above.
[-φωσκ. A]

t = Matt. xxiv. 4.　1 Cor. iii. 10. viii. 9. x. 12. xvi. 10.　Gal. v. 15.　Col. ii. 8.　Heb. iii. 12. xii. 25.
note) Luke viii. 18.　1 Cor. iii. 10.
w here only †.　　x Gal. iii. 13. iv. 5.　Col. iv. 5 only.　Dan. ii. 8 only.
z = 2 Tim. iii. 1.　Heb. x. 32.　1 Pet. iii. 10.　　a Ps. xl. 1.　　b = Gal. i. 4. ch. vi. 13.　　c Luke
xi. 40. xii. 20.　Rom. ii. 20 al6. L.P., exc. 1 Pet. ii. 15.　Job v. 3.

Clem Orig₁(and cat₃)].　επιψαυσεις του χριστου contingeς Christum D¹ mss-in-
Chr-Jer Thdrt(who however cites txt from ἔνια τῶν ἀντιγρ. with approval) Orig-int
Ambrst: txt ABD³FKL[P]ℵ rel [Mcion-e₂ Hipp₂] Clem Orig₂ Ath Chr Damasc
(Archel) Jer Ambr Aug_aliq Vig Pel.
　15. aft ουν ins αδελφοι Aℵ³ vulg copt Pel.　　ακριβως bef πως Bℵ¹ 17 copt [Orig-
cat₂] Chr₁.

same Christ revealed in his awakened
heart. We have then in Scripture an
exhortation to that effect) He (viz. God,
in the Scripture : see ch. iv. 8 note: all
other supplies, such as 'the Spirit in
the Christian' (Stier),—'the Christian
speaking to the Heathen' (Flatt),—'one
may say' (Bornemann) &c. are mere
lame helps out of the difficulty :—as are
all ideas of St. Paul having quoted a
Christian hymn (some in Thdrt.), an
apocryphal writing (some in Jer., Epiph.,
al.), a baptismal formula (Michaelis),—
one of our Lord's unrecorded sayings
(Rhenferd),—or that he means, 'thus
saith the Lord' (some in Jer. al.), or
alludes to the general tenor of Scripture
(Wesley),—or does not quote at all
(Barnes), &c. &c.) saith, Awake, thou
that sleepest, and arise from the dead,
and Christ shall shine upon thee (where
is this citation to be found? In the first
place, by the introduction of ὁ χριστός,
it is manifestly a paraphrase, not an
exact citation. The Apostle cites, and had
a perfect right to cite, the language of
prophecy in the light of the fulfilment of
prophecy : and that he is here doing so,
the bare word 'Christ' shews us beyond
dispute. I insist on this, that it may be
plainly shewn to be no shift in a difficulty,
no hypothesis among hypotheses,—but the
necessary inference from the form of the
citation. This being so,—of what passage
of the O. T. is this a paraphrase? I
answer, of Isa. lx. 1, 2. There, the church
is set forth as being in a state of darkness
and of death (cf. lix. 10), and is exhorted
to awake, and become light, for that her
light is come, and the glory of Jehovah
has arisen upon her. Where need we go
further for that of which we are in search?
It is not true (as Stier), that there is 'no
allusion to sleep or death' in the prophet :
nor is it true again, that ἐπὶ σὲ φανήσεται

κύριος κ. ἡ δόξα αὐτοῦ ἐπὶ σὲ ὀφθήσεται
is not represented by ἐπιφαύσει σοι ὁ
χριστός. The fact is, that Stier has altogether mistaken the context, in saying,—
"The Apostle quotes here, not to justify
the exhortation—'convict, that they may
become light;'—but to exhort—' Become
light, that ye may be able to convict
(shine):'" the refutation of which see
above, on ver. 13). 15.] He now resumes the hortative strain, interrupted by
the digression of vv. 12—14. Take heed
then (there is not any immediate connexion with the last verse : but the οὖν
resumes from the περιπατεῖτε in ver. 8,
and that which followed it there) how ye
walk strictly (the construction is exactly
as in ref. 1 Cor., ἕκαστος δὲ βλεπέτω πῶς
ἐποικοδομεῖ. 'Take heed, of what sort
your ἀκριβῶς περιπατεῖν is:'—the implication being, 'take heed not only that
your walk be exact, strict, but also of
what sort that strictness is—not only that
you have a rule, and keep to it, but that
that rule be the best one.' So that a
double exhortation is involved. See
Ellic. here : and the Fritzschiorum Opuscula, pp. 208 f., note), (namely) not
as unwise, but as wise (qualification
of the ἀκριβῶς περιπατεῖτε, and expansion of the πῶς (μή, subj.): no περιπατοῦντες need be supplied after μή, as
Harl.), buying up for yourselves (the)
opportunity (viz. of good, whenever occurring; let it not pass by, but as merchants
carefully looking out for vantages, make
it your own : see Col. iv. 5. The compound ἐξ- does not suggest the question
'from whom' it is to be bought, as Beng.,
Calv., al., nor imply mere completeness,
as Mey., but rather refers to the 'collection out of' (see reff. Gal.), the buying
up, as we say : culling your times of good
out of a land where there are few such
flowers. The middle gives the reflexive

d Rom. iii. 11,
from Ps. xiii.
2, al. fr.
e Acts xxi. 14
only. elsw.
(ch. vi. 6 al.
fr.) τοῦ θεοῦ.
f Prov. xxiii.

ἀλλὰ ^dσυνίετε τί τὸ ^eθέλημα τοῦ ^eκυρίου. ¹⁸καὶ μὴ ^fμεθύσκεσθε οἴνῳ, ἐν ᾧ ἐστιν ^gἀσωτία, ἀλλὰ ^hπληροῦσθε ⁱἐν πνεύματι, ¹⁹λαλοῦντες ^{kl}ἑαυτοῖς [ἐν] ^{km}ψαλμοῖς καὶ

ABDFK
LPℵ a b
c e f g h
k l m n o
17. 47

30.   Luke xii. 45.   1 Thess. v. 7 only.   (θύειν, 2 Cor. xi. 21.)   Prov. iv. 17.   g Tit. i. 6.   1 Pet. iv. 4
only.   Prov. xxviii. 7.   2 Macc. iv. 6 only.   (-τος, Prov. vii. 11. -τως, Luke xv. 13.)   h = Acts xiii. 52.   Rom.
i. 29.   xv. 13 al.   i constr., Rom. x. 20.   k Col. iii. 16.   l = ch. iv. 32 reff.
m = 1 Cor. xiv. 26.   Col. as above (k) (Luke xx. 42. xxiv. 44.   Acts i. 20. xiii. 33) only.   Isa. lxvi. 20.

17. rec συνιεντες, with D³KL rel Chr Thdrt Damasc_{h.l.}: συνιοντες D¹F latt syr goth Lucif: txt AB[P]ℵ 17. 67² [Syr æth arm] Chr-ms Damasc₁ Jer.   for θελημα, φρονημα ℵ¹.   for κυριου, θεου A 115 D-lat F-lat Syr Thl [Victorin] Jer Aug Pel Gild.—B adds ημων.

19. rec om 1st εν, with ADFKLℵ rel [Eus₁] Cyr-jer Thdrt Damasc [Tert]: ins B[P] 17. 67² vulg D-lat Chr [Victorin] Ambrst Jer Pel.

sense: cf. ref. Dan.), because the days (of your time,—in which you live) are evil (see above. ὁ ἐξαγοραζόμενος τὸν ἀλλότριον δοῦλον, ἐξαγοράζεται κ. κτᾶται αὐτόν. ἐπεὶ οὖν ὁ καιρὸς δουλεύει τοῖς πονηροῖς, ἐξαγοράσασθε αὐτόν, ὥστε καταχρήσασθαι αὐτῷ πρὸς εὐσέβειαν. Severianus, in Cramer's Catena). 17.] On this account (because ye have need so prudently to define your rule of life, and so carefully to watch for opportunities of good : not, because the ἡμέραι are πονηραί (Œc., Thl., De W., Olsh.), which would fritter down the context) be not (better than 'do not become,' which though more strictly the literal sense of μὴ γίνεσθε, puts the *process of degeneracy* too strongly in English) senseless (Tittmann, Syn. p. 143, has discussed the meaning of ἄφρων, 'qui mente non recte utitur'), but understand (συνιέναι, to know intelligently,—γινώσκειν merely to know as matter of fact, as the servant who knew his lord's will and did it not, Luke xii. 47) what is the will of the Lord. 18.] The connexion seems to be : after the general antithesis in ver. 17, μὴ ἄφρονες, ἀλλὰ συνίετε κ.τ.λ., he proceeds to give one prominent instance, in the same antithetical shape. And (καί is subordinate, introducing a particular after a general: so Herod. i. 73, τῶνδε εἵνεκα καὶ γῆς ἱμέρῳ . . . . see Hartung i. 145) be not intoxicated with wine, in which practice (not, ἐν οἴνῳ, but ἐν τῷ μεθύσκεσθαι οἴνῳ—the crime is not in *God's gift*, but in the *abuse* of it : and the very arrangement of the sentence, besides the spirit of it, implies the lawful use of wine—see 1 Tim. v. 23) is profligacy (ἀσωτία, not from ἀ-σώζεσθαι,—as Clem. Alex. Pædag. ii. 1, p. 167 P. (ἀσώτους αὐτοὺς οἱ καλέσαντες πρῶτον εὖ μοι δοκοῦσιν αἰνίττεσθαι τὸ τέλος αὐτῶν, ἀσώστους αὐτοὺς κατὰ ἔκθλιψιν τοῦ σ στοιχείου νενοηκότες), al., but from ἀ—σώζειν: ἀσωτία ἐστὶν ὑπερβολὴ περὶ

χρήματα, Aristot. Eth. Nic. iv. 1. 3. But as spendthrifts are almost of necessity self-indulgent and reckless, the word comes to have the meaning of '*dissoluteness,*' '*debauchery,*' '*profligacy,*' — see Eth. Nic. iv. 1. 36, Tittmann, p. 152, and Trench, N. T. Syn. § 16. Theodotion renders Isa. xxviii. 7 by ἐν τῇ μέθῃ ἠσωτεύθησαν ὑπερόγκως): but (contrast, see above) be filled (antith. to μεθύσκεσθε οἴνῳ;—not to μεθύσκεσθε alone, so that ἐν πνεύματι should be opposed to οἴνῳ: see below) with (ἐν, as ch. i. 23, but also '*in:*' let this be the region in, and the ingredient with which you are filled) the Spirit (the ambiguity in the preposition is owing to the peculiar meaning of πνεῦμα as applied to the Christian :—viz. *his own spirit, dwelt in and informed by the Holy Spirit of God,* see note on ch. iv. 23. If this is so, if you are full of the Spirit, full in Spirit, there will be a joy indeed, but not that of ἀσωτία: one which will find its expression not in drunken songs, but in Christian hymns, and continual thankfulness), speaking to one another (ch. iv. 32; see also the ||, Col. iii. 16. It is perhaps too much to find in this the practice of antiphonal chanting : but it is interesting to remember that in Pliny's letter the Christians are described as ' soliti stato die ante lucem convenire, *carmenque* Christo quasi Deo *dicere secum invicem:*' and that Nicephorus, Hist. xiii. 8 (cited by Eadie), says τὴν τῶν ἀντιφώνων συνήθειαν ἄνωθεν ἀποστόλων ἡ ἐκκλησία παρέλαβε. Conyb. places a full stop at ἑαυτοῖς : but surely both style and sense are thus marred) in (this must be the rendering, whether the preposition is inserted or not) psalms (not to be confined, as Olsh. and Stier, to O. T. hymns; see 1 Cor. xiv. 26 ; James v. 13. The word properly signified those sacred songs which were performed with musical accompaniment (so Basil, Hom. in Ps. xxix. 1, vol. i. p. 124, ὁ ψαλμὸς λόγος

^{kn} ὕμνοις καὶ ^{ko} ᾠδαῖς [^{kp} πνευματικαῖς], ^{kq} ᾄδοντες καὶ ^r ψάλλοντες [ἐν] τῇ ^{ks} καρδίᾳ ὑμῶν τῷ κυρίῳ, 20 ^{tu} εὐχαριστοῦντες ^{tv} πάντοτε ὑπὲρ ^{tv} πάντων ἐν ὀνόματι τοῦ κυρίου ἡμῶν Ἰησοῦ χριστοῦ ^w τῷ θεῷ καὶ πατρί, 21 ^x ὑποτασσόμενοι ἀλλήλοις ἐν ^y φόβῳ ^y χριστοῦ· 22 αἱ γυναῖκες τοῖς

n Col. as above (k) only. Neh. xii. 46.
(-νεῖν, Acts xvi. 25.)
o Col. as above (k). Rev. v. 9. xiv. 3 bis. xv. 3 only.
Exod. xv. 1 al.
p Rom. i. 11

al21. Paul only, exc. 1 Pet. ii. 5 bis †.   q Col. Rev. as above (ko) only. Jer. xxxvii. (xxx.) 19
r Rom. xv. 9, from Ps. xvii. 49. 1 Cor. xiv. 15 bis. James v. 13 only. 1 Kings xvi. 16.   s = Acts
vii. 54. Rom. ii. 15, 29. x. 6. 1 Cor. vii. 37 al.   t 1 Cor. i. 4. 1 Thess. i. 2. 2 Thess. i. 3. P.
u = Luke xvii. 16. xviii. 11. John xi. 41. Paul, Rom. i. 8 & freq. Rev. xi. 17 †. Judith viii. 25. Wisd.
xviii. 2. 2 Macc. i. 11 only.   v 2 Cor. ix. 8. Phil. i. 4. 1 Thess. i. 2. P.   w James i. 27.
x ch. i. 22 reff.   y here only. φ. τ. κυρίου, Acts ix. 31. 2 Cor. v. 11. φ. θεοῦ, Rom. iii. 18. 2 Cor. viii. 1.

om πνευματικαις B D-lat Ambrst-ed (it prob came from Col iii. 16, where none omit it. In such a case, the evidence of B might be sufficient, were it not for the possibility of omn by homœotel). aft πνευμ. ins εν χαριτι A. om 2nd εν Bℵ. for τη καρδια, ταις καρδιαις (see Col iii. 16) ADF[P]ℵ³ [47] latt Syr syr-mg copt goth Bas Chr₂ lat-ff: txt BKLℵ¹ rel syr-txt æth [arm] Chr-txt Thdrt Damasc Thl Œc.
20. for παντων, υμων F. om ημων ℵ. χρ. bef ιησ. B. πατρι και θεω D¹F m D-lat G-lat goth [arm] Victorin Vig.
21. rec (for χριστου) θεου (φοβ. θεου being the more usual expression), with rel Clem Thdrt: κυριου K: txt AB(DF)L[P]ℵ c f k m 17 [47].—D adds, F(not F-lat) pref ιησου.

ἐστὶ μουσικός, ὅταν εὐρύθμως κατὰ τοὺς ἁρμονικοὺς λόγους πρὸς τὸ ὄργανον κρούηται—and Greg. Nyss. in Psal. lib. ii. 3, vol. i. p. 493, Migne, ψαλμός ἐστιν ἡ διὰ τοῦ ὀργάνου τοῦ μουσικοῦ μελῳδία),—as ὕμνοι without it: but the two must evidently here not be confined strictly to their proper meaning) and hymns (see above) and [spiritual] songs (ᾠδή being the general name for all lyrical poetry, and applying especially to such effusions as persons used in the state of drunkenness, the Christian's ᾠδή is to be spiritual (Chr. opposes αἱ σατανικαὶ ᾠδαί), inspired by that fulness of the Spirit which is in him), singing and playing (as well as λαλοῦντες, not explanatory of it: ᾄδοντες and ψάλλοντες corresponding to ὕμνοις and ψαλμοῖς above) in your hearts (Harl. remarks that ἐν καρδίᾳ cannot, being joined with ὑμῶν, represent the abstract 'heartily,' as Chr., Thdrt., Pelag., &c.; but must be rendered as Bullinger, 'canentes intus in animis et cordibus vestris') to the Lord (i. e. Christ —cf. Pliny's letter above),—giving thanks (another additional, not explanatory, clause) always for all things (see Phil. iv. 6: not only for blessings, but for every dispensation of God: Ellic. quotes from Thl.,—οὐχ ὑπὲρ τῶν ἀγαθῶν μόνον, ἀλλὰ καὶ τῶν λυπηρῶν, κ. ὧν ἴσμεν, κ. ὧν οὐκ ἴσμεν· καὶ γὰρ διὰ πάντων εὐεργετούμεθα κἂν ἀγνοῶμεν) in the name (the element in which the εὐχαριστοῦντες must take place. "The name of the Lord is there, where He is named. How He is named, depends on the particular circumstances: it is one thing to be reproached (1 Pet. iv. 14), another to be saved (Acts iv. 12), another to be baptized (Acts x. 48), another to command

(2 Thess. iii. 6), another to pray (John xiv. 13), another to give thanks (cf. Col. iii. 17) in the name of the Lord. . . . . The Apostle says, that all the Christian would do, he must do in the name of Christ (Col. iii. 17)." Harl.: the rest of the note is well worth consulting) of our Lord Jesus Christ to God and the Father (see on ch. i. 3),—being subject to one another (a fourth additional, not subordinate clause. λαλοῦντες,—ᾄδοντες κ. ψάλλοντες, — εὐχαριστοῦντες, — ὑποτασσόμενοι ἀλλήλοις: and then out of this last general injunction are unfolded all the particular applications to the relations of life, ver. 22—ch. vi. 9. It is not so easy to assign precisely its connexion with those which have preceded. It is hardly enough to say that as the first three name three special duties in regard to God, so this last a comprehensive moral duty in regard to man (Ellic.): for the question of the connexion is still unanswered. I would rather regard it (as I see Eadie also does), as a thought suggested by the μὴ μεθ. κ.τ.λ. with which the sentence began—that as we are otherwise to be filled, otherwise to sing and rejoice, so also we are otherwise to behave—not blustering nor letting our voices rise in selfish vaunting, as such men do,—but subject to one another, &c.) in the fear of Christ ('rara phrasis,' Beng.: of Him, whose members we all are, so that any displacement in the Body is a forgetfulness of the reverence due to Him).
22—VI. 9.] The Church, in her relation to Christ, comprehending and hallowing those earthly relations on which all social unity (and hers also) is founded, the Apostle proceeds to treat of the three

z 1 Cor. vii. 2.
xiv. 35.
a = 1 Cor. xi.
3. ch. i. 22.
iv. 15. Col.
i. 18. ii. 10,
19 only. P.
Isa. vii. 8, 9.
b ch. i. 22 reff.
c = John iv.
42. 1 Tim.
iv. 10. 1 John
iv. 14.

^{z} ἰδίοις ^{z} ἀνδράσιν ὡς τῷ κυρίῳ, ^{23} ὅτι ἀνήρ ἐστιν ^{a} κεφαλὴ
τῆς γυναικὸς ὡς καὶ ὁ χριστὸς ^{a} κεφαλὴ τῆς ^{b} ἐκκλησίας,
αὐτὸς ^{c} σωτὴρ τοῦ σώματος. ^{24} ἀλλὰ ὡς ἡ ^{b} ἐκκλησία
^{x} ὑποτάσσεται τῷ χριστῷ, οὕτως καὶ αἱ γυναῖκες τοῖς
ἀνδράσιν ^{d} ἐν παντί. ^{25} οἱ ἄνδρες, ἀγαπᾶτε τὰς γυναῖκας,

ABDFK
LPℵ a b
c e f g h
k l m n o
17. 47

d Phil. iv. 6, 12. 1 Thess. v. 18.

22. rec aft ανδρασιν ins υποτασσεσθε (*prob supplementary gloss, as also* υποτασσεσθωσαν), with KL rel Chr, and, bef ιδ., DF Syr; υποτασσεσθωσαν A[P]ℵ 17. 67²
vulg copt [goth æth arm] Clem₁ Bas Thdrt Damasc [Orig-int₁] lat-ff: om‚B and greek-
mss-in-Jerome("*Hoc quod in lat. exx. additum est*, subditæ sint, *in gr. edd. non
habetur . . . . Sed hoc magis in græco intelligitur quam in latino*").
23. rec ins o bef ανηρ, with b l o [47] Clem: om ABDFKL[P]ℵ rel Damasc.
1st κεφαλη bef εστιν B m vulg(and F·lat) lat-ff.   rec ins και bef αυτος and adds
εστιν, with D²·³KL[P]ℵ³ rel: om ABD¹Fℵ¹ [17] latt Clem [Orig-int Victorin] Ambrst.
ins o bef σωτηρ Aℵ¹ [17] Clem.
24. (αλλα, so BD¹.)   rec (for ως) ωσπερ, with D³KL rel [Orig-cat₁] Thdrt
Damasc₁.₁.: om B Ambrst-ed: txt AD¹F[P]ℵ 17 [47] 67² Clem [Orig-cat₁] Chr
Damasc.   for χρ., κυριω D¹-gr Chr.   rec ins ιδιοις bef ανδρασιν (*from ver 22*),
with AD³KL[P] rel [Clem Orig-int₁]: om BD¹Fℵ 17. 67² [Orig-cat].
25. rec aft γυναικας ins εαυτων (*see below*, ver 28), with DKL rel Chr₁ Thdrt₂
Damasc: [præf P :] υμων F Thdrt₁ [Orig-int₃]: om ABℵ 17 Clem(citing vv 21 to 25)
Orig Chr₂ Cyr.

greatest of those: that of *husband and
wife* (vv. 22—33), that of *parent and
child* (ch. vi. 1—4), that of *master and
servant* (vi. 5—9). See this expanded by
Stier, in his very long note, ii. 316—329.
    22—33.] *Mutual duties of wives
and husbands* arising from the relation
between Christ and the Church.
22.] Wives (supply, as rec. has inserted,
ὑποτάσσεσθε, seeing that the subsequent
address to husbands is in the 2nd person),
to your own husbands (ἰδίοις, as we often
use the word (e. g. 'He murdered his own
father'), to intensify the recognition of
the relationship and suggest its duties: see
1 Cor. vii. 2: also John v. 18), as to the
Lord ('quasi Christo ipsimet, cujus locum
et personam viri repræsentant.' Corn.-a-
lap. in Ellic.: i. e. 'in obeying your husbands, obey the Lord:' not merely as in
all things we are to have regard to Him,
but because, as below expanded, the husband stands peculiarly in Christ's place.
But he is not thus identified in power
with Christ, nor the obedience, in its
nature, with that which is owed to Him):
for a husband (any husband, taken as an
example: the same in sense would be expressed by ὁ ἀνήρ, the husband in each
case, generic: sing. of οἱ ἄνδρες) is head
of his wife, as also (καί, introducing
identity of category) Christ is Head of
the church (see for the sentiment, 1 Cor.
xi. 3 note), (*being*, in His case—see below)
Himself Saviour of the Body (i. e. 'in
Christ's case the Headship is united with,
nay gained by, His having SAVED the

body in the process of Redemption: so
that I am not alleging Christ's Headship
as one entirely identical with that other,
for He has a claim to it and office in it
peculiar to Himself.' 'Vir autem non est
servator uxoris, in eo Christus excellit:
hinc *sed sequitur*.' Bengel. Stier remarks the apparent play on σωτήρ—
σώματος, in reference to the supposed
derivation of σῶμα from σώω (σώζω);
and has noticed that in the only other
place (except the pastoral Epistles) where
St. Paul uses σωτήρ, Phil. iii. 20, 21, it is
also in connexion with σῶμα): but (what
I do say is, that thus far the two Head-
ships are to be regarded as identical, in
the *subjection of the body* to the Head,
as the church is subjected to Christ, so
also (again, identity of category in the
ὑποτάσσ.) let the wives be to their husbands (not ἰδίοις now, as it would disturb
the perspicuity of the comparison) in every
thing (thus only, with Calv., Beng., Mey.,
Ellic., can I find any legitimate meaning
or connexion in the words. All attempts
1) to explain σωτὴρ τοῦ σώμ. also of the
marriage state (Bulling., Beza, 'viri est
quærere quod mulier conservet'), or 2)
to deprive ἀλλά of its adversative force
(Rück., Harl., al.), or 3) refer it to something other than the preceding clause
(De W., Eadie), seem to me unsatisfactory).   25.] I cannot refrain from
citing Chrys.'s very beautiful remarks on
this next passage,—εἶδες μέτρον ὑπακοῆς;
ἄκουσον καὶ μέτρον ἀγάπης. βούλει σοι
τὴν γυναῖκα ὑπακούειν, ὡς τῷ χριστῷ

καθὼς καὶ ὁ χριστὸς ἠγάπησεν τὴν ἐκκλησίαν καὶ ^eἑαυτὸν ^eπαρέδωκεν ὑπὲρ αὐτῆς, ²⁶ ἵνα αὐτὴν ^fἁγιάσῃ ^gκαθαρίσας τῷ ^hλουτρῷ τοῦ ὕδατος ⁱἐν ^jῥήματι, ^{27 k}ἵνα παραστήσῃ αὐτὸς ἑαυτῷ ^lἔνδοξον τὴν ἐκκλησίαν μὴ ἔχουσαν ^mσπίλον

e ver. 2 reff.
f = John xvii.
17, 19. Rom.
xv. 16. 1 Cor.
vi. 11.
1 Thess. v.
23. Rev.
xxii. 11 al.
g = Tit. ii. 14.
Heb. x. 2.

h Tit. iii. 5 only. Cant. iv. 2. Sir. xxxi. (xxxiv.) 25 only. i ch. iv. 19. vi. 2. j (without art).
Rom. x. 17. ch. vi. 17. Heb. vi. 5. xi. 3. P.H. k = (L.P. only. see Matt. xxvi. 53.) 2 Cor. xi.
2. Luke ii. 22. Acts i. 3. ix. 41. xxiii. 33. Rom. vi. 13 bis al7. l Luke vii. 25. xiii. 17. 1 Cor. iv. 10
only. 1 Kings ix. 6 al. m 2 Pet. ii. 13 only †. Jos. Ant. xiii. 11. 3. (-λάς, Jude 12.)

27. rec (for αυτος) αυτην, with D³K rel syrr Chr Thdrt₁, εαυτην m¹ : αυτο 67² : txt ABD¹FL[P]א 17 [47] latt copt goth gr-lat-ff. for εαυτω, αυτω א¹.

τὴν ἐκκλησίαν; προνόει καὶ αὐτὸς αὐτῆς, ὡς ὁ χριστὸς τῆς ἐκκλησίας· κἂν τὴν ψυχὴν ὑπὲρ αὐτῆς δοῦναι δέῃ, κἂν κατακοπῆναι μυριάκις, κἂν ὁτιοῦν ὑπομεῖναι καὶ παθεῖν, μὴ παραιτήσῃ· κἂν ταῦτα πάθῃς, οὐδὲν οὐδέπω πεποίηκας, οἷον ὁ χριστός· σὺ μὲν γὰρ ἤδη συναφθεὶς ταῦτα ποιεῖς, ἐκεῖνος δὲ ὑπὲρ ἀποστρεφομένης αὐτὸν καὶ μισούσης· ὥσπερ οὖν αὐτὸς τὴν ἀποστρεφομένην αὐτὸν καὶ μισοῦσαν καὶ διαπτύουσαν καὶ θρυπτομένην, περὶ τοὺς πόδας αὐτοῦ τῇ πολλῇ ἤγαγε τῇ κηδεμονίᾳ, οὐκ ἀπειλαῖς, οὐδὲ ὕβρεσιν, οὐδὲ φόβῳ, οὐδὲ ἑτέρῳ τινὶ τοιούτῳ· οὕτω καὶ σὺ πρὸς τὴν γυναῖκα ἔχε τὴν σήν· κἂν ὑπερορῶσαν, κἂν θρυπτομένην, κἂν καταφρονοῦσαν ἴδῃς, δυνήσῃ αὐτὴν ὑπὸ τοὺς πόδας ἀγαγεῖν τοὺς σοὺς τῇ πολλῇ περὶ αὐτὴν προνοίᾳ, τῇ ἀγάπῃ, τῇ φιλίᾳ. οὐδὲν γὰρ τούτων τυραννικώτερον τῶν δεσμῶν, καὶ μάλιστα ἀνδρὶ κ. γυναικί. οἰκέτην μὲν γὰρ φόβῳ τις ἂν καταδῆσαι δυνήσεται, μᾶλλον δὲ οὐδὲ ἐκεῖνον· τάχεως γὰρ ἀποπηδήσας οἰχήσεται· τὴν δὲ τοῦ βίου κοινωνόν, τὴν παίδων μητέρα, τὴν πάσης εὐφροσύνης ὑπόθεσιν, οὐ φόβῳ καὶ ἀπειλαῖς δεῖ καταδεσμεῖν, ἀλλ᾽ ἀγάπῃ καὶ διαθέσει. **Husbands, love your wives, as also** (see above) **Christ loved the church and gave Himself for her** (better than 'it;' the comparison is thus brought out as in the original. κἂν πάθῃς τι ὑπὲρ αὐτῆς, μὴ ὀνειδίσῃς· αὐτὸ γὰρ ὁ χρ. τοῦτο ἐποίησε. Chr.) **that** (intermediate purpose, as regarded *her;* see below, ver. 27) **He might sanctify her, having purified her** (ἁγιάσῃ and καθαρίσας might be contemporaneous, and indeed this is the more common usage of past participles with past finite verbs in the N. T. (see ch. i. 9 note). But here, inasmuch as the sanctifying is clearly a gradual process, carried on till the spotless presentation (ver. 27), and the washing cannot be separated from the introductory rite of baptism, it is best to take the **καθαρίσας** as antecedent to the **ἁγιάσῃ**) **by the laver** (not '*washing*,' as E. V.: a meaning the word never has) **of the water** (of which we all know: viz. the *baptismal*

water, see ref. Tit. We can hardly set aside the reference to the purifying bath of the bride previous to marriage:—see below on ver. 27, and cf. Rev. xxi. 2) **in the word** (*what word?* ἐν ὀνόματι πατρὸς κ. υἱοῦ κ. ἁγίου πνεύματος, says Chrys. alluding to the formula in Baptism: and so many fathers:—the '*mandatum divinum*' on which Baptism rests (Storr, Peile):—the '*invocatio divini nominis*' which gives Baptism its efficacy (Erasm.):—the preached *word of faith* (Rom. x. 8) of which confession is made in baptism, and which carries the real cleansing (John xv. 3; xvii. 17) and regenerating power (1 Pet. i. 23; iii. 21 (?))—so Aug. Tract. 80 in Joan. 3, vol. iii. p. 1840, Migne; where those memorable words occur, "Detrahe verbum, et quid est aqua nisi aqua? Accedit verbum ad elementum, et fit sacramentum, etiam ipsum tanquam visibile verbum." And this certainly seems the sense most analogous to St. Paul's usage, in which ῥῆμα is confined to the *divine* word. But we must not join **ἐν ῥήματι** with τῷ λουτρῷ nor with τοῦ ὕδατος; for the former would require τῷ ἐν ῥήματι,—the latter, τοῦ ἐν ῥήματι,—there being no such close connexion as to justify the omission of the article; indeed the specification being here absolutely required, after so common a term as τὸ λοῦτρον τοῦ ὕδατος. So that we are referred back to the verb (**ἁγ.**) and participle (**καθαρίσας**) preceding. The former connexion is not probable, on account of the participle intervening: see also below. The latter is on all accounts the most likely. Thus, *the word*, preached and received, is the conditional element of purification,—the real water of spiritual baptism;—that wherein and whereby alone the efficacy of baptism is conveyed—that wherein and whereby we are regenerated, the process of sanctification being subsequent and gradual), **27.] that** (further purpose of ἑαυτ. παρέδωκεν ὑπὲρ αὐτῆς) **He might Himself present to Himself** (as a bride, see reff. 2 Cor.: not as a sacrifice (Harl.), which is quite against the context. The

n here only †.
Aristoph.
Plut. 1051.
Plato, Symp.
p. 191 A.
o Rom. i. 32
(al. fr. Paul).
3 John 8.
p ch. i. 4 reff.
q = Luke xvii.
10. John xiii.
14. 1 Cor.
xi. 10 al.‡.

ABDFK LP א a b c e f g h k l m n o　17. 47

ἢ ^n ῥυτίδα ἤ τι ^o τῶν τοιούτων, ἀλλ' ἵνα ᾖ ἁγία καὶ
^p ἄμωμος. ^28 οὕτως ^q ὀφείλουσιν καὶ οἱ ἄνδρες ἀγαπᾶν
τὰς ἑαυτῶν γυναῖκας ὡς τὰ ἑαυτῶν σώματα. ὁ ἀγαπῶν
τὴν ἑαυτοῦ γυναῖκα ἑαυτὸν ἀγαπᾷ. ^29 οὐδεὶς γάρ ποτε τὴν
ἑαυτοῦ σάρκα ἐμίσησεν, ἀλλὰ ^r ἐκτρέφει καὶ ^s θάλπει αὐτήν,

r ch. vi. 4 only. 3 Kings xii. 8, 10 al.　　s 1 Thess. ii. 7 only. Deut. xxii. 6.

om η τι א¹(ins א-corr¹ obl).
28. rec om και, with KLא rel syrr Meth Chr Thdrt Damasc: ins ABDF[P] 17 latt
syr copt goth Clem lat-ff.—[και] οι ανδρες bef οφειλουσιν ADF[P] latt copt goth Clem :
txt BKLא rel syrr Meth Chr Thdrt Damasc.　　for σωματα, τεκνα א¹ [το εαυ. σωμα
D¹ Victorin.]
29. for εαυτου σ., σαρκα αυτου א¹.　　(αλλα, so ABD³L[P] a b c h l n o.)

expression sets forth that the preparation
of the Church for her bridal with Christ
is exclusively by His own agency) the
church glorious (the prefixed adjective is
emphatic, which we lose in translation),
not having spot (a late word—τοῦτο
φυλάττον, λέγε δὲ κηλίς—Phryn. Lobeck
28, where see note. It is found in Dion.
Hal., Plut., Lucian, &c. The proper ac-
centuation seems to be as in text, not
σπῖλος. In Anthol. vi. 252, we have
ἄσπιλον, ἀρρυτίδωτον, beginning a hexame-
ter) or wrinkle (ῥυτίς, ἡ συγκεκλυσμένη
σάρξ, Etym. Mag.: from (ἐ)ρύω, see Palm
and Rost, Lex. A classical word, see reff.),
or any of such things, but that she may
be holy (perfect in holiness) and blameless (see on both, note, ch. i. 4). The
presentation here spoken of is clearly, in
its full sense, that future one at the Lord's
coming, so often treated under the image
of a marriage (Matt. xxii. 1 ff.; xxv. 1 ff.;
Rev. xix. 7 ff.; xxi. 2 al. fr.), not any progress of sanctification here below, as Harl.,
Beng., al., maintain (and Calv., commonly
quoted on the other side: for he says on
παραστήσῃ, 'finem baptismi et ablutionis
nostræ declarat: ut sancte et inculpate
Deo vivamus') : however the progress towards this state of spotlessness in this life
may sometimes be spoken of in its fulness
and completion, or with reference to its
proper qualities, not here found in their
purity. Schöttgen quotes a rabbinical
comment on Cant. i. 5 :—' Judæi de syna-
goga intelligunt, et sic explicant: nigra
sum in hoc sæculo, sed decora in sæculo
futuro.' 28.] Thus (two ways of understanding this οὕτως are open to us:
1) as referring back to Christ's love for
the church,—' Thus,' 'in like manner,'
&c., as (being) 'their own bodies:' and
2) as referring forward to the ὡς below,
as very frequently (though Eadie calls it
contrary to grammatical law) in St. Paul
(cf. 1 Cor. iii. 15; iv. 1; ix. 26, al., and
ver. 33 below, where Eadie himself renders,
'so .... as himself'),—' Thus,' 'so,' &c.,

' as (they love) *their own bodies*.' After
weighing maturely what has been said on
one side and the other, I cannot but decide for the latter, as most in accordance
with the usage of St. Paul and with
ver. 33 : also as more simple. The sense
(against Ellic.) remains substantially the
same, and answers much better to the comment furnished by the succeeding clauses :
—husbands ought to love their own wives
as they love their own bodies (= themselves : for their wives are in fact part of
their own bodies, ver. 31): this being illustrated by and referred to the great mystery
of Christ and His church, in which the same
love, and the same incorporation, has place)
ought the husbands also (as well as Christ
in the archetypal example just given) to
love their own (emphatic: see above on
ver. 22) wives, as (with the same affection
as) their own bodies. He that loveth his
own (see above) wife, loveth himself (is
but complying with that universal law of
nature by which we all love ourselves. The
best words to supply before the following
γάρ will be, "And this we all do"): for
(see above) no man ever hated his own
flesh (= ἑαυτόν, but put in this form to
prepare for εἰς σάρκα μίαν in the Scripture proof below. Wetst. quotes from
Seneca, Ep. 14, 'fateor, insitam nobis esse
corporis nostri caritatem'), but nourishes
it up (through all its stages, to maturity:
so Aristoph. Ran. 1189, of Œdipus, ἵνα μὴ
'κτραφεὶς γένοιτο τοῦ πατρὸς φονεύς : and
ib. 1427, οὐ χρὴ λέοντος σκύμνον ἐν πόλει
τρέφειν (at all): ἢν δ' ἐκτραφῇ τις (have
been brought up), τοῖς τρόποις ὑπηρετεῖν)
and cherishes (ref. 1 Thess. It is certainly
not necessary to confine the meaning to
' warming,' as Beng. ('id spectat amic-
tum'), Mey., al.: for it is very forced to
apply the feeding and clothing to the other
member of the comparison (as Grot.: ' nu-
trit eam verbo et spiritu, vestit eam virtutibus'), as must then be done (against
Mey.)) it, as also (does) Christ (nourish
and cherish) the church.　　30.] For

καθὼς καὶ ὁ χριστὸς τὴν ἐκκλησίαν. ³⁰ ὅτι μέλη ἐσμὲν
τοῦ ᵗ σώματος αὐτοῦ [, ἐκ τῆς σαρκὸς αὐτοῦ, καὶ ἐκ τῶν
ᵘ ὀστέων αὐτοῦ]. ³¹ ᵛ ἀντὶ ᵛ τούτου ᵂ καταλείψει ἄνθρωπος πατέρα καὶ μητέρα, καὶ ˣ προσκολληθήσεται πρὸς
τὴν γυναῖκα αὐτοῦ, καὶ ἔσονται οἱ δύο ʸ εἰς σάρκα μίαν.
³² τὸ ᶻ μυστήριον τοῦτο μέγα ἐστίν, ἐγὼ δὲ λέγω ᵃ εἰς

t ch. i. 23 reff.
u Matt. xxiii.
27. Luke xxiv. 39.
John xix. 36, from Num. ix. 12. Heb. xi. 22 only.
v here only.
see Luke xii. 3.
w Matt. xix. 5 ||, from GEN. ii. 24.
1 Thess. iii. 1

al.   x Matt. || as above (w), from l. c.   Acts v. 36 only.   y Matt. || as above (w). xxi.
42. Luke iii. 5.   Rom. ii. 26.   Gen. xv. 6.   z = Paul, Rom. xi. 25.   1 Cor. xv. 51.   1 Tim. iii. 9, 16.
a = Acts ii. 25.   Heb. vii. 14.   1 Pet. i. 11.

rec (for χριστος) κυριος, with D³KL rel Œc : txt ABD¹F [P(omg ὁ)] ℵ b¹ k m o 17 [47]
latt syrr coptt [goth æth arm] gr-lat-ff.

30. om εκ της σαρκος αυτου και εκ των οστεων αυτου (*prob from homœotel : had the
words been insd from LXX, οστ. would prob have come first. See note*) ABℵ¹ 17. 67²
copt æth [Orig-cat] Meth Ambrst : ins DFKL[P]ℵ³ rel vss Iren-gr-int Chr Thdrt
Damasc [Victorin] Jer.

31. rec ins τον bef πατερα and την bef μητερα (*from LXX*), with AD³KL[P]ℵ rel
[Mcion-e₃ Orig₂] Meth Tit : om BD¹F.   rec aft πατερα ins αυτου (*from LXX*),
with AD³KL[P]ℵ³ rel Mcion-e [Meth] : [aft μητ. also P 47 Orig₁ :] om BD¹Fℵ¹ 17.
67² Orig₂ Thdrt₁ Thl-ms Jer(expr after Orig).   [for προσκολλ., κολληθησεται
D¹Fℵ³ Mcion-e₂.]   for προς την γυναικα, τη γυναικι (*so also in Gen* ii. 24, *A al*
Meth Ath Epiph lat-ff) AD¹Fℵ¹ m 17 latt Meth Epiph lat-ff : txt BD³KL [P(omg
προς)] ℵ³ rel Orig₂ Chr Thdrt₂.   om αυτου ℵ¹(ins ℵ-corr¹·³) [Mcion-e₂].

(again a link is omitted; 'the church,
which stands in the relation of marriage
to Him : for, &c.') members **we are of His
Body** [,—(being) **of His flesh, and of His
bones** (see Gen. ii. 23. As the woman
owed her natural being to the man, her
source and head, so we owe our entire
spiritual being to Christ, our source and
head : and as the woman was one flesh
with the man in this natural relation, so
we in our entire spiritual relation, body,
soul, and Spirit, are one with Christ, God
manifested in our humanity,—parts and
members of His glorified Body. Bengel
well remarks, that we are not, as in Gen.,
l. c. ὀστοῦν ἐκ τῶν ὀστέων αὐτοῦ, καὶ
σὰρξ ἐκ τῆς σαρκὸς αὐτ. :—'non ossa
et caro nostra, sed *nos* spiritualiter pro-
pagamur ex humanitate Christi, carnem et
ossa habente')] : **wherefore** (the allusion, or
rather free citation, is still carried on : cf.
Gen. ii. 24 :—i. e. because we are members
of Him in the sense just insisted on. This
whole verse is said (see on ver. 32 below)
not of human marriages, but of Christ and
the church. He is the ἄνθρωπος in the
Apostle's view here, the Church is the
γυνή. But for all this, I would not understand the words, as Meyer, in a prophetical
sense of the future coming of Christ :—
the omission of the article before ἄνθρωπος
sufficiently retains the general aphoris-
matic sense :—but would regard the saying
as applied to that, past, present, and future,
which constitutes Christ's Union to His
Bride the Church : His leaving the Father's
bosom, which is *past*—His gradual prepa-

ration of the union, which is *present :* His
full consummation of it, which is *future.*
This seems to me to be necessary, because
we are as truly now εἰς σάρκα μίαν with
Him, as we shall be, when heaven and
earth shall ring with the joy of the nup-
tials ;— and hence the exclusive future
sense is inapplicable. In this allegorical
sense (see below), Chrys., Jer., and most
of the ancients : Beng., Grot., Mey. (as
above), al., interpret : and Eadie would
have done well to study more deeply the
spirit of the context before he characterized it as 'strange romance,' 'wild and
visionary,' and said, 'there is no hint that
the Apostle intends to allegorize.' That
allegory, on the contrary, is the *key to the
whole*) **shall a man leave father and
mother and shall be closely joined to his
wife, and they two shall become** (see
Matt. xix. 5, note) **one flesh** ('non solum
uti antea, respectu ortus : sed respectu
novæ conjunctionis.' Beng.).   **32.**]
This mystery is great (viz. the matter
mystically alluded to in the Apostle's
application of the text just quoted : the
mystery of the spiritual union of Christ
with our humanity, typified by the close
conjunction of the marriage state. This
meaning of μυστήριον, which is strictly
that in which St. Paul uses the word (see
reff.),—as something passing human comprehension, but revealed as a portion of the
divine dealings in Christ,—is, it seems to
me, required by the next words. It is
irksome, but necessary, to notice the ridi-
culous perversion of this text by the Romish

b – always in Paul. 1 Cor. xi. 11 al³. & in Matt. & Luke (Gosp. vi. 24 al13.). Rev. ii. 25.
Judg. iv. 9. in Mark (xii. 32) [John viii. 10 rec.], & Acts (viii. al3.), with gen. 'except.'
15. iv. 1. ix. 26 bis.
h Matt. xv. 4 ‖ al., from Exod. xx. 12. Deut. v. 16.

χριστὸν καὶ [ᵃ εἰς] τὴν ἐκκλησίαν. ³³ ᵇ πλὴν καὶ ὑμεῖς
οἱ ᶜ καθ' ἕνα ἕκαστος τὴν ἑαυτοῦ γυναῖκα ᵈ οὕτως ἀγαπάτω
ᵈ ὡς ἑαυτόν, ἡ δὲ γυνὴ ᵉ ἵνα φοβῆται τὸν ἄνδρα.

VI. ¹ τὰ τέκνα ᶠ ὑπακούετε τοῖς γονεῦσιν ὑμῶν [ᵍ ἐν
κυρίῳ]· τοῦτο γάρ ἐστιν δίκαιον. ² ʰ Τίμα τὸν πατέρα

c Acts xxi. 19. 1 Cor. xiv. 31. see Mark xiv. 19. [John viii. 9.] d 1 Cor. iii.
e constr., Mark v. 23. f Matt. viii. 27 al. fr. g ch. iv. 17 reff.

32. om 2nd εἰς BK b g h k o Iren-gr-int Tert : ins ADFL[P]ℵ rel latt Orig₂[and int₂] Meth Tit Chr Sevrn-cat Thdrt Chron Cypr Victorin Hil.

33. ins ινα bef εκαστος D¹[P]ℵ³.   εκαστον F [47].   ως εαυ. bef αγαπ. DF.

Chap. VI. 1. om εν κυριω (prob as appearing irrelevant, had it been inserted from ch v. 22 it wd have been ως τω κ., if from Col iii. 20, it wd have stood aft δικαιον : so Mey., and Harless) BD¹F [Clem₁] Cyr-jer [Tert] Cypr Ambrst : ins AD²·³KL[P]ℵ rel vss Orig-cat Chr_expr Thdrt Damasc Jer.

church, which from the Vulgate rendering, 'sacramentum hoc magnum est, ego autem dico in Christo et in Ecclesia,' deduces that 'marriage is a great sacrament in Christ and in His Church' (Encyclical letter of 1832 cited by Eadie). It will be enough to say that this their blunder of 'sacramentum' for 'mysterium,' had long ago been exposed by their own Commentators, Cajetan and Estius): but I (emphatic) say (allege) it with reference to Christ, and [with reference to] the church (i. e. my meaning, in citing the above text, is to call your attention, not to mere human marriage, but to that high and mysterious relation between Christ and His Church, of which that other is but a faint resemblance). 33.] Nevertheless (not to go further into the mystical bearings of the subject—so Meyer) you also (as well as Christ) every one (see reff. and 1 Cor. xiv. 27; Acts xv. 21; Heb. ix. 25), let each (the construction is changed and the verb put into concord with ἕκαστος instead of ὑμεῖς: so Plato, Gorg. p. 503, ὥσπερ κ. οἱ ἄλλοι πάντες δημιουργοὶ βλέποντες πρὸς τὸ ἑκάστου ἔργον ἕκαστος οὐκ εἰκῇ ἐκλεγόμενος προσφέρει κ.τ.λ. ; Rep. p. 346, αἱ ἄλλαι πᾶσαι (τέχναι) οὕτω τὸ αὑτῆς ἑκάστη ἔργον ἐργάζεται, κ.τ.λ. Cic. de Off. i. 41, 'poetæ suum quisque opus a vulgo considerari vult ') so love his own wife as himself, and the wife (best taken as a nominative absolute, as Mey. Otherwise we should rather expect ἵνα δὲ ἡ γυνὴ κ.τ.λ. It is no objection to this (Eadie) that in the resolution of the idiom a verb must be supplied :—but the wife, for her part,—' I order,' or, ' let her see,' cf. note on 2 Cor. viii. 7), that she fear (ὡς πρέπει γυναῖκα φοβεῖσθαι, μὴ δουλοπρεπῶς, (Ec.) her husband.   Ch. VI. 1—4.] See on ch. v. 22. Duties of children and parents. Children, obey your parents [in the Lord

(i. e. Christ : the sphere in which the action is to take place, as usual : ἐν κυρίῳ belonging to ὑπακούετε τ. γον., not to τοῖς γον., as if it were τοῖς ἐν κυρίῳ γον., nor can this be combined, as a second reference, with the other, as by Orig. in Cramer's Catena, understanding 'your fathers in the faith, ὁποῖος ὁ Παῦλος ἦν Κορινθίων.' I should venture however to question whether the Apostle's view was to hint at such commands of parents as might not be according to the will of God, as is very generally supposed (' quia poterant parentes aliquid imperare perversum, adjunxit in Domino.' Jer.): for cf. Col. iii. 20, ὑπακούετε τοῖς γονεῦσιν κατὰ πάντα. I should rather believe, that he regards both parents and children as ἐν κυρίῳ, and the commands, as well as the obedience, as having that sphere and element. How children were to regard commands not answering to this description, would be understood from the nature of the case : but it seems to violate the simplicity of this ὑποτασσόμενοι ἀλλήλοις passage, to introduce into it a by-thought of this kind)]: for this is right (Thdrt., Harl., De W., Mey., al., regard δίκαιον as explained by the next verse, and meaning κατὰ τὸν θεοῦ νόμον. But it seems rather an appeal to the first principles of natural duty, as Est., ' ut a quibus vitam accepimus, iis obedientiam reddamus.' So Beng. Stier, as usual, combines both senses—just, according to the law both of nature and of God. Surely it is better to regard the next verse as an additional particular, not the mere expansion of this).   2.] Honour thy father and thy mother, for such is (' seeing it is,' as Ellic., is rather too strong for ἥτις, throwing the motive to obedience too much on the fact of the promise accompanying it. Whereas the obedience rests on the fact implied in ἐντολή, and the promise comes

σου καὶ τὴν μητέρα, ἥτις ἐστὶν ἐντολὴ πρώτη ⁱ ἐν ἐπαγ-
γελίᾳ, ³ ἵνα ʲᵏ εὖ σοι ᵏ γένηται καὶ ἔσῃ ˡ μακροχρόνιος ἐπὶ
τῆς γῆς. ⁴ καὶ οἱ πατέρες, μὴ ᵐ παροργίζετε τὰ τέκνα
ὑμῶν, ἀλλὰ ⁿ ἐκτρέφετε αὐτὰ ἐν ᵒ παιδείᾳ καὶ ᴾ νουθεσίᾳ
κυρίου.

i — ch. v. 26
reff.
j Matt. xxv. 21,
23. Mark xiv.
7. (Luke xix.
17.) Acts
xv. 29 only.
k here only.
Gen. xii. 13
al.
l here only.
ll. cc. Deut.

xvii. 20 A (-νίζειν, B) only.   m Rom. x. 19 (Col. iii. 21 v. r.) only, from Deut. xxxii. 21. (-ισμός,
ch. iv. 26.)   n ch. v. 29 only. Prov. xxiii. 24.   o 2 Tim. iii. 16. Heb. xii. 5, 7, 8, 11
only. Prov. i. 2, 7. Isa. liii. 5.   p l Cor. x. 11. Tit. iii. 10 only †. Judith viii. 27 (23)
Ald. (-τησις, ΑΒΝ). Wisd. xvi. 6 only. (-ετεῖν,θ Acts xx. 31.)

2. aft την μητερα ins σου F[P] m [47 Orig-cat₁].   om εστιν B 46.   ins τη
bef επαγγελια DF.

3. Ν¹ has written the ver twice : Ν-corr has marked the second for erasure.

4. (αλλα, so ABD¹Ν.)

in to shew its special acceptableness to God) **the first commandment** (in the decalogue, which naturally stands at the head of all God's other commandments ; and which, though not formally binding on us as Christians, is quoted, in matters of eternal obligation (not of positive enactment), as an eminent example of God's holy will) **with a promise** (i. e. with a special promise attached : 'in respect of promise' is too vague, and does not convey any definite meaning in English. The fact certainly is so, and the occurrence of the description of God as ' shewing mercy unto thousands, &c.' after the second commandment, does not, as Jer., al., have thought, present any difficulty—for that is no special promise attached to the commandment. Nor does the fact that no other commandment occurs in the *decalogue* with a promise: see above. The ἐν, as in reff.—in the sphere or department of—characterized by—accompanied with), **that it may be well with thee, and thou be long-lived upon the earth** (he paraphrases the latter portion of the commandment, writing for ἵνα μακρ. γένῃ, ἔσῃ μ.,—and omitting after γῆς, (τῆς ἀγαθῆς, so in Exod., but not in Deut.) ἧς κύριος ὁ θεός σου δίδωσίν σοι: thus adapting the promise to his Christian readers, by taking away from it that which is special and peculiar to the Jewish people. It is surely a mistake, as Jer., Aq., Est., Olsh., to spiritualize the promise, and understand by τῆς γῆς the heavenly Canaan. The very fact of the omission of the special clause removes the words from the region of type into undoubted reality: and when we remember that the persons addressed are τὰ τέκνα, we must not depart from the simplest sense of the words. For the future after ἵνα, see 1 Cor. ix. 18, note: and John vii. 3; Rev. xxii. 14. To consider it as such, is far better than to suppose a change of construction to the direct

future—'and thou shalt be, &c.').

4.] **And ye, fathers** (the mothers being included, as ὑποτασσόμεναι τοῖς ἰδίοις ἀνδράσιν—they being the fountains of domestic rule: not for any other less worthy reason, to which the whole view of the sexes by the Apostle is opposed), **irritate not** (οἷον, says Chrys., οἱ πολλοὶ ποιοῦσιν, ἀποκληρονόμους ἐργαζόμενοι, καὶ ἀποκηρύκτους ποιοῦντες, καὶ φορτικῶς ἐπικείμενοι, οὐχ ὡς ἐλευθέροις ἀλλ᾿ ὡς ἀνδραπόδοις. But the Apostle seems rather to allude to provoking by vexatious commands, and unreasonable blame, and uncertain temper, in ordinary intercourse: cf. Col. iii. 21) **your children, but bring them up** (see on ch. v. 29, where it was used of physical fostering up: and cf. Plato, Rep. p. 538 c, περὶ δικαίων κ. καλῶν, ἐν οἷς ἐκτεθράμμεθα ὡς ὑπὸ γονεῦσι) **in** (as the sphere and element : see Plato above) **the discipline and admonition** ('παιδεία hic significare videtur institutionem per pœnas: νουθεσία autem est ea institutio quæ fit verbis.' Grot. Such indeed is the general sense of παιδεία in the LXX and N. T., the word having gained a deeper meaning than mere 'eruditio,' by the revealed doctrine of the depravity of our nature: see Trench, Syn. § 32. Ellic. remarks, that this sense seems not to have been unknown to earlier writers, e. g. Xen. Mem. i. 3. 5, διαίτῃ τήν τε ψυχὴν ἐπαίδευσε κ. τὸ σῶμα . . . , he *disciplined* &c., but not Polyb. ii. 9. 6, where it is ἀβλαβῶς ἐπαιδεύθησαν πρὸς τὸ μέλλον. **νουθεσία** (a late form for νουθέτησις, see Phryn. Lob. p. 512) is as Cicero, '*quasi lenior objurgatio:*' 'the training by word—by the word of encouragement, when no more is wanted ;—of remonstrance, reproof, or blame where these are required.' Trench, ubi supra) **of the Lord** (i. e. Christ : either objective,—'*concerning the Lord :*'—so Thdrt. and very many of the ancients, and Erasm., Beza (not Est.), &c.; or sub-

5 Οἱ δοῦλοι, ὑπακούετε τοῖς κυρίοις [q] κατὰ σάρκα [r] μετὰ
[s] φόβου καὶ [st] τρόμου, ἐν [u] ἁπλότητι τῆς καρδίας ὑμῶν, ὡς
τῷ χριστῷ, 6 μὴ κατ' [v] ὀφθαλμοδουλείαν ὡς [w] ἀνθρωπάρεσκοι, ἀλλ' ὡς [x] δοῦλοι [x] χριστοῦ, [y] ποιοῦντες τὸ
[y] θέλημα τοῦ θεοῦ, 7 ἐκ [z] ψυχῆς μετ' [a] εὐνοίας δουλεύοντες

ABDFK LPℵ a b c e f g h k l m n o 17. 47

q (Acts ii. 30 v. r.) Rom. i. 3. iv. 1. ix. 3 al. Paul only. = σαρκί, or ἐν σ., 1 Pet. iii. 18 al.
r = ch. iv. 2 reff.
s 1 Cor. ii. 3. 2 Cor. vii. 15. Phil. ii. 12 only. Ps. liv. 5.
t as above (s). Mark xvi. 8 only.
u Col. iii. 22 al6. only. P. 1 Chron. xxix. 17.
v Col. iii. 22 only †.
w Col. iii. 22 only. Ps. lii. 5 only.
x 1 Cor. vii. 22.
y Matt. vii. 21. xii. 50. John iv. 34. (ch. ii. 3.) Heb. x. 7, from Ps. xxxix. 8. 1 John ii. 17 al.
z Col. iii. 23 only. Ezek. xxv. 15. see Mark xii. 30, 33.
a here only †. 1 Macc. xi. 53 al.

5. *κατα σαρκα* bef *κυριοις* (*see Col* iii. 22) AB[P]ℵ m 17 [47] Clem Chr_1 Damasc Thl: txt DFKL rel Chr_2 Thdrt Œc. om *της* ℵ 72. 114-5. 122 [$Orig\text{-}cat_1$]. for *χριστω*, *κυριω* AL 17 copt Chr_1.

6. rec ins *του* bef *χριστου*, with D^3KL rel Chr Thdrt: om ABD^1F[P]ℵ l n^1 17 [47] Damasc Thl-ms Œc.

jective—'*such as the Lord approves* and dictates by His Spirit,'—so De W., Harl., Olsh., Mey., Stier. Conyb. renders '*such training and correction as befits the servants of Christ,*' which surely the words can hardly contain). **5—9.**] See on ch. v. 22. *Duties of masters and slaves.* **Slaves** (or as Conyb., '*Bondsmen.*' There is no reason to render **οἱ δοῦλοι**, *servants*, as in E. V., for by this much of the Apostle's exhortation is deprived of point), **obey your lords according to the flesh** (= τοῖς κατὰ σάρκα κυρίοις, Col. iii. 22: not to be joined with **ὑπακούετε**: nor can it be here said as so often, that κύριος-κατὰ-σάρκα is united in one idea: for in the context, another description of κύριος is brought forward, viz. ὁ χριστός. Chrys. sees in **κατὰ σάρκα** a consolatory hint that the δεσποτεία is πρόσκαιρος καὶ βραχεῖα: Calv., that their real liberty was still their own: Ellic. in citing these, rightly observes, that however they may be doubted, still both, especially the latter, are obviously *deductions* which must have been, and which the Apostle *might* have intended to have been, made) **with fear and trembling** (see reff., and note on 1 Cor. ii. 3: whence it appears that the **φόβος κ. τρόμος** was to be not that of dread, arising from their condition as slaves, but that of *anxiety* to do their duty,—'sollicita reverentia, quam efficiet cordis simplicitas.' Calv.), **in** (as its element) **simplicity** (singleness of view: "so Pind., Nem. viii. 61, speaks of κελεύθοις ἁπλόαις ζωᾶς in contrast with πάρφασις, treachery: in Aristoph. Plut. 1159, it is opposed to δόλιος: in Philo, Opif. 36, 39 (§ 55, 61, vol. i. pp. 38, 41), it is classed with ἀκακία," Harl.) **of your heart, as to Christ** (again—He being the source and ground of all Christian motives and duties), **not in a spirit of** (according to, measuring your obedience by) **eye-service** (τὴν οὐκ ἐξ εἰλικρινοῦς καρδίας προσφερομένην θεραπείαν, ἀλλὰ τῷ σχήματι κεχρωσμένην, Thdrt. Xen. Œc. xii. 20, βασιλεὺς ἵππου ἐπιτυχὼν ἀγαθοῦ παχῦναι αὐτὸν ὡς τάχιστα βουλόμενος ἤρετο τῶν δεινῶν τινα ἀμφ' ἵππους δοκούντων εἶναι, τί τάχιστα παχύνει ἵππον· τὸν δὲ εἰπεῖν λέγεται ὅτι δεσπότου ὀφθαλμός) **as men-pleasers** (on **ἀνθρωπάρεσκοι**, see Lob. on Phryn., p. 621; who, while disapproving of forms such as εὐάρεσκος and δυsάρεσκος, allows ἀνθρωπάρεσκος), **but as slaves of Christ** (ὁ ἄρα ἀνθρωπάρεσκος, οὐ δοῦλος τοῦ χριστοῦ· ὁ δὲ δοῦλος τοῦ χριστοῦ, οὐκ ἀνθρωπάρεσκος. τίς γὰρ θεοῦ δοῦλος ὤν, ἀνθρώποις ἀρέσκειν βούλεται; τίς δὲ ἀνθρώποις ἀρέσκων, θεοῦ δύναται εἶναι δοῦλος; Chrys. The contrast is between **κατ' ὀφθαλμοδουλείαν** and **ὡς δοῦλοι χρ.**, and **ποιοῦντες** κ.τ.λ. is a qualification of **δοῦλοι χριστοῦ**. This is much more natural, than, with Rückert, to make ποιοῦντες κ.τ.λ. carry the emphasis, and ὡς δοῦλ. χρ. to be merely subordinate to it), **doing the will of God** (serving not a *seen* master only (ὀφθαλμοδουλ.), but the great invisible Lord of all, which will be the surest guarantee for your serving your earthly masters, even when unseen); **from your soul with good will doing service** (this arrangement, which is that of Syr., Chr., Jer., Beng., Lachm., Harl., De Wette, seems to me far better than the other (Tischdf., Mey., Ellic., al.) which joins **ἐκ ψυχῆς** to **ποιοῦντες τὸ θέλ. τοῦ θεοῦ**. For 1) these words need here no such qualification as ἐκ ψυχῆς: if the will of God be the real object of the man's obedience, the μὴ κατ' ὀφθαλμοδουλ. will be sufficiently answered: and 2) were it so, it would be more natural to find **ἐκ ψυχῆς** preceding than following the clause,—ἐκ ψυχῆς ποιοῦντες τὸ θέλ. τοῦ θεοῦ, or ἐκ ψυχῆς τὸ θέλ. τοῦ θεοῦ ποιοῦντες, or τὸ θέλ. τοῦ θεοῦ ἐκ ψυχῆς ποιοῦντες, whereas 3) the double qualification, ἐκ

ὡς τῷ κυρίῳ καὶ οὐκ ἀνθρώποις· 8 εἰδότες ὅτι ἕκαστος
ἐάν τι ποιήσῃ ἀγαθόν, τοῦτο b κομίσεται παρὰ κυρίου, εἴτε
c δοῦλος εἴτε c ἐλεύθερος. 9 καὶ οἱ κύριοι, τὰ αὐτὰ ποιεῖτε
πρὸς αὐτούς, d ἀνιέντες τὴν e ἀπειλήν, εἰδότες ὅτι καὶ
αὐτῶν καὶ ὑμῶν ὁ κύριός ἐστιν ἐν οὐρανοῖς καὶ fg προς-
ωπολημψία οὐκ ἔστιν f παρ᾽ αὐτῷ.

b = 2 Cor. v. 10.
Col. iii. 25 al.
Ps. xxxix. 15.
c 1 Cor. xii. 13.
Gal. iii. 28.
Col. iii. 11.
Rev. vi. 15.
18.
xiii. 16. xix.
d Acts xvi. 26.
xxvii. 40.
Heb. xiii. 5
(from Deut.
xxxi. 6)
only.

e Acts iv. [17] 29. ix. 1 only. Job xxiii. 6. iii. 25. James ii. 1 only †.   f Rom. ii. 11 only.   g as above (f). Col.

7. μετα B. rec om ως, with D3KL rel Thdrt: ins ABDF[P]א b c l² m o 17. 67² vss Constt Bas Chr Damasc Antch Thl-ms Ambrst-ed Pel. ανθρωπω B [æth] Damasc.

8. rec (ὁ) εαν τι bef εκαστος, with L(Kא) rel syrr Chr Thdrt Damasc_h.l. Thl Œc: txt ABDF[P] m 17 latt Bas Damasc.—om ὁ BL1א¹ g k¹ Thl-mss.—εαν (ο εαν א³) ποιηση bef εκαστος א¹.—for εαν, αν D¹F a Chr₁: om K n¹.—om τι AD¹FK[P]א m n¹ 17 Bas: ins BD² or ³ L rel.   rec κομιειται (see Col iii. 25), with D3KLא3 rel Bas Chr Thdrt Damasc: txt ABD¹Fא¹ Petr [κομισηται P].   rec ins του bef κυριου, with KL rel Chr Thdrt: om ABDF[P]א 17 [47] Petr Damasc₂.

9. rec (for αυτων κ. υμων) υμων αυτων (the sense of Col iv. 1 helping the omn of κ. αυτων by homœotel.: cf varr), with K rel D-lat Syr ff: και αυτ. υμ. D3F: αυτων κ. ημων 43: ημων αυτων 26. 109: κ. υμ. κ. αυτ. L 67². 115 syr Petr Antch Cypr Ambrst: εαυτ. κ. υμων א¹: υμων κ. εαυτ. א³: txt ABD¹[P] m 17 vulg(and F-lat) copt goth arm Clem Jer.   [τοις ουρ. P:] ουρανω א [47].   for παρ᾽ αυτω, παρα θεω D¹ spec demid(and F-lat) Ambrst-ed Pel: π. τω θεω F: εν αυτω b m o 118 syr-mg [Cypr].

ψυχῆς μετ᾽ εὐνοίας, attached to δουλεύοντες, describes beautifully the source in himself (ἐκ ψυχῆς) and the accompanying feeling towards another (μετ᾽ εὐνοίας) of Christian service. On εὔνοια in this sense, cf. Eur. Androm. 59, εὔνους δὲ καὶ σοί, ζῶντι δ᾽ ἦν τῷ σῷ πόσει: Xen. Œcon. xii. 5, εὔνοιαν πρῶτον ... δεήσει αὐτὸν ἔχειν σοι καὶ τοῖς σοῖς ...; ἄνευ γὰρ εὐνοίας τί ὄφελος ἐπιτρόπου ἐπιστήμης γίνεται; and the other examples in Wetst.) as to the Lord and not to men, 8.] knowing (as ye do; i. e. seeing that ye are aware) that each man if he shall have done (at Christ's coming) any good thing (the reading is in some doubt. If we take the rec., or that of A, &c. we must render 'whatsoever good thing each man shall have done,' and take ὃ ἐάν τι for ὅτι ἄν; so Plato, Legg. ix. p. 864 E, ἣν ἄν τινα καταβλάψῃ: and Lysis. p. 160, ὃς ἄν τις ὑμᾶς εὖ ποιῇ (cited in Mey.). On ἐάν, see Winer, § 42. 6 obs.), this (emphatic: 'this in full,' 'this exactly') he shall receive (see reff. where the same expression occurs—this he shall then receive in its value as then estimated,—changed, so to speak, into the currency of that new and final state) from the Lord (Christ), whether he be slave or free (Chrys. beautifully gives the connexion of thought: ἐπειδὴ γὰρ εἰκὸς ἦν πολλοὺς τῶν δεσποτῶν ἀπίστους ὄντας μὴ αἰσχύνεσθαι μηδὲ ἀμείβεσθαι τοὺς οἰκέτας τῆς ὑπακοῆς, ὅρα πῶς αὐτοὺς παρεμυθήσατο ὥστε μὴ ὑποπτεύειν τὴν ἀνταπόδοσιν, ἀλλὰ σφόδρα

θαρρεῖν ὑπὲρ τῆς ἀμοιβῆς. καθάπερ γὰρ οἱ καλῶς πάσχοντες, ὅταν μὴ ἀμείβωνται τοὺς εὐεργέτας, τὸν θεὸν αὐτοῖς ὀφειλέτην ποιοῦσιν· οὕτω δὴ καὶ οἱ δεσπόται, ἂν παθόντες εὖ παρὰ σοῦ μή σε ἀμείψωνται, μᾶλλον ἡμείψαντο, τὸν θεὸν ὀφειλέτην σοι καταστήσαντες): 9.] and ye masters, do the same things ('jus analogum, quod vocant:' as they are to remember one whom they serve, so (below) are ye—and, 'mutatis mutandis,' to act to them as they to you. This wider sense is better than that of Chrys., τὰ αὐτὰ ποῖα; μετ᾽ εὐνοίας δουλεύετε) with regard to them, forbearing your (usual) threatening (τήν, 'quemadmodum vulgus dominorum solet,' Erasm. par. in Mey.), knowing (as ye do: see ver. 8) that both of them and of yourselves the Master is in the heavens, and respect of persons (warping of justice from regard to any man's individual pre-eminence, see reff. exists not with Him (Wetst. quotes the celebrated lines of Seneca, Thyest. 607, 'vos quibus rector maris atque terræ | jus dedit magnum necis atque vitæ, | ponite inflatos tumidosque vultus: | quicquid a vobis minor extimescit, | major hoc vobis dominus minatur: | omne sub regno graviore regnum est'). 10—20.] General exhortation to the spiritual conflict and to prayer. Henceforward (cf. Gal. vi. 17, note: τὸ λοιπόν (see var. readd.) would be 'finally.' Olsh.'s remark, that the Apostle never addresses his readers as ἀδελφοί in this Epistle, is perfectly cor-

h 2 Cor. xiii. 11.
Phil. iv. 8.
1 Thess. iv. 1.
2 Thess. iii.
1. = Paul only.
i Paul (Rom. iv. 20 al5.) only, exc. Acts ix. 22 (of Paul) and Heb. xi. 34. Ps. li. 7 (9). Judg. vi. 34 AB (not Edvat. F) only. 22 only. only †. only. Sir. xiv. 18. xxii. 53.

10 Τοῦ [h] λοιποῦ, [i] ἐνδυναμοῦσθε ἐν κυρίῳ καὶ ἐν τῷ [j] κράτει τῆς [j] ἰσχύος αὐτοῦ. 11 [k] ἐνδύσασθε τὴν [l] πανοπλίαν τοῦ θεοῦ, [m] πρὸς τὸ δύνασθαι ὑμᾶς στῆναι πρὸς τὰς [n] μεθοδείας τοῦ διαβόλου. 12 ὅτι οὐκ ἔστιν * ἡμῖν ἡ [o] πάλη πρὸς [p] αἷμα καὶ [p] σάρκα, ἀλλὰ πρὸς τὰς [q] ἀρχάς, πρὸς τὰς [q] ἐξουσίας, πρὸς τοὺς [r] κοσμοκράτορας τοῦ [s] σκότους

ABDFK LPℵ a b c e f g h k l m n o 17. 47

j ch. i. 19 reff.   k ch. iv. 24 reff.   l ver. 13.   Luke xi.
2 Kings ii. 21.   m = Matt. v.28. vi. 1 al.   n ch. iv. 14 only (reff.).   o here
(-λαίειν, Job xxxviii. 8 Aq.)   q ch. i. 21 reff.   p Matt. xvi. 17.   1 Cor. xv. 50.   Gal. i. 16.   Heb. ii. 14   p here only †.   r here only †.   s = Col. i. 13. Luke

10. rec το λοιπον (see *Phil* iii. 1, iv. 8; 2 *Thess* iii. 1; 2 *Cor* xiii. 11), with DFKL[P]ℵ[3] rel Chr Thdrt Thl Œc : txt ABℵ[1] 17. 67[2] Cyr Procop Damasc.   rec ins αδελφοι μου bef ενδυναμ. (see *Phil &c. as above*), with KL[P]ℵ[3] rel(a in red) [Syr copt goth], and (omg μου) F [47] 71. 109 vulg syr Thdrt Aug Pel : om A(insg αδελφ. aft ενδ.) BDℵ[1] 17 æth arm Cyr Damasc Lucif Jer Ambrst.   δυναμουσθε B 17.   ins τω bef κυριω ℵ[1](om ℵ-corr[1](?) [3]) 91.

11. aft ενδυσασθαι ins υμας F [vulg goth Orig-int[2]].   for 1st προς, εις DF.   στηναι bef υμας D : αντιστ. K Orig.   μεθοδιας A B[1](Rl [Tischdf]) D[1]FKLℵ e m 17.

12. * ὑμῖν BD[1]F a c Syr [goth æth] Lucif Ambrst : ημιν AD[3]KL[P]ℵ rel vulg syr copt [arm] Thdrt Clem Orig [Eus] Meth [Tert] Cypr Hil Jer Aug Ambr.   om 2nd προς τας F : for π. τ., και D vulg [Orig-int[2]] lat-ff.   rec ins του αιωνος bef τουτου, with D[3]KL[P]ℵ[3](but rubbed out) rel syr-w-ast Mac[1] Ath-ms Chr Thdrt : om ABD[1]Fℵ[1] 17. 67[2] latt copt goth [æth arm] Clem Orig[sæpe] Ath Eus Bas Nyss Cyr[aliq] Tert Cypr Lucif Hil Ambrst Jer Ors.

rect: the ἀδελφοῖς in ver. 23 does not contravene it (as Eadie), but rather establishes it. He there sends his apostolic blessing τοῖς ἀδελφοῖς, but does not directly address them) **be strengthened** (passive, not middle, see reff.—and Fritz. on Rom. iv. 20) **in the Lord** (Christ), **and in the strength of his might** (see on κράτος τῆς ἰσχύος, note, ch. i. 19). **Put on the entire armour** (emphatic: repeated again ver. 13: offensive, as well as defensive. It is probable that the Apostle was daily familiarized in his imprisonment with the Roman method of arming) **of God** (Harl. maintains that the stress is on τοῦ θεοῦ, to contrast with τοῦ διαβόλου below: but there is no distinction made between the armour of God and any other spiritual armour, which would be the case, were this so. τοῦ θεοῦ, as supplied, ministered, by God, who ἅπασι διανέμει τὴν βασιλικὴν πανοπλίαν, Thdrt.), **that ye may be able to stand against** (so Jos. Antt. xi. 5. 7, θαρρεῖν μὲν οὖν τῷ θεῷ πρῶτον, ὡς καὶ πρὸς τὴν ἐκείνων ἀπέχθειαν στησομένῳ: see Kypke, ii. p. 301, and Ellicott's note here) **the schemes** (the instances (concr.) of a quality (abstr.) of μεθόδεια. τί ἐστι μεθόδεια; μεθοδεῦσαί ἐστι τὸ ἀπατῆσαι, κ. διὰ συντόμου ἑλεῖν, Chrys. :—the word is however sometimes used in a good sense, as Diod. Sic. i. 81, ταύτας δὲ οὐ ῥάδιον ἀκριβῶς ἐξελέγξαι, μὴ γεωμέτρου τὴν ἀλήθειαν ἐκ τῆς ἐμπειρίας μεθοδεύσαντος,—'if the geometrician had not investigated, &c.' The bad sense is found in Polyb. xxxviii. 4. 10, πολλὰ δή τινα πρὸς ταύτην τὴν ὑπόθεσιν ἐμπορεύων κ. μεθοδευόμενος, ἐκίνει κ. παρώξυνε τοὺς ὄχλους. See Ellic. on ch. iv. 14) **of the devil. 12.]** For (confirms τ. μεθ. τοῦ διαβ. preceding) **our** (or *'your :'* the ancient authorities are divided) **wrestling** (πάλη must be literally taken—it is a hand to hand and foot to foot 'tug of war'—that in which the combatants close, and wrestle for the mastery) **is not** (Meyer well remarks, that the negative is not to be softened down into *non tam*, or *non tantum*, as Grot., &c.—the conflict which the Apostle means (qu.? better, ἡ πάλη, the only conflict which can be described by such a word —our life and death struggle, there being but *one* such) is absolutely *not* with men but &c. He quotes from Aug., "Non est nobis colluctatio adversus carnem et sanguinem, i. e. adversus homines, quos videtis sævire in nos. Vasa sunt, alius utitur: organa sunt, alius tangit") **against blood and flesh** (i. e. men : see reff.), **but** (see above) **against the governments, against the powers** (see note on ch. i. 21), **against the world-rulers** (*munditenentes*, as Tert. c. Marc. v. 18, vol. ii. p. 58. Cf. John xii. 31 note; xiv. 30; xvi. 11; 2 Cor. iv. 4; 1 John v. 19. The Rabbis (see Schöttg.) adopted this very word קוסמוקרתור, and applied it partly to earthly kings (as on

τούτου, πρὸς τὰ ᵗ πνευματικὰ τῆς ᵘ πονηρίας ἐν τοῖς
ᵛ ἐπουρανίοις. ¹³ διὰ τοῦτο ʷ ἀναλάβετε τὴν ˣ πανοπλίαν
τοῦ θεοῦ, ἵνα δυνηθῆτε ʸ ἀντιστῆναι ἐν τῇ ᶻ ἡμέρᾳ τῇ ᶻ πο-
νηρᾷ καὶ ἅπαντα ᵃ κατεργασάμενοι στῆναι. ¹⁴ στῆτε οὖν

ᵗ ch. v. 19 reff. constr. see note. here only.
ᵘ Matt. xxii. 18. Mark vii. 22. Luke xi. 39. Acts iii. 26. Rom. i. 29. 1 Cor. v. 8
only. Ps. cxl. 4.   ᵛ ch. i. 3 reff.   ʷ Acts vii. 43. xx. 13, 14. xxiii. 31.   2 Tim. iv.
11. Deut. i. 41. Jer. xxvi. (xlvi.) 3.   ˣ ver. 11 reff.   ʸ Matt. v. 39 al.   Paul, Rom.
ix. 19 al6. abs., here only. Esth. ix. 2. Nah. i. 6.   ᶻ ch. v. 16 reff.   ᵃ = Rom. vii.
15, 17, &c. xv. 18 al. Paul only, exc. James i. 3 (20 v. r.). 1 Pet. iv. 3.

13. κατεργασμενοι A.   om στηναι and ουν ver 14 D¹F Cypr [Victorin].

Gen. xiii.), partly to the Angel of Death;
'quamvis te feci κοσμοκράτορα super
homines &c.' So that the word must
be literally understood, as in the places
cited. Cf. Ellicott's note) of this (state
of) darkness (see ch. ii. 2; v. 8, 11),
against the spiritual (armies) (so we have
(Mey.) τὸ πολιτικόν (Herod. vii. 103),
τὸ ἱππικόν (Rev. ix. 16), τὰ ληστρικά
(Polyæn. v. 14), τὰ δοῦλα, τὰ αἰχμάλωτα
&c. Winer, Gr. § 34, remark 3, compares
τὰ δαιμόνια, originally a neuter-adjective
form. See Bernhardy, Synt. p. 326, for
more examples. Stier maintains the abstract meaning, 'the spiritual things:'
but as Ellic. remarks, the meaning could
not be 'spiritales malignitates,' as Beza,
but 'spiritualia nequitiæ,' as the Vulg.,
i. e. 'the spiritual elements,' or 'pro-
perties,' 'of wickedness,' which will not
suit here) of wickedness in the heavenly
places (but what is the meaning? Chrys.
connects ἐν τοῖς ἐπουρανίοις with ἡ
πάλη ἐστὶν—ἐν τοῖς ἐπ. ἡ μάχη κεῖται
. . . . ὡς ἂν εἰ ἔλεγεν, ἡ συνθήκη ἐν
τίνι κεῖται; ἐν χρυσῷ. And so Thdrt.,
Phot., Œc., al. But it is plain that ἐν
will not bear this (Chrys. says, τὸ ἐν,
ὑπέρ ἐστι, καὶ τὸ ἐν, διά ἐστι), though
possibly the order of the sentence might.
Rückert, Matth., Eadie, al., interpret of
the scene of the combat, thus also joining
ἐν τ. ἐπ. with ἔστ. ἡμ. ἡ πάλη. The
objection to this is twofold: 1) that the
words thus appear without any sort of
justification in the context: nay rather
as a weakening of the following διὰ τοῦτο,
instead of a strengthening: and 2) that
according to Eadie's argument, they stultify themselves. He asks, "How can
they (the heavenly places, the scenes of
divine blessing, of Christ's exaltation,
&c.) be the seat or abode of impure
fiends?" But if they are "the scene of"
our "combat" with these fiends, how
can our enemies be any where else but
in them? Two ways then remain: to
join ἐν τοῖς ἐπουρ. a) with τὰ πνευματικὰ τῆς πονηρίας—b) with τῆς πονηρίας only. The absence of an article
before ἐν forms of course an objection to

both: but not to both equally. Were b)
to be adopted, the specifying τῆς would
appear to be required—because the sense
would be, 'of that wickedness,' viz., the
rebellion of the fallen angels, 'which
was (or is) in the heavenly places.' If
a), we do not so imperatively require
the τά before ἐν, because ἐν τοῖς ἐπουρ.
only specifies the locality,—does not distinguish τὰ πνευματικὰ τῆς πονηρ. ἐν
τοῖς ἐπουρ. from any other πνευματικὰ
τῆς πονηρίας elsewhere. So that this
is in grammar the least objectionable
rendering. And in sense it is, notwithstanding what Eàdie and others have
said, equally unobjectionable. That habitation of the evil spirits which in ch.
ii. 2 was said, when speaking of mere
matters of fact, to be in the ἀήρ, is,
now that the difficulty and importance
of the Christian conflict is being forcibly
set forth, represented as ἐν τοῖς ἐπουρανίοις—over us, and too strong for us
without the panoply of God. Cf. τὰ
πετεινὰ τοῦ οὐρανοῦ, Matt. vi. 26; and
reff.). **13.]** Wherefore (since our foes
are in power too mighty for us,—and in
dwelling, around and above us) take up
(i. e. not 'to the battle,' but 'to put on:'
'frequens est ἀναλαμβάνειν de armis;'
Kypke in loc. He refers to Diod. Sic.
xx. 33, ἕκαστοι τὰς πανοπλίας ἀνελάμ-
βανον ἐπὶ τὴν τοῦ φονεύσαντος τιμωρίαν,
—and many places in Josephus. See also
Wetst.) the entire armour of God (see
on ver. 11) that ye may be able to withstand in the evil day (not as Chrys.,
ἡμέραν πονηρὰν τὸν παρόντα βίον φησί
—for then the evil day would be upon the
Christian before he has on the armour;
the ἀεὶ ὁπλίζεσθε of Chr., if taken literally, would be but a poor posture of defence. Nor again can his view stand, ἀπὸ
τοῦ χρόνου παραμυθεῖται· βραχύς, φησίν,
ὁ καιρός—evidently no such point is raised
in the following exhortations, but rather
the contrary is implied—a long and weary
conflict. The right interpretation is well
given by Bengel—"Bellum est perpetuum: pugna alio die minus, alio magis
fervet. Dies malus, vel ingruente morte,

<table>
<tr><td>b Luke xii. 35.
Exod. xii. 11.
see 1 Pet. i.
13.
c Paul, here
only. Luke
xii. 35, 37.</td><td>^{bc} περιζωσάμενοι τὴν ^{bd} ὀσφὺν ὑμῶν ^e ἐν ἀληθείᾳ, καὶ ^f ἐν-
δυσάμενοι ^gον ^g θώρακα τῆς δικαιοσύνης, 15 καὶ ^h ὑποδη-
σάμενοι τοὺς πόδας ^e ἐν ⁱ ἑτοιμασίᾳ τοῦ ^j εὐαγγελίου τῆς</td><td>ABDFK
LPℵ a b
c e f g h
k l m n o
17.47</td></tr>
</table>

xvii. 8. Rev. i. 13. xv. 6 only. Ps. lxiv. 6. Dan. x. 5.   d as above (b). Matt. iii. 4. Mark i. 6. Acts ii. 30. Heb. vii. 5, 10 only. Isa. xi. 5   e = Matt. xi. 8 ‖ L. John xix. 40. 1 Tim. ii. 9. 1 Cor. iv. 21. 1 Chron. xv. 27 B (om Aℵ). f ch. iv. 24 reff.   g 1 Thess. v. 8. Rev. ix. 9, 17 only. Isa. lix. 17.   h Mark vi. 9. Acts xii. 8 only. 2 Chron. xxviii. 15.   i here only. = Ps. ix. 37. see Ezra ii. 68.   j here only. see Matt. iv. 23. Acts xx. 24. Rom. x. 15, from Isa. lii. 7.

14. περιεζωσμενοι D¹F Naz Chr.

vel in vita : longior, brevior, in se ipso sæpe varius, ubi Malus vos invadit, et copiæ malignæ vos infestant, ver. 12"), **and having accomplished all things** (requisite to the combat: being fully equipped and having bravely fought. The words must not be taken in the sense of, ' *omnibus debellatis*,' as if **κατεργασάμενοι** = καταπολεμήσαντες (so Chrys. — ἅπαντα —τουτέστι, καὶ πάθη κ. ἐπιθυμίας ἀτόπους κ. τὰ ἐνοχλοῦντα ἡμῖν ἅπαντα), nor again, understood of *preparation* only (= παρασκευασάμενοι, 1 Cor. xiv. 8) as Erasm., Beza, Bengel, al. To finish, or accomplish, is the invariable Pauline usage of the word when taken in a good sense) **to stand firm** (at your post : as Estius, reporting others,—'ut posteaquam omnia quæ boni militis sunt, perfeceritis, stare et subsistere possitis :'—that you may not, after having done your duty well in battle, fall off, but stand your ground to the end. The other interpretation, ' stare tanquam triumphatores,' is precluded by what has been said above). **14—20.**] *Particulars of the armour, and attitude of the soldier.* **14.**] **Stand therefore** (whether ' ready for the fight,' or ' in the fight,' matters very little : all the aoristic participles are in time antecedent to the στῆτε—and the fight ever at hand), **having girt about your loins with** (ἐν, not instrumental, but *local* : the girt person is within, surrounded by, the girdle : but this is necessarily expressed in English by ' *with*') **truth** (not *truth objective*, which is rather the ῥῆμα θεοῦ below, ver. 17 : but ' *truthfulness*,' subjective truth : to be understood however as based upon the faith and standing of a Christian, necessarily *his* truthfulness *in his place in Christ*. As the girdle (hardly here, however true that may have been, to be regarded as carrying the sword, for that would be confusing the separate images, cf. ver. 17) kept all together, so that an ungirded soldier would be (see Mey.) a contradiction in terms,—just so Truth is the band and expediter of the Christian's work in the conflict, without which all his armour would be but encumbrance. Gurnall's notion (Christian Armour, vol.

i. p. 378), that ' the girdle is used as an ornament, put on uppermost, to cover the joints of the armour, which would, if seen, cause some uncomeliness' (see also Harl. ' fie ift des Chriften Schmuck'), is against the context, and against the use of the phrase ζωνν. τ. ὀσφ. in the N. T.), **and having put on the breastplate of righteousness** (see ref. Isa., and Wisd. v. 19. As in those passages, righteousness *is* the breastplate—the genitive here being one of apposition. The righteousness spoken of is that of Rom. vi. 13—the purity and uprightness of Christian character which is the result of the work of the Spirit of Christ ; the inwrought righteousness of Christ, not merely the imputed righteousness), **and having shod your feet** (as the soldier with his sandals—cf. the frequent description of arming in Homer—ποσσὶ δ' ὑπαὶ λιπαροῖσιν ἐδήσατο καλὰ πέδιλα. The Roman *caliga* may be in the Apostle's mind : see on ver. 11) **with** (local again, not instrumental: see on ver. 14) **readiness** (the article omitted after ἐν) (the uses of ἑτοιμασία (' in classical Greek, ἑτοιμότης, Dem. 1268. 7.' Mey.) in Hellenistic Greek are somewhat curious, and may have a bearing on this passage. In Ps. ix. 17, it has the sense of *inward* ' *preparedness*,'—τὴν ἑτοιμασίαν τῆς καρδίας (τῶν πενήτων)—of *outward*, in Jos. Antt. x. 1. 2, δισχιλίους .... ἵππους εἰς ἑτοιμασίαν ὑμῖν παρέχειν ἕτοιμός εἰμι : of *preparation*, in an active sense, Wisd. xiii. 12, τὰ ἀποβλήματα τῆς ἐργασίας εἰς ἑτοιμασίαν τροφῆς ἀναλώσας ἐνεπλήσθη : in Ezra ii. 68, it answers to the Heb. ןוכמ, a foundation, τοῦ στῆσαι αὐτὸν (the temple) ἐπὶ τὴν ἑτοιμασίαν αὐτοῦ, see also Ps. lxxxviii. 14, δικαιοσ. κ. κρίμα ἑτοιμασία τοῦ θρόνου σου, and Dan. xi. 7 Theod. From this latter usage (which can hardly be a mistake of the translators, as Mey. supposes) some (Beza, Bengel, al.) have believed that as the ὑποδήματα are the lowest part of the panoply, the same meaning has place here : but no good sense seems to me to be gained : for we could not explain it ' pedes militis Christiani *firmantur Evangelio*, ne loco moveatur,' as Beng. Nor again can it

[j] εἰρήνης, 16 [k]* ἐπὶ [k] πᾶσιν [l] ἀναλαβόντες τὸν [m] θυρεὸν τῆς
πίστεως, [n] ἐν ᾧ δυνήσεσθε πάντα τὰ [o] βέλη τοῦ [p] πονηροῦ
[τὰ] [q] πεπυρωμένα [r] σβέσαι. 17 καὶ τὴν [s] περικεφαλαίαν
τοῦ [t] σωτηρίου [u] δέξασθε, καὶ τὴν [v] μάχαιραν τοῦ πνεύμα-

k Luke iii. 20. xvi. 26. 2 Cor. vii. 4. Col. iii. 14. 1 Thess. iii. 7, 9. ἐν π., = 2 Tim. iv. 5. Tit. ii. 9. Heb. xiii. 28. 1 Pet. iv. 11.

l ver. 13 reff. m here only. 2 Kings i. 21. n simply local, see note. o here only. 4 Kings ix. 24. p = Matt. (v. 37?) xiii. 19. (2 Thess. iii. 3?) 1 John ii. 13. v. 18. q 1 Cor. vii. 9. 2 Cor. xi. 29. 2 Pet. iii. 12. Rev. i. 15. iii. 18 only. Prov. x. 20. r Matt. xii. 20 (from Isa. xlii. 3). xxv. 8. Mark ix. 44, &c. 1 Thess. v. 19. Heb. xi. 34. Job xvi. 15. s 1 Thess. v. 8 only. Isa. lix. 17. t Luke ii. 30. iii. 6. Acts xxviii. 28 (Paul) only. Isa. lx. 6. (-ιος, Tit. ii. 11.) u = Luke ii. 28. xvi. 6, 7. xxii. 17 only. v Heb. iv. 12 al. fr. Prov. xii. 18.

16. * ἐν B[P]א m 17 latt $Meth_1$ Naz Cyr-jer Cypr [Lucif Victorin]: επι ADFKL rel goth $Meth_1$ Chr Thdrt $Damasc_1$ [$Orig\text{-}int_1$] Jer Ambrst. δυνασθε D¹F: δυνησεσθαι א. om 2nd τα BD¹F: ins AD²KL[P]א rel.

17. om δεξασθε D¹F Tert Cypr [Lucif Victorin]. (δεξασθαι AD³K[P] abcefghlmo 17.)

mean the *preparation* (*active*) of the Gospel, or *preparedness* to preach the Gospel, as Chrys. and most Commentators ('shod as ready messengers of the glad tidings of peace,' Conyb.), for the persons addressed were not teachers, but the whole church. The only refuge then is in the genitive subjective, '*the preparedness of,*' i. e. arising from, suggested by '*the Gospel of peace;*' and so Œc. (2), Calv., Harl., Olsh., De W., Mey., Ellic., al.) **of the Gospel of peace** (the Gospel whose message and spirit is peace: so ὁ μῦθος ὁ τῆς ἐπιστήμης, Plato, Theæt. p. 147 c: see Bernhardy, p. 161), **besides all** (not as E. V. '*above* all,' as if it were the most important: nor as Beng., al. '*over all,*' so as to cover all that has been put on before:—see especially reff. to Luke. And the *all,* as no τούτοις is specified, does not apply only to 'quæcunque indu*istis*' (Beng.), but generally, to all things whatever. But it is perhaps doubtful, whether **ἐν πᾶσιν** ought not to be read: in which case it will be "*in all things,*" i. e. on all occasions) **having taken up** (see on ver. 13) **the shield** (θυρεός, 'scutum:' οἷόν τις θύρα φυλάττων τὸ σῶμα: the large oval shield, as distinguished from the small and light buckler, ἀσπίς, 'clypeus.' Polybius in his description (vi. 23) of the Roman armour, which should by all means be read with this passage, says of the θυρεός,—οὗ τὸ μὲν πλάτος ἐστὶ τῆς κυρτῆς ἐπιφανείας πένθ' ἡμιποδίων· τὸ δὲ μῆκος, ποδῶν τεττάρων. Kypke quotes from Plutarch, that Philopœmen persuaded the Achæans, ἀντὶ μὲν θυρεοῦ καὶ δόρατος ἀσπίδα λαβεῖν καὶ σάρισσαν. He adduces examples from Josephus of the same distinction,—which Phryn. p. 366, ed. Lob., states to have been unknown to the ancients, as well as θυρεός in this sense at all. See Lobeck's note, and Hom. Od. ι. 240) **of** (genitive of apposition) **faith, in which** (as lighting on it and being quenched in it; or perhaps (as Ellic. altern. with the above), "as protected by and under cover of which") **you shall be able** (not as Mey., to be referred to the last great future fight—but used as stronger than 'in which ye may,' &c., implying the certainty that the shield of faith will at all times and in all combats quench &c.) **to quench all the fiery darts** (cf. Ps. vii. 13, τὰ βέλη αὐτοῦ τοῖς καιομένοις ἐξειργάσατο:—Herod. viii. 52, ὅκως στυπεῖον περὶ τοὺς ὀϊστοὺς περιθέντες ἅψειαν, ἐτόξευον ἐς τὸ φράγμα:—Thucyd. ii. 75, καὶ προκαλύμματα εἶχε δέρρεις καὶ διφθέρας, ὥστε τοὺς ἐργαζομένους καὶ τὰ ξύλα μήτε **πυρφόροις ὀϊστοῖς** βάλλεσθαι, εἰς ἀσφάλειάν τε εἶναι, and other examples in Wetst. Apollodorus, Bibl. ii. 4, uses the very expression, τὴν ὕδραν . . . . . βαλὼν **βέλεσι πεπυρωμένοις** . . . . . Appian calls them πυρφόρα τοξεύματα. The Latin name was *malleoli.* Ammianus Marcellin. describes them as cane arrows, with a head in the form of a distaff filled with lighted material. Wetst. ib. The idea of Hammond, Bochart, al., that *poisoned* darts are meant ('*causing fever*'), is evidently ungrammatical. See Smith's Dict. of Antiq. art. Malleolus, and Winer, Realw. 'Bogen.' If the art. **τά** be omitted, a different turn must be given to the participle, which then becomes predicative: and we must render, '*when inflamed,*' even in their utmost malice and fiery power) **of the wicked one** (see reff. and notes on Matt. v. 37; John xvii. 15. Here, the conflict being personal, the adversary must be not an abstract principle, but a concrete person).

17.] **And take** ('accipite oblatam a Domino.' Beng.) **the helmet** (πρὸς δὲ τούτοις . . . περικεφαλαία χαλκῆ. Polyb. ubi supra) **of** (genitive of apposition as above) **salvation** (the neuter form, from LXX l. c.: otherwise confined to St. Luke. Beng. takes it masculine, '*salutaris,* i. e. Christi,'—but this is harsh, and does not

w ch. v. 26 reff.
x Rom. iv. 11.
2 Cor. ii. 4.
ix. 12 al. fr.
y Phil. iv. 6.
1 Tim. ii. 1.
v. 5. 2 Chron.
vi. 19 al.
z Luke xxi.
36 only.
Ps. xxxiii. 1.
a ch. ii. 22 reff.

τος, ὅ ἐστιν ʷ ῥῆμα θεοῦ, 18 ˣ διὰ πάσης ʸ προσευχῆς καὶ ABDFK
ʸ δεήσεως προσευχόμενοι ᶻ ἐν παντὶ ᶻ καιρῷ ᵃ ἐν πνεύματι, LPℵ a b c e f g h
καὶ ᵇᶜ εἰς ᶜαὐτὸ ᵈ ἀγρυπνοῦντες ἐν πάσῃ ᵉ προσκαρτερήσει καὶ k l m n o 17. 47
ʸ δεήσει περὶ πάντων τῶν ᶠ ἁγίων 19 καὶ ὑπὲρ ἐμοῦ, ἵνα μοι
δοθῇ ᵍ λόγος ʰ ἐν ⁱ ἀνοίξει τοῦ στόματός μου ᵏ ἐν ᵏˡ παρρησίᾳ

b = 1 Pet. iv. 7.   c (w. τοῦτο, Rom. ix. 17. xiii. 6. 2 Cor. v. 5. ver. 22. Col. iv. 8.)   d Mark xiii. 33. Luke
xxi. 36. Heb. xiii. 17 only. Cant. v. 2. (-πνία, 2 Cor. v. 5.)   e here only †. (-ρεῖν, Col. iv. 2.)
f ch. i. 1 reff.   g = 1 Cor. xii. 8.   h see note.   i here only †. (-γειν τὸ στ., Matt. v.
2. Acts viii. 35. x. 34 al. Ezek. xvi. 63.)   k Phil. i. 20. Col. ii. 15. = Paul only.   l ch. iii. 12 reff.

18. rec aft αυτο ins τουτο (*explanatory expansion of* αυτο: αυτον *speaks also for
the reading of but one word*), with D³KL[P] rel Chr-txt Thdrt Damasc-txt: om ABℵ
17 copt goth Bas Chr₂ Damasc₁, αυτον D¹F, *in illum* G-lat, *in illo* D-lat, *in ipso* vulg
(and F-lat).   aft αγρυπνουντες ins παντοτε DF Syr goth Bas [Victorin].   om
προσκαρτερησει και D¹F [Victorin].   ins τη bef δεησει D¹.   for περι, υπερ
D¹F m [47] syr[-txt(txt, syr-mg)] Thdrt.

19. μοι bef δοθη ℵ¹(txt ℵ³).   rec (for δοθη) δοθειη: txt ABDFKL[P]ℵ rel.

correspond to the parallel, 1 Thess. v. 8,
where the helmet is the hope of salvation,
clearly shewing its subjective character.
Here, it is *salvation appropriated*, by
faith), **and the sword of** (furnished, forged,
by: cf. τ. πανοπλ. τ. θεοῦ vv. 11, 13 : not
here the genitive of apposition, for ὅ ἐστιν
follows after) **the Spirit, which** (neuter,
attracted to ῥῆμα: see ch. iii. 13 and
reff. there) **is** (see on ἐστιν, Gal. iv. 24
reff.) **the word of God** (the Gospel: see
the obvious parallel, Heb. iv. 12 : also
Rom. i. 16 : and our pattern for the use
of this sword of the Spirit, Matt. iv. 4,
7, 10); **with** (see reff. : as the state through
which, as an instrument, the action takes
place. The clause depends on στῆτε οὖν,
the principal imperative of the former
sentence—not on δέξασθε, which is merely
a subordinate one, and which besides
(Mey.) would express only how the weapons should be *taken*, and therefore would
not satisfy πάσης and ἐν παντὶ καιρῷ)
all (kind of) **prayer and supplication**
⟨"it has been doubted whether there is
any exact distinction between προσευχή
and δέησις. Chrys. and Thdrt. on 1 Tim.
ii. 1 explain προσευχή as αἴτησις ἀγαθῶν
(see Suicer, Thes. s. v. 1),—δέησις as ὑπὲρ
ἀπαλλαγῆς λυπηρῶν ἱκετεία (so Grot. as
ἀπὸ τοῦ δέους, but see 2 Cor. i. 11): compare Orig. de Orat. c. 33 (vol. i. p. 271).
Alii alia. The most natural and obvious distinction is that adopted by
nearly all recent Commentators, viz. that
προσευχή is a 'vocabulum sacrum' (see
Harl.) denoting prayer in general, '*pre-
catio:*' δέησις a 'vocabulum commune,'
denoting a special character or form of it,
'*petitum,*' *rogatio:* see Fritz. Rom. x. 1,
vol. ii. p. 372. Huther on Tim. l. c."
Ellicott) **praying in every season** (literal:
cf. Luke xviii. 1 note, and 1 Thess. v. 17.

There seems to be an allusion to our
Lord's ἐν παντὶ καιρῷ δεόμενοι, ref.
Luke) **in the Spirit** (the Holy Spirit:
see especially Jude 20, and Rom. viii.
15, 26 ; Gal. iv. 6 :—not, *heartily*, as Est.,
Grot., al.), **and thereunto** (with reference
to their employment which has been just
mentioned. Continual habits of prayer
cannot be kept up without watchfulness
to that very end. This is better than to
understand it, with Chr., &c. of persistence in the prayer itself, which indeed
comes in presently) **watching in** (element
in which : watching, being employed, in)
all (kind of) **importunity and supplication** (not a hendiadys: rather the latter
substantive is explanatory of the former,
without losing its true force as coupled to
it : '*importunity and* (accompanied with,
i. e. exemplified by)· *supplication*') **concerning all saints, and** (καί brings into
prominence a particular included in the
general : see Hartung, i. 145) **for me** (certainly it seems that some distinction between ὑπέρ and περί should be marked :
see Eadie's note, where however he draws
it too strongly. Krüger, § 68. 28. 3, regards the two in later writers as synonymous. So Meyer, who quotes Demosth.
p. 74. 35, μὴ περὶ τῶν δικαίων μηδ' ὑπὲρ
τῶν ἔξω πραγμάτων εἶναι τὴν βουλήν,
ἀλλ' ὑπὲρ τῶν ἐν τῇ χώρᾳ; and Xen.
Mem. i. 1. 17, ὑπὲρ τούτων περὶ αὐτοῦ
παραγνῶναι) **that** (aim of the ὑπὲρ ἐμοῦ)
there may be given me (I do not see the
relevance of a special emphasis on δοθῇ as
Mey., Ellic. That it is a *gift*, would be
of course, if it were prayed for from God)
speech in the opening of my mouth
(many renderings have been proposed.
First of all, the words must be joined
with the preceding, not with the following, as in E. V., Grot., Kypke, De W.,

[m] γνωρίσαι τὸ [m] μυστήριον τοῦ εὐαγγελίου, 20 ὑπὲρ οὗ
[n] πρεσβεύω ἐν [o] ἁλύσει, ἵνα [p] ἐν αὐτῷ [q] παρρησιάσωμαι
[r] ὡς δεῖ με λαλῆσαι.

21 Ἵνα δὲ εἰδῆτε καὶ ὑμεῖς [s] τὰ [st] κατ' ἐμέ, [u] τί πράσσω,

m ch. i. 9 (reff.)
n 2 Cor. v 20
only †. (·εία, Luke xiv. 32.)
o Mark v. 3. &c. ‖ L. Acts xii. 6, 7. xxi. 33. xxviii. 20. 2 Tim. i. 16. Rev.
p see note.
r Col. iv. 4.
s Col. iv. 7

xx. 1 only†.   Wisd. xvii. 17 only.   Exod. xxviii. 22 Aq. Symm. Theod.
q Acts ix. 27 al(6).   1 Thess. ii. 2 only. L.P.   Prov. xx. 9 al.
reff.   t = ch. i. 15.   u — here only.

om του ευαγγελιου BF (Tert) Ambrst [Victorin].
20. παρρησιασωμαι bef εν αυτω ℵ.   for εν αυτω, αυτο B.
21. και υμεις bef ειδητε ADF[P]ℵ latt Thdrt : om και υμεις 17: txt BKL rel syrr

al., which would (see below) be too tame
and prosaic for the solemnity of the passage. Œc. (and similarly Chr. ? see Ellic.)
regards the words as describing *unpre-
meditated* speech: ἐν αὐτῷ τῷ ἀνοῖξαι
ὁ λόγος προΐει. But as Mey., this certainly would have been expressed by ἐν
αὐτῇ τῇ ἀν. or the like. Calv., 'os aper-
tum cupit, quod erumpat in liquidam et
firmam confessionem : ore enim semiclauso
proferuntur ambigua et perplexa responsa,'
and similarly Rück., al., and De W. But
this again is laying too much on the
phrase : see below. The same objection
applies to Beza and Piscator's rendering,
'ut aperiam os meum:' and to taking
the phrase of an opening of his mouth
by God, as (Chrys. ἡ ἅλυσις ἐπίκειται
τὴν παρρησίαν ἐπιστομίζουσα, ἀλλ' ἡ εὐχὴ
ἡ ὑμετέρα ἀνοίγει μου τὸ στόμα, ἵνα
πάντα ἃ ἐπέμφθην εἰπεῖν, εἴπω) Corn.-
a-lap., Grot., Harl., and Olsh. from Ps.
l. 17 and Ezek. xxix. 21. The best rendering is that of Est. ('dum os meum
aperio'), Meyer, Eadie, Ellic., al., '*in* (at)
the opening of my mouth,' i. e. 'when I
undertake to speak :' thus we keep the
meaning of ἀνοίγειν τὸ στόμα (reff. and
Job iii. 1 ; Dan. x. 16), which always carries some solemnity of subject or occasion
with it), **in boldness** ((subjective) freedom
of speech, not as Grot. ('ut ab hac custodia
militari liber per omnem urbem per-
ferre possem sermonem evangelicum,' &c.),
Koppe (objective), *liberty of speech*) **to
make known** (the purpose of the gift of
λόγος ἐν ἀνοίξει τοῦ στόματος) **the mystery
of the gospel** (contained in the gospel : subjective genitive. 'The genitive is somewhat different to τὸ μυστήρ. τοῦ θελήματος,
ch. i. 9 : there it was the mystery in the
matter of, concerning the θέλημα, gen. ob-
jecti,' Ellic.), **on behalf of which** (viz. τοῦ
μυστ. τοῦ εὐαγγ.—for as Meyer remarks,
this is the object of γνωρίσαι, and γνωρίσαι is pragmatically bound to πρεσβεύω)
I am an ambassador (*of Christ* (ref.): *to
whom*, is understood : we need not supply
as Michaelis, to the court of Rome) **in**

chains (the singular is not to be pressed, as
has been done by Paley, Wieseler, al., to
signify the chain by which he was bound
to ' the soldier that kept him ' (Acts xxviii.
20): for such singulars are often used collectively : see Bernhardy, Syntax, p. 58 f.,
Polyb. xxi. 3. 3, παρὰ μικρὸν εἰς τὴν
ἅλυσιν ἐνέπεσον. Wetst. remarks, 'alias
legati, jure gentium sancti et inviolabiles,
in vinculis haberi non poterant.' His
being thus a captive ambassador, was all
the more reason why they should pray earnestly that he might have boldness, &c.),
that (co-ordinate purpose with ἵνα δοθῇ,
not subordinate to πρεσβεύω. See examples of such a co-ordinate ἵνα in Rom. vii.
13 ; Gal. iii. 14 ; 2 Cor. ix. 3. But no
tautology (as Harl.) is involved : see below)
in (the matter of, in dealing with : cf. λήθη
ἐν τοῖς μαθήμασι, Plato, Phileb. p. 252 B :
and see Bernhardy, p. 212: not as in
1 Thess. ii. 2, ἐπαρρησιασάμεθα ἐν τῷ θεῷ
ἡμῶν, where ἐν denotes the source or
ground of the confidence) **it I may speak
freely, as I ought to speak** (no comma at
με, as Koppe—'*that I may have confidence, as I ought, to speak ;*' but the
idea of speaking being already half understood in παρρησίᾳ, λαλῆσαι merely refers
back to it. This last clause is a further
qualification of the παρρησία—that it is a
courage and free-spokenness ὡς δεῖ : and
therefore involves no tautology).

21—24.] CONCLUSION OF THE EPISTLE.

21.] But (transition to another subject : the contrast being between his more
solemn occupations just spoken of, and his
personal welfare) **that ye also** (the καί may
have two meanings: 1) as *I* have been
going at length into the matters concerning *you*, so if *you also* on your part, wish to
know my matters, &c. : 2) it may relate to
some others whom the same messenger was
to inform, and to whom he had previously
written. If so, it would be an argument
for the priority of the Epistle to the Ccolos-
sians (so Harl. p. lx, Mey., Wieseler, and
Wigger's Stud. u. Krit. 1841, p. 432):
for that was sent by Tychicus, and a simi-

v Col. v. 7, 9.
James i. 16,
19. ii. 5.
2 Pet. iii. 15.
see ch. v. 1
reff.　1 Cor.
xv. 58.
w Col. i. 7. iv.
7.
x Eph. iii. 7
reff.
y ch. ii. 21. iv.
1.　Rom. xvi.
11, 12 al. P.
z see ver. 18
reff.
a = 2 Cor. i. 4
(3ce) al. fr.
Isa. lxvi. 13.
b 2 Cor. xiii. 13.
1 Thess. iii. 6.
Jude 2.
c Gal. i. 1 reff.
d absol., Col. iv.
18 reff.
18, 19 only.

πάντα ὑμῖν ᵐγνωρίσει Τύχικος ὁ ᵛἀγαπητὸς ᵛἀδελφὸς
καὶ ʷπιστὸς ʷˣδιάκονος ʸἐν κυρίῳ, ²² ὃν ἔπεμψα πρὸς ὑμᾶς
ᶻεἰς ᶻαὐτὸ ᶻτοῦτο, ἵνα γνῶτε τὰ περὶ ἡμῶν καὶ ᵃπαρακα-
λέσῃ τὰς καρδίας ὑμῶν.

²³ Εἰρήνη τοῖς ἀδελφοῖς καὶ ᵇἀγάπη μετὰ πίστεως ἀπὸ
ᶜθεοῦ ᶜπατρὸς καὶ κυρίου Ἰησοῦ χριστοῦ. ²⁴ ἡ ᵈχάρις
μετὰ πάντων τῶν ἀγαπώντων τὸν κύριον ἡμῶν Ἰησοῦν
χριστὸν ἐν ᵉἀφθαρσίᾳ.

ABDFK
LPℵ a b
c e f g h
k l m n o
17. 47

ΠΡΟΣ ΕΦΕΣΙΟΥΣ.

ꝰ Rom. ii. 7.　1 Cor. xv. 42, 50, 53, 54.　2 Tim. i. 10 (Tit. ii. 7 v. r.) only. P.†　Wisd. ii. 23. vi.

basm [æth arm] Chr Damasc Jer Ambrst.　om παντα D¹F Syr [Victorin].
γνωρισει bef υμιν (see Col iv. 7) BDF[P] m 17 fuld goth Ambrst: txt AKL(ℵ) rel
vulg syr Chr Thdrt Damasc Jer.—ℵ¹ wrote υ bef γνωρ. but marked it for erasure: ℵ³
added μιν but obliterated it.　om διακονος ℵ¹(ins ℵ-corr¹).

23. for αγαπη, ελεος A.

24. rec at end ins αμην, with DKL[P]ℵ³ rel vss gr-lat-ff: om ABFℵ¹ 17. 67² æth
[arm] Jer₁ Ambrst.

SUBSCRIPTION. rec adds απο ρωμης δια τυχικου, with KL rel D²-lat syrr copt Chr
Thdrt Euthal; εγραφη απο ρωμης B²[P]: no subscr in l: txt AB¹D 17, also F(prefixing ετελεσᴿη), and ℵ(adding στιχων τιβ´) [as do LP 47].

lar sentiment occurs there, iv. 7. But I
prefer the former meaning) **may know the
matters concerning me, how I fare** (not,
'*what I am doing*,' as Wolf: Meyer answers well, that he was always doing *one
thing :* but as in Ælian, V. H. ii. 35, where
Gorgias being sick is asked τί πράττοι : or
as in Plut. inst. Lac. p. 241 (Kypke),
where when a Spartan mother asks her
son τί πράσσει πατρίς; he answers, 'all
have perished') **Tychicus** (Acts xx. 4. Col.
iv. 7. 2 Tim. iv. 12. Tit. iii. 12. He
appears in the first-cited place amongst
Paul's companions to Asia from Corinth,
classed with Τρόφιμος as Ἀσιανοί. Nothing more is known of him) **shall make
known all to you, the beloved brother**
(reff.) **and faithful** (trustworthy) **servant**
('*minister*' is ambiguous, and might lead
to the idea of Estius, who says on '*in Domino*,'—'non male hinc colligitur Tychi-
cum sacra ordinatione diaconum fuisse:'
see Col. iv. 7, where he is πιστὸς διάκονος
καὶ σύνδουλος, and note there) **in the
Lord** (belongs to διάκονος, not to both ἀδ.
and διάκ. He διηκόνει ἐν κυρίῳ, Christ's
work being the field on which his labour
was bestowed); **whom I sent to you for
this very purpose** (not '*for the same purpose*,' as E. V.) **that ye may know the
matters respecting us** (see Col. iv. 8, where
this verse occurs word for word, but with
ἵνα γνῷ τὰ περὶ ὑμῶν for these words.
Does not this variation bear the mark of

genuineness with it ? The ἡμῶν are those
mentioned Col. iv. 10) **and that he may
comfort** (we need not assign a reason why
they wanted comfort :—there would probably be many in those times of peril) **your
hearts. 23, 24.]** *Double* APOSTOLIC
BLESSING ; addressed (23) to the brethren,
and (24) to all real lovers of the Lord Jesus
Christ.　**23.]** **Peace** (need not be further specified, as is done by some :—the
Epistle has no special conciliatory view.
It is sufficiently described by being *peace
from God* **to the brethren** (of the Church
or Churches addressed : see Prolegg. to
this Epistle, § ii.: not as Wieseler, ἀδελφοῖς to the Jews, and πάντων below to
the Gentiles : for least of all in this Epistle
would such a distinction be found) **and love
with faith** (faith is perhaps presupposed
as being theirs : and he prays that love
may always accompany it, see Gal. v. 6 :
or both are invoked on them, see 1 Tim. i.
14) **from God the Father and the Lord
Jesus Christ** (see note on Rom. i. 7).
24.] General benediction on all who love
Christ : corresponding, as Mey. suggests,
with the malediction on all who love Him
not, 1 Cor. xvi. 22. **May the grace** (viz.
of God, which comes by Christ) **be with
all who love our Lord Jesus Christ in incorruptibility** (i. e. whose love is incorruptible. The method of exegesis of this
difficult expression will be, to endeavour
to find some clue to the idea in the Apos-

tle's mind. He speaks, in Col. ii. 22, of worldly things which are εἰς φθορὰν τῇ ἀποχρήσει·—ἄφθαρτος is with him an epithet of God (Rom. i. 23. 1 Tim. i. 17): the dead are raised ἄφθαρτοι (1 Cor. xv. 52): the Christian's crown is ἄφθαρτος (1 Cor. ix. 25). ἀφθαρσία is always elsewhere in N. T. (reff.) the *incorruptibility* of future immortality. If we seek elsewhere in the Epistles for an illustration of the term as applied to inward qualities, we find a close parallel in 1 Pet. iii. 4; where the ornament of women is to be ὁ κρυπτὸς τῆς καρδίας ἄνθρωπος ἐν τῷ ἀφθάρτῳ τοῦ πραέος κ. ἡσυχίου πνεύματος —the contrast being between the φθαρτά, ἀργύριον καὶ χρυσίον, and the *incorruptible* graces of the renewed spiritual man. I believe we are thus led to the meaning here;—that the love spoken of is ἐν ἀφθαρσίᾳ;—in, as its sphere and element and condition, *incorruptibility*— not a fleeting earthly love, but a spiritual and eternal one. And thus only is the word worthy to stand as the crown and

climax of this glorious Epistle : whereas in the ordinary (E. V.) rendering, ' *sincerity*,' —besides that (as Mey.) this would not be ἀφθαρσία but ἀφθορία (Tit. ii. 7) or ἀδιαφθορία (see Wetst. on Tit. l. c.), the Epistle ends with an anti-climax, by lowering the high standard which it has lifted up throughout to an apparent indifferentism, and admitting to the apostolic blessing all those, however otherwise wrong, who are only not hypocrites in their love of Christ. As to the many interpretations,— that ἐν is for ὑπέρ (Chr. 2nd alt.), διά (Thl.), μετά (Thdrt.), εἰς (Beza), σύν (Piscator)— that ἐν ἀφθαρσίᾳ is to be taken with χάρις (Harl., Bengel, Stier), that ἐν ἀφθ. means ' in immortality,' as the sphere of the ἀγάπη, cf. ἐν τοῖς ἐπουρανίοις, ch. i. 3,— that it is to be joined with Ἰησοῦ χριστοῦ (' Christum immortalem et gloriosum, non humilem,' Wetst.), that it is short for ἵνα ζωὴν ἔχωσιν ἐν ἀφθαρσίᾳ (Olsh.), &c. &c. (see more in Mey.), none of them seem so satisfactory as that assigned above).

ΠΡΟΣ ΦΙΛΙΠΠΗΣΙΟΥΣ.

a Gal. i. 1. reff.
b Eph. i. 1 reff.
c Rom. xvi. 3.
1 Cor. iv. 15.
Gal. iii. 28 al.
d = Acts xxiii.
15. 1 Cor. i.
2. 2 Cor. i.
1.

I. ¹ Παῦλος καὶ Τιμόθεος, ᵃ δοῦλοι χριστοῦ Ἰησοῦ, πᾶσιν τοῖς ᵇ ἁγίοις ᶜ ἐν χριστῷ Ἰησοῦ τοῖς οὖσιν ἐν Φιλ-ίπποις ᵈ σὺν ᵉ ἐπισκόποις καὶ ᶠ διακονοις. ᵍ χάρις ὑμῖν

ABDFK
LPℵ a b
c e f g h
k l m n J
17.47

e Acts xx. 28. 1 Tim. iii. 2. Tit. i. 7. 1 Pet. ii. 25 only. 2 Chron. xxxiv. 12.   f = Rom. xvi.
1. 1 Tim. iii. 8, 12.

TITLE. Steph η προς τους φιλιππησιους επιστολη : elz παυλου του αποστολιν η προς φιλιππησιους επιστολη, with rel : πρ. φ. επιστ. h k : επ. πρ. φ. l : του αγιου αποστολου παυλου επιστολη προς φιλιππησιους L : [τ. παναγιου π. επ. π. φ. P :] ταυτ' αγορευει παυλος φιλιππησιοισιν f : αρχεται πρ. φ. DF : txt ABKℵ m n o 17 [47].

CHAP. 1. 1. rec ιησ. bef χρ., with FKL[P] rel syrr [æth arm] Chr Thdrt : txt BDℵ coptt. (A uncert.)   for σὺν ἐπισκ., συνεπισκόποις B²D³K 17 Chr Thl Cassiod.

CHAP. I. 1, 2.] ADDRESS AND GREET-ING. **1.**] Timotheus seems to be named as being well known to the Philippians (Acts xvi. 3, 10 ff.), and present with St. Paul at this time. The mention is merely formal, as the Apostle proceeds (ver. 3) in the first person singular. Certainly no *official* character is intended to be given by it, as Huther, al., have thought : for of all the Epistles, this is the least official : and those to the Romans and Galatians, where no such mention occurs, the most so. Observe, there is no ἀπόστολος subjoined to Παῦλος (as in Col. i. 1), probably because the Philippians needed no such reminiscence of his authority. Cf. also 1 and 2 Thess. On δοῦλοι χρ. Ἰησ., see Ellicott. πᾶσιν] both here and in vv. 4, 7, 8, 25 ; ch. ii. 17, 26, is best accounted for from the warm affection which breathes through this whole Epistle (see on ver. 3), not from any formal reason, as that the Apostle wishes to put those Philippians who had not sent to his support, on a level in his affection with those who had (Van Hengel),—that he wishes to set himself above all their party divisions (ch. ii. 3 :

so De W.), &c. σὺν ἐπισκ.] This is read by Chrys. συνεπισκόποις, and he remarks : τί τοῦτο ; μιᾶς πόλεως πολλοὶ ἐπίσκοποι ἦσαν ; οὐδαμῶς· ἀλλὰ τοὺς πρεσβυτέρους οὕτως ἐκάλεσε. τότε γὰρ τέως ἐκοινώνουν τοῖς ὀνόμασι, κ. διάκονος δ ἐπίσκοπος ἐλέγετο (see also var. readd.). But thus the construction would be imperfect, the σύν having no reference. Theodoret remarks, ἐπισκόπους τοὺς πρεσβυτέρους καλεῖ· ἀμφότερα γὰρ εἶχον κατ' ἐκεῖνον τὸν καιρὸν ὀνόματα,—and alleges Acts xx. 28, Tit. i. 5, 7, as shewing the same. See on the whole subject, my note on Acts xx. 17, and the article Bischof, by Jacobson, in Herzog's Realencyclopädie für protestantische Theologie u. Kirche. κ. διακόνοις] See on Rom. xii. 7 ; xvi. 1. Chrys. enquires why he writes *here* to the κλῆρος as well as to the ἅγιοι, and not in the Epistles to the Romans, or Corinthians, or Ephesians. And he answers it, ὅτι αὐτοὶ καὶ ἀπέστειλαν, κ. ἐκαρποφόρησαν, κ. αὐτοὶ ἔπεμψαν πρὸς αὐτὸν τὸν Ἐπαφρόδιτον. But the true reason seems to be, the late date of our Epistle. The ecclesiastical offices were now more plainly distinguished than at

καὶ εἰρήνη ἀπὸ θεοῦ πατρὸς ἡμῶν καὶ Κυρίου Ἰησοῦ χριστοῦ. ^{g Eph. i. 16 reff.}

³ ^g Εὐχαριστῶ τῷ θεῷ μου ^h ἐπὶ πάσῃ τῇ ⁱ μνείᾳ ὑμῶν, ⁴ πάντοτε ἐν πάσῃ δεήσει μου ὑπὲρ πάντων ὑμῶν ^j μετὰ χαρᾶς τὴν ^k δέησιν ^k ποιούμενος, ⁵ ^l ἐπὶ τῇ ^m κοινωνίᾳ ὑμῶν ^m εἰς τὸ εὐαγγέλιον ἀπὸ τῆς πρώτης ἡμέρας ⁿ ἄχρι τοῦ νῦν,

g Eph. i. 16 reff. h dat., 2 Cor. iii. 14 vii. 4. Heb. ix. 15, 26. i Eph. i. 16 reff. j Matt. xiii. 20 ‖. Heb. x. 34 al. 1 Chron. xxix. 22. k Luke v. 33. 1 Tim. ii. 1. l = 1 Cor. i. 4 al. m 2 Cor. ix. 13.

n Rom. viii. 22. 1 Cor. iv. 11. 2 Cor. iii. 14 al.

3. εγω μεν ευχαριστω τω κυριω ημων επι κ.τ.λ. D¹F Ambrst Cassiod. [om τη D.]
4. aft πασῃ ins τη א¹(א³ disapproving) c m 80. aft χαρας ins και F harl² Thdrt-ms. [aft δεησιν ins μου L c k 47 syr basm.]
5. rec om της, with DFKL rel Chr Thdrt Damasc: ins AB[P]א k m.

the time when the two former of those Epistles were written. That to the Ephesians rests on grounds of its own. The simple juxtaposition of the officers with the members of the Church, and indeed *their* being placed *after* those members, shews, as it still seems to me, against Ellicott in loc., the absence of hierarchical views such as those in the Epistles of the apostolic fathers. 2.] See on Rom. i. 7.

3—11.] THANKSGIVING FOR THEIR FELLOWSHIP REGARDING THE GOSPEL (3—5), CONFIDENCE THAT GOD WILL CONTINUE AND PERFECT THE SAME (6—8), AND PRAYER FOR THEIR INCREASE IN HOLINESS UNTO THE DAY OF CHRIST (9—11). 3.] See the similar expressions, Rom. i. 9; 1 Cor. i. 4; Eph. i. 16; Col. i. 3; 1 Thess. i. 2; Philem. 4. ἐπί here with a dative is hardly distinguishable in English from the same preposition with a genitive in Rom. i. 9; Eph. i. 16;—at, or in: the primitive idea of such construction being *addition* by close adherence: 'my whole remembrance of you is *accompanied with* thanks to God.' πάσῃ τῇ μνείᾳ must not be rendered as in E. V. (so even Conyb.) '*every remembrance*,' but my whole remembrance. The expression *comprehends in one* all such remembrances: but the article forbids the above rendering: cf. πᾶσα ἡ πόλις, Matt. xxi. 10; also ib. vi. 29; Mark iv. 1; Luke iii. 3: Winer, § 18. 4. Some (Maldon., Bretschn., al.) take ἐπί as assigning the reason for εὐχαριστῶ (as 1 Cor. i. 4), and μνείᾳ ὑμῶν as meaning, '*your remembrance of me*,' viz. in sending me sustenance. But this is evidently wrong: for the ground of εὐχαριστῶ follows, ver. 5. μνεία here, remembrance, not '*mention*,' which meaning it only gets by ποιεῖσθαι being joined to it, 'to make an *act of* remembrance,' i. e. to *mention*, Rom. i. 9; Eph. i. 16; 1 Thess. i. 2; Philem. 4. 4.] πάν-

τοτε—πάσῃ—πάντων—here we have the overflowings of a full heart. Render—always in every prayer of mine making my prayer for you all with joy: not, as in E. V., '*in every prayer of mine for you all making request with joy.*' For the second δέησις, having the article, is thereby defined to be the *particular* request, ὑπὲρ π. ὑμ.—τὸ μετὰ χαρᾶς μεμνῆσθαι σημεῖον τῆς ἐκείνων ἀρετῆς, Thl.; so that the sense is, that every time he prayed, he joyfully offered up that portion of his prayers which was an intercession for them. See Ellic., who defends the other connexion; but has misunderstood my note. 5.] for (*ground* of the εὐχ., πάντοτε το ποιούμενος having been *epexegetical* of it) your fellowship (with one another: entire accord, unanimous action: not your fellowship *with me*, ὅτι κοινωνοί μου γίνεσθε κ. συμμερισταὶ τῶν ἐπὶ τῷ εὐαγγελίῳ πόνων, Thl.: this must have been further specified, by μετ' ἐμοῦ (1 John i. 3) or the like. Still less must we with Estius, Wetst., al. (and nearly so Chrys.), render ἐπὶ τῇ κοινωνίᾳ, *pro liberalitate vestra erga me*) as regards the Gospel (not '*in the Gospel*,' as E. V. and Thdrt., κοινωνίαν δὲ τοῦ εὐαγγελίου τὴν πίστιν ἐκάλεσε: but thus it would be the genitive, and εἰς τὸ εὐ. can hardly be taken as equivalent to it: cf. κοινωνεῖν εἰς, ch. iv. 15. Their mutual accord was *for the purposes of the Gospel*—i. e. the perfecting, of which he proceeds to treat. "The article τῇ is not repeated after ὑμῶν, because κοινωνία εἰς τὸ εὐ. is conceived as one idea, together." Meyer. Ellic. would understand κοιν. as absolute and abstract, 'fellowship,' not 'contribution:' including, without expressly mentioning, 'that particular manifestation of it which so especially marked the liberal and warm-hearted Christians of Philippi.' and it may well be so, even holding my former interpretation: this was the exhibition of their

6 [o]πεποιθὼς [p]αὐτὸ [pq]τοῦτο, [q]ὅτι ὁ [r]ἐναρξάμενος ἐν ὑμῖν ABDFK
[st]ἔργον [t]ἀγαθὸν [u]ἐπιτελέσει ἄχρι [v]ἡμέρας χριστοῦ Ἰησοῦ, LPℵ a b c e f g h
7 [w]καθώς ἐστιν [x]δίκαιον ἐμοὶ τοῦτο [y]φρονεῖν [z]ὑπὲρ πάν- k l m n o 17. 47

o constr., ver. 25. p Acts xxiv. 15, 20. 2 Cor. vii. 11. Gal. ii. 10 al. q Acts xxiv. 14. Rom. vi. 6 al. fr. Winer, § 23. 5. b. r Gal. iii. 3 only. Deut. ii. 24, 25, 31. s = Rom. xiv. 20. t Eph. ii. 10 reff. u Rom. xv. 28. 2 Cor. vii. 1. viii. 6 al. 1 Kings iii. 12. v 1 Cor. i. 8. 2 Cor. i. 14. ver. 10. ch. ii. 16 al. w = 2 Thess. i. 3. x = 2 Pet. i. 13. y = Gal. v. 10 reff. z = 2 Cor. i. 6 b.

6. rec *αχρις*, with DFKL[P] rel: *αχρι ης* A: txt Bℵ a[1]. rec *ιησ.* bef *χρ.*, with AFK[P]ℵ rel am[2](with demid): txt BD[L] c e k n [vss] Ambrst Aug.

κοινωνία εἰς τὸ εὐαγγ.) **from the first day** (of your receiving it) **until now.** This last clause is by Lachm. and Meyer attached to *πεποιθώς*, but they are surely in error. The reason assigned is, that, if it had belonged to *κοινωνίᾳ*, &c., the article *τῇ* would have been repeated. But the same account which I have quoted from Meyer himself above of its omission after *ὑμῶν* will also apply to its omission here—that the whole *κοινωνία* from the first is taken as one idea, and therefore this feature of it, that it was *ἀπὸ τῆς πρ. ἡμ. ἄχρι τ. νῦν*, need not be specially particularized by the definite article. It is St. Paul's constant habit to place *πέποιθα* first in the sentence (cf. Rom. ii. 19; 2 Cor. ii. 3; Gal. v. 10; ch. ii. 24; 2 Thess. iii. 4; Philem. 26: also Matt. xxvii. 43), pregnant as it is with emphasis, and including the matter of confidence which follows: and we may certainly say that had this clause referred to *πεποιθώς*, it would have followed, not preceded it. Besides which, the emphatic *αὐτὸ τοῦτο* would be rendered altogether vapid, by so long an emphatic clause preceding the verb. Œcum., Beza, and Bengel connect the words with the distantly preceding verb *εὐχαριστῶ*, which (hardly however, as Ellic., on account of the pres. tense and *πάντοτε*) is still more improbable. **πεποιθώς**] parallel with *ποιούμενος*—**being** (i. e. seeing I am) **confident of . . . αὐτὸ τοῦτο**] **this very thing** (it points out sharply and emphatically, implying, as here, that the very matter of confidence is one which will ensure the success of the *δέησις*. Conyb. renders it '*accordingly*,' which is far too weak. As regards the construction, *αὐτὸ τοῦτο* is only a secondary accusative, of reference, not governed directly by *πεποιθώς*. It is immediately resolved into *ὅτι ὁ ἐν. κ.τ.λ.*). **6. ὁ ἐναρξ.**] **He who has begun in you a good work,** viz. God: cf. ch. ii. 13. Wakefield, perversely enough, renders, '*he among you who has begun, &c.*' By '*a good work*,' he refers his confidence to the *general* character of God as the doer and finisher of good: the one good work in his mind being, their *κοινωνία* &c. **ἐν** is **in**, not '*among*:' but the preposition in **ἐναρξάμενος** seems not to be connected with it, cf. reff., where the verb has an absolute meaning, irrespective of any *immanent* working. The **ἄχρι ἡμέρας χρ. Ἰησοῦ** assumes the nearness of the coming of the Lord (*μέχρι τῆς τοῦ σωτῆρος ἡμῶν ἐπιφανείας*, Thdrt.). Here, as elsewhere, Commentators (even Ellic. recently) have endeavoured to escape from this inference. Thus Thl., Œc., refer the saying not only to the then existing generation of Philippians, but *καὶ τοῖς ἐξ ὑμῶν*: Estius, in the case of each man, '*usque ad mortem suam;*' Calov., understanding not the continuance till the day of Christ, but '*terminus et complementum perfectionis, quod habituri isto die erimus:*' and so nearly Calvin, but saying very beautifully,—'Tametsi enim qui ex corpore mortali sunt liberati, non amplius militent cum carnis concupiscentiis, sintque extra teli jactum ut aiunt: tamen nihil erit absurdi, si dicentur esse in profectu, quia nondum pertigerunt quo aspirant: nondum potiuntur felicitate et gloria quam sperarunt: denique nondum illuxit dies, qui revelet absconditos in spe thesauros. Atque adeo quum de spe agitur, semper ad beatam resurrectionem, tanquam ad scopum, referendi sunt oculi.' Doubtless, this is *our* lesson, and must be our application of such passages: but this surely was not the sense in which the Apostle wrote them. **7.**] *Justification of the above-expressed confidence:*—it was fair and right for him to entertain it. **καθώς**] a word of later Greek, never used by the elder Attic writers; = *καθό* (Thuc.), *καθά*, *καθάπερ* (see Phryn. Lobeck, p. 425, and note). It takes up, and justifies by analogy, the confidence of the last verse. **ἐστιν δίκ. ἐμοί**] The usual classical constructions are, *ἐμὲ δίκαιόν ἐστι φράζειν*, Herod. i. 39: *ἐμὲ δίκαιον . . . . προσλαμβάνειν*, Plato, Legg. x. 897; *οὗτος δίκαιός ἐστι φέρεσθαι*, ib. i. 32. But Ellic. remarks, that there is nothing unclassical in the present usage; and compares Plato, Rep. i. 334, *δίκαιον τότε τούτοις τοὺς πονηροὺς ὠφελεῖν.* **τοῦτο φρονεῖν**] viz. the confidence of ver. 6. **ὑπέρ**]

τῶν ὑμῶν, διὰ τὸ ᵃἔχειν με ἐν τῇ ᵃκαρδίᾳ ὑμᾶς ἔν τε τοῖς
ᵇδεσμοῖς μου καὶ ἐν τῇ ᶜἀπολογίᾳ καὶ ᵈβεβαιώσει τοῦ
εὐαγγελίου, ᵉσυγκοινωνούς ᶠμου τῆς ᵍχάριτος πάντας
ὑμᾶς ὄντας. 8 ʰμάρτυς γάρ μου ὁ θεός, ʰ ὡς ⁱἐπιποθῶ
πάντας ὑμᾶς ἐν ʲσπλάγχνοις χριστοῦ Ἰησοῦ 9 καὶ

a 2 Cor. vii. 3.
b ver. 13 (see reff. there),
&c. Col. iv.18.
2 Tim. ii. 9.
Philem. 10,
13. Heb. xi.
36. Nah. i.
13.
c Acts xxii. 1.
xxv. 16.
1 Cor. ix. 3.
2 Cor. vii.

11. ver. 16. 2 Tim. iv. 16. 1 Pet. iii. 15 only †. Wisd. vi. 10 only. d Heb. vi. 16 only. Levit. xxv.
23. Wisd. vi. 18 only. e Rom. xi. 17. 1 Cor. ix. 23. Rev. i. 9 only †. (-νεῖν, ch. iv. 14.)
f double gen., ver. 25. ch. ii. 30. g = Eph. ii. 8. Col. i. 6. h Rom. i. 9. (1 Thess. ii. 10.)
i & constr., 2 Cor. ix. 14. ch. ii. 26. 1 Pet. ii. 2. Ps. cxviii. 131. w. inf., Rom. i. 11. 2 Cor. v. 2. (ch. ii. 26
v. r.) 1 Thess. iii. 6. 2 Tim. i. 4. w. πρός, James iv. 5 only. j = 2 Cor. vi. 12. Col. iii.
12. Philem. 7, 12, 20. Prov. xii. 10.

7. rec om (3rd) ἐν, with AD¹F Thl : ins BD²·³KL[P]‭א‬ rel latt Syr Chr Thdrt Œc
Ambrst Pel.   τῆς χαριτος bef μου DF latt : for μου, μοι k l.

8. for μου, μοι DF(‭א‬-corr?) latt Syr arm Chr Ambrst Pel.   rec aft μου ins
εστιν (possibly from Rom i. 9: no doubt, as Ellic. contends, the Ap. may have twice
used the same formula; but this is not the question), with ADKL[P]‭א‬³ rel syrr copt :
om BF‭א‬¹ 17. 67² latt æth Thdor-mops Chr-ms.   rec ιησ. bef χρ., with FKL rel
syrr copt : om ιησ. D³ basm æth : txt ABD¹G[P]‭א‬ m 17 am(with demid) sah Chr-ms
Damasc-comm Ambrst.

because it is an opinion involving their
good : see ref. Calov. and Wolf understand φρον. ὑπέρ, 'to care for,' and τοῦτο
to refer to the prayer, ver. 4 : but unnaturally.   διὰ τό] reason why he
was justified, &c. as above. με is the
subject, ὑμᾶς the object, as the context
(ver. 8) clearly shews : not the converse,
as Rosenm., al.   ἔν τε . . .] Chrys.
finely says, κ‭αὶ‬ τί θαυμαστόν, εἰ ἐν τῷ
δεσμωτηρίῳ εἶχεν αὐτούς; οὐδὲ γὰρ κατ'
ἐκεῖνον τὸν καιρόν, φησι, καθ' ὃν εἰσῄειν
εἰς τὸ δικαστήριον ἀπολογησόμενος, ἐξ-
επέσατέ μου τῆς μνήμης. οὕτω γάρ ἐστι
τυραννικὸν ὁ ἔρως ὁ πνευματικός, ὡς μηδενὶ παραχωρεῖν καιρῷ, ἀλλ' ἀεὶ τῆς
ψυχῆς ἔχεσθαι τοῦ φιλοῦντος, καὶ μηδεμίαν θλίψιν καὶ ὀδύνην συγχωρεῖν περι-
γενέσθαι τῆς ψυχῆς.   His bonds were his
situation : his defence and confirmation
of the Gospel his employment in that
situation;—whether he refers to a public
defence (2 Tim. iv. 16), or only to that
defence of the Gospel, which he was constantly making in private. However this
may be, the two, ἀπολογ. and βεβαίωσις,
are most naturally understood as referring
to one and the same course of action :
otherwise the τῇ would be repeated before
βεβ. One such ἀπολ. and βεβ. we have
recorded in Acts xxviii. 23 ff. These
words, ἔν τε . . . . εὐαγγελίου, are most
naturally taken with the foregoing (Chrys.,
al., Meyer, De W.), as punctuated in the
text, not with the following (Calv., al.).
συγκοιν. κ.τ.λ., which render a reason for
the whole, διὰ τό to εὐαγγελίου.
συγκ.] See above. ὑμᾶς is thus characterized : ' Ye are fellow-partakers of my
grace :' the grace vouchsafed to me by

God in Christ, see reff. : not the grace of
suffering in Him, as ver. 29 (Meyer), still
less the grace of apostleship, Rom. i. 5,
which the Philippians had furthered by
their subsidies (Rosenm., al.) : ver. 8 decides the χάρις to be spiritual in its
meaning. The rendering gaudii in the
Vulg. must have arisen from reading
χαρᾶς. The repetition of ὑμᾶς, referring
to a ὑμᾶς gone before, is usual in rhetorical sentences of a similar kind. So
Demosth. p. 1225,—ὧν ἀκούοντά με, καὶ
παρὰ τῶν ἀφικνουμένων . . . .,—τίνα με
οἴεσθε ψυχὴν ἔχειν; But Bernhardy, Synt.
p. 275, remarks that the most accurate
writers in verse and prose do not thus
repeat the personal pronoun. No such
pleonasm is found in Homer or Plato.

8.] Confirmation of ver. 7. οὐχ
ὡς ἀπιστούμενος μάρτυρα καλεῖ τὸν θεόν,
ἀλλὰ τὴν πολλὴν διάθεσιν οὐκ ἔχων
παραστῆσαι διὰ λόγου, Thl. after Chrys.
On ἐπιποθῶ, see reff. The preposition indicates the direction of the desire, not its
intensification. On ἐν σπλάγχνοις χριστοῦ
Ἰησοῦ, Bengel remarks, " in Paulo non
Paulus vivit, sed Jesus Christus : quare
Paulus non in Pauli sed in Jesu Christi
movetur visceribus." All real spiritual
love is but a portion of the great love
wherewith He hath loved us, which lives
and yearns in all who are vitally united
to Him.   9—11.] The substance of
his prayer (already, ver. 4, alluded to) for
them. καί refers back to the δέησις
of ver. 4 : ' and this is the purport of my
prayer.' At the same time this purport
follows most naturally, after the expression of desire for them in the last verse.
There is an ellipsis in the sense between

τοῦτο ᵏπροσεύχομαι, ᵏἵνα ἡ ¹ἀγάπη ¹ὑμῶν ἔτι ᵐμᾶλλον
καὶ ᵐμᾶλλον ⁿπερισσεύῃ ἐν ᵒἐπιγνώσει καὶ πάσῃ ᵖαἰσθή-
σει, 10 ᑫεἰς τὸ ʳδοκιμάζειν ὑμᾶς τὰ ˢδιαφέροντα, ἵνα ἦτε
ᵗεἰλικρινεῖς καὶ ᵘἀπρόσκοποι εἰς ᵛἡμέραν χριστοῦ, 11 ʷπε-
πληρωμένοι ˣʸκαρπὸν ʸδικαιοσύνης τὸν διὰ Ἰησοῦ χριστοῦ, εἰς δόξαν καὶ ἔπαινον θεοῦ.

ABDFK
LPℵ a b
c e f g h
k l m n o
17. 47
[P has
several
lacunæ
in vv.
10—15.]

k Matt. xxiv. 20 ‖ Mk.
Mark xiv. 35.
l Cor. xiv. 13.
Col. i. 9. iv.
3. 2 Thess.
i. 11. iii. 1.
(ὅπως, Acts viii. 15.)
l gen. subj.,
1 Cor. xvi. 24.
Col. i. 8.
Philem. 5, 7.
Rev. ii. 4, 19.
m here only.
n constr. (see note), Rom. xv. 13. Col. ii. 7. Sir. xix. 24.   o Eph. i. 17 reff.   p here only. Exod.
xxviii. 3.   Prov. i. 4.   q Eph. i. 12 reff.   r = Luke xii. 56. Rom. ii. 18. Job xxxiv. 3.
s Rom. ii. 18. Gal. ii. 6. Dan. vii. 3.   t 2 Pet. iii. 1 only †. Wisd. vii. 25 only. (-εια, 2 Cor. i. 12. ii. 17.)
u Acts xxiv. 16. 1 Cor. x. 32 only †. P. Sir. xxxv. (xxxii.) 21 only.   v ver. 6 reff.   w = & constr.,
Col. i. 9. Ps. xv. 11 A (not Bℵ F).   see Rev. xvii. 3, 4.   x = John iv. 36. Rom. i. 13. vi. 21, 22. ch. iv.
17. James iii. 18.   y Heb. xii. 11. James iii. 18. Prov. xi. 30.

9. [om και μαλλον P.]   περισσευση (substn of aor : see e. g. vv 24, 26) BD k
m : περισσευοι F : txt AK²Lℵ rel Clem Chr Thdrt Damasc [-σενει K¹P].

10. om υμας ℵ¹(ins ℵ³) m.   αλικρινεις (but corrd) ℵ¹.

11. rec καρπων δικ. των, with [P] rel syrr copt Chr : txt A(B)DFKLℵ f m n 17 [47]
latt sah æth arm Thdrt-comm Damasc Œc Ambrst Pel.—om τον B 116-22.   for
θεον, χριστου D¹ : μοι F(not F-lat) : ejus harl¹.

τοῦτο and ἵνα,—τοῦτο introducing the
substance of the prayer, ἵνα its aim. See,
on ἵνα with προσεύχομαι, note, 1 Cor.
xiv. 13 : and Ellic. here.   ἡ ἀγάπη
ὑμ.] not, 'towards me,' as Chrys. (ὅρα
πῶς φιλούμενος ἔτι μᾶλλον ἐβούλετο φιλεῖσθαι, Thl., Grot., all.,—nor towards
God and Christ (Calov., al.), but either
perfectly general, as Ellic., or, 'towards
one another:' virtually identical with the
κοινωνία of ver. 5. In ἡ ἀγάπη ὑμῶν its
existence is recognized; in μᾶλλον καὶ
μᾶλλον περισσ., its deficiency is hinted
at. ἐν is not to be taken as if ἐπίγνωσις
and αἴσθησις were departments of Love,
in which it was to increase : but they are
rather elements, in whose increase in their
characters Love is also, and as a separate
thing, to increase : q. d. 'that your love
may increase, but not without an increase
in ἐπίγνωσις and αἴσθησις.' For by these
Love is guarded from being ill-judged
and misplaced, which, separate from them,
it would be : and accordingly, on the increase of these is all the subsequent stress
laid.   ἐπίγνωσις is accurate knowledge
of moral and practical truth : αἴσθησις,
perceptivity of the same, the power of apprehending it : "the contrary of that dul-
ness and inactivity of the αἰσθητήρια τῆς
καρδίας (Jer. iv. 19), which brings about
moral want of judgment, and indifference"
(Meyer). De W. renders it well, moral
tact.   10.] Purpose of the increase in
knowledge and perceptiveness : with a
view to your distinguishing things that
are different, and so choosing the good, and
refusing the evil. Meyer's objection to
this rendering—that the purpose is, not
such distinction, but the approval of the
good, is, after all, mere trifling : for the
former is stated as implying the latter.

He would render with Vulg., E. V., Chr.
(τὰ διαφέροντα, τουτέστι, τὰ συμφέροντα),
Thl., Erasm., Grot., Est., Beng., al.,
'approving (or, as Ellic., with Syr., æth.,
'proving,' 'bringing to the test') things
that are excellent,' which certainly is
allowable, such sense of διαφέρω being
justified by Matt. x. 31, and τὰ διαφέροντα for præstantiora occurring Xen.
Hier. i. 3; Dio Cassius xliv. 25. But
the simpler and more usual meaning of
both verbs is preferable, and has been
adopted by Thdrt. (διακρίσεως, ὥστε εἰδέναι τίνα μὲν καλά, τίνα δὲ κρείττονα, τίνα
δὲ παντάπασι τὰ διαφορὰν πρὸς ἄλληλα
ἔχοντα), Beza, Wolf, all., Wies., De Wette,
al.   εἰλικρινεῖς] pure —a double
derivation is given for the word · (1) εἴλη,
κρίνω that which is proved in the sun-
light,—in which case it would be better
written as it is often in our manuscripts,
εἰλ. : and (2) εἶλος (εἰλεῖν, ἴλλειν), κρίνω:
that which is proved by rapid shaking, as
in sifting. This latter is defended by Stall-
baum on Plato, Phæd. p. 66 A, where the
word occurs in an ethical sense as here
(εἰλικρινεῖ τῇ διανοίᾳ χρώμενος αὐτὸ καθ'
αὑτὸ εἰλικρινὲς ἕκαστον ἐπιχειροίη θη-
ρεύειν τῶν ὄντων): see also ib., p. 81 c:
and cf. Ellic.'s note here.   ἀπρόσκοποι]
here as in ref. Acts, used intransitively,
void of offence,—without stumbling ; so
Beza, Calv., De W., Wies., al. The transitive meaning, 'giving no offence' (see ref.
1 Cor.), is adopted by Chr. (μηδένα σκαν-
δαλίσαντες), Thdrt. (?), al., Meyer, al.: but
it has here no place in the context, where
other men are not in question.   εἰς
ἡμέραν χριστοῦ] See above on ver. 6 : but
εἰς is not exactly = ἄχρι; it has more
the meaning of 'for,'—'so that when that
day comes, ye may be found.' Our tem-

12 z Γινώσκειν δὲ ὑμᾶς z βούλομαι, ἀδελφοί, ὅτι a τὰ a κατ᾽
ἐμὲ b μᾶλλον c εἰς d προκοπὴν τοῦ εὐαγγελίου c ἐλήλυθεν,
13 ὥστε τοὺς e δεσμούς μου f φανεροὺς ἐν χριστῷ f γενέσθαι
ἐν ὅλῳ τῷ g πραιτωρίῳ καὶ τοῖς λοιποῖς πᾶσιν, 14 καὶ

z Rom. i. 13.
x. 25 al.
a Acts xxiv. 22.
xxv. 14.
Eph. vi. 21.
Col. iv. 7 al.
b comparat. =
Acts xxv. 10.
xxvii. 13.
2 Cor. vii. 7.

viii. 17.   2 Tim. i. 18 al.   Winer, edn. 6, § 35. 4.   c = Wisd. xv. 5. (not Mark v.
26.   Acts xix. 27.)   d ver. 25.   1 Tim. iv. 15 only †.   Sir. li. 17.   2 Macc. viii. 8
only.   μεγάλην προκ. ποιεῖν τῆς ἐπιβολῆς, Polyb. ii. 43. 7 al.   e ver. 7 reff. plur. masc. here
only.   Judg. xv. 14.   neut., Luke viii. 29.   Acts xvi. 26. xx. 23.   f = Mark xi. 14.   Acts vii.
13.   1 Cor. iii. 13.   Gen. xlii. 16.   g John xviii. 28 (bis) ‖ Mt. Mk., 33. xix. 9.   Acts xxiii. 35 only.

13. γενεσθαι bef εν χριστω DF vulg [arm] Chr-comm Thl : om εν χρ. a¹.   ins
τω bef χριστω ℵ¹(ℵ³ disapproving) 80.   for γενεσθαι, γεγονεναι ℵ¹(txt ℵ-corr¹(?)³).

poral use of 'against' exactly gives it.
    11. πεπληρωμένοι καρπὸν δικαιοσ.]
filled with (the accusative of reference or
secondary government, reff.) **the fruit of
righteousness** (that result of work for
God's glory which is the product of a holy
life : δικαιοσ. being here, the whole purified moral habit of the regenerate and
justified man. Cf. καρπ. τοῦ πνεύματος,
Gal. v. 22,—τ. φωτός, Eph. v. 9,—δικαιοσύνης, James iii. 18) **which is** (specifies the καρπός—that it is not of nor by
man, but) **through Jesus Christ** (by the
working of the Spirit which He sends from
the Father : "Silvestres sumus oleastri et
inutiles, donec in Christum sumus insiti,
qui viva sua radice frugiferas arbores nos
reddit." Calvin) **unto the glory and praise
of God** (belongs to πεπληρωμένοι).

    12—26.] DESCRIPTION OF HIS CONDI-
TION AT ROME : HIS FEELINGS AND
HOPES. And first he explains, 12—18.]
*how his imprisonment had given occasion
to many to preach Christ: how some indeed had done this from unworthy motives,
but still to his joy that, any-how, Christ
was preached.* **12.**] According to
Meyer, the connexion is with ἐπιγνώσει
above, whence γινώσκειν is placed first :—
q. d., 'and as part of this knowledge, I
would have you, &c.' (Ellic. cites this
view as mine also, but erroneously.)
τὰ κατ᾽ ἐμέ] **my affairs** (reff.).   μᾶλ-
λον] **rather** (than the contrary) : not,
'*more now than before,*' as Hoelemann,
which would be expressed by μᾶλλον ἤδη
or νῦν μᾶλλον.   προκοπήν] **advance**
(reff.). The word is common in Polyb.
and later authors, but is condemned by
Phrynichus, ed. Lobeck, p. 85, as unknown
to the Attic writers.   ἐλήλυθεν]
'*evaserunt,*' **have turned out**: so Herod.
i. 120, κ. τά γε τῶν ὀνειράτων ἐχόμενα,
τέλεως ἐς ἀσθενὲς ἔρχεται.   **13.**] **so
that** (effect of this εἰς προκ. ἐληλυθέναι)
my bonds (the fact of my imprisonment)
have become manifest in Christ (φανερ.
ἐν χριστῷ is to be taken together. They
became known, not as a matter simply of
notoriety, but of notoriety *in Christ*, i. e.

in connexion with Christ's cause,—as endured for Christ's sake ;—and thus the
Gospel was furthered) **in the whole prætorium** (i. e. the *barrack of the prætorian
guards* attached to the palatium of Nero
(Dio liii. 16, καλεῖται δὲ τὰ βασίλεια πα-
λάτιον . . . ὅτι ἔν τε τῷ Παλατίῳ (monte
Palatino) ὁ Καῖσαρ ᾤκει, καὶ ἐκεῖ τὸ στρατ-
ήγιον εἶχε. See Wieseler's note, ii. 403 f.):
not the *camp* of the same outside the city
('castra prætorianorum,' Tac. Hist. i. 31 :
Suet. Tiber. 37). That this was so, is
shewn by the greeting sent ch. iv. 22 from
οἱ ἐκ τῆς Καίσαρος οἰκίας, who would
hardly have been mentioned in the other
case. The word '*prætorium*' is also used
of castles or palaces belonging to Cæsar
(Suet. Aug. 72, Tiber. 39, Calig. 37, Tit.
8), or to foreign princes (Acts xxiii. 35,
Juv. x. 161), or even to private persons
(Juv. i. 75): it cannot be shewn ever to
have signified the palatium at Rome, but
the above meanings approach so nearly
to this, that it seems to me no serious
objection can be taken to it. The fact
here mentioned *may* be traced to St. Paul
being guarded by a prætorian soldier,
and having full liberty of preaching the
Gospel (Acts xxviii. 30 f.): but more probably his situation had been changed
since then,—see Prolegg. to this Epistle,
§ iii. 6.   I should now say that the ὅλῳ,
and the τοῖς λοιποῖς πᾶσιν, make it more
probable that the prætorium is to be
taken in the larger acceptation,—the
quadrangular camp now forming part of
Aurelian's city walls,—including also the
smaller camp on the Palatine) **and to all
the rest** (a popular hyperbole :—i. e., to
others, besides those in the prætorium :
not to be taken (Chr., Thdrt., E. V.) as
governed by ἐν and signifying, '*in all
other places.*' The matter of fact interpretation would be, that the soldiers, and
those who visited him, carried the fame of
his being bound for Christ over all Rome),
14.] **and** (so that) **most of** (not
'*many of,*' as E. V., al.) **the brethren in
the Lord** (this is the most natural connexion . see on πέποιθα, -ώς, standing first

h τοὺς πλείονας τῶν ⁱ ἀδελφῶν ⁱ ἐν κυρίῳ ʲ πεποιθότας ABDFK
τοῖς ᵉ δεσμοῖς μου ᵏ περισσοτέρως ˡ τολμᾶν ᵐ ἀφόβως τὸν
λόγον τοῦ θεοῦ ˡ λαλεῖν. 15 τινὲς μὲν καὶ ⁿ διὰ ᵒᵖ φθό-
νον καὶ ᵒ۹ ἔριν, τινὲς δὲ καὶ δι᾽ ʳ εὐδοκίαν τὸν ˢ χριστὸν
ˢ κηρύσσουσιν. 16 οἱ μὲν ᵗ ἐξ ἀγάπης, εἰδότες ὅτι ᵘ εἰς
ᵛ ἀπολογίαν τοῦ εὐαγγελίου ᵘ κεῖμαι, 17 οἱ δὲ ᵗ ἐξ ʷ ἐριθείας
[τὸν] χριστὸν ˣ καταγγέλλουσιν οὐχ ʸ ἁγνῶς, ᶻ οἰόμενοι

LPℵ a b
c e f g h
k l m n o
17. 47

h Acts xix. 32. xxvii. 12.
1 Cor. ix. 19. x. 5, 6 al.
i Eph. vi. 21. Col. iv. 7.
j constr., 2 Cor. x. 7. Philem. 21. Prov. xiv. 16. xxviii. 26.
k Gal. i. 14 reff.
l Rom. xv. 18. see 2 Macc. iv. 2.
m Luke i. 74. 1 Cor. xvi. 10.

Jude 12 only. Prov. i. 33. Wisd. xvii. 4 Bℵ (-βος, ib. AC. Prov. iii. 24 al.) only. n = Matt. xxvii. 18. John vii. 43. x. 19 al. Winer, § 49. c. o Rom. i. 29. Gal. v. 21. 1 Tim. vi. 4. p as above (o). Matt. xxvii. 18 ‖ Mk. Tit. iii. 3. James iv. 5. 1 Pet. ii. 1 only†. Wisd. vi. 23 (25). 1 Macc. viii. 16 only. q as above (o). Rom. xiii. 13. 1 Cor. i. 11. iii. 3. 2 Cor. xii. 20. Tit. iii. 9 only. P.† Sir. xxviii. 11. xl. 5, 9 only. r Matt. xi. 26 ‖. Luke ii. 14. Rom. x. 1. Eph. i. 5, 9. ch. ii. 13. 2 Thess. i. 11 only. Ps. l. 19. s Acts viii. 5. 1 Cor. i. 23 al. t = 2 Cor. ii. 17. ix. 7. 1 Thess. ii. 3. 2 Tim. ii. 22. u Luke ii. 34. 1 Thess. iii. 3. Josh. iv. 6. v ver. 7 reff. w Gal. v. 20 reff. x = Acts iv. 2 al. L.P.† w. person, Acts xvii. 3, 23. Col. i. 28 only. y here only †. (-νός, ch. iv. 8. -νότης, 2 Cor. vi. 6.) z = & constr., here only. 1 Macc. v. 61. 2 Macc. v. 21. οἰόμενοι βλάπτειν, Plato, Apol. Socr. p. 41. (John xxi. 25. James i. 7 only. Job xi. 2. 2 Macc. vii. 24 only.)

14. rec om του θεου, with D³K Chr_{h.l.} Thdrt Damasc Thl Œc Tert: ins AB[P]ℵ k m 17 [47] vulg(and F-lat) Syr [syr-w-ast] copt goth [æth arm] Clem Chr₁(and 2 mss_{h.l.}) Ambrst Pel₁; κυριου F; ins bef τον λογ. f[: aft λαλειν D¹]. (om from περισσ. to κηρυσσουσιν in next ver L.)

15. om 1st και ℵ³ [17 syr æth arm.]   κηρυσσειν ℵ¹(txt ℵ-corr¹, appy).

16, 17. rec transp vv 16 and 17, also the μεν and δε (to suit order in ver 15), with D²K rel syr gr-ff [Victorin]: om ver 17 L: txt ABD¹F[P]ℵ k m 17 [47] latt Syr coptt goth æth arm Bas Tert Ambrst Pel Aug.   om τον BF Chr-ms: ins ADK[P]ℵ (marks for erasure have been placed but removed) rel Chr Thdrt Damasc.

in the sentence, above, ver. 5. And so De W., al. Meyer, Ellic., Winer, § 20. 2, al., take ἐν κυρ. with πεποιθότας, as the element in which their confidence was exercised, as ἐν χριστῷ, ver. 13. To this sense there is no objection: but the other arrangement still seems to me, in spite of Ellic.'s note, more natural. No article is required before ἐν: see reff.) encouraged by (having confidence in) my bonds (εἰ γὰρ μὴ θεῖον ἦν, φησί, τὸ κήρυγμα, οὐκ ἂν ὁ Παῦλος ἠνείχετο ὑπὲρ αὐτοῦ δεδέσθαι, Œc.) are venturing more abundantly (than before) to speak the word of God (it would certainly seem here, from the variations, as if the shorter reading were the original text) fearlessly. 15.] The two classes mentioned here are not subdivisions of the ἀδελφοὶ ἐν κυρίῳ above, who would more naturally be οἱ μέν and οἱ δέ, but the first (καί) are a new class, over and beyond those ἀδελφοί, and the second (in which clause the καί refers to the first) are identical with the ἀδελφοί above. The first were the anti-pauline Christians, of whom we hear so often in the Epistles (see Rom. xiv.; 1 Cor. iii. 10 ff.; iv. 15; ix. 1 ff.; 2 Cor. x. 1 ff.; xi. 1 ff. &c.). καί, besides those mentioned ver. 14. But this does not imply that the καί is to be referred to τινες, as Ellic. represents me;—it introduces a new motive, διὰ κ.τ.λ., and consequently, in my view, a new class of persons. διά, not strictly 'for the sake of,' so

that they set envy (of me) and strife before them as their object—but 'in pursuance of,'—so on account of,—to forward and carry out: see reff. καί (2nd)—besides the hostile ones: introducing (see above) another motive again, differing from that last mentioned. δι᾽ εὐδοκίαν—on account of, in pursuance of, good will (towards me). 16, 17.] The two classes of οἱ μέν, οἱ δέ, answering to hi and illi, take up again those of the preceding verse, the last being treated first. These last indeed (preach Christ: omitted, as having just occurred: see below) out of (induced by, reff.) love (this arrangement is better than with Mey., De W., and Ellic. to take οἱ ἐξ ἀγάπης and οἱ ἐξ ἐριθ. as generic descriptions, as in Rom. ii. 8, of the two classes: for in that case the words τὸν χρ. καταγγέλλουσιν would hardly be expressed in ver. 17, whereas in our rendering they come in naturally, ἐξ ἐριθείας being emphatically prefixed), knowing (motive of their conduct) that I am set (not 'lie in prison:' see reff. :—'am appointed by God') for the defence (as in ver. 7: hardly as Chrys., τουτέστι, ἵνα εὐθύνας μοι ὑποτέμνοντες τὰς πρὸς τὸν θεόν,—helping me in the solemn matter of my account of my ministry to God) of the Gospel: 17.] but the former out of self-seeking (or 'intrigue' (Conyb.): not 'contention,' as E. V., which has arisen from a mistake as to the derivation of the

ᵃ θλίψιν ᵇ ἐγείρειν τοῖς ᶜ δεσμοῖς μου. ¹⁸ ᵈ τί γάρ ; ᵉᶠ πλὴν ᶠ ὅτι ᵍ παντὶ ᵍ τρόπῳ, εἴτε ʰ προφάσει εἴτε ἀληθείᾳ, χριστὸς ʸ καταγγέλλεται, καὶ ⁱ ἐν τούτῳ ⁱ χαίρω, ʲ ἀλλὰ καὶ χαρήσομαι· ¹⁹ οἶδα γὰρ ὅτι τοῦτό μοι ᵏˡ ἀποβήσεται εἰς ˡ σωτηρίαν διὰ τῆς ὑμῶν δεήσεως καὶ ᵐ ἐπιχορηγίας τοῦ πνεύματος Ἰησοῦ χριστοῦ ²⁰ κατὰ τὴν ⁿ ἀποκαραδοκίαν

right margin notes:
a Eph. iii. 13 reff.
b = here only. Prov. xvii. 11.
c ver. 7 reff.
d Rom. iii. 3.
e Eph. v. 33 reff.
f Acts xx. 23.
2 Kings xii. 14.
g dat., here only. 1 Macc.

xiv. 35. w. ἐν, 2 Thess. iii. 16. acc. w. κατά, Rom. iii. 2. h Mark xii. 40 ǁ L. John xv. 22. Acts xxvii. 30. 1 Thess. ii. 5 only. Hos. x. 4. (προφ., ἀληθ., ex. in Wetst.) dat. of manner, 1 Cor. xi. 5. i Col. i. 24. j = ch. iii. 8. Eur. Phœn. 627, μῆτερ, ἀλλά μοι σὺ χαῖρε. k = Luke xxi. 13 (v. 2. John xxi. 9) only. l Job xiii. 16. m Eph. iv. 16 only†. (-γεῖν, Col. ii. 19.) n Rom. viii. 19 only. (-κεῖν, Ps. xxxv. 7 Aq. Jos. B. J. iii. 7. 26. Polyb. xvi. 2. 8.)

rec (for εγειρειν) επιφερειν, with D³K rel syrr: [επεγειρειν P:] txt ABD¹Fℵ 17 latt coptt goth æth arm Antch Damasc(not txt_h.l.) lat-ff.

18. rec om οτι, with DKL rel copt Chr Thdrt Damasc : om πλην B Ath-ms : txt AF[P]ℵ c 17 [47] sah Ath Cyr₁ Thl-marg. (*dum* vulg D-lat goth lat-ff, *dum tamen* Ambrst, *verum tamen* Cypr.) ins εν bef αληθεια D³ m 80. 116 : ℵ¹ has written ε, but marked it for erasure.

19. for γαρ, δε B m o sah. [αποβησεται bef μοι P.] χρ. bef ιησ. DF goth.

word, see note, Rom. ii. 8) **proclaim Christ insincerely** (so Cic. pro leg. Manil. 1, 'in privatorum periculis caste integreque versatus,' — μεγάλων ἀέθλων ἀγνὰν κρίσιν, Pind. Ol. iii. 37), **thinking** (explains οὐχ ἀγνῶς ;—'in that they think.' In the οἰόμενοι is involved, 'they do not succeed in their purpose,' cf. ref. 1 Macc.) **to raise up tribulation for** (me in) **my bonds** (i. e. endeavouring to take opportunity, by my being laid aside, to depreciate me and my preaching, and so to cause me trouble of spirit. The meaning given by Chrys., al., 'to excite the hatred of his persecutors and so render his condition worse, whether by the complaints of the Jews or otherwise,'—seems to me quite beside the purpose. It surely could not, from any circumstances to us unknown (Calvin's excuse, adopted by Ellic., for the *objective* view of θλίψις), make his imprisonment more severe, that some were preaching Christ from wrong motives). **18.**] **What then** (i. e. 'what is my feeling thereupon?' see Ellic.'s note)? **Nevertheless** (i. e. notwithstanding this opposition to myself : see reff. : St. Paul uses πλήν in this sense only. Reading ὅτι after the πλήν, the expression is elliptical, as in ref. Acts. What then ? '(nothing,) except that') **in every way** (of preaching ;—from whatever motive undertaken and however carried out), **in pretext** (with a by-motive, as in ver. 17), **or in verity** ('truth and sincerity of spirit :' the datives are those of the manner and form,—see Winer, § 31. 7. On προφάσει and ἀληθείᾳ, cf. Æschin. cont. Timarch. p. 6, προφάσει μὲν τῆς τέχνης μαθητής, τῇ δὲ ἀληθείᾳ πωλεῖν αὐτὸν προῃρημένος, and other

examples in Wetst.) **Christ IS PROCLAIMED** (then these adversaries of the Apostle can hardly have been those against whom he speaks so decisively in Galatians, and indeed in our ch. iii. 2. These men *preached Christ*, and thus forwarded pro tanto the work of the Gospel, however mixed their motives may have been, or however imperfect their work): **and in this** (ἐν ἀρεταῖς γέγαθε, Pind. Nem. iii. 56 : οὐ γὰρ ἂν γνοίης ἐν οἷς | χαίρειν προθυμῇ κἂν ὅτοις ἀλγεῖς μάτην, Soph. Trach. 1118) **I rejoice, yea and** (on ἀλλὰ καί, see Ellic. It does not seem to me necessary, with him, to place a colon at χαίρω) **I shall** (hereafter) **rejoice: 19.**] **for I know that this** (viz. the greater spread of the preaching of Christ, last mentioned, ver. 18 : not as Thl., Calv., Est., De W., the θλίψιν ἐγείρ. κ.τ.λ., in which case ver. 18 would be (Mey.) arbitrarily passed over) **shall turn out to my salvation ✱** (σωτηρία is variously interpreted : by Chrys. and Thdrt., of *deliverance* from present custody ; by Œc., of *sustenance in life* : by Michaelis, of *victory* over foes : by Grot., of the *salvation of others*. But from the context it must refer to *his own spiritual good*—his own fruitfulness for Christ and glorification of Him, whether by his life or death ;—and so eventually his own *salvation*, in *degree* of blessedness, not in relation to the absolute fact itself), **through your prayer** (his affection leads him to make this addition—q. d. if you continue to pray for me ;—not without the help of your prayers : see similar expressions, 2 Cor. i. 11 ; Rom. xv. 30, 31 ; Philem. 22) **and (your) supply** (to me, by that prayer and its answer) **of the**

o gen. pers.,
　Acts xxviii.
20. 2 Cor. i.
6. Ps. cxlv.
5.
p = ver. 28.
q Luke xvi. 3.
　2 Cor. x. 8.
　1 Pet. iv. 16.
　1 John ii. 28
　only. Ps. xxxiv. 4, 26. lxix. 2.
s Eph. iii. 12 reff.
u = 1 Cor. iii. 22. xv. 19. James iv. 14.

r = Matt. xxiii. 27. Acts iv. 29. xx. 19. Rom. i. 18. 2 Cor. viii. 7 al. fr.
t = Luke i. 46. Acts v. 13. x. 46. 2 Kings vii. 26. (L.P., exc. Matt. xxiii. 5.)
1 Pet. iii. 10 (from Ps. xxxiii. 12).

ABDFK
LPℵ a b
c e f g h
k l m n o
17. 47

v constr., 1 Cor. xi. 6.

καὶ ^o ἐλπίδα μου, ὅτι ^p ἐν οὐδενὶ ^q αἰσχυνθήσομαι, ἀλλ᾿ ἐν ^r πάσῃ ^s παρρησίᾳ ὡς πάντοτε καὶ νῦν ^t μεγαλυνθήσεται χριστὸς ἐν τῷ σώματί μου, εἴτε διὰ ^u ζωῆς εἴτε διὰ θανά- του. ²¹ ἐμοὶ γὰρ ^v τὸ ζῆν χριστὸς καὶ ^v τὸ ἀποθανεῖν

20. for αποκαραδ., καραδοκιαν F h 18. 44. 123 Ath-3·mss.　　　aft ουδενι ins υμων F.
　παρρ. bef πασῃ G¹ coptt.
21. aft χριστος ins εστιν F latt [Syr goth].

spirit of Jesus Christ (the construction obliges us to take ἐπιχορηγίας as parallel with δεήσεως, and as the article is wanting, as also included under the ὑμῶν. Were the sense as E. V., and ordinarily, ' through your prayer and the supply of the Spirit of Jesus Christ,' διὰ or διὰ τῆς would have been repeated, or at least the article τῆς expressed. This I still hold, notwithstanding Ellic.'s note. How such a meaning can be dogmatically objectionable, I am wholly unable to see. Surely, that intercessory prayer should attain its object, and the supply take place in consequence of the prayer, is only in accord with the simplest idea of any reality in such prayer at all. Then again, is τοῦ πνεύματος a subjective genitive, ' supply which the Spirit gives,'—so Thdrt. (τοῦ θείου μοι πν. χορηγοῦντος τὴν χάριν), Calv., De W., Meyer, all. :—or objective, the Spirit being that which is supplied (so Chrys., Thl., Œc., Grot., Beng., al.) ? Decidedly, I think, the latter, on account (1) of St. Paul's own usage of ἐπιχορηγεῖν with this very word πνεῦμα in Gal. iii. 5, which is quite in point here, and (2) perhaps also, but see Ellic., of the arrangement of the words, which in the case of a subjective genitive would have been κ. τοῦ πν. ᾽Ι. χ. ἐπιχορηγίας, as in Eph. iv. 16, διὰ πάσης ἁφῆς τῆς ἐπιχορηγίας.— By a delicate touch at the same time of personal humility and loving appreciation of their spiritual eminence and value to him, he rests the advancement of his own salvation, on the supply of the Holy Spirit won for him by their prayers),　　**20.**] **according to** (for it is ' our confidence, which hath great recompense of reward,' Heb. x. 35 f.) **my expectation** (not, 'earnest' expectation,' which never seems to be the sense of ἀπό in composition : still less is ἀπό superfluous: but καραδοκεῖν signifies to 'attend,' 'look out'—(παρὰ τὴν κάραν ὅλην δοκεῖν ('observare'), Thl. ad loc.) ; and ἀπό adds the signification of 'from a particular position,' or better still that of exhaustion, 'look out until it be fulfilled,'—as in 'exspectare,' ἀπεκδέχομαι, ἀπέχω, &c. See the word

thoroughly discussed the Fritzschiorum Opuscula, p. 150 ff.) **and hope that** (Est., al., take ὅτι argumentatively, because : but thus the expectation and hope will have no explanation, and the flow of the sentence will be broken) **in nothing** (in no point, no particular, see ref. It should be kept quite indefinite, not specified as Chrys. (κἂν ὁτιοῦν γένηται). ' In none ' (of those to whom the Gospel is preached) as Hoelemann, is beside the purpose—no persons are adduced, but only the most general considerations) **I shall be ashamed** (general : have reason to take shame for my work for God, or His work in me), **but** (on the contrary : but perhaps after the ἐν οὐδενί this need not be pressed) **in all** (as contrasted with ἐν οὐδενί above) **boldness** (contrast to shame :—boldness on my part, seeing that life or death are both alike glorious for me—and thus I, my body, the passive instrument in which Christ is glorified, shall any-how be bold and of good cheer in this His glorification of Himself in me) **as always, now also** (that I am in the situation described above, ver. 17) **Christ shall be magnified** (δειχθήσεται ὅς ἐστι, Thdrt. : by His Kingdom being spread among men. So Ellicott, saying rightly that it is more than 'praised,' as in my earlier editions) **in my body** (my body being the subject of life or death,—in the occurrence of either of which he would not be ashamed, the one bringing active service for Christ, the other union with Him in heaven, ver. 21 ff.), **either by** (means of) **life or by** (means of) **death.**
21.] **For** (justification of the preceding expectation and hope, in either event) **to me** (emphatic) **to live** (continue in life, present), **(is) Christ** (see especially Gal. ii. 20. All my life, all my energy, all my time, is His—I live Christ. That this is the meaning, is clear, from the corresponding clause and the context. But many have taken χριστός for the subject, and τὸ ζῆν for the predicate, and others (as Chrys.) have understood τὸ ζῆν in the sense of higher spiritual life. Others again, as Calvin, Beza, &c., have rendered,

ʷκέρδος· ²² εἰ δὲ ᵛτὸ ζῆν ˣἐν σαρκί, ʸτοῦτό μοι ᶻκαρπὸς
C καὶ τι ᵃἔργου, ᵇκαὶ ᶜτί ᵈαἱρήσομαι οὐ ᵉγνωρίζω· ²³ ᶠσυνέχομαι
ABCDF δὲ ἐκ τῶν δύο, τὴν ᵍἐπιθυμίαν ἔχων ʰεἰς τὸ ⁱἀναλῦσαι
KLPℵ a

w ch. iii. 7. Tit. i. 11
only†. Gen. xxxvii. 26
Symm.
x 1 Tim. iii. 16 reff.
y Matt. xv. 11

b c e f g
h k l m n
o 17. 47

al. so ἐκεῖνα, Mark vii. 15.
38. ch. ii. 30. 1 Thess. v. 13.
31. xxiii. 17, 19. Luke vii. 42. Xen. Cyr. i. 3. 17.
e intr., here only. (Eph. i. 9 reff.) Thuc. vii. 44 al.
al. L.P., exc. Matt. iv. 24. Job xxxi. 23.
x. 24. ἐπιθ. πρὸς τὸ ζῆν, Polyb. iii. 63. 6.

z = Rom. i. 13. ver. 11 reff.
b see note, and 1 Cor. v. 2. 2 Cor. ii. 2.
d 2 Thess. ii. 13. Heb. xi. 25 only. Jer. viii. 3.
f Luke iv. 38. Acts vii. 57. 2 Cor. v. 14
g in good sense, Luke xxii. 15. 1 Thess. ii. 17. Prov.
h 1 Thess. iii. 10. 2 Thess. i. 5. ii. 2. iii. 9.

a = Acts xiii. 2. xv-
c = Matt. xxi-

i = here (Luke xii. 36) only†. to depart, Judith xiii. 1. 2 Macc. xii. 7. 3 Macc. ii. 24. (-λυσις, 2 Tim.
iv. 6. Philo in Flacc. § 21, vol. ii. p. 544, τὴν ἐκ τοῦ βίου τελευταίαν ἀνάλυσιν.)

22. [for δε, τε D¹.] aft εργου ins εστιν F latt. αιρησωμαι B(ita cod).
23. rec (for δε) γαρ, with demid(and hal) Syr Thdrt [Orig-int₁]: om copt basm
[arm]: txt ABCDFKL[P]ℵ rel latt syr sah goth gr-lat-ff. om εις DF (latt).

'mihi enim vivendo Christus est et mo-
riendo lucrum,' understanding before τὸ
ζ. and τὸ ἀπ., κατά or the like), and to
die ('to have died,' aorist; the act of
living is to him Christ; but it is the state
after death, not the act of dying, which
is gain to him (the explanation of the two
infinitives given here does not at all affect
their purely substantival character, which
Ellic. defends as against me: τὸ ζῆν is
life and τὸ ἀποθανεῖν is death: but we
must not any the more for that lose sight
of the tenses and their meaning. τὸ
ἀποθνήσκειν would be equally substantival,
but would mean a totally different thing))
(is) gain. This last word has surprised
some Commentators, expecting a repetition of χριστός, or something at all
events higher than mere κέρδος. But it
is to be explained by the foregoing context. 'Even if my death should be the
result of my enemies' machinations, it will
be no αἰσχύνη to me, but gain, and my
παρρησία is secured even for that event.'
22.] But if (the syllogistic, not
the hypothetical 'if:' assuming that it is
so) the continuing to live in the flesh
(epexegesis of τὸ ζῆν above), this very
thing (τοῦτο directs attention to the antecedent as the principal or only subject
of that which is to be asserted: this very
ζῆν which I am undervaluing is) is to
me the fruit of my work (i. e. that in
which the fruit of my apostolic ministry
will be involved,—the condition of that
fruit being brought forth), then (this use of
καί to introduce an apodosis is abundantly
justified: cf. Simonides, fragm. Danae, εἰ
δέ τοι δεινὸν τόγε δεινὸν ἦν, καί κεν ἐμῶν
ῥημάτων λεπτὸν ὑπεῖχες οὖας: Hom. Il.
ε. 897, εἰ δέ τευ ἐξ ἄλλου γε θεῶν γένευ
ὧδ' ἀίδηλος, καί κεν δὴ πάλαι ἦσθα ἐνέρ-
τερος οὐρανιώνων: Od. ξ. 112, αὐτὰρ
ἐπεὶ δείπνησε κ. ἤραρε θυμὸν ἐδωδῇ, καί οἱ
πλησάμενος δῶκε σκύφον, ᾧπερ ἔπινεν.
And the construction is imitated by Virg.
Georg. i. 200, 'si brachia forte remisit,

Atque illum præceps prono rapit alveus
amni.' See Hartung, Partikell. i. 130,
where more examples are given. The
primary sense is 'also,' introducing a new
feature—for whereas he had before said
that death was gain to him, he now says,
but, if life in the flesh is to be the fruit of
my ministry, then (I must add,—this besides arises—), &c.) what (i. e. which of
the two) I shall choose (for myself) I know
not. The above rendering is in the main
that of Chr., Thdrt., Œc., Thl., Erasm.,
Luth., Calv., all., Meyer, De Wette,—and
as it appears to me, the only one which
will suit the construction and sense.
Beza's 'an vero vivere in carne mihi
operæ pretium sit et quid eligam ignoro,'
adopted (except in his omission of the
τοῦτο and his rendering of καρπὸς ἔργου
by 'operæ pretium') by Conyb., is open to
several objections: (1) the harshness of
attaching to οὐ γνωρίζω the two clauses
εἰ . . . ., and τί . . . . : (2) the doubtfulness of such a construction at all as
οὐ γνωρίζω, εἰ . . . . (3) the extreme
clumsiness of the sentence when constructed, "whether this life in the flesh
shall be the fruit of my labour, and what
I shall choose, I know not" (Conyb.):
(4) in this last rendering, the lameness of
the apodosis in the clause εἰ δὲ (τὸ ζῆν ἐν
σαρκὶ τοῦτό) μοι καρπὸς ἔργου, which
would certainly, were τοῦτο to be taken
with τὸ ζῆν, have been καρπός μοι ἔργου
or καρπὸς ἔργου μοι. 23.] But (the
contrast is to the decision involved in
γνωρίζω) I am perplexed (reff. and Acts
xviii. 5 note: held in, kept back from decision, which would be a setting at liberty)
by (from the direction of,—kept in on
both sides) the two (which have been mentioned, viz. τὸ ζῆν and τὸ ἀποθανεῖν: not,
which follow: this is evident by the insignificant position of ἐκ τῶν δύο behind the
emphatic verb συνέχομαι, whereas, had the
two been the new particulars about to be
mentioned, τὸ ἀναλῦσαι and τὸ ἐπιμένειν

καὶ σὺν χριστῷ εἶναι, πολλῷ γὰρ ᵏ μᾶλλον ᵏˡ κρεῖσ-
σον· 24 τὸ δὲ ᵐ ἐπιμένειν ἐν τῇ σαρκὶ ⁿ ἀναγκαιότερον
δι᾽ ὑμᾶς. 25 καὶ τοῦτο ° πεποιθὼς οἶδα ὅτι ᴾ μενῶ
καὶ ᑫ παραμενῶ πᾶσιν ὑμῖν εἰς τὴν ὑμῶν ʳ προκοπὴν
καὶ ˢ χαρὰν τῆς ˢ πίστεως, 26 ἵνα τὸ ᵗ καύχημα ὑμῶν
ᵘ περισσεύῃ ἐν χριστῷ Ἰησοῦ ᵛ ἐν ἐμοὶ διὰ τῆς ἐμῆς

k double compar., Mark vii. 36. 2 Cor. vii. 13.
Winer, edn. 6, § 35. 1.
l = 1 Cor. vii. 9, 38. 1 Pet. iii. 17. 2 Pet. ii. 21. Prov. iii. 14. (1 Cor. xi. 17. xii. 31.
Heb. i. 4 al2.)
kl κρεῖσσον 24 μενειν εν... ABCDF KLPℵ a bcdefg hklmn o17. 47

m Gal. i. 18 reff.   n = Acts xiii. 46. ch. ii. 25.   1 Cor. xii. 12.   2 Cor. ix. 5.   Heb. viii. 3.   Tit. iii. 14 (Acts x. 24) only †.   2 Macc. ix. 21.   o constr., ver. 6.   p = John xx. 22, 23.   1 Cor. xv. 6.
q 1 Cor. xvi. 6.   Heb. vii. 23.   James i. 25 only.   Gen. xliv. 33.   r ver. 12 reff.   s see Rom. xv. 13.   1 Pet. i. 8.   t Paul (Rom. iv. 2 al8.) only, exc. Heb. iii. 6.   Deut. x. 21.   u Rom. iii. 7.   2 Cor. i. 5 al. Tobit iv. 16.   v = Rom. xv. 17. ii. 17 al.

for πολλω, ποτω D¹F Victorin.   Steph om γαρ, with DFKL[P]ℵ¹ rel latt basm goth Orig₁ Bas Chr Thdrt Thl Œc [Victorin] Aug_aliq : ins ABCℵ-corr¹ ᵒᵇˡ f 17 [47] 67² copt Clem Orig₂ Aug_saepe et expr Ambrst Ambr₁.

24. επιμειναι B [Cyr₁₋p] Petr [Orig-cat].   om εν AC[P]ℵ c k o Clem Orig₃ Petr Chr Cyr : ins BDFKL rel Thdrt Damasc Thl Œc.

25. rec συμπαραμενω (corrn on account of the unusual dative follg), with D³KL[P] rel Chr_expr Thdrt Damasc Thl Œc : permanebo latt : txt ABCD¹Fℵ 17. 67².   at end add υμων ℵ¹(ℵ³ disapproving).

[26. περισσευση D.]

it would have been ἐκ δὲ τῶν δύο συνέχομαι), having my desire towards (εἰς belongs to ἔχων, not to ἐπιθυμίαν. The E. V., 'having a desire to,' would be ἐπιθυμίαν ἔχων τοῦ, and entirely misses the delicate sense) departing (from this world—used on account of σὺν χρ. εἶναι following. The intransitive sense of ἀναλύω is not properly such, but as in the Latin solvere, elliptical, to loose (anchor or the like: see reff.) for departure, for return, &c.) and being with Christ (" valet hic locus ad refellendum eorum deliramentum, qui animas a corporibus divisas dormire somniant: nam Paulus aperte testatur, nos frui Christi præsentia quum dissolvimur." Calv.; and similarly Est. Thus much is true: but not perhaps that which some have inferred from our verse, that it shews a change of view respecting the nearness of the Lord's advent—for it is only said in case of his death: he immediately takes it up (ver. 25) by an assurance that he should continue with them: and cf. ver. 6 ; ch. iii. 20, 21, which shew that the advent was still regarded as imminent), for it is by far better (ref. Mark, and examples in Wetst., Plato, Hip. Maj. § 56, οἴει σοι κρεῖττον εἶναι ζῆν μᾶλλον ἢ τεθνάναι : Isocr. Helen. 213 c, οὕτως ἠγανάκτησεν ὥσθ᾽ ἡγήσατο κρεῖττον εἶναι τεθνάναι μᾶλλον : ib. Archidam. 134 c, πολὺ γὰρ κρεῖττον ἐν ταῖς δόξαις αἷς ἔχομεν τελευτῆσαι τὸν βίον μᾶλλον ἢ ζῆν ἐν ταῖς ἀτιμίαις): but to continue (the preposition gives the sense of still, cf. Rom. vi. 1) in my flesh (the article makes a slight distinction from ἐν σαρκί, abstract, ver. 22) is more needful (this comparison contains in itself a mixed construction, be-

tween ἀναγκαῖον and αἱρετώτερον or the like) on account of you (and others—but the expressions of his love are now directed solely to them. Meyer quotes from Seneca, Epist. 98 :—' vitæ suæ adjici nihil desiderat sua causa, sed eorum, quibus utilis est.' Cf. also a remarkable passage from id. Epist. 104 in Wetst.).   25.] And having this confidence (Thl., al., take τοῦτο with οἶδα, and render πεποιθὼς adverbially, ' confidently,'—which last can hardly be, besides that οἶδα will thus lose its reference, τοῦτο .... ὅτι being unmeaning in the context), I know that I shall remain and continue alive (so Herod. i. 30, σφι εἶδε ἅπασι τέκνα ἐκγενόμενα, καὶ πάντα παραμείναντα.   συμπαραμένω (see var. readd.) occurs in Ps. lxxi. 5, and in Thuc. vi. 89) with you all (the dative may either be after the compound verb, or better perhaps a ' dativus commodi') for your advancement and joy in your faith (both προκ. and χαρ. govern τῆς πίσ. which is the subjective genitive; it is their faith which is to advance, by the continuance of his teaching, and to rejoice, as explained below, on account of his presence among them),   26.] that your matter of boasting (not, as Chr., 'mine in you:' nor, as commonly rendered, 'your boasting' (καύχησις). Their Christian matter of boasting in him was, the possession of the Gospel, which they had received from him, which would abound, be assured and increased, by his presence among them) may abound in Christ Jesus (its field, element of increase, it being a Christian matter of glorying) in me (its field, element, of abounding in Christ Jesus, I being the worker of that which

[w] *παρουσίας πάλιν* [x] *πρὸς ὑμᾶς.* 27 [y] Μόνον [z] *ἀξίως τοῦ*
εὐαγγελίου τοῦ χριστοῦ [a] *πολιτεύεσθε, ἵνα εἴτε ἐλθὼν*
καὶ ἰδὼν ὑμᾶς εἴτε [b] *ἀπὼν* * *ἀκούσω* [c] *τὰ* [c] *περὶ ὑμῶν, ὅτι*
[d] *στήκετε ἐν* [e] *ἑνὶ* [e] *πνεύματι,* [f] *μιᾷ* [f] *ψυχῇ* [g] *συναθλοῦντες τῇ*
πίστει τοῦ [h] *εὐαγγελίου,* 28 *καὶ μὴ* [i] *πτυρόμενοι* [k] *ἐν μηδενὶ*

w = 1 Cor. xvi.
17. 2 Cor.
vii. 6, 7. ch.
ii. 12 al.†
2 Macc. viii.
12. xv. 21
only.
x Gal. iv. 18
reff.
y Gal. ii. 10. v.
13.
z Eph. iv. 1

reff.   a Acts xxiii. 1 only†.   2 Macc. vi. 1. xi. 25 only.   (-ευμα, ch. iii. 20.)   b mostly w.
παρών, 1 Cor. v. 3. 2 Cor. x. 1, 11. xiii. 2, 10. Wisd. xi. 11. xiv. 17. alone, Col. ii. 5 only.   Job vi.
13. Wisd. ix. 6 only.   c Luke xxiv. 19, 27. Acts xxiv. 10. ch. ii. 19, 20 al. Col. iv. 8. w. acc.,
ch. ii. 23 al.   d Gal. v. 1 reff.   e Eph. i. 18 reff.   f Acts iv. 32 only. 1 Chron.
xii. 38.   g ch. iv. 3 only †.   h gen. obj., see Col. ii. 12 reff.   i here only †. ἵπποι
... *πτυρόμενοι*, Diod. Sic. xvii. 34.   k ver. 20.

27. om *του χριστου* א[1](ins א-corr[1]) arm-ed.   [om 2nd *του* D.]   om ειτε
απων א[1](ins א-corr[1] obl).   * *ἀκούω* BD[1][P]א [47] basm: ακουσω ACD[3]FKL
א-corr[1] obl rel (*audiam* latt).

furnishes this material) **by means of my
presence again with you.**

27—II. 18.] EXHORTATIONS TO UNITED
FIRMNESS, TO MUTUAL CONCORD, TO HU-
MILITY; AND IN GENERAL TO EARNEST-
NESS IN RELIGION.   **27.**] μόνον,—
i. e. I have but this to ask of you, in the
prospect of my return:—see reff.
πολιτεύεσθε] The πολίτευμα being the
heavenly state, of which you are citizens,
ch. iii. 20. The expression is found in
Jos. (Antt. iii. 5. 8) and in Philo, and is
very common in the fathers: e. g. Ps-
Ignat. Trall. 9, p. 789, ὁ λόγος σὰρξ ἐγένετο,
κ. ἐπολιτεύσατο ἄνευ ἁμαρτίας,—Cyr. Jer.
Catech. Illum. iv. 1, p. 51, ἰσάγγελον βίον
πολιτεύεσθαι. See Suicer in voc.   The
emphasis is on ἀξίως τ. εὐ. τοῦ χρ.
ἵνα εἴτε κ.τ.λ.] This clause is loosely constructed,—the verb ἀκούσω belonging
properly only to the second alternative,
εἴτε ἀπών, but here following on both.
Meyer tries to meet this by understanding ἀκούσω in the former case, '*hear from
your own mouth;*' but obviously, ἰδών is
the real correlative to ἀκούσω, only constructed in a loose manner: the full construction would be something of this kind,
ἵνα, εἴτε ἐλθὼν κ. ἰδὼν ὑμᾶς εἴτε ἀπὼν
κ. ἀκούσας τὰ περὶ ὑμῶν, γνῶ ὅτι στήκετε.
Then τὰ περὶ ὑμῶν, ὅτι στήκετε is another irregular construction—the article
generalizing that which the ὅτι particularizes, as in οἶδά σε, τίς εἶ, and the like.
ἐν ἑνὶ πνεύματι] refers to the unity
of spirit in which the various members
of the church would be fused and blended
in the case of *perfect unity :* but when
Meyer and De W. deny that the Holy
Spirit is meant, they forget that this one
spirit of Christians united for their common faith would of necessity be the Spirit
of God which penetrates and inspires
them: cf. Eph. iv. 3, 4. Then, as this
Spirit is the highest principle in us,—he
includes also the lower portion, the ani-

mal soul ;   μιᾷ ψυχῇ συναθλοῦντες]
These words must be taken together, not
ψυχῇ taken with στήκετε as in apposition
with πνεύματι (Chr., Thl., all.), which
would leave συναθλ. without any modal
qualification. The ψυχή, receiving on the
one hand influence from the spirit, on the
other impressions from the outer world, is
the sphere of the affections and moral energies, and thus is that in and by which
the exertion here spoken of would take
place. συναθλοῦντες either *with one another* (so Chr., Thdrt., Thl., Œc., all., De
W., al.), or *with me* (so Erasm., Luth.,
Beza, Bengel, al., Meyer). The former
is I think preferable, both on account of
the ἑνὶ πν. and μιᾷ ψυχῇ, which naturally
prepare the mind for an *united* effort, and
because *his own* share in the contest which
comes in as a new element in ver. 30, and
which Meyer adduces as a reason for his
view, seems to me, on that view, superfluous; ἐμοί after συναθλοῦντες (cf. ch.
iv. 3) would have expressed the whole.
I would render then as E. V., **striving
together.** τῇ πίστει is a 'dativus commodi'—**for the faith,** cf. Jude 3—not, as
Erasm. Paraphr., '*with the faith,*' 'adju-
vantes decertantem adversus impios evangelii fidem;' for such a personification of
πίστις would be without example : nor
is it a dative of the *instrument* (Beza,
Calv., Grot., al.), which we have already
had in ψυχῇ, and which could hardly be
with τοῦ εὐαγ. added.   **28.**] πτύρω,
akin to πτοέω, πτώσσω, πτήσσω, **to
frighten,** especially said of animals (ref.),
but often also used figuratively, e. g. by
Plato, Axioch. p. 370 A, οὐκ ἄν ποτε
πτυρείης τὸν θάνατον : Ps-Clem. Hom. ii.
39, p. 71, πτύραντες τοὺς ἀμαθεῖς ὄχλους.
ἐν μηδενί] **in nothing,** see on ver. 20.
The ἀντικείμενοι, from the comparison which follows with his own conflict,
and the ὑπὲρ αὐτοῦ πάσχειν, must be the
adversaries of the faith, whether Jews or

1 Gal. v. 17 reff.
m — Col. ii. 23.
attr., Mark
xv. 16. 1 Tim.
iii. 15 al.
n Rom. iii. 25,
26. 2 Cor.
viii. 24 only†.
o Matt. vii. 13.
John xvii. 12.
1 Tim. vi. 9
reff. Jer.
xxvi. (xlvi.)
21.

ὑπὸ τῶν ¹ἀντικειμένων, ᵐ ἥτις ἐστὶν αὐτοῖς ⁿ ἔνδειξις
ᵒ ἀπωλείας, ὑμῶν δὲ σωτηρίας, ᵖ καὶ ᵖ τοῦτο ἀπὸ θεοῦ,
29 ὅτι ὑμῖν ᑫ ἐχαρίσθη τὸ ὑπὲρ χριστοῦ οὐ μόνον τὸ
ʳ εἰς αὐτὸν ʳ πιστεύειν, ἀλλὰ καὶ τὸ ὑπὲρ αὐτοῦ ˢ πάσχειν,
30 τὸν αὐτὸν ᵗᵘ ἀγῶνα ᵗᵛ ἔχοντες οἷον εἴδετε ἐν ἐμοὶ καὶ νῦν
ἀκούετε ἐν ἐμοί. II. ¹ εἴ τις οὖν ʷ παράκλησις ἐν χριστῷ,

ABCDF
KLPℵ a
b c d e f g
h k l m n
o 17. 47

p Rom. xiii.
11. 1 Cor. vi. 6, 8. Eph. ii. 8. 3 John 5.　　　q = Acts iii. 14. 1 Cor. ii. 12.　　　r Gal. ii. 16 reff.
s Gal. iii. 4 reff.　　　t Col. ii. 1.　　u as above (t). 1 Thess. ii. 2. 1 Tim. vi. 12. 2 Tim. iv. 7. Heb. xii.
1 only. Isa. vii. 13.　　v constr. of part., Acts xxvi. 3. Col. iii. 16 al.　　w = Acts xiii. 15. xv.
31. Rom. xii. 8. Heb. xii. 5 al. L.P.H. 1 Macc. x. 24.

28. rec (for εστιν αυτοις) αυτοις μεν εστιν, with KL rel Thdrt: εστιν αυτοις μεν
D³[P 47] syr Chr Thl: αυτοις (alone) o: txt ABCD¹Fℵ 17 am(with fuld tol) Syr
coptt goth Ambrst Pel.　　rec υμιν (corrn to suit αυτοις), with D³KL rel vulg[and
F-lat] syr coptt goth Chr₁ Thdrt Ambrst: ημιν C¹D¹[F] Damasc [Victorin]: txt
ABC²[P]ℵ 17 [47] D-lat Chr-ms Aug.

29. ημιν A 35.　　om 1st το F 3. 68². 73. 120 Œc-comm.

30. [εχον (for εχοντες) B¹.]　　aft οιον ins και D¹F latt [Tert₁] Ambrst Pel: aft
ειδετε, C¹.　　rec ιδετε, with B²D³FKL[P] d m n [47¹ Clem(sic, Treg)] Thl Œc:
txt AB¹CD¹ℵ rel 67² Clem Chr Thdrt Damasc₁

Gentiles, cf. 1 Cor. xvi. 9.　　ἥτις, viz.
τὸ ὑμᾶς μὴ πτύρεσθαι, fem., on account
of ἔνδειξις, following: see a similar ἥτις,
Eph. iii. 13.　　ἔνδ. ἀπωλ., because it
will shew that all their arts are of no
avail against your union and firmness and
hopefulness: and thus their own ruin
(spiritual, as the whole matter is spiritual), in hopelessly contending against
you, is pointed out, not perhaps to themselves as perceiving it, but to themselves
if they choose to perceive it.　　ὑμῶν
δὲ σω.] but (is a sign) of your (see var.
readd.) salvation (spiritual again: not
merely, rescue and safety from them),
and this (viz. the sign, to them of perdition, to you of your salvation: not to be
referred to σωτηρίας, nor merely to ὑμῶν
δὲ σωτ. (Calv., al.), nor to both ἀπωλ. and
σωτ., nor to the following sentence (Clem.
Alex.(Strom.iv.13,vol.i.p.604 P.), Chrys.,
Thdrt., al.), but simply to ἔνδειξις: the
sign is one from God) from God,—because
(proof that the sign is from God, in that
He has granted to you the double proof
of His favour, not only, &c.) to you (first
emphasis) it was granted (second emphasis—'gratiæ munus, signum salutis
(?) est.' Beng. The aorist refers to the
fact in the dealings of God regarded as a
historical whole), on behalf of Christ (the
Apostle seems to have intended immediately to add πάσχειν, but, the οὐ μόνον
κ.τ.λ. coming between, he drops τὸ ὑπὲρ
χριστοῦ for the present, and takes it up
again by and by with ὑπὲρ αὐτοῦ. The
rendering of τὸ ὑπ. χ., absolute, 'to you
it is given in the behalf of Christ' (E. V.),
'quod attinet ad Christi causam,' is manifestly wrong), not only to believe on Him,
but also on his behalf to suffer,

30.] having (the nominative instead of
the dative, the subjective ὑμεῖς being before the Apostle's mind: so Eph. iv. 2,—
Thuc. iii. 36, ἔδοξεν αὐτοῖς . . . . ἐπικα-
λοῦντες: ib. vi. 24, καὶ ἔρως ἐνέπεσε
πᾶσιν . . . . εὐέλπιδες ὄντες: Sallust, Jug.
112, 'populo Romano melius visum . . . .
rati:' see other examples in Kühner, ii.
p. 377. This is far better than with
Lachm., al., to parenthesize ἥτις . . . .
πάσχειν, which unnecessarily breaks the
flow of the sentence) the same conflict
(one in its nature and object) as ye saw
(viz. when I was with you, Acts xvi. 16
ff.) in me (in my case as its example), and
now hear of in me (ἐν ἐμοί, as before, not
'de me.' He means, by report of others,
and by this Epistle).　　II. 1—11.]
Exhortation to unity and humility (1—
4), after the example of Christ (5—11).
1.] He introduces in the fervour
of his affection (ὅρα πῶς λιπαρῶς, πῶς
σφοδρῶς, πῶς μετὰ συμπαθείας πολλῆς,
Chr.) four great points of the Christian
life and ministry, and by them enforces
his exhortation.　　Mey. observes, that the
four fall into two pairs, in each of which
we have first the objective principle of
Christian life (ἐν χριστῷ and πνεύματος),
and next the subjective principle (ἀγάπης
and σπλάγχ. κ. οἰκτιρμοί). And thus
the awakening of motives by these four
points is at the same time (so Chrys.
above) powerful and touching.　　παρά-
κλησις] here, exhortation, not 'comfort,' which follows in παραμύθιον. ἐν
χριστῷ specifies the element of the exhortation.　　παραμύθ.] better comfort, than 'persuasion:' it corresponds
(see above) to σπλ. κ. οἰκτιρ. in the other
pair: see also reff. παραμυθία, the ear-

εἴ τι ˣπαραμύθιον ἀγάπης, εἴ τις ʸκοινωνία πνεύματος, εἴ
ᶻτις ᵃσπλάγχνα καὶ ᵇοἰκτιρμοί, 2 ᶜπληρώσατέ μου τὴν
ᶜχαράν, ᵈἵνα ᵉτὸ ᵉαὐτὸ ᵉᶠφρονῆτε, τὴν αὐτὴν ἀγάπην
ἔχοντες, ᵍσύμψυχοι, ʰτὸ ʰἓν ᶠʰφρονοῦντες, 3 μηδὲν ⁱκατ᾽
ᵏἐριθείαν μηδὲ κατὰ ˡκενοδοξίαν, ἀλλὰ τῇ ᵐταπεινοφροσύνῃ
ἀλλήλους ⁿἡγούμενοι ᵒὑπερέχοντας ἑαυτῶν, 4 μὴ τὰ

CHAP. II. 1. for τι, τις D¹·⁴L [17]. rec (for last τις) τινα, with 57(ed Alter) al (e sil "si in ullis, in perpaucis certe codicibus græcis" Reiche p. 213. Cf also ib. p. 211 note 7): τι b e h m o 4. 18. 37. 46. 72-4. 116-32-9. 219¹ Clem Chr-ed-montf : τε 109 Thdrt-ms : txt ABCDFKL[P]ℵ rel al₆₅(in Reiche) Bas Chr-mss Damasc Thl Œc.

2. for το ἐν, το αυτο ACℵ¹(txt ℵ³) 17 : *id ipsum* vulg Pel.

3. rec (for κατ᾽) κατα, with AD³ rel : txt BCD¹FL[Pℵ] l m n 17 [47]. rec (for μηδε κατα) ἤ, with DFKL[P] rel [syrr goth] Chr Thdrt : txt ABCℵ(but ℵ³ disapproves κατα) m 17 vulg D-lat copt [arm Hil] Victorin Ambrst Aug. προηγουμενοι D¹·²K 80. ins τους bef υπερ. B. υπερεχοντες DF.

lier form, occurs in the same sense 1 Cor. xiv. 3 ; Wisd. xix. 12. **ἀγάπης** is the subjective genitive,—'consolation furnished by love.' **κοιν. πν.**] communion,—fellowship of the *Holy Spirit*, cf. ref. 2 Cor.: not, *'spiritual communion'* (De W., al.). The manuscript evidence in favour of the reading **εἴ τις** is overwhelming; and in Tischendorf's language, "nobis servandum erit τις, nisi malumus grammatici quam editoris partes agere." It is in its favour, that almost all the great MSS. have εἴ τι before παραμύθιον. For if εἴ τις had been a mere mechanical repetition of the preceding, why not in one place as well as in the other ? And if this were once so, and the former τις got altered back to its proper form, why not this also ? The construction may be justified perhaps as analogous to ὄχλου ... ἐχόντων, Mark viii. 1; see also Luke ii. 17; vii. 49 : though, it must be confessed, it is the harshest example of its kind. σπλάγχνα, of *affectionate emotion* in general : **οἰκτιρμοί**, of the *compassionate* emotions in particular. So Tittm. p. 68 a : —tenderness and compassion, Conyb.— 'herzliche Liebe und Barmherzigkeit,' Luth.

I may remark, that the exhortation being addressed to the Philippians, the εἴ τις and εἴ τι are to be taken subjectively— **If there be with you any &c.** **2.**] **πληρώσατε** has the emphasis—'he already had joy in them, but it was not *complete*, because they did not walk in perfect unity:' cf. ch. i. 9. **ἵνα**, of the *purpose*, as always—but here as frequently, of a correlative result, *contemplated as* the purpose :

never, however, without reason : e. g., here the unanimity of the Philippians is the far greater and more important result, to which the πληροῦν μου τὴν χ. is but accessory. **τὸ αὐτὸ φρονῆτε**] This expression (be of the same mind) is more general than τὸ ἓν φρονοῦντες (*'being of one mind'*) below. And this is all that can be reasonably said of the difference between them. In the more fervid portions of such an Epistle as this, we must be prepared for something very nearly approaching to tautology. βαβαί, says Chrys., ποσάκις τὸ αὐτὸ λέγει ἀπὸ διαθέσεως πολλῆς. **τ. αὐτὴν ἀγάπ.** **ἔχοντες**] τουτέστιν, ὁμοίως καὶ φιλεῖν κ. φιλεῖσθαι, Chrys. **σύμψ. τὸ ἓν φρ.**] to be taken together as one designation only : σύμψ. having the emphasis, and defining the τὸ ἓν φρ., **with union of soul, unanimous** (minding one thing). So that the Apostle does not, as Œc., διπλασιάζει τὸ ὁμοφρονεῖν. **3.**] **μηδὲν— φρονοῦντες**, scil. from the last verse :— **entertaining no thought in a spirit of self- seeking** (see note, Rom. ii. 8, on the common mistaken rendering of this word), **nor in a spirit of vainglory** (κενοδοξία, ματαία τις περὶ ἑαυτοῦ οἴησις, Suidas), **but by means of humility of mind** (article either generic or possessive : in the latter case assuming ταπεινοφροσύνη as a Christian grace which you possess. The dative is either modal (ch. i. 18. Rom. iv. 20), or instrumental, or more properly perhaps, causal : see Ellicott's note) **esteeming one another superior to yourselves** (i. e. each

ἑαυτῶν ἕκαστοι [p] σκοποῦντες, ἀλλὰ καὶ τὰ ἑτέρων ἕκαστοι.
5 τοῦτο [f] φρονεῖτε ἐν ὑμῖν ὃ καὶ ἐν χριστῷ Ἰησοῦ, 6 ὃς
ἐν [q] μορφῇ θεοῦ [r] ὑπάρχων οὐχ [s] ἁρπαγμὸν [t] ἡγήσατο τὸ

ABCDF KLPℵ a b c d e f g h k l m n o 17. 47

p = 2 Cor. iv. 18 (Gal. vi. 1 reff.). q here bis. Mark xvi. 12 only. Isa. xliv. 13. r 1 Cor. xi. 7. Gal. i. 14 reff. particip., 1 Cor. ix. 19. Philem. 8. s here only †. (see note.) t = James i. 2. 2 Pet. iii. 15. (ver. 3 reff.) Job xli. 19.

4. for εαυτων, εαυτου C² Thl_1 : ετερου Thl_1. rec (for 1st εκαστοι) εκαστος, with CDKL[P]ℵ rel vss gr-ff [Hil Victorin]: txt ABF 17 vulg spec lat-ff. rec σκοπειτε, with L rel copt Chr Thdrt: σκοπειτω K k 73 syrr Thl [Victorin]: txt ABCDF[P]ℵ c 17 [47] latt goth arm Ath lat-ff. om και D¹FK o latt arm Bas lat-ff(not Aug). for 2nd τα, το D³K a h l n 67² Œc. ins των bef ετερων D¹F b¹ c k o. rec (for 2nd εκαστοι) εκαστος, with KL rel D-lat syrr goth [arm] Chr Cyr Thdrt: om F vulg lat-ff: txt ABD[P]ℵ 17 [47] copt Bas [Victorin]. (C defective.) ACℵ [17] Cyr join 2nd εκαστ. to follg.

5. rec aft τουτο ins γαρ, with DFKL[P]ℵ³ rel latt syr goth Chr Thdrt Damasc Hil Victorin Ambrst: om ABCℵ¹ k m 17 [copt] arm Orig [Eus] Ath &c. rec (for φρονειτε) φρονεισθω, with C³KL[P] rel copt goth arm Orig Eus_2 Ath Cyr_{aliq} Chr $Thdrt_2$ Damasc: φρονειτω εκαστος Cyr_{aliq} Thdot-ancyr: txt ABC¹DFℵ 17. 67² latt $Cyr_{sæpe}$ Hil [Victorin] Ambrst Pel Ruf.

6. om το F 109 Eus_2 Did.

man his neighbour better than himself); **each** (the plural is only found here in the N. T., and unusual elsewhere: it occurs in Thuc. i. 2, ῥᾳδίως ἕκαστοι τὴν ἑαυτῶν ἀπολείποντες,—Hom. Od. ι. 164, πολλὸν γὰρ ἐν ἀμφιφορεῦσιν ἕκαστοι ἠφύσαμεν) **regarding** (cf. both for expressions and sense, Herod. i. 8, πάλαι τὰ καλὰ ἀνθρώποισι ἐξεύρηται . . . ἐν τοῖσιν ἓν τόδε ἐστί, σκοπέειν τινὰ τὰ ἑωϋτοῦ: Thuc. vi. 12, τὸ ἑαυτοῦ μόνον σκοπῶν) **not their own matters, but each also the matters of others** ("this second clause (Mey.) is a feebler contrast than might have been expected after the absolute negation in the first." The καί shews that that first is to be taken with some allowance, for by our very nature, each man must σκοπεῖν τὰ ἑαυτοῦ in some measure). On the nature of the strife in the Philippian church, as shewn by the exhortations here, see Prolegg. § ii. 7. **5—11.**] *The exhortation enforced, by the example of the self-denial of Christ Jesus.* The monographs on this important passage, which are very numerous, may be seen enumerated in Meyer. **Think this in** (not '*among*,' on account of the **ἐν χρ. Ἰ.** following. On the reading, see various readings, and Fritzschiorum Opuscula, p. 49 note) **yourselves, which was** (ἐφρονεῖτο) **also in Christ Jesus** (as regards the dispute, whether the λόγος ἄσαρκος or the λόγος ἔνσαρκος be here spoken of, see below. I assume now, and will presently endeavour to prove, that the Apostle's reference is first to the *taking on Him* of our humanity, and then to his *further humiliation in* that humanity): **who subsisting** (originally: see on ὑπάρχω and εἰμί, Acts xvi. 20. Less cannot be implied in this word than eternal præ-existence. The participle is hardly equivalent to "although he subsisted," as Ellic., still less "inasmuch as he subsisted;" but simply states its fact as a link in the logical chain, "subsisting as He did;" without fixing the character of that link as causal or concessive) **in the form of God** (not merely the *nature* of God, which however is *implied:* but, as in Heb. i. 3, the ἀπαύγασμα τ. δόξης κ. χαρακτὴρ τ. ὑποστάσεως αὐτοῦ—cf. John v. 37, οὔτε εἶδος αὐτοῦ ἑωράκατε, with ib. xvii. 5, τῇ δόξῃ ᾗ εἶχον πρὸ τοῦ τὸν κόσμον εἶναι παρὰ σοί. "Ipsa natura divina decorum habebat infinitum in se, etiam sine ulla creatura illam gloriam intuente." Beng. See also Col. i. 15; 2 Cor. iv. 4. That the divine *nature* of Christ is not here meant, is clear: for He did not with reference to *this* ἐκένωσεν ἑαυτόν, ver. 7) **deemed not his equality** (notice ἴσα, not ἴσον, bringing out equality in nature and essence, rather than in Person) **with God a matter for grasping.** The expression is one very difficult to render. We may observe, (1) that **ἁρπαγμόν** holds * the emphatic place in the sentence: (2) that this fact casts τὸ εἶναι ἴσα θεῷ into the shade, as secondary in the sentence, and as referring to the state indicated by ἐν μορφῇ θεοῦ ὑπάρχων above: (3) that ἁρπαγμός strictly means, as here given, the *act* of seizing or snatching (so in the only place in profane writers where it occurs, viz. Plut. de Puerorum educ. p. 120 A, καὶ τοὺς μὲν Θήβησι κ. τοὺς Ἤλιδι φευκτέον ἔρωτας, κ. τὸν ἐκ Κρήτης καλούμενον **ἁρπαγμόν.** One thing must also be remembered,—that in the word, the leading idea is not 'snatching *from another*,' but 'snatching, grasping, *for one's self*:'—it answers to τὰ ἑαυτῶν σκοποῦντες above),

εἶναι [u]ἴσα [u]θεῷ, 7 ἀλλὰ ἑαυτὸν [v]ἐκένωσεν [q]μορφὴν δούλου [u]John v. 18.
τιμὴν ἴσα
θεοῖς, Diod.

Sic. i. 89. ἴσα τῷ θεῷ σέβειν, Paus. Corinth. 2. τιμὴν δὲ λελόγχασ᾽ ἴσα θεοῖσι, Hom. Odyss. λ. 304,
see 2 Macc. ix. 12. ἴσα, Luke vi. 34. Rev. xxi. 16 only. Wisd. vii. 4 only. -ος, Matt. xx. 12. Mark xiv.
56, 59. Johr as above. Acts xi. 17 only. Ezek. xl. 5. [v = here only. Jos. Antt. viii. 10. 3]
τοὺς θησαυροὺς ἐξεκένωσε. (Rom. iv. 14. 1 Cor. i. 17. ix. 15. 2 Cor. ix. 3 only. Jer. xiv. 2. xv. 9
only.)

7. (αλλα, so BF℘ [47].)

not (ἅρπαγμα) the *thing so seized* or
snatched : but that here, τὸ εἶναι ἴσα θεῷ,
i. e. a *state*, being in apposition with it,
the difference between the *act* (subjective)
and the *thing* (objective) would logically
be very small : (4) that τὸ εἶναι ἴσα θεῷ
is no *new* thing, which He thought it not
robbery to *be*, i. e. to *take upon Him*,—
but His state already existing, *respecting
which* He οὐχ ἡγήσατο &c.: (5) that this
clause, being opposed by ἀλλά to His
great act of self-denial, cannot be a mere
secondary one, conveying an additional
detail of His Majesty in His præ-existent
state, but must carry the whole weight of
the negation of selfishness on His part :
(6) that this last view is confirmed by the
ἡγήσατο, taking up and corresponding to
ἡγούμενοι above, ver. 3. (7) Other renderings have been :—(α) of those who hold
τὸ εἶναι ἴσα θεῷ, as above to be virtually
identical with ἐν μορφῇ θεοῦ ὑπάρχειν before,—Chrys. says, ὁ τοῦ θεοῦ υἱὸς οὐκ
ἐφοβήθη καταβῆναι ἀπὸ τοῦ ἀξιώματος.
οὐ γὰρ ἁρπαγμὸν ἡγήσατο τὴν θεότητα,
οὐκ ἐδεδοίκει μή τις αὐτὸν ἀφέληται τὴν
φύσιν ἢ τὸ ἀξίωμα. διὸ καὶ ἀπέθετο αὐτό,
θαρρῶν ὅτι αὐτὸ ἀναλήψεται· καὶ ἔκρυψεν,
ἡγούμενος οὐδὲν ἐλαττοῦσθαι ἀπὸ τούτου.
διὰ τοῦτο οὐκ εἶπεν οὐχ ἥρπασεν, ἀλλὰ
οὐχ ἁρπαγμὸν ἡγήσατο, ὅτι οὐχ ἁρπάσας
εἶχε τὴν ἀρχήν, ἀλλὰ φυσικήν, οὐ δε-
δομένην, ἀλλὰ μόνιμον κ. ἀσφαλῆ.— And
so in the main, Œc., Thl., Aug.:—Beza,
"*non ignoravit, se in ea re* (quod Deo
patri coequalis esset) *nullam injuriam cuiquam facere, sed suo jure uti : nihilominus
tamen quasi jure suo cessit*"—and so Calvin, but wrongly maintaining for ἡγήσατο
a subjunctive sense : '*non fuisset arbitra-
tus:*' Thdrt., θεὸς γὰρ ὤν, κ. φύσει θεός, κ.
τὴν πρὸς τὸν πατέρα ἰσότητα ἔχων, οὐ
μέγα τοῦτο ὑπέλαβε. τοῦτο γὰρ ἴδιον
τῶν παρ᾽ ἀξίαν τιμῆς τινος τετυχηκότων.
ἀλλὰ τὴν ἀξίαν κατακρύψας, τὴν ἄκραν
ταπεινοφροσύνην εἵλετο, κ. τὴν ἀνθρω-
πείαν ὑπέδυ μορφήν: and so, nearly,
Ambr., Castal., all.;—Luther, Erasm.,
Grot., Calov., all.,—'*He did not as a
victor his spoils, make an exhibition of
&c., but*' .... (β) of those who distinguish
τὸ εἶναι ἴσα θεῷ from ἐν μορφῇ θεοῦ ὑπάρχειν : Bengel,—'*Christus, quum posset
esse pariter Deo, non arripuit, non duxit

*rapinam, non subito usus est illa facul-
tate:*' De Wette, ' *Christ had, when He
began His Messianic course, the glory of
the godhead potentially in Himself, and
might have devoted Himself to manifesting
it forth in His life : but seeing that it lay
not in the purpose of the work of Redemption that He should at the commencement
of it have taken to Himself divine honour,
had He done so, the assumption of it would
have been an act of robbery:*'—Lünemann
(in Meyer): ' *Christus, etsi ab æterno
inde dignitate creatoris et domini rerum
omnium frueretur, ideoque divina indutus
magnificentia coram patre consideret, ni-
hilo tamen minus haud arripiendum sibi
esse autumabat existendi modum cum Deo
æqualem, sed ultro se exinanivit.*' And in
fact Arius (and his party) had led the way
in this explanation : ὅτι θεὸς ὢν ἐλάττων
οὐχ ἥρπασε τὸ εἶναι ἴσα τῷ θεῷ τῷ με-
γάλῳ καὶ μείζονι. See this triumphantly
answered in Chrys. Hom. vi. in loc. Indeed
the whole of this method of interpretation
is rightly charged with absurdity by Chrys.,
seeing that in ἐν μορφῇ θεοῦ ὑπάρχειν we
have already equality with God expressed :
εἰ ἦν θεός, πῶς εἶχεν ἁρπάσαι; κ. πῶς
οὐκ ἀπερινόητον τοῦτο; τίς γὰρ ἂν εἴποι,
ὅτι ὁ δεῖνα, ἄνθρωπος ὤν, οὐχ ἥρπασε τὸ
εἶναι ἄνθρωπος; πῶς γὰρ ἂν τις ὕπερ
ἐστίν, ἁρπάσειεν; (8) We have now to enquire, whether the opening of the passage will bear to be understood of our
Lord *already incarnate.* De Wette, al.,
have maintained that the name χριστὸς
Ἰησοῦς cannot apply to the λόγος ἄσαρκος. But the answer to this is easy, viz.
that that name applies to the *entire historical Person* of our Lord, of whom
the whole passage is said, and not merely
to Him in his præ-existent state. That
one and the same Person of the Son of
God, ἐν μορφῇ θεοῦ ὑπάρχων, afterwards
ἐν ὁμοιώματι ἀνθρώπων ἐγένετο, gathering to itself the humanity, in virtue of
which He is now designated in the concrete, Christ Jesus. So that the dispute
virtually resolves itself into the question
between the two lines of interpretation
given above,—on which I have already
pronounced. But it seems to me to
be satisfactorily settled by the contrast
between ἐν μορφῇ θεοῦ ὑπάρχων and

w = here only.
x Rom. i. 23.
v. 14.　vi. 5.
viii. 3.　Rev.
ix. 7 only.
Ps. cv. 20.
y Rom. i. 3.
Acts xix. 26.　Gal. iv. 4.
xvii. 18.　2 Cor. v. 3.　1 Kings xiii. 15.
39.　2 Cor. ii. 9 only.　Prov. iv. 3. xiii. 1.
vii. 16.　　　e = Rom. iii. 22.
z 1 Cor. vii. 31 only.　Isa. iii. 17 only.
b Matt. xviii. 4. xxiii. 12 al.　Prov. xiii. 7.
d = 2 Tim. ii. 9.　Heb. xii. 4.　2 Macc. xiii. 14.　3 Macc.
a = Matt. i. 18.　Luke
c Acts vii.

ʷ λαβών, ἐν ˣ ὁμοιώματι ἀνθρώπων ʸ γενόμενος, ⁸ καὶ ᶻ σχήματι ᵃ εὑρεθεὶς ὡς ἄνθρωπος ᵇ ἐταπείνωσεν ἑαυτόν, γενόμενος ᶜ ὑπήκοος ᵈ μέχρι θανάτου, θανάτου ᵉ δὲ σταυ-

8. ins τον bef σταυρου ℵ.

μορφὴν δούλου λαβών. These two cannot belong to Christ in the same incarnate state. Therefore the former of them must refer to his *præ-incarnate* state.

　7.] **but emptied Himself** (ἑαυτόν emphatic, — not ἐκένωσεν ἑαυτόν. ἐκένωσεν, contrast to ἁρπαγμὸν ἡγήσ. — he not only did not *enrich* himself, but he *emptied* himself :—He used His equality with God as an opportunity, not for self-exaltation, but for self-abasement. And the word simply and literally means, '*exinanivit*' (vulg.) as above. He emptied Himself of the μορφὴ θεοῦ (not His *essential* glory, but its *manifested* possession : see on the words above : the glory which He had with the Father before the world began, John xvii. 5, and which He resumed at His glorification)—He ceased, while in this state of exinanition, to reflect the glory which He had with the Father. Those who understand ὅς above of the *incarnate* Saviour, are obliged to explain away this powerful word: thus Calv., '*in initio hæc eadem est cum humiliatione de qua postea videbimus:*' Calov., '*veluti deposuit:*' Le Clerc, '*non magis ea usus est, quam si ea destitutus fuisset:*' De W., 'the manner and form of the κένωσις is given by the three following participles' (λαβών, γενόμενος, εὑρεθείς): alii aliter) **by taking the form of a servant** (specification of the *method in which* He emptied Himself: not co-ordinate with (as De W., al.) but *subordinate to* ἐκένωσεν ἑαυτόν. The participle λαβών does not point to that which has preceded ἑαυτ. ἐκέν., but to a simultaneous act, = as in εὖ γ᾽ ἐποίησας ἀναμνήσας με (Plato, Phæd. p. 60 D), see Bernhardy, Synt. p. 383, and Harless on Eph. i. 13. And so of γενόμενος below. The δοῦλος is contrasted with 'equality with God'—and imports '*a servant of God,*'—not *a servant generally,* nor a servant of man and God. And this state, of a *servant of God,* is further defined by what follows) being made (by birth into the world,—'*becoming:*' but we must not render the general, γενόμενος, by the particular, '*being born*') **in the likeness of men** (cf. ἐν ὁμοιώματι σαρκὸς ἁμαρτίας, Rom. viii. 3. He was not a *man, purus putus homo* (Mey.), but the Son of God

manifest in the flesh and nature of men. On the interpretation impugned above, which makes all these clauses refer to acts of Christ, in our *nature,* this word ὁμοιώματι loses all meaning. But on the right interpretation, it becomes forcible in giving another subordinate specification to μορφὴν δούλου λαβών—viz. that He was made in *like form* to *men,* who are θεοῦ δοῦλοι). 8.] My interpretation has hitherto come very near to that of Meyer. But here I am compelled to differ from him. He would join καὶ σχ. εὑρ. ὡς ἄνθρ. to the foregoing, put a period at ἄνθρ., and begin the next sentence by ἐταπείνωσεν without a copula. The main objection to this with me, is, the word εὑρεθείς. It seems to denote the taking up afresh of the subject, and introducing a new portion of the history. Hitherto of the act of laying aside the form of God, specified to have consisted in μορφὴν δούλου λαβεῖν, and ἐν ὁμ. ἀνθρώπων γενέσθαι. But now we take Him up again, this having past; we *find* Him in his human appearance—and what then? we have further acts of self-humiliation to relate. So Van Hengel: "duo enim, ut puto, diversa hic tradit Paulus, et quamnam vivendi rationem Christus inierit, ... et quomodo hanc vivendi rationem ad mortem usque persecutus sit." **And when He was** (having been) **found in having** (guise, outward semblance; e. g. of look, and dress, and speech. σχήματι is a more specific repetition of ὁμοιώμ. above: and is here *emphatic:* 'being found in *habit,* &c. He did not stop with this outward semblance, but . . . .') **as a man** (for He was not *a man,* but God (in Person), with the humanity taken on Him: ὡς ἄνθρωπος—ἢ γὰρ ἀναληφθεῖσα φύσις τοῦτο ἦν· αὐτὸς δὲ τοῦτο οὐκ ἦν, τοῦτο δὲ περιέκειτο, Thdrt.) **He humbled himself** (in His humanity : a further act of self-denial. This time, ἑαυτόν does not precede, because, as Meyer well says,—in ver. 7 the pragmatic weight rested on the *reflexive reference* of the act, but here on the *reflexive act* itself) **by becoming** (see on the aorist participle above. It specifies, *wherein the* ταπείνωσις *consisted*) **obedient** (to God ; as before in the δούλου: not '*capientibus se, dam-*

ρου. ⁹ ᶠδιὸ ᶠκαὶ ὁ θεὸς αὐτὸν ᵍὑπερύψωσεν καὶ ʰἐχαρί- ᶠ= [Rom. i. 24.
σατο αὐτῷ [τὸ] ⁱὄνομα τὸ ὑπὲρ πᾶν ⁱὄνομα, ¹⁰ ⁱνα ᵏἐν ᵍ here only.
τῷ ⁱὀνόματι Ἰησοῦ πᾶν ˡγόνυ ˡᵐκάμψῃ ⁿἐπουρανίων καὶ

iv. 22.]
1 Cor. v. 9.
g here only.
Ps. xxxvi.
35. xcvi. 9.
Song of 3
children,

passim. Dan. iv. 34, 37 Theod.   h Luke vii. 21.   Rom. viii. 32.   Gal. iii. 18. ch. i. 29†.   2 Macc. iii. 33.
i = Eph. i. 21 reff.   k = John xiv. 13.   Eph. v. 20 al.   1 Eph. iii. 14 reff.   m intr.,
Rom. xiv. 11, from Isa. xlv. 24.   n = John iii. 12. 1 Cor. xv. 40 al. (Eph. i. 3 reff.)   Dan. iv.
23 (26) Theod. A Compl. Ald. (οὖρ., B F.)

9. rec om 1st το, with DFKL[P] rel [Clem] Orig₃ Eus₃ Ath₃ Epiph Chr Cyr₃ Thdrt₂
Procl Damasc : ins ABCℵ 17 [Hipp] Dion Eus₂ Cyr[-psæpe] Procop₃.—ins εις bef το
υπερ F, ut sit super Cypr.   aft ιησ. ins χριστου ℵ¹(om ℵ³) [47 syr-w-ast æth
Orig₁].

nantibus et interficientibus,' as Grot. See
Rom. v. 19, Heb. v. 8 f., and ver. 9,—διὸ
καὶ ὁ θεός,—referring to the τῷ θεῷ here
understood) **even unto** (as far as) **death**
(the climax of His obedience. μέχρι θανάτου must not be taken with ἐταπείνωσεν,
as Beng., al., which breaks the sentence
awkwardly), **and that the death of the**
* **cross** (on this sense of δέ, see ref., and note
there :—τουτέστι, τοῦ ἐπικαταράτου, τοῦ
τοῖς ἀνόμοις ἀφωρισμένου, Thl.).
9—11.] *Exaltation of Jesus, consequent
on this His humiliation:*—brought forward as an encouragement to follow His
example. "Quod autem beati sint quicunque sponte humiliantur cum Christo,
probat ejus exemplo: nam a despectis-
sima sorte evectus fuit in summam alti-
tudinem. Quicunque ergo se humiliat,
similiter exaltabitur. Quis nunc submis-
sionem recuset, qua in gloriam regni cœlestis conscenditur?" Calvin. **Wherefore** (i.e.
on account of this His self-humiliation
and obedience : see Heb. ii. 9, note : not
as Calv., *'quo facto,'* trying to evade the
meritorious obedience of Christ thus, 'quod
dictio illativa hic magis consequentiam
sonet quam causam, hinc patet, quod alio-
qui sequetur, hominem divinos honores
posse mereri et ipsum Dei thronum ac-
quirere, quod non modo absurdum sed
dictu etiam horrendum est:' strangely forgetting that herein Christ was not *a man,*
nor an example what we can do, but the
eternal Son of God, lowering Himself to
take the nature of men, and in it rendering
voluntary and perfect obedience) **also** (introduces the result, reff. and Luke i. 35 ;
Acts x. 29) **God** (on His part: reference to
the τῷ θεῷ understood after ὑπήκοος
above) **highly exalted Him** (not only
ὕψωσεν, but ὑπερύψωσεν ; His exaltation being a super-eminent one, cf. ὑπερ-
νικᾶν, Rom. viii. 37, also 2 Cor. xii. 7 ;
2 Thess. i. 3. Not, *'hath* highly exalted :' the reference is to a historical fact,
viz. that of His Ascension), **and gave to
Him** (the Father being greater than the
incarnate Son, John xiv. 28, and having

by His exaltation of Jesus to His throne,
freely bestowed on him the kingly office,
which is the completion of His Mediatorship, Rom. xiv. 9) **the name which is
above every name** (ὄνομα must be kept,
against most Commentators, to its plain
sense of NAME,—and not rendered '*glory,'*
or understood of His office. The name
is, the very name which He bore in His
humiliation, but which now is the highest
and most glorious of all names, τὸ ὄνομα
Ἰησοῦ. Compare His own answer in
glory, Acts ix. 5, ἐγώ εἰμι Ἰησοῦς, ὃν σὺ
διώκεις. As to the construction in the
rec., without the τό before ὄνομα, the
indefinite ὄνομα is afterwards *defined* to
be *that* name, which we all know and
reverence, by τὸ ὑπὲρ κ.τ.λ. The τό before ὄνομα may have been inserted to
assimilate the expression to the more
usual one),   **10.]** that (intent of this
exaltation) **in the name of Jesus** (empha- *
tic, as the ground and element of the act
which follows) **every knee should bend**
(i. e. all prayer should be made (not, as
E. V., '*at* the name of Jesus every knee
should bow,'—which surely the words will
not bear). But *what* prayer? *to* JESUS,
or *to* GOD THROUGH HIM? The only
way to answer this question is to regard
the general aim of the passage. This undoubtedly is, the *exaltation of Jesus.*
The εἰς δόξαν θεοῦ πατρός below is no
deduction from this, but rather an additional reason why we should carry on the
exaltation of Jesus *until this new particular is introduced.* This would lead us
to infer that the universal prayer is to be
to JESUS. And this view is confirmed by
the next clause, where every tongue is to
confess that Jesus Christ is κύριος, when
we remember the common expression,
ἐπικαλεῖσθαι τὸ ὄνομα κυρίου, for prayer :
Rom. x. 12 f. ; 1 Cor. i. 2 (2 Tim. ii. 22) ;
Acts (vii. 59) ix. 14, 21 ; xxii. 16), **of
those in heaven** (angels. Eph. i. 20, 21.
Heb. i. 6) **and those on earth** (men) **and
those under the earth** (the dead: so Hom.
Il. ι. 457, Ζεὺς καταχθόνιος, Pluto ; so

o John iii. 12. 1 Cor. xv. 40 bis. 2 Cor. 1. ch. iii. 19. James iii. 15 only †.
p here only †.
q Rom. xiv. 11. xv. 9. Matt. xi. 25. Isa. l. c. A$\aleph^{3b}$. (ὁμεῖται, B$\aleph$1.)
r = 1 Cor. v. 8. xi. 33. xiv. 39. ch. iv. 1 al. only. Ps. cxxvi. 2.

ABCDF KLP$\aleph$ a b c d e f g h k l m n o 17. 47

ᵒἐπιγείων καὶ ᵖκαταχθονίων, 11 καὶ πᾶσα γλῶσσα ᑫἐξ-
ομολογήσεται ὅτι κύριος Ἰησοῦς χριστὸς εἰς δόξαν θεοῦ
πατρός. 12 ʳὥςτε, ˢἀγαπητοί μου, καθὼς πάντοτε ὑπηκούσατε, μὴ ὡς ἐν τῇ ᵗπαρουσίᾳ μου μόνον, ἀλλὰ νῦν
πολλῷ μᾶλλον ἐν τῇ ᵘἀπουσίᾳ μου ᵛμετὰ ᵛφόβου καὶ
ᵛτρόμου τὴν ʷἑαυτῶν σωτηρίαν ˣκατεργάζεσθε, 13 θεὸς

s w. gen., Matt. xii. 18. Acts xv. 25. Rom. i. 7. xvi. 5, &c. 1 Cor. x. 14
t = ch. i. 26 reff.
u here only †.
v Eph. vi. 5 reff.
w 2nd pers., Rom. vi. 11, 13, 16. 1 Cor. vi. 19. 2 Cor. vii. 11 al.
x = Rom. iv. 15. v. 3. 2 Cor. vii. 10 al.

11. rec εξομολογησηται, with B$\aleph$ rel [Iren$_1$ Clem$_2$] Eus Cyr$_4$: txt ACDFKL[P] a(in lect at end of ms) d e k m [47] Orig$_5$ [Eus$_3$ Cyr$_2$-p] Ath-3-mss [Hil]. om χριστος F(not F-lat) Eus [Novat Hil$_{sæpe}$].

12. for αγαπητοι, αδελφοι A, some lectionaries, demid æth. om ως B 3. 17. 48. 72. 178 Syr copt [æth] arm Chr$_1$ lat-ff. om 1st εν F$\aleph^3$ fuld D-lat G-lat Ambrst. πολ. μαλ. bef νυν DF latt arm [Victorin] Ambrst Pel: om νυν f k 4. 33. 115 Chr-comm Thl. om εν τη απουσ. μου F.

Thdrt.: ἐπουρανίους καλεῖ τοὺς ἀοράτους δυνάμεις, ἐπιγείους δὲ τοὺς ἔτι ζῶντας ἀνθρώπους, καὶ καταχθονίους τοὺς τεθνεῶτας. Various erroneous interpretations have been given—e. g. Chr., Thl., Œc., Erasm. understand by καταχθ., the *devils* —and Chr., Thl. give metaphorical meanings, οἱ δίκαιοι κ. οἱ ἁμαρτωλοί), **11.**] **and every tongue** (of all the classes just named) **shall confess** (result of the πᾶν γόνυ κάμψαι) **that Jesus Christ is Lord** (see the predicate κύριος similarly prefixed in 1 Cor. xii. 3) **to the glory** (so as for such confession to issue in the glory) **of God the Father** (which is the great end of all Christ's mediation and mediatorial kingdom, cf. 1 Cor. xv. 24—28. 'Ut Dei majestas in Christo reluceat, et Pater glorificetur in Filio. Vide Johan. v. et xvii., et habebis hujus loci expositionem.' Calv.). **12—16.**] *After this glorious example, he exhorts them to earnestness after Christian perfection.*

12. ὥςτε] **wherefore**—i. e. as a consequence on this pattern set you by Christ. The **ὑπηκούσατε** answers to γενόμενος ὑπήκοος ver. 8, and **σωτηρία** to the exaltation of Christ. It is therefore better, with Meyer, to refer **ὥςτε** to that which has just preceded, than with De Wette, Wiesinger, al., to all the foregoing exhortations, ch. i. 27 ff. **ὑπηκούσατε**] i. e. *to God*, as Christ above: not as ordinarily, 'to *me*' or '*my Gospel*.' This last De W. grounds on the presence and absence of the Apostle mentioned below: those clauses however do not belong to ὑπηκούσατε, but to κατεργάζεσθε. This is evident by μὴ ὡς and νῦν. In fact it would be hardly possible logically to connect them with ὑπηκούσατε. As it is, they connect admirably with κατεργάζεσθε, see below. **ὡς** is by no means superfluous, but gives the sense **not as if** (it were a matter to be done) **in my presence only,—but now** (as things are at present) **much more** (with more earnestness) **in my absence** (because spiritual help from me is withdrawn from you) **carry out** (bring to an accomplishment) **your own** (emphasis on ἑαυτῶν, perhaps as directing attention to the example of Christ which has preceded,—as He obeyed and won His exaltation, so do *you* obey and carry out *your own* salvation) **salvation** (which is *begun* with justification by faith, but must be carried out, brought to an issue, by sanctification of the Spirit—a life of holy obedience and advance to Christian perfection. For this reason, the E. V., '*work out* your own salvation,' is bad, because ambiguous, giving the idea that the salvation is a thing to be gotten, brought in and brought about, by ourselves) **with fear and trembling** (lest you * should fail of its accomplishment at the last. The expression indicates a state of anxiety and self-distrust: see reff.—δεῖ γὰρ φοβεῖσθαι κ. τρέμειν ἐν τῷ ἐργάζεσθαι τὴν ἰδίαν σωτηρίαν ἕκαστον, μήποτε ὑποσκελισθεὶς ἐκπέσῃ ταύτης. Œc. in Meyer. And the stress of the exhortation is on these words:—considering the immense sacrifice which Christ made for you, and the lofty eminence to which God hath now raised Him, be ye more than ever earnest that you miss not your own share in such salvation. The thought before the Apostle's mind is much the same as that in Heb. ii. 3, πῶς ἡμεῖς ἐκφευξόμεθα τηλικαύτης ἀμελήσαντες σωτηρίας;):

13.] encouragement to fulfil the last exhortation—for you are not left to yourselves, but have the almighty Spirit

γάρ ἐστιν ὁ ⁿ ἐνεργῶν ἐν ὑμῖν καὶ τὸ θέλειν καὶ τὸ ⁿ ἐνεργεῖν ᶻ ὑπὲρ τῆς ᵃ εὐδοκίας. ¹⁴ ᵇ πάντα ποιεῖτε χωρὶς
ᶜ γογγυσμῶν καὶ ᵈ διαλογισμῶν, ¹⁵ ἵνα γένησθε ᵉ ἄμεμπτοι

y Paul (1 Cor.
xii. 6 al15.)
only, exc.
Matt. xiv. 2 ‖.
James v. 16.
Isa. xli. 4.
z = Rom. xv.
8.   a = Eph. i. 4 reff.   b = 1 Cor. x. 31.   c John vii. 12.   Acts vi. 1.   1 Pet.
iv. 9 only.   Exod. xvi. 7, 9.   d = Luke xxiv. 38.   1 Tim. ii. 8.   e Luke i
6. ch. iii. 6.   1 Thess. iii. 13.   Heb. viii. 7 only.   Gen. xvii. 1.   (-τως, 1 Thess. ii. 10.)

13. rec ins ὁ bef θεος, with D²·³L rel : om ABCD¹FK[P]א 17 [Eus] Damasc.
aft ενεργων ins δυναμεις A.   aft ευδοκιας ins αυτου C.

15. for γενησθε, ητε AD¹F latt : txt BCD³KL[P]א rel Chr Thdrt Philo-carp Damasc.

dwelling in you to aid you. "Intelligo," says Calvin, "gratiam supernaturalem, quæ provenit ex Spiritu regenerationis. Nam quatenus sumus homines, jam in Deo sumus, et vivimus, et movemur; verum hic de alio motu disputat, quam illo universali." This working must not be explained away with Pelagius (in Mey.), 'velle operatur *suadendo* et *præmia promittendo:*' it is an efficacious working which is here spoken of : God not only *brings about* the will, but *creates* the will —we owe both the will to do good, and the power, to His indwelling Spirit. ἐν ὑμ. not *among you*, but **in you**, as in ref. 1 Cor., and 2 Cor. iv. 12 ; Eph. ii. 2 ; Col. i. 29. The θέλειν and ἐνεργεῖν are well explained by Calvin : "Fatemur, nos a natura habere voluntatem : sed quoniam peccati corruptione mala est, tunc bona esse incipit, quum reformata est a Deo. Nec dicimus hominem quicquam boni facere, nisi volentem : sed tunc, quum voluntas regitur a Spiritu Dei. Ergo quod ad hanc partem spectat, videmus Deo integram laudem asseri, ac frivolum esse quod sophistæ docent, offerri nobis gratiam et quasi in medio poni, ut eam amplectemur si libeat. Nisi enim efficaciter ageret Deus in nobis, non diceretur efficere bonam voluntatem. De secunda parte idem sentiendum. Deus, inquit, est (ὁ) ἐνεργῶν ἐνεργεῖν. Perducit igitur ad finem usque pios affectus, quos nobis inspiravit, ne sint irriti : sicut per Ezechielem (xi. 20) promittit : Faciam ut in præceptis meis ambulent. Unde colligimus, perseverantiam quoque merum esse ejus donum." ὑπὲρ τῆς εὐδοκίας) **for the sake of His good pleasure,—**i. e. in order to carry out that good counsel of His will which He hath purposed towards you : εὐδοκίαν δὲ τὸ ἀγαθὸν τοῦ θεοῦ προσηγόρευσε θέλημα· θέλει δὲ πάντας ἀνθρώπους σωθῆναι, κ. εἰς ἐπίγνωσιν ἀληθείας ἐλθεῖν, Thdrt. Conyb. would join ὑπὲρ τῆς εὐδ. with the following verse, —'do all things for the sake of good will'—and remarks, ' It is strange that so clear and simple a construction, involving no alteration in the text, should not have

been before suggested.' But surely St. Paul could not have written thus. The sense of εὐδοκία indeed, would be the same as in ch. i. 15 :—but that very passage should have prevented this conjecture. It must have been in that case here as there, δι' εὐδοκίαν, or at all events, ὑπὲρ εὐδοκίας : the insertion of the article where it is generally omitted from abstract nouns after a preposition, as here, necessarily brings in a reflexive sense,—to be referred to the subject of the sentence : and thus we should get a meaning very different from that given by Conyb., viz. : ' Do all things for the sake of (to carry out) *your own* good pleasure.' It has been proposed (I know not by whom, but it was communicated to me by letter : I see it also noticed in Ellic.'s note, and Van Hengel's refutation of it referred to) to take ἑαυτῶν (ver. 12) as = ἀλλήλων, and render " with fear and trembling labour heartily for one another's salvation;" thus connecting the ὥστε with ver. 4. The suggestion is ingenious, and as far as the *mere question* of the *sense* of ἑαυτῶν goes, perhaps allowable ; but see Eph. iv. 32 ; Col. iii. 13, 16 ; 1 Pet. iv. 8, 10 : there are, however, weighty and I conceive fatal objections to it. 1) the emphatic position of ἑαυτῶν, which restricts it to its *proper* meaning : 2) the occurrence of ἑαυτῶν, in the very verse (4) with which it is sought to connect our passage, *in its proper meaning*—μὴ τὰ ἑαυτῶν ἕκαστοι σκοπεῖτε, ἀλλὰ καὶ τὰ ἑτέρων ἕκαστοι : 3) the context, and inference drawn by ὥστε, which this rendering altogether mistakes : see it explained above. **14 ff.**] *More detailed exhortations*, as to the manner of their Christian energizing. γογγυσμός, in every other place in the N. T. (reff.), as also in ref. Exod., signifies murmuring against men, not against God (as Mey.). And the context here makes it best to keep the same sense : such murmurings arising from selfishness, which is especially discommended to us by the example of Christ. This I still maintain as against Ellic. : his rejection of John vii. 12 and 1 Pet. iv. 9, as not applicable, not seeming to me to be

f Matt. x. 16.
Rom. xvi. 19
only.
g = John i. 12.
∑i. 52. Rom.
viii. 16, 21.
ix. 4. 1 John
iii. 1, &c. v.
2 only.

καὶ f ἀκέραιοι, g τέκνα θεοῦ h ἄμωμα i μέσον kl γενεᾶς
km σκολιᾶς καὶ ln διεστραμμένης, ἐν o οἷς φαίνεσθε ὡς p φωστῆρες ἐν κόσμῳ, 16 q λόγον q ζωῆς r ἐπέχοντες, εἰς s καύ-

ABCDF
KLPℵ a
bcdefg
hklmn
o 17.47

h Eph. i. 4 reff. (-μητος, 2 Pet. iii. 14 only.) see DEUT. xxxii. 5.   i adv., Num. xxxv.
5.   Hom. Il. μ. 167.   Od. ξ. 300.   k Acts ii. 40.   Deut. xxxii. 5.   1 Matt. xvii. 17 ᵈ.   m as
above (k).   Luke iii. 5, from Isa. xl. 4.   1 Pet. ii. 18 only.   n as above (l).   Luke xxiii. 2.   Acts
xiii. 8, 10. xx. 30 only.   Prov. vi. 14.   o constr., Matt. i. 21. xiv. 14.   John xv. 6.   Josh. xv. 1.   Winer, edn.
6, § 21. 3.   p Rev. xxi. 11 only.   Gen. i. 14, 16.   q 1 John i. 1 only. see Acts v.
20.   xiii. 26.   r = here only.   Hom. Il. χ. 83, μαζὸν. 494, κοτύλην.   Od. π. 444, οἶνον.   (1 Tim.
iv. 16 reff.)   s Gal. vi. 4 reff.   constr., 1 Cor. ix. 16.

rec (for αμωμα) αμωμητα, with DFKL[P] rel Chr Thdrt Philo-carp Damasc:
txt ABCℵ 17 (Clem) Cyr.   rec (for μεσον) εν μεσω (explanatory corrn), with
D².³KL rel: txt ABCD¹F[P]ℵ 17. 67² Clem.   εν τω κοσμω τουτω in hoc mundo
F D-lat spec Chrom Leo [Orig-int₁].
16. εχοντες ℵ¹(txt ℵ-corr¹).

justified.   διαλογισμῶν] by the same
rule, we should rather understand disputings with men, than doubts respecting
God or duty (Mey.).   It is objected that
the N. T. meaning of διαλογισμός is generally the latter.   But this may be doubted
(see on 1 Tim. ii. 8); and at all events the
verb διαλογίζω, and its cognate διαλέγο-
μαι, must be taken for 'to dispute' in
Mark ix. 33, 34.   I cannot understand
how either word can apply to matters
merely internal, seeing that the primary
object is stated below to be blamelessness, and good example to others: cf.
μέσον γενεᾶς, κ.τ.λ.   15.] ἄμεμπτοι,
without blame, ἀκέραιοι, "pure, simplices,
vulg æth: sinceres (i), Clarom.: ὁ μὴ
κεκραμένος κακοῖς, ἀλλ' ἁπλοῦς καὶ ἀποί-
κιλος, Etym. Mag. . . . .   For the distinction between ἀκέραιος, ἁπλοῦς, and ἄκακος,
see Tittm. Synon. i. p. 27." Ellicott.
On τέκνα θεοῦ, see especially Rom. viii.
14, 15.   ἄμωμα, blameless: unblamed,
and unblamable: Herod. uses it, ii. 177,
of a law: τῷ ἐκεῖνοι ἐς αἰεὶ χρέωνται,
ἐόντι ἀμώμῳ νόμῳ.   The whole clause is
a reminiscence of ref. Deut., where we
have τέκνα μωμητά, γενεὰ σκολιὰ κ. διεστραμμένη.   For the figurative meaning of σκολιός, cf. reff. Acts and 1 Pet.,
and Plato, Legg. xii. p. 945 B, ἄν τίς τι εἴπῃ
σκολιὸν αὐτῶν ἢ πράξῃ,—Gorg. p. 525 A,
πάντα σκολιὰ ὑπὸ ψεύδους κ. ἀλαζονείας,
κ. οὐδὲν εὐθὺ διὰ τὸ ἄνευ ἀληθείας τε-
θράφθαι:—and on διεστραμμένη, — δι-
εστρέφετο ὑπὸ κόλακος, Polyb. viii. 24. 3.
ἐν οἷς, the masculine referring to
those included in γενεά: so Thuc. i. 136,
φεύγει—ἐς Κέρκυραν, ὧν αὐτῶν εὐεργέτης.
See more examples in Kühner, ii. p. 43.
φαίνεσθε, not imperative, as most
of the Fathers, Erasm., Calvin, Grot., al.,
—but indicative, for this is the position
of Christians in the world: see Matt. v.
14; Eph. v. 8.   So De W., Meyer, Wiesinger, &c. &c.   It has been said (Mey.,

Wies., al.) that we must not render φαίνεσθε 'shine,' which would be φαίνετε:
but surely there is but very little difference
between 'appear' and 'shine' here, and
only St. John and St. Peter use φαίνω for
'to shine,' John i. 5; v. 35; 1 John ii. 8;
Rev. i. 16; 2 Pet. i. 19,—not St. Paul,
for whom in such a matter their usage is
no rule.   Ellic. 1) objects that this must
not be alleged against the simple meaning
of the word, and 2) wishes to give the
middle a special use in connexion with
the appearance or rising of the heavenly
bodies.   But we may answer 1) by such
examples as δεινοὶ δέ οἱ ὄσσε φάανθεν,
where Rost and Palm translate the passive
'leuchteten:' and 2) by urging that such a
reference seems here to lay too much
pregnancy of meaning on the word.
φωστῆρες, not 'lights' merely, but lumi-
naries, 'heavenly bodies:' see ref. Gen.:
and Sir. xliii. 7, Wisd. xiii. 2.
ἐπέχοντες] probably as E. V. holding ✳
forth (hardly, as Ellic., "seeing ye hold
forth," but " in that ye hold forth :" the
participle being rather explicative than
causal) to them, applying to them, which
is the one of the commonest meanings
of ἐπέχειν,—see reff.   Various senses have
been given,—e. g. 'holding fast,' Luther,
Estius, Bengel, De Wette, al.: 'in vertice
tenentes,' Erasm.: 'sustinentes,' Calv.:
'possessing,' Meyer, who quotes for this
meaning Herod. i. 104, οἱ δὲ Σκύθαι τὴν
'Ασίαν πᾶσαν ἐπέσχον, and Thuc. ii. 101,
ὁ δὲ τήν τε Χαλκιδικὴν κ. Βοττικὴν κ.
Μακεδονίαν ἅμα ἐπέχων ἔφθειρε,—neither
of which justify it: for in both these
places it is 'to occupy,' not 'to possess:'
as also in Polyb. iii. 112. 8, εὐχαὶ κ. θυσίαι
κ.τ.λ. . . . . ἐπεῖχον τὴν πόλιν.   And this
sense would manifestly be inapplicable.
His objection to the ordinary rendering,
that the subjects of the sentence themselves shine by means of the λόγος τῆς
ζωῆς, surely is irrelevant: for may not

χῆμα ἐμοὶ ᵗ εἰς ᵘ ἡμέραν χριστοῦ, ὅτι οὐκ ᵛ εἰς ᵛʷ κενὸν
ˣ ἔδραμον οὐδὲ ᵛ εἰς ᵛʷ κενὸν ʸ ἐκοπίασα. ¹⁷ ἀλλὰ ᶻ εἰ ᶻ καὶ
ᵃ σπένδομαι ᵇ ἐπὶ τῇ θυσίᾳ καὶ ᶜ λειτουργίᾳ τῆς πίστεως
ὑμῶν, χαίρω καὶ ᵈ συγχαίρω πᾶσιν ὑμῖν· ¹⁸ ᵉ τὸ δ᾽ αὐτὸ
καὶ ὑμεῖς χαίρετε καὶ ᶜ συγχαίρετέ μοι.

t Eph. iv. 30.
  2 Tim. i. 12.
u ch. i. 6 reff.
v Gal. ii. 2 reff.
w 1 Thess.
  ii. 1 reff.
x = Gal. ii. 2
  reff.
y = Rom. xvi.
  6. Gal. iv. 11.
  Job xxxix. 16.
z 2 Cor. iv. 3, 16.

a 2 Tim. iv. 6 only. Num. xxviii. 7 al.
  30. Heb. viii. 6. ix. 21 only. L.P.H. 1 Chron. xxiv. 3.
  26. xiii. 6 only. Gen. xxi. 6 only.

b see note.

e = Matt. xxvii. 44.

c Luke i. 23. 2 Cor. ix. 12. ver.
d Luke i. 58. xv. 6, 9. 1 Cor. xii.

καυχησιν D.   ουδ᾽ B.
17. (αλλα, so BD¹F.) (A def.)   και bef ει (et si) F.   om και συγχαιρω
(homœot) א¹(ins א-corr¹) [Tert Victorin].
18. δε [BP]א [17] 109.

the stars be said 'præbere,' 'prætendere,'
their light, notwithstanding that that
light is *in* them? Chrys., Œc., Thl., interpret it, μέλλοντες ζήσεσθαι, τῶν σωζομένων ὄντες· and Chrys. continues οἱ
φωστῆρές, φησι, λόγον φωτὸς ἐπέχουσιν·
ὑμεῖς λόγον ζωῆς. τί ἐστι, λόγον ζωῆς·
σπέρμα ζωῆς ἔχοντες, τουτέστιν, ἐνέχυρα
ζωῆς ἔχοντες, αὐτὴν κατέχοντες τὴν ζωήν,
τουτέστι σπέρμα ζωῆς ἐν ὑμῖν ἔχοντες :—
Thdrt., ἀντὶ τοῦ τῷ λόγῳ προσέχοντες
τῆς ζωῆς, ungrammatically, for this would
be λόγῳ ζωῆς ἐπέχοντες,—as ὁ δὲ ἐπεῖχεν
αὐτοῖς, Acts iii. 5: cf. also ref. 1 Tim.

εἰς καύχ. ἐμοί] for (result of your
thus walking, *as concerns myself*) a matter
of boasting for me against (temporal:
reserved for) **the day of Christ,** that (ὅτι
οὐ μάτην τὴν ὑπὲρ ὑμῶν ἀνεδεξάμην
σπουδήν, Thdrt.) **I did not run** (the past
tense is from the point of view of that
day. On ἔδραμον, see reff.) **for nothing,
nor labour for nothing** (cf. ref. Job).

17, 18.] These verses are closely
connected with the preceding; not, as
De W., al., with ch. i. 26, which is most
unnatural, and never would occur to any
reader. The connexion is this : in ver. 16
he had tacitly assumed (εἰς ἡμ. χ.) that
he should live to witness their blameless
conduct even till the day of Christ. *Now,*
he puts the other alternative—that the
dangers which surrounded him would
result in his death :—and in that case
equally he rejoiced, &c.   **εἰ καί** implies more probability than καὶ εἰ : in the
former the case is presupposed, in the
latter merely hypothesized. Klotz in
Devar. p. 519 f., gives two examples from
Xen.'s Anabasis: (1) ὁδοποιήσειέ γ᾽ ἂν
αὐτοῖς, καὶ εἰ σὺν τεθρίπποις βούλοιντο
ἀπιέναι (iii. 2. 24), a supposition evidently
thought improbable: (2) ἐγώ, ὦ Κλέανδρε,
εἰ καὶ οἴει με ἀδικοῦντά τι ἄγεσθαι (vi. 4.
27), where as evidently the speaker believes
that Cleander does entertain the thought.
The difference is explained by the common
rules of emphasis. In εἰ καί, the stress is

on εἰ, which is simply '*posito,*' and the
'*even*' belongs to *that which is assumed :*
in **καὶ εἰ**, the stress is on *καί, even,* and
the strangeness belongs not to the thing
simply assumed, but to the making of the
assumption. In the present case then,
the Apostle seems rather to believe the
supposition which he makes.   **σπένδομαι**] not future, but *present;* **If I am
even being poured out,** because the danger
was besetting him *now,* and waxing onward to its accomplishment. He uses the
word literally, with reference to the shedding of his blood. "He represents his
whole apostolic work for the faith of the
Philippians, as a *sacrifice :* if he is put to
death in the course of it, he will be, by
the shedding of his blood, poured out as a
libation upon this sacrifice, as among the
Jews (Num. xxviii. 7; xv. 4 ff. Jos. Antt.
iii. 9. 4. Winer, Realw., s. v. Trankopfer)
and heathens, in their sacrifices, libations
of wine were usual, which were poured
over the offerings (Hom. Il. λ. 775, σπέν-
δων αἴθοπα οἶνον ἐπ᾽ αἰθομένοις ἱεροῖσιν :
cf. also Herod. ii. 39)." Meyer.   Wetst.,
al., would render it '*affundor*' (κατασπέν-
δομαι), and understand it of the pouring
of wine over a live victim destined for
sacrifice—but wrongly.   The θυσία is
the *sacrifice :* i. e. the *deed* of sacrifice, not
the victim, the thing sacrificed.   **λειτουργία, priest's ministration,** without
another article, signifying therefore the
same course of action as that indicated by
θυσία, viz. his apostolic labours : see below.
τῆς πίστεως ὑμ., gen. objective ; **your
faith** *is the sacrifice,* which I, as a priest,
offer to God. The image is precisely as in
Rom. xv. 16, where he is the priest, offering up the Gentiles to God. And the case
which he puts is, that he, the priest, should
have his own blood poured out at, upon
(i. e. in accession to : not *locally* "upon :"
for it was not so among the Jews, see Ellic.
here), his sacrificing and presentation to
God of their faith.   **χαίρω**] not to be
joined with ἐπί, as Chrys., but absolute, **I**

f = ver. 24.
(not 1 Cor.
xv. 19.)
g dat., Acts
xi. 29. 1 Cor.
iv. 17. ch. iv.
16.
h here only†.
Jos. Antt. xi.
6. 9. (-χος,
Prov. xxx.
31.)
i ch. i. 27 reff.
j here only.
Ps. liv. 13
only.
k = Acts x. 41,
47.

19 Ἐλπίζω δὲ f ἐν κυρίῳ Ἰησοῦ Τιμόθεον ταχέως
πέμψαι g ὑμῖν, ἵνα κἀγὼ h εὐψυχῶ γνοὺς i τὰ i περὶ ὑμῶν.
20 οὐδένα γὰρ ἔχω j ἰσόψυχον, k ὅστις l γνησίως i τὰ l περὶ
ὑμῶν m μεριμνήσει· 21 n οἱ n πάντες γὰρ o τὰ ἑαυτῶν o ζητοῦσιν, οὐ τὰ Ἰησοῦ χριστοῦ 22 τὴν δὲ p δοκιμὴν αὐτοῦ
γινώσκετε, ὅτι ὡς q πατρὶ τέκνον q σὺν ἐμοὶ r ἐδούλευσεν
s εἰς τὸ εὐαγγέλιον· 23 τοῦτον t μὲν οὖν ἐλπίζω πέμψαι,

ABCDF
KLPℵ a
b c d e f g
h k l m n
o 17. 47

l here only †. 2 Macc. xiv. 8. (-ος, ch. iv. 8. 1 Tim. i. 2.) m constr.,
1 Cor. vii. 32, 33, 34. ch. iv. 6 (Matt. vi. 34 v. r.) only. Exod. ϵ. 9 (a). n Rom. xi. 32. Eph. iv. 13 reff.
o 1 Cor. x. 24. xiii. 5. p Rom. v. 4 bis. 2 Cor. ii. 9. viii. 2. ix. 13. xiii. 3 only †. Ps. lxvii. 31 Symm.
q change of constr., Eph. v. 27, 33. 1 John ii. 2 al. r = Luke xv. 29. s = Rom. x. 1. ch. i. 5 al.
t 1 Cor. vi. 4, 7. ix. 25 al.

19. for κυριω, χριστω CD¹F copt : txt ABD³KL[P]ℵ rel vulg(and F-lat) vss gr-lat-ff. for υμιν, προς υμας D¹ latt. εκψυχω A.

21. rec χρ. bef ιησ., with BL rel fuld(and demid) syr copt gr-ff Ambrst-ms : om ιησ. K Cypr : txt ACDF[P]ℵ 17 [(47)] vss Clem lat-ff.—rec pref του, with b d f g h n [47] : om ABCDFKL[P]ℵ rel.

22. for εις το ευαγ., εν τοις δεσμοις του ευαγγελιου C.

---

rejoice for myself (οὐχ ὡς ἀποθανούμενος λυποῦμαι ἀλλὰ χαίρω, ὅτι σπονδὴ γίνομαι, Thl.) and congratulate you (so the Vulg. rightly, and all. : not, 'rejoice with you,' as most Commentators (even Ellic.). Meyer well observes that the following verse is decisive against this : for if they rejoiced already, what need of καὶ ὑμεῖς χαίρετε?—congratulate you, viz. on the fact that I have been thus poured out for your faith, which would be an honour and a boast for you. De W.'s objection, after Van Hengel, that to congratulate would be συγχαίρομαι is futile : cf. Æschin. p. 34, τὴν Ἑστίαν ἐπώμοσε τὴν βουλαίαν συγχαίρειν τῇ πόλει ὅτι τοιούτους ἄνδρας ἐπὶ τὴν πρεσβείαν ἐξέπεμψεν : —Demosth. p. 194,—'Ῥοδίοις . . . συγχαίρω τῶν γεγενημένων.) **18.]** and ('but' would be too strong : the contrast is only in the reciprocity) **on the same account** (accusative of reference, governed by χαίρ.) **do ye** (imperative, not indicative, as Erasm., al.) **rejoice** (answer to συγχαίρω above,—for this your honour) **and congratulate me** (answer to χαίρω above,—on this my joy).

19—30.] ADDITIONAL NOTICES RESPECTING THE APOSTLE'S STATE IN HIS IMPRISONMENT: HIS INTENDED MISSION OF TIMOTHEUS AND ACTUAL MISSION OF EPAPHRODITUS. The connexion with the foregoing seems to be,—'and yet this σπένδεσθαι is by no means certain, for I hope to hear news of you soon, nay, to see you myself.' **19. ἐν κυρίῳ**] 'my hope is not an idle one, as a worldly man's might be ; but one founded on faith in Christ.' 1 Cor. xv. 19, to which Meyer refers, is wholly different : see there. **ταχέως,** see ver. 23. **ὑμῖν**] The dative after verbs of

sending, &c. need not be regarded (as De W., al., here) as the dativus commodi, but is similar to that case after verbs of giving—indicating the position of the recipient. I stated in some former editions, that it is in no case equivalent to the mere local πρὸς ὑμᾶς. But Ellic. has reminded me, that this is too widely stated, later writers undeniably using it in this sense. See note on Acts xxi. 16, and cf. such examples as πότερον ἡγόμην Ἀβροκόμῃ, Xen. Eph. iii. 6, and ἤγαγεν αὐτὸν Ἀθανασίῳ τῷ πάππᾳ, Epiph. vit. p. 340 d. See the discussion in Winer, § 31. 5. **κἀγώ**] 'as well as you, by your reception of news concerning me.' **εὐψ.]** may be of **good courage.** The verb is unknown to the classics: the imperative εὐψύχει is found in inscriptions on tombs, in the sense of the Latin 'have pia anima.'

20.] Reason why he would send Timotheus above all others: **for I have none else like-minded** (with myself, not with Timotheus, as Beza, Calv., al.) **who** (of that kind, who) **will really** (emphatic : —with no secondary regards for himself, as in ver. 21) **care for your affairs** (have real anxiety about your matters, to order them for the best): **21.]** for all (my present **companions**) (who these were, we know not : they are characterized, ch. iv. 21, merely as οἱ σὺν ἐμοὶ ἀδελφοί—certainly not Luke—whether Demas, in transition between Philem. 24 and 2 Tim. iv. 10, we cannot say) **seek their own matters, not those of Jesus Christ** (no weakening of the assertion must be thought of, as that of rendering οἱ πάντες, many, or most,—or understanding the assertion, care more about &c. than &c.,—as many Commentators : nor must it be restricted

u ὡς ἂν v ἀφίδω w τὰ w περὶ ἐμέ, x ἐξ x αὐτῆς· 24 πέποιθα δὲ y ἐν κυρίῳ ὅτι καὶ αὐτὸς ταχέως ἐλεύσομαι. 25 za ἀναγκαῖον δὲ zb ἡγησάμην Ἐπαφρόδιτον τὸν ἀδελφὸν καὶ e συνεργὸν καὶ d συνστρατιώτην μου, ὑμῶν δὲ e ἀπόστολον καὶ f λειτουργὸν τῆς g χρείας μου, πέμψαι πρὸς ὑμᾶς, 26 h ἐπειδὴ i ἐπιποθῶν ἦν πάντας ὑμᾶς, καὶ k ἀδημονῶν, διότι ἠκού-

u Rom. xv. 24. 1 Cor. xi. 34.
v here only. = Jonah iv. 5 (Thucyd. vii. 71).
w ch. i. 27 reff.
x Mark vi. 25. Acts x. 33.
xi. 11. xxi. 32. xxiii. 30.
y = ver. 19.
z 2 Cor. ix. 5. 2 Macc. ix. 21.
a ch. i. 24 reff.

b Acts xxvi. 2. ver. 3 al. Job xlii. 6.   c Rom. xvi. 3, 9, 21. ch. iv. 3. Col. iv. 11. Philem. 1,
24. Paul only, exc. 3 John 8 †. 2 Macc. viii. 7. xiv. 5 only.   d Philem. 2 only †. 2 Macc. i. 2. 26.
e = John xiii. 16. 2 Cor. viii. 23. 3 Kings xiv. 6 A &c. [B def.] only.   f Rom. xiii. 6. xv. 16. Heb.
i. 7 (from Ps. ciii. 4). viii. 2 only.   g = Acts xx. 34. xxviii. 10. Rom. xii. 13. ch. iv. 16, 19. Tit.
iii. 14. 2 Chron. ii. 16.   h Luke xi. 6. Acts xiii. 46. 1 Cor. i. 21, 22 al. L.P. (exc. Matt.
xxi. 46 v. r.) Jer. xxxi. [xlviii.] 7 Aq.   i & constr., ch. i. 8 reff.   k Matt. xxvi.
37 ‖ Mk. only †. Job xviii. 20 Aq.

23. rec απιδω, with B² C(-ει-) D³ K(e sil) L[P] rel : txt AB¹D¹Fℵ 17.
24. aft αυτος ins εγω ℵ-corr¹.   at end ins προς υμας AC[P]ℵ¹(ℵ³ disapproving) vulg Syr copt Chr Thl Ambrst Pel Facund.
26. υμας bef παντας B copt.   aft υμας ins ιδειν (supplement. Meyer defends it, seeing no reason why it should have been supplied here, and not in ch i. 8 : but how could it be insd there, seeing that εν σπλαγχνοις χρ. ιησου follows?) ACDℵ¹ a b² f l m n 17 syrr copt æth arm Damasc Thl Cassiod : om BFKL[P]ℵ³ rel Chr Thdrt Victorin

to the *love of ease*, &c., *unwillingness to undertake so long a journey*, as Chr., Œc., Thl.: both οἱ πάντες and the assertion are absolute). **23.**] But the approved worth (reff.) of him ye know (viz. by trial, when we were at Philippi together, Acts xvi. 1, 3,—xvii. 14),—viz.: that as a son (serves) a father, he served with me for (reff.) the Gospel. The construction is this : the Apostle would have written, 'as a son a father, so he *served* me,'—but changes it to 'so he served *with* me,' from modesty and reverence, seeing that we are not servants one of another, but all of God, in the matter of the Gospel. We must not supply σύν before πατρί :—when, in case of several nouns governed by the same preposition, that preposition is omitted before any, it is not before the *first*, cf. Plato, Rep. iii. p. 414, δεῖ ὡς περὶ μητρὸς κ. τροφοῦ τῆς χώρας ἐν ᾗ εἰσι βουλεύεσθαι : and see Bernhardy, Syntax, p. 205. The examples cited by Ellicott to disprove this, do not seem to me to apply : viz. Æsch. Suppl. 313 (311), Eur. Hel. 872 (863) : both are instances of local terms coupled by καί, and both occur in poetry, where the exigencies of metre come into play. Winer takes the construction as above, edn. 6, § 63, ii. 1 [see Moulton's Translation, p. 722]. **μέν** answers to **δέ**, ver. 24 : **οὖν** reassumes ver. 19. **ὡς ἂν ἀφίδω**] as soon as I shall have ascertained. On the force of the preposition, see Heb. xii. 2, note. **ὡς ἄν,** of time, implying uncertainty as to the event indicated : see reff. and Cebes, tab. p. 168, προστάττει δὲ τοῖς εἰσπορευομένοις, τί δεῖ αὐτοὺς ποιεῖν, ὡς ἂν εἰσέλθωσιν εἰς τὸν βίον. See also Klotz, Devar. pp. 759. 63.

The form **ἀφίδω** is supposed by Meyer to be owing to the pronunciation of ἴδω with the digamma. The word signifies here, *see clearly*, as in Herod. viii. 37, ἐπεὶ δὲ ἀγχοῦ τε ἔσαν οἱ βάρβαροι ἐπιόντες καὶ ἀπώρεον τὸ ἱρὸν . . . : following the analogy of ἀπέχω and similar words : the preposition being not intensive (as Ellic. wrongly reports my view), but exhaustive. **τὰ περὶ ἐμέ**, my matters. **24.** **ἐν κυρίῳ**] See above, ver. 19. **καί**, as well as Timothy. **25—30.**] *Of Epaphroditus: his mission: and recommendation of him.* Epaphroditus is not elsewhere mentioned. The name was a common one : see Wetst. h. l., and Tacit. Ann. xv. 55 ; Suet. Domit. 14. There is perhaps no reason for supposing him identical with Epaphras (Col. i. 7 ; iv. 12. Philem. 23), who was a minister of the Colossian church. We must not attempt to give a strict official meaning to each of the words predicated of Epaphroditus. The accumulation of them serves to give him greater recommendation in the eyes of the Philippians. **25.**] συνστρατ. applies to the combat with the powers of darkness, in which the ministers of Christ are the leaders : see besides ref., 2 Tim. ii. 3. **ὑμ. δέ**] the contrast is to μου above. **ἀπόστολον,** not in the ordinary sense of Apostle, so that ὑμῶν should be as ἐθνῶν (ἀπόστολος) in Rom. xi. 13,—but as in ref. 2 Cor. (where see note), almost = ὁ ἀποσταλεὶς ὑφ' ὑμῶν. **λειτουρ.**] minister (in supply) of my want. Cf. λειτουργία below, ver. 30 : and on χρείας, reff., especially Acts xx. 34. λειτουργὸν δὲ αὐτὸν εἴρηκε τῆς χρείας, ὡς τὰ παρ' αὐτῶν

l here only †.
Thucyd. vii.
19. (-ως,
Heb. ii. 14.)
m Matt. ix. 27.
Rom. ix. 15
(from Exod.
xxxiii. 19) al.
n constr., Ps.
lxviii. 27.
Ezek. vii. 26.
o John xvi. 21,
22. 2 Cor.
ii. 3 only.
p Luke vii. 4.
Tit. iii. 13
only †. Wisd.
ii. 6 only.

σατε ὅτι ἠσθένησεν. 27 καὶ γὰρ ἠσθένησεν l παραπλήσιον θανάτῳ· ἀλλὰ ὁ θεὸς m ἠλέησεν αὐτόν, οὐκ αὐτὸν δὲ μόνον, ἀλλὰ καὶ ἐμέ, ἵνα μὴ no λύπην ἐπὶ n λύπην o σχῶ. 28 p σπουδαιοτέρως οὖν ἔπεμψα αὐτόν, ἵνα ἰδόντες αὐτὸν πάλιν χαρῆτε, κἀγὼ q ἀλυπότερος ὦ. 29 r προσδέχεσθε οὖν αὐτὸν r ἐν κυρίῳ s μετὰ t πάσης s χαρᾶς, καὶ u τοὺς τοιούτους v ἐντίμους w ἔχετε, 30 ὅτι διὰ τὸ x ἔργον yz μέχρι

ABCDF
KLPℵ a
b c d e f g
h k l m n
o 17. 47

(-ος, 2 Tim. i. 17.)　　　　q here only †.　　　　r = Rom. xvi. 2.　　　　s = ch. i. 3 al.　　1 Chron.
xxix. 22.　　　　t = ch. i. 20 reff.　　u 1 Cor. xvi. 16, 18 al.　　v Luke vii. 2. xiv. 8.　1 Pet. ii.
4, 6 (from Isa. xxviii. 16) only.　1 Kings xxvi. 21.　　w = Matt. xiv. 5. xxi. 26, 46.　Philem. 17.
x ch. i. 22 reff.　　　　y ver. 8 reff.　　　　z here only.　ἐγγ. εἰς, Job xxxiii. 22.　ἐγγ. ἕως, Ps. cvi. 18.

Ambrst.　　for οτι ησθ., αυτον ησθενηκεναι D¹F latt goth lat-ff. [C¹ uncert.]
27. θανατου B[P]ℵ³ l Chr Thl-ms.　　(αλλα, so ABDℵ c e n 17.)　　rec αυτον bef ηλεησεν, with KL rel vss gr-ff: txt ABC²DF[P]ℵ m¹ 17 latt Phot lat-ff.　　rec (for 2nd λυπην) λυπη (corrn to more usual constr), with K rel Thdrt Phot: txt ABCDFL[P]ℵ a b c k l² o 17 [47] Chr-mss Damasc Thl-ms Œc.　　for σχω, εχω D¹F.
28. σπουδαιοτερον D¹F [-ρος P. C uncert.]　　for ουν, δε F 17 Thl. (not F-lat.)
29. προσδεξασθε A²ℵ 67². 73. 80.
30. rec aft εργον ins του χριστου, with DKL rel, χριστου BF 73. 80; κυριου Aℵ[P] 17 [47], του κυριου 57; του θεου al copt æth Chr-comm: om C.　　for μεχρι, εως DF.

ἀποσταλέντα κομίσαντα χρήματα, Thdrt.

πέμψαι] it was actually a sending *back*, though not so expressed here: see ch. iv. 18.　**26.**] reason for the necessity. The imperfect is, as usual, from the position of the receivers of the letter. **ἀδημ.**] See note on ref. Matt. Whether there was any special reason, more than affection, which made Epaphroditus anxious to return on account of this, we cannot say.　**27.**] **καὶ γάρ** recognizes and reasserts that which has before been put as from another, as "ἔλεγες τοίνυν δή, ὅτι κ.τ.λ." "καὶ γὰρ ἔλεγον, ἔν γε ὄχλῳ." Plato, Gorg. 459: see Hartung, Partikell. i. 137,—for he really *was* sick. **παραπλήσιον** does not involve any ellipsis (De W.) as of ἀφίκετο or the like, but (as Mey.) it stands adverbially as παραπλησίως; so in Polyb. iii. 33. 10, εἰ πεποιήκαμεν παραπλήσιον τοῖς ἀξιοπίστως ψευδομένοις τῶν συγγραφέων: and **θανάτῳ** is the dative of *congruence* after it,—sometimes a genitive, as Plato, Soph. p. 217, λόγων ἐπελάβου παραπλησίων ὧν . . . . διερωτῶντες ἐτυγχάνομεν. **λύπην ἐπὶ λύπην**] for construction, see reff. The dative after ἐπί is more usual: so φόνος ἐπὶ φόνῳ, Eur. Iph. Taur. 197 (189): the accus. giving the sense of accession,— "sorrow coming upon sorrow,"—not, sorrow superimposed upon sorrow. The second λύπην refers to his own distress in his imprisonment, as often implied in this Epistle: see Prolegg. § iii. 4, 5: 'si ad vincula accessisset jactura amici,' Grot. This is better, than with Chrys., al., to refer it to Epaphroditus's sickness,—τὴν

ἀπὸ τῆς τελευτῆς ἐπὶ τῇ διὰ τὴν ἀρρωστίαν,—which does not agree with ἀλυπότερος, ver. 28, implying that λύπη would remain even after the departure of Epaphroditus.　**28.**] **πάλιν** most naturally, considering St. Paul's habit of prefixing it to verbs, belongs to χαρῆτε: and there is here no reason to depart from his usage and attach it to ἰδόντες, as Beza, Grot., De W., all., have done. The **κἀγὼ ἀλυπότερος ὦ** is one of the Apostle's delicate touches of affection. If *they* rejoiced in seeing Epaphroditus, *his own* trouble would be thereby lessened.　**29.**] **οὖν**, as accomplishing the purpose just expressed. The stress is on **προσδέχεσθε**, see ref. There certainly seems to be something behind respecting him, of which we are not informed. If extreme affection had been the sole ground of his ἀδημονεῖν, no such exhortation as this would have been needed.　**τοὺς τοιούτους**] ἵνα μὴ δόξῃ αὐτῷ μόνῳ χαρίζεσθαι, . . . Thl. Then there is an inaccuracy in expression, in reverting back to the [concrete] conduct of Epaphroditus as a reason why οἱ τοιοῦτοι [abstract] should be held in honour.　**30.**] **διὰ τὸ ἔργον**, viz. of the Gospel, or of Christ (see the glosses in var. readd.);—part of which it was to sustain the minister of the Gospel.

μέχρι θ. ἤγγ.] he incurred so serious and nearly fatal a sickness :—not to be understood of danger incurred by the hostility of the authorities, as Chrys., al., also Thdrt.: καθειργόμενον γὰρ πάντως μαθών, καὶ ὑπὸ πλείστων φυλαττόμενον, εἰσελθὼν ἐθεάσατο, τοῦ κινδύνου

ʸ θανάτου ᶻ ἤγγισεν ᵃπαραβολευσάμενος τῇ ᵇ ψυχῇ, ἵνα ᵃ here only †.
ᶜ ἀναπληρώσῃ τὸ ᵈ ὑμῶν ᵉ ὑστέρημα ᵈ τῆς πρός με ᶠ λειτουργίας.

III. ¹ ᵍ Τὸ ᵍ λοιπόν, ἀδελφοί μου, ʰ χαίρετε ʰ ἐν κυρίῳ.
τὰ αὐτὰ γράφειν ὑμῖν ἐμοὶ μὲν οὐκ ⁱ ὀκνηρόν, ὑμῖν δὲ

ᵃ here only †.
(see notes.)
ᵇ = Acts xv.
26. xx. 24
al. Exod.
xxi. 23. dat.,
see note.
ᶜ Gal. vi. 2 reff.
Gen. ii. 21.
ᵈ double gen.,
ch. i. 7, 25.
Acts v. 32.

e 1 Cor. xvi. 17. 2 Cor. viii. 13, 14. ix. 12. xi. 9.   Col. i. 24.   1 Thess. iii. 10. P. only, exc. Luke xxi. 4. Judg.
    xviii. 10.   f = ver. 17 reff.   g Eph. vi. 10 reff.   h ch. iv. 4, 10.
i Matt. xxv. 26.   Rom. xii. 11 only.   Prov. vi. 6, 9.

rec παραβουλευσαμενος, with CKL[P] rel Chr Thdrt Damasc Thl Œc : txt
ADFℵ, παρακολ. B(ita in cod. see table at end of prolegg [not so Tischdf Cod. Vat., who
gives B as txt]).—parabolatus (see notes) D-lat G-lat : tradens vulg(and F-lat) æth
lat-ff (pref in interitum Ambrst) : spernens syrr : postponens copt : obliviscens goth.
αναπληρωσει ℵ d [17 : πληρωσῃ B(sic, Tischdf) 122].   εμε ℵ¹ b c o [47].
CHAP. III. 1. for τα αυτα, ταυτα F-gr ℵ¹(txt ℵ³) [P copt].

καταφρονήσας.   παραβολευσάμενος]
There is, and must ever remain, some
doubt whether to read παραβουλ- or
παραβολευσάμενος. Both words are unknown to Greek writers. The first verb
would signify 'male consulere vitæ,' and
is found not unfrequently in the fathers,
especially Chrys., which makes it all the
more likely to have been introduced here
for the other. This latter would be formed
from παράβολος, 'venturesome,' as περ-
περεύομαι from πέρπερος (1 Cor. xiii. 4),
ἀλογεύομαι from ἄλογος (Cic. ad Att.
vi. 4) : similarly ἀσωτεύομαι, φιλανθρω-
πεύομαι, πονηρεύομαι, &c.   See Lobeck
on Phryn. pp. 67, 591. Thus παραβο-
λεύεσθαι would be used exactly as παραβάλλεσθαι in Polyb. ii. 26. 6, ἔφη δεῖν μὴ
κινδυνεύειν ἔτι, μηδὲ παραβάλλεσθαι τοῖς
ὅλοις, and iii. 94. 4, and παραβάλλεσθαι
ταῖς ψυχαῖς in Diod. Sic. iii. 16. Phryn.
(p. 238, ed. Lob.) says, παραβόλιον· ἀδόκιμον τοῦτο. τῷ μὲν οὖν ὀνόματι οὐ χρῶνται οἱ παλαιοί, τῷ δὲ ῥήματι. φασὶ γὰρ
οὕτω, παραβάλλομαι τῇ ἐμαυτοῦ κεφαλῇ.
ἐχρῆν οὖν κἀπὶ τούτων λέγειν, παραβάλλομαι ἀργυρίῳ. Hence also nurses of the
sick were called parabolani. See various
patristic interpretations, and illustrations,
in Tischendorf and Wetstein.   ἵνα
κ.τ.λ.] that he might fill up (1 Cor. xvi.
17) your deficiency (viz. on account of
your absence) in the ministration to me
(the λειτουργία was the contribution of
money, which had been sent by Epaphroditus. The only ὑστέρημα in this kind
service was, their inability through absence, to minister it to the Apostle themselves : and this Epaphroditus filled up,
and in so doing risked his life in the way
above hinted at, i. e. probably by too
constant and watchful attendance on the
Apostle. So that there is no blame conveyed by τὸ ὑμ. ὑστέρημα, as Chr., ὅπερ
ἐχρῆν πάντας ποιῆσαι, τοῦτο ἔπραξεν αὐ-

τός,—but the whole is a delicate way of
enhancing Epaphroditus's services—'that
which you would have done if you could,
he did for you—therefore receive him
with all joy').
CH. III.1—IV.1.] WARNING AGAINST
CERTAIN JUDAIZERS,—ENFORCED BY HIS
OWN EXAMPLE (1—16): ALSO AGAINST
IMMORAL PERSONS (17—iv. 1).
1.] He appears to have been closing his
Epistle (τὸ λοιπόν, and reff.), but to have
again gone off, on the vehement mention of
the Judaizers, into an explanation of his
strong term κατατομή. Chrys., al., find a
connexion with the foregoing, but it is far-
fetched (ἔχετε Ἐπαφρ., δι' ὃν ἤλγειτε,
ἔχετε Τιμόθ., ἔρχομαι κἀγώ. τὸ εὐαγγέλιον
ἐπιδίδωσι· τί ὑμῖν λείπει λοιπόν;) : the
sense is evidently closed with ch. iii. 30.
τὰ αὐτά] It seems to me that
Wiesinger has rightly apprehended the
reference of this somewhat difficult sentence. The χαίρετε ἐν κυρίῳ, taken up
again by the οὕτως στήκετε ἐν κυρίῳ,
ch. iv. 1, is evidently put here emphatically, with direct reference to the
warning which follows—let your joy (your
boast) be in the Lord. And this same
exhortation, χαίρειν, is in fact the ground-
tone of the whole Epistle. See ch. i. 18,
25; ii. 17; iv. 4, where the πάλιν ἐρῶ
seems to refer back again to this saying.
So that there is no difficulty in imagining
that the Apostle may mean χαίρετε by the
τὰ αὐτά. The word ἀσφαλές is no objection to this : because the χαίρ. ἐν κυρ.
is in fact an introduction to the warning
which follows : a provision, by upholding
the antagonist duty, against their falling
into deceit. And thus all the speculation,
whether τὰ αὐτά refer to a lost Epistle, or
to words uttered (γράφειν?) when he was
with them, falls to the ground. And the
inference from Polycarp's words in his
Epistle to these Philippians, § 3, p. 1008,

k 1 Cor. i. 26 (& note). x. 18.   ἀσφαλές.   2 ᵏ βλέπετε τοὺς ¹ κύνας, ᵏ βλέπετε τοὺς κακοὺς
Col. iv. 17.
l = Matt. vii. 6.   ᵐ ἐργάτας, ᵏ βλέπετε τὴν ⁿ κατατομήν. 3 ἡμεῖς γάρ ἐσμεν
Rev. xxii. 15.
Ps. xxi. 16.   ἡ ᵒ περιτομή, οἱ ᵖ πνεύματι θεοῦ ᑫ λατρεύοντες καὶ ʳ καυ-
m Luke x. 2 al.†
Wisd. xvii.
17. = 2 Cor.   χώμενοι ʳ ἐν χριστῷ Ἰησοῦ, καὶ οὐκ ἐν ˢ σαρκὶ ᵗ πεποι-
xi. 13.
n here only†.   θότες, 4 ᵘ καίπερ ἐγὼ ἔχων ᵛ πεποίθησιν καὶ ἐν σαρκί.
(-τέμνειν,
Levit. xxi. 5.)   εἴ τις ʷ δοκεῖ ἄλλος ᵗ πεποιθέναι ἐν σαρκί, ἐγὼ μᾶλλον,
o see Rom. iii.
30. Gal. ii.
7.   p dat., 1 Cor. xiv. 2, 15.   q absol., Luke ii. 37. Acts xxvi. 7. Heb. ix. 9. x. 2.
r Rom. ii. 17. v. 3.   2 Cor. x. 15 al.   Jer. ix. 23, 24.   s = Rom. ii. 28. Gal. iii. vi. 13.   t constr.,
here only.   Jer. xxxi. [xlviii.] 7. see ch. ii. 24.   u Paul, here only. Heb. v. 8. vii. 5. xii. 17. 2 Pet.
i. 12 only.   v Eph. ii. 12 reff.   w = 1 Cor. iii. 18. viii. 2. xiv. 37. Gal. vi. 3. James i.
26. Winer, § 65. 7. c.

ABCDF
KLPℵ a
b c d e f
g h k l m
n o 17. 47

ins το bef ασφαλες d h k m n 80. 113-4-5-6. 120-1-2-3 Procop Damasc. (A defective.)

3. rec for θεου, θεω (perhaps corrn after such passages as Rom i. 9. 2 Tim i. 3), with D¹(and lat) [P]ℵ³ vulg(with F-lat &c, agst ms₁) Syr goth Thdrt₁ [Orig-int₅] latff : θειω 115 : txt ABCD³FKLℵ¹ rel al₆₀(Tischdf) gr-mss-mentd-by-Aug (" omnes aut pæne omnes ") lat-mss-in-Aug(" exempl. nonnulla" have θεω) syr-mg copt Eus Ath Aug_expr.

4. om και D¹F a n o Aug₁.   αλλος bef δοκει D a latt : δε αλλως δοκει F : om αλλος al₂ Syr Chr-comm Lucif Ambrst.—αλλως m.   for εγω ℵ¹ has πε(txt ℵ-corr¹).

ὃς καὶ ἀπὼν ὑμῖν ἔγραψεν ἐπιστολάς, may be a true one, but does not belong here.

ὀκνηρόν] troublesome : Mey. quotes from Plato, Ep. ii. 310 D, τἀληθῆ λέγειν οὔτε ὀκνήσω οὔτε αἰσχυνοῦμαι. 2.] βλέπετε, not, ' beware of,' as E. V. (βλ. ἀπό, Mark viii. 15 reff.), but as in reff., observe, with a view to avoid : cf. σκοπεῖν, Rom. xvi. 17. τοὺς κύνας] profane, impure persons. The appellation occurs in various references ; but in the Jewish usage of it, uncleanness was the prominent idea : see, besides reff., Deut. xxiii. 18 ; Isa. lvi. 10, 11 ; Matt. xv. 26, 27. The remark of Chrys. is worth noting in connexion with that follows : οὐκέτι τέκνα Ἰουδαῖοι. ποτὲ οἱ ἐθνικοὶ τοῦτο ἐκαλοῦντο, νῦν δὲ ἐκεῖνοι. But I would not confine it entirely to them, as the next clause certainly generalizes further. τοὺς κακοὺς ἐργάτας] cf. δόλιοι ἐργάται, 2 Cor. xi. 13,—ἐργάτην ἀνεπαίσχυντον, 2 Tim. ii. 15,—ἐργάζονται μὲν γάρ, φησιν, ἀλλ' ἐπὶ κακῷ. By ἐργάτας, he seems to point out persons who actually wrought, and professedly for the Gospel, but who were ' evil workmen,' not mere ' evil-doers.'

τ. κατατομήν] ' gloriosam appellationem περιτομῆς, circumcisionis, vindicat Christianis.' Beng. Observe the (I will not say, circumcision, but mere) concision (' amputation :' who have no true circumcision of heart, but merely the cutting off of the flesh. Mey. quotes from Diog. Laert. vi. 24, of Diogenes the Cynic, τὴν Εὐκλείδου σχολὴν ἔλεγε χολήν, τὴν δὲ Πλάτωνος διατριβὴν κατατριβήν. Cf. Gal. v. 12 note. On the thrice repeated article, Erasmus says,

' indicat, eum de certis quibusdam loqui, quos illi noverint') : 3.] for WE are the περιτομή, the real CIRCUMcision (whether bodily circumcised, or not — there would be among them some of both sorts : see Rom. ii. 25, 29 ; Col. ii. 11), who serve (pay religious service and obedience) by the Spirit of God (cf. John iv. 23, 24. The dative is instrumental, Rom. viii. 13,—expressing the agent, whereby our service is rendered : see Rom. v. 5 ; viii. 14 ; xii. 1 ; Heb. ix. 14. The emphasis is on it : for both profess a λατρεία. The θεοῦ is expressed for solemnity), and glory in (stress on καυχώμενοι,—are not ashamed of Him and seek our boast in circumcision, or the law, but make our boast in Him) Christ Jesus, and trust not in the flesh (stress on ἐν σαρκί—' but, in the Spirit—in our union with Christ').

4.] Although (see Hartung, Partik. i. 340 : πίθου γυναικί, καίπερ οὐ στέργων, ὅμως, Æsch. Theb. 709 : προσεκύνησαν, καίπερ εἰδότες, ὅτι ἐπὶ θανάτῳ ἄγοιτο, Xen. Anab. i. 6. 10) I (emphatic. There is no ellipsis, but the construction is regular, καίπερ, as in the above examples, having a participle after it : had it been καίπερ ἔχοντες, this would have been universally seen : now, only one of the οὐ πεποιθότες, viz. ἐγώ, is made the exception ; but the construction is the same) have (not, ' might have,' as E. V. I have it, but do not choose to make use of it : I have it, in the flesh, but I am still of the number of the οὐ πεποιθότες, in spirit) confidence (not, ' ground of confidence,' as Beza, Calv., Grot., &c. : there is no need to soften the assertion, see above :

⁵ ^x περιτομῇ ^y ὀκταήμερος, ἐκ ^z γένους Ἰσραήλ, φυλῆς   ^x constr., 1 Cor.
...βενια   Βενιαμίν, ^a Ἑβραῖος ἐξ Ἑβραίων, ^{bc} κατὰ ^c νόμον Φαρι-   xiv. 20. ch.
C.   ii. 8 al.
ABDFK σαῖος, ⁶ ^b κατὰ ^d ζῆλος ^e διώκων τὴν ^f ἐκκλησίαν, ^b κατὰ   ^y here only †.
LPℵ a b   usually of
c d e f g δικαιοσύνην τὴν ^g ἐν νόμῳ γενόμενος ^h ἄμεμπτος. ⁷ [ἀλλὰ]   persons.
h k l m n   ὁ Λάζαρον
o 17. 47 ἄτινα ἦν ⁱ μοι ^k κέρδη, ταῦτα ^l ἥγημαι διὰ τὸν χριστὸν   μὲν τετραή-
                                                                                μερον, σὲ
                                                                                δὲ τετραετῆ
                                                                                ζωοποιῶν,

Greg. Naz. Orat. xxv. vol. i. p. 465.   z = Acts xviii. 2 al. Esth. ii. 10.   a Acts vi.
1. 2 Cor. xi. 22 only. Gen. (xiv. 13 Heb.) xxxix. 14 al.   b = ch. ii. 3. iv. 11 al.   c Acts
xxii. 12. xxiv. 6. Heb. viii, 4 al.   d 2 Cor. vii. 11. ix. 2 al. Ps. lxviii. 9. neut., here only.
e = Gal. i. 13 reff. particip., ib. i. 23.   f absol., Eph. i. 22 reff.   g Rom. ii. 12. iii. 19.
h ch. ii. 15 reff.   i dat., Rom. xiv. 14. 1 Cor. iv. 3.   k ch. i. 21. Tit. i. 11 only †. Gen.
xxxvii. 26 Symm.   l = Acts xxvi. 2. 2 Cor. ix. 5 al. Job xlii. 6.

5. περιτομή a e g h k l m n o : περιτομῇ f.   ins τον bef νομον F.
6. rec ζηλον, with D^{2.3}KL[P]ℵ³ rel : txt ABD¹Fℵ¹.   aft εκκλησιαν ins θεου F
(122) vulg arm(not ed-1805) Ambrst.
7. om αλλα (so BD¹) AGℵ¹ 17 D-lat Cyr Lucif Ambr Aug.—αλλι τινα F (sic).
μοι bef ην B b c o 238 latt Thdrt Lucif : txt ADFKL[P]ℵ rel syrr copt goth
Chr Victorin.

nor, with Van Hengel, to understand it of the unconverted state of the Apostle) also (over and above) in the flesh. If any other man thinks (δοκεῖ is certainly, as De W., Wiesinger, al., and reff., of *his own judgment of himself*, not of other men's judgment of him, as Meyer, al.: for how can other men's judging of the *fact* of his having confidence be in place here? But it is his own judgment of the existence of the πεποίθησιν ἔχειν which is here in comparison) he has confidence in the flesh, I more: 5.] "predicates of the ἐγώ, justifying the ἐγὼ μᾶλλον," Meyer. He compares himself with them in three particulars : 1. pure Jewish extraction : 2. legal exactitude and position : 3. legal zeal. In circumcision (i. e. 'as regards circumcision :' reff. Many (Erasm., Beng., all.) have taken περιτ. as nominative, and understood it concrete, ' circumcisus,' but wrongly, for the usage applies only collectively, see Winer, edn. 3 (not in edn. 6), § 31. 3), of eight days (Gen. xvii. 12 : as distinguished from those who, as proselytes, were circumcised in after life. For usage, see reff.), of the race of Israel (cf. Rom. xi. 1 ; 2 Cor. xi. 22, οὔτε μὴν ἐκ προσηλύτων γεγέννημαι, ἀλλὰ τὸν Ἰσραὴλ αὐχῶ πρόγονον. Thdrt.), of the tribe of Benjamin (ὥστε τοῦ δοκιμωτέρου μέρους, Chrys. : or perhaps as Calv., merely 'ut moris erat, singulos ex sua tribu censeri'), an Hebrew, of Hebrews (i. e. from Hebrew parents and ancestry (which the word *parents* was of course meant to imply in my earlier editions : not, as Ellic., to limit the assertion to St. Paul's father and mother) on both sides : ἐντεῦθεν δείκνυσιν ὅτι οὐχὶ προσήλυτοs, ἀλλ' ἄνωθεν τῶν εὐδοκίμων Ἰουδαίων. ἐνῆν μὲν γὰρ εἶναι τοῦ Ἰσραήλ, ἀλλ' οὐχ Ἑβραῖον ἐξ

Ἑβραίων. πολλοὶ γὰρ καὶ διέφθειρον ἤδη τὸ πρᾶγμα, καὶ τῆς γλώσσης ἦσαν ἀμύητοι, ἑτέροις μεμιγμένοι ἔθνεσιν. Chrys.: see also Trench, Synonyms, § xxxix. p. 153 ff. So Demosth. adv. Androt. p. 614, δούλους ἐκ δούλων καλῶν ἑαυτοῦ βελτίους κ. ἐκ βελτιόνων: see other examples in Kypke and Wetst.), as regards the law (with reference to relative legal position and observance), a Pharisee (cf. Acts xxiii. 6 ;. xxvi. 5), as regards zeal (for the law), a persecutor of the church (of Christ: on the participle, see ref.: Ellic. holds the pres. part. to have an adjectival force, being predicate to a suppressed verb subst.), as regards righteousness which is in (as its element : consists in the keeping of) the law, become blameless (i. e. having carried this righteousness so far as to have become perfect in it, in the sight of men. Calvin well distinguishes between the real and apparent righteousness in the law—the former before God, never possessed by any man : the latter before men, here spoken of by Paul :—'erat ergo hominum judicio sanctus, et immunis ab omni reprehensione. Rara sane laus, et prope singularis : videamus tamen quanti eam fecerit').

7.] But whatsoever things (emphatic (cf. ταῦτα below) and general : these above mentioned, and all others. The *law itself* is not included among them, but only his κέρδη from this and other sources) were to me gains (different kinds of gain : cf. Herod. iii. 71, περιβαλλόμενος ἑωυτῷ κέρδεα), these (emphatic) I have esteemed, for Christ's sake (see it explained below, vv. 8, 9), as loss ("this *one* LOSS he saw in all of which he speaks : hence no longer the plural, as before κέρδη." Meyer. Ellicott remarks that the singular is regularly used in this formula, referring to

[m] ζημίαν. 8 ἀλλὰ [n] μὲν οὖν καὶ [l] ἡγοῦμαι πάντα [m] ζημίαν
εἶναι διὰ τὸ [o] ὑπερέχον τῆς [p] γνώσεως [p] χριστοῦ Ἰησοῦ τοῦ
κυρίου μου, δι᾽ ὃν [q] τὰ πάντα [r] ἐζημιώθην καὶ [l] ἡγοῦμαι
[s] σκύβαλα εἶναι, ἵνα χριστὸν [t] κερδήσω 9 καὶ [u] εὑρεθῶ ἐν
αὐτῷ, [v] μὴ ἔχων [w] ἐμὴν [w] δικαιοσύνην τὴν [x] ἐκ νόμου, ἀλλὰ
τὴν [y] διὰ [y] πίστεως [z] χριστοῦ, τὴν ἐκ θεοῦ [a] δικαιοσύνην
[b] ἐπὶ τῇ πίστει, 10 [c] τοῦ γνῶναι αὐτὸν καὶ τὴν [d] δύναμιν

ABDFK LPℵ a b c d e f g h k l m n o 17. 47

m Acts xxvii. 10, 21 only. Ezra vii. 26.
n = Luke xi. 28. see Rom. ix. 20. x. 18.
o ch. ii. 3 reff. constr., Rom. viii. 3.
p = 2 Pet. iii. 18.
q acc., Matt. xvi. 26 ‖ Mk. Prov. xix. 19.
r Mt. Mk. as above (q) ‖ L. 1 Cor. iii. 15. 2 Cor. vii. 9 only.
s here only †. Sir. xxvii. 4 only. (-βαλίζειν, ib. xxvi. 28.)
t Matt. xxv. 17, 22 al.†
u = 2 Cor. v. 3. 2 Pet. iii. 14 al.
v so ἐλπ. μὴ ἔχ., Eph. ii. 12.
w see Rom. x. 3.
x Rom. x. 5. see Gal. iii. 21.
y Eph. ii. 8 reff.
z obj. gen., Eph. iii. 12 reff.
a see 2 Cor. v. 21.
b = Luke v. 5. Acts iii. 16. Job xxix. 22.
c Acts xiv. 9. 1 Cor. ix. 10.
d = Acts viii. 10. Rom. i. 16.

8. rec aft *μενουν* ins *γε*, with A[P]ℵ b k m o 17 Did Cyr_3 Thl: om BDFKL rel Bas Chr Cyr Thdrt Damasc Œc Hesych. om 1st *και* ℵ[1](ins ℵ[3]) 80. ins *του* bef *χρ.* B Thdrt. *ιησ.* bef *χρ.* AK[P] b f o [47] vulg(and F-lat) gr-lat-ff. for *μου*, *ημων* A[P] demid(and harl[1]) syr copt æth [arm] Bas Cyr Did Thdrt Lucif Aug. om 2nd *ειναι* (*as superfluous, cf ch* ii. 6) BD[1]Fℵ[1] 17 latt arm [$Orig_2$(and int_1)] Lucif Ambr Hil Pel Ambrst Fulg: ins AD[3]KL[P]ℵ[3] rel goth Cyr_3 Aug.
9. *δικαιοσ.* bef *εμην* ℵ[1](txt ℵ[3]) [om *εμην* L]. for *επι τη π.*, *εν πιστει* D[1], *in fide* latt: om Syr: in L 23. 46 syr gr-lat-ff it is joined with the follg.

Kypke and Elsner in loc. But the reason of this usage in analogous to that given above, and not surely lest *ζημίαι* should be mistaken to mean "punishments." Thus, in the instance from Xen. in Kypke, *ἐπὶ μὲν τοῖς οἰκέταις ἀχθομένους καὶ ζημίαν ἡγουμένους*, the separate deaths of the servants are all massed together, and the loss thought of as *one*).

8.] **But moreover** (not only have I once for all passed this judgment, but I *continue to count*, &c. The contrast is of the present **ἡγοῦμαι** to **ἥγημαι** above) **I also continue to esteem them all** (not, *all things*, which would require *πάντα* or *τὰ πάντα* (see below) *before* *ἡγοῦμαι*, emphatic) **to be loss on account of the super-eminence** (above them all: *τοῦ γὰρ ἡλίου φανέντος, προσκαθῆσθαι τῷ λύχνῳ ζημία.* Chrys. On the neuter adjective (or participle) construction, see ref. and 2 Cor. iv. 17) **of the knowledge of Christ Jesus my Lord** ('quod Dominum suum vocat, id ad exprimendam affectus vehementiam facit.' Calv.), **on whose account** (explained by **ἵνα** . . . . below) **I suffered the loss of** ALL THINGS (now, emphatic and universal. Or, it may be, "them all," as Ellic.: but this almost involves a tautology; and, besides, *τὰ πάντα* stands too far from *ἅτινα* for the *τά* to be reflexive), **and esteem them to be refuse, that I may** (by so disesteeming them: *ἵνα* gives the aim of what went before) **gain Christ** (not, as the rationalizing Grot., 'Christi favorem:' no indeed, it is Christ Himself,—His perfect image, His glorious perfection, which he wishes to win. He has Him now, but not in full: this can only be when his course is finished, and to this time the next words allude) **and be found** (now, and especially at His coming,—'evadam:' —not as Calv., 'Paulum renuntiasse omnibus . . . *ut recuperaret* (ungrammatical) in Christo.' Cf. ref. 2 Cor.) **in Him** (living and being, and included, in Him as my element), **not having** (specification of **εὑρ. ἐν αὐτῷ**,—but not to be joined, as Lachm., al., with **ἐν αὐτῷ**, which would make this latter superfluous) **my own righteousness** (see on ver. 6) **which is of** (arising from) **the law, but that which is through** (as its medium) **the faith of** (in) **Christ** (a construction of this sentence has been suggested to me, which is perhaps possible, and at all events deserves mention. It consists in making *ἐμὴν δικαιοσύνην* predicative; "not having as my righteousness that righteousness which is of the law, but that which is through faith in Christ"), **the righteousness which is of** (answering to **ἐκ νόμου**,—as its source, see Eph. ii. 8) **God on my faith** (built on, grounded on, granted on condition of, my faith. It is more natural to take **ἐπὶ τῇ πίστει** with *δικαιοσύνην*, which it immediately follows, than with Meyer to understand another *ἔχων* to attach it to. The omission of the article is no objection, but is very frequent, where the whole expression is joined as one idea. Chrys., al., join **ἐπὶ τῇ πίστει** with **τοῦ γνῶναι**, as if it were *τοῦ ἐπὶ τ. π. γνῶναι*, which of course is unallowable: Calv., Grot., Bengel, make the infinitive **τοῦ γνῶναι** dependent on **πίστει** ("describit vim et naturam fidei, quod scilicet sit Christi cognitio." Calv.), which is also

τῆς ^eἀναστάσεως αὐτοῦ, καὶ [τὴν] ^fκοινωνίαν τῶν ^gπαθη-
μάτων αὐτοῦ, ^hσυμμορφιζόμενος τῷ θανάτῳ αὐτοῦ, 11 ⁱεἴ
ⁱπως ^kκαταντήσω ^kεἰς τὴν ^lἐξανάστασιν τὴν ἐκ νεκρῶν.
12 ^mοὐχ ^mὅτι ἤδη ἔλαβον ἢ ἤδη ⁿτετελείωμαι, ^oδιώκω

e = Acts i. 22.
Rom. vi. 5.
1 Pet. i. 3 al.‡
f ch. ii. 1 reff.
1 Cor. i. 9.
x. 16 al.
g 2 Cor. i. 5.
Heb. ii. 10.
1 Pet. i. 11.
iv. 13. v. 1†.

h here only †. (·φος, ver. 21.)   i = & constr., Rom. i. 10. xi. 14 (w. opt., Acts xxvii. 12) only.
k Eph. iv. 13 reff.   l here only †. = Polyb. iii. 55. 4.   m = ch. iv. 11 reff.
n = Heb. ii. 10. v. 9. vii. 28. Wisd. iv. 13.   o absol., Luke xvii. 23. Hagg. i. 9.

10. for αναστ., γνωσεως ℵ¹(txt ℵ-corr¹ obl), πιστεως 108.   om 1st αυτου D¹.
om 2nd την ABℵ¹ : ins DFKL[P]ℵ³ rel.   om των [B] ℵ¹(ins ℵ³).   rec συμ-
μορφουμενος (more usual form), with D³KLℵ³ rel Chr Thdrt : συνφορτιζομενος
cooneratus F D-lat goth Iren-int Lucif : txt ABD¹[P]ℵ¹ 17 (67²) Orig-ms, Bas Maced.
11. rec (for την εκ) των (see note), with KL rel copt Thdrt : των εκ F : txt ABD
[P]ℵ 17 latt syrr Bas Chr Damasc Iren-int [Orig-int] Tert Lucif [Victorin] Ambrst.
12. aft ελαβον add η ηδη δεδικαιωμαι D¹F [goth] Iren-int Sing-cler Ambrst (not

inadmissible, for πίστις, as Mey. observes, is never joined with a genitive article and infinitive: and when with a genitive, not the nature but the object of faith is described by it),   10.] (aim and employment of this righteousness,—taking up again the ὑπερέχον τῆς γνώσεως, ver. 8. De W., al., treat τοῦ γν. as parallel with ἵνα κερδήσω, κ.τ.λ. But as Mey. remarks, it is no real parallel, for there is more in ἵνα χρ. κερδήσω &c. than in τοῦ γνῶναι αὐτόν &c. Besides, thus the process of thought is disturbed,—in which, from ἵνα to ἐπὶ τῇ πίστει answers to διὰ τὸν χριστόν above, and from τοῦ γν. to νεκρῶν answers to διὰ τὸ ὑπερέχον τ. γνώσεως αὐτοῦ. See a similar construction, Rom. vi. 6), in order to know Him (know, in that fulness of experimental knowledge, which is only wrought by being like Him), and (not = 'that is to say:' but additional : His Person, and .... and ....) the power of His resurrection (i. e. not 'the power by which He was raised,' but the power which His resurrection exercises on believers—in assuring them of their justification, Rom. iv. 25; 1 Cor. xv. 17 ;—mostly however here, from the context which goes on to speak of conformity with His sufferings and death,—in raising them with Him,—cf. Rom. vi. 4; Col. ii. 12),—and the participation of His sufferings (which is the necessitating condition of being brought under the power of His resurrection, see as above, and 2 Tim. ii. 11), being conformed (the nominative is an anacoluthon, belonging to τοῦ γνῶναι, and referring, as often, to the logical subject) to His Death (it does not appear to me that St. Paul is here speaking, as Mey., al., of his imminent risk of a death of martyrdom, but that his meaning is general, applying to his whole course of suffering and self-denial, as indeed throughout the sentence. This conformity with Christ's death was to take place by means of that

perfect self-abjuration which he here asserts of himself—see Rom. viii. 29; 2 Cor. ii. 14; iv. 10 ff. ; 1 Cor. xv. 31, and especially Gal. ii. 20), if by any means (so Thucyd. ii. 77, πᾶσαν γὰρ ἰδέαν ἐπενόουν, εἴ πως σφίσιν ἄνευ δαπάνης κ. πολιορκίας προσαχθείη: Herod. vi. 52, βουλομένην, εἴ κως ἀμφότεροι γενοίατο βασιλῆες. It is used when an end is proposed, but failure is presumed to be possible: see Hartung, ii. 206; Kühner, ii. 584. ὅμως μετὰ ταῦτα πάντα οὔπω θαρρῶ· ὕπερ ἀλλαχοῦ λέγει· οὐ δοκῶν ἑστάναι βλεπέτω μὴ πέσῃ. κ. πάλιν, φοβοῦμαι μή πως ἄλλοις κηρύξας, αὐτὸς ἀδόκιμος γένωμαι. Chrys.) I may attain (not future, but subjunctive aorist. On the sense, see Acts xxvi. 7; from which alone, it is evident that it does not signify 'live until,' as Van Hengel) unto the resurrection from the dead (viz. the blessed resurrection of the dead in Christ, in which οἱ τοῦ χριστοῦ shall rise ἐν τῇ παρουσίᾳ αὐτοῦ, 1 Cor. xv. 23, see also 1 Thess. iv. 16. But the ἐξ- in ἐξανάστ. does not distinctively point out this first resurrection, but merely indicates rising up, out of the dust ; cf. the verb Mark xii. 19 ‖ L., Acts xv. 5, and the word itself in ref. Polyb.).   12—14.] This seems to be inserted to prevent the misapprehension, that he conceived himself already to possess this knowledge, and to have grasped Christ in all His fulness.   12.] not that (I do not mean, that . . . . , see reff.) I have already acquired (this χριστὸν κερδῆσαι : not the βραβεῖον below (Mey.), which is an image subsequently introduced, whereas the reference here must be to something foregoing, nor τὴν ἀνάστασιν, which has just been stated as an object of his wishes for the future : but as Calv., "nempe ut in solidum communicet Christi passionibus, ut perfectum habeat gustum potentiæ resurrectionis, ut ipsum plane cognoscat ") or am already completed (in spiritual perfection. Philo de

p = Rom. ix. 30. 1 Cor. ix. 24. Exod. xv. 9. Deut. xxviii. 45.   q = Gal. v. 13. 1 Thess. iv. 7.   ellips., Mark x. 40. Luke v. 25.   r = Rom. iii. 28. xiv. 14 al. Wisd. xv. 12.   t = Mark xiii. 16 al. Gen. xix. 17.   6. w. gen., Heb. vi. 10. xiii. 2, 16. elsw., Matt. xvi. 5 ǁ, Mk. James i. 24 only.

δὲ εἰ καὶ ᴾ καταλάβω ᑫἐφ᾽ ᾧ καὶ ᴾ κατελήμφθην ὑπὸ χρισ- ABDFK LPℵ a b τοῦ. ¹³ ἀδελφοί, ἐγὼ ἐμαυτὸν οὐ ʳλογίζομαι ᴾκατειλη- c d e f g h k l m n φέναι· ¹⁴ ˢ ἓν δέ, ᵗ τὰ μὲν ᵗ ὀπίσω ᵘἐπιλανθανόμενος, ᵛ τοῖς o 17. 47 δὲ ᵛ ἔμπροσθεν ·ʷ ἐπεκτεινόμενος, ˣ κατὰ ʸ σκοπὸν ᵒ διώκω

u w. acc. (and Paul), here only.   Deut. iv. 9 al. pass., Luke xii.   s ellips., Rom. xiii. 7.   2 Cor. viii. 15.   Winer, § 66. 1. b.
v here only.   Isa. xli.   w here only †.   x = Acts
26. σκοπείτω τὰ ἔμπρ., ὡς μηδὲν ἡμᾶς λάθῃ, Xen. Anab. vi. 3. 14.   viii. 26.   y here only.   Job xvi. 13.

Tert Hil Ambr Aug Jer Pel).   om 1st και DF ℵ¹(ins ℵ³) vulg goth [æth arm Orig-int,] Tert Hil [Victorin] Ambr Ambrst Jer.   om 2nd και DF l¹ 67² Tert : for και, ει ℵ¹(txt ℵ-corr¹).   rec (for χρ.) του χρ. ιησ., with KL rel : χρ. ιησ. A[P]ℵ c f [47] Chr₁ Thl-ms : ιησ. χρ. a 112 : του χρ. D³ Damasc : txt BD¹F 17 goth æth Clem Mac [Orig-int₁] Tert Sing-cler Hil [Victorin] Jer.

13. om εγω D¹.   [εμαυτω P.]   for ου, ουπω AD¹[P]ℵ b² c g h 17 [47] syr-w-ast copt æth Clem Bas Chr-comm₁ Thdrt Damasc Chron Thl Œc Ambrst Jer_aliq. κατιληφοτα F.

14. for τοις δε, εις δε τα D¹F.   απεκτεινομενος F.

Alleg. iii. 23, vol. i. p. 101, πότε οὖν, ὦ ψυχή, μάλιστα νεκροφορεῖν σαυτὴν ὑπολήψῃ; ἆρά γε οὐχ ὅταν τελειωθῇς καὶ βραβείων κ. στεφάνων ἀξιωθῇς ;), but I pursue (the image of a runner in a course is already before him. So διώκω absolute in Æsch. Theb. 89, ὄρνυται λαὸς . . . ἐπὶ πόλιν διώκων. This is simpler than to suppose that an object, the βραβεῖον, is in his mind, though not expressed. See Ellic.'s note) if (nearly = εἴ πως above) I may also (besides διώκεις —not as Mey., nicht bloß greife (ἔλαβον), fondern auch ergreife: nor does it answer to the καί following, as De W.) lay hold of (Herod. ix. 58, διωκτέοι εἰσί, ἐς ὃ καταλαμφθέντες . . . . δώσουσι δίκας: Lucian, Hermotim. 77, διώκοντες οὐ κατέλαβον) that for which (this seems the simplest rendering, and has been the usual one. Meyer's rendering of ἐφ᾽ ᾧ 'because,' after Chrys., Thdrt., Thl., requires καταλάβω to be absolute, and would more naturally be expressed ἐφ᾽ ᾧ κἀγὼ κατελήμφθην, the emphatic first person hardly admitting of being supplied from the preceding clause : whereas on our rendering the whole forms but one clause, the first person recurring throughout it. Grot.'s, 'quo ut pervenire possem,' Beza's, &c., 'for which reason,'—all keeping καταλάβω absolute, are not open to the above objection) I was also laid hold of (the καί belongs to the verb, not to ἐγώ understood, nor to the ἐφ᾽ ᾧ, as if there might be other ends for which he was apprehended (Ellic.) : see above—and brings out, that in my case there was another instance of the καταλαβεῖν. For the sense, cf. 1 Cor. xiii. 12, ἐπιγνώσομαι καθὼς καὶ ἐπεγνώσθην : and Plato, Tim. p. 39, τῇ δὴ ταὐτοῦ φορᾷ τὰ τάχιστα περιιόντα ὑπὸ τῶν βραδυτέρων ἰόντων ἐφαίνετο καταλαμβάνοντα καταλαμβάνεσ-

θαι. The time referred to by the aorist was his conversion : but we need not, as Chrys., al., press the image of the race, and regard him as flying and overtaken) by Christ.   13.] Emphatic and affectionate re-statement of the same, but not merely so ;—he evidently alludes to some whom he wishes to warn by his example. Brethren, I (emphatic: cf. John v. 30; vii. 17 ; viii. 33; Acts xxvi. 9) do not reckon myself (emphatic) to have laid hold : but one thing (I do : not λογίζομαι, nor διώκω, nor φροντίζω, none of which correspond to the epexegesis following : nor can we say that nothing requires to be supplied (Grot., al.), for even in τοῦτο δέ this would not be so—the sense must have a logical supplement : nor will it do to join ἕν to διώκω (Aug., al.), or to supply ἐστι (Beza)) : forgetting the things behind (me, as a runner in the course ; by which image, now fully before him, the expressions in this verse must be explained : καὶ γὰρ ὁ δρομεὺς οὐχ ὅσους ἤνυσεν ἀναλογίζεται διαύλους, ἀλλ᾽ ὅσους λείπεται .... τί γὰρ ἡμᾶς ὠφελεῖ τὸ ἀνυσθέν, ὅταν τὸ λειπόμενον μὴ προστεθῇ ; Chr. Thdrt. explains it περὶ τῶν τοῦ κηρύγματος πόνων : but this seems insufficient), but ever reaching out towards (as the runner whose body is bent forwards in his course; the ἐπί giving the continual addition of exertion in this direction (Mey.) or perhaps merely the direction itself. ὁ γὰρ ἐπεκτεινόμενος, τοῦτ᾽ ἐστιν, ὁ τοὺς πόδας καίτοι τρέχοντας τῷ λοιπῷ σώματι προλαβεῖν σπουδάζων, ἐπεκτείνων ἑαυτὸν εἰς τὸ ἔμπροσθεν, κ. τὰς χεῖρας ἐκτείνων, ἵνα κ. τοῦ δρόμου πλέον τι ἐργάσηται. Chr.) the things before (i. e. the perfection not yet reached), I pursue (on διώκω absolute, see note, ver. 12) towards the goal (the contrary of ἀπὸ σκοποῦ, beside the

^z εἰς τὸ ^aβραβεῖον τῆς ^bἄνω ^cκλήσεως τοῦ θεοῦ ἐν z εἰς,=2 Thess.
i. 11; or
χριστῷ Ἰησοῦ. ¹⁵ ὅσοι οὖν ^dτέλειοι, τοῦτο ^eφρονῶ- 1 Cor. xi. 17.
Heb. vi. 8.—
μεν. καὶ εἴ τι ^fἑτέρως ^eφρονεῖτε, καὶ τοῦτο ὁ θεὸς ὑμῖν ἐπί, = Luke
xv. 4.
^gἀποκαλύψει. ¹⁶ ^hπλὴν ⁱεἰς ὃ ⁱἐφθάσαμεν, ^kτῷ αὐτῷ a 1 Cor. ix. 24
only †.
(-εύειν,
Col. iii. 14.)
^lστοιχεῖν. b Gal. iv. 26.
Col. iii. 1.

c = (1 Cor. i. 26.)   2 Thess. i. 11.   Heb. iii. 1.   d = 1 Cor. ii. 6. xiv. 20.   Heb. v. 14.
e = 1 Cor. xiii. 11.   Gal. v. 10 reff.   f here only †.   g = Matt. xvi. 17. (-ψις, Eph. i. 7.)
h Eph. v. 33 reff.   i Rom. ix. 31. Dan. iv. 19. xii. 12 Theod. ἐπί, 1 Thess. ii. 16. Dan. iv. 25
Theod. πρός. Eccl. viii. 14.   k dat., Gal. vi. 16.   l (=) Acts xxi. 24. Rom. iv. 12. Gal.
v. 25. vi. 16 only. (Eccles. xi. 6 only.)

rec (for εἰς) επι, with DFKL[P] rel [Petr] Chr Thdrt [Novat Victorin] : txt ABℵ 17
Clem Ath Chron.   om του θεου F vulg-ms Clem Novat Sing-cler [Victorin] Haymo.
for χρ. ιησ., κυριω ιησ. χρ. D¹F.
15. aft τελειοι ins εν χρ. ιησου F(not F-lat).   aft 1st τουτο ins ουν ℵ¹(ℵ³ disapproving).   φρονουμεν Lℵ n mss-in-Jer Clem.   om ο D¹.
16. συνστοιχειν F.   rec aft στοιχειν ins κανονι το αυτο φρονειν (κανονι
*prob to supply τω αυτω, and το αυτο φρονειν as a gloss explaing τω αυτ. στ. : cf Gal
vi. 16 ; ch ii. 2),* with D³KL[P]ℵ³ rel : aft εφθασαμεν ins το αυτο φρονειν D¹F m
Victorin Ambrst, D¹F omg κανονι, m insg it aft αυτω : om ABℵ¹ 17. 67² coptt æth
Thdot-ancyr Hil Aug_sæpe Facund (Sedul).

mark, Plato, Tim. p. 25 al.) **for** (to reach,
with a view to ; or perhaps simply in the
direction of : see reff. for both) **the prize**
(see 1 Cor. ix. 24 ; 2 Tim. iv. 8 ; Rev. ii.
10) **of my heavenly** (reff. and κλῆσις ἐπουράνιος Heb. iii. 1, Ἱερουσ. ἐπουράνιος
Heb. xii. 22. Not, *'from above,'* = ἄνωθεν : but the allusion is to his appointment
having been made directly in heaven, not
by delegation on earth) **calling** (not as we
familiarly use the word,—'calling in life,'
&c.—but to be kept to the *act of his being
called* as an Apostle : q. d. 'the prize consequent on the faithful carrying out of that
summons which I received from God in
heaven') **of God** (who was the caller : but
we must not think of Him, as Grot., al.,
—as the arbiter sitting above and summoning to the course,—for in these last
words the figure is dropt, and ἡ ἄνω κλῆσις represents real matter of fact) **in
Christ Jesus** (to what are these last words
to be referred ? Chrys., al., join them
with διώκω :—ἐν χ. Ἰ. τοῦτο ποιῶ, φησιν.
οὐ γὰρ ἔνι χωρὶς τῆς ἐκείνου ῥοπῆς τοσοῦτον διελθεῖν διάστημα· πολλῆς δεῖ τῆς
βοηθείας, πολλῆς τῆς συμμαχίας. But I
own the arrangement of the sentence thus
seems to me very unnatural—and the constant practice of St. Paul to join θεός and
things said of θεός with ἐν χριστῷ weighs
strongly for the other connexion, viz. that
with τ. κλήσεως τοῦ θεοῦ. The objection
that then τῆς or τοῦ would be required
before ἐν, is not valid ; the unity of the
idea of the κλῆσις ἐν κυρίῳ, 1 Cor. vii. 22,
would dispense with it). **15, 16.**] *Exhortation to them to be unanimous in following this his example.* In order to understand this somewhat difficult passage,

we must remember **(1)** that the description
of his own views and feelings which he holds
up for their imitation (συμμιμηταί μου
γίν.) began with having no confidence in
the flesh, ver. 4, and has continued to ver.
14. Also **(2)** that the description commencing with ὅσοι οὖν τέλειοι, is taken up
again from ver. 3, ἡμεῖς γάρ ἐσμεν ἡ περιτομή, οἱ πνεύματι θεοῦ λατρεύοντες, κ. καυχώμενοι ἐν χ. Ἰησοῦ, κ. οὐκ ἐν σαρκὶ πεποιθότες. These two considerations will keep
us from narrowing too much the **τοῦτο
φρονῶμεν,** and from misunderstanding the
ὅσοι οὖν τέλειοι. As many of us then
(refers to ver. 3 : see above) **as are perfect**
(mature in Christian life, = those described
above, ver. 3), **let us. be of this mind**
(viz. that described as entertained by himself, vv. 7—14) : **and if in any thing**
(accusative of reference : see Kühner,
Gramm. ii. 220 ff.) **ye be differently minded**
(for ἑτέρως, cf. Od. α. 232 ff., μέλλεν μέν
ποτε οἶκος ὅδ' ἀφνειὸς κ. ἀμύμων | ἔμμε-
ναι, ὄφρ' ἔτι κεῖνος ἀνὴρ ἐπιδήμιος
ἦεν· | νῦν δ' ἑτέρως ἐβάλοντο θεοί, κακὰ
μητιόωντες : Demosth. p. 298. 22, εἰ μέν
τι τῶν δεόντων ἐπράχθη, τὸν καιρόν, οὐκ
ἐμέ φησιν αἴτιον γεγενῆσθαι, τῶν δ' ὡς
ἑτέρως συμβάντων ἁπάντων ἐμὲ καὶ τὴν
ἐμὴν τύχην αἰτίαν εἶναι. Hence it gives
the meaning of diversity in a bad sense.
The difference referred to seems to be that
of too much self-esteem as to Christian
perfection : see below), **this also** (as well
as the rest which he has revealed) **will
God reveal to you** (i. e. in the progress
of the Christian life, you will find the
true knowledge of your own imperfection
and of Christ's all-sufficiency revealed to
you by God's Spirit, Eph. i. 17 ff. ὅρα

m here only †.
n (but not =)
Rom. xvi. 17.
Gal. vi. 1 reff.
o Rom. vi. 4.
Eph. iv. 1
reff.
p = 1 Thess. i. 7.   2 Thess. iii. 9.   1 Tim. iv. 12.   Tit. ii. 7.   1 Pet. v. 3.
John viii. 27.   Rom. iv. 6.
q = 2 Thess. iii. 7—9.   r constr.,
ABDFK LPℵ a b c d e f g h k l m n o 17. 47

17 ᵐ Συμμιμηταί μου γίνεσθε, ἀδελφοί, καὶ ⁿ σκοπεῖτε τοὺς οὕτως ᵒ περιπατοῦντας καθὼς ἔχετε ᵖ τύπον ᑫ ἡμᾶς. 18 πολλοὶ γὰρ ᵒ περιπατοῦσιν, ʳ οὓς πολλάκις ᵏ ἔλεγον

πῶς συνεσταλμένως τοῦτό φησιν. ὁ θεὸς ὑμᾶς διδάξει, τουτέστιν, ὑμᾶς πείσει, οὐχὶ διδάξει ἁπλῶς. ἐδίδασκε μὲν γὰρ ὁ Παῦλος, ἀλλ' ὁ θεὸς ἐνῆγε. καὶ οὐκ εἶπεν, ἐνάξει, ἀλλ' ἀποκαλύψει, ἵνα δόξῃ μᾶλλον ἀγνοίας εἶναι τὸ πρᾶγμα. οὐ περὶ δογμάτων ταῦτ' εἴρηται, ἀλλὰ περὶ βίου τελειότητος, κ. τοῦ μὴ νομίζειν ἑαυτοὺς τελείους εἶναι· ὡς ὅ γε νομίζων τὸ πᾶν εἰληφέναι, οὐδὲν ἔχει. Chrys. τοῦτο must not be taken as Œc., Grot., &c. as representing *the fact, that ye* ἑτέρως φρονεῖτε, but is *the thing, respecting which* ye ἐτ. φρ.).

16.] Let not however this diversity, respecting which some of you yet await deeper revelations from God's Spirit, produce any dissension in your Christian unity. **Nevertheless** (notwithstanding that some of you, &c. as above. On πλήν, see Devarius, and Klotz's note, i. 188; ii. 725) **as far as we have attained** (towards Christian perfection: ὁ κατωρθώσαμεν, Thl.: including both knowledge and practice, of both which he spoke above in his own case. On the construction, see reff.), **walk by the same (path)** (reff.: Polyb. xxviii. 5. 6, βουλόμενοι στοιχεῖν τῇ τῆς συγκλήτου προθέσει: see Fritz. ad Rom. iii. p. 142. On the elliptic usage of the infinitive for the imperative see Kühner, ii. p. 342, where many examples are given. It appears from these that the usage occurs in the *2nd person only*: which determines this to be not '*let us walk*,' but 'walk ye'). The exhortation refers to the onward advance of the Christian life—let us go on together, each one in his place and degree of advance, but all in the same path. 17 —IV. 1.] *Exhortation to follow his example* (17): *warning against the enemies of the cross of Christ* (18, 19): *declaration of the high privileges and hopes of Christians* (20, 21), *and affectionate entreaty to stedfastness* (iv. 1). **Be imitators together** (i. e. with one another: so, and not imitators together with those mentioned below (Mey., Wies.), must the word here be rendered. The latter would be allowable as far as the word is concerned, but the form of the sentence determines for the other. συμμιμηταί μου γίνεσθε forms a complete clause, in which συμμιμηταί has the place of emphasis, and in συμμιμηταί the preposition: it is therefore unallowable to pass on the sense

of the συμ. to another clause from which it is separated by καί and another verb. So that instead of καὶ σκοπεῖτε κ.τ.λ. being a reason for this meaning, it is in fact a reason against it) **of me, and observe** (for imitation: τοὺς εὐτέλειαν μᾶλλον ἢ πολυχρηματίαν σκοποῦντας, Xen. Symp. iv. 42) **those who walk in such manner as ye have an example in us.** The construction is much controverted. Meyer and Wiesinger would separate οὕτως and καθώς—*observe those who thus walk* (i. e. as implied above); *as ye have* (emphatic—ye are not in want of) *an example in us* (viz. Paul and those who thus walk). My objection to this is, that if οὕτως and καθώς are to be independent —the three verbs γίνεσθε, σκοπεῖτε, ἔχετε, being thus thrown into three independent clauses, will be all correlative, and the ἔχετε τύπον will not apply to οὕτως περιπατοῦντας, but to the foregoing verbs, thus stultifying the sentence: "*Be &c., and observe &c., as ye have an example* (viz. of being συμμιμηταί μου and of σκοπεῖν τοὺς οὕτως περιπατοῦντας) *in us.*" Besides which, the οὕτως περιπατοῦντας would be (1) very vague as referring back to what *went before*, seeing that no περιπατεῖν has been specified, whereas (2) it is directly related to what *follows*, by the πολλοὶ περιπατοῦσιν of ver. 18. I therefore retain the usual rendering. Meyer's objections to it are, (1) that it is ἔχετε, not ἔχουσιν:—but this does not affect the matter: for, the example including in its reference the τοὺς οὕτως περιπατοῦντας and the Philippians, the 2nd person would be more naturally used, the 3rd making a separation which would not be desirable: —(2) that it is ἡμᾶς, not ἐμέ:—but granting that this does not apply to Paul alone, it certainly cannot, as Mey., be meant to include the τοὺς οὕτ. περ. with him, which would be a way of speaking unprecedented in his writings,—but must apply to himself and his fellow-workers, Timotheus, Epaphroditus, &c. Of course the τύπον is no objection (as De W.) to the proper plural sense of ἡμᾶς, for it is used of that wherein they were all united in one category, as in ἡδεῖς τὴν ὄψιν (Plato), κακοὶ τὴν ψυχήν (Æsch.): see Kühner, ii. 27. 18.] **For** (reason for σκοπεῖτε κ.τ.λ. in the form of warning against others who walk differently) **many walk**

ὑμῖν, νῦν δὲ καὶ κλαίων λέγω, τοὺς ˢἐχθροὺς τοῦ ᵗ σταυ- ˢ accus. attr.,
1 John ii. 25.
ροῦ τοῦ χριστοῦ, ¹⁹ ὧν τὸ ᵘτέλος ᵛἀπώλεια, ὧν ὁ θεὸς Plato, Rep.
iii. 12, p. 402,
ἡ ʷκοιλία, καὶ ἡ ˣδόξα ἐν τῇ ʸαἰσχύνῃ αὐτῶν, οἱ τὰ οὔτε αὐτοί,
οὔτε οὕς
ᶻἐπίγεια ᵃ φρονοῦντες. ²⁰ ἡμῶν γὰρ τὸ ᵇπολίτευμα ἐν φαμεν ἡμῖν
παιδευτέον
οὐρανοῖς ᶜὑπάρχει, ἐξ ᵈοὗ καὶ σωτῆρα ᵉἀπεκδεχόμεθα εἶναι, τοὺς
φύλακας.
Winer, § 59.7.

t Gal. v. 11 reff.   u = Rom. vi. 21.   2 Cor. xi. 15. Heb. vi. 8.   1 Pet. iv. 17. Wisd. iii. 19.
v = Matt. vii. 13. ch. i. 28. Jer. xxvi. (xlvi.) 21.   w = Rom. xvi. 18. Prov. xxiv. 15.   x – Eph.
iii. 13. 1 Thess. ii. 20.   y = 2 Cor. iv. 2. Jude 13. (Luke xiv. 9. Heb. xii. 2. Rev. iii. 18
only. Obad. 10.)   z ch. ii. 10 reff.   a = ch. ii. 2 al.   b here only. (see
note.) 2 Macc. xii. 7 only. (-εύειν, ch. i. 27.)   c Gal. i. 14 reff.   d so Col. ii. 19
(see note).   e Gal. v. 5 reff.

18. ἐλεγομεν D¹.   om και D¹ 55 Syr.
20. for γαρ, δε 80 latt Syr syr-mg goth [æth arm] Clem Orig₂[and int₃] Eus₂
Chr-comm Thl-ed Iren-int lat-ff.

(no need to supply any thing, as κακῶς
(Œc.), or '*longe aliter*' (Grot.), nor to
understand the word '*circulantur*,' as
1 Pet. v. 8 (Storr, al., but inconsistently
with ver. 17),—still less with Calv. '*am-
bulant terrena cogitantes*' (ungrammatical: οἱ τὰ ἐπίγ. φρ.): or to consider the
sentence as broken off by the relative
clause (De W., al.); for περιπατοῦσιν is
a 'verbum indifferens,' as in ver. 17, τοὺς
οὕτως περιπ.) whom I many times (answers to πολλοί) mentioned to you (viz.
when I was with you) but now mention
even weeping (διὰ τί; ὅτι ἐπέτεινε τὸ
κακόν, ὅτι δακρύων ἄξιοι οἱ τοιοῦτοι . . . .
κλαίει τοίνυν ὁ Παῦλος ἐφ᾽ οἷς ἕτεροι
γελῶσι καὶ σπαταλῶσιν. οὕτως ἐστὶ συμ-
παθητικός, οὕτω φροντίζει πάντων ἀνθρώπων. Chrys.), the enemies (the article
designates the particular class intended)
of the cross of Christ (not, as Thdrt.,
Luth., Erasm., all., of the *doctrine* of the
Cross:—nor is there any reason to identify these with those spoken of ver. 2.
Not Judaistic but Epicurean error, not
obliquity of creed but of practice, is here
stigmatized. And so Chrys.,—ἐπειδή τινες ἦσαν ὑποκρινόμενοι μὲν τὸν χριστια-
νισμόν, ἐν ἀνέσει δὲ ζῶντες κ. τρυφῇ·
τοῦτο δὲ ἐνάντίον τῷ σταυρῷ),—of whom
perdition (everlasting, at the coming of
the Lord: see ch. i. 28) is the (fixed,
certain) end; of whom their belly is the
god (cf. the boast of the Cyclops, in Eurip.
Cycl. 334 ff.,—ᾆ 'γὼ οὔ τινι θύω, πλὴν
ἐμοί, θεοῖσι δ᾽ οὔ, | καὶ τῇ μεγίστῃ γαστρὶ
τῇδε δαιμόνων | ὡς τοὔμπιεῖν γε καὶ
φαγεῖν τοὔφ᾽ ἡμέραν, | Ζεὺς οὗτος ἀν-
θρώποισι τοῖσι σώφροσιν. Seneca de be-
nef. vii. 26, 'alius abdomini servit') and
their glory in their shame ("ἡ δόξα is
subjective,—in the judgment of these
men,—and τῇ αἰσχύνῃ objective,—according to the reality of morals. Cf.
Polyb. xv. 23. 5, ἐφ᾽ οἷς ἐχρῆν αἰσχύνεσθαι καθ᾽ ὑπερβολήν, ἐπὶ τούτοις ὡς

καλοῖς σεμνύνεσθαι καὶ μεγαλαυχεῖν.
On εἶναι ἐν, 'versari,' to be found in, or
contained in, any thing, cf. Plato Gorg.
470 E, ἐν τούτῳ ἡ πᾶσα εὐδαιμονία ἐστίν,
—Eur. Phœn. 1310,—οὐκ ἐν αἰσχύνῃ τὰ
σά." Meyer.   Ambr., Hil., Pel., Aug.,
Beng., al., refer the expression to circumcision, taking another meaning for αἰσχύνη ('venter et pudor sunt affinia.'
Beng.), but without reason; and Chrys.,
al., disown the meaning, who regard (it
is not easy to give φρονεῖν, φρόνημα, in
this sense, by one word in English. They
betoken the whole aspect, the *set* of the
thoughts and desires: τὰ ἐπίγεια, are
the substratum of all their feelings) the
things on earth (in opposition to the
things above, cf. Col. iii. 1 ff. The construction is that of logical reference to the
subject of the sentence, setting aside the
strictness of grammatical connexion: so
Thuc. iii. 36,—ἔδοξεν αὐτοῖς . . . . ἐπι-
καλοῦντες, and iv. 108; vi. 24; vii.
42: see more examples in Kühner, ii. 377.
The οἱ serves as τούς above, to indicate and individualize the class).   **20.**]
For (I may well direct you to avoid τοὺς
τὰ ἐπίγεια φρονοῦντας:—*for*—our state
and feelings are wholly alien from theirs)
our (emphatic) **country** (the *state*, to
which we belong, of which we by faith are
citizens,—ἡ πατρίς, Thl.; meaning the
Kingdom of God, the heavenly Jerusalem
(Gal. iv. 26. Col. iii. 1 ff.). This objective meaning of the word is better than the
subjective one, '*our citizenship*' (πολιτεία,
Acts xxii. 28: but they seem sometimes to
be used indifferently, see Palm and Rost's
Lex., and Aristot. Pol. iii. 4, κύριον μὲν
γὰρ τὸ πολίτευμα τῆς πόλεως· πολίτευμα
δ᾽ ἐστὶν ἡ πολιτεία, cf. however, on the
other side, Ellicott: and his note throughout), or, '*our conversation*,' as vulg. E. V.,
which rendering seems to want precedent.
Conyb. renders it '*life*:' but this is insufficient, even supposing it justifiable, as

f 1 Cor. iv. 6.
2 Cor. xi. 13,
14, 15 only †.
1 Kings
xxviii. 8
Symm. Jos.
Antt. vii. 10.
5.
g constr., Rom.
vii. 24.

κύριον Ἰησοῦν χριστόν, ²¹ ὃς ᶠ μετασχηματίσει τὸ ᵍ σῶμα τῆς ʰ ταπεινώσεως ἡμῶν ⁱ σύμμορφον τῷ ᵍ σώματι τῆς δόξης αὐτοῦ, κατὰ τὴν ᵏ ἐνέργειαν ˡ τοῦ δύνασθαι αὐτὸν καὶ ᵐ ὑποτάξαι αὐτῷ τὰ πάντα. IV. ¹ ⁿ ὥστε, ἀδελφοί

ABDFK
LPℵ a b
c d e f g
h k l m n
o 17. 47

h Luke i. 48. Acts viii. 33 (from Isa. liii. 8). James i. 10 only.   i Rom. viii. 29 only †. constr., Matt.
xii. 13. 1 Thess. iii. 13. Winer, § 66. 3. g.   k Eph. i. 19 reff. iii. 7.   l constr., Luke xxii. 6. Acts
xiv. 9. 2 Cor. viii. 11.   m Eph. i. 22 reff.   n = ch. ii. 12 reff.

21. rec ins εις το γενεσθαι αυτο bef συμμορφον, with D²·³KL[P] rel syrr Orig₂[and int₁] Cæs Epiph Chron Victorin Jer : om ABD¹Fℵ latt (copt) goth æth [arm] Eus Ath Cyr[-p] Antch Iren-int Orig-int Tert Cypr [Hil₂].   rec (for αυτω) εαυτω, with D³Lℵ³ rel 67² Thdrt, sibi vulg(and F-lat) Hil Ambr : txt ABD¹F[KP]ℵ¹ b¹ f k o 17 [47] Eus Epiph Chr₁-mss Cyr Thl-mss [Victorin].

giving the English reader the idea of ζωή, and so misleading him. I may remark, in passing, on the unfortunate misconception of St. Paul's use of the plural, which has marred so many portions of Mr. Cony-beare's version of the Epistles, and none more sadly than this,—where he gives the Apostle's noble description of the state and hopes of us Christians, as contrasted with the τὰ ἐπίγ. φρονοῦντες,—all in the singular—'*For my life, &c.,—from whence also I look, &c.*') subsists (the word is more solemn, as indicating priority and fixedness, than ἐστιν would be: see notes, ch. ii. 6, and Acts xvi. 20) in the heavens, from whence (οὗ does not refer to πολίτευμα, as Beng., al.—nor = ὧν, nor to be rendered '*ex quo tempore,*' as Erasm., but ἐξ οὗ is adverbial, '*unde,*' see Winer, § 21. 3, and cf. Xen. Anab. i. 2. 20, ἡμέρας τρεῖς, ἐν ᾧ) also (additional particular, following on heaven being our country) we wait for (expect, till the event arrives : see note on Rom. viii. 19, and a dissertation in the Fritzschiorum Opuscula, p. 150 ff.) a Saviour (emphatic : therefore *we* cannot τὰ ἐπίγ. φρονεῖν, because we are waiting for one to deliver us from them. Or, as Saviour (Ellic.) : but perhaps the other is preferable, as being simpler), (viz.) the Lord Jesus Christ, 21.] (describes *the method, in which* this Saviour shall save us—a way utterly precluding *our* making a God of our body) who shall transform (see 1 Cor. xv. 51 ff. The words assume, as St. Paul always does when speaking incidentally, the ἡμεῖς surviving to witness the coming of the Lord. The change from the dust of death in the resurrection, however we may *accommodate* the expression to it, was not originally contemplated by it ; witness the ἀπεκδεχόμεθα, and the σῶμα τῆς ταπεινώσεως ἡμῶν. It is quite in vain to attempt to escape from this inference, as Ellicott does, by saying that "every moment of a true Christian's life involves such an ἀπεκδοχήν." This is

most true, but in no way accounts for the peculiar expressions used here) the body of our humiliation (beware of the hendiadys, by which most Commentators, and even Conyb. here enervate the Apostle's fine and deep meaning. The *body* is that object, that material, in which our *humiliation* has place and is shewn, by its suffering and being degraded—πολλὰ πάσχει νῦν τὸ σῶμα, δεσμεῖται, μαστίζεται, μυρία πάσχει δεινά, Chrys. He once had such a ταπείνωσις, and has passed through it to His glory—and He shall change us so as to be like Him.—Whereas the rendering '*our vile body*' sinks all this, and makes the epithet merely refer to that which is common to all humanity by nature. It is besides, perhaps, hardly allowable : for ταπείνωσις cannot—unless the exigency of context require it, as in ref. Luke (not in Prov. xvi. 19),—signify mere '*vileness,*' ταπεινότης, but must imply the act whereby the body ταπεινοῦται) (so as to be) conformed to (on this common idiom, εὔφημον, ὦ τάλαινα, κοίμησον στόμα, Æsch. Ag. 1258, al. freq.,—cf. Kühner, ii. 121) the body of His glory (in which, as its object or material, His glory has place and is displayed : see above), according to (after the analogy of) the working of His power also (besides the μετασχήμ. &c. spoken of) to subject to Him all things (*the universe* : see the exception, 1 Cor. xv. 25—27). ταῦτα δὲ ποιήσει, says Thdrt., ἅτε δὴ δύναμιν ἄρρητον ἔχων, κ. ῥᾳδίως κ. τὴν φθορὰν κ. τὸν θάνατον καταπαύων, κ. εἰς ἀθανασίαν τὰ ἡμέτερα σώματα μεταβάλλων, κ. παρασκευάζων ἅπαντας εἰς αὐτὸν ἀποβλέπειν. And Chrys. :—ἔδειξε μείζονα ἔργα τῆς δυνάμεως αὐτοῦ, ἵνα κ. τούτοις πιστεύσῃς. αὐτῷ, used of the αὐτός of the whole sentence, from the position of the writer, not of the agent in the clause itself. IV. 1.] *Concluding exhortation,* referring to what has passed since ch. iii. 17,—not farther back, for there first he turns directly to them in the second

μου ἀγαπητοὶ καὶ ° ἐπιπόθητοι, ᵖ χαρὰ καὶ ᵖ٩ στέφανός
μου, οὕτως ʳ στήκετε ἐν κυρίῳ, ˢ ἀγαπητοί.
² Εὐοδίαν ᵗ παρακαλῶ καὶ Συντύχην ᵗ παρακαλῶ τὸ
αὐτὸ ᵘ φρονεῖν ἐν κυρίῳ. ³ ᵛ ναὶ ʷ ἐρωτῶ καὶ σέ, ˣ γνήσιε
ʸ σύνζυγε, ᶻ συνλαμβάνου αὐταῖς, ᵃ αἵτινες ᵇ ἐν τῷ εὐαγγε-

o here only †.
p 1 Thess. ii.
19.
q Prov. xvi. 31.
Ezek. xvi. 12.
r Gal. v. 1 reff.
s (alone) Paul,
Rom. xii. 19.
2 Cor. xii. 19
only. Heb.
vi. 9. 1 Pet.
ii. 11 al5.
1 John ii. 7
v Philem. 20.

al5. 3 John 2, 5, 11. Jude 3, 17, 20.   t Eph. iv. 1 reff.   u ch. ii. 2 reff.   v Philem. 20.
w = Matt. xv. 23. 1 Thess. iv. 1 reff.   x 2 Cor. viii. 8. 1 Tim. i. 2. Tit. i. 4 only †. Sir. vii. 18
only. (-ίως, ch. ii. 20.)   y here only †. Aristoph. Plut. 945.   z = Luke v. 7 only. Gen.
xxx. 8 F(not A. B def.).   a = Acts x. 41, 47. xiii. 31, 43 al.   b = Rom. i. 9. 2 Cor. viii. 18. x. 14 al.

CHAP. IV. 1. χαρις F(and G, but *gaudium* G-lat).   [om 2nd μου B¹.]   ins
και bef οντως F.   om 2nd αγαπητοι D¹ 108 [goth Victorin].   aft 2nd αγαπητοι
ins μου B 17.
2. (ευοδιαν, so ABDFKLℵ, &c [not P 47].)
3. rec for ναι, και (*error*), with h(e sil) : txt ABDFKL[P]ℵ rel vss gr-lat-ff.
rec συζυγε bef γνησιε, with KL rel syrr Chr Thdrt : εγνησιε γερμανε συνζ. F : txt
ABD[P]ℵ c o 17 [47] latt copt Thl.

person, with ἀδελφοί, as here,—there also
οὕτως occurs, answering to the οὕτως here,
—and there, in the Christian's hopes, vv.
20, 21, lies the ground of the ὥστε here.
ὥστε] 'quæ cum ita sint'—since
we have such a home, and look for such a
Saviour, and expect such a change:—ὥστε
κἂν ὁρᾶτε τούτους χαίροντας, κἂν ὁρᾶτε
δεδοξασμένους, στήκετε, Chrys. Cf. 1 Cor.
xv. 58.   ἐπιπόθ.] longed for. The
word occurs in Appian, vi. 43, ὅρκους τε
ὤμοσεν αὐτοῖς κ. ἔλαβεν, ἐπιποθήτους ἐν
τοῖς ὕστερον πολέμοις πολλάκις γενομένους. For the verb, see ch. i. 8 reff.: for
the substantive, -ησις, 2 Cor. vii. 7, 11.
στέφανος] from ref. 1 Thess., both
χαρά and στέφανος apply to the future
great day in the Apostle's mind. And
indeed even without such reference to his
usus loquendi, it would be difficult to dis-
sociate the "*crown*" from such thoughts
as that in 2 Tim. iv. 8.   οὕτως] see
above : ' as I have been describing :' not
ὡς ἑστήκατε ἀκλινῶς, as Chrys., Thl.,
Œc., Calv., Beng., '*ita, ut statis, state*,'
which would be inconsistent with ch. iii.
17.   ἐν κυρίῳ] as the element wherein
your stedfastness consists.   ἀγαπητοί]
an affectionate repetition : μετ' εὐφημίας
πολλῆς ἡ παραίνεσις, Thdrt. "Doctrinam suo more vehementioribus exhorta-
tionibus claudit, quo eam hominum animis
tenacius infigat. Et blandis appellationi-
bus in eorum affectus se insinuat : quæ
tamen non sunt adulationis, sed sinceri
amoris." Calv.   2—9.] *Concluding
exhortations to individuals* (2, 3), *and to
all* (4—9). 2.] Euodia and Syntyche
(both *women*, cf. αὐταῖς and αἵτινες below)
appear to have needed this exhortation on
account of some disagreement, both however being faithful, and fellow-workers
(perhaps deaconesses, Rom. xvi. 1) with
himself in the Gospel. θαυμάζει μὲν τὰς

γυναῖκας· αἰνίττεται δὲ ὡς ἔριν τινὰ πρὸς
ἀλλήλας ἐχούσας, Thdrt. The repetition
of the verb παρακαλῶ not merely signifies
'vehementiam affectus' (Erasm.), but hints
at the present separation between them.
τὸ αὐτὸ φρονεῖν] see ch. ii. 2, note.
He adds ἐν κυρίῳ, both to shew them
wherein their unanimity must consist, and
perhaps to point out to them that their
present alienation was *not* ἐν κυρίῳ.
3.] ναί assumes the granting of the request
just made, and carries on farther the same
matter, see Philem. 20 and note; but does
not *conjure*, as Grot., al.   γνήσιε
σύνζυγε] true ('*genuine* :'—true, as distinguished from counterfeit : lit. of legitimate worth (γενήσιος)) yoke-fellow.
Who is intended, it is quite impossible
to say. Various opinions have been, (1)
that St. Paul addresses *his own wife*.
So Clem. Alex. Strom. iii. 6 (53), p. 535 P,
καὶ ὅ γε Παῦλος οὐκ ὀκνεῖ ἔν τινι ἐπιστολῇ
τὴν αὐτοῦ προσαγορεύειν σύνζυγον, ἣν
οὐ περιεκόμιζε διὰ τὸ τῆς ὑπηρεσίας εὐ-
σταλές.—Eus. H. E. iii. 30, al. But this
is evidently an error, and Thdrt. says
rightly,—τὸν δὲ σύνζ. τινες ἀνοήτως ὑπέλαβον γυναῖκα εἶναι τοῦ ἀποστόλου, οὐ
προσεσχηκότες τοῖς ἐν τῇ πρὸς Κορινθίους
γεγραμμένοις (1 Cor. vii. 8), ὅτι τοῖς ἀγά-
μοις συνέταξεν ἑαυτόν. Besides which,
the adjective in this case would be feminine,—cf. Eur. Alcest. 326, ποίας τυχοῦσα
συνζύγου ;—and 354, τοιᾶσδ' ἁμαρτάνοντι
συνζύγου : perhaps even if it were of two
terminations (as adjectives in -ιος frequently in the N. T., e.g. οὐράνιος, Luke ii.
13; Acts xxvi. 19 : ὁσίους χεῖρας, 1 Tim.
ii. 8, &c. See Winer, § 11. 1), in which
case Ellic. remarks, it would revert to
three terminations ; but authority for this
statement seems wanting. (2) that he
was the husband, or brother, of Euodia
or Syntyche; so Chrys. doubtfully, and

c ch. i. 27
only †.
d ch. ii. 25 reff.
e Rev. iii. 5.
xiii. 8. xvii.
8. xx. 15.
xxi. 27.
(Exod. xxxii.
32. Ps.
lxviii. 28.
Dan. xii. 1.)
24. Lev. iv. 14.

λίῳ ^c συνήθλησάν μοι, μετὰ καὶ Κλήμεντος καὶ τῶν λοι- ABDFK
πῶν ^d συνεργῶν μου, ὧν τὰ ὀνόματα ἐν ^e βίβλῳ ^e ζωῆς.

4 ^f Χαίρετε ἐν κυρίῳ πάντοτε· πάλιν ἐρῶ, χαίρετε.

5 τὸ ^g ἐπιεικὲς ὑμῶν ^h γνωσθήτω πᾶσιν ἀνθρώποις. ὁ

LPℵ a b
c d e f g
h k l m n
o 17. 47

f ver. 10. ch. iii. 1.   g = 1 Tim. iii. 3 reff   h constr., Acts ix.

om καὶ (bef κλημεντος) D¹F a latt arm (Orig) [Victorin] Ambrst Pel.   om
λοιπων, adding και των λοιπων aft μου, ℵ¹(txt ℵ³).
5. ins τοις bef ανθρ. A.

Thl., al. But then the epithet would hardly be wanted—nor would the expression be at all natural. (3) that he was some fellow-labourer of the Apostle. So Thdrt.,— σύνζυγον καλεῖ, ὡς τὸν αὐτὸν ἕλκοντα τῆς εὐσεβείας ζυγόν, Pelag., all., and De W.,—and of these some (Grot., Calov., al.) have understood *Epaphroditus,* —Estius, *Timotheus,*—Bengel (but afterwards he preferred *Epaphroditus*), Silas, —Luther, the *chief bishop* at Philippi. (4) Others have regarded Σύνζυγε as a proper name : so τινές in Chrys. and Œc., and so Meyer. In this case the γνήσιε would mean, 'who art veritably, as thy name is,' a yoke-fellow. And this might be said by the Apostle, who elsewhere compares the Christian minister to the βοῦς ἀλοῶν. It seems to me that we must choose between the two last hypotheses. The objections to each are about of equal weight : the Apostle no where else calls his fellow-labourers σύνζυγοι,—and the proper name Σύνζυγος is no where else found. But these are no reasons, respectively, against either hypothesis. We may safely say with Chrys., εἴτε τοῦτο, εἴτε ἐκεῖνο, οὐ σφόδρα ἀκριβολογεῖσθαι δεῖ. **συνλαμβάνου αὐταῖς**] help them (Euodia and Syntyche) : but not, as Grot., 'ut habeant, unde se suosque honeste sustentent :' it is *the work of their reconciliation* which he clearly has in view, and in which they would need help. **αἵτινες**] '*utpote quæ*'—seeing that they .... The E. V. here is in error, '*help those women which* ...' The Gospel at Philippi was first received by *women,* Acts xvi. 13 ff., and these two must have been among those who, having believed, laboured among their own sex for its spread. **ἐν τῷ εὐαγ.**] see reff. **μετὰ καὶ Κλήμεντος**] These words belong to συνήθλησαν, not to συνλαμβάνου, and are rather an additional reminiscence, than a part of the exhortation '*as did Clemens also* &c.' q. d. 'not that I mean, by naming those women with distinction, to imply forgetfulness of those others &c., and especially of Clemens.' The insertion of καί between the preposition and substantive is said to

be a habit principally of Pindar,—e. g. ἐν καὶ θαλάσσᾳ, Ol. ii. 28 ; ἐν καὶ τελευτᾷ, Ol. vii. 26 : ἐπὶ καὶ θανάτῳ, Pyth. iv. 330. See Hartung, i. 143. It is not necessary to regard the καὶ—καί as bound together : so that these examples are in point (against Ellic.). Clemens must have been a fellow-worker with the Apostle *at Philippi,* from the context here ; and, from the non-occurrence of any such name among Paul's fellow-travellers, and the fact that οἱ λοιποὶ συνεργοί must have been Philippians,—himself a native of Philippi. It is perhaps arbitrary, seeing that the name is so common, to assume his identity with Clemens afterwards Bishop of Rome, and author of the Epistles to the Corinthians. So Eus. H. E. iii. 4, ὁ Κλήμης, τῆς Ῥωμαίων κ. αὐτὸς ἐκκλησίας τρίτος ἐπίσκοπος καταστάς, Παύλου συνεργὸς κ. συναθλητὴς γεγονέναι πρὸς αὐτοῦ μαρτυρεῖται : see also H. E. v. 6 : so Origen, Com. in Joan. t. vi. 36, vol. iv. p. 153 : and Jer. Script. Eccl., 15, vol. ii. p. 854. Chrys. does not notice any such idea. See on the whole, Ellicott's note. **ὧν τὰ ὀν. ἐν βίβλῳ ζωῆς**] belongs to the λοιποί, whom *he does not name :* whose names are (not a wish, εἴη, as Bengel, nor are they to be regarded as *dead* when this was written) in the book of life (reff., and Luke x. 20). **4—9.**] *Exhortation* to ALL. **4. πάλιν ἐρῶ**] AGAIN I will say it: referring to ch. iii. 1, where see note. It is the groundtone of the Epistle. **5.**] τὸ ἐπιεικές, **your forbearance**, from ἐπί, implying direction, and εἰκός, ἔοικα (not εἴκω, to yield, as Trench, N. T. Syn. 171 : see Palm and Rost's Lex., under the word, as also under ΕΊΚΩ and ἔοικα), *reasonableness of dealing,* wherein not strictness of legal right, but consideration for one another, is the rule of practice. Aristot., Eth. Nic. v. 10. 6, defines it to be that which fills up the necessary deficiencies of *law,* which is *general,* by dealing with particular cases as the law-giver would have dealt with them if he had been by. διό, he adds, δίκαιον μέν ἐστι, καὶ βέλτιόν τινος δικαίου.... καὶ ἔστιν αὕτη ἡ φύσις ἡ τοῦ ἐπιεικοῦς, ἐπανόρθωμα νόμου, ᾗ ἐλλείπει διὰ τὸ καθ-

κύριος [i] ἐγγύς. [6] μηδὲν [k] μεριμνᾶτε, ἀλλ᾽ [l] ἐν παντὶ τῇ [m] προσευχῇ καὶ τῇ [m] δεήσει μετὰ [n] εὐχαριστίας τὰ [o] αἰτήματα ὑμῶν [p] γνωριζέσθω πρὸς τὸν θεόν. [7] καὶ ἡ εἰρήνη τοῦ θεοῦ ἡ [q] ὑπερέχουσα πάντα [r] νοῦν [s] φρουρήσει τὰς καρδίας ὑμῶν καὶ τὰ [t] νοήματα ὑμῶν ἐν χριστῷ Ἰησοῦ.

i = Matt. xxvi. 18. Rev. i. 3. xxii. 10. Joel i. 15.
k constr., ch. ii. 20 reff.
l = Eph. v. 24.
1 Thess. v. 18.
m Eph. vi. 18 reff.
n Eph. v. 4 reff.

o Luke xxiii. 24.　1 John v. 15 only.　Ps. xix. 5 al.　　　p = Luke ii. 15.　Acts ii. 28.　Eph. i.
9 al.　Ezek. xliv. 23.　　q ch. ii. 3 reff.　　　r = Luke xxiv. 45.　Rev. xiii. 18.　Job xxxiii. 16.
s Gal. iii. 23 reff.　　t 2 Cor. ii. 11. iii. 14. iv. 4. x. 5. xi. 3 only. P.†　Baruch ii. 8 only.

6. μετ᾽ Bℵ.

7. for θεου, χριστου A syr-mg Cyr[alic] Procop Ambr₁ Pel-comm.　　for νοηματα, σωματα F D-lat spec tol Chrom Oros [Victorin].

ὅλου. And he describes the ἐπιεικής as ὁ μὴ ἀκριβοδίκαιος ἐπὶ τὸ χεῖρον. See Trench, New Test. Syn., as above.
By the γνωσθήτω πᾶσιν ἀνθρ., the Apostle rather intends, 'let no man know of you any inconsistency with ἐπιείκεια.' The universality of it justifies its application even to those described above, ch. iii. 18 f., —that though warned against them, they were to shew all moderation and clemency towards them: so Chrys. Meyer observes well, that the succession of these precepts seems to explain itself psychologically by the disposition of spiritual joy in the Lord exalting us both above rigorism, and above anxiety of mind (ver. 6). ὁ κύριος ἐγγύς] These words may apply either to the foregoing—'the Lord will soon come, He is the avenger; it is yours to be moderate and clement' (so De Wette, al.): or to the following—'the Lord is near, be not anxious:' so Chrys., Thdrt., all. Perhaps we may best regard it as the transition from the one to the other: Christ's coming is at hand—this is the best enforcer of clemency and forbearance: it also leads on to the duty of banishing anxiety. ὁ κύριος is *Christ*, and the ἐγγύς refers to the παρουσία; see on ch. iii. 20. **6.**] μηδέν has the emphasis. It is the accusative of the object, as τὸ πολλὰ μεριμνᾶν, Xen. Cyr. viii. 7. 12. ἐν παντί] in every thing: see ref. 1 Thess. and note. Meyer remarks that the literally correct rendering of the Vulg. 'in omni (neut.) oratione' led Ambrose wrong, who gives it 'per omnem orationem.' τῇ προσευχῇ καὶ τῇ δεήσει] **by your prayer and your supplication:** or better, **by the prayer and the supplication** appropriate to each thing. On the difference between προσευχή and δέησις, see on Eph. vi. 18, 1 Tim. ii. 1. Not μετὰ τῆς εὐχαριστίας, because the matters themselves may not be recognized as grounds of εὐχαριστία, but it should *accompany* every request. Ellic., who doubts this explanation, thinks it "more simple

to say that εὐχαριστία, 'thanksgiving for past blessings,' is in its nature more general and comprehensive, προς. and δεησ. almost necessarily more limited and specific. Hence, though εὐχαρ. occurs 12 times in St. Paul's Epistles, it is only twice used with the article, 1 Cor. xiv. 26, 2 Cor. iv. 15." But I much prefer the other view. τὰ αἰτήματα] = ὃ ἂν αἰτώμεθα, 1 John v. 15. Plato, Rep. viii. p. 566, speaks of τὸ τυραννικὸν αἴτημα . . . αἰτεῖν τὸν δῆμον φύλακάς τινας τοῦ σώματος. πρὸς τὸν θεόν] unto, 'before,' 'coram:' see Acts viii. 24. **7.**] *Consequence* of this laying every thing before God in prayer with thanksgiving—*peace unspeakable.* καί, and then. ἡ εἰρ. τοῦ θεοῦ, that peace which rests in God and is wrought by Him in the soul, the counterpoise of all troubles and anxieties—see John xvi. 33 . . . . . ἵνα ἐν ἐμοὶ εἰρήνην ἔχητε· ἐν τῷ κόσμῳ θλίψιν ἔχετε. Meyer denies that εἰρήνη ever has this meaning: but he is certainly wrong. The above verse, and John xiv. 27, Col. iii. 15, cannot be fully interpreted on *his* meaning, mere *mutual concord.* It is of course true, that mutual concord, and τὸ ἐπιεικές, are necessary elements of this peace: but it goes far beyond them. See the alternatives thoroughly discussed, as usual, in Ellic.'s note. ἡ ὑπερέχουσα πάντα νοῦν] not as Chrys., ὅταν λέγῃ πρὸς τοὺς ἐχθροὺς εἰρηνεύειν . . . . πῶς οὐχ ὑπὲρ νοῦν ἐστιν ἀνθρώπινον τοῦτο; nor as Estius, "quia omnem expectationem humanam excedit, quod Deus pro inimicis sibi reconciliandis filium suum dederit in mortem:" nor as Calvin, "quia nihil humano ingenio magis adversum, quam in summa desperatione nihilominus sperare:" but as Erasm., all., "res felicior quam ut humana mens queat percipere." νοῦς is the *intelligent faculty*, the perceptive and appreciative power: reff. On the sentiment itself, cf. Eph. iii. 19. φρουρήσει must not with Chrys., Thdrt., Thl., Luth., all. and Vulg., be made *optative*

<table>
<tr><td>

u Eph. vi. 10
reff. ch. iii. 1.
v 1 Tim. iii. 8,
11.   Tit. ii..
2 only.   Prov.
xv. 26.
(-νότης.
1 Tim. ii. 2.)
w = 2 Cor. vii.
11. xi. 2.

</td><td>

8 ^u Τὸ ^u λοιπόν, ἀδελφοί, ὅσα ἐστὶν ἀληθῆ, ὅσα ^v σεμνά,
ὅσα δίκαια, ὅσα ^w ἁγνά, ὅσα ^x προσφιλῆ, ὅσα ^y εὔφημα,
^z εἴ ^z τις ^a ἀρετὴ καὶ ^z εἴ ^z τις ἔπαινος, ταῦτα ^b λογίζεσθε.   9 ^a
καὶ ἐμάθετε καὶ ^c παρέλαβετε καὶ ἠκούσατε καὶ εἴδετε

</td><td>

ABDFK
LPℵ a b
c d e f g
h k i m n
o 17. 47

</td></tr>
</table>

James iii. 17.   Ps. xviii. 9.   x here only †.   Sir. iv. 7. xx. 13 only.   y here only †.   Ps. lxii. 6
    Symm.   (-μία, 2 Cor. vi. 8.)   z = Eph. iv. 29.   a Paul, here only. = 2 Pet. i. (3) 5 bis (1 Pet. ii.
    9) only.   Wisd. viii. 7.   b 1 Cor. xiii. 5.   Ps. cxxxix. 2.   Zech. viii. 17.   c = Gal. i. 9, 12 reff.

8. aft ἔπαινος ins ἐπιστημης *disciplinæ* D¹F vulg(not am¹ tol) Sing-cler Ambrst Pel
(not [Victorin] Aug Fulg Sedul).

in sense : it is not a wish, but a declaration—following upon the performance of the injunction above.   **τὰς καρδίας ὑμῶν κ. τὰ νοήματα ὑμῶν**] The heart is the fountain of the thoughts, i. e. designs, plans (not *minds*, as E. V.): so that this expression is equivalent to '*your hearts themselves, and their fruits.*'   **ἐν χριστῷ 'Ιησοῦ** is not the predicate after φρουρήσει—*shall keep &c. in Christ*, i. e. keep them from falling from Christ (ὥστε μένειν κ. μὴ ἐκπεσεῖν αὐτοῦ τῆς πίστεως, Chrys.): but, as usual, denotes the sphere or element of the φρουρά thus bestowed— that it shall be a Christian security :—the verb φρουρήσει being *absolute.*

8, 9.] *Summary exhortation to Christian virtues not yet specified.*   **8.**] **τὸ λοιπόν** resumes again his intention of closing the Epistle with which he had begun ch. iii., but from which he had been diverted by incidental subjects. It is unnatural to attribute to the Apostle so formal a design as De W. does, of now speaking of man's part, as he had hitherto of God's part :—Chrys. has it rightly,— τί ἐστι τὸ λοιπόν: ἀντὶ τοῦ, πάντα ἡμῖν εἴρηται. ἐπειγομένου τὸ ῥῆμά ἐστι, καὶ οὐδὲν κοινὸν ἔχοντος πρὸς τὰ παρόντα.

This beautiful sentence, full of the Apostle's fervour and eloquence, derives much force from the frequent repetition of ὅσα, and then of εἴ τις.   **ἀληθῆ**] subjective, truthful : not, *true* in matter of fact. The whole regards ethical qualities. ταῦτα γὰρ ὄντως ἀληθῆ, ἡ ἀρετή, ψεῦδος δὲ ἡ κακία. κ. γὰρ ἡ ἡδονὴ αὐτῆς ψεῦδος, κ. ἡ δόξα αὐτῆς ψεῦδος, κ. πάντα τὰ τοῦ κόσμου ψεῦδος. Chrys. **σεμνά**] τὸ σεμνὸν ὄνομα, τὸ καλόν τε κἀγαθόν, Xen. Œc. vi. 14. It is difficult to give it in any one English word : '*honest*' and '*honourable*' are too weak : '*reverend*' and '*venerable,*' '*grave,*' are seldom applied to *things.* Nor do I know any other more eligible.   **δίκαια**] not '*just,*' in respect of others, merely—but **right**, in that wider sense in which δικαιοσύνη is used—before God and man : see this sense Acts x. 22 ; Rom. v. 7.

ἁγνά] not merely '*chaste*' in the ordinary confined acceptation : but pure generally : "castimoniam denotat in omnibus vitæ partibus." Calv.   **προσφιλῆ**] lovely, in the most general sense : no subjects need be supplied, as τοῖς πιστοῖς, or τῷ θεῷ (Chrys.) : for the exhortation is markedly and designedly as *general* as possible.

εὔφημα] again, general, and with reference to general fame—of good report, as E. V. The meaning '*sermones qui bene aliis precantur,*' adopted by Storr and Flatt, though philologically justified, is evidently not general enough for our context.   **εἴ τις ἀρετὴ . . . .**] sums up all which have gone before and generalizes still further. The E. V. '*if there be any virtue,*' &c. is objectionable, not for the reason alleged by Scholefield, Hints, &c. p. 85, as 'expressing a doubt of the existence of the thing in the abstract,' which it does not,—but as carrying the appearance of an *adjuration*, '*by the existence of,*' &c. which conveys a wrong impression of the sense—whatever virtue there is (not 'there *be*,' as Scholef.) &c.

ἀρετή] virtue, in the most general ethical sense : **ἔπαινος**, praise, not '*pro eo quod est laudabile,*' as Calv., al., but as Erasm., 'laus, virtutis comes.' The *disciplinæ*, which follows 'laus' in the Vulg. &c., is a pure interpolation, and beside the meaning : see various readings. **ταῦτα**—viz., all the foregoing—the ἀληθῆ &c.,—the ἀρετή, and the ἔπαινος—these things meditate : let them be your νοήματα.   **9.**] These general abstract things he now particularizes in the concrete as having been exemplified and taught by himself when among them. The first καί is not '*both,*' as E. V., but also,—moreover : which, besides what I have said recommending them above, were also recommended to you by my own example.   **ἐμάθετε**] again, not as E. V. '*have learned,*' &c.—but all aorists, —referring to the time when he was among them. Those things which (not '*whatsoever* things :' we are on generals no longer : nor would he recommend to

ἐν ἐμοί, ταῦτα πράσσετε, καὶ ὁ [d] θεὸς τῆς [d] εἰρήνης [e] ἔσται μεθ᾽ ὑμῶν.

[10] [f] Ἐχάρην δὲ ἐν κυρίῳ [g] μεγάλως, ὅτι [h] ἤδη [h] ποτὲ [i] ἀνεθάλετε [k] τὸ ὑπὲρ ἐμοῦ [l] φρονεῖν· [mn] ἐφ᾽ [m] ᾧ καὶ [ln] ἐφρονεῖτε, [o] ἠκαιρεῖσθε δέ. [11] [p] οὐχ [p] ὅτι [q] καθ᾽ [r] ὑστέρησιν

d Rom. xv. 33.
xvi. 20.
1 Cor. xiv. 33.
2 Cor. xiii. 11.
1 Thess. v. 23.
Heb. xiii. 20.
(2 Thess. iii. 16.)
e Acts vii. 9.
xviii. 10.
Isa. lviii. 11.
f ver. 4. ch. iii. 1.

g here only. 1 Chron. xxix. 9. Neh. xii. 43.   h Rom. i. 10 only.   i here only. trans., Ezek.
    xvii. 24. Sir. i. 18. xi. 22. intr., Ps. xxvii. 7.   k 1 Thess. iii. 3 reff.   l see ch. i. 7.
m Rom. v. 12. 2 Cor. v. 4. ch. iii. 12.   n constr., here only.   o here only†. (-ρῶς, 2 Tim.
    iv. 2.)   p = John vi. 46. 2 Cor. i. 24. iii. 5. ch. iii. 12. ver. 17. 2 Thess. iii. 9 only.
q = ch. ii. 3. Matt. xix. 3. Acts iii. 17.   r Mark xii. 44 only†. (-ημα, ch. ii. 30.)

9. ιδετε D²FKL d h m n [47] Clem Thdrt Thl-ms [: om Victorin].
10. εθαλατε D¹.   for το, του F.

them *all* his own sayings and doings; but the καί expressly provides for their being of the kinds specified above) **ye moreover learned, and received** (reff.: here of receiving not by *word of mouth*, but by knowledge of his character: the whole is not doctrinal, but ethical) **and heard** (again not of preaching, but of his tried and acknowledged Christian character, which was in men's mouths and thus heard) **and saw** (each for himself) **in me** (ἐν ἐμοί will not properly belong to the two first verbs, ἐμάθ. and παρελ., but must be associated by zeugma with them —he himself being clearly the example throughout), **these things** (ταῦτα . . . . ἅ) practise (correlative with, not opposed to, λογίζεσθε above:—*that λογισμός* being eminently practical, and issuing, in the concrete, in the ταῦτα πράσσειν, after Paul's example). **καί] and then :** see ver. 7. On εἰρήνη, see there.

10—20.] *He thanks them for the supply received from Philippi.* **10.**] δέ is transitional; the contrast being between the personal matters which are now introduced, and those more solemn ones which he has just been treating. **ἐν κυρίῳ]** See above, ch. iii. 1, ver. 4. "Every occurrence, in his view, has reference to Christ,—takes from Him its character and form." Wiesinger. **ἤδη ποτέ]** now **at length,** as E. V.: 'tandem aliquando:' χρόνον δηλοῦντός ἐστι μακρόν, Chrys. The ποτέ takes up and makes indefinite the ἤδη : as in δή ποτε, δή που, &c. See Klotz ad Devar. p. 607, 8. But no *reproof* is conveyed by the expression, as Chrys. thinks: see below. **ἀνεθάλετε]** lit. **ye came into leaf;** "metaphora sumta ab arboribus, quarum vis hyeme contracta latet, vere florere incipit," Calv. But it is fanciful to conclude with Bengel, that it *was Spring,* when the gift came : see on a similar fancy in 1 Cor. v. 7. The word is taken transitively (see reff.) by Grot., all.,— '*ye caused to spring again your care for*

me' (see below): but the intransitive only will suit the sense here—**ye budded forth again in caring for my interest** (see below). Your care for *me* was, so to speak, the *life* of the tree ; it existed just as much in winter when there was no vegetation, when ye ἠκαιρεῖσθε, as when the buds were put forth in spring. This is evident by what follows. We must thank Meyer, to whom we owe so much in accuracy of grammatical interpretation, for having followed out the right track here, first indicated by Bengel, and rendered τὸ ὑπὲρ ἐμοῦ as the accusative governed by φρονεῖν. The ordinary way (so Wiesinger and Ellicott recently) has been to regard the words as = τὸ φρονεῖν ὑπὲρ ἐμοῦ, thus depriving the relative ἐφ᾽ ᾧ of any thing to refer to, and producing the logical absurdity (Mey.), ἐφρονεῖτε ἐπὶ τῷ ὑπὲρ ἐμοῦ φρονεῖν, or forcing ἐφ᾽ ᾧ to some unjustified meaning ('*although,*' as Luth., al.,—'*sicut,*' as vulg.,—&c.), or understanding it '*for whom,*' as Calv., al., —contrary to the Apostle's usage, in which (reff.) ἐφ᾽ ᾧ is always neuter. But if we take τὸ ὑπὲρ ἐμοῦ together,—'*my interest,*'—and govern it by φρονεῖν, all will be simple and clear : **I rejoiced, &c. that at last ye flourished in anxiety for my interest : for which purpose** (cf. Plato, Gorg. p. 502 B, ἐφ᾽ ᾧ ἐσπούδακε :—the purpose, namely, *of* flourishing, putting forth the supply which you have now sent. Wiesinger prefers the other, and vindicates it from Meyer's imputation : but to me not convincingly : as neither Ellicott) **ye also were anxious** (all that long time, imperfect), **but had no opportunity** (ἀκαιρέω is a word of later Greek : **εὐκαιρέω,** its opposite, is used by Lucian, Plutarch, Polyb., &c., as also its compounds ἐνευκαιρέω, προσευκαιρέω, &c. See Phryn. ed. Lobeck, p. 125. Wiesinger well remarks that we must not press this ἠκαιρεῖσθε into a definite hypothesis, such as that their financial state was not adequate—that they

s = Heb. v. 8.
t εἰ θέλει με
ἐν τοιούτοις
εἶναι ἐν οἶς
εἰμι, Arrian,
Epict. i. 22.
u ellips., 1 Pet.
ii. 12. iii. 14
al. Ezek.
xiv. 4.
v here only. =
Sir. xl. 18.

λέγω· ἐγὼ γὰρ ˢἔμαθον ᵗἐν ᵘοἷς ᵗεἰμὶ ᵛαὐτάρκης εἶναι. 12 ʷοἶδα καὶ ˣταπεινοῦσθαι, ʷοἶδα καὶ ʸπερισσεύειν. ᶻἐν παντὶ καὶ ᶻἐν πᾶσιν ᵃμεμύημαι καὶ ᵇχορτάζεσθαι καὶ ᶜπεινᾶν καὶ ʸπερισσεύειν καὶ ᵈὑστερεῖσθαι. 13 πάντα ᵉἰσχύω ᶠἐν τῷ ᵍἐνδυναμοῦντί με. 14 ʰπλὴν ⁱκαλῶς

ABDFK
LPℵ a b
c d e f g
h k l m n
o 17. 47

(·κεῖν, Deut. xxxii. 10. -κεια, 1 Tim. vi. 6.)
w = 1 Thess. iv. 4. James iv. 17. Job xxxiv. 19.
x := 2 Cor. xi. 7. Prov. xiii. 7.　　y = ver. 18.　　z see 2 Cor. xi. 6.　　a here only †.　3 Macc. ii. 30.
ᶻ̓ Paul, here only. Matt. xiv. 20. James ii. 16. Rev. xix. 21. Ps. xxxvi. 19.　　c Matt. iv. 2. 1 Cor. iv.
11. xi. 21 al. Prov. xxv. 21.　　d = Luke xv. 14. 2 Cor. xi. 3. Heb. xi. 37. Sir. xiii. 4.　　e = Gal.
v. 6. James v. 16. Wisd. xvi. 20.　　f = ἐν χριστῷ, &c. passim.　　g Eph. vi. 10 reff.
h = Eph. v. 33 reff.　　i Acts x. 33. 1 Cor. vii. 37, 38. James ii. 8, 19. 2 Pet. i. 19. 3 Kings viii. 18.

12. rec (for 1st καὶ) δε, with b d e f : txt ABDFKL[P]ℵ rel vulg syr goth Clem lat-ff. om καὶ (bef περισσευειν) A Syr.

13. rec aft με ins χριστω (gloss: or as in Orig below, filled up from 1 Tim i. 12), with D³KL[P]ℵ³ rel syrr goth (Orig₁) [Eus₂] Ath(elsw ιησ. χρ.) Nyss Chr [cyr-p] Thdrt Damasc : χρῡ F : χῶ ιῡ Orig₃(elsw adds ιησου τω κυρ. ημων) : om ABD¹ℵ 17 vulg (and F-lat) copt æth arm Clem [Eus₅ Victorin] Ambr Ambrst Aug Pel.

had no means of conveyance, &c.—it is perfectly general, and all such fillings up are mere conjecture). **11.**] inserted to prevent misunderstanding of the last verse. οὐχ ὅτι] See ch. iii. 12 : **my meaning is not, that . . . . καθ',** **according to,** i. e. **in consequence of**—see reff., and Od. γ. 106, πλαζόμενοι κατὰ ληΐδ': Herod. ii. 152, κατὰ ληΐην ἐκπλώσαντας : Thuc. vi. 31, 'ut more receptum est penuriæ,' which would be κατὰ τοὺς ὑστεροῦντας (see Rom. iii. 5 al.). **For I** (emphatic : **for my part,** whatever others may feel) **learned** (in my experience, my training for this apostolic work : not ✱ 'have learned :' the aorist is much simpler and more humble—'I was taught :' the present result of this teaching comes below, οἶδα, but not in this word), **in the state in which I am** (not 'in whatsoever state I am' (E. V. : which would be ἐν οἷς ἂν εἰμί,—cf. ὅπου ἂν εἰσεπορεύετο, Mark vi. 56, ὅσοι ἂν ἥπτοντο αὐτοῦ, ib. Winer, § 42. 3. a), nor as Luther, bei ꞷelchen idȷ bin (οἷς masculine), which is against the context. But ἐν οἷς εἰμί does not apply only to the Apostle's present circumstances, but to any possible present ones : 'in which I am at any time :' see next verse) **to find compe-tence** (we have no word for αὐτάρκης. 'Self-sufficing' will express its mean-ing of independence of external help (τελειότης κτήσεως ἀγαθῶν, Plato, Def. p. 412), but is liable to be misunderstood : 'competent' is not in use in this sense, though the abstract noun competence is : the German ɡenüɡſam gives it well). **12.**] See above. **I know** (by this teaching) **also** (the first καί expresses that, besides the general finding of com-petence in all circumstances, he specially

has been taught to suffer humiliation and to bear abundance. See Ellic.'s note) **how to be brought low** (generally : but here especially by need, in humiliation of circumstances. Meyer remarks that 2 Cor. iv. 8 ; vi. 9, 10, are a commentary on this), **I know also** (καί as before, or as an addition to οἶδα καὶ ταπεινοῦσθαι) **how to abound** (ὑψοῦσθαι, as Wies. re-marks, would be the proper general op-posite : but he chooses the special one, which fits the matter of which he is treat-ing) : **in every thing** (not as vulg., E. V., all., 'every where,' nor 'at every time,' as Chrys., Grot.,—nor both, as Thl., &c. :—but as usually in St. Paul : see ref. and note) **and in all things** (not, as Luth., Beng., 'respectu omnium hominum :' ἐν παντὶ πράγματι, φησι, κ. ἐν πᾶσι τοῖς παρεμπίπτουσι, Œc. : the expression con-veys universality, as 'in each and all,' with us) **I have been taught the lesson** ('initiated :' but no stress to be laid, as by Beng., 'disciplina arcana imbutus sum, ignota mundo :' see the last example be-low. Beware (against Wiesinger) of join-ing μεμύημαι with ἐν παντὶ κ. ἐν πᾶσιν, initiated in, &c.; the verb is (against Ellicott) not constructed with ἐν, but with an accusative of the person and the thing (μυεῖν τινά τι), which last accu-sative remains with the passive : so μ' ἀνὴρ ἐμύησ' Ἑλικωνίδα, Anthol. ix. 162, —οἱ τὰς τελετὰς μεμυημένοι, Plato, Symp. p. 209. The present construction, with an infinitive, occurs, Alciphr. ii. 4, κυβερ-νᾷν μυηθήσομαι) **both to be satiated and to hunger** (the forms πεινᾷν, διψᾷν, for -ῆν, seem to have come in with Mace-donian influence : being found first in Aristotle ; see Lobeck in Phryn. p. 61), **both to abound and to be in need.** **13.**] 'After these special notices, he de-

ἐποιήσατε ^k συγκοινωνήσαντές μου τῇ ¹ θλίψει. ¹⁵ οἴδατε
δὲ καὶ ὑμεῖς, Φιλιππήσιοι, ὅτι ἐν ^m ἀρχῇ τοῦ ^m εὐαγγελίου,
ὅτε ⁿ ἐξῆλθον ἀπὸ Μακεδονίας, οὐδεμία μοι ἐκκλησία ^o ἐκοι-
νώνησεν εἰς ^p λόγον ^{qr} δόσεως καὶ ^{qs} λήμψεως, εἰ μὴ ὑμεῖς
μόνοι, ¹⁶ ὅτι καὶ ἐν Θεσσαλονίκῃ καὶ ^t ἅπαξ καὶ ^{tu} δὶς ^v εἰς

k Eph. v. 11.
Rev. xviii.
4 only †.
(-νός, ch. i.
7.)
l Eph. iii. 13
reff.
m Mark i. 1.
m Mark xi. 12.
Luke xvii.
29. Gen.
xxviii. 10.

o Gal. vi. 6 reff.   p 1 Macc. x. 40.   Polyb. xv. 34. 2.   q Sir. xli. 19. xlii. 7.
r James i. 17 only. Prov. xxi. 14.   s here only.   Prov. xv. 27. Sir. as above (q) only.
t 1 Thess. ii. 18.   Neh. xiii. 20.   u as above (t). Mark xiv. 30, 72.   Luke xviii. 12.   Jude 12 only.
v Acts xi. 29.

14. τη θλιψει bef μου DF latt.

15. om δε D¹ f m 72. 115 syr æth-pl Chr Thdrt Thl-mss.   ins οτι bef ουδεμια
(*retaining former* οτι) D¹F.   om μονοι A¹ [arm].

16. om εις AD¹ Syr goth Ps-Ath Œc-txt Victorin: *usibus meis* Ambrst Aug.

clares his *universal* power,—how triumphantly, yet how humbly!' Meyer. **I can
do** (reff.: so μηδὲν ἰσχύειν, Plato Crit.
p. 50 b) **all things** (not '*all these things,*'
τὰ πάντα, as Van Hengel: 'the Apostle
rises above mere relations of prosperous
and adverse circumstance, to the *general,*' De W.) **in** (in union with,—by
means of my spiritual life, which is not
mine, but Christ living in me, Gal. ii. 20:
the E. V. '*through*' does not give this
union sufficiently) **him who strengthens
me** (i. e. *Christ*, as the gloss rightly supplies: cf. 1 Tim. i. 12).   **14.**] 'Cavet,
ne fortiter loquendo contempsisse ipsorum
beneficium videatur.' Calv. μὴ γὰρ ἐπειδή, φησιν, ἐν χρείᾳ οὐ καθέστηκα, νομί-
σητε μὴ δεῖσθαί με τοῦ πράγματος· δέομαι δι' ὑμᾶς. Chrys.   συγκοινωνήσαντές μου τῇ θλίψει] ὅρα σοφίαν, πῶς
ἐπαίρει τὸ πρᾶγμα, Thl.: **in that ye
made yourselves partakers with my present tribulation** (not *poverty:* by their
sympathy for him they suffered with him;
and their gift was a *proof* of this sympathy).   **15—17.**] *Honourable recol-
lection of their former kindness to him.*
15.] δέ contrasts this former service with their present one.   καὶ
ὑμεῖς] 'as well as I myself.' He addresses them *by name* (as 2 Cor. vi. 11)
to mark them particularly as those who
did what follows : but not to the absolute
exclusion of others, as Bengel ('antitheton ad ecclesias aliorum oppidorum'):
others *may* have done it too, for aught
that this appellative implies : that they
did not, is by and by expressly asserted :
ἐν ἀρχῇ τοῦ εὐαγγελίου, *penes vos*, Beng.:
he places himself in their situation ; dates
from (so to speak) *their* Christian era.
This he specifies by ὅτε ἐξῆλθον ἀπὸ
Μακεδονίας. See Acts xvii. 14. By this
is not meant, as commonly understood,
the supply which he received at Corinth
(2 Cor. xi. 9), in order to which De W.,
Wies., al., understand ἐξῆλθον as a plu-

perfect,—but that mentioned below : see
there : ἐξῆλθον being the aorist marking
the simple date : **when I left Macedonia.**
οὐδεμία μοι ἐκκλησία] **no church
communicated with me as to (in) an
account of giving and receiving** (i. e.
every receipt being part of *the department of giving and receiving*, being *one
side* of such a reckoning, ye alone opened
such an account with me. It is true the
Philippians had all the giving, the Apostle all the receiving : the debtor side was
vacant in *their* account, the creditor side
in *his* : but this did not make it any the
less an account of "giving-and-receiving,"
categorically so called. This explanation,
which is Meyer's, is in my view far the
most simple (against Ellic., who apparently has misunderstood it), and preferable to the almost universal one, that his
creditor and their debtor side was that
which he *spiritually* imparted to them :
for the introduction of spiritual gifts does
not belong to the context, and therefore
disturbs it. Similar usages of λῆψις κ.
δόσις occur : e. g. Artemid. i. 44, οἱ διὰ
δόσεως κ. λήψεως ποριζόμενοι : Arrian,
Epict. ii. 9, τὸν φιλάργυρον (ἐπαύξουσιν)
αἱ ἀκατάλληλοι λήψεις κ. δόσεις : Cicero,
Lælio 16, 'ratio acceptorum et datorum.'
See Wetst.) **but you only : 16.**] **for
even in Thessalonica** (which was an early
stage of my ἐξελθεῖν ἀπὸ Μακ., before
the departure was consummated. The
ὅτι gives a reason for and proof of the
former assertion—ye were the only ones,
&c.,—and ye began as early as ἐν Θεσσ., i.e.
when I was at Thessalonica.   In such
brachylogical constructions the preposition of rest, as belonging to the act accomplished, overbears the preposition of
motion, as belonging to it only in its imperfect state ; so οἱ ἐν τῷ Ἡραίῳ κατα-
πεφευγότες, Xen. Hell. iv. 5. 5,—ταῖς
λοιπαῖς ἐν τῇ γῇ καταπεφευγυίαις ἐνέβαλ-
λον, Thuc. iv. 14,—ἀποστελοῦντες . . . .
ἐν τῇ Σικελίᾳ, ib. vii. 17, where ἐς τὴν Σ.

w ch. ii. 25 reff.   τὴν ^wχρείαν μοι ^xἐπέμψατε.   17 ^x οὐχ ^xὅτι ^yἐπιζητῶ τὸ ABDFK
x ver. 11 reff.   LP‭ℵ‬ a b
y = Matt. vi.   ^zδόμα, ἀλλὰ ^yἐπιζητῶ τὸν ^aκαρπὸν τὸν ^bπλεονάζοντα εἰς   c d e f g
32 al. 1 Macc.   h k l m n
vii. 13.
z Matt. vii. 4.   ^pλόγον ὑμῶν.   18 ^cἀπέχω δὲ πάντα καὶ ^dπερισσεύω,   o 17. 47
Luke xi. 13.
Eph. iv. 8   ^eπεπλήρωμαι δεξάμενος παρὰ Ἐπαφροδίτου ^fτὰ παρ᾽ ὑμῶν,
(from Ps.
lxvii. 18)   ^gὀσμὴν ^gεὐωδίας, θυσίαν ^hδεκτὴν ⁱεὐάρεστον τῷ θεῷ.
only. Gen.
xxv. 6.
a ch. i. 11 reff.   19 ὁ δὲ θεός μου ^kπληρώσει πᾶσαν ^lχρείαν ὑμῶν κατὰ
b = Rom. v.
20. vi. 1 al.   τὸ ^mπλοῦτος αὐτοῦ ⁿἐν δόξῃ ἐν χριστῷ Ἰησοῦ.   20 τῷ
P. only, exc.
2 Pet. i. 8.

2 Chron. xxiv. 11.   c = Matt. vi. 2.   Philem. 15.   Gen. xliii. 23.   d ver. 12.   e = Acts
ii. 28.   xiii. 52.   Rom. xv. 13, 14.   2 Cor. vii. 4. ch. i. 11.   f Luke x. 7.   g Eph. v. 2 (reff.) only.
h Luke iv. 19, 24.   Acts x. 35.   2 Cor. vi. 2 only.   Isa. lvi. 7.   Sir. xxxii. (xxxv.) 7.   i Eph. v.
12 reff.   k see Luke iii. 5.   l = ver. 16.   Sir. xxxix. 33.   m Eph. i. 7 reff.
n 1 Tim. iii. 16 reff.

for μοι, μου DL¹[P] Chr₁ Procop Thdrt Thl Œc Ambrst Aug.
17. (αλλα, so AB[P].)   ins τον bef λογον F 121.
18. om παρα επαφροδιτου A: for παρα, απο ‭ℵ‬-corr¹.   for τα, το D¹.   aft
υμ. ins πενφθεν D¹, πεμφθεντα F latt Syr Iren-int [Orig-int] Cypr Victorin.
19. πληρωσαι D¹F b c g m o 17 [47] 67² latt Chr₁ Thdrt Thl lat-ff: txt ABD³
KL[P]‭ℵ‬ rel copt Chr₂ Thdrt-ms.   rec τον πλουτον, with D³KL‭ℵ‬³ rel Cyr: τον
πλουτος m¹: txt ABD¹F[P]‭ℵ‬¹ 17. 67².   for αυτου, υμων D¹.   om 1st εν ‭ℵ‬¹
(ins ‭ℵ‬-corr¹ obl).

in Bekker's text is a correction) **ye sent both once and twice** (the account of the expression being, that when the first arrived, they had sent *once*: when the second, not only once, but twice. So in ref.: and Herod. ii. 121, αὐτῷ κ. δὶς κ. τρὶς ἀνοίξαντι: iii. 148, τοῦτο κ. δὶς κ. τρὶς εἴπαντος Μαιανδρίου. The opposite expression, οὐχ ἅπαξ οὐδὲ δίς, is found in Plato, Clitoph. § 7) **ye sent** (absolute as in ref.) **to** (for the supply of, ref.) **my necessity. 17.]** Again he removes any chance of misunderstanding, as above in ver. 11. It was not for his own sake but for theirs that he rejoiced at their liberality, because it multiplied the fruits of their faith. **Not that** (see above, ver. 11) **I seek** (present, 'it is my character to seek.' The preposition in composition denotes, as so often, the direction; not *studiose*, nor *insuper*) **the gift** (τό—in the case in question), **but I do seek** (the repetition of the verb is solemn and emphatic) **the fruit which** (thereby, in the case before us) **abounds to your account** (this εἰς λόγον refers to the same expression, ver. 15—fruit, μισθόν in the day of the Lord, the result of your labour for me in the Lord. De W., after Van Hengel, doubts whether πλεονάζοντα can be constructed with εἰς, and would therefore separate them by a comma. But surely little would be thus gained, for the εἰς would belong to the whole clause, the connecting link being καρπὸν πλεονάζοντα, so that even thus the idea of πλεονάζοντα must be carried on to εἰς: and perhaps in 2 Thess. i. 3 it is so: see note there). **18.] But** (notwithstanding that the gift is not that which I

desire, I have received it, and been sufficiently supplied by it) **I have** (emphatic, and exactly as in ἀπέχειν τὸν μισθόν—'I have no more to ask from you, but have enough :'—not as Erasm., Beza, Grot., &c. 'I have duly received all you sent') **all** (I want), **and abound** (over and above): **I am filled** (repetition and intensification of περισσεύω), **having received at the hands of Epaphroditus the remittance from you, a savour of fragrance** (a clause in apposition, expressing a judgment,—so frequently in poetry, especially in tragedians,—Il. ω. 735, ἤ τις Ἀχαιῶν ῥίψει, χειρὸς ἑλών, ἀπὸ πύργου, λυγρὸν ὄλεθρον: Eur. Orest. 950, τιθεῖσα λευκὸν ὄνυχα διὰ παρηΐδων, αἱματηρὸν ἄταν. See Kühner, ii. 146. On ὀσμὴ εὐωδίας see Eph. v. 2, note), **a sacrifice acceptable, well pleasing to God** (see Heb. xiii. 16 ; 1 Pet. ii. 5). **19.]** an assurance taken up from τῷ θεῷ above, μου because he (Paul) was the receiver: this was his return to them: 'qui quod servo ejus datur remunerabitur.' Beng. πληρώσει . . . . all refers to vv. 16, 18;—as ye πεπληρώκατέ μου τὴν χρείαν. It is an *assurance*, not a *wish* (-σαι). πᾶσαν,—not only in the department alluded to, but in all. Meyer refers to the beatitudes in Matt. v. and especially St. Luke's χορτασθήσεσθε and γελάσετε, Luke vi. 21, as illustrative. ἐν δόξῃ] to be connected with πληρώσει, not with τὸ πλοῦτος αὐτοῦ: not, *gloriously*, as many Commentators, which is weak and flat in the extreme: but δόξα is the instrument and element by and in which 'all your need' will be supplied: **in glory**, cf. Ps. xvi. 15 LXX: but not only at the

δὲ [o] θεῷ καὶ [o] πατρὶ ἡμῶν ἡ [p] δόξα [p] εἰς τοὺς αἰῶνας τῶν αἰώνων, ἀμήν.

21 Ἀσπάσασθε πάντα [q] ἅγιον ἐν χριστῷ Ἰησοῦ. ἀσπάζονται ὑμᾶς οἱ σὺν ἐμοὶ ἀδελφοί. 22 ἀσπάζονται ὑμᾶς πάντες οἱ [q] ἅγιοι, μάλιστα δὲ οἱ ἐκ τῆς Καίσαρος [r] οἰκίας.

23 Ἡ χάρις τοῦ κυρίου Ἰησοῦ χριστοῦ μετὰ τοῦ [s] πνεύματος ὑμῶν[, ἀμήν].

o Gal. i. 4 reff.
p Gal. i. 5 reff.
q = Acts ix. 13. Rom. i. 7 & passim.
r = 1 Cor. xvi. 15. Gen. l. 8 (but see note).
s Gal. vi. 18. 2 Tim. iv. 22. Philem. 25.

ΠΡΟΣ ΦΙΛΙΠΠΗΣΙΟΥΣ.

20. aft ημων ins ω ℵ[1](om ℵ[3]). om των αιωνων KL [47] 80.
22. om υμας F. om δε L 17 Chr-mss Thdrt Thl Ambrst(και μαλ. æth). for εκ, απο B.
23. rec aft κυριου ins ημων, with D[P] a d f k l fuld(with F-lat al) Syr syr-w-ast copt [æth] gr-lat-ff: om ABFKLℵ rel am D-lat(and G-lat) arm Damasc Thl-mss Œc. rec (for του πνευματος) παντων (*cf* 2 *Cor* xiii. 13. *De W. supposes txt to have come from Gal* vi. 18), with KLℵ[3] rel syrr Chr Thdrt: txt ABDF[P]ℵ[1] 17 [47] 67[2] latt coptt æth arm Damasc lat-ff. om αμην BF [47] 67[2] sah Chr Œc Ambrst: ins ADKL[P]ℵ rel vss.

Subscription. rec adds εγραφη απο ρωμης, with B[2]KL rel syrr copt Chr Thdrt Euthal; rec adds further δι' επαφροδιτου, with KL rel syrr Thdrt: δια τιμοθεου κ. επαφρ. copt: no subscr in 1: εγραφη κ.τ.λ., omg πρ. φιλ., h k m o: txt AB b 17, and D(addg επληρωθη) F(prefg ετελεσθη) ℵ(adding στιχοι σ). [P def.]

coming of Christ (as Meyer, according to his wont), but in the whole glorious imparting to you of the unsearchable riches of Christ, begun and carried on here, and completed at that day. **ἐν χριστῷ Ἰησοῦ**] and this filling (or, 'this glory,' but then *perhaps* τῇ would have been expressed) is, consists, and finds its sphere and element, **in Christ Jesus.** **20.**] The contemplation both of the Christian reward, of which he has been speaking, and of the glorious completion of all God's dealings at the great day,—and the close of his Epistle,—suggests this ascription of praise. **δέ**] **But**—however rich you may be in good works, however strong I may be by Christ to bear all things,—not to us, but to our God and Father be the glory. On **εἰς τοὺς αἰῶνας τῶν αἰώνων**, see note, Eph. iii. 21.

21—23.] Greeting and final benediction. **21.**] **πάντα ἅγιον, every** individual **saint.** The singular has love and affection, and should not be lost as in Conyb., 'Salute all *God's people.*' **ἐν χριστῷ Ἰησοῦ**] belongs more probably to **ἀσπάσασθε,**—see Rom. xvi. 22; 1 Cor. xvi. 19,—than to **ἅγιον,** as in ch. i. 1, where, as Meyer observes, the expression has a diplomatic formality, whereas here there is no reason for so formal an adjunct.

οἱ σὺν ἐμοὶ ἀδελφοί] These must, on account of the next verse, have been his closer friends, perhaps his colleagues in the ministry, such as Aristarchus, Epaphras, Demas, Timotheus. But there has arisen a question, how to reconcile this with ch. ii. 20? And it may be answered, that the lack of ἰσοψυχία there predicated of his companions, did not exclude them from the title ἀδελφοί, nor from sending greeting to the Philippians: see also ch. i. 14.

22.] **πάντες οἱ ἅγιοι,** all the Christians here. **οἱ ἐκ τῆς Καίσαρος οἰκίας**] These perhaps were slaves belonging to the familia of Nero, who had been converted by intercourse with St. Paul, probably at this time a prisoner in the prætorian barracks (see ch. i. 13 note) attached to the palace. This is much more likely, than that any of the actual *family* of Nero should have embraced Christianity. The hint which Chrys., al., find here, εἰ γὰρ οἱ ἐν τοῖς βασιλείοις πάντων κατεφρόνησαν διὰ τὸν βασιλέα τῶν οὐρανῶν, πολλῷ μᾶλλον αὐτοὺς χρὴ τοῦτο ποιεῖν, is alien from the simplicity of the close of an Epistle. The reason of these being specified is not plain: the connexion perhaps between a *colonia*, and some of the imperial household, might account for it. **23.**] See Gal. vi. 18.

ΠΡΟΣ ΚΟΛΑΣΣΑΕΙΣ.

a Rom. xv. 32.
1 Cor. i. 1.
2 Cor. i. 1.
vii. 5. Eph.
i. 1. 2 Tim.
i. 1 only. P.
b = (subst.)
Eph. i. 1 reff.
(adj.) Heb.
iii. 1 (1 Thess.
v. 27 v. r.) only.

I. ¹ Παῦλος ἀπόστολος χριστοῦ Ἰησοῦ ᵃ διὰ θελήματος θεοῦ, καὶ Τιμόθεος ὁ ἀδελφός, ² τοῖς ἐν Κολοσσαῖς ᵇ ἁγίοις καὶ ᶜ πιστοῖς ἀδελφοῖς ᶜ ἐν χριστῷ. χάρις ὑμῖν καὶ εἰρήνη ἀπὸ θεοῦ πατρὸς ἡμῶν.

c Eph. i. 1. Phil. i. 1.

C χαρις
...
ABCDF
KLPℵ a
b c d e f
g h k l m
n o 17. 47

TITLE. elz παυλου του αποστολου η προς κολ. επιστολη, with rel: Steph η πρ. κολ. επ. παυλ.: του αγιου απ. παυλ. επ. πρ. κολ. L: η πρ. κολ. επ. ταυτα διδασκαλη κολασσαευσι παρα παυλου f: πρ. κολ. επ. τ. αγ. απ. παυλ. h: [. . . . π. επ. πρ. κολ. P:] επ. πρ. κολ. k l : αρχεται πρ. κολ. F: txt ABDKℵ b m n o 17 [47] syr-mg-gr copt. [In D this ep follows Eph. Usually in D the subscr of one ep and the title of the next are written in 3 lines προς . . . | επληρωθη αρχεται | προς . . ., here however the middle line is omitted.]

CHAP. I. 1. rec ιησ. bef χρ., with DK rel vulg-ed(with demid tol) Syr æth [arm] Chr Thdrt: txt ABFL[P]ℵ 17 am(with fuld) D-lat syr copt Synops Damasc Ambrst Jer Cassiod.

2. Steph κολασσ. (see prolegomena), with AK[P(but -λοσ- in subscr)] rel syrr copt Orig Synops Nyss Chr-ms Thdrt Euthal Damasc-ms Thl-ms Suid (so also Polyænus Hierocles Herodot-mss Xenoph-mss) : txt B¹(see table)DFLℵ e f n (g 17, in title) latt Clem Chr Thdrt-ms Thl lat-ff (so also Herodot Xenoph Strabo al, and coins in Eckhel). [αδελφ. bef αγ. και πιστ. P.] aft χριστω ins ιησου AD¹F 17 latt Syr lat-ff : om BD³ KL[P]ℵ rel syr æth [arm] Chr Thdrt Damasc. rec aft ημων ins και κυριου ιησου χριστου, with ACFℵ rel vulg-ed(with demid tol) syr-w-ast: [και ιησ. χρ. τ. κυρ. ημ. P:] om BDKL d k 17 am(with fuld harl mar) Syr syr sah æth-rom Chr(expr., καίτοι ἐν ταύτῃ τὸ τοῦ χριστοῦ οὐ τίθησιν ὄνομα) Thlₑₓₚᵣ Orig-intₑₓₚᵣ.

CHAP. I. 1, 2.] ADDRESS AND GREET-ING. 1. διὰ θελήματος θεοῦ] see on reff. καὶ Τιμόθεος] as in 2 Cor. i. 1 (see also Phil. i. 1; Philem. 1, and 2 Thess. i. 1). ὁ ἀδελφός] see on 2 Cor. i. 1. On his presence with the Apostle at the time of writing this Epistle, see Prolegg. to Past. Epp. § i. 5. Chrys. (and similarly Thl.) says on ὁ ἀδελφός, οὐκοῦν καὶ αὐτὸς ἀπόστολος : but there seems no reason for this. 2.] On COLOSSÆ, or COLASSÆ, see Prolegg. § ii. 1. ἁγίοις should be taken (Mey.) as a substantive, not (De W.) with ἀδελφοῖς, in which case πιστοῖς, being already (as Mey.) presupposed in ἁγίοις, would be tame and superfluous :—and καὶ πιστοῖς ἀδελφοῖς ἐν χριστῷ seems to be a specifying clause, 'viz.—to the &c.:' or perhaps added merely on account of the natural diplomatic character of an opening address. ἐν χρ. belongs closely to πιστοῖς ἀδελφοῖς or perhaps rather to ἀδελφοῖς alone, as Phil. i. 14: no article before ἐν χριστῷ being wanted, because no distinction between these and any other kind of brethren is needed—the idea ἀδελφὸς-ἐν-χριστῷ being familiar. χάρις κ.τ.λ.] see Rom. i. 7. 3—29.] INTRODUCTION, but unusually expanded, so as to anti-

3 ^d Εὐχαριστοῦμεν τῷ ^e θεῷ πατρὶ τοῦ ^e κυρίου ἡμῶν
'Ιησοῦ χριστοῦ πάντοτε * περὶ ὑμῶν ^f προσευχόμενοι
4 ^g ἀκούσαντες τὴν ^h πίστιν ὑμῶν ^h ἐν χριστῷ 'Ιησοῦ καὶ
τὴν ⁱ ἀγάπην ἣν ἔχετε ⁱ εἰς πάντας τοὺς ἁγίους 5 διὰ τὴν
^j ἐλπίδα τὴν ^k ἀποκειμένην ὑμῖν ἐν τοῖς ^l οὐρανοῖς, ἣν
^m προηκούσατε ἐν τῷ ⁿ λόγῳ τῆς ^{no} ἀληθείας τοῦ ^o εὐ-

d Eph. v. 20 reff.
e Rom. xv. 6. 2 Cor i. 3. xi. 31. Eph. i. 3. Paul only, exc. 1 Pet. i. 3. Rev. i. 6. see 1 Cor. xv. 24. Gal. i. 4.
f w. περί, ch. iv. 3. Acts viii. 15. Heb. xiii.

18 al. Ps. lxxi. 15. w. ὑπέρ, ver. 9 reff. g constr., Matt. xi. 2. Acts xxiii. 16. Eph. i. 15 al.
h Eph. i. 15 reff. i Rom. v. 8. [Eph. i. 15.] 1 Pet. iv. 8. = ἀγ. ἐν, 1 John iv. 16. l = Gal.
v. 5. Tit. ii. 13. Heb. vi. 18. k Luke xix. 20. 2 Tim. iv. 8. Heb. ix. 27 only. Gen. xlix.
10. Job xxxviii. 23. 2 Macc. xii. 45 only. ἐν τῷ καλῶς ἀποθανεῖν . . . . . τῆς ὅλης αὐτοῖς
δόξης ἀποκειμένης, Jos. Antt. vi. 14. 7. ἐν μόνῳ τῷ δικαίῳ . . . τὴν βεβαιοτάτην ἐλπίδα ἀποκεῖσθαι, ib. viii. 11. 2. l Matt. v. 12. vi. 20. xix. 21. Phil. iii. 20. 1 Pet. i. 4. m here
only †. Xen. Mem. ii. 4. 7. Polyb. x. 5. 5. = Jos. Antt. viii. 12. 3, προακηκοὼς τὰ μέλλοντα. see Gal. v.
21. n Eph. i. 13 reff. o Gal. ii. 5, 14.

3. rec ins και bef πατρι (*from Eph* i. 3), with AC²D³KL[P]א rel vulg(and F-lat); τω
D¹F Chr: om B C¹(appy) harl² syrr copt æth Ambrst Aug Cassiod. om χριστου
B. *ὑπὲρ (*see ver 9, where none vary*) BD¹F m 17 [47] Thl: περι ACD³KL[P]א
rel gr-ff.

4. for χριστω, κυριω Aא¹(txt א³). rec (for ην εχετε) την (*aft Eph* i. 15), with
D³KL rel Syr gr-ff: om B: txt ACD¹F[P]א a m o 17 [47] latt syr copt arm lat-ff.

cipate the great subjects of the Epistle. And herein, 3—8.] *Thanksgiving for the faith, hope, and love of the Colossians, announced to him by Epaphras.*
3.] We (I and Timotheus. In this Epistle, the plural and singular are too plainly distinguished to allow us to confuse them in translating: the plural pervading ch. i., the singular ch. ii., and the two occurring together in ch. iv. 3, 4, and the singular thenceforward. The change, as Mey. remarks, is never made without a pragmatic reason) give thanks to God the Father (πατήρ, like ἥλιος, γῆ, &c. is anarthrous, as indeed often in our own language, from its well-known universal import as a predicate necessarily single of its kind: see Eph. i. 2, 3) of our Lord Jesus Christ, always (I prefer, against De W., Mey., B.-Crus., Eadie, to join πάντοτε to περὶ ὑμ. προσευχ., rather than to εὐχαριστ. For 1) it would come rather awkwardly after so long an interruption as τῷ θ. πατ. τ. κυρ. ἡμ. 'Ιησ. χρ. (see however 1 Cor. xv. 58): and 2) I doubt whether the next clause would begin with περὶ ὑμῶν, so naturally as with πάντοτε περὶ ὑμῶν, which are found together so usually, cf. 1 Cor. i. 4; 1 Thess. i. 3 (2 Thess. i. 2)) praying for you (Meyer's and Eadie's objection to joining πάντοτε with προσευχόμενος is, that it is much more natural to say 'we always give thanks when we pray,' than 'we give thanks, always praying.' But we must remember that 'prayer with thanksgiving' was the Apostle's recommendation (Phil. iv. 6), and doubtless his practice, and that the wider term προσευχόμενος included both): since we heard of (not, *because* we heard: see Eph.

i. 15. The facts which he heard, not the fact of his hearing, were the ground of his thanksgiving) your faith in (not τὴν ἐν: the immediate element of their faith, not its distinctive character, is the point brought out) Christ Jesus, and the love which ye have (these words, dwelling on the fact as reported to him, carry more affectionate commendation than would merely the article τήν of the rec.) towards all the saints, 5.] on account of (not to be joined with εὐχαριστ. as Beng., Eadie, al.: for, as Mey., the ground of such thanksgiving is ever in the spiritual state of the person addressed, see Rom. i. 8; 1 Cor. i. 4 ff.; Eph. i. 15 &c., and this can hardly (against Eadie) be said to be of such a kind: but with ἣν ἔχετε— so Chr.: τοῦτο πρὸς τοὺς πειρασμούς, ὥστε μὴ ἐνταῦθα ζητεῖν τὴν ἄνεσιν. ἵνα γὰρ μή τις εἴπῃ καὶ τί τὸ κέρδος τῆς ἀγάπης τῆς εἰς τοὺς ἁγίους κοπτομένων αὐτῶν; χαίρωμεν, φησίν, ὅτι μεγάλα ἑαυτοῖς προξενεῖτε ἐν τοῖς οὐρανοῖς. So also Calvin, who combats the argument of Est., al., deriving support for the idea of meritorious works from this verse. It is obvious that we must not include τὴν πίστιν ὑμῶν in the reference, as Grot., Olsh., De W., al., have done: for πίστις ἐν χ. 'I. cannot be referred to any such motive: besides, see ver. 8, where he returns again to τὴν ἀγάπην) the hope (on the objective sense of ἐλπίς, see reff.) which is laid up (Kypke quotes Plut. Cæs. p. 715—κοινὰ ἆθλα τῆς ἀνδραγαθίας παρ' αὐτῷ φυλασσόμενα ἀποκεῖσθαι, and Jos. B. J. ii. 8. 11,—ταῖς μὲν ἀγαθαῖς (ψυχαῖς) τὴν ὑπὲρ ὠκεανὸν δίαιταν ἀποκεῖσθαι) for you in the heavens

αγγελίου 6 τοῦ [p] παρόντος εἰς ὑμᾶς, καθὼς καὶ ἐν παντὶ
τῷ κόσμῳ ἐστὶν [q] καρποφορούμενον καὶ [r] αὐξανόμενον
καθὼς καὶ ἐν ὑμῖν, ἀφ᾽ ἧς ἡμέρας ἠκούσατε καὶ [s] ἐπέγνωτε
τὴν [t] χάριν τοῦ θεοῦ [u] ἐν ἀληθείᾳ· 7 καθὼς ἐμάθετε ἀπὸ

ABCDF KLPℵ a b c d e f g h k l m n o 17. 47

p = 2 Pet. i. 12. w. εἰς, here only. w. πρός, Acts xii. 20. 2 Cor. xi. 8. Gal. iv. 18, 20. q Mark iv. 20 ||, 28. Rom. vii. 4, 5. ver. 10 only. Hab. iii. 17. Wisd. x. 7 only. mid., here only. r transit., 1 Cor. iii. 6, 7. 2 Cor. ix. 10. Gen. xvii. 6. pass. (or mid.), 2 Cor. x. 15. ver. 10. 1 Pet. ii. 2. Exod. i. 7. s = 1 Tim. iv. 3. 2 Pet. ii. 21. Job xxxiv. 27. t = John i. 14, &c. Acts xi. 23. 1 Cor. i. 4. 2 Cor. ix. 8. u Matt. xxii. 16. 1 John iii. 18 al. 2 Chron. xix. 9.

6. rec ins και bef εστιν (*to preserve the balance of the sentence, that* καθ. κ. εν π. τ. κ. *might answer to* καθ. κ. εν υμ.), with D³FKL rel latt syrr Chr Thdrt Damasc Ambrst: om ABCD¹[P]ℵ k 17 coptt [æth arm] Aug Sedul. rec om και αυξανομενον (*homœotel*), with D³K rel Damasc-txt: ins ABCD¹FL[P]ℵ a h m o 17 [47] vss gr-lat-ff.

7. rec aft καθως ins και (*to corresp with* καθ. και *above*), with D³KL rel syr gr-ff: om ABCD¹F[P]ℵ 17 latt Syr copt æth arm Ambrst Pel. εμαθατε ℵ.

(reff.), **of which ye heard** (aorist, referring to the time when it was preached among them) **before** (not, *before this letter was written*, as Beng., and usually: nor, as Mey., *before ye had the hope:* nor, as De Wette, al., *before the hope is fulfilled:* nor exactly as Eadie, '*have* (see above) *already heard:*' but 'before,' in the absolute indefinite sense which is often given to the idea of priority, —'ere this'—*olim, aliquando*) **in** (as part of) **the word of the truth** (no hendiadys) **of the Gospel** (the word or preaching whose substance was that truth of which the Gospel is the depository and vehicle),

6.] **which is present** (emphatic: is now, as it was then: therefore not to be rendered as an imperfect, which stultifies the argument, cf. ἐστὶν καρποφ. . . . ἀφ᾽ ἧς ἡμ. below. οὐ παρεγένετο, φησίν, κ. ἀπέστη· ἀλλ᾽ ἔμεινε, κ. ἐστὶν ἐκεῖ, Chrys.) **with you** (pregnant construction,—'came to and remains with:' see reff., and Herod. vi. 24, παρῆν ἐς Ἀσίην, and al. frequently) **as it is also in all the world** (ἐπεὶ δὴ μάλιστα οἱ πολλοὶ ἐκ τοῦ κοινωνοὺς ἔχειν πολλοὺς τῶν δογμάτων στηρίζονται, διὰ τοῦτο ἐπήγαγεν 'καθ. κ. ἐν π. τ. κόσ.' πανταχοῦ κρατεῖ· πανταχοῦ ἕστηκεν. Chrys. The expression **παντὶ τῷ κόσμ.** is no hyperbole, but the pragmatic repetition of the Lord's parting command. Though not yet announced to all nations, it is παρὼν ἐν παντὶ τῷ κόσμῳ—the whole world being the area in which it is proclaimed and working) **bearing fruit and increasing** (the paragraph is broken and unbalanced. The filling up would be, to insert καί after κόσμῳ as in rec. Then it would be, '*which is present with you, as also in all the world, and* καρπ. and αὐξ. (in all the world), *as also among you.*' But neglecting this, the Apostle goes forward, more logically indeed (for the reference in the rec. of κ. ἐστὶν καρπ. to the second member of the foregoing comparison, is harsh), but not so perspicuously, enlarging the παρόντος of his first member into ἐστὶν καρπ. κ. αὐξ. in the second, and then in these words, for fear he should be supposed to have predicated more of the whole world than of the Colossians, returning to καθ. κ. ἐν ὑμ. Again: on **καρπ. κ. αὐξ.**, cf. Thdrt.: καρποφορίαν τοῦ εὐαγγελίου κέκληκε τὴν ἐπαινουμένην πολιτείαν. αὔξησιν δὲ τῶν πιστευόντων τὸ πλῆθος. As Mey. observes, the figure is taken from a *tree*, whose καρποφορία does not exclude its growth: with *corn*, it is otherwise) **as also** (it is καρπ. κ. αὐξ.) **among you, from the day when ye heard** (it) (the Gospel: better thus, than with De W., to go on to **τὴν χάριν τοῦ θεοῦ** for the object of both verbs: ἐπεγν. being not simultaneous with ἠκούσ., and ἐν ἀληθ. not being thus satisfied: see below) **and knew** (ἐπ-, intensitive, but too delicately so to be expressed by a stronger word in our language) **the grace of God in truth** (not adverbial, 'truly,' as Beza, Olsh., Mey., De W., al., which would make ἐν ἀλ. a mere qualification to ἐπέγνωτε: still less, as Storr, al., τὴν χάριν ἀληθῆ, or as Grot., ἐν τῷ λόγῳ τῆς ἀλ.: but generally said, 'truth' being the whole element, in which the χάρις was proclaimed and received: 'ye knew it in truth,'—in its truth, and with true knowledge, which surely differs very appreciably from the adverbial sense (against Ellicott): οὐκ ἐν λόγῳ, φησίν, οὐδὲ ἐν ἀπάτῃ, ἀλλ᾽ ἐν αὐτοῖς τοῖς ἔργοις),

7.] **as** (scil. ἐν ἀληθείᾳ—'in which truth') **ye learnt from Epaphras** (mentioned again ch. iv. 12 as of Colossæ, and Philem. 23, as then a fellow-prisoner with the Apostle. The name *may be* (hardly as Conyb., *is*) identical with Epaphroditus. A person of this latter name is mentioned, Phil. ii. 25, as sent by St. Paul to the church at Philippi, and ib. iv. 18, as having previously brought

Ἐπαφρᾶ τοῦ ἀγαπητοῦ ᵛ συνδούλου ἡμῶν, ὅς ἐστιν πιστὸς
ὑπὲρ ἡμῶν ʷˣδιάκονος τοῦ ˣχριστοῦ, 8 ὁ καὶ ʸ δηλώσας
ἡμῖν τὴν ᶻ ὑμῶν ᶻᵃἀγάπην ᵃᵇἐν πνεύματι. 9 διὰ τοῦτο
καὶ ἡμεῖς ἀφ' ἧς ἡμέρας ἠκούσαμεν οὐ παυόμεθα ᶜ ὑπὲρ
ὑμῶν ᶜᵈπροσευχόμενοι, καὶ ᵈᵉ αἰτούμενοι ᶠἵνα ᵍ πληρωθῆτε
τὴν ʰἐπίγνωσιν τοῦ ⁱ θελήματος αὐτοῦ ʲἐν ᵏ πάσῃ ˡ σοφίᾳ
καὶ ᵐσυνέσει ⁿπνευματικῇ, 10 ᵒπεριπατῆσαι ᵒἀξίως τοῦ

v Paul, ch. iv.
7 only. Matt
xviii. 28, 29,
31, 33. xxiv.
49. Rev. vi.
11. xix. 10.
xxii. 9 only.
Ezra iv. 7, 9.
w = vv. 23, 25.
2 Cor. iii. 6.
Eph. iii. 7.
x 2 Cor. xi. 23.
1 Tim. iv. 6.
y 1 Cor. i. 11.
iii. 13. Heb.
ix. 8. xii.
27. 1 Pet. i.

11. 2 Pet. i. 14 only. Exod. vi. 3.   z = Phil. i. 9 reff.   a see Rom. xv. 30.   b Eph. ii.
22 reff.   c Matt. v. 44. Luke vi. 28. (ver. 3. James v. 16 v. r.) 1 Kings xii. 19.
d Mark xi. 24.   e Eph. iii. 13 reff.   f Phil. i. 9 reff.   g = & constr., Phil. i. 11 reff.
h Eph. i. 17 reff.   i = Eph. v. 17.   j Eph. v. 18.   k Phil. i. 20 reff.
l Eph. i. 8, 17 al.   m Eph. iii. 4 reff.   n Rom. i. 11. 1 Cor. ii. 13. iii. 1 al.†
e Eph. iv. 1 (reff.). 1 Thess. ii. 12 only.

rec (for 2nd ημων) υμων, with CD³FKL[P]א³ rel Chr Thdrt Damasc : txt ABD¹א¹ aˡ
Ambrst-comm('vice apostoli').

9. om και αιτουμενοι (homœotel) BK Ps-Ath Arnob : ins ACDFL[P]א rel vss gr-
lat-ff.   τη επιγνωσει D² m o 80.

10. rec aft περιπατησαι ins υμας (filling up the construction), with D³KL[P]א³ rel
Chr Thdrt Damasc al : txt ABCD¹Fא¹ m 17 Clem.

to him offerings from that church. There
is no positive reason disproving their identity : but probability is against it) our (not
'my') beloved fellow-servant (of Christ,
Phil. i. 1 : not necessarily 'fellow-bonds-
man,' as Conyb. : συναιχμάλωτος, Philem.
23), who is a minister of Christ faithful
on our behalf (the stress of the predicatory sentence is on πιστὸς ὑπὲρ ἡμῶν,
which ought therefore in the translation
not to be sundered. He was one acting
faithfully "vice Apostoli" (Ambrst.), and
therefore not lightly to be set aside in
favour of the new and erroneous teachers),
who also made known to us your love in
the Spirit (viz. the ἀγάπη of which he
described himself in ver. 4 as having
heard ; their love εἰς πάντας τοὺς ἁγίους.
This love is emphatically a gift, and in its
full reference the chief gift of the Spirit
(Gal. v. 22 ; Rom. xv. 30), and is thus in
the elemental region of the Spirit,—as
distinct from those unspiritual states of
mind which are ἐν σαρκί. This love of
the Colossians he lays stress on, as a ground
for thankfulness, a fruit of the hope laid up
for them,—as being that side of their Christian character where he had no fault (or
least fault, see ch. iii. 12—14) to find with
them. He now proceeds, gently and delicately at first, to touch on matters needing
correction).

9—12.] Prayer for their confirmation
and completion in the spiritual life.
9.] For this reason (on account of your
love and faith, &c. which Epaphras announced to us) we also (καί, on our side—
the Colossians having been the subject before ; used too on account of the close correspondence of the words following with

those used of the Colossians above) from the
day when we heard (it) (viz. as in ver. 4)
do not cease praying for you ('precum
mentionem generatim fecit ver. 3 : nunc ex-
primit, quid precetur,' Beng.) and (brings
into prominence a special after a general,
cf. Eph. vi. 18, 19) beseeching that (on ἵνα
after verbs of praying, see note, 1 Cor. xiv.
13) ye may be filled with (accusative, as
in reff.) the thorough knowledge (ἐπίγν.
stronger than γνῶσις : see 1 Cor. xiii. 12) of
His (God's, understood as the object of our
prayer) will (respecting your walk and conduct, as the context shews : not so much His
purpose in Christ, as Chrys. (διὰ τοῦ υἱοῦ
προσάγεσθαι ἡμᾶς αὐτῷ, οὐκέτι δι' ἀγγέλων), Œc., Thl., al. : cf. Eph. i. 9 : but
of course not excluding the great source of
that special will respecting you, His general
will to be glorified in His Son) in all wisdom (seeing that ἐν πάσῃ σοφίᾳ, in the
similar clauses, Eph. i. 8 ; ver. 28, ch. iii.
16, is absolute, I prefer taking it so here,
and not, as Ellic., with πνευματικῇ) and
spiritual understanding (the instrument
by which we are to be thus filled,—the
working of the Holy Spirit, πνευματική.
On σοφία and σύνεσις, the general and
particular, see note Eph. i. 8 : so Bengel
here,—" σοφία est quiddam generalius :
σύνεσις est sollertia quædam, ut quovis tempore aliquid succurrat, quod hic et nunc
aptum est. σύνεσις est in intellectu : σοφία
est in toto complexu facultatum animæ ")
to walk (aim of the foregoing imparting of
wisdom : 'so that ye may walk.' ἐνταῦθα
περὶ βίου κ. τῶν ἔργων φησίν· ἀεὶ γὰρ τῇ
πίστει συζεύγνυσι τὴν πολιτείαν. Chrys.)
worthily of the Lord (Christ, see reff. and
cf. ἀξίως τοῦ θεοῦ, 3 John 6) unto ('with

κυρίου ᵖ εἰς ᵏ πᾶσαν ᑫ ἀρέσκειαν, ἐν παντὶ ʳ ἔργῳ ʳ ἀγαθῷ
ˢ καρποφοροῦντες καὶ ˢ αὐξανόμενοι τῇ ᵍ ἐπιγνώσει τοῦ
θεοῦ, 11 ἐν ᵏ πάσῃ ᵗ δυνάμει ᵘ δυναμούμενοι ᵛ κατὰ τὸ ʷ κράτος τῆς ʷ δόξης αὐτοῦ ᵖ εἰς ᵏ πᾶσαν ˣ ὑπομονὴν καὶ ʸ μακροθυμίαν ᶻ μετὰ χαρᾶς, 12 ᵃ εὐχαριστοῦντες τῷ ᵇ πατρὶ τῷ

ABCDF
KLPℵ a
b c d e f
g h k l m
n o 17. 47

p = Acts xi. 18. Rom. vi. 22. x. 1 al. fr.
q here only. Prov. xxxi. 30 only.
r Eph. ii. 10 reff.
s ver. 6.
t Eph. iii. 16 (dat.).
u here only. Ps. lxvii. 28.
w see Eph. i. 19. vi. 10. 2 Thess. i. 9.
y = 2 Tim. iii. 10. iv. 2. xxix. 22.

Eccl. x. 10 only. Dan. ix. 27 Theod.
2 Thess. i. 9.
Heb. vi. 12. James v. 10. Isa. lvii. 15.
a Eph. v. 20 reff.

x = Luke xxi. 19. Rom. ii. 7. v. 3, 4.
b abs., Acts i. 4, 7. ii. 33. 1 Cor. viii. 6.

v = ver. 29. Eph. iii. 16. 2 Thess. ii. 9.
Heb. xii. 1 al. Ps. ix. 18.
z = Mark iii. 5. Eph. vi. 7 al. 1 Chron.
Eph. ii. 18. 1 John passim.

rec εις την επιγνωσιν, with D³KL rel Thdrt Damasc Thl Œc: εν τη επιγνωσει ℵ³ 6. 10.
34. 47 Chr, *in scientia* vulg Syr Hil Pel: txt ABCD¹F[P]ℵ¹ 17 am(with tol) Clem
Cyr Max. (*The constr* (see note) *being found difficult, was emended either by
inserting* εν, *or substituting the more usual* εις (see Eph. ii. 21, iv. 15), *which had the
additional recommendation of already ending the adjacent participial clauses.
Tischdf* [ed.7] *and Meyer retain rec.*)
     12. ins αμα bef τω πατρι B.   ins θεω και bef πατρι C³ b g k o vss gr-lat-ff; θεω

'a view to,' subjective: or, '*so as to effect*,'
objective: the latter is preferable) **all** (all
manner of, all that your case admits) **well-
pleasing** (the word occurs in Theophr.
Character. 5, which is on ἀρέσκεια as a subjective quality. Mey. quotes from Polyb.
xxxi. 26. 5, πᾶν γένος ἀρεσκείας προσ-
φερόμενος. The meaning is, 'so that (see
above) in every way ye may be well pleasing to God') : **in** (exemplifying element of
the καρπ.; see below) **every good work**
(not to be joined with the former clause, as
Œc., Thl., Erasm., al., to the destruction
of the parallelism) **bearing fruit** (the good
works being the fruits: the περιπατῆσαι
is now further specified, being subdivided
into four departments, noted by the four
participles καρποφοροῦντες, αὐξανόμενοι,
δυναμούμενοι, and εὐχαριστοῦντες. On the
construction, see Eph. iii. 18 note) **and
increasing** (see on ver. 6 above) **by the
knowledge of God** (the instrument of the
increase. This is by far the most difficult
of the three readings (see var. readd.),
the meaning of ἐν and εἰς being very obvious—the former pointing out the element, the latter the proposed measure, of
the increase. And hence, probably, the
variations. It is the knowledge of God
which is the real instrument of *enlargement*, in soul and in life, of the believer—
not a γνῶσις which φυσιοῖ, but an ἐπίγνωσις which αὐξάνει),   **11.**] (corresponding to ἐν παντὶ κ.τ.λ. above) **in**
(not instrumental (Mey.), but betokening
the *element*: all these, ἐν πάσῃ, ἐν παντὶ
.... are subjective, not objective. The instrument of this strength comes in below)
all (departments of every kind of) **strength
being strengthened according to** (in pursuance of, as might be expected from, reff.)
the power of His glory (beware of the
hendiadys, 'his glorious power,' into which

E. V. has fallen here: the attribute of His
glorious majesty here brought out is its
κράτος (see Eph. i. 19, note), the *power*
which it has thus to strengthen. In the
very similar expression Eph. iii. 16, it was
the πλοῦτος τῆς δόξης αὐτοῦ, the *exube-
rant abundance* of the same, from which as
an inexhaustible treasure our strength is to
come) **to** (so as to produce in you, so that
ye may attain to) **all patient endurance**
(not only in tribulations, but generally in
the life of the Spirit. Endurance is the
result of the union of outward and inward
strength) **and long-suffering** (not only
towards your enemies or persecutors, but
also in the conflict with error, which is
more in question in this Epistle. Chrys.'s
distinction, μακροθυμεῖ τις πρὸς ἐκείνους
οὓς δυνατὸν καὶ ἀμύνασθαι· ὑπομένει δὲ
οὓς οὐ δύναται ἀμύνασθαι, though in the
main correct, must not be closely pressed:
see (Mey.) Heb. xii. 2, 3) **with joy** (Mey.
argues that these words must be joined, as
Chr., Œc., Thl., Est., al., with εὐχαριστ.,
because in the other clauses the participles
were preceded by these prepositional qualifications. But this can hardly be pressed,
in the frequent disregard of such close parallelism by our Apostle, and seeing that
εὐχαριστ. does in fact *take up again* μετὰ
χαρᾶς, which if attached to it is flat and
unmeaning: and as De Wette says, by
joining μετὰ χαρ. to εὐχ., we lose the essential idea of joyful endurance,—and the
beautiful train of thought, that joyfulness
in suffering expresses itself in thankfulness
to God. And so Luth., B.-Crus., Olsh.,
Eadie, al.), **giving thanks to the Father**
(the connexion is not, as Chr., Thl., Calov.,
Calv., al., with οὐ παυόμεθα, the subject
being *we*, Paul and Timothy,—but with the
last words (see above), and the subjects
are '*you*,'—τῷ πατρί, viz. of our Lord

^{c} ἱκανώσαντι ἡμᾶς ^{d} εἰς τὴν ^{e} μερίδα τοῦ ^{f} κλήρου τῶν
^{g} ἁγίων ἐν τῷ ^{h} φωτί, ^{13} ὃς ^{i} ἐρρύσατο ἡμᾶς ἐκ τῆς
^{k} ἐξουσίας τοῦ ^{k} σκότους καὶ ^{l} μετέστησεν εἰς τὴν βασιλείαν τοῦ ^{m} υἱοῦ τῆς ^{m} ἀγάπης αὐτοῦ, ^{14} ἐν ᾧ ἔχομεν τὴν
^{n} ἀπολύτρωσιν, τὴν ^{o} ἄφεσιν τῶν ἁμαρτιῶν, ^{15} ὅς ἐστιν

c 2 Cor. iii. 6 only †.
d see πρός, 2 Cor. ii. 16.
e Luke x. 42. Acts viii. 21. xvi. 12.
2 Cor. vi. 15 only. L.P.
Deut. xii. 12.
f = Acts (i. 17) viii. 21. xxvi.
i = & constr., Luke

18. Josh. xii. 7. g Eph. i. 1 reff. h 1 John ii. 9. i 74. Rom. vii. 24. 2 Cor. i. 10. 2 Tim. iii. 11. iv. 17. 2 Pet. ii. 9. Gen. xlviii. 16. see 1 Thess. i. 10 reff.
k Luke xxii. 53. see Acts xxvi. 18. l Luke xvi. 4. Acts xiii. 22. xix. 26. 1 Cor. xiii. 2 only. 3 Kings xv. 13. μετέστησεν εἰς τὴν ἑαυτοῦ βασιλείαν, Jos. Antt. ix. 11. 1. m so Gen. xxxv. 18.
n Eph. i. 7 reff. o Mark i. 4. Luke i. 77. Acts x. 43 al.‡

only א m [syr copt Orig-int]₁: θεω bef τω πατ. F].   for ικανωσαντι, καλεσαντι D¹F
17 goth æth arm Did Ambrst Vig : καλεσαντι και ικανωσ. B.   υμας Bא c 17 am
(with tol) spec syr-mg [goth] æth arm Did Thl Ambrst.   om εν C¹.
[13. υμας P arm goth.]
14. εσχομεν B, accepimus copt. (A def.)   rec aft απολυτρωσιν ins δια του αιματος
αυτου (from Eph i. 7), with rel vulg-ed(with demid) syr [arm] Thdrt Œc Iren-int : om
ABCDFKL[P]א d e l m n o 17 [47] am(with[besides F-lat] fuld) Syr coptt goth [æth]
Ath Bas Nyss Chr Cyr spec lat-ff.   om την αφεσιν D¹. (om την απολ. D-lat.)

Jesus Christ : see reff.) **who made** (his-torical—by His gift of the Spirit through His Son) **us** (Christians) **capable** (not, 'worthy,' as Est. after the Vulg.) **for the share** (participation) **of the inheritance of the saints in the light** (it is much disputed with what ἐν τῷ φωτί is to be joined. Mey., after Chr., Œc., Thl., &c., regards it as instrumental—as the means of the ἱκανῶσαι which has been mentioned. But this seems unnatural, both in sense, and in the position of the words, in which it stands too far from ἱκ. to be its qualifying clause. It connects much more naturally with κλήρου, or perhaps better still with the whole, τὴν μερίδα τ. κλήρου τῶν ἁγ., giving τὸ φῶς as the region in which the inheritance of the saints, and consequently our share in it, is situated. This seems supported by the usage of κλῆρος in Acts viii. 21, οὐκ ἔστι σοι μερὶς οὐδὲ κλῆρος ἐν τῷ λόγῳ τούτῳ —cf. also κλῆρον ἐν τοῖς ἡγιασμένοις, ib. xxvi. 18. And so Thdrt., al., De W., Eadie, al.—Grot., al., would take ἐν τῷ φωτί with ἁγίων : against this the omission of the article is not decisive : but it does not seem so natural, as giving too great prominence to οἱ ἅγιοι ἐν τῷ φωτί as the ἐπώνυμοι of the inheritance, and not enough to the inheritance itself. The question as to whether he is speaking of a present inheritance, or the future glory of heaven, seems best answered by Chrys., δοκεῖ δέ μοι κ. περὶ τῶν παρόντων κ. περὶ τῶν μελλόντων ὁμοῦ λέγειν. The inheritance is begun here, and the meetness conferred, in gradual sanctification : but completed hereafter. We are ἐν τῷ φωτί here : cf. Rom. xiii. 12, 13 ; 1 Thess. v. 5 ; Eph. v. 8 ; 1 Pet. ii. 9 al.) :
13.] *Transition, in the form of a laying*

out into its negative and positive sides, of the ἱκάνωσεν above, to the doctrine concerning Christ, which the Apostle has it in his mind to lay down. **Who rescued us out of the power** (i. e. region where the power extends—as in the territorial use of the words 'kingdom,' 'country,' &c.) **of darkness** (as contrasted with light above : not to be understood of a person, Satan, but of the whole character and rule of the region of unconverted human nature where they dwelt), **and translated** (add to reff. Plato, Legg. vi. p. 762 b, πιστεύοντες τῷ μεθίστασθαι κατὰ μῆνας εἰς ἕτερον ἀεὶ τόπον φεύγοντες, and a very striking parallel noticed by Mey., Plato Rep. vii. p. 518 a, ἔκ τε φωτὸς εἰς σκότος μεθισταμένων κ. ἐκ σκότους εἰς φῶς. The word is strictly local in its meaning) **into the kingdom** (not to be referred, as Mey. always so pertinaciously maintains, exclusively to the *future* kingdom, nor is μετέστησεν proleptic, but a historical fact, realized at our conversion) **of the Son of His Love** (genitive subjective : the Son upon whom His Love rests : the strongest possible contrast to that darkness, the very opposite of God's Light and Love, in which we were. The Commentators compare *Benoni*, 'the son of my sorrow,' Gen. xxxv. 18. Beware of the hendiadys, adopted in the text of the E. V. On the whole, see Ellicott's note) :
14—20.] *Description, introduced by the foregoing, of the pre-eminence and majesty of the Son of God, our Redeemer.*
14.] **In whom** (as its conditional element : as in the frequent expressions, ἐν χριστῷ, ἐν κυρίῳ, &c. : see the parallel, Eph. i. 7) **we have** (see note, ibid.) **Redemption** (this is perhaps better, taking the art. as the idiomatic way of expressing the

[p] εἰκὼν τοῦ θεοῦ τοῦ [q] ἀοράτου, [r] πρωτότοκος [s] πάσης

ABCDF KLPℵ a b c d e f g h k l m n o 17. 47

p 2 Cor. iv. 4. Rom. viii. 29. 1 Cor. xi. 7 al. Gen. i. 26, 27. q Rom. i. 20. 1 Tim. i. 17. Heb. xi. 27 only. Gen. i. 2. Isa. xlv. 3. 2 Macc. ix. 5 only. r Luke ii. 7. Rom. viii. 29. Heb. i. 6. xi. 28. xii. 23. Rev. i. 5 only. Exod. iv. 22. constr., see note. s (Mark xiii. 19. xvi. 15.) Rom. viii. 22. ver. 23 (1 Pet. ii. 13) only. Judith xvi. 14.

15. for *ος*, *ο* F. ins *της* bef *κτισεως* f l n 67^2.

abstract subst., than our Redemption as in my earlier editions. See Ellic.), **the remission** ("on the distinction between ἄφεσις and πάρεσις, see Trench, Synon. § xxxiii." Ellic.) **of our sins** (note, Eph., ut supra. παραπτωμάτων, the more special word, is here replaced by ἁμαρτιῶν the more general: the meaning being the same): **15.**] (The last verse has been a sort of introduction, through our own part in Him, to the Person of the Redeemer, which is now directly treated of, as against the teachers of error at Colossæ. He is described, *in His relation* 1) *to God and His Creation* (vv. 15—17): 2) *to the Church* (18—20). This arrangement, which is Meyer's, is far more exact than the triple division of Bähr,—'Source of creation (15, 16): upholder of creation (17): relation to the new moral creation (18—20)'), **who is** (*now*—in His glorified state—essentially and permanently: therefore not to be understood, as De W. after Erasm., Calv., Beza, Grot., Beng., al., of the *historical* Christ, God manifested in our flesh on earth: nor again with Olsh., Bleek on Heb. i. al., of the eternal Word: but of Christ's present glorified state, in which He is exalted in our humanity, but exalted to that glory which He had with the Father before the world was. So that the following description applies to Christ's whole Person in its essential glory,—now however, by His assumption of humanity, necessarily otherwise conditioned than before that assumption. See for the whole, notes on Phil. ii. 6, and Heb. i. 2 ff.; and Usteri, Paulinisches Lehrbegriff, ii. § 4, p. 286 ff.) **image** (= *the* image) **of the invisible God** (the adjunct **τοῦ ἀοράτου** is of the utmost weight to the understanding of the expression. The same fact being the foundation of the whole as in Phil. ii. 6 ff., that the Son ἐν μορφῇ θεοῦ ὑπῆρχεν, that side of the fact is brought out *here*, which points to His being the visible manifestation of that in God which is invisible: the λόγος of the eternal silence, the ἀπαύγασμα of the δόξα which no creature can bear, the χαρακτήρ of that ὑπόστασις which is incommunicably God's: in one word the ἐξηγητής of the Father whom none hath seen. So that while **ἀόρατος** includes in it not only the *invisibility*, but the incommunicability of God, **εἰκών** also must not be restricted to Christ corporeally visible in the Incarnation, but understood of Him as the manifestation of God in His whole Person and work—præ-existent and incarnate. It is obvious, that in this expression, the Apostle approaches very near to the Alexandrian doctrine of the **λόγος**: how near, may be seen from the extracts from Philo in Usteri: e.g. de somniis, 41, vol. i. p. 656, καθάπερ τὴν ἀνθήλιον αὐγὴν ὡς ἥλιον οἱ μὴ δυνάμενοι τὸν ἥλιον αὐτὸν ἰδεῖν ὁρῶσι, κ. τὰς περὶ τὴν σελήνην ἀλλοιώσεις ὡς αὐτὴν ἐκείνην· οὕτως καὶ **τὴν τοῦ θεοῦ εἰκόνα, τὸν ἄγγελον αὐτοῦ λόγον, ὡς αὐτὸν κατανοοῦσι**: and de Monarch. ii. 5, vol. ii. p. 225, λόγος δέ ἐστιν εἰκὼν θεοῦ, δι' οὗ σύμπας ὁ κόσμος ἐδημιουργεῖτο. See other passages in Bleek on Heb. i. 2. He is, in fact, as St. John afterwards did, adopting the language of that lore as far as it represented divine truth, and rescuing it from being used in the service of error. (This last sentence might have prevented the misunderstanding of this part of my note by Ellic. in loc.: shewing, as it does, that the inspiration of St. Paul and the non-inspiration of Philo, are as fully recognized by me as by himself)), **the first-born of all creation** (such, and not '*every creature*,' is the meaning (so I still hold against Ellic. But see his whole note on this passage, as well worth study): nor can the strict usage of the article be alleged as an objection: cf. below, ver. 23, and Eph. ii. 21 note: the solution being, that **κτίσις**, as our word 'creation,' may be used anarthrous, in its collective sense.

Christ is ὁ πρωτότοκος, THE FIRST-BORN, Heb. i. 6. The idea was well known in the Alexandrian terminology: τοῦτον μὲν γάρ,—viz. τὸν ἀσώματον ἐκεῖνον, θείας ἀδιαφοροῦντα εἰκόνος—πρεσβύτατον υἱὸν ὁ τῶν ὄντων ἀνέτειλε πατήρ, ὃν ἑτέρωθι πρωτόγονον ὠνόμασε, καὶ ὁ γεννηθεὶς μέντοι μιμούμενος τὰς τοῦ πατρὸς ὁδούς, πρὸς παραδείγματα ἀρχέτυπα ἐκείνου βλέπων, ἐμόρφου εἴδη. Philo, de Confus. Ling. 14, vol. i. p. 414. That the word is used as one whose meaning and reference was already known to the readers, is shewn by its being predicated of Christ as compared with two classes so different, the *creatures*, and the *dead* (ver. 18). The first and simplest meaning is that of *priority of birth*. But this, if insisted on, in

[s] κτίσεως, 16 ὅτι [t] ἐν αὐτῷ [u] ἐκτίσθη [v] τὰ πάντα τὰ ἐν τοῖς
οὐρανοῖς καὶ τὰ ἐπὶ τῆς γῆς, τὰ [w] ὁρατὰ καὶ τὰ [q] ἀόρατα,

t = 1 Cor. xv. 22. 2 Cor. v. 19. Gal. ii. 17. Eph. i. 4. iii. 11.
u Mark xiii. 19. Rom. i. 25 al. Deut. iv. 32. v = Rom. viii. 32. xi. 36 al. Job viii. 3. w here only. 2 Kings xxiii. 21. 1 Chron. xi. 23. Job xxxiv. 26. xxxvii. 21 only.

16. om 1st τα K[om παντα also, Treg] 73. 118. om 2nd τα BD[1]F[P]א[1] m 17 Orig$_3$: ins ACD[3]KLא[3] rel Orig$_1$ Eus$_4$ Cyr-jer Chr Cyr Thdrt Damasc. add τε C Marcell-in-Eus Eus$_2$ Ath. om 3rd τα Bא[1] Orig$_3$. (Orig$_{alw}$ Eus Thdrt[alic] quote ειτε

its limited temporal sense, must apply to our Lord's birth from his *human mother*, and could have reference only to those brothers and sisters who were born of her afterwards; a reference clearly excluded here. But a secondary and derived meaning of πρωτότοκος, as a designation of *dignity and precedence, implied by priority*, cannot be denied. Cf. Ps. lxxxviii. 27, κἀγὼ πρωτότοκον θήσομαι αὐτόν, ὑψηλὸν παρὰ τοῖς βασιλεῦσι τῆς γῆς:—Exod. iv. 22, υἱὸς πρωτότοκός μου Ἰσραήλ:—Rom. viii. 29, and Heb. xii. 23, ἐκκλησίᾳ πρωτοτόκων ἀπογεγραμμένων ἐν οὐρανοῖς, where see Bleek's note. Similarly πρωτόγονος is used in Soph. Phil. 180, οὗτος πρωτογόνων ἴσως οἴκων οὐδενὸς ὕστερος. It would be obviously wrong here to limit the sense entirely to this reference, as the very expression below, αὐτὸς ἐστὶν πρὸ πάντων, shews, in which his priority is distinctly predicated. The safe method of interpretation therefore will be, to take into account the two ideas manifestly included in the word, and here distinctly referred to—priority, and dignity, and to regard the technical term πρωτότοκος as used rather with reference to both these, than in strict construction where it stands. "First-born of every creature" will then imply, that Christ was not only first-born of His mother in the world, but first-begotten of His Father, before the worlds, — and that He holds the rank, as compared with every created thing, of first-born in dignity: FOR, &c., ver. 16, where this assertion is justified. Cf. below on ver. 18.

It may be well to notice other interpretations: 1) Meyer, after Tert., Chr., Thdrt., al., Bengel, al., would restrict the term to its temporal sense: 'primogenitus, ut ante omnia genitus:' on this, see above. 2) The Arians maintained that Christ is thus Himself declared to be a κτίσις of God. It might have been enough to guard them from this, that as Chr. remarks, not πρωτόκτιστος, but πρωτότοκος is advisedly used by the Apostle. 3) The Socinians (also Grot., Wetst., Schleierm., al., after Theod. Mops.) holding the mistaken view of the necessity of the strict interpretation of πρωτότοκος—maintain, that Christ must be *one of* those among whom He is πρωτότοκος—and that consequently κτίσις must be the new spiritual creation—which it certainly cannot mean without a qualifying adjective to indicate such meaning—and least of all here, where the physical κτίσις is so specifically broken up into its parts in the next verse. 4) Worst of all is the rendering proposed by Isidore of Pelusium and adopted by Erasm. and Er.-Schmidt, '*first bringer forth*' (πρωτοτόκος, but used only of a *mother*). See on the whole, De W.: and a long note in Bleek on the Hebrews, vol. i. pp. 43—48):

16.] **because** (explanatory of the πρωτ. πάσ. κτίσ.—it must be so, seeing that nothing can so completely refute the idea that Christ himself is included in creation, as this verse) **in Him** (as the conditional element, præ-existent and all-including: not '*by Him*,' as E. V. after Chr. (τὸ ἐν αὐτῷ, δι' αὐτοῦ ἐστιν)—this is expressed afterwards, and is a different fact from the present one, though implied in it. The idea of the schoolmen, that in Christ was the 'idea omnium rerum,' adopted in the main by Schl., Neander, and Olsh. ("the Son of God is the intelligible world, the κόσμος νοητός, i. e. creation in its primitive idea, Himself; He bears in Himself their reality," Olsh.), is, as Meyer rightly observes, entirely unsupported by any views or expressions of our Apostle elsewhere: and is besides abundantly refuted by **ἐκτίσθη**, the historic aorist, indicating the physical *act* of Creation) **was created** (in the act of creation: cf. on **ἔκτισται** below) **the universe** (thus only can we give the force of the Greek singular with the collective neuter plural, which it is important here to preserve, as 'all things' may be thought of individually, not collectively)—(viz.) **things in the heavens and things on the earth** (Wetst. urges this as shewing that the physical creation is not meant: 'non dicit ὁ οὐρανὸς κ. ἡ γῆ ἐκτίσθη, sed τὰ ἐν &c., quo habitatores significantur qui reconciliantur' (cf. the Socinian view of ver. 15 above): the right answer to which is—not with De W. to say that the Apostle is speaking of *living* created things only, for manifestly the whole universe is here

<table>
<tr><td>

x Rom. xii. 6.
1 Cor. iii. 22.
y = here only.
(see Dan. vii.
9.) Test. vii.
Patr. p. 532.
z Eph. i. 21
reff.
a John i. 3.
Heb. i. 2.

</td><td>

^x εἴτε ^y θρόνοι ^x εἴτε ^z κυριότητες ^x εἴτε ^z ἀρχαὶ ^x εἴτε ^z ἐξ-
ουσίαι· ^v τὰ πάντα ^{ab} δι᾽ αὐτοῦ καὶ ^b εἰς αὐτὸν ^u ἔκτισται,
17 καὶ ^c αὐτὸς ^d ἐστὶν ^e πρὸ πάντων, καὶ ^v τὰ πάντα ^t ἐν
αὐτῷ ^f συνέστηκεν, 18 καὶ ^c αὐτός ἐστιν ἡ ^g κεφαλὴ τοῦ

</td><td>

ABCDF
KLPℵ a
b c d e f
g h k l m
n o 17.47

</td></tr>
</table>

b Rom. xi. 36.　1 Cor. viii. 6.　see Heb. ii. 10.　　　c = Luke i. 17.　　　d = John viii. 58.　Ps. lxxxix. 2.
e = John v. 7.　Rom. xvi. 7.　Gal. i. 17.　　f here only.　(2 Pet. iii. 5.) ἐκ γῆς...κ....ὕδατος κ. ἀέρος κ.
πυρὸς .. συνέστη ὅδε ὁ κόσμος, Philo de Plant. Noe 2, vol. i. p. 330. ἐκ τοῦ θεοῦ τὰ πάντα, κ. διὰ θεοῦ
ἡμῖν συνέστηκεν, Aristot. de Mundo, vi. p. 471. see Plato Rep. p. 530 a ; Tim. p. 29 a.　　　g Eph. i. 22 reff.

ορ. ειτε αορ.)　　κεκτισται F : εκτισαι C. (Tert testifies to this ver agst Mcion : aft
κυρ. some of the Gnostics (Thdot Val) insd θεοτητες, see Iren Clem Thdrt.)
17. om τα DF 17¹ Chr-txt.

treated of, there being no reason why *living* things should be in such a declaration distinguished from other things,—but with Mey. to treat τὰ ἐν τ. οὐρρ. κ. τὰ ἐπ. τ. γῆς as an inexact designation of heaven and earth, and all that in them is, Rev. x. 6. In 1 Chron. xxix. 11, the meaning is obviously this, σὺ πάντων τῶν ἐν τῷ οὐρ. κ. ἐπὶ τ. γῆς δεσπόζεις), **things visible and things invisible** (which divide between them the universe : Mey. quotes from Plato, Phæd. p. 79 A, θῶμεν οὖν, εἰ βούλει, ἔφη, δύο εἴδη τῶν ὄντων, τὸ μὲν ὁρατόν, τὸ δὲ ἀειδές. The ἀόρατα are the spirit-world (not, οἷον ψυχή, Chr. : this, being incorporated, would fall under the ὁρατά, for the present purpose), which he now breaks up by εἴτε ... εἴτε ... εἴτε), **whether** (these latter be) **thrones, whether lordships, whether governments, whether authorities** (on εἴτε, ... often repeated, see reff. : and Plato, Rep. p. 493 D, 612 A, Soph. El. 595 f. (Mey.)　These distinctive classes of the heavenly powers occur in a more general sense in Eph. i. 21, where see note.　For δυνάμεις there, we have θρόνοι here.　It would be vain to attempt to assign to each of these their places in the celestial world.　Perhaps, as De W., the Apostle chose the expressions as terms common to the doctrine of the Colossian false teachers and his own : but the occurrence of so very similar a catalogue in Eph. i. 21, where no such object could be in view, hardly looks as if such a design were before him.　Mey. well remarks, " For Christian faith it remains fixed, and it is sufficient, that there is testimony borne to the existence of different degrees and categories in the world of spirits above ; but all attempts more precisely to fix these degrees, beyond what is written in the N. T., belong to the fanciful domain of theosophy."　All sorts of such interpretations, by Teller and others, not worth recording, may be seen refuted in De W.) : **the whole universe** (see above on τὰ πάντα, ver. 16) **has been created** (not

now of the mere act, but of the resulting endurance of creation—leading on to the συνέστηκεν below) **by Him** (instrumental : He is the agent in creation—the act was His, and the upholding is His : see John i. 3, note) **and for Him** (with a view to Him : He is the *end* of creation, containing the reason in Himself why creation is at all, and why it is as it is.　See my Sermons on Divine Love, Serm. I. II.　The fancies and caprices of those who interpret *creation* here *ethically*, are recounted and refuted by Meyer) : **and He Himself** (emphatic, His own Person) **is** (as in John viii. 58, of essential existence : ἦν might have been used, as in John i. 1 : but as Mey. well observes, the Apostle keeps the past tenses for the explanatory clauses referring to past facts, vv. 16, 19) **before all things** (in *time* ; bringing out one side of the πρωτότοκος above : not in *rank*, as the Socinians : of which latter James v. 12, 1 Pet. iv. 8, are no justifications, for if πρὸ-πάντων be taken as there, we must render, ' and He, above all, exists,' ' He especially exists,' προπάντων being adverbial, and not to be resolved.　For the temporal sense, see reff.) **all things** (not ' *omnes*,' as Vulg.), **and in Him** (as its conditional element of existence, see above on ἐν αὐτῷ ver. 16) **the universe subsists** (' keeps together,' ' is held together in its present state :' οὐ μόνον αὐτὸς αὐτὰ ἐκ τοῦ μὴ ὄντος εἰς τὸ εἶναι παρήγαγεν, ἀλλὰ καὶ αὐτὸς αὐτὰ συγκρατεῖ νῦν, Chr.　On the word, see reff. : and add Philo, quis rer. div. hæres. 12, vol. i. p. 481, ὁ ἔναιμος ὄγκος, ἐξ ἑαυτοῦ διαλυτὸς ὢν κ. νεκρός, **συνέστηκε κ.** ζωπυρεῖται προνοίᾳ θεοῦ).

18—20.] *Relation of Christ to the Church* (see above on ver. 15) : **And He** (emphatic; not any angels nor created beings : the whole following passage has a controversial bearing on the errors of the Colossian teachers) **is the Head of the body the church** (not ' the body *of* the church :' the genitive is much more naturally taken as one of apposition, inasmuch

^{h} σώματος, τῆς ^{i} ἐκκλησίας, ὅς ἐστιν ^{j} ἀρχή, ^{kl} πρωτό-
τοκος ἐκ ^{l} τῶν νεκρῶν, ἵνα ^{m} γένηται ^{n} ἐν πᾶσιν αὐτὸς ^{o} πρω-
τεύων· 19 ὅτι ^{p} ἐν αὐτῷ ^{q} εὐδόκησεν πᾶν τὸ ^{rs} πλήρωμα

h = ver. 24.
1 Cor. x. 17.
xii. 12, 27 al.
i abs., Eph. i.
22 reff. gen.
apposition,
see Rom. iv.
11. ch. iii. 24.
m constr.,

j = Rev. iii. 14.   see Gen. xlix. 3.   Deut. xxi. 17.   k ver. 15.   l see Rev. i. 5.   m constr.,
Mark i. 4. ix. 3, 7.   2 Cor. vi. 14.   Heb. v. 12.   Rev. iii. 2. xvi. 10.   Josh. ix. 12.   see Winer, edn. 6, § 45. 5.
n = Phil. iv. 12.   1 Tim. iii. 11 al. fr.   o here only.   Esth. v. 11 BN.   2 Macc. vi. 18.   xiii. 15 only.
p ver. 16.   q Rom. xv. 26.   1 Cor. i. 21.   Gal. i. 15 al.   Ps. lxvii. 16.   r = John i. 16.   Rom.
xv. 29.   Eph. i. 23.   s ch. ii. 9.

18. for ος, ο F m : *qui aut quod* G-lat.   ins η bef αρχη B b [47] 67² : απαρχη
17. 118 Chr Damasc; Œc : εν αρχη Cyr. (17 omits η bef κεφ.)   om εκ ℵ¹.
19. ηυδοκ. AD o Chr Damasc.

as in St. Paul, it is the church which *is*, not which possesses, the body, see reff.): **who** (q. d. 'in that He is :' the relative has an argumentative force : see Matthiæ, Gr. § 477 : in which case it is more commonly found with a particle, ὃς μέν, or ὅς γε) is **the beginning** (of the Church of the First-born, being Himself πρωτότ. ἐκ τ. νεκρ. : cf. ἀπαρχὴ χριστός, 1 Cor. xv. 23, and reff., especially the last. But the word evidently has, standing as it does here alone, a wider and more glorious reference than that of mere temporal precedence : cf. ref. Rev. and note : He is the Beginning, in that in Him is begun and conditioned the Church, vv. 19, 20), **the First-born from** (among) **the dead** (i. e. the first who *arose* from among the dead : but the term πρω-τότοκος (see above) being predicated of Christ in both references, he uses it here, regarding the resurrection as a kind of birth. On that which is implied in πρω-τότ., see above on ver. 15), **that** HE (emphatic, again : see above) **may become** (not, as Est., 'ex quibus efficitur, Christum .... tenere :' but the *aim* and *purpose* of this his priority over creation and in resurrection) **in all things** (reff. Beza, (and so Kypke) argues, that because the Apostle is speaking of the Church, πᾶσιν must be masculine, allowing however that the neuter has some support from the τὰ πάντα which follows. In fact this decides the question : the τὰ πάντα there are a resumption of the πᾶσιν here. The ἐν then is not 'inter,' but of the reference :— 'in all matters :' πανταχοῦ, as Chrys. : because the πάντα which follows applies not only to things concrete, but also to their combinations and attributes) **pre-eminent** (*first in rank :* the word is a transitional one, from priority in time to priority in dignity, and shews incontestably that the two ideas have been before the Apostle's mind throughout. Add to reff., from Wetst., πρωτεύειν ἐν ἅπασι κράτιστον, Demosth. 1416. 25 : and Plut. de puer. educ. p. 9 B, τοὺς παῖδας ἐν πᾶσι τάχιον πρωτεῦσαι).

19.] "Confirmatory of the above-said γίνεσθαι ἐν πᾶσιν αὐτ. πρωτεύοντα—

'of which there can be no doubt, since it pleased &c.'" Meyer.—**for in Him God was pleased** (on the use of εὐδοκέω for δοκέω by the later Greeks, see Fritzsche's note, on Rom. vol. ii. pp. 369—72. The subject here is naturally understood to be God, as expressed in 1 Cor. i. 21; Gal. i. 15 : clearly not Christ, as Conyb., thereby inducing a manifest error in the subsequent clause, 'by Himself He willed to reconcile all things to Himself,' for it was not to Christ but to the Father that all things were reconciled by Him, cf. 2 Cor. v. 19. See a full discussion on the construction, and the subject to εὐδόκησεν, in Ellic.'s note. His conclusion, that πλήρωμα is that subject, I cannot accept) **that the whole fulness** (of God, see ch. ii. 9 ; Eph. iii. 19, and on πλήρωμα, note, Eph. i. 10, 23. We must bear in mind here, with Mey., that the meaning is not active, 'id quod rem implet,' but passive, 'id quo res impletur :' all that fulness of grace which is the complement of the divine character, and which dwells permanently in Christ : 'cumulatissima omnium divinarum rerum copia,' Beza,—as in John i. 16. The various other interpretations have been,— "the essential fulness of the Godhead ;" so Œc., al. ; which is manifestly not in question here,—but is not to be set aside, as Eadie, by saying that 'the divine essence dwelt in Christ unchangeably and not by the Father's consent or purpose : it is His in His own right, and not by paternal pleasure :' for all that is His own right, is His Father's pleasure, and is ever referred to that pleasure by Himself ;— "the fulness of the whole universe ;" so Conyb., and Castellio in Beza. This latter answers well : "Quorsum mentio univer-sitatis rerum ? Nam res ipsa clamat Apostolum de sola ecclesia hic agere, ut etiam 1 Cor. xv. 18 (?) ; Eph. i. 10 ; iv. 6, 20 (?) :"—'the Church itself,' as Seve-rianus in Cramer's Catena, τουτέστιν τὴν ἐκκλησίαν τὴν πεπληρωμένην αὐτοῦ ἐν τῷ χριστῷ,—and Thdrt., πληρ. τὴν ἐκκλη-σίαν ἐν τῇ πρὸς Ἐφεσίους ἐκάλεσεν, ὡς τῶν θείων χαρισμάτων πεπληρωμένην, ταὐ-

t ver. 21. Eph. ii. 16 only †.
u ver. 16.
v here only.
Prov. x. 10 only. see Matt. v. 9. Eph. ii. 15.

^{s} κατοικῆσαι, ^{20} καὶ δι᾽ αὐτοῦ ^{t} ἀποκαταλλάξαι ^{u} τὰ πάντα
εἰς αὐτὸν ^{v} εἰρηνοποιήσας διὰ τοῦ ^{w} αἵματος τοῦ σταυροῦ
αὐτοῦ, δι᾽ αὐτοῦ, ^{x} εἴτε τὰ ἐπὶ τῆς γῆς ^{x} εἴτε τὰ ἐν τοῖς

ABCDF KLPℵ a b c d e f g h k l m n o 17. 47

w sc Rom. iii. 25.   x ver. 16.

20. om 2nd δι᾽ αυτου BD¹FL f [47] latt sah [æth] arm (Orig₃) Chr-txt Cyr₂ Thl lat-ff: ins ACD³K[P]ℵ rel syrr copt goth Eus Chr_aliq Thdrt Damasc Œc.   om της bef γης B [Orig₁].   for εν, επι L d g h l n 91¹. 113-4. 121-2-3 Chr Thdrt Damasc.

την ἔφη εὐδοκῆσαι τὸν θεὸν ἐν τῷ χριστῷ κατοικῆσαι, τουτέστιν αὐτῷ συνῆφθαι,—and similarly B.-Crus., al., and Schleierm., understanding the fulness of the Gentiles and the whole of Israel, as Rom. xi. 12, 25, 26. But this has no support, either in the absolute usage of πλήρωμα, or in the context here. See others in De W.) should dwell, and ('hæc inhabitatio est fundamentum reconciliationis,' Beng.) by Him (as the instrument, in Redemption as in Creation, see above ver. 16 end) to reconcile again (see note on Eph. ii. 16) all things (= the universe: not to be limited to 'all intelligent beings,' or 'all men,' or 'the whole Church:' these πάντα are broken up below into terms which will admit of no such limitation. On the fact, see below) to Him (viz. to God, Eph. ii. 16: not αὐτόν; the writer has in his mind two Persons, both expressed by αὐτός, and to be understood from the context. The aspirate should never be placed over αυτ-, unless where there is a manifest necessity for such emphasis. But we are not (as Conyb.,—also Est., Grot., Olsh., De W.) to understand Christ to be meant: see above), having made peace (the subject is not Christ (as in Eph. i. 15; so Chrys. (διὰ τοῦ ἰδίου σταυροῦ), Thdrt., Œc., Luth., al.), but the Father: He is the subject in the whole sentence since εὐδόκησεν) by means of the blood of (genitive possessive, belonging to, figuratively, as being shed on: 'ideo pignus et pretium nostræ cum Deo pacificationis fuit sanguis Christi, quia in cruce fusus,' Calv.) His Cross,—through Him (emphatic repetition, to bring αὐτός, the Person of Christ, into its place of prominence again, after the interruption occasioned by εἰρην..... αὐτοῦ: not meaning, as Castal. (in Mey.), 'per sanguinem ejus, hoc est, per eum:' for the former and not the latter is explicative of the other),—whether (τὰ πάντα consist of) the things on the earth, or the things in the heavens. It has been a question, in what sense this reconciliation is predicated of the whole universe. Short of this meaning we cannot stop: we cannot hold with Erasm., al., that it is a reconciliation of the various portions of creation to one

another: 'ut abolitis peccatis, quæ dirimebant concordiam et pacem cœlestium ac terrestrium, jam amicitia jungerentur omnia:' for this is entirely precluded by the εἴτε . . . εἴτε: nor, for the same reason, with Schleierm., understand that the elements to be reconciled are the Jews and Gentiles, who were at variance about earthly and heavenly things, and were to be set at one in reference to God (εἰς αὐτόν). The Apostle's meaning clearly is, that by the blood of Christ's Cross, reconciliation with God has passed on all creation as a whole, including angelic as well as human beings, unreasoning and lifeless things, as well as organized and intelligent. Now this may be understood in the following ways: 1) creation may be strictly regarded in its entirety, and man's offence viewed as having, by inducing impurity upon one portion of it, alienated the whole from God: and thus τὰ πάντα may be involved in our fall. Some support may seem to be derived for this by the undeniable fact, that the whole of man's world is included in these consequences (see Rom. viii. 19 f.). But on the other side, we never find the angelic beings thus involved: nay, we are taught to regard them as our model in hallowing God's name, realizing His kingdom, and doing His will (Matt. vi. 9, 10). And again the εἴτε . . . εἴτε would not suffer this: reconciliation is thus predicated of each portion separately. We are thus driven, there being no question about τὰ ἐπὶ τῆς γῆς, to enquire, how τὰ ἐν τοῖς οὐρρ. can be said to be reconciled by the blood of the Cross. And here again, 2) we may say that angelic, celestial creation was alienated from God because a portion of it fell from its purity: and, though there is no idea of the reconciliation extending to that portion, yet the whole, as a whole, may need thus reconciling, by the final driving into punishment of the fallen, and thus setting the faithful in perfect and undoubted unity with God. But to this I answer, a) that such reconciliation (?) though it might be a result of the coming of the Lord Jesus, yet could not in any way be effected by the blood of His Cross: b) that we have no reason to think

οὐρανοῖς.　²¹ καὶ ὑμᾶς ποτὲ ὄντας ⁿ ἀπηλλοτριωμένους y Eph. ii. 12.
iv. 18 only.
καὶ ᶻ ἐχθροὺς τῇ ᵃ διανοίᾳ ἐν τοῖς ᵇ ἔργοις τοῖς ᵇ πονηροῖς, z Ps. lxviii. 8.
z Rom. v. 10.
Heb. i. 13 al.,

from Ps. cix. 1.　　　a = and dat., Eph. iv. 18.　　　b John iii. 19. vii. 7.　2 Tim. iv. 18.　1 John
iii. 12.　2 John 11 only.

21. της διανοιας *sensus* D¹F fuld [της διανοια(sic) P].—add [υμων F syr copt æth :]
ejus D-lat spec, *vestri* G-lat.—*sensu vestro* F-lat.

that the fall of some angels involved the
rest in its consequences, or that angelic
being is evolved from any root, as ours is
from Adam : nay, in both these particulars,
the very contrary is revealed. We must
then seek our solution in some meaning
which will apply to angelic beings in their
essential nature, not as regards the sin of
some among them. And as thus applied,
no reconciliation must be thought of which
shall resemble *ours* in its process—for
Christ took not upon Him the seed of angels, nor paid any propitiatory penalty in
the root of their nature, as including it in
Himself. But, forasmuch as He is their
Head as well as ours,—forasmuch as in
Him they, as well as ourselves, live and
move and have their being, it cannot be
but that the great event in which He was
glorified through suffering, should also
bring them nearer to God, who subsist in
Him in common with all creation. And
at some such increase of blessedness does
our Apostle seem to hint in Eph. iii. 10.
That such increase might be described
as a *reconciliation*, is manifest : we know
from Job xv. 15, that " the heavens are not
clean in His sight," and ib. iv. 18, " His
angels He charged with folly." In fact,
every such nearer approach to Him may
without violence to words be so described,
in comparison with that previous greater
distance which now seems like alienation ;
—and in this case even more properly, as
one of the consequences of that great propitiation whose first and plainest effect was
to reconcile to God, in the literal sense, the
things upon earth, polluted and hostile in
consequence of man's sin. So that our
interpretation may be thus summed up :
all creation subsists in Christ : all creation
therefore is affected by His act of propitiation : sinful creation is, in the strictest
sense, *reconciled*, from being at enmity :
sinless creation, ever at a distance from
his unapproachable purity, is lifted into
nearer participation and higher glorification of Him, and is thus *reconciled*,
though not in the strictest, yet in a very
intelligible and allowable sense. Meyer's
note, taking a different view, that the
reconciliation is the great κρίσις at the
παρουσία, is well worth reading : Eadie's,
agreeing in the main with the above result,

is unfortunately, as so usual with him, over-
loaded with flowers of rhetoric, never more
out of place than in treating lofty subjects
of this kind. A good summary of ancient
and modern opinions is given in De W.

21—23.] *Inclusion of the Colossians in
this reconciliation and its consequences, if
they remained firm in the faith.*
21, 22.] **And you, who were once
alienated** (subjective or objective ? —
' *estranged* ' (in mind), or ' *banished* ' (in
fact) ? In Eph. ii. 12, it is decidedly objective, for such is the cast of the whole
sentence there : so also in ref. Ps. : in Eph.
iv. 18 it describes the objective result, with
regard to the life of God, of the subjective
' being darkened in ·the understanding.'
It is better then here to follow usage, and
interpret objectively—' alienated '—made
aliens) **(from God,**—not ἀπὸ τῆς πολιτείας
τοῦ Ἰσρ., nor ἀπὸ τῆς ζωῆς τ. θεοῦ : for
' God ' is the subject of the sentence), **and
at enmity** (active or passive ? ' *hating
God*,' or ' hated by God ?' Mey. takes
the latter, as necessary in Rom. v. 10 (see
note there). But here, where the διάνοια
and ἔργα τὰ πονηρά are mentioned, there
exists no such necessity : the objective
state of enmity is grounded in its subjective causes ;—and the intelligent responsible being is contemplated in the whole
sentence : cf. εἴ γε ἐπιμένετε κ.τ.λ. below.
I take ἐχθ. therefore actively, ' hostile to
Him ') **in** (dative of reference ; not, as
Mey. is obliged to take it on account of
his passive ἐχθ. of the cause, ' on account
of,' &c. : this is not the fact : our passive
ἔχθρα subsists not on account of any subjective actuality in us, but on account of
the pollution of our parent stock in Adam)
your understanding (intellectual part : see
on Eph. ii. 3, iv. 18. Erasm.'s rendering,
in his Par., ' enemies to reason,' ' etenim
qui carni servit, repugnat rationi,' is clearly
wrong : **διάνοια** is a ' *vox media*,' and cannot signify ' reason :' besides, there is
nothing here about ' carni inservire :' that
of Tert., Ambr., and Jer., ' enemies to
God's will,' rests on the reading αὐτοῦ
after διαν.,—see var. readd.: that of Beza,
Mich., Storr, and Bähr,—' *mente operibus
malis intenta*,' is allowable constructionally : the verb is followed by ἐν, cf. Ps.
lxxii. 8, διενοήθησαν ἐν πονηρίᾳ, Sir. vi.

νυνὶ δὲ ^cἀποκατήλλαξεν ²² ^dἐν τῷ σώματι τῆς ^dσαρκὸς
αὐτοῦ διὰ τοῦ θανάτου, ^eπαραστῆσαι ὑμᾶς ἁγίους καὶ
^{fg}ἀμώμους καὶ ^hἀνεγκλήτους ^{gi}κατενώπιον αὐτοῦ, ²³ ^kεἴ
γε ^lἐπιμένετε τῇ πίστει ^mτεθεμελιωμένοι καὶ ⁿἑδραῖοι, καὶ

c ver. 20. Eph.
ii. 16 only †.
d & constr.,
Eph. ii. 15.
e = ver. 28.
Eph. v. 27
reff.
f Eph. i. 4 reff.
g Jude 24.
h 1 Cor. i. 8.
1 Tim. iii. 10.   Tit. i. 6, 7 only. P.† 3 Macc. v. 31.   i Eph. i. 4 reff.   k Eph. iii. 2 reff.
l Rom. vi. 1. xi. 22, 23. 1 Tim. iv. 16. L.P. [exc. John viii. 7.] Exod. xii. 39 B.   m Eph. iii. 18 reff.
n 1 Cor. vii. 37. xv. 58 only. Ps. lvi. 8 Symm.

ABCDF
KLPℵ a
b c d e f
g h k l m
n o 17. 47

for νυνι, νυν D¹F.   for αποκατηλλαξεν, αποκατηλλαγητε B, αποκατηλλακαται (sic)
17 : αποκαταλλαγεντες D¹F spec Iren-int Hil Ambrst Sedul : txt ACD³KL[P(απεκατ.)]
ℵ rel vulg(and F-lat) syrr copt Chr Thdrt Damasc.
    22. om 1st αυτου F.   aft θανατου ins αυτου A[P]ℵ a b² c h k spec Syr syr-w-ast
[copt æth arm] Chr-comm Iren-int.

37; xxxix. 1, and consequently the article
before ἐν would not be needed : but is impugned by the τοῖς ἔρ. τοῖς πονηροῖς,—
not only wicked works, but *the wicked
works which ye did*) **in your wicked
works** (sphere and element in which you
lived, applying to both ἀπηλλ. and ἐχθ. τῇ
διαν.), **now however** (contrast to the preceding description—the participles forming a kind of πρότασις : so δέον αὐτοὺς
τὴν φρόνησιν ἀσκεῖν μᾶλλον τῶν ἄλλων,
οἱ δὲ χεῖρον πεπαίδευνται τῶν ἰδιωτῶν,
Isocr. ἀντιδ. c. 26 : χρεὼν γάρ μιν μὴ
λέγειν τὸ ἐόν, λέγει δ' ἄν, Herod. v. 50 :
Eur. Alcest. 487 (476). See more examples in Hartung, i. p. 186. It is probably
this δέ which has given rise to the variety
of readings : and if so, the rec. is most
likely to have been original, at least accounting for it) **hath He** (i. e. God, as
before : the apparent difficulty of this may
have likewise been an element in altering
the reading) **reconciled in** (of the *situation* or *element* of the reconciliation, cf.
ver. 24, ἐν τῇ σαρκί μου, and 1 Pet. ii.
24) **the body of his** (Christ's) **flesh** (why so
particularized ? 'distinguitur ab ecclesia,
quæ corpus Christi dicitur,' Beng.,—but
this is irrelevant here : no one could have
imagined that to be the meaning :—'corpus
humanum quod nobiscum habet commune
Filius Dei,' Calv. (and so Grot., Calov.),—
of which the same may be said :—as against
the Docetæ, who maintained the unreality
of the incarnation : so Bcza, al. ; but St.
Paul no where in this Epistle maintains, as
against any adversaries, the doctrine of its
reality. I am persuaded that Mey. is right :
'He found occasion enough to write of the
reconciliation as he does here and ver. 20,
in the angel-following of his readers, in
which they ascribed reconciling mediatorship with God partly to higher spiritual
beings, who were without a σῶμα τῆς σαρκός') **by means of His Death** (that being
the instrumental cause, without which
the reconciliation would not have been
effected) **to** (aim and end, expressed with-

out εἰς τό : as in Eph. i. 4, al. fr.) **present
you** (see Eph. v. 27 and note : not, as a
sacrifice) **holy and unblameable and irreproachable** ('erga Deum . . . . . respectu
vestri . . . . respectu proximi,' Beng. But
is this quite correct ? do not ἀμώμ. and
ἀνεγκλ. both refer to blame from without ? rather with Meyer, ἁγίους represents the positive, ἀμώμ. and ἀνεγκλ. the
negative side of holiness. The question
whether *sanctitas inhærens* or *sanctitas
imputata* is here meant, is best answered
by remembering the whole analogy of St.
Paul's teaching, in which it is clear that
progressive sanctification is ever the end,
as regards the Christian, of his justification by faith. Irrespective even of the
strong testimony of the next verse, I
should uphold here the reference to inherent holiness, the work of the Spirit,
consequent indeed on entering into the
righteousness of Christ by faith : 'locus
est observatio⟨n⟩e dignus, non conferri nobis
gratuitam justitiam in Christo, quin Spiritu etiam regeneremur in obedientiam
justitiæ : quemadmodum alibi (1 Cor. i.
30) docet, Christum nobis factum esse
justitiam et sanctificationem.' Calvin) **before His** (own, but the aspirate is not required : see above on ver. 20 : not, that
of Christ, as Mey., reading ἀποκατηλλά-
γητε : in Eph. i. 4, a different matter is
spoken of) **presence** (at the day of Christ's
appearing) :   **23.** (condition of their
presentation being realized : put in the
form of an assumption of their firmness
in the hope and faith of the Gospel)—**if,
that is** (i. e. 'assuming that,' see note on
2 Cor. v. 3), **ye persist** (more locally
pointed than μένετε ;—usually implying
some terminus ad quem, or if not, perseverance to and rest in the end) **in the
faith** (ref. : also Xen. Hell. iii. 4. 6,
'Αγησίλαος δὲ . . . . ἐπέμεινε (al. ἐνέμ.)
ταῖς σπονδαῖς : more frequently with ἐπί,
see Rost u. Palm sub voce) **grounded** (see
Eph. iii. 18, note : and on the sense, Luke
vi. 48, 49) **and stedfast** (1 Cor. xv. 58,

μὴ °μετακινούμενοι ἀπὸ τῆς ᵖἐλπίδος τοῦ ᑫ εὐαγγελίου
ᑫ οὗ ἠκούσατε, τοῦ κηρυχθέντος ἐν ʳπάσῃ ʳκτίσει τῇ
ˢὑπὸ τὸν οὐρανόν, οὗ ἐγενόμην ᵗἐγὼ ᵗΠαῦλος ᵘδιάκονος.
24 νῦν ᵛχαίρω ᵛἐν τοῖς ʷπαθήμασιν ὑπὲρ ὑμῶν, καὶ
ˣἀνταναπληρῶ τὰ ʸὑστερήματα τῶν ᶻθλίψεων τοῦ χρισ-

o here only.
Deut. xix.
14. xxxii.
30. Ezra ix.
11. Isa. liv.
10 only.
p constr., Acts
xvi. 19. Gal.
v. 5. Eph. i.
18. iv. 4.
q attr., Matt.
xviii.19. Acts

i. 1.   Zeph. iii. 11.   r ver. 15.   s Acts ii. 5. iv. 12.   Deut. xxv. 19.
t Gal. v. 2 reff.   u ver. 7 reff.   v Phil. i. 18.   w = Rom. viii. 18.   2 Cor. i. 6.   2 Tim.
iii. 11 al. †   x here only †.   (ἀναπλ., Gal. vi. 2 reff.)   ἀνταναπληροῦντες πρὸς τὸν εὐπο-
ρώτατον ἀεὶ τοὺς ἀπορωτάτους, Demosth. 182. 22.   y Phil. ii. 30 reff.   z = here
only (see note & Rev. i. 9).

23. rec aft πασῃ ins τῃ, with D³KL[P]ℵ³ rel : om ABCD¹Fℵ¹ m o 17 Chr.   υπ
ουρ., omg τον, F a.   ins κηρυξ και αποστολος και bef διακονος (see 1 Tim ii. 7) A
syr-mg; κηρυξ και æth-rom : for διακ., κηρ. κ. απ. [P]ℵ¹(txt ℵ³).
24. at beg ins os (from preceding termination ?) D¹F latt Ambrst Pel.   rec aft
παθημασιν ins μου, with ℵ³ b d g h k [m-marg] o [47] syr Chr : om ABCDFKL[P]ℵ¹
rel latt syrr copt [goth] Thdrt Damasc Phot lat-ff : ℵ¹ [and m-txt] also om υπερ (ins
ℵ·corr¹ [m-marg]).   αναπληρω F k 108 (Orig ?).

where the thought also of μὴ μετακιν.
occurs), and not (the second of two correlative clauses, if setting forth and conditioned by the first, assumes a kind of
subjective character, and therefore if expressed by a negative particle, regularly
takes μή, not οὐ. So Soph. Electr. 380,
μέλλουσι γάρ σε . . . . ἐνταῦθα πέμψαι,
ἔνθα μήποθ' ἡλίου φέγγος προσόψει.   See
more examples in Hartung, ii. 113 f.)
being moved away (better passive than
middle: cf. Xen. rep. Lac. xv. 1, τὰς δὲ
ἄλλας πολιτείας εὕροι ἄν τις μετακεκινη-
μένας κ. ἔτι νῦν μετακινουμένας: it is
rather their being stirred (objective) by
the false teachers, than their suffering
themselves (subjective) to be stirred, that
is here in question) from the hope (subjective, but grounded on the objective,
see note on Eph. i. 18) of (belonging to,
see Eph. as above: the sense 'wrought
by' (Mey., De W., Ellic.) is true in fact,
but hardly expresses the construction) the
Gospel, which ye heard ("three considerations enforcing the μὴ μετακινεῖσθαι:
the μετακινεῖσθαι would be for the Colossians themselves inexcusable (οὗ ἠκούσ.),
inconsistent with the universality of the
Gospel (τοῦ κηρυχθ. &c.), and contrary
to the personal relation of the Apostle to
the Gospel." Mey. This view is questioned by De W., but it certainly seems
best to suit the context: and cf. Chrys.
πάλιν αὐτοὺς φέρει μάρτυρας, εἶτα τὴν
οἰκουμένην ἅπασαν, and see below),—
which was preached (οὐ λέγει τοῦ κηρυτ-
τομένου, ἀλλ' ἤδη πιστευθέντος κ. κηρυχθέντος, Chr.) in the whole creation (see
Mark xvi. 15. On the omission of the
article before κτίσει see above, ver. 15,
note) which is under the heaven,—of
which I Paul became a minister (κ. τοῦτο
εἰς τὸ ἀξιόπιστον συντελεῖ. μέγα γὰρ

αὐτοῦ ἦν τὸ ἀξίωμα λοιπὸν πανταχοῦ
ἀδομένου, κ. τῆς οἰκουμένης ὄντος διδασκάλου, Chrys.).   24.] Transition from
the mention of himself to his joy in his
sufferings for the Church, and (25—29)
for the great object of his ministry :—all
with a view to enhance the glory, and
establish the paramount claim of Christ.
I now (refers to ἐγενόμην — extending
what he is about to say down to the present time—emphatic, of time, not transitional merely) rejoice in (as the state in
which I am when I rejoice, and the element of my joy itself.   Our own idiom
recognizes the same compound reference)
my sufferings (no τοῖς follows : τοῖς παθήμασιν = οἷς πάσχω) on your behalf
(= ὑπὲρ τ. σώμ. below; so that the preposition cannot here imply substitution,
as most of the Roman Catholic Commentators (not Est., 'propter vestram gentium salutem:' nor Corn.-a-lap., 'pro
evangelio inter vos divulgando'), nor 'because of you,' but strictly 'in commodum
vestri,' that you may be confirmed in the
faith by (not my example merely, as Grot.,
Wolf, al.) the glorification of Christ in my
sufferings), and am filling up (the ἀντί
implies, not 'vicissim,' as Le Clerc, Beza,
Bengel, al.; nor that ἀναπλ. is said of
one who 'ὑστέρημα a se relictum ipse
explet,' and ἀνταναπλ. of one who 'alte-
rius ὑστ. de suo explet,' as Winer (cited
by Mey.), but the compensation, brought
about by the filling up being proportion-
ate to the defect: so in ref. : in Dio Cass.
xliv. 48, ὅσον . . . . ἐνέδει, τοῦτο ἐκ τῆς
παρὰ τῶν ἄλλων συντελείας ἀνταναπλη-
ρωθῇ: in Diog. Laert. x. 48, καὶ γὰρ
ῥεύσις ἀπὸ τῆς τῶν σωμάτων ἐπιπολῆς
συνεχὴς συμβαίνει, οὐκ ἐπίδηλος αἰσθήσει
διὰ τὴν ἀνταναπλήρωσιν, 'on account of
the correspondent supply') the deficiencies

a = ver. 18.
b = 1 Cor.
ix. 17.
(Eph. i. 10
reff.)

τοῦ ἐν τῇ σαρκί μου ὑπὲρ τοῦ ᵃ σώματος αὐτοῦ, ὅ ἐστιν
ἡ ᵃ ἐκκλησία, ²⁵ ἧς ἐγενόμην ἐγὼ ᵘ διάκονος κατὰ τὴν ᵇ οἰ-

ABCDF
KLP𝕹 a
b c d e f
g h k l m
n o 17.47

om τη F.   om αυτου D¹.   for ο, ος CD¹ o : om m : txt ABD²·³FKL[P]𝕹 rel
67².   om η D¹ d 109.

25. aft εγω ins παυλος A[P]𝕹¹ 17. 31. 71. 120 arm.

(plural, because the θλίψεις are thought of individually, not as a mass: those sufferings which are wanting) **of the tribulations of Christ in my flesh** (belongs to ἀνταναπλ., not (as Aug. on Ps. lxxxvi. c. 3, vol. iv. p. 1104, Storr, al.) to τῶν θλίψ. τοῦ χρ., not only because there is no article (τῶν ἐν τῇ σαρκί μου), which would not be absolutely needed, but on account of the context: for if it were so, the clause τῶν θλίψ. τ. χρ. ἐν τῇ σ. μ. would contain in itself that which the whole clause asserts, and thus make it flat and tautological) **on behalf of** (see on ὑπέρ above) **His body, which is the Church** (the meaning being this: all the tribulations of Christ's body are Christ's tribulations. Whatever the whole Church has to suffer, even to the end, she suffers for her perfection in holiness and her completion in Him: and the tribulations of Christ will not be complete till the last pang shall have passed, and the last tear have been shed. Every suffering saint of God in every age and position is in fact filling up, in his place and degree, the θλίψεις τοῦ χριστοῦ, in his flesh, and on behalf of His body. Not a pang, not a tear is in vain. The Apostle, as standing out prominent among this suffering body, predicates this of himself κατ' ἐξοχήν; the ἀναπλήρωσις to which we all contribute, was on his part so considerable, as to deserve the name of ἀνταναπλήρωσις itself—I am contributing θλίψεις which one after another fill up the ὑστερήματα. Notice that of the **παθήματα** τοῦ χριστοῦ not a word is said (see however 2 Cor. i. 5): the context does not concern, nor does θλίψεις express, those meritorious sufferings which He bore in His person once for all, the measure of which was for ever filled by the one sufficient sacrifice, oblation, and satisfaction, on the cross: He is here regarded as suffering with His suffering people, bearing them in Himself, and being as in Isa. lxiii. 9, "afflicted in all their affliction." The above interpretation is in the main that of Chrys., Thl., Aug., Anselm, Calv., Beza, Luth., Melancth., Est., Corn.-a-lap., Grot., Calov., Olsh., De W., Ellic., Conyb. The latter refers to Acts ix. 4, and thinks St. Paul remembered those words when he wrote this: and Vitringa (cit. in Wolf) says well, 'Hæ sunt passiones Christi, quia

Ecclesia ipsius est corpus, in quo ipse est, habitat, vivit, ergo et patitur.' The other interpretations are 1) that the sufferings are such as Christ would have endured, had He remained longer on earth. So Phot. (in Eadie): ὅσα . . . . ἔπαθεν ἂν κ. ὑπέστη, καθ' ὃν τρόπον κ. πρὶν κηρύσσων κ. εὐαγγελιζόμενος τὴν βασιλείαν τῶν οὐρανῶν. 2) That the sufferings are not properly Christ's, but only *of the same nature* with His. Thus Thdrt., after stating Christ's sufferings in behalf of the Church, says, καὶ ὁ θεῖος ἀπόστολος ὡσαύτως ὑπὲρ αὐτῆς ὑπέστη τὰ ποικίλα παθήματα: and so Mey., Schl., Huther, and Winer. But evidently this does not exhaust the phrase here. To resemble, is not to fill up. 3) Storr, al., would render, '*afflictions for Christ's sake*,'—which the words will not bear. 4) Some of the Roman Catholic expositors (Bellarmine, Cajetan, al.) maintain hence the doctrine of indulgences: so Corn.-a-lap. in addition: 'Hinc sequitur non male Bellarminum, Salmeroneum, Franc. Suarez, et alios Doctores Catholicos, cum tractant de Indulgentiis, hæc generalia Apostoli verba extendere ad thesaurum Ecclesiæ, ex quo ipsa dare solet indulgentias: hunc enim thesaurum voluit Deus constare meritis et satisfactionibus non tantum Christi, sed et Apostolorum omniumque Christi Sanctorum: uti definivit Clemens VI. extravagante (on this word, I find in Ducange, glossarium in voce, '*extravagantes* in jure canonico dicuntur pontificum Romanorum constitutiones quæ *extra* corpus canonicum Gratiani, sive *extra* Decretorum libros *vagantur*') *unigenitus*.' But Estius, although he holds the doctrine to be catholic and apostolic, and 'aliunde satis probata,' yet confesses, 'ex hoc Apostoli loco non videtur admodum solide statui posse. Non enim sermo iste, quo dicit Apostolus se pati pro ecclesia, necessario sic accipiendus est, quod pro redimendis peccatorum pœnis quas fideles debent, patiatur, *quod forte nonnihil haberet arrogantiæ:* sed percommode sic accipitur, quomodo proxime dixerat "gaudeo in passionibus meis pro vobis," ut nimirum utraque parte significet afflictiones et persecutiones pro salute fidelium, ipsiusque ecclesiæ promovenda toleratas.' The words in italics are at least an ingenuous confession. Con-

κονομίαν τοῦ θεοῦ τὴν ᶜ δοθεῖσάν μοι ᵈ εἰς ὑμᾶς ᵉ πληρῶσαι
τὸν λόγον τοῦ θεοῦ, ²⁶ τὸ ᶠ μυστήριον τὸ ᵍ ἀποκεκρυμμένον ᵍ ἀπὸ τῶν ᵍ αἰώνων καὶ ἀπὸ τῶν ʰ γενεῶν, νῦν δὲ
ⁱ ἐφανερώθη τοῖς ᵏ ἁγίοις αὐτοῦ, ²⁷ οἷς ἠθέλησεν ὁ θεὸς

c = Rom. xii.
3. xv. 15.
2 Cor. i. 4
al. freq.
d = Rom. xv.
16.
e = Rom. xv.
19. see Acts
xii. 25.
f Eph. i. 9 reff.

g Eph. iii. 9 reff.
i Rom. xvi. 26. 2 Tim. i. 10. Tit. i. 3 al.
h = Luke i. 48, 50. Acts xiv. 16. xv. 21. Eph. iii. 5, 21. Isa. xli. 4.
Jer. xl. (xxxiii.) 6 only.
k = Eph. i. 1 reff.

26. rec νυνι, with ADKL rel Eus Cyr : txt BCF[P]א 17 [47] Did.   (for ν. δε,
o νυν k m 20-marg 23 [47] 49. 57. 80. 177. 213 syr arm Clem.)   φανερωθεν D¹.
(but *manifestatum fuit* D-lat.)   for αγιοις, αποστολοις F.

sult on the whole matter, Meyer's and Eadie's notes) : **of which** (parallel with οὗ above : in service of which, on behoof of which) **I** (emphatic, resuming ἐγὼ Παῦλος above) **became a minister, according to** (so that my ministry is conducted in pursuance of, after the requirements and conditions of) **the stewardship** (see on 1 Cor. ix. 17 ; iv. 1, al.: also Eph. i. 10 ; iii. 2 : not, ' *dispensation*,' as Chrys., Beza, Calv., Est., al.: the simpler meaning here seems best, especially when taken with δοθεῖσαν. ' In domo Dei quæ est ecclesia, sum œconomus, ut dispensans toti familiæ, i. e. singulis fidelibus, bona et dona Dei domini mei,' Corn.-a-lap.) **of God** (of which God is the source and chief) **which was given** (entrusted to) **me towards** (with a view to; ref.) **you** (among other Gentiles ; but as so often, the particular reference of the occasion is brought out, and the general kept back), **to** (object and aim of the stewardship : depends on τ οἰκ. τ. δοθ. μοι) **fulfil the word of God** (exactly as in Rom. xv. 19, to fulfil the duty of the stewardship εἰς ὑμᾶς, in doing all that this preaching of the word requires, viz. ' ad omnes perducere,' as Beng., see also below : a pregnant expression. The interpretations have been very various : ' sermonem Dei vocat promissiones .... quas Deus præstitit misso ad gentes Apostolo qui Christum eis patefaceret,' Beza : 'finem adscribit sui ministerii, ut efficax sit Dei sermo, quod fit dum obedienter accipitur,' Calv.: 'ut compleam prædicationem evang. quam cœpit Christus,' Corn.-a-lap. : ' ut plene ac perfecte annuntiem verbum Dei : vel, secundum alios (Vatabl. al.) ut ministerio meo impleam æternum Dei verbum, i. e. propositum et decretum de vocatione gentium ad fidem : vel denique, quod probabilius est, ut omnia loca impleam verbo Dei,' Est.: ' valet, supplere doctrinam divinam, nempe institutione quam Epaphras inchoavit, profliganda et conficienda,' Fritzsche ad Rom., vol. iii. p. 275, where see much more on the passage : and other interpretations in Eadie, Meyer, and De

W. All the above fail in not sufficiently taking into account the οἶκον. εἰς ὑμᾶς. Chrys. better, εἰς ὑμᾶς, φησί, πληρῶσαι τ. λόγ. τ. θεοῦ (but this connexion can hardly stand) περὶ τῶν ἐθνῶν λέγει. He goes on however to understand πληρῶσαι of perfecting *their faith*, which misses the reference to fulfilling his own office) **26.] (namely) the mystery** (see on Eph. i. 9) **which has been hidden from** (the time of ; ἀπό is temporal, not ' from ' in the sense of ' hidden from ') **the ages and the generations** (before us, or of the world: as many Commentators have remarked, not πρὸ τ. αἰ., which would be ' from eternity,' but the expression is historical, and within the limits of our world), **but now** (in these times) **was manifested** (historical : at the glorification of Christ and the bestowal of the Spirit. This change of a participial into a direct construction is made when the contrasted clause introduced by it is to be brought into greater prominence than the former one. So Thuc. iv. 100, ἄλλῳ τε τρόπῳ πειράσαντες, καὶ μηχανὴν προσήγαγον, ἧπερ εἷλεν αὐτό, τοιάνδε. Herod. ix. 104, ἄλλας τε κατηγεόμενοί σφι ὁδοὺς—καὶ τέλος αὐτοί σφι ἐγένοντο κτείνοντες πολεμιώτατοι. See Bernhardy, p. 473) **to His saints** (all believers, not merely as in Eph. iii. 5, where the reference is different, the Apostles and prophets (see there, and cf. various readings here), as some of the Commentators have explained it (not Thdrt., who expressly says, οἷς ἠβουλήθη ἁγίοις, τουτέστι τοῖς ἀποστόλοις, κ. τοῖς διὰ τούτων πεπιστευκόσι), e. g. Est., Steiger, al., and Olsh., but regarding the Apostles only as the representatives of all believers) : **27.] to whom** (' quippe quibus,' as Mey.: this verse setting forth, not the contents of the mystery before mentioned, but a separate particular, that these ἅγιοι are persons to whom God, &c.) **God willed** (it is hardly justifiable to find in this word so much as Chrys. and others have done— τὸ δὲ θέλειν αὐτοῦ, οὐκ ἄλογον. τοῦτο δε εἶπε χάριτος αὐτοὺς μᾶλλον ὑπευθύνους

ˡ γνωρίσαι τί τὸ ᵐⁿ πλοῦτος τῆς ⁿᵒ δόξης τοῦ ᶠ μυστηρίου
τούτου ἐν τοῖς ἔθνεσιν, ὅ ἐστιν χριστὸς ἐν ὑμῖν, ἡ ᵖ ἐλπὶς
τῆς δόξης,
28 ὃν ἡμεῖς ᵠ καταγγέλλομεν ʳ νουθετοῦντες
πάντα ἄνθρωπον καὶ διδάσκοντες πάντα ἄνθρωπον ˢ ἐν

ABCDF KLPℵ a b c d e f g h k l m n o 17. 47

l = 1 Cor. xii. 3. xv. 1. 2 Cor. viii. 1. Eph. i. 9. 1 Kings xxviii. 15. m (neut.) Eph. i. 7. n Eph. i. 18 reff. o Eph. i. 6 reff. p 1 Tim. i. 1. so ζωή, ch. iii. 4. q Phil. i. 18 reff. r Acts xx. 31 (Paul). Rom. xv. 16. 1 Thess. v. 12, 14. 2 Thess. iii. 15 only. P. Job iv. 3. Wisd. xii. 2 al. s ver. 9. ch. iii. 16.

27. rec (for *τι το*) *τις ο*, with C[P]ℵ b f h k o [47] Chr Thdrt: [*το* only F Hil:] txt ABD²³KL rel Clem Eus Thl-comm Œc. (*τον πλουτον* D¹.) for *τουτου*, *του θεου* D¹F Hil Ambrst: *του* ℵ¹ Clem₁ Chr-txt(with ms): *αυτου* arm Cyr. rec (for *ὃ*) *ος*, with CDKLℵ rel [Eus₂] Chr Cyr Thdrt Damasc, *qui* syrr: txt ABF[P] 17 [47] 67²; *quod* latt goth.

28. om *και διδασκοντες παντα ανθρωπον* (*homœotel*) L [47] 67². 73. 109 Clem₁ Œc-comm: om *παντα ανθρ.* D¹F(and lat) f 17 æth Clem₁ lat-ff. (om 1st *π. ανθρ.* Syr: om

ποιῶν, ἢ ἀφιεὶς αὐτοὺς ἐπὶ κατορθώματι μέγα φρονεῖν—and similarly Calv., Beza, and De W. Such an *inference* from the expression is quite legitimate: but not such an *exposition*. No prominence is given to the doctrine, but it is merely asserted in passing) **to make known** (**γνωρίσαι** is not an interpretation of **ἐφανερώθη**, nor an addition to it, nor result of it, as has been supposed: see on the reference of the verse above) **what** (how full, how inexhaustible this meaning of **τί**, necessarily follows from its being joined with a noun of quantity like **πλοῦτος**) **is the richness of the glory of this mystery among the Gentiles** (*σεμνῶς εἶπε κ. ὄγκον ἐπέθηκεν ἀπὸ πολλῆς διαθέσεως, ἐπιτάσεις ζητῶν ἐπιτάσεων.* Chrys. Beware therefore of all attempts to weaken down the sense by resolving the substantives into adjectives by hendiadys. This the E. V. has here avoided: why not always? Next, as to the meaning of these substantives. All turns on **τῆς δόξης**. Is this the (subjective) glory of the elevated human character, brought in by the Gospel (so Chrys., Thdrt. (Calv.?)): or is it the glory of God, manifested (objective) by His grace in this mystery, revealing His Person to the Gentiles? Neither of these seems to satisfy the conditions of the sentence, in which **τῆς δόξης** reappears below with **ἡ ἐλπίς** prefixed. On this account, we must understand it of the glory *of which the Gentiles are to become partakers* by the revelation of this mystery: i. e. the glory which is begun here, and completed at the Lord's coming, see Rom. viii. 17, 18. And it is the glory of, belonging to, this mystery, because the mystery contains and reveals it as a portion of its contents. The richness of this glory is unfolded and made known by God's Spirit as the Gospel is received *ἐν τ. ἔθν.*, as the most wonderful display of it: the Gentiles having been sunk so low in moral and spiritual degradation. See Chr. and Calv. in Mey.), **which** (mystery: this is more in analogy with St. Paul's own method of speaking than to understand **ὅ** of **τὸ πλοῦτος**: cf. *τὸ ἀνεξιχνίαστον πλοῦτος τοῦ χριστοῦ*, Eph. iii. 8,—and *τὸ τῆς εὐσεβείας μυστήριον, ὃς ἐφανερώθη ἐν σαρκὶ κ.τ.λ.* 1 Tim. iii. 16. Besides which (*τοῦ μυστηρ. τούτου*) (*ἐν τοῖς ἔθνεσιν*) is strictly parallel with, being explained by, (*χριστὸς*) (*ἐν ὑμῖν*)) **is** (consists in) **Christ** (Himself: not to be weakened away into *ἡ τοῦ χρ. γνῶσις* (Thl.),—'doctrina Christi' (Grot.): cf. Gal. ii. 20; Eph. iii. 17; 1 Tim. iii. 16, al.) **among you** (not to be confined to the rendering, 'in you,' individually, though this is the *way in which* Christ is among you: *ἐν ὑμῖν* here is parallel with *ἐν τοῖς ἔθνεσιν* above: before the Gospel came they were *χωρὶς χριστοῦ*, Eph. ii. 12), **the** HOPE (emphatic; explains how Christ among them was to acquaint them *τί τὸ πλοῦτος* &c., viz. by being Himself the HOPE of that glory) **of the glory** (not abstract, 'of glory:' *τῆς δόξης* is, the glory which has just been mentioned). **28.**] **Whom** (Christ) **we** (myself and Timothy: but generally, of all who were associated with him in this true preaching: not, as Conyb., 'I,' which here quite destroys the force: the emphasis is on *ἡμεῖς*. WE preach Christ—not circumcision, not angel worship, not asceticism, as the source of this hope) **proclaim** (as being this *ἐλπὶς τῆς δόξης*), **warning** (see on Eph. vi. 4, and below) **every man, and teaching every man** (I am inclined with Mey. to take *νουθετοῦντες* and *διδάσκοντες* as corresponding in the main to the two great subjects of Christian preaching, repentance and faith: but not too closely or exclusively: we may in fact *include* Thl.'s view,—**νουθ.** *μὲν ἐπὶ τῆς πράξεως*, **διδ.** *δὲ ἐπὶ δογμάτων*,—Steiger's, that the former belongs more to early, the latter to more

πάσῃ σοφίᾳ, ἵνα [t] παραστήσωμεν πάντα ἄνθρωπον [u] τέλειον
ἐν χριστῷ· 29 [v] εἰς ὃ [v] καὶ [w] κοπιῶ [x] ἀγωνιζόμενος [y] κατὰ
τὴν [y] ἐνέργειαν αὐτοῦ τὴν [z] ἐνεργουμένην ἐν ἐμοὶ [a] ἐν
δυνάμει.

II. [1] [b] Θέλω γὰρ ὑμᾶς εἰδέναι, [c] ἡλίκον [d] ἀγῶνα [d] ἔχω

[t] = ver. 22.
Eph. v. 27 reff.
[u] = 1 Cor. ii. 6.
xiv. 20. Heb.
v. 14 al. see
Eph. iv. 13.
[v] = 2 Thess. i.
11.
[w] Matt. vi. 28.
Acts x. 35.
Rom. xvi. 6,
12 bis. 1 Tim.

iv. 10 al.　Ps. cxxvi. 1.　　　x Luke xiii. 24.　John xviii. 36.　ch. iv. 12.　1 Tim. iv. 10.　vi. 12.　2 Tim. iv.
7†.　Sir. iv. 28 al.　Dan. vi. 14 Theod.　　　y Eph. i. 19 reff.　　　z Paul, Rom. vii. 5
al15.　Matt. xiv. 2 ||.　James v. 16 only.　Isa. xli. 4.　　　a Mark ix. 1.　Rom. i. 4.　1 Cor. iv.
20.　xv. 43 al.　　　b 1 Cor. xi. 3.　　　c James iii. 5 bis only †.　　　d Phil. i. 30
(reff.).　1 Thess. ii. 2.

3rd 14. 48. 72 : om εν παση to 3rd ανθρ. (homœotel) a d.)　aft σοφια ins πνευματικη
F(and lat) D-lat.　rec aft χριστ. ins ιησου, with D²˙³KL[P]א³ rel vulg(and F-lat)
syr copt goth [æth arm] Chr_aliq Thdrt lat-ff : [pref, Syr :] om ABCD¹Fא¹ h 17 Clem₂
Chr-comm₂ Ambrst Primas.

advanced instruction, and Huther's, that
the former affects the heart, while the
latter informs the intellect (see Eadie's
note) : for all these belong, the one class
to repentance, the other to faith, in the
widest sense) **in all wisdom** (method of
this teaching : not as Est. (giving the
other but preferring this), 'in perfecta
cognitione Dei et mysteriorum fidei, quæ
est vera sapientia,' and so Aug., Anselm,
al.-latt. : this is usually in the accusative : but the Greek Commentators, *τουτέστι, μετὰ πάσης σοφίας κ. συνέσεως*),
that we may present (see above ver. 22)
every man (notice the emphatic triple
repetition of *πάντα ἄνθρ.*, shewing that
the Apostle was jealous of every the least
invasion, on the part of the false teachers,
of those souls with whom he was put in
charge. At the same time it carries a
solemn individual appeal to those thus
warned and taught : as Chrys., —*τί λέγεις;
πάντα ἄνθρωπον; ναί, φησι, τοῦτο σπου-
δάζομεν· τί γάρ; εἰ καὶ μὴ γένηται τοῦτο,
ἔσπευδεν ὁ μακ. Π. τέλειον ποιῆσαι*. There
is hardly perhaps, as Mey., Bisp., Ellic.,
al., suppose, an allusion to the Judaizers,
those who would restrict the Gospel)
perfect in Christ (element of this perfection, in union with and life in Him,—
comprehending both knowledge and practice. The presentation spoken of is clearly
that at the great day of Christ's appearing) :　29.] His own personal part
in this general work—**for which end**
(viz. the *παραστῆσαι*, &c.) **I also** (*καί*
implies the addition of a new particular
over and above the *καταγγέλλειν*, carrying it onwards even to this) **toil in conflict** (of spirit; in the earnestness with
which he strove for this end, see ch. ii.
1—3 : not, with adversaries : this was so,
but is not relevant here. See Phil. i. 30.
1 Thess. ii. 2), **according to** (after the
proportion of, as is to be expected from)
His (Christ's—see Phil. iv. 13 : not God's,

as Chrys., Grot., Calv., al.) **working which
worketh** (not passive, as Est. See on Gal.
v. 6, Eph. iii. 20, and Fritzsche on Rom.
vii. 5) **in me in power** (reff. : there is no
allusion to miraculous gifts, as Ambrst.,
Mich., al.).

CHAP. II. FIRST PART OF THE EPIS-
TLE. His earnestness in entering into
and forwarding the Christian life among
them, so amply set forth in ch. i., is now
more pointedly directed to warning them
against false teachers. This he does by 1)
*connecting his conflict just spoken of,
with the confirmation in spiritual knowledge of themselves and others whom he
had not seen* (vv. 1—3) : 2) *warning them
against false wisdom which might lead
them away from Christ* (vv. 4—23) : and
that a) *generally and in hints* (vv. 4—
15),—b) *specifically and plain-spokenly*
(vv. 16—23). 1.] **For** (follows on,
and justifies, while it exemplifies, *ἀγωνιζόμενος*, ch. i. 29)—**I would have you
know how great** (emphatic ; not only
that I have an *ἀγών*, but how great it is.
The word is unusual, see reff.) **a conflict**
(of anxiety and prayer, cf. ch. iv. 12 : his
present imprisoned state necessitates this
reference here : he could not be in conflict
with the false teachers) **I have on behalf
of you and those in Laodicea** (who probably were in the same danger of being
led astray, see ch. iv. 16 : on Laodicea, see
Prolegg. to Apocalypse, § iii. 13), **and** (it
would not appear on merely grammatical
grounds, whether this *καί* generalizes from
the two specific instances, you and those
in Laodicea, to the genus, including those
two in the *ὅσοι* (see the two first reff., in the
second of which however ἄλλα is added)—
or adds another category to the two which
have preceded, as in the third ref., *Μακε-
δόνες καὶ . . . καὶ . . . καὶ ὅσοι τῆς Θρηΐκης
τὴν παραλίην νέμονται*. This must be
decided on other grounds, viz. those furnished by the context : see below) **(for) as**

e Acts iv. 6.
Herod. i. 57.
vii. 185.
f here only.
(Acts xx. 25.
Rev. xxii. 4.
Gen. xliii. 3.)
ἰδεῖν,
1 Thess. ii. 17.
iii. 10.
g 1 Tim. iii. 16 reff.
8. Eph. vi. 22.
16. Winer. edn. 6, § 63. i. 2 a. see Acts xxvi. 3.

ὑπὲρ ὑμῶν καὶ τῶν ἐν Λαοδικείᾳ ᵉ καὶ ὅσοι οὐχ ᶠ ἑώρακαν ...και
τὸ ᶠπρόσωπόν μου ᵍ ἐν σαρκί, ² ἵνα ʰⁱ παρακληθῶσιν αἱ
ⁱ καρδίαι αὐτῶν, ᵏ συμβιβασθέντες ἐν ἀγάπῃ καὶ ¹ εἰς
πᾶν ᵐ πλοῦτος τῆς ⁿ πληροφορίας τῆς ° συνέσεως, ¹εἰς

...και
οσοι F
(and G
also).
ABCDK
LℵₐR a b
c d e f g
h k l m n
o 17. 47

h = 1 Thess. iii. 2.　2 Thess. ii. 17.　Deut. iii. 28.　Job iv. 3.　　　i ch. iv.
k Eph. iv. 16 only.　Isa. xl. 14. constr. partic., 2 Cor. ix. 11. ch. iii. 16.　Jude
l ch. i. 29.　　　m neut., Eph. i. 7 reff.

n 1 Thess. i. 5. Heb. vi. 11. xx. 22 only†. (-ρεῖσθαι, ch. iv. 12.)　　o Eph. iii. 4 reff.

CHAP. II. 1. rec (for ὑπερ) περι, with D¹·³FKL rel Chr Thdrt Damasc : txt
ABCD³[P]ℵ 17 [47]. rec εωρακασι (more usual), with D³KLℵ³ rel Cyr : txt
ABCD¹[P]ℵ¹ Thdrt-ms.—εορ. CD³(and E) [P]ℵ d e n. om εν σαρκι ℵ(ins ℵ-corr¹).
2. rec συμβιβασθεντων (grammatical correction), with D³KL rel [syr-mg-gr] : txt
ABCD¹[P]ℵ 17. 67² latt Clem Cyr Œc-schol lat-ff. om και D¹ Hil Ambrst Vig.
rec παντα πλουτον, with KL[P]ℵ³ rel : παντα τον πλουτον D Chr : παν το
πλουτος AC 17 (παν το rendered the substitution of the commoner masculine form still
more obvious) : txt Bℵ¹ 67² Clem.

many as have not seen ("the form ἑώρακαν is decidedly Alexandrian. . . . . The
'ſonſtige Gebrauch Pauli' urged against
it by Mey. is imaginary, as the third person plural does not elsewhere occur in St.
Paul's Epistles." Ellicott) my face in the
flesh (my corporal presence : ἐν σαρκί
must not be joined with the verb, as
Chrys. seems to have done, who adds,
δείκνυσιν ἐνταῦθα, ὅτι ἑώρων συνεχῶς ἐν
πνεύματι; for in ver. 5 the σαρκί is
attached to the Apostle. But it is not
necessary nor natural, with Estius, to see
any 'ταπείνωσις, ut intelligant pluris fa-
ciendam esse præsentiam spiritus quam
carnis.' Rather is the tendency of this
verse the other way—to exalt the importance of the Apostle's bodily presence
with a church, if its defect caused him
such anxiety), that (object of the ἀγών)
their hearts (these are the words on
which the interpretation of the former
καὶ ὅσοι must turn. If αὐτῶν apply to a
separate class of persons, who had not
seen him, whereas the Colossians and Laodiceans had, how are we to bring them
into the ἀγών? In ver. 4 the third person αὐτῶν becomes ὑμᾶς. Where is the
link, on this hypothesis, that binds them
together? The sentence will stand thus :
"I am anxious for you who have seen me,
and for others who have not : for these
last, that &c. &c. This I say that no
man may deceive you." What logical
deduction can there be, from the circumstances of others, to theirs, unless they
are included in the fact predicated of
those others? in a word, unless the ὅσοι
above include the Colossians and Laodiceans? Thus the αὐτῶν extends to the
whole category of those who had never
seen him, and the ὑμᾶς of ver. 4 singles
them specially out from among this category for special exhortation and warning.

This seeming to be the only logical interpretation of the αὐτῶν and ὑμᾶς, the καὶ
above must be ruled accordingly, to be
not copulative but generalizing : see there)
may be confirmed (see reff. It can hardly
be doubted here, where he is treating, not
of troubles and persecutions, but of being
shaken from the faith, that the word, so
manifold in its bearings, and so difficult to
express in English, carries with it the
meaning of strengthening, not of comforting merely. If we could preserve in
'comfort' the trace of its derivation from
'confortari,' it might answer here : but
in our present usage, it does not convey any idea of strengthening. This I
still hold against Ellicott), they being
knit together (so E. V. well : not 'in-
structi,' as vulg. On the construction,
see reff. and Eph. iii. 18 ; iv. 2) in love
(the bond of perfectness as of union : dis-
ruption being necessarily consequent on
false doctrine, their being knit together
in love would be a safeguard against it.
Love is thus the element of the συμβι-
βασθῆναι) and (besides the elementary
unity) unto (as the object of the συμβ.)
all (the) richness of the full assurance
(reff. see also Luke i. 1) of the (Christian)
understanding (the accumulated substantives shew us generally the Apostle's
anxious desire for a special reason to impress the importance of the matter on
them. οἶδά, φησιν, ὅτι πιστεύετε, ἀλλὰ
πληροφορηθῆναι ὑμᾶς βούλομαι, οὐκ εἰς
τὸν πλοῦτον μόνον, ἀλλ' εἰς πάντα τὸν
πλοῦτον, ἵνα καὶ ἐν πᾶσι καὶ ἐπιτετα-
μένως πεπληροφορημένοι ἦτε, Chrys.), unto
(parallel with the former, and explaining πᾶν τὸ πλ. τ. πληρ. τῆς συν. by ἐπίγν.
τοῦ μ. τ. θεοῦ) the thorough-knowledge
(on ἐπίγνωσις and γνῶσις, here clearly
distinguished, see on ch. i. 9) of the
mystery of God (the additions here found

^p ἐπίγνωσιν τοῦ ^q μυστηρίου τοῦ θεοῦ,* ³ ἐν ᾧ εἰσὶν πάντες
οἱ ^{rs} θησαυροὶ τῆς ^t σοφίας καὶ ^t γνώσεως ^{su} ἀπόκρυφοι.

p ch. i. 9.
q Eph. i. 9 reff.
r Epp., 2 Cor. iv.
7. Heb. xi. 26
only. Gospp.,

Matt. ii. 11 al8. Mark x. 21. Luke vi. 45 (bis) al3. Josh. vi. 19. s Isa. xlv. 3. 1 Macc. i. 23.
t 1 Cor. xii. 8. u Mark iv. 22. Luke viii. 17 only. Ps. ix. 8, 9 (29, 30). Dan. xi. 43 Theod.

* rec aft του θεου has καὶ πατρὸς καὶ τοῦ χριστοῦ, with D³KL rel syr(2nd και w. ast.) Thdrt Damasc; εν χριστω Clem₂ Ambrst; του εν χ. 17; ὅ ἐστιν χριστός D¹ Aug; *quod de christo* æth; χριστοῦ B Hil (addg, *deus christus sacramentum est*); και χριστου Cyr; πατρὸς καὶ τοῦ χριστοῦ 47. 73 Syr copt Chr Pel; *patris et domini nostri christi* demid; κ. πατρος τ. χριστου א³ 115; πατρὸς τοῦ χριστοῦ AC b¹ o am (with fuld hal) sah: πατρὸς χριστοῦ א¹: om [D³P] m 67². 71. 80¹. 116 arm(ed-1085).

3. rec ins της bef γνωσεως, with AD³KL[P]א³ rel Clem₁ Orig₃ Eus₁ Chr Thdrt Damasc: om BCD¹א¹ 17 [47] Clem₁ Orig₂ Eus₂ Cyr Did Thl-ms.

in the rec. and elsewhere seem to be owing to the common practice of annotating on the divine name to specify to which Person it belongs. Thus τοῦ θεοῦ having been original, πατρός was placed against it by some, χριστοῦ or τοῦ χριστοῦ by others: and then these found their way into the text in various combinations, some of which from their difficulty gave rise again to alterations, as may be seen in various readings. The reading in text, as accounting for all the rest, has been adopted by Griesb., Scholz, Tischdf. (edn. 2), Olsh., De Wette, al.: τοῦ θεοῦ χριστοῦ by Mey. and Steiger. This latter is also edited, in pursuance of his plan, by Lachm. The shorter reading was by that plan excluded from his present text, as not coming before his notice. In the present digest, the principal differing readings are printed in the same type as that in the text, because I have been utterly unable to fix the reading on any *external* authority, and am compelled to take refuge in that which appears to have been the origin of the rest. One thing is clear, that τοῦ θεοῦ χριστοῦ, which Ellicott adopts 'with some confidence,' is simply one among many glosses, of which it is impossible to say that any has overwhelming authority. Such expressions were not corrected ordinarily by *omission* of any words, but constantly by supplementing them in various ways): in which (mystery, as Grot., Beng., Mey., De W., al. (Bisping well remarks, that the two in fact run into one, as Christ is Himself the μυστήριον τοῦ θεοῦ. He might have referred to ch. i. 27 and 1 Tim. iii. 16)— not '*in whom*,' as E. V. (but 'wherein' in marg.), and so, understanding 'whom' of *Christ*, Chrys., Thdrt., al.: for it is unnatural to turn aside from the main subject of the sentence,—the μυστήριον, and make this relative clause epexegetic

of the dependent genitive merely. To this view the term ἀπόκρυφος also testifies: see below) are all the secret (the * ordinary rendering is, to make ἀπόκρυφοι the predicate after εἰσίν: '*in which are all*, &c. *hidden*.' The objection to this is, that it is contrary to fact: the treasures are not hidden, but revealed. The meaning given by Bähr, B.-Crus., and Robinson (Lex,), 'laid up,' lying concealed, ἀποκείμενα, does not belong to the word, nor is either of the places in the canonical LXX (reff.) an example of it. The rendering which I have adopted is that of Meyer, and I am persuaded on consideration that it is not only the only logical but the only grammatical one also. The ordinary one would require ἀποκεκρυμμένοι, or with ἀπόκρυφοι, a different arrangement of the words ἐν ᾧ ἀπόκρυφοί εἰσιν, or ἐν ᾧ εἰσὶν ἀπόκρυφοι. The objection, that for our rendering οἱ ἀπόκρυφοι would be required (Bähr), shews ignorance of the logic of such usage. Where the whole subject is covered by the extent of the predicate, the latter, even though separated by an intervening clause from the former, does not *require* the specification by the article. It *may* have it, but need not. Thus if all the men in a fortress were Athenians, I *might* say 1) οἱ ἄνδρες ἐν τούτῳ ἐν τῷ τείχει οἱ Ἀθηναῖοι: but I might also say 2) οἱ ἄνδρες ἐν τούτῳ ἐν τῷ τείχει Ἀθηναῖοι. If however, part of the men were Platæans, I *must* use 1), and could not use 2). Here, it is not asserted that 'all the treasures, &c. which are secret, are contained in the mystery,' others being implied which are not secret,—but the implication is the other way: 'the treasures, &c. are all secret, and all contained in the mystery.' Ellicott's rendering of ἀπόκρυφοι as an adverbial predicate, 'hiddenly,' is quite admissible, and tallies better with the

v James i. 22 only. Gen. xxix. 25. Josh. ix. 22. Judg. xvi. 10 A.
w here only †. πιθανολο- γεῖν πει- ρᾶται, Diod. Sic. i. 39.

4 τοῦτο [δὲ] λέγω ἵνα μηδεὶς ὑμᾶς ᵛπαραλογίζηται ἐν ᵂπιθανολογίᾳ. 5 εἰ γὰρ καὶ τῇ σαρκὶ ˣἄπειμι, ʸἀλλὰ τῷ ᶻπνεύματι ᵃσὺν ὑμῖν ᵃεἰμί, ᵇχαίρων καὶ ᵇβλέπων ὑμῶν τὴν ᶜτάξιν καὶ τὸ ᵈστερέωμα τῆς ᵉεἰς χριστὸν ᵉπίσ-

ABCDK LPℵ a b c d e f g h k l m n o 17. 47

a = Luke viii. 38. xxii. 56.   Phil. i. 23.   x Phil. i. 27 reff.   1 Thess. iv. 17.   2 Pet. i. 18 al.   y = 1 Cor. viii. 6.   z = 1 Cor. v. 3.   b cf. Jos. B. J. iii. 10. 2, προθυμίας . . . . ὑμᾶς . . . . εὖ ἔχοντας χαίρω καὶ βλέπων.   c Luke i. 8.   1 Cor. xiv. 40. Heb. v. 6, 11, & vi. 20 (from Ps. cix. 4). vii. 11, &c. only L.P.H.   Job xxxviii. 12.   d here only. Ezek. xiii. 5.   Gen. i. 6, &c.   Ps. xvii. 2.   (-ρεοῦν, Acts xvi. 5.)   e Acts xx. 21. xxiv. 24. xxvi. 18. Philem. 5.   Paul (or of Paul) only.

4. om δε A¹(appy) Bℵ¹ Ambrst Aug. Clem₁ : txt ABCD[P]ℵ¹ m 17 Clem₁. πειθανολ. D²L.

5. aft αλλα ins γε D¹. Aug Ambrst.

rec (for μηδεις) μη τις, with KLℵ³ rel ημας C.   παραλογισητε C²[P] 17.

for στερεωμα, id quod deest (i. e. υστερημα) D-lat tol

classification and nomenclature of predicates, which he has adopted from Donaldson: but I question whether the rendering given above be not both more simple and more grammatical) **treasures** (see Plato, Phileb. p. 15 e, ὥς τινα σοφίας εὑρηκὼς θησαυρόν: Xen. Mem. iv. 2. 9, ἄγαμαί σου διότι οὐκ ἀργυρίου κ. χρυσίου προείλου θησαυροὺς κεκτῆσθαι μᾶλλον ἢ σοφίας: also ib. i. 7. 14) **of wisdom and knowledge** (σοφ., the general, γνῶσις, the particular; see note on Eph. i. 8). **4.**] See summary at the beginning of the chapter. [**But** (the contrast is between the assertion above, and the reason of it, now to be introduced)] **this** (viz. vv. 1—3, not ver. 3 only, as Thl., Calv., al.: for ver. 1 is alluded to in ver. 5,—and vv. 1—3 form a logically connected whole) **I say, in order that** (aim and design of it) **no one may deceive you** (the word is found in this sense in Æsch. p. 16, 33, ἀπάτῃ τινὶ παραλογισάμενος ὑμᾶς,—ib. in Ctesiph. (Wetst.), ἢ τοὺς ἀκούοντας ἐπιλήσμονας ὑπολαμβάνεις ἢ σαυτὸν παραλογίζῃ—also in Diod. Sic., &c., in Wetst. See also Palm u. Rost sub voce) **in** (element in which the deceit works) **persuasive discourse** (add to the ref. Plato, Theæt. p. 162 e, σκοπεῖτε οὖν . . . εἰ ἀποδέξεσθε πιθανολογίᾳ τε κ. εἰκόσι περὶ τηλικούτων λεγομένους λόγους, and see 1 Cor. ii. 4): **5.**] personal ground, why they should not be deceived: **for though I am also** (in εἰ καί the force of the καί does not extend over the whole clause introduced by the εἰ, as it does in καὶ εἰ, but only belongs to the word immediately following it, which it couples, as a notable fact, to the circumstance brought out in the apodosis: so πόλιν μέν, εἰ καὶ μὴ βλέπεις, φρονεῖς δ' ὅμως, οἵᾳ νόσῳ ξύνεστι, Soph. Œd. Tyr. 302. See Hartung, i. 139) **absent** (there is no ground whatever from this expression for

inferring that he had been at Colossæ, as Wiggers supposed, Stud. u. Krit. 1838, p. 181: nor would the mere expression in 1 Cor. v. 3 authorize any such inference were it not otherwise known to be so) **in the flesh** (ver. 1 reff.), **yet** (ἀλλά introduces the apodosis when it is a contrast to a hypothetically expressed protasis: so Hom. Il. α. 81 f., εἴπερ γάρ τε χόλον γε κ. αὐτῆμαρ καταπέψῃ, ἀλλά τε καὶ μετόπισθεν ἔχει κότον, ὄφρα τελέσσῃ. See Hartung, ii. 40) **in my spirit** (contrast to τῇ σαρκί: not meaning as Ambrst. and Grot., 'Deus Paulo revelat quæ Colossis fierent') **I am with you** (reff.) **rejoicing** (in my earlier editions, I referred χαίρων to the fact of rejoicing at being able thus to be with you in spirit: but I see, as pointed out by Ellic., that this introduces a somewhat alien thought. I would now therefore explain it, not exactly as he does, by continuing the σὺν ὑμῖν, but as referring to their general state: rejoicing as such presence would naturally suggest: the further explanation, καὶ βλέπων &c., following) **and** (strictly copulative : there is no logical transposition, as De W., al.: nor is καί explicative, 'rejoicing, in that I see'—as Calv., Est., al.: nor, which is nearly allied, is there any hendiadys, ' I rejoice, seeing,' as Grot., Wolf, al.: nor need ἐφ' ὑμῖν be supplied after χαίρων, as Winer and Fritzsche: but as above. The passage of Jos. in ref. is rather a coincidence of terms than an illustration of construction) **seeing your order** (ἡ συμπᾶσα σχέσις κ. τάξις τῆς οἰκουμένης, Polyb. i. 4. 6 : see also 36. 6; Plato Gorg. p. 504 a. It is often used of the organization of a state, e. g. Demosth. p. 200. 4, ταύτην τὴν τάξιν αἱρεῖσθαι τῆς πολιτείας. Here it imports the orderly arrangement of a harmonized and undivided church. Mey.) **and** (as τάξις was the outward manifestation, so this is the inward fact

τέως ὑμῶν. 6 ὡς οὖν f παρελάβετε τὸν χριστὸν Ἰησοῦν f 1 Cor. xi. 23.
τὸν κύριον, g ἐν αὐτῷ g περιπατεῖτε, 7 h ἐρριζωμένοι καὶ
i ἐποικοδομούμενοι ἐν αὐτῷ καὶ j βεβαιούμενοι [ἐν] τῇ
πίστει k καθὼς ἐδιδάχθητε, l περισσεύοντες [ἐν αὐτῇ] l ἐν
m εὐχαριστίᾳ. 8 n βλέπετε μή τις ὑμᾶς ο ἔσται p ὁ q συλ-

f 1 Cor. xi. 23.
xv. 1. Gal.
i. 9, 12 al. of
Christ, John
i. 11 only.
g constr., Rom.
vi. 4. 2 Cor.
iv. 2. x. 3.
Eph. v. 2 al.
Prov. viii. 20.
w. αὐτῷ,
here only.

h Eph. iii. 18 only. Isa. xl. 24.　　　　　i Eph. ii. 20 reff.　　　　　j Mark xvi. 20. Rom. xv.
8. 1 Cor. i. 6, 8. 2 Cor. i. 21. Heb. ii. 3. xiii. 9 only. Ps. xl. 12. cxviii. 28 only.　　k ch. i. 7.
l constr., Phil. i. 9 reff.　　　m Eph. v. 4 reff.　　　n Gal. v. 15 reff.　　　o indic., Gal.
iv. 10. 1 Thess. iii. 5. Heb. iii. 12.　　　　p constr., Gal. i. 7 reff.　　　q here only †. see
1 Cor. ix. 27.

6. τον κυριον ιησ. χρ. D: τον κυριον ιησ., omg χρ., 17.
7. om εν αυτω ℵ¹(ins ℵ-corr¹) 71.　　　rec aft βεβαιουμενοι ins εν, with ACD³KL[P]ℵ
rel demid(and hal) syrr copt gr-ff: om BD¹ k 17 [47] vulg(and F-lat) Thl Archel
Ambrst.　　　om τη (bef πιστει) AC.　　　aft καθως ins και D¹ latt.　　　om εν αυτη
(passing on to εν ευχ.) ACℵ¹ m 17 [47] am(with fuld tol) copt Archel : ins BD³KL[P]
rel 67² syrr [arm] gr-ff, εν αυτω D¹ℵ³ vulg-ed(with demid) syr-mg Pel.
8. εσται bef υμας ACDℵ : txt BKL[P] rel.　　　συλαγων ℵ¹.

on which it rested) **the solid basis** (ὅτε πολλὰ συναγαγὼν συγκολλήσεις πυκνῶς κ. ἀδιασπαστῶς, τότε στερέωμα γίνεται. Chrys. It does not mean '*firmness*' (Conyb.), nor '*stedfastness*' (E. V.), nor indeed any abstract quality at all : but, as all nouns in -μα, the concrete product of the abstract quality) **of your faith on Christ.** 6.] As then (he has described his conflict and his joy on their behalf—he now exhorts them to justify such anxiety and approval by consistency with their first faith) **ye received** (from Epaphras and your first teachers) **Jesus the Christ the Lord** (it is necessary, in order to express the full sense of τὸν χρ. Ἰησ. τὸν κύρ., to give something of a predicative force both to τὸν χρ. and to τὸν κύρ. : see 1 Cor. xii. 3 (but hardly so strong as "for your Lord," as rendered in my earlier editions : see Ellicott here). The expression ὁ χρ. Ἰησ. ὁ κύρ. occurs only here : the nearest approach to it is in 2 Cor. iv. 5, . . . κηρύσσομεν . . . χριστὸν Ἰησ. κύριον : where also κύρ. is a predicate : but this is even more emphatic and solemn. Cf. also Phil. iii. 8, τὸ ὑπερέχον τῆς γνώσεως χρ. Ἰησοῦ τοῦ κυρ. μου. On the sense, Bisping says well: " Notice that Paul here says, παρελάβετε τὸν χριστόν, and not παρελ. τὸν λόγον τοῦ χρ. True faith is a spiritual communion : for in faith we receive not only the doctrine of Christ, but Himself, into us : in faith He Himself dwells in us : we cannot separate Christ, as Eternal Truth, and His doctrine "), **in Him walk** (carry on your life of faith and practice), **rooted** (see Eph. iii. 18) **and being continually built up in Him** (as both the soil and the foundation—in both cases the conditional element. It is to be noticed 1) how the

fervid style of St. Paul, disdaining the nice proprieties of rhetoric, sets forth the point in hand by inconsistent similitudes : the walking implying motion, the rooting and building, rest; 2) that the rooting, answering to the first elementary grounding in Him, is in the past : the being built up, answering to the continual increase in Him, is present. See Eph. ii. 20, where this latter is set forth as a fact in the past) **and confirmed in the** (or, your) **faith** (dat. of reference : it seems hardly natural with Mey. to take it instrumental, as there is no question of instrumental means in this passage), **as ye were taught, abounding in it** (reff.) **in thanksgiving** (the field of operation, or element, in which that abundance is manifested. " Non solum volo vos esse confirmatos in fide, verum etiam in ea proficere et proficiendo abundare per pleniorem mysteriorum Christi cognitionem : idque cum gratiarum actione erga Deum, ut auctorem hujus totius boni." Est.).
8—15.] See summary, on ver. 1—*general warning against being seduced by a wisdom which was after men's tradition, and not after Christ,—of whose perfect work, and their perfection in Him, he reminds them.* **8.] Take heed lest there shall be** (the future indicative expresses strong fear lest that which is feared should really be the case; so Aristoph. Eccles. 487, περισκοπουμένη κἀκεῖσε καὶ τἀκ δεξιᾶς, μὴ ξυμφορὰ γενήσεται τὸ πρᾶγμα. Hartung, ii. 138: see reff. and Winer, § 56. 2. b α) **any one who** (cf. τινὲς οἱ ταράσσοντες, ref. Gal. and note. It points at some known person) **leads you away as ✱ his prey** (Mey. connects the word in imagery with the foregoing περιπατεῖτε —but this perhaps is hardly necessary after

r here only.
s = Acts iv. 25, from Ps. ii. 1.
Eph. v. 6 al.
t Eph. iv. 22 reff.
u Gal. i. 14 reff.
v Mark vii. 8.
w Gal. iv. 3 reff.
x ch. i. 19 (reff.).

αγωγων διὰ τῆς ʳ φιλοσοφίας καὶ ˢ κενῆς ᵗ ἀπάτης κατὰ τὴν
ᵘᵛ παράδοσιν τῶν ᵛ ἀνθρώπων, κατὰ τὰ ʷ στοιχεῖα τοῦ
ʷ κόσμου καὶ οὐ κατὰ χριστόν, 9 ὅτι ἐν αὐτῷ ˣ κατοικεῖ
πᾶν τὸ ˣ πλήρωμα τῆς ʸ θεότητος ᶻ σωματικῶς 10 καί ἐστε

F (and also G) κοσμου

y here only †. (see note.)   z here only †. (-κός, 1 Tim. iv. 8.)

ABCDF
KLPℵ a
b c d e f
g h k l m
n o 17.4,

the disregard to continuity of metaphor shewn in vv. 6, 7. The meaning 'to rob' (so with τὸν οἶκον, Aristæn. ii. 22), adopted here by Thdrt. (τοὺς ἀποσυλᾷν τ. πίστιν ἐπιχειροῦντας), 'to undermine,' Chrys. (ὥσπερ ἄν τις χῶμα κάτωθεν διορύττων μὴ παρέχῃ αἴσθησιν, τὸ δ' ὑπονοστεῖ), hardly appears suitable on account of the κατὰ . . . . κατά, which seem to imply motion. We have (see Rost and Palm's Lex.) συλαγωγεῖν παρθένον in Heliod. and Nicet., which idea of abduction is very near that here) by means of his (or the article may signify, as Ellic., the current, popular, philosophy of the day: but I prefer the possessive meaning: see below) philosophy and empty deceit (the absence of the article before κενῆς shews the καί to be epexegetical, and the same thing to be meant by the two. This being so, it may be better to give the τῆς the possessive sense, the better to mark that it is not all philosophy which the Apostle is here blaming: for Thdrt. is certainly wrong in saying ἣν ἄνω πιθανολογίαν, ἐνταῦθα φιλοσοφίαν ἐκάλεσε,—the former being, as Mey. observes, the form of imparting,—this, the thing itself. The φιλοσοφ. is not necessarily Greek, as Tert. de præscr. 7, vol. ii. p. 20 ('fuerat Athenis')—Clem. Strom. i. 11, 50, vol. i. p. 346, P. (οὐ πᾶσαν, ἀλλὰ τὴν Ἐπικούρειον), Grot. al. As De W. observes, Josephus calls the doctrine of the Jewish sects philosophy: Antt. xviii. 2. 1,— Ἰουδαίοις φιλοσοφίαι τρεῖς ἧσαν, ἥ τε τῶν Ἐσσηνῶν κ. ἡ τῶν Σαδδουκαίων, τρίτην δὲ ἐφιλοσόφουν οἱ Φαρισαῖοι. The character of the philosophy here meant, as gathered from the descriptions which follow, was that mixture of Jewish and Oriental, which afterwards expanded into gnosticism), according to the tradition of men (this tradition, derived from men, human and not divine in its character, set the rule to this his philosophy, and according to this he ἐσυλαγώγει: such is the grammatical construction; but seeing that his philosophy was the instrument by which, the character given belongs in fact to his ✻ philosophy), according to the elements (see on Gal. iv. 3: the rudimentary lessons: i. e. the ritualistic observances ('nam continuo post exempli loco speciem unam adducit, circumcisionem scilicet,

Calv.) in which they were becoming entangled) of the world (all these belonged to the earthly side—were the carnal and imperfect phase of knowledge—now the perfect was come, the imperfect was done away, and not (negative characteristic, as the former were the affirmative characteristics, of this philosophy) according to Christ (" who alone is," as Bisp. observes, " the true rule of all genuine philosophy, the only measure as for all life acceptable to God, so for all truth in thought likewise: every true philosophy must therefore be κατὰ χριστόν, must begin and end with Him "):   9.] (supply, 'as all true philosophy ought to be ') because in Him (emphatic: in Him alone) dwelleth (now, in His exaltation) all the fulness (cf. on ch. i. 19, and see below) of the Godhead (Deity: the essential being of God: 'das Gott sein,' as Meyer. θεότης, the abstract of θεός, must not be confounded with θειότης the abstract of θεῖος, divine, which occurs in Rom. i. 20, where see Fritzsche's note. θεότης does not occur in the classics, but is found in Lucian, Icaromenippus, c. 9: τὸν μέν τινα πρῶτον θεὸν ἐπεκάλουν, τοῖς δὲ τὰ δεύτερα κ. τὰ τρίτα ἔνεμον τῆς θεότητος. 'The fulness of the Godhead' here spoken of must be taken, as indeed the context shews, metaphysically, and not as 'all fulness' in ch. i. 19, where the historical Christ, as manifested in redemption, was in question; see this well set forth in Mey.'s note. There, the lower side, so to speak, of that fulness, was set forth—the side which is presented to us here, is the higher side. Some strangely take πλήρωμα here to mean the Church—so Heinr. in Mey.: "Ab eo collecta est omnis ex omnibus sine discrimine gentibus ecclesia, eo tanquam οἴκῳ, tanquam σώματι, continetur gubernaturque." Others again hold Christ here to mean the Church, in whom [or which] the πλήρωμα dwells: so τινές in Thdrt. and Chrys.) bodily (i. e. manifested corporeally, in His present glorified Body—cf. on οἰκεῖ above, and Phil. iii. 21. Before His incarnation, it dwelt in Him, as the λόγος ἄσαρκος, but not σωματικῶς, as now that He is the λόγος ἔνσαρκος. This is the obvious, and I am persuaded only tenable interpretation. And so Calov., Est., De W., Mey.,

ἐν αὐτῷ ᵃπεπληρωμένοι, * ὅς ἐστιν ἡ ᵇκεφαλὴ πάσης
ᶜἀρχῆς καὶ ᶜἐξουσίας, ¹¹ ἐν ᾧ καὶ ᵈπεριετμήθητε ᵉπερι-
τομῇ ᶠἀχειροποιήτῳ ἐν τῇ ᵍἀπεκδύσει τοῦ σώματος ʰ τῆς

a -- Eph. iii. 19 reff.
b Eph. i. 22 reff.
c Eph. i. 21 reff.
d Gal. ii. 3 reff.

e Eph. ii. 11 reff. dat., 1 Cor. ix. 7.   f 2 Cor. v. 1. Mark xiv. 58 only †.   g here only †.
(-δύεσθαι, ver. 15.)   h gen., Rom. vi. 6. vii. 23, 24.

10. * ὅ BDF [47¹]: os ACKL[P]א rel Cyr-jer Chr Thdrt Damasc.   om η
D¹F.   ins της bef αρχης א.   for αρχ. κ. εξουσ., εκκλησιας D¹: αρχης εκκλησιας א¹.
11. [om και F.]   rec aft του σωματος ins των αμαρτιων (explanatory, cf Rom vi.
6), with D².³KLא³ rel syrr goth Epiph Chr Thdrt [Cypr] Aug(altern): om ABCD¹F[P]א¹
f 17 latt copt æth[-rom] arm Clem Ath Bas Cyr Thdrt Damasc Thl Orig-int Hil
Ambrst Aug(altern) Fulg Jer Pel.

Eadie, al. Others have been 1) 'really,'
as distinguished from τυπικῶς: so,—resting for the most part on ver. 17, where
the reference is quite different,—Aug.,
Corn.-a-lap., Grot., Schöttg., Wolf, Nösselt, al. 2) 'essentially,' οὐσιωδῶς, as contrasted with the energic dwelling of God
in the prophets: the objection to which
is that the word cannot have this meaning: so Cyr., Thl., Calv., Beza, Usteri,
p. 324, Olsh., al.), and ye are (already—
there is an emphasis in the prefixing of
ἐστε) in Him (in your union with Him,—
'Christo cum sitis semel insiti,' Erasm. in
Mey.) filled up (with all divine gifts—so
that you need not any supplementary
sources of grace such as your teachers are
directing you to,—reff.: τῆς γὰρ ἀπ'
αὐτοῦ χάριτος ἀπελαύσατε, as Thdrt.:
cf. John i. 16, ἐκ τοῦ πληρώματος αὐτοῦ
ἡμεῖς πάντες ἐλάβομεν: not, as Chrys.,
Thl., De W., 'with the fulness of the
Godhead,' which is not true, and would
require ἧς ἐστε καὶ ὑμεῖς ἐν αὐτ. πεπλ.
Nor must ἐστε be taken as imperative,
against the whole context, which is assertive, no less than usage—'verbum ἐστέ
nunquam in N. T. sensu imperandi ad-
hibitum invenio, v. c. ἐστὲ οἰκτίρμονες,
sed potius γίνεσθε, cf. 1 Cor. x. 32; xi. 1;
xv. 58: et Eph. iv. 32; v. 1, 7, 17, &c.
Itaque si Paulus imperare hoc loco quicquam voluisset, scripturus potius erat κ.
γίνεσθε ἐν αὐτῷ πεπληρ.' Wolf. What
follows, shews them that He their perfection, is not to be mixed up with other
dignities, as objects of adoration, for He
is the Head of all such)—who (or, which:
but the neuter seems to have been written
to agree with πλήρωμα) is the Head of
every government and power: 11.]
(nor do you need the rite of circumcision to make you complete, for you have
already received in Him the spiritual substance, of which that rite is but the shadow) in whom ye also were circumcised
(not as E. V. 'are circumcised,'—the
reference being to the historical fact of
their baptism) with a circumcision not

wrought by hands (see Eph. ii. 11, and
Rom. ii. 29. The same reference to spiritual (ethical) circumcision is found in
Deut. x. 16; xxx. 6: Ezek. xliv. 7: Acts
vii. 51), in (consisting in—which found
its realization in) your putting off (=
when you threw off: ἀπεκδ., the putting
off and laying aside, as a garment: an
allusion to actual circumcision,—see below) of the body of the flesh (i. e. as ch. i.
22, the body of which the material was
flesh: but more here: so also its designating attribute, its leading principle, was
fleshliness—the domination of the flesh
which is a σὰρξ ἁμαρτίας, Rom. viii. 3.
This body is put off in baptism, the sign
and seal of the new life. " When ethically circumcised, i. e. translated by μετά-
νοια out of the state of sin into that of
the Christian life of faith, we have no
more the σῶμα τῆς σαρκός: for the body,
which we bear, is disarrayed of its sinful
σάρξ as such, quoad its sinful quality:
we are no more ἐν τῇ σαρκί as before,
when lust ἐνηργεῖτο ἐν τοῖς μέλεσιν (Rom.
vii. 5, cf. ib. ver. 23): we are no more
σάρκινοι, πεπραμένοι ὑπὸ τὴν ἁμαρτίαν
(Rom. vii. 14), and walk no more κατὰ
σάρκα, but ἐν καινότητι πνεύματος (Rom.
vii. 6), so that our members are ὅπλα
δικαιοσύνης τῷ θεῷ (Rom. vi. 13). This
Christian transformation is set forth
in its ideal conception, irrespective of
its imperfect realization in our experience." Meyer. To understand τὸ σῶμα
to signify 'the mass,' as Calv. ('corpus
appellat massam ex omnibus vitiis conflatam, eleganti metaphora'), Grot. ('omne
quod ex multis componitur solet hoc vocabulo appellari'), al.,—besides that it is
bound up very much with the reading
τῶν ἁμαρτιῶν, is out of keeping with
N. T. usage, and with the context, which
is full of images connected with the body),
—in (parallel to ἐν before—then the circumcision without hands was explained,
now it is again adduced with another
epithet bringing it nearer home to them)
the circumcision of Christ (belonging to,

i Rom. vi. 4
only †.
j Mark vii. 4
[8]. Heb.
vi. 2. ix. 10
only †.

σαρκὸς ἐν τῇ ^d περιτομῇ τοῦ χριστοῦ, ^{12 i} συνταφέντες αὐτῷ
ἐν τῷ ^j βαπτισμῷ, ἐν ᾧ καὶ ^k συνηγέρθητε διὰ τῆς πίστεως

sing., here only.   k Eph. ii. 6 reff.

ABCDF
KLPℵ a
b c d e f
g h k l m
n o 17. 47

12. rec βαπτισματι (*usual word*), with ACD³KL[P]ℵ¹ rel, *baptismate* Tert Hil: txt
BD¹Fℵ³ [47] 67² Chr₁, *baptismo* latt Ambrst.   συνηγερθημεν C.

brought about by union with, Christ:
nearly =, but expresses more than '*Christian circumcision*,' inasmuch as it shews
that the root and cause of this circumcision without hands is in Christ, the
union with whom is immediately set forth.
Two other interpretations are given: 1)
that in which Christ is regarded as the
circumciser: ὁ χρ. περιτέμνει ἐν τῷ βαπτίσματι, ἀπεκδύων ἡμᾶς τοῦ παλαιοῦ
βίου, Thl., but not exactly so Chrys., who
says, οὐκέτι φησὶν ἐν μαχαίρᾳ ἡ περιτ.,
ἀλλ' ἐν αὐτῷ τῷ χρ.· οὐ γὰρ χεὶρ ἐπάγει,
καθὼς ἐκεῖ, τ. περιτομὴν ταύτην, ἀλλὰ
τὸ πνεῦμα. Beza combines both—
'Christus ipse nos intus suo spiritu cir-
cumcidit.' 2) that in which Christ is the
circumcised—so Schöttg.: "per circumcisionem Christi nos omnes circumcisi
sumus. Hoc est: circumcisio Christi qui
se nostri causa sponte legi subjecit, tam
efficax fuit in omnes homines, ut nulla amplius circumcisione carnis opus sit, præcipue quum in locum illius baptismus a
Christo surrogatus sit " (i. p. 816). The
objection to both is, that they introduce
irrelevant elements into the context. *The
circumcision which Christ works*, would
not naturally be followed by συνταφέντες
αὐτῷ, union with Him: *that which was
wrought on Him* might be thus followed,
but would not come in naturally in a
passage which describes, not the universal efficacy of the rite once for all
performed on Him, but the actual undergoing of it in a spiritual sense, by each
one of us),   12.] (goes on to connect this still more closely with the
person of Christ—q. d., in the circumcision of Christ, to whom you were united,
&c.)—**buried together** (i. e. ' when you
were buried:' the aorist participle, as so
often, is contemporary with the preceding
past verb) **with Him in your baptism** (the
new life being begun at baptism,—an
image familiar alike to Jews and Christians,—the process itself of baptism is
regarded as the burial of the former life:
originally, perhaps, owing to the practice
of immersion, which would most naturally
give rise to the idea: but to maintain
from such a circumstance that immersion
is *necessary* in baptism, is surely the
merest trifling, and a resuscitation of the
very ceremonial spirit which the Apostle

here is arguing against. As reasonably
might it be argued, from the ἀπέκδυσις
here, that nakedness was an essential in
that sacrament. The things represented
by both figures belong to the essentials of
the Christian life: the minor details of the
sacrament which corresponded to them,
may in different ages or climates be varied;
but the spiritual figures remain. At the
same time, if circumstances concurred,—
e. g. a climate where the former practice
was always safe, and a part of the world,
or time of life, where the latter would be
no shock to decency,—there can be no
question that the external proprieties of
baptism ought to be complied with. And
on this principle the baptismal services of
the Church of England are constructed);
in which (i. e. baptism: not, as Mey.
(and so most expositors), '*in whom*,' i. e.
Christ. For although it is tempting
enough to r ,ard the ἐν ᾧ καί as parallel
with the ἐν ᾧ καί above, we should be
thus introducing a second and separate
leading idea into the argument, manifestly
occupied with one leading idea, viz. the
completeness of your Christian circumcision,—cf. ἀκροβυστία again below,—as
realized in your baptism: whereas on this
hypothesis we should be breaking off from
baptism altogether,—for there would be
no link to connect the present sentence
with the former, but we must take up
again from ἐξουσίας. This indeed is freely
confessed by Mey., who holds that all allusion to baptism *is* at an end here, and that
the following is a benefit conferred by
faith as separate from baptism. But see
below. His objection, that if ἐν ᾧ applied
to baptism, it would not correspond to the
rising again, which should be ἐξ οὗ, or at
all events the unlocal δι' οὗ, arises from the
too precise materialization of the image.
As ἐν before did not necessarily apply to
the mere going under the water, but to the
process of the sacrament, so ἐν now does
not necessarily apply to the coming up out
of the water, but also to the process of the
sacrament. *In it*, we both die and rise
again,—both unclothe and are clothed)
ye were also raised again with Him (not
your material, but your spiritual resurrection is in the foreground: it is bound on,
it is true, to *His* material resurrection, and
brings with it in the background, *yours*:

¹τῆς ^mἐνεργείας τοῦ θεοῦ τοῦ ⁿἐγείραντος αὐτὸν ἐκ [τῶν]
νεκρῶν. ¹³ καὶ ὑμᾶς ^oνεκροὺς ὄντας ἐν τοῖς ^{op}παρα-
πτώμασιν καὶ τῇ ^qἀκροβυστίᾳ τῆς σαρκὸς ὑμῶν, ^rσυν-
εζωοποίησεν ὑμᾶς σὺν αὐτῷ ^sχαρισάμενος ἡμῖν πάντα τὰ

l gen. (see
note), Mark
xi. 22. Acts
iii. 16. Rom.
iii. 22. Gal.
ii. 16, 20 al.
m Eph. i. 19
reff.
n Gal. i. 1 reff.
o Eph. ii. 1, 5.

p Gal. vi. 1 reff.   q Rom. iii. 30 al.   Paul only, exc. Acts xi. 3.   Gen. xvii. 11.   r Eph. ii. 5 only †.
s = Luke vii. 41, 42.   2 Cor. ii. 7, 10. xii. 13.   Eph. iv. 32 (bis). ch. iii. 13 (bis) L.P.† (2 Macc. iii. 33 al.)

om των ACKL[P]א a d f k l m [47] Chr Thl: ins BDF rel 67² Thdrt Damasc.
   13. om εν (*as Eph* ii. 1) BLא¹ f g h k m 17 [47] goth gr-ff_m Tert-ms Ambr: ins
ACDFK[P]א-corr¹ rel.   ins εν bef τη ακροβυστια D¹F.   for συνεζ., εζωοποιη-
σεν D¹F Tert [Hil₂].   rec om 2nd υμας, with DF[P]א³ b c [47] latt copt goth
[arm] Chr: ins ACKLא¹ rel tol syr Thdrt-ms Damasc Œc, ημας B a e g l² m 17.
rec (for ημιν) υμιν, with L[P]א³ (a¹ ?) c d e m 17 vulg æth Thdrt [Hil₂]: txt ABCD
FKא¹ rel vss gr-ff [Tert Hil₂].   at end add ημων D Syr [copt] arm.

but in the spiritual, the material is included and taken for granted, as usual in
Scripture) **by** (means of : the mediate, not
the efficient cause; the hand which held on,
not the plank that saved. I am quite unable to see why this illustration is, as Ellic.
states, "in more than one respect, not
dogmatically satisfactory." Surely it is
dogmatically exact to say that Faith is the
hand by which we lay hold on Christ the
Ark of our refuge) **your faith in** (so
Chrys., Thdrt., Œc., Thl., Erasm., Beza,
Calv., Grot., Est., Corn.-a-lap., Mey., al.,
Beng. ('fides est (opus) operationis divinæ'), al., and Luther. De W. understands faith wrought by God ('durch den
Glauben den Gott wirket,' Luth.: 'mittelst
des Glaubens Kraft der Wirksamkeit
Gottes,' De W.). But both usage and the
context are against this. The genitive after
πίστις is ever (against Ellic. here) of the
object of faith, see reff., and on Eph. i.
19) **the operation of God** (in Christ—that
mighty power by which the Father raised
Him, cf. Rom. viii. 11; ἣν ἐνήργηκεν ἐν
χριστῷ, Eph. i. 20) **who raised Him from
the dead** (πιστεύοντες γὰρ τῇ τοῦ θεοῦ
δυνάμει προσμένομεν τὴν ἀνάστασιν, ἐν-
έχυρον ἔχοντες τοῦ δεσπότου χριστοῦ τὴν
ἀνάστασιν. Thdrt. But there is very
much more asserted than the mere προσ-
μένειν τὴν ἀνάστασιν—the power of God
in raising the dead to life is one and the
same in our Lord and in us—the physical
power exerted in Him is not only a pledge
of the same physical power to be exerted
in us, but a condition and assurance of a
spiritual power already exerted in us,
whereby we are in spirit risen with Christ,
the physical resurrection being included
and taken for granted in that other and
greater one):   **13—15.**] *Application,
first to the (Gentile) Colossians, then to
all believers, of the whole blessedness of
this participation in Christ's resurrection,
and assertion of the antiquation of the*

*law, and subjection of all secondary
powers to Christ.* **And you, who were**
(or perhaps more strictly, **when you were**)
dead (allusion to ἐκ [τῶν] νεκρῶν immediately preceding) **in your trespasses** (see
Eph. ii. 1, notes) **and** (in) **the uncircumcision of** (i. e. which consisted in : this is
better than, with Ellic., to regard the gen.
as simply possessive) **your flesh** (i. e. having
on you still your fleshly sinful nature, the
carnal præputium which now, as spiritual,
you have put away. So that, as Mey.
very properly urges, it is not in ἀκροβυστία, but in τῆς σαρκός, that the ethical
significance lies—ἀκροβυστία being their
state still, but now indifferent), **He** (God
—who, not Christ, is the subject of
the whole sentence, vv. 13—15. See the
other side ingeniously, but to me not convincingly defended in Ellic.'s note here.
He has to resort to the somewhat lame
expedient of altering αὐτῷ into αὑτῷ : and
even then the sentence would labour under
the theological indecorum of making our
Lord not the Resumer of His own Life
merely, but the very Worker of acts which
are by Himself and His Apostles always
predicated of the Father. It will be seen
by the whole translation and exegesis
which follows, that I cannot for a moment
accept the view which makes Christ the
subject of these clauses) **quickened you**
(this repetition of the personal pronoun is
by no means unexampled, cf. Aristoph.
Acharn. 391,—νῦν οὖν με πρῶτον πρὶν
λέγειν ἐάσατε | ἐνσκευάσασθαί μ' οἷον
ἀθλιώτατον: see also Soph. Œd. Col.
1407: Demosth. p. 1225. 16—19. Bernhardy, p. 275 f.) **together with Him**
(Christ : brought you up,—objectively at
His Resurrection, and subjectively when
you were received among His people,—out
of this death. The question as to the
reference, whether to spiritual or physical
resurrection, is answered by remembering
that the former includes the latter), **having**

t Acts iii. 19.
Rev. iii. 5.
vii. 17. xxi.
4 only. Ps.
1. 10.
u = Matt. xii.
30. Rom.
viii. 31. Gal.
iii. 21. v. 23.
x Heb. x. 27 only. Gen. xxii. 17. Exod. xxiii. 27. Job xiii. 24.
xiii. 49. Acts xvii. 33. xxiii. 10. 1 Cor. v. 2. 2 Cor. vi. 7, from Isa. lii. 11. 2 Thess. ii. 7 only. Isa. lvii. 2.
n here only †. 3 Macc. iv. 9. σταυρῷ προσηλῶσαι, Jos. B. J. ii. 14. 9.

ᵖ παραπτώματα, ¹⁴ ᵗ ἐξαλείψας τὸ ᵘ καθ᾽ ἡμῶν ᵛ χειρό- ABCDF
γραφον τοῖς ʷ δόγμασιν ὃ ἦν ˣ ὑπεναντίον ἡμῖν, καὶ αὐτὸ KLPℵ a b c d e f
ʸ ἦρκεν ᶻ ἐκ τοῦ ᶻ μέσου ᵃ προσηλώσας αὐτὸ τῷ σταυρῷ, g h k l m n o 17.47

v here only †.   Tobit v. 3. ix. 5 only.
w Eph. ii. 15 reff. dat., Gal. vi. 11.
ᵧ = Eph. iv. 31 reff.   z Matt.

14. for ημιν, ημων ℵ¹(txt ℵ-corr¹) 114 [υμιν P m¹].   for ηρκεν, ηρεν D¹F a b c
f g h k Orig Thdrt Thl [ηρκται P].   om του A 67².

forgiven (the aorist participle (which aor. 'having forgiven' is in English, we having but one past active participle) is here not contemporaneous with συνεζωοπ. but antecedent: this forgiveness was an act of God wrought once for all in Christ, cf. ἡμῖν below, and 2 Cor. v. 19; Eph. iv. 32) us (he here passes from the particular to the general—from the Colossian Gentiles to all believers) all our transgressions (ἃ τὴν νεκρότητα ἐποίει, Chrys.: but this, though true, makes the χαρισάμ. apply to the συνεζ., which it does not), having wiped out (contemporary with χαρισάμενος—in fact the same act explained in its conditions and details. On the word, see reff., and Plato, Rep. vi. p. 501, τὸ μὲν ἄν, οἶμαι, ἐξαλείφοιεν, τὸ δὲ πάλιν ἐγγράφοιεν: Dem. 468. 1, εἶθ᾽ ὑμεῖς ἔτι σκοπεῖτε εἰ χρὴ τοῦτον (τὸν νόμον) ἐξαλεῖψαι, καὶ οὐ πάλαι βεβούλευσθε;) the handwriting in decrees (cf. the similar expression τὸν νόμον τῶν ἐντολῶν ἐν δόγμασιν, Eph. ii. 15, and notes. Here, the force of -γραφον passes on to the dative, as if it were τὸ γεγραμμένον τοῖς δόγμασιν—cf. Plato, Ep. vii. p. 343 a, κ. ταῦτα εἰς ἀμετακίνητον, ὃ δὴ πάσχει τὰ γεγραμμένα τύποις. This explanation of the construction is negatived by Ellicott, on the ground of χειρόγραφος being "a synthetic compound, and apparently incapable of such a decomposition:" referring to Donaldson, Gram. § 369 (it is § 377). But there it is laid down that in synthetic compounds of this kind, the accent makes the difference between transitive and intransitive, without any assertion that the verbal element may not pass on in the construction. If χειρόγραφον means written by hands, then surely the element in which the writing consists may follow. Meyer would make the dative instrumental: but it can be so only in a very modified sense, the contents taken as the instrument whereby the sense is conveyed. The χειρόγρ. represents the whole law, the obligatory bond which was against us (see below), and is apparently used because the Decalogue, representing that law, was written on tables of stone with the finger of God. The most various interpre-

tations of it have been given. Calv., Beza, al., understand it of the mere ritual law: Calov., of the moral, against πάντα τὰ παραπτ. above: Luther, Zwingl., al., of the law of conscience. Thdrt.'s view is very curious: he interprets τὸ χειρόγρ. to mean our human body,—ὁ τοίνυν θεὸς λόγος, τὴν ἡμετέραν φύσιν ἀναλαβών, πάσης αὐτὴν ἁμαρτίας ἐλευθέραν ἐφύλαξε, κ. ἐξήλειψε τὰ κακῶς ὑφ᾽ ἡμῶν ἐν αὐτῇ γενόμενα τῶν ὀφλημάτων γράμματα. He urges as an objection to the usual interpretation, that the law was for Jews, not Gentiles, whereas the Apostle says καθ᾽ ἡμῶν. But this is answered by remembering, that the law was just as much against the Gentiles as against the Jews: it stood in their way of approach to God, see Rom. iii. 19: through it they would be compelled to come to Him, and by it, whether written on stone or on fleshy tablets, they were condemned before Him. Chrys., Œc., Thl., al., would understand τὸ χειρόγραφον ὃ ἐποίησε πρὸς Ἀδὰμ ὁ θεὸς εἰπὼν ᾗ ἂν ἡμέρα φάγῃς ἀπὸ τοῦ ξύλου, ἀποθάνῃ—but this is against the whole anti-judaistic turn of the sentence) which was hostile to us (the repetition of the sentiment already contained in καθ᾽ ἡμῶν seems to be made by way of stronger emphasis, as against the false teachers, reasserting and invigorating the fact that the law was no help, but a hindrance to us. There does not appear to be any force of 'subcontrarius' in ὑπεναντίος; Mey. refers, besides reff., to Herod. iii. 80, τὸ δ᾽ ὑπεναντίον τούτου εἰς τοὺς πολιήτας πέφυκε—to ὑπεναντιότης, Diog. Laert. x. 77: ὑπεναντίωμα, Aristot. poet. xxvi. 22· ὑπεναντίωσις, Demosth. 1405. 18), and (not only so, but) has taken it (the handwriting itself, thus obliterated) away (i. e. 'from out of the way,' cf. reff.: Dem. de corona, p. 323, τὸ καταψεύδεσθαι κ. δι᾽ ἔχθραν τι λέγειν ἀνελόντας ἐκ μέσου: other places in Kypke, ii. 323: and the contrary expression, Dem. 682. 1,—οὐδὲν ἂν ἦν ἐν μέσῳ πολεμεῖν ἡμᾶς πρὸς Καρδιανοὺς ἤδη), by nailing (contemporary with the beginning of ἦρκεν) it to the cross ("since by the death of Christ on

15 ᵇ ἀπεκδυσάμενος τὰς ᶜ ἀρχὰς καὶ τὰς ᶜ ἐξουσίας ᵈ ἐδει-
γμάτισεν ἐν ᵉ παῤῥησίᾳ, ᶠ θριαμβεύσας αὐτοὺς ἐν αὐτῷ.

b ch. iii. 9 only †.
(·δυσις, ver. 11.)
c = Eph. i. 21
e Eph. iii. 12 reff.

reff.　　d Matt. i. 19 only †.　(παραδειγ., Heb. vi. 6.　Num. xxv. 4.)
f 2 Cor. ii. 14 only †.

15. aft απεκδυσαμενος ins την σαρκα, omg τας αρχας και, F [Novat₁] Hil₁ Pac ; so, but retaining τ. αρχ. κ., Syr goth Hil_sæpe Aug.　　ins και bef εδειγματισεν B.　　εν εαυτω G, *in semetipso* latt lat-ff·: (rec has ἐν αὐτῷ :) εν τω ξυλω (*interpretation of* αὐτῷ) Orig₈ Ath Chr Thdrt Macar Epiph Œc. (*licet in aliis exemplaribus habeatur in semetipso sed apud Græcos habetur in ligno* Orig in Josh. Hom. viii. 3, vol. ii. p. 416.)

the cross the condemnatory law lost its hold on us, inasmuch as Christ by this death bore the curse of the law for mankind (Gal. iii. 13),—in the fact of *Christ* being nailed to the Cross *the Law* was nailed thereon, in so far as, by Christ's crucifixion, it lost its obligatory power and ceased to be *ἐν μέσῳ.*" Meyer. Chrys. finely says, οὐδαμοῦ οὕτως μεγαλοφώνως ἐφθέγξατο. ὁρᾷς σπουδὴν τοῦ ἀφανισθῆναι τὸ χειρ. ὅσην ἐποιήσατο ; οἷον πάντες ἦμεν ὑφ' ἁμαρτίαν κ. κόλασιν, αὐτὸς κολασθεὶς ἔλυσε κ. τὴν ἁμαρτίαν κ. τὴν κόλασιν· ἐκολάσθη δὲ ἐν τῷ σταυρῷ).

15.] The utmost care must be taken to interpret this verse according to the requirements of grammar and of the context. The *first* seems to me to necessitate the rendering of ἀπεκδυσάμενος, not, as the great majority of Commentators, ' *having spoiled* ' (ἀπεκδύσας), a meaning unexampled for the middle, and precluded by the plain usage, by the Apostle himself, a few verses below, ch. iii. 9, of the same word ἀπεκδυσάμενοι,—but ' *having put off*,' ' divested himself of.' Then the *second* must guide us to the meaning of τὰς ἀρχὰς καὶ τὰς ἐξουσίας. Most Commentators have at once assumed these to be the *infernal powers,* or *evil angels :* relying on Eph. vi. 12, where undoubtedly such is the specific reference of these general terms. But the terms *being general,* such specific reference must be determined by the context of each passage,—or, indeed, there may be no such specific reference at all, but they may be used in their fullest general sense. Now the words have occurred before in this very passage, ver. 10, where Christ is exalted as the κεφαλὴ πάσης ἀρχῆς κ. ἐξουσίας : and it is hardly possible to avoid connecting our present expression with that, seeing that in τὰς ἀρχὰς κ. τὰς ἐξουσίας the articles seem to contain a manifest reference to it. Now, what is the context ? Is it in any way relevant to the fact of the law being antiquated by God in the great Sacrifice of the atonement, to say that He, in that act (or, according to others, Christ in that act), spoiled and triumphed over the *in-*

fernal potentates ? Or would the following οὖν deduce any legitimate inference from such a fact ? But, suppose the matter to stand in this way. The law was διαταγεὶς δι' ἀγγέλων (Gal. iii. 19 : cf. Acts vii. 53), ὁ δι' ἀγγέλων λαληθεὶς λόγος (Heb. ii. 2) : cf. also Jos. Antt. xv. 5. 3, ἡμῶν τὰ κάλλιστα τῶν δογμάτων, κ. τὰ ὁσιώτατα τῶν ἐν τοῖς νόμοις δι' ἀγγέλων παρὰ τ. θεοῦ μαθόντων ;—they were the promulgators of the χειρόγραφον τοῖς δόγμασιν. In that promulgation of theirs, God was pleased to reveal Himself of old. That writing, that investiture, so to speak, of God, was first wiped out, soiled and rendered worthless, and then nailed to the Cross—abrogated and suspended there. Thus God ἀπεξεδύσατο τὰς ἀρχὰς κ. τὰς ἐξουσίας—divested Himself of, put off from Himself, that ἀγγέλων διαταγή, manifesting Himself henceforward without a veil in the exalted Person of Jesus. And the act of triumph, by which God has for ever subjected all principality and power to Christ, and made Him to be the only Head of His people, in whom they are complete, was that sacrifice, whereby all the law was accomplished. In that, the ἀρχαί κ. ἐξουσίαι were all subjected to Christ, all plainly declared to be powerless as regards His work and His people, and triumphed over by Him, see Phil. ii. 8, 9 : Eph. i. 20, 21. No difficulty need be created, on this explanation, by the objection, that thus more prominence would be given to angelic agency in the law than was really the fact : the answer is, that the prominence which is given, is owing to the errors of the false teachers, who had evidently *associated the Jewish observances* in some way *with the worship of angels :* St. Paul's argument will go only to this, that whatever part the angelic powers may have *had,* or be supposed to have had, in the previous dispensation, all such interposition was now entirely at an end, that dispensation itself being once for all antiquated and put away. Render then,—putting off (by the absence of a copula, the vigour of the sentence is increased. The participle is con-

g = Matt. vii. 1.
John vii.
24. Rom.
xiv. 3.
James iv. 11.
h so Rom. ii. 1.
xiv. 22.
1 Pet. ii. 12.

16 Μὴ οὖν τις ὑμᾶς g κρινέτω h ἐν i βρώσει * καὶ ἐν
k πόσει ἢ ἐν l μέρει mn ἑορτῆς ἢ no νουμηνίας ἢ np σαββάτων,
17 * ὅ ἐστιν qrs σκιὰ τῶν r μελλόντων, τὸ δὲ s σῶμα

ABCDF
KLPℵa
b c d e f
g h k l m
n o 17. 47

i = Rom. xiv. 17. 1 Cor. viii. 4. 2 Cor. ix. 10. Heb. xii. 16 (John iv. 32. vi. 27 bis, 55. Matt. vi. 19, 20) only. Gen.
ii. 9 al. k John vi. 55. Rom. xiv. 17 only. Dan. i. 10 only. l = 2 Cor. iii. 10. ix. 3
(1 Pet. iv. 16 v. r.) only. Demosth. 638. 5, 668. 24. m Paul, here only. Matt. xxvi. 5 al. fr. in Gospp. Acts
xviii. 21. n 1 Chron. xxiii. 31. 2 Chron. ii. 4. xxxi. 3. o here only.
p plur., Matt. xii. 1, &c. Luke iv. 16 al. q = Heb. viii. 5. x. 1 (Matt. iv. 16. Mark iv. 32. Luke i.
79. Acts v. 15) only ‡. (Job xiv. 2.) r Heb. x. 1. s so Jos. B. J. ii. 2. 5, σκιὰν αἰτησόμενος
βασιλείας, ἧς ἥρπασεν ἑαυτῷ τὸ σῶμα. Philo de conf. ling. 37, vol. i. p. 434, τὰ μὲν ῥητὰ τῶν χρησμῶν
σκιάς τινας ὡσανεὶ σωμάτων εἶναι.

16. * rec ἤ (to suit the rest of the sentence), with ACDFKL[P]ℵ rel vulg syr goth
Orig₂ Eus₂ Mcion-e₂ Aug aliq Ambr : txt B (Syr) copt Orig₁ Jer Aug₁ Tich.—καὶ νουμ.
καὶ σαβ. Syr : et (4 times) Mcion-t. νουμηνια η σαββατω D¹F Mcion-e.—
νεομην. BF l [17].

17. * rec ἅ, with ACDKL[P]ℵ rel vulg(and F-lat) syrr Orig Eus₂ Aug₁ : txt BF spec
copt goth Epiph Ambrst Aug.

temporary with ἦρκεν above, and thus must not be rendered 'having put off') the governments and powers (before spoken of, ver. 10, and ch. i. 16: see above) He (GOD, who is the subject throughout: see also ch. iii. 3 :—not Christ, which would awkwardly introduce two subjects into the sentence) exhibited them (as completely subjected to Christ ;—not only put them away from Himself, but shewed them as placed under Christ. There seems no reason to attach the sense of putting to shame (παραδειγματίσαι) to the simple verb. That this sense is involved in Matt. i. 19, is owing to the circumstances of the context) in (element of the δειγματίσαι) openness (of speech ; declaring and revealing by the Cross that there is none other but Christ the Head πάσης ἀρχῆς κ. ἐξουσίας), triumphing over them (as in 2 Cor. ii. 14, we are said (see note there) to be led captive in Christ's triumph, our real victory being our defeat by Him,—so here the principalities and powers, which are next above us in those ranks of being which are all subjected to and summed up in Him) in Him (Christ : not 'in it,' viz. the cross, which gives a very feeble meaning after the ἐγείραντος αὐτόν, and συνεζωοπ. σὺν αὐτῷ above). The ordinary interpretation of this verse has been attempted by some to be engrafted into the context, by understanding the χειρόγρ. of a guilty conscience, the ἀρχ. κ. ἐξ. as the infernal powers, the accusers of man, and the scope of the exhortation as being to dissuade the Colossians from fear or worship of them. So Neander, in a paraphrase (Denkwürdigkeiten, p. 12) quoted by Conyb. and Howson, edn. 2, vol. ii. p. 478 note. But manifestly this is against the whole spirit of the passage. It was θρησκεία τῶν ἀγγέλων to which they

were tempted—and οἱ ἄγγελοι can bear no meaning but the angels of God.
16—23.] More specific warning against false teachers (see summary on ver. 1), and that first (vv. 16, 17) with reference to legal observances and abstinence.
16.] Let no one therefore (because this is so—that ye are complete in Christ, and that God in Him hath put away and dispensed with all that is secondary and intermediate) judge you (pronounce judgment of right or wrong over you, sit in judgment on you) in (reff.) eating (not, in St. Paul's usage, meat (βρῶμα), see reff. ; in John iv. 32 ; vi. 27, 55, it seems to have this signification. Mey. quotes Il. τ. 210, Od. α. 191, Plato, Legg. vi. p. 783 c, to shew that in classical Greek the meanings are sometimes interchanged. The same is true of πόσις and πόμα) and (or or) in drinking (i. e. in the matter of the whole cycle of legal ordinances and prohibitions which regarded eating and drinking : these two words being perhaps taken not separately and literally,—for there does not appear to have been in the law any special prohibition against drinks,—but as forming together a category in ordinary parlance. If however it is desired to press each word, the reference of πόσις must be to the Nazarite vow, Num. vi. 3) or in respect (reff. : Chrys. and Thdrt. give it the extraordinary meaning of 'in part,'—ἐν μέρει ἑορτῆς· οὐ γὰρ δὴ πάντα κατεῖχον τὰ πρότερα : Mey. explains it, 'in the category of' —which is much the same as the explanation in the text) of a feast or new-moon or sabbaths (i. e. yearly, monthly, or weekly celebrations ; see reff.), 17.] which (if the sing. be read, the relative may refer either to the aggregate of the observances mentioned, or to the last mentioned, i. e. the Sabbath. Or it may be singular by attraction, and refer to all, just as if it

τοῦ χριστοῦ.　¹⁸ μηδεὶς ὑμᾶς ^t καταβραβευέτω　^u θέλων　t here only †.
ἐπιστάμεθα
Στράτωνα

ὑπὸ Μειδίου καταβραβευθέντα, Demosth. Mid. p. 544 ult.　(βραβ., ch. iii. 15.)　　u = (see note)
(1) 2 Pet. iii. 5.　(2) 1 Kings xviii. 22.　2 Kings xv. 26.　3 Kings x. 9.　2 Chron. ix. 8.　Ps. cxlvi. 10.

om του DFKLℵ³ rel Chr Thdrt Damasc Thl : ins ABC[P]ℵ¹ m Œc, ο χριστος Syr.

were plural, see Matt. xii. 4) is (or as in rec. *are*: not, '*was*,' or *were*: he speaks of them in their nature, abstractedly) a shadow (not, a *sketch*, σκιαγραφία or -φημα, which meaning is precluded by the term opposed being σῶμα, not the finished picture,—but literally the *shadow*: see below) of things to come (the blessings of the Christian covenant: these are the substance, and the Jewish ordinances the mere type or resemblance, as the shadow is of the living man. But we must not, as Mey., press the figure so far as to imagine the shadow to be cast back by the τὰ μέλλοντα going before (cf. also Thdrt., somewhat differently, προλαμβάνει δὲ ἡ σκιὰ τὸ σῶμα ἀνίσχοντος τοῦ φωτός· ὡς εἶναι σκιὰν μὲν τὸν νόμον, σῶμα δὲ τὴν χάριν, φῶς δὲ τὸν δεσπότην χριστόν): nor with the same Commentator, interpret τῶν μελλ. of the *yet future* blessings of the state following the παρουσία,—for which ἐστιν (see above) gives no ground. Nor again must we imagine that the *obscurity* (Suicer, al.) of the Jewish dispensation is alluded to, there being no subjective comparison instituted between the two,—only their objective relation stated); but the body (the substance, of which the other is the shadow) belongs to Christ (i. e. the substantial blessings, which those legal observances typified, are attached to, brought in by, found in union with, Christ: see on the whole figure Heb. viii. 5; x. 1). We may observe, that if the ordinance of the Sabbath had been, *in any form*, of lasting obligation on the Christian Church, it would have been quite impossible for the Apostle to have spoken thus. The fact of an obligatory rest of one day, whether the seventh or the first, would have been directly in the teeth of his assertion here: the holding of such would have been still to retain the shadow, while we possess the substance. And no answer can be given to this by the transparent special-pleading, that he is speaking only of that which was *Jewish* in such observances; the whole argument being general, and the axiom of ver. 17 universally applicable.

I cannot see that Ellicott in loc. has at all invalidated this. To hold, as he does, that the sabbath was a σκιά of *the Lord's day*, is surely to fall into the same error as we find in the title of 1 Cor. x. in our authorized bibles,—'The Jewish

Sacraments were types of ours.' The antitype is not to be found in another and a higher type, but in the eternal verity which both shadow forth. An extraordinary punctuation of this verse was proposed by some mentioned by Chrys. : οἱ μὲν οὖν τοῦτο στίζουσι, τὸ δὲ σῶμα, χριστοῦ. ἡ δὲ ἀλήθεια ἐπὶ χριστοῦ γέγονεν· οἱ δὲ, τὸ δὲ σῶμα χριστοῦ μηδεὶς ὑμᾶς καταβραβευέτω· and Aug. ep. 149 (59). 27, vol. ii. p. 841 f., has 'corpus autem Christi nemo vos convincat. Turpe est, inquit . . . ut cum sitis corpus Christi, seducamini umbris.' No wonder that the same father should confess of the passage, 'nec ego sine caligine intelligo.'

18—23.] See above—*warning*, 2ndly, *with reference to angel-worship and asceticism.*　**18.**] Let no one of purpose (such is by far the best rendering of θέλων,—to take it with καταβραβ. and understand it precisely as in ref. 2 Pet. And thus apparently Thl.: θέλουσιν ὑμᾶς καταβραβεύειν διὰ ταπεινοφρος. Mey. pronounces this meaning 'ganȝ unpraȝenð,' and controverts the passages brought to defend it; *omitting however* ref. 2 Pet. So also does Ellicott, believing it to "impute to the false teachers a frightful and indeed suicidal malice, which is neither justified by the context, nor in any way credible." But his own "*desiring to do it*" is hardly distinguishable from that other: nor does it at all escape the imputation of motive which he finds so improbable. But surely it is altogether relevant, imputing to the false teachers not only error, but insidious designs also. Others take θέλων with ἐν ταπ., keeping however its reference as above, and understanding, as Phot. in Œc., τοῦτο ποιεῖν after it. So Thdrt., τοῦτο τοίνυν συνεβούλευον ἐκεῖνοι γίνεσθαι ταπεινοφροσύνη δῆθεν κεχρημένοι,—Calv., 'volens id facere,'—Mey., Eadie, al. This latter, after Bengel, assigns as his reason for adopting this view, that the participles θέλων, ἐμβατεύων, φυσιούμενος, κρατῶν, form a series. This however is not strictly true —for θέλων would stand in a position of emphasis which does not belong to the next two: rather should we thus expect ἐν ταπ. θέλων κ. θρ. τῶν ἀγγ. I cannot help thinking this rendering flat and spiritless. Others again suppose a harsh Hebraism, common in the LXX (reff., especially Ps. cxlvi. 10), but not found

v Eph. iv. 2
reff.
w Acts xxvi. 5.
James i. 26, 27 only †.

ἐν ᵛ ταπεινοφροσύνῃ καὶ ʷ θρησκείᾳ τῶν ἀγγέλων, ἃ ἑόρακεν

ABCDF
KLPℵ a
b c d e f
g h k l m
n o 17. 47

James i. 26, 27 only †.   Wisd. xiv. 18, 27 only.   (-σκός, James i. 26.   -σκεύειν, Wisd. xiv. 16.)

18. om εν ℵ¹(ins ℵ-corr¹).   θρησκια CDF.17.   ℵ¹ has written μελλοντων before αγγελων : marked for erasure by ℵ-corr¹.   rec aft ἅ ins μη (see note), with CD²·³KL[P]ℵ³ rel vulg syrr goth [arm] Orig Chr Thdrt Damasc Lucif Orig-int Aug ; ουκ F : om ĀBD¹ℵ¹ 17. 67² mss-in-Aug spec copt [æth] Orig-edd Tert Lucif Ambrst. (εορακεν, so B¹CD[P]ℵ.)   for αυτου, αυτων ℵ¹(txt ℵ-corr¹·³).

in the N. T., by which θέλειν ἐν is put for בְּ חָפֵץ, 'to have pleasure in.' So Aug., Est., Olsh., al. The principal objection to this rendering here is, that it would be irrelevant. Not the delight which the false teacher takes in his ταπ. &c., but the fact of it as operative on the Colossians, and its fleshly sources, are adduced) **defraud you of your prize** (see reff. Demosth. Mey. points out the difference between **καταβρ.**, a *fraudulent adjudication with hostile intent* against the person wronged, and **παραβραβεύειν**, which is merely, as Thdrt. explains this, ἀδίκως βραβεύειν. So Polyb. xxiv. 1. 12, τινὲς δ' ἐγκαλοῦντες τοῖς κρίμασιν, ὡς παραβεβραβευμένοις, διαφθείραντος τοῦ Φιλίππου τοὺς δικαστάς. Supplying this, which Chrys. has not marked, we may take his explanation : καταβραβευθῆναι γάρ ἐστιν ὅταν παρ' ἑτέρων μὲν ἡ νίκη, παρ' ἑτέρων δὲ τὸ βραβεῖον. Zonaras gives it better, in Suicer ii. 49 : **καταβρ.** ἐστι, τὸ μὴ τὸν νικήσαντα ἀξιοῦν τοῦ βραβείου, ἀλλ' ἑτέρῳ διδόναι αὐτό, ἀδικουμένου τοῦ νικήσαντος. This deprivation of their prize, and this wrong, they would suffer at the hands of those who would draw them away from Christ the giver of the prize (2 Tim. iv. 8. James i. 12. 1 Pet. v. 4), and lower them to the worship of intermediate spiritual beings. The various meanings, —'ne quis brabeutæ potestatem usurpans atque adeo abutens, vos currentes moderetur, perperamque præscribat quid sequi quid fugere debeatis præmium accepturi' (Beng.), — 'nemo adversum vos rectoris partes sibi ultro sumat' (Beza and similarly Corn.-a-lap.), — 'præmium, id est libertatem a Christo indultam, exigere' (Grot.),—are all more or less departures from the meaning of the word) **in** (as the element and sphere of his καταβραβ.) **humility** (αἵρεσις ἦν παλαιὰ λεγόντων τινῶν ὅτι οὐ δεῖ τὸν χριστὸν ἐπικαλεῖσθαι εἰς βοήθειαν, ἢ εἰς προσαγωγὴν τὴν πρὸς τὸν θεόν, ἀλλὰ τοὺς ἀγγέλους· διὰ τάχα τὸν χριστὸν ἐπικαλεῖσθαι πρὸς τὰ εἰρημένα μείζονος ὄντος τῆς ἡμετέρας ἀξίας. τοῦτο δὲ τάχα ταπεινούμενοι ἔλεγον. Zonaras in canon 35 of the Council of Laodicea, in Suicer i.

p. 45. Similarly Thdrt., λέγοντες ὡς ἀόρατος ὁ τῶν ὅλων θεός, ἀνεφικτός τε κ. ἀκατάληπτος, κ. προσήκει διὰ τῶν ἀγγέλων τὴν θείαν εὐμένειαν πραγματεύεσθαι. Aug. Conf. x. 42, vol. i. p. 807, says : "Quem invenirem, qui me reconciliaret tibi ? abeundum mihi fuit ad angelos ? . . . . multi conantes ad te redire, neque per se ipsos valentes, sicut audio, tentaverunt hæc, et inciderunt in desiderium curiosarum visionum, et digni habiti sunt illusionibus." So that no ironical sense need be supposed) **and** (explicative, or appending a specific form of the general ταπεινοφρ.) **worship of the angels** (genitive objective, '*worship paid to the holy angels :*' not subjective, as Schöttg., Luther, Rosenm., al. : cf. Jos. Antt. viii. 8. 4, τοῦ ναοῦ κ. τῆς θρησκείας τῆς ἐν αὐτῷ τοῦ θεοῦ ; Justin M. cohort. ad Græc. § 38, p. 35,—ἐπὶ τὴν τῶν μὴ θεῶν ἐτράπησαν θρησκείαν. With reference to the fact of the existence of such teaching at Colossæ, Thdrt. gives an interesting notice : οἱ τῷ νόμῳ συνηγοροῦντες καὶ τοὺς ἀγγέλους σέβειν αὐτοῖς εἰσηγοῦντο, διὰ τούτων λέγοντες δεδόσθαι τὸν νόμον. ἔμεινε δὲ τοῦτο τὸ πάθος ἐν τῇ Φρυγίᾳ κ. Πισιδίᾳ μέχρι πολλοῦ. οὗ δὴ χάριν κ. συνελθοῦσα σύνοδος ἐν Λαοδικείᾳ τῆς Φρυγίας νόμῳ κεκώλυκε τὸ τοῖς ἀγγέλοις προσεύχεσθαι· κ. μέχρι δὲ τοῦ νῦν εὐκτήρια τοῦ ἁγίου Μιχαὴλ παρ' ἐκείνοις κ. τοῖς ὁμόροις ἐκείνων ἐστὶν ἰδεῖν. The canon of the council of Laodicea (A.D. 360) runs thus : οὐ δεῖ χριστιανοὺς ἐγκαταλείπειν τὴν ἐκκλησίαν τοῦ θεοῦ, κ. ἀπιέναι, κ. ἀγγέλους ὀνομάζειν, κ. συνάξεις ποιεῖν, ἅπερ ἀπηγόρευται. εἴ τις οὖν εὑρεθῇ ταύτῃ τῇ κεκρυμμένῃ εἰδωλολατρείᾳ σχολάζων, ἔστω ἀνάθεμα, ὅτι ἐγκατέλιπε τὸν κύρ. ἡμ. Ἰ. χρ. τ. υἱ. τοῦ θεοῦ, κ. εἰδωλολατρείᾳ προσῆλθε. See, for an account of subsequent legends and visions of the neighbourhood, Conyb. and Hows., ii. p. 480, note, edn. 2),—**standing on the things which he hath seen** (an inhabitant of, *insistens* on, the realm of sight, not of faith : as Aug. above, 'incidens in desiderium curiosarum visionum.' First a word respecting the reading. The μή of the rec. and οὐκ of others, seem to me to

ˣ ἐμβατεύων, ʸ εἰκῇ ᶻ φυσιούμενος ὑπὸ τοῦ ᵃ νοὸς τῆς σαρκὸς αὐτοῦ, ¹⁹ καὶ οὐ ᵇ κρατῶν τὴν ᶜ κεφαλήν, ἐξ ᵈ οὗ πᾶν
τὸ σῶμα διὰ τῶν ᵉ ἀφῶν καὶ ᶠ συνδέσμων ᵍ ἐπιχορηγούμενον

x here only.
  Josh. xix. 49.
1 Macc. xii.
  25 al3. only.
τολμηρὸν
ἐμβατεύειν
τὴν ἀπερι-

νόητον φύσιν, Xen. Conviv. p. 698 Raphel.   y Gal. iii. 4 reff.   z 1 Cor. iv. 6, &c. v.
2. viii. 1. xiii. 4 only †.   a = Rom. i. 28. xii. 2.   b = Acts iii. 11. Cant. iii. 4.
c Eph. i. 22 reff.   d Phil. iii. 20. constr. gender, 1 Tim. iii. 16.   e Eph. iv.
  16 only ‡. (Lev. xiii. 2 al. fr.)   f Acts viii. 23. Eph. iv. 3. ch. iii. 14 only. Isa. lviii. 6.
g Gal. iii. 5 reff.

19. aft κεφαλην ins χριστον D¹ syr arm Novat.

have been unfortunate insertions from misunderstanding the sense of ἐμβατεύων. That it *may* mean 'prying into,' would be evident from the simplest metaphorical application of its primary meaning of treading or entering on: but whether it *does* so mean here, must be determined by the context. And it surely would be a strange and incongruous expression for one who was advocating a religion of *faith*,—whose very charter is μακάριοι οἱ μὴ ἰδόντες κ. πεπιστευκότες,—to blame a man or a teacher for ἃ μὴ ἑόρακεν ἐμβατεύειν, placing the *defect of sight* in the very emphatic forefront of the charge against him. Far rather should we expect that one who διὰ πίστεως περιεπάτει, οὐ διὰ εἴδους, would state of such teacher as one of his especial faults, that he ἃ ἑόρακεν ἐνεβάτευεν, found his status, his standing-point, in the realm of sight. And to this what follows corresponds. This insisting on his own visual experience is the result of fleshly pride as contrasted with the spiritual mind. Of the other meanings of ἐμβατεύειν, that of 'coming into possession of property,' 'inheriting,' might be suitable, but in this sense it is usually constructed with 'εἰς, cf. Demosth. 1085. 24, 1086. 19. The ordinary meaning is far the best here: see reff., and cf. Æsch. Pers. 448—νῆσος . . . . ἢν ὁ φιλόχορος Πὰν ἐμβατεύει, Eur. Electr. 595—κασίγνητον ἐμβατεῦσαι πόλιν (this view I still maintain as against Ellicott)), **vainly** (groundlessly. εἰκῇ must not be joined with ἐμβατ., as De W., Conyb., al.,—for thus the emphasis of that clause is destroyed: see above) **puffed up** (no inconsistency with the ταπεινοφρ. above: for as Thdrt. says, τὴν μὲν ἐσκήπτοντο, τοῦ δὲ τύφου τὸ πάθος ἀκριβῶς περιέκειντο) **by** (as the working principle in him) **the mind** (intent, bent of thought and apprehension) **of his own flesh** (ὑπὸ σαρκικῆς διανοίας, οὐ πνευματικῆς, Chrys. But as usual, this adjectival rendering misses the point of the expression,—the διάνοια is not only σαρκική, but is τῆς σαρκός—the σάρξ, the ordinary sensuous principle, is the fons of the νοῦς—which therefore dwells in

the region of visions of the man's own seeing, and does not in true humility hold the Head and in faith receive grace as one of His members. I have marked αὐτοῦ rather more strongly than by ' *his* ' only : its expression conveys certainly some idea of self-will. On the psychological propriety of the expression, see Ellicott's note), **19.**] **and not** (objective negative source of his error) **holding fast** (see ref. Cant. The want of firm holding of Christ has set him loose to ἐμβατεύειν ἃ ἑόρακεν) **the Head** (Christ: see on Eph. i. 22. Each must hold fast the Head for himself, not merely be attached to the other members, however high or eminent in the Body), **from whom** (better than with Mey., '*from which*,' viz. the Head,— Christ, according to him, being referred to 'nidjt perfönlidj, fondern fadjlidj:' but if so, why not ἐξ ἧς—what reason would there be for any change of gender ? The only cause for such change must be sought in *personal* reference to Christ, as in ref. 1 Tim.; and this view is confirmed by the τ. αὔξησιν τ. θεοῦ below, shewing that the figure and reality are mingled in the sentence. Beng. gives as his first alternative, 'ex quo, sc. tenendo caput :' but this would be δι' οὗ, not ἐξ οὗ. The Head itself is the *Source* of increase : the holding it, the *means*) **all the body** (in its every part: not exactly = '*the whole body*,' in its entirety, which would, if accurately expressed, be τὸ πᾶν σῶμα, cf. τὸν πάντα χρόνον, Acts xx. 18,—ὁ πᾶς νόμος, Gal. v. 14. On the whole passage see Eph. iv. 16, an almost exact parallel) **by means of the joints** (see against Meyer's meaning, ' *nerves*,' on Eph. l. c.) **and bands** (sinews and nerves which bind together, and communicate between, limb and limb) **being supplied** (the passive of the simple verb is found in 3 Macc. vi. 40, Polyb. iv. 77. 2, πολλαῖς ἀφορμαῖς ἐκ φύσεως κεχορηγημένος πρὸς πραγμάτων κατάκτησιν : ib. iii. 75. 3 ; vi. 15. 4, al. The ἐπι, denoting continual accession, suits the αὔξει below) **and compounded** (see on Eph. Notice, as there, the present participles, denoting that the process is now going on. *Wherewith* the body is supplied

h Eph. v. 16   καὶ ʰ συνβιβαζόμενον ⁱ αὔξει τὴν ᵏ αὔξησιν τοῦ θεοῦ. ABCDF
reff.   KLPℵ a
i (-ξειν) Eph. 20 εἰ ˡ ἀπεθάνετε σὺν χριστῷ ᵐ ἀπὸ τῶν ⁿ στοιχείων τοῦ b c d e f
ii. 21 only.   g h k l m
Isa. lxi. 11.   n o 17. 47
k Eph. iv. 16   κόσμου, τί ὡς ζῶντες ἐν κόσμῳ ᵒ δογματίζεσθε 21 Μὴ
only †.
2 Macc. v. 16 only. constr., as John vii. 24.   1 = Gal. ii. 19.   m = Rom. vii. 2. ix. 3.   2 Cor. xi. 3.   2 Thess.
i. 9.   n Gal. iv. 3 reff.   o here only. Esth. iii. 9.   Esdr. vi. 34.   2 Macc. x. 8. xv. 36 only.

αυξη ℵ¹(txt ℵ-corr¹) m 44. 108-9-10. 219.
  20. rec aft ει ins ουν, with ℵ³ rel [vulg] syr [Cyr₁ or ₂-p] Thdrt Ambr Ambrst, *autem*
demid, *enim* Syr: aft αποθανετε(sic) ℵ¹: om ABCDFKL[P]ℵ-corr¹(appy) d k 17 [47]
67² am(with fuld tol) copt goth [æth] arm Cyr Tert Cypr.   rec ins τω bef χριστω,
with k: om ABCDFKL[P]ℵ rel 67² Chr Thdrt Damasc.   ins δια bef τι D¹.
aft τι ins παλιν D¹F; ετι vulg arm.   ins τω bef κοσμω F; *in hoc mundo* D-lat fuld
Ambrst.

and compounded, is here left to be inferred, and need not be, as by some Commentators, minutely pursued into detail.
It is, as Thl., τὸ ζῆν κ. αὔξειν πνευματικῶς,—as Chrys.,—understanding it
however after πᾶν τὸ σῶμα,—ἔχει τὸ
εἶναι, κ. τὸ καλῶς εἶναι. The supply is as
the sap to the vine—as the πᾶσα αἴσθησις
κ. πᾶσα κίνησις (Thl.) to the body) in-
creaseth with (accusative of the cognate
substantive, see Ellic. and Winer, § 32. 2)
the increase of God (i. e. 'the increase
wrought by God,'—God being the first
cause of life to the whole, and carrying
on this growth in subordination to and
union with the Head, Jesus Christ: not
as Chrys., merely = κατὰ θεόν, τὴν ἀπὸ
τῆς πολιτείας τῆς ἀρίστης,—nor to be
tamed down with Calv., al., to "significat, non probari Deo quodvis augmentum,
sed quod ad caput dirigitur." Still less
must we adopt the adjectival rendering,
'godly growth,' Conyb., making that an
attribute of the growth, which is in reality
its *condition of existence*).   The Roman
Catholic Commentators, Corn.-a-lap., Estius, Bisping, endeavour by all kinds of
evasions to escape the strong bearing of
this passage on their following (and out-
doing) of the heretical practices of the
Judaizing teachers in this matter of the
θρησκεία τῶν ἀγγέλων. The latter (Bisp.)
remarks,—"It is plain from this passage,
as indeed from the nature of things, that
the Apostle is not blaming every honouring of the angels, but only such honouring
as put them in the place of Christ. The
true honouring of the angels and saints is
after all in every case an honouring of
Christ their Head." On this I may remark 1) that the word '*honouring*'
(Verehrung) is simply disingenuous, there
being no question of honouring, but of
worship in the strict sense (θρησκεία).
2) That whatever a Commentator may say
in his study, and Romanists may assert
when convenient to them, the honour and
worship actually and practically paid by
them to angels and saints does by very

far exceed that paid to Christ their Head.
Throughout Papal Europe, the worship of
Christ among the body of the middle and
lower orders is fast becoming obliterated,
and supplanted by that of His Mother.
  20.] *Warning against asceticism.*
If ye died (in your baptism, as detailed
above, vv. 11 ff.) with Christ from (a pregnant construction : 'died, and so were set
free from:' not found elsewhere in N. T.:
cf. Rom. vi. 2 ; Gal. ii. 19, where we have
the dative) the elements (cf. ver. 8 : the
rudimentary lessons, i. e. ritualistic observances) of the world (see on ver. 8:
Christ Himself was set free from these,
when, being made under the law, He at His
Death bore the curse of the law, and thus
it was antiquated in Him), why, as *living*
(emphatic, as though you had *not died*,
see Gal. vi. 14) in the world, are ye being
prescribed to (the active use of the verb,
'*to decree*,' is common in the later classics,
and occurs in the LXX, and Apocrypha.
The *person to whom* the thing is decreed or prescribed is put in the *dative*
(2 Macc. x. 8), so that, according to usage,
such person may become the *subject* of
the *passive* verb : cf. Thuc. i. 82, ἡμεῖς
ὑπ' Ἀθηναίων ἐπιβουλευόμεθα (ἐπιβου-
λεύειν τινί),—Herod. vii. 144, αἱ δὲ νῆες
.... οὐκ ἐχρήσθησαν (χρῆσθαί τινι), and
see Kühner, Gram. ii. p. 35. Some, as
Bernhardy, p. 346, and Ellicott, prefer considering this form as *middle*, and give it
the sense of "doceri vos sinitis." It seems
to be of very little consequence which
we call it; the meaning in either case is
almost identical : "why is the fact so?" or,
"why do you allow it?" To my mind, the
passive here carries more keen, because
more hidden, rebuke.   The ἀδικεῖσθε and
ἀποστέρεσθε of 1 Cor. vi. 7 rest on somewhat different ground. There, the voluntary element comes into emphasis, and
the *middle* sense is preferable. See note
there.   I cannot see, with Meyer, why we
should be so anxious to divest the sentence of all appearance of blaming the Colossians, and cast all its blame on the false

p ἅψῃ μηδὲ q γεύσῃ μηδὲ r θίγῃς—22 ἅ s ἐστιν πάντα s εἰς
t φθορὰν u τῇ v ἀποχρήσει—κατὰ τὰ wx ἐντάλματα καὶ wy διδασκαλίας τῶν ἀνθρώπων, 23 z ἅτινά ἐστιν a λόγον b μὲν

p 1 Cor. vii. 1.
2 Cor. vi. 17,
from Isa. lii.
11. Levit.
xi. 8.
q Acts x. 10.
xx. 11. xxiii.
14. 2 Macc. vi. 20.   r Heb. xi. 28. xii. 20 only.   Exod. xix. 12 only.   s Matt. xix. 5. Eph. i.
12 al. fr.   t = Gal. vi. 8 reff.   u dat., Rom. xi. 20, 30.   v here only †.   w Matt.
xv. 9 ‖, from Isa. xxix. 13.   x Matt. as above (w) ‖ Mk. vii.   Job xxiii. 11 (12 BN).   Isa. as above
only.   y Eph. v. 14.   1 Tim. i. 10 reff.   z = ch. iii. 5.   Rom. ix. 4 al.   change of gender, Phil. i. 28.
a here only.   b so μέν (see note) Acts i. 1. iii. 13.   Rom. vii. 12.   Gal. iv. 24.   Winer, § 63. i. 2. e.

teachers. The passive (see above) would
demand a reason for the fact being so—
'Cur ita siti estis, ut . . . ,' which is just
as much a reproach as the middle 'Cur,
sinitis, ut . . .' The *active* renderings,
'*decreta facitis*,' Melancth. (in Eadie),
'*decernitis*,' Ambrst. (ib.), are wrong both
in grammar and in fact.   The reference
to δόγμασιν ver. 14 is plain. They were
being again put under that χειρόγρ. which
was wiped out and taken away) "Handle
not, neither taste, nor even touch" (it
will be understood that these words follow
immediately upon δογματίζεσθε without
a stop, as τὰ δογματιζόμενα;—just as the
inf. in 2 Macc. x. 8. Then as to the
meaning, — I agree with Calv., Beza,
Beng., and Meyer in referring all the
three to *meats*,—on account mainly of
vv. 22, 23 (see below), but also of γεύσῃ
coming as a defining term between the two
less precise ones ἅψῃ and θίγῃς. Others
have referred the three to different objects
ἅψῃ and θίγῃς variously to meats, or unclean objects, or women: γεύσῃ universally to meats. Mey. remarks of the negatives, the relation of the three prohibitions is, that the first μηδέ is '*nec*,' the
second '*ne . . . quidem*.' This would not
be necessary from the form of the sentence,
but seems supported by the word θίγῃς
introducing a climax. Wetst. and the Commentators illustrate ἅψῃ and θίγῃς as applied to meats, by Xen. Cyr. i. 3. 5, ὅταν
μὲν τοῦ ἄρτου ἅψῃ, (ὁρῶ) εἰς οὐδὲν τὴν
χεῖρα ἀποψώμενον, ὅταν δὲ τούτων τινὸς
θίγῃς, εὐθὺς ἀποκαθαίρῃ τὴν χεῖρα εἰς
τὰ χειρόμακτρα)—which things (viz. the
things forbidden) are set (ἐστιν emphatic,
'whose very nature is . . .') all of them
for destruction (by corruption, see reff.)
in their consumption (i. e. are appointed
by the Creator to be decomposed and obliterated with their consumption by us. So
Thdrt.—πῶς . . . νομίζετέ τινα μὲν τῶν
ἐδεσμάτων ἔννομα, τινὰ δὲ παράνομα, κ.
οὐ σκοπεῖτε ὡς μόνιμον τούτων οὐδέν;
εἰς κόπρον γὰρ ἅπαντα μεταβάλλεται:
and similarly Œc.—φθορᾷ γάρ, φησιν,
ὑπόκειται ἐν τῷ ἀφεδρῶνι—Thl., Erasm.,
Luth., Beza, Calv., Grot., Wolf, Olsh.,
Mey., al.   The argument in fact is similar
to that in Matt. xv. 17, and 1 Cor. vi. 13.
    Two other lines of interpretation have

been followed: 1) that which carries the
sense on from the three verbs, "*Handle
not, &c. things which tend to (moral) corruption in their use.*" De W., Baum.-
Crus., al. But this suits neither the collo-
cation of the words, nor ἀποχρήσει, the
'*using up*,' '*consumption*,' which should
thus rather be χρήσει. 2) that which
makes ἅ refer to δόγματα, and renders
'*which δόγματα all tend to (everlasting)
destruction in their observance*;' but this
is just as much against the sense of ἀπό-
χρησις, and would rather require τήρησις,
if indeed τῇ ἀποχρήσει be not superfluous altogether. See these same objections urged at greater length in Meyer's
note)—according to (connects with δογματίζεσθε Μὴ . . . θίγῃς: the subsequent
clause being a parenthetical remark; thus
defining the general term δόγματα to consist in human, not divine commands) the
commands and systems (διδασκαλία is
the wider term comprising many ἐντάλματα.   In reff., the wider term is prefixed:
here, where examples of separate ἐντάλματα have been given, we rise from them
to the system of doctrine of which they are
a part) of men (not merely ἀνθρώπων,
bringing out the individual authors of
them, but τῶν ἀν. describing them gene-
rically as *human*, not divine. This I would
press as against Ellic., who views the τῶν
as the art. of correlation, rendered necessary by τὰ ἐντάλματα.   But even if this
usage were to be strictly pressed with such
a word as ἀνθρώπων, the substantive nearest to it, διδασκαλίας, has no article), such
as (ἅτινα brings us from the general objective, human doctrines and systems, to
the specific subjective, the particular sort
of doctrines and systems which they were
following: q. d., 'and that, such sort of
ἐντ. κ. διδασκ. as . . .') are possessed of
(ἐστιν ἔχοντα does not exactly = ἔχει, but
betokens more the abiding attribute of
these δόγματα—'enjoy,' as we say) a re-
putation (λόγον ἔχειν occurs in various
meanings. Absolutely, it may signify
'*avoir raison*,' as Demosth. adv. Lept. p.
461, ἔστι δὲ τοῦτο οὕτωσι μὲν ἀκοῦσαι λόγον
τινὰ ἔχον, which meaning is obviously out
of place here:—as is also '*to take account
of*,' Herod. i. 62, 'Αθηναῖοι δὲ οἱ ἐκ τοῦ
ἄστεος, ἕως . . . . . λόγον οὐδένα εἶχον.

c here only †.
(see note.)
d ver. 18.
e here only †.
(-δῶς, Prov.
xxi. 26.)
f 1 Thess. iv. 4.

ABCDF
KLPℵ a
b c d e f
g h k l m
n o 17. 47

ᵃἔχοντα σοφίας ἐν ᶜἐθελοθρησκείᾳ καὶ ᵈταπεινοφροσύνῃ καὶ ᵉἀφειδίᾳ σώματος, οὐκ ᶠἐν τιμῇ τινι,—πρὸς ᵍπλησμονὴν τῆς σαρκός;

(τὰ καινὰ τῶν ὑποδημάτων ἐν τιμῇ τινι . . . . ἐστιν, Lucian de merced. cond. 17. Wetst.)   g here only. Exod. xvi. 8 al.

23. ἐθελοθρησκια (for -κεια) CD¹ [P(-ρισκ.)] ℵ e g) 17: A uncert: θρησκια F. aft ταπεινοφροσυνη ins του νοος F(and F-lat) D-lat [syr copt] goth lat-ff.   om 2nd και B spec [Iren-int₁] Hil.   αφειδεια B[Tischdf assigns it to his B³, αφιδεια P] : txt [B¹(Tischdf)] CDFKLℵ rel. (A def.)

But the meaning '*to have the repute of*,' —found Herod. v. 66, Κλεισθένης . . . . ὅσπερ δὴ λόγον ἔχει τὴν Πυθίην ἀναπεῖσαι ('is said to have influenced the Pythia'),—and Plato, Epinomis, p. 987 b, ὁ μὲν γὰρ ἑωσφόρος ἕσπερός τε ὢν αὐτὸς Ἀφροδίτης εἶναι σχεδὸν ἔχει λόγον ('Veneris esse dicitur,' as Ficinus),—manifestly fits the context here, and is adopted by most Commentators) indeed (the μέν solitarium leaves the δέ to be supplied by the reader, or gathered from what follows. It is implied by it, not by the mere phrase λόγον ἔχειν (see the examples above), that they had the repute only without the reality) of wisdom in (element of its repute) voluntary worship (words of this form are not uncommon: so we have ἐθελοπρόξενος, a volunteer or self-constituted proxenus, in Thuc. iii. 70—ἐθελοκωφέω, to pretend to be deaf, Strabo i. p. 36,—ἐθελοδουλεία, voluntary slavery, Plato Symp., p. 184 c, &c. &c.; see Lexx., and Aug., Ep. 149 (59, cited above on ver. 17), says 'sic et vulgo dicitur qui divitem affectat thelodives, et qui sapientem thelosapiens, et cætera hujusmodi.' Mey. cites Epiphan. Hær. xvi. p. 34, explaining the name Pharisees, διὰ τὸ ἀφωρισμένους εἶναι αὐτοὺς ἀπὸ τῶν ἄλλων διὰ τὴν ἐθελοπερισσοθρησκείαν παρ' αὐτῶν νενομισμένην. See many more examples in Wetst. The θρ. was mainly that of *angels*, see above, ver. 18: but the generality of the expression here may take in other voluntary extravagancies of worship also) and humility (see ver. 18) and unsparingness of the body (Plato defines ἐλευθερία, ἀφειδία ἐν χρήσει κ. ἐν κτήσει οὐσίας, Def. p. 412 D: Thuc. ii. 43 has ἀφειδεῖν βίου : Diod. Sic. xiii. 60, ἀφειδῶς ἐχρῶντο τοῖς ἰδίοις σώμασιν εἰς τὴν κοινὴν σωτηρίαν, &c. &c., see Wetst.), not in any honour of it (on the interpretations, see below. τιμή is used by St. Paul of honour or respect bestowed on the body, in 1 Cor. xii. 23, 24: of honourable conduct in matters relating to the body, 1 Thess. iv. 4 (see note there: cf. also Rom. i. 24): and such is the meaning I would assign to it here—these δόγματα have the repute of wisdom for (in) &c., and for (in) unsparingness of the body, not in any real honour done to it—its true honour being dedication to the Lord, 1 Cor. vi. 13),— to the satiating of the flesh ? I connect these words not with the preceding clause, but with δογματίζεσθε above—'*why are ye suffering yourselves* (see on the passive above) *to be thus dogmatized* (in the strain μὴ ἅψῃ &c. according to &c., which are &c.), *and all for the satisfaction of the flesh*'—for the following out of a διδασκαλία, the ground of which is the φυσιοῦσθαι ὑπὸ τοῦ νοὸς τῆς σαρκός, ver. 18? Then after this follow most naturally the exhortations of the next chapter; they are not to seek the πλησμονὴ τῆς σαρκός— not τὰ ἐπὶ τῆς γῆς φρονεῖν, but νεκρῶσαι τὰ μέλη τὰ ἐπὶ τῆς γῆς. The ordinary interpretation of this difficult passage has been, as E. V. '*not in any honour to the satisfying of the flesh,*' meaning thereby, that such commands do not provide for the honour which we owe to the body in the supply of the proper refreshment to the flesh. But two great objections lie against this, and are in my judgment fatal to the interpretation in every shape: 1) that ἡ σάρξ cannot be used in this indifferent sense as equivalent to τὸ σῶμα, in a sentence where it occurs together with τὸ σῶμα, and where it has before occurred in an ethical sense: 2) that πλησμονή will not bear this meaning of mere ordinary supplying, 'satisfying the wants of:' but must imply satiety, 'satisfying to repletion.' The children of Israel were to eat the quails εἰς πλησμονήν, Ex. xvi. 8: cf. also Deut. xxxiii. 23: Lam. v. 6; Hab. ii. 16: also διὰ τὰς ἀλόγους οἰνοφλυγίας κ. πλησμονάς, Polyb. ii. 19. 4. Meyer renders—'*these commands have a repute for wisdom, &c.,—not for any thing which is really honourable* (i. e. which may prove that repute to be grounded in truth), *but in order thereby to the satiation of men's sensual nature:*' and so, nearly, Ellicott. The objections to this are, 1) the strained meaning of τιμή τις, —2) the insertion of '*but*' before πρός, or as in Ellic. '*only*' after it, both which are

III. ¹ Εἰ οὖν ʰ συνηγέρθητε τῷ χριστῷ, ⁱ τὰ ἄνω   ʰ Eph. ii. 6
ᵏ ζητεῖτε, οὗ ὁ χριστός ἐστιν ˡ ἐν ˡ δεξιᾷ τοῦ θεοῦ καθήμενος·   reff. ch. ii. 12.
   i Gal. iv. 26.
² ⁱ τὰ ἄνω ᵐ φρονεῖτε, μὴ τὰ ⁿ ἐπὶ τῆς γῆς. ³ ἀπεθάνετε   Phil. iii. 14. k = Matt. vi.
γάρ, καὶ ἡ ζωὴ ὑμῶν ° κέκρυπται σὺν τῷ χριστῷ ᵖ ἐν τῷ   33. 1 Pet.iii. 11, from Ps. xxxiii. 14.

   1 Macc. ii. 29.

l = Eph. i. 20 reff.   m = Phil. ii. 2 reff.   n see Phil. iii. 19.   o = Rev. ii. 17.   Ps. xxvi. 5.
p = Luke iv. 25, 27. Acts ii. 29. Num. xxiii. 21.

CHAP. III. 1. for τω, εν א¹(txt א-corr¹).   for ου, που F.   for χs, θs (but corrd) א¹.   om εστιν א¹(ins א-corr¹) 120 : εστιν bef ο χρ. 116.
2. for 1st τα, ἃ F.   om της a 67².
3. om 1st τω D.   om 2nd τω KL d e l n o 67².

wholly gratuitous. This same latter objection applies to the rendering of Beza, al., 'nec tamen ullius sunt pretii, *quum ad ea spectant quibus farcitur caro*,'—besides that this latter paraphrase is unwarranted. See other renderings still further off the point in Mey. and De W. Among these I fear must be reckoned that of Conyb., 'are of no value to check (?) the indulgence of fleshly passions,' and that of Bähr and Eadie, regarding λόγον—τινι as participial, and joining ἐστιν with πρός—a harshness of construction wholly unexampled and improbable. The interpretation above given seems to me, after long consideration, the simplest, and most in accord with the context. It is no objection to it that the antithesis presented by οὐκ ἐν τιμῇ τινι is thus not to ἐν ἐθελοθρ. κ.τ.λ., but merely to ἀφειδίᾳ σώματος: for if the Apostle wished to bring out a negative antithesis to these last words only, he hardly could do so without repeating the preposition, the sense of which is carried on to ἀφειδίᾳ.

CHAP. III. 1—IV. 6.] SECOND PART OF THE EPISTLE. *Direct exhortations to the duties of the Christian life—founded on their union with their risen Saviour.*

1—4.] *Transition to the new subject, and grounding of the coming exhortations.* 1.] **If then** (as above asserted, ch. ii. 12, 20 : the εἰ implies no doubt of the fact, but lays it down as ground for an inference, see ch. ii. 20, and cf. Xen. Mem. i. 5. 1) **ye were raised up together with Christ** (not as E. V. '*are risen:*' the allusion, as above, ch. ii. 11—13, is to a definite time, your baptism. And it is important to keep this in view, that we may not make the mistake so commonly made, of interpreting συνηγέρθητε in an *ethical* sense, and thereby stultifying the sentence—for if the participation were an ethical one, what need to exhort them to its ethical realization ? The participation is an objective one, brought about by that faith which was the condition of their baptismal admission into Him. This faith the Apostle exhorts

them to energize in the ethical realization of this resurrection state), **seek the things above** (heavenly, spiritual things: cf. Matt. vi. 33; Gal. iv. 26; Phil. iii. 20) **where Christ is** ('se trouve,' not merely the copula. If you are united to Him, you will be tending to Him ; and He is in heaven),—**seated on the right hand of God** (see Eph. i. 20. Here, as every where, when the present state of Christ is spoken of, the Ascension is taken for granted): **care for the things above (φρονεῖτε,** wider than ζητεῖτε, extending to the whole region of their thought and desire), **not the things on the earth** (cf. οἱ τὰ ἐπίγεια φρονοῦντες, Phil. iii. 19: i. e. matters belonging to this present mortal state—earthly pleasure, pelf, and pride. There is no reason, with Thl., Calv., Schrad., Huther, to suppose him still aiming at the false teachers, and meaning by τὰ ἐπὶ τῆς γῆς, τὰ περὶ βρωμάτων κ. ἡμερῶν (Thl.) : in this part of the Epistle he has dropped the controversial and taken the purely ethical tone). **For ye died** (ch. ii. 12: '*are dead*,' though allowable, is not so good, as merely asserting a state, whereas the other recalls the fact of that state having been entered on. That being made partakers with Christ's death, cut you loose from the τὰ ἐπὶ τῆς γῆς: see Rom. vi. 4—7), **and your life** (that resurrection life (which *is* "your real and true life" as Ellic., objecting to this explanation: The only real life of the Christian is his resurrection life in and with Christ. The fact is, Ellic. has mistaken my meaning in this term: see my remarks on it below), which you now have only in its first fruits, in possession indeed, but not in *full* possession, see below, and cf. Rom. viii. 19—23) **is hidden** (οὔπω ἐφανερώθη, 1 John iii. 2 : is laid up, to be manifested hereafter: that such is the sense, the next verse seems plainly to shew) **with Christ** (who is also Himself hidden at present from us, who wait for His ἀποκάλυψις (1 Cor. i. 7. 2 Thess. i. 7. 1 Pet. i. 7, 13; iv. 13), which shall be also **ours,**

θεῷ· 4 ὅταν ὁ χριστὸς [q] φανερωθῇ, ἡ [r] ζωὴ ἡμῶν, τότε
καὶ ὑμεῖς σὺν αὐτῷ [q] φανερωθήσεσθε [s] ἐν δόξῃ.
5 [t] Νεκρώσατε οὖν τὰ [u] μέλη τὰ [n] ἐπὶ τῆς γῆς, [v] πορ-
νείαν, [wx] ἀκαθαρσίαν, [y] πάθος, [za] ἐπιθυμίαν [a] κακήν, καὶ τὴν

ABCDF KLPℵ a b c d e f g h k l m n o 17. 47

q = 1 John ii. 28. (ch. i. 26 reff.)
r so ἐλπίς, ch. i. 27.
s = 1 Tim. iii. 16 reff.
t Rom. iv. 19. Heb. xi. 12 only †.
u Rom. vi. 13. vii. 5 al. Exod. xxix. 17.
v Matt. v. 32 al. fr. Gen. xxxviii. 24.
w Rom. i. 24. Gal. v. 19 al. Prov. vi. 16.
x Eph. iv. 19.
y Rom. i. 26. 1 Thess. iv. 5 only †. Job xvi. 4 Symm. = Xen. Mem. iii. 10. 8.
z Rom. i. 24. 2 Pet. ii. 18 al.
a Prov. xxi. 26.

4. [ins και bef η ζωη F.] for ημων, υμων (*see note*) CD¹F[P]ℵ k 17 [47] latt goth [æth arm] gr-lat-ff: txt BD²·³KL rel syrr copt Orig [Meth] Dial Œc Hil_1 Ambr. (A uncert.) om συν αυτω A 57 Nyss: ins aft φανερ. 73. 118 vulg.

5. rec aft τα μελη ins υμων, with AC³DFKL[P]ℵ³ rel latt syrr copt goth $Clem_1$ $Damasc_1$ Iren-int Cypr Hil: om BC¹ℵ¹ 17. 67² $Clem_1$ $Orig_5$ Eus Damasc-comm(appy) Sing-cler [Tert]. aft πορνειαν ins και D sah; αποθεμενοι syr arm Jer.

see ver. 4, and Rom. viii. 19) **in God** (with Christ who is εἰς τὸν κόλπον τοῦ Πατρός—it is in Him, as in a great depth, that all things concealed are hidden, and He brings them out as seems good to Him. Notice the solemnity of the repetition of the articles: and so all through these verses). **When Christ shall be manifested** (shall emerge from his present state of hiddenness, and be personally revealed), **who is our** (no emphasis—ἡμῶν applies to Christians generally—see on ὑμ. below) **life** (not as Eadie, 'shall appear in the character of our life' (ὅτ. χρ. ἡ ζωὴ ἡμ. φανερωθῇ): Christ IS personally Himself that life, and we possess it only by union with Him and His resurrection: see John xiv. 19), **then shall ye also** (καί takes out the special from the general—ye, as well as, and among, other Christians: with the reading ἡ ζ. ὑμῶν, the καί would mean, 'as well as Christ') **with Him be manifested in glory** (see on the whole, the parallel 1 John iii. 2. Though the *completed life of the resurrection* seems so plainly pointed out by this last verse as the sense to be given to ἡ ζωή, this has not been seen by many Commentators, who hold it to be *ethical;* hidden, inasmuch as inward and spiritual —ἐν τῷ κρυπτῷ, Rom. ii. 29 (De W.), and ideal: or, inasmuch as it is unseen by the world (Beng., similarly Storr, Flatt, Bisping, al.). The root of the mistake has been the want of a sufficiently comprehensive view of that resurrection life of ours which is now hidden with Christ. It includes in itself both spiritual, ethical, and corporeal: and the realization of it as far as possible, here, is the sum of the Christian's most earnest endeavours: but the life itself, in its full manifestation, is that perfection of body, soul, and spirit, in which we shall be manifested with Him at His appearing. Cf. Thdrt.: ἐκείνου γὰρ ἀναστάντος πάντες ἠγέρθημεν· ἀλλ' οὐδέπω ὁρῶμεν τῶν πραγμάτων τὴν ἔκβασιν. κέκρυπται δὲ ἐν αὐτῷ τῆς ἡμετέρας ἀναστάσεως τὸ μυστήριον).

5—17.] *General exhortations:* and herein (5—11)—*to laying aside of the vices of the old man,*—(12—17) *to realizing the new life in its practical details.* **Put to death therefore** (the **οὖν** connects with the ἀπεθάνετε of ver. 3: follow out, realize this state of death to things on earth—**νεκρώσατε**—notice the aorist implying a definite act:—cf. ἐσταύρωσαν Gal. v. 24, θανατοῦτε Rom. viii. 13, in the same reference) **your members which are on the earth** (literally, as to τὰ μέλη: your feet, hands, &c.: reduce these to a state of death as regards their actions and desires below specified—as regards, in other words, their denizenship of this earth. With this you have no concern—they are members of Christ, partakers of His resurrection, renewed after His image. The metaphorical sense of μέλη, regarding πορν. &c., as 'membra quibus vetus homo, i. e. ratio ac voluntas hominis depravata perinde utitur ac corpus membris.' Beza, —'naturam nostram quasi massam ex diversis vitiis conflatam imaginatur.' Calv., —seems unnecessary. And the understanding of φρονοῦντα with τὰ ἐπὶ τῆς γῆς, as Grot., after Thdrt. (τουτέστι τὴν ἐπὶ τὰ χείρω τοῦ φρονήματος ῥοπήν), is certainly a mistake: cf. τὰ ἐπὶ τῆς γῆς above, ver. 2),—**fornication** (these which follow, are the carnal functions of the earthly members. It is one instance of that form of the double accusative, where the first denotes the whole, the second a part of it, as τὸν δ' ἄορι πλῆξ' αὐχένα, λῦσε δὲ γυῖα, Il. λ. 240,—ποῖόν σε ἔπος φύγεν ἕρκος ὀδόντων; Od. α. 64. See Kühner, ii. p. 230), **impurity** (reff.), **lustfulness** (see Rom. i. 26, whence it would appear that the *absolute* word need not be understood of *unnatural* lust, the specifying genitive ἀτιμίας giving it there that meaning. We may understand it

xb πλεονεξίαν, c ἥτις ἐστὶν d εἰδωλολατρεία, 6 δι᾽ ὃ ἔρχεται ἡ e ὀργὴ τοῦ e θεοῦ. 7 f ἐν οἷς καὶ ὑμεῖς f περιεπατήσατέ ποτε, ὅτε g ἐζῆτε g ἐν τούτοις· 8 νυνὶ δὲ h ἀπόθεσθε καὶ ὑμεῖς τὰ πάντα, ij ὀργὴν ij θυμὸν ik κακίαν, il βλασφημίαν m αἰσχρολογίαν ἐκ τοῦ στόματος ὑμῶν, 9 μὴ n ψεύδεσθε

b Mark vii. 22.
Luke xii. 15.
Paul, Rom. i.
29 al4.
2 Pet. ii. 3,
14 only. Ps.
cxviii. 36.
Ezek. xxii.
27.
c = ch. ii. 23
reff.
d 1 Cor. x.

14. Gal. v. 20. 1 Pet. iv. 3 only †. (-τρης, Eph. v. 5.) e John iii. 36. Rom. i. 18. Eph. v. 6. Rev. xix. 15. Ps. lxxvii. 36. f = Rom. vi. 4. 2 Cor. iv. 2. Eph. ii. 2, 10. v. 2. ch. iv. 5 al. freq. Eccl. xi. 9. g = Rom. vi. 2. ch. ii. 20 (of things). h Eph. iv. 22 reff. i Eph. iv. 31. j Eph. as above (i). Rom. ii. 8. k Eph. as above (i). Rom. i. 29. Tit. iii. 3. l Matt. xii. 31. 1 Tim. vi. 4 al. ˉEzek. xxxv. 12. m here only †. n w. εἰς, here only. Susan. 55 only. w. dat., Acts v. 4.

6. rec for ὅ, ἅ (see *Eph* v. 6), with ABC²D²·³KL[P]ℵ rel vulg(with F-lat) syrr coptt goth [arm] Clem₂ Iren-int Cypr: *quod aut quæ* G-lat: txt C¹(appy) D¹F æth. om ἣ C¹F. rec aft θεου ins επι τους υιους της απειθειας *from Eph* v. 6, *where none omit it*), with AC(D)FKL[P]ℵ rel Clem₁(mss vary): om B (D has it written, contrary to its custom, at the end of the line which should finish with θεου) sah æth[-rom] Clem₁ or ₂ Iren-int Ambrst-txt.

7. [om ποτε P.] rec (for τουτοις) αυτοις, with D³ F[αυτους] KL rel syrr Chr Thdrt: *illis* latt: txt ABCD¹[P]ℵ 17 [47] coptt goth.

8. om και υμεις ℵ¹(ins ℵ-corr¹) [sah]. for τα π., κατα παντα F: *universum aut secundum omnia* G-lat: *omnem* spec Jer Vig: om æth (Clem). at end ins μη εκπορευεσθω F [coptt goth] æth Vig Ambrst.

generally as in Plato, Phædr. p. 265 b, τὸ ἐρωτικὸν πάθος, — 'morbum libidinis,' Beng.), shameful desire (more general than πάθος: as Mey. remarks, π. is always ἐπιθ., but not vice versa. The relation is the same as between πορνεία and ἀκαθαρσία), and covetousness (τὴν πλ. as Beng.—'articulus facit ad epitasin, et totum genus vitii a genere enumeratarum modo specierum diversum complectitur.' On πλεονεξία, see on Eph. iv. 19, and Trench, N. T. Synonyms, § xxiv.), for it is ('quippe quæ sit') idolatry (the πλεονέκτης has set up self in his heart —and to serve self, whether by accumulation of goods or by satiety in pleasure, is his object in life. He is therefore an idolater, in the deepest and worst, namely in the practical significance. τὸ μαμωνᾶ, κύριον ὁ Σωτὴρ προσηγόρευσε, διδάσκων ὡς ὁ τῷ πάθει τῆς πλεονεξίας δουλεύων, ὡς θεὸν τὸν πλοῦτον τιμᾷ, Thdrt.), on which account (on account of the πλεονεξία, which amounts to idolatry, the all-comprehending and crowning sin, which is a negation of God and brings down His especial anger) cometh (down on earth, in present and visible examples) the wrath of God: in which (vices. Mey.'s remark that the reading δι᾽ ὅ makes this ἐν οἷς necessarily refer to the ἐπὶ τοὺς υἱοὺς τ. ἀπειθ. which he reads after θεοῦ, does not apply if δι᾽ ὅ be interpreted as above to refer to πλεονεξία. There does not seem to occur in St. Paul any instance of ἐν, after περιπατεῖν absolute, referring to persons. Cf. 2 Thess. iii. 11 (περιπ. ἀτάκτως), John xi. 54, Eph. ii. 3, which last, if the clause ἐπ. τ. υἱ. τ. ἀπ. were inserted here,

would certainly go far to decide the matter) ye also walked once, when ye lived (before your death with Christ to the world) in these things (the assertion is not tautological: cf. Gal. v. 25, εἰ ζῶμεν πνεύματι, πνεύματι καὶ στοιχῶμεν. When ye were alive to these things, ye regulated your course by them, walked in them. "Vivere et ambulare inter se differunt, quemadmodum potentia et actus: vivere præcedit, ambulare sequitur." Calv.): 8.] but now (that ye are no longer *living* in them: opposed to ποτὲ ὅτε above) do ye also (as well as other believers) put away the whole (τὰ πάντα seems to have a backward and a forward reference—'the whole,—both those things which I have enumerated, and those which are to follow.' The mistake of rendering ἀπόθεσθε, '*have put off*,' which one would hardly look for in a Commentator, occurs in Eadie here—cf. Eph. iv. 22),—anger, wrath (see on Eph. iv. 31), malice (ib.), evil speaking (ib.), abusive conversation (the context makes this more probable here, than '*filthy conversation*' (so E. V.; Clem. Alex., περὶ αἰσχρολογίας, Pæd. ii. 6, p. 198 P.; he however himself uses αἰσχρολογεῖν for to abuse in words, Pæd. iii. 11, p. 296 P.: Chrys., who calls it ὄχημα πορνείας), for these four regard want of charity, of kindness in thought and word, rather than sins of uncleanness, which were before enumerated. And the occasional usage of the word itself bears this out, cf. Plato, Rep. iii. p. 395 end, κακηγοροῦντάς τε καὶ κωμῳδοῦντας ἀλλήλους κ. αἰσχρολογοῦντας: Polyb. viii. 13. 8, ἡ κατὰ τῶν φίλων αἰσ-

o ch. ii. 15
only †.
(-δυσις,
ch. ii. 11.)
p Rom. vi. 6.
Eph. iv. 22.
q = Matt. xvi.
27. Luke
xxiii. 51.
Rom. viii. 13.
2 Chron. xii.
15.
r = Eph. iv. 24
reff.
s = 1 Cor. v. 7.

εἰς ἀλλήλους, °ἀπεκδυσάμενοι τὸν ᵖπαλαιὸν ᵖἄνθρωπον ABCDF
σὺν ταῖς �q πράξεσιν αὐτοῦ, 10 καὶ ʳἐνδυσάμενοι τὸν ˢνέον
τὸν ᵗἀνακαινούμενον εἰς ᵘἐπίγνωσιν ᵛκατ᾽ ʷεἰκόνα τοῦ
ˣκτίσαντος αὐτόν, 11 ὅπου οὐκ ʸἔνι ″Ελλην καὶ ᾽Ιουδαῖος,
ᶻπεριτομὴ καὶ ᶻἀκροβυστία, ᵃΒάρβαρος, Σκύθης, ᵇδοῦ-
λος, ᵇἐλεύθερος, ἀλλὰ τὰ ᶜπάντα καὶ ᶜἐν πᾶσιν χριστός.

KLPℵ a
b c d e f
g h k l m
no 17. 47

t 2 Cor. iv. 16 only †.   (-νωσις, Tit. iii. 5.   -νίζειν, Ps. cii. 5.)   u = Eph. i. 17 reff   v Gal. iv. 28 reff.
w ch. i. 15 reff.   x Eph. ii. 10 reff.   y Gal. iii. 28 reff.   z Gal. v. 6 reff.   a Acts
xxviii. 2, 4.   Rom. i. 4.   1 Cor. xiv. 11 bis only.   Ezek. xxi. 31.   b Eph. vi. 8 al.   c = 1 Cor.
(xii. 6) xv. 28. see Herod. iii. 157.   Polyb. v. 26. 5.

[9. αποδυσαμενοι P.]   10. επενδυσαμενοι ℵ¹.
11. aft ενι add αρσεν και θηλυ (see Gal iii. 28) D¹F vulg-sixt(with hal F-lat) lat-ff.
aft βαρβαρος ins και D¹F latt Syr [goth] æth Petr Jer lat-ff.   aft δουλος ins
και AD¹F latt lat-ff: om BCD³KL[P]ℵ rel syr Clem.   om τα ACℵ¹ 17 Clem Petr
Naz Cyr Œc-txt · ins BDFKL[P]ℵ³ rel Chr Thdrt Damasc.

χρολογία) out of your mouth (these words
most naturally belong to the two last
specified sins, and must be constructed
either with ἀπόθεσθε, which seems best,
or with 'proceeding,' implied in αἰσχρολογίαν),—lie not towards (εἰς the indifferent general preposition of direction:
so κατά with ψεύδομαι in a hostile sense,
James iii. 14. Plato, Euthyd. p. 284 a,
οὐδὲν κατά σου ψεύδεται. We have πρὸς
ἐκεῖνον ψευσάμενοι, Xen. Anab. i. 3. 5)
one another,—having put off (the participles contain the motive for all the preceding, from ἀπόθεσθε—so Thdrt. (τοῦτον
ἀπεκδύσασθε ἐν τῷ βαπτίσματι), Calv.
(postquam exuistis), Mey., al. Vulg.
(exuentes), Luth., Calov., Beng., Olsh.,
De W., Conyb., al., understand them as
contemporary with ἀπόθεσθε, — putting
off.—or, and put off. But surely this is
very flat, and besides would, if it is to
answer to the foregoing, contain a superfluous member, the ἐνδυσάμ. κ.τ.λ. there
being no exhortation to graces in the
former sentence, only dehortation from
vices. Besides, as Mey. remarks, the objective description in ver. 11 belongs to
an assignment of motive, not to a hortative sentence: and the hortative figure
begins ver. 12) the old man (i. e. as Mey.,
'die vorchriftliche Individualität;' the nature which they had before their conversion: see on reff.) with his deeds (habits,
ways of acting: see reff., and cf. Demosth.
126. 21, ἔπραττον ὅπως ἡ πόλις ληφθήσε-
ται, καὶ κατεσκευάζοντο τὴν πρᾶξιν), and
having put on the new (the other was the
negative ground: this is the positive. See
on Eph. iv. 23, and ii. 15), who (the two
are personal: not 'which,'—except in its
old personal sense) is continually being
renewed (notice the present participle.
"The new man is not any thing ready at
once and complete, but ever in a state of

development (by the Holy Spirit, Tit.
iii. 5), by which a new state and nature is
brought about in it, specifically different
from that of the old man." Mey.) towards
perfect knowledge (which excludes all
falsehood, and indeed all the vices mentioned above) according to the image of
Him that created him (the new creation
of the spirit unto fulness of knowledge
and truth, the highest form of which
would be the perfect knowledge of God,
is regarded by the Apostle as analogous to
man's first creation. As he was then
made in the image of God, so now: but it
was then his naturally, now spiritually in
ἐπίγνωσις. Some join κατ᾽ εἰκ. with ἀνακαιν., some with ἐπίγνωσ. The sense
will be the same; but grammatically it is
far better to join it with ἀνακαιν. Thus
the norm and method of the renewal is,
κατ᾽ εἰκ. τ. κτίσαντος αὐτόν (the new
man),—i. e. God, who is ever the Creator, not as Chrys., al., Christ. To understand the whole passage as referring to
a restoration of the image of God in the
first creation, as Calov., Est., and De W.,
is to fall far short of the glorious truth.
It is not to restore the old, but to create
the new, that redemption has been brought
about. Whatever may have been God's
image in which the first Adam was
created, it is certain that the image of
God, in which Christ's Spirit re-creates
us, will be as much more glorious than
that, as the second man is more glorious
than the first): where (viz. in the realm
or sphere of the new man) there is not
(on ἔνι see Gal. iii. 28) Greek and Jew
(difference of nation; with special allusion
also to the antiquation of the Abrahamic
privilege as regarded his natural seed),
circumcision and uncircumcision (difference of legal ceremonial standing),—bar-
barian (having as yet specified by pairs,

12 [r] Ἐνδύσασθε οὖν, ὡς [d] ἐκλεκτοὶ τοῦ [d] θεοῦ ἅγιοι καὶ
ἠγαπημένοι, [e] σπλάγχνα [f] οἰκτιρμοῦ, [g] χρηστότητα, [h] ταπεινοφροσύνην, [gh] πραΰτητα, [gh] μακροθυμίαν, 13 [i] ἀνεχόμενοι
ἀλλήλων καὶ [kl] χαριζόμενοι [lm] ἑαυτοῖς ἐάν τις [n] πρός τινα
ἔχῃ [o] μομφήν· καθὼς καὶ ὁ κύριος [k] ἐχαρίσατο ὑμῖν, [i]
οὕτως καὶ ὑμεῖς· 14 [p] ἐπὶ πᾶσιν δὲ τούτοις τὴν ἀγάπην,

d Rom. viii. 33.
Tit. i. 1. gen,
Rom. i 6, 7.
e = Phil. i. 8
reff.
f Phil. ii. 1 reff.
g Gal. v. 22, 23
reff.
h Eph. iv. 2
reff.
i = Luke ix.
41. 2 Cor.
xi. 1, &c.
Eph. iv. 2.
Isa. xlvi. 4.

k = ch. ii. 13 reff.   l Eph. iv. 32.   m = 1 Cor. vi. 7. ver. 16 al.   n = Acts xxiv. 19. xxv.
19   1 Cor. vi. 1.   o here only†.   p Luke iii. 20. xvi. 26. 2 Chron. xxix. 10.

12. ωσει D¹F.   om του (bef θεου) AD¹F c : ins BCD³KL[P]ℵ rel.   om και
B 17 lect-17 sah Did : ins ACDFKL[P]ℵ rel.   rec οικτιρμων, with K b c [Clem₁]
Orig-ms Thdrt : και οικτιρμον D¹ [Syr arm] : txt ABCD²·³FL[P]ℵ rel Clem Orig Bas
Chr Damasc.   rec πραοτητα, with DFKL rel : txt ABC[P]ℵ 17 Antch Max.
13. εχει FL[P] c f k 17 Thl.   for μομφην, μεμψιν D¹ : οργην F.   rec (for
κυριος) χριστος (*the practice of interpreting the indefinite* κυριος *was so common, that*
χριστος *was far more probably substd, esp as it occurs in Eph* iv. 32), with CD²·³
KL[P]ℵ-corr¹(?)³ rel syrr coptt goth [æth] Clem₂ Chr Thdrt Damasc Ambrst : θεος ℵ¹
17, simly arm Aug₁ : txt ABD¹ F[omg ὁ] latt Aug₁ Pel.   ημιν D¹K a k n 17 Clem
Thdrt (so ℵ³, but corrd).   at end ins ποιειτε D¹F sah [goth] æth Ambrst.

he now brings forward a few single categories, which in the new man were non-
existent as marks of distinction ; see below.
The proper *contrast* to Βάρβαρος would
have been Ἕλλην, which has been already
expressed), **Scythian** (the citations in
Wetst. sufficiently shew, that the Σκύθαι
were esteemed, as Beng., 'barbaris bar-
bariores.' It is remarkable that in one
of those citations, from Polyb., they are
classed with the *Galatians ;* εἰρήνης οὔσης
παρεσπόνδησαν, Σκυθῶν ἔργον κ. Γαλατῶν ἐπιτελοῦντες), **bond, free** (he perhaps
does not say '*bond and free,*' because
these relations actually subsisted : but the
persons in them were not thus regarded
in Christ—no man is, *quoad a Christian,*
δοῦλος, nor (see also Gal. iii. 28) ἐλεύθερος) : but CHRIST (emphatically closes
the sentence) **is all** (every distinctive
category of humanity is done away as
to worth or privilege, and all have been
absorbed into and centre in this one,
χριστοῦ εἶναι, yea χριστὸς εἶναι—His
members, in vital union with Him) **and in
all** (equally sprinkled on, living in, working through and by every class of mankind).   **12.**] **Put on therefore** (as a
consequence of having put on the new
man, to whom these belong) **as the
elect of God** (see reff. and 1 Thess. i. 4),
holy and beloved (it seems best to take,
as Mey., ἐκλεκτοί for the subject, and ἅγ.
and ἠγ. for predicates,—1) because ἐκλεκτοί is a word which must find its ground
independently of us, in the absolute will
of God, and therefore cannot be an adjunctive attribute of ἅγιοι (καὶ) ἠγαπ.—and 2)
because ἐκλεκτοὶ θεοῦ is used in reff. and
ἐκλεκτοί in several other places, as a

substantive), **bowels of compassion** (see
reff., and Luke i. 78. The expression is
a Hebraism : and the account of it to be
found in the literal use of σπλάγχνα as
the seat of the sympathetic feelings : cf.
Gen. xliii. 30), **kindness** (see on Gal. v. 22),
lowliness (towards one another—see on
Eph. iv. 2), **meekness** (Eph. ib. : but here
it is primarily *towards one another ;* not
however excluding but rather implying
meekness towards God as its ground),
long-suffering (ib.), **forbearing one another** (see ib.) **and forgiving each other**
(ἑαυτοῖς is not = ἀλλήλοις, as De W., al. :
but the mutual forgiveness of the Christian
body is put in marked correspondence to
that great act of forgiveness which has
passed upon the whole body, in Christ.
'Forgiving yourselves,' did it not convey
to our ears a wrong idea, would be the
best rendering : doing as a body for yourselves, that which God did once for you
all), **if any have cause of blame** (the
phrase is a classical one—cf. Eur. Orest.
1068, ἐν μὲν πρῶτά σοι μομφὴν ἔχω—
Phœn. 781 ; Soph. Aj. 180, and other examples in Wetst.) : **as also** (καί ; besides,
and more eminent than, the examples
which I am exhorting you to shew of this
grace) **the Lord** (Christ : in Eph. iv. 32,
the forgiveness is traced to its source, ὁ
θεὸς ἐν χριστῷ. Mey. compares the expression ἡ χάρις τοῦ κυρίου ἡμῶν) **forgave**
(see on Eph. iv. 32) **you, so also ye** (scil.
χαριζόμενοι—do not supply an imperative,
by which the construction is unnecesarily
broken. Chrys. carries this χαρίζεσθαι
to an exaggerated extent, when he says
that it extends not only to τὴν ψυχὴν
ὑπὲρ αὐτῶν θεῖναι—τὸ γὰρ 'καθὼς' ταῦτα

q constr., Mark
xii. 42. xv. 42.
Eph. v. 5.
r ch. ii. 19 reff.
s Heb. vi. 1
only. Judg.
ix. 16, 19.
t = John xiv.
27. Phil. iv. 7.
6 reff.

^q ὅ ἐστιν ^r σύνδεσμος τῆς ^s τελειότητος· ¹⁵ καὶ ἡ ^t εἰρήνη ABCDF KLPℵ a
τοῦ χριστοῦ ^u βραβευέτω ἐν ταῖς καρδίαις ὑμῶν, εἰς ἣν b c d e f g h k l m
καὶ ^v ἐκλήθητε ^w ἐν ἑνὶ σώματι· καὶ ^x εὐχάριστοι γίνεσθε. n o 17.47

u here only. Wisd. x. 12. = Polyb. ii. 25. 3 al. fr. (-ειον, Phil. iii. 14.)   v = Gal. i.
w = 1 Cor. vii. 15. Eph. ii. 16.   x here only. Prov. xi. 16 only. = Xen. Cyr. viii. 3. 49.

14. rec (for ὅ) ητις (*grammatical emendation*), with D³KLℵ³ rel : txt ABCF[P]
17(sic) latt Clem₂ Ambrst, os D¹ℵ¹.   for τελει., ενοτητος D¹F Ambrst.

15. om ἡ F [47¹].   rec (for χριστου) θεου (*cf Phil* iv. 7), with C²D³KLℵ³ rel
goth Chr Ambrst : txt ABC¹D¹F[P]ℵ¹ m 17 [47] latt syrr coptt æth arm Clem₂
Damasc Aug Pel.   om ενι B 67² sah (om εν ενι σ. 33-5).   γενεσθε D¹.

ἀπαιτεῖ—καὶ οὐδὲ μέχρι θανάτου μόνον στῆναι δεῖ, ἀλλ᾽ εἰ δυνατὸν καὶ μετὰ ταῦτα ; thinking perhaps on Rom. ix. 3) :

14.] but (the contrast lies between ταῦτα πάντα, which have been individually mentioned, and ἐπὶ πᾶσι τούτοις, that which must over-lie them as a whole) **over** (carrying on the image ἐνδύσασθε—see below. Calvin's '*propter* omnia hæc' is every way wrong :—'in addition to,' as Eadie, al., falls short of the fitness and beauty of the passage, weakening what is really the literal sense into a metaphorical one. The E. V., '*above all these things*,' looks ambiguous, but by repeating '*put on*,' it seems as if our translators meant '*above*' to be taken locally and literally) **all these things** (put on) **love** (the article gives a fine and delicate sense here, which we cannot express—ἡ ἀγάπη is not merely love, but 'the (well-known) love which becomes Christians :' the nearest rendering would perhaps be '*Christian love*,' but it expresses too much), **which thing** (reff. : there is a slight causal force,—'for it is') **is the bond of perfectness** (the idea of an upper garment, or perhaps of a girdle, as Calov. supposed, seems to have been before the Apostle's mind. This completes and keeps together all the rest, which, without it, are but the scattered elements of completeness : πάντα ἐκεῖνά, φησιν, αὕτη συσφίγγει παροῦσα· ἀπούσης δὲ διαλύονται κ. ἐλέγχονται ὑπόκρισις ὄντα κ. οὐδέν, Thl. Wetst. cites from Simplic. in Epictet., p. 208, καλῶς οἱ Πυθαγόρειοι περισσῶς τῶν ἄλλων ἀρετῶν τὴν φιλίαν ἐτίμων, κ. σύνδεσμον αὐτὴν πασῶν τῶν ἀρετῶν ἔλεγον. The genitive after σύνδεσμος is not the genitive of apposition, as in Eph. iv. 3, but of that which is held together by the σύνδεσμος, as in Plato, Rep. x. p. 616 c, εἶναι γὰρ τοῦτο τὸ φῶς ξύνδεσμον τοῦ οὐρανοῦ, οἷον τὰ ὑποζώματα τῶν τριήρων, οὕτω πᾶσαν ξυνέχον τὴν περιφοράν. Those who, as some of the Roman Catholic expositors (not Bisping), find here justification by works, must be very hard put to discover support for that doctrine. The

whole passage proceeds upon the ground of previous justification by faith : see ch. ii. 12, and our ver. 12, ὡς ἐκλ. τ. θ. Some render σύνδεσμος 'the sum total,' or inclusive idea, '𝔍nbegriff :' so Bengel, Usteri, De W., Olsh., al. : and it appears to bear this sense in Herodian iv. 12. 11, πάντα τὸν σύνδεσμον τῶν ἐπιστολῶν,—but not in the N. T. ; and besides, the sense would be logically inconsistent with ἐπὶ πᾶσιν τούτοις, implying that Love does not include, but covers and supplements all the former. Still worse is the wretched adjectival rendering of τῆς τελ. as = τέλειος, 'the perfect band,' as Grot., Erasm.-par., Est., al.) : **and** (simply an additional exhortation, not an inference, 'and so,' as Beng. ; compare Eph. iv. 3, where peace *is* the σύνδεσμος. It is exceedingly interesting to observe the same word occurring in the same trains of thought in the two Epistles, but frequently with different application. See the Prolegg. to this Epistle, §. iv. 7) **let Christ's peace** (the peace which He brings about, which He left as his legacy to us (ref. John), which is emphatically and solely His. This peace, though its immediate and lower reference here is to mutual concord, yet must not on account of the context be limited to that lower side. Its reference is evidently wider, as βραβευέτω shews : see below. It is the whole of Christ's Peace in all its blessed character and effects) **rule** (sit umpire—be enthroned as decider of every thing. Cf. Demosth. 3. 6, 7, ἐξὸν ἡμῖν κ. τὰ ἡμέτερ᾽ αὐτῶν ἀσφαλῶς ἔχειν κ. τὰ τῶν ἄλλων δίκαια βραβεύειν. ib. 1231. 19, τοῦτον τὸν τρόπον ὑμῶν ταῦτα βραβευόντων : and in the later sense of simply to *rule*, Polyb. ii. 25. 3, ἅπαν τὸ γιγνόμενον ὑπὸ τῶν Γαλατῶν θυμῷ μᾶλλον ἢ λογισμῷ βραβεύεται, al., in Schweigh. Lex. Polyb., also in Jos. and Philo. It is forcing the passage, to introduce the idea of a combat and a prize, as Chrys., &c. : and philologically wrong to render, as Calv., '*palmam ferat*,' explaining it '*superior sit omnibus carnis affectibus*.' As much beside the purpose is

16 ὁ ʸλόγος τοῦ χριστοῦ ᶻἐνοικείτω ἐν ὑμῖν ªπλουσίως, ʸ = 1 Cor. i. 5.
ᵇἐν πάσῃ σοφίᾳ ᶜδιδάσκοντες καὶ ᵈνουθετοῦντες ᵉἑαυτοὺς
P. ᵘμνοις ᶠψαλμοῖς ᶠὕμνοις ᶠᾠδαῖς ᵍπνευματικαῖς, ʰ ἐν ʰ τῇ ʰⁱχάριτι

z Rom. viii. 11.
2 Cor. vi. 16.
2 Tim. i. 5,
14 only. Lev.
xxvi. 32.
a 1 Tim. vi.

17. Tit. iii. 6.   2 Pet. i. 11 only †.   b Eph. i. 8. ch. i. 9, 28.   c constr., ch. ii. 2 reff.   d ch. i.
28 reff. P.   e = ver. 13.   f Eph. v. 19 reff.   g Rom. i. 11 [Eph., as above] al20. Paul
only, exc. 1 Pet. ii. 5 bis †.   h ch. iv. 6.   i absol., = Acts xviii. 27.   2 Cor. iv. 15. Gal. v. 4. Eph.
iv. 7. ch. iv. 18 (reff.).

16. for χριστου, θεου AC¹ k o 17 sah Thdrt Thl-marg: κυριου (*from above*) ℵ¹ copt
Clem: txt BC²DFKL[P]ℵ³ rel latt syr goth gr-lat-ff.   rec aft ψαλμοις ins και
(*cf Eph* v. 19), with C²D²·³KL[P] rel demid Syr coptt [æth arm] : om ABC¹D¹Fℵ
latt syr goth Clem Chr₂ Pel.   rec aft υμνοις ins και (*cf Eph* v. 19), with AC³D²·³KL
rel vulg-ed(with fuld-vict) Syr copt [æth arm] Chr : om BC¹D¹Fℵ 17 am(with demid
tol) syr goth Clem.   rec om τη (bef χαριτι), with A(C)D³KLℵ¹ Chr Damasc : ins
BD¹Fℵ³ 672 Clem Chr-comm₂ Thdrt. (In C τι of χαριτι is left out and εν χαρι
marked as wrong.)

Grot.'s 'dijudicet, nempe si quid est inter
nos controversum:' similarly Kypke and
Hammond ('componat omnia vestra cum
aliis dissidia') : against this is ἐν ταῖς καρδίαις ὑμῶν, which makes the office of the
peace spoken of not *adjudicare*, but *præ-
venire lites*) **in your hearts,—to which**
(with a view to which, as your blessed
state of Christian perfection in God—
see Isa. xxvi. 3; lvii. 19: Eph. ii. 14—
17) ye were also (the καί marks the introduction of an additional motive—' to
which, besides my exhortation, ye have
this motive: that,' &c.) **called** (reff.) **in
one body** (as members of one body—oneness of body being the sphere and element
in which that peace of Christ was to be
carried on and realized. This reminiscence
refers to the whole context from ver. 8,
in which the exhortations had been to
mutual Christian graces. διὰ τί γὰρ ἄλλο
ἐσμὲν ἐν σῶμα, ἢ ἵνα ὡς μέλη ὄντες ἀλλήλων ταύτην τηρῶμεν, κ. μὴ διϊστώμεθα:
Thl.): **and be thankful** (to God, who called
you: so the context before and after certainly demands: not ' one to another,' as
Conyb., which though an allowable sense
of εὐχάριστος, breaks the connexion here,
which is as Chrys. on ver. 16—παραινέσας
εὐχαρίστους εἶναι, καὶ τὴν ὁδὸν δείκνυσι.
The ἐκλήθητε was the word which introduced the exhortation—all conduct inconsistent with the ' *calling in one body'* being
in fact unthankfulness to God, who called
us. Jer., Erasm.-not., Calv., al., render it
' *amiable,*' ' *friendly,*' against which the
same objection lies. See Eph. v. 4; and ib.
19, 20: where the same class of exhortations occurs).   **16.**] See the connexion
in Chrys. above. This thankfulness to God
will shew itself in the rich indwelling in
you and outflowing from you of the word
of Christ, be it in mutual edifying converse, or in actual songs of praise. **Let
Christ's word** (the Gospel: genitive subjective; the word which is His—He spoke
it, inspired it, and gives it power) **dwell**

in you (not 'among you,' as Luther, De
W., al.: which does not suit ἐνοικ. As
Ellic. observes, St. Paul's usage (reff.,
remembering that ref. 2 Cor. is a quotation) seems to require that the indwelling
should be individual and personal. Still
we may say with Mey. that the ὑμεῖς
need not be *restricted* to individual Christians: it may well mean the whole community—you, as a church. The word
dwelling in them richly, many would arise
to speak it to edification, and many would
be moved to the utterance of praise.
And to this collective sense of ὑμῖν, ἑαυτοὺς below seems to correspond ; see above
on ver. 13) **richly** (i. e. in abundance and
fulness, so as to lead to the following results), **in all wisdom** (these words seem
to be better taken with the following
than with the foregoing. For 1) ch. i.
28 already gives us νουθ. . . κ. διδ. . . ἐν
πάσῃ σοφίᾳ. 2) ἐνοικείτω has already its
qualifying adverb πλουσίως emphatically
placed at the end of the sentence. 3)
The two following clauses will thus correspond—ἐν πάσῃ σοφίᾳ διδάσκοντες . . .
ἐν τῇ χάριτι ᾄδοντες. And so Beng.,
Olsh., De W., Mey., al.: the usual arrangement has been with E. V., all. (not
Chrys.), to join them with the preceding)
teaching and warning (see on ch. i. 28)
each other (see on ver. 13) **in psalms,** *
hymns, spiritual songs (on the meaning
of the words, see notes, Eph. v. 19. The
arrangement here adopted may be thus
vindicated: ψ. ὕμν. ᾠδ. πν. must be
joined with the preceding, not with the
following, because 1) the instrumental
dative is much more naturally taken after
διδ. κ. νουθ. ἑαυτ., from the analogy of
Eph. v. 19, λαλοῦντες ἑαυτοῖς ψ. κ. ὕμν.
κ. ᾠδ. [πν.], ᾄδοντες κ.τ.λ. 2) ᾄδοντες
here has already two qualifying clauses,
one before and one after, ἐν τῇ χάριτι and
ἐν ταῖς καρδίαις ὑμῶν. Meyer's note here
is important: 'Notice moreover that Paul
here also (see on Eph. ut supra) is not

j Matt. vii. 24.
x. 32. Acts
iii. 23.
k Rom. xv. 18.
2 Cor. x. 11.
1 John iii. 18.
l = John xiv.
13.—ellips., 2
Cor. viii. 15,
from Exod.
xvi. 18. Winer, § 64. 4.
3. Eph. vi. 23.

f ἄδοντες ἐν ταῖς f καρδίαις ὑμῶν τῷ θεῷ· 17 καὶ j πᾶν j ὅ
τι ἂν ποιῆτε ἐν k λόγῳ ἢ ἐν k ἔργῳ, πάντα l ἐν ὀνόματι
κυρίου Ἰησοῦ m εὐχαριστοῦντες τῷ mn θεῷ n πατρὶ δι'
αὐτοῦ.

ABCDF
KLℵ a b
c d e f g
h k l m n
o 17. 47

m Rom. i. 8. xiv. 6 bis. Eph. v. 20 al. fr. (Judith viii. 25.) n Gal. i.

rec (for ταις καρδιαις) τη καρδια (*from Eph* v. 19), with D³KL rel [æth] Clem Thdrt Damasc Thl Œc: txt ABCD¹Fℵ b¹ (m) 67² vss Chr lat-ff. rec (for θεω) κυριω (*from Eph* v. 19), with D³KL rel demid [copt goth] Thdrt Ambrst-ms Pel : χω or κω C² : txt ABC¹D¹Fℵ 17 [47] 67² [vulg syrr sah arm] Clem Chr_aliq Œc Ambrst-ed Paulin. 17. om και D¹F latt goth lat-ff. εαν BFL o: om sah : txt ACDKℵ rel. ποιειτε K²L sah. for κυρ. ιησ., ιησ. χριστου ACD¹F : κυριου L : κυρ.(του κ. ℵ³) ιησ. χρ. ℵ¹ [vulg Syr]: txt BD³K rel am syr goth [arm Clem] Thdrt Damasc Ambrst. (*In the probability of the alteration of our whole passage from Eph* v. 19, 20 (*where there are hardly any varns*), *txt is most likely to have been original.*) rec ins και bef πατρι: (*Eph* v. 20), with DFKL rel latt syr [arm] (Clem): txt ABCℵ Syr coptt goth æth Ambr Paulin.

speaking of 'divine service' properly so called, for this teaching and admonishing is required of his *readers generally* and mutually, and as a proof of their *rich* possession of the word of Christ :—but of the communication of the religious life among one another (e. g. at meals, at the Agapæ, and other meetings, in their family circles, &c.), wherein spiritual influence caused the mouth to overflow with the fulness of the heart, and gave utterance to brotherly instruction and reproof in the higher form of psalms, &c. ; perhaps in songs already known,—or extemporized, according to the peculiarity and productivity of each man's spiritual gift : perhaps sung by individuals alone (which would especially be the case when they were extemporized), or in chorus, or in the form of antiphonal song (Plin. Ep. x. 97)." How common religious singing was in the ancient church, independently of 'divine service' properly so called, see in Suicer, Thes. ii. p. 1568 f. Euseb., H. E. ii. 17, v. 28, testifies to the existence of a collection of rhythmical songs which were composed ἀπαρχῆς by Christians (ψαλμοὶ δὲ ὅσοι κ. ᾠδαί, ἀδελφῶν ἀπαρχῆς ὑπὸ πιστῶν γραφεῖσαι, τὸν λόγον τοῦ θεοῦ τὸν χριστὸν ὑμνοῦσι θεολογοῦντες, v. 28). On singing at the Agapæ, see Tert. Apol. 39, vol. i. p. 477 : "post aquam manualem et lumina, ut quisque de scripturis sanctis vel proprio ingenio potest, provocatur in medium Deo canere"); in grace (*the* grace—of Christ (see reff. for the absolute use of ἡ χάρις)—ἀπὸ τῆς χάριτος τοῦ πνεύματός φησιν ᾄδοντες, Chrys.: so Œc., διὰ τῆς παρὰ τοῦ ἁγίου πνεύματος δοθείσης χάριτος: not as Erasm., Luth., Melancth., Calv. ('pro dexteritate quæ grata sit'), and indeed Chrys. (altern.: ταῖς ἐν χάριτι ᾠδαῖς), Beza, Corn.-a-lap.,

al., '*gracefully*,'—which would be irrelevant as applied to the singing of the heart : see below—nor as Anselm, and De W., Conyb., al., '*thankfully*,' which would be a flat and unmeaning anticipation of εὐχαριστοῦντες below. The article marks 'the grace,' which is yours by God's indwelling Spirit) **singing in your hearts to God** (this clause has generally been understood as qualifying the former. But such a view is manifestly wrong. That former spoke of their teaching and warning one another in effusions of the spirit which took the form of psalms, &c. : in other words, dealt with their intercourse *with one another ;* this on the other hand deals with their own private intercourse *with God.* The second participle is coordinate with the former, not subordinate to it. The mistake has partly arisen from imagining that the former clause related to public worship, in its external form : and then this one was understood to enforce the genuine heartfelt expression of the same. But this not being so, that which is founded on it falls with it. The singing τῷ θεῷ is an analogous expression to that in 1 Cor. xiv. 28,—ἐὰν δὲ μὴ ᾖ διερμηνευτής, ... ἑαυτῷ ... λαλείτω κ. τῷ θεῷ. So the ἐν ταῖς καρδ. ὑμ. describes the method of uttering this praise, viz. by the thoughts only : τῷ θεῷ designates to whom it is to be addressed,—not, as before, to one another, but to God) :

17.] *general exhortation,* comprehending all the preceding spiritual ones. **And every thing whatsoever ye do in word or work** (so far is a 'nominativus pendens') **all things (do) in the name of the Lord Jesus** (not as Chrys., Œc., Thl., &c., τουτέστιν αὐτὸν καλῶν βοηθόν, nor as Thdrt., who treats it as a dehortation from the worship of angels, which they

18 Αἱ γυναῖκες, [o] ὑποτάσσεσθε τοῖς ἀνδράσιν, ὡς [p] ἀνῆκεν
[q] ἐν κυρίῳ. 19 οἱ ἄνδρες, ἀγαπᾶτε τὰς γυναῖκας καὶ μὴ
[r] πικραίνεσθε πρὸς αὐτάς. 20 τὰ τέκνα, [s] ὑπακούετε τοῖς
γονεῦσιν κατὰ πάντα· τοῦτο γὰρ [t] εὐάρεστόν ἐστιν [q] ἐν
κυρίῳ. 21 οἱ πατέρες, μὴ [u] ἐρεθίζετε τὰ τέκνα ὑμῶν, ἵνα

o Eph. i. 22 reff.
p Eph. v. 4. Philem. 8 only +. 1 Macc. xi. 35 al.
q Eph. iv. 17. 1 Thess. iv. 1 al. fr. Paul only.
r Rev. viii. 11. x. 9, 10 only. = Exod. xvi. 20. Job xxvii. 2 Bℵ.
s Matt. viii. 27. Eph. vi. 1 al.
t Eph. v. 10 reff.
u 2 Cor. ix. 2 only. Deut. xxi. 20 Prov. xix. 7.

18. om αι F. rec ins ιδιοις bef ανδρασιν (*from Eph* v. 22), with D²L rel Thdrt: om ABCD¹·³FKℵ c d¹ e k 17 [47] vulg arm Clem Thl Ambrst Pel. aft ανδρ. ins υμων D¹F syr-w-ast [copt goth æth arm] Thl Pel. ins τω bef κυριω F.

19. aft γυναικας ins υμων C²D¹F latt Syr syr-w-ob copt [goth] æth arm lat-ff: pref εαυτων ℵ³: om ABC¹D³KLℵ¹ rel Clem. παραπικραιν. C²K 113-4 Thl-marg.

20. rec εστιν bef ευαρεστον (*after Eph* vi. 1), with FKL rel Chr Thdrt Damasc: txt ABCDℵ m 17 [47] latt. rec (for εν) τω, with rel spec syr copt [æth] Clem: txt ABCDFKLℵ b e f g l m n 17 [47] 67² latt [syr(sic, Treg)] goth Chr Thdrt Damasc.

21. for ερεθιζετε, παροργιζετε (*from Eph* vi. 4) ACD¹FLℵ m 17 [47. syr-mg] Thdrt-ms Thl: txt BD²·³K rel Clem.

were to exclude by their always τὰ ἔργα κοσμῆσαι τῇ μνήμῃ τοῦ δεσπότου χριστοῦ:—but much as the common ἐν χριστῷ—so that the name of Christ is the element in which all is done—which furnishes a motive and gives a character to the whole) **giving thanks to God the Father** (where ἡμῶν is not expressed, the words **θεὸς πατήρ** must be taken as approximating in sense to that more technical meaning which they now bear, without exclusive reference to either our Lord or ourselves,—and should be rendered '*God the Father*') **through Him** (as the one channel of all communication between God and ourselves, whether of grace coming to us, or of thanks coming from us. Cf. His own saying, οὐδεὶς ἔρχεται πρὸς τὸν πατέρα εἰ μὴ δι' ἐμοῦ).

18—IV. 1.] Special exhortations to relative social duties: 18, 19, *to the married:* 20, 21, *to children and parents:* 22—IV. 1, *to slaves and masters.* Seeing that such exhortations occur in Ephesians also in terms so very similar, we are not justified, with Chrys., al., in assuming that there was any thing in the peculiar circumstances of the Colossian church, which required more than common exhortation of this kind. It has been said, that it is only in Epistles addressed to the Asiatic churches, that such exhortations are found: but in this remark the entirely general character of the Epistle to the Ephesians is forgotten. Besides, the exhortations of the Epistle to Titus cannot be so completely severed from these as to be set down in another category, as Eadie has endeavoured to do. See throughout the section, for such matters as are not remarked on, the notes to Eph. v. 22—vi. 9. **18. ὡς ἀνῆκεν**] The verb is in the imperfect—as ἔδει and χρῆν, conveying always in its form a slight degree of blame, as implying the non-realization of the duty pointed out—just as when we say, 'It was your duty to,' &c. See Winer, § 40. 3, end. The words **ἐν κυρίῳ** belong to ἀνῆκεν, not to ὑποτάσσεσθε; as is shewn by the parallel expression in ver. 20: was fitting, in that element of life designated by ἐν κυρίῳ. **19.**] See the glorious expansion of this in Eph. v. 25—33. **πικραίνεσθαι** occurs in the same sense in Demosth. 1464. 18: also in Plato, Legg. p. 731 d,—τὸν θυμὸν πραΰνειν κ. μὴ ἀκραχολοῦντα, γυναικείως πικραινόμενον, διατελεῖν. Kypke illustrates the word from Plutarch, de ira cohibenda, p. 457, 'ubi dicit, animi prodere imbecillitatem quum viri πρὸς γύναια διαπικραίνονται:' and from Eurip. Helen. 303: ἀλλ' ὅταν πόσις πικρὸς | ξυνῇ γυναικί, κ. τὸ δῶμ' ἐστι (lege σῴζεσθαι) πικρόν, θανεῖν κράτιστον. **20.**] See Eph. vi. 1. **κατὰ πάντα,** the exceptions not being taken into account: St. Paul's usual way of stating a general rule. It is best to take **εὐάρεστον,** as Mey. absolutely, as προσφιλῆ, Phil. iv. 8: the Christian qualification being given by the ἐν κυρίῳ: De W., al., understand τῷ θεῷ, which would render that qualification meaningless.

21.] See on Eph. vi. 4, for **πατέρες. μὴ ἐρεθ.**] do not irritate them—τουτό ἐστι, μὴ φιλονεικοτέρους αὐτοὺς ποιεῖτε. ἔστιν ὅπου καὶ συγχωρεῖν ὀφείλετε, Chrys. In ἵνα μὴ ἀθ., it is assumed that the result of such irritation will be to cause repeated punishment, and so eventual desperation, on the part of the child. It would be well if all who have to educate children took to heart Bengel's remark

v here only.
1 Kings xv.
11. 2 Kings
vi.8.
w = Rom. ix.
11. xi. 21.
x Eph. vi. 5
reff.
y Eph. vi. 6
only †.
z Eph. vi. 6
only. Ps. lii.
5 only.
a Eph. vi. 5 al6.
P. 1 Chron.
xxix. 17.
b Eph. vi. 7
(reff.) only.
e = Gal. iv. 5 reff.
Rom. iv. 11. ch. i. 18.
xxii. 11. Ps. cv. 6.

μὴ ᵛ ἀθυμῶσιν. ²² οἱ δοῦλοι, ˢ ὑπακούετε κατὰ πάντα
τοῖς ʷˣ κατὰ ˣ σάρκα κυρίοις, μὴ ἐν ʸ ὀφθαλμοδουλείαις ὡς
ᶻ ἀνθρωπάρεσκοι, ἀλλ᾽ ἐν ᵃ ἁπλότητι καρδίας φοβούμενοι
τὸν κύριον. ²³ ὃ ἐὰν ποιῆτε, ᵇ ἐκ ψυχῆς ᶜ ἐργάζεσθε
ὡς τῷ ᵈ κυρίῳ καὶ οὐκ ᵈ ἀνθρώποις, ²⁴ εἰδότες ὅτι ἀπὸ
κυρίου ᵉ ἀπολήμψεσθε τὴν ᶠ ἀνταπόδοσιν τῆς ᵍ κληρονομίας.
τῷ κυρίῳ χριστῷ ʰ δουλεύετε. ²⁵ ὁ γὰρ ⁱ ἀδικῶν ʲ κομιεῖται

ABCDF
KLℵab
cdefg
hklmn
o17.47

c 1 Cor. xvi. 10. Gal. vi. 10 al. Exod. xxxv. 9.   d dat., Rom. vi. 10 al.
f here only. Isa. xxxiv. 8. (·δομα, Rom. xi. 9.)   g = Eph. i. 14 reff. gen. appos.,
h = Matt. vi. 24 ‖ L. Acts xx. 19. 1 Thess. i. 9. Ps. ii. 11.   i = Rev.
j = 2 Cor. v. 10. Eph. vi. 8 al. Ps. xxxix. 15.

22. [om κατα παντα 47 arm.   κυρ. bef κ. σ. F.]   ins ως bef 1st εν C¹.
οφθαλμοδουλεια (the sing occurs in the similar passage Eph vi. 5) ABDF [47] Damasc
Thl : -λειαι k : κατ᾽ -ειαν (as Eph vi. 5) Chr(txt and comm₁) : txt CKLℵ rel Clem Chr-
comm₁ Thdrt Œc.—for -λει, -λι- CDF b² c e f l n 17.   αλλα B.   rec (for
κυριον) θεον, with D³Kℵ³ rel D-lat copt goth Thdrt : txt ABCD¹FLℵ¹ 17 [47] am(with
(besides F-lat) harl) syrr arm Clem Ambrst.

23. rec (for ο εαν) και παν ο τι εαν (from ver 17), with D²·³KL rel (αν a d¹ f m) Syr
gr-lat-ff ; [και π. ο εαν 47 :] παν οτι εαν 67¹ : παν ο αν 67² : παν ο εαν ℵ³ : txt ABCD¹Fℵ¹
17 latt copt goth Thl-ms lat-ff.   aft κυριω ins δουλευοντες A o 8-pe (copt) Clem.
om και B.

24. for απολ., ληψεσθε AC²[K]Lℵ³ a b¹ c f g h k m (n?) Chr Thdrt.—(λημψ. A c ?)
aft κληρονομιας ins υμων C² m [47] 80. 116 arm Chr-comm Thdrt.   rec aft
τω ins γαρ, with D³KL rel syrr goth [arm] Clem : om ABCD¹ℵ 17 [47] vulg copt Pel
Bede.—του κυριου ημων ιησου χριστου ω δουλευετε F, and, omg ημ. ιησ., D-lat Ambrst.

here ; 'ἀθυμία, fractus animus, pestis juventutis.' Wetst. quotes from Æneas
Tacticus, ὀργῇ δὲ μηθένα μετιέναι τῶν
τυχόντων ἀνθρώπων· ἀθυμότεροι γὰρ
εἶεν ἄν.   22.] See on Eph. vi. 5 ff.
The ὀφθαλμοδουλεῖαι here are the concrete acts of the -εία of Eph. vi. 6, the
abstract spirit.   τὸν κύριον, Him who
is absolutely, and not merely κατὰ σάρκα,
your master. τοῦτο ἐστι φοβεῖσθαι τὸν
θεόν, ὅταν, μηδενὸς ὁρῶντος, μηδὲν πράττωμεν πονηρόν. ἂν δὲ πράττωμεν, οὐχὶ
τὸν θεόν, ἀλλὰ τοὺς ἀνθρώπους φοβού-
μεθα, Chrys.   23.] ἐκ ψυχῆς, as
Chrys., μετ᾽ εὐνοίας, μὴ μετὰ δουλικῆς
ἀνάγκης, ἀλλὰ μετ᾽ ἐλευθερίας κ. προαιρέσεως. The datives may be taken as of
reference, or commodi. In Eph. vi. 7 the
construction is filled up by δουλεύοντες.
Mey. observes against De W., that οὐκ is
an absolute not a mere relative negative :
'doing things unto men' is to be laid
aside altogether, not merely less practised
than the other : "as workers to the Lord
and non-workers to men," Ellic.
24.] = Eph. vi. 8, but more specific as
to the Christian reward. εἰδότες, knowing as ye do . . . The ἀπὸ κυρίου is
emphatically prefixed—'that it is from
the Lord that you shall . . . . .' ἀπό,
as Winer, § 47. b, is distinguished
from παρά, as indicating not immediate
bestowal, but that the Lord is the
ultimate source and conferrer of the in-

heritance—from the Lord—not 'at the
hands of the Lord.' You must look to
Him, not to men, as the source of all
Christian reward. (Eadie, p. 265, has
represented Winer as saying the contrary
of that which he does say.) ἀνταπόδοσις
occurs in Thuc. iv. 81, in the sense of a
mutual exchange of places taken in war :
in Polyb. vi. 5. 3, in that of a compensation, τοῦτο ἱκανὸν ἀνταπόδοσιν ποιήσει
ἐκείνου,—and xx. 7. 2, ὥσπερ ἐπιτηδὲς
ἀνταπόδοσιν ποιουμένη ἡ τύχη : and hence
in that of 'an opposite turn,' xxvii. 2. 4,
ἀνταπόδοσιν λαμβάνει τὰ πράγματα—iv.
43. 5, ἀνταπόδοσιν ποιεῖται ὁ ῥοῦς πρός,
&c. Here the sense would appear to be,
with a marked reference to their present
state of slavery, the compensation.
κληρ., genitive of apposition (reff). The
very word κληρονομία should have kept
the Roman Catholic expositors from introducing the merit of good works here.
The last clause, without the γάρ, is best
taken imperatively, as a general comprehension of the course of action prescribed
in the former part of the verse : serve ye
the Lord Christ. So Vulg. 'domino Christo
servite.'   25.] This verse seems best
to be taken as addressed to the slaves by
way of encouragement to regard Christ as
their Master and serve Him—seeing that
all their wrongs in this world, if they
leave them in His hands, will be in due
time righted by Him, the just judge,

[k] ὃ ἠδίκησεν, καὶ οὐκ ἔστιν [l] προσωποληψία. IV. 1 οἱ k constr., Gal. iv. 12 al.
κύριοι, τὸ δίκαιον καὶ τὴν [m] ἰσότητα τοῖς δούλοις [n] παρ- l Eph. vi. 9. Rom. ii. 11. James ii. 1 only †. see Acts x. 34.
έχεσθε, εἰδότες ὅτι καὶ ὑμεῖς ἔχετε κύριον ἐν οὐρανῷ.
2 Τῇ [op] προσευχῇ [pq] προσκαρτερεῖτε [r] γρηγοροῦντες ἐν m 2 Cor. viii. 13, 14 only. Job xxxvi.

29. Zech. iv. 7 only. n mid., Luke vii. 4. Acts xix. 24. o absol., Matt. xxi. 22. Luke xxii. 45. 1 Cor. vii. 5. Ps. iv. 1. p Acts i. 14. ii. 42. vi. 4. Rom. xii. 12. q as above (o). Mark iii. 9. Acts ii. 46. viii. 13. x. 7. Rom. xiii. 6 only. Numb. xiii. 21 only. Susan. 6 Theod. r Mark xiii. 37. 1 Cor. xvi. 13. 1 Thess. v. 6. Jer. i. 2. 1 Macc. xii. 27.

25. rec (for γαρ) δε (*conseq of former*), with D³KL rel syrr gr-ff: txt ABCD¹Fℵ 17 latt copt goth Clem lat-ff. κομισεται BD³KLℵ³ d m Clem Chr-comm Thdrt Thl; κομισηται k: κομιζεται F: txt ACD¹ℵ¹ rel Damasc (*see on Eph* vi. 8). at end add παρα τω θεω F vulg(not am) [goth] arm Chr lat-ff.

Chap. IV. **1.** παρεχετε C b¹ f 72. 114 Clem Chr₂ Thl-ms. rec ουρανοις (*from Eph* vi. 9), with DFKLℵ³ rel Chr Thdrt: txt ABC²ℵ¹ m 17 Clem Orig Damasc. (C¹ illegible.)

2. [B¹(Tischdf) repeats προσευχη.]

with whom there is no respect of persons. **For he that doeth wrong shall receive** (see, as on the whole, Eph. vi. 8) **that which he did wrongfully** (the tense is changed because in **ἀδικῶν** he is speaking of present practice—in **ἠδίκησεν**, he has transferred the scene to the day of the Lord, and the wrong is one of past time), **and there is not respect of persons** (= εἴτε δοῦλος εἴτε ἐλεύθερος, Eph. vi. 8). At His tribunal, every one, without regard to rank or wealth, shall receive the deeds done in the body. So that in your Christian uprightness and conscientiousness you need not fear that you shall be in the end overborne by the superior power of your masters: there is a judge who will defend and right you: ἐστὶ δικαιοκρίτης ὃς οὐκ οἶδε δούλου κ. δεσπότου διαφοράν, ἀλλὰ δικαίαν εἰςφέρει τὴν ψῆφον, Thdrt. Some, as Thl., Beng., al., suppose the verse spoken *with reference to* the slaves; but οὐκ ἔστιν προσωποληψία is against this, unless we accept Bengel's far-fetched explanation of it: "tenues sæpe putant, sibi propter tenuitatem ipsorum esse parcendum."

Ch. IV. **1.**] Meyer contends for the strict meaning of '*equality*' for **ἰσότητα**, and that it never has the signification of '*fairness*.' But (see examples in Wetst.) the common conjunction of ἴσον κ. δίκαιον would naturally lead to assigning to ἴσον the same transferred meaning which 'æquus' has in Latin, and to ἰσότης the same which 'æquitas' has. I would render then, **equity,—fairness**: understanding by that, an extension of τὸ δίκαιον to matters not admitting of the application of strict rules—a large and liberal interpretation of justice in ordinary matters. In every place cited by Meyer where the word is used ethically and not materially, this rendering is better than his. In Polyb. ii. 38. 8, the case is different: it there imports absolute political equality. Erasm., Corn.-a-lap., al., understand *impartiality* not preferring one above another: but this does not seem to be in question here. Calv. says: 'Non dubito quin Paulus ἰσότητα hic posuerit pro jure analogo aut distributivo: quemadmodum ad Ephesios τὰ αὐτά. Neque enim sic habent domini obnoxios sibi servos, quin vicissim aliquid ipsis debeant: quemadmodum jus analogum valere debet inter omnes ordines.' Thdrt.: ἰσότητα οὐ τὴν ἰσοτιμίαν ἐκάλεσεν, ἀλλὰ τὴν προσήκουσαν ἐπιμέλειαν, ἧς παρὰ τῶν δεσποτῶν ἀπολαύειν χρὴ τοὺς οἰκέτας. Chrys.: τί δέ ἐστιν ἰσότης; πάντων ἐν ἀφθονίᾳ καθιστᾷν, κ. μὴ ἐᾷν ἑτέρων δεῖσθαι, ἀλλ' ἀμείβεσθαι αὐτοὺς τῶν πόνων. Cf. Philem. 16. **παρέχεσθε**] '*supply on your side*:' see Krüger, Griechische Sprachlehre, § 52. 8, who gives several examples of the dynamic middle in this very verb. Ellic. well insists on and explains its force, as referring rather to the powers put forth by the subject, whereas the active simply and objectively states the action. **εἰδότες**] See ch. iii. 24. **καὶ ὑμεῖς**] as well as they: as you are masters to them, so the Lord to you.

2—6.] Special concluding exhortations: and **2—4.**] *to prayer*; see Rom. xii. 12: 1 Thess. v. 17.

2.] **γρηγ. watching in it,** i. e. not remiss and indolent in your occupation of prayer (**τῇ** πρ.), but active and watchful, cheerful also, as ἐν εὐχαριστίᾳ, which defines and characterizes the watchfulness. ἐπειδὴ γὰρ τὸ καρτερεῖν ἐν ταῖς εὐχαῖς ῥᾳθυμεῖν πολλάκις ποιεῖ, διὰ τοῦτό φησι **γρηγοροῦντες**, τουτέστι νήφοντες, μὴ ῥεμβόμενοι. οἶδε γάρ, οἶδεν ὁ διάβολος ὅσον ἀγαθὸν εὐχή· διὸ βαρὺς ἔγκειται. οἶδε δὲ καὶ Παῦλος πῶς ἀκηδιῶσι πολλοὶ εὐχόμενοι.

αὐτῇ ˢἐν ˢᵗεὐχαριστίᾳ, ³ ᵘπροσευχόμενοι ἅμα καὶ ᵛπερὶ ἡμῶν, ᵘἵνα ὁ θεὸς ʷἀνοίξῃ ἡμῖν ʷθύραν τοῦ λόγου ˣλα-λῆσαι τὸ ʸμυστήριον τοῦ χριστοῦ, δι᾽ ὃ καὶ δέδεμαι, ⁴ ἵνα ᶻφανερώσω αὐτὸ ᵃὡς δεῖ με λαλῆσαι. ⁵ Ἐν ᵇσοφίᾳ ˣπεριπατεῖτε πρὸς ᵈτοὺς ᵈἔξω, τὸν καιρὸν ᵉἐξαγοραζό-μενοι. ⁶ ὁ ᶠλόγος ὑμῶν πάντοτε ᶠᵍἐν ᵍχάριτι ʰἅλατι

s ch. ii. 7.
t Eph. v. 4 reff.
u ch. i. 3.
v Phil. i. 9 reff.
w Acts xiv. 27. 1 Cor. xvi. 9. 2 Cor. ii. 12. Rev. iii. 8 (lit.). Isa. xlv. 1.
x inf. of object, ch. i. 22.
y Eph. i. 9 reff. z = 2 Cor. xi.
a Eph. vi. 20. iv. 12. Mark iv. 11.
b = Acts vi. 3. (Sir. prol.)
c ch. iii. 7 reff.
d (Acts xxvi. 11.) = 1 Cor. v. 12. 1 Thess.
e Gal. iii. 13. iv. 5. Eph. v. 16 only. Dan. ii. 8 only.
f 1 Cor. ii. 4.
g ch. iii. 16.
h Matt. v. 13 bis. Mark ix. 50 bis (ἅλς, ib. 49, 50). Luke xiv. 34 bis only. Lev. ii. 13.

ABCDF KLℵ a b c d e f g h k l m n o 17. 47

om εν αυτη ℵ¹(ins ℵ-corr¹).   om εν ευχαριστια D¹ Cypr Ambrst.

3. for αμα, ινα ℵ¹(but corrd) : αρα m.   om [1st] του D¹F.   aft λογου ins εν παρρησια A.   for χριστου, θεου B¹ [L(Treg)] 4. 41. 238 æth.   for ὅ, ὅν BF : txt ACDKLℵ rel vulg(and F-lat) Clem Cyr.

4. aft ινα ins και D¹.

διὸ φησι ᵍρ. ἐν αὐτ. ἐν εὐχαρ.—τοῦτο γάρ φησιν ἔργον ὑμῶν ἔστω, ἐν ταῖς εὐχαῖς εὐχαριστεῖν, κ. ὑπὲρ τῶν φανερῶν κ. ὑπ. τῶν ἀφανῶν, κ. ὑπὲρ ὧν ἑκόντας, κ. ὑπὲρ ὧν ἄκοντας ἐποίησεν εὖ, κ. ὑπὲρ βασι-λείας, κ. ὑπὲρ γεέννης, κ. ὑπὲρ θλίψεως, κ. ὑπὲρ ἀνέσεως. οὕτω γὰρ ἔθος τοῖς ἁγίοις εὔχεσθαι, κ. ὑπὲρ τῶν κοινῶν εὐερ-γεσιῶν εὐχαριστεῖν. Chrys. 3.]
ἡμῶν, not 'me,'—see ch. i. 1, 3. This is plainly shewn here by the singular fol-lowing after. ἵνα] see on 1 Cor. xiv. 13. Here, the idea of final result is prominent : but the purport is also in-cluded. θύραν τ. λόγου] not as Calv., al., *oris apertionem*, Eph. vi. 19; but as in reff., objective, an opening of opportunity for the extension of the Gospel by the word. This would, seeing that the Apostle was a prisoner, naturally be given first and most chiefly, as far as he was concerned, by his liberation : cf. Philem. 22. λαλῆσαι] inf. of pur-pose—so that we may speak. δι᾽ ὃ κ. δ.] for (on account of) which (mystery) I am (not only a minister but) also bound.
4.] The second ἵνα gives the pur-pose of the previous verse, not the purpose of δέδεμαι, as Chrys. (τὰ δεσμὰ φανεροῖ αὐτόν, οὐ συσκιάζει), Bengel ('vinctus sum ut patefaciam : paradoxon'), nor to be joined with προσευχόμενοι, as Beza, De W., al. If that might be so, the door opened, &c.,—then he would make it known as he ought to do—then he would be fulfilling the requirements of that apos-tolic calling, from which now in his im-prisonment he was laid aside. Certainly this is the meaning,—and not, as ordi-narily understood, cf. Chrys., al., that he might boldly declare the Gospel *in his im-prisonment*. 5, 6.] *Exhortations as to their behaviour in the world.*
5. ἐν σοφίᾳ] in (as an element) wisdom

(the practical wisdom of Christian pru-dence and sound sense). πρός, as in οὐδὲν πρὸς Διόνυσον,—εἴ του δέοιτο πρὸς Τιμόθεον πρᾶξαι, Demosth. p. 1185, signifying simply in relation to, in the intercourse of life. Ellic. refers to a good discussion of this preposition in Rost and Palm's Lex. vol. ii. p. 1157. On οἱ ἔξω, see reff. They are those outside the Christian brotherhood. πρὸς τὰ μέλη τὰ οἰκεῖα οὐ τοσαύτης ἡμῖν δεῖ ἀσφαλείας, ὅσης πρὸς τοὺς ἔξω· ἔνθα γὰρ ἀδελφοί, εἰσὶ κ. συγγνῶμαι πολλαὶ κ. ἀγά-παι. Chrys. τ. καιρ. ἐξαγορ.] see on Eph. v. 16. The opportunity *for what*, will be understood in each case from the circumstances, and our acknowledged Christian position as watching for the cause of the Lord. The thought in Eph., ὅτι αἱ ἡμέραι πονηραί εἰσι, lies in the back-ground of the word ἐξαγοραζόμενοι.
6.] Let your speech (πρὸς τοὺς ἔξω still) be always in (as its characteristic element) grace (i. e. gracious, and winning favour : cf. Luke iv. 22), seasoned with salt (not insipid and void of point, which can do no man any good : we must not forget that both these words have their spiritual mean-ing : χάρις, so common an one as to have almost passed out of its ordinary accepta-tion into that other,—the grace which is conferred on us from above, and which our words and actions should reflect :—and ἅλας, as used by our Saviour in reff. (see note on Mark), as symbolizing the unction, freshness, and vital briskness which cha-racterizes the Spirit's presence and work in a man. So that we must beware here of supposing that mere Attic 'sales' are meant, or any vivacity of outward expres-sion only, and keep in mind the *Christian* import. Of the Commentators, Thdrt. comes the nearest,—πνευματικῇ συνέσει κοσμεῖσθε. There seems to be no allusion

ⁱ ἠρτυμένος, ʲ εἰδέναι πῶς δεῖ ὑμᾶς ᵏ ἑνὶ ᵏ ἑκάστῳ ἀποκρίνεσθαι.

⁷ ¹ Τὰ ¹ κατ᾿ ἐμὲ πάντα ᵐ γνωρίσει ὑμῖν Τύχικος ὁ
ⁿ ἀγαπητὸς ⁿ ἀδελφὸς καὶ ⁿ πιστὸς ⁿᵒ διάκονος καὶ ᵖ σύνδουλος ⁿᑫ ἐν κυρίῳ, ⁸ ὃν ἔπεμψα πρὸς ὑμᾶς εἰς ʳ αὐτὸ
τοῦτο, ἵνα γνῷ ˢ τὰ ˢ περὶ ὑμῶν καὶ ᵗ παρακαλέσῃ τὰς ᵗ καρδίας ὑμῶν, ⁹ σὺν Ὀνησίμῳ τῷ πιστῷ καὶ ⁿ ἀγαπητῷ
ⁿ ἀδελφῷ, ὅς ἐστιν ᵘ ἐξ ὑμῶν· πάντα ὑμῖν ᵐ γνωριοῦσιν τὰ
ᵛ ὧδε. ¹⁰ Ἀσπάζεται ὑμᾶς Ἀρίσταρχος ὁ ʷ συναιχμά-

Marginal references:
i Mark ix. 50. Luke xiv. 34 only †. Cant. viii. 2 Symm.
j inf., Mark vii. 4. Acts xv. 10. Heb. v. 5. Rev. xvi. 9.
k Eph. iv. 16 reff.
l Acts xxiv 22. xxv. 14.
Eph. vi. 21. Phil. i. 12.
m 1 Cor. xii. 3. xv. 1. 2 Cor. viii. 1. Eph. i. 9 al. 1 Kings xxviii. 15.
n Eph. vi. 21 (reff.).

o = ch. i. 7, 23. p ch. i. 7 reff. q Phil. i. 14. r Acts xxiv. 15, 20. xxv. 25. 2 Cor.
ii. 3. vii. 11. s Phil. i. 27 reff. t ch. ii. 2 (reff.). u ver. 12.
v Paul, 1 Cor. iv. 2 only. w Rom. xvi. 7. Philem. 23 only †.

---

6. ημων D¹. υμας bef πως δει B[Bch : not Mai Tischdf] d 108.
7. aft τα ins δε א¹(א³ disapproving) [Syr arm]. om και συνδουλος א¹.
8. for γνω and 1st υμων, γνωτε and ημων (as in Eph vi. 22) ABD¹F[P] m 17 [47] æth [arm] Thdrt-txt Jerₗ : txt CD²·³KL(א) rel vulg(and F-lat) syrr copt goth Chr Thdrt-comm lat-ff.—aft γνω ins τε א¹(om א³ who also altered υμων to ημων but corrected it again both here and in ver 9). παρακαλεσαι D¹ : -σει L[P] f : παρακαλεση τε 17.
9. αγαπητω και πιστω DF latt goth Chr lat-ff. γνωρισουσιν BF[P]א³ Damasc, -σωσιν D¹ : γνωριζουσι m : txt ACD³KLא¹ rel Chr. at end add πραττομενα F latt Jer Pel Bede.

---

here to the conservative power of salt : the matter in hand at present is not avoiding corrupt conversation. Still less does the meaning of *wit* belong to this place. A local allusion is *just possible :* Herod. vii. 30 says of Xerxes, Ἄναυα δὲ καλεομένην Φρυγῶν πόλιν παραμειβόμενος, καὶ λίμνην ἐκ τῆς ἅλες γίνονται, ἀπίκετο ἐς Κολοσσάς, πόλιν μεγάλην Φρυγίης).

εἰδέναι] to know—i. e. so that you may know : see ref., "loosely appended infin., expressive of consequence," as Ellicott. See Winer, edn. 6, § 44. 1. Cf. 1 Pet. iii. 15, which however is but one side of that readiness which is here recommended. **7—18.] CLOSE OF THE EPISTLE. 7—9.]** *Of the bearers of the Epistle, Tychicus and Onesimus.*

7.] On Tychicus, see Eph. vi. 21.
ὁ ἀγ. ἀδελφός, as dear to his heart : πιστ. διάκ., as his tried companion in the ministry,—σύνδ. ἐν κυρίῳ, as one with him in the motives and objects of his active work : ὥστε, as Chrys., αὐτῷ πάντοθεν τὸ ἀξιόπιστον ξυνήγαγεν. There is a delicate touch of affection in ἵνα γνῷ τὰ περὶ ὑμ., which can hardly, in the doubtfulness of the reading, be the work of a corrector. It implies that there were painful circumstances of trial, to which the subsequent παρακαλέσῃ also has reference. δείκνυσιν αὐτοὺς ἐν τοῖς πειρασμοῖς ὄντας, Chrys. The objection (Eadie), that thus the εἰς αὐτὸ τοῦτο will announce another purpose from that enounced above in τὰ

κατ᾿ ἐμὲ π. γνωρ., will apply just as much to the other reading ;—for any how the αὐτὸ τοῦτο must include the καὶ παρακαλέσῃ κ.τ.λ. But the fact is, that αὐτὸ τοῦτο may apply exclusively to the *following*, without any reference to what has *preceded :* see Rom. ix. 17 ; the parallel place, Eph. vi. 22 ; Phil. i. 6. **9. σὺν Ὀνησ.]** There can hardly be a doubt (compare ver. 17 with Philem. 2, 10 ff.) that this is the Onesimus of the Epistle to Philemon. When Calv. wrote "vix est credibile hunc esse servum illum Philemonis, quia furis et fugitivi nomen dedecori subjectum fuisset," he forgot that this very term, ἀδελφὸς ἀγαπητός, is applied to him, Philem. 16. ἐξ ὑμῶν] most probably, a native of your town. πάντ. ὑμ. γν. τὰ ὧδε] A formal restatement of τὰ κατ᾿ ἐμὲ π. γν. above. Is it likely, with this restatement, that the same should be again stated in the middle of the sentence, as would be the case with the reading ἵνα γνῶτε τὰ περὶ ἡμῶν ?
10—14.] *Various greetings from brethren.*
10.] Aristarchus was a Thessalonian (Acts xx. 4), first mentioned Acts xix. 29, as dragged into the theatre at Ephesus during the tumult, together with Gaius, both being συνέκδημοι Παύλου. He accompanied Paul to Asia (ib. xx. 4), and was with him in the voyage to Rome (xxvii. 2). In Philem. 24, he sends greeting, with Marcus, Demas, and Lucas, as here. On συναιχμάλωτος, Meyer (after

λωτός μου, καὶ Μάρκος ὁ ˣ ἀνεψιὸς Βαρνάβα, περὶ οὗ
ᵞ ἐλάβετε ᵞ ἐντολάς (ἐὰν ἔλθῃ πρὸς ὑμᾶς, ᶻ δέξασθε αὐτόν),
11 καὶ Ἰησοῦς ὁ λεγόμενος Ἰοῦστος· οἱ ὄντες ᵃ ἐκ ᵃ περιτομῆς οὗτοι μόνοι ᵇ συνεργοὶ ᶜ εἰς τὴν ᵈ βασιλείαν τοῦ ᵈ θεοῦ,
ᵉ οἵτινες ἐγενήθησάν μοι ᶠ παρηγορία. 12 ἀσπάζεται ὑμᾶς

x here only.
Num. xxxvi.
11.　Tobit
vii. 2 (not א)
only.
y John x. 18.
Acts xvii. 15.
2 John 4
only.
z = 2 Cor. vii.
15 al.
a Acts x. 45.
xi. 2.　Rom.
iv. 12.　Gal. ii. 12.　Tit. i. 10 only.
17.　1 Cor. iv. 20 al.

ABCDF
KLPא a
bcdefg
hklmn
o 17. 47

b Phil. ii. 25 reff.

e = Acts x. 41, 47. xiii. 31, 43 al.

c = Phil. ii. 22.

f here only †. (-ρεῖν, Job xvi. 2 Symm.)

d Rom. xiv.

10. δεξασθαι D¹F 17 syrr Thl(but mentions txt) Ambrst.
11. aft συνεργοι ins μου εισιν D¹F latt arm (Dial₈) Ambrst[: pref εισιν P.]

Fritzsche, Rom. vol. i. prolegg. p. xxi) suggests an idea, which may without any straining of probability be adopted, and which would explain why Aristarchus is here συναιχμ., and in Philem. 24, συνεργός, whereas Epaphras is here, ch. i. 7, merely a σύνδουλος, and in Philem. 23 a συναιχμάλωτος. His view is, that the Apostle's friends may have voluntarily shared his imprisonment by turns: and that Aristarchus may have been his fellow-prisoner when he wrote this Epistle, Epaphras when he wrote that to Philemon. συναιχμάλωτος belongs to the same image of warfare as συνστρατιώτης, Phil. ii. 25; Philem. 2.　Μάρκος] can hardly be other than John Mark, cf. Acts xii. 12, 25, who accompanied Paul and Barnabas in part of their first missionary journey, and because he turned back from them at Perga (ib. xiii. 13; xv. 38), was the subject of dispute between them on their second journey. That he was also the Evangelist, is matter of pure tradition, but not therefore to be rejected.

ἀνεψιός] not 'sister's son:' this rendering has arisen from mistaking the definition given by Hesych., ἀνεψιοί, ἀδελφῶν υἱοί,—meaning that ἀνεψιοί are sons of brothers, i. e. cousins. (Ellic. in notes on his translation of the Epistle, suggests that 'sister's-son' may after all be no mistake, but an archaism to express, as the German Geſchwiſterkind, a cousin.) "Pollux dicit, filios filiasque fratrum et sororum, dici ἀνεψιούς, ex his prognatos ἀνεψιαδοῦς, ἀνεψιαδάς, — tertio gradu ἐξανεψιούς, ἐξανεψιάς a Menandro dici." Lobeck on Phrynichus, p. 306. This is decisively shewn in Herod. vii. 5, Μαρδόνιος . . . ὃς ἦν Ξέρξῃ μὲν ἀνεψιός, Δαρείου δὲ ἀδελφεῆς παῖς. It is also used in a wider sense (see Hom. Il. α. 464): but there is no need to depart here from the strict meaning.　περὶ οὗ . . .] What these commands were, must be left in entire uncertainty. They had been sent previous to the writing of our Epistle (ἐλάβετε): but from, or by whom, we know

not. They concerned Marcus, not Barnabas (as Thl., al.): and one can hardly help connecting them, associated as they are with ἐὰν ἔλθῃ, δέξασθε αὐτόν, with the dispute of Acts xv. 38. It is very possible, that in consequence of the rejection of John Mark on that occasion by St. Paul, the Pauline portion of the churches may have looked upon him with suspicion.

11. Ἰησοῦς . . . Ἰοῦστος] Entirely unknown to us. A Justus is mentioned Acts xviii. 7, as an inhabitant of Corinth, and a proselyte: but there is no further reason to identify the two. The surname Justus (צדיק) was common among the Jews: cf. Acts i. 23, and Jos. Vit. 9, 65, 76. **These alone who are of the circumcision** (the construction is of the nature of an anacoluthon, οἱ ὄντες ἐκ π. being equivalent to 'of those of the circumcision.' We have a similar construction frequently in the classics: e. g. ἄμφω δ' ἐξομένω γεραρώτερος ἦεν Ὀδυσσεύς, Il. γ. 211: ὅρκια πιστὰ ταμόντες ὁ μὲν βασιλευέτω αἰεί, Od. ω. 483. See many more examples in Kühner, ii. § 678. 2. This seems far better, with Meyer and Lachmann, than with rec. Ellic. al. to place the stop at περιτομῆς and attach the clause to the three preceding names. For thus we lose (in spite of the assertion by Ellic. that the μόνοι naturally refers the thought to the category last mentioned) the fact that there were other συνεργοί not of the circumcision who had been a comfort to him. The judaistic teachers were for the most part in opposition to St. Paul: cf. his complaint, Phil. i. 15, 17) **are my fellow-workers towards the kingdom of God** (the rest would not be called by this name—so that De W.'s objection to the construction does not apply, that the opponents would not be called συνεργοί; for they *are not* so called), **men that proved** (the passive meaning of ἐγενήθησαν is not safely to be pressed: see notes on Eph. iii. 7; 1 Thess. i. 5, 6; 1 Pet. i. 15. The aor. alludes to some event recently passed: to what precisely, we cannot say)

Ἐπαφρᾶς ὁ ^gἐξ ὑμῶν ^hδοῦλος ^hχριστοῦ Ἰησοῦ, πάντοτε
ⁱἀγωνιζόμενος ὑπὲρ ὑμῶν ἐν ταῖς προσευχαῖς, ἵνα ^{jk}στῆτε
τέλειοι καὶ ^{lm}πεπληροφορημένοι ^kἐν ⁿπαντὶ ⁿθελήματι τοῦ
θεοῦ. 13 ^oμαρτυρῶ γὰρ αὐτῷ ὅτι ἔχει πολὺν ^pπόνον
ὑπὲρ ὑμῶν καὶ τῶν ἐν Λαοδικείᾳ καὶ τῶν ἐν Ἱεραπόλει.
14 ἀσπάζεται ὑμᾶς Λουκᾶς ὁ ^qἰατρὸς ὁ ἀγαπητὸς καὶ

g ver. 9.
h Gal. i. 10 reff.
i ch. i. 29 reff.
j Eph. vi. 13, 14.
k John viii. 44.
Rom. v. 2.
see 1 Cor. xv. 1.
l Rom. xii. 2.
ch. i. 28.
James i. 4.
m Luke i. 1.
Rom. iv. 21.
xiv. 5. 2 Tim. iv. 5, 17
n 2. Gal. iv.
o Acts xxii. 5. Rom. x. 2. Gal. iv.
q Mark ii. 17 ||.

only. Eccles. viii. 11 only.   n see Acts xiii. 22.   o Acts xxii. 5.   Rom. x. 2.   Gal. iv.
15. Gen. xxxi. 48.   p Rev. xvi. 10, 11. xxi. 4 only.   Isa. lxv. 14.   q Mark ii. 17 ||.
v. 26 ||.   Luke iv. 23 only.   Jer. viii. 22.

12. rec om ιησου, with DFK [47] syrr goth [æth] Chr Thdrt Ambrst: ins ABCLℵ
m 17 vulg(not F-lat) copt Aug Pel[: and bef χρ. P 80(Sz) arm.]   for υπερ, περι
D¹F.   ημων ℵ¹.   σταθητε Bℵ¹: ητε c g l² 91. 116-22² Ambrst.   rec
πεπληρωμενοι (more usual), with D³KL[P] rel: txt ABCD¹Fℵ 17. 67².   [om 2nd
εν P.]   om του [P] k [47] 67².   for θεου, χριστου D¹ l.
13. rec (for πολυν πονον) ζηλον πολυν (gloss, see note), with KL rel syrr, πολυν
ζηλον D³ 17 [47]: πολυν αγωνα 6. 67²: txt ABC[P]ℵ copt, πολυν κοπον D¹F, multum
laborem latt lat-ff.

a comfort to me (they are my συνεργοί 'quippe qui . . . .' Hierocles, de nuptiis, apud Stob. (Kypke), has the same
phrase: ἡ γυνὴ δὲ παροῦσα μεγάλη γίνεται κ. πρὸς ταῦτα παρηγορία: so Plutarch, de auditione, p. 43 (id.), νόσημα
παρηγορίας . . . δεόμενον).   12.] On
Epaphras, see ch. i. 7 note. The sentence
is better without a comma at ὑμῶν, both
as giving more spirit to the δοῦλος χ. Ἰ.,
and setting the ἐξ ὑμ. in antithesis to the
ὑπὲρ ὑμῶν below. On ἀγων. besides reff.,
see Rom. xv. 30. By mentioning Epaphras's anxious prayers for them, he works
further on their affections, giving them
an additional motive for stedfastness, in
that one of themselves was thus striving
in prayer for them. ἵνα here gives the
direct aim of ἀγωνιζ. See above on ver.
3—that ye may stand,—perfect and fully
persuaded (see reff.),—in (be firmly settled in, without danger of vacillating or
falling) all the (lit. 'in every:' but we
cannot thus express it in English) will
of God. This connexion, of στῆτε with
ἐν, as Mey., seems better than, as ordinarily (so also De W. and Ellic.), to join
ἐν with the participles. Eadie characterizes it as needless refinement in Mey.
to assert that thus not only a modal=
bestimmung but a local=bestimmung is
attached to στῆτε: but the use of στῆναι
ἐν in the reff. seems to justify it.
13.] πόνος,—an unusual word in the N. T.,
hence the var. readd.,—is usual in the
toil of conflict in war, thus answering to
ἀγωνιζόμ. above: so Herod. vi. 114, ἐν
τούτῳ τῷ πόνῳ ὁ πολέμαρχος Καλλί-
μαχος διαφθείρεται: similarly viii. 89.
Plato, Phædr. 247 b, ἔνθα δὴ πόνος τε κ.
ἀγὼν ἔσχατος ψυχῇ πρόκειται: Demosth.
637. 18, εἰ δ᾽ ἐκεῖνος ἀσθενέστερος ἦν

τὸν ὑπὲρ τῆς νίκης ἐνεγκεῖν πόνον.
On account of this mention of Laodicea
and Hierapolis, some have thought that
Epaphras was the founder of the three
churches. See Prolegg. § ii. 2, 7.
Λαοδικείᾳ] LAODICEA was a city of Phrygia Magna (Strabo xii. 8, Plin. v. 29:
according to the subscription (rec.) of
1 Tim., the chief city of Phrygia Pacatiana), large (ἡ τῆς χώρας ἀρετὴ κ. τῶν
πολιτῶν τινες εὐτυχήσαντες, μεγάλην
ἐποιήσαντο αὐτήν, Strabo) and rich (Rev.
iii. 17; and Prolegg. to Rev. § 13. 13. Tac.
Ann. xiv. 27: 'Laodicea, tremore terræ
prolapsa, nullo a nobis remedio, propriis
opibus revaluit:' δυνατωτέρα τῶν ἐπὶ θα-
λάττῃ, Philostr. Soph. i. 25), on the river
Lycus (hence called Λ. ἡ ἐπὶ Λύκῳ or
πρὸς τῷ Λύκῳ, see Strabo, ib.), formerly
called Diospolis, and afterwards Rhoas;
its subsequent name was from Laodice
queen of Antiochus II. (Steph. Byz.) In
A.D. 62, Laodicea, with Hierapolis and
Colossæ, was destroyed by an earthquake
(Tacit. l. c.), to which visitations the
neighbourhood was very subject (εἰ γάρ
τις ἄλλη κ. ἡ Λαοδίκεια εὔσειστος, κ. τῆς
πλησιοχώρου πλέον, Plin. ib.). There is
now on the spot a desolate village called
Eski-hissar, with some ancient ruins
(Arundel, Seven Churches). Winer, Realw.
Ἱεραπόλει] Six Roman miles north
from Laodicea: famed for many mineral
springs (Strabo, xiii. 4, describes them at
length, also the caverns which exhale
noxious vapour. See also Plin. ii. 95),
which are still flowing (Schubert, i. 283).
Winer, Realw.   14.] This Λουκᾶς has
ever been taken for the Evangelist: see Iren.
iii. 14. 1, p. 201, and Prolegg. to St. Luke,
§ i. In ὁ ἰατρὸς ὁ ἀγαπητός there may
be a trace of what has been supposed,

r Acts ii. 46.
v. 42. viii. 3.
xx. 20.
s Rom. xvi. 5.
1 Cor. xvi. 19.
Philem. 2.
t Acts viii. 28.
xv. 21.
2 Cor. iii. 15.
Exod. xxiv. 7.
u 1 Thess. v.27.
v = 1 Cor. xvi.
2. Rev. ii.
13.
w = Rom. xvi.
22. 1 Thess.
v. 27. 2 Thess.
iii. 14. see
1 Cor. v. 9.
x John xi. 37.
Rev. iii. 9.
xiii. 12,
[15,]16. Eccl.
iii. 14.
y transposn.
w. ἵνα, Gal.
ii. 10 reff.

Δημᾶς. 15 ἀσπάσασθε τοὺς ἐν Λαοδικείᾳ ἀδελφοὺς καὶ Νυμφᾶν καὶ τὴν ʳˢκατ' οἶκον αὐτῶν ˢἐκκλησίαν· 16 καὶ ὅταν ᵗᵘἀναγνωσθῇ ᵛπαρ' ὑμῖν ᵘʷἡ ἐπιστολή, ˣποιήσατε ἵνα καὶ ἐν τῇ Λαοδικέων ἐκκλησίᾳ ᵗἀναγνωσθῇ, καὶ ʸτὴν ἐκ Λαοδικείας ἵνα καὶ ὑμεῖς ᵗἀναγνῶτε. 17 καὶ εἴπατε Ἀρχίππῳ ᶻΒλέπε τὴν ᵃᵇδιακονίαν ἣν ᶜπαρέλαβες ᵈἐν κυρίῳ, ἵνα αὐτὴν ᵇᵉπληροῖς. 18 Ὁ ᶠᵍἀσπασμὸς ᶠʰτῇ ἐμῇ ᶠʰχειρὶ ᶠΠαύλου. ⁱμνημονεύετέ μου τῶν ᵏδεσμῶν. ἡ ˡχάρις ˡμεθ' ὑμῶν.

ABCDF
KLPℵ a
bcdefg
hklmn
o 17. 47

ΠΡΟΣ ΚΟΛΑΣΣΑΕΙΣ.

z = w. ἵνα, 1 Cor. xvi. 10. 2 John 8. w. πῶς, 1 Cor. i. 26. Eph. v. 15.   a Eph. iv. 12 reff.
b Acts xii. 25. see 2 Tim. iv. 5. τὴν διακονίαν ἐκπλήσαντες, Philo in Flacc. § 19, vol. ii. p. 540.   c 1 Cor.
xi. 23. xv. 1, 3. Gal. i. 9, 12 al.   d ch. iii. 18 reff.   e = Matt. iii. 15. Acts xiv. 26 al. Ps. xix. 4.
f 1 Cor. xvi. 21. 2 Thess. iii. 17.   g as above (f). Luke i. 29, 41, 44. xi. 43 ‖. xx. 46 only †.
h as above (f). Gal. vi. 11. Philem. 19.   i = Gal. ii. 10.   k Phil. i. 7 reff.   l absol. in
valedictions, Eph. vi. 24. 1 Tim. vi. 22. 2 Tim. iv. 22. Tit. iii. 15. Heb. xiii. 25 only. elsw. with τοῦ κυρ., &c.
Rom. xvi. 20 [24]. 1 Cor. xvi. 23. 2 Cor. xiii. 13. 1 Thess. v. 28. 2 Thess. iii. 18 al.

15. rec αὐτοῦ (see note), with DFKL rel Chr Thdrt Damasc: αυτης (reading Νύμφαν, as B² accentuates, as a woman) B 67² : txt AC[P]ℵ 17 [47].

16. om η επιστολη B.   om last και D¹ o Ambrst: και bef ινα F.

18. rec at end ins αμην, with DKL[P]ℵ³ rel vss ff : om ABCFℵ¹ 17. 67² æth-rom Ambrst.

SUBSCRIPTION. rec adds εγραφη απο ρωμης δια τυχικου και ονησιμου, with KL rel (of which, b h k m o om πρ. κολ.: aft τυχ. ins και τιμοθεου m): om 1: A adds απο ρωμη(sic): B² adds εγραφη απο ρωμης [so P, adding στιχων ˢ]: η προς κολ. a: txt B¹C 17 æth, and D(addg επληρωθη) F(prefixing ετελεσθη) ℵ(adding στιχων τ).

that it was in a professional capacity that he first became attached to St. Paul, who evidently laboured under grievous sickness during the earlier part of the journey where Luke first appears in his company. Compare Gal. iv. 13 note, with Acts xvi. 6, 10. But this is too uncertain to be more than an interesting conjecture.

Δημᾶς] one of Paul's συνεργοί, Philem. 24, who however afterwards deserted him, from love to the world, 2 Tim. iv. 10. The absence of any honourable or endearing mention here may be owing to the commencement of this apostasy, or some unfavourable indication in his character.

15—17.] Salutations to friends.

15.] καί, before Νυμφᾶν, as so often, selects one out of a number previously mentioned: Nymphas was one of these Laodicean brethren. The var. readings, αὐτοῦ, αὐτῆς, appear to have arisen from the construction (see below) not being understood, and the alteration thus having been made to the singular, but in various genders. αὐτῶν refers to τῶν περὶ Νυμφᾶν: cf. Xen. Mem. i. 2. 62, ἐάν τις φανερὸς γένηται κλέπτων — τούτοις θάνατός ἐστιν ἡ ζημία: and see Bernhardy, p. 288; Kühner ii. § 419 ß. On the ἐκκλησία spoken of, see note, Rom. xvi. 5.

16.] ἡ ἐπιστ., the present letter,

reff. ποιήσ. ἵνα] as ποίει, ὅπως . . . Herod. i. 8. 209,—ὡς σαφέστατά γὰν εἰδείην . . . ἐποίουν, Xen. Cyr. vi. 3. 18.

τὴν ἐκ Λαοδ.] On this Epistle, see Prolegg. to Eph. § ii. 17, 19; and Philem. § iii. 2, 3 [and note on the subscription to 1 Tim.]. I will only indicate here the right rendering of the words. They cannot well be taken, as τινές in Chrys., to mean οὐχὶ τὴν Π. πρὸς αὐτοὺς ἀπεσταλμένην, ἀλλὰ τὴν παρ' αὐτῶν Παύλῳ (so also Syr., Thdrt., Phot. in Œc., Erasm., Beza, Calv., Wolf, Est., Corn.-a-lap., al.), both on account of the awkwardness of the sense commanding them to read an Epistle sent from Laodicea, and not found there, and on account of the phrase τὴν ἐκ so commonly having the pregnant meaning of 'which is there and must be sought from there;' cf. Kühner, ii. § 623 a. Herod. iii. 6. Thucyd. ii. 34; iii. 22; vi. 32; vii. 70, and other examples there. We may safely say that a letter not from, but to the Laodiceans is meant. For the construction of this latter sentence, ποιήσατε again is of course to be supplied.

17.] Archippus is mentioned Philem. 2, and called the Apostle's συνστρατιώτης. I have treated on the inference to be drawn from this passage as to his abode, in the Prolegg. to Philemon, § iii.

1. He was evidently some officer of the church, but *what*, in the wideness of διακονία, we cannot say: and conjectures are profitless (see such in Est. and Corn.-a-lap.). Meyer well remarks, that the authority hereby implied on the part of the congregation to exercise reproof and discipline over their teachers is remarkable : and that the hierarchical turn given to the passage by Thl. and Œc. (ἵνα ὅταν ἐπιτιμᾷ ᾿Αρχ. αὐτοῖς, μὴ ἔχωσιν ἐγκαλεῖν ἐκείνῳ ὡς πικρῷ, . . . ἐπεὶ ἄλλως ἄτοπον τοῖς μαθηταῖς περὶ τοῦ διδασκάλου διαλέγεσθαι, Thl.) belongs to a later age. As to the words themselves,—**Take heed to the ministry which thou receivedst in the Lord** (the sphere of the *reception* of the ministry; in which the recipient lived and moved and promised at his ordination : not, of the ministry itself (τὴν ἐν κυρ.),—nor is ἐν to be diverted from its simple local meaning), **that** (aim and end of the βλέπε,—in order that) **thou fulfil it** (reff.).

18.] AUTOGRAPH SALUTATION.

ὁ . . . . Παύλου] See ref. 1 Cor., where the same words occur. μνημ. . . . .

δεσμ.] These words extend further than to mere pecuniary support, or even mere prayers: they were ever to keep before them the fact that one who so deeply cared for them, and loved them, and to whom their perils of false doctrine occasioned such anxiety, was a prisoner in chains : and that remembrance was to work and produce its various fruits—of prayer for him, of affectionate remembrance of his wants, of deep regard for his words. When we read of ' his chains,' we should not forget that they moved over the paper as he wrote. His *right* hand was chained to the soldier that kept him. See Smith's Dict. of Antiq. under ' Catena.' ἡ χάρις—cf. reff. and ch. iii. 16. 'The grace' in which we stand (Rom. v. 2) : it seems (reff.) to be a form of valediction belonging to the later period of the Epistles of St. Paul.

ΠΡΟΣ ΘΕΣΣΑΛΟΝΙΚΕΙΣ Α.

I. ¹ Παῦλος καὶ Σιλουανὸς καὶ Τιμόθεος τῇ ἐκκλησίᾳ ABDFK LPℵ a b
Θεσσαλονικέων ᵃ ἐν ᵇ θεῷ ᵃᵇ πατρὶ καὶ κυρίῳ Ἰησοῦ χριστῷ. c d e f g h k l m n
ᶜ χάρις ὑμῖν καὶ ᶜ εἰρήνη. o 17. 47

a here (2 Thess. i. 1) only.
b Gal. i. 1 reff.
c Rom. i. 7 al.

TITLE. rec παυλου του αποστολου η προς θεσσ. επιστολη πρωτη: Steph η του αγιου παυλου πρ. θεσσ. πρωτη επ.: του αγ. απ. π. επ. πρ. θ. πρωτη L: αρχεται πρ. θεσσαλονικαιους F: επ. παυλου πρ. θεσσ. πρωτη O: [π. επ. πρ. θεσσ. a P:] θετταλικοις πολιταις ταδε κηρυξ ουρανοφοιτης f: επιστολη πρ. τ. θεσσ. α' l: πρ. θεσσ. επ. α' h k: txt ABKℵ m¹ n 17 [47] and (prefixing αρχεται) D.

CHAP. I. 1. [θεσσαλονικανων P.]   ins και bef πατρι K syr: add ημων A m 116. 8-pe vulg-sixt basm æth arm-marg Did Ambrst Pel.   και κυριου ιησου χριστου A (d) 17 (copt).   rec aft ειρηνη ins απο θεου πατρος ημων και κυριου ιησου χριστου (*from later epistles, e.g.* 1 Cor i. 3, 2 Cor i. 2, &c) with A D[omg ημων] KL[P]ℵ rel fuld(with tol) syr-w-ast (copt): om BF [47] vulg fri Syr basm æth-rom arm Chr-comm Thl Orig-int_expr("... pax. *Et nihil ultra*") Ambrst Pel. (C defective.)

CHAP. I. 1.] ADDRESS AND GREETING. The Apostle names Silvanus and Timotheus with himself, as having with him founded the church at Thessalonica, see Acts xvi. 1 : xvii. 14. Silvanus is placed before Timotheus, then a youth (Acts xvi. 1 f., see further in Prolegg. to 1 Tim. § i. 3, 4), as being one ἡγούμενος ἐν τοῖς ἀδελφοῖς (Acts xv. 22, 32; xviii. 5), and a προφήτης (ib. xv. 32, see also 2 Cor. i. 19; 1 Pet. v. 12). He does not name himself *an Apostle*, probably for (an amplification of) the reason given by De Wette,—because his Apostleship needed not any substantiation to the Thessalonians. For the same reason he omits the designation in the Epistle to the Philippians. This last fact precludes the reasons given,—by Pelt, al., '*id ei tum non jam moris fuisse*,' by Chrys.,—διὰ τὸ νεοκατηχήτους εἶναι τοὺς ἄνδρας, κ. μηδέπω αὐτοῦ πεῖραν εἰληφέναι,—by Estius, Pelt (altern.), and Zwingl., *out of modesty*, not to distinguish himself from Silvanus and Timotheus,—by Jowett, "probably the name 'Apostle,'

which in its general sense was used of many, was gradually, and at no definite period, applied to him with the same special meaning as to the Apostles at Jerusalem." τῇ ἐκκλησίᾳ] So in 2 Thess., Gal., Corr., in the other Epistles, viz. Rom., Eph., Col., Phil., more generally, e.g.,—πᾶσιν τοῖς οὖσιν ἐν Ῥώμῃ ἀγαπητοῖς θεοῦ, κλητοῖς ἁγίοις. This is most probably accounted for by the circumstances of the various Epistles. We may notice that the gen. plur. of the persons constituting the church occurs only in the addresses of these two Epistles. We may render 'of Thessalonians,' or 'of the Thessalonians :' better the former. ἐν θεῷ πατρί] The construction need not be filled up by τῇ or τῇ οὔσῃ, as Chr., al.: nor with Schott, by understanding χαίρειν λέγουσιν, which would be unnecessary, seeing that the apostolic greeting follows. The words form a ("*tertiary*," Ellic.) predication respecting τῇ ἐκκλησίᾳ, or Θεσσαλονικέων, which requires no supplementing. See Winer, edn. 6,

C ευχα-
ρισ...
ABCDF
KLPℵ a
b c d e f g
h k l m n
o 17. 47

² ᵈ Εὐχαριστοῦμεν τῷ ᵈ θεῷ πάντοτε περὶ πάντων ὑμῶν
ᵉ μνείαν [ὑμῶν] ᵉ ποιούμενοι ᵉ ἐπὶ τῶν προσευχῶν ἡμῶν
ᶠ ἀδιαλείπτως, ³ ᵍ μνημονεύοντες ὑμῶν τοῦ ʰⁱ ἔργου τῆς
πίστεως καὶ τοῦ ʲ κόπου τῆς ⁱ ἀγάπης καὶ τῆς ᵏ ὑπομονῆς

d Rom. i. 8.
1 Cor. i. 4.
Col. i. 3.
Phil. i. 3.
Philem. 4.
(Judith viii.
25. 2 Macc.
i. 11.)
e Eph. i. 16
reff.

f Rom. i. 9. ch. ii. 13. v. 17 only†.　1 Macc. xii. 11 al.　　　g w. gen., Luke xvii. 32.　John xvi. 4, 21.　Acts
　　xx. 35 al.　1 Chron. xvi. 15.　　　　　　　h Rom. xiii. 12.　Gal. v. 19.　Eph. iv. 12.　　　i Heb. vi. 10.
j 1 Cor. iii. 8.　xv. 58.　Gen. xxxi. 42.　　　　k so Rom. ii. 7.

2. om 1st υμων C fri : περι π. υμων bef παντοτε a 17. 74. 120.　　　om 2nd υμων
(*because* υμων *preceded?　See Eph* i. 16 *var readd*) ABℵ¹ 17. 67² am (with harl²)
[arm] : ins CDFKL[P]ℵ³ rel latt coptt syrr gr-lat-ff. (om from μνειαν to end of ver m.)
ποιουμενο**ς** C¹(corrd by C¹, appy) d 17, *faciens* D-lat.　　　for ημων, υμων A.
(so also ch ii. 18 for ημας, υμας A¹.)
3. του εργ. της πιστ. bef υμων (*transposn from misunderstandg*) DF latt Syr æth
Ambrst. (το εργον F, των εργων Syr.)　　　τον κοπον and την υπομονην D¹F.

§ 20. 2.　　　ἐν θεῷ πατρί marks them
as not being heathens,—κ. κυρίῳ Ἰησοῦ
χριστῷ, as not being Jews. So De W.
after Chrys.: but perhaps the πατρί
already marks them as Christians.
The ἐν, as usual, denotes *communion* and
participation in, as the element of spiritual life.　χάρις ὑμῖν κ. εἰρήνη]
"Gratia et pax a Deo sit vobis, ut, qui
humana gratia et sæculari pace privati
estis, apud Deum gratiam et pacem ha-
beatis." Anselm (in Pelt). The words
which follow in the rec. are not yet added
in this his first Epistle. Afterwards they
became a common formula with him.
2—III. 13.] FIRST PORTION OF THE
EPISTLE, *in which he pours out his heart
to the Thessalonians respecting all the circumstances of their reception of and adhesion to the faith.*　2—10.] Jowett remarks, that few passages are more characteristic of the style of St. Paul than this
one: both as being the overflowing of his
love in thankfulness for his converts, about
whom he can never say too much: and
as to the very form and structure of the
sentences, which seem to grow under his
hand, gaining force in each successive
clause by the repetition and expansion of
the preceding. See this exemplified in detail in his note.　　　2.] εὐχαριστοῦμεν,
coming so immediately after the mention of
Paul, Silvanus, and Timotheus, can hardly
be here understood of the Apostle alone, as
Pelt, Conyb. and Hows., Jowett, al. For
undoubted as it is that he often, e. g. ch.
iii. 1, 2, where see note, uses the plural of
himself alone, yet it is as undoubted that
he uses it also of himself and his fellow-
labourers—e. g., 2 Cor. i. 18, 19. And so
De W., Lünemann, al., take it here.
πάντοτε περὶ πάντων] We have the same
alliteration Eph. v. 20. These words belong to εὐχαριστ., not to μνείαν ποι. On
these latter words see Rom. i. 9 f.

ἀδιαλείπτως seems by the nearly parallel
place, Rom. i. 9, to belong to μνείαν ὑμ.
ποι., not to μνημονεύοντες, as Lün., Pelt,
al. Such a formula would naturally repeat itself, as far as specifications of this
kind are concerned. Still it must be
borne in mind, that the order there is
slightly different.　3.] μνημον. is not
intransitive, as Erasm.-Schmid, al.: but
as in reff.: '*commemorantes*,' Beza. ὑμῶν
is by Œcum., Calv., al., regarded as the
genitive after μνημον. standing alone, and
ἕνεκα supplied before the other genitives.
But such a construction may be doubted,
and at all events it is much simpler here
to regard ὑμ. as the genitive governed by
τοῦ ἔργου, ... τοῦ κόπου, and τῆς ὑπομονῆς, and prefixed, as belonging to all
three. πίστις, ἀγάπη, ἐλπίς, are the
three great Christian graces of 1 Cor.
xiii. See also ch. v. 8; Col. i. 4, 5 : and
Usteri, paulinisch. Lehrbegriff, p. 236 ff.
τοῦ ἔργου τῆς πίστεως] Simple as
these words are, all sorts of strange meanings have been given to them. Koppe
and Rosenmüller hold τ. ἔργου to be pleonastic: Calv., Calov., al., render (ungrammatical) '*your faith wrought by
God;*' Kypke, '*the reality* (ἔργ. as contrasted with λόγος) *of your faith;*' Chrys.,
Thl., Thdrt., Œc., al., '*the endurance of
your faith in suffering:*' &c. Comparing
the words with the following genitives,
they seem to mean, 'that work (energetic
activity) which faith brings forth' (as
Chrys. ἡ πίστις διὰ τῶν ἔργων δείκνυται:
the gen., as also those following, being
thus a *possessive* one: see Ellicott here):
q. d. 'the activity of your faith:' see
2 Thess. i. 11: or perhaps, as Jowett (but
not so well), "'your work of faith,' i. e. the
Christian life, which springs from faith :"
thus making the gen. one of *origin*.
τοῦ κόπου] probably *towards the sick
and needy strangers*, cf. Acts xx. 35;

τῆς ¹ἐλπίδος τοῦ κυρίου ἡμῶν Ἰησοῦ χριστοῦ ᵐἔμπροσθεν ABCDF
τοῦ ⁿθεοῦ καὶ ⁿπατρὸς ἡμῶν, ⁴ εἰδότες, ἀδελφοὶ °ἠγαπη-
μένοι ὑπὸ θεοῦ, τὴν ᵖἐκλογὴν ὑμῶν· ⁵ ὅτι τὸ ᑫεὐαγγέ-
λιον ᑫἡμῶν οὐκ ʳˢἐγενήθη ˢεἰς ὑμᾶς ἐν ᵗλόγῳ μόνον,

1 accumula-
tion of geni-
tives, 2 Cor.
iv. 4.　Eph. i.
6. iv. 13 al. fr.
m = Matt. x. 32.
ch. ii. 19. iii.
9, 13.
n Gal. i. 4 reff.
o 2 Thess. ii.
13.　Deut. xxxiii. 12.
14 reff.
Luke iii. 2.
p Acts ix. 15.　Rom. ix. 11. xi. 5, 7, 28.　2 Pet. i. 10 only†.
r form, Acts iv. 4.　Col. iv. 11 al.
t 1 Cor. iv. 19, 20. see Col. iii. 17 reff.
s Acts xxviii. 6.　Gal. iii. 14. see πρός, 1 Cor. ii. 3.　ἐπί,
ABCDF
KLPℵ a
b c d e f g
h k l m n
o 17. 47
q 2 Thess. ii.

ᴏᴍ τηϛ ελπιδοϛ A Ambrst-txt : for ελπ., αγαπηϛ 17 : pref και k 19 tol Chr-comm₁
Ambrst-comm.

4. ins του bef θεου ACK[P]ℵ b k m o sah Thl-marg(and comm) : om BDFL rel
gr-ff.

5 aft ευαγ. ins του θεου [C(but om ημων)] ℵ.　　for εις, προς (see 1 Cor ii. 3)
AC²DF Chr Thl : εφ' 46 : txt BKLℵ rel Chr-ins Thdrt Damasc[: εν υμιν P.] (C¹
illegible.)　　μονω (mechanical repetition) DK c d k.

Rom. xvi. 6, 12—not *in the word and
ministry* (De W.), cf. ch. v. 12 : which is
irrelevant here. τῆς ἀγάπ. not as *springing from*, but as *belonging to*, love,—
characterizing it (Lün.) : see above.
τ. ὑπομ. τῆς ἐλπίδος] **your endurance of
hope**—i. e. endurance (in trials) which
belongs to (see above), characterizes, your
hope; and also nourishes it, in turn : cf.
Rom. xv. 4, ἵνα διὰ τῆς ὑπομονῆς, κ. διὰ
τῆς παρακλήσεως τῶν γραφῶν τὴν ἐλπίδα
ἔχωμεν.　　**τοῦ κυρ. ἡμ. Ἰ. χ.**] specifies
the hope—that it is a hope of the coming
of the Lord Jesus Christ (cf. ver. 10). Olsh.
refers the words to all three preceding
substantives—but this seems alien from
St. Paul's style.　On all three Jowett says
well, ' your faith, hope, and love ; a faith
that had its outward effect on your lives :
a love that spent itself in the service of
others : a hope that was no mere transient
feeling, but was content to wait for the
things unseen when Christ should be revealed.'　　**ἔμπρ. τ. θ. κ. πατρ. ἡμ.**]
belongs most naturally to μνημονεύοντες—**making mention . . . . before God :**
not to the genitives preceding (see Rom.
iv. 17 ; xiv. 22), as Thdrt., al.

4.] **εἰδότες** refers back to μνημονεύοντες ; **in that we know**—or **for
we know.** Thdrt., Erasm., Grot., al., take
it for οἴδατε γάρ, or εἰδότες ἐστέ, wrongly
referring it to the Thessalonians : Pelt
joins it with μνείαν ποιούμενοι : but the
construction as above seems the best. **ὑπὸ
θεοῦ** belongs to ἠγαπημένοι, as in 2 Thess.
ii. 13, see also Rom. i. 7 : not to εἰδότες,
as Est. thinks possible (ὑπὸ for παρά ?),
nor to ἐκλογὴν—either as E. V., '*your
election of God*,' which is ungrammatical
(requiring τὴν ὑπ. θ. ἐκ.), or as Œc., Thl.,
all., ὑπὸ θ. τὴν ἐκλ. ὑμ. (εἶναι), which
would introduce an irrelevant emphasis on
ὑπὸ θεοῦ.　**ἐκλογή** must not be softened
down : it is the **election** unto life of individual believers by God, so commonly

adduced by St. Paul (reff. : and 1 Cor. i.
27 ; 2 Thess. ii. 13).　**ὑμῶν**, objective
genitive after ἐκλογήν—knowing that
God ἐξελέξατο ὑμᾶς.　　**5.**] **ὅτι** has
been taken to mean '*videlicet, ut*,' and the
verse to be an epexegesis of ἐκλογήν : but
as Lün. remarks, evidently verses 5, 6 ff.
are meant not to explain *wherein* their
election *consisted*, but to give reasons in
matter of fact for concluding (εἰδότες) the
existence of that election. ὅτι must then
be **because**, and a colon be placed at ὑμῶν.
These reasons are (1) the power and confidence with which he and Silvanus and
Timotheus preached among them (ver. 5),
and (2) the earnest and joyful manner in
which the Thessalonians received it (vv.
6 ff.).　Both these were signs of God's
grace to them—tokens of their election
vouchsafed by Him.　**τὸ εὐαγγ. ἡμ.**, **the
gospel which we preached.**　**ἐγενήθη
εἰς**] See reff., especially Gal. : **came to
you** is perhaps the nearest : εἰς betokens
the direction. πρός, with ἐγέν., would give
nearly the same sense, or perhaps that of
apud, see ref. 1 Cor. &c.　We must not
take ἐγενήθη εἰς ὑμ. for a constr. præg-
nans (ἦλθ. εἰς καὶ ἐγ. ἐν), which with ἦν
it might be : for ἐγενήθη εἰς carries motion in itself without any thing supplied.
On 'the passive form ἐγενήθη, alien to the
Attic, and originally Doric, but common
in the κοινή' (Lün.), see note on Eph. iii. 7 ;
Lobeck on Phryn. p. 108 ff. ; Winer, § 15.　It was attempted in my
earlier editions to press the *passive sense*
in the frequent occurrences of this form
in this Epistle.　But wider acquaintance
with the usage has since convinced me
that this is not possible, and that we must
regard it as equivalent in meaning to the
more usual ἐγένετο.　　The prepositions **ἐν** following indicate the form and
manner in which the *preaching was carried on*, not (as Pelt, al.) that in which
the Thessalonians received it, which is not

ἀλλὰ καὶ ἐν ᵗ δυνάμει καὶ ᵘ ἐν πνεύματι ἁγίῳ καὶ ἐν
ᵛ πληροφορίᾳ πολλῇ, καθὼς οἴδατε οἷοι ʷ ἐγενήθημεν ἐν
ὑμῖν δι᾽ ὑμᾶς. ⁶ καὶ ὑμεῖς ˣ μιμηταὶ ἡμῶν ἐγενήθητε
καὶ τοῦ κυρίου, ʸ δεξάμενοι τὸν λόγον ἐν θλίψει πολλῇ
ᶻ μετὰ ᵃ χαρᾶς πνεύματος ἁγίου, ⁷ ᵇ ὥστε γενέσθαι ὑμᾶς
ᶜ τύπον πᾶσιν τοῖς πιστεύουσιν ἐν τῇ Μακεδονίᾳ καὶ ἐν τῇ

u 1 Cor. ii. 4.
  2 Cor. vi. 6.
v Col. ii. 2.
  Heb. vi. 11.
  x. 22 only †.
  (-ρείσθαι,
  Col. iv. 12.)
w = 1 Cor. i.
  30. 2 Cor.
  vii. 14 al.
x 1 Cor. iv. 16.
  xi. 1. Eph.
  v. 1. ch. ii.
  14. Heb. vi
  12 only †.

y = Luke viii. 13. Acts viii. 14. xi. 1. xvii. 11. 1 Cor. ii. 14. ch. ii. 13. James i. 21. Prov. iv. 10.
z = Phil. i. 4. ii. 29. 1 Chron. xxix. 22. a Rom. xiv. 17. b = Phil. i. 13 al.
c = 1 Tim. iv. 12 reff.

om 3rd εν c e l n o 17. 67² D-lat tol copt Thdrt-ms.   om 4th εν Bℵ 17 tol coptt.
    om 5th εν AC[P]ℵ f 17. 67² am.

6. for θεου, κυριου A.   aft χαρας ins και B.

7. rec τυπους (*alteration to suit υμας*), with ACFKL[P]ℵ rel syr gr-ff : τυπος D³ 49
(*by mistake? or perhaps* (Mill) *a neuter form as* πλουτος?) : txt BD¹ 17 [47] 67² latt
Syr coptt Ambrst Pel.   rec om 2nd εν, with KL rel (c g h m o [47] Chr om τη
also) : ins ABCDF[P]ℵ k 17 latt syrr Thdrt Ambrst Pel.

treated till ver. 6.   δυνάμει is not '*miracles*,' as Thdrt., Œc., all., nor *efficacia et
vis agens in cordibus fidelium* (Bullinger)
(see above), but **power**, viz. of utterance
and of energy.   πν. ἁγίῳ] beware
again of the supposed figure of ἐν διὰ δυοῖν,
by which all character of style and all
logical exactness is lost. Even Conyb. here
has fallen into this error, and rendered
"*power of the Holy Ghost*." It is a
predicate advancing *beyond* ἐν δυνάμει—
not only in force and energy, but **in the
Holy Ghost**—in a manner which could
only be ascribed to the operation of the
Holy Spirit.   πληροφορίᾳ πολλῇ]
much confidence (of faith), see reff. Many
irrelevant meanings have been given : *fulness of spiritual gifts*, which the Thessalonians had received (Lomb., Corn.-a-lap.,
Turretin.) : *certainty of the truth*, felt by
them (Macknight, Benson, al.) : '*fulfilment of the apostolic office*' (Estius). The
confidence (see above) was that in which
*Paul and Silvanus and Timotheus preached
to them*.   καθὼς κ.τ.λ.] Appeal to
their knowledge that the fact was so.
These words restrict the foregoing to the
preachers, as explained above : καὶ τί, φησι,
μακρηγορῶ; αὐτοὶ ὑμεῖς μάρτυρές ἐστε, οἷοι
ἐγενήθημεν πρὸς ὑμᾶς. Œc. This interpretation is fixed by καθώς, referring back to
the whole previous description. The sense
has been variously given : Conyb., '*And
you, likewise know*'—but '*likewise*' surely
confounds the connexion : Pelt, even further from the mark, ... '*ita accipimus,
ut Apostolum exemplum suum Thessaloni-
ensibus imitandum statuamus*.'   οἷοι
ἐγενήθ.] what manner of men we proved,
as Ellic. : not '*quales facti simus*,' see
above in this note : nor as vulg., '*quales
fuerimus;*' the point of the fact appealed
to is, the proof given, what manner of men

they were, by the manner of their preaching. "The ποιότης was evinced in the
power and confidence with which they delivered their message." Ellic. : *the proof
given by the manner of their preaching*.
ἐν ὑμῖν] local merely : **among you.**
δι᾽ ὑμᾶς] for your sakes—convey-
ing the purpose of the Apostle and his colleagues, and in the background also *the
purpose of* GOD—'you know what God
enabled us to be,—how mighty in preaching the word,—for your sakes—thereby
proving that he loved you, and had chosen
you for His own.'   6.] Further proof of
the same, that ye are ἐκλεκτοί, by the
method in which *you received* the Gospel
thus preached by us. καὶ ὑμεῖς corresponds
with τὸ εὐ. ἡμῶν above. It is somewhat
difficult here to fix exactly the point of
comparison, in which they imitated their
ministers and Christ. Certainly it is not
merely, in *receiving the word*—for to omit
other objections, this would not apply at all
to Him :—and therefore, not in any qualifying detail of their *method* of reception
of the word—not in δύναμις, nor in πν. ἁγ.,
nor in πληρ. πολλ.   So far being clear,
we have but one particular left, and that respects the circumstances under which, and
the spirit with which : and here we find a
point of comparison even with Christ Himself : viz. joyful endurance in spirit under
sufferings. This it was in which they imitated the Apostles, and their divine Master,
and which made them patterns to other
churches (see below). For this θλίψις
in which they ἐδέξαντο τὸν λόγον, see Acts
xvii. 5—10 ; ch. ii. 14; iii. 2, 3, 5.
δεξάμενοι] in that ye received. χαρὰ
πνεύματος ἁγίου (ref.), joy wrought by
the Holy Spirit. On the gen. of origin,
see Ellic.'s note here.   7.] *Further specification of the eminence of the Thessalo-*

d — 1 Cor. xiv. 36.
e here only. Joel iii. 14.
Sir. xl. 13 only.
f = Acts viii. 25. xiii. 48, 49. xv. 36. xix. 10, 20.
2 Thess. iii. 1.
g here (Philem. 5 v. r.) only.
see Gal. iii. 26 reff.

Ἀχαΐᾳ. [8] [d] ἀφ' ὑμῶν γὰρ [e] ἐξήχηται ὁ [f] λόγος τοῦ [f] κυρίου οὐ μόνον ἐν τῇ Μακεδονίᾳ καὶ Ἀχαΐᾳ, ἀλλ' ἐν παντὶ τόπῳ ἡ [g] πίστις ὑμῶν ἡ [g] πρὸς τὸν θεὸν [h] ἐξελήλυθεν, ὥστε μὴ [i] χρείαν [i] ἔχειν ἡμᾶς λαλεῖν τι. [9] [k] αὐτοὶ γὰρ περὶ ἡμῶν [l] ἀπαγγέλλουσιν [m] ὁποίαν [n] εἴσοδον ἔσχομεν

ABCDF
KLPℵ a
b c d e f g
h k l m n
o 17.47

h = Matt. ix. 26.   i w. inf., ch. iv. 9 reff.   k = Gal. ii. 2 reff.
l Paul, 1 Cor. xiv. 25 only. Gospp. & Acts, passim. Heb. ii. 12. 1 John i. 2 only. Gen. xiv. 13.   m Acts xxvi. 29. 1 Cor. iii. 13. Gal. ii. 6. James i. 24 only †.   n Acts xiii. 24. ch. ii. 1. Heb. x. 19. 2 Pet. i. 11 only. 1 Kings xvi. 4.

8. [homœotel in A αχαια ver 7 to αχαια.] om γαρ ℵ[1](ins ℵ-corr[1]) k. for κυρ., θεου ℵ[1] [syr-mg basm]. ins εν τη bef αχαια (*repeated from former ver, as* "necessary to mark Ach. as a distinct province." *For this very reason Meyer retains it*) CDFKL[P]ℵ rel latt syrr Cyr Damasc Œc Ambrst Pel : ins τη f k o : om AB c m 17 [47] Chr Thdrt Thl. rec (for αλλ' εν) αλλα και εν (και *insd as being usual after* ου μονον), with D[3]KL rel æth Chr Cyr Thdrt : txt ABCD[1]F[P] m 17 am(with fuld demid) syrr coptt, ℵ[1] has αλλα—, of which ℵ-corr[1] or 3 has made αλλα εν. rec ημας bef εχειν (*for emphasis to contrast with* αυτοι *follg*), with KL rel Chr Damasc : txt ABCDF[P]ℵ (c) m 17 Thdrt. for λαλειν, παλιν C.

9. for ημων, υμων B a h k n o 120-1-2-3 D-lat coptt Chr[1]-ms[1] Thdrt Damasc Œc. rec (for εσχ.) εχομεν (with 17 ?) : txt ABCDFKL[P]ℵ rel latt Chr Thdrt Thl-marg lat-ff.

---

nians' *Christian character.* τύπον, of the whole church as one : see Bernhardy, p. 60. πᾶσιν τοῖς πιστεύουσιν] to the whole of the believers. οἱ πιστεύοντες, like ὁ πειράζων, designates the *kind.* Chrys. understands this participle as if it were πιστεύσασιν :—καὶ μὴν ἐν ὑστέρῳ ἦλθε πρὸς αὐτούς· ἀλλ' οὕτως ἐλάμψατε, φησίν, ὡς τῶν προλαβόντων γενέσθαι διδασκάλους . . . . οὐ γὰρ εἶπεν, ὥστε τύπους γενέσθαι πρὸς τὸ πιστεῦσαι, ἀλλὰ τοῖς ἤδη πιστεύουσι τύπος ἐγένεσθε. But it was not so : for the only church in Europe which was in Christ before the Thessalonian, was the Philippian (Acts xvi. 12—xvii. 1, see ch. ii. 2). Μακ. κ. Ἀχ.] Cf. Rom. xv. 26; Acts xix. 21 : the two Roman provinces, comprehending Northern and Southern Greece. There is no reference, as Thdrt., to the Greeks being ἔθνη μέγιστα κ. ἐπὶ σοφίᾳ θαυμαζόμενα, and so their praise being the greater : these are mentioned simply because the Apostle had been, since their conversion, in Macedonia, and had left Silvanus and Timotheus there,—and was now in Achaia. **8.**] *Proof of the praise in ver. 7.* ἀφ' ὑμῶν is merely local, **from you,** as in ref.; not '*by you*' (as preachers) (ὑφ' ὑμῶν), as Rückert, "locorum Paulinorum 1 Thess. i. 8 et 1 Thess. iii. 1—3 explanatio :" nor '*by your means,*' viz. in saving Silas and myself from danger of our lives and so enabling us to preach (δι' ὑμῶν), as Storr, and Flatt. ἐξήχηται] δηλῶν ὅτι ὥσπερ σάλπιγγος λαμπρὸν ἠχούσης ὁ πλησίον ἅπας πληροῦται τόπος, οὕτω τῆς ὑμετέρας ἀνδρείας ἡ φήμη καθάπερ ἐκείνη σαλπίζουσα ἱκανὴ τὴν οἰκουμένην ἐμπλη-

σαι. Chrys. ὁ λόγ. τ. κυρίου, cannot be as De W. '*the fame of the reception of the Gospel by you:*' the sense seems to be that your ready reception and faith as it were sounded forth the λόγον τοῦ κυρίου, the word of the Lord, the Gospel message, loudly and clearly, through all parts. The logical construction of this verse is somewhat difficult. After the οὐ μόνον ἐν τῇ Μακ. κ. Ἀχ., we expect merely ἀλλ' ἐν παντὶ τόπῳ : but these words appear, followed by a new subject and a new predicate. Either then we must regard this new subject and predicate as merely an epexegesis of the former, ἐξήχηται ὁ λόγ. τοῦ κυρ., or, with Lünemann, we must place a colon at κυρίου, and begin a new sentence with οὐ μόνον. This last is very objectionable, for it leaves ἀφ' ὑμ. . . . . κυρίου standing alone in the most vapid and spiritless manner, with the strong rhetorical word ἐξήχηται unaccounted for and unemphatic. The other way then must be our refuge, and I cannot see those objections to it which Lün. has found. It is quite according to the versatile style of St. Paul, half to lose sight of the οὐ μόνον ἀλλ', and to go on after ἐν παντὶ τόπῳ with a new sentence ; and especially as that new sentence explains the somewhat startling one preceding. πρός, towards, directed towards God as its object (and here, as contrasted with idols, see next verse)—not = the more usual εἰς, to and into, as Ellic. correcting my previous on (ἐπί). De Wette, al., suppose with some probability that the report of the Thessalonians' faith may have been spread by

πρὸς ὑμᾶς, καὶ πῶς °ἐπεστρέψατε πρὸς τὸν θεὸν ἀπὸ
τῶν ᵖ εἰδώλων, ᑫ δουλεύειν θεῷ ʳ ζῶντι καὶ ˢ ἀληθινῷ,
¹⁰ καὶ ᵗ ἀναμένειν τὸν υἱὸν αὐτοῦ ἐκ τῶν οὐρανῶν, ὃν
ᵘ ἤγειρεν ᵘ ἐκ τῶν νεκρῶν, Ἰησοῦν τὸν ᵛ ῥυόμενον ἡμᾶς
ἀπὸ τῆς ʷ ὀργῆς τῆς ἐρχομένης.

II. ¹ Αὐτοὶ γὰρ οἴδατε, ἀδελφοί, τὴν ˣ εἴσοδον ἡμῶν
τὴν πρὸς ὑμᾶς, ὅτι οὐ ʸ κενὴ γέγονεν, ² ἀλλὰ ᶻ προπα-

o = Acts xiv.
15. 2 Cor.
iii. 16. Amos
iv. 6.
p = Acts xv.
20. Rom. ii.
22. 1 John
v. 21 al.
Num. xxv. 2.
q = Acts xx.
19. Gal. iv.
8. Ps. ii. 11.
r Acts xiv. 15.
1 Kings xvii.
36 f.
s John xvii. 3.
1 John v. 20

(3ce) al. Isa. lxv. 16. t here only. Job vii. 2. Isa. lix. 11. Gal. i. 1 al.
v w. ἀπό, Matt. vi. 13. Rom. xv. 31. 2 Thess. iii. 2. 2 Tim. iv. 18 only. Ps. cxxxix. 1. w. ἐκ, Col. i. 13.
w = Matt. iii. 7 ‖ L. Rom. ii. 5. ch. ii. 16. Zeph. ii. 2. x ch. i. 9 reff. y Acts iv. 25. 1 Cor.
xv. 10, 14, 58. Deut. xxxii. 47. z here only †. παρηνόμησαν οὐ προπαθόντες, Thuc. iii.
67. cf. also iii. 82.

10. rec om 2nd των, with ACK Œc: ins BDFL[P]‫א‬ rel Chr Damasc Thdrt Thl.
forαπο, εκ [A]B[P]‫א‬ 17. 73.

Chap. II. 2. rec aft αλλα ins και, with D-lat: om ABCDFKL[P]‫א‬ rel vulg syrr
coptt [arm] Cyr lat-ff.

Christian travelling merchants, such as
Aquila and Priscilla. ὥστε μὴ . . . .]
The report being already rife, we found
no occasion to speak of your faith, or in
your praise. 9.] αὐτοί, the people
ἐν τῇ Μακ. κ. ᾽Αχ., κ. ἐν παντὶ τόπῳ:
see reff., and Bernhardy, p. 288.
περὶ ἡμῶν] concerning us, Paul and Silvanus and Timotheus; not as Lün., 'us
both,' including the Thessalonians. This
he does, to square the following clauses,
which otherwise are not correspondent:
but there are two objections to his view:
(1) the emphatic position of περὶ ἡμῶν,
which seems to necessitate its keeping its
strict meaning: (2) that it would in this
case have been much more naturally ὑμῶν
than ἡμῶν, as the second person has prevailed throughout, and our εἴσοδος to you
was quite as much a matter happening to
you as to us. That καὶ περὶ ὑμῶν, πῶς
should be abbreviated as we find it, will
surely not surprise any one familiar with
the irregularities, in point of symmetry, of
St. Paul's style. The ἀπαγγελλόμενα
here correspond to the two members of
the above proof, verses 5 and 6. ὁποίαν
has no reference to danger, as Chrys., al.
εἴσοδος merely access, in the way of
coming to them: see ch. ii. 1: not of itself facilis aditus, as Pelt. πῶς, merely
how that, introducing matter of fact,—
not 'how,' 'in what manner,' how joyfully and energetically, as Lünem.: if so,
the long specification (πρὸς . . . . ἐρχομένης), which follows the (thus) unemphatic
verb, drags wearily: whereas, regarded as
indicating matter of fact only, the πῶς
is unemphatic, and the matter of fact itself, carrying the emphasis, justifies the
full statement which is made of it.
ζῶντι κ. ἀληθινῷ] ζῶντα μὲν αὐτὸν ὠνόμασεν, ὡς ἐκείνων οὐ ζώντων. ἀληθινὸν

δέ, ὡς ἐκείνων ψευδῶς θεῶν καλουμένων.
Thdrt. 10.] The especial aspect of
the faith of the Thessalonians was hope:
hope of the return of the Son of God from
heaven: a hope, indeed, common to them
with all Christians in all ages, but evidently entertained by them as pointing to
an event more immediate than the church
has subsequently believed it to be. Certainly these words would give them an
idea of the nearness of the coming of
Christ: and perhaps the misunderstanding
of them may have contributed to the notion which the Apostle corrects, 2 Thess.
ii. 1 ff.: see note there. By ὃν ἤγ. ἐκ
τῶν νεκρῶν, that whereby (Rom. i. 4)
Jesus was declared to be the Son of God
with power, is emphatically prefixed to
His name. τὸν ῥυόμενον] who de-
livereth: not = τ. ῥυσόμενον,—still less
as E. V., past, 'who delivered,' but descriptive of His office, = 'our Deliverer,'
as ὁ πειράζων, &c. τῆς ἐρχ.—which is
coming: cf. Eph. v. 6; Col. iii. 6. Ch.
II. 1—16.] He reminds the Thessalonians
of his manner of preaching among them (1
—12, answering to ch. i. 9 a): praises
them for their reception of the Gospel, and
firmness in persecution (13—16, answering to ch. i. 9 b). 1.] γάρ refers
back to ὁποίαν, ch. i. 9: 'not only do
strangers report it, but you know it to be
true.' He makes use now of that knowledge to carry out the description of his
preaching among them, with a view, by
recapitulating these details, to confirm
them, who were as yet but novices, in the
faith. κενή] It is evident from vv.
2 ff., that this does not here apply to the
fruits, but to the character of his preaching: the result does not appear till ver.
13. And within this limitation, we may
observe that the verb is γέγονεν, not

a Matt. xxii. 6.
Luke xi. 45.
xviii. 32.
Acts xiv. 5
only. 2 Kings
xix. 43.
b Acts ix. 27,
28. xiii. 46.
xiv. 3 al3.
Eph. vi. 20
only. L.P.
Prov. xx. 9
al.
c so Acts ix.
27, 28. Eph.

θόντες καὶ ᵃ ὑβρισθέντες, καθὼς οἴδατε, ἐν Φιλίπποις, A B C D F
K L P א a
ᵇ ἐπαρρησιασάμεθα ᶜ ἐν τῷ θεῷ ἡμῶν λαλῆσαι πρὸς ὑμᾶς b c d e f g
h k l m n
τὸ ᵈ εὐαγγέλιον τοῦ ᵈ θεοῦ ἐν πολλῷ ᵉ ἀγῶνι. ³ ἡ γὰρ o 17. 47
ᶠ παράκλησις ἡμῶν οὐκ ἐκ ᵍ πλάνης οὐδὲ ἐξ ʰ ἀκαθαρσίας,
οὐδὲ ἐν ⁱ δόλῳ, ⁴ ἀλλὰ καθὼς ʲ δεδοκιμάσμεθα ὑπὸ τοῦ
θεοῦ ᵏ πιστευθῆναι τὸ εὐαγγέλιον, οὕτως λαλοῦμεν, οὐχ

vi. 20. = ἐπί, Acts xiv. 3.　　　　　　　　　 d Rom. i. 1. xv. 16.　2 Cor. xi. 7. vv. 8, 9.　1 Pet. iv. 17 only. (see Mark i.
14.　Acts xx. 24.　1 Tim. i. 11.)　　　　　 e = Phil. i. 30 (reff.).　　　　　f = Phil. ii. 1 reff.　　　　g = Matt.
xxvii. 64.　Eph. iv. 14 al.　Prov. xiv. 8.　　h Paul (Rom. vi. 19. ch. iv. 7 al.) only, exc. Matt. xxiii. 27.　Hos.
ii. 10.　　　　　i John i. 48.　2 Cor. xii. 16.　1 Pet. ii. 1 al.　Job xiii. 7.　　　　　j = Rom. xiv. 22.　1 Cor. xvi.
3. (see below [m].)　　　k Rom. iii. 2.　1 Cor. ix. 17. constr., Acts xxi. 3.　Gal. ii. 7.

3. rec (for 2nd ουδε) ουτε, with D³KL rel Chr_aliq Thdrt(txt₂) Damasc Thl Œc : txt
ABCD¹F[P]א 17 [47] 67², ουδ' m.

ἐγένετο; to be understood therefore not
of any mere intent of the Apostle at the
time of his coming among them, but of
some abiding character of his preaching.
It cannot then be understood as Koppe,
—'veni ad vos eo consilio .... ut vobis
prodessem, non ut otiose inter vos vive-
rem :' and nearly so Rosenm. It probably expresses, that his εἴσοδος was and
continued 'no empty scheme' ('no light
matter,' as we say; οὐχ ἡ τυχοῦσα, Chrys.),
but an earnest, bold, self-denying endeavour for their good. This he proceeds to
prove.　　　　2.] προπαθόντες, having
previously suffered : reff. On the fact,
see Acts xvi.　　ἐπαρρησιασ.] Lünemann seems to be right (against De W.)
in rendering it we were confident, not
'we were free of speech.' See however,
on the other side, Ellic.'s note.
ἡμῶν, because all true confidence is in
God as our God. This word reproduces
the feeling with which Paul and Silas
opened their ministry among them : διὰ
τὸν ἐνδυναμοῦντα θεὸν τοῦτο ποιῆσαι
τεθαρρήκαμεν. Œcum.　　λαλῆσαι is
infinitive of the object after ἐπαρρησ.—
we had the confidence to speak : as E. V.,
were bold to speak. This seems more
probable than with De W., Mey. on Eph.
vi. 20, and Ellic., to regard it as the
epexegetical inf. "defining still more
clearly the oral nature of the boldness."
Chrys. can hardly be quoted on that side,
as Ellic. doubtfully.　　τοῦ θεοῦ, for
solemnity, to add to the weight of their
εἴσοδος.　　ἐν πολλῷ ἀγῶνι] in (amidst)
much conflict, viz. under outward circumstances conflicting much with our work :
and therefore that work could be no
κενόν, which was thus maintained.
3, 4.] Reasons why he ἐπαρρησιάσατο
λαλῆσαι .... ἐν πολλῷ ἀγῶνι :—viz. the
true and single-minded character of his
ministry, and his duty to God as the
steward of the Gospel.　　3. παρά-
κλησις] exhortation to you, viz. our

whole course of preaching. Supply is,
not 'was ;' cf. λαλοῦμεν below. "The
two senses of παράκλησις, exhortation
and consolation, so easily passing into one
another (compare ver. 11), are suggestive
of the external state of the early church,
sorrowing amid the evils of the world,
and needing as its first lesson to be comforted ; and not less suggestive of the first
lesson of the Gospel to the individual soul, ✳
of peace in believing." Jowett.　　ἐκ]
having its source in.　　πλάνης] here
probably error. "The word is used transitively and intransitively. In the former
case, it is 'imposture' (Matt. xxvii. 64) or
'seduction' (Eph. iv. 14) : in the latter
and more usual, error." Lünem.
ἀκαθαρσίας] hardly, as Chrys., ὑπὲρ μυ-
σαρῶν πραγμάτων οἷον γοήτων κ. μάγων,
—though such a reference is certainly
possible, considering the vile degradation
of that class at the period,—but here apparently of the impure desire of gain,
cf. ver. 5, where ἐν προφάσει πλεονεξίας seems to correspond with ἐξ ἀκαθαρσίας. Still such a meaning seems to
want example. If it be correct, this represents (Lün.) the subjective side, the
motive, as ἐκ πλάνης the objective side,
the ground.　　ἐν δόλῳ] this of the
manner, or perhaps, as Ellic., the ethical
sphere, in which : 'nor did we make use
of deceit to win our way with our παράκλησις.' See 2 Cor. ii. 17.　　4.] καθώς,
according as, in proportion as.
δεδοκιμ.] see reff.,—we have been approved,—thought fit : cf. πιστὸν ἡγήσατο,
1 Tim. i. 12. Lünem. cites Plut. Thes. 12:
ἐλθὼν οὖν ὁ Θησεὺς ἐπὶ τὸ ἄριστον, οὐκ
ἐδοκίμαζε φράζειν αὐτὸν ὅστις εἴη. We
must not introduce any ascertained fitness of them in themselves into the idea
(οὐκ ἂν ἐξελέξατο, εἰ μὴ ἀξίους ἐγίνωσκε
Thl.: so Chr., Œc., Olsh.): it is only
the free choice of God which is spoken
of. On πιστευθ. τὸ εὐαγγ. see reff., and
Winer, edn. 6, § 32. 5.　　οὕτως

ὡς ἀνθρώποις [1]ἀρέσκοντες, ἀλλὰ θεῷ τῷ [m]δοκιμάζοντι τὰς καρδίας ἡμῶν. [5] οὔτε γάρ ποτε [n]ἐν [o]λόγῳ [p]κολακείας [n]ἐγενήθημεν, καθὼς οἴδατε, οὔτε ἐν [q]προφάσει [r]πλεονεξίας, [s]θεὸς [s]μάρτυς, [6] οὔτε [t]ζητοῦντες ἐξ ἀνθρώπων [t]δόξαν, οὔτε ἀφ᾽ ὑμῶν οὔτε ἀπ᾽ ἄλλων, δυνάμενοι ἐν [u]βάρει εἶναι ὡς [v]χριστοῦ [v]ἀπόστολοι, [7] ἀλλ᾽ ἐγενή-

[1] Gal. i. 10 reff.
m = Luke xiv. 19. 1 Cor. iii. 13. 2 Cor. viii. 8. ch. v. 21 al. Prov. xvii. 3.
n see 1 Tim. iv. 15.
o compare Eph. i. 13 reff.
p here only †.
q Mark xii. 46 ‖ (Mt. v. r.) L. John xv.

22. Acts xxvii. 30. Phil. i. 18 only. Hos. x. 4.   r Col. iii. 5 reff.   2 Pet. ii. 3.   s Rom.
i. 9.   2 Cor. i. 23.   Phil. i. 8. ver. 10.   t John v. 44. (vii. 18.)   u = here (Gal. vi. 2 reff.)
only. (see note.)   v 1 Cor. i. 1.   2 Cor. i. 1. xi. 13.   Eph. i. 1.   Jude 17 al.

4. δεδοκειμασμενοι F.   rec ins τω bef θεω (as more usual with art follg), with AD³FKLℵ³ rel : om BCD¹[P]ℵ¹ 67² Clem Bas Œc.

5. om 2nd εν Bℵ³ a 17 [47 Clem-mss,].   ins ο bef θεος F.

6. for υμων, ημων A.   for απ᾽, απο DFL[P] rel : txt ABCℵ (k o m 17 [47], e sil).

answers not to the following ὡς, but to the preceding καθώς, and is emphatic— 'even so.'   ἀρέσκοντες, in the strict sense of the *present tense*,—going about to please,—striving to please.   ὡς belongs to the whole sentence, not merely to ἀνθρ. ἀρέσκ. (as Lün.): for in that case the second member would involve almost too harsh an ellipsis.   ἡμῶν, of us,—not said generally, of all men: but of us, Paul and Silvanus and Timotheus. As Lünem. justly observes against De W., τὰς καρδίας here and τὰς ἑαυτ. ψυχάς below, are conclusive against imagining that St. Paul in this place is speaking of *himself alone*. Yet Conyb. renders it, 'my heart,' and τὰς ἑ. ψ., 'my own life.'

5 ff.] *Proofs again of the assertions of vv.* 3, 4. For neither did we become conversant (see reff. γενέσθαι ἔν τινι, *in re quadam versari;* so οἱ μὲν ἐν τούτοις τοῖς λόγοις ἦσαν, Xen. Cyr. iv. 3. 23. On the impracticability of maintaining a passive sense in the form ἐγενήθημεν, see above, on ch. i. 5) in speech of (consisting of) flattery (not '*incurring repute of flattery,*' as Hamm., Le Clerc, Michael., al. (similarly as to meaning, Pelt), which would be irrelevant, as he is not speaking of what *others thought* of their ministry, but of their own behaviour in it. On κολακ. Lün. quotes Theophrastus, Charr. 2,—τὴν δὲ κολακείαν ὑπολάβοι ἄν τις ὁμιλίαν αἰσχρὰν εἶναι, συμφέρουσαν δὲ τῷ κολακεύοντι,—and Ellic. remarks, "It seems more specifically to illustrate the ἐν δόλῳ of ver. 3, and forms a natural transition to the next words, the essence of κολακεία being self-interest: ὁ δὲ ὅπως ὠφέλειά τις αὐτῷ γίγνηται εἰς χρήματα καὶ ὅσα διὰ χρημάτων, κόλαξ. Aristot. Eth. Nic. iv. 12 ad fin.") as ye know, nor (ἐγενήθημεν) in pretext (employed in that which was meant to be a pretext, not '*in occasione avaritiæ,*' as vulg. and Le Clerc;

nor is πρόφασις '*species,*' as Wolf) of (serving to conceal) avarice; God is witness (τῆς μὲν κολακείας αὐτοὺς ἐκάλεσε μάρτυρας, δῆλα γὰρ τοῖς ἀκούουσι τῶν κολάκων τὰ ῥήματα· τῆς δὲ πλεονεξίας οὐκέτι αὐτούς, ἀλλὰ τὸν τῶν ὅλων ἐπόπτην. Thdrt., and similarly Chrys. But perhaps it is simpler, seeing that no ὑμεῖς is expressed with οἴδατε, to refer θεὸς μάρ. to the whole).   6.] ζητοῦντες belongs to ἐγενήθημεν above.   ἐξ ἀνθρώπων, emphatic: τὴν γὰρ ἐκ θεοῦ καὶ ἐζήτουν κ. ἐλάμβανον. Œc. The real distinction here between ἐκ and ἀπό seems to be, that ἐκ belongs more to the *abstract ground* of the δόξα, ἀπό to the *concrete object* from which it was in each case to accrue. This is strictly correct, not, as Ellic., who has misunderstood my distinction, 'artificial and precarious:' nor is it ever safe to assume identity of meaning, in St. Paul's style, of different prepositions, except where the form of the sentence absolutely requires it. The glory which they sought was not at all to come out of human sources, whether actually from the Thessalonians or from any others.   δυνάμενοι] though we had the power.   ἐν βάρει εἶναι] Thdrt., Est., Grot., Calov., all., refer this to πλεονεξ. mentioned above, and understand it of using the power of living by the gospel, which St. Paul, &c. might have done, but did not: so ἐπιβαρεῖν, ver. 9: 2 Thess. iii. 8; καταβαρεῖν, 2 Cor. xii. 16; ἀβαρῆ ἐμαυτὸν ἐτήρησα, ib. xi. 9. But the words are separated from the πλεονεξία by the new idea beginning at ζητοῦντες, to which, and not to the former clause, this is subordinated. I therefore take them with Chrys. (Œc., Thl., undecided), Ambrst., Erasm., Calv., &c., Olsh., De W., Lün.,— as equivalent to ἐν τιμῇ εἶναι—εἰκὸς γὰρ τοὺς παρὰ θεοῦ πρὸς ἀνθρώπους ἀποσταλέντας, ὡσανεὶ ἀπὸ τοῦ οὐρανοῦ νῦν

w 2 Tim. ii. 24
only τ. see
note.
x Matt. x. 16.
xviii. 20.
Luke ii. 46.　Heb. ii. 12 (from Ps. xxi. 22) al.
xlix. 23 only.　　z Eph. v. 29 only.　Deut. xxii. 6.
lxii. 1 Symm.　　b Gal. i. 15 reff.

y here only.　Gen. xxxv. 8.　4 Kings xi. 2 ‖ Chron.　Isa.
a here only.　Job iii. 21 (AB1C א).　ἱμ., Ps.

ABCDF
KLP א a
b c d e f g
h k l m n
o 17. 47

θημεν * ʷ ἤπιοι ˣ ἐν ˣ μέσῳ ὑμῶν, ὡς ἐὰν ʸ τροφὸς ᶻ θάλπῃ τὰ ἑαυτῆς τέκνα, 8 οὕτως ᵃ ὁμειρόμενοι ὑμῶν ᵇ εὐδοκοῦμεν

---

7. αλλα Bא. 　 * νήπιοι (prob from attaching the ν of the precedg word to ηπιοι. In such a case, where it is almost as likely that the ν of νηπ. may have dropped out, and the evidence is so divided, the sense may fairly be taken as our guide : see note) BC¹D¹Fא¹ a m latt copt æth Clem(from context) Orig₁ₑₓₚᵣ Cyr mss-in-Thl Orig-int₂ Ambrst Pel Aug : ηπιοι AC²D³KL[P]א³ rel syrr sah Clem₁ Orig₁[and int₂] Chr-comm Œc-comm Thdrt-comm Damasc Thl-comm(alt.,—ἢ καὶ νήπιοι).
εμμεσω AC 17. 　 rec αν, with AD³ K(e sil) L[P]א¹ rel Orig₂ Thdrt : txt BCDFא³.
θαλπει KL[P] d f k m.

8. rec ιμειρομενοι, with rel [Eus₁] Cyr : txt ABCDFKL[P]א d e (f k) m n [47] Chrₐₗᵢₑ Damasc-ms Thlₑₓₚᵣ(ὁμειρ. τινὲς δὲ ἱμειρόμενοι ἀνέγνωσαν· οὐκ ἔστι δέ). (17 def.)
ηυδοκουμεν B : ευδοκησαμεν 17, volebamus vulg(and F-lat) syrr coptt Pel :

ἥκοντας πρέσβεις, πολλῆς ἀπολαῦσαι τιμῆς. Chr. 　 **βάρος** is used of importance, dignity,—'weight,' as we say : e. g. Diod. Sic. iv. 61, ἀπὸ τούτων τῶν χρόνων Ἀθηναῖοι, διὰ τὸ βάρος τῆς πόλεως, φρονήματος ἐνεπίμπλαντο, κ. τῆς τῶν Ἑλλήνων ἡγεμονίας ὠρέχθησαν, and in this sense St. Paul's Epistles were called βαρεῖαι, 2 Cor. x. 10. Cf. also βάρος δόξης, where however βάρος is used sensu proprio, as opposed to ἐλαφρόν, 2 Cor. iv. 17. Render therefore, **when we might have stood on our dignity.** Heins., Pisc., Hamm., understand the words of ecclesiastical censures—'quum severitatem exercere apostolicam posset,'—and oppose them to ἔγεν. ἤπιοι below : but see there.
ὡς χρ. ἀπ.] not : 'as the other Apostles' (Grot., Pelt, referring to 1 Cor. ix. 5, but ungrammatical), but **as** (being) **Apostles of Christ.** It is simpler to take ἀπόστολοι here in its wider sense, than to limit the sentence to St. Paul alone.
7.] **ἀλλά** contrasts, not with the mere subordinate clause of the last verse (δυνάμ. κ.τ.λ.), but with its whole sense, and introduces the positive side of their behaviour —q. d. 'so far from being any of the aforesaid, we were . . .' **ἐγενήθ.**, as before, with a reference to God enabling us.
ἤπιοι, mild: so Od. β. 47, πατὴρ δ᾽ ὡς ἤπιος ἦεν : Herodian iv. 1, ἤπιον ἄρχοντα κ. πατέρα : Pausan. Eliac. ii. 18, βασιλέα γὰρ οὐ τὰ πάντα ἤπιον, ἀλλὰ καὶ τὰ μάλιστα θυμῷ χρώμενον Ἀλέξανδρον τοῦ Φιλίππου (Wetst.): see also Herod. iii. 89 : and Ellic.'s note here. Surely the reading νήπιοι, being (1) by far the commoner word, (2) so easily introduced by the final ν of the preceding word, can hardly, in the teeth of the sense, come under consideration : seeing too that the primary authorities are not unanimous. **ἐν μέσῳ ὑμ.**] i. e. 'in

our converse with you ;' but with an allusion to our not lifting ourselves above you ;—ὡς εἶς ἐξ ὑμῶν, Œc. It is best to retain the comma after ὑμῶν, not as Lün., to place a colon : for though there is a break in the construction, it is one occasioned by the peculiar style of the Apostle, which should not be amended by punctuation. The emphasis on **ἑαυτῆς** should not be lost sight of—**as when a** nurse (a suckling mother) **cherishes** (reff.) **her own children.** See Gal. iv. 19, for the same figure. 　 **8.**] **οὕτως** belongs to εὐδοκοῦμεν, and is the apodosis to ὡς above. 　 **ὁμειρόμενοι**] ὁμείρεσθαι is found in reff. only (and in both, the mss. differ), except in the glossaries. Hesych., Phavor., and Phot. explain it by ἐπιθυμεῖν. Thl. says, τουτέστι, προσδεδεμένοι ὑμῖν, κ. ἐχόμενοι ὑμῶν, παρὰ τὸ ὁμοῦ κ. τὸ εἴρω, τὸ συμπλέκω : and Phot. gives ὁμοῦ ἡρμόσθαι as its meaning. But as Lünem. observes after Winer, edn. 6, § 16, B.b), "This is suspicious, 1) because the verb here governs a genitive and not a dative, 2) because there is no instance of a similar verb compounded with ὁμοῦ or ὁμός. Now as in Nicander (Theriaca, ver. 402) the simple form μείρεσθαι occurs in the sense of ἱμείρεσθαι, it can hardly be doubted that μείρεσθαι is the original root, to which ἱμείρεσθαι and ὁμείρεσθαι (having the same meaning) are related, having a syllable prefixed for euphony. Cf. the analogous forms κέλλω and ὀκέλλω,—δύρομαι and ὀδύρομαι,—φλέω and ὀφλέω,—αὔω and ἰαύω, &c., and see Kühner, i. p. 27." It will thus perhaps be best rendered by **loving you, earnestly desiring you.** 　 **εὐδοκ.**] not present, but imperfect, without an augment, as is also generally the aorist εὐδόκησα in N. T. : see Winer, § 12. 3. a : **we delighted** ; 'it was my joy to . . .'

ᶜ μεταδοῦναι ὑμῖν οὐ μόνον τὸ ᵈ εὐαγγέλιον τοῦ ᵈ θεοῦ, ἀλλὰ καὶ τὰς ᵉ ἑαυτῶν ᶠ ψυχάς, διότι ἀγαπητοὶ ἡμῖν ...ἐγενή- θητε C. ἐγενήθητε. 9 ᵍ μνημονεύετε γάρ, ἀδελφοί, τὸν ʰ κόπον ABDFK LPℵ a b ἡμῶν καὶ τὸν ⁱ μόχθον· ʲ νυκτὸς καὶ ʲ ἡμέρας ᵏ ἐργαζό- cdefg hklmn μενοι, ˡ πρὸς τὸ μὴ ᵐ ἐπιβαρῆσαί τινα ὑμῶν, ἐκηρύξαμεν o17.47 ⁿ εἰς ὑμᾶς τὸ ᵈ εὐαγγέλιον τοῦ ᵈ θεοῦ. 10 ὑμεῖς ᵒ μάρ- τυρες καὶ ᵒ θεός, ὡς ᵖ ὁσίως καὶ ۹ δικαίως καὶ ʳ ἀμέμπτως ὑμῖν τοῖς πιστεύουσιν ˢ ἐγενήθημεν, 11 ᵗ καθάπερ οἴδατε,

ᶜ Eph. iv. 28 reff. constr., Rom. i. 11. 2 Macc. viii. 12. Xen. Anab. iv. 5. 5.
ᵈ ver. 2 reff.
ᵉ 1st pers., Rom. viii. 23. 1 Cor. xi. 31 al.
ᶠ = Matt. ii. 20. Acts xv. 26. xx. 24
ᵍ al. Exod. xxi. 23.
ʰ w. acc., Matt. xvi. 9. 2 Tim.

ii. 8 only. 1 Chron. xvi. 12. h see below (i). Matt. xxvi. 10 ‖. 2 Cor. vi. 5 al. Deut. i. 12.
i (in N. T. always w. κόπος) 2 Cor. xi. 27. 2 Thess. iii. 8 only. Num. xxiii. 21. j Mark v. 5. ch.
iii. 10. 2 Tim. i. 3. Isa. xxxiv. 10. k = Matt. xxi. 28. 1 Cor. iv. 12. ch. iv. 11. Exod. v. 18.
l = 2 Cor. iii. 13. m 2 Cor. ii. 5. 2 Thess. iii. 8 only †. n Mark xiii. 10. Luke xxiv. 47.
o ver. 5 reff. p here only †. Wisd. vi. 10 only. q Luke xxiii. 41. 1 Cor. xv. 34. Tit.
ii. 12. 1 Pet. ii. 23 only. Prov. xxviii. 18. r ch. v. 23 only †. (-τος, Phil. ii. 15.)
s constr. (see ch. i. 5), appy here only. t Paul (Rom. iv. 6. xii. 4 al⁸.) only, exc. Heb. iv. 2. Lev.
xxvii. 8. see Heb. v. 4.

cupimus old-lat Jer. rec (for εγενηθητε) γεγενησθε (*corrn in error, from imagining* ευδοκουμεν *to be pres*), with K rel Chr₁ Thdrt: txt ABCDFL[P]ℵ a m 17 [47] Bas Chr₁.
9. [for αδελφ., αγαπητοι P. των κοπων and των μοχθων P b c l 219²(Sz).]
rec aft νυκτος add γαρ, with D³KL rel syr-mg [arm] Chr-txt Thdrt: om ABD¹ F[P]ℵ d k 17 latt syrr coptt [æth] Chr₂ Thl Ambrst Aug. for εις υμας, υμιν ℵ¹ (txt ℵ-corr¹): om εις c.
10. aft μαρτ. ins εστε D¹F vss lat-ff. for ως οσιως, προς αγιος (sic) F(not G).

Conyb. τὰς ἑαυτ. ψυχάς, as remarked above, shews beyond doubt that he is including here Silas and Timotheus with himself. μεταδοῦναι will not strictly apply to τὰς ἑαυ. ψυχ., but we must borrow from the compound verb the idea of giving, or offering. The comparison is exceedingly tender and beautiful: as the nursing-mother, cherishing her children, joys to give not only her milk, but her life, for them,—so we, bringing up you as spiritual children, delighted in giving, not only the milk of the word, but even (and here it was matter of fact) our own lives, for your nourishment in Christ. And that, **because ye became** (the passive form ἐγενήθητε must not be pressed to a passive meaning, as in my earlier editions: see on ch. i. 5) **very dear to us. 9.**] *Proof of the dearness of the Thessalonians to Paul and his companions:* not of ἐγενήθ. ἤπιοι, to which it would be irrelevant,—nor of their readiness to give their lives, &c. (as Ellic.), for this verse does not refer to dangers undergone, but to *labour, in order not to trouble any.* It is no objection to this (Ellic.) that διότι κ.τ.λ. is a subordinate causal member of the preceding sentence, seeing that it is precisely St. Paul's habit to break the tenor of his style by inserting confirmations of such clauses. μνημ. is indic. (γάρ). τ. κόπον κ. τ. μόχθον] a repetition (reff.) to intensify—as we should say **labour and pains**: no distinction can be established. νυκτός first, not merely because the Jews and Athenians ('Athenienses

inter duos occasus,' Plin. N. H. ii. 77) so reckoned it, but *for emphasis*, being the most noteworthy, and the *day* following as matter of course. See besides reff. Acts xx. 31. ἐργαζόμενοι (reff.) in its strict meaning of manual labour—viz., at tent-cloth making, Acts xviii. 3. πρ. τὸ μὴ ἐπιβ.] in order not to burden any of you, viz. by accepting from you the means of sustenance. One can hardly say with Chrys., ἐνταῦθα δείκνυσιν ἐν πενίᾳ ὄντας τοὺς ἄνδρας: for we know St. Paul's strong feeling on this point, 2 Cor. xi. 9, 10. εἰς ὑμᾶς, to you—not quite = ὑμῖν: the latter represents the preaching more as a thing *imparted*, this as a thing *diffused.* On the supposed inconsistency of the statement here with the narrative in Acts xvii., see Prolegomena, § ii. 3, and note.
10—12.] *General summary of their behaviour and teaching among the Thessalonians.* **10.**] ὑμεῖς μάρτ., of the outward appearance. ὁ θεός, of the heart. ὁσίως κ. δικ.] Cf. Plato, Gorg. p. 507 Α, Β,—καὶ μὴν περὶ μὲν ἀνθρώπους τὰ προσήκοντα πράττων δίκαι' ἂν πράττοι, περὶ δὲ θεοὺς ὅσια,—and Polyb. xxiii. 10. 8, παραβῆναι κ. τὰ πρὸς τοὺς ἀνθρώπους δίκαια κ. τὰ πρὸς τ. θεοὺς ὅσια. This distinction, perhaps "precarious" (Ellic.) where the words occur separately, or seem to require no very precise application, is requisite here where both divine and human testimony is appealed to. ὑμῖν τ. πιστ.] not the dat. commodi (Ellic.), nor 'towards you believers,' nor is it governed

u = Luke xx. 37 (‖ Mk.
v. r.). Jude 7.
v w. gen. part., Luke iv. 40. xvi. 5. Acts ii. 3. xvii. 27. xxi. 26 al.
w = Eph. iv. 1 reff.
x = (see note) ch. v. 14 (John xi. 19, 31) only †.

u ὡς ᵛ ἕνα ᵛ ἕκαστον ὑμῶν ὡς πατὴρ τέκνα ἑαυτοῦ ʷ παρακαλοῦντες ὑμᾶς καὶ ˣ παραμυθούμενοι, ¹² καὶ ʸ μαρτυρό-
μενοι ᶻ εἰς τὸ ᵃ περιπατεῖν ὑμᾶς ᵃᵇ ἀξίως τοῦ ᵇ θεοῦ τοῦ
ᶜ καλοῦντος ὑμᾶς εἰς τὴν ἑαυτοῦ βασιλείαν καὶ ᵈ δόξαν.
¹³ καὶ διὰ τοῦτο καὶ ἡμεῖς ᵉ εὐχαριστοῦμεν τῷ θεῷ ᶠ ἀδιαλείπτως, ὅτι ᵍ παραλαβόντες ʰ λόγον ʰⁱ ἀκοῆς παρ' ἡμῶν

ABDFK LPℵ a b c d e f g h k l m n o 17. 47

2 Macc. xv. 9. 80. viii. 53. i. 10 only.
c ch. i. 2 reff. 12 al.
Thucyd. viii. 72. (-θία, 1 Cor. xiv. 3. -θιον, Phil. ii. 1.)
z Acts iii. 19. vii. 19. Rom. i. 11, 20. 1 Cor. x. 6.
b 3 John 6 only.
f Rom. i. 9. ch. i. 2. v. 17 only †.
h = Heb. iv. 2. see Jer. x. 22.
c = Gal. i. 6 reff.
2 Macc. iii. 26 al.
1 = Rom. x. 16.
y Gal. v. 3 reff. Thucyd. vi.
a = Eph. iv. 1 (reff.). om-
d = Rom. v. 2. viii. 18 al.
g 1 Cor. xi. 23. xv. 1. Gal. i. 9,

11. for 1st ως, πως F (qualiter latt, but in ver 10 quam) : εις ο.   [αυτου (for εαυτ.) P.]   om υμας ℵ.

12. rec μαρτυρουμενοι, with D¹F a h l¹ m [47¹] Thdrt Thl : txt BD³KLℵ rel Chr Damasc Œc.—om και μαρτ. A[P] 114 Ambrst-ed.   rec περιπατησαι (aor more usual), with D³KL rel : txt ABD¹F[P]ℵ k m 17.   καλεσαντος Aℵ 73 vulg coptt æth Chr-txt Thdrt Ambrst-ed Vig Pel.

13. rec om 1st και, with DFKL rel [vss] latt Chr Aug : ins AB[P]ℵ syr copt Thdrt-ms Ambrst.   [παρ ημ. bef λογ. ακ. P.]

by ἀμέμπτως, but as Œc., Thl., Lünem., dat. of the *judgment*, as in 2 Pet. iii. 14, σπουδάσατε ἄσπιλοι κ. ἀμώμητοι αὐτῷ εὑρεθῆναι. For otherwise we lose the force of the slight emphasis on ὑμ. τοῖς πιστ., q. d. 'whatever we may have seemed to the unbelieving:' "tametsi aliis non ita videremur," Bengel. See Bernhardy, p. 337 f. The charge of *want of point*, brought by Jowett against the words τοῖς πιστεύουσιν, hence appears to be unfounded. The former verse having referred to external occupation, in which he must have consorted with unbelievers, he here narrows the circle, to speak of his behaviour among the brethren themselves.

11, 12.] *Appeal to the detailed judgment of each one, that this was so.* This ὁσίως κ. δικαίως κ. ἀμέμπτως in their judgment is substantiated by the fact, that οἱ περὶ τὸν Παῦλον busied themselves in establishing every one of them in the faith.

11.] καθάπερ refers what follows to what has gone before, as co-ordinate with it.   ὡς ἕνα ἕκαστ. . . . ὑμᾶς] The construction is that of nouns in apposition, in cases where the one designates the individuals of whom the other is the aggregate. In this case the noun of larger designation generally comes first. The simplest instance that can be given is ταῦτα πάντα, where ταῦτα is the aggregate, πάντα the individualizing noun (whereas in πάντα ταῦτα, ταῦτα is the individuals, and πάντα merely the adjective designation of their completeness): so here ἕνα ἕκαστον ὑμῶν . . . ὑμᾶς differs very little from πάντας ὑμᾶς. As regards the participles, the simplest way of constructing them is to supply ἐγενήθημεν, which has just preceded. Ellicott would rather re-

gard them as an instance of St. Paul's common participial anacolutha, which may also be : but here the construction is simple without such a supposition. Both παρακλ. and παραμυθ. seem here best taken, with Lünem., as applying to *exhortation*, but in a sense nearly allied to consolation : see note on ver. 3. The subject of the exhortation follows, εἰς τὸ κ.τ.λ. : and this would be closely connected with their bearing up under trouble and persecution : cf. vv. 14 ff.   **12. μαρτυρόμ.**] see reff. : it strengthens the two former participles ; **conjuring.** This is the sense of the verb not only in later but in earlier writers also : see reff.   εἰς τὸ . . . belongs to all three participles preceding : the εἰς implying the direction, and, of course, in a subjective sentence, consequently the *purpose* of their action.   καλοῦντος, pres. because the action is extended on to the future by the following words.   βασιλείαν and δόξαν must not be incorporated by the silly ἐν διὰ δυοῖν : God calls us to His *kingdom*, the kingdom of our Lord Jesus, which He shall establish at His coming : and He calls us to His *glory*,—to partake of that glory in His presence, which our Lord Jesus had with Him before the world began ; John xvii. 5, 24. See Rom. v. 2.   **13.**] διὰ τοῦτο is best and most simply referred, with Lünem., to the fact announced in the preceding words—viz. that God καλεῖ ὑμᾶς εἰς, &c. Seeing that He is thus calling you, your thorough reception of His word is to us a cause of thanksgiving to Him. That διὰ τοῦτο is made thus 'to refer to a mere appended clause' (Ellie.) is no objection : see above on ver. 9. It is surely not possible with Jowett,

τοῦ ʲ θεοῦ ᵏ ἐδέξασθε οὐ λόγον ἀνθρώπων ἀλλὰ ¹ καθώς
¹ ἐστιν ἀληθῶς λόγον θεοῦ, ὃς καὶ ᵐ ἐνεργεῖται ᵐ ἐν ὑμῖν
τοῖς πιστεύουσιν. ¹⁴ ὑμεῖς γὰρ ⁿ μιμηταὶ ἐγενήθητε, ἀδελφοί, τῶν ᵒ ἐκκλησιῶν τοῦ ᵒ θεοῦ τῶν οὐσῶν ἐν τῇ Ἰουδαίᾳ
ἐν χριστῷ Ἰησοῦ, ὅτι τὰ αὐτὰ ἐπάθετε καὶ ὑμεῖς ὑπὸ τῶν
ᵖ ἰδίων ᑫ συμφυλετῶν, καθὼς καὶ αὐτοὶ ὑπὸ τῶν Ἰουδαίων,

ʲ arrangt. of words, see Gal. ii. 9.
2 Pet. iii. 2.
k = ch. i. 6 reff.
l see Matt. i. 18.
1 Pet. ii. 15.
m Col. i. 29 reff.
n ch. i. 6 reff.
o Acts xx. 28.
1 Cor. i. 2.
xi. 16.
2 Thess. i. 4

al.　p 2nd pers., Luke vi. 41. 1 Pet. iii. 1.　q here only †. (-λος, Zech. xiii. 7 Aq.)

the words from του θεου (ver 13) to θεου (ver 14) are written twice by ℵ¹ : the second
copy is marked for erasure by ℵ-corr¹. αληθως bef εστιν B ℵ-corr¹ 17 [copt] : om
αληθως (twice) ℵ¹.　[ins του bef 2nd θεου P.]　for υμιν, ημιν ℵ.
　14. rec (for τα αυτα) ταῦτά, with A : txt BDFKL[P]ℵ rel Orig.　om και υμεις
D¹.　for 1st υπο, απο D¹F Orig-ed.　for 2nd υπο, απο F

to refer διὰ τοῦτο 'to the verses both before and after.'　καὶ ἡμεῖς] We also,
i. e. as well as πάντες οἱ πιστεύοντες
ἐν τῇ Μακεδ. κ. ἐν τῇ Ἀχ., ch. i. 7.
παραλαβόντες . . . . ἐδέξασθε] The former verb denotes only the *hearing*, as
objective matter of fact : the latter, the
receiving into their minds as subjective
matter of belief : see reff.　ἀκοῆς
παρ' ἡμῶν is perhaps to be taken together—of hearing (genitive of apposition)
from us—i. e. ' which you heard from us.'
So Est., Pelt, Olsh., Lünem., all. Or
παραλ. παρ' ἡμῶν may be taken together,
as De W., strongly objecting to the construction ἀκοῆς παρ' ἡμῶν, and understanding by λόγος ἀκοῆς the preached
word (Wort der Kunde). Lünem. answers,—that the construction ἀκοῆς παρ'
ἡμῶν is unobjectionable, as ἀκούειν παρά
τινος occurs John i. 41, al., and substantives and adjectives often retain in construction the force of the verbs from which
they are derived (Kühner, ii. 217, cites
from Plato, Alcib. ii. p. 141, οἶμαι δὲ οὐκ
ἀνήκοον εἶναι ἔνιά γε χθιζά τε καὶ πρῴζα
γεγενημένα) :—that De W.'s rendering is
objectionable, because thus no reason is
given for separating παρ' ἡμῶν from
παραλ., and because ἀκοῆς is superfluous
and vapid if the same is already expressed
by παραλαβ. παρ' ἡμῶν. On the other
rendering, which is adopted and defended
also by Ellicott, there is a significant contrast, St. Paul distinguishing himself and
his companions, as mere publishers, from
God, the great Source of the Gospel.
τ. θεοῦ] of (i. e. 'belonging to,' 'coming
from,' not ' *speaking of*,' as Grot., al., see
below) God (i. e. which is God's. But we
must not supply ' *as*,' with Jowett : no
subjective view of theirs being implied in
these words, but simply the objective fact
of their reception of the word from Paul,
Silvanus, and Timotheus).　ἐδέξ.] See
above on παραλ. Ye received it (being)

not (no 'as' must be inserted : he is not
speaking of the *Thessalonians' estimate*
of the word, but (see above) of the fact
of their receiving it as it really was) the
word of men (having man for its author),
but as it is in reality, the word of God,
which (Bengel, al., take ὅς as referring to
θεός : but the Apostle uses always the
active ἐνεργεῖν of God, cf. 1 Cor. xii. 6 :
Gal. ii. 8 ; iii. 5 : Eph. i. 11 : Phil. ii. 13
al.,—and (reff.) the middle (not passive)
of things) is also (besides being merely
heard) active in you that believe.
14.] Proof of this ἐνεργεῖται,—that they
had imitated in endurance the Judæan
churches.　ὑμεῖς γάρ resumes ὑμῖν
above.　μιμηταί] not in intention,
but in fact. (On ἐγενήθητε, see on ch. i.
5.) Calvin suggests the following reason
for his here introducing the conflict of the
Judæan churches with the Jews : ' Poterat
illis hoc venire in mentem : Si hæc vera est
religio, cur eam tam infesti animis oppug-
nant Judæi, qui sunt sacer Dei populus ?
Ut hoc offendiculum tollat, primum admo-
net, hoc eos commune habere cum primis
Ecclesiis, quæ in Judæa erant : postea
Judæos dicit obstinatos esse Dei et omnis
sacræ doctrinæ hostes.' But manifestly
this is very far-fetched, and does not naturally lie in the context : as neither does
Olsh.'s view, that he wishes to mark out the
judaizing Christians, as persons likely to
cause mischief in the Thessalonian church.
The reason for introducing this character of
the Jews here was because (Acts xvii. 5 ff.)
they had been the stirrers up of the persecution against himself and Silas at Thessalonica, to which circumstance he refers below. By the mention of them as the adversaries of the Gospel in Judæa he is carried
on to say that there, as well as at Thessalonica, they had ever been its chief enemies.
And this is a remarkable concidence with
the history in the Acts, where we find him
at this time, in Corinth, in more than usual

r here [and
Luke xi. 49]
only. Ps.
cxviii. 157.
Joel ii. 20.
s Rom. viii. 8.   (1 Cor. vii. 32.) ch. iv. 1.   t Gal. i. 10 reff.

¹⁵ τῶν καὶ τὸν κύριον ἀποκτεινάντων Ἰησοῦν καὶ τοὺς ABDFK
προφήτας, καὶ ἡμᾶς ^r ἐκδιωξάντων, καὶ ^s θεῷ μὴ st ἀρεσ-

ABDFK
LPℵ a b
c d e f g
h k l m n
o 17. 47

15. rec ins ιδιους bef προφητας, with D²·³KL rel syrr goth Chr Thdrt Mcion-t: om
ABD¹F[P]ℵ 17. 67² latt coptt æth [arm] Orig₂ Dial Tert_expr.—(for ημας Steph & Mill
(not rec) have υμας, appy by mistake.)   αρεσαντων F.

conflict with the Jews (Acts xviii. 5, 6,
12).   On ἐν χριστῷ Ἰησοῦ Œc. remarks, εὐφυῶς διεῖλεν· ἐπειδὴ γὰρ καὶ
αἱ συναγωγαὶ τῶν Ἰουδαίων ἐν θεῷ εἶναι
δοκοῦσι, τὰς τῶν πιστῶν ἐκκλησίας καὶ
ἐν τῷ θεῷ καὶ ἐν τῷ υἱῷ αὐτοῦ λέγει
εἶναι.   συμφυλέτης, ὁμοεθνής, Hesych. Herodian says, πολίτης, δημότης,
φυλέτης, ἄνευ τῆς σύν, συνέφηβος δὲ καὶ
συνθιασώτης κ. συμπότης μετὰ τῆς σύν·
ὅτι καὶ πρόσκαιρος αὐτῶν ἡ κοινωνία, ἐπὶ
δὲ τῶν προτέρων οὐχ ὁμοίως.   And this
criticism seems just : the Latins also using
civis meus not concivis, of the enduring
relation of fellow-citizen,—but commilito
meus, not miles meus, of the temporary
relation of fellow-soldier.   See Scaliger, in
Lobeck on Phrynichus, p. 471 (also p. 172).
Ellicott would regard these words merely
as supererogatory compounds belonging to
later Greek.   These συμφυλέται were not
Jews wholly nor in part, but Gentiles
only.   For they are set in distinct contrast here to οἱ Ἰουδαῖοι.   τὰ αὐτὰ
. . . . καθώς] The proper apodosis to τὰ
αὐτά would be ἅ, or ἅπερ.   But such inaccuracies are found in the classics :
Kühner (ii. 571) cites from Plato, Phæd.
p. 86 A, εἴ τις διϊσχυρίζοιτο τῷ αὐτῷ
λόγῳ ὥσπερ σύ : so also Legg. p. 671 C ;
Xen. An. i. 10. 10.   αὐτοί, not ' we
ourselves,' as Erasm., al. : but the members of the Judæan churches mentioned
above.   The same construction occurs in
Gal. i. 22, 23.   15, 16.] Characterization of the Jews as enemies of the Gospel
and of mankind.   Jowett's note is worth
quoting : "Wherever the Apostle had gone
on his second journey, he had been persecuted by the Jews : and the longer he travelled about among Gentile cities, the more
he must have been sensible of the feeling
with which his countrymen were regarded.
Isolated as they were from the rest of
the world in every city, a people within a
people, it was impossible that they should
not be united for their own self-defence,
and regarded with suspicion by the rest of
mankind.   But their inner nature was not
less repugnant to the nobler as well as the
baser feelings of Greece and Rome.   Their
fierce nationality had outlived itself: though
worshippers of the true God, they knew
Him not to be the God of all the nations

of the earth : hated and despised by others,
they could but cherish in return an impo-
tent contempt and hatred of other men.
What wonder that, for an instant (? on all
this see below), the Apostle should have
felt that this Gentile feeling was not wholly
groundless ? or that he should use words
which recall the expression of Tacitus :
' Adversus omnes alios hostile odium ? '
Hist. v. 5."   15. τῶν καί] The repeated καί serves for enumeration.
τὸν κύρ. ἀποκτ. Ἰησ. is thus arranged to
give prominence to τὸν κύρ., and thus enhance the enormity of the deed : it should
be rendered who killed Jesus the Lord,
τὸν κύρ. being in a position of emphasis.
κ. τοὺς προφήτας] belongs to
ἀποκτεινάντων (see Matt. xxiii. 31—37 ;
Acts vii. 52), not to ἐκδιωξ. as De W.
His objection, that all the prophets were
not killed, is irrelevant : neither were they
all persecuted.   The ἰδίους of rec. appears
to have been an early insertion : Tert.
ascribes it to Marcion.   ἐκδιωξ.] drove
out by persecution, viz. from among you,
Acts xvii. 5 ff.,—not for the simple verb
διωξ. (De W.), nor does the preposition
merely strengthen the verb (Lünem.),—
but it retains its proper meaning (ὁ δῆμος
αὐτῶν ἐξεδίωξε τοὺς δυνατούς, οἱ δὲ ἀπελ-
θόντες . . . Thuc. i. 24), and the aorist
refers it to a definite event, as in the case
of ἀποκτεινάντων : when their habit is
spoken of, the participles are present,
e. g. ἀρεσκόντων and κωλυόντων below.
ἡμᾶς refers to Paul and Silas.
θεῷ μὴ ἀρεσκ.] The μή gives a subjective
sense : not exactly that of Bengel, al.,
' Deo placere non quærentium.'   For in
strictness, as Ellicott, the shade of sub-
jectivity is only to be found in the
aspect in which the subject and the participle is presented to the reader : and
therefore can hardly be reproduced in
English.   Compare on the usage, Winer,
edn. 6, § 55. 5, g. β, and Ellicott's
note here.   In πᾶσιν ἀνθρώποις ἐναντίων, most Commentators, and recently
Jowett (see above), have seen the odium
humani generis ascribed to the Jews
by Tacitus (Hist. v. 5), and by several
other classic authors (Juv. Sat. xiv.
103 ff. Diod. Sic. xxxiv. p. 524, &c.).
But it is hardly possible that St. Paul,

κόντων καὶ πᾶσιν ἀνθρώποις ᵘ ἐναντίων, ¹⁶ ᵛ κωλυόντων
ἡμᾶς τοῖς ἔθνεσιν λαλῆσαι ἵνα σωθῶσιν, ʷ εἰς τὸ ˣ ἀνα-
πληρῶσαι αὐτῶν τὰς ἁμαρτίας πάντοτε. ʸ ἔφθασεν δὲ
ʸ ἐπ᾽ αὐτοὺς ἡ ᶻ ὀργὴ ᵃ εἰς τέλος.

¹⁷ Ἡμεῖς δέ, ἀδελφοί, ᵇ ἀπορφανισθέντες ἀφ᾽ ὑμῶν
ᶜ πρὸς καιρὸν ὥρας ᵈ προςώπῳ οὐ ᵈ καρδίᾳ, ᵉ περισσο-

u = Acts xxvi. 9. xxviii. 17.
Tit. ii. 8
(Mark vi. 48 || Mt. xv.
39. Acts xxvii. 4)
only. Prov. xiv. 7.
v = Matt. xix. 14. Acts viii. 36. xvi. 6.
1 Kings xxv. 26.
w ver. 12.

x Gal. vi. 2 reff. Gen. xv. 16.
15. 2 Cor. x. 14.)
xviii. 5. John xiii. 1. Amos ix. 8.
vii. 5. 2 Cor. vii. 8. Gal. ii. 5.
y Matt. xii. 28 || L.
z ch. i. 10 reff. Luke xxi. 23.
b here only †.
d 2 Cor. v. 12.
Eccl. viii. 14. εἰς, Phil. iii. 16 reff. (ch. iv.
a Matt. x. 22. xxiv. 13. Luke
c here only, see John v. 35. 1 Cor.
e Gal. i. 14 reff.

16. σωθησονται F. om τας αμαρτιας B. εφθακεν BD¹ : txt ACD²·³FKL[P]א
rel Orig₂ Eus₄ Chr Thdrt Damasc. η οργη bef επ᾽ αυτους B vulg(and F-lat) Orig₁.
aft η οργη ins του θεου DF latt goth lat-ff.

himself a Jew, should have blamed an exclusiveness which arose from the strict monotheism and legal purity of the Jew : and besides this, the construction having been hitherto carried on by copulæ, but now dropping them, most naturally goes on from ἐναντίων to κωλυόντων, **in that they prevent**, and thus κωλ. specifies wherein the ἐναντιότης consists, viz. in opposing the salvation of mankind by the Gospel. So that the other seems to be irrelevant (so nearly Lünem.).

16. εἰς τό] not of the result merely, '*so that*,'—but of the *intention*, not of the Jews themselves, but of their course of conduct, viewed as having an intent in the divine purposes : as so often in St. Paul.

ἀναπλ.] to bring up the measure of their sins to the prescribed point.

πάντοτε] ταῦτα δὲ καὶ πάλαι ἐπὶ τῶν προφητῶν κ. νῦν ἐπὶ τοῦ χριστοῦ κ. ἐφ᾽ ἡμῶν ἔπραξαν, ἵνα πάντοτε ἀναπληρωθῶσιν αἱ ἁμαρτίαι αὐτῶν, Œcum. The idea is, not of a new measure having to be filled πάντοτε, but of their being πάντοτε employed in filling up *the measure*.

But (this their opposition to God and men shall not avail them: for) **the** (predestined, or predicted, or merited) **wrath** (of God) **came upon them** (he looks *back* on the fact in the divine counsels as a thing in past time, q. d. 'was appointed to come:' not 'has come.' No sense of *anticipation* need be sought in ἔφθασεν in later Greek, except when it governs an accusative of the person, as ch. iv. 15 ; see reff.) **to the utmost** (to the end of it, i. e. the wrath : so that it shall exhaust all its force on them : not 'at last' Wahl, al. : nor to be taken with ἡ ὀργή, the wrath which shall endure to the end (ἡ εἰς τ. ?), as Thl., Œc., al. : nor to be referred to the Jews, 'so as to make an end of them,' De W.

17—III. 13.] *He relates to them how he desired to return after his separation from them : and when that was impracticable, how he sent Timotheus : at whose good*

intelligence of them he was cheered, thanks God for them, and prays for their continuance in love and confirmation in the faith. **17.**] ἡμεῖς δέ resumes the subject broken off at ver. 13 : the δέ introducing a contrast to the description of the Jews in vv. 15, 16. ἀπορφανισθέντες] ὀρφανός is properly used, as with us, of children who have lost their parents. But it is found in a wider sense, e. g. John xiv. 8,—Pind., Isthm. vii. 16, ὀρφανὸν μυρίων ἑτάρων;—Olymp. ix. 92, ὀρφανοὶ γενεᾶς (ὀρφ. τέκνων, Dion. Hal. Antt. i. p. 69, Kypke): Hesych. : ὀρφανός, ὁ γονέων ἐστερημένος καὶ τέκνων (compare the similitude, ver. 7). The word ἀπορφανίζω occurs Æsch. Choëph. 247, of the eagles' brood deprived of their parents. Here it is used in deep affection, the preposition giving the sense of *local* severance, which is further specified by ἀφ᾽ ὑμῶν following. There is no occasion to press the metaphor, as Chrys., al. πρὸς καιρὸν ὥρας] for the space of an hour, i. e. for a very short time : it is a combination of the expressions πρὸς καιρόν and πρὸς ὥραν, see reff. It refers, not to his present impression that the time of separation would still be short (as Flatt and De W.), for this the past participle ἀπορφανισθέντες forbids, but to the time alluded to in that past participle—when we had been separated from you for the space of an hour. προςώπ. οὐ κ.] datives of the manner in which (i. e. as Ellic. 'marking, with the true limiting power of the case, the metaphorical place,' which in the interpretation of the metaphor would be manner or form, 'to which the sense is restricted') no separation in heart took place. περισσοτ. ἐσπ.] the more abundantly (because our separation was so short. Lünem. says well : "Universal experience testifies, that the pain of separation from friends and the desire of return to them are more vivid, the more freshly the re-

τέρως f ἐσπουδάσαμεν τὸ· g πρόςωπον ὑμῶν g ἰδεῖν ἐν ABDFK
πολλῇ h ἐπιθυμίᾳ. 18 διότι ἠθελήσαμεν ἐλθεῖν πρὸς ὑμᾶς, cdefg
ἐγὼ j μὲν i Παῦλος, καὶ k ἅπαξ καὶ k δίς, καὶ l ἐνέκοψεν o 17. 47
ἡμᾶς ὁ σατανᾶς. 19 τίς γὰρ ἡμῶν m ἐλπὶς ἢ n χαρὰ ἢ
n στέφανος op καυχήσεως, q ἢ οὐχὶ καὶ ὑμεῖς, r ἔμπροσθεν
τοῦ κιρίου ἡμῶν Ἰησοῦ s ἐν τῇ αὐτοῦ st παρουσίᾳ; 20 ὑμεῖς
γάρ ἐστε ἡ u δόξα ἡμῶν καὶ ἡ u χαρά. III. 1 διὸ μηκέτι

f Eph. iv. 3 reff.
g ch. iii. 10.
Gen. xliv. 23.
see Col. ii. 1.
Rev. xxii. 4.
h in good sense,
Phil. i. 23
reff.
i Gal v. 2 reff.
j (μέν, solita-
rium), Col. ii.
23 reff.
k Phil. iv. 16
reff.
l Acts xxiv. 4.
Rom. xv. 22.
Gal. v. 7.

1 Pet. iii. 7 only.   Dan. ix. 26 Theod.-Ald. only (ἐκκόπτ., AB).   m so of Christ, 1 Tim. i. 1.   n Phil.
iv. 1.   o Ezek. xvi. 12. xxiii. 42. Prov. xvi. 31.   p Rom. iii. 27. 1 Cor. xv. 21 al. P. only, exc.
James iv. 16.   q = Rom. ii. 4.   r ch. i. 3 reff.   s 1 Cor. xv. 23. ch. iii. 13. v. 23. 1 John
ii. 28.   t = as above (s). Matt. xxiv. 3, &c. ch. iv. 15. 2 Thess. ii. 1, 8. James v. 7, 8 al. (Phil. i. 26 reff.)
u = Eph. iii. 13 reff.

18. rec διο, with D³KL rel Chr Thdrt Damasc : txt ABD¹F[P]‍א m 17. 67².
ανεκοψεν F 121.
    19. for καυχ., αγαλλιασεως A ; exultationis Tert.   om 3rd ἤ ‍א¹.   rec aft ιησου
ins χριστου, with FL rel vulg-ed(with fuld¹ &c) coptt goth [æth arm] Chr Thl Tert
al : om ABDK[P]‍א d e h l 17. 67² am(and fuld²) syrr Thdrt Damasc Œc Ambrst-ed.
    20. om 2nd ἤ ‍א¹ 109.

membrance of the parting works in the
spirit, i. e, the less time has elapsed since
the parting." Therefore the explanation
of Œc. and Thl., after Chrys., is unpsycho-
logical : περισσοτέρως ἐσπουδάσαμεν, ἢ
ὡς εἰκὸς ἦν τοὺς πρὸς ὥραν ἀπολειφθέν-
τας. Luth., Bretschn., De W., and Ellic.
understand it 'the more,' i. e. than if I
had been separated from you in heart :
but the above seems both simpler and
more delicate in feeling) endeavoured
(implies actual setting on foot of measures
to effect it) in much desire (i. e. very
earnestly) to see your face.   18.]
Wherefore (as following up this earnest
endeavour) we would have come (had a
plan to come : "not ἐβουλόμεθα, which
would indicate merely the disposition :
see Philem. 13, 14" (Lün.)) to you, even
I Paul (the introduction of these words
here, where he is about to speak of himself alone, is a strong confirmation of the
view upheld above (on ch. i. 9) that he
has hitherto been speaking of himself and
his companions. The μέν answers to a
suppressed δέ, q. d. περὶ δὲ τῶν ἄλλων οὐ
νῦν ὁ λόγος, or the like. Grot., al., think
the suppressed δέ refers to the rest having
intended it once only, but the Apostle
more times, taking κ. ἅπ. κ. δίς with ἐγ.
μ. Παῦ.), not once only but twice (literally,
'both once and twice :' not used widely
(ἅπ. κ. δίς), but meaning that on two
special occasions he had such a plan : see
ref. The words refer to ἐσπουδάσ., not
to ἐγὼ μ. Π.,—see above), and (not 'but :'
the simple copula, as in Rom. i. 13, gives
the matter of fact, without raising the
contrast between the intention and the
hindrance) Satan (i. e. the devil : not any
human adversary or set of adversaries, as
De W., al. ; whether Satan acted by the

Thessalonian Jews or not, is unknown to
us, but by whomsoever acting, the agency
was his) hindered us (reff.).   19.]
accounts for this his earnest desire to
see them, by the esteem in which he held
them. The words ἔμπρ. τ. κυρ. ἡμ. Ἰησ.
κ.τ.λ. must not be transposed in the rendering ("construi hæc sic debent, τίς γ.
ἡμ. ἐλπ. . . . . ἔμπρ. τ. κυρ. . . . . ἢ οὐχὶ
κ. ὑμ." Grot.) : for the Apostle, after
having asked and answered the question
τίς γὰρ κ.τ.λ., breaks off, and specifies
that wherein this hope and joy mainly
consisted, viz. the glorious prospect of
their being found in the Lord at His
appearing. But he does not look forward
to this as anticipating a reward for the
conversion of the Thessalonians (Est., al.),
or that their conversion will compensate
for his having persecuted the Church before, but from generous desire to be found
at that day with the fruits of his labour,
and that they might be his boast and be
theirs before the Lord : see 2 Cor. i. 14 ;
Phil. ii. 16.   On στέφ. καυχ., see
reff. and Soph. Aj. 460.   ἢ οὐχὶ
καὶ ὑμεῖς] The ἤ, as Ellic., 'introduces
a second and negative interrogation, explanatory and confirmatory of what is
implied in the first :' see Winer, edn. 6,
§ 57. 1. b.   καί, 'as well as others my
converts.'   ἐν τῇ αὐτ. παρ. further
specifies the ἔμπρ. τοῦ κυρίου.   20.]
γάρ sometimes serves to render a reason
for a foregoing assertion, by asserting it
even more strongly, q. d. 'it must be so,
for the fact is certain.' So Soph. Philoct.
746, "δεινόν γε τοὐπίσαγμα τοῦ νοσή-
ματος." "δεινὸν γάρ, οὐδὲ ῥητόν :" see
Hartung, Partikell. i. p. 474. I should
be inclined to ascribe to ver. 20, on this
very account, a wider range than ver. 19

^v στέγοντες ^w εὐδοκήσαμεν ^x καταλειφθῆναι ἐν Ἀθήναις
μόνοι, ² καὶ ἐπέμψαμεν Τιμόθεον τὸν ἀδελφὸν ἡμῶν καὶ
^{yz} συνεργὸν τοῦ ^z θεοῦ ἐν τῷ εὐαγγελίῳ τοῦ χριστοῦ, ^a εἰς
τὸ ^b στηρίξαι ὑμᾶς καὶ ^c παρακαλέσαι ὑπὲρ τῆς πίστεως
ὑμῶν ^{3 d} τὸ μηδένα ^e σαίνεσθαι ἐν ταῖς θλίψεσιν ταύταις·

v] Cor. ix. 12.
xii. 7. ver.
5 only †. Sir.
viii. 17 only.
w Gal. i. 15 reff.
x = [John viii.
9] Acts
xviii. 19 al.
Ruth ii. 11.
y Phil. ii. 25
reff.
z 1 Cor. iii. 9.
a ch. ii. 12 reff.

b Acts xviii. 23.　Rom. i. 11. xvi. 25.　Ps. l. 12 (14).　　　　　　c = Col. ii. 2.　2 Thess. ii. 17.　Deut. iii.
28.　Job iv. 3.　　　　d so inf., w. τό, Rom. iv. 13.　Phil. iv. 10. see note.　　　　　　　e here
only †.　οἱ δέ, σαινόμενοι τοῖς λεγομένοις, ἐδάκρυόν τε κ. ὤμωζον, Diog. Laert. viii. 41. (Kypke.)

CHAP. III. 1. διοτι B: διο και a.　　ηυδοκησαμεν B[P]‭ℵ.
2. rec (for συνεργον του θεου) διακονον του θεου και συνεργον ημων, with D³KL rel
Syr syr(altern) Chr Thdrt Damasc; διακονον τ. θ. A[P]‭ℵ 67². 73 vulg syr(altern) copt
basm [goth] æth Bas Pel-txt; διακονον και συν. του θεου F; συνεργον, omg του θεου,
B (harl¹ διακ. for συνεργ.) arm Pel-comm: txt (from objections to which expression
the variations probably arose) D¹ 17 Ambrst.　　rec aft παρακαλεσαι ins υμας, with
D³KL rel Syr: om ABD¹F[P]‭ℵ m 17 [47] latt copt arm Chr Thdrt₁ Damasc Ambrst
Pel.　　rec (for υπερ) περι, with D³L rel Thdrt₁: txt ABD¹FK[P]‭ℵ 17 [47] Bas
Chr Thdrt₁.
3. rec τω (see note), with a c: τον b¹: ινα F 73: του l 67: txt ABDKL[P]‭ℵ rel Damasc.

embraces: q. d. **you will be our joy in
the day of the Lord: for ye** (at all
times, ye *are*, abstractedly) **our glory and
joy.** This seems to me far better than,
with Ellic., to regard the γάρ as only
'confirmatory and explicative.'
III. 1.] **διό,** because of our affection for
you just expressed; 'hac narratione quæ
sequitur, desiderii illius sui fidem facit,'
Calvin.　**μηκ. στέγοντες**] **no longer
being able to** (μηκέτι gives the subjective
feeling as distinguished from οὐκέτι, which
would describe the mere objective matter
of fact) **bear** (reff.) (our continued absence from you), **we** (I Paul, from above,
ch. ii. 18) **determined** (εὐδοκήσαμεν does
not carry with it any expression of *pleasure* ('promptam animi inclinationem designat,' Calv.), except in so far as we say
'it was our pleasure,'—referring merely
to the resolution of the will) **to be left
behind** (see Acts xvii. 15, 16) **in Athens
alone,　　2.] and sent Timotheus our
brother and fellow-worker with God** (ref.
and Ellic.'s note here) **in** (the field of his
working) **the Gospel of Christ** (there does
not appear to be any special reason for
this honourable mention of Timotheus (as
Chrys., τοῦτο οὐ τὸν Τιμόθεον ἐπαίρων
φησίν, ἀλλ' αὐτοὺς τιμῶν), further than
the disposition to speak thus highly of
him on the part of the Apostle. Such is
the more natural view, when we take into
account the fervid and affectionate heart
of the writer. See, however, note on 1 Tim.
v. 23; with which timid character of
Timotheus such designations as this may
be connected), **in order to confirm you,
and exhort on behalf of** (in order for the
furtherance of) **your faith,　　3.] that
no one might be disquieted** (reff.: Soph.

Antig. 1214, παιδός με σαίνει φθόγγος:
Eur. Rhes. 53, σαίνει μ' ἔννυχος φρυκ-
τώρια, &c. In these places **σαίνω** is a
vox media, conveying the meaning of
agitation, disquieting, which the context
must interpret for better or worse) **in** (in
the midst of) **these tribulations** (which
are happening to us both). The construction of **τὸ μηδένα σαίνεσθαι** is doubted.
Lünem. enters into the matter, as usual,
at length and thoroughly. He first deals
with the rec. τῷ μηδ. σ., and exposes as
ungrammatical the view which would regard it as a *dativus commodi*, as = εἰς
τὸ . . . , rejecting also Rückert's more
grammatical view, that it indicates "*unde
nascituram τὴν παράκλησιν speraverat,
quum Timotheum misit, apostolus.*" Then
as to τὸ μ. σ.,—we may take it either
1) with Matthæi, supplying a second εἰς
from the former εἰς τὸ στηρ. But then
why is not the second εἰς expressed, as
in Rom. iv. 11? Or, 2) with Schott, as
a pendent accusative, in the sense '*quod
attinet, ad.*' But this is a very rare construction, which has been often assumed
without reason (see Bernhardy, pp. 132 ff.),
and therefore should only be resorted to
when no other supposition will help the
construction: 3) Winer, edn. 3 (not in
edn. 6), § 45. 3 anm., whom De W. and
Ellicott follow, makes it dependent on
παρακαλέσαι, and treats it as a further
explanation of ὑπὲρ τῆς πίστεως — viz.
'*to exhort, that none should become un-
stable.*' But if τὸ μηδ. σαίν. depended
on παρακαλέσαι, then παρακαλεῖν, in the
sense of '*to exhort,*' would be followed by
a imple accusative of the thing, which
though perhaps possible, see 1 Tim. vi. 2,
is very harsh. (Consult however Ellicott's

f Luke ii. 34.
Phil. i. 17.
g Matt. xiii. 56.
Mark xiv. 49.
John i. 1 al.
h 2 Cor. xiii. 2.
Gal. v. 21
only. Isa.
xli. 26 only.
i pres., Gal. ii.
14 reff. but
see note.
j = 2 Cor. i. 6.
iv. 8. vii. 5.
2 Thess. i. 6,
7. 1 Tim. v.
10. Heb. xi.
37 (Matt. vii.
14. Mark iii.
9) only. Ps.
ci. 2.

αὐτοὶ γὰρ οἴδατε ὅτι f εἰς τοῦτο f κείμεθα· 4 καὶ γὰρ ὅτε
g πρὸς ὑμᾶς g ἦμεν, h προελέγομεν ὑμῖν ὅτι i μέλλομεν
j θλίβεσθαι, καθὼς καὶ ἐγένετο καὶ οἴδατε. 5 διὰ τοῦτο
k κἀγὼ μηκέτι l στέγων ἔπεμψα m εἰς τὸ γνῶναι τὴν πίστιν
ὑμῶν, μή πως n ἐπείρασεν ὑμᾶς ὁ o πειράζων καὶ p εἰς
κενὸν γένηται ὁ q κόπος ἡμῶν. 6 ἄρτι δὲ ἐλθόντος Τιμο-
θέου πρὸς ἡμᾶς ἀφ' ὑμῶν καὶ r εὐαγγελισαμένου ἡμῖν τὴν
πίστιν καὶ τὴν ἀγάπην ὑμῶν, καὶ ὅτι s ἔχετε st μνείαν ἡμῶν

...καγω
P.
ABDFK
LΝ a b c
d e f g h
k l m n o
17. 47

k = (see note) John i. 31.   Rom. xi. 3.   2 Cor. vi. 17.   l ver. 1 reff.   m ch. ii. 12 reff.
n indic., Gal. iv. 11.   Col. ii. 8.   Winer, edn. 6, § 56. 2. b. β.   o Matt. iv. 3.   p 2 Cor. vi. 1.   Gal.
ii. 2.   Phil. ii. 16 bis.   Isa. lxv. 23.   q 1 Cor. iii. 8. xv. 58.   Gen. xxxi. 42.   r = Luke i. 19. ii.
10.   Rom. x. 15, from Isa. lii. 7.   s 2 Tim. i. 3. elsw. as Eph. i. 16 reff. w. ποιεῖσθαι.   t here
only. see 2 Macc. vii. 20.

4. προϲελεγομεν D¹ : ελεγομεν F.   aft καθωs om και F D-lat.
5. υμων bef πιστιν B m 73.
6. ins υμων bef πιστιν ℵ.   μνειαν bef εχετε DF : ημων bef εχετε 17, mem. nostr.
hab. D-lat vulg(and F-lat).

note, as to the mere mediate dependence
of such clauses on the governing verb in
comparison with the immediate dependence of substantives.) Besides, if τὸ μ. σ.
were a further specification of ὑπὲρ τῆς
πίστεως ὑμῶν, it would not be accusative
but genitive. 4) It only remains that
we should take τὸ μ. σ. as in apposition
with the whole foregoing sentence, εἰς
τὸ στ. ὑ. κ. παρ. τ. πίστ. ὑμ.—so
that τὸ μηδ. σαίν. serves only to repeat
the same thought, which was before positively expressed, in a negative but better
defined form: τό being nearly = τουτέστι. So that the sense is: to confirm
you and exhort you on behalf of your
faith, that is, that no one may be
shaken in these troubles: τὸ μηδ. being
dependent, not on a second εἰς understood, as in (1), but on the first εἰς,
which is expressed. With this view I
entirely agree, only adding, that instead of
making τό = τουτέστι, I would rather say
that τουτέστι might have been inserted
before τὸ μηδένα. αὐτοὶ γὰρ . . .]
Reason why no one should be shaken.
Griesb., al., parenthesize αὐτοὶ—οἴδατε
ver. 4: but wrongly, for διὰ τοῦτο ver. 5,
connects with this sentence immediately.
οἴδατε; probably not for Theodoret's reason: ἄνωθεν ἡμῖν ταῦτα προηγόρευσεν
ὁ δεσπότης χριστός,—but for that given
in ver. 4. εἰς τοῦτο, viz. to θλίβεσθαι,
contained in θλίψεις above: the subject to
κείμεθα being 'we Christians.' 4.]
reason for οἴδατε. πρὸς ὑμ., see reff.
μέλλομεν may be taken either as the
recit. present, or better as representing the
counsel of God, as in ὁ ἐρχόμενος and the
like. The subject to μέλλ., as above, being
'we Christians.' οἴδατε, viz. by experience. 5.] διὰ τοῦτο, because tribu-

lation had verily begun among you (καθὼς
καὶ ἐγένετο). κἀγώ seems to convey
a delicate hint that Timotheus also was
anxious respecting them: or it may have
the same reference as καὶ ἡμεῖς, ch. ii. 13,
—viz. to the other Christians who had heard
of their tribulation. De W. would render,
not, 'therefore I also &c.'—but 'therefore
also, I &c.' But this would require (as
Lün.) διὰ καὶ τοῦτο—or καὶ διὰ τ.
εἰς τὸ γν.] that I (not ' he ') might know
(be informed about) : belongs to the subject of the verb ἔπεμψα. μή πως
κ.τ.λ.] lest perchance the tempter (ref.)
have tempted (not, as Whitby, al., 'seduced') you (indicative betokening the fact
absolute), and our labour might be (subjunctive, betokening the fact conditional)
to no purpose (reff.). Fritz. and De W.
rather harshly take μή πως in two different
meanings,—with the first clause as 'an
forte,' and with the second as 'ne forte.'
6—8.] Of the good news brought
by Timotheus. 6.] ἄρτι δέ is by Lünem.
(and De W. hesitatingly) separated by a
comma from ἐλθόντος, and joined to παρ-
εκλήθημεν ver. 7. But the direct connexion of ἄρτι with an aorist verb is harsher
than with an aorist participle, and παρεκλ.
has already its διὰ τοῦτο, which refers back
to the whole preceding clause as contained
in the τοῦτο. I would therefore join ἄρτι
with ἐλθόντος. But Timotheus having
just now come &c. εὐαγγ.] having
brought good news of: see reff. οὐκ εἶπεν
ἀπαγγείλαντος, ἀλλὰ εὐαγγελισαμένου·
τοσοῦτον ἀγαθὸν ἡγεῖτο τὴν ἐκείνων βεβαίωσιν κ. τὴν ἀγάπην. Chrys. First
their Christian state comforted him,—
then, their constant remembrance of himself. Thdrt. remarks: τρία τέθεικεν ἀξι-
έραστα, τὴν πίστιν, κ. τ. ἀγάπην, κ. τοῦ

ᵗἀγαθὴν πάντοτε, ᵘἐπιποθοῦντες ἡμᾶς ἰδεῖν ᵛκαθάπερ
καὶ ἡμεῖς ὑμᾶς, ⁷διὰ τοῦτο ʷπαρεκλήθημεν, ἀδελφοί,
ˣἐφ' ὑμῖν ʸἐπὶ πάσῃ τῇ ᶻἀνάγκῃ καὶ θλίψει ἡμῶν διὰ τῆς
ὑμῶν πίστεως· ⁸ὅτι νῦν ᵃζῶμεν ᵇἐὰν ὑμεῖς ᶜστήκετε ἐν
κυρίῳ.   ⁹τίνα γὰρ ᵈεὐχαριστίαν δυνάμεθα τῷ θεῷ ᵉἀντ-
αποδοῦναι περὶ ὑμῶν ʸἐπὶ πάσῃ τῇ χαρᾷ ᶠᾗ ᵍχαίρομεν δι'

y = 2 Cor. i. 4. iii. 14. vii. 4 al.   z = 1 Cor. vii. 26. 2 Cor. vi. 4 al.   1 Kings xxii. 2.
a = 2 Cor. xiii. 4. see Rom. vii. 9, or x. 5.   b w. ind., 1 John v. 15. Job xxii. 3.   c Gal. v. 1 reff.
d Eph. v. 4 reff.   e Luke xiv. 14 bis. Rom. xi. 35. xii. 19. 2 Thess. i. 6. Heb. x. 30 only. L.P.H. Ps.
cxv. 12 (3).   f attr., Eph. i. 6 reff.   g so Matt. ii. 10. (John iii. 29.) see Judg. xi. 33.

7. παρακεκλημεθα A 3. 23. 57.   for επι, εν F 109 vulg goth Pel.   rec θλιψ.
και αναγκ., with KL rel [æth] Chr Thdrt Damasc : txt ABDF℘ m 17 [47] latt syrr
copt [goth] arm Ambrst Pel.   for ημων, υμων A B²[(not Tischdf, Cod Vat) copt
arm-ed].   ins και bef δια A [for δια, και D gr].   πιστεως bef υμων A fuld.
8. rec στηκητε, with D℘¹ (b² c e h 17, e sil) : txt A B(ita cod) FKL℘³ rel Chr-ms.
9. for θεω, κυριω D¹F℘¹ copt[not so, Treg].   for υμων, ημων B¹[txt B²·³(Tischdf)].
η εχαιρομεν D¹.

διδασκάλου τὴν μνήμην. δηλοῖ ἡ μὲν
πίστις τῆς εὐσεβείας τὸ βέβαιον· ἡ δὲ
ἀγάπη τὴν πρακτικὴν ἀρετήν· ἡ δὲ τοῦ
διδασκάλου μνήμη, κ. ὁ περὶ αὐτὸν πόθος,
μαρτυρεῖ τῇ περὶ τὴν διδασκαλίαν στοργῇ.
πάντοτε belongs more naturally to
the foregoing : see 1 Cor. i. 4 ; xv. 58 ;
Gal. iv. 18 ; Eph. v. 20. " ἐπιποθεῖν τι
(huc etiam redire structuram ἐπιποθεῖν sq.
infinitivo nemo nescit) idem valet quod
πόθον ἔχειν ἐπί τι, desiderium ferre in aliquid versum, cf. LXX. Ps. xlii. (xli.) 1, ὃν
τρόπον ἐπιποθεῖ ἡ ἔλαφος ἐπὶ τὰς πηγὰς
τῶν ὑδάτων." Fritz. in Rom. i. 11. So
that *direction*, not intensity (which as
Fritz. also remarks, after the analogy of
περιπόθητος, should be expressed by περι-,
not ἐπιποθεῖν) is the force of the preposition.   ἡμεῖς ὑμᾶς] scil. ἰδεῖν ἐπιπο-
θοῦμεν.   7.] διὰ τοῦτο, viz. on account of what has just been mentioned,
from ἄρτι . . . . ;—τοῦτο combining the
whole of the good news in one.   ἐφ'
ὑμῖν, with reference to you: as we say,
over you. *You* were the object of our
consolation : the faith which you shewed
was the means whereby that object was
applied to our minds.   ἐπὶ πάσῃ τῇ
ἀνάγ. κ. θλ. ἡμ.] in (reff., i. e. '*in the
midst of*,'—'*in spite of*') all our necessity
and tribulation : *what* necessity and tribulation does not appear ;—but clearly
some external trouble, not, as De W.,
care and anxiety for you, for this would
be removed by the message of Timotheus.
We may well imagine such external trouble, from Acts xviii. 5—10 :   8.]
for now (not so much an adverb of *time*,
here, as implying the fulfilment of the
condition (ἐάν) which follows : so Eur.
Iph. in Aul. 644 : " συνετὰ λέγουσα μᾶλλον εἰς οἰκτόν μ' ἄγεις." " ἀσύνετα νῦν
ἐροῦμεν, εἰ σέ γ' εὐφρανῶ." See more

examples in Hartung, Partikell. ii. p. 25 ;
Kühner, ii. p. 185) **we live** (the ἀνάγκη and
θλίψις being conceived as a *death*: but not
to be referred to *everlasting* life, as Chrys.
(ζωὴν λέγων τὴν μέλλουσαν), nor weakened to 'vivit qui felix est' (Pelt), but
with direct reference to the infringement
of the powers of life by ἀνάγκ. and θλ., as
Lünem., "we are in full strength and freshness of life, we do not feel the sorrows
and tribulations with which the outer
world surrounds us ") **if ye stand fast in
the Lord.** The conditional form of this
last sentence, with ἐάν, not ἐπεί, carries it
forward as an exhortation for the future
also ; while the solœcistic indicative gives
the Apostle's confident expectation that
such would be the case.   The reading
must not be dismissed, as Ellic., by taking
refuge in Scrivener's assertion that permutations of similar vowels are occasionally
found even in the best MSS.   I have examined the Vatican Codex through the
greater part of the N. T., and can safely
say that these permutations are found only
in such cases as H, I, and EI, and O and Ω
in doubtful inflexions, as ἑώρακ. and ἑόρακ.;
not in cases like the present, nor in any
ordinary occurrences of long and short
vowels. See remarks on Rom. v. 1 ; and
prolegg. to Vol. I. ch. vi. § i. 36, 37.
There were (ver. 10) ὑστερήματα in their
faith, requiring κατάρτισις.   9.] And
this vigour of life shews itself in the
earnest desire of abundant thanksgiving :
so the **γάρ** accounts for, and specifies the
action of, the ζωή just mentioned.
τίνα, what — i. e. what sufficient — ?
ἀνταπ.] reff. : *thanks* is itself a
return for God's favours : see especially
ref. Ps.   ἐπί, may be taken as
above (ref. ʸ), or as **for,—in return for:** the
two meanings in fact run up into one.

h = ch. i. 3 reff.　ὑμᾶς [h] ἔμπροσθεν τοῦ θεοῦ ἡμῶν; [10] [i] νυκτὸς καὶ [i] ἡμέρας　ABDFK
i ch. ii. 9 reff.
j Eph. iii. 20　[j] ὑπερεκπερισσοῦ δεόμενοι [k] εἰς τὸ [l] ἰδεῖν ὑμῶν τὸ [l] πρός-　Lℵ a b c
only †.　Dan.　　　　　　　　　　　　　　　　　　　　　　　　　　d e f g h
iii. 22
Theod.-Ald.　ωπον καὶ [m] καταρτίσαι τὰ [n] ὑστερήματα τῆς πίστεως ὑμῶν.　k l m n o
-compl.　　　　　　　　　　　　　　　　　　　　　　　　　　　　17. 47
(-σσῶς,　[11] [o] αὐτὸς δὲ ὁ [p] θεὸς καὶ [p] πατὴρ ἡμῶν καὶ ὁ κύριος ἡμῶν
ch. v. 13.)
k constr., Phil.　Ἰησοῦς [q] κατευθύναι τὴν ὁδὸν ἡμῶν πρὸς ὑμᾶς.　[12] ὑμᾶς
i. 23 reff.
l ch. ii. 17 reff.　δὲ ὁ κύριος [r] πλεονάσαι καὶ [s] περισσεύσαι τῇ ἀγάπῃ εἰς
m = Matt. iv.
21. (Luke　ἀλλήλους καὶ εἰς πάντας, [t] καθάπερ καὶ ἡμεῖς εἰς ὑμᾶς,
vi. 40.) Gal.
vi. 1. Ezra
iv. 12, 13, 16.
n Phil. ii. 30 reff.　　o ch. iv. 16. v. 23.　2 Thess. ii. 16. iii. 16.　p Gal. i. 4 reff.　q Luke i.
79.　2 Thess. iii. 5 only.　Ps. v. 8.　　　　r trans., here only.　Num. xxvi. 54.　Ps. lxx. 21. (intr., Rom. v. 20
al.)　Paul only, exc. 2 Pet. i. 8.　　　s trans., 2 Cor. iv. 15. ix. 8.　Eph. i. 8 only ‡.　　t ver. 6.

for θεου, κυριου ℵ¹.

11. om ιησ. D¹.　　rec aft ιησους ins χριστος, with D³ᵇFKL rel vulg syrr copt
goth [arm] Ath : om ABD³ªℵ 17 am(with demid harl¹ tol) D-lat æth-rom Ambr Vocat.
for 3rd ημων, υμων ℵ¹.

12. for κυριος, θεος A 73 : κυρ. ιησους D¹F(not F-lat) : om am¹ Syr.　της
αγαπης F.

πάσ. τῇ χαρᾷ, all the joy: i. e.
not the joy from so many different
sources, but the joy in its largeness and
depth: q. d. τῇ χαρᾷ τῇ μεγάλῃ.
ῇ attr. for ἥν,—see Matt. ii. 10 : not as
John iii. 29,—see note there.
ἔμπρ. τ. θεοῦ ἡμ. shews the joy to be of
the very highest and best,—no joy of
this world, or of personal pride, but one
which will bear, and does bear, the searching eye of God, and is *His* joy (John xv.
11). **10.**] νυκτ. κ. ἡμ. see on ch. ii.
9. ὑπερεκπ. : see reff., and cf. Mark
vi. 51. δεόμενοι belongs to the question of ver. 9—q. d., ' what thanks can we
render, &c., proportioned to the earnestness of our prayers, &c.?' So that δεόμενοι would best be rendered **praying as we
do.** εἰς τό—direction, or aim, of the
prayers. καταρτίσαι τὰ ὑστ.] τὰ
ἐλλείποντα πληρῶσαι, Thdrt.: cf. 2 Cor. ix.
12. These ὑστερήματα were consequences
of their being as yet novices in the faith :
partly theoretical, e. g. their want of stability respecting the παρουσία, and of fixed
ideas respecting those who had fallen asleep
in Christ,—partly practical, ch. iv. 1. One
can hardly conceive a greater perverseness
than that of Baur, who takes this passage
for a proof that the Thessalonian church
had been long in the faith. **11—13.**]
*Good wishes, with respect to this his
earnest desire, and to their continued
progress in love and holiness.* **11.**
αὐτός] Not as De W. in contrast with
the δεόμενοι just spoken of,—but as
Chrys., αὐτὸς δὲ ὁ θεὸς ἐκκόψαι τοὺς
πειρασμοὺς τοὺς πανταχοῦ περιέλκοντας
ἡμᾶς, ὥστε ὀρθὴν ἐλθεῖν πρὸς ὑμᾶς,—
i. e. it exalts the absolute power of God
and the Lord Jesus,—if He expedites the
way, it will be accomplished. αὐτός then
is in contrast with *ourselves,* who have

once and again tried to come to you, but
have been hindered by Satan. Lünem.
remarks that ὁ θεός is best taken absolute, and ἡμῶν referred to πατήρ only.
More majesty is thus given to the αὐτὸς ὁ
θεός, although αὐτός refers to the whole.
Cf. 2 Thess. ii. 16, 17. κατευθύναι]
not infinitive, but third person singular
optative aorist. It certainly cannot be
passed without remark, that the two
nominatives should thus be followed, here
and in 2 Thess. ii. 16, 17, by a singular
verb. It would be hardly possible that
this should be so, unless some reason
existed in the subjects of the verb. Mere
unity of will between the Father and
the Son (Lünem.) would not be enough,
unless absolute unity were also in the
writer's mind. Athanasius therefore seems
to be right in drawing from this construction an argument for the unity of the
Father and the Son. πρὸς ὑμᾶς more
naturally belongs to κατευθύναι than to
τὴν ὁδὸν ἡμῶν, in which case it should be
τὴν ὁδ. ἡμ. τὴν πρὸς ὑμ. **12.**] ὑμᾶς
δέ—emphatic—' sive nos veniemus sive
minus,' Bengel. ὁ κύριος may refer
either to the Father, or to Christ. It is
no objection to the former, that τ. θεοῦ κ.
πατρ. ἡμ. is repeated below, any more
than it is to the latter that τ. κυρ. ἡμ. Ἰ.
is so repeated. I should rather understand (still, notwithstanding Ellic.'s note)
it of the Father : see 2 Cor. ix. 8.
πλεονάσαι] transitive, see reff. : **enlarge
you**—not merely in *numbers,* as Thdrt.,
but in *yourselves,* in richness of gifts and
largeness of faith and knowledge—fill up
your ὑστερήματα, ver. 10. περισσεύσαι (reff.), **make you to abound.**
εἰς πάντας] toward all men, not, as
Thdrt., πάντας τοὺς ὁμοπίστους, but as
Est., '*etiam infideles et vestræ salutis*

13 ^uεἰς τὸ ^vστηρίξαι ὑμῶν τὰς καρδίας ^wἀμέμπτους ἐν u Eph. i. 12 reff.
v Rom. i. 11.
^xἁγιωσύνη ^yἔμπροσθεν τοῦ ^pθεοῦ καὶ ^pπατρὸς ἡμῶν ^zἐν xvi. 25. ver.
2. Ps. l. 12 (14).
τῇ ^zπαρουσίᾳ τοῦ κυρίου ἡμῶν Ἰησοῦ μετὰ πάντων τῶν w Phil. ii. 15 reff. constr., Phil. iii. 21 reff.
^aἁγίων αὐτοῦ.

IV. ¹ ^bΛοιπὸν οὖν, ἀδελφοί, ^cἐρωτῶμεν ὑμᾶς καὶ x Rom. i. 4.
2 Cor. vii. 1 only. Ps.
^dπαρακαλοῦμεν ^eἐν κυρίῳ Ἰησοῦ, ἵνα καθὼς ^fπαρελάβετε y = ch. i. 3 reff.
παρ' ἡμῶν ^gτὸ πῶς δεῖ ὑμᾶς ^hπεριπατεῖν καὶ ⁱἀρέσκειν z ch. ii. 19 reff. a see Ps. xxxviii. 7.
ⁱθεῷ, καθὼς καὶ ^hπεριπατεῖτε, ἵνα ^kπερισσεύητε μᾶλλον. Dan. iv. 10

Theod. Jude 14.   b 1 Cor. i. 16. iv. 2.   2 Cor. xiii. 11.   (2 Thess. iii. 1.)   c = Phil. iv. 3. ch.
v. 12.   2 Thess. ii. 1 al.   d = Eph. iv. 1 reff.   e = 2 Cor. ii. 17.   Eph. iv. 17 al.
f = 1 Cor. xi. 23. xv. 1.   Gal. i. 9, 12 al.   g art., Mark ix. 23.   Luke i. 62.   Rom. v. 15.
h = Rom. vi. 4 al. fr.   i ch. ii. 15 reff.   k Rom. iii. 7.   Phil. i. 26. ver. 10 al. fr.   Eccl. iii. 19.

13. τας καρδιας bef υμων DF latt.   αμεμπτως BL [47 Mill] Ps-Ath.   αγιοσυνη
B¹DF: δικαιοσυνη A 23. 57.   rec aft ιησου ins χριστου, with FL rel vulg syrr copt
goth æth-pl [arm] Ps-Ath₄ [Tert]: om ABDKℵ d l m n am æth Damasc Ambr.—om
ιησ. also m.   at end ins αμην (an ecclesiastical lection ending here) AD¹ℵ¹ m vulg
copt æth arm Pel Bede: om BD²FKLℵ³ rel fuld¹ syrr goth Tert Ambrst Vocat.

CHAP. IV. 1. rec ins το bef λοιπον, with B² a c g h k Chr Thdrt: om AB¹DFKℵ rel
Chr-ms Damasc.   om ουν B¹ d¹ k m 17 Syr copt [arm] Chr Thl: autem D-lat.
ins τω bef κυριω [A]ℵ.   rec om 1st ινα, with AD³KLℵ rel syr [æth] Chr
Thdrt Damasc: ins BD¹F m 17 latt Syr [copt goth] arm Chr-ms Ambrst Pel.
rec om καθως και περιπατειτε (see notes), with D³KL rel Syr Chr Thdrt Damasc Thl Œc:
ins ABD¹Fℵ m 17 vulg [syr] copt goth æth arm Ambrst.   περισσευσητε B.

inimicos.' **καθ. κ. ἡμεῖς,** viz. περισ-
σεύομεν τῇ ἀγάπῃ :—ἔχετε γὰρ μέτρον κ.
παράδειγμα τῆς ἀγάπης ἡμᾶς, Thl.
13.] εἰς τὸ στηρίξαι—the further and
higher aim of πλεον. κ. περισσ.—**in order
to confirm** (i. e. εἰς τὸ τὸν κύριον στηρίξαι
—'in order that He may confirm') **your
hearts** (not merely ὑμᾶς: ἐκ γὰρ τῆς
καρδίας ἐξέρχονται διαλογισμοὶ πονηροί,
Chrys.) **unblameable** (i. e. so as to be unblameable: cf. reff. and εἰσδόκε θερμὰ λοῦτρα
θερμήνῃ, Il. ξ. 6,—εὔφημον, ὦ τάλαινα,
κοίμησον στόμα, Æsch. Ag. 1258,—τῶν
σῶν ἀδέρκτων ὀμμάτων τητώμενος, Soph.
Œd. Col. 1200) **in holiness** (belongs to
ἀμέμπτ.,—the sphere in which the blamelessness is to be shewn :—not to στηρίξαι)
before (Him who is) **God and our Father**
(or **our God and Father.** This ensures
the genuineness of this absence of blame
in holiness: that it should be not only
before men, but also before God), **at (in)
the coming,** &c.   ἁγίων—we need
not enter into any question whether these
are angels, or saints properly so called :
the expression is an O. T. one,—Zach.
xiv. 5, LXX,—and was probably meant
by St. Paul to include both. Certainly
(2 Thess. i. 7. Matt. xxv. 31, al.) He
will be accompanied with the angels : but
also with the spirits of the just, cf. ch.
iv. 14.

CHAP. IV. 1—V. 24.] SECOND POR-
TION OF THE EPISTLE : consisting of exhortations and instructions.   1—12.]

Exhortations: and   1—8.] to a holy
life.   1.] **λοιπόν** has no reference to
time, ἀεὶ κ. εἰς τὸ διηνεκές, Chr., Thl.,
but introduces this second portion, thus
dividing it from the first, and implying
the close of the Epistle. St. Paul uses it
towards the end of his Epistles: see in
addition to reff., Eph. vi. 10; Phil. iv. 8.
      οὖν, in furtherance of the wish
of ch. iii. 12, 13: τούτῳ κεχρημένοι τῷ
σκόπῳ προσφέρομεν ὑμῖν τὴν παραίνεσιν.
      ἐρωτῶμεν] in the classics, only
used of asking a question : but in N. T.
(as the Heb. שָׁאַל, Lün., which however, in
the sense of requesting, is rendered in
the LXX by αἰτεῖν) it has both meanings of our verb 'to ask' (reff.).
      παρακ. ἐν κυρ. Ἰησ.] we exhort you in
(as our element of exhortation ; in whom
we do all things pertaining to the ministry
(see Rom. ix. 1): Eph. iv. 17—not 'by,'
as a 'formula jurandi,' which is contrary
to N. T. usage, see Fritzsche on Rom.
ix. 1) the **Lord Jesus, that as ye received**
(see on ch. ii. 13) **from us how** (τό is not
superfluous: it collects and specifies what
follows, q. d.—'the manner of your,' &c.)
ye ought to walk and to please God (i. e.
to please God in your walk and conduct :
—to walk, and thereby to please God), **as
also ye are walking** (this addition, says
Lün., is required as well (see var. readd.)
by internal considerations. For **ἵνα περισσ.** requires the assumption of a prior
commencement (see ver. 10): and such

1 Acts v. 28.
xvi. 24.
1 Tim. i. 5,
18 only †.
m = 2 Cor. i. 5.
n John vi. 40.
see 1 Pet. ii.
15.
o Rom. vi. 19,
22. 1 Cor. i.
30. 2 Thess. ii. 13. 1 Tim. ii. 15. Paul only, exc, Heb. xii. 14. 1 Pet. i. 2. 2 Macc. xiv. 36.
Acts xv. 20. ch. v. 22. Job i. 1, 8. gen. without ἀπό, Acts xv. 29. 1 Tim. iv. 3. 1 Pet. ii. 11.
v. 32 al. fr. Gen. xxxviii. 24. r = Phil. iv. 12. Job xxxiv. 19. s = see note.

ABDFK
LℵＬ a b c
d e f g h
k l m n o
17. 47

p w. ἀπό,
q Matt.

² οἴδατε γὰρ τίνας ¹παραγγελίας ἐδώκαμεν ὑμῖν ᵐ διὰ τοῦ κυρίου Ἰησοῦ. ³ ⁿτοῦτο γάρ ἐστιν ⁿ θέλημα τοῦ θεοῦ, ὁ ᵒἁγιασμὸς ὑμῶν, ᵖἀπέχεσθαι ὑμᾶς ἀπὸ τῆς �q πορνείας, 4 ʳεἰδέναι ἕκαστον ὑμῶν τὸ ἑαυτοῦ ˢσκεῦος ˢκτᾶσθαι ἐν

2. παρεδώκαμεν D¹F: δεδωκ. ℵ m 73. 80. aft κυριου ins ημων D¹F 45 Syr æth Chr Thl Hil. om ιησ. (and not δια τ. κυρ.) 17 : aft ιησ. ins χριστου F a 19. 27. 45 syrr Chr Hil.

3. ins το bef θελημα AF [K(Matth Treg, agst Tischdf)] c Clem [Orig-c] Antch Damasc : om BDL rel Chr Thdrt. om του D¹F l [47]. for της, πασης ℵ³ 73. 115 Syr [arm-ms] Chr Thdrt Thl : πασι(sic) της F.

4. ins ενα bef εκαστον B²(see table) D³ᵃ 73 (vss) Chr. εκαστος AF. κτασθαι

a commencement would not be implied in the preceding text, without καθὼς καὶ περιπατεῖτε. Evidently the Apostle would originally have written ἵνα, καθ. παρ. παρ' ἡμ. τὸ πῶς κ.τ.λ. . . . ., οὕτως καὶ περιπατῆτε : but while writing, altered this his intended expression, that he might not say too little, wishing to notice the good beginning already made by the Thessalonians. The repetition of ἵνα after so long an intervening clause is too natural to have given rise (as De W. thinks) to the insertion) that ye abound yet more, viz.: ἐν τῷ οὕτως περιπατεῖν : not, as Chrys., ἵνα ἐκ πλείονος περιουσίας, μὴ μέχρι τῶν ἐντολῶν ἵστασθε, ἀλλ' ἵνα καὶ ὑπερβαίνητε. **2.**] takes up the καθὼς παρελάβετε of the former verse, and appeals to their memory in its confirmation. See similar appeals in Gal. iv. 13; 1 Cor. xv. 1. παραγγ.] commands, see reff. The stress is on τίνας, to which τοῦτο answers, ver. 3. διὰ τ. κ. Ἰησ.] by, i. e. coming from, παραγγελθείσας διά. So τὰς διὰ τῶν ὀλίγων πολιτείας, Demosth. p. 489: δι' ἑαυτοῦ, of himself, Xen. Cyr. viii. 1. 43 : see Bernhardy, p. 236. **3.**] further specification (γάρ) of the παραγγελίαι : see above. τοῦτο is the subject, not the predicate (as De W.): see Rom. ix. 8: Gal. iii. 7: not superfluous, as Pelt, but emphatically prefixed (so Lünem.). θέλημα τ. θεοῦ serves to take up again the διὰ τ. κυρ. Ἰησοῦ. The article may be omitted, because the predicate θέλημα τ. θ. is not distributed (?): but in this case, τὸ θέλ. would be equally applicable, there being no danger of τὸ θέλ. being mistaken for 'the whole will,' but rather specifying 'that which forms part of the will.' This explanation is not to be abandoned, as Ellic., on account of the merely occasional omission of the article after a noun substantive, mentioned by Middleton and Ellic.: for

the reason of that omission is to be sought rather in logic than in idiom. Rather perhaps should we say that there is in Greek a tendency to omit articles before predicates, even where such an omission cannot be logically pressed. ὁ ἁγ. ὑμ. is in apposition with θέλ. τ. θ. as a 'locus communis,' the will of God respecting us being known to be our sanctification, and then this sanctification being afterwards specified as consisting in ἀπέχεσθαι, &c. Therefore ἁγιασμός must be taken in the most general sense, and that which is afterwards introduced, ἀπέχεσθαι, &c., as a part of our ἁγιασμός. ὑμῶν is the objective genitive, of you. ἀπέχεσθαι and εἰδέναι are not the negative and positive sides of ὁ ἁγ. ὑμ. as Lünem. and Ellic.,—for the negative comes in again in verses 5, 6,—but the latter (εἰδέναι to διεμαρτυράμεθα, ver. 6) further specifies and ensures the former. **4.**] εἰδέναι, know how (reff.). On the meaning of τὸ σκεῦος, there has been * much difference. Very many Commentators understand it of 'the body.' (So, among others, Chrys. (see below), Thdrt., Œc., Thl., Tert., Pelag., Calv., Corn.-a-lap., Beza, Grot., Calov., Ham., Beng., Macknight, Pelt, Olsh., Baumg.-Crus.) But it is fatal to this interpretation, (1) that it must force an untenable meaning on κτᾶσθαι, which can only mean 'to acquire,' not 'to possess.' Chrys., whose sense of Greek usage led him to feel this, tries to fit the meaning 'to acquire' into the sense: ἡμεῖς αὐτὸ κτώμεθα, ὅταν μένῃ καθαρὸν κ. ἐστιν ἐν ἁγιασμῷ ὅταν δὲ ἀκάθαρτον, ἁμαρτία—(so Olsh. also); but this is lame enough, and would not, as De W. remarks, answer for the other member of the sentence, μὴ ἐν πάθει ἐπιθυμίας. (2) that the mere use of σκεῦος, without any explanation, could hardly point at the body. In all the passages ordinarily quoted to support it, the meta-

^oἁγιασμῷ καὶ τιμῇ, ⁵ μὴ ἐν ^tπάθει ^uἐπιθυμίας ^vκαθάπερ

καὶ τὰ ἔθνη τὰ μὴ ^wεἰδότα τὸν θεόν, ^{6 x}τὸ μὴ ^yὑπερ-

t Rom. i. 26.
Col. iii. 5
(reff.) only.
u Rom. i. 24
al. fr.
y here

v ch. iii. 6, 12.
only. Jer. v. 22.

w Gal. iv. 8.   2 Thess. i. 8.   (Jer. iv. 22.)

x art., ver. 1 reff.

bef το ε. σκευος DF goth.   ins εν bef τιμη אּ¹ d.

phor is further explained by the context:
—e.g., Barnab., ep. 7, 11, pp. 744, 760, τὸ
σκεῦος τοῦ πνεύματος αὐτοῦ,—Philo, quod
det. pot. insid. § 46, vol. i. p. 223,
τῆς ψυχῆς ἀγγεῖον τὸ σῶμα,—de migr.
Abr. § 36, vol. i. p. 467, τοῖς ἀγγείοις τῆς
ψυχῆς σώματι κ. αἰσθήσει,—Cic. disp. Tusc.
i. 22 : ' corpus quidem quasi vas est aut
aliquod animi receptaculum,'—Lucret. iii.
441 : ' corpus, quod vas quasi constitit ejus
(sc. animæ).' 2 Cor. iv. 7 is evidently no case
in point, ὀστρακίνοις being there added,
and the body being simply *compared* to an
earthen vessel. (3) that the order of the
words is against it.   In τὸ ἑαυτοῦ σκεῦος,
the emphasis must lie on ἑαυτοῦ—cf. 1 Cor.
vii. 2, ἕκαστος τὴν ἑαυτοῦ γυναῖκα ἐχέτω.
Had the body been meant, this would be
without import, and it would more naturally have been τὸ σκεῦος ἑαυτοῦ (or
αὐτοῦ). (4) But a more fatal objection
than any of the former is, that the context is entirely against the meaning. The
ἁγιασμός has been explained to consist in
ἀπέχεσθαι ἀπὸ τῆς πορνείας. And now
this πορνεία comes to be specified, wherein it consists, and how it may be guarded
against : viz. in carrying on the divinely-
appointed commerce of the sexes in holiness and honour. In fact, the thought
is exactly as in 1 Cor. vii. 2, διὰ τὰς πορνείας ἕκαστος τὴν ἑαυτοῦ γυναῖκα ἐχέτω,
κ. ἑκάστη τὸν ἴδιον ἄνδρα ἐχέτω. Many
have therefore understood σκεῦος in its
literal meaning as applied to τὸ πρᾶγμα,
—i. e. the *woman* (or indeed the *man*, on
the other side, inasmuch as the woman
has ἐξουσία over his body, see 1 Cor. vii.
4. So that thus it would be an exhortation to the woman also : so De Wette).
Thus the context would be satisfied, and
the emphatic position of ἑαυτοῦ (as in
1 Cor. vii. 2);—and κτᾶσθαι would retain
its proper meaning : **that each of you
should know how to acquire his own
vessel** (for this purpose) **in sanctification**
(κτᾶσθαι ἐν ἁγ. belong together) **and
honour.** This sense of σκεῦος is found in
the Jewish books (Megill. Esth. i. 11 :
"In convivio dixerunt aliqui : mulieres
Medicæ sunt pulcriores : alii, Persicæ sunt
pulcriores. Dixit Ahasuerus : Vas meum,
quo ego utor, nec Persicum est nec Medi-
cum, sed Chaldaicum"). And the expression κτᾶσθαι γυναῖκα is common : cf. Xen.
Symp. ii. 10 : ταύτην (Ξανθίππην κέκ-

τημαι: Ruth iv. 10; Sir. xxxvi. 24.
And so Thdr. Mops. (σκεῦος τὴν ἰδίαν
ἑκάστου γαμετὴν ὀνομάζει), some in Thdrt.
(τινὲς τὸ ἑαυτοῦ σκεῦος τὴν ὁμόζυγα ἡρ-
μήνευσαν), Aug. (contr. Jul. iv. 10 (56),
vol. x. p. 765,—' ut sciret unusquisque possidere vas suum, hoc est, uxorem :' cf. also
ib. v. 9 (35), p. 805 : de nupt. et conc. i. 8
(9), p. 418,—' non solum igitur conjugatus
fidelis vase non utatur alieno, sed faciunt
a quibus uxores alienæ appetuntur : sed
nec ipsum proprium in concupiscentiæ
carnalis morbo possidendum sciat.' But
he mistakes κτᾶσθαι for *possidere*, and so
understands the command as given *con-
jugatis fidelibus*), Thom. Aquin., Zwingle,
Est., Heins., Wetst., Schöttg., Michaelis,
Koppe, Schott, De Wette, Lünem., al.
(Much of the foregoing note is from De
W. and Lün.) The objection to the above
view, that thus only *men* would be addressed (Calv., al.) is easily answered (besides as above, under 4) by observing that
in other places also, where πορνεία is in
question, the male only is exhorted, e. g.
1 Cor. vi. 15—18 : the female being included by implication, and bound to interpret on her side that which is said of the
other.   **5.]** ἐν πάθει ἐπιθ.,—πάθει
having the emphasis,—' in the mere *passio*
of lust,'—as Thdr. Mops. (Lün.), ὡς ἂν
τούτο ποιοῦντος οὐκέτι ταύτῃ ὡς γυναικὶ
συνόντος ἀλλὰ διὰ μίξιν μόνην ἁπλῶς,
ὅπερ πάθος ἐπιθυμίας ἐκάλεσεν.
καθ. καί] the καί so usual after particles
of comparison, points to the association in
the same category which the particle supposes : καὶ ἡμῖν ταὐτὰ δοκεῖ ἅπερ καὶ
βασιλεῖ, Xen. Anab. ii. 1. 22. See examples in Hartung, Partikell. ii. 127 : and
cf. ch. ii. 13 ; iii. 6, 12, &c.   τὰ μὴ
εἰδ. τ. θ.] μή, because the Gentiles are
spoken of by the writer from this point
of view. It is not a mere fact which is
stated, but that fact as logically interwoven with the course of the context :
and hence the subjective negative. See
reff.   **6.]** I cannot help regarding it
as most unnatural, to interpret this verse
of a new subject introduced, viz. the not
wronging one another in the business of
life. How such Commentators as De Wette
and Lünem. can have entertained this
view, I am at a loss to imagine. For (1)
the sense is carried on from vv. 4, 5,
without even the repetition of ἕκαστον

z 2 Cor. ii. 11.
vii. 2. xii. 17,
18 only. P.
Ezek. xxii.
27. Hab. ii.
9 only.
a (see note)
2 Cor. vii. 14.
b Rom. xiii. 4
only †. Wisd
xii. 12. Sir.
xxx. 6 only.
c Acts i. 16.
Gal. v. 21
only †.
d Luke xvi. 28.

βαίνειν καὶ ᶻπλεονεκτεῖν ἐν ᵃτῷ πράγματι τὸν ἀδελφὸν ABDFK
αὐτοῦ, διότι ᵇἔκδικος κύριος περὶ πάντων τούτων, καθὼς
καὶ ᶜπροείπαμεν ὑμῖν καὶ ᵈδιεμαρτυράμεθα. 7 οὐ γὰρ
ᶠᵍʰ ἐκάλεσεν ἡμᾶς ὁ θεὸς ᵍⁱ ἐπὶ ᵏ ἀκαθαρσίᾳ, ἀλλ᾽ ʰ ἐν
ᶫ ἁγιασμῷ. 8 ᵐ τοιγαροῦν ὁ ⁿ ἀθετῶν οὐκ ἄνθρωπον
ⁿ ἀθετεῖ, ἀλλὰ τὸν θεὸν τὸν [καὶ] ᵒᵖ δόντα τὸ ᵒ πνεῦμα
αὐτοῦ τὸ ἅγιον ᵖ εἰς ὑμᾶς.

ABDFK
Lℵ a b c
d e f g h
k l m n o
17. 47

Acts ii. 40
al7. 1 Tim. v. 21. 2 Tim. ii. 14. iv. 1. Heb. ii. 6 only. L.P.H. Ezek. xvi. 2. f = Rom. viii. 30. ix.
11. 1 Cor. vii. 15. Eph. iv. 1. 2 Thess. ii. 14 al. g Gal. v. 13. h 1 Cor. vii. 15. Gal.
i. 5. Eph. iv. 4. i Eph. ii. 10. k = Rom. i. 24. vi. 19. Gal. v. 19 al. (see ch. ii. 3.)
1 ver. 3 reff. m Heb. xii. 1 only. Prov. i. 31 al. n = Luke x. 16. John xii. 48. Isa. xxxiii.
1. (see Gal. ii. 21 reff.) o Luke xi. 13. John iii. 34. Acts v. 32. viii. 18. xv. 8. Rom. v. 5 al.
p = Luke xv. 22. see 2 Cor. i. 22.

6. rec ins o bef κυριος, with D³ F[θεος] KLℵ³ rel Clem: om ABD¹ℵ¹ 17.
προειπομεν AKL rel Clem Chr Thdrt: txt BDFℵ n o [47]. διεμαρτυρομεθα D³K
d e f l¹ m n o.

7. αλλα BD³.

8. om 1st τον D¹F. om και ABD³ o 17 D-lat Syr [copt] goth [æth Orig] Ath
Did Chr Thdrt-ms Thl Ambr Ambrst Pel: ins D¹FKLℵ [rel] vulg syr [arm] Clem Thdrt
Damasc Œc Bede. διδοντα (corrn to make the gift of the spirit present) BDFℵ¹
[Orig] Ath Did: txt AKLℵ³ rel 67² vss Clem Chr Thdrt Damasc. αυτο το πν.
το αγ. εις A. rec ημας (to suit the idea that ανθρ. was the Ap. himself), with
A c vulg-ed(and F-lat) syr-txt [æth] Chr: txt BDFKLℵ rel am(with fuld harl² tol)
Syr syr-mg copt goth arm Clem [Orig] Did Chr-ms Damasc Œc.

ὑμῶν to mark the change of topic: and
(2) when the Apostle sums up the whole
in ver. 7, he mentions merely impurity,
without the slightest allusion to the other.
To say that more than one kind of sin
must be mentioned because of περὶ πάντων τούτων, is mere trifling: the πάντα
ταῦτα (not ταῦτα πάντα, which would
collect many individuals into a whole)
generalizes from the sin mentioned to a
wider range. The interpretation which I
impugn, is also that of Zwingle, Calv.,
Grot., Calov., Le Clerc, Wolf, Koppe,
Flatt. I understand the verse, with
Chrys., Thdrt., Œc., Thl., Jer., Erasm.,
Est., Corn.-a-lap., Heins., Whitby, Wetst.,
Kypke, Beng., Michaelis, Pelt, Olsh., all.,
to refer to the sins of uncleanness, and
continue vv. 4, 5:—that he should not
(viz. τινά, contained in the αὐτοῦ following: so that τὸ μὴ . . . is a further specification of ὁ ἁγιασμός, rather than parallel
with εἰδέναι) set at nought (the order of
the sentence requires that ὑπερβ. should
not stand absolutely, as De W., Lün., al.,
for 'transgress' (μὴ νῦν ὑπέρβαιν᾽, ἀλλ᾽
ἐναισίμως φέρε, Eur. Alc. 1077: ὅτε κέν
τις ὑπερβήῃ κ. ἁμάρτῃ, Il. ι. 497), but
transitively: otherwise τινα would have
occurred after ὑπερβαίνειν to mark the
distinction of construction: and ὑπερβ.
with an accusative of person signifies
either 'to pass by' or 'take no notice,'
'posthabere,' as Herod. iii. 89, ὑπερβαίνων
τοὺς προσεχέας: or 'to go beyond' or
'surpass,' as Plato, Tim. 24 D, πάσῃ πάν-

τας ἀνθρώπους ὑπερβεβηκότες ἀρετῇ. Of
these, the former seems most applicable here: see below) or overreach his
brother in the matter (viz of τὸ ἑαυτοῦ
σκεῦος κτᾶσθαι—that there should be
among you none of those strifes on account
of the πάθη ἐπιθυμίας, the 'teterrima
belli causa' in the heathen world. As
Jowett rightly observes, "It is not necessary to suppose that any idea of unchastity
is conveyed by the term πλεονεκτεῖν, any
more than in the tenth commandment,
'Thou shalt not covet thy neighbour's
wife.' The meaning exclusively arises
from the connexion and application of
the word." How τῷ πράγματι can ever
signify τοῖς πράγμασιν, 'business affairs'
(De W., alt.), I cannot imagine; and
it is equally futile (with E. V. arm.)
to take τῷ for τῳ = τινι in the N. T.
"It is probable that the obscurity of
the passage arises partly from the decency in which the Apostle clothes it."
Jowett), because God is the avenger
('righter,' in such cases of setting at
nought and overreaching) of all these
things (viz. cases of ὑπερβασία and πλεονεξία, and by inference, lustful sins like
them) as also (see on ver. 5) we before told
you and constantly testified.   7.]
This verse (see above) is in my view decisive for the above rendering of ver. 6.
There is no mention here of avarice: nor
is it possible to understand ἀκαθαρσία,
when ver. 3 has gone before, of any thing
but carnal impurity. Chap. ii. 3, which is

9 Περὶ δὲ τῆς q φιλαδελφίας οὐ r χρείαν r ἔχετε γράφειν ὑμῖν· αὐτοὶ γὰρ ὑμεῖς s θεοδίδακτοί ἐστε t εἰς τὸ
u ἀγαπᾷν u ἀλλήλους· 10 καὶ γὰρ ποιεῖτε αὐτὸ εἰς πάντας
τοὺς ἀδελφοὺς τοὺς ἐν ὅλῃ τῇ Μακεδονίᾳ. v παρακαλοῦμεν δὲ ὑμᾶς, ἀδελφοί, v περισσεύειν μᾶλλον 11 καὶ

q Rom. xii. 10. Heb. xiii. 1. 1 Pet. i. 22 2 Pet. i. 7 bis, only +. (-φος, 1 Pet. iii. 8.)
r Matt. iii. 14. xiv. 6. John xiii. 10. ch. i. 8. v. 1. Dan. iii. 16. constr., see Heb. v. 12.
s here only +. see John vi. 45, aft. Isa. liv. 13. 1 Cor. ii. 13.
t Phil. i. 23. ch. iii. 10 al.
u John xiii. 34 bis. xv. 12, 17. Rom. xiii. 8. 1 Pet. i. 32. 1 John iii. 11, 23. iv. 7, 11, 12 only.
v ver. 1.

9. εχομεν D¹Fℵ³ b [47²(-ωμεν¹)] 67² latt syr goth Chr Thl lat-ff: ειχομεν B am (with hal harl²) Pel (*corrn on acct of the harsh constr: for which reason also* c 43. 67¹. 73. 80 copt *have* γραφεσθαι *as in ch* v. 1): txt AD³KLℵ¹ rel Syr copt [Orig-c] Thdrt Damasc.

10. om γαρ F [not G]. ins και bef εις B. om 2nd τους AD¹F Chr-ms: for τους, υμων ℵ¹: txt BD²·³KLℵ³ rel [και τους 47]. for αδελφοι, αγαπητοι A.

adduced to shew that it may here represent covetousness, is a very doubtful example: see there. **ἐπί, for the purpose of,—on condition of: ἐν, in,** 'in the element of,' not = εἰς, the *aim:* but **ἁγιασμός** is the whole sphere of our Christian life. **8.**] Hence, the sin of (rejecting) setting at nought such limitations and rules is a fearful one—no less than that of setting at nought God the giver of the Holy Spirit. In **ἄνθρωπον ἀθετεῖ** there is an obvious allusion to ὑπερβαίνειν κ. πλεονεκτεῖν τ. ἀδελφόν above. There is no need to supply any thing after **ἀθετων—ὁ ἀθετῶν** simply describes him who commits the act of rejecting; q. d. **the rejecter**—*what* he rejects, is not to be supplied in the construction, but is clear from the context—viz. τὸν ἀδελφὸν αὐτοῦ. The distinction between ἄνθρωπον (anarthrous) and **τὸν** θεόν, seems to be, that the former is indefinite; **not** (any) **man, but** (definite) **God.** **τὸν [καὶ] δόντα]** q. d. who also is the AUTHOR of our sanctification. [**καί**—'novum hic additur momentum,' Bengel. It introduces a climax, whereby the sin is intensified.] **δόντα**, as being one great definite act of God by His Son. **τὸ πν. αὐτοῦ τὸ ἅγ.]** This form of expression (q. d. 'His own (αὐτοῦ emphatic) Spirit, the Holy One') is probably chosen, and not τὸ ἅγ. πν. αὐτοῦ, for precision, to bring out τὸ ἅγιον as connected with ἁγιασμός preceding. **εἰς ὑμᾶς** is not = ὑμῖν, but gives the idea of direction: see Gal. iv. 6; ch. ii. 9. **9—12.**] *Exhortations to brotherly love* (9, 10 a), *and to honest diligent lives* (10 b—12). **9.**] **δέ** is transitional, the implied contrast being to the sin last spoken of. **φιλαδελφία** (reff.) here refers more immediately (cf. ποιεῖτε αὐτό below) to deeds of kindness by way of relief to poor brethren. **οὐ χρείαν ἔχετε]** This is a not unusual touch of delicate rhetoric with St. Paul (cf. 2 Cor. ix. 1: Philem. 19: ch. v. 1). It conveys tacit but gentle reproof. The knowledge and the practice already exist: but the latter is not quite in proportion to the former. τῷ εἰπεῖν, οὐ χρεία ἐστί, μεῖζον ἐποίησεν ἢ εἰ εἶπεν. Chrys. The construction οὐ χρείαν ἔχετε γράφειν ὑμῖν (defended by De Wette and Winer), has been pronounced inadmissible by Lünemann, such use of the infinitive active being only found where no special personal reference is attached to the verb, as ὑμῖν here: so that this would require ἐμὲ γρ. or γράφεσθαι. He therefore reads ἔχομεν. But with so many corrections (see var. readd.), and with the known irregularities of St. Paul's style in such constructions, it surely is not safe to speak so positively. I should regard the construction, not as analogous with χῶρον οὐχ ἁγνὸν πατεῖν, Soph. Œd. Col. 37; ἄξιος θαυμάσαι, Thuc. i. 38, and the like,—but as a mixed one between ἔχομεν γράφειν and ἔχετε γράφεσθαι. **αὐτοὶ ὑμεῖς**, in opposition to ἡμᾶς, the subject to be supplied from γράφειν: but **αὐτοί** is not *sponte*, which would not agree with **θεοδίδακτοι.** The stress of the sentence is on **αὐτοὶ ὑμεῖς**, not on the **θεο-** in θεοδίδακτοι, as Olsh.,—"where *God* teaches, there, the Apostle says, *he* may be silent:" but as Lün. observes, the **θεο-** comes in over and above as it were; **διδακτοί** would convey the *fact:* θεοδίδακτοι = διδακτοί, κ. ταῦτα παρὰ θεοῦ. And this teaching is practical—its tendency and object being εἰς τὸ ἀγ. ἀλλ.,—to produce mutual love. **10.**] follows up the θεοδίδακτοί ἐστε by a matter of fact, shewing the teaching to have been in some measure effectual. **καὶ γάρ]** the **καί** belongs to ποιεῖτε—'besides being taught it, ye *do* it,'—**ποιεῖτε** carrying the emphasis of the sentence. **αὐτό**, scil. τὸ ἀγαπᾷν ἀλ. **περισσεύειν**, viz. in this ἀγάπῃ. (But there does not seem any reason, with Jowett, to ascribe this

w Rom. xv. 20.
2 Cor. v. 9
only †.
x = Luke
xxiii. 56
(xiv. 4. Acts
xi. 18. xxi.
14) only.
y = here only.
z ch. ii. 9 reff.
a 1 Cor. iv. 12.
Wisd. xv.
17.

ᵂ φιλοτιμεῖσθαι ˣ ἡσυχάζειν καὶ πράσσειν ʸ τὰ ἴδια καὶ
ᶻᵃ ἐργάζεσθαι ταῖς ᵃ χερσὶν ὑμῶν, καθὼς ὑμῖν ᵇ παρηγγεί-
λαμεν, ¹² ἵνα. ᶜ περιπατῆτε ᵈ εὐσχημόνως πρὸς ᵉ τοὺς ἔξω
καὶ μηδενὸς ᶠ χρείαν ᶠ ἔχητε.

ABDFK
LℵＮ a b c
d e f g h
k l m n o
17. 47

¹³ ᵍ Οὐ θέλομεν δὲ ὑμᾶς ᵍʰ ἀγνοεῖν, ἀδελφοί, περὶ τῶν

b Mark vi. 8.　2 Thess. iii. 4, &c.　1 Tim. i. 3. iv. 11. v. 7 al.　Josh. vi. 6.　　　　c = Rom. vi. 4. xiii. 13.　Eph.
iv. 1 al. fr.　　　　d Rom. xiii. 13.　1 Cor. xiv. 40 only †.　(-μων, 1 Cor. vii. 38.)　　　e (see Acts xxvi.
11.)　Mark iv. 11.　1 Cor. v. 12.　Col. iv. 5.　(ἐκτός, Sir. prol.)　　　　f w. gen., Matt. vi. 8. xxvi. 65.　Luke
v. 31 al.　Prov. xviii. 2.　　　　g Rom. i. 13. xi. 25.　1 Cor. x. 1. xii. 1.　2 Cor. i. 8.　　　h Gal. i. 22 reff.

11. rec ins ιδιαις bef χερσιν (gloss, to suit τα ιδια precedg), with AD³KLℵ¹ rel Thdrt
Damasc Œc [Tert₁]: om BD¹Fℵ³ k [47] 67² vss Bas Chr Damasc Thl Ambrst Pel.
[om υμων m.] παρηγ. bef υμιν [L]ℵ³ [47].
13. rec (for θελομεν) θελω, with d [47] syrr copt [Orig-c₁ Eus₁]: txt ABDFKLℵ rel

ἀταξία to their uneasiness about the state
of the dead: much rather (as he also
states: see below) to their mistaken anticipations of the immediate coming of the
Lord.) It would seem as if, notwithstanding their liberality to those without, there
were some defect of quiet diligence and
harmony within, which prompted this exhortation: see 2 Thess. iii. 11, 12. Thdrt.
assigns another reason for it: οὐκ ἐναντία
τοῖς προῤῥηθεῖσιν ἐπαίνοις ἡ παραίνεσις.
συνέβαινε γὰρ τοὺς μὲν φιλοτίμως χορ-
ηγεῖν τοῖς δεομένοις τὴν χρείαν, τοὺς δὲ διὰ
τὴν τούτων φιλοτιμίαν ἀμελεῖν τῆς ἐργα-
σίας· εἰκότως τοίνυν κἀκείνους ἐπήνεσε,
καὶ τούτοις τὰ πρόσφορα συνεβούλευσε.
(So also Est., Benson, Flatt, Schott, and
De W.) Lünem. objects to this, that thus
the Church would be divided into two
sections, the one exhorted to persist and
abound in their liberality, the other to work
diligently to support themselves; whereas
there is no trace in the text of such a division. He therefore would abandon the
idea of a connexion, and treat vv. 11, 12
as applying to a totally distinct subject;
accounting for its introduction in such close
grammatical connexion with ver. 10, by
St. Paul's rapid transitions in the practical
parts of his Epistles. But we may well
answer, that instances are frequent enough
of exhortations being addressed to whole
churches which in their application would
require severing and allotting to distinct
classes of persons. 11. φιλοτιμεῖσθαι
ἡσυχάζειν] to make it your ambition
to be quiet—have no other φιλοτιμία
than that of a quiet industrious holy life.
Thl. (as an alternative) and Calvin would
take φιλοτιμεῖσθαι alone, and understand
it "optima æmulatio, quum singuli bene-
faciendo se ipsos vincere conantur:" but
thus the omission of any copula before
ἡσυχ. would introduce great harshness into
the sentence. πράσσειν τὰ ἴδια] τὰ
ἴδια πράττω κ. τὰ ἴδια πράττει οἱ πολλοὶ

λέγουσιν εἰκῇ, δέον, τὰ ἐμαυτοῦ πράττω,
κ. τὰ σαυτοῦ πράττεις λέγειν, ὡς οἱ παλαιοί, ἢ τὰ ἴδια ἐμαυτοῦ πράττω κ. τὰ ἴδια
σαυτοῦ πράττεις. Phryn. ed. Lob., p. 441:
where see examples in the note.
From ἐργ. τ. χερσ. ὑμ., it appears that the
members of the Thessalonian church were
mostly of the class of persons thus labouring. Observe the present infinitives,
indicative of continued habit.
12.] Purpose of ver. 11. εὐσχη-
μόνως] honourably: ἀτάκτως, 2 Thess.
iii. 6, 11, is the opposite. πρός,
with regard to: as in the proverb
οὐδὲν πρὸς Διόνυσον, — πρὸς Τιμόθεον
πρᾶξαι, Demosth., p. 1185. See Bernhardy, p. 265. τοὺς ἔξω] the unbelieving world (reff.). μηδενός (subjective, as ruled by the χρείαν ἔχητε) is
much better taken neuter than masculine;
for as Lün. observes, to stand in need of
no man, is for man an impossibility.
13—CH. V. 11.] INSTRUCTIONS AND
EXHORTATIONS CONCERNING THE TIME
OF THE END: and herein 13—18.] instructions respecting the resurrection of
the departed at the Lord's coming. We
can hardly help suspecting some connexion between what has just preceded,
and this section. It would certainly seem
as if the preaching of the kingdom of
Jesus at Thessalonica had been partially
misunderstood, and been perverted into a
cause why they should not quietly follow
active life, and why they should be uneasy
about those who fell asleep before that
kingdom was brought in, imagining that
they would have no part in its glories.
Cf. Acts xvii. 7. 13.] οὐ θέλ. κ.τ.λ.,
is with our Apostle (see reff.) a common
formula of transition to the imparting of
weighty information. τ. κοιμ.] those
who are sleeping; so the present is
used in the well-known epitaph, ἱερὸν
ὕπνον | κοιμᾶται· θνήσκειν μὴ λέγε τοὺς
ἀγαθούς. Or we may understand it,

ij κοιμωμένων, ἵνα μὴ ᵏλυπῆσθε καθὼς καὶ ¹οἱ λοιποὶ οἱ
μὴ ἔχοντες ἐλπίδα. ¹⁴ εἰ γὰρ ᵐπιστεύομεν ᵐὅτι Ἰησοῦς
ἀπέθανεν καὶ ⁿἀνέστη, ᵒοὕτως καὶ ὁ θεὸς τοὺς ʲκοιμηθέν-
τας διὰ τοῦ Ἰησοῦ ᵖἄξει σὺν αὐτῷ. ¹⁵ τοῦτο γὰρ ὑμῖν

i pres., 1 Cor.
xi. 30.
j = Matt. xxvii.
52. Acts vii.
60. xiii. 36.
1 Cor. vii. 39.
xv. 6, &c.
Isa. xiv. 8.
k = Matt. xvii.
23. 2 Cor. vi.

10. vii. 9 al. Neh. v. 6.   l = Acts v. 13. Eph. ii. 3. ch. v. 6.   m John xiv. 10. Acts
ix. 26. Rom. x. 9. Job xv. 31.   n = Mark viii. 31 al. fr. Isa. xxvi. 19.   o = Rev.
xi. 5.   p = 2 Tim. iv. 11.

latt goth [æth] gr-lat-ff.   rec κεκοιμημενων, with DFKL rel Orig(mss vary) Hip
Chr Cyr Thdrt Damasc: κοιμημενων 17: txt ABℵ e n 67² Orig-mss [Eus] Chr-ms
Damasc.   λυπεισθε AD¹·²FL b¹ c d [47 Orig-c₁] Cyr.   for καθως, ως D¹Fℵ³
67² Orig Hip.

14. επιστευομεν ℵ¹.   ο θεος bef και B 67² syr[: om και 47 copt Meth.]
κεκοιμημενους F.

'those who (from time to time) fall asleep
(among you),' as suggested in the Journal
of Sacred Lit. for April, 1856, p. 15: but
the other seems simpler. It was an expression (reff.) conveying definite meaning
to the Thessalonians as importing *the
dead in Christ* (ver. 16). No inference
must therefore be drawn from the Apostle's
use of this word, as to the intermediate
state (as De W. after Weizel, *for* the sleep
of the soul,—and Zwingle, Calvin, al.,
against it): for the word is a mere common term. ἵνα μὴ λ.] object of my
not wishing you to be ignorant.
μὴ λυπ. is *absolute*, that ye mourn not:
—not (as Thdrt., Calvin, al.) μὴ λυπ. καθὼς . . . , 'that ye may not mourn (so
much) as others &c.' He forbids λυπεῖσθαι
altogether. But we must remember, *what
sort* of λυπεῖσθαι it was. Surely not absolutely the mourning for *our* loss in their
absence, but for *theirs* (see above), and *in
so far*, for ours also. See Chrysostom's
very beautiful appeal in loc.   οἱ λοι-
ποί] viz. the heathen, and those Jews who
did not believe a resurrection.   οἱ μὴ
ἔχοντες ἐλπίδα] viz., in the *resurrection*.
Lün. cites,—Theocr. Idyll. iv. 42, ἐλπί-
δες ἐν ζωοῖσιν, ἀνέλπιστοι δὲ θανόντες:
Æsch. Eum. 638, ἅπαξ θανόντος οὔτις
ἐστ' ἀνάστασις: Catull. v. 4 ff., 'Soles
occidere et redire possunt: | nobis quum
semel occidit brevis lux | nox est perpetua
una dormienda:' Lucret. iii. 942 f., 'nec
quisquam expergitus exstat | frigida quem
semel est vitai pausa secuta.' Jowett adds
'the sad complaints of Cicero and Quintilian over the loss of their children, and the
dreary hope of an immortality of fame in
Tacitus and Thucydides.' (But when he
goes on to say that the language of the
O. T., though more religious, is in many
passages hardly more cheering, and substantiates this by Isa. xxxviii. 18, 19, it is
surely hardly fair to give the dark side,
without balancing it with such passages as
Ps. lxxiii. 23—26; Prov. xiv. 32. In the

great upward struggle of the ancient church
under the dawn of the revelation of life and
immortality, we find much indeed of the
αἴλινον αἴλινον εἰπέ—but the τὸ δ' εὖ νι-
κάτω has its abundant testimonies also.)
This shews of *what kind* their λύπη was:
viz. a grief whose ground was unbelief in
a resurrection: which regarded the dead
as altogether cut off from Christ's heavenly
kingdom.   14.] *Substantiation* (γάρ)
*of that implied in last verse, that further
knowledge will remove this their grief:*
and that knowledge, grounded on the
resurrection of our Lord.   εἰ] not
'*seeing that*:' but hypothetical: '*posito*,
that we, &c.'   ἀπέθ. κ. ἀνέστη go
together, — forming the same process
through which οἱ κοιμώμενοι are passing.
"The Apostle here, as always, uses the
direct term ἀπέθανε in reference to our
Lord, to obviate all possible misconception: in reference to the faithful he
appropriately uses the consolatory term
κοιμᾶσθαι: see Thdrt. in loc." Ellicott.
οὕτως] The two clauses do not
accurately correspond. We should expect καὶ πιστεύομεν ὅτι οὕτως καὶ οἱ
ἐν Ἰησοῦ κοιμηθέντες ἀναστήσονται, or
the like. Still the οὕτως betokens identity of lot for the two parties concerned, viz., death, and resurrection. In
this they resemble: but in the expressed
particulars here, they differ. Christ's was
simply ἀνέστη: theirs shall be a resurrection through Him, at His coming.
διὰ τ. Ἰησοῦ] I feel compelled to differ
from the majority of modern scholars (not
Ellicott), in adhering to the old connexion
of these words with τ. κοιμηθέντας. I am
quite aware of the grammatical difficulty:
but as I hope to shew, it is not insuperable. But if we join διὰ τ. Ἰησ. with
ἄξει, we obtain a clause which I am
persuaded the Apostle could never have
written,—flat and dragging in the extreme—διὰ τοῦ Ἰησοῦ ἄξει σὺν αὐτῷ—
αὐτῷ referring to Ἰησοῦ already men-

q 1 Cor. ii. 7.
xiv. 6.
3 Kings xxi.
(xx.) 35.
r 2 Cor. iv. 13.
(v. 15.)
Herodian ii. 1.

λέγομεν q ἐν λόγῳ κυρίου, ὅτι r ἡμεῖς οἱ r ζῶντες οἱ s περιλειπόμενοι εἰς τὴν t παρουσίαν τοῦ κυρίου οὐ μὴ u φθά-

ABDFK
LℵA a b c
d e f g h
k l m n o
17. 47

s ver. 17 only†. 2 Macc. i. 31. viii. 14 only. μόνος τῶν πατρῴων περιλειπόμενος φίλων ἔτι,
t = ch. ii. 19 reff. u = here only. (ch. ii. 16 reff.) Wisd. vi. 13.

15. for [2nd] κυριον, ιησου B : χριστου Mcion-t.

tioned in the same clause. Whereas, on
the other connexion, we have Ἰησοῦς and
οἱ κοιμηθέντες διὰ τοῦ Ἰησοῦ set over
against one another, the very article, and
the unemphatic position of the words,
shewing the reference back,—and we have
αὐτῷ naturally and forcibly referring back
to Ἰησοῦς and διὰ τοῦ Ἰησοῦ, in the
preceding clauses. In other words, the
logical construction of the sentence seems
to me so plainly to require the connexion
of διὰ τοῦ Ἰησοῦ with κοιμηθέντας, that
it must be a grammatical impossibility
only, which can break that connexion.
But let us see whether there be such
an impossibility present. οἱ κοιμηθέντες
are confessedly the *Christian* dead, and
none else. They are distinguished by the
Apostle's use of and adhesion to the word,
from the merely θανόντες. What makes
this distinction? Why are they asleep,
and not dead? *By whom* have they
been thus privileged? Certainly, διὰ τοῦ
Ἰησοῦ. We are said πιστεύειν δι' αὐτοῦ
(Acts iii. 16),— εὐχαριστεῖν δι' αὐτοῦ
(Rom. i. 8), εἰρήνην ἔχειν δι' αὐτοῦ (ib.
v. 1), καυχᾶσθαι δι' αὐτοῦ (ib. 11), παρα-
καλεῖσθαι δι' αὐτοῦ (2 Cor. i. 5), &c. &c. :
why not also κοιμᾶσθαι δι' αὐτοῦ? And
when Lünem. objects, that the extent
of the idea οἱ κοιμηθέντες is understood
from the former part of the sentence,
εἰ πιστεύομεν κ.τ.λ.,—this very reason
seems to me the most natural one for the
specification—If we believe that Jesus
died and rose again, then even thus also
those, of whom we say that they sleep,
just because of Jesus, will God, &c. : the
emphasis being on the διά. Jowett
keeps this connexion, merely saying however, "nor will the order of the words
allow us to connect them with ἄξει;" a
reason surely insufficient for it. He is
certainly in error when he continues,
"The only remaining mode is to take
διά for ἐν (?), 'those that are asleep in
Christ.'" ἄξει σὺν αὐτῷ] will
bring (back to us) with Him (Jesus):
i. e. when Jesus shall appear, they also
shall appear with Him, being (as below)
raised at His coming. Of their disem-
bodied souls there is here no mention:
nor is the meaning, as often understood,
that God will bring them (their disem-
bodied souls, to be joined to their raised
bodies) with Him : but the bringing them

with Jesus = their being raised when
Jesus appears. **15.**] *Confirmation
of last verse by direct revelation from the
Lord.* τοῦτο—this which follows :
taken up by ὅτι. ἐν λόγῳ κυρ., in
(virtue of : an assertion made within the
sphere and element of that certainty,
which the word of the Lord gives) the
word of the Lord,—i. e. by direct revelation from Him made to me. τουτέστιν,
οὐκ ἀφ' ἑαυτῶν, ἀλλὰ παρὰ τοῦ χριστοῦ
μαθόντες λέγομεν, Chr. : ἐκ θείας ἡμῖν
ἀποκαλύψεως ἡ διδασκαλία γεγένηται,
Thdrt. That St. Paul had many special
revelations made to him, we know from
2 Cor. xii. 4. Cf. also Gal. i. 12; Eph.
iii. 3; 1 Cor. xi. 23; xv. 3, and notes.
ἡμεῖς οἱ ζῶντες] Then beyond
question, he himself expected to be alive,
together with the majority of those to
whom he was writing, at the Lord's
coming. For we cannot for a moment
accept the evasion of Theodoret (cf. also
Chrys. and the majority of ancient Commentators, down to Bengel, and even
some of the best of the moderns, warped
by their subjectivities : cf. Ellicott here),
—οὐκ ἐπὶ τοῦ ἑαυτοῦ προσώπου τέθεικεν,
ἀλλ' ἐπὶ τῶν κατ' ἐκεῖνον τὸν καιρὸν
περιόντων ἀνθρώπων :—nor the ungrammatical rendering of Turretin and Pelt—
'we, if we live and remain' (ἡμεῖς ζῶντες,
περιλειπόμενοι) :—nor the idea of Œc.,
al., that οἱ ζῶντες are the *souls,* οἱ
κοιμηθέντες the *bodies :*—but must take
the words in their only plain grammatical
meaning, that οἱ ζῶντες οἱ περιλ. are a
class distinguished from οἱ κοιμηθέντες,
by being yet in the flesh when Christ
comes, in which class, by prefixing ἡμεῖς,
he includes his readers and himself. That
this *was* his expectation, we know from
other passages, especially from 2 Cor. v.
1—10, where see notes. It does not seem
to have been so strong towards the end of
his course; see e. g. Phil. i. 20—26. Nor
need it surprise any Christian, that the
Apostles should in this matter of detail
have found their personal expectations
liable to disappointment, respecting a day
of which it is so solemnly said, that no
man knoweth its appointed time, not the
angels in heaven, nor the Son (Mark
xiii. 32), but the Father only. At the
same time it must be borne in mind, that
this inclusion of himself and his hearers

σωμεν τοὺς ⁱ κοιμηθέντας, ¹⁶ ὅτι ^v αὐτὸς ὁ κύριος ^w ἐν
^x κελεύσματι, ^w ἐν φωνῇ ^y ἀρχαγγέλου καὶ ^w ἐν ^z σάλπιγγι
^a θεοῦ ^b καταβήσεται ἀπ᾽ οὐρανοῦ, καὶ οἱ νεκροὶ ^c ἐν χριστῷ
P ζωντες ^d ἀναστήσονται πρῶτον, ¹⁷ ἔπειτα ^r ἡμεῖς οἱ ^r ζῶντες οἱ
^e περιλειπόμενοι ^f ἅμα σὺν αὐτοῖς ^g ἁρπαγησόμεθα ἐν νε-

v = ch. iii. 11 reff. (see note.)
w = Rom. xv. 29. 1 Cor. iv. 21.
2 Thess. i. 8. Ps. xciv. 2.
x here only.
Prov. xxx. 27 only.
Thucyd. ii.

92 init.   y Jude 9 only †.   z Matt. xxiv. 31.   1 Cor. xiv. 8. xv. 52.   Rev. iv. 1 &
passim. Exod. xix. 13 al.   a so 1 Chron. xvi. 42.   Rev. xv. 2.   b John iii. 13. Eph. iv.
9. Prov. xxx. 4.   c = 1 Cor. xv. 18.   Rev. xiv. 13.   d ver. 14.
f ch. v. 10.   g = 2 Cor. xii. 2.   Rev. xii. 5.   John vi. 15.   Acts viii. 39.   e ver. 15.

16. aft νεκροι ins οι F, *mortui qui in Christo sunt* latt goth : om οι νεκροι m Cyr. πρωτοι D¹F latt [Eus₂] Thdrt₁ Cyr Thl-marg [Orig-int₂] lat-ff : txt ABD³KLℵ rel syrr copt goth Orig [Hip Meth] Dial.

17. οι ζωντες bef ημεις K n : om ημεις 80.   om οι περιλειπομενοι F(not F-lat)

among the ζῶντες and περιλειπόμενοι, does not in any way enter into the fact revealed and here announced, which is respecting that class of persons only as they are, and must be, *one portion* of the faithful at the Lord's coming; not respecting the question, *who shall*, and *who shall not* be among them in that day. οἱ περιλειπ. εἰς . . .] Dr. Burton, doubting whether περιλειπόμενοι εἰς τ. π. can mean '*left to the coming*' (but why not? εἰς as defining the terminus temporis is surely common enough, cf. Phil. i. 10; Acts iv. 3, εἰς τέλος John xiii. 1 al. fr.), puts a comma at περιλειπόμενοι, and takes εἰς τὴν π. with οὐ μὴ φθάσωμεν, rendering, *those who are alive at the last day will not enter into the presence of the Lord before those who have died*. But 1) ἡ παρουσία τοῦ κυρίου is never used *locally*, of the *presence* of the Lord, but always *temporally*, of His *coming*: and 2) the arrangement of the sentence would in that case be οὐ μὴ φθ. τοὺς κοιμ. εἰς τ. π. τοῦ κυρ. οὐ μὴ φθάσωμεν] shall not (emphatic—'there is no reason to fear, that . . .') prevent (get before, so that they be left behind, and fail of the prize). 16.] A reason of the foregoing assertion, by detailing the method of the resurrection. Because—(not '*that*,' so as to be parallel with ὅτι above, as Koch) the Lord Himself (not, as De W., '*He, the Lord*'—which would be to the last degree flat and meaningless;—nor as Olsh., 'the Lord *Himself*,' in contrast to any other kind of revelation:—nor as Lünem., as the chief Person and actor in that day, emphatically opposed to His faithful ones as acted on,—but said for solemnity's sake, and to shew that it will not be a mere *gathering* to Him, but HE HIMSELF will descend, and we all shall be summoned before Him) with ('in,' as the element,—the accompanying circumstance) a signal-shout (κέλευσμα is not only '*the shout of battle*,' as Conyb.; but is used

of any signal given by the voice, whether of a captain to his rowers, Thuc. ii. 92 : of a man shouting to another at a distance, Herod. iv. 141 : of a huntsman to his dogs, Xen. Cyneg. vi. 20. Here it seems to include in it the two which follow and explain it), viz. with the voice of an archangel (Christ shall be surrounded with His angels, Matt. xxv. 31 al. To enquire, *which* archangel, is futile : to understand the word of *Christ Himself* (Ambrst., Olsh.) or the Holy Spirit (al.), impossible), and with the trumpet of God (θεοῦ as in reff., the trumpet especially belonging to and used in the heavenly *state* of God; not *commanded by God* (Pelt, Olsh., al.),—nor does θεοῦ import *size* or *loudness* (Bengel, al.), although these qualities of course are understood. On the trumpet as summoning assemblies, cf. Num. x. 2; xxxi. 6; Joel ii. 1 :—as accompanying the divine appearances, Ex. xix. 16; Ps. xlvii. 5; Isa. xxvii. 13; Zech. ix. 14; Matt. xxiv. 31; 1 Cor. xv. 52) shall descend from heaven (cf. Acts i. 11): and the dead in Christ (ἐν χρ. must not, as Pelt, Schott, be joined with ἀναστήσονται: for apart from the question whether this would give *any* admissible meaning, it would bring ἐν χριστῷ into an emphatic position of prominence, which would confuse the whole sentence) shall first rise (πρῶτον has no reference whatever to the *first resurrection* (Rev. xx. 5, 6), here, for *only the Lord's people* are here in question: but answers to ἔπειτα below : *first*, the dead in Christ shall rise : *then*, we, &c.): then we who are living, who remain (as above) shall be caught up (reff. : the great change spoken of 1 Cor. xv. 52, having first suddenly taken place) all together (see Rom. iii. 12, ch. v. 10 note : ἅμα does not belong to σὺν αὐτοῖς) with them (the raised of ver. 16) in (the) clouds (ἔδειξε τὸ μέγεθος τῆς τιμῆς· ὥσπερ γὰρ αὐτὸς ὁ δεσπότης ἐπὶ νεφελῆς φωτεινῆς ἀνελήφθη, οὕτω καὶ οἱ εἰς αὐτὸν

h always w.
εἰς, in N. T.
& LXX (not
Apocrypha,
2 Macc. xii.
30 al.),
Matt. xxv.
(1 v. r.) 6.
Acts xxviii.
15 only.
1 Kings ix.
14.
i Eph. ii. 2 reff.
k = Acts vii. 8.
xvii. 33. xxviii. 14.   1 Cor. xi. 28. xiv. 25 al.   1 = Phil. i. 23.   m = Phil. ii. 12 reff.
n = 2 Cor. i. 4 al. fr.   Isa. lxvi. 13.   o = 2 Cor. vii. 6, 7. Tit. i. 9.   p Acts i. 7. Dan. ii. 21.
q = Matt. xvi. 3. 2 Tim. iii. 1.   r constr., see ch. iv. 9.   s = Matt. ii. 8. Luke i. 3. Acts xviii. 25,
26. xxiii. 15, 20. xxiv. 22 (Eph. v. 15) only. Deut. xix. 18. Wisd. xix. 18 only. Dan. vii. 19 Theod.   t Acts
ii. 20, from Joel ii. 31. 2 Pet. iii. 10 only. Isa. ii. 12. ἡμ. τοῦ κυρ., 2 Thess. ii. 2. see 1 Cor. i. 8. 2 Cor. i. 14 al.
u see Matt. xxiv. 43. 2 Pet. iii. 10. Rev. iii. 3. xvi. 15. Jer. xxix. 10 (xlix. 9).

ABDFK
LΡℵ a b
c d e f g
h k l m n
o 17. 47

φέλαις εἰς ʰ ἀπάντησιν τοῦ κυρίου εἰς ⁱ ἀέρα, καὶ ᵏ οὕτως πάντοτε ˡ σὺν κυρίῳ ˡ ἐσόμεθα. 18 ᵐ ὥστε ⁿ παρακαλεῖτε ἀλλήλους ᵒ ἐν τοῖς λόγοις τούτοις.

V. 1 Περὶ δὲ τῶν ᵖ χρόνων καὶ τῶν ᵖ𐞥 καιρῶν, ἀδελφοί, οὐ ʳ χρείαν ἔχετε ὑμῖν ʳ γράφεσθαι· 2 αὐτοὶ γὰρ ˢ ἀκριβῶς οἴδατε, ὅτι [ἡ] ᵗ ἡμέρα ᵗ κυρίου ὡς ᵘ κλέπτης ἐν νυκτὶ

[Meth₂] Tert Ambr Ambrst-ed : περιλειμενοι(sic) B.   εις υπαντησιν τω χριστω
D¹F latt Orig-int Tert Jer₁.   for παντοτε, παντες D¹.   for συν, εν B.

CHAP. V. 1. for χρειαν εχετε, χρια εστιν F D-lat(and G-lat but not F-lat) arm Tert
Ambrst.   γραφεσθαι bef υμιν ℵ³ [47] 115 [Tert] : του γρ. υμιν ℵ¹.
2. om ἡ (bef ημερα) BDF[P]ℵ 17. 67² : ins AKL rel Eus.

πεπιστευκότες . . . ἐπὶ νεφελῶν ὀχούμενοι ὑπαντήσουσ. τῷ τῶν ὅλων κριτῇ . . . . Thdrt.) **to meet the Lord** (as He descends: so Aug. de civit. Dei xx. 20. 2, vol. vii. p. 688 : ' non sic accipiendum est tanquam in aëre nos dixerit semper cum Domino mansuros, quia nec ipse utique ibi manebit, quia veniens transiturus est, venienti quippe itur obviam, non manenti.' Christ is *on His way to this earth* : and when De W. says that there is no plain trace in St. Paul of Christ's kingdom on earth,—and Lün., that the words shew that the Apostle did not think of Christ as descending down to the earth, surely they cannot suppose him to have been so ignorant of O. T. prophecy, as to have allowed this, its plain testimony, to escape him. **εἰς ἀπάντησιν** occurs (reff.) twice more in the N. T., and each time implies meeting one who was *approaching*—not merely ' meeting with' a person) **into the air** (belongs to **ἁρπαγησόμεθα**, not to εἰς ἀπ. τοῦ κυρ. as in E. V.), **and thus we** (i. e. we and they united, ἡμεῖς ἅμα, σὺν αὐτοῖς, who were the subject of the last sentence) **shall be always with the Lord.** That he advances no further in the prophetic description, but breaks off at our union in Christ's presence, is accounted for, by his purpose being accomplished, in having shewn that they who have died in Christ, shall not be thereby deprived of any advantage at His coming. The rest of the great events of that time—His advent on this earth, His judgment of it, assisted by His saints (1 Cor. vi. 2, 3),—His reign upon earth,— His final glorification with His redeemed in heaven,—are not treated here, but not therefore to be conceived of as alien from the Apostle's teaching. **18.]** ὥστε, so then: reff. **παρακ.**, comfort:

cf. ἵνα μὴ λυπῆσθε, ver. 13. **λόγοις**, not *things*, here or any where : but words : **these words,** which I have by inspiration delivered to you. It will be manifest to the plain, as well as to the scholar-like reader, that attempts like that of Prof. Jowett, to interpret such a passage as this by the rules of mere figurative language, are entirely beside the purpose. The Apostle's declarations here are made in the practical tone of strict matter of fact, and are given as literal details, to console men's minds under an existing difficulty. Never was a place where the analogy of symbolical apocalyptic language was less applicable. Either these details must be received by us as matter of practical expectation, or we must set aside the Apostle as one divinely empowered to teach the Church. It is a fair opportunity for an experimentum crucis : and such test cannot be evaded by Prof. Jowett's intermediate expedient of figurative language.
CH. V. 1—11.] *Exhortation to watch for the day of the Lord's coming, and to be ready for it.* 1—3.] *the suddenness and unexpectedness of that day's coming.*
1.] On **χρόν.** and **καιρ.**, see Acts i. 7, note. They had no need, for the reason stated below : that St. Paul had already by word of mouth taught them as much as could be known. **2.] [ἡ] ἡμέρα κυρίου** is not the *destruction of Jerusalem,* as Hammond, Schöttg., al.,— nor the day of *each man's death,* as Chrys., Œc., Thl., Lyr., al.,—*but the day of the Lord's coming,* the **παρουσία,** which has been spoken of, in some of its details, above. So Thdrt.—ἡ δεσποτικὴ παρουσία. This is plain, by comparing 2 Thess. ii. 2 : 1 Cor. i. 8 ; v. 5 : 2 Cor. i. 14 : Phil. i. 6, 10 ;

οὕτως ἔρχεται. ³ ὅταν λέγωσιν ᵛ Εἰρήνη καὶ ʷ ἀσφά-
λεια, τότε ˣ αἰφνίδιος αὐτοῖς ʸ ἐφίσταται ᶻ ὄλεθρος ὥσπερ
ἡ ᵃ ὠδὶν τῇ ᵇ ἐν ᵇᶜ γαστρὶ ᵇ ἐχούσῃ, καὶ οὐ μὴ ᵈ ἐκφύγωσιν.
⁴ ὑμεῖς δέ, ἀδελφοί, οὐκ ἐστὲ ἐν ᵉ σκότει, ἵνα ᶠ ἡ ἡμέρα
ὑμᾶς ὡς ᵘ κλέπτης ᵍ καταλάβῃ· ⁵ πάντες γὰρ ὑμεῖς ʰ υἱοὶ
φωτός ἐστε καὶ ʰ υἱοὶ ⁱ ἡμέρας. οὐκ ἐσμὲν ᵏ νυκτὸς οὐδὲ
ⁱ σκότους. ⁶ ˡ ἄρα ˡ οὖν μὴ ᵐ καθεύδωμεν ὡς [καὶ] ⁿ οἱ

v Ezek. xiii. 10.
w = Acts v. 23 (Luke i. 4) only. Deut. xii. 10.
x Luke xxi. 34 only †.
Wisd. xvii. 15. 2 Macc. xiv. 17 only.
(-ως, 2 Macc. v. 5. xiv. 22.)
y = Luke xxi. 34. 2 Tim. iv. 6. (Luke xx. 1 al. fr.)
z (=) 1 Cor. v.

5. 2 Thess. i. 9. 1 Tim. vi. 9 only. Prov. xxi. 7. a Matt. xxiv. 8 ‖ Mk. Acts ii. 24 only. Exod.
xv. 14 al. b Matt. i. 18, 23 (from Isa. vii. 14 ﬡ). xxiv. 19 ‖. Rev. xii. 2 only. Exod. xxi. 22.
c = as above (b). Luke i. 31 (Tit. i. 12) only. d = Luke xxi. 36. Rom. ii. 3. 2 Cor. xi. 33. Judg.
vi. 11. e = John iii. 19. Rom. xiii. 12 al. f so 1 Cor. iii. 13. Heb. x. 25.
g = John xii. 35. Numb. xxxii. 23. h Luke v. 6. xvi. 8. John xii. 36. Eph. ii. 2. v. 6.
i = Rom. xiii. 13. 2 Pet. i. 19. k gen., 1 Cor. i. 12. iii. 22, 23 al. l Rom. v. 18 al10. P.
m Paul, Eph. v. 14. ver. 10 only. Gospp. (literally) Matt. viii. 24 & fr. Sir. xxii. 7. n ch. iv.
13 reff.

3. rec aft οταν ins γαρ, with KL[P] rel vulg arm-marg Damasc; δε BDﬡ³ syr copt
Eus Chr Thdrt: om AFﬡ¹ 17 [47] D-lat Syr goth [æth] arm Iren-int [Orig-int] Tert
Cypr Ambrst. λεγουσιν F. επιστεται BLﬡ: φανησεται F D-lat(not F-lat)
Hes(in Aug)₂. (A def.)—επιστ. bef αυτοις B. εκφευξονται D¹F.

4. υμας bef η ημερα (throwing the emphasis on υμας) ADF latt Eus: txt BKL[P]ﬡ
rel goth Epiph Chr Thdrt Damasc.—add εκεινη F latt.—om ἡ c 17. κλεπτας AB
copt. καταλαβοι F.

5. rec om γαρ, with K(e sil) rel am [æth]: ins ABDFL[P]ﬡ c m 17 [47] latt syrr
copt arm Clem Eus Chr Thdrt Thl Ambrst Aug Pel. aft ημερ. ins και D¹F(not
D-lat F-lat) [47] fuld [syrr æth] Chr-ms. εστε D¹F fuld(with mar harl²) Syr
goth Ambrst.

6. om 1st και ABﬡ¹ b 17 am(and F-lat) syr copt æth Clem₂ Antch: ins DFKL[P]ﬡ³
rel vulg Syr Chr Thdrt Ambrst.

---

ii. 16.   It is both the suddenness, and the
terribleness (surely we cannot with Ellic.
omit this element, in the presence of the
image in the next verse) of the Day's
coming, which is here dwelt on: cf. next
verse. οὕτως fills up the comparison
—as a thief in the night (comes), so . . it
comes (not for future, but expressing, as
so often by the present, the absolute truth
and certainty of that predicated—it is its
attribute, to come). 3.] Following
out of the comparison ὡς κλ. ἐν νυκτί, into
detail. λέγωσιν, viz. men in general
—the children of the world, as opposed to
the people of God: cf. ὄλεθρος below. The
vivid description dispenses with any copula.
εἰρ. κ. ἀσφ., scil. ἐστιν, see ref. Ezek.
αἰφνίδ. has the emphasis, becoming
a kind of predicate. ἐφίσταται,
generally used of any sudden unexpected
appearance: see reff., and Acts iv. 1.
It is pressing too close the comparison
ὥσπερ ἡ ὠδὶν κ.τ.λ., when De W. says
that it "assumes the day to be near,—for
that such a woman, though she does not
know the day and the hour, yet has a definite knowledge of the period:" for it is
not the woman, nor her condition, that is
the subject of comparison, but the unexpected pang of labour which comes on her.

4, 5.] But the Thessalonians, and
Christians in general, are not to be thus

overtaken by it.   4.] ἐν σκότει refers
back to ἐν νυκτί above—in the ignorance
and moral slumber of the world which
knows not God. τῷ παραβολικῷ ἐπέμεινε
σχήματι, κ. σκότος μὲν καλεῖ τὴν ἄγνοιαν,
ἡμέραν δὲ τὴν γνῶσιν, Thdrt. τὸν σκο-
τεινὸν κ. ἀκάθαρτον βίον φησί, Chrys.
Both combined give the right meaning.

ἵνα] not 'so that,' here or any
where else: but that,—in order that:
it gives the purpose in the divine arrangement: for with God all results are purposed. ἡ ἡμέρα] not, 'that day,' but
the DAY—the meaning of ἡμέρα as distinguished from σκότος being brought out,
and ἡ ἡμέρα being put in the place of emphasis accordingly. This not having been
seen, its situation was altered, to throw the
first stress on ὑμᾶς, which properly has the
second. That this is so, is plain from what
follows, ver. 5.   5.] You (a) and all
we Christians (b) have no reason to fear,
and no excuse for being surprised by, the
DAY of the Lord; for we are sons of
light and the day (Hebraisms, see reff.:
signifying that we belong to, having our
origin from, the light and the day),
and are not of (do not supply 'sons'
—the genitives are in regular construction after ἐσμεν, signifying possession—
we belong not to) night nor darkness.
See, on the day of the Lord as connected

o = Mark xiii. 37. 1 Cor. xvi. 13 al. fr. (Jer. i. 2.)
p 1 Pet. v. 8.
q Paul, 2 Tim. iv. 5 only. 1 Pet. i. 13. iv. 7. v. 8 only †.
r Luke xii. 45. Eph. v. 18 only. Prov. iv. 17.
s Matt. xxiv. 49. John ii. 10. Acts ii. 15. 1 Cor. vi. 21. Rev. xvii. 2, 6 only. Joel i. 5.
v Eph. vi. 17 only. Isa. lix. 17.

λοιποί, ἀλλὰ ^{ορ} γρηγορῶμεν καὶ ^{ρq} νήφωμεν. 7 οἱ γὰρ
^{m} καθεύδοντες νυκτὸς ^{m} καθεύδουσιν, καὶ οἱ ^{r} μεθυσκόμενοι
νυκτὸς ^{s} μεθύουσιν· 8 ἡμεῖς δὲ ^{k} ἡμέρας ὄντες ^{q} νήφωμεν,
^{t} ἐνδυσάμενοι ^{u} θώρακα πίστεως καὶ ἀγάπης, καὶ ^{v} περικεφαλαίαν ^{w} ἐλπίδα σωτηρίας, 9 ὅτι οὐκ ^{x} ἔθετο ἡμᾶς ὁ
θεὸς ^{x} εἰς ^{y} ὀργήν, ἀλλὰ εἰς ^{z} περιποίησιν σωτηρίας διὰ
τοῦ κυρίου ἡμῶν Ἰησοῦ χριστοῦ, 10 τοῦ ἀποθανόντος

ABDFK LP א a b c d e f g h k l m n o 17. 47

t Eph. iv. 24 reff. u Eph. vi. 14 reff.
w so Rom. v. 2. x Acts xiii. 47. 1 Tim. i. 12. 1 Pet. ii. 8. Jer.
xxv. 12. y Rom. xiii. 4. z = 2 Thess. ii. 14. (Eph. i. 14 reff. -ποιεῖσθαι, Acts xx. 28.)

7. for μεθυσκομενοι, μεθυοντες B [Clem₁].
9. ο θεος bef ημας B m. (αλλα, so BD³א 17.)

8. om και αγαπης א¹.
om χριστου B [æth].

with darkness and light, Amos v. 18 ff. There, its aspect to the ungodly is treated of :—here, its aspect to Christians.
6—8.] *Exhortation to behave as such:* i.e. to watch and be sober—ἐπίτασις ἐγρηγόρσεως τὸ νήφειν· ἔνι γὰρ καὶ ἐγρηγορέναι καὶ μηδὲν διαφέρειν καθεύδοντος, Œc. (after Chrys.) 6.] οἱ λοιποί—i. e. the careless world. 7.] Explanation of the assertion regarding οἱ λοιποί above from the common practice of men. There is no distinction, as Macknight pretends, between μεθυσκόμενοι and μεθύουσιν (' the former denoting the *act* of getting drunk, the latter the *state* of being so '), but they are synonymous, answering to καθεύδοντες and καθεύδουσιν. Nor are the expressions to be taken in a spiritual sense, as Chrys., al. (μέθην ἐνταῦθά φησιν, οὐ τὴν ἀπὸ τοῦ οἴνου μόνον, ἀλλὰ καὶ τὴν ἀπὸ πάντων τῶν κακῶν : ' Spiritual sleep and intoxication belong to the state of darkness,' Baum.-Crus.) : the repetition of the same verbs as subjects and predicates (Lün.) shews that νυκτός is merely a designation of *time*, and to be taken literally. 8.] Contrast (δέ) of our course, who are of the day. And this not only in being awake and sober, but in being *armed*—not only watchful, but as sentinels, on our guard, and *guarded* ourselves. Notice, that these arms are defensive only, as against a sudden attack—and belong therefore not so much to the Christian's conflict with evil, as (from the context) to his guard against being surprised by the day of the Lord as a thief in the night. The best defences against such a surprise are the three great Christian graces, Faith, Hope, Love,—which are accordingly here enumerated : see ch. i. 3, and 1 Cor. xiii. 13. In Eph. vi. 13—17, we have offensive as well as defensive weapons, and the symbolism is somewhat varied, the θώραξ being δικαιοσύνη, πίστις being the θυρεός; while the

helmet remains the same. See on the figure, Isa. lix. 17 ; Wisd. v. 17 ff. We must not perhaps press minutely the meaning of each part of the armour, in the presence of such variation in the two passages. 9.] Epexegesis of ἐλπίδα σωτηρίας—' and we *may* with confidence put on such an hope as our helmet '—for God set us not (' appointed us not ' (reff.) ; keep the aorist meaning,—referring to the time when He made the appointment) to (' with a view to '—so as to issue in, become a prey to) wrath, but to acquisition (περιποιέω, ' to make to remain over and above,' hence ' to keep safe :' opp. to διαφθείρω, Herod. i. 110; vii. 52, &c. Thuc. iii. 102 (L. and S.). Hence περιποίησις, ' a keeping safe :' Plato, Def. 415 c, σωτηρία, περιποίησις ἀβλαβής. If this last remarkable coincidence be taken as a key to our passage, σωτηρίας will be a genitive of apposition, 'a keeping safe, consisting in salvation.' But (reff.) it seems more according to the construction to understand περιπ. simply as acquisition, as it undoubtedly is in ref. 2 Thess. Jowett's note, " περιποιεῖν, to make any thing over: hence περιποίησις, possession," if I understand it rightly, alleges a meaning of the verb which has no existence. ' To make to remain over ' is as different as possible from ' to make over (to another person) ') of salvation through (διὰ . . . refers to περιπ. σωτ. not to ἔθετο) our Lord Jesus Christ, 10.] who died for us, that whether we wake or sleep (in what sense ? surely not in an ethical sense, as above : for they who sleep will be overtaken by Him as a thief, and His day will be to them darkness, not light. If not in an ethical sense, it must be in that of *living* or *dying*, and the sense as Rom. xiv. 8. (For we cannot adopt the trifling sense given by Whitby, al.,—' whether He come in the night, and

* ὑπὲρ ἡμῶν, ἵνα εἴτε [a] γρηγορῶμεν εἴτε [b] καθεύδωμεν [c] ἅμα
σὺν αὐτῷ ζήσωμεν. 11 διὸ [d] παρακαλεῖτε ἀλλήλους, καὶ
[e] οἰκοδομεῖτε [f] εἷς τὸν [f] ἕνα, καθὼς καὶ ποιεῖτε.

12 [g] Ἐρωτῶμεν δὲ ὑμᾶς, ἀδελφοί, [h] εἰδέναι τοὺς [i] κοπιῶντας ἐν ὑμῖν καὶ [k] προϊσταμένους ὑμῶν [l] ἐν κυρίῳ
καὶ [m] νουθετοῦντας ὑμᾶς, 13 καὶ [n] ἡγεῖσθαι αὐτοὺς [o] ὑπερ-

a (ver. 6.) = here only.
(Neh. viii. 3.
b = Matt. ix. 24 only. (ver. 6 reff.)
Dan. xii. 2.
c = ch. iv. 17. Rom. iii. 12.
d = 2 Cor. i. 4.
2 Thess. ii. 17. Isa. lxvi. 13.
e = 1 Cor. viii. 1. x. 23. xiv.
h = here

4, 17. | f 1 Cor. iv. 6. | g = Phil. iv. 3, ch. iv. 1. | 2 Thess. ii. 1 al.
only. see 1 Cor. xvi. 18. | Prov. xxvii. 23. | Gen. xxxix. 6. | i Rom. xvi. 6, 11. | 1 Cor. xv.
10. Gal. iv. 11. | Ps. cxxvi. 1. | k 1 Tim. iii. 4, 5 reff. | l Rom. xvi. 2, 8, 12. | 1 Cor. xvi.
19 al. | m Col. i 28 reff. P. | n = here only. | o here only †. (-σσου, ch. iii. 10
reff. ὑπερπ., Mark vii. 37.)

10. * περί BΝ[1] 17 : υπερ ADFKL[P]Ν[3] rel.　　καθευδομεν KL[P] b c f g h k l
m o Chr Thl (in ver 6 KL have -δομεν).　　ζησομεν A 48 lect-1 : ζωμεν D[1] 73.
12. προισταν ομενους AΝ.　　νουθετουντες A.
13. for και, ωστε F ; ut latt.　　ηγεισθε B b d e f g k l m syr copt goth.
[αυτων P.]　　rec υπερεκπερισσου (more usual word ; cf ch iii. 10), with AD[3]KL[P]Ν

so find us taking our natural rest, or in the day when we are waking.') Thus understood however, it will be at the sacrifice of perspicuity, seeing that γρηγορεῖν and καθεύδειν have been used ethically throughout the passage. If we wish to preserve the uniformity of metaphor, we *may* (though I am not satisfied with this) interpret in this sense : that our Lord died for us, that whether we watch (are of the number of the watchful, i. e. already Christians) or sleep (are of the number of the sleeping, i. e. unconverted) we should live, &c. Thus it would = 'who died that all men might be saved :' who came, not to call the righteous only, but sinners to life. There is to this interpretation the great objection that it confounds with the λοιποί, the ἡμᾶς who are definitely spoken of as set by God not to wrath but to περιποίησιν σωτηρίας. So that the sense **live or die**, must, I think, be accepted, and the want of perspicuity with it. The construction of a subjunctive with εἴτε … εἴτε is not classical : an optative is found in such cases, e. g. Xen. Anab. ii. 1. 14, καὶ εἴτε ἄλλο τι θέλοι χρῆσθαι εἴτ' ἐπ' Αἴγυπτον στρατεύειν . . . . See Winer, edn. 6, § 41, p. 263, Moulton's Engl. transl. 368, note 2. **ἅμα**] **all together** : not to be taken with σύν, see reff. **11.**] *Conclusion from the whole*—**διό**, '*quæ cum ita sint*'—since all this is so : or perhaps in literal strictness, as Ellic., *quamobrem* : which however is exceedingly close to the above meaning. **παρακαλεῖτε**, more naturally **comfort**, as in ch. iv. 18, than '*exhort.*' For as Lün. remarks, the exhortation begun ver. 6 has passed into consolation in vv. 9 10. **οἰκ. εἰς τὸν ἕνα**] **edify the one the other** : see ref. : and cf. (Kypke) Theocr. Idyl. xxii. 65, εἰς ἑνὶ χεῖ-

ρας ἄειρον—Lucian, Asin. p. 169, ἐγὼ δὲ ἕν' ἐξ ἑνὸς ἐπιτρέχων—Arrian, Epict. i. 10, ἐν ἐξ ἑνὸς ἐπισεσώρευκεν. Whitby, Rückert, al., would read **εἰς τὸν ἕνα**, and render '*edify yourselves into one body*' (Whitb. εἰς ἕν)—or '*so as to shew the One, Christ, as your foundation*, on whom the building should be raised' (Rückert : but this should be ἐπὶ τῷ ἑνί). The only allowable meaning of εἰς τὸν ἕνα would be, '*into the One*,' viz., Christ, as in Eph. iv. 13. But the use of τὸν ἕνα for Christ, with any further designation, would be harsh and unprecedented. **12—24.**] *Miscellaneous exhortations, ending with a solemn wish for their perfection in the day of Christ.* **12, 13.**] *In reference to their duties to the rulers of the church among them.* The connexion (δέ, a slight contrast with that which has just passed) is perhaps as Chrys., but somewhat too strongly—ἐπειδὴ εἶπεν οἰκοδομεῖτε εἷς τὸν ἕνα, ἵνα μὴ νομίσωσιν ὅτι εἰς τὸ τῶν διδασκάλων ἀξίωμα αὐτοὺς ἀνήγαγε, τοῦτο ἐπήγαγε, μονονουχὶ λέγων, ὅτι κ. ὑμῖν ἐπέτρεψα οἰκοδομεῖν ἀλλήλους· οὐ γὰρ δυνατὸν πάντα τὸν διδάσκαλον εἰπεῖν. Rather, as the duty of comforting and building up one another has just been mentioned, the transition to those whose especial work this is, is easy, and one part of forwarding the work is the recognition and encouragement of them by the church.

12.] **εἰδέναι** in this sense is perhaps a Hebraism : the LXX (in ref. Prov.) express ידע by ἐπιγινώσκειν. The persons indicated by **κοπιῶντας, προϊσταμένους**, and **νουθετοῦντας**, are the same, viz. the πρεσβύτεροι or ἐπίσκοποι : see note on Acts xx. 17, 28. **ἐν ὑμ.** is **among you**, not as Pelt, al. '(bestowing labour) *on* you.' **ἐν κυρίῳ**, as the element in

p = Acts xiii. 2. ἐκπερισσῶς ἐν ἀγάπῃ διὰ τὸ ᵖ ἔργον αὐτῶν. ᑫ εἰρηνεύετε ABDFK
xiv. 26. xv.
38. Phil. i. ἐν ʳ ἑαυτοῖς. 14 ˢ παρακαλοῦμεν δὲ ὑμᾶς, ἀδελφοί, ᵐ νου- c d e f g
22 al.
Mark ix. 50. θετεῖτε τοὺς ᵗ ἀτάκτους, ᵘ παραμυθεῖσθε τοὺς ᵛ ὀλιγοψύ- o17. 47
Rom. xii. 18. h k l m n
2 Cor. xiii. 11
only. Job v. χους, ʷ ἀντέχεσθε τῶν ˣ ἀσθενῶν, ʸ μακροθυμεῖτε πρὸς
24. Sir. vi. 6.
r = Col. iii. 13 πάντας. 15 ᶻ ὁρᾶτε ᶻ μή τις ᵃ κακὸν ᵃ ἀντὶ ᵃ κακοῦ τινὶ
reff.
s = Eph. iv. 1
reff. ᵃᵇ ἀποδῷ, ἀλλὰ πάντοτε ᶜ τὸ ἀγαθὸν ᵈ διώκετε καὶ εἰς
t here only †.
Deut. xxxii.
10 Aq. (-τως, ἀλλήλους καὶ εἰς πάντας. 16 πάντοτε χαίρετε, 17 ᶠ ἀδια-
2 Thess. iii.

6, 11. -τεῖν, 2 Thess. iii. 7.) u = ch. ii. 11 (reff.). v here only. Prov. xiv. 29. xviii. 14. Isa.
lvii. 15 al. w Matt. vi. 24. Luke xvi. 13. Tit. i. 9 only. Prov. iii. 18. x = 1 Cor. viii.
7. (-νῶν [part.], Rom. xiv. 1. 1 Cor. viii. 11.) y Matt. xviii. 26, 29. Luke xviii. 7. 1 Cor. xiii. 4. Heb.
vi. 15. James v. 7 bis, 8. 2 Pet. iii. 9 only. Prov. xix. 11. z Matt. xviii. 10 al. a Rom. xii.
17. 1 Pet. iii. 9. (Prov. xvii. 13.) b = Matt. vi. 4, 6. Luke xix. 8 al. c Gal. vi. 10 reff.
d = Rom. ix. 30, 31. xii. 13. xiv. 19. 1 Cor. xiv. 1. Heb. xii. 14. 1 Pet. iii. 11, from Ps. xxxiii. 14. Sir. xxvii. 8.
f ch. i. 2. ii. 13. Rom. i. 9 only †. 2 Macc. ix. 4 al.

rel : txt BD¹F. ins και bef ειρην. ℵ¹(ℵ³ disapproving) [goth æth]. for εαυτ.,
αυτοις D¹F[P]ℵ a b¹ d l n o 73 vulg syrr Chr Thdrt (Thl: γράφεται καὶ ἐν αὐτοῖς) :
txt ABD³KL rel copt goth Clem Damasc, ipsis D-lat G-lat Ambrst-ms.
14. [om υμας D¹.] νουθετειν . . παραμυθεισθαι . . αντεχεσθαι F 115 G-lat(altern).
15. αποδοιη D¹ : αποδω D²(appy) Fℵ¹ : txt ABKL[P]ℵ³ rel. om 1st και ADFℵ¹
m 17. 67² Syr copt goth [æth arm] Ambrst-ed Pel : ins BKL[P]ℵ³ rel am(with fuld
al) syr Chr Thdrt Damasc Ambrst-ms.
16. aft χαιρετε ins εν τω κυριω F(not F-lat) harl² [goth] Ambrst.

which, the matter with regard to which, their presidency takes place : = ' in divine things :' οὐκ ἐν τοῖς κοσμικοῖς, ἀλλ' ἐν τοῖς κατὰ κύριον. Thl. 13.] ἡγεῖσθαι ἐν ἀγάπῃ is an unusual expression for to esteem in love ; for such seems to be its meaning. Lün. compares ἔχειν τινὰ ἐν ὀργῇ (Thuc. ii. 18). We have περὶ πολλοῦ ἡγεῖσθαι, Herod. ii. 115 (Job xxxv. 2 does not apply). ὑπερεκπερισσῶς is best taken with ἐν ἀγάπῃ : it will not form a suitable qualification for ἡγεῖσθαι, which is merely a verbum medium. And so Chrys., all. διὰ τὸ ἔργ. αὐτ. may mean, because of the nature of their work, viz. that it is the Lord's work, for your souls : or, on account of their activity in their office, as a recompense for their work. Both these motives are combined in Heb. xiii. 17. The reading εἰρηνεύετε ἐν αὐτοῖς (see var. readd.) can hardly mean, as Chrys., al.,—μὴ ἀντιλέγειν τοῖς παρ' αὐτῶν λεγομένοις (Thdrt.), —but is probably, as De W., a mistaken correction from imagining that this exhortation must refer to the presbyters as well as the preceding : whereas it seems only to be suggested by the foregoing, as enforcing peaceful and loving subordination without party strife : cf. ἀτάκτους below. ἑαυτοῖς not = ἀλλήλοις (see ref. Col. and note there, and cf. Mark ix. 50). 14—22.] General exhortations with regard to Christian duties. There appears no reason for regarding these verses as addressed to the presbyters, as Conybeare in his translation (after

Chrys., Œc., Thl., Est., al.). They are for all : for each to interpret according to the sphere of his own duties. By the ἀδελφοί, he continues the same address as above. The attempt to give a stress to ὑμᾶς (' you, brethren, I exhort,' Conyb.) is objectionable : (1) because in that case the order of the words would be different (ὑμᾶς δέ, ἀδ., παρ., or ὑμᾶς δὲ παρ., ἀδ.), —(2) because the attention has been drawn off from οἱ προϊστάμενοι by εἰρηνεύετε ἐν ἑαυτοῖς intervening. 14. ἀτάκτους] This as ch. iv. 11, 2 Thess. iii. 6, 11, certainly implies that there was reason to complain of this ἀταξία in the Thessalonian church. " ἄτακτος is especially said of the soldier who does not remain in his rank : so inordinatus in Livy." Lün. : hence disorderly. ὀλιγοψύχους] such e. g. as needed the comfort of ch. iv. 13 ff. ἀντέχεσθε] keep hold of (reff.)— i. e. support. οἱ ἀσθενεῖς must be understood of the spiritually weak, not the literally sick : see reff. πρὸς πάντας] not, ' all the foregoing ' (ἀτάκτους, ὀλιγοψύχους, ἀσθενῶν): but all men : cf. next verse. 15.] ὁρᾶτε μή gives a slight warning that the practice might creep on them unawares. It is not addressed to any particular section of the church, but to all ; to each for himself, and the church for each. 16.] Chrys. refers this to ver. 15 : ὅταν γὰρ τοιαύτην ἔχωμεν ψυχὴν ὥστε μηδένα ἀμύνεσθαι, πόθεν ἡμᾶς εὐφρανεῖν, πόθεν, εἰπέ μοι, τὸ τῆς λύπης κέντρον παρεισελθεῖν δυνήσεται ; ὁ γὰρ οὕτω χαίρων τῷ

λείπτως προςεύχεσθε, [18] g ἐν παντὶ h εὐχαριστεῖτε· i τοῦτο
γὰρ θέλημα θεοῦ ἐν χριστῷ Ἰησοῦ εἰς ὑμᾶς. [19] τὸ
πνεῦμα μὴ k σβέννυτε, [20] l προφητείας μὴ m ἐξουθενεῖτε,
[21] πάντα δὲ n δοκιμάζετε· τὸ καλὸν o κατέχετε, [22] ἀπὸ
παντὸς p εἴδους q πονηροῦ r ἀπέχεσθε.   [23] s αὐτὸς δὲ ὁ

g 2 Cor. vii. 16.
Eph. v. 24.
Phil. iv. 6.
h absol., Matt.
xv. 36 ‖ al.†
Wisd. xviii. 2.
i ch. iv. 3.
k Matt. xii. 20.
xxv. 8. Mark
ix. 44, &c.,
from Isa.

lxvi. 24.   Eph. vi. 16.   Heb. xi. 34 only.
m = Luke xviii. 9.   Rom. xiv. 3 al.   Prov. i. 7.
15.   1 Cor. xi. 2. xv. 2.   Heb. iii. 6, 14. x. 23 ‡.
only.   Jer. xv. 3.   πᾶν εἶδος πονηρίας, Jos. Antt. x. 3. 1.
14.   Deut. i. 39.   r ch. iv. 3 reff.

l = Rom. xii. 6.   1 Cor. xii. 10. xiii. 2, 8 al.
n = ch. ii. 4 (2nd) reff.   o = Luke viii.
p Luke iii. 22. ix. 29.   John v. 37.   2 Cor. v. 7
q so καλοῦ τε κ. κακοῦ, Heb. v.
s = ch. iii. 11 reff. (see note.)

18. aft γαρ ins εστιν [A]D¹F [goth: aft θεου m 80(Sz)].   ins του bef θεου A(appy)
א¹(א³ disapproving).   εις υμας bef εν χριστω ιησ. A: om ιησ. L 177.
19. ζβεννυτε B¹D¹F.
21. rec om δε (*perhaps absorbed by* δο *follg : so Meyer*), with Aא¹ b¹ c f g k 17 Syr
copt Orig Chr_aliq Thdrt Œc Tert Ambrst-ms: ins BDFKL[P]א³ rel 67² latt syr goth
[arm] Clem₂ Bas Chr₁ Damasc Thl Ambrst-ed Pel.   δοκιμαζοντες K a b c f g k l²
o syr-txt Bas Chr₁ Cyr Damasc₁ [Orig-int₂].

παθεῖν κακῶς, ὡς κ. εὐεργεσίαις ἀμύνεσθαι τὸν πεποιηκότα κακῶς, πόθεν δυνήσεται ἀνιαθῆναι λοιπόν; But perhaps this
is somewhat far-fetched. The connexion
seems however to be justified as he proceeds : καὶ πῶς οἷόν τε τοῦτό, φησιν ; ἂν
ἐθέλωμεν, δυνατόν. εἶτα καὶ τὴν ὁδὸν
ἔδειξεν. ἀδιαλείπτως προσεύχεσθε κ.τ.λ.
And Thl.: ὁ γὰρ ἐθισθεὶς ὁμιλεῖν τῷ θεῷ
κ. εὐχαριστεῖν αὐτῷ ἐπὶ πᾶσιν ὡς συμ-
φερόντως συμβαίνουσι, πρόδηλον ὅτι χαρὰν ἕξει διηνεκῆ.   17.] See Chrys. and
Thl. above.   προσεύχεσθε, not of the
mere spirit of prayer, as Jowett : but, as in
parallel, Eph. vi. 18, of direct supplications
to God. These may be unceasing, in the
heart which is full of his presence and
evermore communing with Him.
18. ἐν παντί] in every thing,—every
circumstance : see reff., and cf. ὑπὲρ πάντων, Eph. v. 20 : κατὰ πάντα, Col. iii.
22, 23. Chrys., al., explain it '*on every
occasion*' (καιρῷ) ; but 2 Cor. ix. 8, ἐν
παντὶ πάντοτε, precludes this. τοῦτο
perhaps refers back to the three—χαίρ.,
προσεύχ., εὐχαρ., or perhaps, as Ellic. and
most modern expositors, to εὐχαρ. alone.
After γάρ, supply ἐστίν, and understand θέλημα, not '*decree*,' but will, in its
practical reference to your conduct.   ἐν
χρ. Ἰησ.] in, as its medium ; Christ being
the Mediator.   19.] Chrys., Thl., Œc.,
understand this ethically : σβέννυσι δ' αὐτὸ
βίος ἀκάθαρτος. But there can be no
doubt that the *supernatural* agency of the
Spirit is here alluded to,—the speaking in
tongues, &c., as in 1 Cor. xii. 7 ff. It is
conceived of as a flame, which may be
checked and quenched : hence the ζέων
τῷ πνεύματι of Acts xviii. 25, Rom. xii. 11.
The word is a common one with the later
classics applied to *wind* : e.g. Plut. de Is.
and Osir. p. 366 E,—τὰ βόρεια πνεύματα

κατασβεννύμενα κομιδῇ τῶν νοτίων ἐπι-
κρατούντων. Galen. de Theriaca i. 17,
uses the expression of the spirit of life in
children : speaking of poison, he says, τὸ
ἔμφυτον πνεῦμα ῥᾳδίως σβέννυσιν. See
more examples in Wetst.   20.] On
προφητείας, see 1 Cor. xii. 10, note. They
were liable to be despised in comparison
with the more evidently miraculous gift
of tongues : and hence in 1 Cor. xiv. 5,
&c., he takes pains to shew that prophecy
was in reality the greater gift.   21.]
πάντα δὲ δοκιμάζετε refers back to the
foregoing : but try all (such χαρίσματα) :
see 1 Cor. xii. 10 ; xiv. 29 ; 1 John iv. 1.
τὸ καλὸν κατέχετε is best regarded
as beginning a new sentence, and opposed
to ἀπὸ παντ. εἴδ. κ.τ.λ. which follows :
not however as disconnected from the preceding, but suggested by it. In this, and
in all things, hold fast the good.
22. ἀπὸ π. εἴδ. πον. ἀπέχ.] These words
cannot by any possibility be rendered as
in E. V., '*abstain from all appearance
of evil*.' For (1) εἶδος never signifies
'*appearance*' in this sense : (2) the two
members of the sentence would thus not
be logically correspondent, but a new idea
would be introduced in the second which
has no place in the context : for it is not
against being deceived by false *appearance*, nor against giving occasion by behaviour which *appears like* evil, that he
is cautioning them, but merely to distinguish and hold fast that which is good,
and reject that which is evil. εἶδος is
the *species*, as subordinated to the *genus*.
So Porphyr. (in Lünem.) isagoge de quin-
que vocibus 2 : λέγεται δὲ εἶδος καὶ τὸ
ὑπὸ τὸ ἀποδοθὲν γένος· καθ' ὃ εἰώθαμεν
λέγειν τὸν μὲν ἄνθρωπον εἶδος τοῦ ζῴου,
γένους ὄντος τοῦ ζῴου· τὸ δὲ λευκὸν τοῦ
χρώματος εἶδος· τὸ δὲ τρίγωνον τοῦ σχή-

t Phil. iv. 9 reff.
u Eph. v. 26 reff.
v here only †.
(-τελῶς, Deut. xiii. 16
Aq.) constr., see note.
w James i. 4 only. Deut. xxvii. 6 al.
x Job vii. 15 A (not F).
see 1 Cor. ii. 14. xv. 44. Jude 19.
y ch. ii. 10 only †.
x. 5.
d Col. i. 3 reff.

ᵗ θεὸς τῆς ᵗ εἰρήνης ᵘ ἁγιάσαι ὑμᾶς ᵛ ὁλοτελεῖς, καὶ ʷ ὁλό- ABDFK
κληρον ὑμῶν τὸ ˣ πνεῦμα καὶ ἡ ˣ ψυχὴ καὶ τὸ ˣ σῶμα cdefg
ʸ ἀμέμπτως ᶻ ἐν τῇ ᶻ παρουσίᾳ τοῦ κυρίου ἡμῶν Ἰησοῦ hklmn
χριστοῦ ᵃ τηρηθείη. 24 ᵇ πιστὸς ὁ ᶜ καλῶν ὑμᾶς, ὃς καὶ
ποιήσει.
25 Ἀδελφοί, ᵈ προσεύχεσθε ᵈ περὶ ἡμῶν. 26 ἀσπάσασθε
τοὺς ἀδελφοὺς πάντας ᵉ ἐν ᵉᶠ φιλήματι ἁγίῳ. 27 ᵍ ἐνορκίζω

LPℵ a b
cdefg
hklmn
o 17. 47

(·τος, Phil. ii. 15.)   z ch. ii. 19 reff.   a = 1 Cor. vii. 37.   2 Cor. xi. 9 al.   Wisd.
b 1 Cor. i. 9. x. 13.   2 Cor. i. 18.   2 Thess. iii. 3.   2 Tim. ii. 13 al.   c & particip., Gal. v. 8.
e Rom. xvi. 16.   1 Cor. xvi. 20.   2 Cor. xiii. 12.   1 Pet. v. 14.   f as above (e).   Luke
vii. 45. xxii. 48 only.   Prov xxvii. 6.   Cant. i. 2 only.   g here only †.   Neh. xiii. 25 A.   ὁρκ., & constr.,
Mark v. 7.   Acts xix. 13.   ἐξορκ., Matt. xxvi. 63.   Gen. xxiv. 3.   Judg. xvii. 2 A only.

23. αγιασει F copt.   τηρηθειην D¹ : om (leaving a space) F-gr G-lat.
24. ins ο bef πιστος F(not G), fidelis deus F-lat.   ημας A e¹.   ποιησαι
F(not G).
25. ins και bef περι BD¹ m syr goth ⌈arm⌉ Damasc.   for περι, υπερ F[P] Damasc.
27. rec (for ενορκ.) ορκιζω, with D²·³FKL[P]ℵ rel : txt ABD¹E 17 Synops Damasc.

ματος εἶδος. And πονηροῦ is not an adjective, but a substantive:—from every species (or form) of evil. The objection which Bengel brings against this, 'species mali esset εἶδος τοῦ πονηροῦ,' is null, as such articles in construction are continually omitted, and especially when the genitive of construction is an abstract noun. Lün. quotes πρὸς διάκρισιν καλοῦ τε κ. κακοῦ, Heb. v. 14: πᾶν εἶδος πονηρίας, Jos. Antt. x. 3. 1.   23, 24.] αὐτὸς δέ —contrast to all these feeble endeavours on your own part.   εἰρήνη here most probably in its wider sense, as the accomplishment of all these Christian graces, and result of the avoidance of all evil. It seems rather far-fetched to refer it back to ver. 13.   ὁλοτελεῖς seems to refer to the entireness of sanctification, which is presently expressed in detail. Jerome, who treats at length of this passage, ad Hedibiam (ep. cxx.) quæst. xii., vol. i. p. 1004, explains it, 'per omnia vel in omnibus, sive plenos et perfectos:' and so Pelt, 'ut fiatis integri :' and the reviewer of Mr. Jowett in the Journal of S. Lit., April, 1856 : 'sanctify you (to be) entire.' But I prefer the other interpretation : in which case it = ὅλους.   καί introduces the detailed expression of the same wish from the lower side—in its effects.   ὁλόκληρον] emphatic predicate, as its position before the article shews : entire—refers to all three following substantives, though agreeing in gender with πνεῦμα, the nearest. Cf. besides reff., Levit. xxiii. 15, ἑπτὰ ἑβδομάδας ὁλοκλήρους.   τὸ πν. κ. ἡ ψυχ. κ. τὸ σῶμα] τὸ πνεῦμα is the SPIRIT, the highest and distinctive part of man, the immortal and responsible soul, in our common parlance : ἡ ψυχή is the lower or animal soul, containing the passions

and desires (αἰτία κινήσεως ζωικῆς ζώων, Plato, Deff. p. 411), which we have in common with the brutes, but which in us is ennobled and drawn up by the πνεῦμα. That St. Paul had these distinctions in mind, is plain (against Jowett) from such places as 1 Cor. ii. 14. The spirit, that part whereby we are receptive of the Holy Spirit of God, is, in the unspiritual man, crushed down and subordinated to the animal soul (ψυχή) : he therefore is called ψυχικὸς πνεῦμα μὴ ἔχων, Jude 19 : see also note on 1 Cor. as above.   ἀμέμπτως defines and fixes ὁλόκληρον τηρηθ.: that, as Ellic., regarding quantity, this defining quality.   ἐν, for it will be in that day that the result will be seen,—that the ὁλόκληρον τηρηθῆναι will be accomplished.   24.] Assurance from God's faithfulness, that it will be so.   πιστός (reff.)—true to His word and calling : ἀντὶ τοῦ ἀληθής, Thdrt.   ὁ καλῶν] not = ὁ καλέσας, but bringing out God's office, as the Caller of his people : cf. Gal. v. 8.   ποιήσει, viz. that which was specified in the last verse.   25—28.] CONCLUSION.   25.] Cf. Rom. xv. 30; Eph. vi. 19; Col. iv. 3; 2 Thess. iii. 1.   περί is not so definite as ὑπέρ—pray concerning us—make us the subject of your prayers—our person—our circumstances—our apostolic work. Ellic. however remarks, that this distinction is precarious ; and hardly appreciable.   26.] From this verse and the following, it would appear that this letter was given into the hands of the elders.   ἐν, simply 'in,'—the kiss being the vehicle of the salutation : in our idiom, 'with.'   27.] The meaning of this conjuration is, that an assembly of all the brethren should be held, and the

ὑμᾶς τὸν κύριον, [hi] ἀναγνωσθῆναι [ik] τὴν ἐπιστολὴν πᾶσιν

τοῖς ἀδελφοῖς.

[28] Ἡ [l] χάρις τοῦ κυρίου ἡμῶν Ἰησοῦ χριστοῦ μεθ'

ὑμῶν.

ΠΡΟΣ ΘΕΣΣΑΛΟΝΙΚΕΙΣ Α.

h Acts viii. 28
al. fr.   Esdr.
iii. 15.
i Col. iv. 16.
1 Macc. v. 14.
k = Rom. xvi.
22. see 1 Cor.
v. 9.
l see Col. iv. 18
reff.

[om την επιστολην P.]   rec ins αγιοις bef αδελφοις (gloss from the margin), with AKL[P]א³ rel vulg syrr copt goth æth-pl [arm] Chr Thdrt Damasc : om BDFא¹ æth-rom Euthal Ambrst Cassiod.
28. rec at end ins αμην, with AD²·³KL[P]א rel vss Chr Thdrt : om BD¹F o 17. 67² am [arm-zoh] Ambrst.

SUBSCRIPTION. rec adds εγραφη απο αθηνων, with AB²KL rel Syr copt : a Laodicea Ɔ²-lat syr : l o goth have no subscr : εγρ. α. αθ. b h k m : πρ. θεσσ., omg α', 17 : pref του αγιου απ. παυλου L : txt B¹א, and (adding επληρωθη) D, (prefixing ετελεσθη) F. [P uncert.]

Epistle then and there publicly read. The aorist, ἀναγνωσθῆναι, referring to a single act, shews this (but consult Ellic.'s note). On the construction τὸν κύρ. see reff. Jowett offers various solutions for the Apostle's vehemence of language. I should account for it, not by supposing any distrust of the elders, nor by the other hypotheses which he suggests, but by the earnestness of spirit incidental to the solemn conclusion of an Epistle of which he is conscious that it conveys to them the will and special word of the Lord. πᾶσιν] i. e. in Thessalonica, assembled together.   **28.**] See on 2 Cor. xiii. 13.

a 1 Thess. i. 1.
b Gal. i. 1 reff.
c = Eph. i. 16 reff.
d Eph. v. 28 reff.
e Phil. i. 7.
f = here only. Xen. Mem. i. 5. 3. Anab. ii. 3. 25.
g here only †.
αὐξ., Paul elsw. transit. 1 Cor. iii. 6 l. but see Eph. ii. 21.
h see 1 Thess. iii. 12 reff.
i 1 Thess. ii. 11 reff.

ABDFK LPℵ a b c d e f g h k l m n o 17. 47

I. ¹ Παῦλος καὶ Σιλουανὸς καὶ Τιμόθεος τῇ ἐκκλησίᾳ Θεσσαλονικέων ᵃἐν ᵃθεῷ ᵃπατρὶ ἡμῶν καὶ κυρίῳ Ἰησοῦ χριστῷ. ² χάρις ὑμῖν καὶ εἰρήνη ἀπὸ ᵇθεοῦ ᵇπατρὸς καὶ κυρίου Ἰησοῦ χριστοῦ.

³ ᶜΕὐχαριστεῖν ᵈὀφείλομεν τῷ θεῷ πάντοτε περὶ ὑμῶν, ἀδελφοί, ᵉκαθὼς ᶠἄξιόν ἐστιν, ὅτι ᵍὑπεραυξάνει ἡ πίστις ὑμῶν καὶ ʰπλεονάζει ἡ ἀγάπη ⁱἑνὸς ἑκάστου πάντων ὑμῶν εἰς ἀλλήλους, ⁴ ὥστε αὐτοὺς ἡμᾶς ἐν ὑμῖν ᵏἐγ-

k here only †. Ps. li. 1. xcvi. 7. cv. 47.

TITLE. rec παυλου του αποστολου η πρ. θεσσ. επ. δευτερα: του αγ. αποστ. παυλου πρ. θεσσ. επιστ. β′ L : πρ. θεσσ. β′ επ. παυλου o : ανδρασι θεσσαλιης ταδε δευτερα ουρανιος φως f : η πρ. θεσσ. β′ επ. k : πρ. θεσσ. δευτ. επ. h : πρ. θεσσ. επ. β′ l : txt ABℵ m n 17 [47], and (prefixing αρχεται) DF. [P uncert.]

CHAP. I. 1. σιλβανος DF 67². ins και bef πατρι ℵ¹(but corrd) 4. 80. om κυριω F(not F-lat). χριστ. bef ιησ. DF(not F-lat).

2. rec aft πατρος ins ημων (as in other epp), with AFKLℵ rel vulg syrr copt goth [æth arm] Chr Thdrt Ambrst-ven : om BD[P] 17 Thl Ambrst-rom Pel.

3. om last υμων ℵ¹.

4. rec ημας bef αυτους, with ADFKL rel : txt B[P]ℵ m 17. 73.   rec (for εγκ.)

CH. I. 1, 2.] ADDRESS AND GREETING. On ver. 1, see 1 Thess. i. 1, note.

2.] πατρός, absol.: see Gal. i. 1, 3; 1 Tim. i. 2; 2 Tim. i. 2; Tit. i. 4.

3—12.] INTRODUCTION. *Thanksgiving for their increase in faith and love, and their endurance under persecution* (vv. 3, 4): *promise of a rich recompense at Christ's coming* (vv. 5—10), *and good wishes for their Christian perfection* (vv. 11, 12). **3.** καθὼς ἄξιόν ἐστιν] as it is right—refers to the whole preceding sentence. ὅτι, not '*that*,'—εὐχαριστεῖν ὅτι—which would make καθὼς ἄξ. ἐστ. flat and superfluous,—but because, dependent on the clause preceding, καθὼς ἄξ. ἐστιν, it is right, because &c.

"ὀφείλομεν expresses the duty of thanksgiving from its *subjective* side as an inward conviction,—καθὼς ἄξιόν ἐστιν, on the other hand, from the *objective* side, as something answering to the state of circumstances." Lün. ὑπεραυξάνει] 'Frequentavit hujus generis voce Paulus (ὑπερλίαν 2 Cor. xi. 5, ὑπερπλεονάζω 1 Tim. i. 14, ὑπερπερισσεύομαι 2 Cor. vii. 4 (cf. also Rom. v. 20), ὑπερνικάω Rom. viii. 37, ὑπερυψόω Phil. ii. 9), non quod iis delectaretur, sed quia vir vehemens natura duce sua cogitata gravibus verbis enuntiavit.' Fritzsche ad Rom. v. 20. εἰς ἀλλήλους goes with ἀγάπη.

4.] αὐτοὺς ἡμᾶς—as well as our informants, and others who heard about

καυχᾶσθαι ἐν ταῖς [1] ἐκκλησίαις τοῦ [1] θεοῦ ὑπὲρ τῆς [m] ὑπο-
μονῆς ὑμῶν καὶ πίστεως ἐν πᾶσιν τοῖς [n] διωγμοῖς ὑμῶν καὶ
ταῖς θλίψεσιν [o] αἷς [p] ἀνέχεσθε, 5 [q] ἔνδειγμα τῆς [r] δικαίας
[r] κρίσεως τοῦ θεοῦ, [s] εἰς τὸ [t] καταξιωθῆναι ὑμᾶς τῆς
βασιλείας τοῦ θεοῦ, ὑπὲρ ἧς [u] καὶ πάσχετε, 6 [v] εἴπερ
δίκαιον [w] παρὰ θεῷ [x] ἀνταποδοῦναι τοῖς [y] θλίβουσιν ὑμᾶς
θλῖψιν, 7 καὶ ὑμῖν τοῖς [y] θλιβομένοις [z] ἄνεσιν μεθ᾽ ἡμῶν

l 1 Thess. ii. 14 reff.
m Col. i. 11 reff.
n Mark iv. 17 ‖ Mt. x. 30.
Rom. viii. 35.
2 Cor. xii. 10.
2 Tim. iii. 11.
Prov. xi. 19
Lam. iii. 19.
2 Macc. xii. 23 only.
o attr., Eph. i. 6 reff.
p = Eph. iv. 2 reff.

q here only †. (-ξις, Phil. i. 28.)
2. 2 Macc. ix. 18.
36. Acts v. 41 only †.
v Rom. viii. 9, 17 al.
y 1 Thess. iii. 4 reff.
s Phil. i. 23. 1 Thess. iii. 10 al.
Gen. xxxi. 28 compl. 2 Macc. xiii. 12 only.
w = Rom. ii. 13. 1 Cor. iii. 19 al.
z Acts xxiv. 23. 2 Cor. ii. 12. vii. 5. viii. 13 only.
r John v. 30. vii. 24. Rev. xvi. 7. xix. 2. Isa. lviii.
t Luke xx. 35. xxi.
u = Rom. viii. 17.
x 1 Thess. iii. 9 reff.
2 Chron. xxiii. 15

καυχασθαι (more usual word), with DKL rel, καυχησασθαι F : txt AB[P]א 17 Chr-ms. om 2nd ταις D¹F[P]. ενεχεσθε B.
6. ins τω bef θεω A Orthod. ins αυτοις bef τοις θλιβουσιν F vulg D-lat.
7. for ημων, υμων א¹.

you,—see 1 Thess. i. 8. There is ample reason (against Jowett) for the emphasis on αὐτοὺς ἡμᾶς. The fact of an Apostle making honourable mention of them in other churches was one which deserved this marking out, to their credit and encouragement. ἐν ὑμῖν] as the object of our ἐγκαυχ. ἐν ταῖς ἐκκλησίαις τοῦ θεοῦ] i. e. at Corinth and in Achaia. ὑπομονῆς καὶ πίστεως] No ἐν διὰ δυοῖν (Grot., Pelt),—nor is there the slightest necessity, with Lünem., to take πίστις here in a different sense from that in ver. 3. The same faith which was receiving so rich increase, was manifesting itself by its fruit in the midst of persecutions and afflictions. πᾶσιν belongs only to τοῖς διωγμοῖς (ὑμῶν), as is shewn by the article before θλίψεσιν, and by αἷς ἀνέχεσθε, which is parallel with ὑμῶν. αἷς ἀνέχεσθε] attr. for ὧν ἀνέχεσθε,—not for ἃς ἀνέχεσθε, as De W., al., for ἀνέχομαι always governs a genitive in the N. T. ἀνέχ., ye are enduring : the persecutions continued at the time of the Epistle being written. 5—10.] Comfort under these afflictions, to think that they were only part of God's carrying out his justice towards them and their persecutors. 5.] The sentence, in construction, is in apposition with the preceding τῆς ὑπομ. to ἀνέχεσθε,—but in the nominative: ὅ(τι) ἐστίν or the like having to be supplied. In Phil. i. 28 we have the like sentiment, with ἥτις ἐστίν supplied. There is a similar construction in Rom. viii. 3. ἔνδειγμα] cf. ἔνδειξις in ref.—a proof: manifested in you being called on and enabled to suffer for Christ, and your adversaries filling up the measure of their opposition to God. The δικαία κρίσις is, that just judgment which

will be completed at the Lord's coming, but is even now preparing—this being an earnest and token of it. εἰς τὸ κ.τ.λ.] in order to (belongs to the implied assertion of the foregoing clause—'which judgment is even now bringing about &c.' εἰς τό is not merely of the result, as Lün.: nor is it of the purpose of your endurance, αἷς ἀνέχεσθε εἰς τὸ κ.τ.λ., as Estius characteristically, to bring in the Romish doctrine of merit :—but of the purpose of God's dispensation of δικαία κρίσις, by which you will be ripened and fitted for his kingdom. (Ellic. denies this, and would take εἰς τό of the object to which the δικαία κρίσις tended. But surely when we are speaking of the divine proceedings, the tendency involves the purpose, and there is no need for a semi-telic force)) your being counted worthy of the Kingdom of God, on behalf of which (for this meaning of ὑπέρ, see Acts v. 41; ix. 16; Rom. i. 5; xv. 8; 2 Cor. xii. 10; xiii. 8, al.) ye also (καί, as in ref., points out the connexion—q. d. 'ye accordingly') are suffering, 6.] if at least (reff. : it refers back to δικαίας above, and introduces a substantiation of it by an appeal to our ideas of strict justice) it is just with (in the esteem of, reff.) God to requite to those who trouble you, tribulation (according to the strict jus talionis), and to you who are troubled, rest (reff.: literally, relaxation: 'the glory of the kingdom of God on its negative side, as liberation from earthly affliction.' Lün.) with us (viz. the writers, Paul, Silvanus, and Timotheus, who are troubled like yourselves: not 'with us (all) Christians,' as De W., al.,—for all Christians were not θλιβόμενοι, which is the condition of this ἄνεσις in our sentence: still less,

a – Rom. ii. 5. ἐν τῇ ᵃ ἀποκαλύψει τοῦ ᵇ κυρίου Ἰησοῦ ἀπ᾽ οὐρανοῦ μετ
1 Cor. i. 7 al.
b gen., 1 Cor. i. ἀγγέλων δυνάμεως αὐτοῦ ⁸ ᶜ ἐν ᶜᵈ πυρὶ ᵈᵉ φλογὸς ᶠᵍ διδόν-
7. 1 Pet. i. 7,
13. (see
2 Cor. xii. 1.) τος ᵍʰ ἐκδίκησιν τοῖς ⁱ μὴ εἰδόσιν θεὸν καὶ τοῖς μὴ ᵏ ὑπ-
c 1 Cor. iii. 13.
d here (Acts ἀκούουσιν τῷ εὐαγγελίῳ τοῦ κυρίου ἡμῶν Ἰησοῦ, ⁹ ˡ οἵτινες
vii. 30 v. r.)
only. Sir. ᵐ δίκην ⁿ τίσουσιν ᵒ ὄλεθρον αἰώνιον ᵖ ἀπὸ ᑫ προσώπου τοῦ
viii. 10. see
Heb. i. 7.
Rev. i. 14. ii. κυρίου καὶ ἀπὸ τῆς ʳ δόξης τῆς ʳ ἰσχύος αὐτοῦ, ¹⁰ ὅταν
18. xix. 12.
e as above (d) ἔλθῃ ˢ ἐνδοξασθῆναι ἐν τοῖς ᵗ ἁγίοις αὐτοῦ καὶ ᵘ θαυμασθῆ-
& Luke xvi.
24 only.
f = Rev. xviii. ναι ἐν πᾶσιν τοῖς πιστεύσασιν, ὅτι ᵛ ἐπιστεύθη τὸ ʷ μαρτύ-
7.

ABDFK
LPℵ a b
c d e f g
h k l m n
o 17.47

g Ps. xvii. 47.   Ezek. xxv. 14, 17.   (ἀποδιδ., Num. xxxi. 3.)   h Luke xviii. 7, 8. xxi. 22. Acts vii.
   24.   Rom. xii. 19.   2 Cor. vii. 11.   Heb. x. 30.   1 Pet. ii. 14 only.   i 1 Thess. iv. 5. Gal. iv. 8. (Jer.
   ix. 6.)   k = Acts vi. 7. Rom. vi. 17.   l = Acts x. 41, 47. xiii. 31, 43 al. fr.
m Acts (xxv. 15 rec.) xxviii. 4. Jude 7 only. Ezek. xxv. 12.   n here only. Prov. xx. 22. xxiv. 29.
o 1 Thess. v. 3 reff.   p = Col. ii. 20 reff.   q Acts iii. 19.   r Isa. ii. 10, 19, 21. see Eph. i.
   19. vi. 10.   s ver. 12 only. Exod. xiv. 4. Ezek. xxviii. 22. Psa. lxxxviii. 7.   t Eph. i. 1 reff.
u = here only. Wisd. viii. 11. see Rev. xiii. 3. Luke vii. 9.   v pass., 1 Tim. iii. 16.   w = Acts iv.
33. 1 Cor. i. 6. 2 Tim. i. 6.

[for ιησ., ημων ιησ. χριστον L 47 Syr goth Iren-int.   μετα P m 17.]
   8. for πυρι φλογος, φλογι πυρος (*alteration to sense, see reff*) BDF latt syrr copt
[goth] æth arm ancient-writers-in-Iren Mac Thdrt-comm(appy) Thl-marg Œc Tert Aug
Pel : txt AKL[P]ℵ rel syr-mg Chr Thdrt-txt Damasc Thl Ambrst.   διδους D¹F :
dare G-lat Iren-int Tert.   ins τον bef θεον L[P]ℵ³ a b f g.   rec aft ιησου ins
χριστον, with AFℵ rel latt Syr goth Chr Iren-int : om BDKL[P] b d e k l n o 17 [47]
syr copt æth [arm-zoh] Chr-ms Thdrt Damasc Thl Œc.
   9. ολεθριον A 17 [47] 73 Ephr Chr-ms Tert.   om του DF 67² Chr, Thl.
   10. ενθαυμασθηναι D¹F.   rec πιστευουσιν (with a f 17, e sil), *credentibus* G-lat
copt goth Iren-int₁ : txt ABDFKL[P]ℵ rel Ephr Chr Thdrt, *qui crediderunt* vulg syr
Iren-int₁ Ambrst.

'*with us Jews*,' you being Gentiles (Bengel, al.)) at the revelation (manifestation
in His appearing, reff.) of the Lord Jesus
from heaven (cf. 1 Thess. iv. 16) with the
angels of His power (no hendiadys—not
as E. V., 'his mighty angels,' which as
usual, obscures and stultifies the sense:
for the *might of the angels* is no element
here, but His *might*, of which they *are*
the *angels*—serving His power and proclaiming His might) in (the) fire of flame
(further specification of the ἀποκάλυψις
above : does not belong to the following.
On the analogy, see Exod. iii. 2; xix. 18;
Dan. vii. 9, 10) allotting (distributing as
their portion : reff.) vengeance to those
who know not God (the Gentiles, see reff.),
and to those (the τοῖς repeated indicates
a new class of persons) who obey not the
Gospel of our Lord Jesus (the unbelieving
Jews, see Rom. x. 3, 16), which persons
(οἵτινες), generic and classifying, refers
back to their characteristics just mentioned, thus containing in itself the reason
for τίσουσιν &c. following (against Ellic.).
See ὅστις discussed by Hermann, Præf. ad
Soph. Œd. Tyr. pp. vii—xv) shall pay
the penalty of everlasting destruction
from (local, as in Matt. vii. 23, ἀποχω-
ρεῖτε ἀπ᾽ ἐμοῦ οἱ ἐργαζόμενοι τὴν ἀνο-
μίαν,—'apart from,' see reff. (so Pisc.,
Beza, Schott, Olsh., Lünem., al.). It has

been interpreted of *time*,—'*from the time
of the appearing* &c.' (Chr., Œc., Thl.,
&c.), but ἀπὸ προσώπου will not bear
this :—also of the *cause*, which would
make ver. 9 a mere repetition of ἐν τῇ
ἀποκ. to διδόντος ἐκδ. above (so Grot.,
Beng., Pelt, De W., Baumg.-Crus., al.))
the face of the Lord and from the glory
of his Power (i. e. from the manifestation
of his power in the glorification of his
saints (see ref. Isa.). De W. makes
these words, ἀπὸ δόξης κ.τ.λ., an objection to the *local* sense of ἀπό. But it is
not so :—the δόξα being the visible local-
ized result of the ἰσχύς; see next verse)
when He shall have come (follows on
δίκην τίσουσιν &c. above. On the aor.
subj. with ὅταν, see Winer, edn. 6,
§ 42. 5) to be glorified (aor. : by the
great manifestation at His coming) in
(not '*through*' (τουτέστι, διά, Chrys. : so
Œc., Thl., Pelt, al.), nor '*among*:' but
they will be the *element* of His glorification : He will be glorified *in* them, just as
the Sun is reflected in a mirror) his saints
(not angels, but holy men), and to be
wondered at in (see above) all them that
believed (aor. participle, looking back from
that day on the past),—because our testimony to you (ref., not τὸ ἐφ᾽ ὑμ., as ἐφ᾽
belongs immediately to μαρτύριον) was
believed (parenthesis, serving to include

ριον ἡμῶν ˣ ἐφ᾽ ὑμᾶς, ἐν τῇ ʸ ἡμέρᾳ ʸ ἐκείνῃ. 11 ᶻ εἰς ὃ
ᶻ καὶ ᵃ προςευχόμεθα πάντοτε περὶ ὑμῶν, ᵃ ἵνα ὑμᾶς
ᵇ ἀξιώσῃ τῆς ᶜ κλήσεως ὁ θεὸς ἡμῶν καὶ ᵈ πληρώσῃ πᾶσαν
ᵉ εὐδοκίαν ᶠ ἀγαθωσύνης καὶ ᵍ ἔργον ᵍ πίστεως ʰ ἐν δυνάμει,
12 ὅπως ⁱ ἐνδοξασθῇ τὸ ὄνομα τοῦ κυρίου ἡμῶν Ἰησοῦ
ἐν ὑμῖν καὶ ὑμεῖς ἐν αὐτῷ κατὰ τὴν χάριν τοῦ θεοῦ ἡμῶν
καὶ κυρίου Ἰησοῦ χριστοῦ.

x Luke ix. 5.
y 2 Tim. i. 12,
18. iv. 8.
z = Col. i. 29.
a Phil. i. 9 reff.
b = 1 Tim. v.
17. Heb. iii.
3. x. 29 only
(see Luke vii.
7. Acts xv.
38) †.
c = Phil. iii. 14.
Heb. iii. 1
(1 Cor. i. 26).
d = John iii.
29. 2 Cor.
x. 6 al. fr.
e = (see note)

here only. (Eph. i. 5 reff.)   f Gal. v. 22 reff.   g 1 Thess. i. 3.   h Col. i.
29 reff.   i ver. 10.

11. om ημων D¹ am syrr Vig : υμων D³KL e m n : ins υμων bef ο θε. ημων F arm :
ins *sua* vulg(and F-lat).   πληρωσει AK[P] o.   αγαθοσυνης DFL Damasc.
12. rec aft 1st ιησου ins χριστου, with AF[P] b c f h 17 vulg syrr æth-pl [arm]
Chr Ambrst : om BDKLℵ rel coptt [goth] æth-rom Thdrt-ms Damasc Œc.
ημεις A.

the Thessalonians among the πιστεύσαντες),—**in that day** (of which we all know :
to be joined with θαυμασθ., &c., not with
ὅτι ἐπιστεύθη, &c., as Syr., Ambr., Grot.,
al., who also take ἐπιστ. as a future, 'for
in that day our testimony with regard to
you will be substantiated.' Most unwar-
rantable—requiring also ἐπιστώθη instead
of -εύθη. Calvin says, 'repetit in die illa
. . . . ideo autem repetit, ut fidelium vota
cohibeat, ne ultra modum festinent.' I
should rather say, to give more fixity and
definiteness to the foregoing). We may
observe, as against Jowett's view of the
arguments here being merely "they suffer
now ; therefore their enemies will suffer
hereafter :—their enemies will suffer hereafter ; therefore they will be comforted
hereafter,"—that the arguments are nothing of the kind, resting entirely on the
word δίκαιον, bringing in as it does all the
relations of the Christian covenant, of them
to God, and God to them,—and by contrast, of God to their enemies and persecutors.   **11.**] **With a view to which**
(consummation, the ἐνδοξασθῆναι, &c.,
above, in *your case*, as is shewn below :
not '*wherefore*,' as E. V., Grot., Pelt, &c.)
we pray also (as well as wish : had the
καί imported (as Lün.) that the *prayer of
the Apostle* was added on behalf of the
Thessalonians to the fact (?) of the ἐνδοξασθῆναι, it would have been καὶ ἡμεῖς
προς.) **always concerning you, that** (see
note on 1 Cor. xiv. 13) **our God may
count** ʏᴏᴜ (emphatic) **worthy** (not—'*make
you worthy*,' as Luth., Grot., Olsh., al.,
which the word cannot mean. The verb
has the secondary emphasis : see below) **of
your calling** (just as we are exhorted to
walk ἀξίως τῆς κλήσεως ἧς ἐκλήθημεν,
Eph. iv. 1—the calling being taken not
merely as the first act of God, but as the

enduring state produced by that act (see
especially 1 Cor. vii. 20), the normal termination of which is, *glory*. So that κλῆσις
is not 'the good thing to which we are
called,' as Lün. : which besides would require τῆς κλήσεως ἀξιώσῃ : now that τῆς
κλήσεως is sheltered behind the verb, it
is taken as a matter of course, 'your calling,' an acknowledged fact), **and may
fulfil** (complete,—bring to its fulness in
you) **all** (possible) **right purpose of goodness** (it is quite impossible, with many
ancient Commentators, E. V., &c., to refer
εὐδοκίαν to *God*—'*His good pleasure.*'
In that case we must at least have τὴν
εὐδοκίαν—and ἀγαθωσ. will not refer with
any propriety either to God, of whom the
word is never used (occurring Rom. xv. 14;
Gal. v. 22 ; Eph. v. 9 only, and always of
ᴍᴀɴ), or to the Thessalonians (π. ἀγαθω-
σύνην εὐδοκίας). It (εὐδοκία) must then
apply to the Thessalonians, as it does to
human agents in Phil. i. 15. And then
ἀγαθωσύνης may be either a gen. *ob-
jecti*, 'approval of that which is good,'—
or a gen. *appositionis*, a εὐδοκία con-
sisting in ἀγαθωσύνη. The latter I own
seems to me (agst Ellic.) far the best :
as ἀγαθωσύνη is in all the above citations
a subjective quality, and the *approval* of
that which is good would introduce an
element here which seems irrelevant) **and**
(all) **work of faith** (activity of faith : see
ref. 1 Thess. note. The genitive is again
one of apposition), **in power** (belongs to
πληρώσῃ, q. d. *mightily*),—**that** &c. On
ὄνομα, cf. Phil. ii. 9 ff. Lünemann refers
ἐν αὐτῷ to ὄνομα, 'and ye in *it :*' but
surely the expression is one too appropriated in sacred diction, for it to refer
to any but our Lord Himself : cf. 1 Cor.
i. 5 ; 2 Cor. xiii. 4 ; Eph. i. 4 ; iv. 21 ;
Col. ii. 10, al.

k = 1 Thess. iv.
1 reff.
i = John i. 30.
2 Cor. i. 8.
viii. 23.
1 Thess. iii. 2.
m = 1 Thess.
ii. 19 reff.
n Heb. x. 25
only †.
2 Macc. ii. 7
only
(-άγειν,
Matt. xxiv.
31).
o constr., Phil. i. 23.

II. ¹ ᵏ Ἐρωτῶμεν δὲ ὑμᾶς, ἀδελφοί, ¹ ὑπὲρ τῆς ᵐ παρ- ABDFK
ουσίας τοῦ κυρίου ἡμῶν Ἰησοῦ χριστοῦ καὶ ἡμῶν ⁿ ἐπισυν-
αγωγῆς ἐπ᾽ αὐτόν, ² ᵒ εἰς τὸ μὴ ᵖ ταχέως ᑫ σαλευθῆναι
ὑμᾶς ʳ ἀπὸ τοῦ ˢ νοὸς μηδὲ ᵗ θροεῖσθαι, μήτε ᵘ διὰ ᵘ πνεύματος μήτε ᵛ διὰ ᵛ λόγου μήτε δι᾽ ἐπιστολῆς ὡς δι᾽ ἡμῶν,
ʷ ὡς ὅτι ˣ ἐνέστηκεν ἡ ʸ ἡμέρα τοῦ ʸ κυρίου. ³ μή τις

ABDFK
LPℵ a b
c d e f g
h k l m n
o 17. 47

1 Thess. iii. 10.
iv. 31. see Heb. xii. 26, 27.
23, 25. 1 Cor. xiv. 14.
28. xxi. 4. Rom. v 5. Eph. iii. 16 al. L.P.
w 2 Cor. v. 19. xi. 21 only. Winer, edn. 6, ∮ 65. 9.
26. Gal. i. 4. 2 Tim. iii. 1. Heb. ix. 9 only.

p = 1 Tim. v. 22.
r constr. prægn., Rom. vi. 7. vii. 2. ix. 3. 2 Tim. ii 26.
t Matt. xxiv. 6 ‖ Mk. only. Cant. v. 4 only.
(Heb. ix. 14. 1 Pet. i. 22.)
1 Macc. xii. 44.

q = Luke vi. 48. Acts ii. 25 (from Ps. xv. 8).
s = Rom. vii.
u = Acts i. 2. xi.
v ver. 15. Acts xv. 27, 32.
x (=) Rom. viii. 38. 1 Cor. iii. 22. vii.
y see 1 Thess. v. 2 reff.

CHAP. II. 1. om 1st ημων B syr.

2. aft νοος ins υμων D vulg Syr syr-w-ast sah æth [Orig-int₂] Ambrst Jer Pel.
rec for μηδε, μητε (to suit μητε thrice follg : but the sense is diff t), with D³KL[P] rel :
μηποτε 17 : txt ABD¹Fℵ [47] Orig.—μηδε δια λογ. D¹ : μηδε 4 times F, but μητε δια
λογ. F¹.   om ἡ D¹.   om last του F Damasc Thl.   [for δι ημ., παρ᾽ ημ. P.]
     rec (for κυριου) χριστου, with D³K rel goth : txt ABD¹FL[P]ℵ m [47] 67² latt
syrr coptt æth arm Orig Hip Chr Thdrt Damasc Thl Œc Tert Jer Ambrst Pel Aug,
κυριου ιησου 17.

CH. II. 1—12.] DOGMATICAL PORTION
OF THE EPISTLE. *Information* (by way of
correction) *concerning the approach of the
day of the Lord : its prevenient and accompanying circumstances.* This passage
has given rise to many separate treatises :
the principal of which I have enumerated
in the Prolegomena, § v.   1.] But
(passing from those things which he prays
for them, to those which he prays *of* them)
we entreat (reff.) **you, brethren** (to win
their affectionate attention), **in regard to**
(the Vulg., E. V., and many ancient Commentators, render ὑπέρ, '*per*,' '*by*,' and
understand it as introducing a *formula
jurandi*, as in Il. ω. 466, καί μιν ὑπὲρ
πατρὸς . . . λίσσεο. But this construction
is not found in the N. T. ; and it is most
unnatural that the Apostle should thus
conjure them by that, concerning which
he was about to teach them. It is best
therefore to take ὑπέρ, as so often, *not
quite* = περί, but very nearly so, the
meaning '*on behalf of*' being slightly
hinted—for the subject had been mis-
represented, and justice is done to it by
the Apostle ; and so Chrys. (περὶ τῆς
παρουσίας τ. χριστοῦ ἐνταῦθα διαλέγεται
κ. περὶ τῆς ἐπισυναγ. ἡμῶν) al. : see reff.)
**the coming of our Lord Jesus Christ, and
our gathering together** (i. e. the gathering
together of us, announced in 1 Thess.
iv. 17) **to Him** (Lün. condemns *to*, and
would render '*up to*' as 1 Thess. iv. 17 :
but so much does not seem to lie in the
preposition),   2.] **in order that** (aim
of ἐρωτῶμεν) **ye should not be lightly**
(soon and with small reason) **shaken**
(properly of the waves agitated by a storm)
from (see reff.) **your mind** (νοῦς here in

its general sense—your mental apprehension of the subject :—not 'your former
more correct sentiment,' as Est., Corn.-
a-lap., Grot., al.) **nor yet troubled** (reff.),
neither (on μηδέ, which is disjunctive
(δέ), and separates negative from negative,—and **μήτε**, which is adjunctive
(τε), and connects the separate parts of
the same negation, see Winer, Gr. edn.
6, § 55. 6 ; and cf. Luke iv. 3) **by
spirit** (by means of spiritual gift of prophecy or the like, assumed to substantiate
such a view) **nor by word** (*of mouth* :
belongs closely to μήτε δι᾽ ἐπιστ. following,
as is shewn by ver. 15, where they again
appear together) **nor by epistle as by**
(agency of) **us** (pretending to be from us.
Let no pretended saying, no pretended
epistle of mine, shake you in this matter.
That there were such, is shewn by this
parallel position of the clauses with διὰ
πνεύματος, which last agency certainly
was among them. Sayings, and an epistle, to this effect, were ascribed to the
Apostle. So Chrys. : ἐνταῦθα δοκεῖ μοι
αἰνίττεσθαι περϊιέναι τινὰς ἐπιστολὴν
πλάσαντας δῆθεν ἀπὸ τοῦ Παύλου, κ.
ταύτην ἐπιδεικνυμένους λέγειν ὡς ἄρα
ἐφέστηκεν ἡ ἡμέρα τοῦ κυρίου, ἵνα πολλοὺς ἐντεῦθεν πλανήσωσιν.   However
improbable this may seem, our expression
would seem hardly to bear legitimately
any other meaning. Cf. also ch. iii. 17,
and note. It is impossible to understand
the ἐπιστολὴ ὡς δι᾽ ἡμῶν of the first
Epistle, *wrongly understood*, which certainly would have been more plainly expressed, and the Epistle not as here disowned, but explained. Jowett says, " The
most probable hypothesis is, that the Apos-

ὑμᾶς ᶻἐξαπατήσῃ ᵃκατὰ μηδένα ᵃτρόπον· ὅτι ἐὰν μὴ
ἔλθῃ ἡ ᵇἀποστασία πρῶτον καὶ ᶜἀποκαλυφθῇ ὁ ᵈἄν-
θρωπος τῆς ᵈἁμαρτίας, ὁ ᵉυἱὸς τῆς ᵉᶠἀπωλείας, 4 ὁ
ᵍἀντικείμενος καὶ ʰὑπεραιρόμενος ⁱἐπὶ πάντα λεγόμενον

z Rom. vii. 11.
xvi. 18.
1 Cor. iii. 18.
2 Cor. xi. 3.
1 Tim. ii. 14
only. Exod.
viii. 29 B only.
Susan. 56
Theod.
a Acts xv.

11. xxvii. 25. Rom. iii. 2. 2 Macc. xi. 31.
xxix. 19. Jer. ii. 19. (xxxvi. [xxix.] 32 compl.)
d here only.   e John xvii. 12. see Isa. lvii. 4.
h 2 Cor. xii. 7 only. Ps. lxxi. 16.   i = John xiii. 18, from Ps. xl. 9.

b Acts xxi. 21 only.   3 Kings xx. (xxi.) 13 A.   2 Chron.
1 Macc. ii. 15 only.   c vv. 6, 8. see ch. i. 7.
f 1 Tim. vi. 9 reff.   g Gal. v. 17 reff.

3. for αμαρτιας, ανομιας (see vv 7, 8) Bℵ coptt [arm] Orig₂ Cyr-jer Damasc Niceph
Tert (once delinquentiæ, once delicti) Ambrst-ed(iniquitatis) Ambr : txt ADFKL[P]
rel vulg [syrr goth æth] Orig₅ Hip Cyr-jer-ms Chr Thdrt₄ Iren-int.

4. for υπεραιρομ., επαιρομενος F Hip Orig₁ Procop₁(in Niceph): om και υπερ. ℵ¹ :

tle is not referring definitely to any particular speech or epistle, but to the possibility only of some one or other being
used against him." But this seems hardly
definite enough) **to the effect that** ('*as if,*'
or '*as that.*' Lünem. is quite wrong in
saying that ὡς shews that the matter indicated by ὅτι is groundless,—see 2 Cor.
v. 19, and note) **the day of the Lord is
present** (not, '*is at hand :*' ἐνίστημι occurs
six times besides (reff.) in the N. T., and
always in the sense of *being present :* in
two of those places, Rom. viii. 38, 1 Cor.
iii. 22, τὰ ἐνεστῶτα are distinguished expressly from τὰ μέλλοντα. Besides which,
St. Paul could have so written, nor
could the Spirit have so spoken by him.
The teaching of the Apostles was, and of
the Holy Spirit in all ages has been,
that the day of the Lord *is at hand.* But
these Thessalonians imagined it to be already come, and accordingly were deserting
their pursuits in life, and falling into other
irregularities, as if the day of grace were
closed. So Chrys.,—ὁ διάβολος . . . . .
ἐπειδὴ οὐκ ἴσχυσε πεῖσαι ὅτι ψευδῆ τὰ
μέλλοντα, ἑτέραν ἦλθεν ὁδόν, καὶ κατα-
θεὶς ἀνθρώπους τινὰς λυμεῶνας, ἐπεχείρει
τοὺς πειθομένους ἀπατᾶν, ὅτι τὰ μεγάλα
ἐκεῖνα καὶ λαμπρὰ τέλος εἴληφε. τότε
μὲν οὖν ἔλεγον ἐκεῖνοι τὴν ἀνάστασιν ἤδη
γεγονέναι· νῦν δὲ ἔλεγον ὅτι ἐνέστηκεν ἡ
κρίσις καὶ ἡ παρουσία τοῦ χριστοῦ, ἵνα τὸν
χριστὸν αὐτὸν ψεύδει ὑποβάλωσι, καὶ πεί-
σαντες ὡς οὐκ ἔστι λοιπὸν ἀντίδοσις οὐδὲ δικαστήριον καὶ κόλασις καὶ τιμωρία τοῖς κακῶς
πεποιηκόσιν, ἐκείνους τε θρασυτέρους ἐρ-
γάσωνται, καὶ τούτους ταπεινοτέρους. καὶ
τὸ δὴ πάντων χαλεπώτερον, ἐπεχείρουν οἱ
μὲν ἁπλῶς ῥήματα ἀπαγγέλλειν ὡς παρὰ
τοῦ Παύλου ταῦτα λεγόμενα, οἱ δὲ καὶ ἐπι-
στολὰς πράττειν ὡς παρ' ἐκείνου γραφείσας.
Hom. in 2 Thess. i. 1, vol. xi. p. 469).

3.] Let no man deceive you **in
any manner** (not only in either of the foregoing, but in any whatever): for (that day
shall not come) (so E. V. supplies, rightly.
There does not seem to have been any in-

tention on the part of the Apostle to fill
up the ellipsis : it supplies itself in the
reader's mind. Knatchbull connects ὅτι
with ἐξαπατήσῃ, and supplies ἐνέστηκεν
after it : but this is very harsh) **unless
there have come the apostasy first** (of
which he had told them when present, see
ver. 5 : and probably with a further reference still to our Lord's prophecy in Matt.
xxiv. 10—12. There is no need, with
Chrys., Thdrt., Thl., Aug., to suppose
ἀποστασία to mean *Antichrist himself*
(τί ἐστιν ἡ ἀποστασία; αὐτὸν καλεῖ τὸν
ἀντίχριστον ἀποστασίαν, Chr.), nor to regard him as its only cause : rather is he the
chief fruit and topstone of the apostasy),
and there have been revealed (ref. ch. i.
As Christ in his time, so Antichrist in his
time, is '*revealed*'—brought out into
light : he too is a μυστήριον, to be unfolded and displayed : see vv. 8, 9) **the
man of sin** (in whom sin is as it were personified, as righteousness in Christ. The
gen. is called by Ellicott that of the *pre-
dominating quality*), **the son of perdition**
(see ref. John, where our Lord uses the
expression of Judas. It seems merely to
refer to Antichrist himself, whose essence
and inheritance is ἀπώλεια,—not to his
influence over others, as Thdrt. (both :
ὡς κ. αὐτὸν ἀπολλύμενον, κ. ἑτέροις
πρόξενον τούτου γενόμενον), Œc., Pelt,
al.), **he that withstands** (the construction
is not to be carried on by zeugma, as if
ἐπὶ πάντα κ.τ.λ. belonged to ἀντικείμενος as well as to ὑπεραιρόμενος (the
omission of the second article is no proof
of this, as Pelt supposes, but only that
both predicates belong to one and the same
subject), but ἀντικείμενος is absolute, '*he
that withstands* CHRIST,' the ἀντίχριστος,
1 John ii. 18), **and exalts himself above**
(in a hostile sense, reff.) **every one that is
called God** (cf. λεγόμενοι θεοί, 1 Cor. viii. 5.
" The expression includes the *true* God, as
well as the false ones of the heathen—but
λεγόμενον is a natural addition from Christian caution, as πάντα θεόν would have

j Acts xvii. 23
only†. Wisd.
xiv. 20. xv. 17
BℵF(not A)
only. Bel &
Dr. 27 Theod.
k constr., Matt.
ii. 23.
1 Cor. iii. 16,
&c. 2 Cor.
vi. 16 al. Jer.
vii. 4.
m intr., Matt. v. 1.
7. 1 Cor. iv. 9 only†. 1 Macc. x. 34. Xen. Hell. iv. 4. 8.   o w. ὅτι, Acts xx. 31. Eph. ii. 11 only. P. w. ὡς,
2 Macc. x. 6.   p Matt. xiii. 56. Mark vi. 3. ix. 19. Luke ix. 41.   q = 1 Cor.
xvi. 6, 7. Gal. i. 18. iv. 18 al.   r = Rom. i. 18.   s ver. 2.   t ver. 3.
u = Matt. xxvi. 18. Luke i. 20. 1 Tim. vi. 15 al.   v see 1 Tim. iii. 16. Jos. B. J. i. 24. 1, τὸν Ἀντι-
πάτρου βίον οὐκ ἂν ἁμάρτοι τις εἰπὼν κακίας μυστήριον (but see note).

θεὸν ἢ ʲσέβασμα, ὥςτε αὐτὸν ᵏεἰς τὸν ˡναὸν τοῦ θεοῦ ABDFK
ᵐκαθίσαι ⁿἀποδεικνύντα ἑαυτὸν ὅτι ἐστὶν θεός. 5 οὐ
ᵒμνημονεύετε ὅτι ἔτι ᵖ ὢν ᵖᵠ πρὸς ὑμᾶς ταῦτα ἔλεγον ὑμῖν ;
6 καὶ νῦν τὸ ʳκατέχον οἴδατε, ˢεἰς τὸ ᵗἀποκαλυφθῆναι
αὐτὸν ἐν τῷ ἑαυτοῦ ᵘκαιρῷ. 7 τὸ γὰρ ᵛμυστήριον ἤδη

LPℵ a b
c d e f g
h k l m n
o 17. 47

n = Acts ii. 22. xxv.
1 Chron. xxix. 23.

ins ℵ-corr¹ obl.   rec ins ὡς θεον bef καθισαι, with D³[G²]KL rel Syr syr-w-ast Chr
Thdrt₂ : [ινα θεον F :] om ABD¹[P]ℵ 17 vulg coptt [goth] æth arm Orig₃[and int₂]
Hip [Eus₁] Cyr-jer Chr-ms Thdrtₐₗᵢq Damasc Iren-int Tert Cypr Ambrst Aug Ruf.
ἀποδεικνυοντα AF m Orig₁ Cyr-jer Cyr Thdrt₃ Damasc₁ : txt BDKL[P]ℵ rel
Orig₂ Hip [Eus₁] Thdrt₁.
  5. for ων, εμου οντος D¹ Ambrst.
  6. for εαυτ., αυτου AK[P]ℵ¹ c k m 17 Orig₂ Cyr-jer Damasc.
  7. aft ηδη ins γαρ ℵ¹(ℵ³ disapproving) [Orig-int₁(om₂).   aft εως ins αν F.]

been a senseless and indeed blasphemous
expression for a Christian." Lünem.) **or an
object of adoration** (= *numen*, and is a
generalization of θεόν. Cf. the close parallel in Dan. xi. 36, 37 (Theod. and similarly LXX): κ. ὁ βασιλεὺς ὑψωθήσεται
κ. μεγαλυνθήσεται ἐπὶ πάντα θεόν, κ.τ.λ.),
so that he sits (not αὐτὸν . . . . . . καθίσαι, as Grot., Pelt, al., but καθίσαι, intransitive, as in reff.) **in** (*constr. præg-
nans*—'enters into and sits in.' The aor.
usually denotes that one definite act and
not a series of acts is spoken of : but here,
from the peculiar nature of the verb, that
one act is the *setting himself down*, and
the *session* remains after it : cf. Matt. v. 1 ;
xix. 28, &c.) **the temple of God** (this, say
De W. and Lünemann after Irenæus, Hær.
v. 30. 4, p. 330 (cited in Prolegg. § v.
3 note),—cannot be any other than *the
temple at Jerusalem :* on account of the
definiteness of the expression, ὁ ναὸς τοῦ
θεοῦ, and on account of καθίσαι. But
there is no force in this. ὁ ναὸς τοῦ θεοῦ
is used metaphorically by St. Paul in 1 Cor.
iii. 17 bis : and why not here ? see also
1 Cor. vi. 16 ; Eph. ii. 21. From these
✱ passages it is plain that such figurative
sense was familiar to the Apostle. And
if so, καθίσαι makes no difficulty. Its
figurative sense, as holding a place of
power, sitting as judge or ruler, is more
frequent still : see in St. Paul, 1 Cor. vi. 4 :
and Matt. xxiii. 2 : Rev. xx. 4 : to which
indeed we might add the many places
where our Lord is said καθίσαι on the
right hand of God, e. g. Heb. i. 3 ; viii. 1 ;
x. 12 ; xii. 2 ; Rev. iii. 21. Respecting
the *interpretation*, see Prolegomena, § v.)
shewing himself (πειρώμενον ἀποδεικνύναι, Chrys. Hardly that, but the sense of
the *present*, as in ὁ πειράζων—it is his

habit and *office* to exhibit himself as God)
that he is God (not ' *a* god,' nor is it equivalent to ὁ θεός—but designates the divine
dignity which he predicates of himself.
The construction is an attraction, for
ἀποδ. ὅτι αὐτὸς . . . ; and the emphasis is
on ἐστιν, 'that he IS God'). 5.]
conveys a reproach—they would not have
been so lightly moved, if they had remembered this. 6.] **And now** (not *temporal*, but as νυνὶ δέ in 1 Cor. xiii. 13,
'rebus sic stantibus'—'now' in our argument. We must not for a moment
think of the ungrammatical rendering of
Whitby, Masker., Heydenr., Schrader,
Olsh., B.-Crus., and Wieseler, '*that which
at present hinders*,' which must be τὸ
νῦν κατέχον: and for which ver. 7, Rom.
xii. 3, 1 Cor. vii. 17, are no precedent
whatever, not presenting any case of inversion of an adverb from its emphatic
place between an article and a participle. νῦν is a mere adverb of passage, and the stress is on τὸ κατέχον) **ye
know that which hinders** (viz. ' *him* '
—the man of sin : not, *the Apostle from
speaking freely*, as Heinsius,—nor the
coming of Christ) **in order that** (the
aim of κατέχον in God's purposes)—
q. d. ' that which keeps him back, that he
may not be revealed before his,' &c.) **he
may be revealed** (see on ver. 3) **in his own
time** (the time appointed him by God :
reff.). 7.] **For** (explanation of last
verse) **the MYSTERY** (as opposed to the
ἀποκάλυψις of the man of sin) ALREADY
(as opposed to ἐν τῷ ἑαυτοῦ καιρῷ above)
is working (not ' *is being wrought*,' passive,
as Est., Grot., all. I retain the inversion
of the words, to mark better the primary
and secondary emphasis: see below) **of
lawlessness** (i. e. ungodliness—refusal to

ᵂ ἐνεργεῖται τῆς ˣ ἀνομίας, ʸ μόνον ὁ ʳ κατέχων ἄρτι ἕως
ᶻ ἐκ μέσου γένηται, 8 καὶ τότε ᵗ ἀποκαλυφθήσεται ὁ
ᵃ ἄνομος, ὃν ὁ κύριος Ἰησοῦς * ᵇ ἀνελεῖ τῷ ᶜ πνεύματι
τοῦ ᶜ στόματος αὐτοῦ καὶ ᵈ καταργήσει τῇ ᵉ ἐπιφανείᾳ τῆς
ᶠ παρουσίας αὐτοῦ, 9 οὗ ἐστιν ἡ ᶠ παρουσία ᵍ κατ᾽ ᵍʰ ἐνέργειαν τοῦ σατανᾶ ⁱ ἐν πάσῃ ⁱ δυνάμει καὶ ʲ σημείοις καὶ

w absol., Gal.
v. 6 (reff.).
x Matt. vii. 23.
xiii. 41.
Rom. iv. 7 al.
Exod. xxxiv.
9.
y so Gal. ii. 10
(also arrangt.
of words).
z Col. ii. 14
reff.
a Luke xxii.
37 al. L.P.,
exc. 2 Pet. ii.

8. Ezek. xxi. 3 al. fr.   b Paul, Acts xiii. 28. xxii. 20. xxvi. 10 only. Luke xxii. 2 al. Isa.
xi. 4. ἀναλίσκειν, Luke ix. 54. Gal. v. 15 only. Joel ii. 3.   c Ps. xxxii. 6. Isa. l. c.
d Gal. iii. 17 reff. = 1 Cor. xv. 24. 2 Tim. i. 10. Heb. ii. 14.   e 1 Tim. vi. 14. 2 Tim. i. 10. iv. 1,
8. Tit. ii. 13 only. P. 2 Kings vii. 23.   f ver. 1.   g = Col. i. 29. Eph. iii. 7. iv. 16.
h Eph. i. 19 reff.   i Col. i. 29 reff.   j Matt. xxiv. 24 ‖ Mk. John iv. 48. Acts vii. 36
al8. Rom. xv. 19. 2 Cor. xii. 12. Heb. ii. 4 only. Exod. xi. 10.

8. rec om ιησους, with BD³KL¹ rel Orig₁ Mac Cyr-jer Thdrt₁ Damasc_{h.l.} Œc Vig:
ins AD¹FL²[P]א 17 [47] latt syrr coptt [æth] arm Orig₂[and int₁] Hip Constt Ath Bas
Cyr-jer-ms Ephr Chr Thdrt_{sæpe} Damasc Thl Iren-int₁ Tert Jer Fulg Hil Ambr Ambrst
Aug Ruf Primas Pel.   *rec ἀναλώσει, with D³KL rel Orig₁ Mac Cyr-jer Thdrt₁
Damasc₁ Œc Vig: αναλοι א¹ [Orig₃]: ανελοι D¹(appy) Fא³ 17. 67² (Orig₂): ανελει
AB[P] Orig₁ Hip Mac Cyr-jer Ath.   την επιφανειαν D¹ f Cyr-jer-edd.

recognize God's law—see reff. The
genitive is one of apposition : the ἀνομία is
that wherein the μυστήριον consists :—not
a genitive of the working cause, as Thdrt.
(ὡς κεκρυμμένην ἔχοντας τῆς ἀνομίας
τὴν πάγην),—nor must we understand by
the words, Antichrist himself, as Olsh.,
comparing τὸ τῆς εὐσεβείας μυστήριον,
1 Tim. iii. 16,—nor *the unexampled depths
of ungodliness*, as Krebs, al., from Joseph.
B. J. in reff. As to the order of the
words, cf. Arrian, exp. Alex. i. 17. 6, κ.
εὑρέσθαι συγγνώμην τῷ πλήθει τῶν
Θηβαίων τῆς ἀποστάσεως, Lün.) only until
he that now hinders (ὁ κατέχων is placed
before ἕως for emphasis, as in ref. Gal.,
μόνον τῶν πτωχῶν ἵνα μνημονεύωμεν)
be removed (the phrase is used of any
person or thing which is taken out of the
way, whether by death or other removal.
So in reff.: and Plut. Timol. p. 238. 3
(Wetst.). ἔγνω ζῆν καθ᾽ ἑαυτὸν ἐκ μέσου
γενόμενος,—Ter. Phorm. v. 9. 40, 'ea
mortem obiit, e medio abiit.' See also
Herod. viii. 22: and for the opposite, ἐν
μέσῳ εἶναι, Xen. Cyr. v. 2. 26. Various
erroneous arrangements and renderings of
this sentence have been current : of which
the principal have arisen from fancying
that the participle κατέχων requires some
verb to be supplied after it. So Vulg.
('tantum ut qui tenet nunc, teneat, donec
de medio fiat :' so Syr., Erasm., Est., all.),
and E. V. ('only he who now letteth, will
let,' so Beza, Whitby, al.),—κατέχει (so
Bengel, Pelt, al.) :—ἐστίν (so Knatchb.,
Burton, al.)):   **8.**] **and then** (when
he that hinders shall have been removed:
the emphasis is on τότε) **shall be revealed
the lawless one** (the same as the αὐτόν of
ver. 6 : viz. the ἄνθρωπος τῆς ἁμαρτίας),
whom (by this relative clause is introduced

his ultimate fate at the coming of the Lord.
To this the Apostle is carried on by the
fervency of his spirit, and has to return
again below to describe the working of
Antichrist previously) **the Lord Jesus will
destroy by the breath of His mouth**
(from Isa. xi. 4,—πατάξει γῆν τῷ λόγῳ
τοῦ στόματος αὐτοῦ, κ. ἐν πνεύματι διὰ
χειλέων ἀνελεῖ ἀσεβῆ. It is better to
keep the expression in its simple majesty,
than to interpret it, as Thdrt.,—φθέγξε-
ται μόνον, κ. παυωλεθρίᾳ παραδώσει τὸν
ἀλιτήριον. — Thdr-mops, — μόνον ἐπιβοή-
σας. Chrys. on this is fine : καθάπερ γὰρ
πῦρ ἐπελθὸν ἁπλῶς τὰ μικρὰ ζωΰφια καὶ
πρὸ τῆς παρουσίας αὐτῆς πόῤῥωθεν ὄντα
ναρκᾶν ποιεῖ κ. ἀναλίσκει· οὕτω καὶ ὁ
χριστὸς τῷ ἐπιτάγματι μόνον (but see
above) κ. τῇ παρουσίᾳ τὸν ἀντίχριστον
ἀναλώσει. ἀρκεῖ παρεῖναι αὐτόν, καὶ ταῦτα
πάντα ἀπόλωλε) **and annihilate** (not, as
Olsh., '*deprive of his influence*,' nor can
Rev. xix. 19 be brought to bear here)
by the appearance of His coming (not
'the *brightness* of his coming,' as very
many Commentators, and E. V.; but as
Beng.: 'apparitio adventus ipso adventu
prior est, vel certe prima ipsius adventus
emicatio, uti ἐπιφάνεια τῆς ἡμέρας:' the
mere outburst of His presence shall bring
the adversary to nought. Cf. the sublime
expression of Milton,—' far off His coming
shone'):   **9, 10.**] **whose** (refers back
to the ὅν above—going back in time, to
describe the character of his agency)
coming is (the present is not used for the
future, nor is the Apostle setting himself
at the time prophesied of,—but it describes
the essential attribute, as so often) **according to** (such as might be expected from,—
correspondent to) **the working of Satan**
(Satan being the agent who works in the

k ver. 11.
constr., see
Luke xviii.
8, 9. Rom.
vi. 6. vii. 24
al. Ps. cxliii.
8, 11.
1 Eph. iv. 22
reff.
m — Matt.
xviii. 14.
Rom. ii. 12.
1 Cor. i. 18.
2 Cor. ii. 15.
iv. 3. Lev.
xxiii. 30.
o Luke i. 20.
xii. 3. xix.
41. Acts
xii. 23 only.
Gen. xxii. 18.
p = 1 Cor. ii.

^jτέρασιν ^kψεύδους ¹⁰καὶ ἐν πάσῃ ^lἀπάτῃ ^kἀδικίας τοῖς ^mἀπολλυμένοις, ^oἀνθ᾿ ^oὧν τὴν ἀγάπην τῆς ἀληθείας οὐκ ^pἐδέξαντο ^qεἰς τὸ σωθῆναι αὐτούς. ¹¹καὶ διὰ τοῦτο πέμπει αὐτοῖς ὁ θεὸς ^hἐνέργειαν ^rπλάνης, ^qεἰς τὸ πιστεῦ-σαι αὐτοὺς ^sτῷ ψεύδει, ¹²ἵνα ^tκριθῶσιν ἅπαντες οἱ ^uμὴ ^uπιστεύσαντες ^vτῇ ἀληθείᾳ, ἀλλ᾿ ^wεὐδοκήσαντες [ἐν] τῇ ἀδικίᾳ.

¹³Ἡμεῖς δὲ ^xὀφείλομεν ^xεὐχαριστεῖν τῷ θεῷ πάντοτε περὶ ὑμῶν, ἀδελφοὶ ^yἠγαπημένοι ὑπὸ κυρίου, ὅτι ^zεἵλατο

ABDFK
LPℵ a b
c d e f g
h k l m n
o 17.47

14. James i. 21.   Jer. v. 3.   q ver. 2.   r Matt. xxvii. 64.   1 Thess. ii. 3.   1 John iv. 6.   Prov. xiv. 8.
s Rom. i. 25.   t = Matt. vii. 1.   John iii. 17, 18.   James v. 9 al. fr.   u Jude 5.   v = Rom.
ii. 18.   1 Cor. xiii. 6.   Col. ii. 5.   2 Tim. iii. 8.   w w. ἐν, Matt. iii. 17 ‖ Mk. L.   1 Cor. x. 5.   2 Cor. xii.
10.   1 Chron. xxix. 3.   dat. without ἐν, 1 Macc. i. 43.   x ch. i. 3.   y 1 Thess. i. 4.   Deut. xxxiii.
12.   z = Phil. i. 22.   Heb. xi. 25 only.   Deut. xxvi. 18. (see Deut. vii. 6, 7. x. 15.)

10. rec ins της bef αδικ., with DKL[P]ℵ³ rel Hip Chr Thdrt : om ABFℵ¹ 17 Orig₇ Cyr-jer (prob the τη of απατη gave occasion for the insn). rec ins εν bef τοις απολλυμενοις, with D³KL[P]ℵ³ rel syrr Orig₁ : om ADD¹Fℵ¹ 17 latt coptt æth [arm] Orig₅ Cyr-jer Damasc₁ Iren-int Tert Ambrst Aug. aft αληθειας ins χριστου D¹. εξεδεξαντο F. (εδεξ. to σωθηναι, exc 1st ε and ηναι, rewritten by a recent hand in A.)

11. om και D¹ 67² vulg Syr copt æth Chr Cyr-ms Œc Pel. rec πεμψει (see notes), with D³KL[P]ℵ³ rel D-lat(and G-lat) vulg-ed(and F-lat) syrr copt Hip (Orig₂ ?) Thdor-mops Cyr₂ Iren-int Cypr : txt ABD¹Fℵ¹ 67² am(with fuld) Orig₂ Bas Cyr-jer Damasc₁ Iren-int-mss. om αυτους F.

12. (απαντες, so AFℵ 17 Orig₂ Cyr.) αλλα [B]ℵ [Orig₁]. om εν (prob to balance the two members of the sentence) BD¹Fℵ¹ d h m 17 latt sah Orig₂[and int₁] Hip Cyr Cyr-jer Iren-int_{aliq} Tert : ins AD³KL[P]ℵ³ rel syrr copt Orig₂ Chr Thdrt₁ Damasc₁ Cypr Jer.

13. for κυριου, θεου D¹ vulg lat-ff₅ : ins του bef κυριου Aℵ [m] : απο κω F. (ειλατο, so ABDFL[P]ℵ (m ?) 17 [47¹] Thdrt-ms.)

ἄνομος) in (manifested in, consisting in) all (kinds of) **power and signs and won-ders of falsehood** (**πάσῃ** and **ψεύδους** both belong to all three substantives : the varie-ties of his manifested power, and signs and wonders, all have falsehood for their base, and essence, and aim. Cf. John viii. 44), **and in all** (manner of) **deceit** (not, as E. V. 'deceivableness,' for it is the agency of the man of sin—active deceit, of which the word is used) **of unrighteousness** (belonging to, consisting in, leading to, ἀδικία) for (the dativus incommodi) those who are perishing (on their way to per-dition), (WHY? not by God's absolute decree, but) because (in requital for this, that) **they did not** (when it was offered to them) **receive the love of the truth** (the opposite of the ψεῦδος which characterizes all the working of the man of sin : see as before, John viii. 44) **in order to their being saved. 11.] And on this account** (because they did not receive, &c.) **God is sending to them** (not, as E.V., following rec., 'shall send :' the verb is present, because the mystery of iniquity is already working. **✶ πέμπει** must not for a moment be under-stood of permissiveness only on God's part

—He is the judicial sender and doer—it is He who hardens the heart which has chosen the evil way. All such distinctions are the merest folly : whatever God per-mits, He ordains) **the working of error** (is causing these seducing influences to work among them. The E. V. has weakened, indeed almost stultified the sentence, by rendering ἐνέργ. πλάνης 'a strong delu-sion,' i. e. the passive state resulting, in-stead of the active cause), **in order that they should believe the falsehood** (which the mystery of sin is working among them. It is better here to take τῷ definite, refer-ring to what has gone before, than ab-stract),—**that** (the higher or ultimate pur-pose of God) **all might be judged** (i. e. here 'condemned,' by the context) **who did not** (looking back over their time of proba-tion) **believe the truth, but found plea-sure in iniquity.** I have above given the rendering of this important passage. For the history and criticism of its inter-pretation, see the Prolegomena, § v.

13—III. 15.] HORTATORY PORTION OF THE EPISTLE. **13—17.]** Exhortation, grounded on thankfulness to God for their election by Him, to stand fast in the faith;

ὑμᾶς ὁ θεὸς ᵃἀπ᾽ ἀρχῆς εἰς σωτηρίαν ᵇἐν ᵇᶜἁγιασμῷ   a = 1 John
ᵇπνεύματος καὶ πίστει ἀληθείας, ¹⁴ εἰς ὃ ᵈἐκάλεσεν ὑμᾶς   ii. 13. iii. 8.
διὰ τοῦ ᵉεὐαγγελίου ἡμῶν, εἰς ᶠπεριποίησιν ᵍδόξης τοῦ   b 1 Pet. i. 2.
κυρίου ἡμῶν Ἰησοῦ χριστοῦ. ¹⁵ ʰ ἄρα ʰ οὖν, ἀδελφοί,   c 1 Thess. iv.
ⁱστήκετε, καὶ ʲᵏκρατεῖτε τὰς ʲˡπαραδόσεις ᵐἃς ἐδιδάχθητε   3, 4, 7 reff.
εἴτε ⁿδιὰ λόγου εἴτε ⁿδι᾽ ἐπιστολῆς ἡμῶν. ¹⁶ ᵒ αὐτὸς δὲ

a = 1 John ii. 13. iii. 8.
b 1 Pet. i. 2.
c 1 Thess. iv. 3, 4, 7 reff.
d = Rom. viii. 30. Gal. i. 6.
e 2 Cor. iv. 3. 1 Thess. i. 5.
see Rom. ii. 16. xv. 25.
2 Tim. ii. 8.
f = 1 Thess. v. 9. (Eph.

i. 14 reff.)   g = John xvii. 22. Rom. v. 2.   h Rom. v. 18. vii. 3, 25 al⁸. Paul only.
i Gal. v. 1 reff.   j Mark vii. 3, 8.   k = Col. ii. 19. Rev. ii. 13, 14, 15, 25 ‡.
l = Gal. i. 14 reff.   m constr., Mark x. 38. Luke xii. 47. Rev. xvi. 9. Winer, edn. 6, ? 32. 5.
n ver. 2.   o = 1 Thess. iii. 11 reff.

ημας Dᵏᵃ⁸¹ 1 am(with fuld hal F-lat) [arm].   for απ αρχης, απαρχην BF[P 17. 47]
vulg syr Cyr Damasc-comm Did Ambr Pel : txt ADKLℵ rel [copt æth arm] gr-lat-ff.
14. aft εις ο ins και F[P]ℵ m [47] vulg syr arm Ambrst.   for υμας, ημας ABDˡ
Vig.   for [1st] ημων, υμων ℵ¹(txt ℵ-corr¹·³) [om 17].
15. aft παραδοσεις ins ημων Dˡ Ambrst [υμων 17 æth]ₑ

*and prayer that God would enable them to
do so.* **13.**] δέ contrasts Paul, Silvanus,
and Timotheus, with those of whom he has
been recently speaking. **ὀφείλομεν**]
q. d. **find it our duty**: subjective : **are
bound**, as E. V. **ἠγ. ὑπὸ κυρ.**] Lünemann remarks, that as τῷ θεῷ has preceded, and ὁ θεὸς follows, **κύριος** here must
be the Lord Jesus : cf. Rom. viii. 37 : Gal.
ii. 20 : Eph. v. 2, 25. Otherwise, the expression is perhaps more normally used of
the Father, ver. 16 : Eph. ii. 4 : Col. iii.
12 : John iii. 16, al. freq. **ὅτι**] may
enounce either (as Ellicott) the *matter
and grounds* of the thanksgiving, *that
God . . .* , or the *reason* of it, *because
God. . . .* St. Paul does not elsewhere
use **αἱρέομαι** of divine election, but **ἐκλέ-
γομαι** (1 Cor. i. 27, 28. Eph. i. 4) or
προορίζω (Rom. viii. 29. Eph. i. 11). It
is a LXX expression : see reff. **ἀπ᾽
ἀρχῆς** must be taken in the general sense,
as in reff. : not in the special, 'from the
beginning of the gospel,' as Phil. iv. 15.
It answers to πρὸ τῶν αἰώνων 1 Cor. ii. 7,
πρὸ καταβολῆς κόσμου Eph. i. 4, πρὸ
χρόνων αἰωνίων 2 Tim. i. 9, all of which
are spoken of the decrees of God.
εἰς σωτηρίαν] in contrast to the ἀπώλεια
lately spoken of. **ἐν ἁγ. πν. κ. π.
ἀλ.**] the elements in which the εἵλατο εἰς
σωτ. takes place : not, as De W., the aim
(ἐν for εἰς) of the εἵλατο. **πνεύματος**
is the Holy Spirit—**the sanctification of**
(wrought by) **the Spirit**: not, 'sanctification of (your) spirit.' This is the divine
side of the element : the human side follows, the πίστις ἀληθείας, 'your own reception, by faith, of the truth.' **14.**
εἰς ὅ] **to which** (i. e. the being saved in
sanctification of the Spirit and belief of
the truth) **He** (God) **called you through
our Gospel** (our preaching of the Gospel
to you), **in order to** (your) **acquisition**

(see on 1 Thess. v. 9) **of the glory of our
Lord Jesus Christ** (i. e. your sharing in
the glory which He *has ;* see ref. John :
Rom. viii. 17, 29 : not the glory of which
He is the bestower or source, as Pelt., al.
Equally wrong is the interpretation of
Œc., Thl., Corn.-a-lap., al.—ἵνα δόξαν
περιποιήσῃ τῷ υἱῷ αὐτοῦ : of Luther, al.,
"zum herrlichen Eigenthum," 'ut essetis
gloriosa possessio domini nostri J. C. :' for,
not to mention other objections, the whole
context has for its purpose *the lot of the
Thessalonians* as contrasted with that of
those spoken of, vv. 10—12 ;—and the
sense of περιποίησις is indicated by the
parallel 1 Thess. v. 9). **15.**] **Therefore**—seeing that such is God's intent respecting you. Prof. Jowett here describes
the Apostle as being " unconscious of the
logical inconsistency " of appealing to
them to do any thing, after he has just
stated their election of God. Rather we
should say, that he was deeply conscious,
as ever, of the logical necessity of the only
practical inference which man can draw
from God's gracious purposes to him. No
human reasoning powers can connect the
two,—God's sovereignty and man's free-
will : all we know of them is, that the
one is as certain a truth as the other.
In proportion then as we assert the one
strongly, we must ever implicate the other
as strongly : a course which the great
Apostle never fails to pursue : cf. Phil. ii.
12, 13, al. freq. **στήκ.** is a contrast
to σαλευθῆναι, ver. 2. On the sense of
παραδόσεις, as relating to matters of *doctrine*, see Ellic.'s note, and the reff. given
by him. **ἃς** is the accusative of
second reference. **ἐπιστ. ἡμῶν**, as
contrasted with the ἐπιστ. ὡς δι᾽ ἡμῶν
of ver. 2, refers to 1 Thess. **16, 17.**]
αὐτός, as a majestic introduction, in contrast with ἡμῶν, see 1 Thess. iii. 11, and

p Gal. i. 1 reff.
q Eph. ii. 4.
1 John iv. 10,
11. elsw. of
Christ, see
Rom. viii. 37.
Gal. ii. 20.
r = Luke ii. 25.
Rom. xv. 4,
5. 2 Cor. i.
3, &c. (Heb.
vi. 18) al.
L.P.H. Ps.
xciii. 19.
s = Gal. i. 6.
t = Col. ii. 2
reff.

ὁ κύριος ἡμῶν Ἰησοῦς χριστὸς καὶ ὁ [p] θεὸς ὁ [p] πατὴρ
ἡμῶν, ὁ [q] ἀγαπήσας ἡμᾶς καὶ δοὺς [r] παράκλησιν αἰωνίαν
καὶ ἐλπίδα ἀγαθὴν [s] ἐν χάριτι, 17 [t] παρακαλέσαι ὑμῶν τὰς
καρδίας καὶ [u] στηρίξαι ἐν παντὶ [v] ἔργῳ καὶ λόγῳ [v] ἀγαθῷ.

III. [1 w] Τὸ λοιπὸν [x] προσεύχεσθε, ἀδελφοί, [y] περὶ ἡμῶν,
[x] ἵνα ὁ [z] λόγος τοῦ [z] κυρίου [a] τρέχῃ καὶ [b] δοξάζηται καθὼς
καὶ [c] πρὸς ὑμᾶς, [2] καὶ ἵνα [d] ῥυσθῶμεν ἀπὸ τῶν [e] ἀτόπων

ABDFK
LP‭א‬ a b
c d e f g
h k l m n
o 17.47

u = Luke xxii. 32. Rom. i. 11. xvi. 25 al. Ps. l. 12 (14).
x 1 Cor. xiv. 13. Phil. i. 9. Col. i. 9. iv. 3. ch. i. 11.
a = here only. (Gal. ii. 2 reff.) see Ps. cxlvii. 15 (4).
c see 1 Thess. iii. 4 reff.
only. Job iv. 8.

v Eph. ii. 10 reff.
y ch. i. 3 al. fr.
b Rom. xi. 13. see ch. i. 12. Acts xiii. 48.
d 1 Thess. i. 10 reff.

w Eph. vi. 10 reff.
z 1 Thess. i. 8 reff.
e Luke xxiii. 41. Acts xxv. 5. xxviii. 6

16. χρ. ιησ. B : ιησ. ο χρ. A [47].
(appy). om ο (bef θεος) BD¹K 17 [m¹ ?].
AD³(and lat) KL[P] rel vulg(with am &c) syr goth Chr Thdrt Ambr Ambrst : om ο
‭א‬³ : txt BD¹F‭א‬¹ 17 Syr Ambrst Vig.
αιωνιον F.

the 1st και is written above the line by ‭א‬¹
rec (for ο, bef πατηρ) και, with
om ο αγαπ. ημας ‭א‬¹(ins ‭א‬-corr¹).

17. τας καρδιας bef υμων A‭א‬ vss.
copt [æth] Thdrt : om ABD¹F[P]‭א‬ m 17 [47] latt syrr [goth] arm Chr Œc Ambrst.
rec λογω και εργω, with FK [Syr arm] rel : om και λογω 17 : om εργω και d :
txt ABDL[P]‭א‬ c m [47] latt [syr] copt æth Chr Thl Thdrt Œc Ambrst Vig.

rec aft στηριξαι ins υμας, with D³KL rel

CHAP. III. 1. om το F.
goth.
αδελφοι bef προσευχεσθε F f o : π. ημ. bef αδελφ. D 73
for κυριου, θεου F[P] k 17 [vulg(not fuld tol)].

as *ensuring* the efficacy of the wish—q. d.
'and then you are safe.' Our Lord Jesus
Christ is placed first, not merely because
He is the mediator between men and God
(Lün.), but because the sentence is a
climax. **ὁ ἀγ. ἡμ. κ.τ.λ.** probably
refers to ὁ θεὸς κ. ὁ πατ. ἡμ. alone : and
yet when we consider how impossible it
would have been for the Apostle to have
written οἱ ἀγαπήσαντες, and that the
singular verb following undoubtedly refers
to both, I would not too hastily pronounce
this. See note on 1 Thess. iii. 11.
ἀγαπήσας—who loved us—refers to a
single fact—the love of the Father in
sending His Son—or the love of the Father
and Son in our accomplished Redemption.
κ. δούς—and gave—by that act of
Love. **παράκλ. αἰων.**] consolation,
under all trials, and that eternal,—not
transitory, as this world's consolations :
sufficient in life, and in death, and for
ever : cf. Rom. viii. 38 f. This for all time
present : and then **ἐλπ. ἀγ.** for the future.

ἐν χάριτι belongs, not to **ἐλπ. ἀγ.**,
but to **δούς**, and is the medium through,
or element in which, the gift is made.
Better thus than to refer it to both the
participles **ἀγαπ. κ. δούς** ; for ὁ ἀγα-
πήσας as applied to God (or the Lord
Jesus) usually stands absolute, cf. Rom.
viii. 37 ; Gal. ii. 20 ; Eph. v. 2.
παρακαλέσαι] as in 1 Thess. iii. 11,
3 pers. sing. opt. aor. comfort, with reference to your disquiet respecting the

παρουσία. After στηρ. understand ὑμᾶς,
which has been supplied—see var. readd.,
—better than τὰς καρδ. ὑμῶν, which are
not the agents in ἔργον and λόγος. This
latter is not '*doctrine*,' as Chrys., Calv.
('tam in piæ et sanctæ vitæ cursu, quam
in sana doctrina'),—for ἔργον (**work**) and
λόγος (**word**), seeing that παντί applies
to both, must be correlative, and both
apply to matters in which the man is an
agent. Still less must we understand ἐν
as = διά (Chrys., Thl. 2, Beng., al.) : the
sphere, and not the instruments, of the
consolation and confirmation, is spoken of.

CH. III. 1—5.] *Exhortation to pray
for him and his colleagues* (1, 2). *His
confidence that the Lord will keep them*
(3)—*and that they will obey his commands*
(4). *Prayer for them* (5). **1.**] On
τὸ λ. (= λοιπόν), see 1 Thess. iv. 1.
ἵνα] On the use of telic conjunctions with
verbs like προσεύχομαι, see note on 1 Cor.
xiv. 13. **ὁ λ. τ. κυρ.**] the Lord's word
—i. e. the Gospel : see reff. **τρέχῃ**]
Contrast to '*being bound :*' see 2 Tim. ii.
9—may spread rapidly. **δοξ.**] See reff.
The word of the Lord is then glorified,
when it becomes the power of God to
salvation to the believer—see Rom. i. 16.
καθὼς καὶ πρὸς ὑμᾶς] for they
had thus received it : 1 Thess. i. 6.
πρὸς ὑμᾶς] among you (reff.). **2.**]
And in order for that to be the case,
that we may be free to preach it. On
ἄτοπος, Lünem. says, "it is properly used

καὶ πονηρῶν ἀνθρώπων. οὐ γὰρ ᶠπάντων ἡ πίστις.
³ ᵍπιστὸς δέ ἐστιν ὁ κύριος, ὃς ʰστηρίξει ὑμᾶς καὶ ⁱφυ-
λάξει ἀπὸ τοῦ πονηροῦ.   ⁴ ᵏπεποίθαμεν δὲ ἐν κυρίῳ ᵏἐφ'
ὑμᾶς, ὅτι ἃ ˡπαραγγέλλομεν καὶ ποιεῖτε καὶ ποιήσετε.
⁵ ὁ δὲ κύριος ᵐκατευθύναι ὑμῶν τὰς καρδίας εἰς τὴν
ⁿἀγάπην τοῦ ⁿθεοῦ καὶ εἰς τὴν ᵒὑπομονὴν ᵖτοῦ χριστοῦ.

marginal refs: f gen., Acts i. 7. see Matt. — g xx. 23. = 1 Thess. v. 24 reff. — h = ch. ii. 17 reff. — i w. ἀπὸ, Luke xii. 15. 1 John v. 21 only. Ezek. xxxiii. 8. — k = 2 Cor. ii.

3. (Matt. xvii. 43.) see Gal. v. 10.   iii. 11 only. Prov. xxi. 2.   o Rom. ii. 7.   Rev. i. 9. iii. 10 al. fr.   1 1 Thess. iv. 11 reff.   n Luke xi. 42. John v. 42. 1 John ii. 5, 15. iii. 17. iv. 12. v. 3.   p gen., as 2 Cor. i. 5. Col. i. 24. Heb. xi. 26.   m Luke i. 79. 1 Thess. Sir. xii. 11. k = 2 Cor. ii.

3. om εστιν F [fuld], but insd bef η πιστις ver 2 in F vulg D-lat.   for κυριος, θεος (corrn, see 1 Cor i. 9, 10, 13.   2 Cor i. 13) AD¹F latt(not am demid) arm-marg Ambrst: txt BD³KL[P]א rel syrr [copt(sic, Treg) goth] Cyr Jer.—ο κυριος bef εστιν א¹.   aft ος ins και A 37 syr-w-ast [arm] Vocat: pref m.   στηρισει B: τηρησει F.
4. rec aft παραγγελλομεν ins υμιν (corrn, see ver 6), with AD³FKL[P] rel demid [vss]: om BD¹א 17. 67² vulg(with am fuld) Chr₂-comm Ambrst Pel Bede.   aft παραγγ. ins και εποιησατε BF [copt].   om και (bef ποιειτε) AD¹א¹.   for ποιησετε, ποιησατε D¹: ποιησητε 17: om και ποιησετε F.
5. τας καρδιας bef υμων D vss.   rec om 2nd την: ins ABDFKL[P]א rel.

of that which is not in its right place. When of *persons*, it designates one who does or says that which is inappropriate under the circumstances. Thus it answers to *ineptus* in Latin (Cic. de Orat. ii. 4). From 'aptitude,' it passes to its wider ethical meaning, and is used of men who act contrary to divine or human laws. Thus it gets the general signification of **bad or ungodly.** See examples in Kypke, Obss. ii. p. 145,—in Lösner and Wetst." Who are these men? It is obvious that the key to the answer will be found in Acts xviii. They were the Jews at Corinth, who were at that time the especial adversaries of the Apostle and his preaching. And this is confirmed by the clause which he has added to account for their ἀτοπία and πονηρία: οὐ γὰρ πάντων ἡ πίστις—for to all men the (Christian) faith does not belong—all men do not receive it—have no receptivity for it —obviously pointing at Jews by this description. It is more natural to understand the article here as definite, **the faith,** than as abstract: for faith, as such, would not bear much meaning here.
3.] Calvin says, "Ceterum de aliis magis quam de se anxium fuisse Paulum, ostendunt hæc ipsa verba. In eum maligni homines improbitatis suæ aculeos dirigebant, in eum totus impetus irruebat: curam interea suam ad Thessalonicenses convertit, nequid hæc illis tentatio noceat." πιστός seems to be chosen in allusion to πίστις which has just preceded; but the allusion cannot be more than that of sound, as the things spoken of are wholly different.   ὁ κύριος is **our Lord**: see ch. ii. 16, and ver. 5.

δέ, in contrast with the men just mentioned.   στηρίξει] in reference to his wish, ch. ii. 17.   τοῦ πονηροῦ may mean 'the evil one,' as in Matt. xiii. 19: Eph. vi. 16, al.: and so Ellic. But here the assurance seems, as before said, to correspond to the wish ch. ii. 17: and thus στηρίξαι ἐν παντὶ ἔργῳ κ. λόγῳ ἀγαθῷ = στηρίξει κ. φυλάξει ἀπὸ τοῦ πονηροῦ: in which case τ. πον. is *neuter.* We may observe that the words are nearly a citation from the Lord's prayer.
4.] forms a transition to the exhortations which are to follow, vv. 6 ff.
ἐν κυρίῳ, as the element in which his confidence is exercised, shews it to be one assuming that they will act consistently with their Christian profession: and so gives the expectation the force of an exhortation, but at the same time of a hopeful exhortation.   ἐφ' ὑμᾶς (reff.), **with reference to you**—the *direction* of his confidence.   καὶ ποιεῖτε κ. ποιήσετε is all the apodosis—not ὅτι ἃ παραγγ. κ. ποιεῖτε, καὶ ποιήσετε, as Erasm.
5.] There does not appear to be any distrust of the Thessalonians implied by this repeated wish for them, as De W. supposes. Rather is it an *enlargement*, taken up by the δέ (not only so, but) *of the ἃ παραγγέλλομεν κ. ποιεῖτε κ. ποιήσετε.*   ὁ κύρ. is **our Lord,** as before.   ἡ ἀγάπη τ. θεοῦ here, from the fact of his wishing that their hearts may be *directed into it,* must be subjective, *the love of man to God.* The objective meaning, *God's love,* is out of the question. The other subjective meanings, *the love which God works* (Pelt), ... *which God commands* (Le Clerc), are far-fetched.   ἡ ὑπομονὴ τ.

q Acts iii. 6.
1 Cor. v. 1.
vi. 11.
r 2 Cor. viii. 20
only. Mal. ii.
5. (ὑποστ.,
Gal. ii. 12.
Heb. x. 38.)
s ver. 11 only †.
(-ος, 1 Thess.
v. 14.)
t w. adv.,
1 Thess. iv.
12 al. fr.
u ch. ii. 15 reff.
v 1 Cor. xi. 23.
xv. 1, 3.
Gal. i. 9, 12 al.

ABDFK
LPℵ a b
c d e f g
h k l m n
o 17. 47

6 [q] Παραγγέλλομεν δὲ ὑμῖν, ἀδελφοί, [q] ἐν ὀνόματι τοῦ κυρίου Ἰησοῦ χριστοῦ, [r] στέλλεσθαι ὑμᾶς ἀπὸ παντὸς ἀδελφοῦ [s] ἀτάκτως [t] περιπατοῦντος καὶ μὴ κατὰ τὴν [u] παράδοσιν ἣν [v] παρελάβοσαν παρ' ἡμῶν. 7 αὐτοὶ γὰρ οἴδατε πῶς δεῖ [w] μιμεῖσθαι ἡμᾶς, ὅτι οὐκ [x] ἠτακτήσαμεν ἐν ὑμῖν, 8 οὐδὲ [y] δωρεὰν [z] ἄρτον [z] ἐφάγομεν [a] παρά τινος, ἀλλ' ἐν [b] κόπῳ καὶ [b] μόχθῳ [c] νύκτα καὶ [c] ἡμέραν [d] ἐργα-

w here bis. Heb. xiii. 7.   3 John 11 only †.   Wisd. iv. 2 Bℵ. xv. 9 only.   x here
only †.   Xen. Cyr. vii. 2. 6. see above (s).   y = Matt. x. 8.   Rom. iii. 24 al.   Isa. lii. 3.   z = ver.
12.   Mark iii. 20.   Luke vii. 33. xiv. 1, 15 al.   Gen. iii. 19.   a = Acts xxvi. 12 al. fr.   b 1 Thess.
ii. 9 reff.   c Acts xx. 31. xxvi. 7.   Paul only, exc. Mark iv. 27.   Esth. iv. 16. elsw. gen., as Mark v. 5. so
Paul, ch. ii. 9.

6. rec aft κυριου ins ημων, with AD³FKL[P]ℵ rel : om BD¹ Cypr¹(elsw₁ om κυρ.). rec παρελαβε (*corn of plur.* *The less usual form in txt is the preferable one*), with Syr : παρελαβετε BF syr goth [arm Orig] Anton Thdrt₁ Ambrst Sing-cler : παρελαβον D³KL[P]ℵ rel gr-ff (most vss and lat-ff have the plur, but which form, is of course uncert) : txt Aℵ¹ 17 Bas, ελαβοσαν D¹.   for παρ', αφ' B.

[**7.** for εν, παρ P : om 17.]

8. ουτε F.   αλλα ℵ.   νυκτος κ. ημερας BFℵ 17 [47] Chr-ms Damasc₁ : txt ADKL[P] rel.

χριστοῦ has very generally been understood as in E. V., '*the patient waiting for Christ.*' So Œc., Ambr., Erasm., Corn.-a-lap., Beza, all. But ὑπομονή will not bear this meaning. It occurs thirty-four times in the N. T., and always in the sense of **endurance,—patience.** Nor again can the expression mean '*endurance for Christ's sake,*' which the simple genitive will not convey : but it must be, as Chrys. (1) *ἵνα ὑπομένωμεν, ὡς ἐκεῖνος ὑπέμεινεν, the patience of Christ* (gen. possess.),—which Christ shewed. **6—15.**] *Dehortation from disorderly, idle habits of life.* He had given a hint in this direction before, in the first Epistle (v. 14, 15) : he now speaks more plainly, doubtless because their restlessness and excitement concerning the παρουσία had been accompanied by an increase of such habits. His dissuading them from associating with such persons, seems to shew that the core of the Church (as Lün.) was as yet sound in this respect. **6.**] παραγγέλλομεν δέ takes up the assurance of ver. 4, and tests its general form by a special command. ἐν ὀνόμ. κ.τ.λ. strengthens the παραγγ., and does not belong to the following. στέλλεσθαι] lit. 'to take in, or shorten sail :' *ἱστία μὲν στείλαντο, θέσαν δ' ἐν νηῒ μελαίνη,* Il. a. 433 : hence, to draw in or shorten, generally : *πότερά σοι παρρησίᾳ | φράσω τὰ κεῖθεν, ἢ λόγον στελλώμεθα,* Eur. Bacch. 625 :—to conceal : *ἐβουλεύετο μὲν στέλλεσθαι, οὐ μὴν ἠδύνατό γε κρύπτειν τὸ γεγονός,* Polyb. Frag. hist. 39 (from Suidas, voc. στείλασθαι),— *οὐ δυναμένων τὴν ἐκ τῆς συνηθείας καταξίωσιν στέλλεσθαι* ('cohibere

consuetam reverentiam'), ib. viii. 22. 4. So here, 'cohibere vos'—to keep yourselves from: see reff. : obviously without allusion as yet to any formal excommunication, but implying merely avoidance in intercourse and fellowship. The accusative is repeated before the infinitive, probably because the clause ἐν ὀνόμ., &c., intervenes. The παράδοσις refers to the oral instruction which the Apostle had given them when he was present, and subsequently confirmed by writing (1 Thess. iv. 11, 12). παρελάβοσαν] plural, as belonging to the πάντες implied in παντός ; so in ἔβαν οἰκόνδε ἕκαστος. On the form -οσαν, which is said to have been originally Macedonian, and thence is found in the Alexandrian (ἐσχάξοσαν, Lycophr. 21), Lobeck remarks (Phryn. p. 349), "ex modorum et temporum metaplasmis, quos conjunctim tractare solent dialectorum scriptores, nullus diutius viguit eo quo tertiæ aoristi secundi personæ plurales ad similitudinem verborum in μι traducuntur,—εἴδοσαν Niceph., ἐφεύροσαν Anna Comnena, μετήλθοσαν Nicet. (and παρήλθοσαν)." We have ἤλθοσαν ἔθνη, Ps. lxxviii. 1 ; see other examples from LXX in Winer, edn. 6, § 13. 2. f. **7.**] πῶς δεῖ μιμ. ἡμ. is a concise way of expressing 'how ye ought to walk in imitation of us.' ἀτακτέω also occurs in Lysias κατὰ Ἀλκιβ. a. p. 141. 18, in this sense, of 'leading a disorderly life.' **8.**] ἄρτον ἐφάγομεν, a Hebraistic expression for 'got our sustenance :' παρά τινος, 'at any one's expense,' from any one as a gift : there seems to be an allusion in the construction to the original sense of δωρεάν.

ζόμενοι, [d] πρὸς τὸ μὴ [d] ἐπιβαρῆσαί τινα ὑμῶν· 9 [e] οὐχ
[e] ὅτι οὐκ [f] ἔχομεν [f] ἐξουσίαν, ἀλλ' ἵνα [g] ἑαυτοὺς [h] τύπον
δῶμεν ὑμῖν [i] εἰς τὸ [w] μιμεῖσθαι ἡμᾶς. 10 καὶ γὰρ ὅτε
[k] ἦμεν [k] πρὸς ὑμᾶς, τοῦτο [l] παρηγγέλλομεν ὑμῖν, ὅτι εἴ
τις οὐ θέλει [d] ἐργάζεσθαι, μηδὲ ἐσθιέτω. 11 [m] ἀκούομεν
γάρ τινας [n] περιπατοῦντας [o] ἐν ὑμῖν [p] ἀτάκτως, μηδὲν
[q] ἐργαζομένους, ἀλλὰ [r] περιεργαζομένους· 12 [s] τοῖς δὲ
[s] τοιούτοις [l] παραγγέλλομεν καὶ [t] παρακαλοῦμεν [t] ἐν κυρίῳ
Ἰησοῦ χριστῷ, ἵνα [u] μετὰ [v] ἡσυχίας [d] ἐργαζόμενοι τὸν
ἑαυτῶν [w] ἄρτον [w] ἐσθίωσιν. 13 ὑμεῖς δέ, ἀδελφοί, μὴ [x] ἐγ-
κακήσητε [y] καλοποιοῦντες. 14 εἰ δέ τις οὐχ ὑπακούει τῷ

d absol., 1 Thess. ii. 9 reff.
e = John vi. 46. 2 Cor. i. 24. iii. 5. Phil. iii. 12. iv. 11, 17 only.
f Matt. vii. 29. John xix. 10, 11. 1 Cor. ix. 6. Sir. ix. 13.
g 1st person, Rom. viii. 23. 1 Cor. xi. 31. 1 Thess. ii. 8 al.
h = Phil. iii. 17 reff.
i Phil. i. 23 reff.
k 1 Thess. iii. 4 reff.
l ver. 4.
m = Matt. xi. 2. Acts xxiii. 16. Eph. i. 15 al.
n ver. 6.
o = John xi. 54. Eph. ii. 3.
p ver. 6 (reff.) only +.
q Matt. vii. 23. Gal. vi. 10. Ps. xiv. 2.
r here only +. Sir. iii. 23 only. Polyb. xviii. 34. 2. see 1 Tim. v. 13 reff.
s Rom. xvi. 18. 2 Cor. xi. 13 al.
t 1 Thess. iv. 1.
u Mark iii. 5 al. 1 Chron. xxix. 22.
v Acts xxii. 2. 1 Tim. ii. 11, 12 only. Sir. xxviii. 16. (-ιος, 1 Tim. ii. 2.)
w ver. 8.
x Eph. iii. 13 reff.
y here only. Levit. v. 4 Ald. (καλῶς π. AB) only. see Mark iii. 4 al.

10. om *τουτο* ℵ¹.   for *ου*, *μη* D¹.

11. *εν υμιν* bef *περιπατ*. D syr copt [æth arm].   om *ατακτως* 67².   [om *αλλα περιεργ*. 47. 109(Sz).]

12. rec **δια του** *κυρ*. **ημ.** *ιησου χρ*., with D³KLℵ³ syrr [æth] Chr Thdrt Damasc₁ Thl Œc: txt AB(D¹)F[P]ℵ¹ 17 latt copt goth Damasc₁ lat-ff (*said by De Wette to be a corrn from* 1 *Thess* iv. 1: *but is not rec rather a corrn to the more usual form?*).

13. rec *εκκακ*.: txt ABℵ m [47], *ενκακειτε* D¹.   *καλον ποιουντες* F: *το καλον ποι*. h 73. 113-marg 114-21-2². 219² Chr$_{aliq}$.

ἐργαζόμ. belongs to *ἄρτον ἐφ*. as a contrast to *δωρεάν*: **but by working**, &c. The sentence may also be taken as De W. and Ellic., regarding **ἐν κόπῳ κ. μόχ.** as the contrast to **δωρεάν**, and **ἐργαζ. νύκτ. κ. ἡμ.** as a parallel clause to **ἐν κόπ. κ. μόχ.**   **9.**] See 1 Cor. ix. 4 ff., where he treats of his abstinence from this his apostolic power.   **οὐχ ὅτι, my meaning is not, that . . . .** See reff. and Hartung, Part. ii. 153.   **ἑαυτούς** is used in the plural for *ἡμᾶς αὐτούς* and *ὑμᾶς αὐτούς* for shortness, but never in the singular for *ἐμαυτόν* or *σεαυτόν*, where no such reason exists: see Bernhardy, Syntax, p. 272.   **10.**] **καὶ γάρ**,—and we carried this further: we not only set you an example, but inculcated the duty of diligence by special precept. The **γάρ** is co-ordinate with that in ver. 7. The *καί* does not bring out *ὅτε ἦμεν πρ. ὑμᾶς* as a new feature, as Thdrt., for of this period the last three verses have treated—but it brings out **τοῦτο**, on which the stress lies, as an additional element in the reminiscence. This seems to me clearly to be the force here, and not the merely conjunctive, as Ellic. maintains.   **τοῦτο**, viz. what follows.   **εἴ τις** *κ.τ.λ.*] Schöttgen and Wetst. quote this saying from several places in the rabbinical books.   **11.**] *Ground for reminding them of this his saying.*   **περιεργαζομένους**] **being busybodies; or, being active about trifles;** 'busy only with what is not their own business' (Jowett: who refers to Quintilian's 'non agere sed satagere'): see reff. So in the charge against Socrates, Plato, Apol. § 3, *Σωκράτης ἀδικεῖ κ.* **περιεργάζεται** *ζητῶν τά τε ὑπὸ γῆς κ. τὰ ἐπουράνια, κ. τὸν ἥττω λόγον κρείττω ποιῶν, κ. ἄλλους ταὐτὰ ταῦτα διδάσκων.*   **12.**] **παρακαλοῦμεν**, scil. *αὐτούς*.   **ἐν κυρ.** see on ver. 6.   **μετὰ ἡσυχ.** may be taken either subjectively,—**with a quiet mind**;—or objectively, **with quietness, i. e.** in outward peace. The former is most probable, as addressed to the offenders themselves.   **ἑαυτῶν**, emphatic—that which they themselves have earned.   **13.**] **δέ**—ye who are free from this fault. On *ἐγκ*. and *ἐκκ*. see notes on 2 Cor. iv. 1 and Gal. vi. 9.   **καλοποιοῦντες**, from the context, cannot mean '*doing good*' (*to others*), but **doing well**, living diligently and uprightly: see also Gal. vi. 9, where the same general sentiment occurs. Chrys.'s meaning is surely far-fetched: *στέλλεσθε μέν, φησιν, ἀπ' αὐτῶν κ. ἐπιτιμᾶτε αὐτοῖς, μὴ μὴν περιίδητε λιμῷ διαφθαρέντας.*   **14.**] Many Commentators (Luth., Calv., Grot., Calov., Le Clerc, Beng., Pelt, Winer, al.) have joined **διὰ τῆς ἐπιστολῆς** with

z = 1 Cor. xvi.
3. 2 Cor. x.
9, 11. ch. ii.
2, 15 (see note).
a = Rom. xvi.
22. Col. iv.
16. 1 Thess.
v. 27. see
1 Cor. v. 9.
b here only.
Ps. iv. 6 only.
ἐσημειώ-
σαντο τὸν
τόπον,Polyb.
xxii. 11. 12.
c 1 Cor. v. 9, 11

λόγῳ ἡμῶν ^z διὰ ^a τῆς ἐπιστολῆς, τοῦτον ^b σημειοῦσθε ABDFK
μὴ ^c συναναμίγνυσθαι αὐτῷ, ἵνα ^d ἐντραπῇ· 15 καὶ μὴ ὡς
ἐχθρὸν ^e ἡγεῖσθε, ἀλλὰ ^f νουθετεῖτε ὡς ἀδελφόν. 16 g αὐτὸς
δὲ ὁ ^h κύριος τῆς ^h εἰρήνης δῴη ὑμῖν τὴν εἰρήνην ⁱ διὰ
παντὸς ἐν ^k παντὶ ^k τρόπῳ. ὁ ^l κύριος ^l μετὰ πάντων
ὑμῶν.
17 Ὁ ^m ἀσπασμὸς ⁿ τῇ ἐμῇ ⁿ χειρὶ Παύλου, ὅ ἐστιν

ABDFK
LPℵ a b
c d e f g
h k l m n
o 17. 47

only. Hos. vii. 8 A (συμμίγν., B) only.   d = 1 Cor. iv. 14.   Tit. ii. 8 only.   Ps. xxxiv. 26 al.   (Matt. xxi. 27 ‖ Mk. al.)   e Acts xxvi. 2.   2 Cor. ix. 5.   Phil. ii. 3 al.   Job xix. 11.   f Col. i. 28 reff. P.
g = 1 Thess. iii. 11 reff. (see note.)   h Phil. iv. 9 reff.   i Matt. xviii. 10. Acts ii. 25. x. 2. Rom.
xi. 10 (from. Ps. lxviii. 24) al.   k Phil. i. 18 reff.   l here only. Ruth ii. 4.   m = 1 Cor.
xvi. 21. Col. iv. 18 only. (Matt. xxiii. 7 ‖ al.†)   n 1 Cor. Col. as above (m).   Gal. vi. 11.   Philem. 19.

14. υμων B b¹ m æth Chr-in-Thl_{expr} Thl.   δι᾽ επιστολης F.   [σημειουσθαι
DFPℵ d 17.]   rec (aft σημ.) ins και, with D¹FKL[P] rel vulg syrr [æth arm] Bas
Ambrst Aug_{sæpe} : om A(appy) BD³ℵ 17 copt goth Chr Tert.   (συναναμιγνυσθαι, so
AB(D¹F)ℵ D-lat copt goth Tert.)
15. om και D¹ Tert.
16. for κυρ., θεος F[L] d f g vulg-sixt Thl Ambrst Pel.   om την A 67².
for τροπω, τοπω (more usual expression, see 1 Cor i. 2 &c) A¹D¹F 17 latt goth Chr-
montf Ambrst Pel : txt A²BD³KL[P]ℵ rel syrr copt Thdrt Damasc.

what follows, and explained it (usually, see below),—' note that man by an Epistle (to me).' But τῆς is decidedly against this rendering,—unless we suppose that it signifies ' your' answer to this. (Bengel and Pelt, taking τῆς ἐπ. for this Epistle, would render, 'notate nota censoria, hanc Epist., ejus admonendi causa, adhibentes eique incultantes' (Beng.),—' Eum hac epistola freti severius tractate' (Pelt): but both these require σημειοῦσθε to be diverted from its simple meaning.) The great objection to the above connexion is that St. Paul has already pointed out the manner of treating such an one, ver. 6, and is not likely to enjoin a further reference to himself on the subject. It is far better therefore, with Chrys. (there seems no reason for qualifying this by apparently, as Ellic.), Est., Corn.-a-lap., Beza, Hamm., Whitby, Schott, Olsh., De W., Baum.-Crus., Lün., Ellic., all., to join διὰ τῆς ἐπ. with the preceding τῷ λόγ. ἡμ., and render it our word by this Epistle, as ἡ ἐπιστολή is undoubtedly used in reff., and the word is that in ver. 12.   σημειοῦσθε] mark, see ref. Polyb.: the ordinary meaning of the word : put a σημεῖον on him, by noticing him for the sake of avoidance. On what is called the dynamic middle, see Krüger, Sprachlehre, § 52. 8. 4.
15.] καί is more delicate than ἀλλά or δέ would be : q. d. ' and I know that it will follow as a consequence of your being Christians, that ye will, &c.'   ὡς in the first clause seems superfluous: it is perhaps inserted to correspond with the other clause, or still further to soften the ἐχθρὸν ἡγεῖσθε. So ὥσπερ, Job xix. 11;

xxxiii. 10.   16.] Concluding wish. On αὐτὸς δέ, see on ch. ii. 16. ὁ κύριος τῆς εἰρήνης] As the Apostle constantly uses ὁ θεὸς τῆς εἰρ. for the God of Peace (see Rom. xv. 33; xvi. 20: 2 Cor. xiii. 11, al.), we here must understand our Lord Jesus Christ.   ἡ εἰρήνη must not be understood only of peace with one another : for there has been no special mention of mutual disagreement in this Epistle : but of peace in general, outward and inward, here and hereafter, as in Rom. xiv. 17. See Fritz. on Romans, vol. i. p. 22. The stress is on ὑμῖν—May the Lord of Peace give you (that) Peace always in every way (whether it be outward or inward, for time or for eternity).   μετὰ πάντων ὑ.] therefore with the ἀτάκτως περιπατοῦντες also (Lün.) : not as Jowett, pleonastic. The man who was to be admonished as an ἀδελφός, would hardly be excluded from the Apostle's parting blessing.   17, 18.] CONCLUSION.
17.] Autographic salutation. The Epistle, as it follows from this, was not written with the Apostle's own hand, but dictated. So with other Epistles; see Rom. xvi. 22 : 1 Cor. xvi. 21 : Col. iv. 18.   ὅ which circumstance : not attraction for ὅς. The whole of vv. 17, 18, not merely the benediction, are included. By the words οὕτως γράφω, we must not conceive that anything was added, such as his signature,—or as Œc., οἷον τὸ ἀσπάζομαι ὑμᾶς, ἢ τὸ ἔῤῥωσθε, ἤ τι τοιοῦτον : they are said of that which he is writing at the time. His reason for this caution evidently was, the ἐπιστολὴ ὡς δι᾽ ἡμῶν, spoken of ch. ii. 2. And the words ἐν πάσῃ ἐπιστολῇ must

^oσημεῖον ἐν πάσῃ ἐπιστολῇ. οὕτως γράφω. ¹⁸ ἡ ^pχάρις ^{o = Luke ii.}
τοῦ κυρίου ἡμῶν Ἰησοῦ χριστοῦ μετὰ πάντων ὑμῶν.   ^{12. 2 Cor.
xii. 12.
4 Kings xix.
19.
p see Col. iv. 18
reff.}

ΠΡΟΣ ΘΕΣΣΑΛΟΝΙΚΕΙΣ Β.

18. om ημων F : om τ. κυρ. ημ. Syr.   rec at end ins αμην, with ΛDFKL[P]א³ rel [vss] : om Bא¹ 17. 67² fuld(with harl tol) [arm-zoh] Ambrst.

SUBSCRIPTION. rec adds εγραφη απο αθηνων, with ΛB²KL[P] rel : απο ρωμης f g h : απο ρω. η απο αθ. b : no subscr in l o : προς θεσσ. β′ επληρωθη αρχεται προς τειμοθεον α′ D : ετελεσθη προς θ. β′ αρχεται προς τ:μ. α′ F : txt B¹(א) 17 goth æth.—(om β′ א, but adds στιχων ρπ.)   (After this in ΑBK[P]א 5. 9. 16 [17. 47] 137-89-96 the Ep to Heb follows : so also, apparently, in C, see Tischdf. Cod. Eph. proleg. p. 15.)

not, with Lün., be limited to any future Epistles which he might send to the Thessalonians, but understood of a caution which he intended to practise in future with all his Epistles : or at least with such as required, from circumstances, this identification. Thus we have (1 Thess. being manifestly an exception, as written before the rule was established) Gal. written with his own hand (see note on Gal. vi. 11); 1 Cor. authenticated (xvi. 21); 2 Cor. sent by Titus and therefore perhaps not needing it (but it may have existed in xiii. 12, 13 without being specified) ; Rom.

not requiring it as not insisting on his personal authority (but here again the concluding doxology may have been autographic): Col. authenticated (iv. 18): Eph. apparently without it (but possibly vi. 24 may have been autographic) : Phil. from its character and its bearer Epaphroditus not requiring it (but here again iv. 23 may be autographic) : and the Epistles to individuals would not require such authentication, not to mention that they are probably all autographic—that to Philemon certainly is, see ver. 19 there. (So for the most part De Wette.)

ΠΡΟΣ ΤΙΜΟΘΕΟΝ Α.

a Rom. xvi. 26.
1 Cor. vii. 6
(25). 2 Cor.
viii. 8. Tit.
i. 3 (ii. 15)
only †. Esdr.
i. 18 (16).
b Luke i. 47.
epp., ch. ii. 3. Tit. i. 3. ii. 10. iii. 4. Jude 25 only. Ps. lxiv. 5. see ch. iv. 10.
2 Cor. viii. 8. Phil. iv. 3. Tit. i. 4 only †. Sir. vii. 18 only. (-ως, Phil. ii. 20.)
17. 2 Cor. vi. 13. Phil. ii. 22. ver. 18. 2 Tim. i. 2. ii. 1. Tit. i. 4. Philem. 10. 3 John 4.
ii. 20. ver. 4. ch. (ii. 7, 15) iii. 13 (iv. 12). 2 Tim. i. 13. Tit. iii. 15. James ii. 5. elsw., ἐν τῇ π.
c = Col. i. 27.
e = 1 Cor. iv. 14,
f Gal.

Ι. ¹ Παῦλος ἀπόστολος χριστοῦ Ἰησοῦ, ᵃ κατ᾽ ᵃ ἐπιταγὴν ᵇ θεοῦ ᵇ σωτῆρος ἡμῶν, καὶ χριστοῦ Ἰησοῦ τῆς
ᶜ ἐλπίδος ἡμῶν, ² Τιμοθέῳ ᵈ γνησίῳ ᵉ τέκνῳ ᶠ ἐν ᶠ πίστει·

ADFKL
Pℵ a b c
d e f g h
k l m n o
17. 47

TITLE. εἰς παυλου του αποστ. η πρ. τιμ. επιστολη πρωτη : Steph η πρ. τιμ. επ. πρω. :
πρ. τιμ. πρωτης επιστολης(sic) παυλου L : [π. επ. πρ. τιμ. α P :] txt A[K]ℵ h m n o 17
[47], and (prefg αρχεται) DF.

CHAP. I. 1. rec ιησ. bef χριστου, with AKL rel [Syr æth arm] : txt DF[P]ℵ 17
[fuld(with demid)] syr copt goth Damasc Ambrst.   for επιταγην, επαγγελιαν ℵ.
ins του bef σωτηρος D¹ 43.—του σωτ. ημ. θῦ m 80. 116. 213.[—for σωτ., πατρος
P b¹.]   rec και κυριου ιησ. χρ., with D³KLℵ rel Thdrt Damasc : txt AD'F[P] 17
latt syrr sah Chr-comm Ambr Ambrst Cass. (Cursives vary in the similar phrase in
ver 2.)

CHAP. I. 1, 2.] ADDRESS AND GREET-
ING. 1. κατ᾽ ἐπιτ.] See reff., especially
Tit. : a usual expression of St. Paul, and
remarkably enough occurring in the doxology at the end of the Epistle to the Romans, which there is every reason to think
was written long after the Epistle itself.
It is a more direct predication of divine
command than διὰ θελήματος θεοῦ in the
earlier Epistles.   θεοῦ σωτῆρος ἡμ.]
Apparently an expression belonging to the
later apostolic period,—one characteristic
of which seems to have been the gradual
dropping of the article from certain well-
known theological terms, and treating
them almost as proper names (see, however, Ellicott's note).   Thus in Luke i. 47
it is ἐπὶ τῷ θεῷ τῷ σωτῆρί μου : and indeed in almost every place in the pastoral
Epistles except this, σωτήρ has the article.
In ref. Jude, the expression is the same as
here.   καὶ χρ. Ἰησ.] See a similar
repetition after δοῦλος χρ. Ἰησοῦ in Rom.
i. 4 & 6. The Apostle loves them in his
more solemn and formal passages—and

the whole style of these Epistles partakes
more of this character, as was natural in
the decline of life.   τῆς ἐλπίδος ἡμῶν]
It is not easy to point out the exact
reference of this word here, any further
than we may say that it gives utterance
to the fulness of an old man's heart in the
near prospect of that on which it naturally was ever dwelling.   It is the ripening and familiarization of χριστὸς ἐν ὑμῖν
ἡ ἐλπὶς τῆς δόξης of ref. Col.   See also
Tit. i. 2.   I am persuaded that in many
such expressions in these Epistles, we
are to seek rather a psychological than a
pragmatical explanation. Theodoret notices the similar occurrence of words in
Ps. lxiv. (lxv.) 6, ἐπάκουσον ἡμῶν ὁ θεὸς
ὁ σωτὴρ ἡμῶν, ἡ ἐλπὶς πάντων τῶν
περάτων τῆς γῆς—which is interesting,
as it might have suggested the expression
here, familiar as the Apostle was with
O. T. diction. Ellic. refers, for the same expression, to Ignat. Trall. § 2, p. 676.
2. γνησίῳ τ.] Cf. Acts xvi. 1 : 1 Cor. iv.
14—17 ; and Prolegg. to this Epistle, § i.

ᵍ χάρις, ᵍ ἔλεος, ᵍ εἰρήνη ἀπὸ θεοῦ πατρὸς καὶ χριστοῦ ᵍ 2 Tim. i. 2
Ἰησοῦ τοῦ κυρίου ἡμῶν. ³ ʰ Καθὼς ⁱ παρεκάλεσά σε
ᵏ προσμεῖναι ἐν Ἐφέσῳ, πορευόμενος εἰς Μακεδονίαν, ἵνα
ˡ παραγγείλῃς ᵐ τισὶν μὴ ⁿ ἑτεροδιδασκαλεῖν, ⁴ μηδὲ ᵒᵖ προσ-

i = (under like circumst.) 2 Cor. viii. 6. ix. 5. xii. 18.
Paul) only. (Matt. xv. 32 ‖ Mk. Acts xi. 23. xiii. 43. ch. v. 5 only. Judg. iii. 25 A. Wisd. iii. 9 only.)
1 Luke ix. 21. Acts i. 4. iv. 18. xv. 5. Paul, 1 Cor. vii. 10 & passim. 1 Kings xxiii. 8. m = 1 Cor. iv.
18. 2 Cor. iii. 1. x. 2. Gal. i. 7. ii. 12. vv. 6, 19. ch. iv. 1. v. 15. vi. 10, 21. 2 Tim. ii. 18. n ch. vi.
3 only†. Ignat. ad Polyc. c. 3, p. 721. o = & constr., Paul, ch. iii. 8. iv. 1, 13. Tit. i. 14
only. Acts viii. 6, 10, 11. xvi. 14. Heb. ii. 1. 2 Pet. i. 19. p Tit. i. 14.

2. rec aft πατρος ins ημων, with D³KL[P]א³ rel syrr sah [æth]: om AD¹Fא¹ 17
latt copt goth arm Orig-int Ambrst-ed Pel.

1 ff. γνησίῳ, true, genuine—cf. Plato, Politic. p. 293, οὐ γνησίας οὐδ' ὄντως οὔσας . . . . . ἀλλὰ μεμιμημένας ταύτην. ἐν πίστει] When Conyb. says, "'in faith,' not 'in the faith,' which would require τῇ" (so Ellic., without the protest),—he forgets (1) the constant usage by which the article is omitted after prepositions in cases where it is beyond doubt in the mind of the writer and must be expressed in translation: (2) the almost uniform anarthrousness of these Epistles. He himself translates the parallel expression in Tit. i. 4, 'mine own son according to our common faith,' which is in fact supplying the article. Render therefore in the faith: joining it with γνησίῳ τέκνῳ: and compare reff. ἔλεος and εἰρήνη are found joined in Gal. vi. 16, in which Epistle are so many similarities to these (see Prolegg. to these Epistles, § i. 32, note). The expression θεὸς πατήρ, absolute, is found in St. Paul, in Gal. i. 1, 3: Eph. vi. 23: Phil. ii. 11: Col. iii. 17 (τῷ θ. π.): 1 Thess. i. 1: 2 Thess. i. 1: 2 Tim. i. 2: Tit. i. 4. So that it belongs to all periods of his writing, but chiefly to the later. 3—20.] From specifying the object for which Timotheus was left at Ephesus (vv. 3, 4), and characterizing the false teachers (5—7), he digresses to the true use of the law which they pretended to teach (8—10), and its agreement with the gospel with which he was entrusted (11): thence to his own conversion, for the mercies of which he expresses his thankfulness in glowing terms (12—17). Thence he returns to his exhortations to Timotheus (18—20). On these repeated digressions, and the inferences from them, see Prolegg. ch. vii. § i. 36 f. 3.] The sentence begins As I exhorted thee, &c., but in his negligence of writing, the Apostle does not finish the construction: neither verse 5, nor 12, nor 18, will form the apodosis without unnatural forcing. παρεκάλεσα] Chr. lays stress on

the word, as implying great mildness—ἄκουε τὸ προσηνές, πῶς οὐ διδασκάλου κέχρηται ῥωμῇ, ἀλλ' οἰκέτου σχεδόν· οὐ γὰρ εἶπεν ἐπέταξα οὐδὲ ἐκέλευσα, οὐδὲ παρήνεσα, ἀλλὰ τί; παρεκάλεσά σε. This has been met (Huther, al.), by remarking that he says διεταξάμην to Titus, Tit. i. 5. The present word however was the usual one to his fellow-helpers, see reff.: and διεταξάμην there refers rather to a matter of detail—'as I prescribed to thee.' The sense of προσμεῖναι, to tarry, or stay at a place, is sufficiently clear from ref. Acts. The προσ- implies a fixity when the word is absolutely used, which altogether forbids the joining προσμεῖναι with πορευόμενος understood of Timotheus, as some have attempted to do. The aorist προσμεῖναι refers to the act of remaining behind when the Apostle departed; the present would have marked an endurance of stay. Various endeavours have been made to escape from the difficulties of the fact implied. Schneckenburger would read προσμεῖνας: others would take προσμεῖναι as imperative, most unnaturally. No one can doubt, that the straightforward rendering is, As I besought thee to tarry in Ephesus, when I was going to Macedonia . . . . . And on this straightforward rendering we must build our chronological considerations. See the whole subject discussed in the prolegomena, ch. vii. § ii.: and cf. Ellicott's note here. πορευόμενος, present, when I was on my way. ἵνα, &c. object of his tarrying. παραγγείλῃς, see reff. τισίν] so constantly (reff.) in these Epistles: sometimes οἱ ἀντιλέγοντες Tit. i. 9, or πολλοί ib. 10. Huther infers from τισί, that the number at this time was not considerable: but this is hardly safe. "The indefinite pronoun is more probably slightly contemptuous: 'le mot τινες a quelque chose de méprisant,' see Arnaud, on Jude 4, compare Gal. ii. 12." Ellicott. ἑτεροδιδασκαλεῖν] There seems to be in ἑτερο-, as in ἑτεροζυγοῦντες

q ch. iv. 7.   ἔχειν ^q μύθοις καὶ ^{rs} γενεαλογίαις ^t ἀπεράντοις, ^u αἵτινες   ADFKL
2 Tim. iv. 4.   Pℵ a b c
Tit. i. 14.   d e f g h
2 Pet. i. 16 only†. Sir. xx. 19 only.   r Tit. iii. 9.   s Tit. as above (r) only. 1 Chron. v. 7 compl. vii. 5 & 7   k l m n o
Ald. compl. ix. 22 Ald. only. (-γεῖν, Heb. vii. 6.)   t here only. Job xxxvi. 26 only.   u = Acts   17. 47
x. 41, 47. Paul, passim.

2 Cor. vi. 14, the idea of *strange*, or *incongruous*, not merely of different: cf. also ἑτερόγλωσσος, 1 Cor. xiv. 21. And the compound -διδασκαλεῖν, not -διδάσκειν, brings in the sense of '*acting as a teacher:*' **not to be teachers of strange things.** Eusebius has the substantive, H. E. iii. 32 —διὰ τῆς τῶν ἑτεροδιδασκάλων ἀπάτης,— in the sense of heretical teachers—which however is too fixed and developed a meaning to give here. We have καλοδιδάσκαλος, Tit. ii. 3. The meanings of 'other teaching' and 'false teaching,' when we remember that the faith which St. Paul preached was incapable (Gal. i. 8, 9) of any the least compromise with the errors subsequently described, lie very close to one another. **προσέχειν, to give attention to:** see reff. : "as it were, a mean term between ἀκούειν and πιστεύειν, compare Polyb. iv. 84. 6, διακούσαντες οὐδὲν προσέσχον; Jos. B. J. vii. 5. 3, οὔτε προσεῖχον οὔτε ἐπίστευον." Ellicott.

μύθοις] We can only judge from the other passages in these Epistles where the word occurs, what kind of fables are alluded to. In Tit. i. 14, we have μὴ προσέχοντες Ἰουδαϊκοῖς μύθοις. In our ch. iv. 7, they are designated as βέβηλοι καὶ γραώδεις. In 2 Tim. iv. 4, they are spoken of absolutely, as here. If we are justified in identifying the 'fables' in Tit. with these, they had a Jewish origin : but merely to take them, as Thdrt., for the Jewish traditional comments on the law (μύθους δὲ οὐ τὴν τοῦ νόμου διδασκαλίαν ἐκάλεσεν, ἀλλὰ τὴν ἰουδαϊκὴν ἑρμηνείαν τὴν ὑπ' αὐτῶν καλουμένην δευτέρωσιν (מִשְׁנָה, mischna), does not seem to satisfy the βέβηλοι καὶ γραώδεις. And consequently others have interpreted them of the gnostic mythology of the Æons. So Tert. adv. Valentinianos, ch. 3, vol. ii. p. 545: 'qui ex alia conscientia venerit fidei, si statim inveniat tot nomina æonum, tot coniugia, tot genimina, tot exitus, tot eventus, felicitates, infelicitates dispersae atque concisae divinitatis, dubitabiturne ibidem pronuntiare, has esse fabulas et genealogias indeterminatas, quas apostoli spiritus his iam tunc pullulantibus seminibus haereticis damnare praevenit ?' And Iren., in his præf. p. 1, assumes these words in the very outset, almost as his motto—ἐπεὶ τὴν ἀλήθειαν παραπεμπόμενοί τινες ἐπεισάγουσι λόγους ψευδεῖς κ. γενεαλογίας ματαίας αἵτινες ζητήσεις μᾶλλον παρέχουσι, καθὼς ὁ ἀπόστολος φησιν, ἢ οἰκοδομὴν θεοῦ τὴν

ἐν πίστει .... Others again (as Suidas's definition, μῦθος, λόγος ψευδής, εἰκονίζων τὴν ἀλήθειαν) would give an entirely general meaning to the word,—'false teaching' of any kind. But this is manifestly too lax : for the descriptions here (ver. 7, e. g.) point at a Jewish origin, and a development in the direction of γενεαλογίαι ἀπέραντοι. It does not seem easy to define any further these μῦθοι, but it is plain that any transitional state from Judaism to gnosticism will satisfy the conditions here propounded, without inferring that the full-blown gnosticism of the second century must be meant, and thus calling in question the genuineness of the Epistle. On the whole subject, see Prolegg. ch. vii. § i. 8 ff.   **γενεαλ. ἀπερ.**] De W. in his note on Tit. i. 14, marks out well the references which have been assigned to this expression : "**γενεαλογίαι** cannot be 1) *properly genealogical registers*,—either for a pure genealogico-historical end (Chr., Œc., Thl., Ambr., Est., Calov., Schöttg., Wolf), or for a dogmatico-historical one, to foster the religious national pride of Jews against Gentiles, cf. Phil. iii. 4 f. (Storr, Flatt, Wegsch., Leo), or to ascertain the descent of the Messiah (Thdrt., Jer., Wegsch. : according to Nicol. Lyr., to shew that Jesus was not the Messiah), least of all genealogies of Timotheus himself (Wetst.),—for all this does not touch, or too little touches religious interests : nor are they 2) *gentile theogonies* (Chr. gives this as well as the former interpretation : also Œc., Thl., Elsn.) ; nor again 3) *pedigrees of the cabalistic sephiroth* (Vitring. Obss. 1, v. 13: see Wolf), which will hardly suit γενεαλ. : nor 4) *Essenian genealogies of angels* (Mich., Heinr., al.), of the existence of which we have no proof ; nor 5) *allegorizing genealogies*, applications of psychological and historical considerations to the genealogies contained in the books of Moses ; as in Philo (Dähne, Stud. u. Krit. 1853, 1008),—a practice too peculiar to Philo and his view : but most probably 6) *lists of gnostic emanations* (Tert. contr. Val. 3,—præscr. 33, Iren. præf. (see above), Grot., Hamm., Chr., Mosh., Mack, Baur, al.), &c." But again, inasmuch as γενεαλογίαι are coupled in Tit. iii. 9 with μάχαι νομικαί, it seems as if we must hardly understand the ripened fruits of gnosticism, but rather the first beginnings of those genealogies in the abuse of Judaism. See Prolegg.

ˢᵛ ζητήσεις ʷ παρέχουσιν ˣ μᾶλλον ἢ ʸ οἰκονομίαν θεοῦ τὴν
ᶻ ἐν πίστει· ⁵ τὸ δὲ ᵃ τέλος τῆς ᵇ παραγγελίας ἐστὶν

ᵛ John iii. 25.
Acts xv. 2.
xxv. 20.
Paul, ch. vi.
4. 2 Tim. ii.

23. Tit. iii. 9 only †.   w Paul, Gal. vi. 17. Col. iv. 1. ch. vi. 17 only. = Matt. xxvi. 10 al. Isa.
vii. 13.   x John iii. 19. Acts xxvii. 11. 2 Tim. iii. 4.   y Eph. i. 10 reff.   z ver.
2 reff.   a = Rom. x. 4. 1 Pet. i. 9 only. (Phil. iii. 19 reff.)   b ver. 18. 1 Thess. iv. 2 reff.

4. εκζητησεις Aℵ 17.   elz οικοδομιαν, with D³ : οικοδομην D¹ Iren(in Epiph) : *ædificationem* latt Syr syr-mg goth Iren-int lat-ff : txt AFKL[P]ℵ rel syr copt æth [arm] Chr Thdrt. [Dr. Bloomfield's statement, ed. 9, that A has οἰκοδομίαν, and that Chr and Thdrt seem not to have been aware of any other reading, is contrary to fact. A reads οἰκονομίαν, and so do Chr and Thdrt : see both cited in the notes.]   om την F.

"It is curious that Polybius uses both terms in similarly close connexion, Hist. ix. 2. 1." Ellicott.   ἀπεράντοις may be used merely in popular hyperbole to signify the tedious length of such genealogies. The meaning '*profitless*' (Chr., ἤτοι πέρας μηδὲν ἔχουσαι, ἢ οὐδὲν χρήσιμον, ἢ δυσκατάληπτον ἡμῖν, and so Thdrt.; see below) would be a natural deduction from the other, and is therefore hardly to be so summarily set aside as it has been by De W., al. αἵτινες, of the kind which.   ζητήσεις] objective, **questions**: not subjective, '*questionings:*' see reff. in these Epistles, in which ζητήσεις are not themselves, but lead to, ἔρεις, μάχαι, &c.   παρέχουσιν] minister, as E. V., is the best rendering: '*afford,*' '*give rise to,*' '*furnish:*' see below.   μᾶλλον ἤ is a mild way of saying καὶ οὐ: see reff.   οἰκονομίαν θεοῦ . . . .] This has been taken two ways: 1) objectively: *the dispensation* (reff.) *of God* (towards man) *which is* (consists) *in* (the) *faith:* in which case παρέχουσιν must bear something of a transferred meaning,—zeugmatic, as the grammarians call it,—as applied to οἰκονομίαν, implying, "rather than they *set forth,*" &c. And to this there can be no objection, as the instances of it are so common. This meaning also suits that of οἰκονομία in the reff., even 1 Cor. ix. 17, where the οἰκονομία is the objective matter wherewith the Apostle was entrusted, not his own subjective fulfilment of it. 2) subjectively :—'*the exercising of the stewardship of God in faith:*' so Conyb. : or as paraphrased by Storr (in Huther) ζητοῦντας αὐτοὺς ποιοῦσι, μᾶλλον ἢ οἰκονόμους θεοῦ πιστούς. But to this there is the serious objection, that οἰκονομία in this subjective sense, '*the fulfilment of the duty of an οἰκονόμος,*' wants example: and even could this be substantiated, οἰκονομίαν παρέχειν, in the sense required, would seem again questionable. I would therefore agree with Huther and Wiesinger (and Ellicott) in the objective sense —the dispensation of God.   Then τὴν ἐν

πίστει has also been variously taken. Chrys. says, καλῶς εἶπεν, οἰκονομίαν θεοῦ· μεγάλα γὰρ ἡμῖν δοῦναι ἠθέλησεν ὁ θεός, ἀλλ᾽ οὐ δέχεται ὁ λογισμὸς τὸ μέγεθος αὐτοῦ τῶν οἰκονομιῶν. διὰ πίστεως οὖν τοῦτο γίνεσθαι δεῖ. And Thdrt. : αἱ μὲν περιτταὶ ζητήσεις ἀνόνητοι, ἡ δὲ πίστις φωτίζει τὸν νοῦν, καὶ ἐπιδείκνυσι τὰς θείας οἰκονομίας. But the words will hardly bear either of these. The only legitimate meaning seems to be—**which is in faith**, i. e. finds its sphere, and element, and development among men, in faith. Thus ἐν πίστει stands in contrast to ζητήσεις, in which the οἰκονομία θεοῦ *does not* consist; and the way for the next sentence is prepared, which speaks of πίστις ἀνυπόκριτος as one of the means to the great end of the Gospel.   **5.]** But (contrast to the practice of these pretended teachers of the law) **the end** (purpose, aim: Chrys. quotes τέλος ἰατρικῆς ὑγιεία) **of the commandment** (viz. of the ＊ law of God in (ver. 11) the gospel: not, although in the word there may be a slight allusion to it,—of that which Timothy was παραγγέλλειν, ver. 3. This commandment is understood from the οἰκονομία just mentioned, of which it forms a part) **is Love** (as Rom. xiii. 10. We recognize, in the restating of former axiomatic positions, without immediate reference to the subject in hand, the characteristic of a later style of the Apostle) **out of** (arising, springing from, as its place of birth—the heart being the central point of life: see especially ref. 1 Pet.) **a pure heart** (pure from all selfish views and leanings: see Acts xv. 9: on the psychology, see Ellicott's note: and Delitzsch, Biblische Psychologie, iv. 12, p. 204) **and good conscience** (is this συνείδησις ἀγαθή, 1) a conscience good by being freed from guilt by the application of Christ's blood,—or is it 2) a conscience pure in motive, antecedent to the act of love? This must be decided by the usage of this and similar expressions · in these Epistles, where they occur several times (reff. and 1 Tim. iii. 9. 2 Tim. i. 3. 1 Tim.

c Mark x. 30, & Luke x.
27, from Deut. vi. 5.
Rom. vi. 17.
2 Tim. ii. 22.
1 Pet. i. 22.
d Matt. v. 8.
e Acts xxiii. 1 (Paul.) ver. 19. 1 Pet. iii. 16, 21.
g Rom. xii. 9.

ἀγάπη c ἐκ d καθαρᾶς c καρδίας καὶ ef συνειδήσεως e ἀγαθῆς
καὶ πίστεως g ἀνυποκρίτου 6 ὧν h τινὲς i ἀστοχήσαντες
k ἐξετράπησαν εἰς l ματαιολογίαν, 7 θέλοντες εἶναι m νομοδιδάσκαλοι, μὴ n νοοῦντες μήτε ἃ λέγουσιν, μήτε περὶ

ADFKL
Pℵ a b c
d e f g h
k l m n o
17. 47

f = Acts xxiv. 16.   Heb. xiii. 18 al.   (Eccles. x. 20.)   Wisd. xvii. 11 only.
2 Cor. vi. 6.   2 Tim. i. 5.   James iii. 17.   1 Pet. i. 22 only †.   Wisd. v. 18.   xviii. 16 only.   h = ver.
3 reff.   i ch. vi. 21.   2 Tim. ii. 18 only †. constr., here only.   ἀστοχοῦσι τοῦ μετρίου κ. πρέποντος,
Plut. de Def. Orac. p. 414, Wetst.   k ch. v. 15. vi. 20.   2 Tim. iv. 4.   Heb. xii. 13 only.   Amos v. 8 only.
l here only †.   (-γος, Tit. i. 10.)   m Luke v. 17.   Acts v. 34 only †.   n = Matt. xv. 17.   Eph. iii.
4, 20 al.   Prov. i. 2, 6.

5. om αγαθης F.

---

iv. 2. Tit. i. 15). From those examples it would appear, as De W., that in the language of the pastoral Epistles *a good conscience* is joined with *soundness in the faith*, a *bad conscience* with *unsoundness*. So that we can hardly help introducing the element of *freedom from guilt by the effect of that faith on the conscience*. And the earlier usage of St. Paul in Acts xxiii. 1, compared with the very similar one in 2 Tim. i. 3, goes to substantiate this) **and faith unfeigned** (this connects with τὴν ἐν πίστει above; it is faith, not the pretence of faith, the mere 'Scheinglaube' of the hypocrite, which, as in Acts xv. 9, καθαρίζει τὰς καρδίας, and as in Gal. v. 6, δι᾽ ἀγάπης ἐνεργεῖται: Wiesinger well remarks that we see from this, that the general character of these false teachers, as of those against whom Titus is warned, was not so much error in doctrine, as leading men away from the earnestness of the loving Christian life, to useless and vain questionings, ministering only *strife*): **6.**] (the connexion is—it was by declining from these qualities that these men entered on their paths of error) **of which** (the καθαρὰ καρδία, — συνείδησις ἀγαθή, and πίστις ἀνυπόκριτος—the sources of ἀγάπη, which last they have therefore missed by losing them) **some having failed** (reff.: 'missed their mark:' but this seems hardly precise enough: it is not so much to miss a thing at which a man is aiming, as to leave unregarded one at which he ought to be aiming: as Schweigh. Lex. Polyb., 'rationem alicujus rei non habere, et respectu ejus sibi male consulere.' Thus Polyb. i. 33. 10, τῆς μὲν πρὸς τὰ θηρία μάχης δεόντως ἦσαν ἐστοχασμένοι, τῆς δὲ πρὸς τοὺς ἱππεῖς, πολλαπλασίους ὄντας τῶν παρ᾽ αὐτοῖς, ὁλοσχερῶς ἠστόχησαν: v. 107. 2, πρὸς μὲν τὸ παρὸν ἐνδεχομένως ἐβουλεύσατο, τοῦ δὲ μέλλοντος ἠστόχησε: see also vii. 14. 3) **turned aside to** (ἐξ-., away from the path leading to the τέλος, ver. 5, in which they should have been walking: the idiom is often found in the examples cited by Wetst.: e. g. Plato, Phædr., δεῦρ᾽ ἐκτραπόμενος κατὰ τὸν

Ἰλισσὸν ἴωμεν,—Thuc. v. 65, τὸ ὕδωρ ἐξέτρεπε κατὰ τὴν Μαντινικήν,—and in Polyb., ἐκτρέπεσθαι εἰς ὀλιγαρχίαν, vi. 4. 9,—εἰς τὴν συμφυῆ κακίαν, ib. 10. 2 and 7: and in Hippocr. de temp. morbi, even nearer to our present phrase,—εἰς μακρολογίαν ἐξετράποντο) **foolish speaking** (of what kind, is explained ver. 7, and Tit. iii. 9, which place connects this expression with our ver. 4. It is the vain questions arising out of the law which he thus characterizes. Herod. (ii. 118) uses μάταιος λόγος of an *idle tale*, an *empty fable* :— εἰρομένου δέ μευ τοὺς ἱρέας, εἰ μάταιον λόγον λέγουσι οἱ Ἕλληνες τὰ περὶ Ἴλιον γενέσθαι), **wishing to be** (giving themselves out as, without really being: so Paus. i. 4. 6, αὐτοὶ δὲ Ἀρκάδες ἐθέλουσιν εἶναι τῶν ὁμοῦ Τηλέφῳ διαβάντων ἐς τὴν Ἀσίαν. Cf. Palm and Rost's Lex. sub voce) **teachers of the law** (of what law? and in what sense? To the former question, but one answer can be given. The law is that of Moses; *the law*, always so known. The usage of νομοδιδάσκαλος (reff.) forbids our giving the word, as coming from a Jew, any other meaning. That this is so, is also borne out by Tit. i. 14. Then as to the sense in which these men professed themselves teachers of the law. (1) Clearly not, as Baur, by their very antinomianism,—teachers of the law by setting it aside: this would at best be an unnatural sense to extract from the word, and it is not in any way countenanced by vv. 8 ff. as Baur thinks: see below. (2) Hardly, in the usual position of those Judaizing antagonists of St. Paul against whom he directs his arguments in Rom., Gal., and Col. Of these he would hardly have predicated ματαιολογία, nor would he have said μὴ νοοῦντες κ.τ.λ. *Their* offence was not either of these things, promulgating of idle fables, or ignorance of their subject, but one not even touched on here—an offence against the liberty of the Gospel, and its very existence, by reintroducing the law and its requirements. (3) We may see clearly by the data furnished in these pastoral Epistles, that it

τίνων [o] διαβεβαιοῦνται· 8 [p] οἴδαμεν δὲ ὅτι [q] καλὸς ὁ [q] νόμος, ἐάν τις αὐτῷ [r] νομίμως [s] χρῆται, 9 [p] εἰδὼς τοῦτο,

o Tit. iii. 8 only †.
p Paul, Rom. ii. 2. iii. 19. vii. 14 (w. νόμος). viii. 22, 28. 1 Cor. viii. 1, 4. 2 Cor. v. 1 (Heb. x. 30. 1 John iii. 2, 14. v. 15, 18, 19, 20) οἴδατε, & εἰδότες, & εἰδώς, Paul, passim.
q Rom. vii. 16. καλός, Paul16 in other epp., in pastoral Epp., 24 times.
r 2 Tim. ii. 5 only †.
s = Acts xxvii. 17. 1 Cor. vii. 21, 31. ix. 12, 15. ch. v. 23. Prov. x. 26.

[7. **τινος** P.] **8.** [**αυτον** P.] χρη**ση**ται A[P] 73 Clem.

was with a different class of adversaries that the Apostle had in them to deal: with men who corrupted the material enactments of the moral law, and founded on Judaism not assertions of its obligation, but idle fables and allegories, letting in latitude of morals, and unholiness of life. It is against this *abuse of the law* that his arguments are directed: no formal question arises of the *obligation* of the law: these men struck, by their interpretation, at the root of all divine law itself, and therefore at that root itself does he meet and grapple with them. (See more in Prolegg.) Hence the following description), **understanding neither** (notice **μήτε . . . . μήτε**, making the two branches of the negation parallel, not progressively exclusive, as would be the case with μηδέ: they understand as little about the one as about the other) **the things which they say** (the actual diatribes which they themselves put forth, they do not understand: they are not honest men, speaking from conviction, and therefore lucidly: but men depraved in conscience (Tit. i. 14, 15), and putting forth things obscure to themselves, for other and selfish purposes), **nor concerning what things they make their affirmations** (nor those objective truths which properly belong to and underlie the matters with which they are thus tampering. This explanation of the sentence is called in question by De W., on the ground of the parallel expression in Tit. iii. 8, περὶ τούτων βούλομαί σε διαβεβαιοῦσθαι, in which he maintains that in διαβεβαιοῦσθαι περί τινος, περί τινος represents the mere *thing asserted*, not the objective matter *concerning which* the assertion is made,—and he therefore holds our sentence to be a mere tautology, —**ἃ** λέγουσιν answering exactly to περὶ τίνων διαβεβαιοῦνται. But in reply we may say, that there is not the slightest necessity for such a construction in the passage of Titus: see note there. And so Huth., Wies. Cf. Arrian. Epict. ii. 21, τί δ' ἐροῦσι καὶ περὶ τίνων ἢ πρὸς τίνας, καὶ τί ἔσται αὐτοῖς ἐκ τῶν λόγων τούτων, οὐδὲ καταβραχὲς πεφροντίκασι).

8 ff.] On the other hand the law has its right use:—not that to which they put it, but to testify against sins in practice: the catalogue of which seems to be here introduced, on account of the lax moral practice of these very men who were, or were in danger of, falling into them: not, as Baur imagines, because they were antinomians and set aside the (moral) law. They did not set it aside, but perverted it, and practised the very sins against which it was directed. **Now** (slight contrast to last verse, taking up the matter on general grounds) **we know** (see ref.: especially Rom. vii. 14: a thoroughly pauline expression) **that the law is good** (Rom. vii. 16: not only, as Thdrt., ὠφέλιμον, but in a far higher sense, as in Rom. vii. 12, 14: good abstractedly, — in accordance with the divine holiness and justice and truth; see ver. 18, ch. iv. 4) **if a man** (undoubtedly, in the *first place*, and mainly, a *teacher:* but not (as Bengel, De W., and Ellic.) to be confined to that meaning: all that is here said might apply just as well to a private Christian's thoughts and use of the law, as to the use of it by teachers themselves) **use it lawfully** (i. e. not, as most expositors, *according to its intention as law* (ἐάν τις ἀκολουθῇ αὐτοῦ τῷ σκόπῳ, Thdrt.), and as directed against the following sins *in Christians:* but clearly, from what follows, as De W. insists (see also Ellic.), and as Chrys. obscurely notices amongst other interpretations, **νομίμως** *in the Gospel sense:* i. e. as *not binding on*, nor *relevant to Christian believers*, but only *a means of awakening repentance in the ungodly and profane.* Chr.'s words are: τίς δὲ αὐτῷ **νομίμως** χρήσεται; **ὁ εἰδὼς ὅτι οὐ δεῖται αὐτοῦ.** His further references of νομίμως, 'as leading us to Christ,'—as 'inducing to piety not by its injunctions but by purer motives,' &c., are not in place here), **being aware of this** (belongs to **τις**, the teacher, or former of a judgment on the matter. **εἰδώς** implies both the possession and the application of the knowledge: 'heeding,' or 'being aware of'), **that for a just man** (in what sense? in the mere sense of '*virtuous*,' '*righteous*,' in the world's acceptation of the term? in Chrys.'s third alternative, δίκαιον ἐνταῦθα καλεῖ τὸν κατωρθωκότα τὴν ἀρετήν? or as Thl., ὃς δι' αὐτὸ τὸ καλὸν τήν τε πονηρίαν μισεῖ καὶ τὴν ἀρετὴν περιπτύσσεται? All such meanings are clearly excluded by ver. 11, which sets the

t = Luke ii. 34.
Phil. i. 17.
1 Thess. iii. 3.
u = Luke xxii.
37 ℓ. 2 Thess.
ii. 8 (1 Cor.
ix. 21).
v Tit. i. 6, 10.
Heb. ii. 8
only †.

ὅτι δικαίῳ νόμος οὐ ^t κεῖται, ^u ἀνόμοις· δὲ καὶ ^v ἀνυποτάκ- A D F K L
τοις, ^{wx} ἀσεβέσιν καὶ ^{xy} ἁμαρτωλοῖς, ^z ἀνοσίοις καὶ ^a βεβή- P ^{abc}_{defgh}
λοις, ^b πατρολῴαις καὶ ^b μητρολῴαις, ^c ἀνδροφόνοις, ^{klmno}
10 ^d πόρνοις, ^e ἀρσενοκοίταις, ^f ἀνδραποδισταῖς, ^g ψεύσταις, 17. 47

1 Kings xv. 12 Symm.   w Rom. iv. 5. v. 6.   1 Pet. iv. 18.   2 Pet. ii. 5. iii. 7.   Jude 4, 15 bis only.   Prov.
xxi. 30.   (-βεῖν, 2 Pet. ii. 6.   βεια, 2 Tim. ii. 16.)   x 1 Pet. iv. 18.   Prov. xi. 31.   (Jude 15.)
y Rom. iii. 7 al. fr.   Ps. xlix. 16.   z 2 Tim. iii. 2 only.   Ezek. xxii. 9.   Wisd. xii. 4.   2 Macc. vii. 34.   viii. 32
only.   a ch. iv. 7. vi. 20.   2 Tim. ii. 16.   Heb. xii. 16 only.   Levit. x. 10 al.   (-λοῦν, Matt. xii. 5.)
b here only †.   c here only †.   2 Macc. ix. 28 only.   d Eph. v. 5 reff.   e 1 Cor. vi. 9
only †. see Levit. xviii. 22.   f here only †.   g Paul, Rom. iii. 4.   Tit. i. 12 only.   otherwise,
John (viii. 44 al.) only.   Prov. xix. 22.

9. for ανομοις δε, αλλ' ανομοις τε F.   ins και bef ασεβεσιν D¹ [47] syrr goth
Lucif.   ins και bef ανοσιοις F [Syr goth Lucif₁].   rec πατραλ. and μητραλ.,
with rel Thl : πατραλ. but μητρολ. K g n : txt ADFL [P(-ωλ-, bis)] ℵ d f h k l m 17
[47] Thdrt-ms Œc, πατριλ. μητραλ. o.

whole sentence in the full light of Gospel doctrine, and necessitates a corresponding interpretation for every term used in it. δίκαιος therefore can only mean, righteous in the *Christian sense,* viz. by *justifying faith and sanctification of the Spirit,*— '*justitia per sanctificationem,*' as De Wette from Croc.,—one who is included in the actual righteousness of Christ by having put Him on, and so not *forensically amenable to the law,*—partaker of the inherent righteousness of Christ, inwrought by the Spirit, which unites him to Him, and so not *morally needing it*) the law (as before : not, '*a law*' in general, as will be plain from the preceding remarks : nor does the omission of the article furnish any ground for such a rendering, in the presence of numerous instances where νόμος, anarthrous, is undeniably 'the Law' of Moses. Cf. Rom. ii. 25 bis ; ib. 27 ; iii. 28, 31 bis ; v. 20; vii. 1 ; x. 4 : Gal. ii. 19; vi. 13,— to say nothing of the very many examples after prepositions. And of all parts of the N. T. anarthrousness need least surprise us in these Epistles, where many theological terms, having from constant use become technical words, have lost their articles. No such compromise as that of Bishop Middleton's, that the Mosaic law is *comprehended* in νόμος, will answer the requirements of the passage, which strictly deals with the Mosaic law and with nothing else : cf. on the catalogue of sins below. As De Wette remarks, this assertion = that in Rom. vi. 14, οὐ γὰρ ἐστὲ ὑπὸ νόμον, ἀλλὰ ὑπὸ χάριν,—Gal. v. 18, εἰ πνεύματι ἄγεσθε, οὐκ ἐστὲ ὑπὸ νόμον) is not enacted (see very numerous instances of νόμος κεῖται in Wetst. The following are some : Eur. Ion 1046, 7, ὅταν δὲ πολεμίους δρᾶσαι κακῶς | θέλῃ τις, οὐδεὶς ἐμποδὼν κεῖται νόμος : Thucyd. ii. 37, νόμων . . . ὅσοι τε ἐπ' ὠφελείᾳ τῶν ἀδικουμένων κεῖνται : Galen. a. Julian. (Wetst.), νόμος οὐδεὶς κεῖται κατὰ τῶν ψευδῶς ἐγκα-

λούντων), but for lawless (reff. : not as in 1 Cor. ix. 21) and insubordinate (reff. Tit. : it very nearly = ἀπειθής, see Tit. i. 16 ; iii. 3,—this latter being more subjective, whereas ἀνυποτάκτ. points to the objective fact. This first pair of adjectives expresses opposition to *the law,* and so stands foremost as designating those for whom it is enacted), for impious and sinful (see especially ref. 1 Pet. This second pair expresses opposition to *God,* whose law it is—ἀσεβής being the man who does not reverence Him, ἁμαρτωλός the man who lives in defiance of Him), for unholy and profane (this last pair betokens separation and alienation from God and His law alike— those who have no share in His holiness, no relation to things sacred. "The ἀσεβής is unholy through his lack of *reverence :* the ἀνόσιος, through his lack of *inner purity.*" Ellic.), for father-slayers and mother-slayers (or it may be taken in the wider sense, as Ellic., 'smiters of fathers:' so Hesych. : ὁ τὸν πατέρα ἀτιμάζων, τύπτων ἢ κτείνων. In Demosth. κατὰ Τιμοκράτους, p. 732. 14, the word is used of ἡ τῶν γονέων κάκωσις : cf. the law cited immediately after. And Plato, Phæd. 114 a, apparently uses it in the same wide sense, as he distinguishes πατράλοιαι and μητράλοιαι from ἀνδροφόνοι.

Hitherto the classes have been general, and (see above) arranged according to their opposition to the law, or to God, or to both : now he *takes the second table of the decalogue and goes through its commandments,* to the ninth inclusive, *in order.* πατρολῴαις καὶ μητρολῴαις are the transgressors of the *fifth*), for manslayers (the *sixth*), for fornicators, for sodomites (sins of abomination against both sexes : the *seventh*); for slave-dealers (εἴρηται ἀνδραποδιστὴς παρὰ τὸ ἄνδρα ἀποδίδοσθαι, τουτέστι πωλεῖν, Schol. Aristoph. Plut. ver. 521. The etymology is wrong, but the meaning as he states : cf.

ʰ ἐπιόρκοις, καὶ ⁱ εἴ τι ᵏ ἕτερον τῇ ˡᵐ ὑγιαινούσῃ ˡⁿ διδασ-
καλίᾳ ᵒ ἀντίκειται, ¹¹ κατὰ τὸ ᵖ εὐαγγέλιον τῆς ᵖ δόξης
τοῦ ᑫ μακαρίου θεοῦ, ὃ ʳ ἐπιστεύθην ἐγώ. ¹² ˢ χάριν ˢ ἔχω

ʰ here only +.
(-κεῖν, Matt.
v. 33. -κία,
Wisd. xiv.
25.)
i & constr.,
2 Cor. v.

17. Eph. iv. 29. Phil. ii. 1.   k = Rom. viii. 39. xiii. 9.   l 2 Tim. iv. 3. Tit. i.
9. ii. 1. see ch. vi. 3.   m = as above (l). 2 Tim. i. 13. Tit. i. 13. ii. 2 (Luke v. 31 al.) only. ὑγ.
περὶ θεῶν δόξαι, Plut. de audiend. Poetis, p. 20 F, Wetst. τοὺς ὑγ. λόγους, Philo de Abr. 38, vol.
ii. p. 32.   n = as above (l). Matt. xv. 9 ‖, from Isa. xxix. 13.   Eph. iv. 14. Col. ii. 22. ch. iv. 1,
6 (13), 16 (v. 17). vi. 1. 2 Tim. iii. 10 (16). Tit. ii. 7, 10 only.   o Luke xiii. 17. xxi. 15. 1 Cor.
xvi. 9. Gal. v. 17. Phil. i. 28. 2 Thess. ii. 4. ch. v. 14 only. Zech. iii. 1.   p 2 Cor. iv. 4 only.
see 1 Thess. ii. 2 reff.   q Paul, Rom. iv. 7, 8 (from Ps. xxxi. 1, 2). xiv. 22. 1 Cor. vii. 40. Tit.
ii. 13. but of God, ch. vi. 15 only.   r = & constr., Rom. iii. 2. 1 Cor. ix. 17. Gal. ii. 7. 1 Thess.
ii. 4. Tit. i. 3.   s Luke xvii. 9. 2 Tim. i. 3 (Philem. 7 v. r.). Heb. xii 28 only. 2 Macc. iii. 33.

10. εφιορκοις D¹.   om αντικειται A.   at end add τη D¹ vulg arm Bas lat-ff.

12. rec at beg ins και, with DKL rel syrr goth Damasc Œc-txt Lucif Ambrst : om AF[P]א 17. 67². 73. 80 vulg copt æth arm Chr Thdrt Pel Vig Bede.

Xen. Mem. i. 2. 6, τοὺς λαμβάνοντας τῆς ὁμιλίας μισθὸν ἀνδραποδιστὰς ἑαυτῶν ἀπεκάλει : and Pollux. Onomast. iii. 78, ἀνδραποδιστής, ὁ τὸν ἐλεύθερον καταδουλούμενος ἢ τὸν ἀλλότριον οἰκέτην ὑπαγόμενος. (Ellic.) The Apostle puts the ἀνδραποδιστής as the most flagrant of all breakers of the *eighth* commandment. No theft of a man's goods can be compared with that most atrocious act, which steals *the man himself*, and robs him of that free will which is the first gift of his Creator. And of this crime all are guilty, who, whether directly or indirectly, are engaged in, or uphold from whatever pretence, the making or keeping of slaves), **for liars, for perjurers** (breakers of the *ninth* commandment. It is remarkable that he does not refer to that very commandment by which the law wrought on himself when he was alive without the law and sin was dead in him, viz. the *tenth*. Possibly this may be on account of its more spiritual nature, as he here wishes to bring out the grosser kinds of sin against which the moral law is pointedly enacted. The subsequent clause however seems as if he had it in his mind, and on that account added a concluding general and inclusive description), **and if any thing else** (he passes to sins themselves from the committers of sins) **is opposed** (reff.) **to the healthy teaching** (i. e. that moral teaching which is spiritually sound : = ἡ κατ᾽ εὐσέβειαν διδασκαλία, ch. vi. 3, where it is parallel with ὑγιαίνοντες λόγοι οἱ τοῦ κυρ. ἡμ. Ἰησ. χριστοῦ. "The formula .... stands in clear and suggestive contrast to the sickly (ch. vi. 4) and morbid (2 Tim. ii. 17) teaching of Jewish gnosis." Ellic.)—**according to** (belongs, not to ἀντίκειται, which would make the following words a mere flat repetition of τῇ ὑγιαιν. διδασκ. (see ch. vi. 1, 3)—nor to διδασκαλία, as Thl.,—τῇ ὑγ. διδ. τῇ οὔσῃ κατὰ τὸ εὐαγγ.,—all. (see D¹ in digest),—for certainly in this case the speci- fying article must have been inserted,—and thus also the above repetition would occur ; —but to the whole preceding sentence,— the entire exposition which he has been giving of the freedom of Christians from the moral law of the decalogue) **the gospel of the glory** (not, '*the glorious gospel,*' see ref. 2 Cor. : all propriety and beauty of expression is here, as always, destroyed by this adjectival rendering. The gospel is 'the glad tidings of the glory of God,' as of Christ in l. c., inasmuch as it reveals to us God in all His glory, which glory would be here that of justifying the sinner without the law by His marvellous provision of redemption in Christ) **of the blessed God** (μακάριος, used of God, is called unpaulinifch by De Wette, occurring only in 1 Tim. (ref.) : in other words, one of those expressions which are peculiar to this later date and manner of the Apostle. On such, see Prolegomena), **with which I** (emphatic) **was** (aorist, indicating simply the past ; pointing to the time during which this his commission had been growing into its fulness and importance) **entrusted** (not these τινές. ὃ ἐπιστεύθην is a construction only and characteristically pauline : see reff. The connexion with the following appears to be this : his mind is full of thankfulness at the thought of the commission which was thus entrusted to him : he does not regret the charge, but overflows with gratitude at the remembrance of Christ's grace to him, especially when he recollects also what he once was ; how nearly approaching (for I would not exclude even that thought as having contributed to produce these strong expressions) some of those whom he has just mentioned. So that he now goes off from the immediate subject, even more completely and suddenly than is his wont in his other writings, as again and again in these pastoral Epistles : shewing thereby, I believe, the tokens of advancing age, and of that faster hold of individual habits of

t Eph. vi. 10
reff.
u = Acts xxvi.
2. 2 Cor. ix.
5. ch. vi. 1.
Job xlii. 6.
v = 1 Thess. v.
9 reff.
w = Eph. iv.
12 reff.
x John vi. 62.
ix. 8. Gal.
iv. 13 only.
Judg. xviii. 29.
i. 6 al.
ver. 16. Matt. v. 7. Rom. xi. 30, 31. 1 Cor. vii. 25. 2 Cor. iv. 1. 1 Pet. ii. 10. Prov. xxi. 10. Hos. ii. 23 (25) A.
c = Acts xvii. 23 (Paul). Rom. ii. 4. x. 3. Sir. v. 15.   d Rom. iii. 3. iv. 20. xi. 20, 23. Heb. iii. 19†. Wisd.
xiv. 25 only.   e here only†.

τῷ ^tἐνδυναμώσαντί με χριστῷ Ἰησοῦ τῷ κυρίῳ ἡμῶν, ADϝKL
ὅτι πιστόν με ^uἡγήσατο, ^vθέμενος ^vεἰς ^wδιακονίαν, Ρℵabc defgh
13 ^xτὸ πρότερον ὄντα ^yβλάσφημον καὶ ^zδιώκτην καὶ klmno 17.47
^aὑβριστήν· ἀλλὰ ^bἠλεήθην, ὅτι ^cἀγνοῶν ἐποίησα ἐν
^dἀπιστίᾳ. 14 ^eὑπερεπλεόνασεν δὲ ἡ χάρις τοῦ κυρίου

y Acts vi. 11.   2 Tim. iii. 2.   2 Pet. ii. 11.   Rev. xiii. 5 only.   Isa. lxvi. 3 only.   Wisd.
z here only†.   Hos. vi. 8 Symm.   a Rom. i. 30 only.   Prov. vi. 17 al.   b pass.,

ενδυναμουντι ℵ¹ 17. 72.   om με ℵ¹.
13. rec for το, τον, with D³KL rel : txt AD¹F[P]ℵ 17 [47] 67² Dial Chr-ms.
aft οντα ins με A 73.   (αλλα, so ADFL[P]ℵ rel.)—D¹ adds δια τουτο.   for εν,
τη D¹.

thought and mannerisms, which characterizes the decline of life):   (12 ff.]
See summary, on ver. 3.) **I give thanks**
(χάριν ἔχειν (reff.) is only used by the
Apostle here and in 2 Tim. ref.) **to Him
who enabled me** (viz. for His work :
not only as Chr., in one of his finest passages,—φορτίον ὑπῆλθε μέγα, καὶ πολλῆς
ἐδεῖτο τῆς ἄνωθεν ῥοπῆς. ἐννόησον γὰρ
ὅσον ἦν πρὸς καθημερινὰς ὕβρεις, λοιδορίας, ἐπιβουλάς, κινδύνους, σκώμματα,
ὀνείδη, θανάτους ἵστασθαι, καὶ μὴ ἀπο-
κάμνειν, μηδὲ ὀλισθαίνειν, μηδὲ περιτρέ-
πεσθαι, ἀλλὰ πάντοθεν βαλλόμενον μυ-
ρίοις καθ' ἑκάστην ἡμέραν τοῖς βέλεσιν,
ἀτενὲς ἔχοντα τὸ ὄμμα ἑστάναι καὶ ἀκατά-
πληκτον,—see also Phil. iv. 13,—for he
evidently is here treating of the divine
enlightening and strengthening which he
received for the ministry : cf. Acts ix. 22,
where the same word occurs—a coincidence not to be overlooked. So Thdrt. :
οὐ γὰρ οἰκείᾳ δυνάμει χρώμενος ταύτην
τοῖς ἀνθρώποις προσφέρω τὴν διδασκαλίαν, ἀλλ' ὑπὸ τοῦ σεσωκότος ῥωννύμενός
τε καὶ νευρούμενος), **Christ Jesus our
Lord** (not to be taken as the dativus commodi after ἐνδυναμώσαντι, but in apposition with τῷ ἐνδυν.), **that** (not, 'because :' it is the main ground of the χάριν
ἔχω : the specification of τῷ ἐνδυναμώσαντι introducing a subordinate ground)
He accounted me faithful (cf. the strikingly similar expression, 1 Cor. vii. 25,
γνώμην δίδωμι ὡς ἠλεημένος ὑπὸ κυρίου
πιστὸς εἶναι :—He knew me to be such an
one, in His foresight, as would prove faithful to the great trust), **appointing me** (cf.
ref. 1 Thess. The expression is there
used of that appointment of God in His
sovereignty, by which our course is marked
for a certain aim or end : and so it is best
taken here,—not for the act of '*putting
me into*' the ministry, as E. V. But the
present sense must be kept : not '*having
appointed*,' **θέμενος** constituting the *ex-

ternal proof of πιστόν με ἡγήσ.) **to the
ministry** (what sort of διακονία, is declared, Acts xx. 24, ἡ διακονία ἣν ἔλαβον
παρὰ τοῦ κυρίου Ἰησοῦ, διαμαρτύρασθαι
τὸ εὐαγγέλιον τῆς χάριτος τοῦ θεοῦ),
13.] (and all the more is he thankful,
seeing that he was once a direct opponent
of the Gospel) **being before** (the participle
is slightly concessive : as Ellic. from Justiniani, 'cum tamen essem ;' almost equivalent to 'though I was') **a blasphemer** (see
Acts xxvi. 9, 11) **and persecutor and in-
sulter** (one who added insult to persecution. See on **ὑβριστής**, Trench, N. T.
Synonyms, p. 112 f. The facts which justified the use of such a term were known
to St. Paul's conscience : we might well
infer them, from his own confessions in
Acts xxii. 4, 19, and xxvi. 9—12. He describes himself as περισσῶς ἐμμαινόμενος
αὐτοῖς) : **howbeit** ("ἀλλά has here its full
and proper seclusive ('aliud jam hoc esse,
de quo sumus dicturi,' Klotz., Devar. ii.
p. 2), and thence often antithetical force.
God's mercy and St. Paul's want of it are
put in sharp contrast." Ellic.) **I had mercy
shewn me** (reff.), **because I did it igno-
rantly** (so Rom. x. 2, of the Jews, (ζῆλον
θεοῦ ἔχουσιν, ἀλλ' οὐ κατ' ἐπίγνωσιν. Cf.
also as a most important parallel, our Lord's
prayer for His murderers, Luke xxiii. 34)
in unbelief (ἀπιστία was his *state*, of which
his ignorance of what he did was a *consequence*. The clause is a very weighty one
as applying to others under similar circumstances : and should lead us to form our
judgments in all charity respecting even
persecutors—and if of them, then surely
even with a wider extension of charity to
those generally, who lie in the ignorance of
unbelief, whatever be its cause, or its effects),   **14.] but** (contrast still to his
former state, and epexegetical of ἠλεήθην ;
—not to ἠλεήθ.,—'not only so, but,' as
Chr., De W., al.) **the grace of our Lord**
(His mercy shewn to me—but not in

ἡμῶν μετὰ [f] πίστεως καὶ ἀγάπης τῆς [f] ἐν χριστῷ Ἰησοῦ.
15 [gh] πιστὸς ὁ [h] λόγος καὶ [i] πάσης [k] ἀποδοχῆς ἄξιος, ὅτι
χριστὸς Ἰησοῦς [lm] ἦλθεν εἰς τὸν [l] κόσμον [m] ἁμαρτωλοὺς
[m] σῶσαι, ὧν [n] πρῶτός εἰμι ἐγώ· 16 ἀλλὰ διὰ τοῦτο [o] ἠλεήθην, ἵνα [p] ἐν ἐμοὶ [n] πρώτῳ [q] ἐνδείξηται χριστὸς Ἰησοῦς

f Eph. i. 15.
Col. i. 4.
2 Tim. i. 13.
iii. 15. P.
g = Acts xiii.
34 (from Isa.
lv. 3) al.
h ch. iii. 1. iv.
9. 2 Tim. i.
11. Tit. i. 9.
iii. 8. Rev.
xxi. 5. xxii.

6 only.   i Phil. i. 20 reff.   k ch. iv. 9 only †.   ἀποδοχῆς ἀξιοῦται παρ' ἐνίοις
(of a *writer*), Polyb. ii. 56. 1.   ὁ λόγος ἀποδοχῆς τυγχάνει, id. i. 5. 5. (see Wetst.)   l John i.
9. xii. 46. xvi. 28.   m here only. see Matt. xviii. 11 ‖ L.   n = Mark xii. 28, 29.
o ver. 13.   p = Matt. xvii. 12. 1 Cor. ix. 15.   q Eph. ii. 7 reff.

15. om τον ℵ.

16. for πρωτω, πρωτον L a[1] c m o coptt [arm] Thdrt : om D[1] æth Aug[1].   rec
ιησ. bef χρ., with KL[P]ℵ rel syrr copt [æth arm] : om χρ. F l Serap : txt AD k 17
[47] vulg [sah] goth Thdrt[1] lat-ff.

strengthening me for His work, endowing
me with spiritual gifts, &c., as Chr., al. :
for the ἠλεήθην is the ruling idea through
the whole, and he recurs to it again ver.
16, never having risen above it to that of
his higher gifts) **superabounded** (to be
taken not comparatively, but superlatively,
see Rom. v. 20, note) **with** (accompanied
by) **faith and love** (see the same pauline
expression, Eph. vi. 23, and note there)
which are (τῆς probably improperly used
by attraction for τῶν : there is no reason
why πίστις as well as ἀγάπη should not
be designated as ἐν χριστῷ Ἰησοῦ) **in** (as
their element, and, as it were, *home*) **Christ
Jesus** (all these three abounded—grace,
the objective side of God's ἔλεος to him :—
Christian faith and love—the contrast to
his former hatred and unbelief,—God's
gifts, the subjective side. This is much
better than to regard μετὰ πίστεως καὶ
ἀγάπης as giving that wherein the χάρις
ὑπερεπλεόνασεν) :   **15.**] **faithful**
(worthy of credit : ἀντὶ τοῦ, ἀψευδὴς καὶ
ἀληθής, Thdrt. Cf. Rev. xxi. 5, οὗτοι οἱ
λόγοι ἀληθινοὶ καὶ πιστοί εἰσιν : similarly
xxii. 6 [or, one belonging to those who
are of the πίστις]. The formula πιστὸς ὁ
λόγος is peculiar to the pastoral Epistles,
and characteristic I believe of their later
age, when certain sayings had taken their
place as Christian axioms, and were thus
designated) **is the saying, and worthy of
all** (all possible, i. e. universal) **reception**
(see reff. Polyb., and Wetst. and Kypke,
h. l. A word which, with its adjective
ἀποδεκτός (ch. ii. 3 : v. 4), is confined to
these Epistles. We have the verb, οἱ μὲν
οὖν ἀποδεξάμενοι τὸν λόγον αὐτοῦ ἐβαπ-
τίσθησαν, Acts ii. 41), **that Christ Jesus
came into the world** (an expression otherwise found only in St. John. But in the
two reff. in Matt. and Luke, we have
the ἦλθεν) **to save sinners** (to be taken in
the most general sense, not limited in any
way), **of whom** (sinners ; not, as Wegscheider, σωζομένων or σεσωσμένων : the

aim and extent of the Lord's mercy intensifies the feeling of his own especial unworthiness) **I am** (not, '*was*') **chief** (not, 'one
of the chief,' as Flatt,—nor does πρῶτος
refer to *time*, which would not be the fact
(see below) : the expression is one of the
deepest humility : αὐτὸν ὑπερβαίνει τῆς
ταπεινοφροσύνης ὅρον, says Thdrt. : and
indeed it is so, cf. Phil. iii. 6 ; 1 Cor. xv. 9;
Acts xxiii. 1 ; xxiv. 16 ; but deep humility
ever does so : it is but another form of
ἐμοὶ τῷ ἁμαρτωλῷ, Luke xviii. 13 : other
men's crimes seem to sink into nothing
in comparison, and a man's own to be the
chief and only ones in his sight) :
16.] **howbeit** (as E. V. : "not resumptive,
but as in ver. 13, seclusive and antithetical, marking the contrast between
the Apostle's own judgment on himself,
and the mercy which God was pleased to
shew him." Ellic.) **for this purpose I had
mercy shewn me, that in me** (as an
example ; "in my case :" see reff. and cf.
εἰς ὑποτύπωσιν below) **first** (it can hardly
be denied that in πρώτῳ here the senses
of '*chief*' and '*first*' are combined. This
latter seems to be necessitated by μελλόντων below. Though he was not in time
'the first of sinners,' yet he was the first
as well as the most notable example of
such marked long-suffering, held up for
the encouragement of the church) **Christ
Jesus might shew forth** (dynamic middle :
see note on ref. Eph., and Ellicott there)
the whole of His (not merely '*all*' (all
possible, πᾶσαν) : nor 'all His' (Conyb.,
Ellic. : πᾶσαν τὴν . . . .), but '*the whole*,'
'the whole mass of μακροθυμία, of which
I was an example ; ὁ ἅπας seems to be
found here only. If the rec. reading be in
question, in all other cases where ὁ πᾶς
occurs with a substantive in the N. T., it is
one which admits of partition, and may
therefore be rendered by 'all the ' or 'the
whole :' e. g. Acts xx. 18, πῶς μεθ' ὑμῶν
τὸν πάντα χρόνον ἐγενόμην : see also
ref. Wetst. has two examples from Polyb.

r see 1 Cor. xiii. 2.
s Paul, Gal. iii. 28. Eph. vi. 13 only.
t Rom. ii. 4. 1 Pet. iii. 20.
2 Pet. iii. 15 al. Prov. xxv. 15.

ʳ τὴν ˢ ἅπασαν ᵗ μακροθυμίαν, ᵘ πρὸς ᵛ ὑποτύπωσιν ʷ τῶν ADFKL
μελλόντων ˣ πιστεύειν ˣ ἐπ᾽ αὐτῷ ʸ εἰς ʸ ζωὴν αἰώνιον. ᴾℵ a b c d e f g h
17 τῷ ᶻ δὲ ᵃ βασιλεῖ τῶν ᵃᵇ αἰώνων, ᶜ ἀφθάρτῳ, ᵈ ἀοράτῳ, k l m n o 17. 47
ᵉ μόνῳ ᵉ θεῷ, ᶠ τιμὴ καὶ ᶠ δόξα εἰς ᵍ τοὺς αἰῶνας τῶν αἰώνων,

u = Acts iii. 10.　　2 Cor. viii. 19. x. 4 al.　　　　v 2 Tim. i. 13 only †.　　　　w constr. (w. τύπος), 1 Cor. x. 6.
x w. dat. (Matt. xxvii. 42 v. r.)　Luke xxiv. 25 only in N. T., exc. Rom. ix. 33.　x. 11.　1 Pet. ii. 6, all from Isa.
xxviii. 16.　　　　y = Acts xi. 18.　Rom. vii. 10.　　　　z Rom. xvi. 25.　Jude 24.　　　　a Rev. xv.
3 v. r. only.　Tobit xiii. 6, 10. see Sir. xxxvi. 17.　　　　b = Heb. i. 2. xi. 3.　　　c Rom. i. 23.　1 Cor.
ix. 25. xv. 52.　1 Pet. i. 4, 23. iii. 4 only †.　Wisd. xii. 1. xviii. 4 only.　　　d Col. i. 15, 16 reff.　　　e John
v. 44. (xvii. 3.　Rom. xvi. 27.)　Jude 25 only.　　　　　f of God, Paul, here only. (δόξα, Gal. i. 5.)　2 Pet. i.
17.　Rev. iv. 9, 11. v. 12.　　　　g Gal. i. 5 reff.

rec for απασαν, πασαν, with DKL[P] rel : txt AFℵ d m 17 Serap Chr₁.　　　　aft μακροθ.
ins αυτου D Syr coptt æth Thdrt₁ Aug₁.　　　　aft μελλοντων ins αγαθων [see Heb
ix. 11] ℵ¹(but marked for erasure).

17. for αφθαρτ., αθανατω D¹ vulg syr-mg [goth æth] lat-ff : aft αορ. add αθανατω
F.　　rec aft μονω ins σοφω (see Rom xvi. 27), with D²·³KL[P]ℵ³ rel syr Nyss Naz
Thl-comm : om AD¹Fℵ¹ (m ?) 17 latt Syr coptt æth arm Eus Cyr Thdrt₂(from comm,
he plainly did not read σοφ.) Chr-comm Œc-comm [Novat.　　　　om και P c d e f g l
n o 115-21-3].

in which ὁ πᾶς has the meaning of '*the
utmost:*' τῆς πάσης ἀλογιστίας ἐστὶ σημεῖον,— and τῆς ἁπάσης (as here) ἀτο-
πίας εἶναι σημεῖον) long-suffering (not,
generosity, magnanimity: nor is the idea
of *long*-suffering here irrelevant, as some
have said : Christ's mercy gave him all that
time for repentance, during which he was
persecuting and opposing Him, — and
therefore it was his *long*-suffering which
was so wonderful), for an example (cf.
2 Pet. ii. 6, ὑπόδειγμα μελλόντων ἀσεβεῖν
τεθεικώς. Wetst. has shewn by very copious
extracts, that ὑποτύπωσις is used by later
writers, beginning with Aristotle, for a
sketch, an *outline,* afterwards to be filled
up. This indeed the recorded history of
Paul would be,—the filling up taking place
in each man's own case : see ref. 2 Tim.,
note. Or the meaning 'sample,' 'ensample,'
as in 2 Tim. i. 13, will suit equally well) of
(to, see Ellicott's note, and Donaldson, Gr.
Gr. § 450) those who should (the time of
μελλόντων is not the time of writing the
Epistles, but that of the mercy being
shewn : so that we must not say "who
shall," but "who *should*") believe on
Him (the unusual ἐπ᾽ αὐτῷ is easily accounted for, from its occurrence in so very
common a quotation as πᾶς ὁ πιστεύων
ἐπ᾽ αὐτῷ οὐ καταισχυνθήσεται, see reff.
The propriety of the expression here is,
that it gives more emphatically the ground
of the πιστεύειν—brings out more the
reliance implied in it—almost q. d., 'to
rely on Him for eternal life.' Ellicott has,
in his note here, given a full and good
classification of the constructions of πιστεύω in the N. T.) to (belongs to πιστεύειν
(see above) as its aim and end (cf. Heb. x.
39) : not to ὑποτύπωσιν, as Bengel suggests) life eternal :　　　　17.] but (δέ

takes the thought entirely off from himself and every thing else, and makes the
following sentence exclusive as applied to
God. 'Ex sensu gratiæ fluit doxologia.'
Bengel. Compare by all means the very
similar doxology, Rom. xvi. 25 ff.: and
see, on their similarity, the inferences in
the Prolegomena, ch. vii. § i. 33, and note)
to the King (this name, as applied to God,
is found, in N. T., only in Matt. v. 35
(not xxv. 34 ff.) and our ch. vi. 15.　See
below) of the ages (i. e. of eternity : cf. the
reff. Tobit, where the same expression occurs, and Sir.—θεὸς τῶν αἰώνων : also Ps.
cxliv. 13, ἡ βασιλεία σου βασιλεία πάντων
τῶν αἰώνων,—מַלְכוּת כָּל־עֹלָמִים.　Comparing
these with the well-known εἰς τοὺς αἰῶνας
τῶν αἰώνων, εἰς τοὺς αἰῶνας, and the like,
it is far more likely that οἱ αἰῶνες here
should mean eternity, than the ages of this
world, as many have understood it.　The
doxology is to the Father, not to the
Trinity (Thdrt.), nor to the Son (Calov.,
al.) : cf. ἀοράτῳ), incorruptible (in ref.
Rom. only, used of God), invisible (reff. :
see also ch. vi. 16 : John i. 18.　Beware
of taking ἀφθάρτῳ, ἀοράτῳ with θεῷ, as
recommended by Bishop Middleton, on the
ground of the articles being wanting before these adjectives.　It is obvious that
no such consideration is of any weight in
a passage like the present.　The abstract
adjectives of attribute are used almost as
substantives, and stand by themselves,
referring not to βασιλεῖ immediately, but
to Him of whom βασιλεύς is a title, as
well as they : q. d. 'to Him who is the
King of the ages, the Incorruptible, the
Invisible, . . .'), the only God (σοφῷ has
apparently come from the doxology at the
end of Romans, where it is most appropriate), be honour and glory to the ages

ἀμήν. 18 ταύτην τὴν ʰ παραγγελίαν ⁱ παρατίθεμαί σοι,
ᵏ τέκνον Τιμόθεε, κατὰ τὰς ˡ προαγούσας ἐπὶ σὲ ᵐ προφητείας, ἵνα ⁿ στρατεύῃ ᵒ ἐν αὐταῖς τὴν ᵖ καλὴν ᑫ στρατείαν,
19 ʳ ἔχων ʳ πίστιν καὶ ˢ ἀγαθὴν ˢ συνείδησιν, ἣν ᵗ τινὲς
ᵘ ἀπωσάμενοι ᵛ περὶ τὴν πίστιν ʷ ἐναυάγησαν· 20 ˣ ὧν

h ver. 5. 1 Thess.
iv. 2 reff.
i = (Matt. xiii.
24 al.) 2 Tim.
ii. 2 only.
k ver. 2 reff.
l = Heb. vii.
18. lit., Matt.
xxi. 9. ch. v.
24 al. fr.
i Cor. xii.
m Rom. xii. 6.

10, &c. 1 Thess. v. 20. ch. iv. 14.   n Luke iii. 14. 1 Cor. ix. 7. 2 Cor. x. 3. James
iv. 1. 1 Pet. ii. 11 only. Judg. xix. 8 B(pass., A). Isa. xxix. 7.   o = 1 Thess. iv. 15.
p = ch. vi. 12. 2 Tim. iv. 7. see John x. 11. 1 Pet. iv. 10.   q 2 Cor. x. 4 only †.   r Matt.
xxi. 21. Mark xi. 22. Acts xiv. 9. Rom. xiv 22. 1 Cor. xiii. 2. Philem. 5. James ii. 1, 14, 18.
s ver. 5 reff.   t ver. 3 reff.   u Acts vii. 27, 39. xiii. 46. Rom. xi. 1, 2 only. L.P. Ezek. xliii. 9.
v so ch. vi. 21. 2 Cor. ii. 18. Tit. ii. 7.   w 2 Cor. xi. 25 only †.   x 2 Tim. i. 15. ii. 17.

18. απαγγελιαν F.   στρατευση D¹א¹ Clem.   [τ. καλ. στρ. bef εν αυτ. L : om
εν αυτ. k.]
19. [ins την bef 1st πιστιν P.]   εναυγαγησαν A.

of the ages (the periods which are made
up of αἰῶνες, as these last are of years,—
as years are of days : see note, Eph. iii.
21 : and Ellic. on Gal. i. 5), Amen.
18 ff.] He now returns to the matter which
he dropped in ver. 3, not indeed formally,
so as to supply the apodosis there neglected,
but virtually : the παραγγελία not being
the one there hinted at, for that was one
not given to Timotheus, but to be given by
him. Nor is it that in ver. 5, for that is
introduced as regarding a matter quite different from the present—viz. the aberra-
tions of the false teachers, who do not here
appear till the exhortation to Timotheus is
over. What this command is, is plain
from the following. **This command I
commit** (as a deposit, to be faithfully
guarded and kept : see ref. 2 Tim. and ch.
vi. 20 : Herod. vi. 86, beginning) **to thee,
son Timotheus** (see on ver. 2), **according
to** (in pursuance of : these words belong
to παρατίθεμαί σοι, not as Œc., Flatt, al.,
to ἵνα στρατεύῃ below) **the former prophecies concerning thee** (the directions, or,
prophecies properly so called, of the Holy
Spirit, which were spoken concerning Timotheus at his first conversion, or at his admission (cf. ch. iv. 14) into the ministry,
by the προφῆται in the church. We have
instances of such prophetic intimations in
Acts xiii. 1, 2,—(xi. 28,)—xxi. 10, 11. By
such intimations, spoken perhaps by Silas,
who was with him, and who was a προφήτης (Acts xv. 32), may St. Paul have
been first induced to take Timotheus to
him as a companion, Acts xvi. 3. All other
meanings, which it has been attempted to
give to προφητείας, are unwarranted, and
beside the purpose here : as e. g. 'the good
hopes conceived of thee,' Heinrichs. The
ἐπὶ σέ belongs to προφητείας, the preposition of motion being easily accounted
for by the reference to a subject implied in
the word), **that thou mayest** (purpose, and
at the same time purport, of the παραγγελία : cf. note, 1 Cor. xiv. 13 ; and Elli-

cott on Eph. i. 16) **war** (στρατεύεσθαι,
of the whole business of the employed soldier ; not merely of fighting, properly so
called) **in them** (not as De W. 'by virtue
of them,' but as Mack, Matth., and Wies.,
'in,' as clad with them, as if they were
his defence and confirmation. This is not
zu künstlich, as Huther, seeing that the
whole expression is figurative) **the good
warfare** (not, as Conyb., 'fight the good
fight,'—by which same words he renders
the very different expression in 2 Tim. iv.
7, τὸν ἀγῶνα τὸν καλὸν ἠγώνισμαι. It is
the whole campaign, not the fight alone,
which is here spoken of), **holding fast**
(more than 'having ;' but we must hardly,
as Matth., carry on the metaphor and think
of the shield of faith Eph. vi. 16, such continuation being rendered unlikely by the
unmetaphorical character of τὴν ἀγαθὴν
συνείδησιν) **faith** (subjective : cf. περὶ τὴν
πίστιν below) **and good conscience** (cf.
ver. 5),—**which** (latter, viz. good conscience—not, both) **some having thrust
from them** (there is something in the word
implying the violence of the act required,
and the importunity of conscience, reluc-
tant to be so extruded. So Bengel : 're-
cedit invita : semper dicit, noli me lædere')
made shipwreck (the similitude is so common a one, that it is hardly necessary to
extend the figure of a shipwreck beyond
the word itself, nor to find in ἀπωσάμενοι
allusions to a rudder, anchor, &c. See examples in Wetst.) **concerning** (see reff., and
cf. Acts xix. 25, οἱ περὶ τὰ τοιαῦτα ἐργάται,
also Luke x. 40. The same is elsewhere
expressed by ἐν,—so Diog. Laërt. v. 2. 14,
ἐν τοῖς ἰδίοις μάλα νεναυαγηκός,—Plut.
Symp. i. 4, ἐν οἷς τὰ πλεῖστα ναυαγεῖ
συμπόσια. See other examples in Kypke :
Winer, edn. 6, § 49. i. : and Ellicott's
note here) **the faith** (objective) : **of whom**
(genitive partitive : among whom) **is
Hymenæus** (there is a Hymenæus mentioned 2 Tim. ii. 17, in conjunction
with Philetus, as an heretical teacher.

y = 1 Cor. v. 5.
Luke xxiii.
25. 1 Chron.
xii. 27.
z 1 Cor. xi. 32.
2 Cor. vi. 9.
2 Tim. ii. 25.
Heb. xii. 6,
7, 10.   Rev. iii. 19.   Prov. xix. 18.
b ch. i. 3 reff.   c Rom. i. 8. 1 Cor. xi. 18.

ἐστιν Ὑμέναιος καὶ Ἀλέξανδρος, οὓς ʸ παρέδωκα τῷ
Σατανᾷ, ἵνα ᶻ παιδευθῶσι μὴ ᵃ βλασφημεῖν.

II. ¹ ᵇ Παρακαλῶ οὖν ᶜ πρῶτον πάντων ᵈ ποιεῖσθαι

ADFKL
PN a b c
d e f g h
k l m n o
17. 47

a absol., Acts xxvi. 11 (Paul). Matt. ix. 3 al.   2 Macc. x. 34,
d Phil. i. 4.

CHAP. II. 1. παρακαλει D¹F sah lat-ff₅.   om 1st παντων F Orig₁.

There is no reason to distinguish him from this one : nor any difficulty occasioned (De W.) by the fact of his being here παραδο-θεὶς τῷ σατανᾷ, and there mentioned as overthrowing the faith of many. He would probably go on with his evil teaching in spite of the Apostle's sentence, which could carry weight with those only who were sound in the faith) and **Alexander** (in all probability identical with Ἀλέξανδρος ὁ χαλκεύς, 2 Tim. iv. 14. There is nothing against it in what is there said of him (against De Wette). He appears there to have been an adversary of the Apostle, who had withstood and injured him at his late visit to Ephesus: but there is no reason why he should not have been still under this sentence at that time): **whom I delivered over to Satan** (there does not seem to be, as almost always taken for granted, any necessary assertion of excommunication properly so called. The delivering to Satan, as in 1 Cor. v. 5, seems to have been an apostolic act, for the purpose of active punishment, in order to correction. It might or might not be accompanied by extrusion from the church : it appears to have been thus accompanied in 1 Cor. v. 5 :—but the two must not be supposed identical. The upholders of such identity allege the fact of Satan's empire being conceived as including all outside the church (Acts xxvi. 18 al.) : but such expressions are too vague to be adduced as applying to a direct assertion like this. Satan, the adversary, is evidently regarded as the buffeter and tormentor, cf. 2 Cor. xii. 7—ever ready, unless his hand were held, to distress and afflict God's people,—and ready therefore, when thus let loose by one having power over him, to execute punishment with all his malignity. Observe that the verb is not perfect but aorist. He did this when he was last at Ephesus. On the ecclesiastical questions here involved, Ellic. has, as usual, some very useful references) **that they may be disciplined** (the subj. after the aorist indicates that the effect of what was done still abides; the sentence was not yet taken off, nor the παίδευσις at an end. παιδεύω, as in reff., *to instruct by punishment, to discipline*) **not to blaspheme** (God, or Christ, whose holy name

was brought to shame by these men associating it with unholy and unclean doctrines).

Ch. II. 1—15.] *General regulations respecting public intercessory prayers for all men* (1—4): *from which he digresses into a proof of the universality of the gospel* (4—7)—*then returns to the part to be taken by the male sex in public prayer* (8): *which leads him to treat of the proper place and subjection of women* (9—15). **I exhort then** ('οὖν is without any logical connexion,' says De W. Certainly,—with what immediately precedes ; but the account to be given of it is, that it takes up the general subject of the Epistle, q. d., 'what I have then to say to thee by way of command and regulation, is this :' see 2 Tim. ii. 1. "The particle οὖν has its proper collective force ('ad ea, quæ antea posita sunt, lectorem revocat.' Klotz.) : 'continuation and retrospect,' Donaldson, Gr. § 604." Ellic.), **first of all** (to be joined with παρακαλῶ, not, as Chr. (τί δ' ἐστὶ τὸ πρῶτον πάντων ; τουτέστιν, ἐν τῇ λατρείᾳ τῇ καθημερινῇ), Thl., Calv., Est., Bengel, Conyb., E. V., and Luther, with ποιεῖσθαι, in which case, besides other objections, the verb would certainly have followed all the substantives, and probably would have taken πρῶτον πάντων with it. It is, in order and importance, his first exhortation) **to make** (cf. ref. Phil. It has been usual to take ποιεῖσθαι *passive :* and most Commentators pass over the word without remark. In such a case, the appeal must be to our sense of the propriety of the middle or passive meaning, according to the arrangement of the words, and spirit of the sentence. And thus I think we shall decide for the middle. In the prominent position of ποιεῖσθαι, if it were passive, and consequently objective in meaning, 'that prayer, &c. be made,' it can hardly be passed over without an emphasis, which here it manifestly cannot have. If on the other hand it is middle, it is subjective, belonging to the person or persons who are implied in παρακαλῶ : and thus serves only as a word of passage to the more important substantives which follow. And in this way the Greek fathers themselves took

def δεήσεις, ef προσευχάς, g ἐντεύξεις, eh εὐχαριστίας, ὑπὲρ   e Phil. iv. 6.
                                                    f Phil. as above
πάντων ἀνθρώπων, 2 ὑπὲρ βασιλέων καὶ πάντων τῶν   (e). ch. v. 5.
                                                  2 Chron.vi.19.
ἐν i ὑπεροχῇ ὄντων, ἵνα k ἤρεμον καὶ l ἡσύχιον βίον   g ch. iv. 5
                                                    only †.
                                                    2 Macc. iv.

8 only. ἐντεύξεις ἐποιεῖτο πρὸς τὸν βασιλέα, Polyb. v. 35. 4. see Rom. viii. 26, 34. xi. 2.
h = Eph. v. 4 reff.   i 1 Cor. ii. 1 only.   l Kings ii. 3 A.   2 Macc. xiii. 6 only.   (ἔχειν, Rom. xiii. 1.)
k here only †. (-ία, Job iv. 16 Symm.)   i 1 Pet. iii. 4 only.   Isa. lxvi. 2 only. (-ία, vv. 11, 12.)

2. om 1st ἐν F k 109² lect-7.   ἠρεμιον F.

it : e. g. Chrys.—πῶς ὑπὲρ παντὸς τοῦ κόσμου, καὶ βασιλέων, κ.τ.λ. ποιούμεθα τὴν δέησιν) supplications, prayers, intercessions (the two former words, δεήσεις and προσευχαί, are perhaps best distinguished as in Eph. vi. 18, by taking προσευχή for prayer in general, δέησις for supplication or petition, the special content of any particular prayer. See Ellicott's note cited there, and cf. ref. Phil. ἐντεύξεις, judging from the cognate verbs ἐντυγχάνω, and ὑπερεντυγχάνω (reff. Rom.), should be marked with a reference to 'request concerning others,' i. e. intercessory prayer. (Ellic. denies this primary reference, supporting his view by ch. iv. 5, where, he says, such a meaning would be inappropriate. But is not the meaning in that very place most appropriate? It is not there intercession for a person : but it is by ἔντευξις, prayer on its behalf and over it, that πᾶν κτίσμα is hallowed. The meaning in Polybius, copiously illustrated by Raphel, an interview or appointed meeting, compellatio aliqua de re, would in the N. T., where the word and its cognates are always used in reference to prayer, for persons or things, necessarily shade off into that of pleading or intercession.) Very various and minute distinctions between the three have been imagined :—e. g. Theodoret :—δέησις μέν ἐστιν ὑπὲρ ἀπαλλαγῆς τινῶν λυπηρῶν ἱκετεία προσφερομένη· προσευχὴ δέ, αἴτησις ἀγαθῶν· ἔντευξις δέ, κατηγορία τῶν ἀδικούντων :—Origen, περὶ εὐχῆς, § 14 (not 44, as in Wetst. and Huther), vol. i. p. 220,—ἡγοῦμαι τοίνυν, δέησιν μὲν εἶναι τὴν ἐλλείποντός τινι μεθ' ἱκετείας περὶ τοῦ ἐκείνου τυχεῖν ἀναπεμπομένην εὐχήν· τὴν δὲ προσευχήν, τὴν μετὰ δοξολογίας περὶ μειζόνων μεγαλοφυέστερον ἀναπεμπομένην ὑπὸ τοῦ· ἔντευξιν δέ, τὴν ὑπὸ παρρησίαν τινὰ πλείονα ἔχοντος περὶ τινων ἀξίωσιν πρὸς θεόν· κ.τ.λ. The most extraordinary of all is Aug.'s view, that the four words refer to the liturgical form of administration of the Holy Communion—δεήσεις being " precationes . . . quas facimus in celebratione sacramentorum antequam illud quod est in Domini mensa incipiat benedici:—orationes (προσευχαί), cum benedicitur et sanctifica-

tur : . . . interpellationes vel . . . postulationes (ἐντεύξεις), fiunt cum populus benedicitur : . . . . quibus peractis, et participato tanto sacramento, εὐχαριστία, gratiarum actio, cuncta concludit." Ep. cxlix. (lix.) 16, vol. ii. p. 636 f.), thanksgivings, for all men (this gives the intercessory character to all that have preceded. On the wideness of Christian benevolence here inculcated, see the argument below, and Tit. iii. 2); for (i. e. 'especially for'—this one particular class being mentioned and no other) kings (see Tit. iii. 1; Rom. xiii. 1 ff.; 1 Pet. ii. 13. It was especially important that the Christians should include earthly powers in their formal public prayers, both on account of the object to be gained by such prayer (see next clause), and as an effectual answer to those adversaries who accused them of rebellious tendencies. Jos. (B. J. ii. 10. 4) gives the Jews' answer to Petronius, Ἰουδαῖοι περὶ μὲν Καίσαρος καὶ τοῦ δήμου τῶν Ῥωμαίων δὶς τῆς ἡμέρας θύειν ἔφασαν, and afterwards (ib. 17. 2), he ascribes the origin of the war to their refusing, at the instigation of Eleazar, to continue the sacrifices offered on behalf of their Gentile rulers. See Wetst., who gives other examples : and compare the ancient liturgies—e. g. the bidding prayers, Bingham, book xv. 1. 2 : the consecration prayer, ib. 3. 1, and on the general practice, ib. 3. 14. 'Kings' must be taken generally, as it is indeed generalized in the following words : not understood to mean ' Cæsar and his assessors in the supreme power,' as Baur, who deduces thence an argument that the Epistle was written under the Antonines, when such an association was usual) and all that are in eminence (not absolutely in authority, though the context, no less than common sense, shews that it would be so. Cf. Polyb. v. 41. 3,—τοῖς ἐν ὑπεροχαῖς οὖσι περὶ τὴν αὐλήν. He, as well as Josephus (e. g. Antt. vi. 4. 3), uses ὑπεροχαί absolutely for authorities : see Schweigh. Lex. Polyb. Thdrt. gives a curious reason for the addition of these words : μάλα σοφῶς τὸ κοινὸν τῶν ἀνθρώπων προστέθεικεν, ἵνα μή τις κολακείαν νομίσῃ τὴν ὑπὲρ τῶν βασιλέων

m Tit. iii. 3 only ‡.
2 Macc. xii. 38.
n = Phil. i. 20 reff.
o Paul, ch. iii. 16. iv. 7, 8. vi. 3, 5, 6, 11.
-βής, Acts x. 2.
q = Rom. xiv. 21.
s = Luke xvi. 15.

ᵐ διάγωμεν ἐν ⁿ πάσῃ ᵒ εὐσεβείᾳ καὶ ᵖ σεμνότητι. ³ τοῦτο γὰρ ᑫ καλὸν καὶ ʳ ἀποδεκτὸν ˢ ἐνώπιον τοῦ ᵗ σωτῆρος ἡμῶν ᵗ θεοῦ, ⁴ ὃς πάντας ἀνθρώπους θέλει σωθῆναι καὶ

ADFKL
PℵabC defgh klmno
17. 47

2 Tim. iii. 5.   Tit. i. 1 only.   Acts iii. 12.   2 Pet. i. 3, 6, 7. iii. 11 only.   Isa. xi. 2.   (-βεῖν, ch. v. 4.
-βῶς, 2 Tim. iii. 12.)   p ch. iii. 4.   Tit. ii. 7 only †.   2 Macc. iii. 12 only.   (-νός, ch. iii. 8.)
2 Cor. viii. 21.   Isa. v. 20.   r ch. v. 4 only †.   (-δοχή. ch. i. 15. -δέχεσθαι, Acts ii. 41.)
Acts iv. 19. ch. v. 4.   1 John iii. 22.   3 Kings iii. 10.   t ch. i. 1 reff.

om πασῃ D¹.   [ευλαβεια P.]
3. om γαρ Aℵ¹ 17. 67² coptt Cyr₂.

εὐχήν. The succeeding clause furnishes reason enough : the security of Christians would often be more dependent on inferior officers than even on kings themselves), that (aim of the prayer—not, as Heydenreich and Matthies,—subjective, that by such prayer Christian men's minds may be tranquillized and disposed to obey,—but objective, that we may obtain the blessing mentioned, by God's influencing the hearts of our rulers: or as Chrys., that we may be in security by their being preserved in safety) we may pass (more than 'lead' (ἄγειν): it includes the whole of the period spoken of:—thus Aristoph. Vesp. 1006 (see also Eccles. 240), ὥσθ' ἡδέως διάγειν σε τὸν λοιπὸν χρόνον,—Soph. Œd. Col. 1615, τὸ λοιπὸν ἤδη τὸν βίον διάξετον: see numerous other examples in Wetst.) a quiet (the adjective ἤρεμος is a late word, formed on the classical adverb ἠρέμα, the proper adjective of which is ἠρεμαῖος, used by Plato, Rep. p. 307 a, Legg. 734 a &c. Cf. Palm and Rost's Lex. sub voce) and tranquil life (ἐκείνων γὰρ πρυτανευόντων εἰρήνην, μεταλαγχάνομεν καὶ ὑμεῖς τῆς γαλήνης, καὶ ἐν ἡσυχίᾳ τῆς εὐσεβείας ἐκπληροῦμεν τοὺς νόμους, Thdrt. On the distinction between ἤρεμος, tranquil from trouble without, and ἡσύχιος, from trouble within, see Ellicott's note) in all ('possible,' 'requisite') piety (I prefer this rendering to 'godliness,' as more literal, and because I would reserve that word as the proper one for θεοσέβεια : see ver. 10 below. εὐσέβεια is one of the terms peculiar in this meaning to the pastoral Epistles, the second Epistle of Peter (reff.), and Peter's speech in Acts iii. 12. See Prolegg., and note on Acts iii. 12) and gravity (so Conyb. : and it seems best to express the meaning. For as Chrys.,—εἰ γὰρ μὴ ἐσώζοντο, μηδὲ εὐδοκίμουν ἐν τοῖς πολέμοις, ἀνάγκη καὶ τὰ ἡμέτερα ἐν ταραχαῖς εἶναι καὶ θορύβοις. ἢ γὰρ καὶ αὐτοὺς ἡμᾶς στρατεύεσθαι ἔδει, κατακοπέντων ἐκείνων· ἢ φεύγειν πανταχοῦ καὶ πλανᾶσθαι : and thus the gravity and decorum of the Christian life would be broken up). 3, 4.] For this (viz.

ποιεῖσθαι δεήσεις κ.τ.λ. ὑπὲρ πάντων ἀνθρώπων, &c. ver. 1 : what has followed since being merely the continuation of this) is good and acceptable (both adjectives are to be taken with ἐνώπιον, &c., not as De W. and Ellic. 'καλόν, good in and of itself:' compare ref. 2 Cor., καλὰ οὐ μόνον ἐνώπιον κυρίου, ἀλλὰ καὶ ἐνώπιον ἀνθρώπων. I still hold, against Ellicott, to this connexion, shrinking from the crude and ill-balanced form of the sentence which the other would bring in. ἀποδεκτόν, peculiar (cf. ἀποδοχή, ch. i. 15) to these Epistles. See 2 Cor. vi. 2) in the sight of our Saviour (a title manifestly chosen as belonging to the matter in hand, cf. next verse. On it, see ch. i. 1) God who (i. e. seeing that He) willeth all men to be saved (see ch. iv. 10: Tit. ii. 11. πάντας ἀνθρώπους is repeated from verse 1. Chrys.'s comment is very noble : μιμοῦ τὸν θεόν. εἰ πάντας ἀνθρώπους θέλει σωθῆναι, εἰκότως ὑπὲρ ἁπάντων δεῖ εὔχεσθαι. εἰ πάντας αὐτὸς ἠθέλε σωθῆναι, θέλε καὶ σύ. εἰ δὲ θέλεις, εὔχου. τῶν γὰρ τοιούτων ἐστὶ τὸ εὔχεσθαι. Huther rightly remarks, that Mosheim's view, "nisi pax in orbe terrarum vigeat, fieri nullo modo posse ut voluntati divinæ quæ omnium hominum salutem cupit, satisfiat," destroys the true context and train of thought : see more below. Wiesinger remarks σωθῆναι,—not σῶσαι, as in Tit. iii. 5, as adapted to the mediatorial effect of prayer, not direct divine agency : but we may go yet further, and say that by θέλει πάντας ἀνθρ. σωθῆναι is expressed human acceptance of offered salvation, on which even God's predestination is contingent. θέλει σῶσαι πάντας could not have been said : if so, He would have saved all, in matter of fact. See the remarks, and references to English and other divines, in Ellicott's note. Calvin most unworthily shuffles out of the decisive testimony borne by this passage to universal redemption. "Apostolus simpliciter intelligit nullum mundi vel populum vel ordinem salute excludi ; quia omnibus sine exceptione evangelium proponi Deus velit.

εἰς ^{uv} ἐπίγνωσιν ^v ἀληθείας ἐλθεῖν. ⁵ εἷς γὰρ θεός, εἷς καὶ u = Rom. iii.
20. Eph. i.
^w μεσίτης θεοῦ καὶ ἀνθρώπων, ἄνθρωπος χριστὸς Ἰησοῦς, 17 reff.
v 2 Macc. ix. 11.
v 2 Tim. ii. 25.
⁶ ὁ ^x δοὺς ^x ἑαυτὸν ^y ἀντίλυτρον ὑπὲρ πάντων, τὸ ^z μαρτύ- iii 7. Tit. i.
1. Heb. x.

26. see ch. iv. 3.   w Gal. iii. 19, 20 reff.   x = Gal. i. 4.   Tit. ii. 14.   1 Macc. vi. 44.
y here only †. (λύτρ , Matt. xx. 28.)   z = 1 Cor. i. 6. ii. 1.   2 Tim. i. 8.

5. ιησ. bef χρ. K b f 114-5 Syr [æth arm Marcell Eus₂] Chr Thdrt-ms Thl.
6. om υπερ L.   for το, και ℵ¹ : om το μαρτυριον A: pref οὗ D¹F 80. 115 vulg-

.... De hominum generibus, non singulis personis sermo est; nihil enim aliud intendit, quam principes et extraneos populos in hoc numero includere." As if kings and all in eminence were not in each case individual men, **and to come to** (the) **certain knowledge** (on ἐπίγνωσις, fuller and more assured than γνῶσις, see 1 Cor. xiii. 12: Col. i. 11; ii. 2) **of** (the) **truth** (the expression is a favourite one in these Epistles, see reff. This realization of the truth is in fact identical with σωτηρία, not only (Huther) as that σωτηρία is a *rescue* from life in untruth, but in its deepest and widest sense of *salvation*, here and hereafter: cf. John xvii. 3, αὕτη ἐστὶν ἡ αἰώνιος ζωή, ἵνα γινώσκωσίν σε τὸν μόνον ἀληθινὸν θεόν ..... and ib. 17, ἁγίασον αὐτοὺς ἐν τῇ ἀληθείᾳ).
5.] **For** (further grounding of the acceptableness of prayer for *all* men,—in the UNITY of God. But this verse is joined by the γάρ directly to the preceding, not to ver. 1. Chrys. gives it rightly—δεικνὺς ὅτι σωθῆναι θέλει πάντας) **there is** ONE **God** (He is ONE in essence and one in purpose—not of different minds to different nations or individuals, but of one mind towards all. Similarly Rom. iii. 30, and, which is important for the understanding of that difficult passage, Gal. iii. 20. The double reference, to the unity in essence and unity of purpose, for which I have contended there, is plain and unmistakeable here), ONE **Mediator** (see reff. It occurs, besides the places in the Gal., only in the Epistle to the Heb., viii. 6; ix. 15; xii. 24. There is no necessity that the idea should, as De W. and Schleierm., be connected with that of a mutual covenant, and so be here far-fetched as regards the context (borrowed from the places in the Heb., according to De W.): the word is used as standing alone, and representing the fact of Christ Jesus being the only *go-between*, in whatever sense) **also** (the εἷς prefixed to the καί for emphasis) **of** (between) **God and men** (if one only goes between, then that One must be for *all*), (the) **man Christ Jesus** (why ἄνθρωπος? Thdrt. answers, ἄνθρωπον δὲ τὸν χριστὸν ὠνόμασεν, ἐπειδὴ μεσίτην ἐκάλεσεν· ἐνανθρωπήσας γὰρ ἐμεσίτευσεν: and so most Commen-

tators. But it is not here the Apostle's object, to set forth the nature of Christ's mediation as regards its being brought about;—only as regards its unity and universality for mankind. And for this latter reason he calls him here by this name MAN,—that He gathered up all our human nature into Himself, becoming its second Head. So that the ἄνθρωπος in fact carries with it the very strongest proof of that which he is maintaining. Notice it is not ὁ ἄνθρωπος, though we are obliged inaccurately thus to express it: in personality, our Lord was not *a man*, but in nature He was man. It might be rendered, "Christ Jesus, Himself man."
I should object, as against Ellicott, to introduce *at all* the indefinite article: not *individual* but *generic* humanity is predicated: and "a man" unavoidably conveys the idea of human individuality. It is singularly unfortunate that Ellic. should have referred to Augustine, Serm. xxvi. as cited by Wordsw., in corroboration of the rendering "a man:" the Latin *homo* being of course as incapable of deciding this as the Greek ἄνθρωπος, and "*a man*" being only Bp. Wordsworth's translation of it. Nay, the whole tenor of the passage of Augustine (ed. Migne, vol. v. p. 174) precludes such a rendering. The stupidity of such writers as Baur and the Socinians, who regard such an expression as against the deity of Christ, is beyond all power of mine to characterize. In the face of εἷς θεός, εἷς **μεσίτης θεοῦ καὶ ἀνθρώπων**, to maintain gravely such a position, shews utter blindness from party bias even to the plainest thoughts expressed in the plainest words), **who gave himself** (reff., especially Tit.) **a ransom** (ἀντί-, as in ἀντιμισθία, Rom. i. 27; 2 Cor. vi. 13: ἀντάλλαγμα, Matt. xvi. 26, expresses more distinctly the reciprocity which is already implied in the simple word in each case. That the main fact alluded to here is the *death* of Christ, we know: but it is not brought into prominence, being included in, and superseded by the far greater and more comprehensive fact, that He gave HIMSELF, in all that He undertook for our redemption: see Phil. ii. 5—8) **on behalf of all** (not of a

a Gal. vi. 9.
ch. vi. 15.
Tit. i. 3 only.
χρώμενοι
τοῖς ἰδίοις
καιροῖς.
Polyb. i. 30.
10.
43. Dan. iii. 4. Sir. xx. 14 only.
h = ch. v. 14. Tit. iii. 8.

ριον ᵃκαιροῖς ᵃ ἰδίοις, 7 ᵇ εἰς ὃ ᵇᶜ ἐτέθην ἐγὼ ᶜᵈ κῆρυξ καὶ
ᶜ ἀπόστολος (ᵉ ἀλήθειαν λέγω, οὐ ᵉᶠ ψεύδομαι), ᶜ διδάσκαλος
ᶜ ἐθνῶν ᵍ ἐν πίστει καὶ ἀληθείᾳ.   8 ʰ Βούλομαι οὖν προς-

ADFKL
Pℵ a b c
d e f g h
k l m n o
17. 47

b ch. i. 12 reff.   c 2 Tim. i. 11.   d 2 Tim. as above (c). 2 Pet. ii. 5 only. Gen. xli.
e Rom. ix. 1.   f Gal. i. 20 reff.   g ch. i. 2 reff.

sixt(with harl¹, not F-lat) Ambrst.   aft ιδιοις ins εδοθη D¹F harl¹ Ambrst.
7. for εις ὁ, εν ω F latt.   for ετεθην, επιστευθην A.   rec aft λεγω ins εν
χριστω (from Rom ix. 1), with D³KLℵ¹ rel goth [arm] Thdrt : om AD¹F[P]ℵ³ c n
[47] 67² latt syrr coptt æth Chr Damasc Thl Œc Ambrst Pel.   for πιστει, πνευματι
A : γνωσι ℵ.

portion of mankind, but of *all men;* the
point of ver. 1, ὑπὲρ **πάντων** ἀνθρώπων),
—**the testimony** ('that which was (to be)
testified:' so St. John frequently uses
μαρτυρία, 1 John v. 9—11: "an accusative in apposition with the preceding sentence." Ellicott. This oneness of the
Mediator, involving in itself the universality of Redemption, was the great subject of Christian testimony : see below) **in
its own seasons** (reff. ; in the times which
God had appointed for it. On the *temporal dative,* see Ellicott's note), **for** (towards) **which** (the μαρτύριον) **I was
placed as a herald** (pastoral Epistles and
2 Pet. only: but see 1 Cor. i. 21, 23 ; ix. 27 ;
xv. 14) **and apostle** (the proclaiming this
universality of the Gospel was the one
object towards which my appointment as
an apostle and preacher was directed.
Those who hold the spuriousness of our
Epistle regard this returning to himself
and his own case on the part of the writer
as an evidence of his being one who was
acting the part of Paul. So Schleierm.
and De W. They have so far truth on
their side, that we must recognize here a
characteristic increase of the frequency of
these personal vindications on the part of
the Apostle, as we so often have occasion
to remark during these Epistles :—the disposition of one who had been long opposed
and worried by adversaries to recur continually to his own claims, the assertion of
which had now become with him almost,
so to speak, a matter of stock-phrases.
Still, the propriety of the assertion here is
evident : it is only in the manner of it
that the above habit is discernible. See
more on this in the Prolegomena. The
same phrase occurs verbatim in ref. 2
Tim.),—**I speak the truth, I lie not**—(in
spite of all that Huther and Wiesinger say
of the evident appropriateness of this
solemn asseveration here, I own I am unable to regard it as any more than a strong
and interesting proof of the growth of a
habit in the Apostle's mind, which we already trace in 2 Cor. xi. 31, Rom. ix. 1,

till he came to use the phrase with less
force and relevance than he had once done.
Nothing can be more natural than that
one whose life was spent in strong conflict
and assertion of his Apostleship, should
repeat the fervour of his usual asseveration,
even when the occasion of that fervour had passed away. Nor can I consent
to abandon such a view because it is designated "questionable and precarious" by
Ellic., who is too apt in cases of difficulty,
to evade the real conflict of decision by
strong terms of this kind)—**a teacher
of the Gentiles** (it was especially in this
latter fact that the ὑπὲρ πάντων ἀνθρώπων
found its justification. The historical
proof of his constitution as a teacher of
the Gentiles is to be found in Acts ix. 15,
xxii. 21, xxvi. 17; but especially in Gal.
ii. 9) **in (the) faith and (the) truth** (do
these words refer subjectively to his own
conduct in teaching the Gentiles, or objectively to that in which he was to instruct them ? The former view is taken
by Thdrt. and most Commentators : μετὰ
τῆς προσηκούσης πίστεως καὶ ἀληθείας
τοῦτο πᾶσι προσφέρω: the latter by
Heydenreich, al. Huther (also Ellic.)
takes the words as signifying the *sphere
in which* he was appointed to fulfil his
office of διδ. ἐθνῶν,—πίστις being *faith,*
the subjective relation, and ἀλήθεια *the
truth,* the objective good which is appropriated by faith : Wiesinger, as meaning
that he is, in the right faith and in the
truth, the διδ. ἔθν. Bengel regards them
merely as another asseveration belonging
to the assertion that he is διδ. ἔθν.,—'in
faith and truth I say it.' This latter at
once discommends itself, from its exceeding flatness : though Chrys. also seems to
have held it—ἐν πίστει πάλιν· ἀλλὰ μὴ
νομίσῃς ἐπειδὴ ἐν πίστει ἤκουσας, ὅτι
ἀπάτη τὸ πρᾶγμά ἐστι. καὶ γὰρ ἐν ἀληθείᾳ φησίν. εἰ δὲ ἀλήθεια, οὐκ ἔστι ψεῦδος.
In judging between these, we must take
into account the usage of ἀλήθεια above,
ver. 4, in a very similar reference, when it
was to be matter of teaching to all men.

εὔχεσθαι τοὺς ἄνδρας ἐν παντὶ τόπῳ, ⁱ ἐπαίροντας ᵏ ὁσίους
ⁱ χεῖρας ˡ χωρὶς ὀργῆς καὶ ˡᵐ διαλογισμοῦ. ⁹ ⁿ ὡσαύτως
καὶ γυναῖκας ᵒ ἐν ᵖ καταστολῇ ᑫ κοσμίῳ ʳ μετὰ ˢ αἰδοῦς

i Luke xxiv.
50. Ps. lxii.
4 (6).
k Acts ii. 27.
xiii. 34, 35.
Tit. i. 8.
Heb. vi. 26.
Rev. xv.

4. xvi. 5 only. Prov. xxii. 11. θεοῖς . . . ὁσίας δεξιὰς κ. ἀριστερὰς ἀνίσχοντες, Demosth. Meid. 611
(Wolf.). l Phil. ii. 14. m ÷ Phil. as above (l). Luke xxiv. 38. n = ch. iii. 8, 11. Tit. ii.
3, 6. Prov. xxvii. 15. o = Matt. vi. 29. Tit. i. 6. p here only. Isa. lxi. 3 only. see note.
q ch. iii. 2 only. Eccl. xii. 9 only. r Mark iii. 5, &c. 1 Chron. xxix. 22. s here (Heb.
xii. 28 v. r.) only †.

8. [τους ανδρας bef προσευχ. DF vulg coptt goth Orig₁(txt₄) Eus₃.] διαλογισμων
Fℵ³ a c 17 [47] 67² syrr copt Orig₄ Eus Mac Bas Thdrt₂ Damasc-comn Jer: txt
ADKL[P]ℵⁱ rel vulg spec [sah] goth [arm] Orig₃[and int₄] Chr. (*The plur is every
where used in the N. T. except here and Luke* ix. 46, 47 : *hence appy the alteration.*)
9. om 1st και A[P]ℵ¹ 17 Clem. rec in τας bef γυναικας (*to suit τους ανδρας
above*), with [D²]KL rel Chr Thdrt : om AD¹F[P]ℵ 17. 67² Clem Orig₂. κοσμιως

There it undoubtedly is, though anarthrous, *the truth* of God. I would therefore take it similarly here, as Wiesinger,
—the sphere in which both his teaching
and their learning was to be employed—
the truth of the Gospel. Then, if so, it is
surely harsh to make ἐν πίστει subjective,
especially as the ἐν is not repeated before
ἀληθείᾳ. It too will most properly be objective,—and likewise regard that in which,
as an element or sphere, he was to teach
and they to learn : *the faith.* This ἐν π.
κ. ἀλ. will be, not the object of διδάσκαλ.,
but the sphere or element in which he is
the διδάσκαλος). **8.**] See summary
at beginning of chapter. **I will then** ("in
βούλομαι the active wish is implied : it is
no mere willingness or acquiescence," Ellic.
On the distinction between βούλομαι and
θέλω, see Donaldson, Cratyl. § 463, p. 650
f. ed. 2 : and Ellic. on ch. v. 14) **that the
men** (the E. V. by omitting the article,
has entirely obscured this passage for its
English readers, not one in a hundred of
whom ever dream of a distinction of the
sexes being here intended. But again
the position of τοὺς ἄνδρας forbids us from
supposing that such distinction was the
Apostle's main object in this verse. Had
it been so, we should have read τοὺς ἄνδρας προσεύχεσθαι. As it now stands, the
stress is on προσεύχεσθαι, and τοὺς ἄνδρας
is taken for granted. Thus the main subject of ver. 1 is carried on, the duty of
PRAYER, in general—not (as Schleierm.
objects) one portion merely of it, the allotting it to its proper offerers) **pray in
every place** (these words ἐν παντὶ τόπῳ
regard the general duty of praying, not
the particular detail implied in τοὺς ἄνδρας: still less are we to join τοὺς ἄνδρας
(τοὺς) ἐν παντὶ τόπῳ. It is a *local* command respecting prayer, answering to the
temporal command ἀδιαλείπτως προσεύχεσθε, 1 Thess. v. 17. It is far-fetched
and irrelevant to the context to find in
the words, as Chr., Thdrt., al., Pel.,

Erasm., Calv., Beza, Grot., al., the Christian's freedom from prescription of place
for prayer—πρὸς τὴν νομικὴν διαγόρευσιν
τέθεικεν· οὐ γὰρ (vulgo ὃς γὰρ) τοῖς
Ἱεροσολύμοις περιέγραψε τὴν λατρείαν,
Thdrt.: and Chrys., ὅπερ τοῖς Ἰουδαίοις
θέμις οὐκ ἦν), **lifting up holy hands** (see
LXX, ref. Ps.: also Ps. xxvii. 2, xliii. 20;
Clem. Rom. Ep. 1 to Corinthians, ch. 29,
p. 269: προσέλθωμεν αὐτῷ ἐν ὁσιότητι
ψυχῆς, ἁγνὰς καὶ ἀμιάντους χεῖρας αἴροντες
πρὸς αὐτόν. These two passages, as Huther observes, testify to the practice in the
Christian church. The form ὁσίους
with a feminine is unusual : but we must
not, as Winer suggests (edn. 6, § 11.
1), join it to ἐπαίροντας. His own instances, στρατιὰ οὐράνιος, Luke ii. 13,—
Ἶρις . . . ὅμοιος, Rev. iv. 3, furnish some
precedent : and the fact that the ending
-ιος is common to all three establishes an
analogy. "Those hands are holy, which
have not surrendered themselves as instruments of evil desire: the contrary are
βέβηλοι χεῖρες, 2 Macc. v. 16: compare,
for the expression, Job xvii. 9, Ps. xxiii. 4,
and in the N. T., especially James iv. 8,
καθαρίσατε χεῖρας καὶ ἁγνίσατε καρδίας."
Huther. See classical passages in Wetst.)
without (separate from, "putting away,"
as Conyb.) **wrath and disputation** (i. e.
in tranquillity and mutual peace, so literally, *sine disceptatione*, as vulg., see
note on ref. Phil. Ellic.'s objection, that
we should thus import from the context
a meaning unconfirmed by good lexical
authority, is fully met by the unquestion-
able usage of the verb διαλογίζω in the
N. T. for to *dispute*. At the same time,
seeing that the matter treated of is *prayer,*
where *disputing* hardly seems in place,
perhaps *doubting* is the better sense ;
which, after all, is a disputation within
one's self). **9.**] So also (ὡσαύτως,
by the parallel passage, Tit. ii. 3, seems
to be little more than a copula, not
necessarily to refer to the matter which

† Acts xxvi. 25 (Paul). ver.

καὶ ᵗ σωφροσύνης ᵘ κοσμεῖν ἑαυτάς, μὴ ᵒ ἐν ᵛ πλέγμασιν ADFKL

15 only †.
2 Macc. iv. 37 καὶ ʷ χρυσῷ ἢ ˣ μαργαρίταις ἢ ʸ ἱματισμῷ ᶻ πολυτελεῖ,
only.
u Matt. xii. 44   10 ἀλλ' ὃ ᵃ πρέπει γυναιξὶν ᵇ ἐπαγγελλομέναις ᶜ θεοσέβειαν,
L. xxiii.

P℣ a b c
d e f g h
k l m n o
17. 47

29. xxv. 7.
Luke xxi. 5.   Tit. ii. 10.   1 Pet. iii. 5.   Rev. xxi. 2, 19 only.   Ezek. xvi. 11, 13.   v here only.   Isa. xxviii.
5 Aq. Theod.   w Paul, Acts xvii. 29.   1 Cor. iii. 12 only.   Matt. ii. 11 al.   Sir. xlv. 10.   x Matt.
vii. 6. xiii. 45, 46.   Rev. xvii. 4. xviii. 12, 16. xxi. 21 bis only †.   y Luke vii. 25. ix. 29.   John xix.
24, from Ps. xxi. 18.   Acts xx. 33 only.   Ps. xliv. 9.   z Mark xiv. 3.   1 Pet. iii. 4 only.   Prov. i. 13.
a Eph. v. 3 reff.   b = ch. vi. 21 (Tit. i. 2 reff.) only ‡.   c here only.   Job xxviii. 28.   Gen. xx.
11. (-βής, John ix. 31.)

D¹Fℵ³ 17 Orig-ms₁ : -ιων K.   [transp αιδ. and σωφρ. D.]   καταπλεγμασιν A.
    rec (for 3rd καὶ) η, with D²KL rel G-lat(altern) syr [sah] goth Clem [Orig₁
Cypr₂] : om [P] 17 [æth] : txt AD¹Fℵ Syr (copt) Orig₁.   χρυσιω (from 1 Pet iii.
3) AF[P] 17 [47] Chr-ms Thl-ms : txt DKLℵ rel Clem Orig.

has been last under treatment) **I will
that women** (without the article, the
reference to τοὺς ἄνδρας above is not so
pointed : i.e. we need not imagine that the
reference is necessarily to the same matter
of detail, but may regard the verse (see
below) as pointing to the general duties
and behaviour of women, as not belonging
to the category of οἱ προσευχόμενοι ἐν
παντὶ τόπῳ) **adorn themselves** (there is
no need, as Chrys. and most Commentators, to supply προσεύχεσθαι to complete
the sense : indeed if I have apprehended
the passage rightly, it would be altogether
irrelevant. The ὡσαύτως serving merely
as a copula (see above) the προσεύχεσθαι
belonging solely and emphatically to τοὺς
ἄνδρας,—the question, 'what then are
women to do?' is answered by insisting
on modesty of appearance and the ornament of good works, as contrasted (ver.
12) with the man's part. The public assemblies are doubtless, in ver. 12, still before the Apostle's mind, but in a very
slight degree. It is the general duties of
women, rather than any single point in
reference to their conduct in public worship, to which he is calling attention :
though the subject of public worship led
to his thus speaking, and has not altogether disappeared from his thoughts.
According to this view, the construction
proceeds direct with the infinitive κοσμεῖν,
without any supposition of an anacoluthon,
as there must be on the other hypothesis)
in orderly (ref.) **apparel** (cf. Tit. ii. 3,
note : "in seemly guise," Ellic. καταστολή, originally 'arrangement,' 'putting
in order,' followed in its usage that of its
verb καταστέλλω. We have in Eur.
Bacch. 891, αὐτὸν (τὸν πλόκαμον) πάλιν
καταστελοῦμεν,—'we will re-arrange the
dishevelled lock :' then Aristoph. Thesm.
256, ἴθι νῦν κατάστειλόν με τὰ περὶ τὼ
σκέλη—clothe, dress me. Thus in Plut.
Pericl. 5, we read of Anaxagoras, that his
καταστολὴ περιβολῆς, 'arrangement of
dress,' was πρὸς οὐδὲν ἐκταραττομένη

πάθος ἐν τῷ λέγειν. Then in Jos. B. J.
ii. 8. 4, of the Essenes, that their καταστολὴ καὶ σχῆμα σώματος was ὅμοιον τοῖς
μετὰ φόβου παιδαγωγουμένοις παισίν,
which he proceeds to explain by saying
οὔτε δὲ ἐσθῆτας, οὔτε ὑποδήματα ἀμεί-
βουσι, πρὶν ἢ διαρραγῆναι, κ.τ.λ. So
that we must take it as meaning 'the apparel,' the whole investiture of the person.
This he proceeds presently to break up
into detail, forbidding πλέγματα, χρυσόν,
μαργαρίτας, ἱματισμὸν πολυτελῆ, all
which are parts of the καταστολή. This
view of the meaning of the word requires
ἐν καταστολῇ κοσμίῳ to belong to κοσμεῖν,
and then to be taken up by the ἐν following, an arrangement, as it seems to me,
also required by the natural construction
of the sentence itself) **with shamefastness**
(not, as modern reprints of the E. V.,
'shamefacedness,' which is a mere unmeaning corruption by the printers of a
very expressive and beautiful word : see
Trench, N. T. Synonyms, § xx.) **and self-
restraint** (I adopt Conybeare's word as,
though not wholly satisfactory, bringing
out the leading idea of σωφροσύνη better
than any other. Its fault is, that it is a
word too indicative of *effort*, as if the un-
chaste desires were continually breaking
bounds, and as continually held in check :
whereas in the σώφρων, the safe-and-
sound-minded, no such continual struggle
has place, but the better nature is established in its rule. Trench (ubi supra)
has dealt with the two words, setting
aside the insufficient distinction of Xenophon, Cyr. viii. 1. 31,—where he says of
Cyrus, διῄρει δὲ αἰδῶ καὶ σωφροσύνην
τῇδε, ὡς τοὺς μὲν αἰδουμένους τὰ ἐν τῷ
φανερῷ αἰσχρὰ φεύγοντας, τοὺς δὲ σώφρονας καὶ τὰ ἐν τῷ ἀφανεῖ. "If," Trench
concludes, "αἰδώς is the 'shamefastness,'
or tendency which shrinks from over-
passing the limits of womanly reserve and
modesty, as well as from the dishonour
which would justly attach thereto, σωφροσύνη is that habitual inner self-govern-

δι' ^d ἔργων ^d ἀγαθῶν. ¹¹ γυνὴ ἐν ^e ἡσυχίᾳ ^f μανθανέτω
ἐν ^g πάσῃ ^h ὑποταγῇ. ¹² διδάσκειν δὲ γυναικὶ οὐκ ⁱ ἐπι-
τρέπω, οὐδὲ ^k αὐθεντεῖν ἀνδρός, ἀλλ' εἶναι ἐν ^e ἡσυχίᾳ.
¹³ Ἀδὰμ γὰρ πρῶτος ^l ἐπλάσθη, εἶτα Εὖα. ¹⁴ καὶ

d = Acts ix. 36.
Rom. xiii. 3.
2 Cor. ix. 8.
ch. v. 10 al.
e 2 Thess. iii.
12 reff.
f absol., 1 Cor.
xiv. 31.
g Phil. i. 20
reff.

2 Cor. ix. 13. Gal. ii. 5. ch. iii. 4 only †. (-τάσσειν, Tit. ii. 5.)
61. Acts xxvi. 1 al. Job xxxii. 14.
20 only. Gen. ii. 7, 8.
k here only †. (-τῆς, Wisd. xii. 6.)
i Luke viii. 32 ‖ Mt. ix. 59,
1 Rom. ix.

12. rec γυναικι δε διδασκειν, with KL rel syr [sah æth] Thdr-mops Chr Thdrt
Damasc Ambr, and, omg δε, k Did: txt ADF[P]א m 17 latt goth arm [Orig-c₁] Cypr
Ambrst Jer. [αλλα A 17.]

ment, with its constant rein on all the passions and desires, which would hinder the temptation to this from arising, or at all events from arising in such strength as should overbear the checks and hindrances which αἰδώς opposed to it." Ellic. gives for it, "sober-mindedness," and explains it, "*the well-balanced state of mind, arising from habitual self-restraint.*" See his notes, here, and in' his translation), **not in plaits** (of hair: cf. 1 Pet. iii. 3, ἐμπλοκῇ τριχῶν, and see Ellicott's note) **and gold** (καὶ περιθέσεως χρυσίων, 1 Pet. l. c., perhaps, from the καί, the gold is supposed to be twined among, or worn with, the plaited hair. See Rev. xvii. 4), **or pearls, or costly raiment** (= ἐνδύσεως ἱματίων, 1 Pet. l. c.),—but, **which is becoming for women professing** (ἐπαγγέλλεσθαι is ordinarily in N. T. 'to promise,' see reff. But the meaning 'to profess,' 'præ se ferre,' is found in the classics, e. g. Xen. Mem. i. 2. 7, ἐθαύμαζε δέ, εἴ τις ἀρετὴν ἐπαγγελλόμενος ἀργύριον πράττοιτο: cf. Palm and Rost's Lex., and the numerous examples in Wetst.) **godliness** (θεοσέβεια is found in Xen. An. ii. 6. 26, and Plato, Epinomis, pp. 985 d, 989 e. The adjective θεοσεβής is common enough), — **by means of good works** (not ἐν again, because the adornment lies in a different sphere and cannot be so expressed. The adorning which results from good works is brought about by (διά) their practice, not displayed by appearing to be invested with them (ἐν). Huther's construction, after Thdrt., Œc., Luth., Calv., and Mack and Matthies,—ἐπαγγελλ. θεοσέβειαν δι' ἔργων ἀγαθῶν,—is on all grounds objectionable: —1) the understanding ὅ as ἐν τούτῳ ὅ or καθ' ὅ, which of itself might pass, introduces great harshness into the sentence: —2) the junction of ἐπαγγελλομέναις δι' is worse than that of κοσμεῖν δι', to which he objects:—3) the arrangement of the words is against it, which would thus rather be γυναιξὶν δι' ἔργων ἀγαθῶν θεοσέβειαν ἐπαγγελλομέναις:—4) he does not see that his objection, that the adorn-

ment of women has been already specified by ἐν καταστολῇ κ.τ.λ., and therefore need not be again specified by δι' ἔργων ἀγ., applies just as much to his own rendering, taking ὅ for καθ' ὅ or ἐν τούτῳ ὅ).

11.] Let a woman learn (in the congregation, and every where : see below) **in silence in all** (possible) **subjection** (the thought of the public assemblies has evidently given rise to this precept (see 1 Cor. xiv. 34) ; but he carries it further than can be applied to them in the next verse): **but** (the contrast is to a suppressed hypothesis of a claim to do that which is forbidden: cf. a similar δέ, 1 Cor. xi. 16) **to a woman I permit not to teach** (in the church (primarily), or, as the context shews, any where else), **nor to lord it over** (αὐθέντης μηδέποτε χρήσῃ ἐπὶ τοῦ δεσπότου, ὡς οἱ περὶ τὰ δικαστήρια ῥήτορες, ἀλλ' ἐπὶ τοῦ αὐτόχειρος φονέως, Phryn. But Euripides thus uses it, Suppl. 442 : καὶ μὴν ὅπου γε δῆμος αὐθέντης χθονός, ὑποῦσιν ἀστοῖς ἥδεται νεανίαις. The fact is that the word itself is originally a 'vox media,' signifying merely 'one who with his own hand' .... and the context fills up the rest, αὐθέντης φόνου, or the like. And in course of time, the meaning of 'autocrat' prevailing, the word itself and its derivatives henceforth took this course, and αὐθεντέω, -ία, -ημα, all of later growth, bore this reference only. Later still we have αὐθεντικός, *from first authority* ('id enim αὐθεντικῶς, nuntiabatur,' Cic. ad Att. x. 9). It seems quite a mistake to suppose that αὐθέντης arrived at its meaning of a despot by passing through that of a murderer) **the man, but** (supply ("βούλομαι, not κελεύω, which St. Paul does not use." Ellic.) '*I command her :*' the construction in 1 Cor. xiv. 34, is the same) **to be in silence. 13.]** *Reason of this precept, in the original order of creation.* **For Adam was first** (not of all men, which is not here under consideration, and would stultify the subsequent clause :—but first in comparison with Eve) **made** (see ref. Gen., from which

m Eph. v. 6.
James i. 26
only. Job
xxxi. 27.
n 2 Thess. ii. 3
reff.
o Luke xxii.
44. Acts
xxii. 17.
p Gal. iii. 19
reff.
ch. v. 14.)

'Αδὰμ οὐκ ᵐ ἠπατήθη, ἡ δὲ γυνὴ ⁿ ἐξαπατηθεῖσα ᵒ ἐν ᵖ παραβάσει ᵒ γέγονεν, 15 �q σωθήσεται δὲ ʳ διὰ τῆς ˢ τεκνο-γονίας, ἐὰν μείνωσιν ᵗ ἐν πίστει καὶ ἀγάπῃ καὶ ᵘ ἁγιασμῷ μετὰ ᵛ σωφροσύνης.

14. rec απατηθεισα (*on this reading, critical considerations are somewhat uncertain. On the one hand,* ἐξαπ. *may have come from* Rom vii. 11. 2 Cor xi. 3 : *on the other,* ἀπ. *may be a corrn to suit* ἠπατήθη *above. And this latter, as lying so much nearer the corrector's eye, seems the more prob : especially as in* Gen iii. 13 *it stands* ὁ ὄφις ἠπάτησέν με), with D³KLℵ³ rel 67² : txt AD¹F[P]ℵ¹ c 17 Bas Chr₁.

15. for δε, γαρ D¹ : om a¹.

the word ἐπλάσθη seems to be taken : cf. 1 Cor. xi. 8, 9, and indeed that whole passage, which throws light on this), **then Eve. 14.**] *Second reason*—as the woman was *last in being,* so she was *first in sin*—indeed *the only victim* of the Tempter's deceit. **And Adam was not deceived** (not to be weakened, as Thdrt. τὸ οὐκ ἠπατήθη, ἀντὶ τοῦ, οὐ πρῶτος, εἴρηκεν : nor, as Matthies, must we supply ὑπὸ τοῦ ὄφεως : nor, with De W., Wiesinger, al., must we press the fact that the woman only was *misled* by the senses. Bengel and Huther seem to me (but cf. Ellicott) to have apprehended the right reference : 'serpens mulierem decepit, mulier virum non decepit, sed ei persuasit.' As Huther observes, the ἠπάτησεν, in the original narrative, is used of the woman only. We read of no communication between the serpent and the *man.* The "subtlest beast of all the field" knew his course better : *she* listened to the lower solicitation of sense and expediency : he to the higher one of conjugal love) : **but the woman** (not now *Eve,* but generic, as the next clause shews : for Eve could not be the subject to σωθήσεται) **having been seduced** BY DECEIT (stronger than ἀπατηθεῖσα, as *exoro* than *oro* : implying the full success of the ἀπάτη) **has become involved** (the thought is—the present state of transgression in which the woman (and the man too : but that is not treated here) by sin is constituted, arose (which was not so in the man) from her originally having been *seduced by deceit*) **in transgression** (here as always, breach of a positive command : cf. Rom. iv. 15). **15.**] **But** (contrast to this her great and original defect) **she** (general) **shall be saved through** (brought safely through, but in the higher, which is with St. Paul the only sense of σώζω, see below) **her child-bearing** (in order to understand the fulness of the meaning of σωθήσεται here, we must bear in mind the history itself, to

which is the constant allusion. The curse on the woman for her παράβασις was, ἐν λύπαις τέξῃ τέκνα (Gen. iii. 16). Her τεκνογονία is that in which the curse finds its operation. What then is here promised her ? Not only exemption from that curse in its worst and heaviest effects : not merely that she shall safely bear children : but the Apostle uses the word σωθήσεται purposely for its higher meaning, and the construction of the sentence is precisely as ref. 1 Cor.—αὐτὸς δὲ σωθήσεται, οὕτως δὲ ὡς διὰ πυρός. Just as that man should be saved through, as passing through, fire which is his trial, his hindrance in his way, in spite of which he escapes,—so she shall be saved, through, as passing through, her child-bearing, which is her trial, her curse, her (not means of salvation, but) hindrance in the way of it.   The other renderings which have been given seem to me both irrelevant and ungrammatical. Chrys., Thl., al., for instance, would press τεκνογονία to mean the Christian education of children : Heinrichs, strangely enough, holds that her τέκνογ. is the *punishment* of her sin, and that being undergone, she shall be saved διὰ τῆς τ., i. e. by having paid it. Conyb. gives it '*women will be saved by the bearing of children,*' i. e., as he explains it in his note, "are to be kept in the path of safety (?) by the performance of the peculiar functions which God has assigned to their sex." Some, in their anxiety to give διά the instrumental meaning, would understand διὰ τῆς τεκνογ. ' by means of *the Child-bearing,*' i. e. ' the Incarnation :' a rendering which needs no refutation. I see that Ellicott maintains this latter interpretation : still I find no reason to qualify what I have above written. 1 Cor. iii. 15 seems to me so complete a key of Pauline usage of σώζεσθαι διά, that I cannot abandon the path opened by it, till far stronger reason has been shewn than he here alleges. In his

III. [w] Πιστὸς ὁ λόγος· εἴ τις [x] ἐπισκοπῆς [y] ὀρέγεται, [w ch. i. 15 reff. x = Acts i. 20, from Ps. cviii. 8.] [z] καλοῦ [z] ἔργου [a] ἐπιθυμεῖ. [2] δεῖ οὖν τὸν [b] ἐπίσκοπον [c] ἀνεπίλημπτον εἶναι, [d] μιᾶς γυναικὸς [d] ἄνδρα, [e] νηφάλιον, [(Luke xix. 44. 1 Pet. ii. 12 [v. 6 v. r.]]

only.) [y ch. vi. 10. Heb. xi. 16 only †. (act., Job viii. 20 Symm.) [z Matt. v. 16. xxvi.] 10 ‖ Mk. John x. 32, 33. Epp., ch. v. 10, 25. vi. 18. Tit. ii. 7, 14. iii. 8, 14. Heb. x. 24. 1 Pet. ii. 12 only. a constr., Acts xx. 33 only (Paul). Prov. xxiii. 3, 6. b Acts xx. 28. Phil. i. 1. Tit. i. 7. 1 Pet. ii. 25 only. 4 Kings xi. 18. Job xx. 29. Isa. lx. 17. c ch. v. 7. vi. 14 only †. d Tit. i. 6. e ver. 11. Tit. ii. 2 only †. (-φεὶν, 1 Thess. v. 6.)

CHAP. III. 1. for πιστος, ανθρωπινος (probably introduced from the humanus of some of the latin vss : see Ellic here, and cf var readd, ch i. 15) D : G-lat has both.
2. [for ουν, δε F Syr : om æth arm.]　　rec νηφαλεον, with D³K a e f n [47] Damasc: -λαιον FL[P]ℵ³ d o : txt AD¹ℵ¹ rel Orig.sæpe Naz.

second edition he has not in any way strengthened his argument, nor has he taken any notice of the Pauline usage which I allege. After all, it is mainly a question of exegetical tact: and I own I am surprised that any scholar can believe it possible that St. Paul can have expressed the Incarnation by the bare word ἡ τεκνογονία. He himself in this same Epistle, v. 14, uses the cognate verb, of the ordinary bearing of children : and these are the only places where the compound occurs in the N. T.), if they (generic plural as before singular) have remained (shall be found in that day to have remained—a further proof of the higher meaning of σωθήσεται) in faith and love and holiness (see reff., where the word is used in the same reference, of holy chastity) with selfrestraint (see above on ver. 9).

CH. III. 1—13.] Precepts respecting overseers (presbyters) (1—7), and deacons (8—13).　　1.] Faithful is the saying (see on ch. i. 15, from the analogy of which it appears that the words are to be referred to what follows, not, as Chrys., Thl., Erasm., al., to what has preceded): if any man seeks (it does not seem that he uses ὀρέγεται with any reference to an ambitious seeking, as De W. thinks : in Heb. xi. 16 the word is a 'vox media,' and even in ch. vi. 10, the blame rests, not on ὀρεγόμενοι, but on the thing sought; and in Polyb. ix. 20. 5, the word is used as one merely of passage, in giving directions respecting the office sought: κελεύοντες ἀστρολογεῖν κ. γεωμετρεῖν τοὺς ὀρεγομένους αὐτῆς (τῆς στρατηγίας). So that De W.'s inference respecting ambition for the episcopate betraying the late age of the Epistle, falls to the ground) the overseership (or, bishopric; office of an ἐπίσκοπος; but the ἐπίσκοποι of the N. T. have officially nothing in common with our Bishops. See notes on Acts xx. 17, 28. The identity of the ἐπίσκοπος and πρεσβύτερος in apostolic times is evident from Tit. i. 5—7: see also note on Phil. i. 1, the article Bischof in Herzog's

Real-Encyclopädie, and Ellic.'s note here), he desires a good work (not 'a good thing:' but a good employment: see 1 Thess. v. 13 : 2 Tim. iv. 5 : one of the καλὰ ἔργα so often spoken of (reff.)). It behoves then (οὖν is best regarded as taking up καλὸν ἔργον, and substantiating that assertion : "bonum negotium bonis committendum," Bengel) an (τόν generic, singular of τοὺς ἐπισκόπους) overseer to be blameless (Thucyd. v. 17, Πλειστοάναξ δὲ . . . . νομίζων . . . κἂν αὐτὸς τοῖς ἐχθροῖς ἀνεπίληπτος εἶναι . . . . ., where the Schol. has, μὴ ἂν αὐτὸς παρέξων κατηγορίας ἀφορμήν. Thdrt. draws an important distinction : μηδεμίαν πρόφασιν μέμψεως παρέχειν δικαίαν· τὸ γὰρ ἀνεπίληπτον, οὐ τὸ ἀσυκοφάντητον λέγει· ἐπεὶ καὶ αὐτὸς ἀπόστολος παντοδαπᾶς συκοφαντίας ὑπέμεινεν), husband of one wife (two great varieties of interpretation of these words have prevailed, among those who agree to take them as restrictive, not injunctive, which the spirit of the passage and the insertion of μιᾶς surely alike forbid. They have been supposed to prohibit either 1) simultaneous polygamy, or 2) successive polygamy. 1) has somewhat to be said for it. The custom of polygamy was then prevalent among the Jews (see Just. Mart. Tryph. 134, p. 226, —διδασκάλοις ὑμῶν οἵτινες καὶ μέχρι νῦν καὶ τέσσαρας κ. πέντε ἔχειν ὑμᾶς γυναῖκας ἕκαστον συγχωροῦσι : and Jos. Antt. vii. 2 (so cited in Suicer and Huther, but the reference is wrong), πάτριον ἐν ταύτῳ πλείοσιν ἡμῖν συνοικεῖν), and might easily find its way into the Christian community. And such, it is argued, was the Apostle's reference, not to second marriages, which he himself commands ch. v. 14, and allows in several other places, e. g. Rom. vii. 2, 3 : 1 Cor. vii. 39. But the objection to taking this meaning is, that the Apostle would hardly have specified that as a requisite for the episcopate or presbyterate, which we know to have been fulfilled by all Christians whatever : no instance being adduced of polygamy being practised in the Chris-

f Tit. i 8. ii. 2, f σώφρονα, g κόσμιον, h φιλόξενον, i διδακτικόν· 3 μὴ ADFKL
5 only†.   Pℵ a b c
(-φρόνως,   d e f g h
Tit. ii. 12.)   g ch. ii. 9 only.   Eccles. xii. 9 only.   h Tit. i. 8.   1 Pet. iv. 9 only†.   (-νία, Rom.   k l m n o
xii. 13.)   i 2 Tim. ii. 24 only†.   17. 47

tian church, and no exhortations to abstain from it. As to St. Paul's command
and permissions, see below. Still, we must
not lose sight of the circumstance that the
earlier Commentators were unanimous for
this view. Chrys. is the only one who
proposes an alternative :—τὴν ἀμετρίαν
κωλύει, ἐπειδὴ ἐπὶ τῶν Ἰουδαίων ἐξῆν καὶ
δευτέροις ὁμιλεῖν γάμοις, κ. δύο ἔχειν κατὰ
ταὐτὸν γυναῖκας. Thdrt.: τὸ δὲ μιᾶς γυναικὸς ἄνδρα, εὖ μοι δοκοῦσιν εἰρηκέναι
τινές. πάλαι γὰρ εἰώθεισαν καὶ Ἕλληνες
κ. Ἰουδαῖοι κ. δύο κ. τρισὶ κ. πλείοσι γυ-
ναιξὶ νόμῳ γάμου κατὰ ταὐτὸν συνοικεῖν.
τινὲς δὲ καὶ νῦν, καίτοι τῶν βασιλικῶν
νόμων δύο κατὰ ταὐτὸν ἄγεσθαι κωλυόντων γυναῖκας, καὶ παλλακίσι μίγνυνται
κ. ἑταίραις. ἔφασαν τοίνυν τὸν θεῖον ἀπόστολον εἰρηκέναι, τὸν μιᾷ μόνῃ γυναικὶ
συνοικοῦντα σωφρόνως, τῆς ἐπισκοπικῆς
ἄξιον εἶναι χειροτονίας. οὐ γὰρ τὸν δεύτερον, φασίν, ἐξέβαλε γάμον, ὅ γε πολλάκις τοῦτο γενέσθαι κελεύσας. And similarly Thl., Œc., and Jer.   2) For the view
that *second marriages* are prohibited to
aspirants after the episcopate,—is, the
most probable meaning (see there) of ἑνὸς
ἀνδρὸς γυνή in ch. v. 9,—as also the wide
prevalence in the early Church of the idea
that, although second marriages were not
forbidden to Christians, abstinence from
them was better than indulgence in them.
So Hermas Pastor, ii. 4. 4, p. 921 f.,
'Domine, si vir vel mulier alicujus dis-
cesserit, et nupserit aliquis eorum, num-
quid peccat?' 'Qui nubit, non peccat:
sed si per se manserit, magnum sibi con-
quirit honorem apud Dominum :' and
Clem. Alex. Strom. iii. 12 (81), p. 548 P.,
ὁ ἀπόστολος (1 Cor. vii. 39, 40) δι᾽
ἀκρασίαν κ. πύρωσιν κατὰ συγγνώμην
δευτέρου μεταδίδωσι γάμου, ἐπεὶ κ. οὗτος
οὐχ ἁμαρτάνει μὲν κατὰ διαθήκην, οὐ γὰρ
κεκώλυται πρὸς τοῦ νόμου, οὐ πληροῖ δὲ
τῆς κατὰ τὸ εὐαγγέλιον πολιτείας τὴν
κατ᾽ ἐπίτασιν τελειότητα. And so in
Suicer, i. p. 892 f., Chrys., Greg. Naz. (τὸ
πρῶτον (συνοικέσιον) νόμος, τὸ δεύτερον
συγχώρησις, τὸ τρίτον παρανομία. τὸ δὲ
ὑπὲρ τοῦτο, χοιρώδης. Orat. xxxvii. 8,
p. 650),—Epiphanius (δευτερόγαμον οὐκ
ἔξεστι δέχεσθαι ἐν αὐτῇ (τῇ ἐκκλησίᾳ) εἰς
ἱερωσύνην. Doct. compend. de fide, p.
1104), Orig.,—the Apostolical Canon xvii.
(ὁ δυσὶ γάμοις συμπλακεὶς μετὰ τὸ βάπτισμα, ἢ παλλακὴν κτησάμενος, οὐ δύναται
εἶναι ἐπίσκοπος, ἢ πρεσβύτερος, ἢ διάκονος,
ἢ ὅλως τοῦ καταλόγου τοῦ ἱερατικοῦ), &c.

Huther cites from Athenagoras the expression εὐπρεπὴς μοιχεία applied to
second marriage. With regard to the
Apostle's own command and permissions
of this state (see above), they do not come
into account here, because they are confessedly (and expressly so in ch. v. 14)
for those whom it was not contemplated
to admit into ecclesiastical office. 3)
There have been some divergent lines of
interpretation, but they have not found
many advocates. Some (e. g. Wegscheider)
deny altogether the formal reference to
1) or 2), and understand the expression
only of a chaste life of fidelity to the
marriage vow: "that neither polygamy,
nor concubinage, nor any offensive deu-
terogamy, should be able to be alleged
against such a person." But surely this
is very vague, for the precise words μιᾶς
γυναικὸς ἀνήρ. Bretschneider maintains
that μιᾶς is here the indefinite article, and
that the Apostle means, an ἐπίσκοπος
should be the husband of a wife. This
hardly needs serious refutation. Winer
however has treated it, edn. 6, § 18. 9
note, shewing that by no possibility can
the indefinite εἷς stand where it would
as here cause ambiguity, only where unity
is taken for granted. Worse still is the
Romanist evasion, which understands the
μία γυνή of the Church.   The view
then which must I think be adopted, especially in presence of ch. v. 9 (where see
note) is, that to candidates for the episcopate (presbytery) St. Paul forbids second
marriage. He requires of them pre-eminent chastity, and abstinence from a
licence which is allowed to other Christians. How far such a prohibition is to
be considered binding on us, now that the
Christian life has entered into another
and totally different phase, is of course an
open question for the present Christian
church at any time to deal with. It must
be as matter of course understood that
regulations, in all *lawful* things, depend,
even when made by an Apostle, on circumstances : and the superstitious observance
of the letter in such cases is often pregnant
with mischief to the people and cause of
Christ) **sober** (probably in the more extended sense of the word ('vigilantem animo,' Beng. : διεγηγερμένον, καὶ προσκοπεῖν
τὸ πρακτέον δυνάμενον, Thdrt. τουτέστι
διορατικόν, μυρίους ἔχοντα πάντοθεν
ὀφθαλμούς, ὀξὺ βλέποντα, καὶ μὴ ἀμβλύ-
νοντα τὸ τῆς διανοίας ὄμμα, κ.τ.λ. Chrys.),

^k πάροινον, μὴ ^l πλήκτην, ἀλλ᾽ ^m ἐπιεικῆ, ⁿ ἄμαχον, ^o ἀφιλάργυρον, 4 τοῦ ἰδίου οἴκου καλῶς ^p προϊστάμενον,

k Tit. i. 7 only †.
l Tit. i. 7 only †.
Ps. xxxiv. 15 Symm.

m Phil. iv. 5.   Tit. iii. 2.   James iii. 17.   1 Pet. ii. 18 only.   Ps. lxxxv. 5 only.   n Tit. iii. 2 only †.
o Heb. xiii. 5 only †.
only. P.   Prov. xxvi. 17.   p here bis. ver. 12. ch. v. 17.   Rom. xii. 8.   1 Thess. v. 12.   Tit. iii. 8, 14

3. rec aft πληκτ. ins μη αισχροκερδη (*from Tit* i. 7), with rel [syr-mg]: om ADFK L[P]א n 17 [47] 67² latt syrr coptt goth [æth arm] gr-lat-ff.   αλλα A[P]א [17].
4. προιστανομενον א.

as in 1 Thess. v. 6, 8;—a pattern of active sobriety and watchfulness: for all these adjectives, as far as διδακτικόν, are descriptive of *positive* qualities: μὴ πάροινον giving the negative and more restricted opposite), self-restrained (or, discreet; see above on ch. ii. 9), orderly ('quod σώφρων est intus, id κόσμιος est extra,' Beng.: thus expanded by Theodoret: καὶ φθέγματι καὶ σχήματι καὶ βλέμματι καὶ βαδίσματι· ὥστε καὶ διὰ τοῦ σώματος φαίνεσθαι τὴν τῆς ψυχῆς σωφροσύνην), hospitable (loving, and entertaining strangers: see reff. and Heb. xiii. 2. This duty in the early days of the Christian church was one of great importance. Brethren in their travels could not resort to the houses of the heathen, and would be subject to insult in the public deversoria), apt in teaching (τὰ θεῖα πεπαιδευμένον, καὶ παραινεῖν δυνάμενον τὰ προσήκοντα, Thdrt.: so we have τοὺς ἱππικοὺς βουλομένους γενέσθαι, Xen. Sympos. ii. 10 : not merely *given to* teaching, but able and skilled in it. All *might teach*, to whom the Spirit imparted the gift: but *skill* in teaching was the especial office of the minister, on whom would fall the ordinary duty of instruction of believers and refutation of gainsayers):   3—7.] (His *negative qualities* are now specified; the positive ones which occur henceforth arising out of and explaining those negative ones):
3.] not a brawler (properly, '*one in his cups*,' 'a man rendered petulant by much wine:' τὸ τοίνυν παρ᾽ οἶνον λυπεῖν τοὺς παρόντας, τοῦτ᾽ ἐγὼ κρίνω παροινίαν, Xen. Sympos. vi. 1. And perhaps the literal meaning should not be lost sight of. At the same time the word and its cognates were often used without reference to wine: see παροινέω, -ία, -ιος, in Palm and Rost's Lex. As πλήκτης answers to πάροινος, it will be best to extend the meaning to signify rather the character, than the mere fact, of παροινία), not a striker (this word also may have a literal and narrower, or a metaphorical and wider sense. In this latter it is taken by Thdrt.: οὐ τὸ ἐπιτιμᾶν εἰς καιρὸν κωλύει· ἀλλὰ τὸ μὴ δεόντως τοῦτο ποιεῖν. But perhaps the coarser literal sense is better, as setting forth more

broadly the opposite to the character of a Christian ἐπίσκοπος), but (this contrast springs out of the two last, and is set off by them) forbearing (reasonable and gentle : φέρειν εἰδότα τὰ πρὸς αὐτὸν πλημμελήματα, Thdrt. See note on Phil. iv. 5, and Trench, N. T. Syn. § xliii.; but correct his derivation, as in that note), not quarrelsome (cf. 2 Tim. ii. 24. Conyb.'s '*peaceable*' is objectionable, as losing the negative character), not a lover of money ('*liberal*,' Conyb.: but this is still more objectionable : it is not the positive virtue of liberality but the negative one of abstinence from love of money, which, though it may lead to the other in men who *have* money, is yet a totally distinct thing. Thdrt.'s explanation, while true, is yet characteristic of an ἐπίσκοπος of later days : οὐκ εἶπεν ἀκτήμονα· σύμμετρα γὰρ νομοθετεῖ· ἀλλὰ μὴ ἐρῶντα χρημάτων. δυνατὸν γὰρ κεκτῆσθαι μέν, οἰκονομεῖν δὲ ταῦτα δεόντως, καὶ μὴ δουλεύειν τούτοις, ἀλλὰ τούτων δεσπόζειν):
4.] (This positive requisite again seems to spring out of the negative ones which have preceded, and especially out of ἀφιλάργυρον. The negatives are again resumed below with μὴ νεόφυτον) presiding well over his own house (ἰδίου, as contrasted with the church of God below, οἴκου, in its wide acceptation, '*household*,' including all its members), having children (not '*keeping* (or *having*) *his children*' (ἔχοντα τὰ τέκνα), as E. V. and Conyb. The emphatic position of τέκνα, besides its anarthrousness, should have prevented this mistake : cf. also Tit. i. 6,—μιᾶς γυναικὸς ἀνήρ, τέκνα ἔχων πιστά, κ.τ.λ.) in subjection (i. e. who are in subjection) with all gravity ('*reverent modesty*,' see ch. ii. 2. These words are best applied to the *children*, not to the head of the house, which acceptance of them rather belongs to the rendering impugned above. It is the σεμνότης of the children, the result of his προστῆναι, which is to prove that he *knows how* to preside over his own house,—not his own σεμνότης in governing them : the matter of fact, that he has children who are in subjection to him in all gravity,—not his own keeping or endeavouring to keep

τέκνα ἔχοντα ἐν [q] ὑποταγῇ [r] μετὰ [s] πάσης [t] σεμνότητος.
5 εἰ δέ τις τοῦ ἰδίου οἴκου [p] προστῆναι οὐκ οἶδεν, πῶς [u] ἐκκλησίας [u] θεοῦ [v] ἐπιμελήσεται; 6 μὴ [w] νεόφυτον, ἵνα μὴ
[x] τυφωθεὶς εἰς [y] κρῖμα [z] ἐμπέσῃ τοῦ [a] διαβόλου. 7 δεῖ δὲ

H δει δε ... ADFH KLPℵ a b c d e f g h k l m n o 17. 47

q ch. ii. 11 reff. r Mark iii. 5 al. fr. 1 Chron. xxix. 22. s Phil. i. 20 reff. t ch. ii. 2. Tit. ii. 7 only +. 2 Macc. iii. 12 only. u 1 Cor. i. 2. x. 32. xi. 16, 22. xv. 9. Gal. i. 13. 1 Thess. ii. 14. 2 Thess. i. 4. ver. 15. P. v Luke x. 34, 35 only. Gen. xliv. 21. (-λεια, Acts xxvii. 3. -λῶς, Luke xv. 8.) w here only. Job xiv. 9. Ps. cxxvii. 3. cxliii. 12. Isa. v. 7 only. x ch. vi. 4. 2 Tim. iii. 4 only +. y = Mark xii. 40 ‖ L. Rom. iii. 8 al. fr. z Matt. xii. 11. Luke x. 36. xiv. 5. ch. vi. 9. Heb. x. 31 only. Prov. xxviii. 10. a = Paul, Eph. iv. 27. vi. 11. 2 Tim. ii. 26 only. Matt. iv. 1. Heb. ii. 14 al. fr. Job i. 6, &c. (adj., ver. 11.)

7. rec aft δει δε ins *αυτον*, with DKL[P] rel: om AFHℵ 17 copt.

them so. Want of *success* in ruling at home, not want of will to rule, would disqualify him for ruling the church. So that the distinction is an important one): **but** (contrast, as in ch. ii. 12, to the suppressed but imagined opposite case) **if any man knows not** (the use of **εἰ οὐ** here is perfectly regular: see Ellicott's note) **how to preside over his own house** (shews, by his children being insubordinate, that he has no skill in domestic government), **how shall he** (this future includes '*how can he*,' but goes beyond it—appealing, not to the man's power, which conditions his success, but to the resulting matter of fact, which will be sure to substantiate his failure) **take charge of** (so Plato, Gorg. p. 520 a: *οἱ φάσκοντες προεστάναι τῆς πόλεως καὶ ἐπιμελεῖσθαι*) **the church of God** (*ὁ τὰ σμικρὰ οἰκονομεῖν οὐκ εἰδώς, πῶς δύναται τῶν κρειττόνων καὶ θείων πιστευθῆναι τὴν ἐπιμέλειαν;* Thdrt. See the idea followed out popularly in Chrys.)? **6.**] (the negative characteristics are resumed) **not a novice** (*νεόφυτον τὸν εὐθὺς πεπιστευκότα καλεῖ· ἐγὼ γάρ, φησίν, ἐφύτευσα. οὐ γάρ, οὕς τινες ὑπέλαβον, τὸν νέον τῆς ἡλικίας ἐκβάλλει*, Thdrt. So Chr. (*νεοκατήχητος*), Thl. (*νεοβάπτιστος*). An objection has been raised to this precept by Schleierm., that it could hardly find place in the apostolic church, where all were *νεόφυτοι*. Matthies answers, that in Crete this might be so, and therefore such a precept would be out of place in the Epistle to Titus, but the Ephesian church had been many years established. But De W. rejoins to this, that the precepts are perfectly general, not of particular application. The real reply is to be found, partly by narrowing the range of *νεόφυτος*, partly in assigning a later date to these Epistles than is commonly held. The case here contemplated is that of one very recently converted. To ordain such a person to the ministry would, for the reason here assigned, be most unadvisable. But we cannot imagine that such period need be extended at the most to more than three or four years, in cases of men of full age who became Christians; and surely such a condition might be fulfilled in any of the Pauline churches, supposing this Epistle to bear any thing like the date which I have assigned to it in the Prolegg. ch. vii. § ii.), **lest being besotted with pride** (from **τῦφος**, smoke, steam, and hence metaphorically, the pother which a man's pride raises about him so that he cannot see himself or others as they are. So *τὰ τῆς ψυχῆς, ὄνειρος καὶ τῦφος*, Marc. Antonin. ii. 17: *τὸν τῦφον ὥσπερ τινὰ καπνὸν φιλοσοφίας εἰς τοὺς σοφιστὰς ἀπεσκέδασε*, Plut. Mor. (p. 580 c. Palm. Lex.) Hence **τυφοῦσθαι**, which is used only in this metaphorical sense, to be thus blinded or bewildered with pride or self-conceit. So *τετυφωμένος ταῖς εὐτυχίαις*, Strabo xv. p. 686,—*ἐπὶ πλούτοις τε καὶ ἀρχαῖς*, Lucian, Necyom. 12. See numerous other examples in Palm and Rost's Lex., from whence the above are taken) **he fall into the judgment of the devil** (these last words are ambiguous. Is *τοῦ διαβόλου* (1) the genitive objective (as Rom. iii. 8), '*the judgment into which the devil fell*,'—or (2) the genitive subjective, '*the judgment which is wrought by the devil?*' (1) is held by Chrys. (*εἰς τὴν καταδίκην τὴν αὐτήν, ἣν ἐκεῖνος ἀπὸ τῆς ἀπονοίας ὑπέμεινε*), Thdrt. (*τῇ τοῦ διαβόλου τιμωρίᾳ περιπεσεῖται*), Thl., Œc., Pel., Calv. ('in eandem cum diabolo condemnationem ruat.' See below under (2)), Beza, Est., Grot. ('id est, pœna qualis diabolo evenit, qui de cœlo dejectus est, 2 Pet. ii. 4, nempe ob superbiam, Sir. x. 13'), Beng., Wolf ('repræsentato diaboli exemplo'), Heinr., Heydenreich, Mack, De W., Wiesinger, al.: and by Ellicott. (2) by Ambr. (apparently: 'Satanas præcipitat eum'), Heumann, Matthies ("if a Christian church-overseer allowed himself to be involved in a charge of pride, the adversary (*in concreto* living men, his instruments) might by it have reason as well for the accusation of the individual as for inculpation of the congregation, cf.

καὶ ^b μαρτυρίαν καλὴν ἔχειν· ἀπὸ ^c τῶν ^c ἔξωθεν, ἵνα μὴ
εἰς ^d ὀνειδισμὸν ^{ze} ἐμπέσῃ καὶ ^{ef} παγίδα τοῦ ^a διαβόλου.

b = Paul, Acts xxii. 18. Tit. i. 13 only. John i. 7, 19 al.

c Matt. xxiii. 25. Luke xi. 39, 40. (Paul usually, οἱ ἔξω, Col. iv. 5 reff.) 1 Pet. iii. 3. Rev. xi. 2 only. Ezek.
xli. 17. (ἔξωθεν, Paul, 2 Cor. vii. 5 only.)
33. xi. 26. xiii. 13 only.　　　e ch. vi. 9. Prov. xii. 13.　　d Rom. xv. 3, from Ps. lxviii. 9. Heb. x.
from Ps. lxviii. 22. ch. vi. 9. 2 Tim. ii. 26 only.　　　　　　　f Luke xxi. 35. Rom. xi. 9,

εχειν bef καλην DF latt.　　[ins εις bef παγιδα D¹ vulg-ed.]

ch. v. 14, Eph. iv. 27," cited by Huther),
Calv. (as an alternative : " activam significationem non rejicio, fore ut diabolo
causam sui accusandi præbeat." He adds,
" sed verior Chrysostomi opinio "), Beza
(altern.), Huther.　　It is hardly worth
while recounting under this head, the
views of those who take **τοῦ διαβόλου**
for *a slanderer*, inasmuch as **ὁ διάβολος**
never occurs in this sense in the N. T.
(on διάβολος, adjective, in this sense,
see below, ver. 11).　This is done in both
verses 6 and 7, by Luther (ßäfterer),
Rosenm., Michaelis, Wegsch., Flatt : in
verse 6 and not in verse 7, by Erasm.,
Mosheim, al.　In deciding between the
above, one question must first be answered : are we obliged to preserve the
same character of the genitive in verses 6
and 7 ? because, if so, we must manifestly
take (2) : for (ὀνειδισμὸν κ.) παγίδα τοῦ
διαβόλου (see below) cannot bear any
other meaning than ' *the* (reproach and)
snare which the devil lays.' This question must be answered, not by any mere
consideration of uniformity, but by careful
enquiry into the import of the substantive
κρῖμα.　I conceive we cannot understand
it here otherwise than as a *condemnatory
sentence*.　The word is a *vox media* ; οὐκ
εὔκριτον τὸ κρῖμα, Æsch. Suppl. 392 : but
the dread here expressed of *falling into it*
necessarily confines it to its adverse sense.
This being so, Bengel's remark is noticeable :—" diabolus potest *opprobrium* in-
ferre, *judicium* non potest : non enim ju-
dicat, sed judicatur."　To this Huther
answers, that we must not consider the
κρῖμα of the devil as necessarily parallel
with God's κρῖμα, any more than with
man's on his neighbour.　" To understand," he continues, " the κρῖμα τοῦ διαβόλου, we must compare Eph. ii. 2, where
the devil is called τὸ πνεῦμα τὸ νῦν
ἐνεργοῦν ἐν τοῖς υἱοῖς τῆς ἀπειθείας : so
that whatever the world does to the reproach (zur Schmach) of Christ's Church,
is the doing of the spirit that works in the
world, viz. of the devil."　But surely this
reply is quite inadequate to justify the use
of the decisive κρῖμα : and Huther himself has, by suggesting ' *reproach*,' evaded
the real question, and taken refuge in the
unquestioned meaning of the next verse.

He goes on to say, that only by understanding this of a *deed* of the Prince of the
antichristian world, can we clearly establish a connexion with the following verse,
pointed out as it is by δέ.　But this is still
more objectionable : δὲ καί disjoins the
two particulars, and introduces the latter
as a separate and additional matter.　From
the use of the decisive word κρῖμα, I infer
that it cannot be an act of the adversary
which is here spoken of, but an act in
which ὁ ἄρχων τοῦ κόσμου τούτου κέκριται.　Then as to uniformity with ver. 7,
I should not be disposed to make much
account of it.　For one who so loved similarity of external phrase, even where different meanings were to be conveyed, as
St. Paul, to use the genitives in κρῖμα
τοῦ διαβόλου and παγὶς τοῦ διαβόλου in
these different meanings, is surely nothing
which need cause surprise.　τοῦ διαβόλου
is common to both : the devil's condemnation, and the devil's snare, are both alike
alien from the Christian, in whom, as in
his divine Master, the adversary should
find nothing, and with whom he should
have nothing in common.　The κρῖμα τοῦ
διαβόλου is in fact but the consummation
of that state into which the παγὶς τοῦ
διαβόλου is the introduction.　I therefore unhesitatingly adopt (1)—*the condemnation into which Satan fell through
the same blinding effect of pride*).
7.] Moreover (δέ, bringing in the contrast of addition ; ' *more than this*,' ....
καί, the addition itself of a new particular) **he must have a good testimony** (reff.) **from those without** (lit.
' *those from without* :' the unusual θεν
(reff.) being added as harmonizing with
the ἀπό, the testimony coming ' from
without'), **lest he fall into** (a question
arises which must be answered before we
can render the following words.　Does
ὀνειδισμόν (1) stand alone, ' *into reproach,
and the snare of the devil*,' or is it (2) to
be joined with παγίδα as belonging to
διαβόλου ?　For (1), which is the view of
Thl., Est., Wolf, Heyden., Huther, Wiesinger, al. (and Ellic. doubtfully), it is alleged, that ὀνειδισμόν is separated from
καὶ παγίδα by ἐμπέσῃ.　But this alone
cannot decide the matter.　The Apostle
may have intended to write merely εἰς

g Rom. xvi. 1.
Phil. i. 1.
h ch. ii. 9 reff.
i Phil. iv. 8.
ver. 11. Tit.
ii. 2 only. Prov. iii. 6.
m = ch. i. 19.

8 g Διακόνους h ὡσαύτως i σεμνούς, μὴ j διλόγους, μὴ

οἴνῳ πολλῷ k προσέχοντας, μὴ l αἰσχροκερδεῖς, 9 m ἔχον-

ADFHK
LPℵ a b
c d e f g
h k l m n
o 17. 47

8. om σεμνους ℵ¹ 109. 219².

ὀνειδισμὸν ἐμπέσῃ τοῦ διαβόλου. Then in adding καὶ παγίδα, we may well conceive that he would keep εἰς ὀν. ἐμπ. for uniformity with the preceding verse, and also not to throw κ. παγίδα into an unnatural prominence, as would be done by placing it before ἐμπέσῃ. We must then decide on other grounds. Wiesinger, seeing that the ὀνειδισμὸς τοῦ διαβόλου, if these are to be taken together, must come immediately from οἱ ἔξωθεν, objects, that he doubts whether any where the devil is said *facere per se* that which he *facit per alterum*. But surely 1 John iii. 8 is a case in point: ὁ ποιῶν τὴν ἁμαρτίαν ἐκ τοῦ διαβόλου ἐστίν, ὅτι ἀπ᾽ ἀρχῆς ὁ διάβολος ἁμαρτάνει. εἰς τοῦτο ἐφανερώθη ὁ υἱὸς τοῦ θεοῦ, ἵνα λύσῃ τὰ ἔργα τοῦ διαβόλου, —and indeed Eph. ii. 2, τὸ πνεῦμα τὸ νῦν ἐνεργοῦν ἐν τοῖς υἱοῖς τῆς ἀπειθείας. Huther supports this view by ch. v. 14: but I am unable to see how that verse touches the question: for whether the ὀνειδισμός belong to τοῦ διαβ. or not, it clearly must come in either case from οἱ ἔξωθεν. One consideration in favour of this view has not been alleged:—that ἡ παγὶς τοῦ διαβόλου seems, from 2 Tim. ii. 26, to be a familiar phrase with the Apostle, and therefore less likely to be joined with another governing substantive. For (2), we have Thdrt. (τῶν ἔξωθεν τῶν ἀπίστων λέγει. ὁ γὰρ καὶ παρ᾽ ἐκείνοις πλείστην ἔχων πρὸ τῆς χειροτονίας διαβολήν, ἐπονείδιστος ἔσται, καὶ πολλοῖς ὀνείδεσι περιβαλεῖ τὸ κοινόν, καὶ εἰς τὴν προτέραν ὅτι τάχιστα παλινδρομήσει παρανομίαν, τοῦ διαβόλου πάντα πρὸς τοῦτο μηχανωμένου), al.,—Bengel ("diabolus potest antistiti malis testimoniis laboranti plurimum excitare molestiæ, per se et per homines calumniatores"), De W., al. The chief grounds for this view are, (a) grammatical—that the εἰς is not repeated before παγίδα. I am not sure, whether we are right in applying such strict rules to these Pastoral Epistles: but the consideration cannot but have some weight. (b) contextual—that the Apostle would hardly have alleged the mere ἐμπεσεῖν εἰς ὀνειδισμόν as a matter of sufficient importance to be parallel with ἐμπ. εἰς παγίδα τοῦ διαβόλου. This latter, I own, inclines me to adopt (2), but I would not by any means speak strongly in repudia-

tion of the other) the reproach and the snare of the devil (reff. This latter is usually taken as meaning, the danger of relapse (cf. Thdrt. cited above): so Calv.: "ne infamiæ expositus, perfrictæ frontis esse incipiat, tantoque majore licentia se prostituat ad omnem nequitiam: quoô est diaboli plagis se irretire. Quid enim spei restat ubi nullus est peccati pudor?" Grot. gives it a different turn: 'ne contumeliis notatus quærat se ulcisci.' These, and many other references, may well be contained in the expression, and we need not, I think, be at the pains precisely to specify any one direction which the evil would take. Such an one's steps would be shackled—his freedom hampered—his temper irritated—his character lost—and the natural result would be a fall from his place, to the detriment not of himself only, but of the Church of Christ).

8—13.] *Precepts regarding deacons and deaconesses* (see below on ver. 11). **8.**] The construction continues from the preceding—the δεῖ εἶναι being in the Apostle's mind as governing the accusatives. **In like manner** (the ὡσαύτως seems introduced by the similarity of character,—not merely to mark an additional particular) **the deacons** (mentioned as a class, besides here, only Phil. i. 1, where, as here, they follow the ἐπίσκοποι. Phœbe, Rom. xvi. 1, is a διάκονος of the church at Cenchrea. The term or its cognates occur in a vaguer sense, but still indicating a special office, in Rom. xii. 7: 1 Pet. iv. 11. The connexion of the ecclesiastical deacons with the seven appointed in Acts vi. is very doubtful: see Chrysostom's and Œc.'s testimony, distinguishing them, in note there. But that the ecclesiastical order sprung out of similar necessities, and had for its field of work similar objects, can hardly be doubted. See Suicer, διάκονος: Winer, Realw.: Neander, Pfl. u. Leit. i. p. 54 note) (**must be**) **grave, not of double speech** (= δίγλωσσος, Prov. xi. 13 (Ellic. adds διχόμυθος, Eurip. Orest. 890), not quite as Thl. ἄλλα φρονοῦντας κ. ἄλλα λέγοντας, but rather as Thdrt. (and Thl., additional), ἕτερα τούτῳ, ἕτερα δὲ ἐκείνῳ λέγοντας), **not addicted** (applying themselves, reff.) **to much wine** (= μὴ οἴνῳ πολλῷ δεδουλωμένας, Tit. ii. 3), **not greedy of gain** (hardly, as E. V., to be

C ριον της... ACDFH KLPℵ a b c d e f g h k l m n o 17. 47

τας τὸ [n] μυστήριον τῆς πίστεως ἐν [o] καθαρᾷ [op] συνειδήσει.
10 [q] καὶ οὗτοι [q] δὲ [r] δοκιμαζέσθωσαν πρῶτον, εἶτα [s] δια-
κονείτωσαν, [t] ἀνέγκλητοι ὄντες. 11 γυναῖκας [u] ὡςαύτως

n = 1 Cor. ii. 7. see ver. 16. Rom. xi. 25 and note.
o 2 Tim. i. 3 only. see Heb. ix. 14.
p ch. i. 5 reff.
q Paul, Rom. xi. 3. 2 Tim. iii. 12 only. Matt. x. 18. xvi. 18 al.
r = Luke xiv. 19. 1 Cor. ii. 13. 2 Cor. viii. 8. 1 Thess. v. 21. Prov. xvii. 3.
s = ver. 13. 1 Pet. iv. 11 only.
t 1 Cor. i. 8. Col. i. 22. Tit. i. 6, 7 only. P. † 3 Macc. v. 31.
u ver. 8.

9. for εν καθ. συνειδ., και καθαρας συνειδησεως ℵ[1].
10. αυτοι H 73. for ειτα, και ουτω D[1] vulg goth Jer Ambrst.

doubly rendered,—'*greedy* of *filthy* lucre,' —so also Thdrt., ὁ ἐκ πραγμάτων αἰσχρῶν κ. λίαν ἀτόπων κέρδη συλλέγειν ἀνεχόμενος. It would appear from Tit. i. 11, διδάσκοντες ἃ μὴ δεῖ αἰσχροῦ κέρδους χάριν, that all κέρδος is αἰσχρόν which is set before a man as a by-end in his work for God: so likewise in 1 Pet. v. 2,—ἐπισκοποῦντες μὴ . . . . . μηδὲ αἰσχροκερδῶς . . . . . 'nor with a view to gain,' such gain being necessarily base when thus sought. This particular of the deacons' character assumes special importance, if we connect it with the collecting and distributing alms. Cyprian, Ep. 54 (12 ad Corn. Pap. § 1, Migne, Patr. Gr. vol. iii. p. 797), stigmatizes the deacon Felicissimus as 'pecuniæ commissæ sibi fraudator'), **holding the mystery of the** (or **their**) **faith** (that great objective truth which man of himself knows not, but which the Spirit of God reveals to the faithful: cf. Rom. xvi. 25 f.: 1 Cor. ii. 7—10: and even Him who in fact *is* that mystery, the great object of all faith: see note on ver. 16, τὸ τῆς εὐσεβείας μυστήριον. That expression makes it probable that τῆς πίστεως is here to be taken subjectively: *the*, or *their, faith:* the apprehension which appropriates to them the contents of God's revelation of Christ. That revelation of the Person of Christ, their faith's μυστήριον, they are to hold. See Ellic.'s note) **in pure conscience** (see reff. and ch. i. 19. From those passages it appears, that we must not give the words a special application to their official life as deacons, but understand them of earnestness and singleness of Christian character: —being in heart persuaded of the truth of that divine mystery which they profess to have apprehended by faith). **10.**] **And moreover** (the δέ introduces a caution —the slight contrast of a necessary addition to their mere present character. On this force of καὶ . . . δέ, see Hartung, i. 182: Ellic., here. There is no connexion in καὶ . . . δέ with the former requirements regarding ἐπίσκοποι) **let these** (who answer, in their candidateship for the diaconate, to the above character) **be put to the proof first** (viz. with regard to their blamelessness of life, cf. ἀνέγκλ. ὄντες below: e. g. by testimonials, and publication of their intention to offer themselves: but no formal way is specified, only the reality insisted on), **then let them act as deacons** (or, *minister:* but more probably here in the narrower technical sense, as in reff.(?) Not '*be made* deacons,' as Conyb.: the word is of *their* act in the office, not of their reception of it, which is of course understood in the background), **if they are** (found by the δοκιμή to be) **irreproachable. 11.**] **(The) women in like manner** (who are these? Are they (1) women who were to serve as deacons,—deaconesses?—or (2) wives of the deacons?—or (3) wives of the deacons and overseers?—or (4) women in general? I conceive we may dismiss (4) at once, for Chrys.'s reason: τί γὰρ ἐβούλετο μεταξὺ τῶν εἰρημένων παρεμβαλεῖν τι περὶ γυναικῶν;—(3) upheld by Calv., Est., Calov., and Mack, may for the same reason, seeing that he returns to διάκονοι again in ver. 12, be characterized as extremely improbable,—(2) has found many supporters among modern Commentators: Luth., Beza, Beng. (who strangely adds, 'pendet ab *habentes* ver. 9'), Rosenm., Heinr., Huther, Conyb., al., and E. V. But it has against it (*a*) the omission of all expressed reference to the deacons, such as might be given by αὐτῶν, or by τάς: (*b*) the expression of ὡσαύτως, by which the διάκονοι themselves were introduced, and which seems to mark a new ecclesiastical class: (*c*) the introduction of the injunction respecting the deacons, ἔστωσαν μιᾶς γυναικὸς ἄνδρες, as a new particular, which would hardly be if their wives had been mentioned before: (*d*) the circumstance, connected with the mention of Phœbe as διάκονος of the church at Cenchrea in Rom. xvi. 1, that unless these are deaconesses, there would be among these injunctions no mention of an important class of persons employed as officers of the church. We come thus to consider (1), that these γυναῖκες are *deaconesses,*—*ministræ,* as Pliny calls them in his letter to Trajan (see note on Rom. xvi. 1). In this view the ancients are, as far as I know, unanimous. Of the mo-

v = 2 Tim. iii.
3. Tit. ii. 3
only. Esth.
vii. 4 (vv. 6,
7 reff.).
w ver. 2.
x 2 Tim. iv. 5
reff.
y vv. 4, 5.

u σεμνάς, μὴ ᵛ διαβόλους, ʷ νηφαλίους, πιστὰς ˣ ἐν πᾶσιν. ᴬᶜᴰᶠᴴ
12 u διάκονοι ἔστωσαν ʷ μιᾶς γυναικὸς ʷ ἄνδρες, τέκνων
καλῶς ʸ προϊστάμενοι καὶ τῶν ἰδίων οἴκων. 13 οἱ γὰρ

ᴷᴸᴾℵ a
b c d e f
g h k l m
n o 17.47

11. σεμνους A.   Steph νηφαλεους, with D³K e l¹ m n o [47] Damasc: -λαιους
FL[P] d f 39. 72. 93. 123 : txt ACD¹Hℵ rel.
12. aft διακ. ins δε F.   καλων [D¹]F[not G].

derns, it is held by Grot., Mosh., Mich., De W., Wiesinger, Ellicott. It is alleged against it—(a) that thus the return to the διάκονοι, verse 12, would be harsh, or, as Conyb. "on that view, the verse is most unnaturally interpolated in the midst of the discussion concerning the deacons." But the ready answer to this is found in Chrys.'s view of verse 12, that under διά-κονοι, and their household duties, he comprehends in fact both sexes under one: ταῦτα καὶ περὶ γυναικῶν διακόνων ἁρμότ-τει εἰρῆσθαι : (b) that the existence of deaconesses as an order in the ministry is after all not so clear. To this it might be answered, that even were they no where else mentioned, the present passage stands on its own grounds; and if it seemed from the context that such persons were indicated here, we should reason from this to the fact of their existence, not from the absence of other mention to their non-indication here. I decide then for (1): that these women are dea-conesses) (must be) grave, not slan-derers (corresponds to μὴ διλόγους in the males, being the vice to which the female sex is more addicted. Cf. Eurip. Phœn. 298 ff., φιλόψογον δὲ χρῆμα θηλειῶν ἔφυ, | σμικρὰς τ᾽ ἀφορμὰς ἣν λάβωσι τῶν λόγων, | πλείους ἐπεισφέρουσιν· ἡδονὴ δέ τις | γυναιξί, μηδὲν ὑγιὲς ἀλλήλαις λέγειν. διάβολος in this sense (reff.) is peculiar in N. T. to these Epistles), sober (see on ver. 2, corresponding to μὴ οἴνῳ πολλῷ προσέχοντας), faithful in all things (corresponds to μὴ αἰσχροκερδεῖς : trusty in the distribution of the alms committed to them, and in all other ministrations).

12.] General directions respect-ing those in the diaconate (of both sexes, the female being included in the male, see Chrys. cited above), with regard to their domestic condition and duties, as above (verses 4, 5) respecting the episco-pate. Let the deacons be husbands of one wife (see on this above, ver. 2), ruling well over children (the emphatic position of the anarthrous τέκνα, as above ver. 4, makes it probable that the having children to rule is to be considered as a qualification : see Tit. i. 6, note. Chrys.

gives a curious and characteristic reason for the precept : πανταχοῦ τίθησι τὴν τῶν τέκνων προστασίαν, ἵνα μὴ ἀπὸ τού-του οἱ λοιποὶ σκανδαλίζωνται) and their own houses. 13.] The importance of true and faithful service in the dia-conate. For those who served well the office of deacon (the aor. participle, not the perf., because the standing-point of the sentence is at first the great day, when their διακονία has passed by. In fact this aor. participle decides between the inter-pretations: see below) are acquiring (the Apostle having begun by placing himself at the great day of retribution, and conse-quently used the aor. participle, now shifts, so to speak, the scene, and deals with their present conduct : q. d., 'Those who shall then be found to have served well, &c. . . . . . are now, &c.' On περιποιέω and περιποίησις, see notes, Eph. i. 14 : 1 Thess. v. 9) for themselves (emphatic—besides the service they are rendering to the church) a good standing-place (viz. at the great day : cf. ch. vi. 19, ἀποθησαυρίζον-τας ἑαυτοῖς θεμέλιον καλὸν εἰς τὸ μέλλον, ἵνα ἐπιλάβωνται τῆς ὄντως ζωῆς :—and Dan. xii. 3 (Heb. and E. V.), where how-ever the metaphor is different. The interpretations of βαθμόν, a step, or place to stand on (in LXX, the threshold, or step, before a door: see reff.), have been very various. (1) Ambr., Jer., Pel., Thl., Erasm., Bull, Beza, Corn.-a-lap., Est., Grot., Lightf., Beng., Wolf, Mosh., Schött., Wordsw., al., understand it of a degree of ecclesiastical preferment, scil. from the office of deacon to that of presbyter, and take καλόν for a compara-tive. Against this is (a) the forcing of καλόν ; (b) the improbability that such a rise upwards through the ecclesiastical offices was known in the Apostle's time : (c) the still greater unlikelihood, even if it were known, that he would propose as a motive to a deacon to fulfil his office well, the ambitious desire to rise out of it. (2) Mack, Matth., Olsh., Huther, al., following Calv. and Luther, understand by it a high place of honour in the esteem of the church (see on παρρησία below): "qui probe functi fuerint hoc ministerio, non parvo

καλῶς ^z διακονήσαντες ^a βαθμὸν ἑαυτοῖς καλὸν ^b περι-
ποιοῦνται, καὶ ^c πολλὴν ^{cd} παρρησίαν ἐν ^e πίστει τῇ ^e ἐν
χριστῷ Ἰησοῦ. ¹⁴ Ταῦτά σοι γράφω, ἐλπίζων ἐλθεῖν

...ιησου
H.
ACDFK
LPℵ a b
c d e f g
h k l m n
o 17. 47

z ver. 10.
a here only.
1 Kings v. 5.
4 Kings xx.
9, 10 B, 11.
Sir. vi. 36
only.

b Luke xvii. 33. Acts xx. 28 only. Gen. xxxi. 18. Isa. xxxi. 5. (-ποίησις, Eph. i. 14.)   c Philem. 8.
d Eph. iii. 12 reff. = 1 John iii. 21. Heb. iv. 16.   e Gal. iii. 26. Eph. i. 15. Col. i. 4. 2 Tim. iii. 15.

13. for τη εν, την εν F.
14. ελπιζω [for -ζων] F h¹ m.   om προς σε F 67² arm.

honore dignos esse." Calv. Against this is (a) that there is not a more distinct reference made to the estimation of the church; indeed that the emphatic ἑαυτοῖς (see above) is altogether against such reference : (b) that thus again an unworthy motive would be set before the deacons: (c) that again (see below) παρρησία will not on this interpretation, bear any legitimate rendering. (d) the aor. part. διακονήσαντες, as before. (3) Musc., al., take it *spiritually*, as meaning *progress in the faith*. Chrys. is claimed for this view, but this is somewhat doubtful. His words are, τουτέστι, προκοπὴν καὶ παρρησίαν πολλὴν τὴν ἐν πίστει χρ. Ἰησοῦ ὡσεὶ ἔλεγεν, οἱ ἐν τοῖς κάτω δείξαντες ἑαυτοὺς διεγηγερμένους, ταχέως καὶ πρὸς ἐκεῖνα ἀνελεύσονται : where, notwithstanding that προκοπήν would seem to mean subjective progress, Thl.'s explanation of ἐκεῖνα,—τὰ ἀνώτερα, the higher office, seems best to fit the sentence : and thus προκοπή must be objective,—*preferment*. But (a) the whole (especially βαθμὸν περιποιοῦνται) is of too objective a character thus to be interpreted of a merely subjective process—besides that (b) thus also the *present* περιποιοῦνται would require a present participle διακονοῦντες. (4) Thdrt. (below), Croc., Flatt, Heinrichs (modified: see below), De W., Wiesinger, understand it nearly as above—of the station or standing-place which the faithful deacon acquires before God, with reference to his own salvation. The opinions of these Commentators are, however, somewhat various as to the exact time to which the standing on this βαθμός is to be referred. Thdrt. says : εἰ καὶ ἐλάττονα, φησί, τιμὴν ἔχουσι κατὰ τόνδε τὸν βίον, ἀλλ' οὖν εἰδέναι προσήκει, ὡς τὴν ἐγχειρισθεῖσαν πεπληρωκότες διακονίαν, τὸν τιμιώτατον βαθμὸν ἐν τῷ μέλλοντι λήψονται βίῳ, καὶ τῆς πρὸς τὸν δεσπότην χριστὸν ἀπολαύσονται παρρησίας. Heinrichs, with whom De W. and Wiesinger are disposed to agree, understands that they procure to themselves a good *expectation of salvation*: a βαθμός i. e. in *this life, with reference to* the future one. I believe, from the form of the sentence, that the truth will be found by combining

the two views. The διακονήσαντες, as above stated, is used with reference to their finished course at that day. The περιποιοῦνται transfers the scene to the present time. The βαθμός is that which they are now securing for themselves, and will be found standing on at that day : belonging therefore in part to both periods, and not necessarily involving the idea of different degrees of blessedness, though that idea (cf. 1 Cor. iii. 15) is familiar to St. Paul,—but merely predicating the soundness of the ground on which these διάκονοι will themselves stand) **and much confidence** (this also is variously understood, according as βαθμός is interpreted. Those who think of *ecclesiastical preferment*, render παρρησία 'freedom of speech as regards the faith (obj.),' i. e. in teaching ('*majore fiducia aliis Evangelium prædicabunt*,' Grot.), or in resisting error,—or, 'libertas ingenue agendi,' as Est. : or 'a wide field for spiritual action,' as Matthies. To these there might be no objection, but for the adjunct to παρρησία, ἐν πίστει τῇ ἐν χριστῷ Ἰησοῦ. Thus defined, παρρησία must necessarily have a subjective reference,—i. e. to the confidence towards God possessed by those who have made good advance in faith in Christ, as in reff. And so Thdrt. (above), Ambr., Croc., Cocc., Flatt, Calv., Beza (these two understand it more generally, of the confidence wrought by a good conscience), Bengel, Wies., De W., Ellic., al.) **in (the) faith** (subjective, from what follows) **which is in** (see reff. ἐν denotes more the repose of faith *in*, εἰς the reliance of faith *on*, Christ) **Christ Jesus.**

14—16.] CLOSE OF THE ABOVE DIRECTIONS *by a solemn statement of their object and its glorious import.* **These things** (the foregoing precepts, most naturally: hardly, as Bengel, 'totam epistolam') **I write** (expressed in the epistolary aorist, Philem. 19, 21 : but in the present, 1 Cor. xiv. 37 : 2 Cor. i. 13 ; xiii. 10 : Gal. i. 20. (1 John i. 4 : ii. 1, &c.)) **to thee, hoping** ('though I hope:' "part. ἐλπίζων per καίπερ seu similem particulam esse resolvendum, nexus orationis docet." Leo, cited by Huther) **to come to thee sooner**

f John xiii. 27.
xx 4. Heb.
xiii. 19, 23
only. Wisd.
xiii. 9.
1 Macc. ii. 40.
1 Pet. ii. 5.
28 reff.

πρός σε ᶠτάχιον· 15 ἐὰν δὲ ᵍβραδύνω, ἵνα εἰδῇς πῶς δεῖ ἐν ʰοἴκῳ ʰθεοῦ ⁱἀναστρέφεσθαι, ʲἥτις ἐστὶν ᵏἐκκλησία

g 2 Pet. iii. 9 only. Deut. vii. 10.
i = Eph. ii. 3 reff.
k ver. 5 reff. Paul only.

h = (Matt. xii. 4 ‖) Heb. x. 21. 1 Pet. iv. 17. see
j Acts x. 41, 47. xiii. 31, 43 al. Paul, passim. attr., Phil. i.

ACDFK
LPℵ a b
c d e f g
h k l m n
o 17. 47

for ταχιον, εν ταχει ACD¹[P] 17 : ταχειον o : txt D³FKLℵ rel Chr Thdrt Damasc.
15. [om δε F.]   ιδης A(appy) D¹F.   aft δει ins σε D¹ vulg arm Orig lat-ff.
ειτις (itacism) C[P].

(than may seem) (on the comparative,—which must not be broken down into a positive, as it is by almost all the Commentators,—see John xiii. 27 note, and Winer, edn. 6, § 35. 4. Also Acts xvii. 21; xxv. 10; xxvii. 13: Heb. xiii. 19, 23, which last is exactly parallel with this. Some supply it,—before this Epistle come to thee: or, before thou shalt have need to put these precepts into practice: but the above seems simpler, and suits better the usage elsewhere): but if I should delay (coming) (from ἐλπίζων to βραδύνω may be regarded as parenthetical, the ἵνα belonging immediately to γράφω), that thou mayest know how thou oughtest to conduct thyself (reff. Huther would take πῶς δεῖ ἀναστρέφεσθαι generally,—'how men ought to behave themselves;' alleging, that in the preceding, there is no direct prescription how Timotheus is himself to act, and that if we supply σε (as D¹ in digest), we confine the reference of οἶκος θεοῦ to the Ephesian church. The latter objection need not detain us long. If the church in general is the house of God, then any portion of it may clearly partake of the title and the dignity. To the former, we may reply, that in fact, the whole of what has preceded does regard Timotheus's own behaviour. He was to see to all these things—to take care that all these precepts were observed) in the house of God (see reff. also Heb. iii. 2, 5, 6, and notes : 1 Cor. iii. 16: 2 Cor. vi. 16: Eph. ii. 22:—that congregation among whom God dwells, by His Spirit);—for such (the house of God : the ἥτις brings out into prominence the appository explanation, and specially applies it to the antecedent) is the congregation (ἐκκλησίας οὐ τοὺς οἴκους λέγει τοὺς εὐκτηρίους, κατὰ τὴν τῶν πολλῶν συνήθειαν, ἀλλὰ τῶν πιστῶν τὸν σύλλογον. Theod.-mops.) of the living God (thus designated for solemnity, and to shew his personal and active presence among them), the pillar (see below) and basement (= θεμέλιος, 2 Tim. ii. 19 : 'firmamentum.' It is a climax, not as Bengel, "instar unius vocabuli solidissimum quiddam exprimentis :" the στύλος is the intermediate, the ἑδραίω-

μα the final support of the building : as Wahl,—" omne id, cui ut primario et præ ceteris insigni innititur aliquid ") of the truth (these latter words are variously referred : being (1) by Camero, Er-Schmid., Limborch, Le Clerc, Schöttg., Beng., Mosh., Rosenm., Heinr., Wegsch., Heydenr., Flatt, al. (see in Wolf. Not Chillingworth, as stated in Bloomf. : see below), joined with the following sentence, putting a period at ζῶντος, and proceeding στύλος καὶ ἑδραίωμα τῆς ἀληθείας καὶ ὁμολογουμένως μέγα ἐστὶν τὸ μυστ. κ.τ.λ. To this I can only say, that if any one imagines St. Paul, or any other person capable of writing this Epistle, able to have indited such a sentence, I fear there is but little chance in arguing with him on the point in question. To say nothing of its abruptness and harshness, beyond all example even in these Epistles, how palpably does it betray the botching of modern conjectural arrangement in the wretched anti-climax—στύλος καὶ ἑδραίωμα (rising in solemnity) τῆς ἀληθείας, καὶ (what grander idea, after the basement of the whole building, does the reader suppose about to follow?) ὁμολογουμένως μέγα! These two last words, which have (see below) their appropriate majesty and grandeur in their literal use at the emphatic opening of such a sentence as the next, are thus robbed of it all, and sink into the very lowest bathos; the metaphor being dropped, and the lofty imagery ending with a vague generality. If a sentence like this occurred in the Epistle, I should feel it a weightier argument against its genuineness than any which its opponents have yet adduced. (2) by Gregory of Nyssa (de vita Mosis: vol. i. p. 385, οὐ μόνον Πέτρος καὶ Ἰάκωβος καὶ Ἰωάννης στύλοι τῆς ἐκκλησίας εἰσὶ ... ὁ θεῖος ἀπόστολος ... καὶ τὸν Τιμόθεον στύλον καλὸν ἐτεκτήνατο, ποιήσας αὐτόν, καθὼς φησὶ τῇ ἰδίᾳ φωνῇ, στύλον καὶ ἑδραίωμα τῆς ἀληθείας), Chillingworth (Religion of Protestants, &c., ch. iii. 76: but he allows as possible, the reference to the Church : "if you will needs have St. Paul refer this not to Timothy, but to the Church, I will not contend about it any further, than to say, Possibly it may be otherwise "),—by others

kl θεοῦ ¹ ζῶντος, ᵐ στύλος καὶ ⁿ ἑδραίωμα τῆς ἀληθείας. ¹ Acts xiv. 15 (Paul).
2 Cor. iii. 3. vi.

16. ch. iv. 10. Heb. iii. 12. ix. 14. x. 31. xii. 22.   Rev. vii. 2. xv. 7.   Hos. i. 10.   m Gal. ii.
9. Rev. iii. 12. x. 1 only.   3 Kings vii. 41.   n here only†.   (-αῖος, Col. i. 23.)

mentioned in Wolf, and in our own days by Conybeare, it is taken as referring to TIMOTHEUS :—" *that thou mayest know how to conduct thyself in the house of God, which is* &c. . . . . *as a pillar and basement of the truth.*" In the very elaborate discussion of this passage by Suicer (s. v. στύλος), he cites those fathers who seem more or less to have favoured this idea. Of these we must manifestly not claim for it those who have merely used the word στύλος or *columna* of an Apostle or teacher, or individual Christian,—as that is justified, independently of our passage, by Gal. ii. 9 : Rev. iii. 12 :—but Greg. Naz. applies the very words to Eusebius of Samosata (Ep. xliv. 1, vol. iii. (Migne) p. 39), and to Basil (Orat. xviii. 1, vol. i. p. 330): and Basil in the Catena says, εἰσὶ καὶ στύλοι τῆς Ἱερουσαλημ οἱ ἀπόστολοι, κατὰ τὸ εἰρημένον, στύλος καὶ ἑδραίωμα τῆς ἀληθείας: and in the Epistle of the churches of Lyons and Vienne, Euseb. v. 1, it is said of Attalus, στύλον καὶ ἑδραίωμα τῶν ἐνταῦθα ἀεὶ γεγονότα. Other cognate expressions, such as τὸ στερέωμα τῆς πίστεως (Chrys., of St. Peter, Hom. xxxii. vol. v. p. 199; and Basil, of Eusebius, as above), πίστεως ἔρεισμα (Greg. Naz., of Basil, Or. xviii. as above), τὸ τῆς ἐκκλησίας στήριγμα (Thl. on Luke xxii., of St. Peter), θρησκείας στηρίγματα (of Pastors, Nicephorus Hist. vii. 2), are adduced by Suicer. The principal modern reasons for adopting this view have been (a) polemical—as against Roman Catholic infallibility of the Church, or (b) for refinement of symbolism, seeing that in Gal. ii. 9, Rev. iii. 12, *men* are compared to pillars (see this very copiously illustrated in Suicer). On both of these I shall treat expressly below. To the *grammatical* construction of the sentence thus understood, there is no objection. The nominative στύλος after δεῖ would be not only allowable, but necessary, if it expressed, not a previous predicate of the understood σε, but the character which by the ἀναστρέφεσθαι he was to become or shew forth : cf. Plato and Demost. in Kühner, § 646, 2 anm., who however has not apprehended the right reason of the idiom. But to the sentence itself thus arranged and understood, there are weighty, and I conceive fatal objections : to wit, (c) if στύλος κ.τ.λ. had been meant to apply to Timotheus, it would hardly have been possible that σε should be omitted. He would thus be the

prominent object in the whole passage, not as now the least prominent, lurking behind ἀναστρέφεσθαι to make way for greater things. (d) I can hardly think, that, in this case, στύλος would have been anarthrous. Though 'a pillar' might be the virtual meaning, σε, τὸν στύλον, or σε ἀναστρέφεσθαι, ... ὁ στύλος, would certainly be the Greek expression. (e) In this case also, the καὶ ὁμολογουμένως which follows would most naturally refer, not to the great deposit of faith in Christ which is entrusted to the church to keep,—but to the very strong and unusual expression which had just been used of a young minister in the church,—' and confessedly great is the dignity of the least of the ministers of Christ : for,' &c. (3) The reference to THE CHURCH is upheld by Chrys. (οὐχ ὡς ἐκεῖνος ὁ ἰουδαϊκὸς οἶκος θεοῦ. τοῦτο γάρ ἐστι τὸ συνέχον τὴν πίστιν καὶ τὸ κήρυγμα· ἡ γὰρ ἀλήθειά ἐστι· τῆς ἐκκλησίας καὶ στύλος καὶ ἑδραίωμα. This inversion of the sentence may have arisen from taking τῆς ἀληθείας as a genitive of apposition), Thdrt. (οἶκον θεοῦ καὶ ἐκκλησίαν τῶν πεπιστευκότων τὸν σύλλογον προσηγόρευσε. τούτους ἔφη στύλον καὶ ἑδραίωμα τῆς ἀληθείας. ἐπὶ γὰρ τῆς πέτρας ἐρηρεισμένοι καὶ ἀκλόνητοι διαμένουσι, καὶ διὰ τῶν πραγμάτων κηρύττοντες τὴν τῶν δογμάτων ἀλήθειαν), Theodor.-mops. (as cited above, on ἐκκλησία, as far as σύλλογον, then he proceeds, ὅθεν καὶ στύλον αὐτὴν καὶ ἑδραίωμα τῆς ἀληθείας ἐκάλεσεν, ὡς ἂν ἐν αὐτῇ τῆς ἀληθείας τὴν σύστασιν ἐχούσης), Thl., Œc., Ambr., Pel., the Roman Commentators, Luth., Calv. (" nonne Ecclesia mater est piorum omnium, quæ ipsos regenerat Dei verbo, quæ educat alitque tota vita, quæ confirmat, quæ ad solidam perfectionem usque perducit? eadem quoque ratione columna veritatis prædicatur : quia doctrinæ administrandæ munus, quod Deus penes eam deposuit, unicum est instrumentum retinendæ veritatis, ne ex luminum memoria pereat "), Beza, Grot. ("veritatem sustentat atque attollit ecclesia, efficit ne labatur ex animis, efficit ut longe lateque conspiciatur"), Calov., Wolf, &c. DeWette, Huther, Wiesinger, al. And this interpretation agrees with 2 Tim. ii. 19: see note there. But there is brought against it the objection, that there is thus introduced confusion of metaphor. The ἐκκλησία, which was the οἶκος above, now becomes στύλος, a part of the οἶκος. This is not difficult to answer. The

16 καὶ ° ὁμολογουμένως ᵖ μέγα ἐστὶν τὸ τῆς ᑫ εὐσεβείας
pr μυστήριον, ὃς ˢ ἐφανερώθη ᵗ ἐν ᵗ σαρκί, ᵘ ἐδικαιώθη ἐν

ACDFK LPℵ a b c d e f g h k l m n o 17. 47

o here only. Hos. xiv. 5 compl. only. Jos. Antt. ii. 9. 6 init. al. in Wetst. p Eph. v. 32. q ch. ii. 2 reff. r see 1 Thess. ii. 7. s w. μυστ., Rom. xvi. 26. Col. i. 26 (reff.). see 1 John i. 2. 2 Tim. i. 10. t 2 Cor. x. 3. Gal. ii. 20. Eph. ii. 11. Phil. i. 22, 24. Col. ii. 1. Philem. 16. u = Matt. xi. 19? see note.

16. On the famous disputed reading in this verse, I give an analysis of the present state of the evidence:—I. rec **θεος**, i. e. $\overline{\Theta C}$, with the follg: (not A, nor C: see below) D³K (F has $\overline{OC}$ without any apparent stroke in the O) L[P] (ℵ⁵ (cent xii.) has written ΘЄ above the OC of the codex) rel. The testimonies of the fathers for **θεος** are very doubtful. Few make a *direct citation of* the passage as thus read: those which seem to do so being naturally explained on the supposition of their supplying θεός as the subject of ὅς. The readg **θεος** is *directly supported* by Chrysostom, Theodoret, Euthalius, Macedonius (who has been charged by some of the Latins with introducing the reading), Damascenus, Theophylact, Œcumenius. Those *supposed to favour* the reading are Ignatius (ad Eph. 19, p. 660,—θεοῦ (but the Syriac has υἱοῦ) ἀνθρωπίνως φανερουμένου: al ὡς ἀνθρώπου φαινομένου), the Apostolic Constitutions(θεὸς κύριε ὁ ἐπιφανεὶς ἡμῖν ἐν σαρκί) Hippolytus(agst Noetus: θεὸς ἐν σώματι ἐφανερώθη) Gregory Thaumaturgus or rather Apollinaris(in Phot: θεὸς ἐν σαρκὶ φανερωθείς). The testimonies of Athanasius, Nyssen, Cyr, usually adduced in favour of θεός, are either uncertain from various readings, or inapplicable (see below). II. **ος**, i. e. OC, is found in the follg: A(this is now *matter of certainty.* The black line at present visible in the O, is a modern retouching of an older but not original fainter one, due apparently to the darkening of the stroke of an Є seen through from the other side. I have examined the page, and find that a portion of the virgula of the Є, seen through, and now corroded through, extends nearly through the Θ, not however quite in, but somewhat above, its centre, as Sir Frederick Madden has observed to me. It was to complete this that Junius made a dot. See also Ellicott's note, Past. Epp. edn 2, p. 103. Besides which, the mark of abbreviation above the line is modern, not corresponding with those in the MS. Sir Frederick Madden now informs me that a very powerful microscope has been applied by Professor Maskelyne, at his request, to the passage in the MS, and the result has been that *no trace of either virgula in the* O *or mark of contraction over it, can be discovered.* It is to be hoped therefore, that A will never again be cited on the side of rec) C(see Tischendorf, prolegg to his edn of the Codex Ephremi, p. 30)Fℵ¹ 17. 73. 181 mss mentd by Liberatus (Cent VI) Victor Tununensis (Cent VI)

house contains in itself both στύλος and ἑδραίωμα—the pillar and the basement both belong to the house. Why may not the στύλος be taken collectively? the very word ἐκκλησία, occurring since, has pluralized the idea—the building consists of the κλητοί, who are so many στύλοι—why should it not in the aggregate be described as the στύλος? This seems to me far better than, with some in Suicer, to suppose a monumental pillar, or base of an image, to be meant. The way in which the congregation of the faithful is the pillar and basement of the truth is admirably given by Thdrt. and Calvin above: viz. in that it is the element in which and medium by which the truth is conserved and upheld). **16.**] **And** (follows on the preceding: it is indeed worth all thy care to conduct thyself worthily in this house of God—for that truth which is there conserved and upheld is great and glorious above all others, being (see below) none other in fact than THE LORD HIMSELF, in all His gracious manifestation * and glorious triumph) **confessedly** ('as is acknowledged on all hands:' so Thucyd. vi. 90, Ἴβηρας καὶ ἄλλους τῶν ἐκεῖ ὁμολογουμένως νῦν βαρβάρων μαχιμωτάτους: Xen. Anab. ii. 6. 1, Κλέαρχος ὁμολογουμένως ἐκ πάντων τῶν ἐμπείρως αὐτοῦ ἐχόντων δόξας γενέσθαι ἀνὴρ καὶ πολεμικός, κ.τ.λ.: see other examples in Palm and Rost, Lex., and in Wetst. In this word there is a reference to the ἐκκλησία as the upholder of the truth: *confessedly among the* κλητοί. But we must not therefore take the word in a formal sense, 'as we confess,' and then *in consequence* regard the following words as a portion of a confession or song of praise (see below). The adverb is of too general signification for this special reference) **great is the mystery** (see ver. 9: that which was hidden from man until God revealed it, historically, in Redemption) **of piety** (see ch. ii. 2, note: 'of the religious life.' In order to comprehend fully what follows, we must endeavour to realize the train of thought in the Apostle's mind at the time. This '*mystery*' of the life of God in man, is in fact the unfolding of Christ to and in

ᵛ πνεύματι, ʷ ὤφθη ἀγγέλοις, ˣ ἐκηρύχθη ἐν ἔθνεσιν, ʸ ἐπι- ᵛ see 1 Pet. iii.
18.

w = & constr.,
x passive, 1 Cor.

Matt. xvii. 3 ‖.   Luke i. 11. xxii. 43. xxiv. 34.   1 Cor. xv. 5, &c.   Exod. iii. 2.
xv. 12.   2 Cor. i. 19.   (Col. i. 23.)   y = passive, Rom. x. 10.   2 Thess. i. 10 only.

& Hincmar (Cent IX), who charge Macedonius with introducing θεός,—goth syr(or
syr-mg) coptt,—Cyr(de recta fide ad Theodosium, τὸ μέγα τῆς εὐσεβείας μυστήριον,
τουτέστι χριστός..... οἶμαι οὐχ ἕτερον τὸ τῆς εὐσεβείας μυστήριον
ἢ αὐτὸς ἡμῶν ὁ ἐκ τοῦ θεοῦ πατρὸς λόγος, ὃς ἐφανερώθη &c. That Cyril read ὅς as in
the mss, and not θεος as in the present edd, is testified by Œc and Photius h. l. and by
the scholia of several mss of the N. T.) Thdor-mops(Acts of the Council of Constantinop,
Mansi ix. 221) Epiph₂ Pseud-Chrys(but ὅ quod a) Gelasius of Cyzicum (or rather
Macarius of Jerusalem (Cent IV) cited by Gelas. in the Acts of the Nicene Council)
Jerome(on Isa. liii. 11):—ὅς or ὅ is read in Syr.   III. ὅ (correction to agree with
μυστηριον) D¹(accg to Wetstein and Griesbach and recently Tischendorf) latt lat-ff
exc Jerome.—The reading ὅς seems to be supported by the follg: Barnabas(epist. 12,
p. 764, Ἰησοῦς οὐχ ὁ υἱὸς ἀνθρώπου ἀλλ' ὁ υἱὸς τοῦ θεοῦ τύπῳ καὶ ἐν σαρκὶ φανερωθείς)
Theodotus(ὁ σωτὴρ ὤφθη κατιὼν τοῖς ἀγγέλοις) Justin ? to Diognetus(ἀπέστειλε λόγον
ἵνα κόσμῳ φανῇ, ὃς .... διὰ ἀποστόλων κηρυχθεὶς ὑπὸ ἐθνῶν ἐπιστεύθη) Clem-alex in
Œcum(ὃ μυστήριον· μεθ' ἡμῶν εἶδον οἱ ἄγγελοι τὸν χριστόν) Orig(Ἰησοῦς ἐν δόξῃ
ἀναλαμβάνεσθαι λέγεται) Orig-int(Is qui verbum caro factus apparuit positis (or
positus) in carne, sicut Apostolus dicit quia (perhaps qui ?) manifestus est in carne,
justificatus &c) Greg-Nyss(τὸ μυστήριον ἐν σαρκὶ ἐφανερώθη. καλῶς τοῦτο λέγων, οὗτος
ὁ ἡμέτερος λόγος) Basil(τοῦ μεγάλου μυστηρίου ὅτι ὁ κύριος ἐφανερώθη ἐν σαρκί) Nesto-
rins in Arnob-jun(τὸ ἐν τῇ Μαρίᾳ γεννηθὲν ... ἐφανερώθη γάρ, φησίν, ἐν σαρκί, ἐδικαιώθη
&c) Didymus(secundum quod dictum est : manifestatur in carne, on 1 John iv.).—Now
that it may be fairly said, that merely external considerations have settled this question,
we are not driven to combine internal considerations.   Still the grounds which have
confirmed me in deciding for ὅς, may be seen detailed in the note.

him : the key-text to our passage being
Col. i. 27, οἷς ἠθέλησεν ὁ θεὸς γνωρίσαι τί
τὸ πλοῦτος τῆς δόξης τοῦ **μυστηρίου**
τούτου ἐν τοῖς ἔθνεσιν, **ὅ ἐστιν χριστὸς
ἐν ὑμῖν**, ἡ ἐλπὶς τῆς δόξας. This was the
thought in St. Paul's mind; that the
great revelation of the religious life is,
CHRIST. And in accordance with his
practice in these Epistles, written as I
believe, far on in his course, and after
the figures and results of deep spiritual
thoughts had been long familiar to him, he
at once without explanation, or apology as
beforetime in Col. i. 27, or expression of
the χριστός justifying the change of gender in the relative, joins the deep and
latent thought with the superficial and
obvious one, and without saying that the
mystery is in fact Christ, passes from the
mystery to the Person of Christ as being
one and the same. Then, thus passing,
he is naturally led to a summary of those
particulars wherein Christ has been revealed as a ground for the εὐσέβεια of His
Church. And, the idea of μυστήριον being
prominent before him, he selects especially those events in and by which Christ
was manifested forth—came forth from
that secrecy in which he had beforetime
been hidden in the counsels of God, and
shone out to men and angels as the Lord of
life and glory. Let me say in passing, that
it should be noticed, in a question which
now happily no longer depends on internal

considerations, how completely the whole
glorious sentence is marred and disjoined
by the substitution of θεός. It is not the
objective fact of God being manifested, of
which the Apostle is speaking, but the life
of God lived in the church,—the truth, of
which the congregation of believers is the
pillar and basement,—as identical (John
xiv. 6) with Him who is its centre and
heart and stock—as unfolded once for all
in the unfolding of Him. The intimate
and blessed link, furnished by the ὅς, assuring the Church that it is not they that
live, but Christ that liveth in them, is lost
if we understand μυστήριον merely as a
fact, however important, historically revealed. There is hardly a passage in the
N. T., in which I feel more deep personal
thankfulness for the restoration of the
true and wonderful connexion of the original text)—**who** (thus, and not 'which,'
nor 'He who,' should we render, preserv-
ing the same transition, from the mystery,
to Him of whom now all that follows is
spoken. ὅς is, as stated in Ellicott, and
of course implied here, "a relative to an
omitted though easily recognized antecedent, viz. Christ") **was manifested in the
flesh** (it has been often maintained of late,
e. g. by Mack, Winer, Huther, Wiesinger,
Conyb., al., that these sentences, from
their parallelism and concinnity, are taken
from some hymn or confession of the ancient church. We cannot absolutely say

z Rom. v. 13.   στεύθη ᶻ ἐν κόσμῳ, ᵃ ἀνελήμφθη ᵇ ἐν δόξῃ. IV. ¹ ᶜ Τὸ δὲ   ACDFK
1 Cor. viii. 4.   LPℵ a b
xiv. 10.
Phil. ii. 15.   Col. ii. 20.   1 Pet. v. 9.   2 Pet. i. 4.   ἐν τῷ κ., Gospp. & 1 John; but Paul, 2 Cor. i. 12.   Eph. ii. 12 only. c d e f g
a = Mark xvi. 19.   Acts i. 2, &c. x. 16 only.   4 Kings ii. 9, 10, 11.   b = Luke ix. 31.   1 Cor. xv. 43.   2 Cor. h k l m n
iii. 7, &c.   Phil. iv. 19.   Col. iii. 4 only. L.P   c see Acts xvi. 7.   o 17. 47

that it may not have been so: but I
should on all grounds regard it as very
doubtful. I can see no reason why the
same person who wrote the rhetorical passages, Rom. viii. 38, 39; xi. 33—36; 1 Cor.
xiii. 4—7, and numerous others, might
not, difference of time and modified mental characteristics being allowed for, have
written this also. Once written, it would
be sure to gain a place among the choice
and treasured sayings of the Church,
and might easily find its way into liturgical use: but I should be most inclined
to think that we have here its first expression. The reason which some of the above
Commentators adduce for their belief,—
the abrupt insulation of the clauses disjoined from the thought in the context,
has no weight with me: I on the other
hand feel that so beautiful and majestic
a sequence of thoughts springing directly
from the context itself, can hardly be a
fragment pieced in, but must present the
free expansion of the mind of the writer
in the treatment of his subject. On the
sense of this clause, cf. John i. 14, ὁ λόγος
σὰρξ ἐγένετο,—and 2 Tim. i. 10. This is
put first in the rank, as being the preliminary to all the rest. It is followed by
the next clause, because the assertion and
assurance of Christ's perfect unsinning
righteousness was the aim of his manifestation in our flesh all those thirty years
which preceded His public ministry: see
below), was justified (i. e. approved to
be righteous,—according to the uniform
Pauline usage: not as De W., al., 'proved
to be what he was.' The Apostle is following the *historical order of events
during the manifestation of our Lord on
earth.* That this is so, is manifest by the
final clause being, ἀνελήμφθη ἐν δόξῃ. I
take these events then in their order, and
refer this to our Lord's baptism and
temptation, in which His righteousness
★ was approved and proved) in the Spirit
(He was dwelt on by the Spirit in His
baptism—led up by the Spirit to His great
trial, and ἐν πνεύματι, the Spirit of God
being His Spirit (but cf. Ellicott's note),
that of which he said τὸ πνεῦμα μὲν πρό-
θυμον, ἡ δὲ σὰρξ ἀσθενής, He was proved
to be righteous and spotless and separate
from evil and its agent. See Rom. i. 3, 4,
where another proof of this His spiritual
perfection is given, viz. the great and
crowning one of the Resurrection from
the dead. Some have thought of that

proof here also: others, of the continued
course of His miracles, *especially* the Resurrection: Bengel of the Resurrection
and Ascension, by which He entered into
His glory: alii aliter. But I prefer keeping the historical order, though I would
by no means limit the δικαίωσις to that
time only: *then* it was chiefly and prominently manifested), was seen by angels
(viz. by means of His Incarnation, and
specifically, when they came and ministered to Him after His temptation. This
seems to be regarded as the first, or at all
events is the first recorded occasion on
which they ministered to Him. And thus
Chrys. and Thdrt.'s remark may apply:
τὴν γὰρ ἀόρατον τῆς θεότητος φύσιν οὐδὲ
ἐκεῖνοι ἑώρων, σαρκωθέντα δὲ ἐθεάσαντο,
Thdrt.:—μεθ᾽ ἡμῶν, as Chrys. This, one
of the particulars of the glory and manifestation of the incarnate Saviour, is,
though not immediately concerning the
mystery of piety as upheld in the Church,
cited as belonging to the *unfolding* of that
mystery in Christ), was preached among
the nations (that preaching commencing
with the sending out of the Apostles, and
though not then, in the strict technical
sense, carried on ἐν ἔθνεσιν, yet being
the beginning of that which waxed onward till it embraced all nations. See
and compare Rom. xvi. 26 (Eph. iii. 8).
So that we are still proceeding with our
Lord's ministry, taking ἔθνεσιν in that
wider sense in which the Jews themselves
are numbered among them (so also Chrys.,
Huther), and the fact itself as the great
commencement of the proclamation of
Christ to men), was believed on in the
world (including all that winning of faith
first from His disciples (John ii. 11),
then from the Jews (ib. 23, viii. 30), and
Samaritans (iv. 41, 42): see also id. x.
42. Our clause bears with it a reminiscence of his own great saying, John iii.
16 ff.,—οὕτως γὰρ ἠγάπησεν ὁ θεὸς τὸν
κόσμον ὥστε τὸν υἱὸν αὐτοῦ τὸν μονογενῆ
ἔδωκεν, ἵνα πᾶς ὁ πιστεύων εἰς αὐτὸν μὴ
ἀπόληται ἀλλ᾽ ἔχῃ ζωὴν αἰώνιον. οὐ
γὰρ ἀπέστειλεν ὁ θεὸς τὸν υἱὸν αὐτοῦ εἰς
τὸν κόσμον ἵνα κρίνῃ τὸν κόσμον, ἀλλ᾽
ἵνα σωθῇ ὁ κόσμος δι᾽ αὐτοῦ. ὁ πιστεύων
εἰς αὐτὸν οὐ κρίνεται· ὁ δὲ μὴ πιστεύων
ἤδη κέκριται κ.τ.λ.), was received up in
glory (at His Ascension (against De Wette,
who understands it of *celestial precedence*
(von einem himmlischen Vorgange): but
qu. his meaning?): cf. reff.   ἐν δόξῃ is

^{cd} πνεῦμα ^e ῥητῶς ^d λέγει, ὅτι ἐν ^{fg} ὑστέροις ^f καιροῖς ^h ἀπο- στήσονταί ⁱ τινὲς τῆς πίστεως, ^k προσέχοντες ^l πνεύμασιν

...προς-
εχοντες
ACDFK
b.
LPNac
defgh
klmno
17. 47

only †. later Gr. writers freq. see Wetst.   f here only. see 1 Pet. i. 5.   g adj. here (Matt. xxi.
31 v. r.) only. 1 Chron. xxix. 29 only. (-ρον adv., Matt. iv. 2.)   h = Luke viii. 13. Heb. iii.
12. 1 Macc. i. 15.   i = ch. i. 3 reff.   k ch. i. 4 reff.   l = 1 Cor. xii. 10. xiv.
32. 1 John iv. 1. 3 Kings xxii. 21.

d Acts xxi. 11.
Rev. ii. 7,
&c. xiv. 13.
xxii. 17.
e here

best taken as a pregnant construction—was taken up into, and reigns in, glory. It is this distinct reference to the fact of our Lord's personal Ascension, which in my mind rules the whole sentence and makes it, whatever further reference each clause may have, a chain of links of the divine manifestation of the Person of Christ, following in chronological order from His incarnation to His assumption into glory. The order and connexion of the clauses has been very variously understood, as may be seen in Wolf, and in De Wette. The triple antithesis, so characteristic of St. Paul, can hardly escape any reader : ἐν σαρκί, ἐν πνεύματι,—ἀγγέλοις, ἔθνεσιν,—ἐν κόσμῳ, ἐν δόξῃ : but further it is hardly worth while to reproduce the distinctions which some have drawn, or motives for arrangement which they have supposed).

CH. IV. 1—16.] Of future false teachers (1—6); directions to Timotheus in reference to them (7—11); general exhortations to him (12—16).   1.] But (contrast to the glorious mystery of piety which has been just dwelt on) the Spirit (viz. the Holy Spirit of prophecy, speaking in the Apostle himself, or in others,—or, which is most probable, in both—in the general prophetic testimony which He bore throughout the church : cf. γίνωσκε, spoken from the same point of prophetic foresight, 2 Tim. iii. 1. Some (even Wiesinger) have supposed the Apostle to refer to some prophetic passage of the O. T., or to the general testimony of the O. T. prophecies (Dan. vii. 25; viii. 23; xi. 30), or those of our Lord (Matt. xxiv. 4 ff., 11), or of the Apostles (2 Thess: ii. 3 ff. 1 John ii. 18. 2 Pet. iii. 3. Jude 18), or all these combined. But in the two former cases, we should hardly have had τὸ πνεῦμα λέγει, but ἡ γραφή, or ὁ κύριος, or the like ; τὸ πνεῦμα implying rather the present agency of the Spirit: and the latter is only a less clear way of putting the explanation given above : for why should writings be referred to, when the living men were yet testifying in the power of the Spirit among them ? Besides, see the way in which such written prophecies are referred to, in Jude 17) expressly ('plainly,' 'in so many words:' ῥητῶς is a postclassical word, found once in Polyb. (iii. 23. 5 : given by Schweigh., Lex., and Palm and Rost, wrongly, ii. 23. 5; and by Lid-

dell and Scott, in conseq., Polyb. without a reference), ὑπὲρ δὲ Σικελίας τἀναντία διαστέλλονται ῥητῶς, and often in later writers—cf. examples ın Wetst., especially Sext. Empir.,—ὁ Ξενοφῶν ἐν τοῖς ἀπομνημονεύμασι ῥητῶς φησιν, ἀπαρνεῖσθαι αὐτὸν (τὸν Σωκράτην) τὸ φυσικόν; see also Plut. Brut. 29), saith, that in after times (not as E. V. 'in the latter times,' which though not quite so strong as 'in the last times,' yet gives the idea of close connexion with them : whereas here the Apostle speaks only of times subsequent to those in which he was writing : see the difference in 2 Tim. iii. 1: and compare Acts xx. 29) certain men (not the false teachers: rather, those who will be the result of their false teaching) shall depart (or decline: not ✳ by formal apostasy, or the danger would not be that which it is here represented: but subjectively, declining in their own minds and lives from holding Christ in simplicity) from the faith (objective—the doctrine which faith embraces, as so often), giving heed to (see reff.: the participle contains the reason and process of their declension) seducing spirits (πνεύμασιν, as Huther remarks, is in contrast with τὸ πνεῦμα, ver. 1;—it is to be understood as in 1 John iv. 1 and 6, in which last verse we have the cognate expression τὸ πνεῦμα τῆς πλάνης. Wolf's 'spiritualibus seductoribus,' or 'doctoribus seducentibus' is quite inadmissible. The spirits are none other than the spirits of evil, tempting, energizing in, seducing, those who are described, just as the Spirit directs and dwells in those who abide in the faith), and teachings of dæmons (doctrines taught by, suggested by, evil spirits: gen. subjective: cf. σοφία δαιμονιώδης, James iii. 15, and Tert. de præscr. hær. c. 7, vol. ii.p.19, "Hæ sunt doctrinæ hominum et dæmoniorum, prurientibus auribus natæ:" see Col. ii. 22. So Thdrt. (Chrys. is vague), and the fathers generally : (Grot., vaguely,) Wolf, Beng·¹, Olsh., De W., Huther, Wiesinger, Conyb., Ellic. Two wrong interpretations have been given: (1) understanding the genitive as objective, 'teachings concerning dæmons;' so Mede, Works, p. 626 ff., supporting his view by διδαχαὶ βαπτισμῶν, Heb. vi. 2, &c., and Heydenreich ('a characteristic designation of the essene-gnostic false teachers, who had so much to say of the higher spirit-world, of the æons,

m Matt. xxvii.
63. 2 Cor.
vi. 8. 2 John
7 (bis) only.
Job xix. 4.
Jer. xxiii. 32 only.
xvii. 18. James ii. 19.
q r here only †.

^{m} πλάνοις καὶ ^{n} διδασκαλίαις ^{o} δαιμονίων, ^{2} ἐν ^{p} ὑποκρίσει ACDFK
^{q} ψευδολόγων, ^{r} κεκαυτηριασμένων τὴν ἰδίαν ^{s} συνείδησιν, defgh

n ch. i. 10 reff.   o Paul, 1 Cor. x. 20 (bis), 21 (bis) only. Gospp., passim. Acts
Rev. ix. 20. xvi. 14 only.   Ps. xcv. 5.   p Paul, Gal. ii. 13 only. (see reff. there.)
s ch. i. 5 reff.   Tit. i. 15.

ACDFK
LPℵ a c
defgh
k l m n o
17. 47

CHAP. IV. 1. [πλανης P a c f k m o 115-6 lect-14^2 vulg arm Just$_1$ Clem-ms$_1$ Orig$_2$.]
om και D^1 lat-ff.   διδασκαλιας [P^1] ℵ^1[-εας] m.
2. κεκαυστηριασμενων ALℵ d m o Orig-ed Cyr$_1$ Thdrt^1 : txt CDFK[P] rel Clem
Orig [Cyr$_1$-p].

&c.:' in Huther)—but against the context, in which there is no vestige of allusion to idolatry (notwithstanding all that is alleged by Mede), but only to a false and hypocritical asceticism: (2) applying δαιμονίων to the false teachers, who would seduce the persons under description (so Mosheim, Mack, al., and even Calvin— 'quod perinde est ac si dixisset, attendentes pseudo-prophetis et diabolicis eorum dogmatibus'); but this is without example harsh and improbable. The student may refer, as a curiosity, to the very learned disquisition of Mede on these δαιμόνια: —not merely for the really valuable information which it contains, but also as a lesson, to assure the ground well, before he begins to build with such pains) in the (following in the . . . , ἐν giving the element, in which: see below) hypocrisy of those who speak lies (the whole clause belongs to τινὲς ἀποστήσονται, the previous one, προσέχοντες . . . . δαιμονίων, being complete in itself. Bengel gives the construction well: 'construe cum *deficient.* Hypocrisis ea quæ est *falsiloquorum,* illos auferet. τινές, *aliqui,* illi sunt seducti; *falsiloqui,* seductores : falsiloquorum, genitivus, unice pendet ab *hypocrisi.* τὸ *falsiloquorum* dicit relationem ad alios : ergo antitheton est in ἰδίαν, *sua.*' This is much better than to join the gen. ψευδολόγων with δαιμονίων (so Wegscheider and Conyb., but understanding that which is said of the dæmons as meant of those who follow them), or with διδασκαλίαις (Estius,— ' doctrinis, inquam, hominum in hypocrisi loquentium mendacium '),—as making the sentence which follows apply to the false *teachers* (cf. κωλυόντων), whom the τινές follow. And so De W., Huther, Wiesinger: and Mede himself, book iii. ch. 2, p. 677), of men branded (with the foul marks of moral crime : so Cic., Catil. i. 6, ' quæ nota domesticæ turpitudinis non inusta vitæ tuæ est?' Livy, iii. 51, 'ne Claudiæ genti eam inustam maculam vellent :' Plato, Gorg. 524 ε, ὁ 'Ραδάμανθυς . . . . πολλάκις τοῦ μεγάλου βασιλέως ἐπιλαβόμενος ἢ ἄλλου ὁτουοῦν βασιλέως ἢ δυνάστου κατεῖδεν οὐδὲν ὑγιὲς ὂν τῆς ψυχῆς, ἀλλὰ διαμεμαστιγωμένην καὶ οὐλῶν μεστὴν ὑπὸ ἐπι-

ορκιῶν καὶ ἀδικίας. See more examples in Wetst. and Kypke. καυτηριάζω is properly to burn in a mark with a *καυτήρ,* a branding-instrument of hot iron. Thl. explains : ἐπεὶ συνίσασιν ἑαυτοῖς ἀκαθαρσίαν πολλήν, διὰ τοῦτο τὸ συνειδὸς αὐτῶν ἀνεξαλείπτους ἔχει τοὺς καυτῆρας τοῦ ῥυπαροῦ βίου. Thdrt. gives an explanation more ingenious than correct : κεκ. δὲ τὴν ἰδ. συν. αὐτοὺς κέκληκε, τὴν ἐσχάτην αὐτῶν ἀπαλγησίαν διδάσκων. ὁ γὰρ τοῦ καυτήρος τόπος νεκρωθεὶς τὴν προτέραν αἴσθησιν ἀποβάλλει. The idea rather seems to be as Bengel, "qui ipsi in sua sibi conscientia, inustis ei perfidiæ maculis, infames sunt :" cf. Tit. i. 15 ; iii. 11, where αὐτοκατάκριτος seems to express much the same. Or, as Ellic., ' they knew the brand they bore, and yet, with a show of outward sanctity (compare ὑποκρίσει), they strove to beguile and seduce others, and make them as bad as themselves.' The genitive still depends on ὑποκρίσει, as does κωλυόντων also) on their own conscience (τὴν ἰδίαν, as Beng. above—these false teachers are not only the organs of foul spirits, but are themselves hypocritical liars, with *their own* consciences seared by crime. The accusative is one of reference : cf. ch. vi. 5), hindering from marrying (this description has been thought by some to fit the Jewish sects of Essenes and Therapeutæ, who abstained from marriage, Jos. B. J. ii. 8. 2 : Philo de vit. contempl. 4, 8, vol. ii. pp. 476, 482 : cf. Col. ii. 18 ff. But as De W. remarks, the abstinence by and by mentioned seems too general to suit the idea that they were Jews (see below) : besides that the Epistle does not describe them as *present*—but as *to come* in after times), (commanding) (see a like ellipsis (*zeugma*), in which a second but logically necessary verb is omitted, and must be supplied from the context,—in ch. ii. 12, 1 Cor. xiv. 34. Bengel quotes a similar construction from Chrys., ταῦτα λεγω, οὐ κηδεύειν κωλύων, ἀλλὰ μετὰ συμμετρίας τοῦτο ποιεῖν) to abstain from meats (compare Col. ii. 16. It does not appear here from what sort of food this abstinence would be enjoined : but probably the eating of flesh is alluded to.

³ ᵗ κωλυόντων γαμεῖν, ᵘ ἀπέχεσθαι ᵛ βρωμάτων, ἃ ὁ θεὸς
ʷ ἔκτισεν εἰς ˣ μετάλημψιν ʸ μετὰ ʸᶻ εὐχαριστίας τοῖς πιστοῖς
καὶ ᵃᵇ ἐπεγνωκόσιν τὴν ᵇ ἀλήθειαν. ⁴ ὅτι πᾶν ᶜ κτίσμα θεοῦ
ᵈ καλόν, καὶ οὐδὲν ᵉ ἀπόβλητον, ʸ μετὰ ʸᶻ εὐχαριστίας λαμ-
βανόμενον· ⁵ ᶠ ἁγιάζεται γὰρ ᵍ διὰ ᵍ λόγου θεοῦ καὶ ʰ ἐν-

t = Luke xxiii.
2. Acts viii.
36. 1 Cor.
xiv. 39.
1 Thess. ii.
16. 1 Kings
xxv. 26.
u w. gen., Acts
xv. 29. 1 Pet.
ii. 11. Jer.
vii. 10 compl.
w. ἀπό,

Acts xv. 20.　1 Thess. iv. 3.　v. 22. constr., ch. ii. 12.　1 Cor. xiv. 34.　　v plur., Matt. xiv. 15.⎦ L.　Mark
vii. 19.　Luke iii. 11.　1 Cor. vi. 13 bis.　Heb. ix. 10.　xiii. 9 only.　Mal. i. 12 al.　　　　　　w 1 Cor.
xi. 9.　Eph. iii. 9.　Col. i. 16 al.　Deut. iv. 32.　　　　　x here only †.　(μεταλαβεῖν τροφῆς, Acts
xxvii. 33.)　.y Phil. iv. 6.　　　z Eph. v. 4 reff.　　　a Col. i. 6 reff.　　　　　b see
2 John 1 al.　　　c James i. 18.　Rev. v. 13.　viii. 9 only †.　Wisd. ix. 2 al.　　　　d GEN. i. 31.
e here only †.　Levit xix. 7 Aqu.　　f = 1 Cor. vii. 14.　Exod. xxix. 37.　　　　　　g see 3 Kings
xvii. 1.　Sir. xlviii. 3.　　　h ch. ii. 1 reff.

[3. at end add αυτου D¹.　　4. om θεου P.]

Euseb. H. E. iv. 29, quotes from Irenæus
(i. 28. 1, p. 107), ἀπὸ Σατυρνίνου καὶ Μαρ-
κίωνος οἱ καλούμενοι Ἐγκρατεῖς ἀγαμίαν
ἐκήρυξαν, ἀθετοῦντες τὴν ἀρχαίαν πλάσιν
τοῦ θεοῦ, καὶ ἠρέμα κατηγοροῦντες τοῦ
ἄρρεν καὶ θῆλυ εἰς γένεσιν ἀνθρώπων πε-
ποιηκότος· καὶ τῶν λεγομένων παρ' αὐτοῖς
ἐμψύχων ἀποχὴν εἰσηγήσαντο, ἀχαριστοῦν-
τες τῷ πάντα πεποιηκότι θεῷ. These seem
to be the persons here pointed at : and
though the announcement of their success
in after time is prophetic, we may fairly
suppose that the seeds of their teaching
were being sown as the Apostle wrote. The
existence of gnosticism in its earlier form
is certainly implied in ch. vi. 20 : and in
2 Tim. ii. 17, 18, we find that denial of the
resurrection which characterized all the
varieties of subsequent gnosticism. See
the whole subject discussed in the Prolegg.
ch. vii. § i. 12 ff.), which God made for
participation with thanksgiving for (dat.
commodi) those who believe, and have
received the (full) knowledge of the
truth. This last description of the worthy partakers of God's bounties is well
illustrated by Calvin : 'Quid ergo ? annon
solem suum quotidie oriri facit Deus super
bonos et malos (Matt. v. 45) ? annon ejus
jussu terra impiis panem producit ? annon
ejus benedictione etiam pessimi aluntur ?
est enim universale illud beneficium quod
David Psal. civ. 14 decantat. Respondeo,
Paulum de usu licito hic agere, cujus ratio
coram Deo nobis constat. Hujus minime
compotes sunt impii, propter impuram con-
scientiam quæ omnia contaminat, quemadmodum habetur ad Titum, i. 15. Et
sane, proprie loquendo, solis filiis suis Deus
totum mundum et quicquid in mundo est
destinavit, qua ratione etiam vocantur
mundi hæredes. Nam hac conditione constitutus initio fuerat Adam omnium dominus, ut sub Dei obedientia maneret. Proinde rebellio adversus Deum jure quod illi
collatum fuerat, ipsi una cum posteris spo-
liavit. Quoniam autem subjecta sunt
Christo omnia, ejus beneficio in integrum

restituimur, idque per fidem . . . . Poste-
riore membro definit quos vocat fideles,
nempe qui notitiam habent sanæ doctrinæ.'
On μετὰ εὐχαριστίας, see 1 Cor. x. 30:
and below on ver. 4.　　4, 5.] Reason
for the above assertion. Because (ὅτι is
more the objective,—γάρ, which follows,
the subjective causal particle: ὅτι introduces that which rests on a patent fact, as
here on a Scripture quotation,—γάρ, that
which is in the writer's mind, and forms
part of his own reasoning) every thing
which God has made is good (in allusion
to ref. Gen.　See also Rom. xiv. 14, 20);
and nothing (which God has made) is to
be rejected (Wetst. cites Hom. Il. γ. 65,
οὗτοι ἀπόβλητ' ἐστὶ θεῶν ἐρικυδέα δῶρα—
on which the Schol.,—ἀπόβλητα, ἀποβο-
λῆς ἄξια· τὰ ὑπὸ θεῶν, φησί, δεδομένα
δῶρα οὐκ ἔστι μὲν ἀρνήσασθαι) if received
with thanksgiving ("properly, even without this condition, all things are pure :
but he did not rise to this abstraction,
because he was regarding meats not
per se, but in their use, and this latter
may become impure by an ungodly frame
of mind." De Wette): for (see on ὅτι and
γάρ above) it (this subject is gathered out
of the preceding clause by implication,
and = 'every κτίσμα which is partaken
of with thanksgiving') is hallowed (more
than ' declared pure,' or even than ' rendered pure :' the latter it does not want,
the former falls far short of the work of
the assigned agents. The emphasis is on
ἁγιάζεται, and a new particular is introduced by it—not purity merely, but holiness,—fitness for the godly usage of Christian men.　To this, which is more than
mere making or declaring pure, it is set
apart by the εὐχαριστία; so that the
minus is proved by the majus. There is
certainly a slight trace of reference to the
higher consecration in the Lord's Supper.
The same word εὐχαριστία is common to
both.　Ordinary meals are set apart for
ordinary Christian use by asking a blessing on them : that meal, for more than

i = here (Rom. xvi. 4) only.
Jer. xliii. (xxxvi.) 25.
j = 1 Cor. iii.
5. Eph. iii. 7. Col. i. 23 al.
k 2 Cor. xi. 23. Col. i. 7.
l here only †. 17. Luke i. 3. 2 Tim. iii. 10 only †. 2 Macc. viii. 11. ix. 27 only. γραώδη μυθολογίαν, Strabo, i. p. 32 A. Wetst.

τεύξεως. ⁶ Ταῦτα ⁱ ὑποτιθέμενος τοῖς ἀδελφοῖς, καλὸς ἔσῃ ʲᵏ διάκονος ᵏ χριστοῦ Ἰησοῦ, ˡ ἐντρεφόμενος τοῖς λόγοις τῆς πίστεως, καὶ τῆς καλῆς ᵐ διδασκαλίας ᾗ ⁿ παρηκολούθηκας. ⁷ τοὺς δὲ ᵒ βεβήλους καὶ ᵖ γραώδεις ᑫ μύ-

m ch. i. 10 reff.　o ch. i. 9 reff.　n Mark xvi.
q ch. i. 4 reff.　p here

ACDFK LP‎א a c d e f g h k l m n o 17. 47

6. rec ιησ. bef χριστου, with D³ rel am Syr [æth] Chr Thdrt-ms Aug : txt ACD¹F KL[P]‎א e g m latt syr copt [goth] arm Ambrst Pel.　for η, ης A 80 8-pe. [παρηκολουθησας CF.]

ordinary use, by asking on it its own peculiar blessing) **by means of the word of God and intercession** (*what* 'word of God?' how to be understood? treating the plainer word first, the ἔντευξις is evidently intercession (see on ch. ii. 1) *on behalf of the κτίσμα partaken of*—that it may be 'sanctified to our use.' This, bound on as **λόγου θεοῦ** is to ἐντεύξεως by the non-repetition of the preposition, may serve to guide us to its meaning. And first, negatively. It cannot mean any thing which does not form part of the εὐχαριστία: such as God's word in the Scripture just cited (Mack), or in any other place (Grot., al.): or God's word in the foundation-truths of Christianity. Then, positively: it must mean in some sense the εὐχαριστία, or something in it. But not, as Wahl and Leo, the 'word addressed to God,' 'oratio ad Deum facta,' which would be an unprecedented meaning for λόγος θεοῦ: the only way open for us is, that the εὐχαριστία itself, or some part of it, is in some sense *the word of God.* This may be (1) by its consisting in whole or in part of Scripture words, or (2) by the effusion of a Christian man, speaking in the power of God's Spirit, being known as λόγος θεοῦ. This latter is perhaps justified by the reff.: but still it seems to me hardly probable, and I should prefer the former. (So Ellic. also.) It would generally be the case, that any form of Christian thanksgiving before meat would contain words of Scripture, or at all events thoughts in exact accordance with them: and such utterance of God's revealed will, bringing as it would the assembled family and their meal into harmony with Him, might well be said ἁγιάζειν the βρώματα on the table for their use. Many of the Commentators quote from the Constt. Ap. vii. 49, p. 1057, Migne, the following grace before meat, used in the primitive times: εὐλογητὸς εἶ κύριε ὁ τρέφων με ἐκ νεότητός μου, ὁ διδοὺς τροφὴν πάσῃ σαρκί· πλήρωσον χαρᾶς καὶ εὐφροσύνης τὰς καρδίας ἡμῶν, ἵνα πάντοτε πᾶσαν αὐτάρκειαν ἔχοντες, περισσεύωμεν εἰς πᾶν ἔργον ἀγαθὸν ἐν χριστῷ

Ἰησοῦ τῷ κυρίῳ ἡμῶν, δι' οὗ σοὶ δόξα τιμὴ καὶ κράτος εἰς τοὺς αἰῶνας, ἀμήν. Here almost every clause is taken from some expression of Scripture).　**6—11.**] *Recommendatory application to Timotheus of what has been just said, as to form part of his teaching, to the avoidance by him of false and vain doctrine, and to the practice of godliness.* **These things** (hardly, as Rosenm., Heinr., Heyd., ch. iii. 16 f., nor as Chrys.', ποῖα; ἅπερ εἶπεν· ὅτι τὸ μυστήριον μέγα ἐστίν, ὅτι τὸ τούτων ἀπέχεσθαι δαιμόνιόν ἐστιν, ὅτι διὰ λόγου καὶ ἐντεύξεως θεοῦ ἁγιάζεται—but simply the matter treated since the beginning of the chapter,—the coming apostasy after these ascetic teachers and the true grounds of avoiding it. This best suits the following context and the ὑποτιθέμενος, which certainly would not be used of the μέγα μυστήριον) **suggesting** (or counselling, cf. Il. θ. 36, βουλὴν δ' Ἀργείοις ὑποθησόμεθ', ἥτις ὀνήσει: Herod. i. 156, Κροῖσος μὲν δὴ ταῦτά τε οἱ ὑπετίθετο: ... Palm and Rost's Lex. sub voce, 2, c; and Ellic.'s note here) **to the brethren, thou wilt be a good servant of Christ Jesus, ever training thyself in** (the idea of ἐντρέφομαι is not '*nourish oneself with*,' but to grow up amongst, or to be trained in: cf. Eur. Phœn. 368, γυμνάσιά θ', οἷσιν ἐνετράφην: so ἐντρέφεσθαι νόμοις, ἔθεσιν, ὅπλοις, μουσικῇ, λόγοις, τρυφῇ, Plato, Plutarch, al.: see Palm and Rost's Lex. The present, as Chrys., denotes *continuance* in this training, τὸ διηνεκὲς τῆς εἰς τὰ τοιαῦτα προσοχῆς δηλῶν, and again, μηρυκώμενος (*ruminans*), συνεχῶς τὰ αὐτὰ στρέφων, ἀεὶ τὰ αὐτὰ μελετῶν. Cf. 2 Tim. iii. 14) **the words of the faith** (the fundamental doctrines of the Gospel), **and of the good instruction** (not '*words of the faith and good doctrine,*' as Conyb. The repetition of the article forbids this, severs the ᾗ παρηκολούθηκας from τοῖς λόγοις τῆς πίστεως, and attaches it to καὶ τῆς καλῆς διδασκαλίας only) **the course of which thou hast followed** (I have thus endeavoured to give **παρηκολούθηκας** :—'hast

θους ^rπαραιτοῦ· ^sγύμναζε δὲ σεαυτὸν ^tπρὸς ^uεὐσέβειαν· ⁸ἡ γὰρ ^vσωματικὴ ^wγυμνασία ^xπρὸς ὀλίγον ἐστὶν ^yὠφέ-λιμος· ἡ δὲ ^uεὐσέβεια ^xπρὸς πάντα ^yὠφέλιμός ἐστιν, ^zἐπαγγελίαν ἔχουσα ^{za}ζωῆς ^aτῆς ^aνῦν καὶ τῆς ^bμελλού-

r = & constr., Acts xxv. 11 (Paul). ch. v. 11. 2 Tim. ii. 23. Tit. iii. 10. 2 Macc. ii. 31.
s Heb. v. 14. xii. 11.
u ch. ii. 2 reff.

only †. 2 Macc. x. 15 only. (see below [w].)
v Luke iii. 22 only †. 4 Macc. i. 32. (-κῶς, Col. ii. 9.)
note) here only. (James iv. 14. Heb. xii. 10.)
z 2 Tim. i. 1. a here only. see ch. vi. 17. 2 Tim. iv. 10. Tit. ii. 12. also Rom. iii. 26. viii. 25. xi.
5. 2 Cor. viii. 14. 2 Pet. iii. 7.
t = Rom. iii. 26 al. see note.
w here only †. (see above [s].)
y past. epp. only. 2 Tim. iii. 16. Tit. iii. 8 †.
x = (see note)
b = Rom. viii. 38. Heb. vi. 5.

7. for μυθους, θυμους C.   om (2nd) δε D¹[P] 113-7 am(with fuld): *exercens* Ambrst.

8. om 1st προς א¹.   επαγγελιας K d e g h l m o syr[-txt] goth [arm] Euthal Œc₂.

followed along, by tracing its course and accompanying it :' see reff.; and Ellic.'s note).   **7.**] **But profane and anile** (Baur understands this epithet to refer to the gnostic idea of an *old universal mother*, the σοφία or ἀχαμώθ (see Irenæus, i. 4. 1 ff. pp. 18 f.) : but Wiesinger well replies that this will not suit the word γραώδης (from γραῦς, εἶδος, as θεοειδής), which must be subjective,—nor βέβηλος, which on this supposition would not be appro-priate) **fables** (see notes on ch. i. 4 and 7, and Prolegg.) **decline** (lit. 'excuse thyself from,' see reff., Luke xiv. 18, 19, and Palm and Rost's Lex.): **but exercise thyself for piety** (τουτέστι, πρὸς πίστιν καθαρὰν καὶ βίον ὀρθόν· τοῦτο γὰρ εὐσέβεια· γυμνα-σίας ἄρα χρεία καὶ πόνων διηνεκῶν· ὁ γὰρ γυμναζόμενος καὶ ἀγῶνος μὴ ὄντος ἀγω-νίζεται ἱδρῶτος ἄχρι. Thl. (not Thdrt., as Huther). πρός, with a view to, as an athlete with a view to the games: cf. Soph. El. 456, πρὸς εὐσέβειαν ἡ κόρη λέγει, —and the common expressions πρὸς ἡδο-νὴν λέγειν, δρᾶν, δημηγορεῖν, &c.: Soph. Antig. 1170, τἄλλ' ἐγὼ καπνοῦ σκιᾶς οὐκ ἂν πριαίμην ἀνδρὶ πρὸς τὴν ἡδονήν) : **8.**] **for the exercise** (gymnastic training: see below) **of the body is to small ex-tent** ('*for but little*,'—in reference only to a small department of a man's being : not as in ref. James, '*for a short time*,' as the contrast πρὸς πάντα below shews) **profitable** (to what sort of exercise does he allude? Ambr., Thom.-Aq., Lyra, Calv., Grot., Heydenr., Leo, Matthies, al., take it as alluding to corporal austeri-ties for religion's sake: 'hoc nomine appellat quæcunque religionis causa sus-cipiuntur externæ actiones, ut sunt vi-giliæ, longa inedia, humi cubatio, et si-milia,' Calv. But against this are two considerations : 1) that these are not now in question, but the immediate subject is the excellence of being trained and thoroughly exercised in piety : 2) that if they were, it would hardly be consistent with his previous severe characterization of these austerities, ver. 3, to introduce them

thus with even so much creditable mention. Wiesinger has taken up this meaning again and contended very strongly for it, maintaining that the πρὸς ὀλίγον ὠφέλιμος must be *moral*, not corporeal. But it may fairly be answered, if it be moral, then it cannot be said to be πρὸς ὀλίγον, for it would contribute to εὐσέβεια. And indeed he may be refuted on his own ground : he says that the σωματ. γυμνασία *must be-long to* εὐσέβεια : for that if it meant bodily exercise merely, πνευματικὴ γυμνα-σία, not εὐσέβεια, would be the proper contrast to it. But surely we may say, if σωματικὴ γυμν. does *belong to* εὐσέβεια, how can it form a contrast to it? On *his* hypothesis, not on the other, we should require πνευματικὴ γυμνασία as the con-trast. A part cannot be thus contrasted with the whole.   It is therefore far better to understand the words, as Chrys., Thl., Thdrt. (οἱ τῆς τοῦ σώματος, φησίν, εὐεξίας ἐπιμελούμενοι πρὸς ὀλίγον ταύτης ἀπολαύουσιν), Pel., Corn.-a-lap., Estius, Wolf, al., Bengel, Mack, De W., Huther, of mere gymnastic bodily exercise, of which the Apostle says, that it has indeed its uses, but those uses partial only.   Bengel adds, perhaps more ingeniously than conclu-sively, "Videtur Timotheus juvenis inter-dum usus fuisse aliqua exercitatione cor-poris (ch. v. 23) quam Paulus non tam prohibet quam non laudat."   Two curious interpretations of the expression have been given; one by Chrys., as a sort of after-thought: ὃ δὲ λέγει, τοιοῦτόν ἐστι· μηδὲ εἰς γυμνασίαν ποτὲ καταθῇς σεαυτὸν δια-λεγόμενος πρὸς ἐκείνους, ἀλλὰ ταῦτα τοῖς αὐτοῦ παραλίνει. οὐ γάρ ἐστι πρὸς τοὺς διεστραμμένους μαχόμενον ὀνῆσαί τί ποτε, —the other by Braun (Selecta sacra i. 10. 156, cited by Huther), who under-stands by it the ceremonial law): **but piety** (the first member of the antithesis contained the *means*, ἡ σωματικὴ γυμ-νασία : this, the end, εὐσέβεια;—that which is sought by γυμνασία πρὸς εὐ-σέβειαν) **is profitable for all things** (not one portion only of a man's being, but

σης. 9 ᶜπιστὸς ὁ λόγος καὶ ᶜπάσης ᶜἀποδοχῆς ᶜἄξιος· 10 ᵈεἰς τοῦτο γὰρ [καὶ] ᵉκοπιῶμεν καὶ * ᶠὀνειδιζόμεθα, ὅτι ᵍἠλπίκαμεν ἐπὶ ʰⁱθεῷ ʰζῶντι, ὅς ἐστιν ⁱσωτὴρ πάντων

ACDFK LPℵ a c defgh klmno 17. 47

c ch. i. 15 reff.
d Rom. xiv. 9.
2 Cor. ii. 9 al.
e Rom. xvi. 6.
1 Cor. iv. 12.
Eph. iv. 28.
Col. i. 29.
Ps. cxxvi. 1.
f Matt. v. 11 ‖ L. Rom. xv. 3, from Ps. lxviii. 9. 1 Pet. iv. 14 al. g w. ἐπί and dat., Rom. xv. 12, from Isa. xi. 10. ch. vi. 17 (bis, v. r.) only. acc.,ch. v. 5. 1 Pet. i. 13. (iii. 5 v. r.) ἐν, 1 Cor. xv. 19. ch. vi. 17 only. dat. only, Matt. xii. 21. εἰς, John v. 45. 2 Cor. i. 10. 1 Pet. iii. 5. h ch. iii. 15 reff. i see ch. i. 1 reff.

9. om πασης ℵ¹ [Syr].
10. rec bef κοπ. ins καὶ (possibly conformation to Col i. 29), with FKL rel Chr₁ Thdrt Thl Œc : om ACD[P]ℵ 17 [47] 67² vulg Syr copt [goth æth] arm Chr Ambrst Pel. * ἀγωνιζόμεθα (possibly a substitution, as agreeing better with κοπιωμεν: see Col i. 29) ACFKℵ¹ c 17 [47] Chr₁ Cyr : ονειδιζομεθα DL[P]ℵ³ rel vss Chr₃-edd Thdrt Damasc lat-ff. ηλπισαμεν D¹ 17. επι θεον ζωντα D¹.

every portion of it, bodily and spiritual, temporal and eternal), **having** (seeing that it has) **promise of the life** (we may, as far as the construction is concerned, take ζωῆς, as Ellic., abstract, *of life*, and then divide it off into τῆς νῦν and τῆς μελλούσης. But see below), **which is now and which is to come** (how is the genitive ζωῆς to be taken? is it the objective genitive, giving the substance of the promise, LIFE, in its highest sense? in this case it would be ἐν τῷ νῦν αἰῶνι καὶ ἐν τῷ μέλλοντι. And seeing it is not that, but τῆς νῦν κ. τῆς μελλούσης, we should have to understand ζωή in two different meanings,—long and happy life here, and eternal life hereafter—it bears a promise of this life and of the life to come. This to say the least is harsh. It would be better therefore to take ἐπαγγελία as '*the promise*,' in the sense of 'the chief blessedness promised by God,' the blessed contents of His promise, whatever they be, and ζωῆς as the possessive genitive: the best promise belonging to this life and to that which is to come. It may be said, this also is harsh; and to some extent I acknowledge it,—it is not however a harshness in *thought*, as the other, but only in construction, such as need not surprise us in these Epistles. The concrete ἐπαγγελία instead of the abstract is already familiar to us, Luke xxiv. 49 : Acts i. 4; xiii. 32, al.: and the possessive genitive after ἐπαγγ. is justified by Rom. xv. 8, ἐπαγγ. τῶν πατέρων, and by the arrangement of the sentence). 9.] **Faithful is the saying, and worthy of all acceptation** (see on ch. i. 15. The words refer to what *follows*, not as Heinr. to ch. iii. 16, nor as De W., Huther, Wies., al., to what went immediately before : see on γάρ below. The connexion is with καὶ τῆς μελλούσης. Piety has the promise of that life attached to it, according to the well-known Christian saying which follows. Otherwise verse 10 comes in disjointedly and unaccount-

ably) : **for** (γάρ is introduced from a mixture of two constructions, rendering a reason for καὶ τῆς μελλούσης, as if πιστὸς ὁ λόγος had not been inserted. We have the same construction in 2 Tim. ii. 11, where Huther, though he regards the γάρ as decisive against it here, refers the πιστὸς ὁ λόγος to what follows) **to this end** (viz. the σωτηρία implied in that which follows, introduced by ὅτι,—as in reff. : thus alone can the saying as a πιστὸς λόγος cohere together : and so Thdrt., Thl., Beza, Grot., Beng., Mosh., Wegsch., Leo, Wahl :—not, as De W., Huther, Ellic., al., for the obtaining of the promise mentioned above (De W. claims Thdrt. and Bengel for this meaning, but wrongly : the former says, τί δήποτε, &c. εἰ μὴ τίς ἐστι τῶν πόνων ἀντίδοσις ; ἀλλὰ γάρ ἐστιν ἀντίδοσις. ἀΐδιος γὰρ θεὸς ἀγωνοθετεῖ τοῖς ἀθλοῦσι, καὶ πάντων ἐστὶν ἀνθρώπων σωτὴρ κ.τ.λ. ; and the latter, 'hoc nomine, hoc fine, hac spe,' referring to ἠλπίκαμεν)) **we** (Christians in general) **[both] toil** (more than labour (ἐργαζόμεθα) : it gives the idea of 'toil and moil :' see reff.) **and suffer reproach** (climax : we might toil and be had in honour, but as it is, we have both fatigue and shame to bear. The reading ἀγωνιζόμεθα is very strongly supported, but appears to have been introduced from Col. i. 29), **because we have fixed our hope** (the same perfect occurs John v. 45 : 2 Cor. i. 10 : ch. v. 5, vi. 17 : it refers to the time when the strong resolve and waiting began, and to its endurance since that time) **on** (for construction see reff., and Ellicott's note here. Thus in Polyb. i. 12. 6, τὰς . . . . . ἀγορὰς . . . . . ἐφ' οἷς εἶχον τὰς μεγίστας ἐλπίδας) **the living** (inserted for emphasis and solemnity, to bring out the fact that the God in whom we trust is a veritable personal agent, not a creature of the imagination) **God, who is the Saviour of all men** (cf. ch. ii. 4 ; Tit. ii. 11 : His will is that all men should be saved, and He has made full and sufficient provision for the salvation of all : so that,

ἀνθρώπων, ^k μάλιστα πιστῶν. ^{11 l} Παράγγελλε ταῦτα
καὶ δίδασκε. ¹² μηδείς σου τῆς ^m νεότητος ⁿ καταφρονείτω,
ἀλλὰ ^o τύπος γίνου τῶν πιστῶν, ἐν λόγῳ, ἐν ^p ἀνα-
στροφῇ, ἐν ἀγάπῃ, ἐν πίστει, ἐν ^q ἁγνείᾳ. ¹³ ἕως ἔρχομαι,

k Acts xx. 38.
xxv. 26.
xxvi. 3. Gal.
vi. 10. Phil.
iv. 22. ch. v.
8, 17. 2 Tim.
iv. 13. Tit. i.
10 Philem.
16 2 Pet. ii.
10 only.

1 l Thess. iv. 11 reff. constr., 2 Thess. iii. 4.
   only. Gen. vii. 21.   m Mark x. 20 ‖ (Mt. v. r.) L. Acts xxvi. 4 (Paul)
      vi. 2. Heb. xii. 2.   2 Pet. ii. 10 only. Wisd. xiv. 30.   n Matt. vi. 24. xviii. 10. Luke xvi. 13. Rom. ii. 4. 1 Cor. xi. 22. ch.
   7. 2 Thess. iii. 9. Tit. ii. 7. 1 Pet. v. 3.   o = Phil. iii. 17. 1 Thess. i.
      13. 1 Pet. i. 15 al5. 2 Pet. ii. 7. iii. 11 only †. Tobit iv. 14 AB (om ℵ).   p Gal. i. 13. Eph. iv. 22. Heb. xiii. 7. James iii.
q ch. v. 2 only. 2 Chron. xxx. 19.   2 Macc. v. 8 Ed-vat (not AB) only.

12. rec aft εν αγαπη ins εν πνευματι, with KL[P] rel Thdrt Damasc: om ACDFℵ
17 [47] latt syrr copt [goth] æth arm Clem Chr Ambrst Jer Aug.

as far as salvation stands in Him, He is the
Saviour of all men. And it is in virtue of
this universality of salvation offered by God,
that we have rested our hopes on Him and
become πιστοί), **especially them that believe** (in these alone does that universal
salvation, which God has provided, become
actual. He is the same σωτήρ towards and
of all: but these alone appropriate His
σωτηρία. Bengel rightly observes, 'Latet
nervus argumenti a minori ad majus:'
but he applies the σωτὴρ πάντων to *this
life*, and μάλιστα πιστῶν to the life to
come. So also Chrys.: εἰ δὲ τοὺς ἀπίστους σώζει ἐνταῦθα, πολλῷ μᾶλλον τοὺς
πιστοὺς ἐκεῖ. But this does not seem to
suit the context, nor the higher sense to
which σωτήρ is every where in the N. T.
confined, and most especially in these
Epistles, where it occurs very frequently.
The true 'argumentum a minori ad majus'
lies in this—"if God be thus willing for all
to be saved, how much more shall he save
them that put their trust in Him." For the
expression, see reff., and especially Gal. vi.
10). **11.]** Command (see ch. i. 3)
these things (viz. those insisted on since
ver. 7) **and teach them.** **12—16.]**
General exhortations to Timotheus. **Let
✱no one despise thy youth** (as to the construction, Chrys. (μηδεὶς διὰ τὴν νεότητα
καταφρονήσῃ σου), Leo, Mack, Matthies,
take σοῦ as immediately governed by
καταφρονήσῃ, and τῆς νεότητος as a second
genitive — '*thee for thy youth.*' But
though I cannot think with Huther that
such a construction would be illegitimate
(for in what does καταφρονέω differ in
logical reference from κατηγορέω?—cf. εἰ
... παρανόμων ... ἤμελλον αὐτοῦ κατ-
ηγορεῖν, Demosth. Meid. p. 515. 26), yet
ver. 15 seems to rule in favour of the simpler construction, where we have σου preceding its governing substantive with no
such ambiguity. As to the matter of the
youth of Timotheus, see Proleg. ch. vii.
§ ii. 35, note; and remember, that his age
relative to that of the Apostle himself,
whose place he was filling, rather than his

absolute age, is evidently that which is
here meant. By the ἕως ἔρχομαι, we see
that this comparison was before the Apostle's mind. The interpretation of Bengel,
' " talem te gere quem nemo possit tanquam
juvenem contemnere:" libenter id faciunt
senes inanes,' thus endeavouring to elimi-
nate the *fact*, of Timotheus's youth, is
forced, and inconsistent with the τῆς. It
is quite true (cf. what follows—ἀλλὰ τύπος γίνου, &c.) that the exhortation is to
him, not to the Ephesian church: but it
is grounded on the *fact of his youth*, in
whatever light that fact is to be interpreted);—**but become** (by gaining their
respect for the following acts and qualities)
a pattern of the believers (the comma
after **πιστῶν**, in which I have followed
Lachmann, gives more force and independence to the clause adversative to μηδεὶς
κ.τ.λ., and then leaves the specifications
to follow),—**in word** (the whole of thine
utterances, in public and private: ἐν λόγῳ
is elsewhere contrasted, as in Col. iii. 17,
with ἐν ἔργῳ), **in behaviour** (the other
outward sign of the life within: ἐν ἔργῳ,
Col. l. c., but expressing more—' in quoti-
diana consuetudine,' as Beng. The ἀνα-
στροφή may testify, in cases where no
actual deed is done), **in love, in faith** (the
two great springs of Christian conduct,
the one it is true set in motion by the
other,—cf. Gal. v. 6, πίστις δι' ἀγάπης
ἐνεργουμένη,—but both, leading principles of the whole man), **in purity** (probably, not chastity, in the more restricted
sense, though in ch. v. 2 it certainly has
this meaning from the context: but in
the wider and higher meaning which the
context here requires, all believers being
in view, of general holiness and purity.
Cf. for this,—ἁγνός, ch. v. 22: 2 Cor. vii.
11: James iii. 17,—ἁγνίζω, James iv. 8:
1 Pet. i. 22. From these passages the
quality would appear definable as *simplicity of holy motive* followed out in *consistency of holy action*). **13.] Till I
come** (not as De W., as long as thou in
my absence presidest over the Ephesian

[r] πρόσεχε τῇ [s] ἀναγνώσει, τῇ [t] παρακλήσει, τῇ [u] διδασκαλίᾳ. [14] μὴ [v] ἀμέλει τοῦ ἐν σοὶ [w] χαρίσματος, ὃ ἐδόθη
σοι διὰ [x] προφητείας [y] μετὰ [z] ἐπιθέσεως τῶν χειρῶν τοῦ
[a] πρεσβυτερίου. [15] ταῦτα [b] μελέτα, [c] ἐν τούτοις [c] ἴσθι·

14. [for χαρισμ., χρισματος P.]   πρεσβυτερου ℵ¹ m.

church : for this supposes the Apostle to be the normal president of that Church and Timotheus his locum-tenens, which was not the case. Timotheus was put there with a special commission from the Apostle : that commission would cease at the Apostle's coming, not because he would resume residence and presidence, but because he would enforce and complete the work of Timotheus, and thus, the necessity for special interference being at an end, the church would revert to the normal rule of its own presbytery), attend to the (public, see below) reading ("scripturæ sacræ, in ecclesia. Huic adjunguntur duo præcipua genera, adhortatio, quæ ad agendum, et doctrina, quæ ad cognoscendum pertinet, ch. vi. 2 fin. Rom. xii. 7 ff." Beng. This is certainly the meaning; cf. Luke iv. 16 ff.: Acts xiii. 15 : 2 Cor. iii. 14,—not that of Chrys. (ἀκούωμεν ἅπαντες, καὶ παιδευώμεθα μὴ ἀμελεῖν τῆς τῶν θείων γραφῶν μελέτης), Grot., Calv. ("certe fons omnis sapientiæ est Scriptura, unde haurire debent pastores quicquid proferunt apud gregem"), al., who understand private reading. Whether the O. T. Scriptures alone, or in addition to them the earlier gospels were at this time included in this public reading, cf. Just. Mart. Apol. i. (ii.) 67, p. 83 (τὰ ἀπομνημονεύματα τῶν ἀποστόλων ἢ τὰ συγγράμματα τῶν προφητῶν ἀναγινώσκεται, μέχρις ἐγχωρεῖ), cannot be determined with any certainty), to the (also public) exhortation, to the (also public) teaching (cf. Bengel above. Chrys. takes παρακλήσει as social, διδασκαλίᾳ as public,— τῇ παρακλήσει τῇ πρὸς ἀλλήλους, τῇ διδασκαλίᾳ τῇ πρὸς πάντας — so Grot, ' in monendis aliis privatim, docendis publice :' but why so ?).   14.] Do not neglect (= ἀναζωπυρεῖν, 2 Tim. i. 6,— do not suffer to decay and smoulder by carelessness : ' negligunt qui non exercent, nec putant se posse excidere,' Bengel) the spiritual gift which is in thee (see more at length in 2 Tim. i. 6. The spiritual gift is that of teaching and ruling the church. Thdrt. says, too narrowly (and so nearly Ellic.), χάρισμα τὴν διδασκαλίαν

ἐκάλεσε : it was not teaching only, but the whole grace of God given him for the office to which he was set apart by special ordination), which was given thee (by God, 1 Cor. xii. 4, 6) by means of prophecy (not as Mack, 'on account of prophecies,' alleging the plural in ch. i. 18. That verse (see note) refers to the same fact as this—viz. that, either at the first conversion of Timotheus, or at his ordination to the ministry (and certainly the latter seems here to be pointed at), the Holy Spirit spoke, by means of a prophet or prophets, His will to invest him with χαρίσματα for the work, and thus the gift was said to be conferred, as to its certainty in the divine counsels, by such prophecy—'ita jubente per os prophetarum Spiritu Sancto,' Beza. All attempts to make διά bear other meanings (' potest tamen sic accipi ut idem valeat quod εἰς προφητείαν, i. e. ad prophetandum ; vel ἐν προφητείᾳ ita ut quod sit hoc donum exprimat apostolus,' Beza) are illegitimate and needless : see Acts xiii. 1, 2, 3, which is a case precisely analogous : the gift was in Paul and Barnabas διὰ προφητείας, μετὰ ἐπιθέσεως χειρῶν. Bengel strangely joins προφητείας with πρεσβυτερίου, parenthesizing μετὰ ἐπιθ. τ. χειρῶν, alleging that ' impositio manus proprie fit per unam personam et quidem digniorem : prophetia vero fiebat etiam per æquales,' &c. But this certainly was not so : see below), with laying on of the hands (see on Acts vi. 6. Neander, Pfl. u. Leit. i. 267. There is no real difference, as De W. thinks, between this and 2 Tim. i. 6. There was a special reason there for putting Timotheus in mind of the fact that the Apostle's own hands were laid on him : but that fact does not exclude this. See references on the χειροθεσία in Ellicott's note) of the presbytery (reff. : of the body of elders who belonged to the congregation in which he was ordained. Where this was, we know not : hardly in Lystra, where he was first converted : might it not be in Ephesus itself, for this particular office ?).   15.] These things (viz. the things enjoined vv. 12—14) do thou

ἵνα σοῦ ἡ ^d προκοπὴ φανερὰ ᾖ πᾶσιν. ¹⁶ ^e ἔπεχε σεαυτῷ
καὶ τῇ ^f διδασκαλίᾳ. ^g ἐπίμενε αὐτοῖς· τοῦτο γὰρ ποιῶν,
καὶ σεαυτὸν ^h σώσεις καὶ τοὺς ⁱ ἀκούοντάς σου.

V. ¹ Πρεσβυτέρῳ μὴ ^k ἐπιπλήξῃς, ἀλλὰ ^l παρακάλει
ὡς πατέρα· νεωτέρους, ὡς ἀδελφούς· ² ^m πρεσβυτέρας,
ὡς μητέρας· νεωτέρας, ὡς ἀδελφάς, ἐν ⁿ πάσῃ ^o ἁγνείᾳ.

d Phil. i. 12, 25 only †. Sir. li. 17. 2 Macc. viii. 8 only.
e = Luke xiv. 7. Acts iii. 5 (& constr.) only. Sir. xxxi. (xxxiv.) 2. (Acts xix. 22.
g Rom. vi. 1. xi. 22, 23. Col. i. 23. Exod. xii. 39 B.
k here only †. Jos. Antt. xii. 4. 2. Polyb. i. 12. 7 al. (-πληξις, 2 Macc. vii. 33.)
m fem., here only. Zech. viii. 4.
xxx. 19.
h = ch. ii. 15.
n = Phil. i. 20 reff.
Phil. ii. 16 only.)
f ch. i. 10 reff.
i 2 Tim. ii. 14.
1 = ch. ii. 1 al. fr.
o ch. iv. 13 only. 2 Chron.

15. rec ins εν bef πασιν (*from misunderstanding?*), with D³KL[P] rel æth Chr(explaining μὴ ἐν τῷ βίῳ μόνον ἀλλὰ καὶ ἐν τῷ λόγῳ) Thdrt Damasc : om ACD¹FℵR 17 latt syrr copt goth arm Clem Cyr lat-ff.

16. ins εν bef αυτοις D¹ vulg(not tol) goth lat-ff.　om σου ℵ¹.

CHAP. V. 1. om ως πατερα ℵ¹.

care for, in these things be (employed) (Wetst. cites Plut. Pomp. p. 656 b, ἐν τούτοις ὁ Καῖσαρ . . . . ἦν : Lucret. iii. 1093, 'versamur ibidem, atque insumus usque:' Hor. Ep. i. 1. 11, 'quod verum atque decens curo et rogo et omnis in hoc sum.' To which I may add a more striking parallel, Hor. Sat. i. 9. 2, 'Nescio quid meditans nugarum, et totus in illis'), **that thy progress** (ref.: προκοπή is branded as a "vox non immerito a grammaticis contemta" by Lobeck, Phryn. p. 85 : towards perfection ; certainly in the Christian life, as Heydenr., De W.: this is *implied*; but the more direct meaning is, 'with reference to the duties of thine office:' and especially as respects the caution given ver. 12, that no man despise thy youth) **may be manifest to all.** **16.]** **Give heed to thyself** (summary of ver. 12. On ἔπεχε, see Ellicott's note) **and to thy teaching** (summary of ver. 13. "Duo sunt curanda bono pastori: ut docendo invigilet, ac se ipsum purum custodiat. Neque enim satis est, si vitam suam componat ad omnem honestatem, sibique caveat ne quod edat malum exemplum, nisi assiduum quoque docendi studium adjungat sanctæ vitæ: et parum valebit doctrina, si non respondeat vitæ honestas et sanctitas." Calv.). **Continue** (reff.) **in them** (most naturally, the ταῦτα of ver. 15 : but the words are ambiguous and puzzling. Grot. gives a curious interpretation : '*mane apud Ephesios*,' which is certainly wrong : Bengel, as an alternative, refers it to τοὺς ἀκούοντας below, which is no better. I have punctuated it so as to connect this clause with what follows, and thus to render it not quite so harsh, seeing that it then will assume the form of a recapitulatory conclusion) ; **for doing this** ('*in* doing this,' as E. V., better than '*by* doing this,' which asserts too

much) **thou shalt save** (in the day of the Lord : the highest meaning, and no other, is to be thought of in both cases) **both thyself and those that hear thee** (thyself, in the faithful discharge of the ministry which thou hast received of the Lord : thy hearers, in the power of thine influence over them, by God's word and ordinances). **Ch. V. 1—25.]** GENERAL DIRECTIONS TO HIM FOR GOVERNING THE CHURCH. **1, 2.]** *Injunctions respecting his behaviour to the elder and younger of either sex.* **πρεσβυτέρῳ**] The reference to an *office* was called in question as early as Chrys. ἆρα τὸ ἀξίωμα νῦν φησιν; οὐκ ἔγωγε οἶμαι, ἀλλὰ περὶ παντὸς γεγηρακότος. This indeed is evident from the quadruple specification in these verses. So even Mack, though he maintains that the νεώτεροι of Acts v. 6 were official. Leo, as cited by Wiesinger, gives well the connexion with the last chapter : "quum supra scripsisset, nemini licere ex juventute Timothei ejus despiciendi occasionem sumere, nunc jam ipsum hortatur Timotheum, ut semper memor suæ νεότητος ita se gerat erga seniores uti revera deceat virum juniorem." But this connexion must not be too closely pressed. Some important general instructions have intervened since the μηδείς σου τῆς νεότητος καταφρονείτω. **ἐπιπλήξῃς**] Thus Il. μ. 211, "Εκτορ, ἀεὶ μέν πώς μοι ἐπιπλήσσεις ἀγορῆσιν ἐσθλὰ φραζομένῳ. **ἀλλὰ παρακάλει**] ὡσανεὶ πρὸς πατέρα, φησί, προσενεχθείης ἁμαρτάνοντα, οὕτω πρὸς ἐκεῖνον διαλέγου, Chrys. **νεωτέρους**] understand παρακάλει. Thus the prohibition, μὴ ἐπιπλήξῃς, applies to all, all being included in the παρακάλει which is the other and adopted alternative. **ὡς ἀδελφούς**] as on an equality with them, not lording it over them. **ὡς ἀδελφάς**] 'Hic respectus egregie adjuvat castitatem,' Bengel.

p Paul. here only, exc. Eph. vi. 2, from Exod. xx. 12. Epp., 1 Pet. ii. 17 bis only.

3 Χήρας [p] τίμα τὰς [q] ὄντως χήρας. 4 εἰ δέ τις χήρα
τέκνα ἢ [r] ἔκγονα ἔχει, [s] μανθανέτωσαν πρῶτον τὸν ἴδιον
οἶκον [t] εὐσεβεῖν, καὶ [u] ἀμοιβὰς [v] ἀποδιδόναι τοῖς [w] προ-

ACDFK LPℵ a c d e f g h k l m n o 17. 47

q Mark xi. 32. Paul, 1 Cor. xiv. 25. Gal. iii. 21. vv. 5, 16. ch. vi. 19 only. Num. xxii. 37 only. r here only. Deut. vii. 13 al. freq. in LXX. s = & constr., Phil. iv. 11. Tit. iii. 14. see ver. 13. t Acts xvii. 23 only †. (see ch. ii. 2 reff.) u here only †. Isa. i. 23 Symm. οἷς . . . ἀπέδωκ' ἀμοιβὰς οὐ καλάς, Eurip. Orest. 468. (see Wetst.) v Rom. xii. 17. 1 Thess. v. 15 al. w 2 Tim. i. 3 only †. Sir. viii. 4. 2 Macc. viii. 19. xi. 25 only.

4. εγγονα D[1] 44. 109. μαθετωσαν D[1]. των ιδιων οικων D[1]. [ενσεβειν

μηδὲ ὑποψίαν, φησί, δῷς. ἐπειδὴ γὰρ αἱ πρὸς τὰς νεωτέρας γενόμεναι ὁμιλίαι δυσκόλως διαφεύγουσιν ὑποψίαν, δεῖ δὲ γίνεσθαι παρὰ τοῦ ἐπισκόπου καὶ τοῦτο, διὰ τοῦτο "ἐν πάσῃ ἁγνείᾳ" προστίθησι. Chrys. See similar sentiments from profane writers in Wetst. The Commentators cite the apologist Athenagoras (legat. pro christ. 32, p. 310): καθ' ἡλικίαν τοὺς μὲν υἱοὺς κ. θυγατέρας νοοῦμεν, τοὺς δὲ ἀδελφοὺς ἔχομεν καὶ ἀδελφάς· καὶ τοῖς προβεβηκόσι τὴν τῶν πατέρων καὶ μητέρων τιμὴν ἀπονέμομεν. "The rule of Jerome (Ep. 52 (2). 5, vol. i. p. 259) is simple: 'omnes puellas et virgines Christi aut æqualiter ignora aut æqualiter dilige.'" Ellic. **3—16.**] *Directions concerning widows.* This whole passage is somewhat difficult, and has been very variously understood. The differences will be seen below. **3. τίμα**] Is this to be interpreted generally, '*honour*' merely, or with reference to the context? The best guide to an answer will be what follows. If the command be merely to hold them in honour, why should the destitute be held in more honour than those who had families? The command χήρας τίμα would surely apply to all alike. But seeing that it *does not* apply to all alike, we must necessarily limit its general meaning to that particular in which the one would be honoured, and the other not. Thus without giving or seeking for an unusual meaning to τίμα, we may fairly interpret it of this particular kind of honour, viz. being inscribed on the Church's κατάλογος (ver. 9) as a fit object of charitable sustenance. That such a roll existed in the very earliest days of the church, we know from Acts vi. 1. Cf. also Ignat. ad Polyc. c. 4, p. 721 f.: Justin M. Apol. i. 67, p. 84: Euseb. H. E. vi. 43. Thus Huther and De W., and Ellic., after Grot., Calv., all. **τὰς ὄντως χήρας**] cf. ver. 16 below,—**those who are really in a widowed** (destitute) **state**, as contrasted with those described ver. 4. But then the enquiry has been made, Is this ὄντως χήρα to be defined by mere external circumstances, or not rather by the religious character, described below, ver. 5? Or are we to bind (as Chrys., al.) the two together? In a certain sense, I believe we must thus unite them. The Apostle commands, 'Honour (by placing on the list) those who are widows indeed:' for it is these especially, they who are destitute of earthly friends, who are most likely to carry out the true religious duties of a widow. Thus, without the two qualifications being actually united, the former is insisted on as ordinarily ensuring the latter. **4.**] The case of the χήρα who is not ὄντως χήρα, having earthly relations answerable for her support. **ἔκγονα**] τέκνα τέκνων, Hesych.; **grandchildren**: not as E. V. '*nephews;*' at least, not in its present sense. **μανθανέτωσαν**] What is the subject? (1) The ancient Commentators mostly understand αἱ χῆραι, implied in τὶς χήρα: so vulg. (*discat:* also D-lat, 2 cursives have μανθανέτω), Chr. (see below), Thdrt., Œc., Jer., Pel., Ambr., Luth., Calv., Grot., Calov., Huther, al. (2) But some of the ancients took τὰ τέκνα ἢ ἔκγονα as the subject: e. g. Œc. 2, Thl., and so Beza, Wolf, Mosh., Wegscheid: Heydenr., Flatt, Mack, De W., Wiesinger, Ellicott. There is much to be said for both views; and as we advance, we shall give the interpretations on both hypotheses, (1) and (2). **πρῶτον**] Either, '*first of all duties,*' which seems supported by ver. 8 below; or *first,* before applying to the church for sustenance. These meanings will apply to both the above alternatives: whether we understand the subject to be the *widows,* or the *children and grandchildren.* **τὸν ἴδιον οἶκον εὐσεβεῖν**] On hypothesis (1),—*to behave piously towards,* i. e. *to rule religiously* (Luth.; so vulg.), their own household. This seems somewhat to force εὐσεβεῖν, see below; while the sense of τὸν ἴδιον οἶκον is thus the simple and usual one, as the widow in question would be the head of the household. On hypothesis (2), *to behave piously towards,* i. e. *to honour with the honour which God commands,* their own family, i. e. the widowed mother or grandmother who is one of their own family. This sense of εὐσεβής, εὐσέβεια, and εὐσεβέω, is common enough (see especially Palm and Rost's Lex.): the reference

γόνοις· τοῦτο γάρ ἐστιν [xy] ἀποδεκτὸν [x] ἐνώπιον τοῦ θεοῦ.
[5] ἡ δὲ [z] ὄντως χήρα καὶ [a] μεμονωμένη [b] ἤλπικεν [b] ἐπὶ τὸν
θεόν, καὶ [c] προσμένει ταῖς [d] δεήσεσιν καὶ ταῖς [d] προς-
ευχαῖς [e] νυκτὸς καὶ [e] ἡμέρας· [6] ἡ δὲ [f] σπαταλῶσα [g] ζῶσα
[g] τέθνηκεν. [7] καὶ ταῦτα [hi] παράγγελλε, [i] ἵνα [j] ἀνεπί-

x ch. ii. 3.
y as above (x) only †.
(-δοχή, -δέχεσθαι, Acts ii. 41.)
ch. i. 15.
z ver. 3 reff.
a here only †.
Gen. xlix. 6 Aqu.
b see ch. iv. 10

reff.　　c = Acts xiii. 43 (of Paul). see Acts xi. 23.　　d ch. ii. 1 reff.　　e Paul, 1 Thess. ii.
9. iii. 10.　2 Tim. i. 3.　Mark v. 5.　Rev. iv. 8 al.　Isa. xxxiv. 10.　　f James v. 5 only.　Ezek.
xvi. 49.　Sir. xxi. 15 only.　(-λη, Sir. xxvii. 13.　κατασπαταλάω, Prov. xxix. 21.　Amos vi. 4 [cf. Wetst.].)
g see Rev. iii. 1.　πένης ἀποθανών, φροντίδων ἀπηλλάγη, ζῶν γὰρ τέθνηκε, Stob. 238, Wetst.　　h ch.
iv. 11.　Josh. vi. 6.　　i Mark vi. 8.　2 Thess. iii. 12.　　j ch. iii. 2.　vi. 14 only †.

D.] 　rec ins καλον και (from ch ii. 3) bef αποδεκτον, with (d, e sil) m o copt goth
[arm] : om ACDFKL[P]א rel vulg syrr [æth] gr-lat-ff. (17 def.)
5. om τον [CFP]א¹.—for θεον, κυριον D¹א¹ Aug Fulg.
7. om και א³ [Syr copt].

being generally (not always, it is true) to
superiors,—those who demand σέβας,—
those who·stand in the place of God. This
sense of τὸν ἴδιον οἶκον is not so usual,
but not therefore to be rejected. To dishonour their widowed mother or grandmother, would be to dishonour their own
family, in that one of its members who
most required respect. καὶ ἀμοιβὰς
ἀποδιδόναι τοῖς προγόνοις] On hypothesis
(1), as Chrys., ἀπῆλθον ἐκεῖνοι· οὐκ ἠδυ-
νήθης αὐτοῖς ἀποδοῦναι τὴν ἀμοιβήν·
οὐ γὰρ δὴ καὶ αὐτὴ ἐγέννησας ἐκείνους,
οὐδὲ ἀνέθρεψας. ἐν τοῖς ἐκγόνοις αὐτοῦ
ἀμείβου· ἀπόδιδο τὸ ὀφείλημα διὰ τῶν
παιδῶν. But surely it is a very strange
way of requiting one's progenitors for their
care of us, to be kind towards our own
children : and besides, what would this
have to do with the question, whether or
not the widow was to be put on the charity
roll of the church ? But on hypothesis (2),
this sentence certainly becomes more clear
and natural. Let them, the children or
grandchildren, learn first to be piously
grateful to (these members of) their own
families, and to give back returns (a return in each case) to their progenitors (so
called, although living, because, the mother
and grandmother having been both mentioned, πρόγονοι was the only word which
would include them in one category).
τοῦτο γὰρ . . . .] see ch. ii. 3.
5.] see above on ver. 3. 　　 ἡ
ὄντως χήρα, as opposed to the widow just
described ; κ. μεμονωμένη, as contrasting
her condition with that of her who has
children or grandchildren. Thus what
follows is said more for moral eulogy of
such a widow, than as commending her to
the charity of the church : but at the
same time, as pointing out that one who
thus places her hopes and spends her time,
is best deserving of the Church's help.
ἤλπικεν, ch. iv. 10, has set and
continues to set her hope. 　ἐπὶ τὸν

θεόν, on God as its portion and ultimate
aim,—as distinguished from ἐπὶ τῷ θεῷ,
ch. iv. 10, on God as its present stay.
προσμένει] compare reff., and the
similar use of προσκαρτερεῖν, Rom. xii. 12,
Col. iv. 2. ταῖς δεήσ. κ. ταῖς προς-
ευχ.] see on ch. ii. 1. The articles may
refer to the public prayers of the Church,
or may be possessive—'to her supplications and her prayers:' or may serve
merely to designate the two great divisions of prayer. νυκτ. κ. ἡμ.] so St.
Luke of Anna the prophetess, ii. 37,—
νηστείαις κ. δεήσεσιν λατρεύουσα νύκτα
καὶ ἡμέραν. 6.] Contrast (δέ) to the
character just described : and that certainly
with a view to point out that this kind of
widow is no object for the charity of the
Church, as not being at all a partaker of
the life unto God. σπαταλῶσα]
Wetst. from the glossaries, gives σπαταλᾷ,
λίαν τρυφᾷ, ἀσώτως ζῇ. In the Anthol.,
iv. 28. 14, we have coupled πᾶν τὸ βρό-
των σπατάλημα κ. ἡ πολύολβος ἐδωδή.
It appears to be allied to σπαθάω (σπάω),
—see Aristoph., Nub. 53, and Schol. (in
Wetst.); and, Ellic., here. ζῶσα
τέθνηκεν] while alive in the flesh, has no
real life in the Spirit : see ref.—and Matt.
viii. 22 : Eph. v. 14. Wetst. quotes many
such expressions from profane writers:
one, as compared with this passage, remarkably illustrative of the moral difference between Christianity and heathenism:
Soph. Antig. 1183,—τὰς γὰρ ἡδονὰς
ὅταν | προδῶσιν ἄνδρες, οὐ τίθημ᾿ ἐγὼ |
ζῆν τοῦτον, ἀλλ᾿ ἔμψυχον ἡγοῦμαι νεκρόν.
The very expression is found in Stobæus;
see reff. I cannot help regarding the idea
as in the background,—'and, if devoid of
spiritual life, then not to be taken into
account by the Church.' 7.] ταῦτα
most naturally applies to the characters
just given of widows, not more generally :
and in that case ἵνα ἀνεπίληπτοι (see
reff.) ὦσιν must refer to the widows also,

λημπτοι ὦσιν. ⁸ εἰ δέ τις ᵏ τῶν ᵏ ἰδίων καὶ ˡ μάλιστα [τῶν]
ᵐ οἰκείων οὐ ⁿ προνοεῖ, τὴν ᵒ πίστιν ᵒᵖ ἤρνηται, καὶ ἔστιν
ᑫ ἀπίστου ʳ χείρων. ⁹ χήρα ˢ καταλεγέσθω μὴ ᵗ ἔλαττον

(marginal references, left)
k John i. 11.
xiii. 1. Acts
iv. 23. xxiv.
23 only.
2 Macc. xii.
22.
l ch. iv. 10 reff.
m Gal. iv. 10.
Eph. ii. 19 only.   Isa. iii. 6.
o Rev. ii. 13.
iii. 13, 14. vii. 35.   2 Pet. ii. 1.   1 John ii. 22, 23.   Jude 4.   Rev. iii. 8‡.   (Gen. xviii. 15.)
vi. 6. vii. 12, &c. x. 27. xiv. 22, &c.   2 Cor. vi. 14, 15.   Tit. i. 15.
29 al. †   Wisd. xv. 18 only.
t adv. here only.   (-σσων, John ii. 10.   Rom. ix. 12, from Gen. xxv. 23.   Heb. vii. 7 only.)

n Rom. xii. 17, from Prov. iii. 4.   2 Cor. viii. 21 only P.   2 Macc. xiv. 9
p = Paul, 2 Tim. ii. 12, 13. iii. 5.   Tit. i. 16. ii. 12 only.   Matt. x. 33 bis.   Luke xii. 9.   Acts
q — 1 Cor.
r Paul, 2 Tim. iii. 13 only.   Heb. x.
s here only.   Deut. xxv. 16.   2 Macc. vii. 30 only.   Xen. Hell. iii. 4 15.

(marginal references, right)
b νοει
την...
ACDFK
LPℵ a b
c d e f g
h k l m n
o 17. 47

8. om (2nd) των ADˡFℵ : ins CD²·³KL[P] rel Chr Thdrt Damasc. (17 def.)
προνοειται (corrn, the active occurring only here in N. T.) DˡFℵ¹.

not to the τέκνα and ἔκγονα, or to these
and the widows together, as Heydenr., or
more widely still, as Grot., al. This narrower reference is confirmed by the next
verse, which takes up the duty of the
relations, being connected not by γάρ, but
by δέ.   8.] τίς, not only of the τέκνα
ἢ ἔκγονα above, or any persons connected
with widows,—but the saying is perfectly
general, grounding their duties on an
axiomatic truth. Agreeably with their
former interpretation, Chrys., &c. regard
τίς as meaning 'a widow:' Calv. and
Thdrt. unite both, widows and children.

οἱ ἴδιοι seem to be generally any
connexions,—οἱ οἰκεῖοι, those more immediately included in one's own family as
dwelling in the same οἶκος—see reff.
Mack is certainly wrong in regarding
οἰκεῖοι (without τῆς πίστεως) as meaning
those connected by the faith. The omission of the article (see var. readd.) would
make the two belong to one and the same
class.   οὐ προνοεῖ, viz. in the way
noted above,—of support and sustenance.
Notice εἰ οὐ, in its regular usage, the
negation being closely connected with the
verb: "neglects to provide." On the
construction of προνοεῖν, see Ellic.'s note.

τὴν πίστιν ἤρνηται] 'fides enim
non tollit officia naturalia, sed perficit et
firmat.' Bengel. The Roman-Catholic
Commentator Mack has some good remarks here, on the faith of which the
Apostle speaks: "Faith, in the sense of
the Apostle, cannot exist, without including love: for the subject-matter of faith
is not mere opinion, but the grace and
truth of God, to which he that believes
gives up his spirit, as he that loves gives
up his heart: the subject-matter of faith
is also the object of love. Where therefore Love is not, nor works, there is not,
nor works, Faith either: so that he who
fulfils not the offices of love towards his
relatives, is virtually an unbeliever."
ἀπίστου χείρων] For even among heathens the common duties of family piety
are recognized: if therefore a Christian
repudiates them, he lowers himself be-

neath the heathen. Cf. Matt. v. 46, 47.
Also, as Calv. suggests in addition, the
Christian who lives in the light of the
Gospel, has less excuse for breaking those
laws of nature which even without the
Gospel are recognized by men.   According to hypothesis (1) or (2) above, this general statement applies to the widows or to
their children and grandchildren: not, as
Matthies, to their *mutual* relations, about
which the context contains no hint. But
surely it would be very harsh to understand it of the widows: and this forms
an additional argument for hypothesis (2).

9—16.] *Further regulations respecting widows.*   9.] Is χήρα subject or predicate? 'let a widow καταλεγέσθω,' or 'let a woman καταλεγέσθω
χήρα?' I own, from the arrangement of
the words, I am inclined to believe the
latter to be the case. The verb καταλεγέσθω introduces the new particular. Had
χήρα then been the subject, the verb,
having the emphasis, must have preceded.
As it is, χήρα has the emphasis, as it
would have, were it the predicate, spoken
of those of whom the κατάλογος consisted.
I render therefore,—Let a woman be inserted in the catalogue as a widow.
But now, for what purpose? κατα-
λέγειν is to enrol on a list or roll: so
Aristoph. Acharn. 1029: ὅταν στρατιώ-
τας καταλέγωσι . . .,—Lysistr., ὁ δὲ Δημό-
στρατος | ἔλεγεν ὁπλίτας καταλέγειν Ζα-
κυνθίων: Xen. Rep. Lac. iv. 3, τούτων
δ' ἕκαστος ἄνδρας ἑκατὸν καταλέγει: Lysias, p. 172. 37, οὐ τοίνυν οὐδ' εἰς τὸν
κατάλογον 'Αθηναίων καταλέξας οὐδένα
φανήσομαι: see other examples in Palm
and Rost's Lex., and in Wetst. But *what
catalogue* are we to understand? (In replying to this question I agree in the main
with De Wette, from whose note the substance of the following remarks is adopted.)
Hardly, (1) that of those who are to receive relief from the Church (so Chrys.
h. l., Thdrt., Œc., Thl., Jer., Erasm.,
Calv., Est., Wolf, Neand., al.): for thus
the rule, that she is to be *sixty years of
age*, would seem a harsh one, as many

ἐτῶν ἑξήκοντα γεγονυῖα, ⁿἑνὸς ἀνδρὸς γυνη, 10 ἐν ᵛἔργοις
ᵛκαλοῖς ʷμαρτυρουμένη, εἰ ˣἐτεκνοτρόφησεν, εἰ ʸἐξενοδό-

u see ch. iii. 2,
12.
v ch. iii. 1 reff.
w = Acts vi. 3.
x. 22. xxii.

12. Heb. xi. 2, 39.   x here only†. Arrian, Epict. l. 23, διατί ἀποσυμβουλεύεις τῷ σοφῷ
τεκνοτροφεῖν;   y here only†. Herod. vi. 127.

[9. ενος ανδρος γυνη bef γεγονυια P Syr arm.   10. for καλ., αγαθοις P.]

widows might be destitute at a far earlier age: as also the rule that she must not have been *twice married*, especially as the Apostle himself below commands second marriage for the younger widows. Again, the duties enjoined in ver. 10 presuppose some degree of competence, and thus, on this hypothesis, the widows of the poorer classes would be excluded from sustenance by charity,—who most of all others would require it. Also, for the reason alleged in ver. 11, *sustenance* can hardly be in question—for then the re-marrying would simply take them off the roll, and thus be rather a benefit, than a detriment to the Church. Nor again (2) can we understand the roll to be that of the *deaconesses*, as Pelag., Beza, Schleierm., Mack, al.: although the Theodosian code, founded on this interpretation, ordained "nulla nisi emensis LX annis secundum præceptum Apostoli ad Diaconissarum consortium transferatur," xvi. 2. 27 (De W.). For a) the age mentioned is unfit for the work of the deaconesses' office, and in the council of Chalcedon the age of the deaconesses was fixed at 40: b) not only widows but virgins were elected deaconesses (Balsamon, ad Can. xix. conc. Niceni, παρθένοι . . . . . τεσσαρακονταετοὺς ἡλικίας γενόμεναι, ἠξιοῦντο καὶ χειροτονίας διακονισσῶν εὑρισκόμεναι πάντως ἄξιαι. Suicer, i. 865): (3) it is implied in ver. 12, that these widows were bound not to marry again, which was not the case with the deaconesses. It seems therefore better to understand here *some especial band of widows*, sustained perhaps at the expense of the church, but not the only ones who were thus supported:—set apart for ecclesiastical duties, and bound to the service of God. Such are understood here by Chrys. himself in his homily on the passage (311 in div. N. T. loc. 3, vol. iii. p. 523, Migne),—καθάπερ εἰσὶ παρθένων χοροί, οὕτω καὶ χηρῶν τὸ παλαιὸν ἦσαν χοροί, καὶ οὐκ ἐξῆν αὐταῖς ἁπλῶς εἰς τὰς χήρας ἐγγράφεσθαι. οὐ περὶ ἐκείνης οὖν λέγει τῆς ἐν πενίᾳ ζώσης καὶ δεομένης βοηθείας, ἀλλὰ περὶ ταύτης τῆς ἑλομένης χηρείαν. They are also mentioned as τάγμα χηρῶν, τὸ χηρικόν, πρεσβύτιδες, προκαθήμεναι: i. e. such widows as corresponded in office for their own sex in some measure to the presbyters,—sat unveiled in the assemblies in a separate

place, by the presbyters, and had a kind of supervision over their own sex, especially over the widows and orphans: were vowed to perpetual widowhood, clad with a 'vestis vidualis,' and ordained by laying on of hands. This institution of the early church, which was abolished by the eleventh canon of the council of Laodicea (in the translation of Dionys. Exiguus,—'mulieres quæ apud Græcos presbyteræ appellantur, apud nos autem viduæ seniores, univiræ, et matriculariæ nominantur, in ecclesia tanquam ordinatas constitui non debere'), is sufficiently affirmed by Chrys. l. c. Epiphan. hær. lxxix. 4, vol. ii. (Migne), p. 1060 f., and long before by Tert. de veland. virg. 9, vol. ii. p. 902: 'ad quam sedem (viduarum) præter annos LX non tantum univiræ, i. e. nuptæ aliquando, eliguntur, sed et matres et quidem educatrices filiorum.' De W. imagines he finds also a trace of it in Herm. Pastor, i. vision 2. 4, p. 900: 'καὶ Γραπτὴ μὲν ('Grapte diaconissa fuisse videtur.' Hefele, not.) νουθετήσει τὰς χήρας καὶ τοὺς ὀρφανούς:' and in Lucian de morte peregrini, Opp. iii. 335 Reig.,—ἔωθεν μὲν εὐθὺς ἦν ὁρᾶν παρὰ τῷ δεσμωτηρίῳ περιμένοντα γραίδια, χήρας τινὰς καὶ παιδία ὀρφανά. He also refers to the dissertation of Mosheim on this place, in which he has thoroughly gone into all the bearings of the subject and maintained the above view. So also Grot., Fritzsch., and Michaelis: so Wiesinger,—and in a somewhat modified shape, Huther, repudiating the idea of formal ordination and setting apart of widows so early as the apostolic age. In this he is probably right. De W. makes the allusion to this 'institute of widows' one proof of the post-apostolic date of the Epistle: but on this see Prolegg. ch. vii. § i. 27. **Let a woman be enrolled a widow, who is not less than sixty years old** (γεγονυῖα is joined by the vulg. ('quæ fuerit unius viri uxor'), Jer., Luth., Calv., Beza, Grot., Mack, al., to the next clause: but against this is usage (ὅτε ἐγένετο ἐτῶν δώδεκα, Luke ii. 42: cf. also Plato, Legg. vi. p. 765, ἐτῶν μὲν γεγονὼς μὴ ἔλαττον ἢ πεντήκοντα, and see other examples in Wetst.), and the fact that μιᾶς γυναικὸς ἄνδρα stands alone in ch. iii. 2. Besides, if it belonged to the next clause, it would have in it any place but the *first*), **the wife of one husband** (cf. ch. iii. 2.

χησεν, εἰ ^z ἁγίων ^a πόδας ^{ab} ἔνιψεν, εἰ ^c θλιβομένοις ^d ἐπήρ-
κεσεν, εἰ παντὶ ^e ἔργῳ ^e ἀγαθῷ ^f ἐπηκολούθησεν. 11 νεω-
τέρας δὲ χήρας ^g παραιτοῦ· ^h ὅταν γὰρ ⁱ καταστρηνιάσουσιν

ACDFK
LPℵ a b
c d e f g
h k l m n
o 17. 47

z Eph. i. 1 reff.
a John xiii. 5, &c. only.
Gen. xviii. 4.
b as above (a). Matt. vi. 17.
xv. 2. Mark vii. 3. John ix. 7, &c. only.
only †. 1 Macc. viii. 26.
it. 21) only. Isa. lv. 3.
6, § 42. 5.

c 1 Thess. iii. 4. = Paul only, exc. Heb. xi. 37.
e = Eph. ii. 10. ch. ii. 10 reff.
g ch. iv. 7 reff.
i here only †. constr., James ii. 13.

d ver. 16 bis
f = here (Mark xvi. 20. ver. 24. 1 Pet.
h w. ind., Mark iii. 11. Rev. iv. 9. viii. 1. Winer, edn.
(στρηνιάω, Rev. xviii. 7, 9. στρῆνος, Rev. xviii. 3.)

11. rec καταστρηνιασωσι (corrn to suit οταν. The txt could hardly arise from the transcriber's eye having glanced on to θελ-ουσιν, as Ellic), with CDKLℵ rel : txt AF[P] Chr-ms.

Here, as contemporaneous polygamy is out of the question, and thus one element of difficulty in the other case is eliminated, we can hardly understand any thing other than that the πρεσβῦτις should have been the wife of only one husband : i. e., not married a second time : so Tertull. ad uxor. i. 7, vol. i. p. 1286 : "digamos non sinit præsidere, ... viduam allegi in ordinem nisi univiram non concedit." So that the parallel expressions here and in ch. iii. 2 will be consistently interpreted. See the mistaken views of Thdrt. (τὸ σωφρόνως ἐν γάμῳ βιοῦν νομοθετεῖ), &c., treated of under ch. iii. 2), **having a good character** (testimony from without, cf. reff. and ch. iii. 7) **in** (the element or region in which that μαρτυρία is versed) **good works** (reff.), **if** (' the conditions have as yet been expressed by participles in agreement with the noun : the construction is now changed for the hypothetical.' De W.: but εἰ does not depend immediately on καταλεγέσθω: the intervening clauses must be taken for granted. So that it may more properly be said to be dependent on μὴ . . . . μαρτυρουμένη :—such an one, if in addition she, &c.) **she** (at any time—keep the aor.) **brought up children** (her own? or those of others? If (1), the barren might seem hardly dealt with :· if (2), the word must be somewhat forced aside from its ordinary meaning (see τεκνοτροφία in Palm and Rost's Lex.: where in the examples cited, die Kindererzeugung mitinbegriffen ist). Still this latter, considering that ἐξενοδόχησεν is the next good work specified, seems most probable: and so, but for the most part combining it with the other, Beng., De W., Huther, Wiesinger, al. Grot. understands it, 'si nec abortum sibi fecerit, nec ob paupertatem exposuerit liberos . . . , sed omnes sibi natos educaverit, et quidem honeste ac pie :' Calv.,—' non sterilitatem hic damnari a Paulo, sed matrum delicias, quæ sobolis alendæ tædia devorare recusant'), **if she** (at any time) **received strangers** (practised hospitality. This clearly points out a person above the rank of the poor and indigent : though Chrys. pithily replies, κἂν πένης ᾖ, οἰκίαν

ἔχει. οὐ γὰρ δὴ αἴθριος μένει. One is glad to hear that all the Christian widows at Constantinople were so well off. But it can hardly have been so in the apostolic age. Cf. ch. iii. 2 : Tit. i. 8 : Rom. xii. 13 : Heb. xiii. 2), **if she** (at any time) **washed the feet of the saints** ('synecdoche partis, pro omni genere officiorum humilitatis,' Beng. εἰ τὰς ἐσχάτας ὑπηρεσίας τοῖς ἁγίοις ἀνεπαισχύντως ἐξετέλεσε, Thl. Still, we must not dismiss from our consideration the external act itself: as Thdrt. ἐποίουν γὰρ τοῦτο πάλαι: see John xiii. 14, and note, in which, though a formal ceremony in obedience to our Saviour's words is repudiated, the principle of humbly serving one another, which would lead to such an act on occasion presented, is maintained), **if she** (at any time) **relieved** (cf. Herod. i. 91, καιομένῳ αὐτῷ ἐπήρκεσε :— Eur. Hec. 963, τί χρὴ τὸν εὖ πράσσοντα μὴ πράσσουσιν εὖ | φίλοις ἐπαρκεῖν ;— and examples in Wetst. It is more rarely found with an accus. : see Palm and Rost's Lex.) **the distressed** (not merely the poor, as Beng., but those afflicted in any way; cf. example from Herod. above), **if she followed every good work** (Chrys. in his fine homily on this passage, cited above, § 15, says : τί ἐστιν ἐν παντὶ ἔργ. ἀγ. ἐπηκολούθ. ; ὥστε καὶ εἰς δεσμωτήριον εἰσιέναι καὶ τοὺς δεδεμένους ἐπισκέπτεσθαι, καὶ ἀρρωστοῦντας ἐπισκοπεῖν, καὶ θλιβομένους παραμυθεῖσθαι, καὶ ὀδυνωμένους παρακαλεῖν, καὶ πάντα τρόπον τὰ κατὰ δύναμιν εἰσφέρειν ἅπαντα, καὶ μηδὲν ὅλως παραιτεῖσθαι τῶν εἰς σωτηρίαν καὶ ἀνάπαυσιν τῶν ἀδελφῶν γινομένων τῶν ἡμετέρων. Bengel's idea, ' Antistitum et virorum est, bonis operibus præire, Tit. iii. 8, 14 : mulierum, subsequi, adjuvando pro sua parte,' is ingenious, but wrong : cf. Plato, Rep. p. 370 c,—ἀλλ' ἀνάγκη τὸν πράττοντα τῷ πραττομένῳ ἐπακολουθεῖν μὴ ἐν παρέργου μέρει).

11.] **But younger widows decline** (to place on the κατάλογος, see above on verse 9 : not 'avoid,' for fear of scandal, as Chrys. in the homily above cited : nor both of these combined, as Huther : nor 'decline as objects for the alms of the church,' as some above. Baur's idea (Paulus u. s. w.

τοῦ Χριστοῦ, ʲ γαμεῖν θέλουσιν, ¹² ᵏ ἔχουσαι ¹ κρῖμα, ὅτι τὴν πρώτην ᵐ πίστιν ᵐⁿ ἠθέτησαν· ¹³ ἅμα δὲ καὶ ° ἀργαὶ ᵖ μανθάνουσιν ᑫ περιερχόμεναι τὰς οἰκίας· οὐ μόνον δὲ

j of the woman, ver. 14.
1 Cor. vii. 28 (36) only †.
(2 Macc. xiv. 25 bis only.)
k = ver.
m = Polyb. viii. 2. 5 al. fr.
o Gospp., Matt. (xii. 36. xx.
p constr., here

20. John ix. 41. xv. 22, 24.　　1 = Rom. ii. 2.　Gal. v. 10 reff.
n Mark vii. 9.　Gal. ii. 21. iii. 15.　Heb. x. 28 al.　Ps. lxxxviii. 34.
3, 6ʲ only.　Epp., Tit. i. 12.　James in. 20.　2 Pet i. 8 only.　Wisd. xv. 15.
only. see ver. 4 reff.　　q Acts xix. 13. xxviii. 13.　Heb. xi. 37 only.　Job i. 7.

p. 497), that χήρας is the predicate,—'the younger women decline as widows,' refuse to put on the list of widows, is not justified by the construction, nor does it derive any support from the rendering given above of χήρα καταλεγέσθω, verse 9): for when they shall wax wanton (a very full account of the usage of ἐάν and ὅταν with the indic. is given in Klotz, Devar. ii. pp. 468 ff. Ellicott sums it up by saying that in such cases the whole conditional force is restricted to the particle, and there is no necessary internal connexion between the verb in the protasis and that in the apodosis. He does not hold this to be applicable here, and therefore prefers the rec. reading) against (στρηνιάω, and στρῆνος, see reff.—from στρηνής (strenuus), 'strong,' — 'to be strong,' whence κατα-στρ., to be strong against,—to rebel against (see Ellic. here): and in the particular matter here treated, 'to become wanton against') Christ (their proper bridegroom: Jerome's expression, ep. 123 (11) ad Ageruchiam (Gerontiam) 3, vol. i. p. 901, which the Commentators blame as too strong, in fact gives the sense well,—"quæ fornicatæ sunt (-cantur ?) in injuriam viri sui Christi." Thl. similarly, but too vaguely,—ὅταν καθυπερηφανεύσονται τοῦ χριστοῦ, μὴ ἀποδεχόμεναι αὐτὸν νυμφίον), they desire to marry (again),—having (bearing on themselves, as a burden: see reff. and Gal. v. 10) judgment (from God: and as the context necessarily implies, condemnation: but we must not so express it in a version: that which is left to be fixed by the context in the original, should be also left in a translation. The meaning 'bringing on themselves the imputation of having,'&c., given by De W. and upheld by Huther, al., appears to me to be ungrammatical), because they set at nought their first faith (i. e. broke, made void, their former promise. So Chrys., interpreting it, τὰς πρὸς τὸν χριστὸν καταπατῆσαι συνθήκας, Hom. var. ut supra: and again, πίστιν τὴν συνθήκην λέγει, Hom. in loc.: Thdrt. τῷ χριστῷ συνταξάμεναι σωφρόνως ζῆν ἐν χηρείᾳ, δευτέροις ὁμιλοῦσι γάμοις: Thl. ἐψεύσαντο τὴν συμφωνίαν τὴν πρὸς χριστόν. Tert. de monogam. 13, vol. ii. p. 948,—"quod primam fidem resciderunt, illam videlicet a qua in viduitate inventæ et professæ eam

non perseverant." Aug. in Ps. lxxv. 12, § 16, vol. iv. p. 968: "Quid est 'primam fidem irritam fecerunt ?' voverunt et non reddiderunt." Having devoted themselves to widowhood as their state of life, and to the duties of the order of πρεσβύτιδες as their occupation, they will thus be guilty of a dereliction of their deliberate promise. Of the later vows of celibacy, and ascetic views with regard to second marriages, there is no trace: see below. Calv. (al.) interprets τὴν πρώτην πίστιν ἠθέτησαν of falling away from the faith,—'quia a fide baptismi et Christianismo prorsus deficiant,' and defends this view against that given above, calling it 'nimis frigidum :' but as it seems to me quite unsuccessfully. He expresses well, however, the difference between this addiction to single life and the later compulsory vows: 'non ideo cœlibes se fore promittebant olim viduæ, ut sanctius agerent vitam quam in conjugio : sed quod non poterant marito et ecclesiæ simul esse addictæ :'—see the rest of his note). 13.] Moreover they also learn to be idle (so Syr., Chr., Thl., Beza, Huther, Winer, Ellic. ("It is needless to say that Winer does not conceive 'an ellipsis of οὖσαι for εἶναι.' Bloomf.,—a mistake of which such a scholar could not be capable." Ellic. edn. 1), al. ;—a harsh construction, but, it is said, not without example: however, the only one cited is from Plato, Euthyd. p. 276 b: οἱ ἀμαθεῖς ἄρα σοφοὶ μανθάνουσι, where the word σοφοί does not occur in Bekker's text, and seems on critical grounds very suspicious. Still, I conceive that the present sentence will admit of no other construction, on account of the emphatic position of ἀργαί, which is further heightened by οὐ μόνον δὲ ἀργαί below. De W. objects to it, that idleness is the cause, not the effect, of going about, &c.: but it may well be answered, that not only does a spirit of idleness give rise to such going about, but such going about confirms the habit of idleness. Bengel would lay the stress on μανθάνουσιν—'reprehenditur discendi genus: sequiturque species, —discunt, quæ domos obeundo discuntur,' i. e. statum familiarum curiose explorant.' But μανθ. does not seem to bear this meaning. The usual interpretation has been to take περιερχ. as an infin., 'learn

r here only †.　 ^o ἀργαί, ἀλλὰ καὶ ^r φλύαροι καὶ ^s περίεργοι, λαλοῦσαι   ACDFK
(-ρεῖν,
3 John 10.)   ^t τὰ μὴ δέοντα.   14 ^u βούλομαι οὖν νεωτέρας ^v γαμεῖν,   LPℵ a b
s Acts xix. 19   c d e f g
only. (-γέω,   ^w τεκνογονεῖν, ^x οἰκοδεσποτεῖν, μηδεμίαν ^{yz} ἀφορμὴν ^z διδόναι   h k l m n
Sir. xli. 22.   o 17. 47
-γάζεσθαι,
2 Thess. iii.   τῷ ^a ἀντικειμένῳ ^b λοιδορίας ^c χάριν.   15 ἤδη γάρ ^d τινες
11. Σωκρά-
της περιερ-   ^e ἐξετράπησαν ^f ὀπίσω τοῦ Σατανᾶ.   16 εἴ τις [^g πιστὸς ἢ]
γάζεται,
Plato, Apol. Socr. 19 b.)   t so Tit. i. 11.   u = ch. ii. 8. Tit. iii. 8.   v ver. 11.
w here only †.   (-νία, ch. ii. 15.)   x here only †.   (-της, Matt. xx. 25.)   y Gal. v. 13 reff.
z 1 Cor. v. 12   a absol., 1 Cor xvi. 9. Phil. i. 28. 2 Thess. ii. 4 (ch. i. 12. Luke xiii. 17. xxi. 15). L.P. Isa.
lxvi. 6.   b i Pet. iii. 9 only. Prov. xx. 18. (-ρος, 1 Cor. v. 11. -ρεῖν, John ix. 28.)   c Paul,
Gal. iii. 19. Eph. iii. 1, 14. Tit. i. 5, 11. Gospp., Luke vii. 47 only. 1 John iii. 12. Jude 16 only.   3 Kings xiv. 16
A, &c. (B def.) Sir. xxxiv. (xxxi.) 6.   d = ch. i. 1, 3 reff.   e ch. i. 6 reff.   f Acts v.
37. xx. 30. Rev. xiii. 3. Judg. ii, 19.   g = Eph. i. 1 reff.

14. ins τας bef νεωτερας D¹ m 73. 80.

15. om ver 67².   εξετραπησαν bef τινες AF : txt CDKL[P] rel vulg syrr copt
[æth arm] gr-lat-ff.

16. [for τις, δε P.]   om πιστος η (passing from πιστ. to πιστ.?) ACF[P]ℵ 17
[47] am(with harl¹) copt arm (Ath) : ins DKL rel fuld(with tol harl²) syrr Chr Thdrt
Damasc Ambrst. (om η πιστη vulg-ed F-lat Ambr Aug Pel₃—demid G-lat æth have si

---

to go about:' so vulg., Luth., &c.: but
the objection to this is, that μανθάνω
with a participle always means to be aware
of, take notice of, the act implied in the
verb: e. g. διαβεβλημένος ὑπὸ Ἀμάσιος
οὐ μανθάνεις, Herod. iii. 1) going about
from house to house (lit. "the houses,"
viz. of the faithful. For the construction
compare Matt. ix. 35, περιῆγεν ὁ Ἰησοῦς
τὰς πόλεις): but not only (to be) idle,
but also gossips (περιοδεύουσαι τὰς οἰκίας,
οὐδὲν ἀλλ' ἢ τὰ ταύτης εἰς ἐκείνην φέ-
ρουσι, καὶ τὰ ἐκείνης εἰς ταύτην. Thl.
'Ex otio nascebatur curiositas, quæ ipsa
garrulitatis est mater.' Calv.) and busybodies (reff.), speaking (not merely 'saying:' the subject-matter, as well as the
form, is involved in λαλοῦσαι) things
which are not fitting (his fear is, that
these younger widows will not only do the
Church's work idly, but make mischief by
bearing about tales and scandal).   I will
(consult Ellic.'s note on βούλομαι. We
may generally state that θέλω is the resting inclination of the will, βούλομαι its
active exertion) then ("οὖν has here its
proper collective force, 'in consequence of
these things being so, I desire.'" Ellic.)
that younger widows (such, and not the
younger women, is evidently the Apostle's
meaning. (χήρας is supplied in several
cursives, Chr., Thdrt., Jer.) The whole
passage has concerned widows—and to
them he returns again, ver. 16) marry
(not as Chrys., ἐπειδὴ αὐταὶ βούλονται
βούλομαι κἀγώ. . . . . ἔδει μὲν οὖν τὰ τοῦ
θεοῦ μεριμνᾶν, ἔδει τὴν π·στιν φυλάττειν.
ἐπειδὴ δὲ ἐκεῖνα οὐ γίνεται, βέλτιον ταῦτα
γενέσθαι (so also, characteristically, the
R.-Cath. Mack): for it is not younger
widows who have been taken into the catalogue of πρεσβύτιδες of whom he is speaking, but younger widows in general:

Chrys.'s interpretation would make the
Apostle contradict himself. The οὖν on
which Mack lays stress as favouring this
meaning, simply infers from the temptations of young widows just described. There
is no inconsistency here with the view expressed in 1 Cor. vii. 39, 40 : the time and
circumstances were different), bear children, govern households (i. e. in their
place, and with their share of the duties:
οἰκουρεῖν, as Chrys. Both these verbs
belong to later Greek: cf. Lobeck on
Phryn., p. 373), give no occasion (start-
ing-point, in their behaviour or language)
to the adversary (who is meant? Chrys.
and the ancients for the most part understand, the devil (μὴ βουλόμενος τὸν
διάβολον ἀφορμὴν λαμβάνειν): and so,
lately, Huther, defending it by his interpretation of λοιδορίας χάριν (see below).
But St. Paul's own usage of ἀντικείμενος
(reff., see also Tit. ii. 8) is our best guide.
Ordinarily using it of human adversaries,
he surely would here have mentioned ὁ διάβολος, had he intended him. And the understanding him to be here meant brings
in the next verse very awkwardly, as he
there has an entirely new part assigned
him. Understand therefore, any adversary, Jew or Gentile, who may be on the
watch to get occasion, by the lax conduct
of the believers, to slander the Church)
for the sake of reproach (to be joined with
ἀφορμήν: the ἀφορμή, when taken advantage of by the adversary, would be used
λοιδορίας χάριν, for the sake and purpose
of reproaching the people of God. Mack
would join λ. χ. with βούλομαι,—most unnaturally: 'I will, on account of the reproach which might otherwise come on the
Church, νεωτέρας γαμεῖν &c.:'—Leo,—
with τῷ ἀντικειμένῳ,—which would more
naturally be τῷ λοιδορίας χάριν ἀντικει-

^g πιστὴ ἔχει χήρας, ^h ἐπαρκείτω αὐταῖς, καὶ μὴ ⁱ βαρείσθω
ἡ ἐκκλησία, ἵνα ταῖς ^k ὄντως χήραις ^h ἐπαρκέσῃ.

¹⁷ Οἱ καλῶς ^l προεστῶτες πρεσβύτεροι ^m διπλῆς ⁿ τιμῆς
^o ἀξιούσθωσαν, ^p μάλιστα οἱ ^q κοπιῶντες ἐν λόγῳ καὶ ^r δι-

h here (bis) and ver. 10 only †.
1 Macc. viii. 26.
i Matt. xxvi. 43 (‖ Mk. v. r.). Luke ix. 32. xxi. 34. 2 Cor. i.
m Matt.
n = Acts xxviii. 10?
Sir. xxxviii. 1.
p ch. iv. 10 reff.

8. v. 4 only †. Isa. i. 4 Aqu. Symm., &c.
xxiii. 15. Rev. xviii. 6 (bis) only. Isa. xl. 2.
o = 2 Thess. i. 11. Heb. iii. 3. x. 29 only (see Luke vii. 7. Acts xv. 38) ‡.
q Rom. xvi. 6. 1 Cor. iv. 12. Col. i. 29. ch. iv. 10. Ps. cxxvi. 1.
k ver. 3.
l ch. iii. 4, 5 reff.
r ch. i. 10 reff.

quis fideles(-em æth) habet viduas(-am æth).)   ἐπαρκεισθω AF‌‌ℵ 17. (επαρικ. F.
17. om εν F [syr.   for και διδ., διδασκαλιας P.]

μένῳ.   λοιδορία must be kept to its true sense, *reproach* brought on the Gospel; not forced, as Huther, for the sake of his view of ὁ ἀντικείμενος, to that of disgrace brought on the church by the fall of the widows);—**for already** ('particula provocat ad experientiam,' Beng.) **some** (widows) **have been** (we are obliged here to give a *perfect* rendering in English. Our language will not, as the habit of mixed ·constructions in the Greek permits, bear the placing an indefinite past event in a definite portion of time such as ἤδη expresses) **turned away** (out of the right path, ref.) **after** (so as to follow) **Satan** ('eoque occasionem dedere calumniæ,' Beng. When De W. doubts whether St. Paul's experience could have been long enough to bear out such an assertion—and thus impugns the genuineness of the Epistle,—this is very much a matter of dates: and even taking the earliest commonly assigned, the assertion might be strictly true, applying as it does not only to Ephesus, but to the far wider range of his apostolic ministry).   **16.]** Not a repetition of vv. 4, 8, but an extension of the same duty to more distant relatives than those there spoken of. **If any believing [man or] woman has widows** (in [his or] her family—dependent in any degree, however distant—e. g. as sister, or sister-in-law, aunt, niece, cousin, &c.), **let such person relieve them** (see above, ver. 10), **and let the church not be burdened** (with their support: "later and less correct form for βαρύνειν;" see Ellic.), **that it may relieve those who are widows in reality** (really χῆραι — destitute of help).

17—25.] *Directions respecting* (17—19) *presbyters;* (20—25) *church discipline: and certain matters regarding his own official and personal life.*
17.] Let the presbyters who well preside (not, as in some former editions, *have well presided :* the perf. of ἵστημι has the *present* signification throughout. I owe the correction of this inadvertence to Bishop Ellicott. Preside, viz. over their portion

of the Church's work. Chrys. has well expressed the meaning, but not all the meaning; for wisdom and ability must be taken also into account :—τί δε ἐστι, καλῶς προεστῶτας. ἀκούσωμεν τοῦ χριστοῦ λέγοντος· ὁ ποιμὴν ὁ καλὸς τὴν ψυχὴν αὐτοῦ τίθησιν ὑπὲρ τῶν προβάτων. ἄρα τοῦτό ἐστι καλῶς προεστάναι, μηδενὸς φείδεσθαι τῆς ἐκείνων κηδεμονίας ἕνεκα, **be held worthy of double** (not, as compared with the *widows*, as Chr.,—(alt. 1: διπλῆς τῆς πρὸς τὰς χήρας, ἢ τῆς πρὸς τοὺς διακόνους, ἢ ἁπλῶς διπλῆς τιμῆς, πολλῆς λέγει), Thl. (1), Constt.-ap. (ii. 28, p. 674, Migne), Erasm., Calv., al.,—the *deacons*, as Chr. (2, see above), Thl. (2),—the *poor*, as Flatt, &c.—but as compared with those who have not distinguished themselves by καλῶς προεστάναι; and evidently, as Chrys. 3, it is not to be taken in the mere literal sense of *double*, but implies increase generally—see reff., and below) **honour** (so Plato, Legg. v. p. 378 D, τίμιος μὲν δὴ καὶ ὁ μηδὲν ἀδικῶν· ὁ δὲ μηδ' ἐπιτρέπων τοῖς ἀδικοῦσιν ἀδικεῖν πλέον ἢ διπλασίας τιμῆς ἄξιος ἐκείνου : and see other examples in Wetstein. From the general tenor of those, as well as from the context here, it is evident that not merely honour, but *recompense* is here in question : but the word need not be *confined* to that meaning: honour, and honour's fruit, may be both included in it. Grot. conceives an allusion to the double portion of the firstborn (Deut. xxi. 17) : Elsner, to the double share of provision which used to be set before the presbyters in the Agapæ (Heydr., Baur: cf. Constt.-apost. as above). But as De W. remarks, that practice was much more probably owing to a misunderstanding of this passage): **especially those that labour in (the) word and teaching** (therefore the preaching of the word, and teaching, was *not the office of all* the πρεσβύτεροι. Conyb. rightly remarks, that this is a proof of the early date of the Epistle. Of these two expressions, λόγος would more properly express *preaching ;* διδασκαλία, the work of *instruction*, by

δασκαλία. 18 ˢλέγει γὰρ ἡ ˢγραφὴ Βοῦν ᵗἀλοῶντα οὐ
ᵘφιμώσεις· ᵘκαὶ ἄξιος ὁ ᵛἐργάτης τοῦ μισθοῦ αὐτοῦ.
19 κατὰ πρεσβυτέρου ʷκατηγορίαν μὴ ˣπαραδέχου, ʸἐκτὸς
ʸεἰ μὴ ᶻἐπὶ δύο ἢ τριῶν μαρτύρων. 20 τοὺς [δὲ] ἁμαρ-

18. ου φιμ. bef β. αλ. AC[P] m 17 vulg [Syr] copt [æth] arm Chr Thdrt Ambrst: txt DFKLℵ rel syr goth Damasc Tert.—κημωσεις D. for τ. μισθου, της τροφης (appy) ℵ¹.

20. rec om δε, with D³KL[P]ℵ rel vulg syrr copt gr-lat-ff : ins AD¹ demid(with F-lat) G-lat goth Thl : aft αμαρτ., F.

---

catechetical or other means). **18.]**
Ground for the above injunction. See the first citation ('*an* (or '*the*,' an anarthrous emphatic word) *ox while treading,*' &c., not, '*the ox that treadeth,*' &c., as E. V.) treated by the Apostle at more length, 1 Cor. ix. 9. It is doubted whether the words ἄξιος ὁ ἐργάτ. κ.τ.λ. are a citation at all. Some have referred them to Levit. xix. 13 : Deut. xxiv. 14, which passages however say nothing of the kind, being special directions about paying a labourer's wages before night. Thdrt. and Thl. suppose it to be quoted from the New Testament ; i.e. from our Lord's saying, reff. Matt., Luke. But it is very unlikely that the Apostle should cite these under the title of ἡ γραφή : and Calvin's view seems most probable, that he adduces the sentiment, as our Lord Himself does, as a popular and well-known saying (so Wolf and Huther). This verse it is which makes it extremely probable, that τιμή above refers to the honorarium of pecuniary recompense. **19.]** See the summary above. **Against a presbyter** (Chrys., Thl., are certainly wrong in supposing that age, not office is again here indicated : the whole passage is of presbyters by office—cf. ver. 22 below) **entertain not an accusation, except** (reff. pleonastic expressions such as ἐκτὸς εἰ μή, χωρὶς εἰ or εἰ μή, are found in later writers, such as Plutarch, Dio Cassius, &c. : we have πλὴν εἰ μή in Demosth. 141. 21, 719. 1 : Aristot. de Anim. i. 5. 9, al. See Lobeck on Phrynichus, p. 459) **before** (lit. *in presence of;* and perhaps we ought to press the meaning : but from the occurrence of ἐπὶ στόματος δύο μαρτ. κ.τ.λ. in ref. Deut., it is more likely figurative, '*in the presence of,*' signifying merely '*vorhandenseyn,*' their presence in the case) **two or three witnesses** (De W. asks, —but were not these required in every case, not only in that of a presbyter ? Three answers are given : one by Chrys.

(τὸ δὲ ἐπὶ ἄλλων, φησί, μάλιστα δὲ κατὰ πρεσβυτέρου), Thdrt. (συμβαίνει γὰρ ἐκκλησίας αὐτὸν προστασίαν πεπιστευμένον καὶ λυπῆσαι τῶν ἁμαρτανόντων τινάς, εἶτα ἐντεῦθεν ἐκείνους δεομένους διατεθέντας συκοφαντίαν ὑφῆναι. δεῖ τοίνυν ἀπαντῆσαι τῶν μαρτύρων τὸν ἀριθμόν), and so Calvin at more length : the other by Huther, that Timotheus was not constituted judge in private men's matters, only over the officers of the church in faults with which they might be charged as regarded the execution of their duty: a third by Bengel,—'privatus poterat, lege Mosis, citari uno teste, non condemnari : presbyterum ne citari quidem Paulus jubet, &c.' But this is manifestly a distinction without point—the κατηγορίαν παραδέχεσθαι being used not of mere citation, but of entertaining the charge as a valid one : in other words, as including citation and conviction as well. So nearly Grotius, but bringing out a different distinction, which is manifestly here not in question—'poterat ad unius testis dictum vir plebeius capi aut contra eum inquisitio incipi : non ita autem contra Senatorem, cui æquiparatur Presbyter.' The first reason seems the more probable : that he is only recalling the attention of Timotheus to a known and prescribed precaution, which was in this case especially to be always observed. Somewhat otherwise Ellicott : see his note). **20.** [**But**] **those who are doing wrong** (if δέ is read, these are the sinning presbyters, and cannot well be any others. Without the particle, the application may be doubted. De W., Wiesinger, and Ellic., following a few others (Aret., Heinr., Matthies, al.), maintain the *general* reference. So appears Chrys. to have done, understanding πρεσβ. merely of age, and going on without any further remark, and so (apparently) Thdrt. But, even thus, the other view is the more likely, from the strong language used in ver. 21, and the

τάνοντας ᵃ ἐνώπιον ᵃ πάντων ᵇ ἔλεγχε, ἵνα καὶ οἱ λοιποὶ
φόβον ᶜ ἔχωσιν. ²¹ ᵈ διαμαρτύρομαι ᵉ ἐνώπιον τοῦ θεοῦ
καὶ χριστοῦ Ἰησοῦ καὶ τῶν ᶠᵍ ἐκλεκτῶν ᶠ ἀγγέλων, ἵνα
ταῦτα ʰ φυλάξῃς χωρὶς ⁱ προκρίματος, μηδὲν ποιῶν κατὰ
ᵏ πρόσκλισιν. ²² ˡ χεῖρας ᵐ ταχέως μηδενὶ ˡ ἐπιτίθει,

a see Gal. ii. 14.
b = Matt.
  xviii. 15.
1 Cor. xiv.
  24. Eph. v.
  11. 2 Tim.
  iv. 2. Tit. i.
  9, 13. ii. 15.
  Prov. x. 7.
c ver. 12 reff.
d Luke xvi. 28.
  Acts ii. 40

a l7. 1 Thess. iv. 6. 2 Tim. ii. 14. iv. 1. Exod. xix. 21. see note, Heb. ii. 6. e = Gal. i. 20. ch.
  vi. 13. 2 Tim. ii. 14. iv. 1. f here only. g Rom. viii. 33. xvi. 13. Col. iii.
  12. 2 Tim. ii. 10. Tit. i. 1 al. Prov. xvii. 3. h = Rom. ii. 26. Gal. vi. 13. 2 Tim. i. 12, 14.
  i here only †. (-κρίνειν, Wisd. vii. 8.) k here only †. Clem. ad Cor. i. § 47, 50, pp. 318, 312.
  1 = Acts vi. 6. viii. 17, 19. xiii. 3. Num. xxvii. 18. m = 2 Thess. ii. 2.

21. rec (for χρ. ιησ.) κυριου ιησ. χρ., with D³KL[P] rel syrr goth Chr : txt AD¹Fℵ
17 latt coptt æth arm Clem Ath Bas Thdrt Hil Ambr.   προσκλησιν (prob from
confusion of ι & η so freq in mss : cf Luke xiv. 13) ADL[P] rel Ath Chr(ἵνα σε μηδεὶς
προκαταλάβῃ μηδὲ προοικειώσηται) : txt FKℵ c h [47²] latt(in alteram partem decli-
nando) syrr goth Clem Bas Thdrt Damasc Thl(τουτέστιν κατὰ προσπάθειαν προσκλινό-
μενος τῷ ἑτέρῳ μέρει).
22. επιτιθου D¹.

return again to the subject in ver. 22 ;
and so most Commentators. The pres.
part. is no argument against it (against
De W. and Wiesinger) : 'those who are
(detected in) sinning,' who are proved to
be living in sin, may well be intended by
it : the fact of their being ἁμαρτάνοντες
is not ascertained till they have been
charged with fault, and the evidence of
the witnesses taken) **reprove in the presence of all** (not all *the presbyters*, the
'consessus presbyterorum :' see on καὶ οἱ
λοιποὶ below : but the whole congregation. Had it not been for ecclesiastical
considerations, we should never have heard
of such a limited meaning for ἐνώπιον
πάντων), **that the rest also** (not, the
other presbyters, which would have certainly been pointed out if intended,—but
in its usual sense of ' the rest,' generally :
the καὶ seems to make this even plainer :
that the warning may not be confined to
a few, but may also spread over the whole
church) **may have fear** (see Deut. xiii. 11 :
fear, on seeing the public disgrace consequent on sin. ἔχωσιν, as above, ver. 12).

21.] I adjure thee (see reff., especially 2 Tim. iv. 1) **in the presence of
God, and of Christ Jesus** (on the supposed
reference to one Person only, see Ellic.'s
note) ; **and of the elect angels** (the holy
angels, who are the chosen attendants and
ministers of God. Thus ἐκλεκτῶν is an
epithet distributed over the whole extent
of ἀγγέλων, not one designating any one
class of angels above the rest, as De W.
Bengel says rightly, ἐκλεκτῶν, " epitheton,
Timothei reverentiam acuens :—the angels, God's chosen ministers." Various
meanings have been proposed : *good angels as distinguished from bad* (so Thl.,
Ambr., Grot., Est., Wolf, al.),—but οἱ
ἄγγελοι without any such designation, are

ever good angels :—*the guardian angels*
of Timotheus and the Ephesian church
(Mosheim) : ' those especially selected by
God as His messengers to the human race,
as Gabriel ' (Conyb.),—which, if we suppose these to be any particular class of
angels, would be the best ; but I doubt
ἐκλεκτός, absolute, ever bearing this meaning, and much prefer that upheld above.
Calvin says : " electos vocat angelos non
tantum ut a reprobis discernat, sed excel-
lentiæ causa, ut plus reverentiæ habeat
eorum testimonium." There is a parallel
form of adjuration in Jos. B. J. ii. 16. 4,
where Agrippa is endeavouring to persuade
the Jews to remain in the Roman allegiance : μαρτύρομαι δ' ἐγὼ ὑμῶν τὰ ἅγια
καὶ τοὺς ἱεροὺς ἀγγέλους τοῦ θεοῦ, καὶ
πατρίδα τὴν κοινήν. Schleiermacher
thinks this mention of one class of angels
as '*elect*,' inconsistent with the Apostle's
warning against genealogies and idle questions : but with the above interpretation
such objection falls to the ground. Baur
would explain the expression by the gnostic notion of angels more immediately
connected with our Lord, alluded to by
Irenæus, i. 4. 5, p. 21, οἱ ἡλικιῶται αὐτοῦ ἄγγελοι : see ib. 7. 1, p. 32. But Irenæus' text
is μετὰ τῶν ἡλικιωτῶν αὐτοῦ τῶν ἀγγέλων,
which hardly justifies the interpretation :
and if it did, the whole lies too far off the
matter in our text, to be brought to bear
upon it), **that thou keep these things** (viz.
the injunctions, vv. 19, 20. De W., taking
ver. 20 generally, is obliged, although he
confesses that the connexion with ver. 19
would be best if only vv. 19, 21 came together, to explain ταῦτα of ver. 20 only,
see below) **without prejudice** ('præ-judi-
cium'—previous condemnation before hearing a man's case : a word only found
here), **doing nothing according to par-**

n Gal. vi. 6 reff. μηδὲ ⁿ κοινώνει ἁμαρτίαις ᵒ ἀλλοτρίαις. σεαυτὸν ᴾ ἁγνὸν
= & constr.,
Rom. xv. 27. ᑫ τήρει· ²³ μηκέτι ʳ ὑδροπότει, ἀλλὰ οἴνῳ ὀλίγῳ ˢ χρῶ,
2 John 11.
Isa. xliv. 11
(9) Ald. διὰ τὸν ᵗ στόμαχον καὶ τὰς ᵘ πυκνάς σου ᵛ ἀσθενείας.
compl. Wisd.

ADFKL
Pℵ a b c
d e f g h
k l m n o
17. 47

vi. 23 (25).
o Acts vii. 6.   Paul, Rom. xiv. 4. xv. 20.   2 Cor. x. 15, 16.   Ps. cviii. 11.   p Paul, 2 Cor. vii. 11. xi. 2.   Phil.
    iv. 8. Tit. ii. 5. Prov. xv. 26.   q = 1 Cor. vii. 37.   2 Cor. xi. 9.   1 Thess. v. 23.   James i. 27.   Wisd. x. 5.
r here only †. Herod. i. 71.   s ch. i. 8.   t here only †.   u Luke v. 33.   Acts xxiv. 26
    only ‡.   Ezek. xxxi. 3 A.   2 Macc. viii. 8 only.   v = Matt. viii. 17.   Gal. iv. 13 al. fr.   2 Macc. ix. 21, 22.

[αλλοτρ. bef αμαρτ. P.]
23. (αλλα, so AD¹F[P]ℵ 17.)   [ολιγον P.]   rec (aft στομ.) ins σου, with
D³FKL rel vss [Clem Eus₁] Ath Chr Thdrt Damasc [Orig-int₁] Ambrst-ms al : om
AD¹[P]ℵ 17 (arm) Ambrst-ed Gaud.   ins δια bef τας πυκν. F.

tiality (bias towards, as the other was bias against, an accused presbyter. Diod. Sic., iii. 27, uses the word in its literal sense : τὸ δένδρον διὰ τὴν γινομένην πρὸς αὐτὸ πλεονάκις πρόσκλισιν τοῦ ζώου, τετριμμένον ἐστί :—Diog. Laert., prooem. 20, in its metaphorical : εἰ δὲ αἵρεσιν νοοῖμεν πρόσκλισιν ἐν δόγμασιν. Thdrt. says well, δύο παρακελεύεται· μήτε τῇ τῶν κατηγόρων ἀξιοπιστίᾳ πιστεύσαντα κατακρίνειν, ἢ φιλαπεχθημόνως διακείμενον τοῦτο ποιεῖν πρὸ τῆς ἀκριβοῦς ἐξετάσεως. μήτε τῶν ἐλέγχων προφανῶς γενομένων ἀναβάλλεσθαι τὴν ψῆφον τῇ πρὸς τὸν κρινόμενον χάριτι τὸ δίκαιον διαφθείροντα). 22 f.] The same subject is continued, and direction given whereby the scandal just dealt with may be prevented : viz. by *caution in ordaining* at first. The reference is primarily to presbyters : of course extending also in its spirit to all other church offices. This reference, which is maintained by Chrys., Thdrt., Thl., Grot., Est., Flatt, Mack, al., is denied by De W., Wiesinger, and Huther : the two former (as also Hammond, Ellic.) understanding the command of receiving back into the church excommunicated persons, or heretics, which from later testimonies (Cypr., the Nicene council, &c.) they shew to have been the practice : Huther, rightly rejecting this idea, yet interprets it of laying on of hands as merely conveying ecclesiastical blessing on many various occasions. But surely this is too vague and unimportant for the solemn language here used. Regarding the whole, to v. 25, as connected, and belonging to one subject, I cannot accept any interpretation but the obvious and ordinary one : see especially ch. iv. 14 : 2 Tim. i. 6. **Lay hands hastily on no one, nor be partaker in other men's sins** (as he would do by being the means of negligently admitting into the ministry unfit and ungodly persons, being properly held responsible for the consequence of those bad habits of theirs which more care might have ascertained. ἁμαρτίας points to the former ἁμαρτάνοντας) : — **keep THYSELF**

(highly emphatic : not merely others over whom thou art called to preside and pronounce judgment in admitting them to the ministry. And the emphasis is peculiarly in place here, as applying to that which has just preceded. If he were to admit improper candidates to the ministry from bias or from negligence, his own character, by his becoming a partaker in their sins, would suffer : whatever thou doest therefore, be sure to maintain, by watchful care and caution, *thyself* above all stain of blame) **pure** (not here to be referred to personal purity and chastity, though that of course would be the most important of all elements in carrying out the precept : but as above. On the *word*, see Ellic.). **No longer** (habitually) **drink water, but use a little wine, on account of thy stomach, and thy frequent illnesses** (the question, why this injunction is here inserted, has never been satisfactorily answered. Est., Grot., al., De W., Ellic., al., take it as a modification of σεαυτὸν ἁγνὸν τήρει, so as to prevent it from being misunderstood as enjoining asceticism. But on our explanation of the words, and I may add on any worthy view of the context, such a connexion will at once be repudiated. Chrys. has caught the right clue, when he says δοκεῖ δέ μοι καὶ ἄλλως ἐπίνοσος εἶναι. καὶ τοῦτο δείκνυσι λέγων, διὰ τὰς πυκνάς σου ἀσθενείας, ἀπό τε τοῦ στομάχου, ἀπό τε τῶν ἄλλων μερῶν : but she has not followed it up. Timotheus was certainly of a feeble bodily frame, and this feebleness appears, from other hints which we have respecting him, to have affected his character. See especially 1 Cor. xvi. 10, 11, and note there. Is it not very possible, that such feebleness, and perhaps timidity, may have influenced him as an overseer of the church, and prevented that keen-sighted judgment and vigorous action which a bishop should ever shew in estimating the characters of those who are candidates for the ministry ? If this was so, then it is quite natural that in advising him on this point, St. Paul should throw in a hint, in

24 τινῶν ἀνθρώπων αἱ ἁμαρτίαι ^wπρόδηλοί εἰσιν, ^xπρο-
άγουσαι εἰς ^yκρίσιν· τισὶν δὲ καὶ ^zἐπακολουθοῦσιν.
25 ^aὡσαύτως καὶ τὰ ^bἔργα τὰ ^bκαλὰ ^wπρόδηλα· καὶ τὰ
^cἄλλως ἔχοντα κρυβῆναι οὐ δύνανται.

w Heb. vii. 14
only †.
Judith viii.
29. 2 Macc.
iii. 17. xiv.
39 only.
x ch. i. 18 reff.
y Paul, 2 Thess.
i. 5 only.
Matt. v. 21
c here only. Esth.

al. fr.　　　　z ver. 10 reff.　　　　a ch. ii. 9 al.　　　　b ch. iii. 1 reff.
i. 19. ix. 27. Job xi. 12.

25. aft ωσαυτως ins δε AF goth [Orig-int₁] : om DKL[P]ℵ rel vulg syrr coptt [æth
arm] gr-lat-ff.　　　rec (for τα ε. τα κ.) τα καλα εργα, with KL rel Chr Thdrt : txt
ADF[P]ℵ m 17 latt syrr copt goth Thl Ambr Aug Pel.　　　rec aft προδηλα ins
εστι, with KL rel : εισιν DF[P] c k o 17. 67¹ : om Aℵ 67². rec δυναται (gramml
corrn), with FKLℵ rel Chr : txt AD[P] e g k m 17 [47] Thdrt.

fatherly kindness, that he must not allow
these maladies to interfere with the efficient discharge of his high office, but take
all reasonable means of raising his bodily
condition above them. I feel compelled
to adopt this view, from the close connexion of the next verse with the whole
preceding passage, and the exceedingly
unnatural isolation of this, unless it bears
such a reference. It is impossible to
avoid remarking, that the characteristic,
but unnecessary anxiety of Ellicott to rescue the apostolic Timotheus from any imputation of feebleness of character, has
blinded him to the delicate connexion of
thoughts here, as frequently in the second
Epistle). 24.] The same subject continued : τὸν περὶ τῆς χειροτονίας ἀναλαμβάνει λόγον. Thdrt. If my view of the
last verse is correct, the connexion will be
found in the fact, that the conservation
of himself in health and vigour would
ensure his being able to deal ably and
firmly with the cases which should come
before him for decision. To guide him
still further in this, the Apostle subjoins
this remark, indicating two classes of characters with which he would have to deal
in judging, whether favourably or unfa-
vourably. Of some men the sins (connects with ἁμαρτίαις ἀλλοτρίαις, ver. 22)
are evident (there does not seem to be
any relation of time in πρόδηλοι, 'manifest beforehand,'—for thus the meaning
would be,—as in πρόδηλος πότμος, κίν-
δυνος, &c., that the sins were manifest
before they were committed, which would
reduce this case to the other (see below) :
but the προ- seems rather of place than of
time,—πρὸ τῶν ὀφθαλμῶν,—openly manifest,—notorious by common report), going
before them (so that the man's bad report comes to the person appointed to
judge, before the man himself : not transitive, as Heinrichs,—' peccata in judicium
eos vocant ') to judgment (i. e. so that
when they come before thee to be judged
of as candidates, their sins have arrived

before them): but some men again they
(their sins) follow (i. e. after-proof brings
out the correctness or otherwise of the
judgment. Their characters come before
thee unanticipated by adverse rumour :
but thou mayest by examination discover those flaws in their conduct which
had been skilfully concealed — the sins
which, so to speak, follow at their heels.
Therefore be watchful, and do not let the
mere non-existence of previous adverse
rumour lead thee always to presume fitness for the sacred office). 25.] So
also (in like manner on the other side
of men's conduct) the good works (of
some) are openly manifest: and those
which are otherwise situated (which are
not πρόδηλα) cannot be hidden (will come
out, just as the sins in ver. 24, on examination. The tendency of this verse is
to warn him against hasty condemnation,
as the former had done against hasty approval. Sometimes thou wilt find a man's
good character go before him, and at once
approve him to thee : but where this is not
so, do not therefore be rash to condemn—
thou mayest on examination soon discover,
if there really be any good deeds accompanying him : for they are things which
cannot be hidden—the good tree like the
bad will be known by his fruits, and that
speedily, on enquiry). I have abstained
from detailing all the varieties of interpretation of these verses, following as they do
those already specified on verses 20—22.
They may be seen shortly enumerated in
De W. and Ellicott, and commented on at
somewhat tedious length in Wiesinger.
Chrys., al., confuse the context by understanding κρίσις of eternal judgment, and
the sentiment as equivalent to ἐκεῖ πάντα
γυμνά ἐστιν. And so even Ellicott, who
in objecting to the above interpretation
(which is also Bp. Wordsworth's) charges
it somewhat naïvely with failure in explaining the context. That it only does
explain it satisfactorily, is, in my view,
the decisive consideration in its favour.

d Matt. xi. 29,
30. Acts xv.
10. Gal. v.
1. Rev. vi.
5 only.
Levit. xxvi.
13. Isa. ix. 4.
e Tit. ii. 9.
Prov. xxii. 7.
f = Rom. xiii.
7.
g ch. i. 12 reff.
h Rom. ii. 24, from Isa. lii. 5. James ii. 7. Rev. xiii. 6.
iii. 8. Tit. iii. 2   1 = Tit. i. 6 reff.

i ch. i. 10 reff.
m ch. iv. 12 reff.

k = as above (h). Rom.
n = Eph. vi. 7.

ADFKL
PℵabС
defgh
klmno
17. 47

VI. ¹ Ὅσοι εἰσὶν ὑπὸ ᵈ ζυγὸν δοῦλοι, τοὺς ᵉ ἰδίους ᵉ δεσπότας πάσης ᶠ τιμῆς ἀξίους ᵍ ἡγείσθωσαν, ἵνα μὴ τὸ
ʰ ὄνομα τοῦ θεοῦ καὶ ἡ ⁱ διδασκαλία ʰᵏ βλασφημῆται. ² οἱ
δὲ ˡ πιστοὺς ἔχοντες δεσπότας, μὴ ᵐ καταφρονείτωσαν, ὅτι
ἀδελφοί εἰσιν· ἀλλὰ μᾶλλον ⁿ δουλευέτωσαν, ὅτι ˡ πιστοί

CHAP. VI. 1. δουλου F: -λειας b¹ k 73 sah.   aft δουλ. π is written by ℵ¹, but
marked and erased.   for θεου, κυριου D¹ 17 vulg goth Ambrst Pel Gelas.
βλασφημειται KL 17 [47¹].

CH. VI.] *The Apostle's exhortations
are continued, and pass from ecclesiastical
to civil relations :* and first to the duties of
Christian slaves. This chapter has been
charged (Schleierm., al.) with want of coherence. But to a careful observer the
thread of connexion is very plain. I have
endeavoured to indicate it as we pass on.
Such a thread being detected, the idea of
Schleierm. (partly approved by De W.) of
its being a clumsy compilation out of the
Epistles to Titus and 2 Tim. hardly requires refutation.   1.] Let as many
as are slaves under the yoke (I have
adopted the rendering of De W. and
Huther, attaching δοῦλοι to the predicate,
as the simpler construction. The other,
' *as many slaves as are under the yoke,*'
making ὑπὸ ζυγόν emphatic as distinguishing either 1) those *treated hardly,* or 2)
those who were *under unbelieving masters,*
has undoubtedly something to be said for
it, but does not seem to me so likely, from
the arrangement of the words. Had ὑπὸ
ζυγόν been intended to bring out any distinction, it would have more naturally preceded εἰσίν. I take then ὑπὸ ζυγὸν δοῦλοι
as the predicate : ' bondsmen under yoke ')
hold their own (ἰδίους, as in Eph. v. 22, al.,
to bring out and emphasize the relation ;
see note there) masters worthy of all
(fitting) honour, that the name of God
and his doctrine (cf. Tit. ii. 10, where,
writing on the same subject, he admonishes
slaves ἵνα τὴν διδασκαλίαν τὴν τοῦ σωτῆρος ἡμῶν θεοῦ κοσμῶσιν ἐν πᾶσιν.
Hence it would appear that the article
here is possessive, and ἡ διδασκ. corresponding to τὸ ὄνομα) be not spoken
evil of (Chrys. gives the sense well :
ὁ ἄπιστος ἂν μὲν ἴδῃ τοὺς δούλους διὰ
τὴν πίστιν αὐθάδως προφερομένους, βλασ-
φημήσει πολλάκις ὡς στάσιν ἐμποιοῦντο τὸ
δόγμα· ὅταν δὲ ἴδῃ πειθομένους, μᾶλλον
πεισθήσεται, μᾶλλον προσέξει τοῖς λεγομένοις. This verse obviously applies only
to those slaves who had unbelieving masters. This is brought out by the reason

given, and by the contrast in the next
verse, not by any formal opposition in
terms. The account to be given of the
absence of such opposition is, that this
verse contains the general exhortation, the
case of Christian slaves under *unbelieving*
masters being by far the most common.
The *exception* is treated in the next verse).
2.] But (see above) let those who
have believing masters not despise them
because (belongs to καταφρονείτωσαν only,
containing the ground of their contempt,—
not to the exhortation μὴ καταφρονείτωσαν) they (the masters, not the slaves)
are brethren, but all the more serve
them (μᾶλλον has the emphatic position :
cf. Eph. v. 11, where it merely signifies
'rather,' and the verb has the emphasis,
μᾶλλον δὲ καὶ ἐλέγχετε. Cf. also Hom.
Od. ο. 369, φίλει δέ με κηρόθι μᾶλλον :
and in the same sense ἐπὶ μᾶλλον, Herod.
i. 94,—ἐπεί τε δὲ οὐκ ἀνίεται τὸ κακόν,
ἀλλ' ἐπὶ μᾶλλον ἔτι βιάζεσθαι, iii. 104 ;
iv. 181. "The slaves who were under
heathen masters were *positively* to regard their masters as deserving of honour ;
—the slaves under Christian masters were,
negatively, not to evince any want of respect. The former were not to regard their
masters as their inferiors, and to be insubordinate ; the latter were not to think them
their equals, and to be disrespectful."
Ellicott), because those who receive (mutually receive : the interchange of service
between them in the Christian life being
taken for granted, and this word purposely
used to express it. So Eur. Andr. 742 ff.,
κἂν . . . τολοιπὸν ᾖ | σώφρων καθ' ἡμᾶς,
σώφρον' ἀντιλήψεται. | θυμούμενος δέ,
τεύξεται θυμουμένων, ἔργοισι δ' ἔργα διά-
δοχ' ἀντιλήψεται. This sense, in the active,
also occurs Theogn. 110, οὔτε κακοὺς εὖ
δρῶν, εὖ πάλιν ἀντιλάβοις. And Plut.
Pericl. circa init. has it with the middle and
the genitive construction,—τῇ διαλύσει τῇ
αἰσθήσει, κατὰ πάθος τῆς πληγῆς ἀντι-
λαμβανομένῃ τῶν προστυγχανόντων . . . ;
and so Porphyr. de abstinentia, i. 46, μήτε

εἴσιν καὶ ἀγαπητοὶ οἱ τῆς [o] εὐεργεσιας [p] ἀντιλαμβανόμενοι.
[q] ταῦτα [q] δίδασκε καὶ [r] παρακάλει.
3 Εἴ τις [s] ἑτεροδιδασκαλεῖ, καὶ μὴ [t] προσέρχεται [u] ὑγιαίνουσιν [v] λόγοις τοῖς τοῦ [v] κυρίου ἡμῶν Ἰησοῦ χριστοῦ καὶ τῇ κατ' [w] εὐσέβειαν [u] διδασκαλίᾳ,
4 [x] τετύφωται, μηδὲν ἐπιστάμενος, ἀλλὰ

o Acts iv. 9 only. Ps. lxxvii. 11.
p = here (Luke i. 54, from Isa. xli. 9 Acts xx. 35) only. L.P. see note.
q ch. iv. 11. see ch. v. 7.
r Tit. ii. 15.
s ch. i. 3 only †. Ignat. ad Polyc. c. 3, p. 721. Philo de Gigant. 9, vol. i. p. 267.
t = and Paul, here only. γνώμη προσέρχεσθαι,
u ch. i. 10 reff.
v Acts xx. 35.
w ch. ii. 2 reff.
x ch. iii. 6. 2 Tim. iii. 4 only †.

2. εχοντας AD[1]F k m [47[1]]. om οτι αδελφοι εισιν ℵ[1] c: om οτι to δουλευετωσαν n. for ευεργεσιας, ευσεβειας F 46.
3. [for προσερχ.] προσεχετε ℵ[1]. [aft ευσεβ. ins ουση D[1].]

ἐσθίων πλειόνων ἡδονῶν ἀντιλήψεται. On other senses, see below) **the benefit** (of their μᾶλλον δουλεύειν. There is an apt and interesting passage in Seneca, de beneficiis, iii. 18: 'Quæritur a quibusdam, an beneficium dare servus domino possit?' This question he answers in the affirmative: 'servos qui negat dare aliquando domino beneficium, ignarus est juris humani: refert enim, cujus animi sit qui præstat, non cujus status:' and at some length explains when, and how, such benefits can be said to be bestowed. The passage is remarkable, as constituting perhaps one of those curious indications of community of thought between the Apostle and the philosopher which could hardly have been altogether fortuitous. For instance, when Seneca proceeds thus, "Quidquid est quod servilis officii formulam excedit, quod non ex imperio sed ex voluntate præstatur, beneficium est," we can hardly forbear connecting the unusual sense here of εὐεργεσία after the μᾶλλον δουλευέτωσαν, with the moralist's discussion) **are faithful and beloved.** Very various meanings and references have been assigned to these last words. Chrys., Thl., Grot., Kypke, al., interpret εὐεργεσίας of the kindness of the master to the slave ("*quia fideles sunt et dilecti qui beneficii participes sunt* (vulg.): primum, quia fide in Deum sunt præditi: deinde diligendi eo nomine quod curam gerant, ut vobis benefaciant: id est ut vos vestiant, pascant, ab injuriis protegant." Grot.). On the other hand, Ambr. (?), Lomb., Th.-Aq., Calv., Beza, Bengel, al., understand it of God's grace in redemption. But thus, if we make οἱ τῆς εὐεργ. ἀντιλ. the subject, as by the article it must be, the sentence will express nothing but a truism: if we escape from this by turning those words into the predicate (as E. V., "because they are faithful and beloved, partakers of the benefit"), we are violating the simplest rules of grammar. **These things** (viz. those immediately preceding, relating to slaves) **teach and exhort**

3—5.] *Designation of those who oppose such wholesome teaching*—fervid indeed, and going further (see Prolegg.) than strict adherence to the limits of the context would require, but still suggested by, and returning to the context: cf. ver. 5 fin. and note. **If any man is a teacher of other ways** (see on ch. i. 3: sets up as an adviser of different conduct from that which I have above recommended), **and does not accede to** (so a convert to the true faith was called προσήλυτος: and we have in Origen, ii. 255 (Wolf), προσιόντας τῷ λόγῳ in the sense of just converted, and in ib. 395, προσερχομένους τῷ θείῳ λόγῳ. So also Irenæus, in two places cited by Wolf: see also Philo in reff. There was therefore no need for Bentley's conjecture, προσέχεται (see itacism in ℵ, var. read.) or προσέχει, or προσίσχεται, though the use of these is commoner: see ch. i. 4 reff. Cf. also Ellic.'s note) **wholesome words** (reff.), **(namely) those of our Lord Jesus Christ** (either, precepts given by Him respecting this duty of subjection, such as that Matt. xxii. 21,—which however seems rather far-fetched: or words agreeing with His teaching and expressing His will, which is more probable), **and to the doctrine which is according to** (after the rules of) **piety,—he is** (the apodosis begins here, not as Mack, al., with the spurious ἀφίστασο, ver. 5) **besotted with pride** (see ch. iii. 6, note), **knowing** (being one who knows: not, '*although* he knows') **nothing** (not οὐδέν, which would be used to express the bare fact of absolute ignorance or idiotcy), **but mad after** (so Plato, Phædr. p. 228, ἀπαντήσας δὲ τῷ νοσοῦντι περὶ λόγων ἀκοήν, ἰδὼν μὲν ἰδὼν ἥσθη ὅτι ἕξοι τὸν συγκορυβαντιῶντα. Bengel and Wetst. quote from Plut. de laud. propr. p. 546 f, νοσεῖν περὶ δόξαν,—de ira cohib. p. 460 d, ν. περὶ σφραγίδια πολυτελῆ, *insanire amore gloriæ*, vel *sigillorum pretiosorum*. See more examples in Kypke. "περί with a *genitive* serves to mark an object as the central point, as it were, of the ac-

^y νοσῶν περὶ ^z ζητήσεις καὶ ^a λογομαχίας, ἐξ ὧν γίνεται ^b φθόνος, ^b ἔρις, ^c βλασφημίαι, ^{de} ὑπόνοιαι ^d πονηραί, 5 ^f διαπαρατριβαὶ ^{gh} διεφθαρμένων ἀνθρώπων τὸν ^h νοῦν καὶ ⁱ ἀπεστερημένων ^j τῆς ^j ἀληθείας, νομιζόντων ^k πορισμὸν εἶναι τὴν ^l εὐσέβειαν. 6 Ἔστιν δὲ ^k πορισμὸς μέγας ἡ ^l εὐσέβεια μετὰ ^m αὐταρκείας. 7 οὐδὲν γὰρ ⁿ εἰσηνέγκαμεν

Marginal references (left):
y here only †. Wisd. xvii. 8 bis only. see note.
z ch. i. 4 reff.
a here only †. (-χεῖν, 2 Tim. ii. 14.)
b Phil. i. 15 reff.
c = Eph. iv. 31. Col. iii. 8 al.
d Sir. iii. 24.
e here only †.

Right margin: ADFKL Pℵ a b c d e f g h k l m n o 17. 47

Sir. as above (d) only. (-νοεῖν, Acts xiii. 25.)   f here only †.   g Luke xii. 33. 2 Cor. iv. 16. Rev. viii. 9. xi. 18 only. Ps. xiii. 1. διεφθαρμένον τοὺς ὀφθαλμούς, Demosth. 1269. 6.   h see 2 Tim. iii. 8. i = here only ‡. (Mark x. 19. 1 Cor. vi. 7, 8. vii. 5. James v. 4 only. Mal. iii. 5 al.)   j 2 Tim. iii. 8. iv. 4. Tit. i. 14.   k here bis only †. Wisd. xiii. 19. xiv. 2 only. δυσὶ κεχρῆσθαι μόνοις πορισμοῖς, γεωργίᾳ καὶ φειδοῖ, Plut. Cat. Maj. § 25. (-ίζειν, Wisd. xv. 12.)   l ch. ii. 2 reff.   m 2 Cor. ix. 8 only †. (-κης, Phil. iv. 11.)   n = Luke v. 18, 19. Heb. xiii. 11 only. Numb. xxxi. 54.

4. for γινεται, γεννωνται D¹ Lucif.   φθονοι D¹ latt copt goth Ambrst-ed Pel. ερεις DFL [47] latt syr copt [goth] Damasc Luc Ambr Ambrst Pel.

5. rec (for διαπαρατρ.) παραδιατριβαι, with b Thl : διατριβαι K d 1 : txt ADFL[P]ℵ rel Clem Bas Chr Thdrt Hesych Suid Damasc Œc.   απεστραμμενων απο της D¹ : destitutorum a D-lat G-lat Lucif.   rec at end ins αφισταστο απο των τοιουτων, with [D³]KL[P] rel tol² spec syrr æth-pl [arm] gr-ff [Cypr Lucif₁] Ambrst : om AD¹Fℵ 17. 67² latt coptt goth æth-rom Lucif Ambr Bede.

6. aft ευσεβεια ins θεου F.

---

tivity (e. g. 1 Cor. xii. 1, the πνευμ. δῶρα formed as it were the centre of the ἄγνοια): the further idea of any *action* or *motion* round it is supplied by περί with the accusative. Cf. Winer, edn. 6, § 47. *e* : Donalds. Gr. § 482." Ellicott) questionings (reff.) and disputes about words (see ref. The word is found only in ecclesiastical writers: see Wetst. Calv. explains it well, " contensiosas disputationes de verbis magis quam de rebus, vel, ut vulgo loquuntur, sine materia, aut subjecto "), from which cometh envy, strife, evil speakings (the context of such passages as Col. iii. 8, shews that it is not *blasphemy*, properly so called (ἐκ δὲ τῆς ἔριδος ἡ κατὰ τοῦ θεοῦ βλασφημία τολμᾶται, Thdrt.), but mutual slander and reproach which is here meant), wicked suspicions (not *concerning God* (περὶ θεοῦ ἃ μὴ δεῖ ὑποπτεύομεν, Chrys.), but of one another : not " 'opiniones malæ,' quales Diagoræ, non esse Deum," as Grot.), incessant quarrels (δια- gives the sense of continuance ; παρατριβή, primarily '*friction*,' is found in later writers in the sense of irritating provocation, or hostile collision : so Polyb. ii. 36. 5, τὰ μὲν οὖν κατὰ Καρχηδονίους καὶ Ῥωμαίους ἀπὸ τούτων ἤδη τῶν καιρῶν ἐν ὑποψίαις ἦν πρὸς ἀλλήλους καὶ παρατριβαῖς :—xxiii. 10. 4, διὰ τὴν πρὸς τὸν Φιλοποίμενα παρατριβήν : see also iv. 21. 5 ; xxi. 13. 5 ; xxiv. 3. 4. According to the other reading, παρά would give the sense of useless, vain, perverse, and διατριβή would be disputation, thus giving the sense 'perverse disputings,' as E. V. Chrys., Œc., Thdrt., explain our word ἀπὸ μεταφορᾶς τῶν

ψωραλέων προβάτων (Œc.) : and Chrys. says, καθάπερ τὰ ψωραλέα τῶν προβάτων παρατριβόμενα νόσου καὶ τὰ ὑγιαίνοντα ἐμπίπλησιν, οὕτω καὶ οὗτοι οἱ πονηροὶ ἄνδρες) of men depraved in mind (reff. ; and see Ellic. on the psychology and construction) and destitute of the truth, who suppose that godliness is gain (lit., 'a gainful trade,' as Conyb. : see reff. :—and therefore do not teach contentment and acquiescence in God's providence, as in ver. 6 : but strive to make men discontented, and persuade them to use religion as a means of worldly bettering themselves).   6.] He then goes off, on the mention of this erroneous view, to shew how it really stands with the Christian as to the desire of riches : its danger, and the mischief it has occasioned. But (although they are in error in thus thinking, there *is* a sense in which such an idea is true ('eleganter et non sine ironica correctione in contrarium sensum eadem verba retorquet.' Calv.), for) godliness accompanied with contentment (see above, and Phil. iv. 11) is great gain (alluding, not to the Christian's reward in the next world, as Thdrt.,—τὴν γὰρ αἰώνιον ἡμῖν πορίζει ζωήν, Erasm., Calv., al.,—but as Chrys., Thl., Ambr., al.,—the πορισμός is in the very fact of possessing piety joined with contentment, and thus being able to dispense with those things which we cannot carry away with us).   7.] Reason why this is so. For we brought nothing into the world, because neither can we carry any thing out (the insertion of δῆλον or ἀληθές, or substitution of ἀλλά or καί for ὅτι, betray themselves as having

εἰς τὸν κόσμον, ὅτι οὐδὲ ᵒ ἐξενεγκεῖν τὶ δυνάμεθα· ⁸ ἔχοντες
δὲ ᵖ διατροφὰς καὶ ᑫ σκεπάσματα, τούτοις ʳ ἀρκεσθησόμεθα.
⁹ Οἱ δὲ ˢ βουλόμενοι πλουτεῖν ᵗ ἐμπίπτουσιν εἰς ᵘ πειρασμὸν καὶ ᵗ παγίδα καὶ ᵛ ἐπιθυμίας πολλὰς ʷ ἀνοήτους καὶ
ˣ βλαβεράς, ʸ αἵτινες ᶻ βυθίζουσιν τοὺς ἀνθρώπους εἰς
ᵃ ὄλεθρον καὶ ᵇ ἀπώλειαν. ¹⁰ ᶜ ῥίζα γὰρ πάντων τῶν

o = Luke xv.
22. Acts v.
6, &c. (Mark
viii. 23. Heb.
vi. 8) only.
Exod. xii. 39.
p here only †.
1 Macc. vi.
49 only.
q here only †.
r = Luke iii.
14. Heb.
xiii. 5.
3 John 10, but
w. ἐπί. (2 Cor.

xii. 9 al.)‡	2 Macc. v. 15.		s = James iv. 4.			t ch. iii. (6) 7 reff.	Prov. xiii.
u Matt. vi. 13. xxvi. 41 ‖ al. fr. Paul, 1 Cor. x. 13. Gal. iv. 14 only.				v Rom. i. 24 al. fr.
w Rom. i. 14. Gal. iii. 1, 3. Tit. iii. 3 only. L.P. Prov. xvii. 28.			x here only. Prov. x. 26 (only?).
y = Acts x. 41, 47 al. fr.					z Luke v. 7 only†. 2 Macc. xii. 4 only. (-θος, 2 Cor. xi. 25.)
a 1 Cor. v. 5. 1 Thess. v. 3. 2 Thess. i. 9 only. P. Prov. xxi. 7.			b Paul, Rom. ix. 22. Phil. i.
28. iii. 19. 2 Thess. ii. 3. 2 Pet. ii. 1 al⁵. Rev. xvii. 8, 11. Isa. xiv. 23.			c = Heb. xi. 15,
from Deut. xxix. 18. Sir. i. 20.

7. rec ins δηλον bef οτι (see note), with D³KL[P]ℵ³ rel syrr Bas Mac Chr Thdrt
Damasc : αληθες D¹ syr-mg, *verum quoniam* D-lat Ambrst, *haud dubium quod* vulg,
in veritate quod goth : αλλ' Polyc(ἀλλ' οὐδὲ ἐξ. τι ἔχομεν) Cypr Aug Paulin : και coptt
æth arm : txt AFℵ 17.

8. διατροφην DFK[P Orig] : *victum* D-lat G-lat lat-ff.	αρκεσθησωμεθα K d n
Chr-ms Damasc.

9. aft παγιδα ins του διαβολου D¹F latt [(not am) goth] Chr Antch Thdrt-txt Ambr
Chrom Cæs-arel.

all sprung from the difficulty of the
shorter and original construction. The
meaning appears to be, — we were appointed by God to come naked into the
world, to teach us to remember that we
must go naked out of it. But this sense
of ὅτι is not without difficulty. De W.
cites Il. π. 35, γλαυκὴ δέ σε τίκτε θά-
λασσα, πέτραι τ' ἠλίβατοι, ὅτι τοι νόος
ἐστὶν ἀπηνής,—and Od. χ. 36, ὦ κύνες, οὔ
μ' ἔτ' ἐφάσκεθ' ὑπότροπον οἴκαδ' ἱκέσθαι |
δήμου ἄπο Τρώων, ὅτι μοι κατεκείρετε
οἶκον, in both which it has nearly the
sense required, of '*seeing that.*' The sentiment is found in Job i. 21, Eccl. v. 14 :
and in words remarkably similar, in
Seneca, Ep. 102. 24, 'non licet plus ef-
ferre, quam intuleris.' See other examples
in Wetst.) :—	**8.**] but (contrast to
the avaricious, who forget this, or knowing it do not act on it : not as De W., =
οὖν, which would be a direct inference
from the preceding verse) having (if we
have) food (the δια- gives the sense of
'sufficient for our continually recurring
wants,'—'the needful supply of nourishment :' the plur. corresponds to the plur.
ἔχοντες, and implies ' in each case ') and
covering (some take it of both clothing
and dwelling : perhaps rightly, but not
on account of the plural : see above :—
Chrys., al., of clothing only,—τοιαῦτα
ἀμφιέννυσθαι, ἃ σκεπάσαι μόνον ἡμᾶς
ὀφείλει καὶ περιστεῖλαι τὴν γύμνωσιν.
These words occur together (Huther) in
Sextus Empiricus ix. 1), with these (so
ἀγαπάω, στέργω, χαίρω, &c. take a dative
of the cause or object of the feeling. See
ref. Luke, and Matthiæ, § 403) we shall

be sufficiently provided (the fut. has an ✶
authoritative sense : so in Matt. v. 48, and
Xen. Hell. ii. 3. 34, cited by Huther,
ὑμεῖς οὖν, ἐὰν σωφρονῆτε, οὐ τούτου, ἀλλ'
ὑμῶν φείσεσθε :—but is not therefore equivalent to an imperative, 'let us be content :' for its sense is not properly subjective but objective—'to be sufficed,' or
'sufficiently provided :' and it is passive,
not middle).	**9.**] But (contrast to
the last verse) they who wish to be rich
(not simply, 'they who *are rich :*' cf.
Chrys.: οὐχ ἁπλῶς εἶπεν, οἱ πλουτοῦντες,
ἀλλ', οἱ βουλόμενοι· ἐστὶ γάρ τινα καὶ
χρήματα ἔχοντα καλῶς οἰκονομεῖν κατα-
φρονοῦντα αὐτῶν), fall (reff.) into temptation (not merely ' *are tempted,*' but are
involved in, cast into and among temptations; "in ἐμπίπτειν is implied the
power which the πειρασμός exercises over
them." Huther) and a snare (being entangled by the temptation of getting rich
as by a net), and many foolish and hurtful
lusts (foolish, because no reasonable account can be given of them (see Ellic. on
Gal. iii. 1): hurtful, as inflicting injury
on all a man's best interests), such as
sink men (mankind, generic) into destruction and perdition (temporal and eternal,
but especially the latter : see the usage in
reff. of both words by St. Paul : not mere
moral degradation, as De W.).	**10.**]
For the love of money is the (not ' *a*,' as
Huther, Conyb., and Ellicott, after Middleton. A word like ῥίζα, a recognized
part of a plant, does not require an article
when placed as here in an emphatic position : we might have ἡ γὰρ ῥίζα, or ῥίζα
γάρ : cf. 1 Cor. xi. 3 (which, notwith-

κακῶν ἐστιν ἡ ^d φιλαργυρία, ἧς ^e τινὲς ^f ὀρεγόμενοι ^g ἀπεπλανήθησαν ἀπὸ τῆς πίστεως καὶ ἑαυτοὺς ^h περιέπειραν ⁱ ὀδύναις πολλαῖς. 11 Σὺ δέ, ὦ ^j ἄνθρωπε [τοῦ] ^j θεοῦ, ταῦτα ^k φεῦγε· ^{lm} δίωκε δὲ ^m δικαιοσύνην, ⁿ εὐσέβειαν, ^o πίστιν, ^o ἀγάπην, ^{op} ὑπομονήν, ^q πραϋπάθειαν. 12 ^{rs} ἀγωνίζου τὸν ^{rt} καλὸν ^{ru} ἀγῶνα τῆς πίστεως, ^v ἐπιλαβοῦ τῆς

Marginal readings (left):

d here only. Jer. viii. 10 compl. Gr. (not A) only. (-ρος, 2 Tim. iii. 2.)
e ch. i. 3 reff.
f ch. iii. 1. Heb. xi. 16 only †. (act., Job viii. 20 Symm.)
g Mark xiii. 22 only. Prov. vii. 21. 17 only.

Marginal readings (right column): ADFKL ℵ a b c d e f g h k l m n o 17. 47

h here only †. Jos. B. J. iv. 7. 4 end.   i Rom. ix. 2 only. Jer. viii. 18.   j 2 Tim. iii. 17 only.   Josh. xiv. 6. 4 Kings iv. 7 al.   k = (Paul only) 1 Cor. vi. 18. x. 14. 2 Tim. ii. 22. Sir. xxi. 2.
l = 1 Thess. v. 15 reff. Xen. Cyr. viii. 1. 39. Thuc. ii. 63.   m Rom. ix. 30. 2 Tim. ii. 22.
n vv. 3, 5, 6.   o 2 Tim. iii. 10. Tit. ii. 2. 2 Pet. i. 6, 7.   p Col. i. 11 reff.   q here only †. Philo de Abr. 37, vol. ii. p. 31, εἴκουσι διὰ τὴν τοῦ δεσπότου πραϋπάθειαν.   r 2 Tim. iv. 7. Eur. Alc. 648.   s Col. i. 29 reff.   t ch. i. 18 reff.   u Phil. i. 30 reff.   v Paul, ver. 19 only. Luke ix. 47. Heb. ii. 16. viii. 9 al. Prov. iv. 13.

10. [om των D¹. (P def., but there is space enough.)]   for πολλαις, ποικιλαις ℵ¹. [P def.]
    11. om του Aℵ¹ 17 : ins DFKL[P]ℵ³ rel gr-ff.   om ευσεβειαν ℵ¹ [47. (P def.)]
    rec (for πραυπαθειαν) πραοτητα, with DKLℵ³ (πραϋτ. D¹ℵ³) rel Chr Thdrt : txt AF [P(. . . αν)] ℵ¹ Petr Ephr Hesych (perhaps alluded to in Ign Trall 8, p. 681, τὴν πραϋπάθειαν ἀναλαβόντες).

standing what Ellic. has alleged against it, still appears to me to be strictly in point to shew that for which it is here adduced), **παντὸς ἀνδρὸς ἡ κεφαλὴ ὁ χριστός ἐστιν, κεφαλὴ δὲ γυναικὸς ὁ ἀνήρ, κεφαλὴ δὲ τοῦ χριστοῦ ὁ θεός.** Here in the first clause it is requisite to throw παντὸς ἀνδρός into emphasis : but had the arrangement been the same as that of the others, we should have read κεφαλὴ (not ἡ κεφ.) παντὸς ἀνδρὸς ὁ χριστός : but no one would therefore have thought of rendering ' *a* head ') **root of all evils** (not, is the only root whence all evils spring : but is the root whence all (manner of evils may and as matter of fact do arise. So that De W.'s objections to the sentiment have no force : for neither does it follow (1) that the covetous man cannot possibly retain any virtuous disposition,— nor (2) that there may not be other roots of evil besides covetousness: neither of these matters being in the Apostle's view. So Diogenes Laert. vit. Diogen. (vi. 50), τὴν φιλαργυρίαν εἶπε μητρόπολιν πάντων τῶν κακῶν: and Philo de judice 3, vol. ii. p. 346, calls it ὁρμητήριον τῶν μεγίστων παρανομηματων. See other examples in Wetst.) : **after which** (φιλαργυρία, see below) **some lusting** (the method of expression, if strictly judged, is somewhat incorrect : for φιλαργυρία is of itself a desire or ὄρεξις, and men cannot be properly said ὀρέγεσθαι after it, but after its object ἀργύριον. Such inaccuracies are, however, often found in language, and we have examples of them in St. Paul elsewhere : e. g. ἐλπὶς βλεπομένη, Rom. viii. 24,—ἐλπίδα . . . . ἣν καὶ αὐτοὶ οὗτοι προσδέχονται, Acts xxiv. 15) **wandered away from the faith** (ch. i. 19 ; iv. 1), **and pierced themselves through** (not all

round' or 'all over,' as Beza, Elsner, al. : the περί refers to the thing pierced *surrounding the instrument piercing* : so περιπ. τὴν κεφαλὴν περὶ λόγχην, Plut. Galb. 27 : see Palm and Rost, and Suicer, sub voce) **with many pains** (the ὀδύναι being regarded as the weapons). ἄκανθαί εἰσιν αἱ ἐπιθυμίαι—καὶ καθάπερ ἐν ἀκάνθαις, ὅθεν ἄν τις ἅψηται αὐτῶν, ἥμαξε τὰς χεῖρας καὶ τραύματα ἐργάζεται· οὕτω καὶ ἀπὸ τῶν ἐπιθυμιῶν τὸ αὐτὸ πείσεται ὁ ταύταις ἐμπεσών, κ. τὴν ψυχὴν ἀλγηδόσι περιβαλεῖ. Chrys.).   **11—16.]** *Exhortation and conjuration to Timotheus, arising out of these considerations.*

11.] But (contrast to τινές above) **thou** (emphatic), **O man of God** (the designation of prophets in the O. T. : cf. LXX, 1 Kings ix. 6, 7, 8, 10, al. ; and hence perhaps used of Timotheus as dedicated to God's service in the ministry : but also not without a solemn reference to that which it expresses, that God, and not riches (see the contrast again ver. 17) is *his* object of desire), **flee these things** (φιλαργυρία and its accompanying evils) : but (the contrast is to the following these things, underlying the mention of them) **follow after** (ref. 2 Tim., where both words occur again) **righteousness** (see Ellic.'s note and references), **piety** (so δικαίως, εὐσεβῶς, Tit. ii. 12), **faith** (not mere rectitude in keeping trust, for all these words regard the Christian life), **love, patience** (under afflictions : stedfast endurance : better than ' *stedfastness* ' (Conyb.), which may be an *active* endurance), **meek-spiritedness** (ref. : we have πραϋπαθέω in Philo de profugis, 1, vol. i. 547, —πραϋπαθής in Basil. M. These two last qualities have reference to his behaviour towards the opponents of the Gospel) :

^w αἰωνίου ^w ζωῆς, ^x εἰς ἣν ^x ἐκλήθης, καὶ ^y ὡμολόγησας
τὴν ^t καλὴν ^z ὁμολογίαν ^a ἐνώπιον πολλῶν μαρτύρων.
¹³ ^b Παραγγέλλω σοι ^c ἐνώπιον τοῦ θεοῦ τοῦ ^d ζωογο-
νοῦντος τὰ πάντα, καὶ χριστοῦ Ἰησοῦ τοῦ ^e μαρτυρήσαντος
^f ἐπὶ Ποντίου Πιλάτου τὴν ^t καλὴν ^z ὁμολογίαν, ¹⁴ ^g τη-

w Acts xiii. 46
(Paul). Tit.
i. 2. iii. 7 al.
x 1 Cor. i. 9.
Col. iii. 15.
2 Thess. ii.
14. 1 Pet. ii.
9, 21. v. 10.
y = John xii.
42. Acts
xxiii. 8.
Rom. x. 10.
z (=) 2 Cor. ix.

13. Heb. iii. 1. iv. 14. x. 23 only. P.H. ‡ (Levit. xxii. 18 al.)   à = Rom. xii. 17.   2 Cor. viii.
21. ch. v. 20. 3 John 6.   b Acts x. 42. xvi. 18 al. fr.   Josh. vi. 6.   c ch. v. 21 reff.
d Luke xvii. 33. Acts vii. 19 only.   Exod. i. 17, 18, 22.   e = (but see note) here only. see Acts
xxiii. 11. constr., Rev. i. 2. xxii. 16, 20.   f = (see note) Mark xiii. 9. Acts xxiii. 30. xxiv. 19,
20. xxv. 9, 10, 26. xxvi. 2. 1 Cor. vi. 1, 6. μαρτυρήσας ἐπὶ τῶν ἡγεμόνων, Clem. Rom. ad Cor. i. 5,
p. 220.   g = Matt. xix. 17. John xiv. 15. Paul, here only. see 1 Cor. vii. 19.

12. rec aft εις ην ins και, with o (d h l m, e sil) syr-w-ast Thl Œc Ambrst-ms : om
ADFKL[P]א rel latt Syr coptt [goth] æth arm Petr Ephr Chr Thdrt Damasc Pel.
13. παραγγελλων, omg (as also א¹ 17) σοι, F.   om 1st του א : om του θεου 109.
rec ζωοποιουντος, with KLא rel Cyr-jer : txt ADF[P] 17 Ath Cyr Thdrt_{aliq} Œc-
comm.   ιησ. bef χρ. Fא Syr [coptt arm-ed æth] Did Thl Tert.

12.] Strive the good strife (see ref.
and ch. i. 18 : 1 Cor. ix. 24 ff. : Phil. iii.
12 ff.) of the faith (not ' of faith,' abstract
and subjective : but that noble conflict
which the faith,—the profession of the
soldier of Christ, entails on him), **lay hold
upon** (as the aim and object of the life-
long struggle ; the prize to be gained : so
that the second imperative is, as Winer
well observes, edn. 6, § 43, not the mere
result of the first, as in ' divide et impera,' but correlative with it and contemporaneous : ' strive . . . , and while doing
so, endeavour to attain ') **everlasting life,
to which thou wast called** (here apparently the image is dropped, and the
realities of the Christian life spoken of.
Some have supposed an allusion to the
athletes being summoned by a herald : but
it seems far-fetched—and indeed inaccurate : for it was to the *contest*, not to
the *prize*, that they were thus summoned),
and didst confess (we must not supply
εἰς ἥν again before ὡμολόγησας, with
Mack, al.,—'*in reference to which*,'—a
most unnatural construction : but regard
it, with De W., as simply coupled to
ἐκλήθης) **the good confession** (of faith in
Christ : *the* confession, which every servant of Christ must make, on taking upon
himself His service, or professing it when
called upon so to do. From the same
expression in the next verse, it would
seem, that the article rather represents
the notoriousness of the confession, ' bonam illam confessionem,' than its definite general character. There is some
uncertainty, to what occasion the Apostle here refers; whether to the baptism
of Timotheus,—so Chrys. (?), Œc., Thl.
(alt.), Ambr., Grot., Beng., &c. : to his
ordination as a minister,—so Wolf, al. :
to his appointment over the church at
Ephesus,—so Mack : to some confession

made by him under persecution,—so, justifying it by what follows, respecting our
Lord, Huther, al. Of these the first appears to me most probable, as giving the
most general sense to ἡ καλὴ ὁμολογία,
and applying best to the immediate consideration of αἰώνιος ζωή, which is the
common object of all Christians. The reference supposed by Thdrt. (πάντας παρ'
αὐτοῦ δεξαμένους τὸ κήρυγμα μάρτυρας
εἶχε τῆς καλῆς ὁμολογίας), Calv., al., to
Timotheus's *preaching*, is clearly inadmissible) **before many witnesses.**
13.] I charge thee (ch. i. 3) **in the presence of God who endues all things ✱
with life** (for the sense, see reff. : most
probably a reference to αἰώνιος ζωή above :
hardly, as De W., al., after Chrys., to the
resurrection, reminding him that death
for Christ's sake was not to be feared : for
there is here no immediate allusion to
danger, but only to the duty of personal
firmness in the faith in his own religious
life), **and of Christ Jesus,** who testified
('*testari confessionem* erat Domini, *con-
fiteri confessionem* erat Timo-nei,' Bengel.
See Ellicott's note) **before Pontius Pilate**
(De W., al. (and Ellicott : see below on
ὁμολογ.) would render it, as in the Apostles' creed, '*under Pontius Pilate :*' but
the immediate reference here being to
His *confession,* it seems more natural to
take the meaning, ' coram :' and so Chrys.,
who as a Greek, and familiar with the
Creed, is a fair witness)—**the good confession** (viz. that whole testimony to the
verity of his own Person and to the Truth,
which we find in John xviii., and which
doubtless formed part of the oral apostolic
teaching. Those who render ἐπί, ' under,'
understand this *confession* of our Lord's
sufferings and death—which at least is
far-fetched. There is no necessity,
with Huther, to require a strict parallel

h James i. 27.
1 Pet. i. 19.
2 Pet. iii. 14 only †. Job xv. 15 Symm.
i ch. iii. 2. v. 7 only †.
k of time, Matt. xi. 23. Acts x. 30. xx. 7 al. Job viii. 2.

ρῆσαί σε τὴν ^g ἐντολὴν ^h ἄσπιλον, ⁱ ἀνεπίλημπτον, ^k μέχρι
τῆς ^l ἐπιφανείας τοῦ κυρίου ἡμῶν Ἰησοῦ χριστοῦ, 15 ἣν
^m καιροῖς ^m ἰδίοις ⁿ δείξει ὁ ^o μακάριος καὶ ^p μόνος ^q δυνάστης,
ὁ ^{rs} βασιλεὺς τῶν βασιλευόντων καὶ ^s κύριος τῶν ^t κυριευ-
όντων, 16 ὁ μόνος ἔχων ^u ἀθανασίαν, φῶς ^v οἰκῶν ^w ἀπρός-

ADFKL
PℵA b c
d e f g h
k l m n o
17. 47

1 2 Thess. ii. 8.   2 Tim. i. 10. iv. 1, 8.   Tit. ii. 13 only.   2 Kings vii. 23.   m Gal. vi. 9. ch. ii. 6.   Tit. i. 3 only.
n John ii. 18. xiv. 8.   o ch. i. 11 reff. of God, there only.'   p ch. i. 17.   q Luke i. 52.   Acts viii. 27
only.   Levit. xix. 15.   2 Macc. xii. 15.   r of the Father, Matt. v. 35. ch. i. 17.   s Rev. xvii. 14. xix.
16. see Deut. x. 17.   Ps. cxxxv. 3.   t Luke xxii. 25.   Rom. vi. 9, 14. vii. 1. xiv. 9.   2 Cor. i. 24 only. L.P. Gen.
iii. 16.   u 1 Cor. xv. 53, 54 only †.   Wisd. viii. 13 al4.   v Paul only, but elsw. w. prep.,
Rom. vii. 17, 18, 20. viii. 9, 11.   1 Cor. iii. 16. vii. 12, 13. constr., Prov. x. 31.   w here only †.

14. om σε D¹ 43 Did.   [aft ασπιλ. ins και D 115.]   χρ. bef ιησ. ℵ.
16. ins και bef φως D¹ vulg Did₁ Ambrst Aug Pel.   for απροσ., αορατον 67².

between the circumstances of the confession of our Lord and that of Timotheus,
nor to infer in consequence of this verse
that his confession must have been one
before a heathen magistrate: it is the *fact*
of a confession having been made in both
cases that is put in the foreground—and
that our Lord's was made in the midst of
danger and with death before him, is a
powerful argument to firmness for his servant in his own confession. Another rendering of this verse is given by Mack, al. :
it makes τὴν καλὴν ὁμολογίαν governed
by παραγγέλλω, and understands by it the
same confession as in verse 12 : ‘I enjoin
on thee,—in the presence . . . . and of
Christ Jesus who bore testimony before
Pontius Pilate—the good confession.’ But
this is quite inadmissible. For it is opposed both to the sense of παραγγέλλω, and
to the following context, in which ἡ ἐντολή, not ἡ καλὴ ὁμολογία, is the thing to
be observed), **that thou keep** (preserve : cf.
ἄσπιλον below, and ch. v. 22) **the commandment** (used not to designate any
special command just given, but as a
general compendium of the rule of the
Gospel, after which our lives and thoughts
must be regulated: cf. παραγγελία in the
same sense, ch. i. 5) **without spot and
without reproach** (both epithets belong to
τὴν ἐντολήν, not to σε, as most Commentators, some, as Est., maintaining that ἀνεπίληπτος can be used of persons only. But
this De W. has shewn not to be the case :
we have ἡ ἀνεπίληπτος τέχνη in Philo de
opif. 22, vol. i. p. 15 : ἀνεπιληπτότερον τὸ
λεγόμενον in Plato, Phileb. p. 43 c. Besides, the ordinary construction with τηρεῖν
is that the qualifying adjective should belong to its object: cf. ch. v. 22 : James i.
27 : 2 Cor. xi. 9. The commandment, entrusted to thee as a deposit (cf. ver. 20),
must be kept by thee unstained and un-
reproached. Consult Ellic.'s note) **until
the appearance** (reff.) **of our Lord Jesus
Christ** (τουτέστι, says Chrys., μέχρι τῆς

σῆς τελευτῆς, μέχρι τῆς ἐξόδου. But surely
both the usage of the word ἐπιφάνεια and
the next verse should have kept him from
this mistake. Far better Bengel : " fideles
in praxi sua proponebant sibi diem Christi
ut appropinquantem : nos solemus nobis
horam mortis proponere." We may fairly
say that whatever impression is betrayed
by the words that the coming of the Lord
would be in Timotheus's lifetime, is chas-
tened and corrected by the καιροῖς ἰδίοις of
the next verse. *That*, the certainty of the
coming in God's own time, was a fixed
truth respecting which the Apostle speaks
with the authority of the Spirit : but the
day and hour was hidden from him as from
us : and from such passages as this we see
that the apostolic age maintained that
which ought to be the attitude of all ages,
constant expectation of the Lord's return)
15, 16.] **which in His own times** (reff. :
τουτέστι τοῖς προσήκουσι, τοῖς ὀφειλομέ-
νοις, Chrys. " Numerus pluralis servan-
dus, brevitatem temporum non valde coarc-
tans ;" Bengel) **He shall manifest** (make
visible, cause to appear ; " display," Ellic.)
(who is) the blessed (ἡ αὐτομακαριότης,
Chrys). **and only Potentate** (Baur, al.,
believe the polytheism or dualism of the
Gnostics to be hinted at in μόνος : but
this is very unlikely. The passage is not
polemical : and cf. the same μόνος in John
xvii. 3), **the King of kings and Lord of
lords** (this seems the place,—on account
of this same designation occurring in reff.
Rev. applied to our Lord,—to enquire
whether these verses 15, 16 are said of
the Father or of the Son. Chrys. holds
very strongly the latter view : but surely
the καιροῖς ἰδίοις, compared with καιρούς, οὓς
ὁ πατὴρ ἔθετο ἐν τῇ ἰδίᾳ ἐξουσίᾳ, Acts i. 7,
determines for the former : so also does
ὃν εἶδεν οὐδεὶς κ.τ.λ. verse 16, which
Chrys. leaves untouched), **who only has
immortality** (Huther quotes (Ps-)Justin
M., quæst. ad Orthod. 61, p. 464: μόνος
ἔχων τὴν ἀθανασίαν λέγεται ὁ θεός, ὅτι οὐκ

ιτον, ὃν εἶδεν οὐδεὶς ἀνθρώπων οὐδὲ ἰδεῖν δύναται, ᾧ ˣτιμὴ
καὶ ʸκράτος αἰώνιον, ἀμήν.

¹⁷ Τοῖς πλουσίοις ἐν ᶻτῷ νῦν ᶻαἰῶνι ªπαράγγελλε μὴ
ᵇὑψηλοφρονεῖν, μηδὲ ᶜἠλπικέναι ἐπὶ πλούτου ᵈἀδηλότητι,
ἀλλ᾽ * ἐν τῷ θεῷ τῷ ᵉπαρέχοντι ἡμῖν πάντα ᶠπλουσίως

x in doxol., Paul, ch. i. 17 only. Rev. iv. 9. v. 13 al.
y in doxol., 1 Pet. iv. 11. v. 11. Jude 25. Rev. i. 6. v. 13.
z 2 Tim. iv. 10. Tit. ii. 12 only. see ch.

iv. 8.   a ch. i. 3 reff.   b Rom. xi. 20 only †. see Rom. xii. 16.   c ch. iv. 10 reff.
d here only †. (-λος, 1 Cor. xiv. 8. -λως, 1 Cor. ix. 26.) ἡ ἀδ. τῶν προςδοκωμένων, Polyb. xxxvi. 4. 2.
e = Acts xxviii. 2. (Col. iv. 1 mid.)   f Col. iii. 16. Tit. iii. 6. 2 Pet. i. 11 only †.

ιδεν A Did.   ανθρωπων bef ουδεις F goth.   om και F[P] n 72. 93.
116-22.   ins το bef κρατος א.
17. for αιωνι, καιρω א¹ : του νυν αιωνος D vulg Syr coptt Bas [Orig-int₁] Jer Ambrst
Pel.   υψηλα φρονειν א.   for ηλπικεναι, ελπιζειν F Damasc.   πλουτω D¹
73.   * ἐπί (as above) AD¹F[P]א 17 [47] 67² Orig-mss Chr Thl : εν D³KL rel
Orig Thdrt Damasc.   om τω (bef θεω) D¹Fא Orig-mss Thl : ins AD³KL[P] rel
Orig.   rec aft θεω add τω ζωντι (see ch iv. 10), with D(om τω D¹) KL rel latt(inclg
vulg-ed fuld-vict) syrr Orig Chr₁ Thdrt lat-ff₅ : om AF[P]א 17 [47] 67² am(with
fuld¹ demid tol harl) coptt æth arm Orig-mss Bas Jer₂.   ins τα bef παντα A m 17
Bas Chr.   rec πλουσιως bef παντα,.with rel : om παντα F : txt ADKL[P]א m 17
[47] latt syrr coptt [arm] Orig Bas Antch Chr Thdrt Thl Damasc Œc Pel.

ἐκ θελήματος ἄλλου ταύτην ἔχει, καθάπερ
οἱ λοιποὶ πάντες ἀθάνατοι, ἀλλ᾽ ἐκ τῆς
οἰκείας οὐσίας.   Bengel remarks : 'Ad-
jectivum immortalis non exstat in N. T.
sed ἄφθαρτος, incorruptibilis : neque ἀθάνατος aut ἀθανασία habent LXX. Utrumque habet Sapientiæ liber qui semper
Græcus fuit'), dwelling in light unapproachable (ἄλλο τὸ φῶς αὐτὸς καὶ ἄλλο
ὃ οἰκεῖ· οὐκοῦν καὶ τόπῳ ἐμπεριείληπται;
ἄπαγε· οὐχ ἵνα τοῦτο νοήσωμεν, ἀλλ᾽
ἵνα τὸ ἀκατάληπτον τῆς θείας φύσεως
παραστήσῃ, φῶς οἰκεῖν αὐτὸν εἶπεν ἀπρός-
ιτον, οὕτω θεολογήσας ὡς ἦν αὐτῷ δυνατόν.
Chrys.), whom no one of men (ever) saw,
nor can see (the Commentators quote
Theophilus ad Autol., i. 5, p. 341 : εἰ
τῷ ἡλίῳ ἐλαχίστῳ ὄντι στοιχείῳ οὐ
δύναται ἄνθρωπος ἀτενίσαι διὰ τὴν ὑπερβάλλουσαν θέρμην καὶ δύναμιν, πῶς οὐχὶ
μᾶλλον τῇ τοῦ θεοῦ δόξῃ ἀνεκφράστῳ οὔσῃ
ἄνθρωπος θνητὸς οὐ δύναται ἀντωπῆσαι;
These words, as compared with John i.
18, seem to prove decisively that the whole
description applies to the Father, not to
the Son), to whom be honour and power
everlasting, Amen (see ch. i. 17, where a
similar ascription occurs).   Some of the
Commentators (Mack, Schleierm.) think
that verses 15, 16 are taken from an ecclesiastical hymn : and Mack has even arranged it metrically. See ch. iii. 16,
2 Tim. ii. 11 ff., notes.
17—19.] Precepts for the rich. Not a
supplement to the Epistle, as commonly
regarded : the occurrence of a doxology is
no sufficient ground for supposing that
the Apostle intended to close with it : cf.
ch. i. 17. Rather, the subject is resumed

from verses 6—10. We may perhaps make
an inference as to the late date of the
Epistle, from the existence of wealthy
members in the Ephesian church.
17.] To those who are rich in this present world (no τοῖς before ἐν τῷ νῦν αἰ.,
because πλούσιοι-ἐν-τῷ-νῦν-αἰῶνι is the
designation of the persons spoken of.
Had there been a distinction such as
Chrys. brings out,—εἰσὶ γὰρ καὶ ἄλλοι
πλούσιοι ἐν τῷ μέλλοντι (τῷ δὲ διορισμῷ
ἀναγκαίως ἐχρήσατο· εἰσὶ γὰρ πλούσιοι
καὶ τοῦ μέλλοντος αἰῶνος, οἱ τὸν μόνιμον
πλοῦτον καὶ διαρκῆ κεκτημένοι. Thdrt.),
the τοῖς would have been more naturally
prefixed. Such a distinction would besides have been improbable, as drawing a
line between the two characters, which it
is the object of the exhortation to keep
united in the same persons. See the distinction in Luke xii. 21) give in charge
not to be high-minded (ταῦτα παραινεῖ,
εἰδὼς ὅτι οὐδὲν οὕτω τίκτει τῦφον, καὶ
ἀπόνοιαν, καὶ ἀλαζονείαν, ὡς χρήματα,
Chrys.), nor to place their hope (i. e. to
have hoped, and continue to be hoping :
see on ch. iv. 10) on the uncertainty
(reff.) of riches (not — τῷ πλούτῳ τῷ
ἀδήλῳ, but far more forcible, hyper-
bolically representing the hope as reposed
on the very quality in riches which least
justified it. On the sense, Thdrt. says,
ἄδηλον γὰρ τοῦ πλούτου τὸ κτῆμα· νῦν
μὲν γὰρ παρὰ τούτῳ φοιτᾷ, νῦν δὲ πρὸς
ἐκεῖνον μεταβαίνει· καὶ πολλοὺς ἔχων
κυρίους, οὐδενός ἐστι κτῆμα. An uncertain
author, in the Anthology, having com-
plained of the fickleness of Fortune, says,
μισῶ τὰ πάντα τῆς ἀδηλίας χάριν), but

g Heb. xi. 25 only †.
(-λαύειν, Prov. vii. 18. Wisd. ii. 6.)
h Acts xiv. 17 only †.
i = Luke xii. 21. Rom. x. 12.
j Eph. ii. 4. ii. 41. 1. vi. 1.

εἰς g ἀπόλαυσιν, 18 h ἀγαθοεργεῖν, i πλουτεῖν j ἐν k ἔργοις
k καλοῖς, l εὐμεταδότους εἶναι, m κοινωνικούς, 19 n ἀποθησαυρίζοντας ἑαυτοῖς o θεμέλιον καλὸν p εἰς τὸ p μέλλον, ἵνα
q ἐπιλάβωνται τῆς r ὄντως ζωῆς. 20 Ὦ Τιμόθεε, τὴν

ADFKL
Pℵ a b c
d e f g h
k l m n o
17. 47

k ch. iii. 1 reff. l here only †. m here only †. Demosth. 182. 17. = Polyb.
n here only †. Sir. iii. 4. see Matt. vi. 19, 20. Tobit iv. 9. o see 1 Cor. iii. 11. Heb.
p Luke xiii. 9 only. q ver. 12. r ch. v. 3 reff.

18. πλουτιζειν F.
19. αποθησαυριζειν D vulg Ambrst-ed.   τον μελλοντα F.   rec (for οντως)
αιωνιου, with D³KL[P] rel mar Chr : txt AD¹Fℵ 17 latt syrr coptt æth arm Constt
Clem Orig Bas Nyss Naz Thdrt Euthal Œc Ambrst Aug Jer Pel, αιωνιου οντως m.

in (see var. readd. : no distinction of meaning need be sought between ἐπί and ἐν : see Winer, ch. 6, § 50. 2) **God** ('transfertur Ejus officium ad divitias, si spes in iis locatur,' Calv.), **who affordeth us all things richly** (πλοῦτος of a nobler and higher kind is included in His bounty: that βούλεσθαι πλουτεῖν which is a bane and snare in its worldly sense, will be far better attained in the course of his abundant mercies to them who hope in Him. And even those who would be wealthy without Him are in fact only made rich by His bountiful hand : 'alias nemo foret πλούσιος,' Beng.) **for enjoyment** (for the purpose of enjoying : cf. ch. iv. 3, εἰς μετάλημψιν. The term ἀπό-λαυσις, the reaping enjoyment from, and so having done with (cf. ἀπέχω &c.), forms a contrast to ἠλπικέναι ἐπί, in which riches are not the subject of ἀπόλαυσις, but are looked on as a reliance for the future) ;—**to do good** (ref. : 'to practise benevolence,' as Conyb.), **to be rich in good works** (honourable deeds : ἀγαθός is good towards another, καλός good in itself, noble, honourable),—**to be free-givers, ready-contributors** (Chrys. takes κοινω-νικούς for affable, communicative,—ὁμιλη-τικούς, φησι, προσηνεῖς : so also Thdrt. : τὸ μὲν (εὐμεταδ.) ἐστι τῆς τῶν χρημάτων χορηγίας· τὸ δὲ τῆς τῶν ἠθῶν μετριότη-τος· κοινωνικοὺς γὰρ καλεῖν εἰώθαμεν τοὺς ἄτυφον ἦθος ἔχοντας. But it seems much better to take it of communicating their substance, as the verb in Gal. vi. 6, and κοινωνία in Heb. xiii. 16, where it is coupled with εὐποιΐα), (**by this means**) ('therefrom,' implied in the ἀπό) **laying up for themselves as a treasure** (hoarding up, not uncertain treasure for the life here, but a substantial pledge of that real and endless life which shall be hereafter. So that there is no difficulty whatever in the conjunction of ἀποθησαυρίζοντας θεμέ-λιον, and no need for the conjectures κει-μήλιον (Le Clerc) or θέμα λίαν καλόν (! Lamb-Bos). For the expression, cf.

ch. iii. 13) **a good foundation** (reff., and Luke vi. 48) **for the future** (belongs to ἀποθησαυρίζοντας), **that** (in order that, as always : not the mere *result* of the preceding : 'as it were,' says De W., 'setting foot on this foundation,' or firm ground) **they may lay hold of** (ver. 12) **that which is really** (reff.) **life** (not merely the goods of this life, but the possession and substance of that other, which, as full of joy and everlasting, is the only true life).

20, 21.] CONCLUDING EXHORTATION TO TIMOTHEUS. **O Timotheus** (this personal address comes with great weight and solemnity : 'appellat familiariter ut filium, cum gravitate et amore,' Beng.), **keep the deposit** (entrusted to thee : reff. 2 Tim. (μὴ μειώσῃς· οὐκ ἔστι σά· τὰ ἀλλότρια ἐνεπιστεύθης· μηδὲν ἐλαττώσῃς, Chrys. I cannot forbear transcribing from Mack and Wiesinger the very beautiful comment of Vincentius Lirinensis in his Commonito-rium (A.D. 434), § 22 f. p. 667 f. : "O Timothee, inquit, depositum custodi, devitans profanas vocum novitates (reading καινοφω-νίας—see var. readd.). 'O!' exclamatio ista et præscientiæ est pariter et caritatis. Prævidebat enim futuros, quos etiam prædolebat, errores. Quid est 'depositum custodi?' Custodi, inquit, propter fures, propter inimicos, ne dormientibus hominibus superseminent zizania super illud tritici bonum semen quod seminaverat filius hominis in agro suo. 'Depositum,' inquit, 'custodi.' Quid est 'depositum?' id est quod tibi creditum est, non quod a te inventum : quod accepisti, non quod excogitasti : rem non ingenii sed doctrinæ, non usurpationis privatæ sed publicæ traditionis : rem ad te perductam, non a te prolatam, in qua non auctor debes esse sed custos, non institutor sed sectator, non ducens sed sequens. 'Depositum,' inquit, 'custodi :' catholicæ fidei talentum inviolatum illibatumque conserva. Quod tibi creditum est, hoc penes te maneat, hoc a te tradatur. Aurum accepisti, aurum redde. Nolo mihi pro aliis alia sub-

^s παραθήκην φύλαξον, ^t ἐκτρεπόμενος τὰς ^u βεβήλους
^v κενοφωνίας καὶ ^w ἀντιθέσεις τῆς ^w ψευδωνύμου ^x γνώσεως,
²¹ ἣν ^y τινὲς ^z ἐπαγγελλόμενοι ^a περὶ τὴν πίστιν ^b ἠστό-
χησαν. ²² Ἡ ^c χάρις μετὰ σοῦ.

ΠΡΟΣ ΤΙΜΟΘΕΟΝ Α.

s 2 Tim. i. 12,
14 (both
times w.
φυλάττειν)
only. Levit.
vi. 2, 4.
2 Macc. iii.
10, 15 only.
t ch. i. 6 reff.
u ch. i. 9 reff.
v 2 Tim. ii. 16
(there also w.
βεβ.) only †.

w here only †.   x see Rom. xv. 14.   1 Cor. i. 5 al.   y = ch. i. 3 reff.   z = ch. ii.
10 (Tit. i. 2 reff.) only ‡.   a so ch. i. 19. (and constr.) 2 Tim. ii. 18.   b ch. i. 6.   2 Tim.
ii. 18 only †.   c absol., Col. iv. 18 reff.

20. [om ω P.]   rec παρακαταθηκην, with b f g [Hip] Chr : txt ADFKL[P]א rel
(syr-mg-gr coptt) Clem Ign Thdrt Damasc Œc.   καινοφωνιας (*itacism*) F 73 Epiph
Bas Chr, *vocum novitates* latt Iren-int Ps-Ath-int Tert [Hil Lucif].

22. for μετα σου, μεθ' υμων (*see 2 Tim* iv. 22, *Tit* iii. 15, *where there is hardly any
variation in mss*) AF[P]א 17 g G-lat(altern) copt : txt DKL rel vss gr-lat-ff.
rec at end ins αμην, with D²KL[P]א³ rel [vss] : om AD¹Fא¹ 17 fuld¹ [arm].

SUBSCRIPTION.—rec προς τιμ. πρωτη εγραφη απο λαοδικειας, ητις εστι μητροπολις
φρυγιας της πακατιανης, with KL rel syr (καπατιανης KL e g k o) : om subscr b l m :
απο αθηνων δια τιτου του μαθητου αυτου copt : απο μακεδονιας 6 : απο Νικοπολεως 114 :
txt A(addg (qu. A² ?) [εγραφη] απο Λαοδικειας) א(adding στιχων σν) [P(adding εγρ.
απο νικοπολεως . . . .)] 17 D-lat² Syr Euthal, πρ. τιμ. α′ επληρωθη D, επληρωθη επ. πρ.
τιμ. α′ F.

jicias, nolo pro auro aut impudenter plum-
bum, aut fraudulenter æramenta supponas :
nolo auri speciem, sed naturam plane
. . . . . Sed forsitan dicit aliquis : nullusne
ergo in ecclesia Christi profectus habebitur
religionis ? Habeatur plane, et maximus
. . . . sed ita tamen, ut vere profectus sit
ille fidei, non permutatio. Siquidem ad
profectionem pertinet, ut in semetipsa una-
quæque res amplificetur, — ad permuta-
tionem vero, ut aliquid ex alio in aliud
transvertatur. Crescat igitur oportet et
multum vehementerque proficiat tam sin-
gulorum quam omnium, tam unius hominis
quam totius ecclesiæ ætatum et seculorum
gradibus, intelligentia, scientia, sapientia :
sed in suo duntaxat genere, in eodem
scilicet dogmate, eodem sensu, eademque
sententia. Imitetur animarum religio
rationem corporum, quæ licet annorum
processu numeros suos evolvant et expli-
cent, eadem tamen quæ erant permanent
. . .''), viz., the sound doctrine which thou
art to teach in thy ministry in the Lord,
cf. Col. iv. 17. This is the most probable
explanation. Some regard it as the ἐντολή above, ver. 14 : some as meaning the
grace given to him for his office, or for his
own spiritual life : but ch. i. 18, compared
with 2 Tim. ii. 2, seems to fix the meaning
as above. Herodotus has a very similar
use of the word, ix. 45, ἄνδρες Ἀθηναῖοι,
παραθήκην ὑμῖν τάδε τὰ ἔπεα τίθεμαι.
And with this the following agrees : for it
is against *false doctrine* that the Apostle
cautions him), **turning away from** (cf.
ἀποτρέπον, 2 Tim. iii. 5) **the profane**

babblings (empty discourses : so also
2 Tim. ii. 16) **and oppositions** (apparently,
dialectic antitheses and niceties of the
false teachers. The interpretations have
been very various : Chrys. says, ὁρᾷς πῶς
πάλιν κελεύει μηδὲ ὁμόσε χωρεῖν πρὸς
τοὺς τοιούτους ; ἐκτρεπόμενός, φησιν, τὰς
ἀντιθέσεις. ἆρα εἰσὶν ἀντιθέσεις, πρὸς
ἃς οὐδὲ ἀποκρίνεσθαι χρή ;—understanding by ἀντιθ., sayings of theirs opposed to
this teaching. But this can hardly be.
Grot., 'nam ipsi inter se pugnabant :' but
this is as unlikely. Pelag., Luth., al.,
understand 'disputations :' Mosheim, the
dualistic oppositions in the heretical systems : Mack, the contradictions which the
heretics try to establish between the various doctrines of orthodoxy : Baur, the
oppositions between the Gospel and the
law maintained by Marcion. On this
latter hypothesis, see Prolegomena. There
would be no objection philologically to
understanding 'propositions opposed to
thee ;' and τοὺς ἀντιδιατιθεμένους, cf. 2
Tim. ii. 25, would seem to bear out such
meaning : but seeing that it is coupled
with κενοφωνίας, it is much more probably something entirely subjective to the
ψευδώνυμος γνῶσις) **of that which is
falsely-named** (ὅταν γὰρ πίστις μὴ ᾖ,
γνῶσις οὐκ ἔστι. Chrys.) **knowledge** (the
true γνῶσις, being one of the greatest
gifts of the Spirit to the Church, was soon
counterfeited by various systems of hybrid
theology, calling themselves by this honoured name. In the Apostle's time, the
misnomer was already current : but we

are not therefore justified in assuming that it had received so definite an application, as afterwards it did to the various forms of Gnostic heresy. All that we can hence gather is, that the true spiritual γνῶσις of the Christian was already being counterfeited by persons bearing the characteristics noticed in this Epistle. Whether these were the Gnostics themselves, or their precursors, we have examined in the Prolegomena to the Pastoral Epistles),

21.] **which** (the ψευδών. γνῶσις) **some professing** (ch. ii. 10) **erred** (reff. : the indefinite past, as marking merely the event, not the abiding of these men still in the Ephesian church) **concerning the** faith. **22.**] Concluding benediction : **The grace** (of God,—ἡ χ., the grace for which we Christians look, and in which we stand) **be with thee.** On the subscription we may remark, that the notice found in A al., owes it origin probably to the notion that this was the Epistle from Laodicea mentioned Col. iv. 16. So Thl.: τίς δὲ ἦν ἡ ἀπὸ Λαοδικείας; ἡ πρὸς Τιμόθεον πρώτη· αὕτη γὰρ ἐκ Λαοδικείας ἐγράφη. The further addition in rec. al. betrays a date subsequent to the fourth century, when the province of Phrygia Pacatiana was first created. See Smith's Dict. of Geography, art. Phrygia, circa finem.

ΠΡΟΣ ΤΙΜΟΘΕΟΝ Β.

ADFKL
PℵΑbc
defgh
klmno
17.47

I. ¹ Παῦλος ἀπόστολος χριστοῦ Ἰησοῦ ᵃ διὰ θελήματος θεοῦ ᵇ κατ᾽ ᶜ ἐπαγγελίαν ᶜ ζωῆς τῆς ἐν χριστῷ
Ἰησοῦ, ² Τιμοθέῳ ἀγαπητῷ ᵈ τέκνῳ.   ᵈ χάρις, ᵈ ἔλεος,

a 1 Cor. i. 1.
2 Cor. i. 1.
-viii. 5. Eph.
i. 1. Col. i. 1
Rom. xv. 32
only. P.
b = 2 Cor. xi.
21. 1 Tim. i.

1 (reff.).   c 1 Tim. iv. 8.   d 1 Tim. i. 2 reff.

TITLE. elz π. τ. αποστ. η πρ. τ. επ. δευτερα: Steph η πρ. τ. επ. δευτ.: του αγ. απ.
π. επ. β′ πρ. τιμ. L: [π. επ. πρ. τιμ. β′ P:] txt AKℵ h k m n o 17, and (prefg αρχεται)
DF.

CHAP. I. 1. rec ιησ. bef χρ., with AL rel Syr goth [æth arm]: txt DFK[P]ℵ d e g n
17 [47] demid syr coptt Damasc Ambrst Cassiod.   επαγγελιας ℵ o(omg ζωης).

CHAP. I. 1, 2.] ADDRESS AND GREET-
ING.   1. διὰ θελ. θεοῦ] Cf. reff.
κατ᾽ ἐπαγγ. ζωῆς] according to (in pursuance of, with a view to the fulfilment of)
the promise (ref.) of life which is in
Christ Jesus (all this is to be taken with
ἀπόστολος, not with θελήματος.   Thdrt.
explains it well, ὥστε με τὴν ἐπαγγελθεῖσαν
αἰώνιον ζωὴν τοῖς ἀνθρώποις κηρύξαι.
Chrysostom sees, in this mention of the
promise of life in Christ, a consolation to
Timotheus under present troubles: ἀπὸ
τῆς ἀρχῆς ποιεῖται τὴν παραμυθίαν — εἰ
ἐπαγγελία ἐστί, μὴ ζήτει αὐτὴν ἐνταῦθα·
ἐλπὶς γὰρ βλεπομένη οὐκ ἔστιν ἐλπίς.
And this idea seems to be borne out by the
strain of the subsequent portion of the
Epistle, which is throughout one of confirmation and encouragement.   So Bengel,
—"nervus ad Timotheum hortandum, ver.
10, cap. ii. 8").   2. ἀγαπητῷ τέκνῳ]
"Can it be accidental," says Mack, "that
instead of γνησίῳ τέκν., as Timotheus is
called in the first Epistle, i. 2, and Titus
i. 4,—here we have ἀγαπητῷ? Or may a
reason for the change be found in this, that
it now behoved Timotheus to stir up afresh
the faith and the grace in him, before he
could again be worthy of the name γνησίον
τέκνον in its full sense?"   This may be

too much pressed: but certainly there is
throughout this Epistle an altered tone
with regard to Timotheus—more of mere
love, and less of confidence, than in the
former: and this would naturally shew
itself even in passing words of address.
When Bengel says, "in Ep. i., scripserat,
genuino: id compensatur hic versu 5," he
certainly misses the delicate sense of ver.
5: see below.   To find in ἀγαπητῷ more
confidence, as Heyd. (and Chrys., maintaining that οἱ κατὰ πίστιν ὅταν ὦσιν
ἀγαπητοί, δι᾽ οὐδὲν ἕτερόν εἰσιν, ἀλλ᾽ ἢ
δι᾽ ἀρετήν), can hardly be correct: the
expression of feeling is different in kind,
not comparable in degree: suiting an
Epistle of warm affection and somewhat
saddened reminding, rather than one of
rising hope and confidence.   I regret to
be, on this point, at issue throughout
this second Epistle, with my friend Bishop
Ellicott, who seems to me too anxious to
rescue the character of Timotheus from
the slightest imputation of weakness:
thereby marring the delicate texture of
many of St. Paul's characteristic periods,
in which tender reproof, vigorous re-
assurance, and fervent affection are ex-
quisitely intermingled.   See reff.
and notes.

e Gal. i. 1 reff.
f = Luke xvii.
9. 1 Tim. i.
12. Heb. xii.
28 only.
L.P.H.
2 Macc. iii.
33.
g Matt. iv. 10
(from Deut.
vi. 13. x. 20).
Acts vii. 7.
Rom. i. 9 al.
h 1 Tim. v. 4
only †. Sir.
viii. 4.
2 Macc. viii.
19. xi. 25 only.
2 only†. (-ως, Rom. i. 9.)
m Paul, Rom. x. 1. 2 Cor. i. 11 al9. 2 Chron. vi. 19, &c.
14 al. freq.
s = Heb. xi. 29. 2 Pet. i. 9.

ᵈ εἰρήνη ἀπὸ ᵉ θεοῦ ᵉ πατρὸς καὶ χριστοῦ Ἰησοῦ τοῦ κυρίου ἡμῶν.

3 ᶠ Χάριν ᶠ ἔχω τῷ θεῷ, ᾧ ᵍ λατρεύω ἀπὸ ʰ προγόνων ἐν ⁱ καθαρᾷ ⁱʲ συνειδήσει, ὡς ᵏ ἀδιάλειπτον ἔχω τὴν περὶ σοῦ ˡ μνείαν ἐν ταῖς ᵐ δεήσεσίν μου ⁿ νυκτὸς καὶ ⁿ ἡμέρας, 4 ᵒ ἐπιποθῶν σε ἰδεῖν, ᵖ μεμνημένος σου τῶν δακρύων, ἵνα χαρᾶς q πληρωθῶ, 5 ʳ ὑπόμνησιν ˢ λαβὼν τῆς ἐν σοὶ

C χαριν
...
ACDFK
LPN a b
c d e f g
h k l m n
o 17. 47

i 1 Tim. iii. 9 only. see Heb. ix. 14.　　j 1 Tim. i. 5 reff.　　k Rom. ix.
l μ. ἔχειν, 1 Thess. iii. 6. elsw., as Eph. i. 16 reff., w. ποιεῖσθαι.
n 1 Tim. v. 5 reff.　　o 1 Thess. iii. 6 reff.
q = Luke ii. 40. Acts iii. 28. xiii. 52. Paul, Rom. xv. 13,
r 2 Pet. i. 13. iii. 1 only †. Wisd. xvi. 11. 2 Macc. vi. 17 only. (-μιμνήσκειν, ch. ii. 14.)
2 Pet. i. 9.

2. for χρ. ιησ., κυριου ιησ. χρ. (retaining του κυ. below) א¹ k m [17. (P def.)]

3. aft θεω ins μου D¹ 17 sah goth Orig Ambrst Pel Cassiod: om ACD³FKLא rel vulg(with am fuld, agst demid hal) syrr copt Chr Thdrt. [P def., but there is space enough.]　λατρευων C¹.

4. επιποθω F copt [arm]. (G-lat has both.)

5. rec λαμβανων, with DKLא³ rel Chr Thdrt Damasc Thl Œc: txt (see note) ACFא¹ 17. [P def.]

3—5.] *Thankful declaration of love and anxiety to see him.* **I give thanks** (reff.) **to God whom I serve from my ancestors** (i. e. as Bengel, "majores, innuit, non Abrahamum &c., quos patres, nunquam προγόνους appellat: sed progenitores proximos." The reason for the profession may perhaps be found in the following mention of the faith of the mother and grandmother of Timotheus, which was already in the Apostle's mind. We may observe that he does not, as De W. charges him, place on the same ground the Jewish and Christian service of God: but simply asserts what he had before asserted, Acts xxiii. 1, xxiv. 14,—that his own service of God had been at all times conscientious and singlehearted, and that he had received it as such from his forefathers) **in pure conscience, how** (not '*that*;' as Chrys. (εὐχαριστῶ τῷ θεῷ ὅτι μέμνημαί σου, φησίν, οὕτω σε φιλῶ), Luth., E. V., al.,—nor '*when*,' as Calv. ('quoties tui recordor in precibus meis, id enim facio continenter, simul etiam de te gratias ago'],—nor '*since*,' '*seeing that*,' as Heyd., Flatt, al., —nor '*as*,' as De W., Huther, Ellic., al.: but as in the parallel, Rom. i. 9, the construction is a mixed one between μάρτυς μου ἐστὶν ὁ θεός, ὡς ἀδιάλ. ἔχω, and εὐχαριστῶ ἀδιάλειπτον ἔχων: and hence the meaning 'how' must be retained, and with it the involution of construction, which is characteristic of one with whom expressions like these had now become fixed in diction, and liable to be combined without regard to strict logical accuracy) **unceasing I make my mention** (not 'mention' only, on account of the article, which specifies the μνεία as a thing constantly happening) **concerning thee** (so Herod. i. 36, παιδὸς μὲν περὶ τοῦ ἐμοῦ μὴ μνήσθητε ἔτι:—Xen. Cyr. i. 6. 12, οὐδ' ὁτιοῦν περὶ τούτου ἐπεμνήσθη:—Plato, Laches, p. 181 a, ὅδ' ἐστὶ Σωκράτης, περὶ οὗ ἑκάστοτε μέμνησθε: and Heb. xi. 22) **in my prayers, night and day** (see Luke ii. 37 note: belongs to ἀδιάλειπτ. ἔχω κ.τ.λ., not to δεήσεσιν, much less, as Mack, al., to the following, for which 1 Thess. ii. 9, iii. 10 are no precedents, as here such an arrangement would deprive the participle ἐπιποθῶν of its place of emphasis); **longing** (ἐπί, as the prep. in composition so often, seems to mark not intensification, but direction: see Ellic.'s note). **to see thee, remembering thy tears** (shed at our parting), **that I may be filled with joy** (the expressions in this verse are assurances of the most fervent personal love, strengthened by the proof of such love having been reciprocal. From these he gently and most skilfully passes to a tone of fatherly exhortation and reproof): **having remembrance** (the aor. participle may be taken either (1) as dependent on ἵνα, and the condition of πληρωθῶ,—or, which is more probable, (2) as in apposition with ἐπιποθῶν and μεμνημένος) **of the unfeigned faith** (which was) (Ellic. objects to '*was*,' and would render '*is*;' see note above on ver. 2. But I do not see how St. Paul could be said ὑπόμνησιν λαβεῖν of a thing then present. Surely the remembrance is of the time when they parted, and the faith then existing. But the sentence does not require any temporal filling up—'the unfeigned faith

^tἀνυποκρίτου πίστεως, ^uἥτις ^vἐνώκησεν πρῶτον ἐν τῇ
^wμάμμῃ σου Λωΐδι καὶ τῇ μητρί σου Εὐνίκῃ, ^xπέπεισμαι
δὲ ὅτι καὶ ἐν σοί. ^{6 y}δι᾽ ἣν ^yαἰτίαν ^zἀναμιμνήσκω σε
^aἀναζωπυρεῖν τὸ ^bχάρισμα τοῦ θεοῦ, ὅ ἐστιν ἐν σοὶ διὰ

t 1 Tim. i. 5 reff.
u Acts x. 41, 47 al. fr. Paul, passim.
v Rom. viii. 11. 2 Cor. vi. 16. Col. iii. 16. ver. 14 only. Lev. xxvi. 32.
y Paul, ver. 12. Tit.
z Mark xi.

w here only †.   x constr., Rom. viii. 38. xiv. 14. xv. 14. ver. 12.   y Paul, ver. 12. Tit.
i. 13 only. Luke viii. 47. Acts x. 21. xxii. 24. xxiii. 28. Heb. ii. 11 only. L.P.H.   z Mark xi.
21. xiv. 72. 1 Cor. iv. 17. 2 Cor. vii. 15.   Heb. x. 32 only. Gen. viii. 1 Ed-vat. [B def.]   (-μνησις, Luke
xxii. 19.)   a here only. LXX. intr., Gen. xlv. 27. 1 Macc. xiii. 7 only. Clem. I. ad Cor. § 27,
p. 268. Ign. Eph. § 1, p. 644.   b 1 Tim. iv. 14 (reff.).

ενοικησεν D¹ 17. [P def.]
6. for αναμ., υπομιμνησκω D.   for χαρ., θελημα ℵ¹.   for θεου, χριστου A.

in thee' is quite enough, and is necessarily thrown into the past by the ὑπόμνησιν λαβών. See more below) in thee
(there is perhaps a slight reproach in
this ὑπόμνησιν and τῆς ἐν σοί, as if it
were a thing once certain as fact, and
as matter of memory, but now only, as
below, resting on a πέπεισμαι ὅτι: and
in presence of such a possible inference,
and of ὑπόμνησιν, I have ventured therefore to render τῆς ἐν σοί, 'which was
in thee,' viz. at the time of τὰ δάκρυα,
—its present existence being only by and
by introduced as a confident hope) such
as dwelt first (before it dwelt in thee) in
thy grandmother (μάμμην τὴν τοῦ πατρὸς ἢ μητρὸς μητέρα, οὐ λέγουσιν οἱ
ἀρχαῖοι, ἀλλὰ τίτθην (l. τήθην). Phryn.,
p. 133, where see Lobeck's note. It is
thus used, as he shews, by Josephus, Plutarch, Appian, Herodian, &c., and Pollux
says (iii. 17), ἡ δὲ πατρὸς ἢ μητρὸς μήτηρ τήθη καὶ μάμμη καὶ μάμμα. But he
adduces all the stricter philologists as
agreeing with Phrynichus) Lois (not elsewhere mentioned), and thy mother Eunice
(Τιμόθεος, υἱὸς γυναικὸς Ἰουδαίας πιστῆς,
πατρὸς δὲ Ἕλληνος, Acts xvi. 1: see also
ch. iii. 15. Both these were probably converts on Paul's former visit to Lystra,
Acts xiv. 6 ff.), but (the δέ gives the
meaning 'notwithstanding appearances.'
It is entirely missed by Ellic., and not
fairly rendered in the E. V., 'and;' see
note below) I am persuaded that (supply
ἐνοικεῖ, not ἐνοικήσει, as Grot., al.) also
in thee (there is undoubtedly a want of
entire confidence here expressed; and
such a feeling will account for the mention of the faith of his mother and grandmother, to which if he wavered, he was
proving untrue. This has been felt by
several of the ancient Commentators;
e. g. Thdrt.,—τῇ μετ᾽ εὐφημίας μνήμῃ τῶν
προγόνων ὁ θεῖος ἀπόστολος κρατύνει τὴν
πίστιν ἐν τῷ μαθητῇ. οὐδὲν γὰρ οὕτως ὀνί-
νησιν ὡς οἰκεῖον παράδειγμα. καὶ ἐπειδὴ
συμβαίνει τινὰς ἐξ εὐσεβῶν γενομένους
μὴ ζηλῶσαι τὴν τῶν προγόνων εὐσέβειαν,

ἀναγκαίως ἐπήγαγε "Πέπεισμαι δὲ ὅτι
καὶ ἐν σοί." εἶτα τοῦτο αὐτὸ τῆς παραινέσεως ὑποβάθραν ποιεῖται).   6—14.]
Exhortation to Timotheus to be firm in
the faith, and not to shrink from suffering: enforced (9—11) by the glorious
character of the Gospel, and free mercy
of God in it, and (11—13) by his own
example. For which cause (reff.: viz.
because thou hast inherited, didst once
possess, and I trust still dost possess, such
unfeigned faith;—ταῦτα περὶ σου πεπεισ-
μένος, Thdrt.) I put thee in mind to stir
up (see examples in reff. and in Wetst.
The metaphorical use of the word was so
common, that there is hardly need to
recur to its literal sense. Cf. especially,
Iambl. vit. Pythagor. c. 16: ἀπεκάθαιρε
τὴν ψυχήν, καὶ ἀνεζωπύρει τὸ θεῖον ἐν
αὐτῇ. At the same time it is well to
compare, as Chrys. does, 1 Thess. v. 19,
τὸ πνεῦμα μὴ σβέννυτε. He adds, ἐν
ἡμῖν γάρ ἐστι καὶ σβέσαι καὶ ἀνάψαι
τοῦτο. ὑπὸ μὲν γὰρ ἀκηδίας καὶ ῥαθυμίας
σβέννυται, ὑπὸ δὲ νήψεως καὶ προσοχῆς
διεγείρεται) the gift of God (χάρισμα,
singular, as combining the whole of the
gifts necessary for the ministry in one
aggregate (τὴν χάριν τοῦ πνεύματος, ἣν
ἔλαβες εἰς προστασίαν τῆς ἐκκλησίας,
Chrys.): not 'the gift of the Spirit imparted to all believers:' see 1 Tim. iv. 14,
note. Of those ministerial gifts, that of
παῤῥησία would be most required in this
case, "videtur Timotheus, Paulo diu
carens, nonnihil remisisse: certe nunc ad
majora stimulatur." Bengel), which is in
thee by means of the laying on of my
hands (these words, especially when compared with 1 Tim. iv. 14, mark the sense
of χάρισμα to be as above, and not the
general gifts of the Spirit which followed
the laying on of hands after baptism.
Any apparent discrepancy with that passage, from the Apostle here speaking of
the laying on of his own hands alone,
may be removed by regarding the Apostle
as chief in the ordination, and the presbytery as his assistants, as is the case with

c = Rom. viii.
15. 2 Cor.
iv. 13. Eph.
i. 17.
d here only.
Levit. xxvi.
36 A. Ps.
liv. 4. (-λος,
Matt. viii. 26. -λιαν, John xiv. 27.)
|| Mk. Rom. i. 16. Heb. ii. 11 al. Job xxxiv. 19 Bℵ. Isa. i. 29 Aℵ1.3b only.

τῆς ᵇἐπιθέσεως τῶν ᵇχειρῶν μου. ⁷ οὐ γὰρ ἔδωκεν ἡμῖν
ὁ θεὸς ᶜπνεῦμα ᵈδειλίας, ἀλλὰ δυνάμεως καὶ ἀγάπης
καὶ ᵉσωφρονισμοῦ. ⁸ μὴ οὖν ᶠἐπαισχυνθῇς τὸ ᵍμαρτύ-

e here only †. (see note.)   f vv. 12, 18. Luke ix. 26 (bis)
g = 1 Tim. ii. 6 reff.

ACDFK
LPℵ a b
c d e f g
h k l m n
o 17. 47

Bishops at the present day. As to the διὰ τῆς ἐπιθ., we can only appeal, against the Roman-Catholic expositors, e. g. Mack, to the whole spirit of St. Paul's teaching, as declaring that by such an expression he does not mean that the inward spiritual grace is operated merely and barely by the outward visible sign,—but is only asserting, in a mode of speech common to us all, that the solemn dedication by him of Timotheus to God's work, of which the laying on of his hands was the sign and seal, did bring with it gifts and grace for that work. In this sense and in this alone, the gift came διὰ τῆς ἐπιθέσεως, that laying on being the concentrated and effective sign of the setting apart, and conveying in faith the answer, assumed by faith, to the prayers of the church. That the Apostle had *authority* thus to set apart, was necessary to the validity of the act, and thus to the reception of the grace :—but the authority did not *convey* the grace. I may just add that the 'indelibility of orders,' which Mack infers from this passage, is simply and directly refuted by it. If the χάρισμα τὸ ἐν σοί required ἀναζωπυρεῖσθαι, if, as Chrys. above, ἐν ἡμῖν ἐστι καὶ σβέσαι καὶ ἀνάψαι τοῦτο,—then plainly it is *not* indelible).

7.] **For** (q. d., 'and there is reason for my thus exhorting thee, seeing that thou hast shewn a spirit inconsistent with the character of that χάρισμα.' The particle is passed over by Ellicott) **God did not give** (when we were admitted to the ministry: not '*has not given*' (δέδωκεν)) **us the Spirit** (q. d., 'the spirit which He gave us was not:' see Rom. viii. 15 and note. The usage of πνεῦμα without the art. in the sense of the spirit of man dwelt in by the Spirit of God, and as the Spirit of God working in the spirit of man, as e. g. continually in Rom. viii. (vv. 4, 5, 9 bis, 13, 14), in 1 Cor. ii. 4; cf. 1 Cor. vi. 17, forbids our rendering πνεῦμα '*a spirit*' (subjective), as Conyb. al.) **of cowardice** (the coincidence in sound with the πνεῦμα δουλείας of Rom. viii. 15, is remarkable, and the most decisive of all testimonies against De Wette's unworthy and preposterous idea that this passage is an imitation from that. Rather I should account the circumstance a fine and deep indication of genuineness :—the habitual asser-

tion of the one axiom having made even its sound and chime so familiar to the Apostle's ear, that he selects, when enouncing another like it, a word almost reproducing that other. There is also doubtless a touch of severity in this δειλίας, putting before Timotheus his timidity in such a light as to shame him : οὐχ ἵνα δειλιῶμεν τοὺς ὑπὲρ τῆς εὐσεβίας κινδύνους, Thdrt.), **but** (the spirit) **of power** (as opposed to the weakness implied in δειλία), **and love** (as opposed to that false compliance with men, which shrinks from bold rebuke :—that lofty self-abandonment of love for others, which will even sacrifice repute, and security, and all that belongs to self, in the noble struggle to do men good), **and correction** (the original meaning of σωφρονισμός, '*admonition* ✳ *of others that they may become* σωφρ.,' τὸ σωφρονίζειν τινά, cf. Tit. ii. 4,—must be retained, as necessary both on account of that usage of the verb, and on account of the context. It is this bearing bold testimony before others, from which Timotheus appears to have shrunk: cf. μὴ οὖν ἐπαισχυνθῇς τὸ μαρτύριον, ver. 8. It also suits the construction of the other two genitives (against Huther), which both express *that which the Spirit inspires a man with*. For the meaning itself, cf. Palm and Rost's Lex. We have examples of it in Hippodamus (Stob. 43. 93, p. 250),—τοὶ μὲν νέοι δέονται σωφρονισμῶ καὶ καταρτύσιος : Plut. Cat. maj. 5,—ἐπὶ διορθώσει καὶ σωφρονισμῷ τῶν ἄλλων : Appian, de rebus Punicis viii. 65, —εἰσὶ γὰρ οἳ καὶ τόδε νομίζουσιν, αὐτὸν ἐς 'Ρωμαίων σωφρονισμὸν ἐθελῆσαι γείτονα καὶ ἀντίπαλον αὑτοῖς φόβον ἐς ἀεὶ καταλιπεῖν. The word in after times became a common one for *discipline* or *ecclesiastical correction*: see examples under σωφρονίζω and -ισμός in Suicer. Some, retaining this proper meaning, understand by it that the Spirit σωφρονίζει ἡμᾶς : so (alt.) Chrys., Thl. (ἢ ἵνα σωφρονισμὸν ἔχωμεν τὸ πνεῦμα) ; but this does not suit the construction of the other genitives, in which it is not power over us, or love towards us, that is meant, but power and love *wrought in us* as towards others, and opposed to cowardice and fear of man. Thl. gives as another alternative the right meaning—ἢ ἵνα καὶ ἄλλοις ὦμεν σωφρο-

ριον τοῦ κυρίου ἡμῶν μηδὲ ἐμὲ τὸν ʰ δέσμιον αὐτοῦ, ἀλλὰ ﹐ ᶦ συγκακοπάθησον τῷ ʲ εὐαγγελίῳ κατὰ ᵏ δύναμιν θεοῦ ⁹ τοῦ ˡ σώσαντος ἡμᾶς καὶ ᵐⁿ καλέσαντος ⁿᵒ κλήσει ἁγίᾳ,

h = (Paul) Eph. iii. 1. iv. 1.
Philem. 1, 9.
i ch. ii. 3 only†.
(κακοπαθ., ch. ii. 9.)
j dat., Phil. i. 27.
m = Gal.

k = 2 Cor. viii. 3. Eph. iii. 20. Heb. vii. 16.
i. 6 reff.   n 1 Cor. vii. 20. Eph. iv. 1.
6. Judith xii. 10 A (ℵ def.) only.

l Tit. iii. 5. see 1 Tim. i. 1 reff.
o Eph. i. 18. Phil. iii. 14. Jer. xxxviii. (xxxi.)

8. om ημων ℵ¹(ins ℵ-corr¹) [add ιησ. χρ. 47 syr-w-ast].   ins του bef θεου D¹ 17.

νισταὶ καὶ παιδευταί. The making σω-φρονισμός = σωφροσύνη, as E. V. and many Commentators, is surely not allowable, though Chrys. puts it doubtfully as an alternative. The only way in which it can come virtually to that, is by supposing the σωφρονισμός to be exercised *by our-selves over ourselves*, as Thdrt.: ἵνα σω-φρονίσωμεν τῶν ἐν ἡμῖν κινουμένων παθη-μάτων τὴν ἀταξίαν. But this does not seem to me to suit the context so well as the meaning given above. **8.] Be not then** (seeing that God gave us such a Spirit, not the other) **ashamed of** (for construction see reff. I cannot see, with Ellic., that the aor. subjunc. with μή, 'ne te pudeat unquam,' as Leo, implies in matter of fact that "Timothy had as yet evinced no such feeling." Surely, grant-ing that such is the primary construc-tional inference from the words, it would be just in keeping with the delicate tact of the Apostle, to use such form of admo-nition, when in fact the blame had been already partly incurred. See note on ver. 1) **the testimony of our Lord** (i. e. the testimony which thou art to give concern-ing our Lord, gen. objective: not '*the testimony which He bore*,' gen. subjective, as Corn.-a-lap., al.,—nor, as Chrys. (appa-rently), '*the martyrdom of our Lord*,' nor must we, with Mack, lay stress on κυρίου, and understand the μαρτύριον to be especially this, that Jesus *is the Lord*. The ἡμῶν is added, hardly for the reason Bengel gives, 'hunc opponit Cæsari, quem sui sic appellabant,' which would hardly have been thus expressed, requiring more prominence to be given to ἡμῶν,—but because, being about to introduce *himself*, he binds by this word Timotheus and himself together), **nor of me His prisoner** (I would hardly say, with De W., Huther, al., that this refers only to the services which the Apostle expected from Timo-theus in coming to him at Rome: such thought may have been in his mind, and may have mingled with his motive in making the exhortation: but I believe the main reference to be to his duty as up-holding St. Paul and his teaching in the face of personal danger and persecution. It is impossible to deny that the above

personal reference does enter again and again: but I cannot believe it to be more than secondary. On the expression, τὸν δέσμιον αὐτοῦ, see Eph. iii. 1 note: the gen. implies not possession, but the reason for which he was imprisoned, cf. Philem. 13, δεσμοὶ τοῦ εὐαγγελίου), **but suffer hardship with me for the Gospel** (this is the meaning (ref.), and not '*suffer hard-ship together with the Gospel*,' as Thdrt. (τῶν κηρύκων τὸ πάθος τοῦ εὐαγγελίου προσηγόρευσε πάθος), Calv. (?), Grot. ('προσωποποιεῖ evangelium, eique sensum tribuit, quomodo alibi legi, morti, pec-cato'): for St. Paul, speaking of his own bonds, ch. ii. 9, says, ὁ λόγος τοῦ θεοῦ οὐ δέδεται. This συγκακοπάθησον extends the sphere of his fellow-suffering with the Apostle beyond his mere visiting Rome) **according to the power of God** (*what* power? that which God has manifested in our salvation, as described below (gen. subj.), or that which God imparts to us (gen. obj.),—*God's power*, or *the power which we get from God*? On all grounds, the former seems to me the juster and worthier sense: the former, as implying indeed the latter *à fortiori*—that God, who by his strong hand and mighty arm has done all this for us, will help us through all trouble incurred for Him. Chrys. gives this meaning very finely: ἐπεὶ φορτικὸν ἦν τὸ εἰπεῖν, κακοπάθησον, πάλιν αὐτὸν παραμυθεῖται λέγων, οὐ κατὰ τὰ ἔργα ἡμῶν τουτέστι, μὴ τῇ δυνάμει λογίζου τῇ σῇ, ἀλλὰ τῇ τοῦ θεοῦ ταῦτα φέρειν. σὸν μὲν γὰρ τὸ ἐλέσθαι καὶ προ-θυμηθῆναι, θεοῦ δὲ τὸ κουφίσαι καὶ παῦσαι. εἶτα καὶ τῆς δυνάμεως αὐτοῦ δείκνυσι τὰ τεκμήρια. πῶς ἐσώθης ἐννόει, πῶς ἐκλήθης. ὥσπερ φησὶν ἀλλαχοῦ, κατὰ τὴν ἐνέργειαν αὐτοῦ τὴν ἐνεργουμένην ἐν ἡμῖν. οὕτω τοῦ ποιῆσαι τὸν οὐρανὸν μείζων δύναμις αὕτη ἦν, τὸ πεῖσαι τὴν οἰκουμένην), **who saved us** (all believers: there is no reason for limiting this ἡμᾶς to Paul and Timotheus. It is painful to see such Commentators as De Wette so blinded by a preconceived notion of the spuriousness of the Epistle, as to call this which follows 'eine ganz allge-meine überflüssige Erinnerung an die christlichen Heilsthatsachen.' I need hardly

οὐ [p] κατὰ τὰ ἔργα ἡμῶν, ἀλλὰ [q] κατὰ ἰδίαν [q] πρόθεσιν
καὶ [r] χάριν τὴν [r] δοθεῖσαν ἡμῖν ἐν χριστῷ Ἰησοῦ [s] πρὸ
[t] χρόνων [t] αἰωνίων, 10 [u] φανερωθεῖσαν δὲ νῦν διὰ τῆς [v] ἐπιφανείας τοῦ σωτῆρος ἡμῶν Ἰησοῦ χριστοῦ, [w] καταρ-
γήσαντος μὲν τὸν θάνατον, [x] φωτίσαντος δὲ ζωὴν καὶ

ACDFK LPℵ a b c d e f g h k l m n o 17. 47

p Rom. ii. 6 al. fr. Ps. xxvii. 4.
q Rom. viii. 28. Eph. i. 11 (reff.). iii. 11.
r Gal. ii. 9 reff.
s = 2 Cor. xii. 2. Tit. i. 2. John xii. 1. Amos i. 1. iv. 7.
t Rom. xvi. 25. Tit. i. 2 only. see Gen. ix. 12.
u = Col. i. 26 reff.
v 2 Thess. ii. 8. 1 Tim. vi. 14. ch. iv. 1, 8. Tit. ii. 13 only. P. 2 Kings vii. 23.
w = 2 Thess. ii. 8 reff. (Gal. iii. 17 reff.)
x = 1 Cor. iv. 5 only. Neh. ix. 12, 19. Jos. Antt. viii. 5. 3. trans., John i. 9. Rev. xxi. 3. intr., Rev. xxii. 5.

9. (**κατα** [2nd], so AC[P]ℵ b k 17 : καθ' F.) αιωνιαν ℵ^1[: προ χρ. αι. bef εν χρ. ιησ. P : om εν χρ. ιησ. h].

10. φανερωθεντος K [-θησαν 47]. επιφανιας CD^{1}F. χρ. bef ιησ. AD^{1}ℵ^1 sah : txt CD^{3}FKL[P]ℵ^3(appy) rel vulg syrr copt goth [æth arm] Orig lat-ff. [add του D. ins την bef ζωην D^1 : νυν o.]

say to the reader who has been hitherto following the course and spirit of the passage, that it is in the strictest coherence, as indeed is shewn by Chrys. above. 'Be not cowardly nor ashamed of the Gospel, but join me in endurance on its behalf, according to God's power, who has given such proofs of that power and of its exercise towards us, in saving us,—calling us in Christ,—destroying death—&c., of which endurance I am an example (11—13)—which example do thou follow' (13, 14)), **and called us** (this, as indeed the whole context, shews that it is the Father who is spoken of: see note on Gal. i. 6), **with an holy** (*τουτέστιν, ἁγίους ἐξειργάσατο ἁμαρτωλοὺς ὄντας καὶ ἐχθρούς*, Chrys. **κλῆσις** expressing the *state*, rather than merely the summoning into it (as does '*vocation*' also), ἁγία is its quality) **calling** (see Eph. iv. 1; i. 18: Rom. viii. 28—30, and notes), **not according to** (after the measure of, in accordance with) **our works: but according to** (after the measure of, in pursuance of) **his own purpose** (*τουτέστιν οὐδενὸς ἀναγκάζοντος, οὐδενὸς συμβουλεύοντος, ἀλλ' ἐξ ἰδίας προθέσεως, οἴκοθεν ἐκ τῆς ἀγαθότητος αὐτοῦ ὁρμώμενος*, Chrys. *οὐκ εἰς τὸν ἡμέτερον ἀποβλέψας βίον, ἀλλὰ διὰ μόνην φιλανθρωπίαν*, Thdrt. "Originem tam vocationis nostræ quam totius salutis designat: non enim erant nobis opera quibus Deum præveniremus: sed totum a gratuito ejus proposito et electione pendet." Calv.), **and** (according to) **the grace which was given to us** (this expression, which properly belongs only to an *actual imparting*, is used, because, as De W., that which God determines in Eternity, is as good as already accomplished in time. No weakening of *δοθεῖσαν* into *destinatam* must be thought of) **in Christ Jesus** (as its element and condition, see Eph. i. 4; iii. 11) **before the periods of ages** (see reff.; *τουτέστιν, ἀνάρχως*, Chrys. It is hardly possible in the presence of Scripture analogy to take the expression *πρὸ χρόνων αἰωνίων* as 'meaning (? Conyb.) the Jewish dispensation:' still less, as Dr. Burton, that 'the scheme of redemption was arranged by God immediately after the fall, before any ages or dispensations.' Even Calvin's interpretation, 'perpetuam annorum seriem a mundo condito,' fails to reach the full meaning. In the parallel, Rom. xvi. 25, the mystery of redemption is described as having been *χρόνοις αἰωνίοις σεσιγημένον*,—which obviously includes ages previous to the *καταβολὴ κόσμου* as well as after it;—see Eph. iii. 11, compared with i. 4: 1 Cor. ii. 7), **but** (contrast to the concealment from eternity in the manifestation in time) **manifested now** (*νυνὶ τοῖς προορισθεῖσι τὸ πέρας ἐπέθηκε*, Thdrt. See Col. i. 26; Tit. i. 3) **by the appearing** (in the flesh: here only used thus, see reff.: but not referring to the birth only: 'His whole manifestation') **of our Saviour Jesus Christ, who abolished** ('*when He made of none effect*,' Ellic., objecting to my rendering, as confounding an anarthrous participle with one preceded by the article. But, *pace tanti viri*, and recognizing to the full the distinction, I must hold that the slightly ratiocinative force of the anarthrous participle is more accurately represented by "who abolished," than by introducing the temporal element contained in "when He." The bald literal rendering, '*abolishing* (not, '*having abolished*;' the aor. participles are synchronous throughout) *as He did*,' is most nearly approached by '*who abolished*:' and it is an approximation to the sense, not grammatical purism, which must be our object) (indeed) **death** (cf. especially 1 Cor. xv. 26. By the death of Christ, Death has lost his sting, and is henceforth of no more account: consequently the mere act of natural death is evermore treated by the

ʸ ἀφθαρσίαν διὰ τοῦ εὐαγγελίου, ¹¹ ᶻ εἰς ὃ ᶻ ἐτέθην ἐγὼ
ᶻ κῆρυξ καὶ ᶻ ἀπόστολος καὶ ᶻ διδάσκαλος ᶻ ἐθνῶν· ¹² ᵃ δι'
ἣν ᵃ αἰτίαν καὶ ταῦτα πάσχω· ἀλλ' οὐκ ᵇ ἐπαισχύνομαι,
οἶδα γὰρ ᾧ ᶜ πεπίστευκα, καὶ ᵈ πέπεισμαι ὅτι ᵉ δυνατός
ἐστιν τὴν ᶠ παραθήκην μου φυλάξαι ᵍ εἰς ʰ ἐκείνην τὴν

y Rom. ii. 7.
1 Cor. xv. 42,
&c. Eph. vi.
24. P.† Wisd.
ii. 23. vi. 18,
19 only.
z 1 Tim. ii. 7
(reff.).
a ver. 6.
b ver. 8.
c w. dat.,
Acts xxvii.

25. Rom. iv. 3 (from Gen. xv. 6). x. 16. Tit. iii. 8 al. d ver. 5. e Rom. xi. 23. see Rom.
xiv. 4. 2 Cor. ix. 8. f (in N. T. always w. φυλ.) ver. 14. 1 Tim. vi. 20 only. Levit. vi. 2,
4. 2 Macc. iii. 10, 15 only. g = Eph. iv. 30. Phil. ii. 16 b. h ver. 18. 2 Thess. i.
10. ch. iv. 8.

11. om 2nd καὶ C[P] c d.   om ἐθνων Aℵ¹ 17.
12. [om 1st καὶ ℵ¹ 73(Sz).]   om μου D¹ a k.

Lord Himself and his Apostles as of no
account : cf. John xi. 26 ; Rom. viii. 2,
38 ; 1 Cor. xv. 55 ; Heb. ii. 14 : and its
actual and total abolition foretold, Rev.
xxi. 4. **θάνατον** must be kept here to its
literal sense, and its spiritual only so far
understood as involved in the other. The
delivering from the *fear of death* is manifestly not to the purpose, even did διὰ τοῦ
εὐαγγ. belong to both participles. Notice
τὸν θάνατον. As Bengel says, 'Articulus
notanter positus.' As if he had said,
'Orcum illum.' ζωήν and ἀφθαρσίαν below have no articles), **but** (contrast to the
gloom involved in θάνατον) **brought to
light** (threw light upon, see ref. 1 Cor.,
and thus made visible what was before
hidden : ἀντὶ τοῦ προμηνύσαντος, Thdrt.)
life (i. e. the new and glorious life of the
Spirit, begun here below and enduring for
ever : the only life worthy of being so
called) **and incorruptibility** (immortality
—of the new life, not merely of the risen
body : that is not in question here, but is,
though a glorious yet only a secondary
consequence of this ἀφθαρσία; see Rom.
viii. 11) **by means of the** (preaching of
the) **Gospel** (which makes these glorious
things known to men. These words are
better taken as belonging only to φωτ.
δὲ ζω. κ. ἀφθ., not to καταργ. μὲν τὸν
θάν. For this former is an absolute act of
Christ, the latter a manifestation to those
who see it), **for which** (viz. the εὐαγγέλιον,
the publication of this good news to men)
**I was appointed a herald, and an apostle,
and a teacher of the Gentiles** (see the
same expression, and note, in 1 Tim. ii. 7.
The connexion in which he here introduces
himself is noticed above, on ver. 8. It is
to bring in his own example and endurance
in sufferings, and grounds of trust, for a
pattern to Timotheus) : **on which account**
(viz. because I ἐτέθην, as above) **I also**
(besides doing the active work of such a
mission. Or καί may be taken with ταῦτα,
as Ellic.,—'even these things') **am suffering these things** (viz. the things implied

in τὸν δέσμιον αὐτοῦ, ver. 8, and further
specified by way of explanation and encouragement to Timotheus below, ver.
15) : **but I am not ashamed** (cf. μὴ
ἐπαισχυνθῇς, ver. 8), **for I know whom
I have trusted** (hardly to be formally
expressed so strongly as De W. '*in whom
I have put my trust*' (εἰς ὃν πεπ.), though
the meaning, in the spiritual explanation,
is virtually the same : the metaphor here
is that of a pledge deposited, and the de- *
positor *trusting* the depositary : and it is
best to keep to the figure. The ᾧ refers
to God, as Tit. iii. 8 : Acts xxvii. 25 ?),
and am persuaded that He is able (reff.
as used of God) **to keep my deposit** (how
are the words to be taken,—and what is
meant by them ? Does **μου** import, the deposit which *He* has entrusted to *me*, or the
deposit which *I* have entrusted to *Him* ?
Let us consider the latter first. In this
case **μου** is the gen. subjective. Now what
is there which the Apostle can be said to
have entrusted to God ? Some say, (a) his
eternal reward, the crown *laid up* for him,
ch. iv. 8 ; so Thl., Beza, Calov., Wolf
(' hoc est κληρονομία quæ dicitur τετηρη-
μένη ἐν οὐρανοῖς, 1 Pet. i. 4 : habes hic
τὸ φυλάσσειν ') : but then we should have
this reward represented as a matter not of
God's free grace, but of his own, delivered
to God to keep : (b) his *soul*, as in 1 Pet.
iv. 19 : Luke xxiii. 46 : so Grot. (' Deus
apud nos deponit verbum suum : nos
apud Deum deponimus spiritum nostrum'),
Beng. (' anima nostra : nos ipsi, et portio
nostra cœlestis. Paulus, decessui proximus,
duo deposita habebat : alterum Domino,
alterum Timotheo committendum '), Conyb. and others (see this treated below) :
(c) his *salvation*, so Ambr., Calv., Huther,
al. (see ib.) : (d) the believers who had
been converted by his means, as Chrys. and
Thl. (alt.), and as in the Ep. ad Heron. of
the Pseudo-Ignatius, 7, p. 916,—φύλαξόν
μου τὴν παραθήκην.... παρατίθημί σοι τὴν
ἐκκλησίαν Ἀντιοχέων, which hardly needs
refutation, as altogether unsupported by

i 1 Tim. i. 16　h ἡμέραν.　　13 i ὑποτύπωσιν　k ἔχε　lm ὑγιαινόντων　mn λόγων, ACDFK
only †.　　　　　　　　　　　　　　　　　　　　　　　　　　　　　　LPℵ a b
k 1 Tim. i. 19.
iii. 9. see note.　　　　l 1 Tim. i. 10 reff.　　　m 1 Tim. vi. 3.　　　n = Acts xviii. 15. Tit. i. 9. ii. c d e f g
8. Heb. ii. 2.　1 John ii. 7.　　　　　　　　　　　　　　　　　　　　　　　　　　h k l m n
　　　　　　　　　　　　　　　　　　　　　　　　　　　　　　　　　　　　　　　o 17. 47

the context. Then, under the former head,
which would make μου a gen. possessive,
we have the following meanings assigned :
—(e) the *Holy Spirit*, as Thdrt. (ὅσην παρ-
έσχε μοι τοῦ πνεύματος χάριν ἀκήρατον
φυλάξει μέχρι τῆς αὐτοῦ παρουσίας) :—
(f) *the faith, and its proclamation to the
world.* So Chrys. (τί ἐστι παρακαταθήκη :
ἡ πίστις, τὸ κήρυγμα : but only as an
alternative, see above), Ellic. ; not Grot.
as De W. see above : (g) the *apostolic office*
(Corn.-a-lap., Heinrichs, De W., al.)
which the Apostle regarded as a thing entrusted to him, a stewardship, 1 Cor. ix.
17 : (h) the *faithful* who had been converted by him, in the (alternative in Chrys.
and Thl.) view of their having been *committed to him by Christ :* (i) *his own soul,*
as entrusted to him by God ; as Bretschneider, al., after Josephus, B. J. iii. 8.
5, where speaking against suicide, he says,
εἰλήφαμεν παρ' αὐτοῦ τὸ εἶναι . . . . . .
ψυχὴ ἀθάνατος ἀεί, καὶ θεοῦ μοῖρα τοῖς
σώμασιν ἐνοικίζεται. εἶτα ἂν μὲν ἀφανίσῃ
τις ἀνθρώπου παρακαταθήκην, ἢ διάθηται
κακῶς, πονηρὸς εἶναι δοκεῖ καὶ ἄπιστος.
And even more strikingly Philo, quis
rerum div. hæres, 26, vol. i. p. 491 :—τοῦτ'
ἔπαινός ἐστι τοῦ σπουδαίου, τὴν ἱερὰν ἣν
ἔλαβε παρακαταθήκην, ψυχῆς, αἰσθήσεως,
λόγου, θείας σοφίας, ἀνθρωπίνης ἐπιστήμης, καθαρῶς καὶ ἀδόλως, μὴ ἑαυτῷ, μόνῳ
δὲ τῷ πεπιστευκότι φυλάξαντος. And Hermas Pastor, ii. 3, p. 918 : "qui ergo men-
tiuntur, abnegant Dominum, non redden-
tes Domino depositum, quod acceperunt."
On all these, and this view of the παραθήκη
generally, I may remark, that we may fairly
be guided by the same words παραθήκην
φύλαξον in ver. 14 as to their sense here.
And from this consideration I deduce an
inference precisely the contrary to that of
De Wette. He argues from it, that παραθήκη must necessarily have the same meaning in both places, without reference to the
verb with which it is joined : and consequently that because in ver. 14 it signifies
a matter entrusted to Timotheus, therefore
here it must signify a matter entrusted to
St. Paul. But this surely is a very lax and
careless way of reasoning. The analogy
between the two verses, if good for any
thing, goes farther than this. As, in ver.
14, παραθήκην φυλάξαι is said of the subject of the sentence, viz. Timotheus, keeping a deposit entrusted to him,—so here
παραθήκην φυλάξαι must be said of the
subject of the sentence, viz. God, keeping
a deposit entrusted to Him. Otherwise,

while keeping the mere word παραθήκη to
the same formal meaning in both places,
we shall, most harshly and unnaturally,
be requiring the phrase παραθήκην φυλάξαι to bear, in two almost consecutive
verses, two totally different meanings.
The analogy therefore of ver. 14, which
De W. uses so abundantly for his view,
makes, if thoroughly considered, entirely
against it, and in fact necessitates the
adoption of the first alternative, viz. the
objective genitive,—and the *deposit committed by the Apostle to God.* And when
we enquire what this deposit was, we have
the reply, I conceive, in the previous
words, ᾧ πεπίστευκα (see this especially
shewn in the quotation from Philo above,
where the πεπιστευκώς is *God*, not man).
He had entrusted HIMSELF, body, soul,
and spirit, to the keeping of his heavenly
Father, and lay safe in his hands, confident of His abiding and effectual care.
A strong confirmation of this view is
gained,—notwithstanding what Ellic. says
of the moral reference there, and not
here : for the parallel is to be sought not
between φυλάξαι and ἁγιάσαι, but between φυλάξαι and τηρῆσαι, which is a
very close one,—from 1 Thess. v. 23, αὐτὸς
δὲ ὁ θεὸς τῆς εἰρήνης ἁγιάσαι ὑμᾶς ὁλοτελεῖς, καὶ ὁλόκληρον ὑμῶν τὸ πνεῦμα καὶ
ἡ ψυχὴ καὶ τὸ σῶμα ἀμέμπτως ἐν τῇ παρουσίᾳ τοῦ κυρίου ἡμῶν Ἰησοῦ χριστοῦ
τηρηθείη) **for** (with reference to, as an
object ;—'against,' as we say, in a temporal sense : not simply '*until*') **that day**
(viz. the day of the παρουσία ; see reff.,
and cf. especially ch. iv. 8).　　　**13.**]
The utmost care is required, in interpreting this verse, to ascertain the probable meaning of the words in reference
to the context. On the right appreciation of this depends the question, whether
they are to be taken in their strict meaning, and simple grammatical sense, or to
be forced to some possible but far-fetched
rendering. It has been generally, as far
as I know by all the Commentators,
assumed that ὑποτύπωσιν ἔχε = ἔχε
(= κάτεχε, see reff.) τὴν ὑποτύπωσιν,
and that then ὑγιαινόντων λόγων is to
be taken as a subject. gen. after ὑποτύπ. ;
i. e. as in E. V., '*Hold fast the form of
sound words :*' thus making the exhortation perfectly general,—equivalent in fact
to the following one in ver. 14. But to
this there are several objections. The
want of the art. before ὑποτύπωσιν might
indeed be got over : a definite word em-

^o ὧν παρ᾽ ἐμοῦ ἤκουσας ^p ἐν πίστει καὶ ἀγάπῃ ^q τῇ ἐν
χριστῷ Ἰησοῦ· ¹⁴ τὴν ^r καλὴν ^s παραθήκην ^s φύλαξον
^t διὰ ^t πνεύματος ἁγίου τοῦ ^u ἐνοικοῦντος ἐν ἡμῖν.

o attr., Eph. i.
6 reff.
p 1 Tim. i. 2
reff.
q 1 Tim. i. 14
r 1 Tim. i. 18
reff.

s ver. 12.　　　t Acts i. 2. xi. 28. xxi. 4.　Rom. v. 5.　Eph. iii. 16.　2 Thess. ii. 2.　Heb. ix. 14.　1 Pet. i. 22.
u ver. 5 reff.

14. rec παρακαταθηκην, with b f g [47] : txt ACDFKL[P]א rel. (in ver 12. b g k al
have παρακαταθ.)

phatically prefixed to its verb is frequently anarthrous. But (1) this sense of
ἔχε can hardly be maintained in its present
unemphatic position. The sense is found
(or something approaching to it, for it
would require to be stronger here than
in either place) in the reff. : but in both,
the verb *precedes* the substantive, as indeed always throughout the N. T. where
any stress whatever is to be laid on it.
Cf., for some examples of both arrangements, (a) ἔχω preceding, with more or
less reference to its sense of having or
holding, as a matter to be taken into
account, Matt. v. 23; viii. 9 ‖, xi. 15 ‖
(always thus), al.,—Mark ix. 50, x. 21,
xi. 22, al.,—Luke iii. 11, viii. 6, xi. 5, al.,—
John iii. 15, 16, 29, 36, al.,—Acts ii. 44,
47, ix. 14, 31, &c.,—Rom. ii. 20, iv. 2,
vi. 22 (cf. ver. 21), xii. 6, &c. : and (b)
ἔχω following its substantive, with always
the stress on the subst., and not on the
verb, Matt. iii. 14, v. 46, viii. 20, &c.,—
Mark iii. 22, 26, viii. 14—18, &c.,—Luke
iii. 8, viii. 13, &c.,—John ii. 3, iv. 17
(instances of *both* arrangements, and each
in full significance), &c.,—Rom. xiv. 22,
&c. I cannot therefore assent to the view,
which would give ἔχε the chief emphasis
in the sentence, but must reserve that
emphasis for ὑποτύπωσιν. Then (2) there
is an objection to taking ὑποτύπωσιν
as '*a form*' with a subjective genitive,—
a '*form consisting of sound words.*' The
word is once only used (ref.) elsewhere,
and that in these Epistles, as a ' pattern,'
'specimen :' and there can hardly be a
doubt that so uncommon a word must be
taken, as again used by the same writer,
in the same meaning, unless the context
manifestly point to another. (3) A third
objection, not so important as the other
two, but still a valid one, will be that
according to the usual rendering, the
relative ὧν would much more naturally be
ἥν, referring as it ought to do in that case
to ὑποτύπωσιν, the object of ἔχε, not to
the λόγοι of which that ὑποτύπωσις was
composed. This being so, we shall have
the rendering so far,—Have (take) 'an ensample of (the) healthy words which thou
heardest of me in faith and love which are

in Christ Jesus. Then two questions arise
for us : to what (1) does ὑποτύπωσιν ἔχε
refer ? I answer,—to the saying immediately preceding, οἶδα γὰρ κ.τ.λ. This
was one of those πιστοὶ λόγοι or ὑγιαίνοντες λόγοι, of which we hear so often
in these Epistles; one which, in his timidity, Timotheus was perhaps in danger
of forgetting, and of which therefore the
Apostle reminds him, and bids him take it
as a specimen or pattern of those sound
words which had been committed to him
by his father in the faith. To what (2)
do the words ἐν πίστει κ. ἀγάπῃ τῇ ἐν
χρ. Ἰησ. refer ? Certainly not, as Thdrt.,
to παρ᾽ ἐμοῦ, taking ἐν as = περὶ (τὴν παρ᾽
ἐμοῦ περὶ πίστεως κ. ἀγάπης γεγενημένην
διδασκαλίαν) : not, again, to ἔχε, to which
in our understanding of ὑποτύπωσιν ἔχε,
such a qualification would be altogether
inapplicable : but to ἤκουσας, reminding
Timotheus of the readiness of belief, and
warmth of affection, with which he had at
first received the wholesome words from
the mouth of the Apostle, and thus tacitly
reproaching him for his present want of
growth in that faith and love; q. d. Let
me in thus speaking, 'I know whom I
have believed &c.,' call to thy mind, by
one example, those faithful sayings, those
words of spiritual health, which thou once
heardest with such receptivity and ar-
dour as a Christian believer. (I am bound
to add, that Chrys., having too much
sense of the import of the Greek arrangement, does not fall into the ordinary mistake of making ἔχε = κάτεχε and emphatic, but, as will be seen, understands
it, "From the ὑγιαίνοντες λόγοι which
I delivered thee, take thine examples and
maxims on every subject." But that
would rather require ὑγιαίνοντας λόγους
οὓς . . . I subjoin his words; καθάπερ
ἐπὶ τῶν ζωγράφων ἐνετυπωσάμην, φησίν,
εἰκόνα σοι τῆς ἀρετῆς, καὶ τῶν τῷ θεῷ
δοκούντων (εὐδοκούντων ?) ἁπάντων, ὥσπερ
τινὰ κανόνα κ. ἀρχέτυπον κ. ὅρους κατα-
βαλὼν εἰς τὴν σὴν ψυχήν. ταῦτα οὖν
ἔχε, κἂν περὶ πίστεως, κἂν περὶ ἀγάπης,
κἂν περὶ σωφρονισμοῦ δέῃ τι βουλεύ-
σασθαι, ἐκεῖθεν λάμβανε τὰ παραδείγματα. Ellic.'s note seems not altogether

^v = Matt. v. 42.
Tit. i. 14.
Heb. xii. 25.
Wisd. xvi. 3.
^w gen., 1 Tim.
i. 20. ch. ii.
17.
^x form, Eph. i.
17 reff.
^y here only.
Isa. xlvii. 6.
^z = Acts x. 2.
xvi. 15, 31.

15 Οἶδας τοῦτο ὅτι ^v ἀπεστράφησάν με πάντες οἱ ἐν τῇ Ἀσίᾳ, ^w ὧν ἐστιν Φύγελος καὶ Ἑρμογένης. 16 ^{xy} δῴη ^y ἔλεος ὁ κύριος τῷ Ὀνησιφόρου ^z οἴκῳ, ὅτι πολλάκις με ^a ἀνέψυξεν καὶ τὴν ^b ἅλυσίν μου οὐκ ^c ἐπαισχύνθη, 17 ἀλλὰ γενόμενος ἐν Ῥώμη ^{de} σπουδαιότερον ἐζήτησέν με καὶ εὗρεν.

ACDFK
LPℵ a b
c d e f g
h k l m u
o 17. 47

1 Cor. i. 16.　1 Tim. iii. 4 al.　　　　　a here only. intr. in LXX, Exod. xxiii. 12.　2 Kings xvi. 14 al. (ψυξις, Acts
iii. 20.)　　　b Eph. vi. 20 reff.　　　　　　　c ver. 8.　　　　　d 2 Cor. viii. 17 bis, 22 only.　Ezek.
xli. 25.　(-ως, Luke vii. 4.　Phil. ii. 28.　Tit. iii. 13.)　　　e compar., Phil. i. 12 reff.

15. rec φυγελλος, with A rel copt Orig Thdrt : txt CDFKL[P]ℵ c e m n 17 latt syrr [sah] goth arm Bas Chr Damasc [Tert₁] Ambrst Jer Pel.

16. rec επηισχυνθη, with Kℵ(ℵ³ altered to txt but erased αι) rel Chr: txt ACDL[P] c d f k¹ m o 17 [47] Bas Œc Thdrt-ed.—ου καταισχυνθη F.

17. σπουδαιως (corrn appy, the comparative not appearing appropriate ?) CD¹F[P]ℵ
17. 67² Orig Bas : txt D³KL rel Chr Thdrt Damasc, σπουδαιοτερως A 73.　　ανεζη-τησεν C[: επεζ. 31. 47 : εξεζ. l.]

perspicuous. He does not enter into the difficulty : and his "not for κάτεχε, though somewhat approaching it in meaning," leaves the student under some doubt as to whether he does or does not agree with the E. V.) Then as following on this single example, the whole glorious deposit is solemnly committed to his care :—being a servant of One who will keep that which *we* have entrusted to HIM, do thou in thy turn keep that which HE, by my means, has entrusted to *thee* :　　14.] that goodly deposit keep, through the Holy Spirit who dwelleth in us (not thee and me merely, but all believers : cf. Acts xiii. 52. Chrys. remarks : οὐ γάρ ἐστιν ἀν-θρωπίνης ψυχῆς οὐδὲ δυνάμεως, τοσαῦτα ἐμπιστευθέντα, ἀρκέσαι πρὸς τὴν φυλακήν. διὰ τί : ὅτι πολλοὶ οἱ λῃσταί, σκότος βαθύ· ὁ διάβολος ἐφέστηκεν ἤδη κ. ἐφεδρεύει).

15—18.] *Notices of the defective adherence of certain brethren.* These notices are intimately connected with what has pre-ceded. He has held up to Timotheus, as an example, his own boldness and con-stancy : and has given him a sample of the faithful sayings which ruled his own con-duct, in ver. 12. He proceeds to speak of a few of the discouragements under which in this confidence he was bearing up : and, affectionate gratitude prompting him, and at the same time by way of an example of fidelity to Timotheus, he dilates on the exception to the general dereliction of him, which had been furnished by Onesiphorus. **Thou knowest this, that all who are in Asia** (it does not follow, as Chrys., that εἰκὸς ἦν, ἐν Ῥώμῃ εἶναι πολλοὺς τότε τῶν ἀπὸ τῶν Ἀσίας μερῶν : this would rather require οἱ ἀπὸ τῆς Ἀσίας : but he uses the expression with reference to him to whom he was writing, who was in Asia) **repudiated me** ('not as E. V., 'are turned

away from me' (perf.) : the act referred to took place at a stated time, and from what follows, that time appears to have been on occasion of a visit to Rome. They were ashamed of Paul the prisoner, and did not seek him out, see ch. iv. 16 : —ἔφυγον τοῦ ἀποστόλου τὴν συνουσίαν διὰ τὸ Νέρωνος δέος, Thdrt. : but perhaps not so much from this motive, as from the one hinted at in the praise of Onesiphorus below. The πάντες must of course apply to all of whom the Apostle *had had trial* (and not even those without exception, vv. 16—18) : the E. V. gives the idea, that *a general apostasy* of all in Asia from St. Paul had taken place. On ASIA, i. e. the proconsular Asia, see note, Acts xvi. 6), **of whom** is (ἐστιν is hardly to be pressed as indicating that *at the present moment* Phygelus and Hermogenes were in Rome and were shunning him : it merely includes them in the class just mentioned) **Phygelus and Hermogenes** (why their names are specially brought forward, does not appear. Suetonius, Domit. c. 10, mentions a certain Hermo-genes of Tarsus, who was put to death by Domitian 'propter quasdam in historia figuras').　　　16.] **May the Lord give mercy** (an expression not found elsewhere in N. T.) **to the house of Onesiphorus** (from this expression, here and in ch. iv. 19, and from what follows, ver. 18, it has been not improbably supposed, that Onesi-phorus himself was no longer living at this time. Some indeed, as Thdrt. (οὐ μόνον αὐτῷ ἀλλὰ καὶ παντὶ τῷ οἴκῳ τὸν θεῖον ἀντέδωκεν ἔλεον), Calv. ("ob eum toti familiæ bene precatur. Unde colli-gimus Dei benedictionem non tantum super caput justi sed super totam domum residere"), al., take it as merely an exten-sion of the gratitude of the Apostle from

18 xf δῴη αὐτῷ ὁ κύριος gh εὑρεῖν h ἔλεος παρὰ κυρίου ἐν i ἐκείνῃ τῇ i ἡμέρᾳ. καὶ ὅσα ἐν Ἐφέσῳ k διηκόνησεν e βέλτιον σὺ γινώσκεις.

II. 1 Σὺ οὖν, 1 τέκνον μου, m ἐνδυναμοῦ n ἐν τῇ χάριτι ο τῇ ἐν χριστῷ Ἰησοῦ, 2 καὶ ἃ ἤκουσας παρ᾽ ἐμοῦ p διὰ πολλῶν μαρτύρων, ταῦτα q παράθου πιστοῖς ἀνθρώποις, οἵτινες r ἱκανοὶ ἔσονται καὶ ἑτέρους διδάξαι. 3 s συγ-

f = Rom. xv. 5. Rev. iii. 21. vi. 4 & passim.
g = Luke ix. 12. Acts vii. 11. [Rom. iv. 1.] Gen. vi. 8.
h here only. Numb. xi. 15.
i ver. 12.
k trans., 2 Cor. iii. 3. viii. 19, 20. 1 Pet. i. 12. iv. 10 only†.

l 1 Tim. i. 2 reff.   m Acts ix. 22.   Rom. iv. 20.   Eph. vi. 10 al3.   Paul, or of Paul, exc. Heb. xi. 34.   Ps. li. 7.   n = Eph. vi. 10.   o 1 Tim. i. 14 reff.   p = Rom. ii. 27. iv. 11.   2 Cor. ii. 4 al.   (Winer, edn. 6, § 47. i.) διὰ μαρτύρων κλαίειν, Philo, leg. ad Cai. § 29, vol. ii. p. 573.
q = 1 Tim. i. 18 only.   (Matt. xiii. 24 al.)   r = and constr., 1 Cor. xv. 9.   s ch. i. 8 only†.

18. ελεον (not in ver 16) D³K e n. [ελεος bef ευρειν P.]   for κυριου, θεω D¹ : κυριω D³ Chr-ms Thdrt₁[: om παρα κυρ. P].

Onesiphorus to his household : but ch. iv. 19 is against this. Thdrt. indeed (as also Chrys.) understands that Onesiphorus was *with him* at this time : but the aorists here (cf. γενόμενος) will hardly allow that), **because on many occasions he refreshed me** (from ψύχω, not from ψυχή. Any kind of refreshing, of body or mind, may be implied), **and was not ashamed of** (ver. 8) **my chain** (reff.): **but when he was in Rome, sought me out with extraordinary diligence** (literally : with more diligence than could have been looked for. Or perhaps, **the more diligently**: scil. because I was in chains. *They* all ἀπεστράφησάν με : *he* not only did not this, but earnestly sought me) **and found me.**

18.] **May the Lord grant to him to find mercy from the Lord** (the account to be given of the double κύριος, κυρίου, here is simply this—that δῴη ὁ κύριος had become so completely a formula, that the recurrence was not noticed. This, which is Huther's view, is far better than to suppose the second κυρ. merely = ἑαυτοῦ, or to enter into theological distinctions between κύριος as the Father, and παρὰ κυρίου as from the Son, the Judge) **in that day** (see on ver. 12): **and how many services he did** (to me : or, to the saints : the general expression will admit of either) **in Ephesus** (being probably an Ephesian, cf. ch. iv. 19), **thou knowest well** (the comparative is not for the positive, here or any where : but the signification is, 'better, than that I need remind thee').

Ch. II. 1—26.] *Exhortations to Timotheus, founded on the foregoing examples and warnings.* **1.**] **Thou therefore** (οὖν follows, primarily on his own example just propounded (cf. συγκακοπάθησον below), and secondarily on that of Onesiphorus, in contrast to those who had been ashamed of and deserted him), **my child,**

be strengthened (reff. The *pres.* indicates an abiding state, not a mere insulated act, as παράθου below. The verb is passive, not middle : see reff., and Fritzsche on Rom. iv. 20) **in the grace which is in Christ Jesus** (τουτέστι διὰ τῆς χάριτος τοῦ χριστοῦ, Chrys. But more than that : the grace of Christ, the empowering influence in the Christian life, being necessary for its whole course and progress, is regarded as the *element in* which it is lived : cf. αὐξάνετε ἐν χάριτι, 2 Pet. ult. χάρις must not be taken, with Ambr., Calov., Mack, al., for his *ministerial office*), **and the things which thou heardest from me with many witnesses** (i. e. with the intervention, or (as Conyb.) attestation of many witnesses: διά (reff.) imports the agency of the witnesses as contributing to the whole matter treated of : so διὰ πολλῶν δακρύων, and διὰ προφητείας, 1 Tim. iv. 14. These witnesses are not, as Chrys., Thdrt., the congregations whom Timotheus had heard the Apostle teaching (ἅπερ ἤκουσάς μου πολλοὺς διδάσκοντος, Thdrt.), or as Clem. Alex. in Œc., testimonies from the law and prophets : nor as Heydenr., the other Apostles : much less, as he gives in another alternative, the Christian martyrs : but *the presbyters and others present at his ordination*, cf. 1 Tim. iv. 14 ; vi. 12 ; and ch. i. 6. No word such as μαρτυρούμενα or βεβαιούμενα (Heydenr.) need be supplied), **these deliver in trust** (cf. παραθήκην above, ch. i. 14) **to faithful men** (i. e. not merely 'believers,' but 'trustworthy men,' men who τὴν καλὴν παραθήκην φυλάξονται) **such as shall be** (not merely 'are,' but 'shall be'—give every hope of turning out) **able to teach them to** (so I take ἑτέρους, not as a first, but as a second accusative after διδάξαι, the first being included in ταῦτα above) **others also (καὶ** carries the mind on to a

t = John x. 11. κακοπάθησον ὡς ᵗ καλὸς ᵘ στρατιώτης χριστοῦ Ἰησοῦ. ACDFK
1 Tim. iv. 6.
1 Pet. iv. 10. 4 οὐδεὶς ᵛ στρατευόμενος ʷ ἐμπλέκεται ταῖς τοῦ βίου ˣ πρα- LPℵ a b
u Paul, here c d e f g
only. h k l m n
(συνστρ., γματείαις, ἵνα τῷ ʸ στρατολογήσαντι ᶻ ἀρέσῃ. 5 ἐὰν δὲ o 17. 47
Philem. 2.)
v 1 Tim. i. 18 reff. w 2 Pet. ii. 20 only. Prov. xxviii. 18 only. x here only. 1 Chron. xxviii.
21. (-τεύεσθαι, Luke xix. 13.) y here only †. Jos. B. J. v. 9. 4. z Rom. viii. 8. Gal. i. 10 reff.

CHAP. II. 3. rec (for συγκακοπαθ.) συ ουν κακοπαθησον, with C³D²·³KL rel goth gr-ff (Bloomf.'s assertion that Syr *must have read* σὺ οὖν, is contrary to fact, see Ellic: and his express citation of B for that reading, when B *does not contain this Ep. at all,* is, it is to be feared, but a sample of the value of his statements in such matters): txt AC¹D¹F[P]ℵ 17 Syr syr-mg-gr copt arm, *labora* latt Ambrst Aug Pel Gild. συνστρατιωτης D¹. rec ιησ. bef χρ., with D³KL rel Syr [æth] gr-ff: txt ACD¹F[P] m 17 [47] latt syr copt goth [arm-ed] Aug Ambrst Pel.

4. aft στρατευομενος ins τω θεω F vulg [Orig-int] Cypr Ambrst-txt Gild Jer Pel ; *domino* goth: θεου arm-ed-marg.

further step of the same process—implying 'in their turn.' These ἕτεροι would be *other trustworthy men* like themselves). The connexion of this verse with the foregoing and the following has been questioned. I believe it to be this: ' The true keeping of the deposit entrusted to thee will involve thy handing it on unimpaired to others, who may in their turn hand it on again. But in order to this, thou must be strong in grace—thou must be a fellow-sufferer with me in hardships—thou must strive lawfully—thou must not be entangled with this life's matters.' So that ver. 2 serves to prepare him to hear of the necessity of endurance and faithful adhesion to his duty as a Christian soldier, considering that he has his deposit not only to keep, but to deliver down unimpaired. It is obviously a perversion of the sense to regard this verse as referring (as Bengel, 'παράθου, antequam istinc ad me proficiscare') merely to his journey to Rome — that *during that time* he should, &c.: the ἔσονται, and the very contemplation of a similar step on the part of these men at a future time, are against such a supposition.

Mack constructs a long argument out of this verse to shew that there are *two sources* of Christian instruction in the Church, written teaching and oral, and ends with affirming that those who neglect the latter for the former, have always shewn that in reality set up their own opinion above all teaching. But he forgets that these two methods of teaching are in fact but one and the same. *Scripture* has been *God's way of fixing tradition,* and rendering it trustworthy at any distance of time ; of obviating the very danger which in this Epistle we see so imminent, viz. of one of those teachers, who were links in this chain of transmission, becoming inefficient and transmitting it inadequately. This very Epistle is therefore a warning to us not to trust oral tradition, seeing that it was so dependent on men, and to accept no way of conserving it but that which God's providence has pointed out to us in the canonical books of Scripture.

3.] **Suffer hardship with me** (Conyb. happily renders it, 'Take thy share in suffering.' The συγ- binds it to what precedes and follows, referring primarily to the Apostle himself, though doubtless having a wider reference to all who similarly suffer: see above, on the connexion of ver. 2), **as a good soldier of Jesus Christ.** 4.] **No soldier when on service is** (suffers himself to be: the passive sense predominates: 'is,' as his normal state. Or the verb may be middle, as Ellic., '*entangleth himself,*' and vulg., '*implicat se*') **entangled** (ref. ; ἐν βιαίοις ἐνπλακέντων πόνοις, Plato, Legg. vii. p. 814 e. Grot. quotes from Cicero 'occupationibus implicatus:' and we have in de Off. ii. 11, 'qui contrahendis negotiis implicantur') **in the businesses of life** (cf. Plato, Rep. vi. p. 500, οὐδὲ γάρ που .... σχολὴ τῷ γε ὡς ἀληθῶς πρὸς τοῖς οὖσι τὴν διάνοιαν ἔχοντι κάτω βλέπειν εἰς ἀνθρώπων πραγματείας: Arrian, Epict. iii. 22 (Wetst.), ὡς ἐν παρατάξει, μήποτ' ἀπερίσπαστον εἶναι δεῖ, ὅλον πρὸς τῇ διακονίᾳ τοῦ θεοῦ ... οὐ προσδεδεμένον καθήκουσιν ἰδιωτικοῖς, οὐδ' ἐμπεπλεγμένον σχέσεσιν: Ambros. de Offic. i. 36 (184), vol. iii. p. 49, 'si is, qui imperatori militat, a susceptionibus litium, actu negotiorum forensium, venditione mercium prohibetur humanis legibus, quanto magis, &c.:' Ps-Athanas. quæst. in Epistolas Pauli 117: εἰ γὰρ ἐπιγείῳ βασιλεῖ ὁ μέλλων στρατεύεσθαι οὐκ ἀρέσει, ἐὰν μὴ ἀφήσῃ πάσας τὰς τοῦ βίου φροντίδας, πόσῳ μᾶλλον μέλλων στρατεύεσθαι τῷ ἐπουρανίῳ βασιλεῖ; see other examples in Wetst. "Vox Græca πραγμάτεια (אישמקרפ), pro mercatura,

καὶ ᵃ ἀθλῇ τις, οὐ ᵇ στεφανοῦται ἐὰν μὴ ᶜ νομίμως ᵃ ἀθλή- ᵃ here (bis) only †.
σῃ. ᵇ τὸν ᵈ κοπιῶντα ᵉ γεωργὸν δεῖ πρῶτον τῶν καρπῶν (-λησις, Heb. x. 32.)

ᵇ Heb. ii. 7, 9

(from Ps. viii. 5) only.   c 1 Tim. i. 8 only † (see note).   d Matt. vi. 28. Acts xx. 35
(Paul). Rom. xvi. 6 al. Job xxxix. 16.   e Paul, here only. Matt. xxi. 33, &c. and ↓. John
xv. 1. James v. 7 only. Jer. xiv. 4.

5. om δε A : *nam* vulg.   6. πρωοτερον (ω marked for erasure) ℵ¹(txt ℵ³).

sæpius occurrit in Pandectis Talmudicis." Schöttgen. On the whole matter, consult Grotius's note), that he may please him who called him to be a soldier (who originally enrolled him as a soldier : the word signifies *to levy soldiers*, or *raise a troop*, and ὁ στρατολογήσας designates the commander of such troop. So ἀντὶ τῶν ἀπολωλότων ἀνδρῶν στρατολογήσαντες ἐξ ἁπάσης φυλῆς, Dion. Hal. xi. 24. The same writer uses στρατολογία for a *muster*, a levy of soldiers,— vi. 44 ; ix. 38. The ' cui se probavit' of the vulgate is unintelligible, unless as Grot. suggests, it is an error for ' *qui se probavit.*' The taking of these precepts according to the letter, to signify that no minister of Christ may have a secular occupation, is quite beside the purpose : for 1) it is not ministers, but all soldiers of Christ who are spoken of : 2) the position of the verb ἐμπλέκεται shews that it is not the fact of the *existence* of such occupation, but the being *entangled* in it, which is before the Apostle's mind : 3) the Apostle's own example sufficiently confutes such an idea. Only then does it become unlawful, when such occupation, from its engrossing the man, becomes a hindrance to the work of the ministry,— or from its nature is incompatible with it).

5.] The soldier must serve on condition of not dividing his service : now we have another instance of the same requirement : and in the conflicts of the arena there are certain laws, without the fulfilment of which no man can obtain the victory. But (the above is not the only example, but) if any one also (q. d. to give another instance) strive in the games (it is necessary to adopt a periphrasis for ἀθλῇ. That of E. V. ' *strive for masteries,*' is not definite enough, omitting all mention of the games, and by consequence not even suggesting them to the ordinary reader. The vulg. gives it ' certat in agone :' and Luth., merely ꜩämpfet : so also Ostervald and Diodati : Scio,— ' lidia en los juegos publicos.' The word ἀθλεῖν, in the best Attic writers, means ' to work,' ' to endure,' and ἀθλεύειν, ' to contend in the games.' (See however Ellic.'s note.) This usage belongs to later Greek : see Palm and Rost's Lex.), he is not crowned

(even in case of his gaining the victory ? or is the word inclusive of all efforts made to get the crown,— ' he has no chance of the crown ?' rather the former, from ἀθλήσῃ below), unless he have striven (this seems to assume the getting of the victory) lawfully (according to the prescribed conditions (not merely of the contest, but of the preparation also, see Ellic.). It is the usual phrase : so Galen, comm. in Hippocr. i. 15 : οἱ γυμνασταὶ καὶ οἱ νομίμως ἀθλοῦντες, ἐπὶ μὲν τοῦ ἀρίστου τὸν ἄρτον μόνον ἐσθίουσιν, ἐπὶ δὲ τοῦ δείπνου τὸ κρέας : Arrian, Epict. iii. 10,—εἰ νομίμως ἤθλησας, εἰ ἔφαγες ὅσα δεῖ, εἰ ἐγυμνάσθης, εἰ τοῦ ἀλείπτου ἤκουσας (Wetst., where see more examples). Compare the parallel place, 1 Cor. ix. 24.—τί ἐστιν, ἐὰν μὴ νομίμως ; οὐκ, ἐάν τις τὸν ἀγῶνα εἰσέλθῃ, ἀρκεῖ τοῦτο, οὐδὲ ἐὰν ἀλείψηται, οὐδὲ ἐὰν συμπλακῇ, ἀλλὰ ἂν μὴ πάντα τὸν τῆς ἀθλήσεως νόμον φυλάττῃ, καὶ τὸν ἐπὶ σιτίων, καὶ τὸν ἐπὶ σωφροσύνης καὶ σεμνότητος, καὶ τὸν ἐν παλαίστρᾳ, καὶ πάντα ἁπλῶς διέλθοι τὰ τοῖς ἀθληταῖς προσήκοντα, οὐδέποτε στεφανοῦται Chrys.). 6.] Another comparison shewing the necessity of active labour as an antecedent to reward. The husbandman who is engaged in labour (who is actually employed in gathering in the fruit : not κοπιάσαντα) must first partake of the fruits (which he is gathering in : the whole result of his ministry, not here further specified. The saying is akin to βοῦν ἀλοῶντα μὴ φιμώσεις —the right of first participation in the harvest belongs to him who is labouring in the field : do not thou therefore, by relaxing this labour, forfeit that right. By this rendering, keeping strictly to the sense of the *present* part., all difficulty as to the position of πρῶτον is removed. Many Commentators (Calv., E. V. marg., al., Grot., al., take πρῶτον for ' *ita demum*') not observing this have supposed, in the sense, a transposition of πρῶτον, and given it as if it were τὸν γεωργὸν δεῖ, κοπιῶντα πρῶτον, τῶν καρπῶν μεταλ., or as Wahl and Winer (so in older editions of his grammar, e. g. edn. 3, p. 458 : but now, edn. 6, § 61. 5, he merely states the two renderings, without giving an opinion),—τὸν

f Acts ii. 46.
(xxiv. 25
w. acc.)
xxvii. 33.
Heb. vi. 7.
xii. 10 only †.
Sir. xviii. 9 al.
(-λημψις,
1 Tim. iv. 3.)
g = Matt.
xxiv. 15. Eph. iii. 4, 20. Isa. xlvii. 7.
23. Luke ii. 47. Prov. ii. 2.
xviii. 5. 1 Chron. xvi. 12.
n John vii. 42. Rom. i. 3.
p Phil. iv. 3 1 Thess. iii. 2.
r = Phil. ii. 8. Heb. xii. 4. 2 Macc. xiii. 14. 3 Macc. vii. 16.

f μεταλαμβάνειν. 7 g νόει ὃ λέγω· δώσει γάρ σοι ὁ κύριος
h σύνεσιν i ἐν πᾶσιν. 8 k μνημόνευε Ἰησοῦν χριστὸν lm ἐγηγερμένον m ἐκ νεκρῶν, n ἐκ σπέρματος Δαυείδ, κατὰ τὸ
ο εὐαγγέλιόν ο μου, 9 p ἐν ᾧ q κακοπαθῶ r μέχρι s δεσμῶν

ACDFK
LPℵ a b
c d e f g
h k l m n
o 17. 47

h Paul (1 Cor. i. 19. Eph. iii. 4. Col. i. 9. ii. 2) only, exc. Mark xii.
i ch. iv. 5 reff.   k w. acc., Matt. xvi. 9.   1 Thess. ii. 9. Rev.
l constr. particip., Acts vii. 12. xix. 35. xxiv. 10.   m Gal. i. 1 reff.
o Rom. ii. 16. xvi. 25 only. see 2 Cor. iv. 3. 1 Thess. i. 5.   2 Thess. ii. 14.
q ch. iv. 5.   James v. 13 only. Jonah iv. 10 only. (-θεια, James v. 10.)
s Phil. i. 7 reff.

7. rec for ὅ, ἅ, with DKLℵ³ rel vulg syr copt [arm]: txt ACF[P]ℵ¹ 17 Syr goth
[æth] Chr-comm.   rec δωη (*probably change for the sake of softening, and
rendering more likely, the exprn. The choice between the readings is difficult, the
rec having a claim, as the harder one: but the authority for txt is strong*), with KL[P]
rel syrr Chr Thdrt, δωει C³: txt AC¹DFℵ 17. 67² latt copt [goth] arm Damasc Hil
Ambrst Pel Vig-taps.

8. μνημονευειν χρ. ιησ. D¹ 111.

γ. τὸν θέλοντα τῶν κ. μεταλ., δεῖ πρῶτον κοπιᾷν: but in both cases κοπιάσαντα
would seem to be, if not absolutely required, yet more natural. Thdrt. and
Œc. understand πρῶτον of the preference
which the teacher has over the taught,
—πρὸ γὰρ τῶν κεκτημένων οἱ γηπόνοι
μεταλαγχάνουσι τῶν καρπῶν. Ambr., Pel.,
Mosh. believe the bodily support of ministers to be imported by τῶν κ. μεταλ.:
but Chrys. answers this well, οὐκ ἔχει
λόγον· πῶς γὰρ οὐχ ἁπλῶς γεωργὸν εἶπεν,
ἀλλὰ τὸν κοπιῶντα; but his own idea
hardly seems to be contained in the
words,—πρὸς τὴν μέλλησιν ἵνα μηδεὶς
δυσχεραίνῃ, ἤδη, φησίν, ἀπολαμβάνεις, ἢ
ὅτι ἐν αὐτῷ τῷ κόπῳ ἡ ἀντίδοσις: and
certainly there is no allusion to that of
Athanasius (in De W.), that it is the duty
of a teacher first to apply to himself that
which he teaches to others: nor to that
of Bengel, 'Paulus Timothei animam ex-
coluit, c. i. 6, ergo fructus ei imprimis ex
Timotheo debentur'). 7.] Under-
stand (νοῖεν . . . "ist die innerlich tiefe,
sittlich ernste Verstandesthätigkeit." Beck,
Biblische Seelenlehre, p. 56. It is the
preparatory step to συνιέναι,—id. ib. note,
and p. 59,—which is "ein den Zusammen-
hang mit seinen Grunden und Folgen
begreifendes Erkennen") what I say (ἐπεὶ
οὖν τὰ παραδείγματα ἔθηκε τὸ τῶν στρατιωτῶν κ. ἀθλητῶν κ. γεωργῶν, καὶ πάντα
ἁπλῶς αἰνιγματωδῶς . . . ἐπήγαγε, νόει
ἃ λέγω, Chrys.: so also Thdrt., all.: not
as Calv., who denies the above, "hoc non
addidit propter similitudinum obscuri-
tatem, sed ut ipse suggereret Timotheo
quanto præstantior sit sub Christi auspiciis militia, et quanto amplior merces:"
this would not agree with σύνεσιν δώσει):
for the Lord (Christ) shall give thee
thorough understanding (on σύνεσις, see

citation from Beck above) in all things
(i. e. thou art well able to penetrate the
meaning and bearing of what I say: for
thou art not left to thyself, but hast
the wisdom which is of Christ to guide
thee. There is perhaps a slight intimation that he might apply to this fountain of wisdom more than he did :—' the
Lord, if thou seekest it from Him').
8—13.] This statement and substantiation of two of the leading facts of the
gospel, seems, especially as connected with
the exhortations which follow on it vv.
14 ff., to be aimed at the false teachers
by whose assumption Timotheus was in
danger of being daunted. The Incarnation and Resurrection of Christ were two
truths especially imperilled, and indeed,
denied, by their teaching. At the same
time these very truths, believed and per-
sisted in, furnished him with the best
grounds for stedfastness in his testimony
to the Gospel, and attachment to the
Apostle himself, suffering for his faithfulness to them: and on his adherence to
these truths depended his share in that
Saviour in whom they were manifested,
and in union with whom, in His eternal
and unchangeable truth, our share in
blessedness depends. **Remember, that
Jesus Christ has been raised up from** *
the dead (the accus. after μνημόνευε imports that it is the *fact respecting* Jesus
Christ, not so much He Himself, to
which attention is directed (see reff.).
Ellic. takes exactly the other view, citing
in its favour Winer, § 45. 4, who however implicitly maintains my rendering,
by classing even 1 John iv. 2, 2 John 7,
with Heb. xiii. 23, γινώσκετε τὸν ἀδ.
Τιμόθεον ἀπολελυμένον, which he renders
"ihr wisset, daß . . . entlassen ist." Ellic.
refers to my note on 1 John iv. 2, as if

ὡς ^{t} κακοῦργος, ἀλλὰ ὁ λόγος τοῦ θεοῦ οὐ δέδεται. ^{10} διὰ
τοῦτο ^{u} πάντα ^{uv} ὑπομένω διὰ τοὺς ^{w} ἐκλεκτούς, ἵνα καὶ

t Luke xxiii.
32, 33, 39
only. Prov.
xxi. 15. Sir.
xi. 33. xxx.

(xxxiii.) 26 only.   u 1 Cor. xiii. 7.   v constr., Heb. x. 32. xii. 2, 3. James i.
12. Wisd. xvi. 22.   w Rom. viii. 33. xvi. 18. Col. iii. 12. 1 Tim. v. 21. Tit. i. 1 al. Prov. xvii. 3.

9. aft εν ω ins και F.   (αλλα, so ACD¹א 17.)   om ου א¹.

it were inconsistent with the rendering here: but the verb there is ὁμολογεῖν, not μνημονεύειν, which I conceive makes all the difference. According to Ellic.'s rendering, unless we refer ἐν ᾧ to Christ, which he does not, the context becomes very involved and awkward. The gen. is more usual in later Greek (see Luke xvii. 32: John xv. 20; xvi. 4, 21: Acts xx. 35, &c.)—but the accus. in classical, see Palm and Rost sub voce, and cf. Herod. i. 36, Æschyl. Pers. 769 (783 Dindorf), Soph. Ag. 1273, Philoct. 121, Eur. Androm. 1165 (1141 Matthiæ), &c.), (Jesus Christ, who was) **of the seed of David** (this clause must be taken as = τὸν ἐκ σπέρμ. Δαυίδ, and the unallowable and otherwise unaccountable ellipsis of the article may probably be explained, as De W., by the words being part of a recognized and technical profession of faith. Compare Rom. i. 3, which is closely parallel.   Mack's attempt to join ἐκ σπέρμ. Δ. to ἐγηγερμένον ἐκ νεκρ., 'that Jesus Christ was raised from the dead in His flesh, as He sprung from David,' is hardly worth refutation), **according to my Gospel** ('the Gospel entrusted to me to teach,' as in reff. Here the expression may seem to be used with reference to the false teachers,—but as in the other places it has no such reference, I should rather incline to regard it as a solemn way of speaking, identifying these truths with the preaching which had been the source of Timotheus's belief.   Baur, in spite of ἐν ᾧ &c. following, understands this εὐαγγ. μου of the *Gospel of St. Luke*, as having been written under the authority of St. Paul. See Prolegg. to St. Luke's Gospel in Vol. I. § iii. 6, note), **in which** ('cujus annuntiandi munere defungens,' Beza: see reff.) **I suffer hardship** (see ver. 3) **even unto** (consult Ellic.'s note and his references on μέχρι) **chains** (see ch. i. 16) **as a malefactor** ('κακοπαθῶ, κακοῦργος— malum passionis, ut si præcessisset malum actionis,' Bengel), **but the word of God is not bound** (δεσμοῦνται μὲν αἱ χεῖρες, ἀλλ' οὐχ ἡ γλῶττα, Chrys.: similarly Thdrt. But we shall better, though this reference to himself is not precluded (cf. ch. iv. 17: Acts xxviii. 31), enlarge the words to that wider acceptation, in which he rejoices, Phil. i. 18.   As regarded himself, the

word of God *might* be said to be bound, inasmuch as he was prevented from the free proclamation of it: his person was not free, though his tongue and pen were. This more general reference Chrys. himself seems elsewhere to admit (as cited in Heydenr.): ὁ διδάσκαλος ἐδέδετο καὶ ὁ λόγος ἐπέτετο· ἐκεῖνος τὸ δεσμωτήριον ᾤκει, καὶ ἡ διδασκαλία πτερωθεῖσα πανταχόσε τῆς οἰκουμένης ἔτρεχε.   The purpose of adding this seems to be, to remind Timotheus, that *his* sufferings and imprisonment had in no way weakened the power of the Gospel, or loosened the ties by which he (Timotheus) was bound to the service of it: hardly as Chrys.: εἰ ἡμεῖς δεδεμένοι κηρύττομεν, πολλῷ μᾶλλον ὑμᾶς τοὺς λελυμένους τοῦτο ποιεῖν χρή).   **10.]** **For this reason** (what reason? 'quia me vincto evangelium currit,' says Bengel: and with this agree Huther, De W., al.   But neither 1) is this sound logic, nor 2) is it in accordance with the Apostle's usage of διὰ τοῦτο . . . . ἵνα. 1) The fact, that the word of God is not bound, is clearly not the reason why he suffers these things for the elect: nor can we say with Huther, that the *consciousness* of this fact is that in which he endures all.   De W. takes the predominant idea to be, the dispersion and success of God's word, in and by which the Apostle is encouraged to suffer.   But this would certainly, as Wolf says, render the connexion 'dilutior et parum cohærens.' 2) In 1 Tim. i. 16, διὰ τοῦτο ἠλεήθην . . . . ἵνα, and Philem. 15, διὰ τοῦτο ἐχωρίσθη . . . ἵνα, the reference of δ. τ. is evidently to what follows: cf. also Rom. iv. 16, 2 Cor. xiii. 10.   I would therefore refer the words to the following, and consider them, as in the above instances, as a marked way of indicating the reason presently to be given: 'for this purpose, ... that;' so Chrys., Thdrt., Wolf, Wiesinger, al.) **I endure all things** (not merely suffer (obj.): but readiness and persistence (subj.) are implied in the word, and the universal πάντα belongs to this subj. meaning—'I am enduring, ready to bear, all things') **for the sake of the elect** (see reff., especially Tit. i. 1. The Apostle does not, as De W., refer merely to those elect of God who are not yet converted, but generally to the whole category, both those who are

αὐτοὶ σωτηρίας ˣτύχωσιν ʸτῆς ʸἐν χριστῷ Ἰησοῦ μετὰ
ᶻδόξης ᶻαἰωνίου. ¹¹ ᵃπιστὸς ὁ ᵃλόγος· εἰ γὰρ ᵇᶜσυναπ-
εθάνομεν, καὶ ᵇᵈσυνζήσομεν· ¹² εἰ ᵉὑπομένομεν, καὶ ᶠσυμβα-
σιλεύσομεν· εἰ ᵍἀρνησόμεθα, κἀκεῖνος ᵍἀρνήσεται ἡμᾶς·
¹³ εἰ ʰἀπιστοῦμεν, ἐκεῖνος ⁱπιστὸς μένει· ᵍἀρνήσασθαι
γὰρ ἑαυτὸν οὐ δύναται.

x = Luke xx. 35. Acts xxvi. 22 (Paul). Heb. xi. 35. 2 Macc. iv. 6. ; Rom. iii. 24. viii. 39. 1 Tim. i. 14. iii. 13. ver. 1. ch. i. 1, 13. iii. 15. z 1 Pet. v. 10. see 2 Cor. iv. 17.

ACDFK LPℵ a b c d e f g h k l m n o 17. 47

a 1 Tim. i. 15 reff.   b 2 Cor. vii. 3.   c Mark xiv. 31. 2 Cor. as above (b) only †. Sir. xix. 10 only.
d Rom. vi. 8. 2 Cor. as above (b) only †.   e Matt. x. 22. xxiv. 13 ‖ Mk. James v. 11. 1 Pet. ii. 20.   f 1 Cor.
iv. 8 only †.   g = 1 Tim. v. 8 reff.   h Matt. xvi. 11, 16. Luke xxiv. 11, 41. Acts xxviii. 24. Rom.
iii. 3 only †. Wisd. x. 7 al. (-τος, 1 Tim. v. 8.)   i = 1 Thess. v. 24 reff.

11. συνζησωμεν CL[P] m¹ o [47¹].
12. συμβασιλευσωμεν ACL[P].   rec αρνουμεθα, with DKL[P]ℵ³ rel syr goth :
txt ACℵ¹ 17 vulg(not demid) Chr Thl Cypr Tert.--om κ. συμβ. to πιστ. next ver F.
13. rec om γαρ, with Kℵ³ rel vulg D-lat syr goth [arm] Damasc lat-ff : ins A[appy]
CDFL[P]ℵ¹ e g l m 17 [47] Syr copt Chr Thdrt Ath.

already turned to him, and those who are yet to be turned: cf. the parallel declaration in Col. i. 24, ἀνταναπληρῶ τὰ ὑστερήματα τῶν θλίψεων τοῦ χριστοῦ . . . . ὑπὲρ τοῦ σώματος αὐτοῦ, ὅ ἐστιν ἡ ἐκκλησία), that they also (as well as ourselves, with reference to what is to follow, the certainty that we, who suffer with Him, shall reign with Him:—De W. (see above) says, 'those yet unconverted, as well as those already converted:' and the mere καὶ αὐτοί might seem to favour this view; but it manifestly is not so) may obtain the salvation which is in (as its element and condition of existence) Christ Jesus with eternal glory (salvation here, in its spiritual presence and power—χάριτί ἐστε σεσωσμένοι, Eph. ii. 5 : and glory hereafter, the full development and expansion of salvation, Rom. viii. 21). Faithful is the saying (see on reff.: another of those current Christian sayings, probably the utterances originally of the Spirit by those who spoke προφητείας in the Church,—and, as in 1 Tim. iii. 16, bearing with it so much of balance and rhythmical arrangement, as to seem to be a portion of some hymn): for (Chrys., Œc., al., regard this γάρ as rendering a reason why the λόγος is πιστός, understanding πιστ. ὁ λ. of what has gone before, viz. the certainty that ὁ ζωῆς οὐρανίου τυχών, καὶ αἰωνίου τεύξεται. But this is most unnatural. The γάρ is not merely explicative, as Grot., Huther, al., but as in 1 Tim. iv. 9, renders a reason for the πιστός,—in the assertion of the fact in well-known words: for the fact is so, that if &c.) if we died with Christ (on account of the aorist, pointing to some one definite event, the reference must be to that participation in Christ's death which takes place at baptism in all

those who are His, and which those who follow Him in sufferings emphatically shew that they then did really take on them: see Rom. vi. 3, 4, 8 : Col. ii. 12. Certainly, if the aor. stood alone, it might be taken proleptically, looking back on life from that future day in which the συνζήσομεν will be realized : but coupled as it is with the present ὑπομένομεν and the future ἀρνησόμεθα, we can hardly take it otherwise than literally as to time, of an event already past, and if so, strictly as in the parallel Rom. vi. 8, where the reference is clear, we shall also live with Him (hereafter in glory): if we endure (with Him : the συν must be supplied, cf. εἴπερ συνπάσχομεν, Rom. viii. 17), we shall also reign with Him (see Rom. v. 17; viii. 17. In the former pair, death and life are opposed : in this, subjection (ὑπο-μ.) and dominion. See the interesting anecdote of Nestor, quoted from the martyrology by Grotius: if we shall deny (Him), He also will deny us (see Matt. x. 33): if we disbelieve (not, His Resurrection, as Chrys.: εἰ ἀπιστοῦμεν ὅτι ἀνέστη, οὐδὲν ἀπὸ τούτου βλάπτεται ἐκεῖνος: nor His Divinity, as Œc.(2) ὅτι θεὸς ἐστί, but Him, generally. Ellic.'s note (which see) has convinced me that ἀπιστία seems always in the N. T. to imply not 'untrueness,' 'unfaithfulness,' but definitely 'unbelief:' see note on Rom. iii. 3, in Vol. II. edn. 5), He remains faithful (to His own word cited above): for He cannot deny Himself (i. e. if we desert faith in Him, He will not break faith with us; He having declared that whosoever denies Him shall be denied by Him, and we having pledged ourselves to confess Him,—we may become unbelieving, and break our pledge, but He will not break His: as He has said, it shall surely be. See Rom. iii. 3. Chrys. gives

¹⁴ Ταῦτα ʲ ὑπομίμνησκε ᵏ διαμαρτυρόμενος ᵏ ἐνώπιον τοῦ
κυρίου μὴ ˡ λογομαχεῖν, ἐπ᾽ οὐδὲν ᵐ χρήσιμον, ⁿ ἐπὶ ᵒ κατα-
στροφῇ τῶν ᵖ ἀκουόντων. ¹⁵ ۹ σπούδασον σεαυτὸν ʳ δόκιμον ˢ παραστῆσαι τῷ θεῷ, ᵗ ἐργάτην ᵘ ἀνεπαίσχυντον,

j Luke xxii. 61.
John xiv. 26.
Tit. iii. 1.
2 Pet. i. 12.
3 John 10.
Jude 5 only †.
(-μνησις,
ch. i. 5.)
k 1 Tim. v. 21
reff.
n = Gal. v. 13. Eph.
p 1 Tim. iv. 16.
q Gal.
r Rom. xiv. 18. xvi.
s = Eph. v. 27 reff.
u here only †.

l here only †.　(-χία, 1 Tim. vi. 4.)　　m here only.　Gen. xxxvii. 26 al.
ii. 10.　1 Thess. iv. 7.　　　o 2 Pet. ii. 6 only.　Gen. xix. 29.
ii. 10.　Eph. iv. 3.　1 Thess. ii. 17.　ch. iv. 9, 21.　Heb. xi. al.　Isa. xxi. 3.
10.　1 Cor. xi. 19.　2 Cor. x. 18. xiii. 7.　James i. 12 only.　Gen. xxiii. 16.
t = Paul, 2 Cor. xi. 13.　Phil. iii. 2.　1 Tim. v. 18.　Matt. xx. 1 ff. †　Sir. xix. 1 al.

14. [for υπομιμν., υπομνησκε P.]　διαμαρτυρομενος C 238 Thdrt.　om του
D¹ 112.　for κυριου, θεου CFℵ b c m syr-mg copt arm Chr Thl Ambrst.　λογομαχει
[for -χειν] AC¹ latt æth Orig-int lat-ff : txt CˢDFKL[P]ℵ rel syrr copt goth Clem
Chr Thdrt Damasc [Orig-int₁].　rec for επ᾽ ουδ., εις ουδεν, with DKLℵ³ rel
Chr₄ₗᵢ۹ Thdrt₂ : επ ουδενι γαρ F lat-ff : txt AC[P]ℵ¹ 17.
15. for θεω, χριστω A[L] Damasc.

a curious explanation : ἀληθής ἐστι, βέ-
βαιός ἐστιν, ἄν τε εἴπωμεν, ἄν τε μὴ εἴπωμεν . . . . ἐκεῖνος γὰρ ὁ αὐτὸς μένει καὶ
ἀρνουμένων καὶ μὴ ἀρνουμένων. ἀρνήσασθαι γὰρ ἑαυτὸν οὐ δύναται, τουτέστι,
μὴ εἶναι. ἡμεῖς λέγομεν ὅτι οὐκ ἔστιν, εἰ
καὶ μὴ τὸ πρᾶγμα οὕτως ἔχει. οὐκ ἔχει
φύσιν μὴ εἶναι, οὐ δυνατόν· τουτέστιν, εἰς
τὸ μὴ εἶναι αὐτὸν χωρῆσαι. ἀεὶ μένει, ἀεὶ
ἔστιν αὐτοῦ ἡ ὑπόστασις, μὴ τοίνυν ὡς
χαριζόμενοι αὐτῷ, οὕτω διακεώμεθα, ἢ ὡς
καταβλάπτοντες. But manifestly there
is no such motive as this last brought forward, nor is the assertion ἐκεῖνος μένει, but
ἐκ. πιστὸς μένει. Mack proposes another
alternative,—'If we fall from the faith
and forfeit our own salvation, He still
carries forward His own gracious will, in
saving mankind by the Gospel.' But that
given above seems best to suit the context).

14—26.] *Application of the above
general exhortations to the teaching and
conversation of Timotheus, especially with
reference to the false teachers.* 14.]
These things (those which have just preceded vv. 8—13) **call to their minds**
(reff.: the minds viz. of those among
whom thou art ministering, as the context
shews : see a similar ellipsis in Tit. iii. 8),
**testifying to them before the Lord not to
contend with words** (see 1 Tim. vi. 4.
The var. reading λογομάχει changes the
whole arrangement, and attaches διαμαρτ.
ἐνώπιον τοῦ κυρίου to the preceding.
The chief objections to this are 1) that
ὑπομίμνησκε διαμαρτυρόμενος ἐνώπ. τοῦ
κυρίου is a very lame and inconsistent
junction of terms, the strong emphasis of
the διαμ. κ.τ.λ. not agreeing with the far
weaker word ὑπομίμνησκε : 2) that in the
other places where διαμαρτύρομαι occurs
in St. Paul, it precedes an exhortation,
e. g. 1 Tim. v. 21; ch. iv. 1, and μαρτύρομαι Eph. iv. 17),—(a thing) useful
(χρήσιμον is in apposition with the pre-

ceding sentence, as καθαρίζον in the rec.
reading of Mark vii. 19 : see Winer, edn.
6, § 59. 9. b) **for no purpose** (the reading ἐπ᾽ οὐδέν, which has been put by,—cf.
Ellic. here,—on account of the rec. illustrating St. Paul's love of prepositional
variation, does in fact illustrate it quite as
much, ἐπί having dat. and accus. in the
same sentence, cf. Ps. cxvii. 9 Ed-vat[B¹
def.] ℵ³ᵃ &c. χρήσιμος is constructed with
εἰς in LXX : e. g., Ezek. xv. 4 ; Wisd. xiii.
11. Cf. also Wisd. xv. 15), (**but practised**)
to (on condition of following from it as
a necessary consequence as if it had been
by covenant attached to it) **the ruin** (the
opposite of οἰκοδομή, cf. καθαίρεσις, 2 Cor.
xiii. 10) **of them that hear.** 15.]
The connexion is close :—by averting them
from vain and unprofitable things, approve
thine own work, so that it may stand in
the day of the Lord. **Strive** (reff.) **to
present thyself** (emphatic, as distinguished
from those alluded to in the preceding
verse) **to God approved** (reff.: tested by
trial, and found to have stood the test.
Not to be joined with ἐργάτην, as Mack),
a workman (a general word, of any kind
of labourer, used (see reff.) of *teachers*
perhaps from the parable in Matt. xx.)
unshamed (by his work being found unworthy : cf. Phil. i. 20,—ἐν οὐδενὶ αἰσχυνθήσομαι, and 1 Cor. iv. 4 : " cui tua
ipsius conscientia nullum pudorem incu-
tiat." Beng. Κypke quotes from Jos. Antt.
xviii. 9 [it should be xviii. 7. 1, see Moulton's Winer, p. 296, note 1], μηδὲ δευτε-
ρεύειν ἀνεπαίσχυντον ἡγοῦ, 'neque credas id
pudore vacare, si secundum teneas locum.'
Chrys., al., would take the word actively,
' not being ashamed of his work,' τουτέστι,
μηδὲν ὅλως αἰσχύνου πράττειν τῶν εἰς εὐσέβειαν ἡκόντων, κἂν δουλεῦσαι δέῃ, κἂν
ὁτιοῦν παθεῖν, Chrys.: and so Agapetus,
in Wetst., παρ᾽ ἄλλῳ εὑρεθέντα μηδαμῶς
παρορᾷ, ἀλλὰ μανθάνει μὲν ἀνεπαίσχύν-

v here only.
Prov. iii. 6.
xi. 5 only.
w 2 Cor. vi. 7.
Eph. i 13.
James i. 18.
(see Gal. ii.
14.)

ᵛ ὀρθοτομοῦντα τὸν ʷ λόγον τῆς ἀληθείας. ¹⁶ τὰς δὲ ᵡ βεβήλους ʸ κενοφωνίας ᶻ περιΐστασο· ᵃ ἐπὶ πλεῖον γὰρ ᵇ προκόψουσιν ᶜ ἀσεβείας, ¹⁷ καὶ ὁ λόγος αὐτῶν ὡς ᵈ γάγ-

ACDFK
LPℵ a b
c d e f g
h k l m n
o 17. 47

x 1 Tim. i. 9 reff.
xxv. 7) only ‡.
52. Rom. xiii. 12. Gal. i. 14. ch. iii. 9, 13 only †.
παρανομίας, Jos. B. J. vi. 2. 2. (-πή, 1 Tim. iv. 15.)
only. Jer. v. 6. (-βεῖν, 2 Pet. ii. 6. -βῆς, 1 Tim. i. 9.)

y 1 Tim. vi. 20 (there also w. βεβ.) only †.
a Acts iv. 17. xx. 9. xxiv. 4 (Paul). ch. iii. 9 only. Jer. ii. 12.
Ps. xliv. 4 Alius in Hexapl. προΰκοψαν εἰς τοσοῦτον
c Rom. i. 18. xi. 26. Tit. ii. 12. Jude 15, 18
d here only †.

z = Tit. iii. 9 (John xi. 42. Acts
b Luke ii.

16. καινοφωνιας F D-lat Chr Lucif Ambrst Aug. (G-lat has both.) ασεβεις [for -βειας] D¹K ; ασεβεια D³.

τως : but the above seems more according to the context. The opposite to ἐργ. ἀνεπαίσχυντος is ἐργάτης δόλιος, 2 Cor. xi. 13), **rightly administering** (the *meaning* of ὀρθοτομέω is very variously derived and explained,—'recte secare' being unquestionably the *rendering*. (1) Melanchthon, Beza, Grot., al., suppose the meaning deduced from the *right division of the victims*, Levit. i. 6 ff.: (2) Vitringa (de Synagog. p. 714, De W.), Calv., al., from the *cutting and distributing of bread* by the steward or father of a household : 'ac si pater alendis filiis panem in frusta secando distribueret.' (3) Pricæus, 'a *lapicidis*, quos melius ἐργάτας vocaveris quam vietimarios illos. Eurip. de Neptuno Trojam ædificante, λαΐνους πύργους πέριξ ὀρθοῖς ἔτεμνε κανόσιν,'—Apuleius, '*non*, inquit, *e monte meo afferam lapidem directim cæsum*, i. e. ὀρθοτετμημένον. Glossarium, *directum*, κατὰ κανόνα ὀρθωθέν :' (4) Thdrt. (ἐπαινοῦμεν τῶν γεωργῶν τοὺς εὐθείας τὰς αὔλακας ἀνατέμνοντας), Lamb-Bos, al., from *plowers*, who are said τέμνειν τὴν γῆν, σχίζειν and ἐπισχίζειν ἀρούρας : (5) Most Commentators, from the more general form of the last explanation, the *cutting* a *way* or a *road* : as 'καινοτομεῖν, novam viam secare, nova via incedere,' so 'ὀρθοτομεῖν, rectam viam secare,' but here used transitively, the λόγος τῆς ἀληθείας being itself the ὁδός : so in Prov. xi. 5, δικαιοσύνη ἀμώμους ὀρθοτομεῖ ὁδούς, and Eurip. Rhes. 422, εὐθεῖαν λόγων τέμνων κέλευθον : Gal. ii. 14, ὀρθοποδεῖν πρὸς τὴν ἀλήθειαν τοῦ εὐαγγελίου. So De W.: but Huther objects, and I think with reason, that in all these places the idea of a *way* is expressly introduced, and that without such expression we cannot supply the idea in λόγον. (6) Huther's own view, that, the original meaning being 'rightly to divide,' the idea of τέμνειν was gradually lost, as in καινοτομεῖν, so that the word came to signify 'to manage rightly,' 'to treat truthfully without falsifying,' seems to approach the nearest to the requirements of the context : the

opposite being, as he observes, καπηλεύειν τὸν λόγον τοῦ θεοῦ, 2 Cor. ii. 17. (7) The meaning given by Chrys. and Œc.— τέμνε τὰ νόθα, καὶ τὰ τοιαῦτα μετὰ πολλῆς τῆς σφοδρότητος ἐφίστασο καὶ ἔκκοπτε, does not seem to belong to the word. (8) It is plain that the patristic usages of it, as e. g. in the Clementine Constt. vii. 33 (Grot.) ὀρθοτομοῦντας ἐν τοῖς κυρίου δόγμασι,—Clem. Alex., Strom. vii. 16 (104), p. 896 P., τὴν ἀποστολικὴν καὶ ἐκκλησιαστικὴν ὀρθοτομίαν τῶν δογμάτων, —Greg.-Naz. apol. fugæ, pp. 23, 28 (Kypke, from Fuller), opposing to ὀρθοτομεῖν, κακῶς ὁδεύειν,—have *sprung from this passage*, and cannot be cited as precedents, only as interpretations) **the word of the** (the art. seems here better expressed : cf. ver. 18 below, and the usage throughout these Epistles, e. g. 1 Tim. iii. 15; iv. 3; vi. 5; ch. iii. 8; iv. 4; Tit. i. 14) **truth. 16.]** But (contrast not to the ὀρθοτομεῖν merely, but to the whole course of conduct recommended in the last verse) **profane babblings** (see ref. 1 Tim.) **avoid** (= ἐκτρέπεσθαι, 1 Tim. vi. 20: so Origen has περιΐστασθαι κινδύνους (in Hammond) : Joseph. B. J. ii. 8. 6, of the Essenes, τὸ ὀμνύειν αὐτοῖς περιΐσταται : Lucian, Hermotim. c. 86, οὕτως ἐκτραπήσομαι καὶ περιστήσομαι, ὥσπερ τοὺς λυττῶντας τῶν κυνῶν : Marc. Antonin. iii. 4, χρὴ μὲν οὖν καὶ τὸ εἰκῆ καὶ μάτην ἐν τῷ εἱρμῷ τῶν φαντασιῶν περιΐστασθαι : see other examples in Wetst. The meaning seems to come from a number of persons falling back from an object of fear or loathing, and standing at a distance round it. Beza's sense, 'cohibe, i. e. observa et velut obside, nempe ne in ecclesiam irrepant,' has no countenance from usage): **for they** (the false teachers : not the κενοφωνίαι : cf. ὁ λόγος αὐτῶν below) **will advance** (intransitive, see reff.,—not transitive, governing ἀσεβείας in the accus.: see below) **to a worse pitch of impiety** (cf. ref. Jos., and Diodor. Sic. xiv. 98, ὁ δὲ βασιλεὺς οὐ βουλόμενος τὸν Εὐαγόραν προκόπτειν ἐπὶ πλεῖον ....), **and their word will eat**

γραινα [e] νομὴν ἕξει. [f] ὧν ἐστιν Ὑμέναιος καὶ Φίλητος, e (see note) =
18 [g] οἵτινες [hi] περὶ τὴν ἀλήθειαν [ik] ἠστόχησαν, λέγοντες
[τὴν] ἀνάστασιν ἤδη γεγονέναι, καὶ [l] ἀνατρέπουσιν τὴν
[m] τινῶν πίστιν. 19 ὁ [n] μέντοι [o] στερεὸς [p] θεμέλιος τοῦ
θεοῦ ἕστηκεν, ἔχων τὴν [q] σφραγῖδα ταύτην [r] Ἔγνω κύριος

e (see note) = here (John x. 9) only ‡.
f gen., 1 Tim. i. 19. ch. i. 15.
g = Acts x. 41, 47 al. Paul, passim.
h so 1 Tim. i. 19.
i 1 Tim. vi. 21.
n John iv.

k 1 Tim. i. 6 reff. l Tit. i. 11 only. Prov. x. 3. m 1 Tim. i. 3 reff. n John iv.
27 al4. James ii. 8. Jude 8 only. o Heb. v. 12, 14. 1 Pet. v. 9 only. Deut. xxxii. 13.
p 1 Cor. iii. 11. Heb. vi. 1 al. Ps. lxxxvi. 1. q Rom. iv. 11. 1 Cor. ix. 2 only, exc. Rev. (v. 1 and
al12). Cant. viii. 6. r Gal. iv. 9 reff. Num. xvi. 5.

18. om 2nd την Fℵ 17. την πιστ. την τινων ανατρ. D goth : την πιστ. τιν. αν.
F : αν. την πιστιν τιν. ℵ³ 17 : αν. την π. την τιν. ℵ¹.
19. for θεου, κυριου ℵ¹ : χριστου 91. aft κυρ. ins παντας ℵ¹(ℵ³ disapproving).

(νομή (pasture, ref. John. Aristot. Hist.
An. 10), from νέμεσθαι (τὸ φῦμα ἐκραγὲν
ἐνέμετο πρόσω, Herod. iii. 133), is the
medical term for the consuming progress
of mortifying disease: cf. νομαὶ σαρκὸς
θηριώδεις, Plut. Mor. p. 165 e: τὸ ἕλκος
θᾶττον ποιεῖται νομήν, Polyb. i. 81. 6,
and Hippocrates and Galen in Wetst. It
is also used of the devastating progress of
fire, as in Polyb. i. 48. 5, τὴν μὲν νομὴν
τοῦ πυρὸς ἐνεργον συνέβαινε γίγνεσθαι,
and xi. 5. 5, τὸ πῦρ λαμβάνει νομήν) as a
gangrene (γάγγραινα, from γράω, γραίνω,
to eat into, is defined by Hippocrates (in
Wetst.) to be the state of a tumour between
inflammation and entire mortification—
ἕπεται ταῖς μεγάλαις φλεγμοναῖς ἡ καλου-
μένη γάγγραινα, νέκρωσίς τε οὖσα τοῦ
πάσχοντος μορίου, καὶ ἢν μὴ διὰ ταχέων
τις αὐτὴν ἰάσηται, νεκροῦται ῥᾳδίως τὸ
πάσχον τοῦτο μόριον, ἐπιλαμβάνει τε τὰ
συνεχῆ, καὶ ἀποκτείνει τὸν ἄνθρωπον. Sometimes it is identical with καρκῖνος, a can-
cer): of whom is (ref.) Hymenæus (see
note, 1 Tim. i. 20) and Philetus (of him
nothing further is known), men who concerning the truth went astray (cf. 1 Tim.
vi. 21), saying that the resurrection has
already taken place (cf. Tert. de resurr.
carnis, c. 19, vol. ii. p. 820,—"resurrectionem quoque mortuorum manifeste adnun-
tiatam in imaginariam significationem dis-
torquent, adseverantes ipsam etiam mortem
spiritaliter intelligendam. Non enim hanc
esse in vero quæ sit in medio dissidium
carnis atque animæ, sed ignorantiam Dei,
per quam homo mortuus Deo non minus in
errore jacuerit quam in sepulcro. Itaque
et resurrectionem eam vindicandam, qua
quis adita veritate sed animatus et revivi-
ficatus Deo, ignorantiæ morte discussa,
velut de sepulcro veteris hominis eruperit:
. . . . exinde ergo resurrectionem fide con-
secutos cum domino esse, cum eum in baptismate induerint." So also Irenæus, ii.
31. 2, p. 164, "esse autem resurrectionem
a mortuis, agnitionem ejus quæ ab eis dicitur veritatis." (See Ellicott's note.) This
error, which belonged to the Gnostics subsequently, may well have been already
sown and springing up in the apostolic age.
If the form of it was that described by Tertullian, it would be one of those instances
of wresting the words of St. Paul himself
(cf. Col. ii. 12: Rom. vi. 4, al.) of which
St. Peter speaks 2 Pet. iii. 16. See on
this Aug. Ep. lv. (cxix.) 4, vol. iii. p. 206.
Thdrt. (so also Pel.) gives a curious and
certainly mistaken meaning,—τὰς ἐκ παι-
δοποιΐας διαδοχὰς ἀνάστασιν οἱ δυσώνυμοι
προσηγόρευον: (so Aug. Hær. 59, de Se-
leucianis, vol. viii. p. 42,—"Resurrectionem non putant futuram, sed quotidie fieri
in generatione filiorum:") Schöttg. another, but merely as a conjecture,—that
the resurrection of some of the bodies of the
saints with Christ (Matt. xxvii. 52) may
have been by them called 'the Resurrection of the dead'), and are overturning
(ref.) the faith of some. 19.] Firm endurance, notwithstanding this overturning
of the faith of some, of the church of God:
its signs and seals. Nevertheless (cf.
Ellicott) God's firm foundation standeth
(not, as E. V. ungrammatically, 'the foundation of God standeth sure.' But what
is ὁ στερεὸς θεμ. τ. θεοῦ? Very various
interpretations have been given. παρασα-
λεῦσαι, says Thdrt., οὐ δύνανται τὴν τῆς
ἀληθείας κρηπῖδα. ὁ θεὸς γὰρ τοῦτον
τέθεικε τὸν θεμέλιον: Cocceius, Michaelis,
Ernesti, explain it the fundamental doctrine of the Resurrection: Ambr., the
promises of God: Bengel, Vatabl., fidem
Dei immotam: Bretschn., al., Christ, 1 Cor.
iii. 11: Heinrichs, Rosenm., the Christian
religion: Calv., Calov., Wolf, Corn.-a-
lap., al., Dei electionem. Rather, as
Mosh., Kypke, Heydenr., Mack, De W.,
Huther, Wiesinger, al., ἐκκλησία τεθεμε-
λιωμένη ὑπὸ θεοῦ—the congregation of
the faithful, considered as a foundation of
a building placed by God,—the οἰκία
spoken of in the next verse. So Estius:
"Ipsa ecclesia rectissime firmum ac solidum Dei fundamentum vocatur, quia super

τοὺς ὄντας ˢ αὐτοῦ, καὶ ᵗ ᾿Αποστήτω ἀπὸ ἀδικίας πᾶς ὁ
ᵘ ὀνομάζων τὸ ὄνομα κυρίου. ²⁰ ἐν μεγάλῃ δὲ οἰκίᾳ οὐκ
ἔστιν μόνον ᵛʷ σκεύη χρυσᾶ καὶ ἀργυρᾶ, ἀλλὰ καὶ ˣ ξύλινα
καὶ ʸ ὀστράκινα, καὶ ʷᶻ ἃ μὲν ʷ εἰς τιμήν, ʷᶻ ἃ δὲ ʷ εἰς
ᵃ ἀτιμίαν. ²¹ ἐὰν οὖν τις ᵇ ἐκκαθάρῃ ἑαυτὸν ἀπὸ τούτων,
ἔσται ʷ σκεῦος ʷ εἰς τιμήν, ᶜ ἡγιασμένον, ᵈ εὔχρηστον τῷ

ACDFK LPℵ a b c d e f g h k l m n o 17. 47

s gen., Rom. xiv. 8. 1 Cor. i. 12. iii. 23. Num. l. c. **t** = 1 Tim. iv. 1 reff. Num. xvi. 27. Isa. lii. 11. **u** = Rom. xv. 20 only. (Eph. i. 21 reff.) Isa. xxvi. 13. **v** Matt. xii. 29. Heb. ix. 21. Rev. ii. 27. xviii. 12 bis, al. Exod. iii. 22. **w** Rom. ix. 21. xi. 32. **y** 2 Cor. iv. 7 only. Levit. vi. 28 (in both places w. σκ.). 35. Luke xxiii. 33 al. Polyb. i. 7. 3. **a** Rom. i. 26. ix. 21. 1 Cor. xi. 14. xv. 43. 2 Cor. vi. 8. xi. 21 only. P. Isa. xxii. 18. **b** 1 Cor. v. 7 only. Deut. xxvi. 13. Judg. vii. 4 B only. **x** Rev. ix. 20 only. Lev. **z** Matt. xiii. 18. xxi. **c** Acts xx. 32. xxvi. 18 (both Paul). Rom. xv. 16 al. Isa. x. 17. 16 Ald. xxxi. 13. Wisd. xiii. 13 only. **d** ch. iv. 11. Philem. 11 only. Prov. xi.

rec (for κυριου) χριστου, with c e: txt ACDFKL[P]ℵ rel vss gr-lat-ff. (17 def.)
21. εκκαθερη A.   om εσται σκευος ℵ¹(ins ℵ-corr¹).   rec ins και bef ευχρη-
στον, with C¹D²·³KL[P]ℵ³ rel vulg syr [sah æth arm] Orig₃[and int₂] Thdrt₁: om
C²D¹Fℵ¹ f 17 Syr copt goth Ephr Chr Thdrt₁ Œc [Orig-int₂] Ambrst Aug₂. (A uncert.)

petram, i. e. Christum, a Deo firmiter fun-
data, nullis aut Satanæ machinis aut ten-
tationum fluctibus subverti potest aut
labefactari: nam etsi quidam ab ea de-
ficiunt, ipsa tamen in suis electis per-
severat usque in finem." He then cites
1 John ii. 19: Matt. xxiv. 24: John x. 28:
Rom. viii. 35, 39: and proceeds, "Ex his
admodum fit verisimile, firmum Dei fundamentum intelligi fideles electos: sive,
quod idem est, ecclesiam in electis."
Against the tottering faith of those just
mentioned, he sets the στερεὸς θεμ., and
the ἔστηκεν. It cannot be moved: Heb.
xii. 28), **having** ("*seeing it hath*,' part.
with a very faint causal force, illustrating
the previous declaration: cf. Donalds. Gr.
§ 615." Ellic.) **this seal** (probably in allusion to the practice of engraving inscriptions over doors (Deut. vi. 9; xi. 20) and
on pillars and foundation stones (Rev. xxi.
14). The seal (inscription) would indicate
ownership and *destination:* both of which
are pointed at in the two texts following)
(1) **The Lord knoweth** (see 1 Cor. viii. 3,
note: 'novit amanter (?), nec nosse de-
sinit,' as Bengel) **them that are His** (the
LXX runs: ἐπέσκεπται καὶ ἔγνω ὁ θεὸς
τοὺς ὄντας αὐτοῦ καὶ τοὺς ἁγίους, καὶ
προσηγάγετο πρὸς ἑαυτόν): **and** (2) **Let
every one that nameth the name of the
Lord** (viz. *as* his Lord: not exactly equivalent to 'calleth on the name of the Lord')
stand aloof from iniquity (the passage in
Isa. stands, ἀπόστητε, ἀπόστητε, ἐξέλθατε
ἐκεῖθεν, καὶ ἀκαθάρτου μὴ ἅψησθε, ...
ἀφορίσθητε οἱ φέροντες τὰ σκεύη κυρίου.
It is clearly no reason against this passage being here *alluded to,* that (as
Conyb.) it is *expressly cited* 2 Cor. vi. 17.
Ellic. remarks, that it is possibly in continued allusion to Num. xvi. 26, ἀπο-
σχίσθητε ἀπὸ τῶν σκηνῶν, τῶν ἀνθρώπων
τῶν σκληρῶν τούτων). **20.**] Those

who are truly the Lord's are known to
Him and depart from iniquity: but in
the visible church there are many unworthy members. This is illustrated by
the following similitude. **But** (contrast
to the preceding definition of the Lord's
people) **in a great house** (= ἐν τῇ οἰκου-
μένῃ πάσῃ, Chrys., who strenuously up-
holds that view; so also Thdrt. and the
Greek Commentators, Grot., al.: but far
better understood of the church, for the
reason given by Calv.: "contextus quidem huc potius nos ducit, ut de ecclesia
intelligamus: neque enim de extraneis disputat Paulus, sed de ipsa Dei familia :"
also Cypr., Aug., Ambr., all. The idea
then is much the same as that in the parable of the drag-net, Matt. xiii. 47—49:
not in the parable of the tares of the
field, as De W.: for there it is expressly
said, ὁ ἀγρὸς ἐστὶν ὁ κόσμος) **there are
not only vessels of gold and silver, but
also of wood and earthenware; and some
for honour, some for dishonour** (viz. in
the use of the vessels themselves: not,
as Mack, al., to bring honour or dishonour
on the house or its inhabitants. Estius,
anxious to avoid the idea of heretics being
in the church, would understand the two
classes in each sentence as those distinguished by gifts, and those not so distinguished: and so Corn.-a-lap., al.: but
this seems alien from the context: cf.
especially the next verse. On the comparison, see Ellic.'s references). **21.**]
Here the thing signified is mingled with
the similitude: the voluntary act described belonging, not to the vessels, but
to the members of the church who are designated by them. **If then** (οὖν deduces
a consequence from the similitude: q. d.
'his positis') **any man** (member of the
church) **shall have purified himself** (not ✱
as Chrys., παντελῶς καθάρῃ: but as

δεσπότῃ, ᶜ εἰς πᾶν ᵉ ἔργον ᵉ ἀγαθὸν ᶠ ἡτοιμασμένον. ²² τὰς
δὲ ᵍ νεωτερικὰς ἐπιθυμίας ʰ φεῦγε, ʰⁱᵏ δίωκε δὲ ʰⁱˡ δικαιοσύνην,
ʰ πίστιν, ʰ ἀγάπην, ᵐ εἰρήνην ᵐ μετὰ τῶν ⁿ ἐπικαλουμένων
τὸν κύριον ᵒ ἐκ ᵒ καθαρᾶς ᵒ καρδίας. ²³ τὰς δὲ ᵖᑫ μωρὰς

e Paul, 2 Cor.
ix. 8. Col. i.
10. 1 Tim. v.
10. ch. iii. 17.
Tit. i. 16. iii.
1 al6. Acts
ix. 36. Heb.
xiii. 21.
f Gospp., Matt.
iii. 3 (from
g here
h = 1 Tim. vi.
1 so Rom. vi. 13 al.

Isa. xl. 3) al. fr. Epp., 1 Cor. ii. 9. Philem. 22. Heb. xi. 16 only. Rev. viii. 6 al.
only †. αὐθάδεια νεωτερική, Jos. Antt. xvi. 11. 7. ν. ζῆλοι, Polyb. x. 24. 7.
11 (reff.). i Rom. ix. 30. 1 Tim. as above. k 1 Thess. v. 15.
m see note. 1 Macc. vi. 49, 58. x. 4. n Acts vii. 59. Rom. x. 12 (&c.). mostly w. ὄνομα, Acts ii. 21
(from Joel ii. 32) al. o 1 Tim. i. 5 reff. p Tit. iii. 9. q Gospp. Matt. (only)
v. 22 al6. 1 Cor. i. 25, 27. iii. 18. iv. 10. Tit. iii. 9 only. Isa. xxxii. 6.

for 2nd εις, προς DF [47].
22. αγαπην bef πιστιν F.   for των, παντων F 73 : παντων των AC 17 syr [sah]
æth Chr-txt Thdrt Isid : txt DKL[P]א rel vulg Syr copt goth [arm] Chr-comm
Damasc Thl Œc Ambrst.   for επικαλ., αγαπωντων A.

Bengel, 'purgando sese *exierit* de numero horum :' the ἐκ corresponds to the ἀπο below, and I have attempted to give that in the following) **from among these** (viz. the latter mentioned vessels in each parallel ; but more especially the σκεύη εἰς ἀτιμίαν, from what follows), **he shall be a vessel for honour** (Chrys. remarks : ὁρᾷς ὅτι οὐ φύσεως οὐδὲ ὑλικῆς ἀνάγκης ἐστὶ τὸ εἶναι χρυσοῦν ἢ ὀστράκινον. ἀλλὰ τῆς ἡμετέρας προαιρέσεως (?) ; ἐκεῖ μὲν γὰρ τὸ ὀστράκινον οὐκ ἂν γένηται χρυσοῦν, οὐδὲ τοῦτο εἰς τὴν ἐκείνου καταπεσεῖν εὐτέλειαν δυνήσεται· ἐνταῦθα δὲ πολλὴ μεταβολὴ καὶ μετάστασις. σκεῦος ὀστράκινον ἦν ὁ Παῦλος, ἀλλ' ἐγένετο χρυσοῦν. σκεῦος χρυσοῦν ἦν (?) ὁ Ἰούδας, ἀλλ' ἐγένετο ὀστράκινον), **hallowed** (not to be joined, as Calv. and Lachmann, who expunges the comma after τιμήν, — with εἰς τιμήν, seeing that εἰς τιμήν stands absolutely in the former verse. ἡγιασμένος (reff.) is a favourite word with our Apostle to describe the saints of God), **useful** (see instances of the meaning of this epithet· in the two N. T. reff.) **for the master** (of the house), **prepared for every good work** (κἂν μὴ πράττῃ, ἀλλ' ὅμως ἐπιτήδειόν ἐστι, δεκτικόν. δεῖ οὖν πρὸς πάντα παρεσκευάσθαι, κἂν πρὸς θάνατον, κἂν πρὸς μαρτύριον· κἂν πρὸς παρθενίαν, κἂν πρὸς ταῦτα πάντα. Chrys.).   22.] Exhortations, taken up again from ver. 16, on the matter of which the intervening verses have been a digression. **But** (contrast to the last-mentioned character, ver. 21, in the introduction of νεωτ. ἐπιθ.) **youthful lusts** (not 'cupiditates rerum novarum,' as Salmasius ; see against him Suicer, vol. i. p. 1167,—νεωτερικαὶ οὐχ αὗται εἰσὶν αἱ τῆς πορνείας μόνον, ἀλλὰ πᾶσα ἐπιθυμία ἄτοπος, νεωτερική. ἀκουέτωσαν οἱ γεγηρακότες, ὅτι οὐ δεῖ τὰ τῶν νεωτέρων ποιεῖν. κἂν ὑβριστὴς ᾖ τις, κἂν δυναστείας ἐρᾷ, κἂν χρημάτων, κἂν σωμάτων, κἂν ὁτουοῦν δήποτε, νεωτερικὴ ἡ ἐπιθυμία, ἀνόητος· οὔπω τῆς καρδίας βε-

βηκυίας οὐδὲ τῶν φρενῶν ἐν βάθει τεθεισῶν, ἀλλ' ἐωρημένων, ἀνάγκη ταῦτα πάντα γίι νεσθαι. Chrys.; and Thdrt., τουτέστ- τρυφήν, γέλωτος ἀμετρίαν, δόξαν κενήν, καὶ τὰ τούτοις προσόμοια. See also Basil. Cæs. in Suicer, as above) **fly from, but** (contrast to the hypothesis of the opposite course to that recommended above) **follow after righteousness** (moral rectitude, as contrasted with ἀδικία, ver. 19 : not, as Calov., 'the righteousness which is by faith ;' far better Calvin : 'hoc est, rectam vivendi rationem.' See the parallel, 1 Tim. vi. 11), **faith, love, peace with** (μετά belongs to εἰρήνην, not to δίωκε ; cf. Heb. xii. 14, εἰρήνην διώκετε μετὰ πάντων : also Rom. xii. 18) **those who call upon the Lord** (Christ, see 1 Cor. i. 2) **out of a pure heart** (these last words belong to ἐπικαλουμένων, and serve to designate the earnest and single-minded, as contrasted with the false teachers, who called on Him, but not out of a pure heart : cf. ch. iii. 5, 8, and especially Tit. i. 15, 16. Chrys. draws as an inference from this, μετὰ δὲ τῶν ἄλλων οὐ χρὴ πρᾶον εἶναι, which is directly against ver. 25 : Thdrt. far better, drawing the distinction between *love* and *peace* : ἀγαπᾶν μὲν γὰρ ἅπαντας δυνατόν, ἐπειδήπερ τοῦτο καὶ ὁ εὐαγγελικὸς παρακελεύεται νόμος, Ἀγαπᾶτε τοὺς ἐχθροὺς ὑμῶν· εἰρηνεύειν δὲ οὐ πρὸς ἅπαντας ἔνεστι, τῆς γὰρ κοινῆς τοῦτο προαιρέσεως δεῖται· τοιοῦτοι δὲ πάντες οἱ ἐκ καθαρᾶς καρδίας τὸν δεσπότην ἐπικαλούμενοι. See Rom. xii. 18).
    23.] But (contrast again to the hypothesis of the contrary of the last exhortation) **foolish** (Tit. iii. 9) **and undisciplined** (ἀπαίδευτος can hardly be ✱ wrested from its proper sense and made to mean 'unprofitable πρὸς παιδείαν,' but, as in reff., must mean *lacking* παιδεία, shewing want of wholesome discipline. Grot. limits it too narrowly, when he says, 'Intelligit hic Paulus quæstiones immodestas : nam et Græci pro ἀκόλαστον dicunt ἀπαί-

r here only.
Prov. viii. 5.
xv. 14.
■ 1 Tim i. 4
reff.
t = 1 Tim. iv.
7 reff.
u Paul, Acts
xxii. 3, 28.
Rom. ix. 11.
1 Cor. iv. 15.
Gal iv. 23,
24, 29.

καὶ ʳ ἀπαιδεύτους ᵖˢ ζητήσεις ᵗ παραιτοῦ, εἰδὼς ὅτι ᵘ γεννῶ-
σιν ᵛ μάχας· ²⁴ ʷ δοῦλον δὲ κυρίου οὐ δεῖ ˣ μάχεσθαι,
ἀλλὰ ʸ ἤπιον εἶναι πρὸς πάντας, ᶻ διδακτικόν, ᵃ ἀνεξίκα-
κον, ²⁵ ἐν ᵇ πραΰτητι ᶜ παιδεύοντα τοὺς ᵈ ἀντιδιατιθεμένους,
ᵉ μήποτε δώῃ αὐτοῖς ὁ θεὸς ᶠ μετάνοιαν ᶠ εἰς ᵍʰ ἐπίγνωσιν

ACDFK
LPℵ a b
c d e f g
h k l m n
o 17. 47

Philem. 10 only. Heb. i. 5, from Ps. it. 7. 1 John ii. 29 al. fr.   v 2 Cor. vii. 5. Tit. iii. 9. James iv. 1
only. ≈ Gen. xiii. 7.   w = Gal. i. 10 reff.   x John vi. 52. Acts vii. 26. James iv. 2 only. Gen.
xxvi 20.   y 1 Thess. ii. 7 only †.   z 1 Tim. iii. 2 only †.   a here only †. (·κία, Wisd.
ii. 19.)   b Gal. v. 23 reff.   c 1 Tim. i. 20 reff.   d here only †.   e = here
only (not Gen. xxiv. 5). see Luke iii. 15.   f 2 Cor. vii. 10.   g Eph. i. 17 reff.   h 1 Tim.
ii. 4 reff.

24. (αλλα, so ADFℵ 17.)   for ηπιον, νηπιον (see 1 Thess ii. 7) D¹F [æth].
25. for εν, συν F latt [Orig-int₂] (cum in modestia D-lat).   rec πραοτητι, with
D³KL rel: πριχοτητι F: txt ACD¹[P]ℵ 17 [47] 67² Ephr Bas Chr-mss.   αντι-
διαθεμενους C: αντικειμενους F.   rec (for δοη) δω, with D³KL[P]ℵ³ rel: txt
ACD¹Fℵ Ephr Chr-ms Isid.   om μετανοιαν ℵ¹.   at end ins ελθειν A.

δευτον (sine disciplina): quia idem est
κολάζειν et παιδεύειν") questionings decline (reff.), being aware that they gender
strifes (reff.): but (contrast to the fact of
μάχαι) the (better than a, as De W. The
meaning being much the same, and δοῦλον
in the emphatic place representing τὸν
δοῦλον, the definite art., in rendering, gives
the emphasis, and points out the individual
servant, better than the indefinite) servant
of the Lord (Jesus; see 1 Cor. vii. 22. It
is evident from what follows, that the servant of the Lord here, in the Apostle's view,
is not so much every true Christian,—however applicable such a maxim may be to
him also,—but the minister of Christ, as
Timotheus was: cf. διδακτικόν, &c. below)
must not strive (the argument is in the
form of an enthymeme:—'propositionem
ab experientia manifestam relinquit. As-
sumptio vero tacitam sui probationem in-
cludit, eamque hujusmodi: servum oportet
imitari Dominum suum.' Estius), but be
gentle (ref.) towards all, apt to teach
(ref.:—so E. V. well: for, as Bengel, 'hoc
non solum soliditatem et facilitatem in
docendo, sed vel maxime patientiam et
assiduitatem significat.' In fact these
latter must be, on account of the contrast
which the Apostle is bringing out, regarded as prominent here), patient of
wrong (so Conyb., and perhaps we can
hardly find a better expression, though
'wrong' does not by any means cover the
meaning of the κακόν: 'long-suffering'
would be unobjectionable, were it not that
we have μακρόθυμος, to which that word is
already appropriated. Plutarch, Coriolan.
c. 15, says, that he did not repress his
temper, οὐδὲ τὴν ἐρημίᾳ ξύνοικον, ὡς
Πλάτων ἔλεγεν, αὐθάδειαν εἰδὼς ὅτι δεῖ
μάλιστα διαφεύγειν ἐπιχειροῦντα πράγ-
μασι κοινοῖς καὶ ἀνθρώποις ὁμιλεῖν, καὶ
γενέσθαι τῆς πολλὰ γελωμένης ὑπ' ἐνίων

ἀνεξικακίας ἐραστήν), in meekness correcting (not 'instructing,' see reff., and
note on ἀπαιδεύτους, ver. 23) those who
oppose themselves (better than as Ambrst., *
'eos qui diversa sentiunt:' to take the
general meaning of διατίθεσθαι, satisfies
the context better, than to supply τὸν
νοῦν. The Vulg., 'eos qui resistunt veri-
tati,' particularizes too much in another
way), if at any time (literally, 'lest at any
time:' but μήποτε in later Greek sometimes loses this aversative meaning and is
almost equivalent to εἴποτε. Cf. Viger,
p. 457, where the annotator says of μήποτε,
'vocula tironibus saepissime crucem figens,
cum significat fortasse, vel si quando,' and
he then cites this passage. The account
to be given of the usage is that, from μή
being commonly used after verbs of fearing,
&c.,—then after verbs expressing anxiety
of any kind (φροντίζω, μὴ . . . Xen.:
σκοπῶ, μὴ ο . . Plato: ὑποπτεύειν, μὴ
. . . Xen.: αἰσχύνομαι, μὴ . . . Plato) its
proper aversative force by degrees became
forgotten, and thus it, and words compounded with it, were used in later Greek
in sentences where no such force can be
intended. De W. refers to Kypke for examples of this usage from Plut. and Athenæus: but Kypke does not notice the word
here at all) God may give them repentance
(because their consciences were impure (see
above on ver. 22) and lives evil. Cf. Ellic.'s
remarks on μετάν.) in order to the knowledge of (the) truth (see note, 1 Tim.
ii. 4), and they may awake sober (from
their moral and spiritual intoxication: so
ἐκνήφ., in ref. 1 Cor., and this same word
in Jos.: the θρῆνοι there, as the ensnare-
ment by the devil here, being regarded as
a kind of intoxication. There is no one
word in English which will express ἀνα-
νήψαι: Conyb. has paraphrased it by
'escape, restored to soberness' ('return

h ἀληθείας, ²⁶ καὶ ⁱ ἀνανήψωσιν ᵏ ἐκ τῆς τοῦ ¹ διαβόλου
¹ παγίδος ᵐ ἐζωγρημένοι ὑπ' ⁿ αὐτοῦ εἰς τὸ ⁿ ἐκείνου
θέλημα.

i here only †.
ἐκ θρήνων
ἀνανήφειν,
Jos. Antt. vi.
11. 10.
(ἐκνήφ.,
1 Cor. xv. 34.)
m Luke

k constr. praegn., 2 Thess. ii. 2.   Rom. vi. 7. vii. 2. ix. 3.
v. 10 only.   2 Chron. xxv. 12.   n see note.

1 1 Tim. iii. 6, 7 reff.

26. ἀνανηψουσιν C [17. 47¹] : αναλημψωσιν D¹ : ανανηψωσιν A-corr n o. (A¹ erased.)
[εζωγρισμενοι P.]

to soberness,' Ellic.) : perhaps the E. V.,
'recover themselves,' is as near an approach to the meaning as we can get.
We have the word used literally by Plutarch, Camillus, c. 23 : ὁ Κάμιλλος . . . .
περὶ μέσας τὰς νύκτας προσέμιξε τῷ
χάρακι . . . . ἐκταράττων ἀνθρώπους κακῶς ὑπὸ μέθης κ. μόλις ἐκ τῶν ὕπνων
ἀναφέροντας πρὸς τὸν θόρυβον. ὀλίγοι
μὲν οὖν ἀνανήψαντες ἐν τῷ φόβῳ κ. δια-
σκευασάμενοι, τοὺς περὶ τὸν Κάμιλλον
ὑπέστησαν . . . . Sir Thomas North renders it, 'There were some notwithstanding did bustle up at the sudden noise.'
See also examples in Wetst.) **out of the
snare of the devil** (gen. subj., 'the snare
which the devil laid for them.' There is
properly no confusion of metaphor, the
idea being that these persons have in a
state of intoxication been entrapped, and
are enabled, at their awaking sober, to
escape. But the construction is elliptic,
ἀνανήψωσιν ἐκ = ἐκφύγωσιν ἀνανήψαντες ἐκ), **having been** (during their spiritual μέθη) **taken captive by him unto**
(for the fulfilment of, in pursuance of)
the will of Him (viz. God : that Other,
indicated by ἐκείνου. Thus I am now
persuaded the words must be rendered :
αὐτοῦ, referring to the devil, and it being
signified that the taking captive of these
men by him only takes place as far as God
permits ; according to His will. Rendering it thus, as do Aret., Estius, and Ellicott, I do not hold the other view, which
makes αὐτοῦ and ἐκείνου both refer to the
devil, to be untenable. I therefore give
my note much as it stood before, that the
student may have both sides before him.
The difficulty is of course to determine
whether the pronouns are used of the
∗ same person, or of different persons. From
the Greek expositors downwards, some
have held a very different rendering of
the words from either of those here indicated : Thl. e. g.,—ἐν πλάνῃ, φησί, νήψον-
ται, ἀλλὰ ζωγρηθέντες ὑπὸ θεοῦ εἰς τὸ
ἐκείνου θέλημα, τουτέστι τοῦ θεοῦ, ἴσως
ἀνανήψουσιν ἀπὸ τῶν ὑδάτων τῆς πλάνης.
This, it is true, does not get rid of the
difficulty respecting the pronouns, but it
pointed a way towards doing so : and thus
Wetst., Bengel, and Mack, understand

αὐτοῦ to apply to the δοῦλος κυρίου,—
ἐκείνου to God—'taken prisoners by God's
servant according to His will.' (Bengel
however, as Beza, Grot., joins εἰς τὸ ἐκ.
θέλ. with ἀνανήψωσιν, which is unnatural,
leaving ἐζωγρ. ὑπ' αὐτοῦ standing alone.)
The great objection to this is, the exceeding confusion which it introduces into the
figure, in representing men who are just
recovering their sense and liberty, as ἐζωγρημένοι,—and in applying that participle, occurring as it does just after the
mention of παγίς, not to that snare, but
to another which does not appear at all.
Aret. and Estius proposed the rendering
given above ;—'taken captive by the devil
according to God's will,' i. e. as Est.,
'quamdiu Deus voluerit, cujus voluntati nec diabolus resistere potest.' De W.
charges this with rendering εἰς as if it were
κατά, but the charge is not just : for the
permitting the devil to hold them captive,
on this view, would be strictly εἰς, 'in
pursuance of,' 'so as to follow,' God's purpose. The real objection perhaps is, that
it introduces a new and foreign element,
viz. the fact that this capture is overruled
by God—of which matter there is here
no question. There is no real difficulty
whatever in the application of αὐτοῦ and
ἐκείνου to the same person. Kühner,
§ 629, anm. 3, gives from Plato, Cratyl.
p. 430, δεῖξαι αὐτῷ ἂν μὲν τύχῃ, ἐκείνου
εἰκόνα, ἂν δὲ τύχῃ, γυναικός (where the
reason for the use of ἐκείνου, viz. to emphasize the pronoun, is precisely as here :
see below) : from Lysias, c. Eratosth. p.
429, ἕως ὁ λεγόμενος ὑπ' ἐκείνου καιρὸς
ἐπιμελῶς ὑπ' αὐτοῦ ἐτηρήθη (which cases
of ἐκεῖνος followed by αὐτός must not be
dismissed, as Ellic., as inapplicable : they
shew at all events that there was no absolute objection to using the two pronouns
of the same person. See below). But
he does not give an account of the idiom,
which seems to be this : ἐκεῖνος, from its
very meaning, always carries somewhat
of emphasis with it ; it is therefore unfit
for mere reflexive or unemphatic use, and
accordingly when the subject pointed out
by ἐκεῖνος occurs in such unemphatic
position, ἐκεῖνος is replaced by αὐτός.
On the other hand, where emphasis is

III. 1 Τοῦτο δὲ γίνωσκε, ὅτι ἐν [o] ἐσχάταις ἡμέραις
[p] ἐνστήσονται καιροὶ [q] χαλεποί. 2 ἔσονται γὰρ οἱ ἄνθρωποι [r] φίλαυτοι, [s] φιλάργυροι, [tu] ἀλαζόνες, [tv] ὑπερήφανοι,
[w] βλάσφημοι, [t] γονεῦσιν [tx] ἀπειθεῖς, [y] ἀχάριστοι, [z] ἀνόσιοι,

ACDFK LPℵ a b c d e f g h k l m n o 17. 47

o so Acts ii. 17. James v. 3. 1 Pet. i. 5. 1 John ii. 18. (Jude 18.) Isa. ii. 2.
p Paul (Rom. viii. 38. 1 Cor. iii. 22. vii. 26. Gal. i. 4. 2 Thess. ii. 2) only, exc. Heb. ix. 9. 1 Macc. xii. 44.
q Matt. viii. 28 only. Isa. xviii. 2 only. Wisd. iii. 19 al.
r here only (see note) †.
s Luke xvi. 14 only †.
t Rom. i. 30.
u Rom. as above (t) only. Job xxviii. 8. Prov. xxi. 24. Hab. ii. 5 only. (-νεια, James iv. 16.)
v Luke i. 51. Rom. i. 30. James iv. 6. 1 Pet. v. 5 (from Prov. iii. 34) only. Ps. cxviii. 21, 51. (-νία, Mark vii. 22.)
w 1 Tim. i. 13 reff.
x Luke i. 17. Acts xxvi. 19. Rom. i. 30. Tit. i. 16. iii. 3 only. Deut. xxi. 18.
y Luke vi. 35 only †. Wisd. xvi. 29. Sir. xxix. 17, 25 only.
z 1 Tim. i. 9 (reff.) only.

Chap. III. 1. *γινωσκετε* AF 17 æth-rom Aug: txt CDKL[P]ℵ rel vulg(and F-lat) syrr copt goth æth-pl gr-lat-ff.
2. om *οι* ℵ 72. 114-5. *αλαζοντες* F. for *αχαριστοι*, *αχριστοι* C[1]: *αχρηστοι* K m.

required, *ἐκεῖνος* is repeated: e. g. Soph. Aj. 1039, *κεῖνος τὰ κείνου στεργέτω, κἀγὼ τάδε*. And this emphatic or unemphatic use is not determined by priority of order, but by logical considerations. So here in *ἐζωγρημένοι ὑπ' αὐτοῦ*, the *αὐτοῦ* is the mere reflex of *διαβόλου* which has just occurred,—whereas in *εἰς τὸ ἐκείνου θέλημα*, the *ἐκείνου* would, according to this rendering, bring out and emphasize the danger and degradation of these persons, who had been, in their spiritual *μέθη*, just taken captive at the pleasure of *ἐκεῖνος*, their mortal foe. Still, it now seems to me it is better to adhere to the common meaning of the two pronouns, even though it should seem to introduce a new idea. The novelty however may be somewhat removed by remembering that God's sovereign power as the giver of repentance was already before the Apostle's mind).

Ch. III. 1—9.] *Warning of bad times to come, in which men shall be ungodly and hypocritical:—nay, against such men as already present, and doing mischief.*

1.] **But** (the contrast is in the dark prophetic announcement, so different in character from the hope just expressed) **this know, that in the last days** (see 1 Tim. iv. 1, where the expression is somewhat different. The period referred to here is, from all N. T. analogy (cf. 2 Pet. iii. 3: Jude 18), that immediately preceding the coming of the Lord. That day and hour being hidden from all men, and even from the Son Himself, Mark xiii. 32,—the Spirit of prophecy, which is the Spirit of the Son, did not reveal to the Apostles its place in the ages of time. They, like the subsequent generations of the Church, were kept waiting for it, and for the most part wrote and spoke of it as soon to appear; not however without many and sufficient hints furnished by the Spirit, of an interval, and that no short one, first to elapse. In this place, these last days are set before Timotheus as being on their way, and indeed their premonitory symptoms already appearing. The discovery which the lapse of centuries and the ways of providence have made to us, *χρονίζει ὁ κύριός μου ἐλθεῖν*, misleads none but unfaithful servants: while the only modification in the understanding of the premonitory symptoms, is, that *for us*, He with whom a thousand years are as one day has spread them, without changing their substance or their truth, over many consecutive ages. Cf. ref. 1 John,—where we have the still plainer assertion, *ἐσχάτη ὥρα ἐστίν*) **grievous times shall come** (we can hardly express *ἐνστήσονται* nearer in English: '*instabunt*,' of the Vulg., though blamed by De W., is right, in the sense in which we use 'instant' of the present month or year (Ellic. quotes Auct. ad Herenn. ii. 5, 'dividitur (tempus) in tempora tria, præteritum, instans, consequens'); '*aderunt*' of Grot. and Bengel amounts in fact to the same. See note on 2 Thess. ii. 2): **2.] for** (reason for *χαλεποί*) **men** (*οἱ* generic: the men who shall live in those times) **shall be selfish** (*οἱ πάντα πρὸς τὴν ἑαυτῶν ὠφέλειαν ποιοῦντες*, Theod-Mops. Aristotle, in his chapter *περὶ φιλαυτίας*, Eth. Nicom. ix. 8, while he maintains that there is a higher sense in which *τὸν ἀγαθὸν δεῖ φίλαυτον εἶναι*,—allows that *οἱ πολλοί* use the word of *τοὺς ἑαυτοῖς ἀπονέμοντας τὸ πλεῖον ἐν χρήμασι, καὶ τιμαῖς, καὶ ἡδοναῖς ταῖς σωματικαῖς*: and adds, *δικαίως δὴ τοῖς οὕτω φιλαύτοις ὀνειδίζεται*), **covetous** (ref.: we have the subst., 1 Tim. vi. 10, and the verb, 2 Macc. x. 20), **empty boasters** (*ἀλαζόνες, καυχώμενοι ἔχειν ἃ μὴ ἔχουσιν*, Theod-Mops.: see ref. and definitions from Aristotle in note), **haughty** (*μεγάλα φρονοῦντες, ἐπὶ τοῖς οὖσιν*, Theod-Mops.: ref. and note), **evil speakers** (*κατηγορίαις χαίροντες*, Theod-Mops. Not 'blasphemers,' unless, as in ref. 1 Tim., the context specifies to what the evil-speaking refers), **disobedient to parents** ('character temporum colligendus imprimis etiam ex juventutis moribus.' Bengel), **ungrateful,**

3 ᵃ ἄστοργοι, ᵇ ἄσπονδοι, ᶜ διάβολοι, ᵈ ἀκρατεῖς, ᵉ ἀνήμεροι, ᶠ ἀφιλάγαθοι, ⁴ ᵍ προδόται, ʰ προπετεῖς, ⁱ τετυφωμένοι, ʲ φιλήδονοι ᵏ μᾶλλον ἢ ˡ φιλόθεοι, ⁵ ἔχοντες ᵐ μόρφωσιν ⁿ εὐσεβείας τὴν δὲ δύναμιν αὐτῆς ᵒ ἠρνημένοι. καὶ τούτους ᵖ ἀποτρέπου. ⁶ ἐκ τούτων γάρ εἰσιν οἱ ᵠ ἐνδύνοντες εἰς τὰς οἰκίας καὶ ʳ αἰχμαλωτίζοντες ˢ γυναικάρια ᵗ σεσωρευ-

a Rom. i. 31 only †.
Æschin. p. 47. 29.
b here (Rom. i. 31 rec.) only †.
c = 1 Tim. iii. (6, 7 reff.)
11. Tit. ii. 3 only. Esth. vii. 4.
d here only. Prov. xxvii. 20 (only?).

e here only †. only †. 2 Macc. v. 15. x. 13, 22 only.
i 1 Tim. iii. 6. vi. 4 only †.
l here only †. Arist. Rhet. ii. 17. 6.
o = 1 Tim. v. 8 reff.
r Luke xxi. 24. Rom. vii. 23. 2 Cor. x. 5 only. 3 Kings viii. 46.
Aristoph. Acharn. 517: ἀνθρωπάρια, id. Plut. 416.

f here only †. see Tit. i. 8.
h Acts xix. 36 only. Prov. x. 14. xiii. 3.
j here only †. Polyb. xl. 6. 10.
m Rom. ii. 20 only †.
p here only †. Sir. xx. 29. see ch. iv. 4.

g Luke vi. 16. Acts viii. 52
Sir. ix. 18 only.
k 1 Tim. i. 4 reff.
n 1 Tim. ii. 2 reff.
q here only †.
s here only †. ἀνδράρια, t Rom. xii. 20 (from Prov. xxv. 21, 22) only.

3. ασπονδοι bef αστοργοι D m 73 [arm] Chr lat-ff : om αστοργοι ℵ : om both 238 Syr.
6. [ενδυοντες (for -νοντες) P h.]　　rec αιχμαλωτευοντες, with D³KL rel Orig-ed Damasc : txt ACD¹F[P]ℵ 17[-τενον(sic Treg) 47] Orig-mss Chr Thdrt Thl Œc. rec ins τα bef γυναικαρια, with a d f o : om ACDFKL[P]ℵ rel gr-ff.

unholy (ref. ἐπιμέλειαν τοῦ δικαίου μὴ ποιούμενοι, Theod-Mops., and Beza's 'quibus nullum jus est nec fas' are perhaps too wide : it is rather 'irreligious'), without natural affection (ref. and note), implacable (it does not appear that the word ever means 'truce-*breakers*,' οὐ βέβαιοι περὶ τὰς φιλίας, οὐδὲ ἀληθεῖς περὶ ἃ συντίθενται,—as Theod-Mops. In all the places where it occurs in a subjective sense, it is, '*that will make*' or '*admit no truce:*' e. g., Æsch. Agam. 1235, ἄσπονδόν τ' ἀρὰν φίλοις πνέουσαν : Eur. Alcest. 426, τῷ κάτωθεν ἀσπόνδῳ θεῷ : Demosth. p. 314. 16, ἄσπονδος κ. ἀκήρυκτος πόλεμος : the same expression, ἄσπ. πόλεμος, occurs in Polyb. i. 65. 6. For the primary objective sense, 'without σπονδή,' see Thucyd. i. 37 ; ii. 22 ; v. 32, and Palm and Rost's Lex.), calumniators (reff.), incontinent (we have the subst. ἀκρασία, 1 Cor. vii. 5), inhuman (ὠμοί, ἀπάνθρωποι, Œc.), no lovers of good (ἐχθροὶ παντὸς ἀγαθοῦ, Thl.), traitors, headlong (either in action, 'qui præcipites sunt in agendo,' Beng. : or in passion (temper), which would in fact amount to the same), besotted by pride (see note, 1 Tim. iii. 6), lovers of pleasure rather than lovers of God (τὸν λαὸν . . . φιλήδονον κ. φιλοπαθῆ μᾶλλον ἢ φιλάρετον κ. φιλόθεον. Philo de agric. § 19, vol. i. p. 313), having a (or the ?) form (outward embodiment : the same meaning as in ref., but here confined, by the contrast following, to the mere outward semblance, whereas there, no contrast occurring, the outward embodiment is the real representation. "The more correct word would be μόρφωμα (Æsch. Ag. 873, Eum. 412), μόρφωσις being properly active, e. g., σχηματισμὸς κ. μόρφωσις τῶν δενδρῶν, Theophr. de caus. plant. iii. 7. 4 : there is, however, a tendency in the N. T.,

as in later writers, to replace the verbal nouns in -μα by the corresponding nouns in -σις : cf. ὑποτύπωσις, ch. i. 13." Ellicott) of piety, but having repudiated (not pres., '*denying*,' as E. V.,—'*renouncing*,' as Conyb. ; their condemnation is, that they are living in the semblance of God's fear, but *have repudiated* its reality) the power of it (its living and renewing influence over the heart and life). Cf. throughout this description, Rom. i. 30, 31. Huther remarks, "We can hardly trace any formal rule of arrangement through these predicates. Here and there, it is true, a few cognate ideas are grouped together : the two first are connected by φίλος : then follow three words betokening high-mindedness : γονεῦσιν ἀπειθεῖς is followed by ἀχάριστοι : this word opens a long series of words beginning with ἀ privative, but interrupted by διάβολοι : the following, προδόται, προπετεῖς, seem to be a paronomasia : the latter of these is followed by τετυφωμένοι as a cognate idea : a few more general predicates close the catalogue. But this very interpenetration serves to depict more vividly the whole manifoldness of the manifestation of evil." And from these turn away (ref.: cf. ἐκτρέπεσθαι, 1 Tim. vi. 20. This command shews that the Apostle treats the symptoms of the last times as not future exclusively, but in some respects present : see note above, ver. 1) : 6.] for (reason of the foregoing command, seeing that they are already among you) among the number of these are they who creep (εἶδες τὸ ἀναίσχυντον πῶς ἔδειξε διὰ τοῦ εἰπεῖν, ἐνδύνοντες· τὸ ἄτιμον, τὴν ἀπάτην, τὴν κολακείαν, Chrys. Cf. Aristoph. Vesp. 1020, εἰς ἀλλοτρίας γαστέρας ἐνδύς. Bengel interprets it 'irrepentes clanculum') into (men's) houses and take captive (as it were prisoners ;

u and constr.,　μένα ἁμαρτίαις, ᵘ ἀγόμενα ἐπιθυμίαις ᵛ ποικίλαις, ⁷ πάντοτε ACDFK
Rom. viii. 14.　　　　　　　　　　　　　　　　　　　　　　　　　　　　　LPℵ a b
Gal. v. 18.　μανθάνοντα καὶ μηδέποτε ʷ εἰς ʷˣʸ ἐπίγνωσιν ʸ ἀληθείας c d e f g
v Matt. iv. 24
‖ Mk. L. Tit.　　　　　　　　　　　　　　　　　　　　　　　　　　　　h k l m n
iii. 3 (also w.　ʷ ἐλθεῖν δυνάμενα.　⁸ ᶻ ὃν τρόπον δὲ Ἰαννῆς καὶ Ἰαμβρῆς o 17. 47
ἐπιθ.). Heb.
ii. 4. xiii. 9.　James i. 2.　1 Pet. i. 6.　iv. 10 only‡.　1 Chron. xxix. 2.　　w 2 Macc. ix. 11.　　x Eph.
x. 17 reff.　　　　　y ch. ii. 25.　1 Tim. ii. 4.　Tit. i. 1.　　z Paul, here only.　Matt. xxiii. 37 ‖ L.　Acts
i. 11. vii. 28 only.　Isa. xxxviii. 19.

aft επιθυμιαις ins και ηδοναις A syr Chr-txt Thdrt₁.

8. ιωαννης C¹ : *Jamnes* am(with fuld demid) Cypr Lucif Opt Aug.　　μαμβρης
F latt goth gr-ff(not Chr Thdrt Damasc) lat-ff(not Aug₁).

a word admirably describing the influence
acquired by sneaking proselytizers over
those presently described : attach to themselves entirely, so that they follow them as
if dragged about by them. a late word, said
to be of Alexandrian or Macedonian origin,
and condemned by the Atticist : see Ellicott) **silly women** (the diminutive denotes
contempt) **laden with sins** (De W. alone
seems to have given the true reason of the
insertion of this particular. The stress is on
σεσωρευμένα : they are burdened, their consciences oppressed, with sins, and in this
morbid state they lie open to the insidious
attacks of these proselytizers who promise
them ease of conscience if they will follow
them), **led about by lusts of all kinds** (I
should rather imagine, from the context,
that the reference here is not so much to
'fleshly lusts' properly so called,—though
from what we know of such feminine
spiritual attachments, ancient (see below)
and modern, such must by no means be
excluded,—as to the ever-shifting (ποικίλη)
passion for change in doctrine and manner
of teaching, which is the eminent characteristic of these captives to designing spiritual teachers—the running after fashionable men and fashionable tenets, which
draw them (ἄγουσι) in flocks in the most
opposite and inconsistent directions), **evermore learning** (always with some new
point absorbing them, which seems to them
the most important, to the depreciation of
what they held and seemed to know before),
and never (on μηδ., see Ellicott) **able to
come to the thorough knowledge** (reff.,
and notes : the decisive and stable apprehension, in which they might be grounded
and settled against further novelties) **of
the truth** (this again is referred by Chrys.,
all., to moral deadening of their apprehension by profligate lives : ἐπειδὴ ἑαυτὰς
κατέχωσαν ταῖς ἐπιθυμίαις ἐκείναις καὶ τοῖς
ἁμαρτήμασιν, ἐπωρώθη αὐτῶν ἡ διάνοια.
It may be so, in the deeper ground of the
psychological reason for this their fickle
and imperfect condition : but I should
rather think that the Apostle here indicates
their character as connected with the fact
of their captivity to these teachers.

With regard to the fact itself, we have
abundant testimony that the Gnostic
heresy in its progress, as indeed all new
and strange systems, laid hold chiefly of
the female sex : so Irenæus i. 13. 3, p. 61,
of the Valentinian Marcus, μάλιστα περὶ
γυναῖκας ἀσχολεῖται, and in ib. 6, p. 63 f.,
καὶ μαθηταὶ δὲ αὐτοῦ τινες . . . ἐξαπατῶντες
γυναικάρια πολλὰ διέφθειραν : and Epiphanius, Hær. xxvi. 12, vol. i. p. 93, charges
the Gnostics with ἐμπαίζειν τοῖς γυναικα-
ρίοις and ἀπατᾶν τὸ αὐτοῖς πειθόμενον
γυναικεῖον γένος, then quoting this passage.
Jerome, Ep. cxxxiii. ad Ctesiphontem 4,
vol. i. p. 1031 f., collects a number of instances of this : "Simon Magus hæresin
condidit Helenæ meretricis adjutus auxilio :
Nicolaus Antiochenus omnium immundi-
tiarum repertor choros duxit fœmineos :
Marcion Romam præmisit mulierem quæ
decipiendos sibi animos præpararet. Apel-
les Philumenem suarum comitem habuit
doctrinarum : Montanus . . . . Priscam et
Maximillam . . . . primum auro corrupit,
deinde hæresin polluit . . . : Arius ut orbem
deciperet, sororem principis ante decepit.
Donatus . . . Lucillæ opibus adjutus est :
Agape Elpidium . . . cæcum cæca duxit
in foveam : Priscilliano juncta fuit Galla."

The general answer to Baur,—
who again uses this as a proof of the
later origin of these Epistles,—will be
found in the Prolegomena, ch. vii. § i.
De Wette remarks, "This is an admirable
characterization of zealous soul-hunters
(who have been principally found, and are
still found, among the Roman Catholics)
and their victims. We must not however
divide the different traits among different
classes or individuals : it is their combination only which is characteristic."
" Diceres, ex professo Paulum hic vivam
monachismi effigiem pingere." Calvin).

8.] **But** (q. d. it is no wonder that
there should be now such opponents to the
truth, for their prototypes existed also
in ancient times) **as Jannes and Jambres
withstood Moses** (these are believed to be
traditional names of the Egyptian magicians mentioned in Exod. vii. 11, 22.
Origen says (in Matt. comment. 117, vol.

ᵃἀντέστησαν Μωυσεῖ, οὕτως καὶ οὗτοι ᵃἀνθίστανται ᵇτῇ
ἀληθείᾳ, ἄνθρωποι ᶜᵈκατεφθαρμένοι τὸν ᵈνοῦν, ᵉἀδόκιμοι
ᶠπερὶ τὴν ᶠπίστιν. ⁹ ἀλλ᾽ οὐ ᵍπροκόψουσιν ᵍἐπὶ πλεῖον·
ἡ γὰρ ʰἄνοια αὐτῶν ⁱἔκδηλος ἔσται πᾶσιν, ὡς καὶ ἡ
ἐκείνων ἐγένετο. ¹⁰ σὺ δὲ ᵏπαρηκολούθησάς μου τῇ

a Paul, Rom.
ix. 19. xiii.
2 bis. Gal. ii.
11. Eph. vi.
13. ch. iv. 15.
Matt. v. 39.
Luke xxi. 15
al. Job xli. 2.
b = 2 Thess. ii.
12 reff.
c here (2 Pet.
ii. 12 v. r.)

only. Gen. vi. 12.   d see 1 Tim. vi. 5 reff.   e Rom. i. 28.   1 Cor. ix. 27.   2 Cor. xiii. 5,
6, 7. Tit. i. 16. Heb. vi. 8 only. Prov. xxv. 4. Isa. i. 22 only.   f 1 Tim. i. 19. vi. 21. see ch.
ii. 18.   g ch. ii. 16 reff.   h Luke vi. 11 only. Prov. xxii. 15.   i here
only †. 3 Macc. iii. 19.   k 1 Tim. iv. 6 reff.

ins τω bef μωυσει F[P] 73. 80. (μωσει, A c l m.)   for ουτοι, αυτοι F.   αντι-
στανται D¹, αντεστησαν 17. 238 : αντιστησονται Chr-comm.
    9. for ανοια, διανοια A.   for εσται, εστιν F. (G-lat has both.)
    10. rec παρηκολουθηκας, with DKL[P] rel Chr Thdrt Damasc : txt ACℵ 17, ηκολου-

iii. p. 916), "quod ait, 'sicut Jannes et
Mambres (see var. readd.) restiterunt
Mosi,' non invenitur in publicis scripturis,
sed in libro secreto, qui suprascribitur
Jannes et Mambres liber." But Thdrt.'s
account is more probable (τὰ μέντοι τούτων
ὀνόματα οὐκ ἐκ τῆς θείας γραφῆς μεμάθη-
κεν ὁ θεῖος ἀπόστολος, ἀλλ᾽ ἐκ τῆς ἀγρά-
φου τῶν Ἰουδαίων διδασκαλίας), especially as the names are found in the Tar-
gum of Jonathan on Exod. vii. 11; Num.
xxii. 22. Schöttgen has (in loc.) a long
account of their traditional history : and
Wetst. quotes the passages at length.
They were the sons of Balaam—prophesied to Pharaoh the birth of Moses, in
consequence of which he gave the order
for the destruction of the Jewish children,
—and thenceforward appear as the coun-
sellors of much of the evil,—in Egypt,
and in the desert, after the Exodus,—
which happened to Israel. They were
variously reported to have perished in the
Red Sea, or to have been killed in the
tumult consequent on the making the
golden calf, which they had advised. Origen, contra Cels. iv. 51, vol. i. p. 543,
mentions the Pythagorean Noumenius
as relating the history of Jannes and
Jambres : so also Euseb. præp. evang. ix.
8, vol. iii. (Migne), p. 412. Pliny, H.
Nat. xxx. 1, says, "Est et alia Magices
factio, a Mose et Jamne et Jotape Judæis
pendens, sed multis millibus annorum post
Zoroastrem." The later Jews, with some
ingenuity, distorted the names into Joannes and Ambrosius), **thus these also
withstand the truth, being men corrupted** (reff. : the Lexx. quote καταφθα-
ρεὶς τὸν βίον from a fragment of Menan-
der) **in mind, worthless** (not abiding the
test, 'rejectanei') **concerning the faith**
(in respect of the faith : περὶ τὴν πίστιν
is not, as Huther, equivalent to περὶ τῆς
πίστεως, but expresses more the local
meaning of περί : '*circa*,' as the Vulg.

here has it. In 1 Tim. i. 19, περὶ τὴν
πίστιν ἐναυάγησαν, we have the local
reference brought out more strongly, the
faith being, as it were, a rock, on, round
which they had been shipwrecked).
   9.] **Notwithstanding** (Ellic. well remarks
that ἀλλά here after an affirmative sentence should have its full adversative
force) **they shall not advance further** (in
ch. ii. 16, it is said, ἐπὶ πλεῖον προκόψουσιν ἀσεβείας : and it is in vain to deny
that there is an apparent and literal inconsistency between the two assertions.
But on looking further into them, it is
manifest, that while there the Apostle is
speaking of an immediate spread of error,
here he is looking to its ultimate defeat
and extinction : as Chrys., κἂν πρότερον
ἀνθήσῃ τὰ τῆς πλάνης, εἰς τέλος οὐ
διαμενεῖ) : **for their folly** (unintelligent
and senseless method of proselytizing and
upholding their opinions (see ref. Luke),
—and indeed folly of those opinions themselves) **shall be thoroughly manifested**
(ref. πάντ᾽ ἐποίησεν ἔκδηλα, Demosth.
24. 10) **to all, as also that of those
men was** (Exod. viii. 18; ix. 11 : but most
probably the allusion is to their traditional
end).
   10—17.] *Contrast, by way of reminding
and exhortation, of the education, knowledge, and life of Timotheus with the character just drawn of the opponents.* **But
thou followedst** (ref. not, as Chrys., Thl.,
Œc., al., τούτων σὺ μάρτυς,—for some of
the undermentioned occurred before the
conversion of Timotheus, and of many of
them this could not be properly said,—but
'followedst as thy pattern :' 'it was my
example in all these things which was set
before thee as thy guide—thou wert a fol-
lower of me, as I of Christ.' So Calvin
('laudat tanquam suarum virtutum imita-
torem, ac si diceret, jam pridem assue-
factus es ad mea instituta, perge modo
qua cœpisti'), Aret., De W., Huther,

l 1 Tim. i. 10 reff.
m here only. = Esth. ii. 20.
ἀγωγὴ τοῦ βίου, Polyb. iv. 74. l & 4. see note.
n = Acts xi. 23. 2 Macc. iii. 8.
o 1 Tim. vi. 11.
Tit. ii. 2. 2 Pet. i. 6, 7.
4. xii. 12 al. Ps. ix. 18.
u l Cor. x. 13. 1 Pet. ii. 19 only. Job ii. 10. Prov. vi. 33.
p Col. i. 11.
s 2 Thess. i. 4 reff.
q Gal. v. 22 reff.
r Luke viii. 15. 2 Cor. i. 6. vi.
t = Rom. viii. 18. 2 Cor. i. 6, Col. i. 24 †.
v Col. i. 13 reff.
w l Tim. iii. 10 reff.

¹ διδασκαλίᾳ, τῇ ᵐ ἀγωγῇ, τῇ ⁿ προθέσει, τῇ ° πίστει, τῇ ᵖᑫ μακροθυμίᾳ, τῇ ° ἀγάπῃ, τῇ ᵒᵖʳ ὑπομονῇ, ¹¹ τοῖς ˢ διωγμοῖς, τοῖς ᵗ παθήμασιν, οἷά μοι ἐγένετο ἐν ᾽Αντιοχείᾳ, ἐν ᾽Ικονίῳ, ἐν Λύστροις· οἵους ˢ διωγμοὺς ᵘ ὑπήνεγκα καὶ ᵛ ἐκ πάντων με ᵛ ἐρρύσατο ὁ κύριος· ¹² ʷ καὶ πάντες ʷ δὲ

ACDFK LPℵ a b c d e f g h k l m n o 17. 47

θησας F.   μοι D¹.   for αγωγη, αγαπη D¹.   om τη αγαπη A 179 Thl.
11. εγενοντο A 72 lectt 7 18 : txt CDFKL[P]ℵ rel.   for ερρυ., ερυσατο AD¹ d.
for κυριος, θεος D.

Wiesinger, all. The *aorist* is both less obvious and more appropriate than the *perfect:* this *was* the example set before him, and the reminiscence, joined to the exhortation of ver. 14, bears something of reproach with it, which is quite in accordance with what we have reason to infer from the general tone of the Epistle. Whereas the *perfect* would imply that the example had been really ever before him, and followed up to the present moment : and so would weaken the necessity of the exhortation) **my teaching, conduct** (reff.: and add 2 Macc. iv. 16 ; vi. 8 ; xi. 24: τῇ διὰ τῶν ἔργων πολιτείᾳ, Thdrt. All these words are dependent on μου, not to be taken (Mack) as applying to Timotheus, 'Thou followedst my teaching in thy conduct, &c.,' which would introduce an unnatural accumulation of encomia on him, and would besides assume that he had been persecuted (cf. τοῖς διωγμοῖς), which there is no reason to suppose), **purpose** (ref. τοῦτο περὶ προθυμίας καὶ τοῦ παραστήματος τῆς ψυχῆς, Chrys. Ellic. remarks, that in all other passages in St. Paul's Epistles, πρόθεσις is used with reference to God), **faith** (ὁποίαν ἔχω περὶ τὸν δεσπότην διάθεσιν, Thdrt.), **long-suffering** (ὅπως φέρω τὰ τῶν ἀδελφῶν πλημμελήματα, Thdrt. : or perhaps, as Chrys., πῶς οὐδὲν τούτων ἐτάραττε,— his patience in respect of the false teachers and the troubles of the time), **love** (ὅπερ οὐκ εἶχον οὗτοι, Chrys.), **endurance** (πῶς φέρω γενναίως τῶν ἐναντίων τὰς προσβολάς, Thdrt.), **persecutions** ('to these ὑπομονή furnished the note of transition.' Huth.), **sufferings** (not only was I persecuted, but the persecution issued in infliction of suffering), such (sufferings) **as befell me in Antioch** (of Pisidia), **in Iconium, in Lystra** (why should these be especially enumerated ? Thdrt. assigns as a reason, τοὺς ἄλλους καταλιπὼν τῶν ἐν τῇ Πισιδίᾳ καὶ τῇ Λυκαονίᾳ συμβεβηκότων αὐτῷ κινδύνων ἀνέμνησε. Λυκάων γὰρ

ἦν καὶ αὐτὸς πρὸς ὃν ἔγραφε, καὶ ταῦτα τῶν ἄλλων ἦν αὐτῷ γνωριμώτερα. And so Chrys., and many both ancient and modern. It may be so, doubtless : and this reason, though rejected by De W., Huther, Wiesinger, al., seems much better to suit the context and probability, than the other, given by Huther, al., that these persecutions were the first which befell the Apostle in his missionary work among the heathen. It is objected to it, that during the former of these persecutions Timotheus was not with St. Paul. But the answer to that is easy. At the time of his conversion, they were recent, and the talk of the churches in those parts : and thus, especially with our rendering, and the aor. sense of παρηκολούθησας, would be naturally mentioned, as being those sufferings of the Apostle which first excited the young convert's attention to make them his own pattern of what he too must suffer for the Gospel's sake. Baur and De Wette regard the exact correspondence with the Acts (xiii. 50; xiv. 5, 19; xvi. 3) as a suspicious circumstance. Wiesinger well asks, would they have regarded a discrepancy from the Acts as a mark of genuineness ?); **what persecutions** (there is a zeugmatic construction here—understand, 'thou sawest ; in proposing to thyself a pattern thou hadst before thee . . .' (I cannot see how, as Ellic. asserts, this rendering vitiates the construction. Doubtless his rendering, '*such persecutions as,*' is legitimate, but it seems to me feeble after the preceding οἷα.) Heydenr., Mack, al., understand these words as an exclamation : οἵους διωγμ. ὑπήνεγκα! I need hardly observe that such an exclamation would be wholly alien from the character and style of the Apostle) **I underwent, and out of all the Lord delivered me** (ἀμφότερα (both clauses of the sentence) παρακλήσεως· ὅτι καὶ ἐγὼ προθυμίαν παρειχόμην γενναίαν, καὶ (ὅτι) οὐκ ἐγ-

οἱ ˣ θέλοντες ʸ εὐσεβῶς ζῆν ἐν χριστῷ Ἰησοῦ ᶻ διωχθήσον-
ται. ¹³ πονηροὶ δὲ ἄνθρωποι καὶ ᵃ γόητες ᵇ προκόψουσιν
ᵇ ἐπὶ τὸ ᶜ χεῖρον, ᵈ πλανῶντες καὶ ᶜ πλανώμενοι. ¹⁴ σὺ δὲ
ᶠ μένε ᶠ ἐν ᵍ οἷς ἔμαθες καὶ ʰ ἐπιστώθης, εἰδὼς παρὰ τίνων

x John v. 35, 40. Heb.
xiii. 18.
y Tit. ii. 12 only †. Xen. Mem. ii. 2. 13. (see 1 Tim. i.² 2 reff.)
z = Matt. v. 10

al. fr. Ps. vii. 1. 2 Macc. v. 8.   a here only †. (-τεια, 2 Macc. xii. 24. λόγοι γοητικοί, Prov. xxvi.
22 Aq.) see note.   b ver. 9.   c Paul, 1 Tim. v. 8 only. Mark v. 25. Heb. x. 29 al.† Wisd. xv.
18 only.   d Matt. xxiv. 4, &c.   1 John ii. 26. Rev. ii. 20 al. Deut. xiii. 5.   e Tit. iii. 3 reff.
f 1 Cor. vii. 20, 24. 1 John ii. 28 and passim. Eccles. vii. 16. 2 Macc. viii. 1.   g attr., Matt. xxiv.
50. Luke ii. 20 al. fr. Paul, Rom. vi. 16 bis. 2 Cor. ii. 10, &c.   h here only.   3 Kings viii. 26.

12. ζην bef ευσεβως A[P]א m 17 syr copt [æth] Orig₂ [Eus₁] Ath₁ : txt CDFKL rel
latt Syr goth [arm(Petr) Eus₁] Ath₂ Chr Thdrt Thl [Orig-int₂ Hil₁].
13. for χειρον, πλειον 67².   γοηται D¹ : γοηταις D².³F.
14. rec τινος (applying it to Paul alone : see ch ii. 2), with C³DKL rel vulg(and
F-lat) syrr copt goth æth [arm] Chr Thdrt Damasc Hil Aug : txt AC¹F[P]א 17
Ambrst.

κατελείφθην. Chrys.).   **12.**] **Yea, and**
(or, **and moreover.** I have explained this
καί . . . . δέ on 1 Tim. iii. 10. 'They who
will, &c., must make up their minds to this
additional circumstance,' viz. persecution)
all who are minded (purpose: see reff. :
'whose will is to,' Ellic. : hardly so strong
as 'who determine,' Conyb. Nor can it be
said that θέλοντες is emphatic, as Huth.
It requires its meaning of 'purpose' to be
clearly expressed, not slurred over : but
that meaning is not especially prominent)
to live piously (ref.) **in Christ Jesus** ('extra Jesum Christum nulla pietas,' Beng. :
and this peculiar reference of εὐσέβεια (cf.
1 Tim. iii. 16) should always be borne in
mind in these Epistles) **shall be persecuted.** **13.**] **But** (on the other hand :
a reason why persecutions must be expected, and even worse and more bitter as
time goes on. The opposition certainly,
as seems to me (see also Wiesinger and
Ellicott), is to the clause immediately
preceding, not, as De W. and Huther
maintain, to ver. 10 f. There would thus
be no real contrast : whereas on our view,
it is forcibly represented that the breach
between light and darkness, between εὐσέβεια and πονηρία, would not be healed,
but rather widened, as time went on)
evil men (in general,—over the world :
particularized, as applying to the matter
in hand, by the next words) **and seducers**
(lit. *magicians*, in allusion probably to
the Egyptian magicians mentioned above.
Jos. contra Apion. ii. 16, has the word in
this sense,—τοιοῦτός τις ἡμῶν ὁ νομοθέτης,
οὐ γόης, οὐδ' ἀπατεών. Demosth. p. 374.
20, puts into the mouth of Æschines, respecting Philip, ἄπιστος, γόης, πονηρός.
See Wetst., and Suicer in voc., and consult Ellic.'s note here) **shall grow worse
and worse** ('advance in the direction of
worse :' see above, ver. 9. There the *dif-
fusion* of evil was spoken of : here its *in-*

tensity), **deceiving and being deceived**
(πλανώμενοι is not middle (as Bengel,
'qui se seducendos permittunt') but passive : rather *for contrast's sake*, as the
middle would be vapid, than for the reason given by Huther, that if so, it would
stand first, because he that deceives others
is first himself deceived : for we might
say exactly the same of the passive. Nor
is the active participle to be assigned to
the γόητες and the passive to the πονηροί,
as Bengel also : both equally designate
both. But his remark is striking and
just, 'Qui semel alios decipere cœpit, eo
minus ipse ab errore se recipit, et eo faci-
lius alienos errores mutuo amplectitur').

14.] **But do thou continue in the
things which** (the object to ἔμαθες, and
the remoter object to ἐπιστώθης, must,
in the construction, be supplied out of the
ἐν οἷς) **thou learnedst** (= ἤκουσας παρ'
ἐμοῦ, ch. ii. 2) **and wert convinced of**
(so Homer, Od. φ. 217 f., where Odysseus
shews his scar,—εἰ δ' ἄγε δὴ καὶ σῆμα
ἀριφραδὲς ἄλλο τι δείξω, | ὄφρα μὲ εὖ
γνῶτον, πιστωθητόν τ' ἐνὶ θυμῷ, and
Soph. Œd. Col. 1040, σὺ δ' ἡμῖν, Οἰδίπους,
| ἔκηλος αὐτοῦ μίμνε, πιστωθεὶς ὅτι | ἢν
μὴ θάνω 'γὼ πρόσθεν, οὐχὶ παύσομαι.
The Vulg. ' credita sunt tibi,' followed by
Luth., Beza, Calv., besides the Roman-
Catholic expositors, would require ἐπιστεύ-
θης, cf. 1 Cor. ix. 17 al.), **knowing** (as
thou dost) **from what teachers** (viz. thy
mother Lois and grandmother Eunice,
ch. i. 5 : cf. ἀπὸ βρέφους below : not Paul
and Barnabas, as Grot., nor the πολλοὶ
μάρτυρες of ch. ii. 2. If the singular
τίνος, then the Apostle must be meant)
thou learnedst them, and (knowing) **that**
(the Vulg. renders ὅτι *quia*, and thus
breaks off the connexion with εἰδώς :
and so also Luth., 'unb weil' . . . . .
Bengel (adding, 'ætiologia duplex. Si-
milis constr. διὰ . . . . καὶ ὅτι, Joh. ii.

i here only.
k Luke i. 41,
44. ii. 12, 16.
xviii. 15.
Acts vii. 19.
1 Pet. ii. 2
only †. Sir.
xix. 11.
1 Macc. i. 61.
2 Macc. vi. 10
only.
15. Esth. vi. 1.
p ch. ii. 10 reff.
xix. 17.   Num. v. 18.

ἔμαθες, [15] καὶ ὅτι [l]ἀπὸ [ik]βρεφους ⌊τα⌋ [l]ἱερὰ [m]γράμματα
οἶδας τὰ δυνάμενά σε [n]σοφίσαι εἰς σωτηρίαν διὰ [o]πίστεως
[p]τῆς [o]ἐν χριστῷ Ἰησοῦ. [16] πᾶσα γραφὴ [q]θεόπνευστος
καὶ [r]ὠφέλιμος [r]πρὸς [s]διδασκαλίαν, πρὸς [t]ἐλεγμόν, πρὸς

ACDFK
LPℵ a b
c d e f g
h k l m n
o 17. 47

l adj., 1 Cor. ix. 13 (bis) only. Josh. vi. 7.   2 Macc. viii. 23.   m = John v. 47. vii.
n = here (2 Pet. i. 16) only.   Ps. xviii. 7. civ. 22. cxviii. 98.   o Eph. i. 15 reff.
q here only †.   r 1 Tim. iv. 8 reff.   s ver. 10.   t here only.   Lev.
4 Kings xix. 3 al.

15. om 1st τα C²D¹Fℵ 17 Damasc₁ : ins AC¹D³KL[P] rel Clem [Hip].   οιδες D.
16. om και vulg Syr copt Clem (Orig₂(?) : see note) Thdor-mops(in Facund) Tert Ambrst Pel Cassiod : ins ACDFKL[P]ℵ rel [am(with fuld) syr goth æth arm] Orig Chr Thdrt Damasc [Hil].   rec ελεγχον, with DKL[P] rel Orig Chr Thdrt Damasc : txt ACFℵ [Clem₁].

24,—ἐπιγνοὺς . . . . καὶ ὅτι, Act. xxii. 29'). But the other construction is much more natural) **from a child** (ἀπὸ πρώτης ἡλικίας, Chrys. The expression carries the learning back to his extreme infancy : see Ellic. here) **thou hast known the** (with or without the art., this will be the rendering) **holy scriptures** (of the O. T. This expression for the Scriptures, not elsewhere found in the N. T. (hardly, as Huther, John vii. 15), is common in Josephus : see Wetst.: cf. also reff. 2 Macc.) **which are able** (not as Bengel, "'quæ poterant :' vis præteriti ex nosti redundat in participium :" for οἶδας is necessarily *present* in signification : '*thou hast known . . . which were*' would be a solœcism) **to make thee wise** (reff. So Hes. Op. 647,— οὔτε τι ναυτιλίης σεσοφισμένος, οὔτε τι νηῶν : Diog. Laert. v. 90, in an epigram, ἀλλὰ διεψεύσθης, σεσοφισμένε) **unto** (towards the attainment of) **salvation, by means of** (the instrument whereby the σοφίσαι is to take place : not to be joined to σωτηρίαν, as Thl., Bengel, al. ; not so much for lack of the art. τήν prefixed, as because the τῆς ἐν χ. Ἰησ. would thus become an unnatural expansion of the merely subordinate πίστεως) **faith, namely that which** (σωτηρία διὰ πίστεως being almost a technical phrase, it is best to keep πίστις here abstract, and then to particularize) **is in** (which rests upon, is reposed in) **Christ Jesus. 16.**] The immense value to Timotheus of this early instruction is shewn by a declaration of the profit of Scripture in furthering the spiritual life. There is considerable doubt about the construction of this clause, **πᾶσα . . . . ὠφέλιμος.** Is it to be taken, (1) **πᾶσα γραφὴ** (subject) **θεόπνευστος** (predicate) (ἐστιν), **καὶ ὠφ.,** i. e. '*every Scripture* (see below) *is* **θεόπνευστος** *and* **ὠφέλιμος**:' or (2) **πᾶσα γραφὴ θεόπνευστος** (subject) **καὶ ὠφέλ.** (ἐστιν) (predicate), i. e. *Every* **γραφὴ θεόπνευστος** *is also* **ὠφέλιμος?** The former is followed by

Chrys. (πᾶσα οὖν ἡ τοιαύτη θεόπνευστος) Greg.-Nyss. (διὰ τοῦτο πᾶσα γραφὴ θεόπνευστος λέγεται), Ath., Est. ('duo affirmantur : omnem scripturam esse divinitus inspiratam, et eandem esse utilem,' &c.), all., by Calv., Wolf, al. : by De W., Wiesinger, Conyb., &c., and the E. V. The latter by Orig. (πᾶσα γραφὴ θεόπνευστος οὖσα ὠφέλιμός ἐστι, in Jesu nave Hom. xx. 3, vol. ii. p. 444: repeated in the Philocal. c. 12, vol. xxv. p. 65, ed. Lomm.), Thdrt. (θεόπνευστον δὲ γραφὴν τὴν πνευματικὴν ὠνόμασεν), al. : by Grot. ('bene expressit sensum Syrus : omnis Scriptura quæ a Deo inspirata est, etiam utilis,' &c.), Erasm. ('tota Scr. quæ nobis non humano ingenio, &c., magnam habet utilitatem,' &c.), Camerar., Whitby, Hammond, al. : by Rosenm., Heinr., Huther, &c. and the Syr. (above), Vulg. ('omnis Scriptura divinitus inspirata utilis est,' &c.), Luth. (denn alle Schrift von Gott eingegeben ist nütze u. s. w.), &c. In deciding between these two, the following considerations must be weighed : (*a*) the requirement of the context. The object of the present verse plainly is to set before Timotheus the value of his early instruction as a motive to his remaining faithful to it. It is then very possible, that the Apostle might wish to exalt the dignity of the Scripture by asserting of it that it was θεόπνευστος, and then out of this lofty predicate might unfold καὶ ὠφέλ., &c.—its various uses in the spiritual life. On the other hand it may be urged, that thus the two epithets do not hang naturally together, the first consisting of the one word θεόπνευστος, and the other being expanded into a whole sentence : especially as in order at all to give symmetry to the whole, the ἵνα ἄρτιος ᾖ κ.τ.λ. must be understood as the purposed result of the θεοπνευστία as well as the ὠφέλεια of the Scriptures, which is hardly natural : (*b*) the requirements of the grammatical construction of καί, which must on all grounds be retained as genuine.

ᵘ ἐπανόρθωσιν, πρὸς ᵛ παιδείαν τὴν ἐν δικαιοσύνῃ· 17 ἵνα

ᵘ here only †.
Esdr. viii. 52.
34 only. ᵛ Eph. vi. 4. Heb. xii. 5, 7, 8, 11 only. 1 Macc. xiv.
Prov. xv. 10.

om προς επανορθωσιν F (added on marg of G) [Orig-int₁].

Can this καί be rendered 'also,' and attached to ὠφέλιμος? There seems no reason to question its legitimacy, thus taken. Such an expression as this, πᾶς ἀνὴρ πλεονέκτης, καὶ εἰδωλολάτρης, though a harsh sentence, would be a legitimate one. And constructions more or less approximating to this are found in the N. T.: e.g., Luke i. 36, Ἐλισάβετ ἡ συγγενίς σου καὶ αὐτὴ συνειληφυῖα: Acts xxvi. 26, πρὸς ὃν καὶ παρρησιαζόμενος λαλῶ: xxviii. 28, αὐτοὶ καὶ ἀκούσονται: Rom. viii. 29, οὓς προέγνω καὶ προώρισεν: Gal. iv. 7, εἰ δὲ υἱὸς καὶ κληρονόμος. In all these, καί introduces the predicatory clause, calling special attention to the fact enounced in it. Cf. also such expressions as καὶ τοῦτο μὲν ἧττον καὶ θαυμαστόν, Plato, Symp. p. 177 b,—σκέψαι τάλαν, ὡς καὶ καταγέλαστον τὸ πρᾶγμα φαίνεται, Aristoph. Eccl. 125,—ᾗ μᾶλλον καὶ ἐπετίθεντο, Thuc. iv. 1. I own on the whole the balance seems to me to incline on the side of (2), unobjectionable as it is in construction, and of the two, better suited to the context. I therefore follow it, hesitatingly, I confess, but feeling that it is not to be lightly overthrown. See on the whole, Ellicott, who takes the same view. **Every Scrip-** * **ture** (not 'every writing:' the word, with or without the art., never occurs in the N. T. except in the sense of 'Scripture;' and we have it, as we might expect in the later apostolic times, anarthrous in 2 Pet. i. 20, πᾶσα προφητεία γραφῆς. Where it occurs anarthrous in the Gospels, it signifies a passage of Scripture, 'a Scripture,' as we say : e.g. John xix. 37. It is true, that πᾶσα γραφή might be numbered with those other apparent solœcisms, πᾶσα οἰκοδομή, Eph. ii. 21, πᾶσα Ἱεροσόλυμα, Matt. ii. 3, where the subst. being used anarthrous, πᾶς = πᾶς ὁ: but, in the presence of such phrases as ἑτέρα γραφὴ λέγει (John l. c.), it is safer to keep to the meaning, unobjectionable both grammatically and contextually, 'every Scripture'—i. e. 'every part of (= in the sense, 'all') Scripture') **given by inspiration of God** (as γραφή answers to γράμματα above, so θεόπνευστος to ἱερά. De W. has well illustrated the word: "θεόπνευστος 'divinitus inspirata,' Vulg., is an expression and idea connected with πνεῦμα (properly breath), the power of the divine Spirit being con-

ceived of as a breath of life : the word thus amounts to 'inspired,' 'breathed through,' 'full of the Spirit.' It (the idea) is common to Jews, Greeks, and Romans. Jos. contra Apion. i. 7, τῶν προφητῶν τὰ μὲν ἀνωτάτω καὶ τὰ παλαιότατα κατὰ τὴν ἐπίπνοιαν τὴν ἀπὸ τοῦ θεοῦ μαθόντων. Æschyl. Suppl. 18; ἐπίπνοια Διός, and similarly Polyb. x. 2. 12. Plato, Republ. vi. 499 b, legg. v. 738 c: Phocyl. 121, τῆς δὲ θεοπνεύστου σοφίης λόγος ἐστὶν ἄριστος: Plut. mor. p. 904, τοὺς ὀνείρους τοὺς θεοπνεύστους : Cic. pro Arch. 8, 'poetam .... quasi divino quodam spiritu af-(l. in-)flari:' de nat. deor. ii. 66, 'nemo vir magnus sine aliquo afflatu divino unquam fuit :' de div. i. 18, 'oracula instinctu divino afflatuque funduntur.' First of all, θεόπνευστος is found as a predicate of persons : ὁ θεόπνευστος ἀνήρ Wetst. (from Marcus Ægyptius), cf. Jos. and Cic. in the two passages above,—2 Pet. i. 21, ὑπὸ πνεύματος ἁγίου φερόμενοι ἐλάλησαν ἀπὸ θεοῦ ἄνθρωποι: Matt. xxii. 43, Δαυεὶδ ἐν πνεύματι καλεῖ αὐτὸν κύριον: then it was also applied to things, cf. the last passage of Cicero, and Phocyl., Plutarch, above." On the meaning of the word as applied to the Scriptures, see Prolegg. to Vol. I. 'On the inspiration of the Gospels:' and compare Ellicott's note here. As applied to the prophets, it would not materially differ, except that we ever regard one speaking *prophecy*, strictly so called, as more immediately and thoroughly the mouthpiece of the Holy Spirit, seeing that the future is wholly hidden from men, and God does not in thi case use or inspire *human testimony to facts*, but suggests the *whole substance* of what is said, *direct* from Himself) **is also** (besides this its quality of inspiration : on the construction, see above) **profitable for** (towards) **teaching** (ἃ γὰρ ἀγνοοῦμεν ἐκεῖθεν μανθάνομεν, Thdrt. This, the *teaching of the person* reading the Scriptures, not the *making him a teacher*, as Estius characteristically, is evidently the meaning. It is not Timotheus's ability as a teacher, but his stability as a Christian, which is here in question), **for conviction** (ἐλέγχει γὰρ ἡμῶν τὸν παράνομον βίον, Thdrt. The above remark applies here also), **for correction** (παρακαλεῖ γὰρ καὶ τοὺς παρατραπέντας ἐπανελθεῖν εἰς τὴν εὐθεῖαν ὁδόν, Thdrt. So Philo, Quod Deus immut. 37,

w here only †.
x 1 Tim. vi. 11
　only.　Josh.
　xiv. 6.
y ch. ii. 21
　(reff.).
z Acts xxi. 5
　only †.
a 1 Tim. v. 21
　reff.
b 1 Pet. iv. 5.
　see Acts x.
42.　Rom. xiv. 9.
(see note), Deut. iv. 26.

ʷ ἄρτιος ᾖ ὁ τοῦ ˣ θεοῦ ˣ ἄνθρωπος, ʸ πρὸς πᾶν ʸ ἔργον
ʸ ἀγαθὸν ᶻ ἐξηρτισμένος. IV. 1 ᵃ Διαμαρτύρομαι ᵃ ἐνώπιον τοῦ θεοῦ καὶ χριστοῦ Ἰησοῦ τοῦ μέλλοντος
ᵇ κρίνειν ᵇ ζῶντας καὶ ᵇ νεκρούς, καὶ τὴν ᶜ ἐπιφάνειαν αὐτοῦ καὶ τὴν βασιλείαν αὐτοῦ, 2 ᵈ κήρυξον τὸν ᵈ λόγον,

ACDFK
LPℵ a b
t d e f g
h k l m n
o 17. 47

c 2 Thess. ii. 8.　1 Tim. vi. 14.　ch. i. 10.　ver. 8.　Tit. ii. 13 only.　2 Kings vii. 23. constr.
d here only. see Rom. x. 8 al.

17. for αρτιος, τελιος D¹.　εξηρτιμενος F: εξηρτημ. K c n o.

CHAP. IV. 1. rec aft διαμαρτυρομαι ins ουν εγω, with D³K[L(sic, Treg)] rel [syr]:
om ACD¹F[P]ℵ 17. 67² latt Syr copt [goth] æth arm Ath Cyr lat-ff.　rec aft και
ins του κυριου, with D³KL Syr syr-w-ast: om ACD¹F[P]ℵ [47] am(with fuld
demid) copt goth [æth arm] Bas Did Cyr lat-ff. (om του θεου και 17.)　rec ιησ.
bef χρ., with D³KL rel syrr æth [arm] Ath Chr Thdrt: txt ACD¹F[P]ℵ [47] am
(with fuld demid) copt goth Bas Did Cyr lat-ff.　κριναι F b 17. 67². 73 Thdrt Thl.
　rec κατα την επιφ., with D³KL[P]ℵ³ rel syrr goth Thdrt Damasc: txt ACD¹
Fℵ¹ 17. 67² am(with fuld harl tol) copt Cyr (Chr also refers to it: κατα (?) τὴν ἐπιφ.
αὐ. κ. τ. βασ. αὐτοῦ. κρίνειν, πότε; ἐν τῇ ἐπιφανείᾳ αὐτοῦ τῇ μετὰ δόξης, τῇ μετὰ
βασιλείας. ἢ τοίνυν τοῦτο λέγει ὅτι οὐχ οὕτως ἥξει ὡς νῦν, ἢ ὅτι διαμαρτύρομαί σοι τὴν
ἐπιφάνειαν αὐτ. κ. τ. βασ.) Cæs-arel Fulg-Bede.

vol. i. p. 299, ἐπὶ .. τῇ τοῦ παντὸς ἐπανορ-
θώσει βίου: similarly Polyb. p. 50, 26 al.
freq. in Raphel: so Epictetus, ib.), for discipline (ref. Eph. and note) in (if the construction is filled out, the παιδείαν is abstract, and the τὴν ἐν particularizes; discipline, viz. that which . . . . .) righteousness (which is versed in, as its element and
condition, righteousness, and so disciplines
a man to be holy, just, and true): that
(result of the profitableness of Scripture:
reasons why God has, having Himself inspired it, endowed it with this profitableness) the man of God (ref. 1 Tim. and note)
may be perfect (ready at every point:
' aptus in officio,' Beng.), thoroughly made
ready (see note on ref. Acts. It is blamed
by the etymologists as an ἀδόκιμον. Jos.
Antt. iii. 2. 2, has πολεμεῖν πρὸς ἀνθρώπους τοῖς πᾶσι καλῶς ἐξηρτισμένους) to
every good work (rather to be generally
understood than officially: the man of God
is not only a teacher, but any spiritual
man: and the whole of the present passage
regards the universal spiritual life. In
ch. iv. 1 ff. he returns to the official duties
of Timotheus: but here he is on that which
is the common basis of all duty).
CH. IV. 1—8.] Earnest exhortation to
Timotheus to fulfil his office; in the near
prospect of defection from the truth, and
of the Apostle's own departure from life.
I adjure thee (ref.) before God, and
Christ Jesus, who is about to judge
living and dead (λέγει τοὺς ἤδη ἀπ-
ελθόντας καὶ τοὺς τότε καταλειφθησο-
μένους ζῶντας, Thl.: so also Thdrt., and
Chrys., alt. 2: not as Chrys., alt. 1, ἁμαρ-

τωλοὺς λέγει καὶ δικαίους), and by (i. e.
' and I call to witness,' as in Deut. iv. 26,
διαμαρτύρομαι ὑμῖν τόν τε οὐρανὸν καὶ
τὴν γῆν, the construction being changed
from that in the first clause. This is
better than with Huther, to take the
accusatives as merely acc. jurandi, as in
1 Cor. xv. 31; James v. 12. With κατά,
it would be, ' at His, &c. :' cf. Matt. xxvii.
15; Acts xiii. 27; Heb. iii. 8) his appearing (reff.) and his kingdom (these two,
τ. ἐπιφ. αὐτοῦ κ. τ. βασ. αὐτοῦ, are not
to be taken as a hendiadys, as Bengel,—
' ἐπιφάνεια est revelatio et exortus regni '
—but each has its place in the adjuration:
—His coming, at which we shall stand
before Him;—His kingdom, in which we
hope to reign with Him),　2.] proclaim (notice the sudden and unconnected
aorists. Ellic. well observes after Schoe-
mann, Isæus, p. 235, that the use of the
imper. aor. seems often due, both in the
N. T. and in classical authors, to the
"lubitus aut affectus loquentis") the
word (of God. The construction after
διαμ. is carried on in 1 Tim. v. 21 with
ἵνα: in our ch. ii. 14 with infinitives:
here with simple imperatives, which is
more abrupt and forcible), press on (ἐπί-
στηθι is generally referred to the last
clause—' be diligent in preaching:' μετ'
ἐπιμονῆς κ. ἐπιστασίας λάλησον, as Thl.:
and Thdrt., οὐχ ἁπλῶς καὶ ὡς ἔτυχεν
αὐτὸν κηρύττειν παρεγγυᾷ, ἀλλὰ πάντα
καιρὸν ἐπιτήδειον πρὸς τοῦτο νομίζειν.
De W. doubts this meaning being justified, and would rather keep the verb to its
simpler meaning ' accede (ad cœtus Chris-

^e ἐπίστηθι ^f εὐκαίρως ^g ἀκαίρως, ^h ἔλεγξον, ⁱ ἐπιτίμησον, e = here only.
see note,
^k παρακάλεσον, ἐν ^l πάσῃ ^m μακροθυμίᾳ καὶ ⁿ διδαχῇ. 3 ἔσ- also ver. 6,
and Jer.
xxvi. (xlvi.)
ται γὰρ καιρὸς ὅτε τῆς ^o ὑγιαινούσης ^o διδασκαλίας οὐκ 14.
f Mark xiv. 11
^p ἀνέξονται, ἀλλὰ κατὰ τὰς ἰδίας ἐπιθυμίας ἑαυτοῖς ^q ἐπι- only †. Sir.
xviii. 22
σωρεύσουσιν ^r διδασκάλους ^s κνηθόμενοι τὴν ^t ἀκοήν, 4 καὶ only. (-ρος,
Heb. iv. 16.

-ρεῖν, Mark
vi. 31. -ρία, Matt. xxvi. 16.)   g here only †.   Sir. xxxv. (xxxii.) 4.   (-ρος, Sir. xx. 19.   -ρεῖσθαι,
Phil. iv. 10.)   h = Matt. xviii. 15.   1 Cor. xiv. 24.   Eph. v. 11.   Tit. i. 9, 13.   ii. 15.   Prov. x. 10.
i Paul, here only.   Gospp. (exc. John) passim, and Jude 9, from Zech. iii. 2.   k absol., 1 Cor. iv. 13.   Tit.
i. 9.   1 = Phil. i. 20 reff.   m = Col. i. 11 reff.   n Paul, Rom. vi. 17. xvi.
17.   1 Cor. xiv. 6, 26.   Tit. i. 9 only.   Matt. vii. 28 al.   Ps. lix. tit. only.   o 1 Tim. i. 10 reff.
p Acts xviii. 14.   2 Cor. xi. 1, &c.   Heb. xiii. 22.   Job vi. 26.   q here only †.   (Symm., Cant. ii.
4.   Job xiv. 17.)   r Eph. iv. 11 reff.   s here only †. see note.   t = 1 Cor.
xii. 17.   Heb. v. 11.   2 Pet. ii. 8.   2 Macc. xv. 39.

2. ακαιρ. bef ευκαιρ. C.   παρακαλ. bef επιτιμ. FN¹ m latt goth Orig Ambr
Ambrst Pel Aug.   for πασῃ, μασῃ(sic) N.
3. ενεξονται C.   for κατα, προς D[P].   rec τας επιθ. τας ιδ., with KL rel copt
Chr Damasc Aug : txt ACDF[P]N g m 17 [47] latt goth Ephr Thdrt Thl Œc lat-ff.
επισωρ. bef εαυτ. F m 73 vulg arm lat-ff.   for κνηθομενοι, τερπομενοι 67².

tianos)," as Bretsch. and so Huther. But
there seems no need to confine the sense
so narrowly. The quotations in De W.
himself justify the meaning of 'press on,'
'be urgent,' generally : not perhaps in
preaching only, but in the whole work of
the ministry. Cf. Demosth. p. 1187. 6,
ἐπειδὴ . . . . ἐφειστήκει δ᾽ αὐτῷ Καλλί-
στρατος καὶ Ἰφικράτης . . . . οὕτω δὲ
διέθεσαν ὑμᾶς κατηγοροῦντες αὐτοῦ, —
'pressed upon him,' 'urgebant eum :' id.
p. 70. 16, διὰ ταῦτ᾽ ἐγρήγορεν ἐφέστηκεν,
. . . . .) in season, out of season (μὴ καιρὸν ἔχε ὡρισμένον, ἀεί σοι καιρὸς ἔστω·
μὴ ἐν εἰρήνῃ, μὴ ἐν ἀδείᾳ, μηδὲ ἐν ἐκκλησίᾳ καθήμενος μόνον· κἂν ἐν τοῖς κινδύ-
νοις, κἂν ἐν δεσμωτηρίῳ ᾖς, κἂν ἅλυσιν
περικείμενος, κἂν μέλλῃς ἐξιέναι ἐπὶ θάνατον, καὶ παρ᾽ αὐτὸν τὸν καιρὸν ἔλεγξον,
μὴ ὑποσταλῇς ἐπιτιμῆσαι· τότε γὰρ καὶ
ἡ ἐπιτίμησις ἔχει καιρόν, ὅταν ὁ ἔλεγχος
προχωρήσῃ, ὅταν ἀποδειχθῇ τὸ ἔργον,
Chrys. I cannot forbear also transcribing
a very beautiful passage cited by Suicer i.
146 from the same father, Hom. xxx. vol. v.
p. 221: ἂν δ᾽ ἄρα τοῖς αὐτοῖς ἐπιμένωσι
καὶ μετὰ τὴν παραίνεσιν, οὐδὲ οὕτως ἡμεῖς
ἀποστησόμεθα τῆς πρὸς αὐτοὺς συμβουλῆς.
καὶ γὰρ καὶ κρῆναι, κἂν μηδεὶς ὑδρεύηται,
ῥέουσι· καὶ οἱ ποταμοί, κἂν μηδεὶς πίνῃ,
τρέχουσι. δεῖ τοίνυν καὶ τὸν λέγοντα,
κἂν μηδεὶς προσέχῃ, τὰ παρ᾽ ἑαυτοῦ πάντα
πληροῦν· καὶ γὰρ νόμος ἡμῖν, τοῖς τὴν
τοῦ λόγου διακονίαν ἐγκεχειρισμένοις, παρὰ
τοῦ φιλανθρώπου κεῖται θεοῦ, μηδέποτε
τὰ παρ᾽ ἑαυτοῦ ἐλλιμπάνειν, μηδὲ σιγᾶν,
κἂν ἀκούῃ τις, κἂν παρατρέχῃ. This
latter passage gives the more correct
reference,—not so much to his opportunities, as the former, but to theirs (as
Ellic. quotes from Aug. on Ps. cxxviii.,
vol. iv. p. 1689, "sonet verbum Dei vo-
lentibus opportune, nolentibus impor-

tune"). Bengel, from Pricæus, gives examples of similar expressions : "Nicetas
Choniates, παιδαγωγῷ ἐμβριθεῖ ἐοικώς, εὐ-
καίρως ἀκαίρως ἐπέπληττεν. Julian : ἐπο-
ρεύετο ἐπὶ τὰς τῶν φίλων οἰκίας ἄκλητος
κεκλημένος. Virgilii : 'digna indigna
pati,' Terentii : 'cum milite isto præsens
absens ut sies.' " So fanda nefanda, plus
minus, nolens volens, &c.), convict, rebuke (reff.), exhort, in (not 'with ;' it is
not the accompaniment of the actions,
but the element, the temper in which
they are to be performed) all (possible)
long-suffering and teaching (not subjective, 'perseverance in teaching,' as Conyb. ; but 'teaching' itself : it (objective)
is to be the element in which these acts
take place, as well as μακροθυμία (subjective). The junction is harsh, but not
therefore to be avoided. Of course, hendiadys (= ἐν πάσῃ μακροθυμίᾳ διδαχῆς,
Grot., Rosenm.) is out of the question.
On διδαχή and διδασκαλία, see Ellicott's
note). 3, 4.] Reason why all these
will be wanted. For there shall be a
time when they (men, i. e. professing
Christians, as the context shews) will not
endure (not bear—as being offensive to
them : reff.) the healthy doctrine (reff. :
viz. of the Gospel), but according to (after
the course of) their own desires (instead
of, in subjection to God's providence) will
to themselves (emphatic) heap up (one
upon another : τὸ ἀδιάκριτον πλῆθος
ἐδήλωσε, Chrys. There is no meaning of
'heap upon themselves,' 'to their own
cost,' as Luth., 'werden sie ihnen selbst
Lehrer auflaben :' so Heydenr. also)
teachers, having itching ears (ζητοῦντές
τι ἀκοῦσαι καθ᾽ ἡδονήν, Hesych. : 'sermones quærunt vitia sua titillantes,' Grot.
This in fact amounts to the same as
Chrys.'s, τῆς ἡδονῆς χάριν λέγοντας

u Acts iii. 26. ch. i. 15.
Tit. i. 14 al.
v 1 Tim. i. 4 reff.
w 1 Tim. i. 6 reff.
x Paul, 1 Thess. v. 6, 8 only. 1 Pet. i. 13. iv. 7. v. 8 only †.
y Col. i. 16. Phil. iv. 12.

ἀπὸ μὲν τῆς ἀληθείας τὴν [t] ἀκοὴν [u] ἀποστρέψουσιν, ἐπὶ δὲ τοὺς [v] μύθους [w] ἐκτραπήσονται. 5 σὺ δὲ [x] νῆφε [y] ἐν πᾶσιν, [z] κακοπάθησον, [a] ἔργον ποίησον [b] εὐαγγελιστοῦ, τὴν [c] διακονίαν σου [d] πληροφόρησον. 6 ἐγὼ γὰρ ἤδη [e] σπένδομαι καὶ ὁ καιρὸς τῆς ἐμῆς [f] ἀναλύσεως [g] ἐφέστηκεν·

ACDFK LPℵ a b c d e f g h k l m n o 17. 47

1 Tim. iii. 11. ch. ii. 7. Tit. ii. 9. Heb. xiii. 18.   z ch. ii. 9. James v. 13 only. Jonah iv. 10 only. (-θεια, James v. 10.)   a = Acts xv. 38. Phil. i, 22 al.   b Acts xxi. 8. Eph. iv. 11 only †.
c Eph. iv. 22 reff.   d = ver. 17 (Luke i. 1. Rom. iv. 21. xiv. only ‡. (Eccles. viii. 11 only.)   e Phil. ii. 17 only. 1 Chron. xi. 18.   f here only. τὴν ἐκ τοῦ βίου ἀνάλυσιν, Philo in Flacc. 21, vol. ii. p. 544. (-λύειν, Phil. i. 23.)   g = (Paul) 1 Thess. v. 3. Luke xxi. 34. L.P.   Wisd. vi. 5, 8. see Acts xxviii. 2. ver. 2.

5. om κακοπαθησον ℵ[1].   aft κακοπαθησον ins ως καλος στρατιωτης χρ. ιησου A.
6. for εμης αναλ., αναλ. μου ACF [P(της ανα . . .)] ℵ m 17 [47] copt arm Eus Ath Ephr Pallad Cypr₁ : txt DKL rel am(with demid F-lat) syrr [Eus-8-mss₁] Chr Thdrt Euthal-mss Damasc₁ Thl Œc Cypr₁.

καὶ τέρποντας τὴν ἀκοὴν ἐπιζητοῦντες, though De W. draws a distinction between them. Plut. de superst. p. 167 b (Wetst.), μουσικὴν φησὶν ὁ Πλάτων . . . ἀνθρώποις οὐ τρυφῆς ἕνεκα καὶ κνήσεως ὤτων δοθῆναι : see more examples in Wetst.), and shall avert their ears from the truth, and be turned aside (ref. and note) to fables (the art. seems to imply that they would be at least *like* the fables already believed: see 1 Tim. i. 4, and cf. Ellic. here). 5 ff.] He enforces on Timotheus the duty of worthily fulfilling his office, *in consideration of his own approaching end.* For this being introduced, various reasons have been given :— (1) he himself would be no longer able to make head against these adverse influences, and therefore must leave Timotheus and others to succeed him : so Heydenr., Huther, al. : (2) "ego quamdiu vixi manum tibi porrexi : tibi meæ assiduæ exhortationes non defuerunt, tibi mea consilia fuerant magno adjumento, et exemplum etiam magnæ confirmationi : jam tempus est ut tibi ipse magister sis atque hortator, natareque incipias sine cortice : cave ne quid morte mea in te mutatum animadvertatur," Calv. : similarly Grot. : (3) "causa quæ Timotheum moveat ad officium : Pauli discessus et beatitudo : finis coronat opus." Beng., and so Chrys., Hom. in loc., in a very beautiful passage, too long for transcription : (4) to stir up Timotheus to imitation of him : so Pel., Ambr., Heinr., al. (in De W.) There seems no reason why any one of these should be chosen to the exclusion of the rest : we may well, with Flatt, combine (1) and (4), at the same time bearing (2) and (3) in mind :—'I am no longer here to withstand these things : be thou a worthy successor of me, no longer depending on, but carrying out for thyself my directions : follow my steps, inherit

their result, and the honour of their end.'
5.] But (as contrasted with the description preceding) **do thou** (emphatic) **be sober** (it is difficult to give the full meaning of **νῆφε** in a version. The reference is especially to the clearness and wakefulness of attention and observance which attends on sobriety, as distinguished from the lack of these qualities in intoxication. 'Keep thy coolness and presence of mind, that thou be not entrapped into forgetfulness, but discern and use every opportunity of speaking and acting for the truth,' Mack : cf. also Ellic.) **in all things, suffer hardship** (reff.), **do the work of an Evangelist** (reff. : here probably in a wider sense, including all that belongs to a preacher and teacher of the Gospel), **fill up the measure of** (fill up, in every point ; leaving nothing undone in. Beza's rendering, 'ministerii tui plenam fidem facito, i. e. veris argumentis comproba te germanum esse Dei ministrum,'—so Calv. 'ministerium tuum probatum redde,'—is justified by usage (reff.), but hardly in accordance with ver. 17 : see there) **thy ministry.** 6.] For the connexion, see above. **For I am already being offered** (as a drink-offering : i. e. the process is begun, which shall shed my blood. '*Ready to be offered*' (E. V., Conyb., so also Matthies, Est., al.) misses the force of the present. Grot. would render it 'jam nunc aspergor vino, id est, præparor ad mortem :' but such a meaning for σπένδομαι does not seem to be justified : see ref. Phil. That σπένδομαι is there followed by ἐπὶ τῇ θυσίᾳ κ.τ.λ., and here stands absolutely, is surely no reason why this usage should not be as significant and as correct as that ; against De W.), **and the time of my departure** (ἀνάλυσις (ref.) is merely this, and not *dissolutio*, as Vulg., Matthies,—nor as Elsner (so also Wolf) imagines, is there any allusion to guests

7 τὸν [hi] ἀγῶνα τὸν [i] καλὸν [ik] ἠγώνισμαι, τὸν [l] δρόμον [h] Phil. i. 30
[m] τετέλεκα, τὴν πίστιν [n] τετήρηκα· 8 [o] λοιπὸν [p] ἀπόκειταί
μοι ὁ τῆς δικαιοσύνης [q] στέφανος, ὃν [r] ἀποδώσει μοι ὁ
κύριος ἐν [s] ἐκείνῃ τῇ [s] ἡμέρᾳ, ὁ [t] δίκαιος [tu] κριτής, οὐ μόνον
δὲ ἐμοί, ἀλλὰ καὶ πᾶσιν τοῖς [v] ἠγαπηκόσιν τὴν [w] ἐπι-

reff.
i 1 Tim. vi. 12.
Eur. Alc. 648.
k Col. i. 29
reff.
l Acts xiii. 25.
xx. 24 (both
Paul) only.
Jer. viii. 6.
m = Paul, here
only. Matt.

vii. 28 al.   Sir. vii. 25. see Gal. v. 16.   n = Paul, Eph. iv. 3 only. see 1 Tim. vi. 14.   o = Acts
xxvii. 20.   1 Cor. i. 16.   2 Cor. xiii. 11 al.   p Col. i. 5 reff.   q 1 Cor. ix. 25. James i.
12.   1 Pet v. 4.   Rev. ii. 10.   Prov. iv. 9.   r = Rom. ii. 6.   Rev. xxii. 12 al. Ps. l. 12 (14).
s ch. i. 12, 18.   2 Thess. i. 10.   t Ps. vii. 11. 2 Macc. xii. 6.   u = Paul, here only. Acts x.
42.   Heb. xii. 23.   James v. 9.   v = 1 Pet. iii. 10, from Ps. xxxiii. 12. Ps. xxxix. 16.
w ver. 1.

7. for τ. αγ. τ. κα., τον καλον αγωνα ACFℵ m 17 vulg Ath Chr₁ Cypr Pel : txt
DKL [P τον α . . . . καλον] rel syrr copt goth Orig₃ Eus lat-ff.
8. om πασιν D¹ 67² vulg(and F-lat) Syr Ambrst : om τοις ηγαπηκοσιν ℵ¹ : txt
ACD³FKL[P]ℵ³ rel syr copt goth Chr_expr Thdrt Ps-Ath Damasc Cypr Archel Jer
Aug_aliq.

breaking up (ἀναλύοντες) from a banquet and making libations (σπένδοντες) :—'allusisse Apostolum ad σπονδάς crediderim ἀναλυόντων e convivio, sensumque esse, sese ex hac vita molestiisque exsatiatum abiturum, libato non vino sed sanguine suo.' He quotes from Athenæus i. 13, ἔσπενδον ἀπὸ τῶν δείπνων ἀναλύοντες. But against this we have only to oppose that most sound and useful rule, that an allusion of this kind must never be imagined unless where necessitated by the context : and certainly here there is no trace of the idea of a banquet having been in the mind of the Apostle, various as are the images introduced) is at hand (not, is present, 'ift vorhanden,' Luth.: which would be ἐνέστηκεν, see 2 Thess. ii. 2 note):

7.] I have striven the good strife (it is hardly correct to confine ἀγών to the sense of 'fight:' that it may be, but its reference is much wider, to any contest, see note on ref. 1 Tim.: and here probably to that which is specified in the next clause : see especially Heb. xii. 1), I have finished my race (see reff.: the image belongs peculiarly to St. Paul. In Phil. iii. 12 ff. he follows it out in detail. See also 1 Cor. ix. 24 ff.: Heb. xii. 1, 2. Wetst. quotes Virg. Æn. iv. 653, "Vixi, et quem dederat cursum fortuna, peregi"), I have kept the faith (not, as Heydenr., 'my plight to observe the laws of the race:' but as Bengel rightly observes, "res bis per metaphoram expressa nunc tertio loco exprimitur proprie." The constant use of ἡ πίστις in these Epistles in the objective technical sense, must rule the expression here. This same consideration will preclude the meaning 'have kept my faith,' 'my fidelity,' as Raphel, Kypke, al.) : 8.] henceforth (perhaps this adverb expresses λοιπόν better than any other. It appears to be used in later Greek, from Polybius downwards, in this

sense of 'proinde,' 'itaque:' cf. Polyb. ii. 68. 9; iv. 32. 5; x. 45. 2) there is laid up (reff.) for me the (not 'α,' as E. V.) crown (reff., and cf. Phil. iii. 14) of righteousness (i. e. the bestowal of which is conditional on the substantiation and recognition of righteousness—q. d. 'a crown among the righteous :' τὸν τοῖς δικαίοις ηὐτρεπισμένον λέγει, Thdrt.: and so De W. after Chrys., δικαιοσύνην ἐνταῦθα πάλιν τὴν καθόλου φησὶν ἀρετήν. This is better than with Huther, al., to take the gen. as one appositionis, as in James i. 12, ὁ στ. τῆς ζωῆς: and 1 Pet. v. 4, ὁ τῆς δόξης στ.: both these, ζωή and δόξα, may well constitute the crown, but it is not easy to say how δικαιοσύνη can. Thdrt.'s alternative, τὸν δικαίᾳ ψήφῳ δωρούμενον (so Heydenr., Matth., al.), is equally objectionable. There is, as Calv. has shewn, no sort of inconsistency here with the doctrines of grace : "neque enim gratuita justificatio quæ nobis per fidem confertur, cum operum remuneratione pugnat quin potius rite conveniunt ista duo, gratis justificari hominem Christi beneficio, et tamen operum mercedem coram Deo relaturum. Nam simulatque nos in gratiam recipit Deus, opera quoque nostra grata habet, ut præmio quoque (licet indebito) dignetur." See further on this point Estius's note, and Conc. Trident. Canones, Sess. vi. c. 16, where the remarkable expression is quoted from the Epist. of Pope Cælestinus I. 12, "Dei tanta est erga omnes homines bonitas, ut eorum velit esse merita, quæ sunt ipsius dona"), which the Lord (Christ : cf. ἐπιφάν. αὐτοῦ below) shall award (more than 'give:' see reff., and Matt. vi. 4, 6, &c., xvi. 27 : the idea of requital should be expressed. Compare however Ellicott's note) me in that day (reff.), the righteous (subj., 'just;' but the word 'righteous' should be kept as answering to 'righteousness' above) judge (see Acts x. 42. In

x ch. ii. 15 reff.
y 1 Cor. iv. 19.
Phil. ii. 19,
24 al.
4 Kings i. 11.
* Matt. xxvii.
46 ‖ Mk.
Acts ii. 27.
2 Cor. iv. 9.
ver. 16 al.
Ps. xi. 10.
a 1 John iii. 15.
b 1 Tim. vi. 17.
Tit. ii. 12
only. see
1 Tim. iv. 8
e ch. ii. 21 reff.

φάνειαν αὐτοῦ. ⁹ ˣ Σπούδασον ἐλθεῖν πρός με ʸ ταχέως. ACDFK
LPℵ a b
¹⁰ Δημᾶς γάρ με ᶻ ἐγκατέλιπεν, ᵃ ἀγαπήσας τὸν ᵇ νῦν c d e f g
h k l m n
ᵇ αἰῶνα, καὶ ἐπορεύθη εἰς Θεσσαλονίκην, Κρήσκης εἰς o 17. 47
Γαλατίαν, Τίτος εἰς Δαλματίαν· ¹¹ Λουκᾶς ἐστιν μόνος
μετ᾽ ἐμοῦ. Μάρκον ᶜ ἀναλαβὼν ᵈ ἄγε μετὰ σεαυτοῦ·
ἔστιν γάρ μοι ᵉ εὔχρηστος εἰς ᶠ διακονίαν. ¹² Τυχικὸν

c = Acts xx. 13 14. xxiii. 31, both of Paul. Exod. iv. 20.   d = 1 Thess. iv. 14.
f = Eph. iv. 12. Col. iv. 17. 1 Tim. i. 12. ver. 5‡. (Esth. vi. 3 A. 1 Macc. xi. 58 only.)

9. πρ. εμε D.
10. [με bef γαρ D¹.]   εγκατελειπεν ACD³FL[P] o 17 [47] : κατελ. D¹.
for γαλατιαν, γαλλιαν Cℵ 73. 80. 123 am¹ æth-rom Ath Eus Epiph(οὐ γὰρ ἐν τῇ Γαλατίᾳ,
ὥς τινες πλανηθέντες νομίζουσιν, ἀλλὰ ἐν τῇ Γαλλίᾳ).   δελματιαν C n o 67² :
δερματιαν A. [om τ. ε. δ. L.]
11. συν εμοι μονος D¹ latt [syr] goth Iren-int Ambrst.   αγαγε A d f 31-8 [47]
72. 238 Thdrt Damasc : txt CDFKLℵ rel Chr. [P def.]

this assertion of just judgment, there is nothing, as De W. imagines, to controvert the doctrines of grace : see above);—and (but) not only to me (better than 'not to me only,' E. V., &c. (οὐδὲ ἐμοὶ μόνῳ), which though true, does not correctly represent the sense), but also to all who have loved (who shall then be found to have loved and still to be loving, see Winer, edn. 6, § 40. 4 a : loved, i. e. (reff.) looked forward with earnest joy to) His appearing (ver. 1).

9—22.] Request to come to Rome. Notices of his own state and that of others : greetings.

9 ff.] Do thine endeavour (so also Tit. iii. 12) to come to me quickly (this desire that Timotheus should come to him, appears in ch. i. 4, 8 : its reason is now specified) : for (I am almost alone) Demas (mentioned Col. iv. 14 with Luke, as saluting the Colossians, and Philem. 24, also with Luke (and others), as one of the Apostle's συνεργοί) deserted me, loving (ἀγαπήσας (used perhaps in contrast to ver. 8 above) is contemporary with ἐγκατέλιπεν—'through love of:' so Ellic. also, who has hardly represented me rightly, when he quotes me as holding the temporal sense of the participle) this present world (τῆς ἀνέσεως ἐρασθείς, τοῦ ἀκινδύνου καὶ τοῦ ἀσφαλοῦς, μᾶλλον εἵλετο οἴκοι τρυφᾶν, ἢ μετ᾽ ἐμοῦ ταλαιπωρεῖσθαι καὶ συνδιαφέρειν μοι τοὺς παρόντας κινδύνους, Chrys.), and went to Thessalonica ('his birthplace,' says De W.: cf. οἴκοι, Chrys., above: but how ascertained ? He may have gone there for the sake of traffic, which idea the ἀγαπήσας τὸν νῦν αἰῶνα would seem to support), Crescens (not named elsewhere. He is said traditionally to have preached the Gospel in Galatia (Constt. apost. vii. 46, p. 1056), and, more

recently (in Sophronius), to have founded the church at Vienne in Gaul : this latter interpretation of Γαλατίαν (τὰς Γαλλίας οὕτως ἐκάλεσεν, see var. readd.) Thdrt. also adopts. All this traditional fabric is probably raised by conjecture on this passage. Winer, Realw.) to Galatia (see Prolegg. to Gal. § ii. 1), Titus (Prolegg. to Titus, § i.) to Dalmatia (part of the Roman province of Illyricum (Suet. Aug. 21. Tib. 9), on the coast of the Adriatic (Plin. iii. 22. Strabo, vii. p. 315), south of Liburnia (Plin. iii. 26), Winer, Realw. See the art. Dalmatia in Dr. Smith's Dict. of Geography. Thdrt. says, referring to ἀγαπήσας τὸν νῦν αἰῶνα, οὗτοι (Crescens and Titus) τῆς κατηγορίας ἐκείνης ἐλεύθεροι· ὑπ᾽ αὐτοῦ γὰρ ἀπεστάλησαν τοῦ κηρύγματος ἕνεκα. But this hardly agrees with ἐπορεύθη, which must be understood with both names : see also the contrast in ver. 12. They had certainly left the Apostle of their own accord : why, does not appear) : Luke (see Prolegg. to Luke's Gospel, § i.) is alone with me (De W.'s question, 'where then was Aristarchus (Acts xxvii. 2. Col. iv. 10. Philem. 24) ?' is one which we have no means of answering : but we may venture this remark : a forger, such as De W. supposes the writer of this Epistle to be, would have taken good care to account for him). Mark (Col. iv. 10, note : Philem. 24. John Mark, Acts xv. 38) take up (on thy way : so ἀναλαμβάνειν implies in the two first reff., and probably also here) and bring with thee : for he is to me useful for the ministry (for help to me in my apostolic labours : not, as Conyb., 'his services are profitable to me,' adding in a note below, "διακονίαν, not, 'the ministry,' as E. V. :" —no such conclusion can be drawn from the omission of the art. after a preposi-

...απεσ-
τειλα d.
ACDFK
LPℵ a b
c e f g h j
k l m n o
17. 47

δὲ ἀπέστειλα εἰς Ἔφεσον. ¹³ τὸν ᵍ φελόνην ὃν ʰ ἀπέλιπον
ἐν Τρωάδι παρὰ Κάρπῳ ἐρχόμενος φέρε, καὶ τὰ ⁱ βιβλία,
μάλιστα τὰς ᵏ μεμβράνας. ¹⁴ Ἀλέξανδρος ὁ ¹χαλκεὺς
πολλά μοι κακὰ ᵐ ἐνεδείξατο· ⁿ ἀποδώσει αὐτῷ ὁ κύριος

g here only †.
h = Paul, ver.
20. Tit. i. 5
only. (Heb.
iv. 6, 9. x.
26. Jude 6
only.)
2 Macc. x. 19.
i = Luke iv. 17,
20. Neh.

viii. 1, &c.   j 1 Tim. iv. 10 reff.   k here only †.   l here only.   Gen. iv. 22.
m = Tit. ii. 10. iii. 2.   Heb. vi. 10, 11. see Eph. ii. 7 (reff.).   n ver. 8 reff.

13. απελειπον ACFL[P] 17.   [aft μαλιστα ins δε D¹ k m vulg.

14. κακα bef μοι LP m.]   rec (for αποδωσει) αποδωη, with D³KL rel am(with
tol) Orthod Thdrt(πρόῤῥησίς ἐστιν, οὐκ ἀρά) Damasc₁(elsw₁ -δωσει, but there περὶ
ἀρᾶς ὑπ' ἀποστόλων γενομένης) Thl(ἀντὶ τοῦ ἀποδώσει· μᾶλλον γὰρ προφητεία ἐστὶν ἢ
ἀρά) Jer : txt ACD¹Fℵ m 17. 67² vulg Chr Eulog(in Phot) Damasc₁(see above) Œc
Aug(non ait reddat sed reddet). [P def.   om 2nd o K(so ver 18) b k. (P def.)]

tion, and least of all in these Epistles.
Cf. θέμενος εἰς διακονίαν, ref. 1 Tim.—
Grot. suggests, 'forte ob Latini sermonis
consuetudinem') : but (apparently a slight
contrast is intended to those above, who
ἐπορεύθησαν of their own accord) Tychicus (see Eph. vi. 21 note) I sent to Ephesus (on the various attempts to give an
account of this journey, and its bearing
on the question, whether Timotheus was
at Ephesus at this time, see Prolegg. to
this Epistle, § i. 5).   13.] The cloak
(φελόνης is said to be a corrupted form
of φαινόλης, lat. pænula, a thick outer
cloak : but as early as Chrys., there has
been a doubt whether this is the meaning
here. He says, φελόνην ἐνταῦθα τὸ ἱμά-
τιον λέγει, τινὲς δέ φασι τὸ γλωσσόκομον
(bag or case, John xiii. 29) ἔνθα τὰ βιβλία ἔκειτο : and so Syr. and all. : but it is
against this idea, as indeed Bengel remarks, that the books should be afterwards mentioned. It would be unnatural, in case a bag of books had been left
behind, to ask a friend to bring the bag,
also the books, and especially the parchments : 'the bag of books and parchments
which I left' would be its most obvious
designation.   A long discussion of the
meanings of φελόνης, and of the question
whether it is rightly supposed to be a corruption from φαινόλης, may be found in
Wolf ad loc. : see also Ellic. The Jews
also had the word פֵּילְיוֹן for a cloak) which
I left (behind me: οἱ δι' ἀσθένειαν ἀπο-
λειφθέντες, Xen. Mem. iv. 1. 32 : for what
reason, is not clear : but in St. Paul's life
of perils, it may well be conceived that
he may have been obliged to leave such
things behind, against his intention) in
Troas (respecting his having been at Troas
lately, see Prolegg. to Past. Epp. § ii. 16,
30, 31) with ('chez') Karpus when
thou art coming (setting out to come)
bring, and the books (i. e. papyrus rolls:
on these, and on μεμβράνας, see Dict. of
Antiquities, art. Liber.   τί δὲ αὐτῷ βιβ-

λίων ἔδει μέλλοντι ἀποδημεῖν πρὸς τὸν
θεόν; καὶ μάλιστα ἔδει, ὥστε αὐτὰ τοῖς
πιστοῖς παραθέσθαι, καὶ ἀντὶ τῆς αὐτοῦ
διδασκαλίας ἔχειν αὐτά. Chrys. This may
have been so : but there is nothing inconsistent with his near prospect of death,
in a desire to have his cloak and books
during the approaching winter), especially the parchments (which as more
costly, probably contained the more valuable writings : perhaps the sacred books
themselves. On a possible allusion to
these books, &c., which the Apostle had
with him in his imprisonment at Cæsarea, see note, Acts xxvi. 24).
14.] Alexander the smith (Eustathius,
on Hom. Od. γ. p. 139 (Wetst.), says,
χαλκεὺς δὲ ὁ πρὸ βραχέων χρυσόχοος,
κατὰ ὄνομα γενικὸν ἀπὸ πρώτου φανέντος
μετάλλου. διὸ καὶ ὁ Ἥφαιστος χαλκεὺς
ἐλέγετο, καὶ χαλκεύειν τὸ οἱανοῦν ἐλατὴν
ὕλην σφύρᾳ παίειν. Similarly the Etymol.
(ib.),—ἀπὸ γὰρ τοῦ πρώτου φανέντος
μετάλλου πάντας τοὺς δημιουργοὺς ἐκά-
λουν οὕτως οἱ παλαιοί. See ref. Gen.,
and 2 Chron. xxiv. 12. Perhaps the
same with the Alexander of 1 Tim. i. 20,
where see note. There is nothing here
said, inconsistent with his being an Ephesian resident. It has been indeed supposed that he was at Rome, and that the
following caution refers to Timotheus's
approaching visit : but the aor. ἐνεδείξατο
seems to suit better the other hypothesis.
It must ever remain uncertain, whether
the Alexander whom we find put forward
by the Jews in the Ephesian tumult, Acts
xix. 33, 34, is this same person: nothing
in that narrative is against it. The title
ὁ χαλκεύς may be intended to mark another Alexander : but it may also be a
mere cursory designation of the same
person) did to me much evil (such, as in
E. V., is the nearest representation in our
language of the phrase κακὰ ἐνδείξασθαι.
Cf. Gen. l. 15, μή ποτε μνησικακήσῃ ἡμῖν
Ἰωσὴφ καὶ ἀνταπόδομα ἀνταποδῷ ἡμῖν

κατὰ τὰ ἔργα αὐτοῦ. 15 ὃν καὶ σὺ ᵒφυλάσσου· ᵖλίαν
γὰρ ᑫἀντέστη τοῖς ἡμετέροις λόγοις. 16 ἐν τῇ πρώτῃ
μου ʳἀπολογίᾳ οὐδείς μοι ˢσυνπαρεγένετο, ἀλλὰ πάντες
με ᵗἐγκατέλιπον· μὴ αὐτοῖς ᵘλογισθείη· 17 ὁ δὲ κύριός μοι
ᵛπαρέστη καὶ ʷἐνεδυνάμωσέν με, ἵνα δι᾽ ἐμοῦ τὸ ˣκήρυγμα

ACDFK LPℵ a b c e f g h k l m n o 17. 47

o w. acc., = Acts xxi. 25. 2 Kings xx. 10. p Paul, 2 Cor. xi. 5. xii. 11 only, but ὑπὲρ λ. Matt. ii. 16 al. q ch. iii. 8 reff. r Phil. i. 7 reff. = Acts xxii. 1. xxv. 16. s Luke xxiii. 48 only. Ps. lxxxii. 8 only. t ver. 10. u = Rom. ii. 26. iv. 4, 8, from Ps. xxxi. 2. 2 Cor. v. 19. Paul, esp. v = Rom. xvi. 2 only. Jer. xv. 11. w ch. ii. 1 reff. x Matt. xii. 41 ∥ L. Rom. xvi. 25. 1 Cor. i. 21. ii. 4. xv. 14. Tit. i. 3 only. 2 Chron. xxx. 5. Prov. ix. 3. Jon. iii. 2. Esdr. ix. 3 only.

[om *τα* 47. (P def.)] om *αυτου* ℵ[1]. [P def.]

15. rec (for *ανεστη*) *ανθεστηκεν*, with D[3]KL [P(. . *στηκεν*)] ℵ[3] rel: *ανθηστη* F: txt ACD[1]ℵ[1] 17.

16. for *συνπαρ.*, *παρεγενετο* ACFℵ[1] k 17 [Eus 4-mss$_1$] Chr$_1$ Euthal-mss. *εγκατελειπον* ACD[3]FL[P] 17 [47[1]].

17. om *μοι* A.

πάντα τὰ κακὰ ἃ ἐνεδειξάμεθα εἰς αὐτόν—and ver. 17, *ἄφες αὐτοῖς . . . . ὅτι πονηρά σοι ἐνεδείξαντο.* In both these places *ἐνδείξασθαι* represents the Hebrew verb גָּמַל, 'affecit:' similarly the Song of the Three Children, ver. 19, *ἐντραπείησαν πάντες οἱ ἐνδεικνύμενοι τοῖς δούλοις σου κακά*: and 2 Macc. xiii. 9, *τοῖς δὲ φρονήμασιν ὁ βασιλεὺς βεβαρβαρωμένος ἤρχετο, τὰ χείριστα τῶν ἐπὶ τοῦ πατρὸς αὐτοῦ γεγονότων ἐνδειξόμενος τοῖς Ἰουδαίοις.* This usage is easily explained. From the primary sense of the middle verb '*to manifest,*' applied to a *subjective quality* (reff. Tit., Heb., and *εὔνοιαν*, Aristoph. Plut. 785,—*γνώμην*, Herod. viii. 141: al. in Lexx.), we have idiomatically the same sense applied to *objective facts* in Hellenistic Greek: Palm and Rost give from Plutarch, *ἐνδείξασθαι φιλανθρωπίας*, a phrase intermediate between the two usages. Then in rendering *ἐνδείξασθαί τινι κακά*, it is for us to enquire, whether we shall be best expressing the mind of the original by changing the subjective *ἐνδείξασθαι* into an objective verb, or by changing the objective subst. *κακά* to a subjective quality (*κακίαν*):—and the answer to this is clear. The *κακά* were facts which we must not disguise. The *ἐνδείξασθαι*, not the *κακά*, is used in an improper and secondary meaning; and therefore in rendering the phrase in a language which admits of no such idiom, it is the verb which must be made objective to suit the substantive, not vice versâ. Conyb.'s rendering, '*charged me with much evil,*' as also his alternative, '*manifested many evil things* (?) *against me,*' would, it seems to me, require the active verb): **the Lord shall requite him according to his works** (the optative of the rec. makes no real difficulty it is not personal revenge, but zeal for the cause of the Gospel which the wish would express, cf. ver. 16 below, where his own personal feelings were concerned): **whom do thou also beware of** (see above, on Alexander); **for he exceedingly withstood our** (better than 'my,' seeing that *μοι* occurs in the same sentence, and immediately follows. The plural may be used because the *λόγοι* were such as were common to all Christians—arguments for, or declarations of, our common faith) **words.**

16.] In my first defence (open self-defence, before a court of justice, see reff. For a discussion of this whole matter, see the Prolegg. and Ellic.'s note. I will only remark here, that any other defence than one made *at Rome*, in the latter years of the Apostle's life, is out of the question) **no one came forward with me** ("verbum *συμπαραγίνεσθαι* indicat patronos et amicos, qui alios, ad causam dicendam vocatos, nunc præsentia sua, nunc etiam oratione (not in the time of Cicero, who clearly distinguishes, De Orat. ii. 74, between the orator or *patronus*, and the *advocati:* speaking of the former he says, 'orat reus, urgent advocati ut invehamur, ut maledicamus, &c.' But in Tacit. Annal. xi. 6, the orators are called *advocati*) adjuvare solebant. Id Cicero, cap. 29, pro Sulla, *adesse supplici*, et cap. 14, pro Milone, simpliciter *adesse* dicit. Græci dicunt nunc *παραγίνεσθαι*, nunc *παρεῖναι*, nunc *συμπαρεῖναι*." Wolf. So Demosth., *κατὰ Νεαίρας*, 1369. 17, *συμπαραγενόμενος αὐτῷ δοκιμαζομένῳ*), **but all men deserted me: may it not be laid to their charge** (by God: reff. *τὴν πατρικὴν περὶ αὐτῶν ἔδειξεν εὐσπλαγχνίαν. οὐ κακοηθείας ἦν, ἀλλὰ δειλίας ἡ ὑποχώρησις*, Thdrt.): **but the Lord** (Jesus) **stood by me, and strengthened** ('*put strength in:*' a word especially used of and by our Apostle, reff.) **me, that by my means the**

^y πληροφορηθῇ καὶ ἀκούσωσιν πάντα τὰ εονη· καὶ ^z ἐρύ- ^{y = ver. 5 (reff.).}
σθην ἐκ ^aστόματος ^{ab} λέοντος. ¹⁸ ^z ῥύσεταί με ὁ κύριος ^{z w. ἐκ, Col. i. 13 reff. w.}
ἀπὸ παντὸς ^c ἔργου ^c πονηροῦ, καὶ σώσει εἰς τὴν βασι- ^{ἀπό, 1 Thess. i. 10 reff.}

PSA. xxi. 21. (see Ps. lvi. 4.)   b Heb. xi. 33.   1 Pet. v. 8.   Rev. iv. 7 al5. only.   ^{a here only.}
21 reff. see 2 Cor. ix. 8.   2 Thess. ii. 17.   ^{c Col. i.}

for πληροφορηθη, πληρωθη F k 73 Œc-comm.   rec ακουση (gramml corrn), with
KL rel Chr Thdrt: txt ACDF[P]א 17 Eus Euthal.   rec ερρυσθ., with DFL[P]
rel: txt ACא m.

18. rec ins και bef ρυσεται, with D³FKL[P] rel syrr æth: om ACD¹א 67² vulg copt

proclamation (of the Gospel) might be delivered in full measure (see on ver. 5) and all the Gentiles might hear (one is tempted, with Thdrt., al., to interpret this of his preservation for further missionary journeys (Thdrt. thinks this defence happened *during* his journey to Spain): but the spirit of the whole context seems to forbid this, and to compel us to confine this πληροφορία to the effect of the single occasion referred to,—his acquittal before the 'corona populi,' in whose presence the trials took place: so Bengel—"una sæpe occasio maximi est momenti : *gentes*—quarum Roma caput." And so Huther and Wiesinger, and in the main, De W.): **and I was delivered from the mouth of the lion** (the Fathers mostly understood this of *Nero:* so Chrys, Thdrt., Thl., Œc., Euseb., &c. : see Suicer, ii. p. 233. And Esth. (add.) xiv. 13, E. V., is quoted, "where Esther says concerning Artaxerxes, Put a word into my mouth ἐνώπιον τοῦ λέοντος." Whitby :—or, seeing that according to the chronology adopted by some, he was not in Rome at the time (see Prolegomena to Past. Epp. § ii. 33), of his *locum tenens, Helius Cæsareanus:* so Pearson, Annales Paulini, p. 24,—or of the *Jewish accuser,* as Wieseler, Chron. ii. p. 476. But these are hardly probable : nor again is it, that the Apostle was literally in danger of being thrown to wild beasts, and established his right as a Roman citizen to be exempted from that punishment (Bengel's objection to this, 'ex ore *leonum* diceret, si proprie bestias innueret,' is of no force: as the popular cry 'Christianos ad leonem' shews: see also ref. Psalm, of which doubtless the words were a reminiscence) : nor again is the idea (Calv., Ellic., al.), that the expression is figurative for *great danger,—the jaws of death,* or the like: for the Apostle *did not fear* death, but looked forward to it as the end of his course, and certainly would not have spoken of it under this image. The *context* seems to me to demand another and very different interpretation. None stood with him—all forsook him : but the Lord stood by

him and strengthened him : *for what ?* that he might *witness a good confession,* and that the κήρυγμα might be expanded to the utmost. The result of this strengthening was, that he was delivered ἐκ στόματος λέοντος : he was strengthened, *witnessed a good confession, in spite of desertion and discouragement.* Then let us pass on to his confidence for the future, the expression of which is bound on to this sentence by ῥύσεται, indicating the identity of God's deliverance,—and **παντός** indicating the *generalization of the danger of which this was a particular case.* And how is the danger generally described ? as **πᾶν ἔργον πονηρόν** : and it is implied that the falling into such danger would preclude him from enduring to Christ's heavenly kingdom. It was then an ἔργον πονηρόν from which he was on this occasion delivered. What ἔργον πονηρόν ? The *falling into the power of the tempter ;* the giving way, in his own weakness and the desertion of all, and betraying the Gospel for which he was sent as a witness. The *lion* then is the *devil ;* ὁ ἀντίδικος ἡμῶν διάβολος ὡς λέων ὠρυόμενος περιπατεῖ ζητῶν τίνα καταπίῃ, 1 Pet. v. 8).   18.] The **Lord (Jesus) shall deliver me from every evil work** (see above : from every danger of faint-heartedness, and apostasy : so, even without adopting the above meaning of ἐκ στόματος λέοντος, Chrys., καὶ γὰρ καὶ τοῦτο τὸ δυνηθῆναι μέχρις αἵματος ἀντικαταστῆναι πρὸς τὴν ἁμαρτίαν, καὶ μὴ ἐνδοῦναι, ἑτέρου λέοντός ἐστι ῥύσασθαι, τοῦ διαβόλου. So also Grot., De W., al. The meaning adopted by Huther, Wiesinger, al., that the ἔργα πονηρά are *the works of his adversaries* plotting against him, is totally beside the purpose : he had no such confidence (ver. 6), nor would his conservation to Christ's heavenly kingdom depend in the least upon such deliverance. Besides which, the correspondence of this declaration of confidence to the concluding petition of the Lord's Prayer cannot surely be fortuitous, and then πονηροῦ, here joined to ἔργου as neuter, must be subjective, evil resulting

λείαν αὐτοῦ τὴν ᵈἐπουράνιον· ᵉ ᾧ ἡ ᵉδόξα εἰς τοὺς ᵉαἰῶνας
τῶν αἰώνων, ἀμήν.

19 Ἄσπασαι Πρίσκαν καὶ Ἀκύλαν καὶ τὸν Ὀνησιφόρου
ᶠοἶκον. 20 Ἔραστος ἔμεινεν ἐν Κορίνθῳ, Τρόφιμον δὲ
ᵍἀπέλιπον ἐν Μιλήτῳ ἀσθενοῦντα. 21 ʰσπούδασον πρὸ
ⁱχειμῶνος ἐλθεῖν. ἀσπάζεταί σε Εὔβουλος καὶ Πούδης
καὶ Λίνος καὶ Κλαυδία καὶ οἱ ἀδελφοὶ πάντες.
22 Ὁ κύριος [Ἰησοῦς χριστὸς] μετὰ τοῦ ᵏπνεύματός
σου. ἡ ˡχάρις μεθ' ὑμῶν.

ΠΡΟΣ ΤΙΜΟΘΕΟΝ.

d 1 Cor. xv. 40,
&c. Phil ii.
10. Heb. xi.
16. xii. 22
al4. 2 Macc.
iii. 39.
e Gal. i. 5 reff
f ch. i. 16 reff.
g ver. 13.
h ver. 9.
i = Matt. (xvi
3) xxiv. 20 ll
Mk. John x.
22 (Acts
xxvii. 20)
only.
k Gal. vi 18.
Phil iv. 23.
Philem. 25.
l Col. iv. 18
reff.

ACDFK
LPℵ a b
c e f g h
k l m n o
17. 47

arm Chr-ms lat-ff. (17 def.)   [εαυτου D¹F.]   for ᾧ, αυτω A k.   om ἡ F.
[19. πρισκιλλαν 47 fuld(with harl¹) syrr.]
20. [om δε P a o 238(Sz).]   απελειπον CL[P] 17 [47]. (A uncert.)
μηλωτα A (C¹ ?) : [μηλιτω P o :] μεληπω 17. [ασθ. bef εν μιλ. D 238(Sz) vulg Syr.]
21. ασπαζονται F vulg(not am fuld F-lat) [æth].   om παντες ℵ¹ [17].
22. om 1st clause 67². om ιησ. χρ. F(not F-lat) ℵ¹ 17 8-pe æth : om χριστος
A 31. 114 : ins CDKL[P]ℵ³ rel.   for η χ. μεθ' υμ. [ημων 47 some-mss-of-vulg],
ερρωσο εν ειρηνη D¹[: om æth-rom.]   rec at end ins αμην, with DKL[P]ℵ³ rel
vulg syrr copt : om ACFℵ¹ 17. 67² æth [arm-zoh] Ambrst.

SUBSCRIPTION. rec προς τ. δευτερα της εφεσιων εκκλησιας πρωτον επισκοπον
χειροτονηθεντα εγραφη απο ρωμης οτε εκ δευτερου παρεστη παυλος τω καισαρι νερωνι,
similarly KL rel : txt C 17, and ℵ(adding στιχων ρπ) : πρ. τ. β D(addg επληρωθη)
F(prefg ετελεσθη) : so also A(addg απο λαοδικειας) [and P(adding εγρ. απυ ρωμης
στιχων ρπ)].

from our *falling* into temptation, not evil
happening to us from without. It is
hardly necessary to observe, that πονηροῦ
here cannot be gen. masc., 'of the evil
one,'—as Pelagius and Mosheim, in De
W.), and shall preserve me safe (σώσει
in its not uncommon, pregnant sense of
'bring safe :' cf. σώζειν πόλινδε, Il. ε.
224 ; ἐς οἴκους, Soph. Philoct. 311 ; ἐς
τὴν Ἑλλάδα, Xen. An. vi. 4. 8 : 6. 23, al.
freq.) unto his kingdom in heaven
(though it may be conceded to De W.
that this expression is not otherwise found
in St. Paul, it is one to which his existing
expressions easily lead on : e. g. Phil. i.
23, compared with iii. 20): to whom be
the glory unto the ages of ages, Amen
(it is again objected, that in St. Paul we
never find doxologies ascribing glory to
Christ, but always to God. This however
is not strictly true : cf. Rom. ix. 5. And
even if it were, the whole train of thought
here leading naturally on to the ascription
of such doxology, why should it not occur
for the first and only time ? It would
seem to be an axiom with some critics,
that a writer can never use an expression
once only. If the expression be entirely
out of keeping with his usual thoughts
and diction, this may be a sound infer-

ence : but this is certainly not the case
in the present instance. Besides, the petition of the Lord's Prayer having been
transferred to our Lord as its fulfiller
(cf. John xiv. 13, 14), the doxology,
which seems to have come into liturgical
use almost as soon as the prayer itself
(see Matt. vi. 13 var. readd.), would naturally suggest a corresponding doxology
here).
19—21.] *Salutations and notices.* Salute Prisca and Aquila (see notes, Acts
xviii. 2: Rom. xvi. 3) and the house of
Onesiphorus (himself probably deceased.
See on ch. i. 16). Erastus (Acts xix. 22,
an Erastus was sent forward into Macedonia by the Apostle from Ephesus,—and
Rom. xvi. 23, an Erastus sends greeting,
who is described as the οἰκονόμος τῆς
πόλεως (Corinth). This latter would
seem to be the person here mentioned)
abode in Corinth (on the inferences to be
drawn from this, see Prolegg to Past. Epp.
§ ii. 30 f.), but Trophimus (he accompanied the Apostle from Greece into Asia,
Acts xx. 4. He was an Ephesian, id. xxi.
29, and was with the Apostle in Jerusalem on his last visit there) I left (not
'*they* (the Asian brethren who came to
Rome) *left*,' as Hug) in Miletus (see

again this discussed in Prolegg. to this Epistle, § i. 5. Various conjectures have been made to escape the difficulty here presented: ἐν Μελίτῃ (Baronius, Beza, Grot., Est., &c.)—a Miletus in *Crete* (Michaelis, Schrader)) sick. **Endeavour to come before winter** (when the voyage would be impossible, and so the visit thrown over to another year. See also on ver. 13). **Eubulus** (otherwise unknown) **greets thee, and Pudens** (see excursus at the end of the Prolegg. to this Epistle on Pudens and Claudia), **and Linus** (Iren. iii.

3. 3, p. 176, οἱ ἀπόστολοι . . . . Λίνῳ τὴν τῆς ἐπισκοπῆς (at Rome) λειτουργίαν ἐνεχείρισαν. τούτου τοῦ Λίνου Παῦλος ἐν ταῖς πρὸς Τιμόθεον ἐπιστολαῖς μέμνηται. So also Euseb. H. E. iii. 4), **and Claudia** (see excursus as before), **and all the brethren.**

22.] CONCLUDING BLESSING. **The Lord [Jesus Christ] be with thy spirit** (reff.): **(the) grace (of God) be with you** (the members of the church where Timotheus was : see Prolegg.).

ΠΡΟΣ ΤΙΤΟΝ.

I. ¹ Παῦλος ᵃ δοῦλος ᵃ θεοῦ, ἀπόστολος δὲ Ἰησοῦ
χριστοῦ κατὰ πίστιν ᵇ ἐκλεκτῶν ᵇ θεοῦ καὶ ᶜᵈ ἐπίγνωσιν
ᵈ ἀληθείας τῆς κατ' ᵉ εὐσέβειαν, ² ᶠ ἐπ' ἐλπίδι ᵍ ζωῆς

TITLE. rec παυλου του απ. η πρ. τιτ. επιστολη : του αγιου απ. π. επ. πρ. τιτ. L :
[παυλου επ. πρ. τιτ. P : π. απ. επ. πρ. τιτ. H :] txt Aℵ k l m n o 17, and prefg αρχεται
DF.

CHAP. I. 1. χρ. bef ιησ. A 106-8 fuld(with tol) syr copt Ambrst-ed Cassiod : om
ιησ. D¹ : txt D³FHKL[P]ℵ rel.

2. for επ' (εφ' D¹), εν FH : om c m 17.   [προεπηγγειλατο 47.]

CHAP. I. 1—4.] ADDRESS AND GREET-
ING.   1.] The occurrence of δοῦλος
θεοῦ, not elsewhere found in the superscriptions of St. Paul's Epistles, is a mark of
genuineness: a forger would have been sure
to suit every expression of this kind to the
well-known habits of the Apostle.   ἀπ.
δέ] δέ further defines—a servant of God,
—this is general :—but a more particular
designation also belongs to the present
matter.   κατὰ πίστιν has been variously
rendered: (1) 'according to the faith of,'
&c., so E. V., Luth., Matthies, al.: (2)
similarly Calv., Beza, Aret., 'mutuus est
inter meum apostolatum et fidem electorum
Dei consensus :' (3) 'so as to bring about
faith in,' &c.,—as De W., justifying it by
κατὰ τὴν ληίην ἐκπλώσαντες, Herod. ii.
152, κατὰ θέαν ἥκειν, Thuc. vi. 31,—so
also Thdrt. (ὥστε πιστεῦσαι τῆς ἐκλογῆς
ἀξίους, Œc. 2, Thl. 1, Jer., Grot., al., but
see below). We may at once say that (1)
and (2) are inadmissible, as setting up a
standard which the Apostle would not have
acknowledged for his Apostleship, and as
not suiting ἐπίγνωσιν below, which also
belongs to the κατά.   Nor do the instances

given to justify (3) apply here : for as
Huther has observed, in them it is the
acquisition of the noun which is spoken of :
so that here it would be to get, not to produce faith. The best sense seems to be
that which he gives,—that of reference,
'with regard to,' i. e. to bring about,
cherish, and perfect : nearly in the same
sense as εἰς ὑπακοὴν πίστεως, Rom. i. 5.
See also 2 Tim. i. 1.   I would render then
'for :' Paul, a servant of God, but an
Apostle of Jesus Christ, for (on this sense
of κατά, destination, see Ellic.'s note)
the faith of the elect of God (those whom
God has chosen of the world—reff.: and
their faith is the only true faith—the only
faith which the apostolic office would sub-
serve) and the thorough knowledge (reff.
and notes: subjective, and κατά as before
—to promote the knowledge. Thl. gives as
an alternative,—διότι ἐπέγνων τὴν ἀλή
θειαν, διὰ τοῦτο ἐπιστεύθην κ.τ.λ.) of the
truth—which is according to (belongs to,
—is conversant in and coincident with :
for as Chrys., ἐστιν ἀλήθεια πραγμάτων
ἀλλ' οὐ κατ' εὐσέβειαν, οἷον τὸ εἰδέναι τὰ
γεωργικά, τὸ εἰδέναι τέχνας, ἀληθῶς ἐστιν

ᵍ αἰωνίου, ἣν ʰ ἐπηγγείλατο ὁ ⁱ ἀψευδὴς θεὸς ᵏˡ πρὸ χρό-
νων ˡ αἰωνίων, ³ ᵐ ἐφανέρωσεν δὲ ⁿ καιροῖς ⁿ ἰδίοις τὸν
λόγον αὐτοῦ ἐν ᵒ κηρύγματι ὃ ᵖ ἐπιστεύθην ἐγὼ ᑫ κατ'
...του ᑫ ἐπιταγὴν τοῦ ᑫ σωτῆρος ἡμῶν ᑫ θεοῦ, ⁴ Τίτῳ ʳ γνησίῳ
σωτη H.
ACDFIₕ ʳ τέκνῳ κατὰ ˢ κοινὴν πίστιν. χάρις καὶ εἰρήνη ἀπὸ θεοῦ
KLPℵ a
bcefg πατρὸς καὶ χριστοῦ Ἰησοῦ τοῦ ᵗ σωτῆρος ἡμῶν.
hklmn
o 17. 47

h = Mark xiv. 11. Acts vii. 5. Rom. iv. 21. Heb. x. 23 al. (1 Tim. ii. 10.) Esth. iv. 7.
i here nly †. Wisd. vii. 17 only.
k John xii. 1. 2 Cor. xii. 2. Amos i. 1. iv. 7.
l Rom. xvi.
o 2 Tim. iv. 7 reff.
q 1 Tim. i. 1 reff.
t add. to Ἰησ. χρ.

25. 2 Tim. i. 9. m Col. i. 26 reff. n Gal. vi, 9. 1 Tim. ii. 6. vi. 15 only.
p and constr., Rom. iii. 2. 1 Cor. ix. 17. Gal. ii. 7. 1 Thess. ii. 4. 1 Tim. i. 11.
r 1 Tim. i. 2 reff. s = Acts ii. 44. iv. 32. Jude 3 only. Wisd. vii. 3.
Paul, pastl. epp. (2 Tim. i. 10. ch. ii. 13. iii. 6) only. other epp., 2 Pet. (i. 1, 11. ii. 20. iii. 18) only.

4. rec (for [1st] καὶ) ελεος (see 1 Tim i. 2; 2 Tim i. 2), with AC²KL rel syr Thdrt : txt C¹DF[P]ℵ 17 latt Syr copt æth arm Chr_expr Damasc_expr Orig-int_expr Ambrst (υμιν και 17). rec (for χρ. ιησ.) κυριου ιησ. χρ., with D³FKL[P] rel syrr Chr : txt ACD¹ I_bℵ 17 vulg copt goth arm Thdrt-ms [Orig-int₁] Pel Jer.

εἰδέναι· ἀλλ' αὕτη κατ' εὐσέβειαν ἡ ἀλήθεια. κατά cannot, as De W., import the *aim,* 'which *leads to* εὐσ.:' it does not *lead to* it, but rather runs parallel with) **piety,** **2.**] in hope (on condition of, in a state of, see note on ἐφ' ᾧ, Rom. v. 12) **of life eternal** (to what are the words ἐπ' ἐλπίδι ζ. αἰ. to be referred? Not back to ἀπόστολος, regarding them as a co-ordinate clause with κατὰ πίστιν κ.τ.λ. (not for the reason assigned by Huther, that thus καί would be required, cf. the similar sentence, Rom. xvi. 25, 26,—but because such a personal reference would not agree with ver. 3 below, where his preaching, not his prospects, is in question) :—not to κατὰ πίστιν καὶ ἐπίγ. τ. ἀλ. as subordinate to it—nor to εὐσέβειαν, nor to any one *portion* of the preceding sentence: for by such reference we develope an inferior member of the former sentence into what evidently is an expansion of the main current of thought, and thus give rise to a disproportion :—but to the whole, from κατὰ πίστιν to εὐσέβ., as subordinate to that whole, and further conditioning or defining it: q. d., that the elect of God may believe and thoroughly know the truth which is according to piety, in hope of eternal life), **which** (eternal life: not ἀλήθεια, nor ἐλπίς) **God who cannot lie** (so μαντήϊον ἀψευδές, Herod. i. 49: Eur. Orest. 364, ἀψευδὴς θεός, ὅς μοι τάδ' εἶπεν ἐμφανῶς παρασταθείς: see Wetst. and cf. Heb. vi. 18) **promised from eternal ages** (the very distinct use of πρὸ χρόνων αἰωνίων in 2 Tim. i. 9, where the meaning '*from ancient times*' is precluded, should have kept Commentators from endeavouring to fix that sense on the words here. The solution of the difficulty, that no promise was actually made till the race of man existed, must be found by regarding, as in 2 Tim. l. c., the construction as a

mixed one,—compounded of the actual promise made in time, and the divine purpose from which that promise sprung, fixed in eternity. Thus, as there God is said to have given us grace in Christ from eternal ages, meaning that the gift took place as the result of a divine purpose fixed from eternity, so here He is said to have promised eternal life from eternal ages, meaning that the promise took place as the result of a purpose fixed from eternity. So Thdrt. ταῦτα γὰρ ἄνωθεν μὲν καὶ πρὸ αἰώνων ἐδέδοκτο τῷ τῶν ὅλων θεῷ· δῆλα δὲ πεποίηκεν, ὅτε ἐδοκίμασε), **3.**] but (contrast to the eternal and hidden purpose, and to the promise, just mentioned) **manifested in its own seasons** (not, '*His own seasons*' (Ellic. al.), cf. ref. Gal. :—the times belonging to it, τουτέστι, τοῖς ἁρμόζουσι, τοῖς ὠφελημένοις, Thl.,—fixed by Him for the manifestation) **His word** (we naturally expect the same object as before, viz. ζωὴν αἰώνιον : but we have instead, τὸν λόγον αὐτοῦ,—not to be taken in apposition with ἥν, as Heinrichs :—i. e. the Gospel, see Rom. xvi. 25) **in** (as the element or vehicle of its manifestation) **the proclamation** (see 2 Tim. iv. 17) **with which** (on the construction, see reff.) **I was entrusted according to** (in pursuance of, reff.) **the command of our Saviour God:** **4.**] **to Titus** (see Prolegg. § i.) **my true** (genuine, see on 1 Tim. i. 2) **child according to** (in respect of, or agreeably to, in conformity with the appointed spread and spiritually generative power of that faith) **the common faith** (common to us both and to all the people of God : hardly as Grot., 'Judæis, qualis Paulus, et Græcis qualis Titus:' for there is no hint of such a distinction being brought out in this Epistle): **grace and peace from God the Father** (see on 1 Tim. i. 2), **and Christ Jesus our Saviour** (reff.).

u Eph. iii. 1 reff.
v = Paul,2 Tim. iv. 13, 20 only. (Heb. iv. 6, 9. x. 26. Jude 6 only.)
2 Macc. x. 19.
w = Luke xviii. 22. ch. iii. 13 (James i. 4, 5. ii. 15) only. Wisd. xix. 4.
x here only †.

5 Τούτου ᵘχάριν ᵛἀπέλιπόν σε ἐν Κρήτῃ, ἵνα τὰ ʷλείποντα ˣἐπιδιορθώσῃ καὶ ʸκαταστήσῃς ᶻκατὰ πόλιν πρεσβυτέρους ὡς ἐγὼ σοὶ ᵃδιεταξάμην, 6 ᵇεἴ τις ἐστὶν ᶜἀνέγκλητος, ᵈμιᾶς γυναικὸς ἀνήρ, τέκνα ἔχων ᵉπιστά, μὴ ᶠἐν ᵍκατηγορίᾳ ʰἀσωτίας ἢ ⁱἀνυπότακτα. 7 δεῖ γὰρ ᵏτὸν ⁱἐπίσκοπον ᶜἀνέγκλητον εἶναι ὡς θεοῦ ᵐοἰκονόμον,

d κος ανηρ...
ACDFIb KLPℵ a bcdef ghklm no17.47

y = Acts vi. 3. Heb. v. 1 al. Gen. xli. 34.
xx. 13 (of Paul). mid., Acts vii. 44. xxiv. 23. 1 Cor. vii. 17. xi. 34 only.
iv. 8. c 1 Tim. iii. 10 reff. d 1 Tim. iii. 2.
f = 1 Tim. ii. 9. g 1 Tim. v. 19 reff.
7. 2 Macc. iv. 6 only.
k = Matt. xiii. 3. xv. 20 bis. John xii. 24. xv. 6 al. freq.
iii. 2. 1 Pet. ii. 25 only. 4 Kings xi. 18. Job xx. 29. Isa. lx. 17.
iv. 10. (Gal. iv. 2. Esth. viii. 9.)
z = Acts xv. 21, 36. xx. 23 (Paul).
b = Eph. iv. 29. Phil.
a = Acts no 17.47
e = Acts x. 45. xvi. 1. 2 Cor. vi. 15 al.
h Eph. v. 18. 1 Pet. iv. 4 only. Prov. xxviii.
i 1 Tim. i. 9. ver. 10. Heb. ii. 8 only†. i Kings ii. 12 Symm.
1 Acts xx. 28 (Paul). Phil. i. 1. 1 Tim.
m = 1 Cor. iv. 1. 1 Pet.

5. rec κατελιπον, with D³KL[P]ℵ³ rel : txt ACD¹FIbℵ¹ 17 Orig Bas-mss (-λειπον ACFIbL[P 47]).   επιδιορθωσης A : επανορθωσης D¹ : δειορθωσης F : txt CD³K[Ib] L[P]ℵ rel Orig Chr Thdrt.
6. ανηεγκλητος (but η marked and erased) ℵ¹.

5—9.] *Reason stated for Titus being left in Crete—to appoint elders in its cities. Directions what sort of persons to choose for this office.* **5.] For this reason I left thee behind** (reff.: ἀπέλ. gives the mere fact of leaving behind when Paul left the island ;—κατέλ. would convey the idea of more permanence: cf. Acts xviii. 19; xxiv. 27. This difference may have occasioned the alteration of the reading from ecclesiastical motives, to represent Titus as permanent bishop of Crete) **in Crete** (on the island, and the whole matter, see Prolegg.) **that thou mightest carry forward the correction** (already begun by me: ἐπι implying the furtherance, addition of διορθώματα. The middle voice, as so often, carries only so far the subjective sense, that whereas the active would state the *mere fact* of διόρθωσις, the middle implies that the subject uses his own agency : *facit per se:* see Krüger, Griechische Sprachlehre, p. 363, who calls this the *dynamic* middle. So Polybius, xxx. 5. 13, τὰ μὲν οὖν κατὰ τοὺς Καννίους . . . . . ταχέως οἱ Ῥόδιοι **διωρθώσαντο**) **of those things which are defective** (' quæ ego per temporis brevitatem non potui expedire,' Beng.: ὁ γὰρ τῆς εὐσεβείας λόγος παρεδίδοτο πᾶσι παρ᾽ αὐτοῦ, ἐλείπετο δὲ οἰκονομῆσαι τὰ κατὰ τοὺς πεπιστευκότας, καὶ εἰς ἁρμονίαν αὐτοὺς καταστῆσαι ταῖς ἐκκλησιαστικαῖς διατυπώσεσι. Theodr-Mops. in Huther), **and** (καί brings out, among the matters to be attended to in the ἐπιδιόρθωσις, especially that which follows) **mightest appoint city by city** (reff.) **elders** (see 1 Tim. iv. 14: note on Acts xx. 17. Thl. remarks, τοὺς ἐπισκόπους οὕτως ἐνταῦθά φησιν, ὡς καὶ ἐν τῇ πρὸς Τιμόθεον· κατὰ πόλεις δέ φησιν. οὐ γὰρ ἐβούλετο πᾶσαν τὴν νῆσον ἐπιτετράφθαι ἑνί, ἀλλ᾽ ἑκάστην πόλιν τὸν ἴδιον ποιμένα

ἔχειν· οὕτω γὰρ καὶ ὁ πόνος κουφότερος, καὶ ἡ ἐπιμέλεια ἀκριβεστέρα), **as I prescribed** (reff.) **to thee** (" διεταξάμην refers as well to the *fact* of appointing elders, as to the *manner* of their appointment,— which last particular is now expanded in directions respecting the characters of those to be chosen." De W.): **6.] if any man is blameless** (see 1 Tim. iii. 10. No intimation is conveyed by the εἴ τις, as Heinr. and Heydenr. suppose, that such persons would be rare in Crete : see besides reff. Matt. xviii. 28; 2 Cor. xi. 20), **husband of one wife** (see note on 1 Tim. iii. 2), **having believing children** ('nam qui liberos non potuit ad fidem perducere, quomodo alios perducet?' Beng.: and similarly Chrys., Thl. πιστοί implies that they were not only 'ad fidem perducti,' but 'in fide stabiliti'), **who are not under** (involved in) **accusation of profligacy** (see Eph. v. 18, note) **or insubordinate** (respecting the reason of these conditions affecting his household, see 1 Tim. iii. 4. I have treated in the Prolegg. ch. vii. § i., the argument which Baur and De W. have drawn from these descriptions for dating our Epistles in the second century). **7 ff.] For it behoves an** (τόν, as so often (reff.), generic, *the*, i. e. every : our English idiom requires the indefinite article) **overseer** (see note, 1 Tim. iii. 2; here most plainly identified with the presbyter spoken of before. So Thdrt.: ἐντεῦθεν δῆλον, ὡς τοὺς πρεσβυτέρους ἐπισκόπους ὠνόμαζον) **to be blameless, as God's steward** (see 1 Tim. iii. 15, to which image, that of a responsible servant and dispensator (1 Pet. iv. 10) in the house of God, the allusion perhaps is, rather than to that of 1 Cor. iv. 1. There is clearly no allusion to the ἐπίσκ.'s *own household*, as Heydenr. supposes. Mack

μὴ ⁿ αὐθάδη, μὴ ^o ὀργίλον, μὴ ^p πάροινον, μὴ ^q πλήκτην,
μὴ ^r αἰσχροκερδῆ, ⁸ ἀλλὰ ^s φιλόξενον, ^t φιλάγαθον, ^u σώφρονα, δίκαιον, ^v ὅσιον, ^w ἐγκρατῆ, ^{9 x} ἀντεχόμενον τοῦ
κατὰ τὴν ^y διδαχὴν ^z πιστοῦ ^{za} λόγου, ἵνα δυνατὸς ᾖ καὶ

n 2 Pet. ii. 10 only. Gen.
xlix. 3, 7.
Prov. xxi. 24 only.
o here only. Prov. xxi. 29.
xxii. 24. xxix. 22 only.
p 1 Tim. iii. 3 only †.
q 1 Tim. iii. 3 only †. Ps. xxxiv. 15 Symm.   r 1 Tim. iii. 8 only †. (-δός,
1 Pet. v. 2.) see ver. 11.   s 1 Tim. iii. 2. 1 Pet. iv. 9 only †. (-νία, Rom. xii. 13.)   t here
only †. Wisd. vii. 22 only.   u 1 Tim. iii. 2. ch. ii. 2, 5 only †.   v 1 Tim. ii. 8 reff.
w here only †. Sir. xxvi. 15 al. (-τεια, Gal. v. 23. -τεύεσθαι, 1 Cor. vii. 9.)   x Matt. vi. 24. Luke
xvi. 13. 1 Thess. v. 14 only. Prov. iii. 18.   y pastl. epp., 2 Tim. iv. 2 (reff.) only.
z = 1 Tim. i. 15 reff.   a Acts xviii. 15. 2 Tim. i 13. ch ii. 8 al.

9. aft ινα ins και F 17. 73.

well remarks, meaning perhaps however more than the words convey, "*God's steward;*—consequently spiritual superiors are not merely servants and commissioned agents of the Church. According to the Apostle's teaching, church government does not grow up out of the ground"), **not self-willed** (ἐπίσκοπος ἑκόντων ἄρχων, οὐκ ὀφείλει αὐθάδης εἶναι ὥστε αὐτογνώμως καὶ αὐτοβούλως καὶ ἄνευ γνώμης τῶν ἀρχομένων πράττειν. τυραννικὸν γὰρ τοῦτο, Thl. σεμνότης δ' ἐστὶν αὐθαδείας ἀνὰ μέσον τε καὶ ἀρεσκείας, ἐστὶ δὲ περὶ τὰς ἐντεύξεις. ὅ τε γὰρ αὐθάδης τοιοῦτός ἐστιν οἷος μηθενὶ ἐντυχεῖν μηδὲ διαλεγῆναι, ἀλλὰ τοὔνομα ἔοικεν ἀπὸ τοῦ τρόπου κεῖσθαι· ὁ γὰρ αὐθάδης αὐτοάδης τίς ἐστιν, ἀπὸ τοῦ αὐτὸς αὐτῷ ἀρέσκειν, Aristot. Magn. Moral. i. 29: see also Theophr. Char. c. xvi. (αὐθάδειά ἐστιν ἀπήνεια ὁμιλίας ἐν λόγοις): Suicer i. p. 572: and Ellic.'s note here), **not soon provoked** (οἱ μὲν οὖν ὀργίλοι ταχέως μὲν ὀργίζονται, καὶ οἷς οὐ δεῖ, καὶ ἐφ' οἷς οὐ δεῖ, καὶ μᾶλλον ἢ δεῖ· παύονται δὲ ταχέως ὃ καὶ βέλτιστον ἔχουσι, Aristot. Eth. Nic. iv. 5: this meaning, and not Thdrt.'s, ὀργίλον δέ, τὸν μνησίκακον,—must be taken), **not a brawler, not a striker** (for both these, see 1 Tim. iii. 3, notes), **not greedy of gain** (1 Tim. iii. 8, note), but **hospitable** (1 Tim. iii. 2, note, and 3 John 5), **a lover of good** (cf. the opposite ἀφιλάγαθος, 2 Tim. iii. 3. It is hardly likely to mean a lover of *good men*, coming so immediately after φιλόξενον. Thl. explains it, τὸν ἐπιεικῆ, τὸν μέτριον, τὸν μὴ φθονοῦντα. Dionys. Areop., Ep. viii. 1, p. 597, calls God τὸν ὑπεράγαθον καὶ φιλάγαθον—and Clem. Alex., Pæd. iii. 11, p. 291 P., classes together ἀνδρία, σωφροσύνη, φιλαγαθία), **self-restrained** (see 1 Tim. ii. 9, note. I am not satisfied with this rendering, but adopt it for want of a better: "discreet is perhaps preferable." See Ellic. on 1 Tim. as above], **just, holy** (see on these, and their distinction, in notes on Eph. iv. 24: 1 Thess. ii. 10), **continent** (τὸν πάθους κρα-

τοῦντα, τὸν καὶ γλώττης καὶ χειρὸς καὶ ὀφθαλμῶν ἀκολάστων· τοῦτο γὰρ ἐστὶν ἐγκράτεια, τὸ μηδενὶ ὑποσύρεσθαι πάθει, Chrys., and id. Epist. ii. ad Olympiad., vol. iii. p. 560 (Migne), ἐγκρατεύεσθαι ἐκεῖνόν φαμεν . . . τὸν ὑπό τινος ἐπιθυμίας ἐνοχλούμενον, καὶ κρατοῦντα ταύτης. See Suicer i. p. 998 ff., for a full explanation of the subsequent technical usages of the word. Here, the sense need not be limited to sexual continence, but may be spread over the whole range of the indulgences), **holding fast** (see reff.: constantly keeping to, and not letting go,—φροντίζοντα, ἔργον τοῦτο ποιούμενον, Chrys. Then how are we to take the following words? Is **τοῦ κατὰ τὴν διδαχὴν πιστοῦ λόγου** equivalent to (1) τοῦ λόγου τοῦ κατὰ τὴν διδαχὴν πιστοῦ, or (2) τοῦ πιστοῦ λόγου τοῦ κατὰ τὴν διδαχήν? (1) is taken by Wiesinger and Conyb. (*the words which are faithful to* (?) *our teaching*): (2) by Chrys., Thl., and almost all Commentators, and I believe rightly. For (α) it is hard to believe that even in these Epistles, such a sentence could occur as ἀντεχόμενον (τοῦ-κατὰ-τὴν-διδαχὴν-πιστοῦ) λόγου: had this been intended, it would certainly have stood τοῦ λ. τοῦ κατὰ τὴν διδ. πιστοῦ: (β) the epithet **πιστός**, absolute, is so commonly attached to λόγος in these Epistles (1 Tim. i. 15; iii. 1; iv. 9: 2 Tim. ii. 11: ch. iii. 8) as to incline us, especially with the above reason, to take it absolutely here also. I therefore render accordingly) **the faithful** (true, trustworthy, see note on 1 Tim. i. 15) **word** (which is) **according to** (measured by, or in accordance with) **the instruction** (which he has received) (διδαχή may be *active*, as Calv., 'qui in ecclesiæ ædificationem sit utilis:' Luth., 'daß lehren kann.' But thus we should have a tautological sentence, in which the practice, and the result of the practice (ἵνα κ.τ.λ.) would have the same power to instruct predicated of them: besides that ἀντεχόμενον would require some forcing to make it apply in this sense of

b absol., 1 Cor.
iv. 13. 2 Tim.
iv. 2 al.
c = 1 Thess.
iv. 18. 2 Cor.
vii. 6, 7.
d 1 Tim. i. 10
reff.
e Acts xiii. 45.
xxviii. 19.
Rom. x. 21.
Hos. iv. 4.
f 1 Tim. v. 20
reff.
g ver. 6 reff.

ᵇ παρακαλεῖν ᶜ ἐν τῇ ᵈ διδασκαλίᾳ τῇ ᵈ ὑγιαινούσῃ καὶ
τοὺς ᵉ ἀντιλέγοντας ᶠ ἐλέγχειν.   10 εἰσὶν γὰρ πολλοὶ
[καὶ] ᵍ ἀνυπότακτοι ʰ ματαιολόγοι καὶ ⁱ φρεναπάται, ᵏ μάλιστα ˡᵐ οἱ ˡ ἐκ ᵐ περιτομῆς, οὓς δεῖ ⁿ ἐπιστομίζειν, 11 ᵒ οἵτινες ὅλους ᵖ οἴκους ᑫ ἀνατρέπουσιν διδάσκοντες ʳ ἃ μὴ δεῖ
ˢ αἰσχροῦ ᵗ κέρδους ᵘ χάριν.   12 εἶπέν τις ἐξ αὐτῶν ᵛ ἴδιος

ACDFIᵦ
KLPℵ a
b c d e f
g h k l m
n o 17.47

h here only.   (-γία, 1 Tim. i. 6.)   i here only †.   (ᵗᾶͷ, Gal. vi. 3.)   k 1 Tim. iv. 10 reff.
l Rom. ii. 8. iii. 26. iv. 14 al.   m Acts x. 45. xi. 2. Rom. iv. 12   Gal. ii. 12.   Col. iv. 11 only.   n here
only †.   o = Acts x. 41, 47. Paul, freq.   p = Acts x. 2.   1 Cor. i 6.   2 Tim. i. 16 al.
q 2 Tim. ii. 18 only. Prov. x. 3.   r so 1 Tim. v. 13.   s 1 Cor. xi. 6. xiv. 35. Eph. v. 12 only. P.   Gen.
xli. 3, &c. only. see ver. 7.   t Phil. i. 21 reff.   u Eph. iii. 1 reff.   v = 1 Thess. ii.
14 al.   (ἰδ. προφ , ib. ver. 15 v. r.)

for εν τη διδασκ. τη υγιαιν., τους εν παση θλιψει A.   om τη υγιαινουση Iᵦ Lucif:
τη υγιαιν. διδ. m 106-8-12.   aft ελεγχειν ins μη χειροτονειν διγαμους μηδε
διακονους αυτους ποιειν μηδε γυναικας εχειν εκ διγαμιας, μηδε προσερχεσθωσαν εν τω
θυσιωστηριω λειτουργειν το θειον, τους αρχοντας τους αδικοκριτας, και αρπαγας, και
ψευστας, και ανελεημονας ελεγχε, ως θεου διακονος 96. 109-gr.

10. om 1st και (as unnecessary, and appearing to disturb the sense) ACIᵦ[P]ℵ a k
17 [47] am²(with demid) syrr copt goth [æth arm] Clem Ambrst-ed Aug : ins DFKL
rel vulg Chr Damasc Lucif Hil Jer.   ins και bef ματαιολ. F[P] Syr copt æth Œc
Jer₁.   aft μαλιστα ins δε CD demid [æth] Thl Jer₁.   ins της bef περιτομης
CDⁱ[Iᵦℵ 17] Frag-tisch.

11. aft χαριν ins τα τεκνα οτι τους ιδιους γονεις υβριζοντες η τυπτοντες επιστομιζε και
ελεγχε, και νουθετει ως πατηρ τεκνα και ειρηνης επισκοπος 96. 109-gr.

'constantly using.' The passive acceptation of διδαχή is therefore preferable :
and the meaning will be much the same
as in 2 Tim. iii. 14, μένε ἐν οἷς ἔμαθες, —
cf. 1 Tim. iv. 6, οἱ λόγοι τῆς πίστεως καὶ
τῆς καλῆς διδασκαλίας ᾗ παρηκολούθηκας. So Ellic. also), that he may be able
both to exhort (believers) in (the element
of his παράκλησις) healthy teaching
(the teaching which is healthy), and
to reprove (see ver. 13 below) the gainsayers.

10—16.] By occasion of the last clause,
the Apostle goes on to describe the nature
of the adversaries to whom he alludes,
especially with reference to Crete.

10.] For (explains τοὺς ἀντιλέγοντας of
ver. 9) there are many [and] insubordinate (ver. 6 above. The joining πολύς
with another adjective by καί is a common idiom. So Herod. viii. 61, πολλὰ
τε καὶ κακὰ ἔλεγε : Aristoph. Lys. 1159,
πολλῶν κἀγαθῶν : Plato, Rep. x. p. 325,
πολλά τε καὶ ἀνόσια εἰργασμένος : Xen.
Mem. ii. 9. 6, συνειδὼς αὑτῷ πολλὰ καὶ
πονηρά. Matthiæ, § 444) vain talkers
(see 1 Tim. i. 6, and ch. iii. 9) and deceivers (see Gal. vi. 3 : deceivers of men's
minds), chiefly (not only — there were
some such of the Gentile converts) they
of the circumcision (i. e. not Jews, but
Jewish Christians : for he is speaking of
seducers within the Church : cf. ver. 11.
On the Jews in Crete, see Jos. Antt. xvii.
12. 1 : B. J. ii. 7. 1 : Philo, Leg. ad Cai.

§ 36, vol. ii. p. 587), whose mouths (ἐλέγχειν
σφοδρῶς, ὥστε ἀποκλείειν αὐτοῖς τὰ στό-
ματα, Thl.) it is necessary to stop (we
hardly need introduce here the figure of
a bit and bridle, seeing that ἐπιστομίζειν
is so often used literally of 'stopping the
mouth,' without any allusion to that figure :
e. g. Aristoph., Eq. 841, ἐμοὶ γάρ ἐστ'
εἰργασμένον τοιοῦτον ἔργον ὥστε | ἀπαξ-
άπαντας τοὺς ἐμοὺς ἐχθροὺς ἐπιστομίζειν :
Plato, Gorg., p. 329 d,—αὐτὸς ὑπὸ σοῦ
ἐμποδισθεὶς ἐν τοῖς λόγοις ἐπεστομίσθη
αἰσχυνθεὶς ἃ ἐννοεῖ εἰπεῖν : and see other
examples in Wetst. And Plut., Alcib. 2,
speaks of τὸν αὐλὸν ἐπιστομίζειν καὶ
ἀποφράττειν. Cf. Palm and Rost's Lex.) :
such men as ("inasmuch as they," Ellic. :
which perhaps is logically better) over-
turn (ref. 1 Tim. : so, literally, Plato, Rep. v.
p. 471 b, οὔτε τὴν γῆν ἐθελήσουσι κείρειν
αὐτῶν, ... οὔτε οἰκίας ἀνατρέπειν : and
fig., Demosth. 778. 22, ἀνατρέψειν οἴει
τὰ κοινὰ δίκαια, and so often) whole
houses (cf. Juv. Sat. x. 5 : "evertere
domos totas optantibus ipsis | Di faciles."
Here it will mean, "pervert whole families." Thl. says, μοχλοὶ γάρ εἰσι τοῦ
διαβόλου, δι' ὧν καθαιρεῖ τοὺς τοῦ θεοῦ
οἴκους), teaching things which are not
fitting (on the use of ἃ οὐ δεῖ (things
which are definitely improper or forbidden), and ἃ μὴ δεῖ (things which are
so either in the mind of the describer, or
which, as here, derive a seeming contingency from the mode in which the subject

αὐτῶν προφήτης Κρῆτες ἀεὶ [w] ψεῦσται, κακὰ [x] θηρία, [y] γα-
στέρες [z] ἀργαί. 13 ἡ [a] μαρτυρία αὕτη ἐστὶν ἀληθής. [b] δι'
...αιτιαν ἣν αἰτίαν [c] ἔλεγχε αὐτοὺς [d] ἀποτόμως, ἵνα [e] ὑγιαίνωσιν ἐν
[I b.]
ACDFK τῇ πίστει, 14 μὴ [f] προσέχοντες [g] Ἰουδαϊκοῖς [f] μύθοις καὶ
LPℵ a b
c d e f g ἐντολαῖς ἀνθρώπων [h] ἀποστρεφομένων τὴν ἀλήθειαν.
h k l m n
o 17. 47

w 1 Tim. i. 10 reff.
x met., here only. see 1 Cor. xv. 32.
y = here only. (1 Thess. v. 3 reff.)
z 1 Tim. v. 13 reff.
a 1 Tim. iii. 7 reff.

b 2 Tim. i. 6 reff.   c ver. 9.   d 2 Cor. xiii. 10 only†.   Wisd. v. 22 only.   e 1 Tim.
i. 10 reff.   f 1 Tim. i. 4 reff.   g here only†. (-κῶς, Gal. ii. 14.)   h 2 Tim. i. 15 reff.

12. aft ειπεν ins δε Fℵ¹ copt.   om εξ 67².   om (2nd) αυτων F Clem.
13. αληθ. bef εστ. D vulg [copt] lat-ff.   om εν ℵ¹(ins ℵ-corr¹) [47] 219.
14. ενταλμασιν F Thdrt[: γενεαλογιαις 47.]

is presented), see Ellic.'s note here and
his references to Herm. on Viger, 267,
and Krüger, Sprachlehre, § 67. 4. 3) for
the sake of base gain (cf. 1 Tim. vi. 5).
12.] One of them (not, of the
πολλοί spoken of above,—nor, of the οἱ ἐκ
περιτομῆς: but of the inhabitants of
Crete, to which both belonged), their
own prophet (see below) said, "The
Cretans are always liars, evil beasts,
slow bellies" (Thl. says: ὁ μὲν οὖν εἰρη-
κώς, Ἐπιμενίδης ἐστίν, ἐν τοῖς μάλιστα
τῶν παρ' Ἕλλησι σοφῶν θειασμοῖς καὶ
ἀποτροπιασμοῖς προσέχων, καὶ μαντικὴν
δοκῶν κατορθοῦν. And so also Chrys.,
Epiph., and Jer. But Thdrt. ascribes the
verse to Callimachus, in whose Hymn to
Zeus, ver. 8, the words Κρῆτες ἀεὶ ψεῦσται are found. To this however Jer. (as
also Epiph.) answers, "integer versus de
Epimenide poeta ab Apostolo sumptus est,
et ejus Callimachus in suo poemate usus
est exordio." EPIMENIDES was a native
of Phæstus in Crete (Ἐπιμ. ὁ Φαίστιος,
Plut. Solon 12: or Cnossus, Diog. Laert.
i. 109, Κρὴς τὸ γένος, ἀπὸ Κνώσσου.
He makes his father's name to have been
Φαίστιος:—πατρὸς μὲν ἦν Φαιστίου, οἱ
δέ, Δωσιάδου, οἱ δὲ Ἀγησάρκου), and lived
about 600 B.C. He was sent for to
Athens to undertake the purification of
the city from the pollution occasioned by
Cylon (see artt. 'Epimenides' and 'Cylon,'
in the Dict. of Biogr. and Mythol.), and
is said to have lived to an extreme old
age, and to have been buried at Lace-
dæmon (Diog. Laert. i. 115). The appellation 'prophet' seems to have belonged
to him in its literal sense : see Cicero, de
Divin. i. 18,—"qui concitatione quadam
animi, aut soluto liberoque motu futura
præsentiunt, ut Baris Bœotius, ut Epimenides Cres:" so also Apuleius, Florid.
ii. 15. 4,—"necnon et Cretensem Epime-
nidem, inclytum fatiloquum et poetam :"
see also id. Apol. 449. Diog. Laert. also
gives instances of his prophetic power,
and says, λέγουσι δέ τινες ὅτι Κρῆτες
αὐτῷ θύουσιν ὡς θεῷ.   On the character

here given of the Cretans, see Prolegg. to
this Epistle, § ii. 9 ff. As to the words,
—κακὰ θηρία is abundantly illustrated
out of various writers by Wetst., Kypke,
and Raphel: γαστέρες ἀργαί is said of
those who by indulging their bodily ap-
petites have become corpulent and indolent : so Juv. Sat. iv. 107, "Montani
quoque venter adest abdomine tardus").
13.] This testimony is true.
Wherefore (ἐπειδὴ ἦθος αὐτοῖς ἐστιν ἰτα-
μὸν καὶ δολερὸν καὶ ἀκόλαστον, Chrys.)
reprove them sharply (ὅταν ψεύδωνται
προχείρως καὶ δολεροὶ ὦσι καὶ γαστρίμαρ-
γοι καὶ ἀργοί, σφοδροῦ καὶ πληκτικοῦ τοῦ
λόγου δεῖ· προσηνείᾳ γὰρ οὐκ ἂν ἀχθείη
ὁ τοιοῦτος, Chrys. ἀπότομος, 'cut off,'
'abrupt:' hence, met., 'rugged,' 'harsh;'
so Eur. Alcest. 985, οὐδέ τις ἀποτόμου
λήματός ἐστιν αἰδώς: Soph. Œd. Tyr.
876, ἀπότομον ὤρουσεν εἰς ἀνάγκαν), that
(in order that : De W. takes ἵνα κ.τ.λ.,
for the substance of the rebuke, as in
παραγγέλλειν ἵνα and the like (?) : but
there appears to be no sufficient reason
for this) they may be healthy in the
faith (not, 'in faith,' as Conyb.: even
were no article expressed after ἐν, it might
be 'in the faith:' when that article is
expressed, the definite reference can never
be overlooked. The Κρῆτες indicated
here, who are to be thus rebuked in order
to their soundness in the faith, are manifestly not the false teachers, but the ordinary believers: cf. ver. 14), 14.]
not giving attention to (ref.) Jewish
fables (on the probable nature of these,
see 1 Tim. i. 4 note: and on the whole
subject, the Prolegg. to these Epistles, § i.
12 ff. They were probably the seeds of
the gnostic mythologies, already scattered
about and taking root) and commandments (cf. 1 Tim. iv. 3 : Col. ii. 16, 22 :
and our next verse, by which it appears
that these commandments were on the
subject of abstinence from meats and
other things appointed by God for man's
use) of men turning away (or the pres.
part. may express habitual character—

i here bis. John xviii. 28.
Heb. xii. 15.
Jude 8 only.
Ezek. xiv. 11.
k = 1 Tim. v. 8 reff.
l 1 Tim. i. 5 reff. iv. 2.
m = John ix. 22. Rom. x. 9.
n = 1 Tim. v.
8 reff.
xxi. 8)
q 2 Tim. ii. 21 (reff.).

15 πάντα καθαρὰ τοῖς καθαροῖς· τοῖς δὲ ⁱ μεμιαμένοις καὶ ᵏ ἀπίστοις οὐδὲν καθαρόν, ἀλλὰ ⁱ μεμίανται αὐτῶν καὶ ὁ νοῦς καὶ ἡ ˡ συνείδησις. 16 θεὸν ᵐ ὁμολογοῦσιν εἰδέναι, τοῖς δὲ ἔργοις ⁿ ἀρνοῦνται, ᵒ βδελυκτοὶ ὄντες καὶ ᵖ ἀπειθεῖς καὶ ᑫ πρὸς ᑫ πᾶν ἔργον ᑫ ἀγαθὸν ʳ ἀδόκιμοι.

Η απισ-
τοις ου-
δεν...
ACDFH
KLPℵ a
b c d e f
g h k l m
n o 17.47

o here only. Prov. xvii. 15. Sir. xli. 5 B (-υρός, ACℵ). 2 Macc. i. 27 only. (-ύσσεσθαι, Rev. xxi. 8)
p Luke i. 17. Acts xxvi. 19 (Paul). Rom. i. 30. 2 Tim. iii. 2. ch. iii. 3 only. L.P. Num. xx. 10.
r 2 Tim. iii 8 reff.

15. rec aft παντα ins μεν, with D³KLℵ³ rel syr : γαρ Syr copt (Orig) : om ACD¹F[P]ℵ¹ 17. 67² latt Orig Tert Ambrst-ed Jer Aug Pel Fulg. rec μεμιασμενοις, with D³ [rel], and (accg to our edd) Clem Orig all : txt ACD(μεμιανμ.) F(μεμειαμ.) KL[P]ℵ (μεμιαμμ.) d f [17. 47] Chr.
16. [for απειθ., ανθαδεις P.] om και ℵ¹ [copt]. om αγαθον ℵ¹(ins ℵ-corr¹).

whose description it is that they turn away—in idiomatic English, the participial clause being merely epithetal, not ratiocinative (agst Ellicott), "who turn away") from (ref.) **the truth. 15.]** *The Apostle's own answer to those who would enforce these commandments.* **All things** (absolutely—all things with which man can be concerned) **are pure to the pure** (οὐδὲν ὁ θεὸς ἀκάθαρτον ἐποίησεν· οὐδὲν γὰρ ἀκάθαρτον, εἰ μὴ ἡ ἁμαρτία μόνη. ψυχῆς γὰρ ἅπτεται καὶ ταύτην ῥυποῖ, Chrys. 'Omnia externa iis qui intus sunt mundi, munda sunt,' Bengel. Cf. Matt. xxiii. 26: Luke xi. 41. There is no ground whatever for supposing this to be a maxim of the false teachers, quoted by the Apostle, any more than the πάντα μοι ἔξεστιν of 1 Cor. vi. 12, where see note. The maxim here is a truly Christian one of the noblest order. **τοῖς καθαροῖς** is the dat. commodi,—'for the pure to use,' not, as often taken, 'in the judgment of the pure.' This is plainly shewn by the use of the same dative in Rom. xiv. 14, where to render it 'in the judgment of' would introduce an unmeaning tautology: τῷ λογιζομένῳ τι κοινὸν εἶναι, ἐκείνῳ κοινόν—'to him (for his use) it is really κοινόν.' As usual in these Epistles (see Prolegg. § i. 38), *purity* is inseparably connected with soundness in the faith, cf. Acts xv. 9,—and 1 Tim. iv. 3, where our τοῖς καθαροῖς is expanded into τοῖς πιστοῖς καὶ ἐπεγνωκόσιν τὴν ἀλήθειαν), **but to the polluted and unbelieving** (cf. the preceding remarks) **nothing is pure, but both** (or 'even,' as E. V. :— but the other seems preferable, on account of the close correspondence of καὶ ὁ νοῦς with καὶ ἡ συνείδησις) **their mind** (their rational part, Eph. iv. 17, which presides over and leads all the determinate acts and thoughts of the man) **and their conscience is polluted** (cf. Dion. Hal. de Thucyd. 8,— κράτιστον δὲ πάντων τὸ μηδὲν ἑκουσίως ψεύδεσθαι, μηδὲ μιαίνειν τὴν αὑτοῦ συνείδησιν. **And therefore, uncleanness tainting their rational acts and their reflective self-recognitions, nothing can be pure to them** : every occasion becomes to them an occasion of sin, every creature of God an instrument of sin ; as Mack well observes, "the relation, in which the sinful subject stands to the objects of its possession or of its inclination, is a sinful one." Philo de legg. spec. ad 6 et 7 dec. cap. § 337, vol. ii. p. 333 f., has a sentence which might be a comment on our verse :—ἀκάθαρτος γὰρ κυρίως ὁ ἄδικος καὶ ἀσεβὴς .... πάντα φύρων καὶ συγχέων διά τε τὰς ἀμετρίας τῶν παθῶν καὶ τὰς τῶν κακῶν ὑπερβολάς· ὥστε ὧν ἂν ἐφάψηται πραγμάτων πάντα ἐστὶν ἐπίληπτα τῇ τοῦ δρῶντος συμμεταβάλλοντα μοχθηρίᾳ. καὶ γὰρ κατὰ τὸ ἐναντίον αἱ πράξεις τῶν ἀγαθῶν ἐπαινεταί, βελτιούμεναι ταῖς τῶν ἐνεργούντων ἀρεταῖς, ἐπειδὴ πέφυκέ πως τὰ γινόμενα τοῖς δρῶσιν ἐξομοιοῦσθαι. Here again, the reference of the saying has been variously mistaken—ἡ ῥυπαρὰ διάνοια κακῶς περὶ τούτων λογιζομένη ἑαυτῇ συμμιαίνει ταῦτα, Œc.: and similarly Chrys., Thl., al. : 'non placent Deo quæ agunt etiam circa res medias, quia actiones tales ex animo Deus æstimat,' Grot. : 'iis nihil prodest externa ablutio et ciborum dierumque observatio,' Baldwin, Croc. in De W.).

16.] *Expansion of the last clause, shewing* (cf. Dion. Hal. above) *their ἑκουσίως ψεύδεσθαι.* **They make confession** (openly, in sight of men : but not so only —their confession is a true one so far, that they *have the knowledge,* and *belie* it : not 'they *profess,*' as E. V. : ὁμολογοῦσιν necessarily contains an implication of the subjective truth of the thing given out) **that they know God, but in** (or, by) **their works they deny (Him)** (not '*it:*' see 2 Tim. ii. 12), **being abominable** (cf. βδέλυγμα ἐνώπιον τοῦ θεοῦ, Luke xvi. 15. In ref. Prov. βδελυκτὸς παρὰ θεῷ is

II. ¹ Σὺ δὲ λάλει ἃ ˢπρέπει τῇ ᵗὑγιαινούσῃ ᵗδιδασκα-
λίᾳ, ² ᵘπρεσβύτας ᵛνηφαλίους εἶναι, ʷσεμνούς, ˣσώφρο-
νας, ᵗὑγιαίνοντας τῇ ʸπίστει, τῇ ʸἀγάπῃ, τῇ ʸᶻὑπομονῇ·
³ ᵃπρεσβύτιδας ᵇὡσαύτως ἐν ᶜκαταστήματι ᵈἱεροπρεπεῖς,
ᵉμὴ ᶠδιαβόλους, ᵉμηδὲ οἴνῳ πολλῷ ᵍδεδουλωμένας,
ʰκαλοδιδασκάλους, ⁴ ἵνα ⁱσωφρονίζουσιν τὰς νέας ʲφιλάν-

ˢ Matt. iii. 15.
1 Cor. xi. 13.
ᵛ Eph. v. 3.
1 Tim. ii. 10.
Heb. ii. 10.
vii. 26 only.
Ps. xcii. 7.
ᵗ 1 Tim. i. 10 reff.
ᵘ Luke i. 18.
Philem. 9 only. Job xxix. 8.
ᵛ 1 Tim. iii. 2, 11

only †. (-φειν, 2 Tim. iv. 5.)
2. ch. i. 8. ver. 5 only †.
a here only †.
καταστήματι.
f = 1 Tim. iii. 11. 2 Tim. iii. 3 only.
vi. 18, 22. 1 Cor ix. 19. Gal. iv. 3. 2 Pet. ii. 19 only.
(-ισμός, 2 Tim. i. 7.)
j here only †.

w Phil. iv. 8. 1 Tim. iii. 8, 11 only. Prov. xv. 26.
y 1 Tim. vi. 11. 2 Tim. iii. 10. 2 Pet. i. 6, 7.
b = 1 Tim. ii. 9 reff.
d here only †. Jos. Antt. xi. 8. 5.
c here only †. — Jos. Antt. xv. 7. 5, ἀτρεμαίῳ τῷ
e John iv. 15. xiv. 27. Acts iv. 18.
g Acts vii. 6, from Gen. xv. 13. 1 Cor. vii. 15. pass., Rom.
h here only †.

x 1 Tim. iii.
z Col. i. 11 reff.

i here only †.

CHAP. II. 1. aft δε ins α ℵ.
[2. νηφαλαιους D¹GLP d f o 47¹: -λεους D³K a b(?) e l m n: -λειους F.]
3. κατασχηματι F[not G]. ιεροπρεπει [for -πεις] CH² m 17 latt syrr copt arm
Clem Bas Thdrt Ambrst Jer Pel Sedul. for μηδε, μη DFHKL[P]ℵ³ rel: txt ACℵ¹.
4. rec σωφρονιζωσι, with CDKLℵ³ rel: txt AFH[P]ℵ¹ o. [om φιλοτεκνους K.]

joined with ἀκάθαρτος) and disobedient, and for (towards the accomplishing of) every good work worthless (ref.).

Ch. II. 1—III. 11.] *Directions to Titus, how to exhort the believers of various classes, and how to comport himself.* For intermediate divisions, see below.

1.] But (contrast to the persons just described: 'on the other hand') do thou speak (not what they speak, ch. i. 11: but) the things which befit the healthy teaching (that teaching which is sound and wholesome, not teaching ἃ μὴ δεῖ): viz., that the aged men (not = πρεσβυτέρους, which implies eldership, and not old age only) be sober (see note on 1 Tim. iii. 2), grave (1 Tim. iii. 4, note), self-restrained (a better word for σώφρων would be a valuable discovery: see above on ch. i. 8, and 1 Tim. ii. 9: '*discreet*' is good, but not adequate), healthy in their faith, in their love, in their patience (see ref. 1 Tim., where the same three are joined together. The datives are of the element or condition: the same was expressed with ἐν, ch. i. 13: ἵνα ὑγιαίνωσιν ἐν τῇ πίστει. The articles should not be overlooked. The occurrence of τῇ ἀγάπῃ and τῇ ὑπομονῇ prevents us from rendering τῇ πίστει objective as in ch. i. 13, and compels us to take the subjective and reflective meaning). 3.] The aged women (= πρεσβύτεραι, 1 Tim. v. 2, there being in this case here no official term to occasion confusion) likewise (after the same general pattern, to which the separate virtues above mentioned belong) in deportment (cf. Porphyr. de abst. in Wetst.,—τὸ δὲ σεμνὸν κἄκ τοῦ καταστήματος ἑωρᾶτο. πορεία τε γὰρ ἦν εὔτακτος, καὶ βλέμμα καθεστηκὸς ἐπετηδεύετο, ὡς ὅτε βουληθεῖεν μὴ σκαρδαμύττειν· γέλως δὲ σπά-

νιος, εἰ δέ που γένοιτο, μέχρι μειδιασμοῦ. ἀεὶ δὲ ἐντὸς τοῦ σχήματος αἱ χεῖρες. The κατάστημα would thus include *gesture and habit*,—more than καταστολή of 1 Tim. ii. 9), reverend (two examples, of those given by Wetst., seem nearest to touch the meaning of the word here as connected with outward deportment:—the one from Jos. Antt. xi. 8. 5, describing the High Priest Jaddus going forth to meet Alexander the Great,—πυθόμενος δ' αὐτὸν οὐ πόῤῥω τῆς πόλεως, πρόεισι μετὰ τῶν ἱερέων καὶ τοῦ πολιτικοῦ πλήθους, ἱεροπρεπῆ καὶ διαφέρουσαν τῶν ἄλλων ἐθνῶν ποιούμενος τὴν ὑπάντησιν .... τὸ μὲν πλῆθος ἐν ταῖς λευκαῖς ἐσθῆσι, τοὺς δὲ ἱερεῖς προεστῶτας ἐν ταῖς βυσσίναις αὐτῶν, τὸν δὲ ἀρχιερέα ἐν τῇ ὑακινθίνῃ καὶ διαχρύσῳ στολῇ: the other from Plato, Theages, § 3, p. 262, Θεαγὴς ὄνομα τούτῳ, ὦ Σώκρατες. Καλόν γε, ὦ Δημόδοκε, τῷ υἱεῖ τὸ ὄνομα ἔθηκες καὶ ἱεροπρεπές), not slanderers (see reff. 1 Tim. and note), nor yet enslaved (so προσέχοντας, 1 Tim. iii. 8) to much wine (this vice may be included in the character given of the Cretans above, ch. i. 12), teachers of that which is good, that they school (see on σωφρονισμός, 2 Tim. i. 7.

The occurrence of ἵνα here with a pres. indic. in the best MSS. is remarkable—especially as the only other instances of this construction in St. Paul, 1 Cor. iv. 6 and Gal. iv. 17 (see notes there), may be accounted for on the hypothesis of an unusual (provincial) formation of the subjunctive, being both verbs in -όω. If this reading is to stand, it would shew that that hypothesis is unnecessary, and that St. Paul did really write the indic. pres. after ἵνα: see also 1 John v. 20. Cf. Winer, edn. 6, § 41 b. 1. c. If he did thus

k ver. 2.
l ÷ 2 Cor. xi.
2. 1 Pet. iii.
2. Prov. xix.
13.
m here only†.
n = Matt. xx.
15. Rom. v.
7. 1 Pet. ii.
18. 1 Kings
xxv. 15.
o Eph. i. 22
reff.
p = 2 Pet. ii. 2
al. see 1 Tim.
vi. 1 reff.
v. 13. Tit. ii. 6.
4, 21.

δρους εἶναι, ἱ φιλοτέκνους, ⁵ᵏ σώφρονας, ˡ ἁγνάς, ᵐ οἰκουργούς, ⁿ ἀγαθάς, ᵒ ὑποτασσομένας τοῖς ἰδίοις ἀνδράσιν, ἵνα
μὴ ὁ λόγος τοῦ θεοῦ ᵖ βλασφημῆται. ⁶ τοὺς νεωτέρους
ᵇ ὡσαύτως ᑫ παρακάλει ʳ σωφρονεῖν, ⁷ ˢ περὶ πάντα ᵗ σεαυτὸν
ᵗ παρεχόμενος ᵘ τύπον ᵛ καλῶν ᵛ ἔργων, ἐν τῇ ʷ διδασκαλίᾳ ˣ ἀφθορίαν, ʸ σεμνότητα, ⁸ ᶻ λόγον ᵃ ὑγιῆ, ᵇ ἀκατά-

...αγα-
θας H.
ACDFK
LPℵ a b
c d e f g
h k l m n
o 17. 47

q = and constr., Rom. xii. 1. 2 Cor. ii. 8. vi. 1 al.   r Mark v. 15 ‖ L. Rom. xii. 3. 2 Cor.
v. 13. Tit. ii. 6.   1 Pet. iv. 7 only†.   s = Luke x. 41. Acts xix. 25. Phil. iii. 23. 1 Tim. i. 19. vi.
4, 21.   t refl. pron. aft. mid. voice, John xix. 24. Isa. vii. 11. Xen Cyr. viii. 1. 39, παράδειγμα . . . τοιόνδε
ἑαυτὸν παρείχετο. Winer, edn. 6, § 38. 6.   u - Phil. iii. 17. 1 Thess. i. 7. 2 Thess. iii.
9. 1 Tim. iv. 12. 1 Pet. v. 3.   v 1 Tim. iii. 1 reff.   w ver. 1.   x here only.
y 1 Tim. ii. 2 reff.   z = 2 Tim. i.'13 reff.   a = (and Paul) here only. see ver. 1 reff., and Prov.
xxxi. (at end of xxiv.) 8.   b here only†. 2 Macc. iv. 47 only.

5. rec οικουρους [for -ργους], with D³HKL[P]ℵ³ rel [syr-mg-gr] Clem : txt ACD¹
Fℵ¹.   aft θεου ins και η διδασκαλια C 5 syr arm.   υποτασσομεναι [for -αις] ℵ¹
(txt ℵ-corr).

7. [παντων P.]   for σεαυτον, εαυτον D¹ Chr Damasc.—παντας εαυτον m¹ n 1
Thdrt Damasc. (So *might* the words in AC be divided, but vulg Syr read them as in
text.)   τυπον bef παρεχ. ℵ¹ 120.   rec αδιαφθοριαν, with D³Lℵ³ rel [syr-mg-
gr] Chr : αφθονιαν F : txt ACD¹K[P]ℵ¹ 17 [47] Damasc Œc-comm.   aft αφθορ.
ins αγνειαν C h² 73. 80 syr arm Jer Chrom.   Steph aft σεμνοτητα ins αφθαρσιαν,
with D³KL rel syr [mg-gr arm] Chr-ms Thdrt : om ACD¹[FP]ℵ 17 [47].

write it, it may be questioned whether he intended to convey any sense very distinct from the pres. subj. : perhaps more immediate and assumed sequence may be indicated : but it is hardly possible to join logically in the mind a causal particle with a pres. indic.) **the young women to be lovers of their husbands, lovers of their children, discreet** (this term certainly applies better to women than *self-restrained :* there is in this latter, in their case, an implication of *effort*, which destroys the spontaneity, and brushes off, so to speak, the bloom of this best of female graces. See, however, note on 1 Tim. ii. 9. The word is one of our greatest difficulties), **chaste, workers at home** (the word is not found elsewhere, and has perhaps on that account been changed to the more usual one οἰκουρούς. It is hardly possible that for so common a word οἰκουργούς should have been substituted. If the rec. is retained, 'keepers at home' will be signified : so Dio Cass. lvi. p. 391 (Wetst.), πῶς οὐκ ἄριστον γυνὴ σώφρων, οἰκουρός, οἰκονόμος, παιδοτρόφος; see Elsner's note on the word, in which he shews that, as might be expected, the ideas of 'keeping at home' and 'guarding the house' are both included : so Chrys.: ἡ οἰκουρὸς γυνὴ καὶ σώφρων ἔσται· ἡ οἰκουρὸς καὶ οἰκονομικὴ· οὔτε περὶ τρυφήν, οὔτε περὶ ἐξόδους ἀκαίρους, οὔτε περὶ ἄλλων τῶν τοιούτων ἀσχοληθήσεται), **good** (Thl. joins this with οἰκουρούς—οἰκουρὸς ἀγαθή. So also Syr. But it seems better to preserve the series of single epithets till broken in the next clause by the construction. As a single epithet (reff.) it seems to provide,

as Heydenr., that their keeping, or working, at home, should not degenerate into churlishness or niggardliness), **in subjection to their own** (inserted to bring out and impress the duties they owe to them —so in Eph. v. 22) **husbands, that the word of God** (the Gospel) **be not ill-spoken of** (τὸ γὰρ προφάσει θεοσεβείας καταλιμπάνειν τοὺς ἄνδρας, βλασφημίαν ἔφερε τῷ κηρύγματι, Thdrt.). **6 ff.]** **The younger men in like manner exhort to be self-restrained** (see above ver. 5, and 1 Tim. ii. 9, note), **shewing thyself** (the use of σεαυτόν with παρέχεσθαι is somewhat remarkable, but borne out by Xen. in reff. The account of it seems to be, that παρέχεσθαι τύπον would be the regular expression for 'to set an example,' the personal action of the subject requiring the middle (see Krüger, p. 363) : and, this being so, the form of such expression is not altered, even where ἑαυτόν is expressed in apposition with τύπον. Cf. Ellic.'s note) **in** ('*about*,' '*in reference to*' (reff.) : a meaning of περὶ with the acc. derived from its local meaning of '*round about :*' see Winer, edn. 6, § 49, i.) **all matters** (not masc. sing.) **an example** (κοινὸν διδασκαλεῖον καὶ ὑπόδειγμα ἀρετῆς ἢ τοῦ σοῦ βίου λαμπρότης ἔστω, οἷόν τις εἰκὼν ἀρχέτυπος πᾶσι προκειμένη τοῖς βουλομένοις ἐναπομάξασθαι τῶν ἐν αὐτῇ καλῶν, Thl.) **of good works** (reff.), **– in thy teaching** (παρεχόμενος) **incorruption** (it is difficult exactly to fix the reference of ἀφθορία (or ἀδιαφθορία, which means much the same). It may be objective of the *contents* of the teaching—that it should set forth purity as

γνωστον, ἵνα ὁ [c] ἐξ [cd] ἐναντίας [e] ἐντραπῇ μηδὲν [f] ἔχων
λέγειν περὶ ἡμῶν [g] φαῦλον. 9 δούλους [h] ἰδίοις [h] δεσπόταις
[i] ὑποτάσσεσθαι, [k] ἐν πᾶσιν [l] εὐαρέστους εἶναι, μὴ [m] ἀντιλέγοντας, 10 μὴ [n] νοσφιζομένους, ἀλλὰ [o] πᾶσαν [p] πίστιν
[q] ἐνδεικνυμένους ἀγαθήν, ἵνα τὴν [w] διδασκαλίαν τὴν τοῦ
[r] σωτῆρος ἡμῶν [r] θεοῦ [s] κοσμῶσιν [k] ἐν πᾶσιν. 11 [t] ἐπ-

c Mark xv. 39 only. 4 Kings ii. 7.
d 1 Thess. ii. 15 reff.
e = 1 Cor. iv. 14. 2 Thess. iii. 14 only. (Luke xviii. 2 al.) Ps. xxxiv. 26.
f constr., Luke vii 40. Acts xxiii. 17, 18, 19. Eph. iv. 28.
g Paul, Rom. ix. 11 only. John iii. 20. v. 29. James iii. 14 only. Prov. xxii. 8.
h 1 Tim. vi. 1. Prov. xxii. 7.
i ver. 5.
k 2 Tim. iv. 5 reff.
l Eph. v. 10 reff.
m ch. i. 9. Acts xiii. 45. Rom. x. 21 (from Isa. lxv. 2) al. L.P., exc. John xix. 12.
n Acts v. 2, 3 only. Josh. vii. 1. 2 Macc. iv. 32 only.
o Phil. i. 20 reff.
p = Matt. xxiii. 23. Rom. iii. 3 al. Prov. xii. 22.
q Rom. ii. 15. 2 Cor. viii 24 al. Paul only, exc. Heb. vi. 10, 11. Gen. l. 15, 17.
r 1 Tim. i. 1 reff.
s 1 Tim. ii. 9 reff.
t Luke i. 79. Acts xxvii. 20. ch. iii. 4 only. Num. vi. 25. (-νεια, ver. 13.)

8. rec περι [ ]μων bef λεγειν, with K[L(Treg)] rel [arm] Chr Aug: txt ACDF L[(Tischdf) P]ℵ m 17 [47] latt syrr [copt æth Orig] Thdrt Ambrst.—rec υμων, with A h [47] copt Thdrt: txt CDFKL[P]ℵ rel latt syrr [arm] gr-lat-ff.

9. δουλοι D[1], *servi subditi sint* D-lat. δεσποταις bef ιδιοις AD[P] latt syrr copt: txt CFKLℵ rel Chr Thdrt Damasc.

10. μηδε C[2]D[1]F 17. rec πιστιν bef πασαν, with KL rel copt Chr Thdrt Damasc: om πιστιν ℵ[1] 17: txt ACD[P]ℵ[3] m syr [arm] lat-ff.—πασ. ενδεικν. πιστιν F. rec om 2nd την, with KL[P] rel Damasc: ins ACDFℵ 17 Chr Thdrt. [om θεου P.]

its character and aim: or subjective, that *he should be, in his teaching*, pure in motive, uncorrupted: so Wiesinger, comparing 2 Cor. xi. 3, μή πως . . . φθαρῇ τὰ νοήματα ὑμῶν ἀπὸ τῆς ἁπλότητος τῆς εἰς τὸν χριστόν. Huther takes it of the *form* of the teaching, that it should be pure from all expressions foreign to the character of the Gospel. This is perhaps hardly satisfactory: and the first interpretation would bring it too near in meaning to λόγον ὑγιῆ which follows), **gravity, a discourse** (in its contents and import) **healthy, not to be condemned, that he of the opposite part** (τὸν ἐξ ἐναντίας φησὶ καὶ τὸν διάβολον καὶ πάντα τὸν ἐκείνῳ διακονούμενον, Chr. But the former idea is hardly before the Apostle's mind, from ver. 5, in which *the Gospel being evil spoken of* was represented as the point to be avoided. Cf. also 1 Tim. vi. 1, and v. 14: 2 Tim. ii. 25. It is rather the heathen or Jewish adversaries of the Gospel, among whom they dwelt) **may be ashamed** (reff.), **having nothing** (μηδέν, because, following the ἔχων, it is subjective to him, the adversary. We should say, οὐδέν ἐστιν ὅ τι ἂν λέγῃ,—but μηδὲν ἔχων λέγειν: in the former the objective fact, in the latter the subjective deficiency, is brought out) **to say of us** (Christians: not 'me and thee') (**that is**) **evil** (in our acts: φαῦλος is never used with λέγειν, nor of words, in the N. T., but always of *deeds*: 'having no evil thing to report of us'—no evil, whether seen in our demeanour, or arising from our teaching). **9.**] (παρακάλει) **Slaves to be in subjection to their own** (see above on ver. 5) **masters,—in all things to give satisfaction** (this, the servants' own phrase among ourselves, expresses perhaps better than any other the meaning of εὐαρέστους εἶναι. '*To be acceptable*' would seem to bring the slave too near to the position of a friend), **not contradicting** (in the wide sense, not merely in words, see especially ref. John), **not purloining** (ref. νοσφιζόμενον, ὑφαιρούμενον, ἰδιοποιούμενον, Suid. τὸ δ' αὐτὸ καὶ σφετερίζεσθαι, Eustath.), **but manifesting** (see ref. 2 Cor.) **all** (possible, reff.) **good faith; that they may adorn in all things** (not '*before all men*,' as Heydenr., al.: cf. ἐν πᾶσιν above) **the doctrine of our Saviour, God** (see on 1 Tim. i. 1. Not Christ, but the Father is meant: in that place the distinction is clearly made. On this '*adorning*' Calvin remarks, "Hæc quoque circumstantia notanda est (this is hardly worthy of his usually pure latinity), quod ornamentum Deus a servis accipere dignatur, quorum tam vilis et abjecta erat conditio, ut vix censeri soliti sint inter homines. Neque enim famulos intelligit quales hodie in usu sunt, sed mancipia, quæ pretio empta tanquam boves aut equi possidebantur. Quod si eorum vita ornamentum est Christiani nominis, multo magis videant qui in honore sunt, ne illud turpitudine sua maculent." Thl. strikingly says, κἂν γὰρ τῷ δεσπότῃ διακονῇς ἀλλ' ἡ τιμὴ εἰς θεὸν ἀνατρέχει, ὅτι καὶ ἀπὸ τοῦ φόβου ἐκείνου ἡ πρὸς τὸν δεσπότην εὔνοια τὴν ἀρχὴν ἔχει). **11—15.**] *Ground of the above exhortations in the moral purpose of the Gospel respecting us* (11—14): *and consequent exhortation to Titus* (15).

ἐφάνη γὰρ ἡ χάρις τοῦ θεοῦ ^uσωτήριος πᾶσιν ἀνθρώποις, ACDFK
12 ^vπαιδεύουσα ἡμᾶς, ἵνα ^wἀρνησάμενοι τὴν ^xἀσέβειαν
καὶ τὰς ^yκοσμικὰς ἐπιθυμίας, ^zσωφρόνως καὶ ^aδικαίως

u here only †. Wisd. i. 14
only. (-ιον, Eph. vi. 17.)
v 1 Tim. i. 20 reff.
w 1 Tim v. 8 reff.
y Heb. ix. 1 only †. only. 1 Pet. ii. 23.

LPℵ a b
c d e f g
h k l m n
o 17. 47

x 2 Tim. ii. 16.   Rom. i. 18. xi. 26.   Jude 15, 18 only.   Jer. v. 6.   (-βεῖν, -βής, Jude 15.)
z here only †.   Wisd. ix. 11 only.   a Paul, 1 Cor. xv. 34.   1 Thess. ii. 10
Luke xxiii. 41 only.   Deut. i. 16.

11. rec ins ἡ bef σωτηριος (to fill out the construction), with C³D².³KL[P] rel Clem
Cyr-jer-mss Nyss Chr Thdrt Procl Damasc : om AC¹D¹ℵ syrr.—for σωτηριος, σωτηρος
ℵ¹ : του σωτηρος ημων (see ch iii. 4) F vulg copt æth Epiph [Lucif₂].
12. om τας D¹.

11.] **For** (reasons for the above exhortations from ver. 1 : not as Chrys., al., only
for vv. 9, 10. The latter clause of ver. 10,
it is true, gives occasion to this declaration ; but the reference of these verses is
far wider than merely to slaves) **the grace
of God** (that divine favour to men, of
which the whole process of Redemption
was a proof: not to be limited to *Christ's
Incarnation*, as Œc. and Thdrt.: though
certainly this may be said for their interpretation, that *it* may *also* be regarded as
a term inclusive of all the blessings of Redemption : but it does not follow, that of
two such inclusive terms, the one may be
substituted for the other) **was manifested,
bringing salvation** (not, 'as bringing salvation :' σωτήριος is not predicate after
ἐπεφ., but παιδεύουσα which follows:
σωτήριος is still part of the subject, and
to make this constructionally clearer, the
art. ἡ has been inserted) **to all men** (dat.
belonging to σωτήριος, not to ἐπεφάνη,
which verb is used absolutely, as in ch. iii.
4 : cf. σωτὴρ πάντων ἀνθρώπων, 1 Tim.
iv. 10 : see also ib. ii. 4), **disciplining us**
(see note on 1 Tim. i. 20. There is no
need to depart from the universal New
Testament sense of παιδεύουσα, and soften
it into '*teaching* :' the education which
the Christian man receives from the grace
of God, is a discipline, properly so called,
of self-denial and training in godliness,
accompanied therefore with much mortification and punitive treatment. Luther
has well rendered παιδεύουσα ἡμᾶς by
' und züchtiget uns.' Corn.-a-lap. (cited
in Mack) explains it also well : " tanquam
pueros rudes erudiens, corrigens, for-
mans, omnique disciplina instituens et
imbuens, perinde ut pædagogus puerum
sibi commissum tam in litteris quam in
moribus: hoc enim est παιδεύειν, inquit
Gell. ii. 13. 13 "), that (by the ordinary
rendering, "*teaching us, that*," we make
ἵνα introduce merely the *purport* of the
teaching : and so, following most Commentators, De W., and I am surprised to
see, Huther, although I suppose representing in some measure the philological

fidelity of Meyer, under whose shelter his
commentary appears. There must have
been some defect of supervision here.
Wiesinger only of the recent Commentators, after Mack and Matthies, keeps
the telic meaning of ἵνα. The Greek
Commentators, as might be expected, adhere to the propriety of their own language. So Chrys. (ἦλθεν ὁ χριστός, ἵνα
ἀρνησώμεθα τὴν ἀσέβειαν), Thl. (παιδεύει
γὰρ ἡμᾶς, ἵνα τοῦ λοιποῦ σωφρόνως
ζήσωμεν), Thdrt. (τούτου χάριν ἐνηνθρώ-
πησεν . . . . ἵνα . . . .). The truth is,
that **παιδεύειν** is one of those verbs, the
purpose and purport of which mutually
include each other. The form and manner of instructive discipline itself conveys
the aim and intent of that discipline. So
that the meaning of ἵνα after such a verb
falls under the class which I have discussed in my note to 1 Cor. xiv. 13, which
see. Our English 'that,' which would be
dubious after '*teaching*,' keeps, after 'disciplining,' its proper telic force), **denying**
(not, 'having denied:' the aor. part. ἀρνησάμενοι is, as so often, not prior to, but
contemporaneous with, the aor. ζήσωμεν
following. (This, against Ellic., requires
pressing here. The whole life being
summed up in ζήσωμεν, aor., not ζῶμεν,
pres., the aor. part. ἀρνησάμενοι must be
so rendered, as to extend over all that sum,
not as if it represented some definite act
of abnegation anterior to it all.) διὰ τοῦ
ἀρνήσασθαι, says Thl., τὴν ἐκ διαθέσεως
ὁλοψύχου ἀποστροφὴν σημαίνει. " Has
(cupiditates) abnegamus, cum eis consen-
sum negamus, cum delectationem quam
suggerunt, et actum ad quem sollicitant,
abnuimus, imo ex mente et animo radi-
citus evellimus et extirpamus." S. Bernard, Serm. xi. (Mack)) **impiety and the
lusts of the world** (the τάς gives universality—'*all* worldly lusts.' **κοσμικάς**,
belonging to the κόσμος, the world which
ἐν τῷ πονηρῷ κεῖται, and is without God :
see 1 John ii. 15—17 and Ellicott's note
here), **we might live soberly** (our old
difficulty of rendering σώφρων and its derivatives recurs. 'Soberly' seems here to

καὶ ᵇ εὐσεβῶς ζήσωμεν ἐν ᶜ τῷ νῦν ᶜ αἰῶνι, 13 ᵈᵉ προσδεχό-   ᵇ 2 Tim. iii. 12
μενοι τὴν ᶠ μακαρίαν ᵉᵍ ἐλπίδα καὶ ʰ ἐπιφάνειαν τῆς δόξης   only †. Xen.
                                                                        Mem. ii. 2.
                                                                      13. (see 1 Tim.

c 1 Tim. vi. 17. 2 Tim. iv. 10 only. see 1 Tim. iv. 8.   d = Mark xv. 43. Luke ii. 25, 38 al. Paul, =
  here and Acts as below (e) only. see Rom. xvi. 2. Phil. ii. 29.   e Acts xxiv. 15.   f of
  things, Acts xx. 35 only. elsw. (passim) of persons. see 1 Tim. i. 11 reff.   g = Gal. v. 5. Heb.
  vi. 18 al.   h 2 Tim. i. 10 reff.

express the *adverb* well, though 'sober' by no means covers the meaning of the *adjective*. The fact is, that the peculiar meaning which has become attached to ' sober,'—so much so, as almost to deprive it of its more general reference to life and thought,—has not taken possession of the adverb) **and justly** (better than '*righteously*,'—'righteous,' by its forensic objective sense in St. Paul, introducing a confusion, where the question is of moral rectitude) **and piously in the present life** (" Bernard, Serm. xi. : *sobrie* erga nos, *juste* erga proximum, *pie* erga Deum, Salmer. p. 630 f. : dicimus in his verbis Apostolum tribus virtutibus, sobrietatis, pietatis et justitiæ, summam justitiæ Christianæ complecti. Sobrietas est ad se, justitia ad proximum, pietas erga Deum .... sobrie autem agit, cum quis se propter Deum diligit: juste, cum proximum diligit : pie, cum charitate Deum colit." Mack. Wolf quotes from Lucian, Somn. p. 8, the same conjunction: τὴν ψυχὴν .... κατακοσμήσω .... σωφροσύνη, δικαιοσύνη, καὶ εὐσεβίᾳ .... ταῦτα γάρ ἐστιν ὁ τῆς ψυχῆς ἀκήρατος κόσμος. These three comprising our παιδεία in faith and love, he now comes to *hope*):
*   **looking for** (this expectation being an abiding state and posture,—not, like ζήσωμεν, the life following on and unfolded from the determining impulse co-ordinate with the ἀρνήσασθαι,—is put in the *pres.*, not in the *aor.*) **the blessed hope** (here, as in reff. Gal. and Acts, Col. i. 5 al., nearly objective,—the hope, as embodying the thing hoped for : but keep the vigour and propriety both of language and thought, and do not tame down the one and violate the other, with Grot., by a metonymy, or with Wolf, by a hypallage of μακαρία ἐλπίς for ἐλπιζομένη μακαριότης) **and manifestation** (ἐλπίδα κ. ἐπιφ. belong together) **of the glory** (δύο δείκνυσιν ἐνταῦθα ἐπιφανείας· καὶ γάρ εἰσι δύο· ἡ μὲν προτέρα χάριτος, ἡ δὲ δευτέρα ἀνταποδόσεως, Chrys. Nothing could be more unfortunate than the application here of the figure of hendiadys in the E. V. : see below) **of the great God** (the Father : see below) **and of our Saviour Jesus Christ** (as regards the sense, an exact parallel is found in Matt. xvi. 27, μέλλει γὰρ ὁ υἱὸς τοῦ ἀνθρώπου ἔρχεσθαι ἐν τῇ δόξῃ τοῦ πατρὸς αὐτοῦ, compared with Matt. xxv.

31, ὅταν ἔλθῃ ὁ υἱὸς τοῦ ἀνθρώπου ἐν τῇ δόξῃ αὐτοῦ. See also 1 Pet. iv. 13. The glory which shall be revealed at the appearing of our Saviour Jesus Christ is *His own* glory, *and* that of *His Father* (John xvii. 5; 1 Thess. iii. 13). This sense having been obscured by the foolish hendiadys, has led to the asking (by Mr. Green, Gr. Test. Gram., p. 216), "What intimation is given in Scripture of a glorious appearing of God the Father and our Lord *in concert?*" To which the answer is, that no such appearing is even hinted at in this passage, taken as above. What is asserted is, that the δόξα shall be that τοῦ μεγάλου θεοῦ καὶ σωτῆρος ἡμῶν Ἰησοῦ χριστοῦ. And we now come to consider the meaning of these words. Two views have been taken of them : (1) that τοῦ μεγάλου θεοῦ καὶ σωτῆρος ἡμῶν are to be taken together as the description of Ἰησοῦ χριστοῦ,—'*of Jesus Christ, the great God and our Saviour :*' (2) that as given above, τοῦ μεγάλου θεοῦ describes the Father, and σωτῆρος ἡμῶν Ἰησοῦ χριστοῦ the Son. It is obvious that in dealing with (1), we shall be deciding with regard to (2) also. (1) has been the view of the Greek orthodox Fathers, as against the Arians (see a complete collection of their testimonies in Dr. Wordsworth's "Six Letters to Granville Sharp on the use of the definite article in the Greek text of the N. T." Lond. 1802), and of most ancient and modern Commentators. That the former so interpreted the words, is obviously not (as it has been considered) decisive of the question, if they can be shewn to bear legitimately another meaning, and that meaning to be the one most likely to have been in the mind of the writer. The case of ἵνα in the preceding verse (see note there), was wholly different. There it was contended that ἵνα with a subjunctive, has, and can have, but one meaning: and this was upheld against those who would introduce another, *inter alia*, by the fact that the Greek Fathers dreamt of no other. The argument rested not on this latter fact, but on the logical force of the particle itself. And similarly here, the passage must be argued primarily on its own ground, not primarily on the consensus of the Greek Fathers. No one disputes that it *may* mean that which they have inter-

i here only.
Neh. ix. 32.
Dan. ii. 45.
ix. 4 al.
j ch. i.⁴ reff.
k Gal. i. 4.   1 Tim. ii. 6.   1 Macc. vi. 44.   (= παραδιδ., Gal. ii. 20.   Eph. v. 25.)   1 Luke xxiv. 21.   1 Pet.
i. 18 only.   Ps. cxxix. 8.

τοῦ ¹μεγάλου ¹θεοῦ καὶ ¹σωτῆρος ἡμῶν Ἰησοῦ χριστοῦ, ACDFK
14 ὃς ᵏἔδωκεν ἑαυτὸν ὑπὲρ ἡμῶν, ἵνα ¹λυτρώσηται ἡμᾶς LPℵ a b
                                                        c d e f g
                                                        h k l m n
                                                        o 17. 47

13. χριστου bef ιησ. ℵ¹[F(not F-lat) copt].
14. υπερ ημων bef εαυτον D Lucif.—αυτον ℵ¹ 238.

preted it : and there were obvious reasons
why they, having licence to do so, should
choose this interpretation.   But it is our
object, not being swayed in this or any
other interpretation, by doctrinal considerations one way or the other, to enquire, not what the words *may* mean, but
what they *do* mean, as far as we may be
able to ascertain it.   The main, and indeed the only reliance of those who take
(1), is the omission of the article before
σωτῆρος.   Had the sentence stood τοῦ μεγ.
θεοῦ καὶ τοῦ σωτῆρος ἡμῶν Ἰ. χ., their
verdict for (2) would have been unanimous.
That the insertion of the article would
have been decisive for (2), is plain : but
is it equally plain, that its omission is decisive for (1)?   This must depend entirely
on the nature and position of the word
thus left anarthrous.   If it is a word which
had by usage become altogether or occasionally anarthrous,—if it is so connected,
that the presence of the article expressed, is
not requisite to its presence in the sense,
then the state of the case, as regards
the omission, is considerably altered.   Now
there is no doubt that σωτήρ was one
of those words which gradually dropped
the article and became a quasi proper
name : cf. 1 Tim. i. 1 (I am quite aware
of Bp. Middleton's way of accounting for
this, but do not regard it as satisfactory) ;
iv. 10 ; which latter place is very instructive as to the way in which the designation from its official nature became
anarthrous.   This being so, it must hardly
be judged as to the expression of the art.
by the same rules as other nouns.   Then
as to its structural and contextual connexion.   It is joined with ἡμῶν, which is
an additional reason why it may spare the
article : see Luke i. 78 : Rom. i. 7 : 1 Cor.
i. 3 (1 Cor. ii. 7 ; x. 11) : 2 Cor. i. 2, &c.
Again, as Winer has observed (edn.
6, § 19, 5 b, remark 1), the prefixing of
an appositional designation to the proper
name frequently causes the omission of
the article.   So in 2 Thess. i. 12 : 2 Pet.
i. 1 : Jude 4 : see also 2 Cor. i. 2 ; vi. 18 :
Gal. i. 3 : Eph. i. 2 ; vi. 23 : Phil. i. 2 ; ii.
11 ; iii. 20 &c.   If then σωτήρ ἡμῶν Ἰησοῦς
χριστός may signify 'Jesus Christ our
Saviour,'—on comparing the two members
of the clause, we observe, that θεοῦ has

already had its predicate expressed in τοῦ
μεγαλιν ;and that it is therefore natural
to expect that the latter member of the
clause, likewise consisting of a proper name
and its predicate, should correspond logically to the former : in other words, that
τοῦ θεοῦ καὶ σωτῆρος ἡμῶν Ἰη. χρ. would
much more naturally suit (1) than τοῦ
μεγάλου θεοῦ καὶ σωτῆρος ἡμ. Ἰη. χρ.
In clauses where the two appellative members belong to one expressed subject, we
expect to find the former of them without
any predicative completion.   If it be replied to this, as I conceive on the hypothesis of (1) it must be, that τοῦ μεγάλου is an epithet alike of θεοῦ and
σωτῆρος, 'our great (God and Saviour),'
I may safely leave it to the feeling of any
scholar, whether such an expression would
be likely to occur.   Let us now consider,
whether the Apostle would in this place
have been likely to designate our Lord
as ὁ μέγας θεὸς καὶ σωτὴρ ἡμῶν.   This
must be chiefly decided by examining the
usages of the expression θεὸς ὁ σωτὴρ
ἡμῶν, which occurs six times in these
Epistles, once in Luke (i. 47), and once
in the Epistle of Jude.   If the writer
here identifies this expression, 'the great
God and our Saviour,' with the Lord
Jesus Christ, calling Him 'God and our
Saviour,' it will be at least probable that
in other places where he speaks of "God
our Saviour," he also designates our Lord
Jesus Christ.   Now is that so ?   On the
contrary, in 1 Tim. i. 1, we have κατ' ἐπιταγὴν θεοῦ σωτῆρος ἡμῶν, καὶ χριστοῦ
Ἰησοῦ τῆς ἐλπίδος ἡμῶν : where I suppose
none will deny that the Father and the
Son are most plainly distinguished from
one another.   The same is the case in
1 Tim. ii. 3—5, a passage bearing much
(see below) on the interpretation of this
one : and consequently in 1 Tim. iv. 10,
where ἐστιν σωτὴρ πάντων ἀνθρώπων
corresponds to θέλει πάντας σωθῆναι in
the other.   So also in Tit. i. 3, where the
σωτὴρ ἡμῶν θεός, by whose ἐπιταγή the
promise of eternal life was manifested,
with the proclamation of which St. Paul
was entrusted, is the same αἰώνιος θεός,
by whose ἐπιταγή the hidden mystery
was manifested in Rom. xvi. 26, where
the same distinction is made.   The only

ἀπὸ πάσης ᵐⁿ ἀνομίας καὶ ᵐᵒ καθαρίσῃ ἑαυτῷ ᵐ λαὸν ᵖ περι- ᵐ Εzεκ. xxxvii. 23.

n Paul, Rom.
iv. 7. vi. 19. 2 Cor. vi. 14. 2 Thess. ii. 7. Matt. vii. 23 al. Exod. xxxiv. 9.   o = Acts xv. 9. Eph.
v. 26. James iv. 8. Sir. xxxviii. 10.   p here only. Exod. xix. 5. Deut. vii. 6. xiv. 2. xxvi.
18 (alw. w. λαός, and never occ. elsw., exc. Mal. iii. 17 Aq. -σιασμός, Ps. cxxxiv. 4. Eccles. ii. 8).

place where there could be any doubt is
in our ver. 10, which possible doubt however is removed by ver. 11, where the
same assertion is made, of the revelation of
the hidden grace of God (the Father).
Then we have our own ch. iii. 4—6, where
we find τοῦ σωτῆρος ἡμῶν θεοῦ in ver. 4,
clearly defined as *the Father*, and διὰ
Ἰησοῦ χριστοῦ τοῦ σωτῆρος ἡμῶν in ver.
6. In that passage too we have the expression ἡ χρηστότης καὶ ἡ φιλανθρωπία
ἐπεφάνη τοῦ σωτῆρος ἡμ. θεοῦ, which is
quite decisive in answer to those who object
here to the expression ἐπιφάνειαν τῆς
δόξης as applied to the Father. In the
one passage of St. Jude, the distinction
is equally clear : for there we have μόνῳ
θεῷ σωτῆρι ἡμῶν διὰ Ἰησοῦ χριστοῦ τοῦ
κυρίου ἡμῶν. It is plain then, that the
usage of the words ' *God our Saviour*' does
not make it probable that the whole expression here is to be applied to the Lord
Jesus Christ. And in estimating this probability, let us again recur to 1 Tim. ii. 3, 5,
a passage which runs very parallel with the
present one. We read there, εἷς γὰρ θεός,
| εἷς καὶ μεσίτης θεοῦ καὶ ἀνθρώπων,
ἄνθρωπος χριστὸς Ἰησοῦς, ὁ δοὺς ἑαυτὸν
ἀντίλυτρον κ.τ.λ. Compare this with τοῦ
μεγάλου θεοῦ | καὶ σωτῆρος ἡμῶν Ἰησοῦ
χριστοῦ, ὃς ἔδωκεν ἑαυτὸν ὑπὲρ ἡμῶν ἵνα
λυτρώσηται κ.τ.λ. Can there be a reasonable doubt, that the Apostle writing two
sentences so closely corresponding, on a
point of such high importance, would have
in his view the same distinction in the
second of them, which he so strongly lays
down in the first ? Without then considering the question as closed, I would submit that (2) satisfies all the grammatical
requirements of the sentence : that it is
both structurally and contextually more
probable, and more agreeable to the
Apostle's way of writing : and I have
therefore preferred it. The principal advocates for it have been, the pseudo-Am-
brose (i. e. Hilary the deacon, the author
of the Commentary which goes by the
name of that Father : whose words are
these, "hanc esse dicit beatam spem cre-
dentium, qui exspectant adventum gloriæ
magni Dei quod revelari habet judice
Christo, in quo Dei Patris videbitur potestas et gloria, ut fidei suæ præmium con-
sequantur. Ad hoc enim redemit nos
Christus, ut" &c.), Erasm. (annot. and
paraphr.), Grot., Wetst., Heinr., Winer

(ubi supra, end), De W., Huther (the
other view,—not this as stated in my
earlier editions, by inadvertence,—is taken
by Ellicott). Whichever way taken, the
passage is just as important a testimony
to the divinity of our Saviour : according
to (1), by asserting His possession of Deity
and right to the appellation of the Highest : according to (2), even more strikingly,
asserting His equality in glory with the
Father, in a way which would be blasphemy if predicated of any of the sons of
men), **who** (our Saviour Jesus Christ), gave
Himself (" the forcible ἑαυτόν, ' Himself, His whole self, the greatest gift ever
given,' must not be overlooked : cf. Beve-
ridge, Serm. 93, vol. iv. p. 285." Ellicott)
for us (' on our behalf,' not ' *in our stead :*'
reff.), **that He might** (by this assertion of
the Redeemer's purpose, we return to the
moral aim of verses 11, 12, more plainly
indicated as in close connexion with Christ's
propitiatory sacrifice) **redeem** (λυτροῦσθαι,
' *to buy off* with a price,' the *middle* including personal agency and interest, cf.
καθαρίσῃ ἑαυτῷ below. So in Diod. Sic.
v. 17, of the Balearians, ὅταν τινὲς γυναῖκες ὑπὸ τῶν προσπλεόντων λῃστῶν
ἁλῶσιν, ἀντὶ μιᾶς γυναικὸς τρεῖς ἢ τέτ-
ταρας ἄνδρας διδόντες λυτροῦνται. Polyb.
xvii. 16. 1, of King Attalus and the Si-
cyonians, where only personal *agency* is
implied in the middle, τὴν ἱερὰν χώραν
τοῦ Ἀπόλλωνος **ἐλυτρώσατο** χρημάτων
αὐτοῖς οὐκ ὀλίγων. See note, 1 Tim. ii. 6 :
and cf. ref. 1 Pet., where the price is stated
to have been the precious blood of Christ)
us from all lawlessness (see reff. and especially 1 John iii. 4, ἡ ἁμαρτία ἐστὶν ἡ
ἀνομία) **and might purify** (there is. no
need to supply ἡμᾶς, though the sense is
not disturbed by so doing. By making
λαόν the direct object of καθαρίζῃ, the
purpose of the Redeemer is lifted off from
our particular case, and generally and objectively stated) **to Himself** (' dat. commodi') **a people** (object : not, as De W.,
Wies., al., predicate, ' (us) for a people')
peculiarly His (see note on Eph. i. 14,
and cf. the reff. here in the LXX, from
which the expression is borrowed. See
also 1 Pet. ii. 9, and Ellicott here. The
ἐξειλεγμένον of Chrys., though expressing
the fact, says too much for the word,—as
also does the *acceptabilis* of the Vulg. :
egregium of Jerome, too little : the οἰκεῖον
of Thdrt. is exact : that which περίεστιν

q = Acts (i. 13) οὔσιον, q ζηλωτὴν r καλῶν r ἔργων. 15 ταῦτα λάλει καὶ ACDFK
xxi. 20. xxii.   LPℵa b
3. 1 Cor.   s παρακάλει καὶ t ἔλεγχε u μετὰ v πάσης w ἐπιταγῆς· μη- cdefg
xiv. 12. Gal.   hklmn
i. 14 al.
1 Pet. iii. 13 δεῖς σου x περιφρονείτω. III. 1 y ὑπομίμνησκε αὐτοὺς o17. 47
(Luke vi. 15)
only. (Exod.   z ἀρχαῖς za ἐξουσίαις b ὑποτάσσεσθαι, c πειθαρχεῖν, d πρὸς
xx. 5 al.)
2 Macc. iv. 2.
r 1 Tim. iii. 1 πᾶν d ἔργον d ἀγαθὸν e ἑτοίμους εἶναι, 2 μηδένα f βλασφη-
reff.
s = 1 Tim. vi. 2. μεῖν, g ἀμάχους εἶναι, h ἐπιεικεῖς, i πᾶσαν j ἐνδεικνυμένους
t 1 Tim. v. 20
reff.
u = Mark iii. 5. k πραΰτητα πρὸς πάντας ἀνθρώπους. 3 ἦμεν γὰρ ποτὲ
1 Chron.
xxix. 22. Paul, passim.   v = Phil. i. 20 reff.   w 1 Tim. i. 1 reff.   x here only †. περι-
φρονῶ, ἴσον τῷ καταφρονῶ, Schol. Aristoph. Nub. 225. see 1 Tim. iv. 12.   y 2 Tim. ii. 14 reff
z Eph. i. 21 reff.   a = Rom. xiii. 1.   b ch. ii. 5, 9. Eph. i. 22 reff.   c Acts v. 29,
32. xxvii. 21 only †. Esdr. viii. 94 (90). Sir. xxx. (xxxii.) 28 only.   d see 2 Tim. ii. 21 reff.
e Paul, 2 Cor. ix. 5. x. 6, 16 only. 1 Pet. iii. 15 al. Ps. xvi. 12.   f = Rom. iii. 8 al. 4 Kings xix. 6 A.
g 1 Tim. iii. 3 only †.   h Phil. iv. 5. 1 Tim. iii. 3. James iii. 17. 1 Pet. ii. 18 only. Ps. lxxxv. 5 only.
i ch. ii. 15.   j ch. ii. 10 reff.   k Gal. v. 23. vi. 1 reff.

15. for λαλει, διδασκε A.

CHAP. III. 1. aft υπομιμνησκε ins δε A Syr arm.   rec aft αρχαις ins και, with
D3KL[P] rel [vss] : om ACD1Fℵ 17.   aft πειθαρχειν ins και A: pref F [Syr] :
in both places arm.   αγαθους ℵ1 k.
2. for μηδενα, μη F : G-lat has both : μηδεν K.   ενδεικνυσθαι ℵ1.   rec
πραοτητα, with DFKLℵ3 rel : txt AC[P] 17. 672 : σπουδην τα(sic) ℵ1.

αὐτῷ), zealous (an ardent worker and promoter) of good works. 15.] gathers up all since ver. 1, where the general command last appeared, and enforces it on Titus. In ch. iii. 1, the train of thought is again resumed. These things (the foregoing : not, the following) speak and exhort (in the case of those who believe and need stirring up) and rebuke (in the case of those who are rebellious) with all imperativeness (μετὰ αὐθεντίας καὶ μετὰ ἐξουσίας πολλῆς, Chrys.—τουτέστι, μετὰ ἀποτομίας, Thl.). Let no man despise thee (addressed to Titus, not to the people, as Calv. ('populum ipsum magis quam Titum hic compellat') : 'so conduct thyself in thine exhortations, with such gravity, and such consistency, and such impartiality, that every word of thine may carry weight, and none may be able to cast slight on thee for flaws in any of these points'). III. 1, 2.] Rules concerning behaviour to those without. Put them in mind (as of a duty previously and otherwise well known, but liable to be forgotten) to be in subjection to governments, to authorities, to obey the magistrate (πειθαρχεῖν here probably stands absolutely, not, as Huther, connected with the dat. ἀρχαῖς ἐξ. So Xen. Cyr. viii. 1. 4, μέγιστον ἀγαθὸν τὸ πειθαρχεῖν φαίνεται εἰς τὸ καταπράττειν τὰ ἀγαθά. The other construction has however the reff. in its favour), to be ready towards every good work (the connexion seems to be as in Rom. xiii. 3, where the rulers are said to be οὐ φόβος τῷ ἀγαθῷ ἔργῳ, ἀλλὰ τῷ κακῷ. Compare also the remarkable coincidence in the sentiment of Xen. quoted

above. Jerome in loc., Wetst., De W., al., suppose these exhortations to subjection to have found their occasion in the insubordination of the Jews on principle to foreign rule, and more especially of the Cretan Jews. In the presence of similar exhortations in the Epistle to the Romans and elsewhere, we can hardly perhaps say so much as this: but certainly Wetst.'s quotations from Diod. Sic., al., seem to establish the fact of Cretan turbulence in general. The inference drawn by Thdrt., al., from these last words,—οὐδὲ γὰρ εἰς ἅπαντα δεῖ τοῖς ἄρχουσι πειθαρχεῖν, does not seem to be legitimately deduced from them), to speak evil of no one (these words set forth the general duty, but are perhaps introduced owing to what has preceded, cf. 2 Pet. ii. 10 : Jude 8), to be not quarrelsome (ref. and note), forbearing (ib., and note on Phil. iv. 5. " The ἐπιεικής must have been, it is to be feared, a somewhat exceptional character in Crete, where an ἔμφυτος πλεονεξία, exhibited in outward acts of aggression, καὶ ἰδίᾳ καὶ κατὰ κοινόν (Polyb. vi. 46—9), is described as one of the prevailing and dominant vices." Ellicott), manifesting all meekness towards all men (from what follows, πάντας ἀνθρ. is evidently to be taken in the widest sense, and especially to be applied to the heathen without : see below). 3.] For (reason why we should shew all meekness, &c. : οὐκοῦν μηδενὶ ὀνειδίσῃς, φησί· τοιοῦτος γὰρ ἦς καὶ σύ, Chrys. ὃ καὶ ὁ λῃστὴς πρὸς τὸν ἕτερον λῃστὴν ἔλεγεν, ὅτι ἐν τῷ αὐτῷ κρίματί ἐσμεν. Thl.) we (Christians) also (as well as they) were (emphatically prefixed) once without

καὶ ἡμεῖς [l] ἀνόητοι, [m] ἀπειθεῖς, [n] πλανώμενοι, [o] δουλεύοντες
ἐπιθυμίαις καὶ [p] ἡδοναῖς [q] ποικίλαις, ἐν [r] κακίᾳ καὶ [s] φθόνῳ
[t] διάγοντες, [u] στυγητοί, μισοῦντες ἀλλήλους· 4 ὅτε δὲ ἡ
[v] χρηστότης καὶ ἡ [w] φιλανθρωπία [x] ἐπεφάνη τοῦ [y] σωτῆρος
ἡμῶν [y] θεοῦ, 5 οὐκ [z] ἐξ ἔργων τῶν [a] ἐν δικαιοσύνῃ ἃ ἐποι-

l Luke xxiv. 25. Rom. i. 14. Gal. iii. 1, 3. 1 Tim. vi. 9 only. L.P. Prov. xvii. 28. m ch. i. 16 reff. n 1 Cor. vi. 9. xv. 33. Gal. vi. 7. 2 Tim iii. 13. Heb. v. 2. James v. 19. Hos. iv. 12. o Gal. iv. 8, 9 reff. p Paul, here only. Luke viii. 14. James iv. 1, 3. 2 Pet ii. 13 only. Numb. xi. 8. Prov. xvii. 1. Wisd. vii. 2. xvi. 20 only. see 2 Tim. iii. 4. q 2 Tim. iii. 6 (there also w. ἐπιθ.) reff. r Eph. iv. 31 reff. s Phil. i. 15 reff. t 1 Tim. ii. 2 only ‡. 2 Macc. xii. 38. u here only †. (-γεῖν, 2 Macc. v. 8.) v Eph. ii. 7 reff. w Acts xxviii. 2 only †. 2 Macc. vi. 22. xiv. 9 only. (-πῶς, Acts xxvii. 3.) x ch. ii. 11 reff. y 1 Tim. i. 1 reff. z = Rom. iii. 20 al. fr. Paul. a so ἐν θεῷ, ἐν κυρίῳ, John iii. 21. 1 Cor. vii. 39. xi. 11 al.

3. [*και ημ.* bef *ποτε* P tol Orig$_1$(expr, and int$_1$) Lucif$_1$.] aft *ανοητοι* ins *και* D vulg(but not am) Syr [Orig$_1$(and int$_1$) Lucif$_1$]. aft *δουλευοντες* ins *εν* ℵ^1(ℵ^3 disapproving). for *στυγητοι*, *μισητοι* D^1 : *στυγηται* ℵ^1. at end ins *αποστερουντες μισθον μισθωτου, και εκχυνομενοι αιμα ιδρωτων αυτων, ων η κρισις ανιλεως τω μη ποιησαντι ελεος* 96. 109.

5. rec for ἅ, ὧν (*correction for elegance*), with C^{2}D^{3}KL[P] rel Ath(many mss) Cyr-jer Ps-Ath Chr Thdrt$_3$: txt AC^{1}D^{1}Fℵ 17 Clem Cyr$_{sæpe}$. (C is deficient from *εποιη-*

understanding (of spiritual things, see Eph. iv. 18), **disobedient** (to God, ch. i. 16: he is no longer speaking of *authorities*, but has passed into a new train of thought), **led astray** (so Conyb.: the passive sense should be kept, as best answering to N. T. usage, ref. 2 Tim.: reff. Heb. and James, which Huther quotes for the neuter sense, are both better rendered passive. Ellic. advocates the neuter '*going astray*'), **slaves to divers lusts and pleasures** (see reff.: an unusual word in N. T., though so common in secular Greek), **passing our lives** (in ref. 1 Tim. *βίον* is expressed) **in malice** (reff.) **and envy,—hateful, hating one another** (the sequence, if there be any, seems to be in the converse order from that assumed by Thl., *ἄξιοι μίσους ἦμεν, ὡς ἀλλήλους μισοῦντες*. It was our natural hatefulness which begot mutual hatred. Or perhaps the two particulars may be taken separately, as distinct items in our catalogue of depravities). **4.**] **But when the goodness** (reff.) **and love-towards-men** (I prefer this literal rendering of *φιλανθρωπία* to any of the more usual ones: cf. Diog. Laert. Plat. iii. 98, *τῆς φιλανθρωπίας ἐστὶν εἴδη τρία· ἓν μὲν διὰ τῆς προσηγορίας γινόμενον, οἷον ἐν οἷς τινὲς τὸν ἐντυγχάνοντα πάντα προσαγορεύουσι καὶ τὴν δεξιὰν ἐμβάλλοντες χαιρετίζουσιν· ἄλλο εἶδος, ὅταν τις βοηθητικὸς ᾖ παντὶ τῷ ἀτυχοῦντι· ἕτερον εἶδός ἐστι τῆς φιλανθρωπίας ἐν ᾧ τινὲς φιλοδειπνισταί εἰσι.* The second of these is evidently that here intended, but Huther's view of the correspondence of this description of God's kindness to us with that which we are required (ver. 2) to shew to others, appears to me to be borne out: and thus His *φιλανθρωπία* would parallel *πραΰτητα πρὸς πάντας ἀνθρώπους* above, and the fact of its being 'love *toward men*' should be expressed. Bengel's remark also is worth notice: "Hominum vitia plane contraria enumerantur versu 3." The junction of *χρηστὸς, -ότης*, with *φιλάνθρωπος, -ία*, is very common: see the numerous quotations in Wetst.) **of our Saviour, God** (the Father: cf. *διὰ Ἰησ. χρ.* below, and see note on ch. ii. 13), **was manifested** (viz. in Redemption, by the Incarnation and Satisfaction of the Redeemer),—**not by virtue of** (*ἐξ*, as the ground out of which an act springs. Cf. besides the frequent *ἐκ πίστεως, ἐξ ἔργων*,—Matt. xii. 37 bis: Rom. i. 4: 2 Cor. xiii. 4) **works wrought in** (I have thus represented the *τῶν ἐν*:—*ἔργων* (general, '*any works*') *τῶν ἐν δικ.* (viz. '*which were*,' particularizing out of those, '*in righteousness*') **ἐν δικ.** *in* righteousness, as the element and condition in which they were wrought) **righteousness which we** (emphatic) **did** (not, '*have done*,' as E. V., nor '*had done*,' as Conyb.,—which in fact obscures the meaning: for God's act here spoken of was a definite act in time—and its application to us, also a definite act in time (see below): and if we take this *ἐποιήσαμεν* pluperfect, * we confine the Apostle's repudiation of our works, as moving causes of those acts of God, to the *time previous to those acts*. For aught that this pluperfect would assert, our salvation might be prompted on God's part by future works of righteousness which He foresaw we should do. Whereas the simple aoristic sense throws the whole into the same time,—"His goodness, &c. was manifested . . . . not for works which we did . . . . He

b Eph. v. 26 only. Cant.
iv. 2. Sir.
xxxi.
(xxxiv.) 25
only.
Col. iii. 10.) ἤσαμεν ἡμεῖς, ἀλλὰ κατὰ τὸ αὐτοῦ ἔλεος ἔσωσεν ἡμᾶς
διὰ ᵇλουτροῦ ᶜπαλιγγενεσίας καὶ ᵈἀνακαινώσεως πνεύ- ACDFK
LPℵab
cdefg
hklmn
o17.47

c Matt. xix. 28 only †.   Jos. Antt. xi. 3. 9.   Philo passim.   d Rom. xii. 2 only †.   (-νοῦσθαι,

σαμεν to εσωσεν.)   rec τον αυ. ελεον, with D³KL rel Chr : txt AD¹F[P]ℵ 17 [47]
67² Clem Max Ath Cyr-jer Thdrt Damasc.—τ. ελ. bef αυτ. DF.   ins του bef
λουτρου A : om CDFKL[P]ℵ rel Orig₍ₛₐₑₚₑ₎ Ath Cyr-jer.   ins δια bef πνευματος
D¹F [Lucif₁].

saved us,"—and renders the repudiation
of human merit universal. On the construction, cf. Thl.: ἔσωσεν ἡμᾶς οὐκ
ἐξ ἔργων ὧν ἐποιήσαμεν, ἀντὶ τοῦ οὔτε
ἐποιήσαμεν ἔργα δικαιοσύνης, οὔτε ἐσώθη-
μεν ἐκ τούτων, ἀλλὰ τὸ πᾶν ἡ ἀγαθότης
αὐτοῦ ἐποίησε), but according to (after
the measure of, in pursuance of, after the
promptings of : see Ellic.'s note) His compassion He saved us (this ἔσωσεν must be
referred back to the definite objective act
of God in Redemption, which has been
above mentioned. On the part of God,
that act is one—in the application of it to
individuals, it is composed of many and
successive acts. But this ἔσωσεν, being
contemporaneous with ὅτε ἐπεφάνη above,
cannot apply, as De Wette, to our individual salvation alone. At the same time,
standing as it does in a transitional position, between God's objective act and the
subjective individual application of it, it no
doubt looks forward as well as backward—
to individual realization of salvation, as well
as to the divine completion of it once for
all in Christ. Calvin, h. l., refers the completeness of our salvation rather to God's
looking on it as subjectively accomplished
in us : " De fide loquitur, et nos jam salutem adeptos esse docet. Ergo utcunque
peccato impliciti corpus mortis circumfera-
mus, certi tamen de salute nostra sumus,
si modo fide insiti simus in Christum, secundum illud (Joh. v. 24) : 'Qui credit in
filium Dei, transivit de morte in vitam.'
Paulo post tamen, fidei nomine interposito
nos re ipsa nondum adeptos esse ostendit,
quod Christus morte sua præstitit. Unde
sequitur, ex parte Dei salutem nostram
impletam esse, cujus fruitio in finem usque
militiæ differtur." The ἡμᾶς here is not
all mankind, which would be inconsistent
with what follows,—nor all Christians,
however true that would be,—but the
same as are indicated by καὶ ἡμεῖς above,
—the particular Christians in the Apostle's
view as he was writing—Titus and his
Cretan converts, and himself) by means
of the laver (not 'washing,' as E. V.: see
the Lexx. : but always a vessel, or pool in
which washing takes place. Here, the
baptismal font : see on Eph. v. 26) of re-

generation (first, let us treat of παλιγγενεσία. It occurs only in ref. Matt., and
there in an objective sense, whereas here
it is evidently subjective. There, it is
the great second birth of heaven and earth
in the latter days : here, the second birth
of the individual man. Though not occurring elsewhere in this sense, it has its
cognate expressions, — e. g. ἀναγεννάω,
1 Pet. i. 3, 23 : γεννηθῆναι ἄνωθεν, John
iii. 3 &c. Then, of the genitive. The
font is the 'laver of regeneration,' because it is the vessel consecrated to the
use of that Sacrament whereby, in its
completeness as a Sacrament (see below),
the new life unto God is conveyed. And
inasmuch as it is in that font, and when
we are in it, that the first breath of that
life is drawn, it is the laver of,—belonging
to, pertaining to, setting forth,—regeneration.   Observe, there is here no
figure : the words are literal : Baptism is
taken as in all its completion,—the outward
visible sign accompanied by the inward spiritual grace ; and as thus complete, it not
only represents, but is, the new birth. Cf.
Calvin : " Solent Apostoli a Sacramentis
ducere argumentum, ut rem illic signifi-
catam probent, quia principium illud valere debet inter pios, Deum non inanibus
nobiscum figuris ludere, sed virtute sua
intus præstare quod externo signo demon-
strat. Quare Baptismus congruenter et
vere lavacrum regenerationis dicitur. Vim
et usum Sacramentorum recte is tenebit
qui rem et siguum ita connectet, ut signum non faciat inane aut inefficax : neque
tamen ejus ornandi causa Spiritui sancto
detrahat quod suum est." The font then,
the laver of regeneration, representing the
external portion of the Sacrament, and
pledging the internal ;—that inward and
spiritual grace, necessary to the completion of the Sacrament and its regenerating
power, is not, as too often, left to follow
as a matter of course, and thus baptismal
regeneration rendered a mere formal and
unmeaning thing, 'ex opere operato,'—
but is distinctly stated in the following
words) and (understand διά again : so
Thdrt. apparently,—Bengel ('duæ res com-
memorantur : lavacrum regenertionis,

μᾱτος ἁγίου 6 e οὗ f ἐξέχεεν ἐφ᾽ ἡμᾶς g πλουσίως, διὰ e attr., Eph. i.
6 reff.
Ἰησοῦ Χριστοῦ τοῦ h σωτῆρος ἡμῶν, 7 ἵνα i δικαιωθέντες f = Acts ii. 17,
18 (from Joel
ii. 28, 29), 33.
τῇ ἐκείνου k χάριτι l κληρονόμοι γενήθωμεν κατ᾽ m ἐλπίδα x. 45. Jer.
xiv. 16.

g Col. iii. 16. 1 Tim. vi. 17. 2 Pet. i. 11 only †.   h ch. i. 4 reff.   i — Acts xiii. 39 (Paul). Rom.
ii. 13 al. Paul passim. elsw., Luke xviii. 14. James ii. 21, 24, 25 only. Ps. cxlii. 2.   k = Rom.
xi. 6 al.   l = Rom. iv. 13, 14. viii. 17. Gal. iv. 7. James ii 5.   m ch. i. 2 reff.

6. for οὖ, ὃ D¹ lect-17.   [for σωτηρος, κυριου P 31.]
7. δικαιωθεντος(sic) א‎.   rec (for γενηθωμεν) γενωμεθα, with D³KLא³ rel Cyr-
jer : txt ACD¹F[P]א¹ (o) 17 Chr Ath.

quæ baptismi in Christum periphrasis,— et renovatio Spiritus sancti'), al. On the other hand, most Commentators (see Ellic. here) take ἀνακαινώσεως as a second gen. after λουτροῦ : and for the purpose of making this clearer, the τοῦ seems to have been inserted before λουτροῦ (see var. readd.). The great formal objection to this is, the destruction of the balance of the sentence, in which παλιγγενεσίας would be one gen., and ἀνακαινώσεως πνεύματος ἁγίου the other. The far greater contextual objection is, that thus the whole from παλ. to ἁγίου would be included under λουτροῦ, and baptism made not only the seal of the new birth, but the sacrament of progressive sanctification) the renewal (ἀνακαίνωσις, see reff., is used of the gradual renewal of heart and life in the image of God, following upon the new birth, and without which the birth is a mere abortion, not leading on to vitality and action. It is here treated as potentially involved in God's act ἔσωσεν. We must not, as Huther, al., for the sake of making it contemporaneous with the λουτρόν, give it another and untenable meaning, that of mere incipient spiritual life) of (brought about by ; genitive of the efficient cause) the Holy Spirit (who alone can renew unto life in progressive sanctification. So that, as in 1 Pet. iii. 21, it is not the mere outward act or fact of baptism to which we attach such high and glorious epithets, but that complete baptism by water and the Holy Ghost, whereof the first cleansing by water is indeed the ordinary sign and seal, but whereof the glorious indwelling Spirit of God is the only efficient cause and continuous agent. 'BAPTISMAL REGENERATION' is the distinguishing doctrine of the new covenant (Matt. iii. 11) : but let us take care that we know and bear in mind what ' baptism ' means : not the mere ecclesiastical act, not the mere fact of reception by that act among God's professing people, but that, completed by the divine act, manifested by the operation of the Holy Ghost in the heart and through the life),   6.]

which (attr. ; not = ἐξ οὗ, as Heydenr. οὗ, viz. the Holy Spirit, not λουτροῦ, as even De W. confesses, who yet maintains the dependence of both genitives on λουτροῦ) He poured out (reff.) on us richly (again, it is mere waste of time to debate whether this pouring out be the one general one at Pentecost, or that in the heart of each individual believer : the one was God's objective act once for all, in which all its subjective exemplifications and applications were potentially enwrapped) through (as its channel and medium, He having purchased it for us, and made the pouring out possible, in and by His own blessed Sacrifice in our nature) Jesus Christ our Saviour (which title was used of the Father above : of Him,—ultimately : of our Lord, immediately : " Pater nostræ salutis primus auctor, Christus vero opifex, et quasi artifex," as Justiniani in Ellicott, whose own remarks are well worth consulting),
7.] in order that (this ἵνα, in the form of the sentence, may express the aim either of ἔσωσεν (Beng., De W., Huther, Ellic.) or of ἐξέχεεν : more naturally, I believe, of the latter (Wiesinger) : and for these reasons, that ἔσωσεν seeming to have its full pregnant meaning as it stands, (1) does not require any further statement of aim and purpose : but ἐξέχεεν being a mere word of action, is more properly followed by a statement of a reason why the pouring out took place : and (2) that this statement of aim and purpose, if it applies to ἔσωσεν, has been already anticipated, if ἔσωσεν be understood as including what is generally known as σωτηρία. Theologically, this statement of purpose is exact : the effusion of the Spirit has for its purpose the conviction of sin and manifestation of the righteousness of Christ, out of which two spring justifying faith) having been justified (the aor. part. here (expressed in English by ' having been ') is not contemporaneous with the aor. subj. below. Ordinarily this would be so : but the theological consideration of the place of justification in the Christian life, illustrated by such passages as Rom.

n 1 Tim i. 15 reff.
o = 1 Tim. ii. 8. v. 14.
p 1 Tim. i. 7 only †.
q here only.
Prov. xxxi. 21.
t Acts xvi. 34.

m ζωῆς ^mαἰωνίου. ^{8 n}Πιστὸς ὁ λόγος, καὶ περὶ τούτων ACDFK
^oβούλομαί σε ^p διαβεβαιοῦσθαι, ἵνα ^q φροντίζωσιν ^rκαλῶν
^r ἔργων ^s προΐστασθαι οἱ ^tπεπιστευκότες ^tθεῷ. ταῦτά ἐστιν

LPℵ a b
c d e f g
h k l m n
o 17. 47

r 1 Tim. iii. 1 reff.　　s Rom. xii. 8. 1 Tim. iii. 4 al. P.　Prov. xxvi. 17. = ver. 14 only.
Gal. iii. 6 (from Gen. xv. 6). 1 John v. 10.

8. for πιστος, αληθης 67². 　　 rec ins τω bef θεω, with rel: om ACDFKL[P]ℵ
Thdrt Damasc Thl. (17 def.)

v. 1, δικαιωθέντες οὖν ἐκ πίστεως εἰρήνην ἔχωμεν πρὸς τ. θεόν, κ.τ.λ., seems to determine here the aor. part. to be antecedent to γενήθωμεν) **by His** (ἐκείνου, referring to the more remote subject, must be used here not of our Lord, who has just been mentioned, but of the Father: and so, usually, χάρις θεοῦ (Acts xi. 23; xx. 24, 32: Rom. v. 15: 1 Cor. i. 4, &c.) is the efficient cause of our justification in Christ) **grace, we might be made** (perhaps passive, see however on 1 Thess. i. 5) **heirs** (see especially Gal. iii. 29) **according to** (in pursuance of, consistently with, so that the inheritance does not disappoint, but fully accomplishes and satisfies the hope; not '*through*' (?) as Conyb., referring to Rom. viii. 24, 25, where, however, the thought is entirely different) **the hope of eternal life** (I cannot consent, although considerable scholars (e. g. De W., Ellic.) have maintained the view, to join the gen. ζωῆς with κληρονόμοι, in the presence of the expression, in this very Epistle, ἐπ' ἐλπίδι ζωῆς αἰωνίου, ch. i. 2. The objection brought against joining ἐλπίδα with ζωῆς here is that thus κληρονόμοι would stand alone. But it *does* thus stand alone in every place where St. Paul uses it in the spiritual sense; viz. Rom. iv. 14; viii. 17 bis (θεοῦ is a wholly different genitive): Gal. iii. 29; iv. 1, 7: and therefore why not here? Chrys.'s two renderings, both of which Huther quotes for his view, will suit mine just as well: κατ' ἐλπίδα, τουτέστι, καθὼς ἠλπίσαμεν, οὕτως ἀπολαύσομεν, ἢ ὅτι ἤδη καὶ κληρονόμοι ἐστέ. The former is the one to which I have inclined: the latter would mean, "we might be heirs, according to the hope"—i. e. in proportion as we have the hope, realize our heirship—"of eternal life"). **8—11.**]
General rules for Titus. **8.**] **Faithful is the saying** (reff.: viz. the saying which has just been uttered, ὅτε ἡ χρηστότης κ.τ.λ. This sentence alone, of those which have gone before, has the solemn and somewhat rhythmical character belonging for the most part to the "faithful sayings" of the apostolic church quoted in these Epistles), **and concerning these**

things (the things which have just been dwelt on; see above) **I would have thee positively affirm** ('confirmare,' Vulg.; 'asseverare,' Beza: cf. Polyb. xii. 12. 6, διοριζόμενος καὶ διαβεβαιούμενος περὶ τούτων. The διά implies persistence and thoroughness in the affirmation), **in order that** (not, 'that,' implying the *purport* of that which he is διαβεβαιοῦσθαι, nor is what follows the πιστὸς λόγος, as would appear in the E. V.: what follows is to be the result of thorough affirmation of vv. 4—7) **they who have believed** (have been brought to belief and endure in it: the present would perhaps express the sense, but the perfect is to be preferred, inasmuch as πιστεύειν is often used of the hour and act of commencing belief: cf. Acts xix. 2: Rom. xiii. 11) **God** (trusted God, learned to credit what God says: not to be confounded with πιστ. εἰς, John xiv. 1, 1 Pet. i. 8, 21—or πιστ. ἐν, Mark i. 15 (not used of God), or πιστ. ἐπί, Rom. iv. 5. There appears no reason for supposing with De W. that these words describe merely the Gentile Christians) **may take care to** (φροντίζειν with an inf. is not the ordinary construction: it commonly has ὅπως, ἵνα, ὡς, εἰ, μή, or a relative clause. We have an instance in Plut. Fab. Max. c. 12, τὰ πραττόμενα γινώσκειν ἐφρόντιζεν. See Palm and Rost, sub voce) **practise** (a workman presides over, is master and conductor of, his work: and thus the transition in προΐστασθαι from presiding over to conducting and practising a business was very easy. Thus we have, tracing the progress of this transition, οὗτοι μάλιστα προειστήκεισαν τῆς μεταβολῆς, Thuc. viii. 75: πῶς οὐ φανερὸν ὅτι προστάντες τοῦ πράγματος τὰ γνωσθένθ' ὑφ' ὑμῶν ἀποστερῆσαί με ζητοῦσιν, Demosth. 869, 2: Ἀσπασία οὐ κοσμίου προεστῶσα ἐργασίας, Plut. Pericl. 24: τέχνης προΐστασθαι,—ᾧ τοῖσιν ἐχθροῖς.... προϋστήτην φόνου, Soph. El. 968: χειρὶ βιαίᾳ προστῆναι τοῦ πανουργήματος, Synes. Ep. 67, p. 211 d. See Palm and Rost, sub voce) **good works: these things** (viz. same as τούτων before, the great truths of vv. 4 —7, this doctrine; not, as Thl., ἡ φροντὶς

καλὰ καὶ ᵘὠφέλιμα τοῖς ἀνθρώποις. ⁹ ᵛμωρὰς δὲ ᵛζητή-
σεις καὶ ʷγενεαλογίας καὶ ˣἔρεις καὶ ʸμάχας ᶻνομικὰς
ᵃπερὶίστασο· εἰσὶν γὰρ ᵇἀνωφελεῖς καὶ ᶜμάταιοι. ¹⁰ ᵈαἱρε-
τικὸν ἄνθρωπον μετὰ μίαν καὶ δευτέραν ᵉνουθεσίαν ᶠπαρ-
αιτοῦ, ¹¹ εἰδὼς ὅτι ᵍἐξέστραπται ʰὁ τοιοῦτος, καὶ ἁμαρτάνει ὢν ⁱαὐτοκατάκριτος.

¹²Ὅταν πέμψω Ἀρτεμᾶν πρός σε ἢ Τυχικόν, ᵏσπού-
δασον ἐλθεῖν πρός με εἰς Νικόπολιν· ἐκεῖ γὰρ ˡκέκρικα
H Zηναν ᵐπαραχειμάσαι. ¹³ Ζηνᾶν τὸν ⁿνομικὸν καὶ Ἀπολλὼ

ÄCDFH
KLPℵa
bcdef
ghklm
n o17.47

only †.   a = 2 Tim. ii. 16 (John xi. 42. Acts xxv. 7) only ‡.
only. Prov. xxviii. 3.   Jer. ii. 8.   c Acts xiv. 15.   1 Cor. iii. 20 (from Ps. xciii. 11). xv.
17.   James i. 26.   1 Pet. i. 18 only.   d here only †.   e Eph. vi. 4 reff.   f = 1 Tim.
iv. 7 reff.   g here only.   Deut. xxxii. 20. see 1 Tim. i. 6 reff.   h Paul, 1 Cor. v.
5.   2 Cor. ii. 6, 7. xii. 2, &c.   i here only †.   k 2 Tim. ii. 15 reff.   l = Acts
xx. 16 (of Paul).   1 Cor. v. 3. vii. 37 al.   2 Macc. xi. 25.   m Acts xxvii. 12. xxviii. 11.   1 Cor. xvi.
6 only †.   n ver. 9 reff.

rec ins τα bef καλα, with D³[P] rel Thdrt: om ACD¹FKLℵ m Chr Damasc. (17 def.)
9. for γενεαλ., λογομαχιας F.   for ερεις, εριν D¹Fℵ¹. [17 def.]
10. νουθεσιαν bef και δευτεραν (DF) syr Chr Thdrt₁ : txt ACKL[P]ℵ rel vulg(and
F-lat) Eus Ath. (17 def.)—for και, ή F.—for δευτεραν, δυο D¹ copt Iren-int₁ Jer₁
(remarks, in mss. latt. legi Post unam et alteram corrept.).
[11. εξεστρεπται AF.   12. om εις F.   for εκει, και P.]
13. απολλωνα F : απολλων D²H¹[ℵ].

καὶ ἡ προστασία τῶν καλῶν ἔργων, ἡ αὐτὰ τὰ καλὰ ἔργα, which would be a tautology: see 1 Tim. ii. 3) are good and profitable for men.   **9.**] Connexion: —maintain these great truths, but foolish questionings (ref. and note), and genealogies (ref. and note, and ch. i. 14, note), and strifes (the result of the genealogies, as in 1 Tim. i. 4) and contentions about the law (see again 1 Tim. i. 7. The subject of contention would be the justification, or not, of certain commandments of men, out of the law: or perhaps the mystical meaning of the various portions of the law, as affecting these genealogies) avoid (stand aloof from, see 2 Tim. ii. 16, note): for they are unprofitable and vain ("ματ. is here and James i. 26, as in Attic Greek, of two terminations: the fem. occurs 1 Cor. xv. 17: 1 Pet. i. 18." Ellicott).   **10.**] An heretical man (one who founds or belongs to an αἵρεσις—a self-chosen and divergent form of religious belief or practice. When St. Paul wrote 1 Cor., these forms had already begun to assume consistency and to threaten danger: see 1 Cor. xi. 19. We meet with them also in Gal. v. 20, both times as αἱρέσεις, divisions gathering round forms of individual self-will. But by this time, they had become so definite and established, as to have their acknowledged adherents, their αἱρετικοί. See also 2 Pet. ii. 1. For a history of the subsequent usage and meanings of the word, see Suicer, vol. i. pp. 119 ff. "It should be observed," says Conyb., "that these early heretics united moral depravity with erroneous teaching: their works bore witness against their doctrine"), after one and a second admonition (reff. and note on ref. Eph.), decline (intercourse with: ref. and note: there is no precept concerning excommunication, as the middle παραιτοῦ shews: it was to be a subjective act), knowing that such an one (a thoroughly Pauline expression: see reff.) is thoroughly perverted (ref. Deut.: and compare 1 Tim. i. 6; v. 15: 2 Tim. iv. 4), and is a sinner (is living in sin: the present gives the force of habit), being (at the same time) self-condemned (cf. 1 Tim. iv. 2, note, —with his own conscience branded with the foul mark of depravity: see Conyb. above).

12—14.] VARIOUS DIRECTIONS. **12.**] Whenever I shall have sent (πέμψω, not fut. ind. but aor. subj.) Artemas (not elsewhere named: tradition makes him afterwards bishop of Lystra) to thee, or Tychicus (see Eph. vi. 21, note: Col. iv. 7), hasten (make it thine earnest care) to come to me to Nicopolis (on the question which of the three cities of this name is here meant, see Prolegg. to Pastoral Epistles, § ii. 30, note): for there I have determined to spend the winter.   Forward on their journey ((see below) the word here has the sense of 'enable to proceed forward,' viz. by furnishing with neces-

[o] σπουδαίως [p] πρόπεμψον, ἵνα μηδὲν αὐτοῖς [q] λείπῃ.
14 [r] μανθανέτωσαν δὲ καὶ οἱ [s] ἡμέτεροι [t] καλῶν [t] ἔργων
[t] προΐστασθαι [u] εἰς τὰς [vw] ἀναγκαίας [wx] χρείας, ἵνα μὴ ὦσιν
[y] ἄκαρποι. 15 Ἀσπάζονταί σε οἱ μετʼ ἐμοῦ πάντες.
ἄσπασαι τοὺς [z] φιλοῦντας ἡμᾶς [a] ἐν πίστει. ἡ [b] χάρις μετὰ
πάντων ὑμῶν.

ACDFH KLPℵ a b c d e f g h k l m n o 17. 47

ΠΡΟΣ ΤΙΤΟΝ.

o Luke vii. 4 only +. Wisd. ii. 6 only. (-ος, 2 Tim. i. 17.) p Acts xv. 3. xx. 38. xxi. 5. Rom. xv. 24. L.P., exc. 3 John 6 +. 1 Macc. xii. 4. Jos. Antt. xx. 2. 5. q ch. i. 5 reff. r = and constr., 1 Tim. v. 4. Phil. iv. 11. s = here only. t ver. 8. u = Phil. iv. 16. v = 1 Cor. xii. 22. Phil. i. 24 al.+ Wisd. xvi. 3. w Demosth. p. 668 end. x Phil. iv. 16 reff. plur., Acts xx. 34. Rom. xii. 13. Sir. xxxviii. 1. y Paul, 1 Cor. xiv. 14. Eph. v. 11 (reff.) only. = 2 Pet. i. 8. z Paul, 1 Cor. xvi. 22 only. Matt. x. 37 al. fr. a 1 Tim. i. 2 reff. b Col. iv. 18 reff.

for σπουδ., ταχεως F. λιπη D[1][ℵ] b g[2] m [17. 47] Thdrt-ed.
15. for ασπασαι, ασπασασθε A. aft η χαρις ins του κυριου D: τ. θεου F [vulg (not demid)] Ambrst Pel. rec at end ins αμην, with D[3]FHKL[P]ℵ[3] rel [vulg syrr copt]: om ACD[1]ℵ[1] 17 fuld æth-rom [arm] Ambrst Jer Pel.

Subscription: rec προς τιτον της κρητων εκκλησιας πρωτον επισκοπον χειροτονηθεντα εγραφη απο νικοπολεως της μακεδονιας, similarly H[with a long addition]KL rel syr: no subscr in k l m: πρ. τιτ. εγραφη απο νικοπολεως A: [πρ. τιτ. εγραφη απο .... στιχων .. P:] txt C 17, and D(addg επληρωθη) F(prefg ετελεσθη επιστολη) ℵ(adding στιχων ϟϛ).

saries for the journey: so in ref. 3 John) **with zeal Zenas the lawyer** (Ζηνᾶς = Ζηνόδωρος. Probably a Jewish scribe or jurist (Matt. xxii. 35, note) who had been converted, and to whom the name of his former occupation still adhered, as in the case of Ματθαῖος ὁ τελώνης. Hippolytus and Dorotheus number him among the seventy disciples, and make him to have been subsequently bishop of Diospolis. There is an apocryphal 'Acts of Titus' bearing his name. Winer, Realw.) and **Apollos** (see on Acts xviii. 24: 1 Cor. i. 12; xvi. 12), **that nothing may be wanting to them.** 14.] **Moreover** (connexion of δὲ καί: the contrast in the δέ is, 'and I will not that thou only shouldest thus forward them, though I use the singular number; *but* see that the other brethren *also* join with thee in contributing to their outfit'), **let also our people** (our fellow-believers who are with thee) **learn to practise** (see note, ver. 8) **good works, contributions to** (εἰς, for the supply of) **the necessary wants which arise** (such is the force of **τάς**: such wants as from time to time are presented before Christians, requiring relief in the course of their Father's work in life), **that they may not be unfruitful** (implying, that in the supply by us of such ἀναγκαῖαι χρεῖαι, our ordinary opportunities are to be found of bearing fruit to God's praise).

15.] Salutations: greetings: Apostolic benedictions. **All that are with me salute thee. Salute those that love us in the faith** (not '*in faith:*' see note, 1 Tim. i. 2. This form of salutation, so different from any occurring in St. Paul's other Epistles, is again [see on ch. i. 1] a strong corroboration of genuineness. An apocryphal imitator would not have missed the Apostle's regular formulæ of salutation). **God's** (ἡ) **grace be with all of you** (of the Cretan churches. It does not follow *from this* that the letter was to be imparted to them: but in the course of things it naturally would be thus imparted by Titus). On the subscription in the rec., making our Epistle date from Nicopolis, see in Prolegg. § ii. 30 ff.

ΠΡΟΣ ΦΙΛΗΜΟΝΑ.

<table>
<tr><td>ADFKL
Pℵ a b c
d e f g h
k l m n o
17. 47</td><td>¹ Παῦλος ^a δέσμιος ^b χριστοῦ Ἰησοῦ καὶ Τιμόθεος ὁ
ἀδελφὸς Φιλήμονι τῷ ^c ἀγαπητῷ καὶ ^d συνεργῷ ἡμῶν
² καὶ Ἀπφίᾳ τῇ ἀδελφῇ καὶ Ἀρχίππῳ τῷ ^e συνστρα-</td><td>^a Acts xxiii. 18
(of Paul).
Eph. iii. 1.
iv. 1. 2 Tim.
i. 8. ver. 9.
^b gen., Matt.
xxv. 34. John</td></tr>
</table>

vi. 45.   Winer, edn 6, § 30. 2.   c Acts xv. 25.   Rmo. i. 7. xvi. 5, 8 al.
d ver. 24.   Phil. ii. 25.   e Phil. ii. 25 only †.   Xen. Anab. i. 2. 26.

TITLE. rec παυλου του αποστολου η προς φιλημονα επιστολη : παυλου (pref του αγ. αποστ. L al) επιστ. πρ. φιλ. KL[P]: παυλος επιστελλει ταδε βεβαια φιλημονι πιστω f: txt Aℵ h m n o 17 [47], and (prefg αρχεται) DF.

CHAP. I. 1. for δεσμ., αποστολος D¹.   ιησ. bef χρ. D¹L a d f h k [am(with tol)] syrr arm Chr Thl Thdrt Damasc Ambr Cassiod.   [om ὁ D¹F, ον G.]   aft αγαπητω ins αδελφω D¹ Ambrst.

2. αφφια D¹ : αμφια F [47. (A def.)]   rec (for αδελφη) αγαπητη, with D³KL rel Syr syr(pref αδελφη w. ob) Thdor-mops_expr Chr Thdrt Damasc : txt AD¹F[P]ℵ 17 am(with tol harl¹) copt arm Hesych Jer. (*It seems much more prob that the transcriber shd have carelessly written αγαπητη again, than that αδ. shd have been substd to avoid repetn.*)   (συνστρατιωτη, so ADFℵ 17.)

Vv. 1–3.] ADDRESS AND GREET-ING.   1.] δέσμιος χ. Ἰ., prisoner of Christ Jesus, i. e. one whom He (or His cause) has placed in bonds: cf. τοῖς δεσμ. τοῦ εὐαγγελίου, ver. 13. He does not designate himself as ἀπόστολος, or the like, as writing familiarly, and not authoritatively. Τιμόθ.] see Pro-legg. to 1 Tim. § i. 10.   συνεργῷ] for construction, see Rom. xvi. 3, 9, 21. We cannot say when or how, but may well infer that it was at Colossæ, in build-ing up the church there, while the Apos-tle was at Ephesus : see Prolegg. to Col. § ii. 7.   ἡμῶν] Storr (cited in Koch) remarks, "In epistolarum inscriptione, quamvis pronomina et verba tertiæ per-sonæ usitatiora sint, interdum tamen etiam pronomina et verba primæ personæ ut ἡμῶν l. n., et ver. 2 (cf. 1 Tim. i. 1), ἡμῖν 2 Pet. i. 1: ἐμοί Gal. i. 2 et ἐλάβομεν

Rom. i. 5 (cf. Tit. i. 3) reperire licet. Cf. Cic. epp. ad diversos lib. iv. ep. 1, et lib. iii. ep. 2. Nempe verbum, quod ad omis-sum vocabulum χαίρειν intelligi debet, cum in tertia, tum in prima persona ac-cipi potest, ut in laudatis inscriptionibus latinis S. P. D. et L. D. legere licet . '(ego) M. T. C. et Cicero *meus* salutem plurimam *dicimus*,' et '(ego) M. T. C. Appio Pulchro, ut spero, censori, salutem *dico*:' cum legamus alias, v. c., lib. xvi. ep. 3, lib. xiv. ep. 14, *dicunt*, vel v. c., ep. 1–5, *dicit*." Ἀπφία is the Latin name Appia, also written Ἀππ., see Acts xxviii. 15: cf. Kühner, Gramm. § 44. She appears to have been the wife of Phi-lemon (Chrys., Thdrt.); certainly, as well as Archíppus, she must have belonged to his family, or they would hardly be thus specially addressed in a private letter con-cerning a family matter.   Ἀρχίππῳ]

f Col. iv. 15 reff.
g Rom. i. 8. 1 Cor. i. 4. Phil. i. 3. 1 Thess. i. 2. 2 Thess. i. 3. (2 Macc. i. 11.)
h Eph. i. 16 reff.
i Rom. i. 10. Eph. ι. 16. 1 Thess. i. 2 only. ἐπὶ τῶν δεήπ- νων, Diod. Sic. iv. 3.
k constr., Matt. xi. 2. Acts xxiii. 16. Gal. i. 13. Eph. i. 15. Col. i. 4.

τιώτῃ ἡμῶν, καὶ τῇ ᶠ κατ᾽ οἶκον σου ᶠ ἐκκλησίᾳ. ³ χάρις
ὑμῖν καὶ εἰρήνη ἀπὸ θεοῦ πατρὸς ἡμῶν καὶ κυρίου Ἰησοῦ
χριστοῦ·

⁴ ᵍ Εὐχαριστῶ τῷ ᵍ θεῷ μου πάντοτε ʰ μνείαν σου
ʰ ποιούμενος ⁱ ἐπὶ τῶν ⁱ προσευχῶν μου, ⁵ ᵏ ἀκούων ˡ σου τὴν
ˡ ἀγάπην καὶ τὴν ᵐⁿ πίστιν ἣν ᵐ ἔχεις ⁿ εἰς τὸν κύριον Ἰησοῦν καὶ εἰς πάντας τοὺς ᵒ ἁγίους, ⁶ ὅπως ἡ ᵖ κοινωνία
τῆς πίστεώς σου ᑫ ἐνεργὴς γένηται ʳ ἐν ˢ ἐπιγνώσει παντὸς

c... ACDFK LP℟ a b c d e f g h k l m n σ17. 47

l gen. subj., Phil. i. 9 reff.   m 1 Tim. i. 19 reff.
n = Col. ii. 5 reff. πρός, 1 Thess. i. 8.   o Eph. i. 1 reff.   p = Phil. ii. 1 (reff.).   q 1 Cor.
xvi. 9. Heb. iv. 12 only †.   Polyb. xi. 23. 2.   r = Phil. i. 9.   s = Eph. i. 17 reff.

3. om ημων ℵ¹.
5. πιστιν και την αγαπην (see Eph i. 15, Col i. 4, 1 Thess i. 3) D m 73. 116 [fuld¹]
Syr [æth] arm Ambrst.   rec for [1st] εις, προς (see note), with D³FKL[P]ℵ rel
syr G-lat(ad dominum . . . et in omnes) : txt ACD¹ 17 copt.   aft ιησ. ins χριστον
D¹ æth.
6. [ινα πως F.]   for κοινωνια, διακονια ℵ¹.   ins εργου bef αγαθου F b² c e g

Cf. Col. iv. 17.   συνστρατιώτῃ] see
reff. and 2 Tim. ii. 3.   He was perhaps
Philemon's *son* (so Michael., Olsh., al.):
or a family friend (ἕτερόν τινα ἴσως φίλον,
Chrys.: so Thl.): or the minister of the
family (ὁ δὲ Ἄρχιππος τὴν διδασκαλίαν
αὐτῶν ἐπεπίστευτο, Thdrt.): the former
hypothesis being perhaps the most probable, as the letter concerns a family
matter: but see on next clause. To what
grade in the ministry he belonged, it is
idle to enquire: nor does Col. iv. 17 furnish us with any data.   τῇ κατ᾽ οἶκ.
σ. ἐκκλ.] This appears to have consisted
not merely of the family itself, but of a
certain assembly of Christians who met in
the house of Philemon: see the same expression in Col. iv. 15, of Nymphas: and in
Rom. xvi. 3—5; 1 Cor. xvi. 19, of Aquila
and Prisca.   Meyer remarks the *tact* of
the Apostle in associating with Philemon
those connected with his *house*, but not
going *beyond* the limits of the house.
The former part is noticed also by Chrys.:
συμπαραλαμβάνει κ. ἕτερον (-ρους) μεθ᾽
ἑαυτοῦ ὥστε κἀκεῖνον ὑπὸ πολλῶν ἀξιού-
μενον μᾶλλον εἶξαι κ. δοῦναι τὴν χάριν.
4—7.] Recognition of the Christian character and usefulness of
Philemon.   4.] See Rom. i. 8:
1 Cor. i. 4. πάντοτε belongs to εὐχαριστῶ
(Eph. i. 16), not to μνείαν ποιούμενος.
The first part., ποιούμενος, expands εὐχαριστῶ,—the 2nd, ἀκούων, gives the ground
of the εὐχαριστία—for that I hear . . . .
5.] It is far better (with Thdrt.,
Grot., De W., all.) to take ἀγάπη and
πίστις as to be distributed between εἰς
τὸν κύριον Ἰησοῦν and εἰς πάντας τοὺς
ἁγίους, than, with Meyer, to insist on
the ἥν as a bar to this, and interpret

πίστις in the wider sense (?) of '*fidelity*,'
or with Ellic. to split up πίστις into spiritual faith towards the Lord, and practical faith towards the saints.   ἥν is
naturally in concord with the nearest
subst. The πρός of the rec. has perhaps
been a correction for reverence sake.
εἰς is '*towards*,' but more as contributing
to—'towards the behoof of:' whereas
πρός is simple direction: cf. ver. 6.
6.] ὅπως belongs, as usually constructed,
to the former clause, εὐχαριστῶ—προσευχῶν μου. The mixing of prayer and
thanksgiving in that clause does not exclude the idea of intercessory prayer, nor
does (as Meyer maintains) the subsequent
clause make against this: the ἀκούων
κ.τ.λ. was the reason why he ηὐχαρίστει
ἐπὶ τῶν προσευχῶν αὐτοῦ, and ὅπως
κ.τ.λ. the aim of his doing so. To join
ὅπως κ.τ.λ. with ἣν ἔχεις is flat in the
extreme, and perfectly inconceivable as a
piece of St. Paul's writing.   In order
that the communication of thy faith
(with others) may become effectual in
(as the element in which it works) the
thorough knowledge (entire appreciation
and experimental recognition (by us))
of every good thing (good gifts and
graces,—cf. Rom. vii. 18, the negation of
this in the carnal man) which is in us, to
(the glory of; connect with ἐνεργὴς γένηται) Christ [Jesus]. This seems the only
simple and unobjectionable rendering. To
understand ἡ κοιν. τῆς π. σου, 'fides tua
quam communem nobiscum habes,' as
Bengel (and indeed Chrys., Thl., al.), is
very objectionable: to join εἰς χρ. ['Ιησ.]
with πίστεως (Calv., Est., al.) still more
so: to render ἐπίγνωσις passively, '*recognition by others*' ('παθητικῶς sumitur

ἀγαθοῦ τοῦ ἐν ἡμῖν ᵗεἰς χριστὸν ['Ιησοῦν]. ⁷ ᵘχαρὰν
γὰρ πολλὴν ᵘἔσχον καὶ ᵛπαράκλησιν ἐπὶ τῇ ἀγάπῃ ʷσου,
ὅτι τὰ ˣʸσπλάγχνα τῶν ᶻἁγίων ʸᵃἀναπέπαυται διὰ
σοῦ, ἀδελφέ. ⁸ διὸ πολλὴν ἐν χριστῷ ᵇπαρρησίαν ᶜἔχων
ᵈἐπιτάσσειν σοι τὸ ᵉἀνῆκον, ⁹ διὰ τὴν ἀγάπην μᾶλλον
ᶠπαρακαλῶ. ᵍΤοιοῦτος ὤν, ᵍὡς Παῦλος ʰπρεσβύτης
νυνὶ δὲ καὶ ⁱδέσμιος ⁱχριστοῦ 'Ιησοῦ, ¹⁰ ᶠπαρακαλῶ σε
περὶ τοῦ ἐμοῦ ᵏτέκνου, ὃν ¹ἐγέννησα ἐν τοῖς ᵐδεσμοῖς,

t w. ἐνεργέω, Gal. ii. 8 bis.
u 3 John 4.
v = 2 Thess. ii. 6 reff.
w gen. subj., ver. 5.
x = vv. 12, 20. 2 Cor. vi. 12.
vii. 15. Phil. i. 8. Prov. xii. 20.
y ver. 20.
z ver. 5.
a = Matt. xi. 28. 1 Cor. xvi. 18.
2 Cor. vii. 13. 1 Chron.

xxii. 9, 18.   b Eph. iii. 12 reff.   c l Tim. iii. 13.   d Mark 1. 27. vi.
27, 39. ix. 25. Luke iv. 36. viii. 25, 31. xiv. 22. Acts xxiii. 2 only. Esth. i. 8. w. acc., here only.
e Eph. v. 4. Col. iii. 18 only†. 1 Macc. xi. 35 al.   f = Eph. iv. l reff.   g not as Acts xxvi. 29.
h Luke i. 18. Tit. ii. 2 only. Job xv. 10 al.   i ver. 1.   k = 1 Tim, i. 2 reff.   l = 1 Cor.
iv. 15.   m Phil. i. 7 reff.

l² vulg(with fuld, agst am F-lat) Pel.   om του AC 17.   rec υμιν (*from a
tendency, Meyer thinks, in transcribers of epp to use the 2nd person*), with F[P]א
rel syrr copt Thl Jer: om εν ημ. am(with demid): txt ACDKL a b d e f g k l n fuld
(with tol harl² mar² hal) syr-mg arm Chr Thdrt Œc Pel-comm Ambrst.   om ιησ.
ACא¹ 17 copt æth-rom Ambrst Jer: ins DFKL[P]א³ rel latt [syr arm] gr-lat-ff (bet
χρ., Syr).
  7. Steph χαριν, with KL[P] rel Chr-ms Thdrt Damasc Thl(χαριν, τουτεστι χαραν:
simly Hesych and Erotianus: see also 2 Cor i. 15): txt ACDFא a o 17 [47] vss Chr
[Orig-int,] lat-ff.   rec (for πολλην εσχον) εχομεν πολλην, with D³KL rel syrr
Chr Damasc Thl Œc: πολλην εσχομεν D¹ Jer: πολλην εχομεν m [47]: πολλην εχω
a: txt ACF[P]א 17 vulg copt arm Thdrt Ambrst Pel.   om και παρακλησιν א.
  for επι, εν D¹[L] 145.
  8. πολλ. παρρ. εχω εν χριστω ιησ. D¹ vulg Jer.
  9. for αγαπην, αναγκην A.   for νυνι, νυν A 67². 73 Thl.   rec ιησ. bef χρ.,
with D³FKL rel [vulg syrr arm]: om ιησ. D¹: txt AC[P]א 17 copt æth Ambr
Ambrst Jer.
  10. ins εγω bef εγεννησα A m 68 Chr₁: om CDFKL[P]א rel (εγω may, as Meyer,
have been omd from similarity of εγω εγεν., but εγε- may also have occasioned its
insertion).   rec aft δεσμοις ins μου, with CD³KL[P]א³ rel vss gr-ff: om AD¹Fא¹
17 latt Ambr Ambrst Jer Pel.

habetque innotescendi significationem,'
Grot.: so Erasm., Beza, Est., all.) worst
of all. The interpretation given above,
I find in the main to be that of De W.,
Meyer, and Koch. 7.] If we read
χάριν with the rec., it will be best interpreted by 2 Cor. i. 15, as a benefit,—an
outpouring of the divine χάρις—not χάρ.
ἔχειν in the sense of 1 Tim. i. 12: 2 Tim.
i. 3, *to give thanks,* for then it seems
always to be followed by a dative. The
γάρ gives a reason for the prayer of ver. 6
as De W., not, as Meyer, for the thanksgiving of ver. 4: see above.   ὅτι
κ.τ.λ.] further specification of τῇ ἀγάπῃ
σου, whose work consisted in ministering
to the various wants and afflictions of the
saints at Colossæ. ἀδελφέ is skilfully
placed last, as introducing the request
which follows.
8—21.] PETITION FOR THE FAVOUR-
ABLE RECEPTION OF ONESIMUS.
8.] διό relates to διὰ τ. ἀγάπ. below, and
refers back to the last verse; it is not to
be joined to the participial clause as Chrys.,
al.: it was not on account of ver. 7 that

St. Paul had confidence to command him,
but that he preferred beseeching him.
ἐν χριστῷ as usual, the element in which
the παρρησία found place.   τὸ ἀνῆκον, a delicate hint, that the reception of
Onesimus was to be classed under this category—that which is fitting (reff.).
9. τὴν ἀγάπην] is not to be restricted to
'this thy love' (of ver. 7: so Calv., al.),
or 'our mutual love' (Grot., al.), but is
quite general—'that Christian love, of
which thou shewest so bright an example:'
ver. 7.   τοιοῦτος ὤν] reason for the
μᾶλλον—'I prefer this way, as the more
efficacious, being such an one, &c.' The
'cum sis talis' of the Vulgate is evidently
a mistake. I believe Meyer is right in
maintaining that τοιοῦτος cannot be taken
as preparatory to ὡς, 'such an one, as . . .'
as in E. V., and commonly. I have therefore punctuated accordingly, as has Ellic.
The rendering will be: Being such an
one (as declared in διὸ . . . . παρακαλῶ,)—
as (1) Paul the aged and (2) now a prisoner also of Christ Jesus (*two* points
are made, and not *three* as Chrys., all.—

n = Gal. i. 13 reff.
o here only. Hos. viii. 8.
p 2 Tim. ii. 21.
q = Luke xxiii. 11 (7, 15.
Acts xxv. 21) only †.
r Matt. xxvii. 46. Mark vii. 12. Rom. vii. 18 al.
u = Luke iv. 42.
w gen., see ver. 1 reff.

Ὀνήσιμον, 11 τὸν ⁿ ποτέ σοι ᵒ ἄχρηστον, νυνὶ δὲ σοὶ
καὶ ἐμοὶ ᵖ εὔχρηστον, ὃν ᑫ ἀνέπεμψά σοι, 12 αὐτόν,
ʳ τουτέστι τὰ ἐμὰ ˢ σπλάγχνα, 13 ὃν ἐγὼ ἐβουλόμην ᵗ πρὸς
ἐμαυτὸν ᵘ κατέχειν, ἵνα ὑπὲρ σοῦ μοι ᵛ διακονῇ ἐν τοῖς
ᵐ δεσμοῖς τοῦ ᵂ εὐαγγελίου, 14 χωρὶς δὲ τῆς σῆς ˣ γνώμης

ACDFK LPℵ a b c d e f g h k l m n o 17. 47

s ver. 7. 　　t = Matt. xiii. 56. Mark ix. 19 a. Luke ix. 41. John i. 1. 1 Cor. xvi. 6, 7 al.
　Gen. xxiv. 56. xlii. 19. 　　v = Matt. xxvii. 55. Acts xix. 22. Rom. xv. 25. Heb. vi. 10.
　　　x = Acts xx. 3. 2 Macc. iv. 39.

11. ins και bef 2nd σοι Fℵ(ℵ³ marked it for erasure but removed the marks) b [17. 47] vulg Syr [æth].　　for ανεπ., επεμψα D d 17. 91 [arm] Chr.　　rec om 3rd σοι, with D³FKL[P]ℵ³ rel am(with fuld) syr goth: ins ACD¹ℵ¹ 17 Syr copt [æth] arm Jer Pel, προς σε demid Chr Ambrst.

12. rec at beg ins συ δε (*see above*), with DFKL[P]ℵ³ rel vss: om ACℵ¹ 17 [æth].

　　rec at end ins προσλαβου (*corrn to supply the sense, which is completed in ver* 17: *cf varr of posn*), with CDKL[P]ℵ³ rel vulg [syrr goth æth]: also aft συ δε m 73. 116 copt: also aft αυτον G-lat arm Thdrt: om AFℵ¹ 17.

13. ηβουλ. ℵ.　　rec διακονη bef μοι (*transposn to avoid concurr of σου μοι*), with KL rel syrr copt [æth] Chr_{h.l.}: txt ACDF[P]ℵ 17 [47] latt goth [arm] Thdrt Thl Ambrst Jer Pel.

Παῦλος πρεσβύτης going together, and the fact of his being a prisoner, adding weight (καί). The fact of πρεσβύτης is interesting, as connected with the date of this Epistle and those to Eph. and Col.: see Prolegg. to Eph. § iv.), **I beseech thee,** &c.　　If we read ἐγώ before ἐγέννησα, the repetition of ἐμοῦ—ἐγώ will serve, as Meyer remarks, to mark more forcibly the character of his *own* child, and ἐν τοῖς δεσμοῖς gives more weight still to the entreaty. 'Ονήσιμον is not (with Erasm.-Schmid) to be treated as if it were a play on the name, ὃν ἐγένν. . . . . ὀνήσιμον, '*profitable to me:*' but simply to be regarded as an accusative by attraction.　　**11.**] Here there certainly appears to be a play on the name —'quondam .... parum suo nomini respondens,—nunc in diversum mutatus.' Erasm. (No play on χριστός (as Koch, al.) must be thought of, as too far-fetched, and because the datives σοί and ἐμοί fix the adjectives to their ordinary meanings.) He had been ἄχρηστος in having run away, and apparently (ver. 18) defrauded his master as well. Meyer quotes from Plato, Lys. p. 204 Β: φαῦλος κ. ἄχρηστος: and from ib. Rep. p. 411 Β: χρήσιμον ἐξ ἀχρήστου ἐποίησεν. On account of the σοὶ καὶ ἐμοί, εὔχρηστον must not be limited to the sense of outward profit, but extended to a spiritual meaning as well—profitable to me, as the fruit of my ministry,—to thee as a servant, and also as a Christian brother (ver. 16).　　**12.**] There does not appear to be any allusion to the fact of sonship in τὰ ἐμὰ σπλάγχνα, as Chrys., Thdrt. (ἐμός ἐστιν υἱός, ἐκ τῶν ἐμῶν γεγέννηται σπλάγχνων), al.: for thus the spiritual

similitude would be confused, being here introduced materially. But the expression more probably means, mine own heart— 'as dear to me as mine own heart.' Meyer compares the expressions in Plautus,— '*meum corculum,*' Cas. iv. 4. 14,—'meum mel, *meum cor,*' Pœn. i. 2. 154. Cf. also, ' Hic habitat tuus ille hospes, mea viscera, Thesbon,' Marius Victor, in Suicer, Thes. ii. 998, and examples of both meanings in Wetst., Suicer, and Koch.　　The construction (see var. readd.) is an anacoluthon: the Apostle goes off into the relative clause, and loses sight, as so often, of the construction with which he began: taking it up again at ver. 17.　　**13.**] ἐγώ, emphatic, I, for my part.　　ἐβουλόμην, nearly as ηὐχόμην, in Rom. ix. 3 (though in that place there certainly is, as Ellic. remarks, a more distinct reference to a suppressed conditional clause),—was wishing,—had a mind, = could have wished, in our idiom.　　ἠθέλησα, ver. 14, differs from ἐβουλόμην, (1) in that it means simply willed, as distinguished from the stronger wished, (2) in that it marks the time immediately preceding the return of Onesimus, whereas the imperfect spreads the wish over the period previous. I was (long) minded .... but (on considering) I was not willing.　　ὑπὲρ σοῦ] For, wert thou here, thou wouldst minister to me: I was minded therefore to retain him in thy place. διακονῇ, pres. subj. representing the ἐβουλόμην as a still continuing wish.　　ἐν τοῖς δεσμ. τοῦ εὐαγγελίου] explained well by Thdrt., ὀφείλεις μοι διακονίαν ὡς μαθητὴς διδασκάλῳ, κ. διδασκάλῳ τὰ θεῖα κηρύττοντι: not without allusion also to the fetters which the

οὐδὲν ἠθέλησα ποιῆσαι, ἵνα μὴ [y] ὡς [z] κατὰ [z] ἀνάγκην [a] τὸ
ἀγαθόν σου ᾖ, ἀλλὰ κατὰ [b] ἑκούσιον· 15 [c] τάχα γὰρ
διὰ τοῦτο [d] ἐχωρίσθη [e] πρὸς [e] ὥραν, ἵνα [f] αἰώνιον αὐτὸν [g] ἀπέχῃς, 16 οὐκέτι ὡς δοῦλον, ἀλλ' [h] ὑπὲρ δοῦλον,
[i] ἀδελφὸν [i] ἀγαπητόν, [k] μάλιστα ἐμοί, [l] πόσῳ δὲ [l] μᾶλλον
σοί, καὶ [m] ἐν [m] σαρκὶ καὶ [n] ἐν [n] κυρίῳ. 17 εἰ οὖν με [o] ἔχεις
[p] κοινωνόν, [q] προςλαβοῦ αὐτὸν ὡς ἐμέ. 18 εἰ δέ τι [r] ἠδί-
κησέν σε ἢ [s] ὀφείλει, τοῦτο ἐμοὶ [t] ἐλλόγα· 19 [u] ἐγὼ [u] Παῦλος

y = Rom. ix. 32 (see note). z here only (see note). ἐξ ἀν, 2 Cor. ix. 7. Heb. vii. 12. a Gal. vi. 10 reff. b here only. καθ' ἑκ., Num. xv. 3. see Thucyd. viii. 27. c Rom. v. 7 only †. Wisd. xiii. 6. xiv. 19 only. d absol., 1 Cor. vii. 11, 15 bis. e John v. 35. 2 Cor. vi. 8. Gal. ii. 5 only. see 1 Thess. ii. 17. f constr., Mark iv. 28. John viii. 7. Acts xii. 10 al. Ps. xiv. 2. Winer, edn. 6, § 54. 2. g = Matt. vi. 2. Phil. iv. 18. Gen. xliii. 23. h = Matt. x. 37. Acts xxvi. 13. i Eph. vi. 21. Col. iv. 7, 9. k 1 Tim. iv. 10 reff. l Rom. xi. 12, 24. Heb. ix. 14 al. m 1 Tim. iii. 16 reff. n = Rom. xvi. 2, &c. Phil. ii. 29. o = Phil. ii. 29 reff. p 1 Cor. x. 18, 20. 2 Cor. i. 7 al. Isa. i. 23. q = Acts xxviii. 2. Rom. xiv. 1, 3. Ps. xxvi. 10. lxxii. 24. r = Matt. xx. 13. 1 Cor. vi. 8. s = Matt. xviii. 28, &c. Luke xvi. 5, 7. Deut. xv. 2. t here only. -γεῖν, Rom. v. 13 only †. u Gal. v. 2 reff.

14. om 2nd κατα D latt Ambr Ambrst Jer_1 Pel. (κατ', 1st, DF [c m]; 2nd, F.)
[**15.** aft εχωρ. ins σου P.]
16. αλλα D¹א m 17.—om αλλ' υπερ δουλον (*homœotel*) F. om αδελφον א¹: αγαπητ. bef αδελφ. 174. [om δε P Syr.]
17. rec (for με) εμε, with K a f: txt [A]CDFL[P]א rel Chr Thdrt Damasc Thl Œc.
18. rec ελλογει, with D²·³KL(א³? but txt restored) rel: txt ACD¹F[P]א 17.

Gospel had laid on himself. **14.] But without thy decision** (= consent: so χωρὶς τῆς αὐτοῦ γνώμης, Polyb. iii. 21. 7; xxi. 8. 7: μετὰ τῆς τοῦ Δ. γνώμ., id. ii. 11. 5) **I was willing** (see above) **to do nothing** (general expression, but meant to apply only to the particular thing in hand; = 'nothing in the matter'), **that thy good** (service towards me: but not in this particular only: the expression is general—the particular case would serve as an *example* of it) **might be not as** (appearing as if it were: 'particula ὡς, substantivis, participiis, totisque enuntiationibus præposita, rei veritate sublata aliquid opinione, errore, simulatione niti declarat.' Fritz. on Romans, ii. p. 360) **of** (after the fashion of, according to: ᾔδει ὅτι πάντες κατ' ἀνάγκην αὐτῷ κοινωνήσουσι τῶν πραγμάτων, Polyb. iii. 67. 5) **necessity, but of free will. 15.] τάχα** is delicately said, to conciliate Philemon: so Chrys., καλῶς τὸ **τάχα**, ἵνα εἴξῃ ὁ δεσπότης· ἐπειδὴ γὰρ ἀπὸ αὐθαδείας γέγονεν ἡ φυγὴ κ. διεστραμμένης διανοίας, κ. οὐκ ἀπὸ προαιρέσεως, λέγει **τάχα**. And Jerome says, 'occulta sunt quippe judicia Dei, et temerarium est quasi de certo pronunciare.' He refers to Gen. xlv. 5, where Joseph suggests the purpose which God's providence had in sending him down into Egypt. **ἐχωρίσθη]** εὐφήμως καὶ τὴν φυγὴν χωρισμὸν καλεῖ, ἵνα μὴ τῷ ὀνόματι τῆς φυγῆς παροξύνῃ τὸν δεσπότην, Thl.: similarly Chrys. **πρὸς ὥραν]** much has been built upon this as indicating that the Epistle was written not so far from Colossæ as Rome: but without ground: the contrast is between πρὸς ὥραν and αἰώνιον. **αἰώνιον** agrees with αὐτόν: see reff.: and imports οὐκ ἐν τῷ παρόντι μόνον καιρῷ, ἀλλὰ κ. ἐν τῷ μέλλοντι, as Chrys. **ἀπέχῃς]** see reff., and note on Matt. vi. 2—**mayest have him for thine own—possess him fully, entirely.** So Antonin., xi. 1, says that the λογικὴ ψυχή does not bear fruit for others to reap, &c., but ὅπου ἂν καταληφθῇ, πλῆρες κ. ἀπροσδεὲς ἑαυτῇ τὸ προτεθὲν ποιεῖ ὥστε εἰπεῖν, Ἐγὼ **ἀπέχω** τὰ ἐμά. **16.]** And that, in a different relation from the one before subsisting. But οὐκέτι ὡς δοῦλον does not imply his manumission; rather the contrary: the stress is on **ὡς** and **ὑπέρ**—'no longer *as* a slave (though he be one), but *above* a slave.' **μάλιστα**, 'of all other men,' of all those without thy house, with whom he has been connected: but πόσῳ μᾶλλον σοί, with whom he stands in so near and lasting a relation. **17.]** takes up again the sentiment (and the construction) broken off at the end of ver. 12. The κοινωνία referred to is that shewn by the ἀγάπη of him, common to both, mentioned in the last verse: but extending far wider than it, even to the community of faith, and hope, and love between them as Christian men: not that of goods, as Bengel: 'ut tua sint mea et mea tua.' **18.] δέ**, in contrast to the favourable reception bespoken for him in the last verse. 'Confessus erat Onesimus Paulo, quæ fecerat,' Bengel. οὐκ εἶπον, εἴ τι ἔκλεψε"

^v ἔγραψα τῇ ἐμῇ ^v χειρί, ἐγὼ ^w ἀποτίσω· ἵνα μὴ λέγω
σοι ὅτι καὶ σεαυτόν μοι ^x προσοφείλεις. ²⁰ ^y ναί, ἀδελφέ,
ἐγὼ σοῦ ^z ὀναίμην ἐν κυρίῳ· ^a ἀνάπαυσόν μου τὰ
^a σπλάγχνα ^b ἐν χριστῷ. ²¹ ^c πεποιθὼς τῇ ^d ὑπακοῇ σου
ἔγραψά σοι, εἰδὼς ὅτι καὶ ^e ὑπὲρ ἃ λέγω ποιήσεις. ²² ἅμα
δὲ καὶ ^f ἑτοίμαζέ μοι ^g ξενίαν· ἐλπίζω γὰρ ὅτι ^h διὰ τῶν
προσευχῶν ὑμῶν ⁱ χαρισθήσομαι ὑμῖν

Left margin notes:
v Gal. vi. 11 reff.
w here only. Exod. xxi. 19.
x here only †. Herod. vi. 59 (Schweigh.). Xen. Cyr. iii. 2. 7.
Hell i. 5. 4. Demosth. 650. 23.
y Phil. iv. 3.
x here only †.
Sir. xxx. 2 only. Xen. Anab. i. 1. 38.

Right margin notes:
...πεποι- θὼς F
(and also G).
ACDKL P א a b c d e f g h k l m n o
17. 47

a ver. 7 reff.   b Rom. xvi. 7, 9, 10 al. fr.   c constr., Phil. i. 14 reff.
d Rom. i. 5 al6.   1 Cor. vii. 15. x. 5, 6.   Heb. v. 8.   1 Pet. i. 2, 14, 22 only.   2 Kings xxii. 36 only.   e ver. 16.
f 2 Tim. ii. 21.   1 Cor. ii. 9.   Heb. xi. 16.   Gen. xxiv. 31.   g Acts xxviii. 23 only †.   Ælian. Var. Hist. iii. 37.
h = Rom. xii. 3.   Gal. i. 18.   i = Acts iii. 14. xxvii. 24.   1 Cor. ii. 12. L.P.†   2 Macc. iii. 33 al.

19. for αποτισω, αποδωσω D¹ scholl (reddam latt).   at end ins ἐν κυριω D¹.
20. rec (for χριστω) κυριω (repetn from foregoing), with D³K rel [vulg(with am demid, not fuld)]: txt ACD¹FL[P]א a m 17 syrr copt [goth] æth arm Chr Œc-comm Thdrt-ms Thl Ambr Ambrst Jer Pel.
21. rec ὅ (appy corrn to suit circumstance, only one request having been made), with DKL rel vss gr-lat-ff: txt AC[P]א 17. 73 syr copt.

ἀλλὰ τί; εἴ τι ἠδίκησεν. ἅμα κ. τὸ ἁμάρτημα ὡμολόγησε, καὶ οὐχ ὡς δούλου ἁμάρτημα ἀλλὰ ὡς φίλου πρὸς φίλον, τῷ τῆς ἀδικίας μᾶλλον ἢ τῷ τῆς κλοπῆς ὀνόματι χρησάμενος, Chrys. ἢ ὀφείλει is said of the same matter, and is merely explanatory of ἠδίκησεν: τοῦτο referring to both verbs. The weight of manuscript testimony to ἐλλόγα overbears the mere assertion of Fritzsche (on Rom. v. 13)—'λογᾶν est dicturire (Luc. Lexiph., p. 15), sed ἐλλογᾶν vox nulla est:'—that reckon, or impute to me: hardly perhaps, notwithstanding the engagement of the next verse, with a view to actual repayment, but rather to inducing Philemon to forego exacting it.
19.] The inference from this is, that the whole Epistle was autographic: for it would be most unnatural to suppose the Apostle to break off his amanuensis here, and write this engagement with his own hand. ἵνα μὴ λέγω] "est σχῆμα παρασιωπήσεως sive reticentiæ, cum dicimus nos omittere velle, quod maxime dicimus," Grot. ἵνα μή does not exactly, as Meyer, give the purpose of St. Paul in ἔγραψα—ἀποτίσω: but rather that of an understood clause,—'yield me this request, lest I should have to remind thee, &c.' Ellic. paraphrases, 'repay: yes I say this, not doubting thee, but not wishing to press on thee all the claim that I might justly urge.' καὶ τοῦτο ἀπὸ ἀγάπης καὶ κατὰ τὸν τῆς φιλίας λόγον, καὶ τοῦ σφόδρα θαρρεῖν ἦν, Chrys. And this may well be the right view. καὶ σεαυτόν] οὐ τὰ σαυτοῦ μόνον, Chr. δι' ἐμοῦ γάρ, φησί, τῆς σωτηρίας ἀπήλαυσας· καὶ ἐντεῦθεν δῆλον, ὡς τῆς ἀποστολικῆς διδασκαλίας ἠξιώθη ὁ Φιλήμων,

Thdrt. 20.] ναί, as so often when we make requests, asserts our assent with the subject of the request: so Phil. iv. 3, al. ἐγώ and σοῦ are both emphatic—and the unusual word ὀναίμην, thus thrown into the background, is an evident allusion to the name 'Ονήσιμος. "The form ὀναίμην is similarly used by Ignatius (Polyc. 1, 6, pp. 720, 725; Magn. 12, p. 672, al.),—once (Eph. 2, p. 645), curiously enough, but apparently by mere accident, after a mention of an Onesimus." Ellicott. (Lobeck, on Phryn., p. 12, gives a complete account of the forms and tenses of this verb which are in use.) The sentiment itself is a reference to σεαυτόν μοι προσοφείλεις :—this being so, let me have profit of thee. ἐν κυρίῳ,—not in worldly gain, but in the Lord—in thine increase and richness in the graces of His Spirit. ἀνάπαυσον . . . .] refresh (viz. by acceding to my request) my heart (as above—the seat of the affections. τὰ σπλάγχνα μου must not for a moment be imagined, with Jer., Est., Schrader, al., to designate Onesimus, who was so called in ver. 12: which would be most unnatural) in Christ (as ἐν κυρίῳ above). 21.] Serves to put Philemon in mind of the apostolic authority with which he writes: and hints delicately (perhaps: but this may be doubtful: compare Ellic. here) at the manumission of Onesimus, which he has not yet requested. καί, also, besides doing what I say. 22. ἅμα δὲ καί] But at the same time (as thou fulfillest my request), also . . . . . We may, perhaps, take this direction as serving to secure the favourable reception of Onesimus: for the Apostle would himself come

²³ Ἀσπάζεταί σε Ἐπαφρᾶς ὁ ^k συναιχμάλωτός μου ἐν χριστῷ Ἰησοῦ, ²⁴ Μάρκος, Ἀρίσταρχος, Δημᾶς, Λουκᾶς, οἱ ^l συνεργοί μου. ²⁵ ἡ ^m χάρις τοῦ ^m κυρίου ἡμῶν Ἰησοῦ χριστοῦ μετὰ τοῦ ⁿ πνεύματος ὑμῶν.

k Rom. xvi. 7.
Col. iv. 10
only †.
l Rom. xvi. 3,
9, 21. 1 Cor.
iii. 9 al8.
Paul only,
exc. 3 John
8 †. 2 Macc.
viii. 7. xiv.
5 only.
m see Col. iv.
18 reff.
n Gal. vi. 18.
Phil. iv. 23.
2 Tim. iv. 22.

ΠΡΟΣ ΦΙΛΗΜΟΝΑ.

23. rec ασπαζονται, with D'·³KL rel : txt ACD¹[P]א m [47] vulg Syr copt [goth] æth arm Chr Thdrt Thl Ambrst Jer Pel.
25. om ημων [P]א 17. 31. 47. 116.		rec at end ins αμην, with CD³KL[P]א rel : om AD¹ 17 arm Jer.

SUBSCRIPTION. rec adds εγραφη απο ρωμης [with P, and further] δια ονησιμου οικετου, with K [47] : FG are deficient after ver 20 : but G (not F) after a vacant space notes προς λαουακησας (*Laudicenses* G-lat) αρχεται επιστολη : του αγιου αποστ. παυλ. επ. πρ. φιλημ. και απφιαν δεσποτας του ονησιμου και προς αρχιππον τον διακονον της εν κολοσσαις εκκλησιας εγραφη απο ρωμης δια ονησιμου οικετου L b : om l : A deficient : εγρ. απ. ρ. δ. ο. οικ. h k m : txt C 17, and D(addg επληρωθη), א(adding στιχων, without numeral). [P adds στιχων μη, 47 στ. λϛ.]

and see how his request had fared : πολλὴ γὰρ ἦν ἡ χάρις κ. ἡ τιμὴ Παύλου ἐνδη· μοῦντος, Παύλου μετὰ ἡλικίαν, Παύλου μετὰ δεσμούς, Chrys. Or it may be, as Ellic., that Philemon was not to consider the Epistle as a mere petition for Onesimus, but as containing special messages on other matters to himself. ὑμῶν and ὑμῖν refer to those named in vv. 1, 2.

23—25.] CONCLUSION. See on Col. iv. 10, 12, 14, where the same persons send greeting. Ἰησοῦς ὁ λεγόμενος Ἰοῦστος (Col. iv. 11) does not appear here.
25.] For this form of salutation, see reff. On all matters regarding the date and circumstances of writing the Epistle, see the Prolegomena.

REVISIONS

The references in this revision to Arndt and Gingrich are to Arndt, William F., and Gingrich, F. Wilbur. A *Greek-English Lexicon of the New Testament and Other Early Christian Literature*. The University of Chicago Press, Chicago, 1957. (This is a translation and adaptation of Walter Bauer's *Griechisch-Deutsches Worterbuch zu den Schriften des Neuen Testaments und der ubrigen urchristlichen literatur*.)

Gal. 1:2. For the location of the churches, see the note on Acts 16:6-9.

Gal. 2:1. Since chronological sequence is important to Paul's argument, it is better, with most interpreters, to understand the fourteen years as reckoned after the three, or seventeen years after the conversion.

Gal. 2:7. The word *Gospel* is not repeated here, showing that the emphasis is on the contrast between circumcision and uncircumcision. This is best understood in geographical terms. Paul continued to preach the Gospel to the Jew as well as to the Greek (Rom. 1:16), but his sphere of labor was outside Palestine even as Peter's lay within it. When Paul tried to preach in Jerusalem, he was admonished by the Lord to go far hence to the Gentiles (Acts 22:21).

Gal. 2:10. This restriction about remembering the poor is not an unrelated adjunct. The poor of the Jerusalem church are meant. Preoccupation with the work among Gentiles distant from the holy land might mean a slackening of the interest Paul and Barnabas already manifested (the present tense in μνημονεύωμεν

437

may be explained as an indirect reference to the famine visit, Acts 11:29, 30).

Gal. 5:22. πίστις here means faithfulness rather than faith.

Gal. 6:5. βαστάσει may be explained as an ethical future—*must bear.*

Gal. 6:11. For several reasons it is well to hold that at this point the apostle began to write with his own hand, taking the pen from the scribe. He seems to call attention to the change in the ἴδετε. He deliberately wrote the rest of the epistle in large letters for emphasis. (See Ramsay, *Paul's Epistle to the Galatians,* pp. 464-466.)

Eph. 2:14. Very likely the language of Paul reflects the barrier which separated the court of the Gentiles from the inner court. This wall bore an inscription at intervals, as follows: "No foreigner is to enter within the railing and enclosure round the Temple. Whoever is caught will be responsible to himself for his death which will ensue." The archaeologist Clermont-Ganneau discovered several of these inscriptions in 1871 (Cobern, *New Archaeological Discoveries,* p. 355).

Eph. 2:20. Almost certainly the construction is a genitive of apposition—the foundation which consists in apostles and prophets. This conclusion ought not to be rejected because of apparent conflict with I Corinthians 3:11. In the soteriological sense, Christ alone is the foundation, but apostles and prophets are instrumental in the building up of the Church (Eph. 4:11-13). Christ Himself authorized such language in His prophecy to Peter (Matt. 16:18).

Eph. 3:15. Most modern translators and commentators favor the rendering, "from whom every family in heaven and on earth is named" or something similar. A few suggest "all fatherhood." But the construction is the same as in 2:20. If πᾶσα οἰκοδομὴ can mean "the whole building," surely πᾶσα πατριὰ can mean "the whole family." There seems to be no warrant for taking πατριὰ as equivalent to an abstract πατρότης meaning fatherhood. It is doubtful that Paul is thinking of angelic and human families. *Father* has its usual redemptive sense, so that the Church in its earthly and heavenly portions is seen as undivided. (See Weymouth's translation, also the helpful comments of

R. C. H. Lenski in *The Interpretation of St. Paul's Epistle to the Galatians, to the Ephesians, and to Philippians*, p. 491.)

Eph. 4:12. The view of Alford, in agreement with Meyer and Ellicott, suffers from the necessity of disturbing the order of the clauses. It is better, with the Nestle text, to omit the comma after ἁγίων. Then Paul may be understood as teaching that the various gifted men are given to the Church for the strengthening of the saints with a view to *their* work of ministry, which in turn has in view the building up of the Body of Christ. There may be a certain awkwardness in representing the same people as working and being built up, but this is true to fact.

Eph. 4:30. Alford's comment on the grieving of the Spirit is unfortunate. Where is the authority for contending that the language implies that the Spirit may be led to depart? His inability to depart (the sealing surely implies this) makes all the more pathetic the Spirit's position. He is involved in an unhappy situation in which He can only grieve.

Eph. 5:14. This may be a fragment of an early Christian hymn. The use of ὁ Χριστὸς makes a quotation from the Old Testament improbable. On the other hand, it is unexpected to have anything but a quotation introduced by λέγει.

Phil. 1:19. Since these words about salvation are a quotation from Job 13:16, it is natural to assume that Paul had Job's situation in mind and was thinking of his own as parallel in some degree. The best rendering of σωτηρία then will probably be *vindication*. Whether this comes by life or death, Paul is conscious of his integrity. (See the extended note in Michael, Moffatt *Commentary*.)

Phil. 2:6. It is perilous to assume that ἁρπαγμὸς can have only an active meaning, in view of the fact that other words with similar ending are used in a passive sense. (See the discussion in Gifford, *The Incarnation*, pp. 59-71.)

Phil. 2:7. Alford does not appear to take a view damaging to the Person of Christ. The same cannot be said, unfortunately, for his remarks on the *kenosis* under Hebrews 1:4.

Phil. 2:8. The rendering, "the death of the cross," fails to reckon with the absence of the article. Paul's emphasis is not upon the fact of Christ's death on the historic cross of Calvary, but on the shameful, reproachful character of such a death. Jesus died a cross-death as opposed to death by other means which would not involve humiliation.

Phil. 2:10. It is in the combination of Jesus and Lord that we are to find the significance of the name which is above every name. (See Acts 2:36; Rom. 10:9; I Cor. 12:3.) A name once despised is now seen to be linked by God's action with the designation most honored.

Phil. 2:12. The comment about the meaning of fear and trembling is unfortunate. Paul's exhortation does not have in view the maintenance of salvation but the manifestation of its power in the life as seen by men. Fear and trembling express the distrust of one's own ability to do this successfully, leading to the necessity of depending on God for strength.

Phil. 2:16. Usage favors the meaning *hold fast* for ἐπέχω. (See Moulton and Milligan.)

Phil. 3:5. In calling himself a Hebrew of Hebrews it is quite possible that Paul intends to convey the thought that despite his birth in the Dispersion, his family, having come to Tarsus only shortly before from Palestine, continued to use the Hebrew (Aramaic) tongue as well as observe the customs of the nation of the Jews.

Phil. 4:11. It is not wise to insist that the English auxiliary word *have* be omitted in rendering the Greek aorist tense. Moulton's conclusion is sound. "Outside narrative we (in English usage) use the periphrastic *have* tense as an *indefinite* past; and it thus becomes the inevitable representative of the Greek aorist when no time is clearly designed" (*Prolegomena*, pp. 135, 136).

Col. 2:2. Practically all modern editors include Χριστοῦ after Θεοῦ, on the basis of the strong attestation of B and P46. The antecedent of Χριστοῦ is almost certainly *mystery* rather than *God*.

Col. 2:3. It is well to find the antecedent of ἐν ᾧ in *Christ*. The difficulty which Alford feels about the word *hidden* may be solved in some such way as this: the word coming, as it does, at the end of the clause, gets a certain emphasis. These treasures are hidden from the mind of the unregenerate man, and are so rich and profound that even to the Spirit-taught they are not fully comprehended.

Col. 2:8. The rendering, *leads you away as his prey,* makes the persons (of the Colossian believers) the object of the robbery rather than their spiritual treasures. Alford's argument for abduction, based on the force of κατά, is misguided. (See Field, *Select Passages of the Greek Testament.*)

Col. 2:8. Many moderns accept in place of the old rendering, *the elements of the world,* the new translation, *the elementary spirits of the universe* (see Arndt and Gingrich). The argument that the στοιχεῖα must be personal because they are put over against Christ is blunted by the consideration that *the tradition of men* is also set over against Christ, and it is not personal.

Col. 2:15. Alford's attempt to identify the principalities and powers with the good angels through whom the Law was communicated is dubious in view of the remainder of the verse, which accords far better with the notion of conquest over hostile forces.

Col. 2:18. For a good handling of this difficult verse, see the discussion by Beare in *The Interpreter's Bible.*

Col. 3:16. A comma should be inserted (as in Nestle) after ἑαυτούς. Teaching and admonishing are not intended to be connected with the use of hymns and spiritual songs.

I Thess. 2:3. Uncleanness does not refer to a mercenary motive, but to the sensuality which was so prevalent in connection with ancient religions.

I Thess. 4:4. See the treatment of σκεῦος by W. F. Arndt and F. W. Gingrich in *A Greek-English Lexicon of the New Testament* (p. 761); George Milligan, *St. Paul's Epistles to the Thessalonians* (pp. 48, 49).

II Thess. 2:4. It is strange that Alford should seek to avoid the literal sense here after contending so strongly for the "literal details" in I Thessalonians 4:13-18 (see remarks under v. 18). For an exposition of the literal position on the passage before us, see Milligan, *St. Paul's Epistles to the Thessalonians.*

II Thess. 2:7. The proposal to take ἕως after μόνον involves a serious disturbance of the order of the sentence. It is possible that μόνον ὁ κατέχων ἄρτι should be construed as a parenthetical statement (*only the restrainer is restraining now*), in which case the last four words of the verse will relate back to the mystery of lawlessness, and could be translated, *until it develop out of the midst*, i.e., attain a state of ripeness which is the necessary preparation for the denouement of the lawless one which is indicated in the following verse. The element of uncertainty here is whether ἐκ μέσου will bear the sense demanded on this construction.

II Thess. 2:11. πέμπει is probably a futuristic present.

I Tim. 1:5. The commandment is best understood of that which Timothy is enjoined to pass on to these teachers.

I Tim. 3:16. There is no real objection to taking the adverb in the sense of *by confession* rather than in the more general sense of *admittedly*. The words which are thus introduced define *the truth* of the previous verse and seem to form the substance of an early Christian confession of faith.

I Tim. 3:16. Due to the evident parallelism between *flesh* and *spirit* here, it is preferable, if not actually necessary, to refer *spirit* to Christ Himself rather than to the Holy Spirit. Though He appeared in the flesh and lived among men, He was thoroughly vindicated in His own consciousness as to His sinlessness, despite the charges leveled against Him. See the discussion in Plummer, *The Pastoral Epistles* (*The Expositor's Bible*), also in Spicq, *Les Epitres Pastorales*.

I Tim. 4:1. Despite Alford's mild statement on those who depart from the faith, one must not overlook the fact that the word used is a strong one—*apostatize*.

I Tim. 4:12. Since the word about Timothy's youth has been urged against Paul's authorship of the epistle, it is helpful to consider the use of the word *youth* in antiquity. It was used of men forty and more years of age. (See Simpson, *The Pastoral Epistles*, p. 69.)

I Tim. 6:8. On the contrary, the verb expresses subjective contentment. If the construction were objective, food and raiment would become the subject of the verb, followed by a dative to indicate those benefited. (See examples in Arndt and Gingrich.)

I Tim. 6:13. The reference seems general. We may think of Paul's description of God, with H. P. Liddon in *Explanatory Analysis of St. Paul's First Epistle to Timothy* (p. 84), as the Giver and Upholder of all life.

II Tim. 1:7. Not correction but self-discipline is the force of σωφρονισμός. There is no ground for objection to rendering πνεῦμα *a spirit* in this passage, contra Alford.

II Tim. 1:12. Alford's view of the deposit may be correct, but it suffers under the difficulty that the word must then be taken in a sense different from its other occurrences in the Pastorals, where it refers to the Gospel message and the obligation to declare it.

II Tim. 2:8. Jesus Christ is the object of the imperative, and ἐγηγερμένον is a predicate accusative. The verb in question may take either the genitive or the accusative as a direct object. (See Matt. 16:9.)

II Tim. 2:21. Alford is certainly right in concluding that strict grammar points to the purifying of oneself from the vessels of dishonor as the natural conclusion, but this is a rather strange use of the figure. Purging oneself seems to call for cleansing from wrong motives and practices. (See C. Spicq in *Les Epitres Pastorales*, pp. 358, 359; also the R.S.V.)

II Tim. 2:23. Here ἀπαιδεύτους must be understood, not in the sense of the undisciplined, but uncultured, shading off into senseless or stupid. (See Arndt and Gingrich.)

II Tim. 2:25. Alford follows the older English versions in his rendering of ἀντιδιατιθεμένους, but the translation gives a wrong impression. (See the correction in Frederick Field's notes in *Notes on Select Passages of the Greek Testament*, pp. 130, 131.) The simple rendering *opponents* is accurate and sufficient.

II Tim. 2:26. It is the tendency of most modern translations and exegetes to refer both pronouns to the Devil. (See F. Field's note in *Notes on Select Passages of the Greek Testament*, pp. 131, 132.) The passage will probably always remain controversial.

II Tim. 3:16. For a crisp exposition of the other viewpoint on the translation, see E. K. Simpson, *The Pastoral Epistles.* It is well known that the R.S.V. has returned to the rendering of the A.V.

Titus 2:4. For σωφρονίζωσιν here, Arndt and Gingrich suggest *encourage* or *advise.*

Titus 2:13. Despite the length of the comment here, it is doubtful that Alford has taken the right position. The use of the one article is highly important. (For other substantiating data, see E. K. Simpson's *The Pastoral Epistles,* pp. 108, 109.)

Titus 3:5. Again, in discussing ἐποιήσαμεν, Alford shows his tendency to render the aorist too rigidly in terms of the English past tense.